EVERY PERSON
in the
OLD
TESTAMENT

Every Person
in the
Old
Testament

Lynn F. Price

First Printing: March, 2002

International Standard Book Number:
0-88290-709-3

Horizon Publishers' Catalog and Order Number:
1958

Printed and distributed
in the United States of America by

Horizon
Publishers
& Distributors, Incorporated

Mailing Address:
P.O. Box 490
Bountiful, Utah 84011-0490

Street Address:
50 South 500 West
Bountiful, Utah 84010

Local Phone: (801) 295-9451
Toll Free: 1 (866) 818-6277
FAX: (801) 295-0196

E-mail: horizonp@burgoyne.com
Internet: http://www.horizonpublishers.biz

Contents

Old Testament People

People Whose Names Begin With:

Charts

KEY TO UNDERSTANDING THE TEXT

People are entered alphabetically. Their names are first entered in capital letters and are bolded, followed b the scriptural reference(s) that pertain to that person, i.e., **AARON**. *Ex. 4:14-16, 27-30; Ex. 5;1-3, etc.* At the beginning of their actual narrtive, their names are bolded and underlined; i.e., **Aaron** When more than one person has the same name, they are entered according to the scriptural reference that appears first in the Old Testament. For instance, Eber (1) who is first referred to in Gen. 10:21, comes before Eber (2) who is first referred to in 1 Chr. 8:12. The Old Testament does not necessarily present information in the "Who, What, Why, When, Where and How" format to which we have become accustomed. Therefore, scriptural references given sometimes show a verse number followed by bracketed verses, i.e., Hanan (6): *Neh. 10:10 (1, 10, 28-31).* Hanan is mentioned by name in verse 10. However, verses 1, 28-31, provide information that pertains to him.

When a person has more than one name, each additional name is in **bold-face** type the first time it is used. When multiple people share the same name, scan down the scriptural references, beginning with the first entry with that name, until you come to the reference that pertains to the particular person you wish to find. When a person has multiple references, those references are all listed at the beginning of that person's entry in the order they appear in the Old Testament. They are also noted in the body of the text. However, because some scripture verses are a repeat of other scripture verses, scriptural references may be combined in the body of the text and, thus, may not always be in the exact order in which they appear in the Old Testament.

Sometimes (as in the case of Baanah (2)) there is only one text entry but two references cited. That means both references said essentially the same thing. However, the second reference may include a slight difference in a given fact (i.e., a number cited), name changes, spelling variations, additions or deletions. The differences presented in the second scripture are indicated by being encased in parentheses; i.e., **SENAH** *Ezra 2:35; Neh. 7:38* . . . "The men of the children of Senaah . . . numbered 3,630 (3,930)." In Ezra, it says 3,630, however, in Nehemiah, it says 3,930.

Not every reference for each group of people, i.e., the Canaanites, has been included since the references are so numerous. Also, it was my calculated guess as to whether names listed on the Ancestral Charts should be listed vertically or horizontally—that is, whether people were actually "sons" or whether they were sons in the sense of being grandsons, great-grandsons, etc. Nevertheless, I have tried to connect them visually to the correct ancestor as far as possible. Because descendants are listed in different ways from time to time, dual ancestral lines are sometimes given, as in the cases of Levi's descendants—Gershon, Kohath and Merari. Many people mentioned in the Old Testament have not been included on any ancestral chart, however, because there was no clear indication of any specific connection. To follow an ancestral line on the charts, follow the names that are in all capital letters to the final name on each line that has only the first letter capitalized. If a person is included on a chart, the chart number is given at the end of that person's entry.

The version of the Old Testament used for this project was the authorized King James version which includes a bible dictionary (BD) and which has explanatory notes and cross references to the Standard Works of The Church of Jesus Christ of Latter-day Saints, published by The Church of Jesus Christ of Latter-day Saints in Salt Lake City, Utah, U.S.A. Once in a while readers are referred to the *New Testament,* Bible Dictionary (BD), to *Joseph Smith's History* (JS-H) located after the *Pearl of Great Price* in the combined scriptures or to other scriptural references: *Joseph Smith's "New Translation of the Bible"* (JST); the *Book of Mormon* (B of M), the *Doctrine and Covenants* (D&C), or the *Pearl of Great Price.* They are bracketed and written in italics as are explanatory comments so as to not confuse the reader as to what is from the Old Testament and what is supplemental information.

In spite of the many challenges and the potential for error in combining all references to a particular person into one entry, it is my hope that this book will prove useful to those who read or merely refer to the Old Testament scriptures from time to time as they seek to identify in their own minds who these people were. They lived. They were real. They helped shape this world for us. They interacted with the Lord. They recorded their communications with Him and their experiences. For all of that, we owe these ancient people a debt of gratitude.

FOREWORD

The Old Testament presented some unique challenges to extracting and doing a synopsis on every person mentioned therein. One challenge was the number of pages to read. Another was the vast number of people chronicled in this volume of scripture. A complicating factor is that, not only are there several different people all of whom share a common name (two or three people with the same name may even be referred to in one single verse of scripture), but also the fact that many people were known and referred to by more than one name. For instance, Jehoiachin was also called Jeconiah and Coniah; Joshua is referred to as Oshea, Hoshea, Jehoshua and Jeshua at different times. Also, many people are merely referred to in passing with nothing really being said about them. Additionally, descendants of a person, citizens of a particular city, and cities themselves, may all be referred to by the same name sometimes making it difficult to determine whether the name in question is a person, a people, or a place.

Another obstacle is the similarity of many names, which makes it difficult to track a given person (i.e., Ahaziah, Amaziah, Azariah, Azaziah). Thus, it was a challenge to try to pull all references to a given individual together. It is possible that in some cases references to two different individuals may have erroneously been combined under one person and that references for one person may be entered under two different entries. However, great effort has been given to minimize that happening.

Another challenge was the fact that syllables to some names are reversed from time to time: i.e., Ammiel and Eliam sometimes refer to the same person. Likewise, Harhas and Hasrah have the syllables reversed. Occasionally, the Bible, itself, appears to refer to the wrong person as in 2 Sam. 21:8, which refers to Saul's daughter Michal when it likely should refer to Saul's daughter Merab.

Adding to the confusion is the different listings of a given person's genealogy. One time a person may be referred to as the son of someone and the next time he may be referred to as the son of someone else (possibly because they have skipped generations in some listings). In the Old Testament, son (or daughter) may refer to son, grandson, great-grandson, i.e., any male (or female, if the person is a woman) descendant in a given genealogy line. Likewise, the "father" of someone may be the father or the grandfather or the great-grandfather, etc., of that person. And "brother" (or sister, as the case may be) may be a cousin or nephew/niece, etc.

Because men frequently had multiple wives, the listings of their children also varies. One scripture may list the sons of someone one way, another listing another way, and a third listing yet another way. Also, names may be added or deleted, spellings of names changed, and alternative names used.

One major challenge was simply the ambiguity of certain passages of scripture. Consider 1 Chr. 4:18-19, for instance: "And his wife Jehudijah bare Jered the father of Gedor, and Heber the father of Socho, and Jekuthiel the father of Zanoah. And these are the sons of Bithiah the daughter of Pharaoh which Mered took. And the sons of his wife Hodiah the sister of Naham, the father of Keilah the Garmite, and Eshtemoa the Maachathite." It is not clear who "his" refers to when it says "his wife Jehudijah." There is no clarification in the Old Testament as to whose wife Jehudijah actually was. It is also not clear what is meant by "these are the sons of Bithiah the daughter of Pharaoh which Mered took." It is again unclear who "his" is when referring to "his wife Hodiah." Hopefully, *Every Person in the Old Testament* will help minimize the challenges readers of the Old Testament encounter in their reading.

A special thank-you is extended to John Hawkes, Assistant General Manager of Horizon Publishers, and Sam Richardson, graphic artist, for their help, encouragement and assistance in bringing the publication of this book to completion. A huge thanks is also extended to my husband, Dick, for his patience, long-suffering and encouragement. Without his support, I would never have been able to complete this project.

NAMES THAT BEGIN WITH "A"

AARON. *Ex. 4:14-16, 27-30; 5:1-3; 6:20, 23; 7-12; 17:10-12; 18:12; 19:24; 24:1, 9-14; 27:21; 28-30; 32:1-5, 21; 40:12-15, 31; Lev. 1-27; Num. 8; 12; 17; 18; 20; 33:39; Deut. 9:20; 1 Chr. 6:3-15; 12:27-28; 23:13; 24:1; 27:17; Ezra 7:1-5; Ps. 105:26; 106:16; Micah 6:4.*

Aaron was Moses' brother and was sent by the Lord to be Moses' mouthpiece in Egypt. *(Ex. 4:14-16, 27-30; Ps. 105:26.)* They asked Pharaoh to let the children of Israel travel three days into the wilderness so they could make a sacrifice unto their God. Pharaoh said, "No," and increased their burden. *(Ex. 5:1-3).*

Aaron, the son of Amram and Jochebed, married Elisheba, daughter of Amminadab (of the tribe of Judah). Their sons were Nadab, Abihu, Eleazar and Ithamar. *(Ex. 6:20, 23.)* Nadab and Abihu died before Aaron and had no children. *(1 Chr. 24:1.)*

The Lord told Moses that He would speak to him; and he, in turn, was to instruct Aaron as to what he should say to Pharaoh. Aaron was 83 years old and Moses was 80 years old when they spoke to Pharaoh. *(Ex. 7:2, 7.)* When Aaron cast down his rod, it became a serpent. Pharaoh's magicians duplicated that act, but Aaron's rod swallowed up the magicians' rods. *(Ex. 7:10-12.)* Aaron smote the rivers and ponds with his rod and the waters turned to blood. *(Ex. 7:20.)* When he stretched his rod over the streams and rivers, frogs came forth. *(Ex. 8:6.)* He stretched forth the rod and the dust turned to lice. *(Ex. 8:16-17.)* The Lord then sent flies. *(Ex. 8:24.)* After the Lord killed the Egyptians' cattle *(Ex. 9:6)*, Aaron and Moses took ashes of the furnace and Moses sprinkled the ashes up toward heaven and it became boils. *(Ex. 9:8-10.)* The next plague was thunder, rain, hail and fire. *(Ex. 9:18-34.)* The rod was stretched forth over the land of Egypt and the Lord sent locusts. When Pharaoh again hardened his heart, the Lord caused a thick darkness to cover the land of Egypt for three days. *(Ex. 10:22.)*

The Lord told Moses that He would yet bring one more plague upon the Egyptians, the death of all the firstborn. Nevertheless, Pharaoh continued to harden his heart and would not let the people go. *(Ex. 11:5-10.)*

The Lord instituted the Passover. And the children of Israel did all that the Lord commanded Moses and Aaron. *(Ex. 12.)*

Aaron helped hold Moses' arms up during Joshua's battle with Amalek and Joshua and the children of Israel were able to "discomfit" Amalek. *(Ex. 17:10-12.)* Aaron and the elders of Israel joined Moses and Moses' father-in-law in eating bread when Jethro brought Zipporah and Moses' sons to Moses in the wilderness. *(Ex. 18:12.)*

The Lord instructed Moses to take Aaron with him up to Mount Sinai. *(Ex. 19:24.)*

Aaron, Nadab, Abihu and seventy of the elders of Israel went with Moses unto the mount as commanded by the Lord. They saw the God of Israel. ". . . and there was under his feet as it were a paved work of a sapphire stone, and as it were the body of heaven in his clearness. And upon the nobles of the children of Israel he laid not his hand: also they saw God, and did eat and drink." When the Lord told Moses to come unto Him in the mount and receive tables of stone, and a law and commandments, he rose up "and his minister Joshua" also rose up and went with him. Moses instructed the elders of Israel to tarry where they were and that Aaron and Hur would be with them to take care of any problems in his absence. *(Ex. 24:1, 9-14.)*

Aaron and his sons were charged to keep the light burning always in the tabernacle of the congregation from evening to morning before the Lord. *(Ex. 27:21.)* The Lord gave Moses instructions regarding Aaron and his sons, Nadab, Abihu, Eleazar and Ithamar, who were to be consecrated and anointed to minister in the priest's office. Specific instructions were given regarding their garments and their responsibilities. *(Ex. 28-30.)*

While Moses was in the mount, the people came to Aaron and asked him to make them gods that they could worship. He had them bring their golden earrings and he melted the gold and made a golden calf. Aaron was chastised by Moses for making the golden calf. *(Ex. 32:1-5, 21.)*

Aaron and his sons were washed and anointed and given an everlasting priesthood. *(Ex. 40:12-15, 31.)* Instructions pertaining to Aaron and his sons were given to Moses who then instructed them regarding their responsibilities. According to instructions received from the Lord, Aaron and his sons were washed and anointed and dressed in the holy garments. *(Lev. 1-27.)* The Lord instructed Moses to have Aaron offer the Levites before the Lord for an offering of the children of Israel. The Levites were not given a land of inheritance, but were to minister in the service of the tabernacle. The Lord said the Levites are His in place of the firstborn of every family, and that He has given the Levites as a gift to Aaron and to his sons to do the service of the children of Israel in the tabernacle. In lieu of a land of inheritance, the Levites were to be supported by the tithes of the people. *(Num. 8, 18.)*

Aaron and Miriam complained against Moses for having married an Ethiopian woman. The Lord chastised them and caused Miriam to become leprous. *(Num. 12.)*

The children of Israel envied Aaron and Moses. *(Ps. 106:16.)* The Lord instructed Moses to have each tribe place a rod in the tabernacle of witness. The rod the Lord chose, which indicated His choice to preside over the tabernacle, would blossom. Thus, the people could cease murmuring against Moses and Aaron. Aaron's rod budded and brought forth buds, bloomed blossoms, and yielded almonds. The Lord told Moses to keep Aaron's rod in the tabernacle for a token against the rebels. *(Num. 17.)*

Miriam died and was buried in Kadesh. While in Kadesh, the people complained against Aaron and Moses because of a lack of water, plants and fruit trees. The Lord instructed Moses to take his rod and Aaron, gather the people together, and speak to the rock so that it would bring forth water. The Lord was displeased that they struck the rock with the rod rather than speak to it and said that "therefore ye shall not bring this congregation into the land which I have given them." When the king of Edom refused to let the children of Israel pass through Edom, they journeyed to mount Hor. As the time approached for Aaron to die, the Lord instructed Moses to take him and Eleazar, Aaron's son, up unto mount Hor and to place Aaron's garments upon Eleazar. This was done. Aaron then died in the top of the mount. The people mourned 30 days for him. *(Num. 20.)* He was 123 years old. *(Num. 33:39.)*

Moses reminded the children of Israel that the Lord was very angry with Aaron when he allowed them to make a golden calf and was going to destroy him but Moses had pleaded in his behalf. *(Deut. 9:20.)*

When David became king and went to Ziklag, all Israel rejoiced and sent their troops to support him. Jehoiada was leader of the Aaronites and took 3,700 men with him. Zadok, a young man of valor, took 22 captains from his father's house with him. *(1 Chr. 12:27-28.)*

When David numbered the Levites at the time he made Solomon king, he divided them into courses among the sons of Levi. Amram's sons were Aaron and Moses. Aaron and his family were separated out because they were assigned to forever sanctify the most holy things, to burn incense before the Lord and to minister unto Him and bless His name *(1 Chr. 23:13)*. The sons of Aaron and the rest of the sons of Levi were divided into groups by David and assigned their duties by lot. *(1 Chr. 24:1.)*

Aaron's descendant Zadok was prince of the tribe of Levi at the time of David. His descendants from Eleazar to Ezra are given in Ezra 7:1-5 with some modification from the listing in 1 Chr. 6:4-15.

Micah chastised the children of Israel and said that in spite of the Lord's sending Moses, Aaron and Miriam to help them, and leading them out of Egyptian bondage, they still turned away from Him. *(Micah 6:4.)* (Charts 7b., 7d.; 8d., 8f.)

ABAGTHA. *Esth. 1:10.*

Abagtha was one of the seven chamberlains serving in the presence of king Ahasuerus who was sent to bring queen Vashti to him.

ABDA. *1 Kgs. 4:6.*

Abda was the father of Adoniram, which Adoniram was over the tribute in Solomon's court.

ABDEEL. *Jer. 36:26.*

Abdeel was the father of Shelemiah, which Shelemiah, along with the king's son Jerahmeel, and Seraiah the son of Azriel, was commanded by Jehoiakim (Eliakim) to arrest Baruch and Jeremiah for voicing the Lord's warnings against the people.

ABDI (1). *1 Chr. 6:44; 2 Chr. 29:12.*

Abdi, a descendant of Levi through Merari, son of Malluch and the father of Kishi (Kish), was one of those whom David set over the service of song in the house of the Lord. (Chart 7e.)

ABDI (2). *Ezra 10:26.*

Abdi was one of the sons of Elam who took wives from among the Canaanites and other groups. He agreed to do as Ezra said and separate himself from his foreign wives.

ABDIEL. *1 Chr. 5:15.*

Abdiel, father of Ahi and son of Guni, was a descendant of Gad. (Chart 13b.)

ABDON (1). *Judg. 12:13-15.*

Abdon was the son of Hillel, a Pirathonite. He judged Israel eight years. He had 40 sons and 30 nephews. When he died, he was buried in Pirathon in the land of Ephraim in the mount of the Amalekites. (Chart 20.)

ABDON (2). *1 Chr. 8:23, 25.*

Abdon, a descendant of Benjamin, was a son of Shashak who was a son of Beriah. (Chart 16g.)

ABDON (3). *1 Chr. 8:30-32; 9:36.*

Abdon, of the tribe of Benjamin, was the firstborn son of the father of Gibeon. His mother was Maachah. His brothers were Zur, Kish, Baal, Nadab, Gedor, Ahio, Zacher and Mikloth. *(1 Chr. 8:30-32.)* Abdon's father is referred to as Jehiel (Abiel), the father of Gibeon. His brothers are listed again. However, Ner is added and Zacher's name is given as Zechariah. *(1 Chr. 9:36.)* (Chart 16k.)

ABDON (4). *2 Chr. 34:20.* See **Achbor (2)**.

ABED-NEGO. *Dan. 1:7.* See **Azariah (19)**.

ABEL. *Gen. 4:2-4, 8.*

Abel was the second son mentioned in the Old Testament born to Adam and Eve. He was a keeper of sheep. His offering of the firstlings of his flock was acceptable to the Lord. When Abel and Cain were talking in the fields, Cain rose up and killed Abel. *(Note: Moses 5:2-3, 13, 16-17 in the Pearl of Great Price state that Adam and Eve had other sons and daughters prior to the births of Cain and Abel.)* (Chart 1.)

ABI (Abijah (2)). *2 Kgs. 18:2.2; 2 Chr. 29:1.*

Abi was the mother of Hezekiah, the daughter of Zachariah and wife of Ahaz. *(2 Kgs. 18:2.)* Her name is given as **Abijah**. Her father was Zechariah (Zachariah). *(2 Chr. 29:1.)*

ABIA. *1 Chr. 3:10.* See **Abijam**.

ABIAH (1). *1 Sam. 8:2-3; 1 Chr. 6:28.*

Abiah, the second son of the prophet Samuel, was a wicked judge in Israel and took bribes and perverted judgment, as did his brother Joel. *(1 Sam. 8:2-3.)* Abiah was a descendant of Levi through Kohath. His brother was Vashni (Joel). *(1 Chr. 6:28.)* (Charts 7d.; 20.)

ABIAH (2) (Daughter of Machir). *1 Chr. 2:21, 24.*

Abiah, the **Daughter of Machir** (granddaughter of Manasseh), married Hezron when Hezron was 60 years old. She bore him Segub. After Hezron's death, Abiah bore Hezron's son Ashur. (Chart 15b.)

ABIAH (3). *1 Chr. 7:8.*

Abiah was a son of Becher and a grandson of Benjamin. His brothers were Zemira, Joash, Eliezer, Elioenai, Omri, Jerimoth, Anathoth and Alameth. (Chart 16c.)

ABI-ALBON (Abiel (2)). *2 Sam. 23:31; 1 Chr. 11:32.*

Abi-albon the Arbathite was one of David's mighty men *(2 Sam. 23:31)* and one of the valiant men of the armies. His name is given as **Abiel**. *(1 Chr. 11:32.)* (Chart 17.)

ABIASAPH (Ebiasaph). *Ex. 6:24; 1 Chr. 6:23, 37; 9:19.*

Abiasaph was a son of Korah, a grandson of Izhar (Amminadab), a great-grandson of Kohath and a great-great-grandson of Levi. *(Ex. 6:24.)* **Ebiasaph** (Abiasaph), son of Elkanah (the son of Assir) was the father of Assir. *(1 Chr. 6:23, 37.)* Ebiasaph, a Levite, was the son of Korah and the father of Kore. *(1 Chr. 9:19.)* *(Note: The terms son, grandson, etc., are used loosely and denote a male descendant.)* (Chart 7d.)

ABIATHAR. *1 Sam. 22:20; 30:7; 2 Sam. 8:17; 15:24-36; 20:25; 1 Kgs. 1:7; 2:26-27, 35; 4:4; 1 Chr. 15:11-12; 18:16; 27:34.*

Abiathar was the son of Ahimelech the priest. When Saul's servant Doeg slew all the priests in Nob, Abiathar escaped and fled after David. *(1 Sam. 22:20.) (Note: The Bible Dictionary states that Abiathar's father was Ahijah or Ahimelech. The implication is they are one and the same.)*

Abiathar, at David's request, brought David the ephod which he, Abiathar, had brought with him, and David inquired of the Lord whether or not he should pursue the Amalekites. He was instructed to do so. *(1 Sam. 30:7.)*

Abiathar was one of the priests when David was king. *(2 Sam. 8:17.) (Note: Abiathar and Ahimelech are apparently reversed in this scripture as it says Ahimelech was the son of Abiathar whereas in 1 Sam. 22:20 we are told that Ahimelech was the father of Abiathar.)*

Abiathar and Zadok, the priests, were with David when he and his household fled from Jerusalem to escape from Absalom. They carried the ark of God with them. David told them to return the ark to the city and to inform him as to the will of God: should he or should he not return from the wilderness. He instructed them to take their sons, Jonathan and Ahimaaz, with them. David instructed his friend, Hushai, to also go back to the city, volunteer to be a servant unto Absalom, and not to only defeat the counsel Ahithophel would be giving to Absalom, but to feed information he gleaned to Abiathar and Zadok. Jonathan, Abiathar's son, and Ahimaaz, Zadok's son, were to carry information back to David. *(2 Sam. 15:24-36.)* Abiathar and Zadok were the priests. *(2 Sam. 20:25.)*

Abiathar supported and helped Adonijah in his bid to wrest the kingdom from David. *(1 Kgs. 1:7.)* When Solomon became king, he ordered Abiathar to leave and go to Anathoth, saying he was worthy of death, but because he bore the ark of the Lord before David, and because he had been afflicted in all wherein David had been afflicted, he would not kill him. Solomon appointed Zadok to be high priest "in the room of Abiathar." *(1 Kgs. 2:26-27, 35; 4:4.)*

After the Lord smote Uzza for touching the ark of God with his hand in an attempt to steady it, David realized that only the Levites should carry the ark. Thus, he assembled the chiefs of the sons of the Levites and hundreds of their brethren and instructed them and Zadok and Abiathar, the priests, to sanctify themselves so they could bring the ark of God "unto the place that I *[David]* have prepared for it." *(1 Chr. 15:11-12.)*

Abiathar was the father of Abimelech (Ahimelech), which Abimelech was a priest along with Zadok. *(1 Chr. 18:16.)*

Abiathar was a counselor to king David along with Jehoiada following Ahithophel. *(1 Chr. 27:34.)* (Chart 7b.)

ABIDA. *Gen. 25:4.*

Abida was a son of Midian and a grandson of Abraham and Keturah. His brothers were Ephah, Epher, Hanoch and Eldaah. (Chart 3f.)

ABIDAN. *Num. 1:11, 36-37; 2:22-23; 7:60.*

Abidan was the son of Gideoni and was of the tribe of Benjamin. He was appointed by the Lord to stand at the head of the tribe of Benjamin as Moses organized Israel in preparation for war. The number of males in the tribe of Benjamin who were 20 years old or older who could go to war totaled 35,400. *(Num. 1:11, 36-37.)* Abidan was instructed to have the tribe of Benjamin pitch their tents on the north side of the encampment, along with the tribes of Ephraim and Manasseh. *(Num. 2:22-23.)* When the altar of the tabernacle was anointed and dedicated, Abidan made his offering on the ninth day. *(Num. 7:60.)*

ABIEL (1) (Jehiel (1), the Father of Gibeon). *1 Sam. 9:1; 14:51; 1 Chr. 8:29-32; 9:35-39.*

Abiel, son of Zeror, was the father of Kish and the grandfather of Saul. He was a Benjamite. *(1 Sam. 9:1.)* He was the father of Ner and the grandfather of Abner, Ner's son. *(1 Sam. 14:51.)* The **father of Gibeon** was of the tribe of Benjamin. His sons include: Abdon, Zur, Kish, Baal, Nadab, Gedor, Ahio, Zacher and Mikloth. His wife was Maachah. *(1 Chr. 8:29-32.)* *(Note: Gibeon might refer to a place rather than to a person since no son by the name of Gibeon is listed as a son of Abiel, i.e., the father of Gibeon.)* The father of Gibeon was **Jehiel** (Abiel). Maachah was his wife. Abdon was his firstborn. The rest of his sons are again named, with the addition of Ner. Zacher's name is given as Zechariah. *(1 Chr. 9:35-39.)* *(Note: Again, no son by the name of Gibeon is mentioned among the listing of Jehiel's sons.)* (Chart 16k.)

ABIEL (2). *1 Chr. 11:32.* See **Abi-albon**.

ABIEZER (1). *2 Sam. 23:27; 1 Chr. 11:28; 27:12.*

Abiezer (or **Abi-ezer**) the Anethothite (or Antothite) was one of David's mighty men *(2 Sam. 23:27)* and one of the valiant men of the armies. *(1 Chr. 11:28.)* He was of the Benjamites and was assigned by David to be over the course of 24,000 who served for the ninth month. *(1 Chr. 27:12.)* (Chart 17.)

ABIEZER (2). *1 Chr. 7:18.*

Abiezer was the son of Hammoleketh, who was a sister of Peresh (Gilead). Thus, he was a grandson of Machir and a great-grandson of Manasseh. His brothers were Ishod and Mahalah. (Chart 15a.)

ABIGAIL (1). *1 Sam. 25:3-42; 27:3; 30:5, 18; 2 Sam. 2:2; 3:3; 1 Chr. 3:1.*

Abigail was the wife of Nabal, a churlish and evil man. She was beautiful and intelligent. When David was bent upon destroying Nabal because he refused to give him and his men some food, Abigail quickly came to him with 200 loaves and 200 bottles of wine, plus sheep, parched corn, raisin clusters and cakes of figs, and pleaded that David not do what he was planning to do. When Nabal learned what Abigail had done "his heart died within him, and he became as a stone," and died about ten days later. When David learned that Nabal was dead, he asked Abigail to be his wife. *(1 Sam. 25:3-42.) (Note: He also took Ahinoam for a wife. His first wife, Michal, the daughter of Saul, had been given by Saul to Phalti for a wife.)* Abigail and Ahinoam dwelt with David in Gath. *(1 Sam. 27:3.)* The Amalekites burned Ziklag and took Abigail and Ahinoam captive along with the other people of Ziklag. David and his men slew the Amalekites and rescued the people, including his wives. *(1 Sam. 30:5, 18.)* Abigail and Ahinoam went to Hebron to dwell with David. *(2 Sam. 2:2.)* Abigail was the mother of Chileab, David's secondborn son in Hebron. *(2 Sam. 3:3.)* Chileab was also called Daniel. *(1 Chr. 3:1.)*

ABIGAIL (2). *2 Sam. 17:25; 1 Chr. 2:16-17.*

Abigail, David's sister, was the daughter of Nahash and was a sister to Zeruiah, Joab's mother. She was the wife of Ithra the Israelite (Jether the Ishmeelite) and the mother of Amasa. *(2 Sam. 17:25; 1 Chr. 2:16-17.) (Note: There is some question regarding Nahash because Zeruiah and Abigail were David's sisters and David's father was Jesse. Maybe Nahash was their mother. The scripture does not say.)* (Charts 8d., 8e.)

ABIHAIL (1). *Num. 3:35.*

Abihail was the father of Zuriel and was of the house of Merari, which Merari was a son of Levi.

ABIHAIL (2). *1 Chr. 2:29.*

Abihail was the wife of Abishur, who was the great-great-grandson of Hezron and Abiah. She bore Abishur two sons: Ahban and Molid.

ABIHAIL (3). *1 Chr. 5:14.*

Abihail, the son of Huri, was a descendant of Gad. (Chart 13b.)

ABIHAIL (4). *2 Chr. 11:18.*

Abihail was the daughter of Eliab, David's brother. She was one of king Rehoboam's 18 wives, and was his father Solomon's cousin. She bore him Jeush, Shamariah and Zaham. (Charts 8d., 8f.)

ABIHAIL (5). *Esth. 2:15; 9:29.*

Abihail was queen Esther's father and Mordecai's uncle.

ABIHU. *Ex. 6:23; 24:1, 9-10; 28:1; 40:12-15; Lev. 1-27; 10:1-2; Num. 3:2, 4; 26: 60-61; 1 Chr. 6:3; 24:1-2.*

Abihu was one of Aaron and Elisheba's sons. His brothers were Nadab, Eleazar and Ithamar. *(Ex. 6:23; 1 Chr. 6:3.)* He was instructed to accompany Moses, Aaron, Nadab and seventy of the elders of Irael unto the mount to worship God. They all saw the God of Israel. *(Ex. 24:1, 9-10.)* The Lord instructed Moses to consecrate and anoint Abihu, along with his father and brothers, to minister in the priest's office. They were to keep a light burning always in the tabernacle of the congregation. *(Ex. 28:1.) (Also see Ex. 27:21.)* He and his father and brothers were washed and anointed and given an everlasting priesthood. *(Ex. 40:12-15.)*

Throughout Leviticus *(chaps. 1-27)*, instructions pertaining to Aaron and his sons were given to Moses who then instructed Aaron and his sons regarding their responsibilities. They were washed and anointed and dressed in the holy garments. *(Lev. 8:6-9, 13.)* Abihu and Nadab offered "strange" fire before the Lord and the Lord slew them with fire. *(Lev. 10:1-2.)* Abihu was Aaron's secondborn son. His brother Nadab was the firstborn. They died when they offered "strange fire" before the Lord. Neither of them had any children. *(Num. 3:2, 4; 26: 60-61; 1 Chr.24:1-2.)* (Chart 7b.)

ABIHUD. *1 Chr. 8:3, 7.*

Abihud was a son of Bela (Belah) who was a son of Benjamin. (Chart 16d.)

ABIJAH (1). *1 Kgs. 14:1-18.*

Abijah was the son of Jeroboam. He became ill and his father sent his mother in disguise to the prophet Ahijah to find out what would become of the child. Ahijah forecast the ruin of Jeroboam's house and told her that Abijah would die when her feet again entered her city. He also told her that Abijah would be the only one of Jeroboam's family who would actually be buried in a grave because he was the only one of Jeroboam's family in whom the Lord God of Israel found some good thing.

ABIJAH (2). *1 Chr. 29:1.* See **Abi.**

ABIJAH (3). *1 Chr. 24:10.*

Abijah was from the sons of Aaron. When David made the divisions of the sons of Aaron, there was one principal household for Eleazar and one taken for Ithamar. Eleazar had 16 sons and there were eight sons of Ithamar. These 24 sons who were chief of the fathers were divided by lot. Abijah drew the eighth lot.

ABIJAH (4). *Neh. 10:7; 12:4, 17.*

Abijah was among the priests who covenanted and sealed the covenant to marry in Israel, honor the Sabbath, pay tithes and keep the commandments. *(Neh. 10:7.)*

He was one of the men (priests and Levites) who left Babylonian captivity and went to Jerusalem with Zerubbabel. Abijah was the father of Zichri who was one of the priests who was a chief of the fathers in the days of Joiakim. *(Neh. 12:4, 17.)*

ABIJAH (5). *2 Chr. 11:20-22.* See **Abijam**.

ABIJAM (Abia, Abijah (5)). *1 Kgs. 14:31; 15:1-8; 1 Chr. 3:10; 2 Chr. 11:20-22; 12:16; 13; 14:1.*

Abijam was the son of Rehoboam and he reigned after Rehoboam died. *(1 Kgs. 14:31.)* He reigned over Judah in the eighteenth year of Jeroboam's reign over the rest of Israel. He reigned for three years. His mother was Maachah, the daughter of Abishalom (Absalom). He walked in wickedness as did his father. There was continual war between him and Jeroboam. He died and was buried in the city of David. His son Asa reigned in his stead. *(1 Kgs. 15:1-8.)*

Abijam was also called **Abia** *(1 Chr. 3:10)* and **Abijah**. Abijah, Attai, Ziza and Shelomith were sons of Maachah (the daughter of Absalom) and Rehoboam. Rehoboam loved Maachah more than his other wives and planned to eventually make Abijah king. *(2 Chr. 11:20-22.)*

Rehoboam died and Abijah reigned in his stead. *(2 Chr. 12:16.)* He began his reign in the 18th year of Jeroboam's reign and reigned three years. *(Note: 2 Chr. 13:2 states that Abijah's mother's name was Michaiah and that she was the daughter of Uriel of Gibeah. That is contrary to scripture verses cited above.)* There was war between Abijah and Jeroboam. Abijah reminded Jeroboam and the children of Israel who followed Jeroboam that the Lord was with the house of David, not with those who worshipped false gods. The Lord struck Jeroboam and he died. The children of Israel fled before Judah, but the Lord delivered them into Judah's hands. Abijah waxed mighty. He had 14 wives and begat 22 sons and 16 daughters. The rest of Abijam's history is recorded in the writings of the prophet Iddo which have been lost. *(2 Chr. 13.)*

Abijah died and his son Asa reigned in his stead. *(2 Chr. 14:1.)* (Chart 1.)

ABIMAEL. *Gen. 10:28.*

Abimael was a son of Joktan, a third great-grandson of Shem and a fourth-great-grandson of Noah. He was a nephew of Peleg, in whose days the earth was divided. (Chart 2b.)

ABIMELECH (1). *Gen. 20:2-18; 21:22-34; 26:1-31.*

Abimelech was the king of Gerar. He took Sarah not knowing she was Abraham's wife. The Lord appeared to him in a dream and told him Sarah was Abraham's wife and to restore her to him. The Lord also told him that Abraham was a prophet and that he would pray for him. Abimelech did as the Lord told him to do. Abraham prayed for him; and God "healed" him and his wife and maidservants and they were then able to bear children. The Lord had closed their wombs because of Sarah. *(Gen. 20:2-18.)* Abimelech and Abraham made a covenant of peace with each other. *(Gen. 21:22-34.)*

Because of a famine in the land, Isaac went to see Abimelech. He and his people were told that Rebekah was Isaac's sister. He eventually sensed that she was his wife and he chastised Isaac for not telling them and placing them in jeopardy had someone chosen to "lightly lien" with her. Isaac was sent away. His servants dug wells and the herdmen of Gerar "strove" with Isaac's servants over the water. Abimelech told Isaac that he knew the Lord was with him. He made a covenant with Isaac that Isaac would do him no harm. *(Gen. 26:1-31.) (Note: Under "Abimelech," the Bible Dictionary suggests that the account of Abraham and Sarah and Isaac and Rebekah might be the same story preserved in two different forms.)*

ABIMELECH (2). *Judg. 8:31; 9:1-54; 2 Sam. 11:21.*

Abimelech was the son of Gideon and a concubine. *(Judg. 8:31.)*

Abimelech was the son of Jerubbaal (Gideon). He solicited help from his mother's brethren and slew his 70 brothers. However, one brother, Jotham, escaped. Abimelech's mother's brethren conspired with others to have Abimelech reign over them rather than Gideon's other 70 sons. They donated 70 pieces of silver with which Abimelech hired "vain and light persons" to follow him. Then, all the men of Shechem and all the house of Millo met and made Abimelech their king. Following three years of his wicked reign, the men of Shechem turned against him. Zebul, the ruler of Shechem and one of Abimelech's officers, sent messengers to Abimelech informing him of Gaal's gathering against him. When Gaal and his brethren were defeated by Abimelech, Zebul banned them from living in Shechem. Abimelech then fought against the city and burned the men and women who had taken refuge in the house of the pagan god Berith. He was finally slain at Thebez when a certain woman dropped a piece of millstone upon his head and broke his skull. He quickly summoned his armorbearer and asked him to put a sword through him so that it wouldn't be said that he was slain by a woman. It was done, and he died. *(Judg. 9:1-54.)*

Abimelech was the son of Jerubbesheth (Gideon). He was slain by a woman who dropped a piece of millstone upon him from the wall in Thebez. *(2 Sam. 11:21.)* (Chart 20.)

ABIMELECH (3). *1 Chr. 18:16*. See **Ahimelech (3)**.

ABIMELECH (4). *Ps. 34:Subtitle*. See **Achish**.

ABIMELECH'S ARMORBEARER. *Judg. 9:54.*

Abimelech's Armorbearer thrust his sword through Abimelech at Abimelech's request so it would not be said that he was slain by a woman.

ABIMELECH'S MOTHER'S BRETHREN. *Judg. 9:1-4.*

Abimelech's Mother's Brethren conspired with others to have Abimelech reign over them rather than Gideon's other 70 sons. They donated 70 pieces of silver with which Abimelech hired "vain and light persons" to follow him and slay his brothers.

ABINADAB (1). *1 Sam. 7:1-2; 2 Sam. 6:3; 1 Chr. 13:7-10.*

Abinadab was the father of Eleazar. He dwelled in Kirjath-jearim. The ark was brought to his house when retrieved from the Philistines and remained there for 20 years. *(1 Sam. 7:1-2.)* When David retrieved the ark from the house of Abinadab, Abinadab's sons Uzzah and Ahio drove the new cart as they took it to the city of David. Uzzah was slain by the Lord when he touched the ark to steady it. *(2 Sam. 6:3; 1 Chr. 13:7-10.)*

ABINADAB (2). *1 Sam. 16:8; 17:13.*

Abinadab, Jesse's second son—one of David's elder brothers—passed before Samuel the prophet, but Samuel said he was not the one the Lord had chosen to be anointed king. *(1 Sam. 16:8.)* He and two of his brothers, Eliab and Shammah, followed Saul to the battle. *(1 Sam. 17:13.)* (Charts 8d., 8e.)

ABINADAB (3) (Also see Ishui). *1 Sam. 31:2-13; 1 Chr. 8:33; 9:39; 10:2, 12.*

Abinadab was one of Saul's sons. He was slain in a battle against the Philistines along with his brothers Jonathan and Malchi-shua. His father died in the same battle. Their bodies were hung on the wall of Beth-shan. Valiant men from Jabesh-gilead, under cover of night, retrieved their bodies and burned them at Jabesh, burying their bones under a tree at Jebesh. His death was foretold by Samuel, who was dead but was "called up" by the witch of En-dor. *(1 Sam. 31:2-13. See 1 Sam. 28:19, also.)*

Abinadab's brothers were Jonathan, Malchi-shua and Esh-baal. *(1 Chr. 8:33; 9:39.)*

The Philistines defeated Israel, wounded Saul and slew Abinadab, Jonathan and Malchi-shua. Fearing what the Philistines would do to him, Saul fell upon his own sword when his armorbearer refused to kill him. The Philistines cut Saul's head off, but faithful followers retrieved his body and those of his sons and carried them back to Jabesh where they buried their bones under an oak in Jabesh. *(1 Chr. 10:2, 12.)* (Chart 16 l.)

ABINADAB (4). *1 Kgs. 4:11.*

Abinadab was the father-in-law of Taphath, Solomon's daughter. His son was one of Solomon's 12 officers who provided victuals for the king and his family one month each year.

ABINADAB'S SON. *1 Kgs. 4:11.*

Abinadab's Son was one of twelve officers over Israel who provided victuals for king Solomon and his family one month each year. His wife was Solomon's daughter Taphath.

ABINOAM. *Judg. 4:6.*

Abinoam was the father of Barak, which Barak helped Deborah deliver Israel from Canaanite bondage.

ABIRAM (1). *Num. 16:1-33; Deut. 11:6; Ps. 106:17.*

Abiram and Dathan, son's of Eliab (son/grandson of Reuben), along with On and Korah, rebelled against Moses. The Lord caused the earth to open up and they, and all their families and goods, were swallowed up. *(Num. 16:1-33; Ps. 106:17.)* Moses reminded the Israelites about what the Lord did to Abiram and his brother Dathan because of their disobedience. *(Deut. 11:6.)* (Chart 5a.)

ABIRAM (2). *1 Kgs. 16:34.*

Abiram was the firstborn of Hiel the Bethelite who rebuilt Jericho in fulfillment of the curse pronounced by Joshua *(Josh. 6:26).* His youngest brother was Segub.

ABISHAG. *1 Kgs. 1:3-4, 15; 2:13-25.*

Abishag was a fair young Shunammite. As David grew old and feeble, his servants suggested that a young virgin be brought to him to wait upon him and to "lie in thy bosom, that my lord the king may get heat." Abishag was selected and brought to the king. She waited upon David, "but the king knew her not." *(1 Kgs. 1:3-4, 15.)*

Following David's death, Adonijah came to Bath-sheba and asked her to petition king Solomon to let him, Adonijah, have Abishag for his wife. Solomon had Adonijah put to death that very day. *(1 Kgs. 2:13-25.)*

ABISHAI. *1 Sam. 26:6-9; 2 Sam. 2:18-24; 10:2-4, 7-14; 16:9-11; 19:21-22; 20:5-7; 23:18; 1 Chr. 2:16; 11:20; 18:12; 19:11-15.*

Abishai, the son of Zeruiah, brother to Joab, went with David down to Saul's camp. He pointed out to David that God had delivered Saul into his hands and offered to kill Saul for him. David refused to have Saul killed. *(1 Sam. 26:6-9.)*

Abishai was with his two brothers, Joab and Asahel, when David's servants engaged in "games" with Abner's men, slaying all twelve of them. Abishai, Joab and Asahel pursued Abner. After Abner slew Asahel, Abishai and Joab continued to pursue Abner. *(2 Sam. 2:18-24.)*

When the children of Ammon insulted the messengers David had sent to console Hanun upon the death of his father Nahash, David sent Joab and the host of mighty men against the children of Ammon and their allies. Joab and his troops went against the Syrians. Joab placed Abishai over the rest of the troops and had them battle against the children of Ammon. The children of Ammon fled from before Abishai when the Syrians fled from before Joab. *(2 Sam. 10:2-4, 7-14; 1 Chr. 19:11-15.)*

Abishai went with David when David fled Jerusalem to escape his son Absalom. When Shimei, a Benjamite of the house of Saul, cursed David and threw stones at him, Abishai wanted to "take off his head." However, David said that if his own son could seek his life, Shimei could certainly curse and throw stones at him, "for the Lord hath bidden him." *(2 Sam. 16:9-11.)* When Shimei came and apologized to David for his earlier behavior and asked for forgiveness, Abishai thought he should be put to death. David rebuked Abishai and forgave Shimei. *(2 Sam. 19:21-22.)*

David sent Amasa (his sister Abigail's son) to assemble all the men of Judah to pursue Sheba who had led all the tribes of Israel away except for Judah and told him to return in three days. When he failed to return, David instructed Abishai to take David's servants and pursue after Sheba. He took Joab and his men, and the Cherethites and the Pelethites, and all the mighty men. *(2 Sam. 20:5-7.)*

Abishai is listed as one of David's 37-plus mighty men. He slew 300 men with his spear. *(2 Sam. 23:18; 1 Chr. 11:20.)* He, Joab and Asahel were the three sons of Zeruiah, David's sister. *(1 Chr. 2:16.)* Abishai slew 18,000 Edomites in the valley of salt. *(1 Chr. 18:12.)* (Charts 8d.; 17.)

ABISHALOM. *1 Kgs. 15:2.* See **Absalom**.

ABISHUA (1). *1 Chr. 6:4-5; Ezra 7:1-5.*

Abishua, the father of Bukki, was the son of Phinehas and was Aaron's great-grandson. *(1 Chr. 6:4-5.)* His descendants and forefathers are listed from Aaron through Ezra with some modification from 1 Chr. 6:4-15. *(Ezra 7:1-5.)* (Chart 7b.)

ABISHUA (2). *1 Chr. 8:4.*

Abishua was a son of Bela who was a son of Benjamin. Other sons of Bela were Addar, Gera, Abihud, Naaman, Ahoah, Gera, Shephuphan and Huram. *(Note: This listing of Bela's sons differs from that in 1 Chr. 7:7.)* (Chart 16d.)

ABISHUR. *1 Chr. 2:28-29.*

Abhisur was one of Shammai's sons. His brother was Nadab. He was the great-great-great-great-grandson of Judah. His wife was Abihail. His sons were Ahban and Molid. (Chart 8c.)

ABITAL. *2 Sam. 3:4; 1 Chr. 3:3.*

Abital was the mother of Shephatiah, David's fifthborn son in Hebron.

ABITUB. *1 Chr. 8:11.*

Abitub was a son of Shaharaim, a descendant of Benjamin. His mother was Hushim. His brother was Elpaal. (Chart 16g.)

ABNER. *1 Sam. 14:50; 17:55-57; 20:25; 26:5-12; 2 Sam. 2:8-32; 3:7-32; 4:1-2, 12; 1 Kgs. 2:5-6, 32; 1 Chr. 26:28; 27:21.*

Abner was the captain of Saul's army. He was the son of Ner, Saul's uncle. Thus, he was Saul's cousin. *(1 Sam. 14:50.)* After David slew Goliath, Saul inquired of Abner as to whose son David was. Abner didn't know but was instructed to find out. Abner brought David to Saul. *(1 Sam. 17:55-57.)*

Abner sat by Saul's side at dinner *(1 Sam. 20:25)* and he was asleep in the trench beside Saul when David took Saul's spear and cruse of water, sparing Saul's life. *(1 Sam. 26:5-12.)*

Upon Saul's death, David was anointed king over Judah. However, Abner took Saul's son Ish-bosheth to Mahanaim and made him king over the rest of Israel. Abner and 12 men from the tribe of Benjamin challenged Joab and 12 of David's followers to a "game." David's followers slew all of Abner's 12 men. When Abner left, Asahel pursued after him. Abner ended up slaying Asahel because Asahel would not give up his pursuit of him. Abner's men and Joab's men gathered to fight, but Abner called for peace and Joab agreed. Through it all, Abner lost 360 men; David lost 19 plus Asahel. *(2 Sam. 2:8-32.)*

Abner was accused by Ish-bosheth of going in unto Rizpah, his father's concubine. Abner became angry with Ish-bosheth because of his accusation and decided to join with David. Joab didn't trust Abner and was angry with Abner for killing his brother Asahel, so he slew him. David mourned Abner's death. He was buried in Hebron. *(2 Sam. 3:7-32.)*

Ish-bosheth was slain by Baanah and Rechab. In retaliation, David had them slain, and the head of Ish-bosheth was buried in the sepulchre of Abner in Hebron. *(2 Sam. 4:1-2, 12.)*

David reminded Solomon that Joab caused the death of Abner and Amasa and charged him to deal appropriately with him. *(1 Kgs. 2:5-6, 32.)*

All that Abner, Samuel the seer, Saul and Joab had won in battle and dedicated to the house of the Lord was under the hand of Shelomith and his brethren. *(1 Chr. 26:28.)*

Jaasiel, son of Abner, was the prince of the tribe of Benjamin when David was king. *(1 Chr. 27:21.)* (Chart 16k.)

ABRAM (Abraham). *Gen. 11:26, 29, 31; Abr. 2:3-5; Gen. 12:1-5, 6-7, 10-12; Abr. 2:14; 2:22-25; Gen. 13-17; 18:20-32; 19:27-29; 20-23; 24:1-9; 25; Ex. 2:24; Neh. 9:7-8; Ezek. 33:24-33; Micah 7.*

Abram was a son of Terah, a seventh great-grandson of Shem and an eighth-great-grandson of Noah. His wife was Sarai (his half-sister—*Gen. 20:12*). His brothers were Nahor and Haran. Terah took Abram, Sarai, Lot and his wife, away from Ur of the Chaldees and traveled to Haran, where they subsequently dwelled. *(Gen. 11:26, 29, 31.) (Note: A little different perspective is given in the Book of Abraham [Abr. 2:3-5] in the Pearl of Great Price. This scripture indicates that Abraham was instructed by the Lord to leave Ur and his kindred and go to a different land. Abram took Sarai, Lot and his wife, and "my father followed after me, unto the land which we denominated Haran." His father had been an idol worshipper and after arriving in Haran, he "turned again unto his idolatry," and remained in Haran while the Lord led Abraham and his group to the land of Canaan.)*

The Lord instructed Abram to leave the land of his kindred and his father's house and go to a land that He would show him. He promised Abram that he would make a great nation of him—that through him all the nations of the earth would be blessed. Abram was 75 years old when he left Haran. *(Note: In Abr. 2:14, we learn that Abraham was 62 years old when he left Haran.)* Again, he took Sarai and Lot with him when he left. They were led to the land of Canaan. When they were in a place called Sichem, unto the plain of Moreh, the Lord told Abram that that land would be given unto him and his seed. Abram built an altar unto the Lord. Because of a famine in the land, Abram moved to Egypt for a time. He told his wife that because she was "a fair woman to look upon" the Egyptians would kill him to get her. Thus, He told her to say she was his sister so that he could live for her sake and it would be well with her. Sarai was taken into Pharaoh's house. The Lord plagued Pharaoh's house because of Sarai. When Pharaoh discovered that Sarai was Abram's wife, he told Abram to take her away, and then sent Abram and Sarai on their way. *(Gen. 12:1-5, 6-7, 10-12.) (Note: We get a slightly different perspective regarding this experience from the Book of Abraham in the Pearl of Great Price. These verses indicate that because Sarai was "a very fair woman to look upon," the Lord instructed Abraham to say that Sarai was his sister so he wouldn't be killed [Abr. 2:22-25].)*

Abram and all who were with him (including Lot) left Egypt and went back to Beth-el, where he had been earlier. He was very rich in cattle, silver and gold. Both he and Lot had many flocks and herds and so the land could not handle all of them. Additionally, strife developed between Abram's herdsmen and those of Lot. Thus, they decided to go separate ways. Abram told Lot to choose which of the land he wanted, that on his left hand or that to the right, and he would take the other. Lot chose all of the plain of Jordan, which included the cities of Sodom and Gomorrah, which was "well watered every where." Abram dwelled in Canaan. After Lot departed, the Lord told Abram to look to the east, north, south and west, "For all the land which thou seest, to thee will I give it, and to thy seed for ever." He also told Abram that his seed would be as the dust of the earth, impossible to number. Abram moved his tent to the plain of Mamre in Hebron and built an altar unto the Lord. *(Gen. 13.)*

A war involving several kings developed during which the kings of Sodom and Gomorrah fell and Lot, who was dwelling in Sodom, was taken captive. A person who escaped told Abram about Lot's capture. Abram armed his trained servants and, together with Mamre, Eshcol and Aner who were confederate with him, they rescued Lot and his goods, and the women and the other people. Upon their return, the king of Sodom went out to meet him and told him to keep the goods but to please return the people to him. Abram declined to keep anything "Save only that which the young men have eaten, and the portion of the men which went with me, Aner, Eshcol, and Mamre; let them take their portion." Following Abram's successful battle to rescue Lot, Melchizedek, king of Salem, brought forth bread and wine. He blessed Abram. Abram gave him tithes of all. *(Gen. 14.)*

The word of the Lord came to Abram in a vision during which he was told that he would have an heir "that shall come forth out of thine own bowels" *(Gen. 15:4)* and that his seed would be so great that he could not number them any more than he could number the stars in the sky. Abram, had no children and he inquired as to how this was to be so. The Lord instructed Abram to take a three-year-old heifer, a three-year-old she goat, a three-year-old ram, a turtledove and a young pigeon. He divided the animals, but not the birds. When the fowls came down upon the carcases, Abram drove them away. A deep sleep fell upon Abram and a great darkness fell upon him. The Lord told Abram, "Know of a surety that thy seed shall be a stranger in a land that is not theirs, and shall serve them; and they shall afflict them four hundred years." *(Gen. 15:13.)* The Lord also told him that He would judge that nation, and afterward Abram's people would come out with great substance. *(Gen. 15:14.)* He further assured him that "in the fourth generation they shall come hither again. In that same day, the Lord made a covenant with Abram, stating "Unto thy seed have I given this land, from the river of Egypt unto the great river, the river Euphrates . . ." *(Gen. 15:18).* Abram was also told that he would go down to his fathers in peace and that he would live to a good old age. *(Gen. 15:15.)*

Sarai was barren so she told Abram to go in unto her handmaid, Hagar, that he might obtain children by her. This Abram did. However, when Hagar conceived, she despised Sarai. Sarai lamented to Abram. He told her to do with Hagar as it pleased her to do. When Sarai dealt "hardly" with her, she fled. An angel of the Lord found her by a fountain of water in the wilderness and instructed her to return to her mistress and to submit herself under her hands. The angel told her that her seed would be multiplied exceedingly, that it shall not be numbered for multitude. The angel instructed her to name her son Ishmael, "because the Lord hath heard thy affliction." She was told that he would be a wild man and his hand would be against every man and every man's hand against him, but that he would dwell in the presence of all his brethren. Abram was 86 years old when Ishmael was born. *(Gen. 16.)*

When Abram was 99 years old the Lord appeared unto him and again told him that he would be a father of many nations. He changed him name from Abram to **Abraham**. *(Gen. 17:5.)* He told Abraham that he would establish his everlasting covenant with him and his seed. He was told once more that the land of Canaan would be given to him and his posterity for an everlasting possession. The law of circumcision was given as a covenant between the Lord and Abraham. Every man child born into Abraham's house, every male that was bought with his money, and every male infant that was eight days old, was to be circumcised. The Lord also gave Sarai a new name: Sarah. He told Abraham that she would be blessed to have a son. Because Sarah was 90 years old, Abraham "fell upon his face, and laughed, and said in his heart, 'Shall a child be born unto him that is an hundred years old? And shall Sarah, that is ninety years old, bear?" He told the Lord that he wished Ishmael would live righteously. The Lord assured Abraham that Sarah would indeed have a son and they should call him Isaac, and that he would establish His covenant with him for an everlastinig covenant, and with his seed after him. He reminded Abraham that he had blessed Ishmael greatly and that he would make him fruitful and would mulitply him exceedingly, "twelve princes shall he beget, and I will make him a great nation," but He reiterated that His covenant would be established with Isaac. Abraham had all the males in his household circumcised. Abraham was 99 years old and Ishmael was 13 years old when they were circumcised. *(Gen. 17.)*

The Lord informed Abraham that he was preparing to destroy Sodom and Gomorrah because their sin was so very grievous. Lot was still living there and

Abraham was concerned about him and asked if there were 50 righteous people there, would the Lord destroy the city. The Lord said if there were 50 righteous people, He would not destroy the city. Abraham querried, "If there were 40?" "If there were 30?" "If there were 20?" "If there were 10?" Each time, the Lord said if there were that many righteous people to be found, He would not destroy the city. Unfortunately, there were not that many righteous people to be found in Sodom. *(Gen. 18:20-32.)*

Abraham got up early in the morning and went to the place where he stood before the Lord and as he looked toward Sodom and Gomorrah, he beheld the smoke of the cities as they burned. But, the Lord remembered Abraham and sent Lot out of the area before destroying the city. *(Gen. 19:27-29.)*

Abraham moved to Gerar. He told Abimelech, king of Gerar, that Sarah was his sister. Abimelech took Sarah but was visited by the Lord in a dream and was informed that Sarah was Abraham's wife and to restore her to him. The Lord said that Abraham was a prophet and that he would pray for him, which Abraham did. When asked why he said Sarah was his sister, he explained his concerns and said she was the daughter of his father but not of his mother. Sarah was his half-sister. *(Gen. 20.)*

Abraham was 100 years old when Isaac was born. He circumcised Isaac when he was eight days old. *(Gen. 21: 2-5.)* At Sarah's request, Abraham cast Hagar and Ishmael out because Ishmael mocked Sarah. This grieved Abraham, but the Lord told him to do as Sarah asked. His seed would be blessed through Isaac, but the Lord said He would also make a nation through Ishmael because he was also Abraham's seed. Abraham gave them bread and water and sent them away. *(Gen. 21:9-14.)* Abraham and Abimelech made a covenant. Abraham stayed in the Philistines' land many days. *(Gen. 21:22-34.)*

The Lord commanded Abraham to sacrifice Isaac. He took two of his young men, Isaac, and some wood and went to where the Lord had told him to go. When Isaac inquired as to where the lamb for the burnt offering was, Abraham told him the Lord would provide. He had the young men wait while he and Isaac went off to build an altar. He bound Isaac and laid him on the altar. As he stretched forth his hand to slay him with a knife, the angel of the Lord stopped him. A ram, caught in the thicket by his horns, was provided for the offering. Abraham called the place, Jehovah-jireh—"In the mount of the Lord it shall be seen." *(Gen. 22:1-14.)* The Lord promised Abraham that because he had not withheld his son from him, he would multiply his seed as the stars of heaven and as the sand upon the sea shore. His seed would possess the gate of his enemies and "in thy seed shall all the nations of the earth be blessed." Abraham returned to the two young men and they all journeyed to Beer-sheba and lived there. *(Gen. 22:15-19.)*

When Sarah died at the age of 127 years, Abraham negotiated with Ephron for the purchase of a burial site for her. He purchased the field of Ephron, which was in Machpelah, which was before Mamre. He buried her in the cave which was in the field. *(Gen. 23.)*

Abraham sent his eldest servant unto the city of Nahor, the land of his countrymen, to find a wife for Isaac as he commanded him that he should not take a wife for Isaac from among the Canaanites. *(Gen. 24:1-9.)*

Abraham took Keturah for a wife. She bore him several children. Abraham gave all he had to Isaac. However, to his children conceived by his concubines, he gave them gifts and sent them away from Isaac. *(Gen. 25:5-6.)* Abraham lived 175 years. He was buried by Isaac and Ishmael in the cave of Machpelah beside his wife Sarah. *(Gen. 25:7-10.)*

God heard the groaning of the children of Israel as they suffered under Egyptian bondage and remembered the covenant He had made with Abraham, Isaac and Jacob. *(Ex. 2:24.)*

The children of Israel praised the Lord, recalling that He had changed Abram's name to Abraham and had given him and his seed the land of the Canaanites, Hittites, Amorites, Perizzites, Jebusites and Girgashites for an inheritance. *(Neh. 9:7-8.)*

The children of Israel thought erroneously that because Abraham, one person, had inherited certain lands from the Lord they, because of their vast numbers, would possess the land promised to them in spite of their rejection of the Lord. However, the Lord said He would lay the land to waste—then they would know that a prophet had been among them. *(Ezek. 33:24-33.)*

Micah lamented the fallen state of Israel, but expressed confidence that in the latter days the Lord will have compassion and will show mercy on Israel, pardoning her iniquity, and "wilt perform the truth to Jacob and the mercy to Abraham," which the Lord had sworn unto their fathers from the days of old. *(Micah 7:20.)* (Charts 1.; 2b-d.; 3a-f.; 5a.; 8a.; 9a.; 10a.; 11a.; 12a.; 13a.; 14a.; 15a.; 16a.; 21.)

ABRAHAM'S ELDEST SERVANT. *Gen. 24:2-66.*

<u>Abraham's Eldest Servant</u> was instructed to go back to the land of Abraham's kindred to find a wife for Isaac as Isaac was not to take a wife from among the Canaanites. He did as instructed and brought Rebekah, Nahor's granddaughter and Abraham's grandniece, back to Isaac to be his wife.

ABSALOM (Abishalom). *2 Sam. 3:3; 13; 14; 15:1-16, 34; 16:15-23; 17; 18:9-18; 1 Kgs. 15:2; 1 Chr. 3:2; 2 Chr. 11:20; Ps. 3. Title.*

<u>Absalom</u> was David's thirdborn son in Hebron. His mother was Maacah *(spelled Maachah in 1 Chr. 3:2)*, the daughter of king Talmai of Geshur. *(2 Sam. 3:3.)* He had a sister named Tamar who was very fair. Amnon, son of David and Ahinoam *(2 Sam. 3:3)*, loved her. Following the counsel of his cousin Jonadab, Amnon devised a plan to get her alone and then used force to lie with her. After forcing her to lie with him, Amnon hated her and had her shut out. She put ashes on her head and tore her garment. Absalom counseled her, "but hold now thy peace, my sister: he is thy brother; regard not this thing." So Tamar remained in her

brother's house. However, in retaliation, Absalom had his servants kill Amnon. Then, Absalom fled and went to his grandfather Talmai, the son of Ammihud, king of Geshur. *(2 Sam. 13.)*

Through Joab's intervention, Absalom was brought back to Jerusalem after a three-year exile. However, David refused to see him. After another two years, Absalom sent for Joab because he wanted him to approach David to get them reunited. Joab refused to respond to Absalom's request to come to him. Following a second request, and a second lack of response from Joab, Absalom had his servants set fire to Joab's fields. Joab then came to Absalom and did as he bid. Thus, Absalom and David were finally reunited. Absalom was a very good-looking man. Absalom had three sons and one daughter, Tamar. *(2 Sam. 14.)*

Absalom turned against his father and gained the support of the people. David took his household, leaving behind 10 concubines to keep house, and fled Jerusalem to escape from Absalom. *(Note: Psalm 103 was written when David fled from Absalom.)* Absalom's supporters included Ahithophel the Gilonite, David's counselor. David sent Hushai the Archite to be a spy in Absalom's household, and told him, "then mayest thou for me defeat the counsel of Ahithophel." *(2 Sam. 15:1-16, 34.)* Absalom and his followers arrived in Jerusalem and Hushai volunteered to be his servant as David had requested. Absalom queried him, but Hushai assured him that just as he served his father, he would now serve him. Ahitophel counseled Absalom to "Go in unto thy father's concubines, which he hath left to keep the house." Absalom took his father's concubines. "And the counsel of Ahithophel, which he counseled in those days, was as if a man had inquired at the oracle of God: so was all the counsel of Ahitophel both with David and with Absalom." *(2 Sam. 16:15-23.)* Absalom rejected Ahitophel's counsel, which was good counsel, and followed Hushai's bad counsel, which is what David hoped would happen. Absalom, himself, led troops against David. He made his cousin Amasa (Abigail's son) captain of the host in lieu of his cousin Joab (Zeruiah's son). *(2 Sam. 17.)*

As Absalom pursued David, his head got caught in an oak tree and he was left hanging there when the mule he was riding went out from under him. A certain man observed the situation and reported it to Joab. Joab, unhappy that the man had not slain Absalom, thrust three darts through Absalom's heart, contrary to David's charge to deal kindly with Absalom for David's sake. Joab's 10 armorbears also gathered around Absalom and slew him. They cast Absalom's body into a big pit and piled a large pile of stones on him. *(2 Sam. 18:9-18.) (Note: 2 Sam. 14:27 states that Absalom had three sons and one daughter, Tamar. 2 Sam. 18:18 quotes Absalom as saying, "I have no son to keep my name in remembrance.")*

Abishalom (Absalom) was the father of Maachah who was Rehoboam's wife. *(1 Kgs. 15:2;2 Chr. 11:20.) (Note: Either the daughter referred to in 2 Sam. 14:27 should have read "Maachah" rather than "Tamar" or Absalom had more than one daughter or, possibly, Tamar and Maachah are one and the same.)* (Charts 8e., 8f.)

ABSALOM'S SERVANTS. *2 Sam. 13:28-29.*

Absalom's Servants were instructed by Absalom to kill Amnon when he gave the word. The servants did as commanded and slew Amnon.

ABSALOM'S SHEEPSHEARERS. *2 Sam. 13:23-28.*

Absalom had **Sheepshearers** in Baal-hazor. Absalom talked David into letting all of his sons, including Amnon, accompany him to Baal-hazor where he planned to have Amnon slain.

ACHAN (Achar). *Josh. 7:1-26; 22:20; 1 Chr. 2:7.*

Achan was the son of Carmi who was the son of Zabdi (Zimri), the son of Zerah of the tribe of Judah. When Israel destroyed Jericho, Achan kept some silver and gold and some garments and hid them in his tent, bringing condemnation upon Israel. The Lord instructed Joshua as to how to find the guilty person and had Joshua destroy Achan and all his household. They were stoned and then burned. *(Josh. 7:1-26.)*

The ten princes in Israel and Phinehas reminded the tribes of Reuben, Gad and the one-half tribe of Manasseh that the Lord's wrath fell upon others as well as upon Achan when Achan sinned and, thus, they feared for their own welfare if these tribes had fallen away as evidenced by their having built an altar. *(Josh. 22:20.)*

Achar (Achan) was "the troubler of Israel, who transgressed in the thing accursed." *(1 Chr. 2:7.)* (Chart 8g.)

ACHBOR (1). *Gen. 36:38.*

Achbor was the father of king Baal-hanan, which Baal-hanan reigned following Saul of Rehoboth's reign over the Edomites.

ACHBOR (2) (Abdon (4)). *2 Kgs. 22:12-20; 2 Chr. 34:20-28; Jer. 26:22; 36:12.*

Achbor was the son of Michaiah. He was commanded by king Josiah to accompany the high priest Hilkiah, Shaphan and others to inquire of the Lord concerning the book of the law which Hilkiah had found in the house of the Lord. They inquired of the prophetess Huldah who prophesied wrath upon the people because of their wickedness but blessings upon king Josiah because of his righteousness—his eyes would not see the evil the Lord promised to bring upon the people. *(2 Kgs. 22:12-20.)* **Abdon** (Achbor), the son of Micah (Michaiah), was commanded by king Josiah to accompany others to inquire of the Lord concerning the book of the law. *(2 Chr. 34:20-28.)*

Achbor was the father of Elnathan who was sent by king Jehoiakim to bring the prophet Urijah back from Egypt so he could be killed for preaching against Jerusalem. *(Jer. 26:22.)* His son Elnathan was one of the princes in Jerusalem at the time of king Jehoiakim when Jeremiah had Baruch read the prophecies he had recorded from Jeremiah's dictation. *(Jer. 36:12.)*

ACHISH (Abimelech (4)). *1 Sam. 21:10-15;27; 28:1-2; 29; 1 Kgs. 2:39-40; Ps. 34: subtitle.*

Achish was the king of Gath. David fled from Nob to Gath because Saul knew he was in Nob and had had all the priests in Nob slain because Ahimelech had helped David. David feared Achish so he feigned madness. *(1 Sam. 21:10-15.)* Achish was the son of Maoch. David lived in Gath among the Philistines for 16 months. *(1 Sam. 27.)*

As the Philistines gathered to fight with Israel, Achish told David that he knew David and his men would "assuredly go out with me to battle." *(1 Sam. 28:1-2.)* David was willing to help Achish, but Achish sent him away when the Philistines told him they didn't trust David's loyalty and did not want him to go with them into battle. *(1 Sam. 29.)* Abimelech (Achish) was he who drove David away. *(Ps. 34: subtitle.)*

When Solomon was king, two of Shimei's servants fled to Achish, son of Maachah (Maoch). Because Shimei left the area and went to Gath to retrieve the servants from Achish, Solomon had him killed. *(1 Kgs. 2:39-40.)*

ACHISH'S SERVANTS. *1 Sam. 21:11.*

Achish's Servants pointed out to king Achish that David was the man people referred to when they sang about someone having slain his ten thousands and Saul his thousands. Thus, David feared the king and feigned madness.

ACHSAH. *Josh. 15:16-17; Judg. 1:12-13; 1 Chr. 2:49.*

Achsah was the daughter of Caleb. Caleb said that anyone who captured the city of Kirjath-sepher could have Achsah for a wife. Othniel, Caleb's nephew, took the city and Achsah became his wife. *(Josh. 15:16; Judg. 1:12-13.)*

Achsah was the daughter of Caleb and his concubine Maachah. *(1 Chr. 2:49.)* *(Note: there is some confusion regarding Caleb, her father. The footnote to Josh. 15:17 indicates it refers to Caleb the son of Jephunneh. However, 1 Chr. 2:49 indicates that Achsah was the daughter of Caleb (Chelubai), son of Hezron. It would appear they are one and the same.)* (Charts 8k., 8n.)

ADAH (1). *Gen. 4:19-21.*

Adah was one of Lamech's wives. She bore two sons: Jabal and Jubal. (Chart 1.)

ADAH (2). *Gen. 36:2-4.*

Adah, the daughter of Elon the Hittite, was one of Esau's wives. She bore Eliphaz. (Charts 3b-c.)

ADAIAH (1). *2 Kgs. 22:1.*

Adaiah of Boscath was the father of Jedidah, grandfather of Josiah, and father-in-law of Amon. (Note: King Amon was the father of Josiah—*2 Kgs. 21:24.*)

ADAIAH (2). *1 Chr. 6:41.* See Iddo (2)

ADAIAH (3). *1 Chr. 8:21.*

Adaiah, a descendant of Benjamin, was a son of Shimhi. (Chart 16h.)

ADAIAH (4). *1 Chr. 9:12-13; Neh. 11:12.*

Adaiah, the son of Jeroham, was one of the priests in Jerusalem whose genealogy was written in the book of the kings of Israel and Judah, who were carried away captive into Babylon because of their transgression. They were "very able men for the work of the service of the house of God."*(1 Chr. 9:12-13.)* He was among those who were elected by lot to dwell in Jerusalem after the children of Israel were allowed to return from Babylonian captivity. He and his brethren, who were chief of the fathers, numbered 242. *(Neh. 11:12.)* (Chart 7g.)

ADAIAH (5). *2 Chr. 23:1-15.*

Adaiah was the father of Maaseiah who was one of the captains of hundreds Jehoiada the priest rallied to make Joash king over Judah and to slay Athaliah.

ADAIAH (6). *Ezra 10:29.*

Adaiah, a son (or descendant) of Bani, was one of the Israelites who took foreign wives, causing Ezra to cry unto the Lord in behalf of Israel, fearing that the Lord would totally destroy the children of Israel due to this latest iniquity. Adaiah and his brothers agreed to put away their foreign wives.

ADAIAH (7). *Ezra 10:39 (18-19, 39, 44).*

Adaiah, a son (or descendant) of Bani, and his brothers were some of the men in Israel who took foreign wives but gave them up when Ezra feared the wrath of God would destroy Israel for this iniquity.

ADAIAH (8). *Neh. 11:5.*

Adaiah, son of Joiarib and father of Hazaiah of the children of Perez, dwelled in Jerusalem after leaving Babylon. (Chart 8b.)

ADALIA. *Esth. 9:8.*

Adalia was one of Haman's ten sons who was slain by the Jews and, at queen Esther's request, was hung on the gallows by king Ahasuerus.

ADAM (Michael (10), "Ancient of Days"). *Gen. 1:26-27; 2:5-7, 16-17, 19; 3:6-8, 17, 20, 21-24; 4:1-2, 25; Moses 5:2-3, 13- 16-17; Gen. 5:3, 5; 1 Chr. 1:1-28; Dan. 7:9-14; D&C 116; 138:38; Dan. 10:13. D & C 27:11; 107:53-4. Dan 12:1.*

Adam was the first man created by God and was created in God's own image. *(Gen. 1:26:27.)* Man was created spiritually before being created mortally. Adam was told he could partake of anything in the Garden of Eden except of the fruit from the tree of the knowledge of good and evil because if he partook of that fruit, he would surely die. Adam gave every animal and creature its name. He is first mentioned by name in Gen. 2:19. *(Gen. 2:5-7, 16-17, 19.)*

Adam and Eve partook of the fruit from the tree of the knowledge of good and evil after the serpent (Lucifer) convinced Eve that she should eat it. Their eyes were then open and they knew they were naked. They made aprons out of fig leaves. He and Eve hid from the Lord God when they heard His voice. The Lord cursed the ground for Adam's sake. Adam called his wife Eve "because she was the mother of all living." The Lord clothed Adam and Eve in coats of skins and had them driven out of the Garden of Eden. *(Gen. 3:6-8, 17, 20, 21-24.)*

Adam begat Cain and Abel. After Cain killed Abel, Adam begat Seth. *(Gen. 4:1-2, 25.). (Note: In Moses 5:2-3, 13, 16-17, in the Pearl of Great Price, we are told that Adam and Eve had other sons and daughters prior to the births of Cain and Abel. These sons and daughters divided two by two in the land and they also had sons and daughters. These sons and daughters of Adam and Eve loved Satan more than they loved God.)* Adam was 130 years old when he begat Seth. He died when he was 930 years old. *(Gen. 5:3, 5.)*

Adam's genealogies and family ties down through Abraham are given. *(1 Chr. 1:1-28.)*

Adam, the **Ancient of days**, was beheld in vision by Daniel. *(Dan. 7:9-14.) (Revelation recorded in the Doctrine and Covenants Sections 116; 138:38, tells us Adam is the Ancient of Days as spoken of by Daniel and was a prince and the patriarch of the human family.)* The Lord spoke to Daniel in a vision and told him that when the prince of the kingdom of Persia withstood Him, **Michael** came to help Him. *(Dan. 10:13.) (Doctrine and Covenants 27:11 and 107:53-54, tell us that Michael (the Archangel) also refers to Adam.)* Daniel prophesied that in the last days, Michael will deliver Israel from their troubles. It will occur during a "time of trouble, such as never was since there was a nation even to that same time." *(Dan. 12:1.)* (Charts 1.; 21.)

ADBEEL. *Gen. 25:13.*

Adbeel was one of Ishmael's twelve sons. He was a grandson of Abraham and Hagar, Sarah's handmaid. (Chart 3e.)

ADDAN (Addon). *Ezra 2:59; Neh. 7:61.*

Addan, Tel-melah, Tel-harsa, Cherub and Immer had decendants go up to Jerusalem who could not declare their lineage so they were regarded as polluted and were put from the priesthood. These included 652 children of Delaiah, Tobiah and Nekoda and the children of the priests: Habaiah, Koz and Barzillai. *(Ezra 2:59; Neh. 7:61.) (Note: Addan's name is spelled **Addon** in Neh. 7:61.)*

ADDAR. *1 Chr. 8:3.*

Addar was a son of Bela who was a son of Benjamin. (Chart 16d.)

ADDON (See Addan)

ADER. *1 Chr. 8:15.*

Ader, a descendant of Benjamin, was a son of Beriah, who was a son of Elpaal, who was a son of Shaharaim and Hushim. (Chart 16g.)

ADIEL (1). *1 Chr. 4:36-38.*

Adiel is listed among the descendants of Shimei who were the "princes in their families." (Chart 6a.)

ADIEL (2) (Azareel (1)). *1 Chr. 9:12; Neh. 11:13.*

Adiel, the father of Maasiai and the son of Jahzerah (a descendant of Immer), was one of the priests in Jerusalem whose genealogy was written in the book of the kings of Israel and Judah, who were carried away captive into Babylon because of their transgression. *(1 Chr. 9:12; Neh. 11:13.) (Note the variations in the genealogy between 1 Chr. 9:12 and Neh. 11:13. In 1 Chr. 9:12, it lists the genealogy as: Maasiai, son of Adiel; son of Jahzerah; son of Meshullam; son of Meshillemith; son of Immer. In Neh. 11:13, the genealogy is given as: Amashai (Maasiai), son of Azareel (1) (Adiel); son of Ahasai (Jahzerah); son of Meshillemoth (Meshillemith); son of Immer. Meshullam is ommitted.)* (Chart 7g.)

ADIEL (3). *1 Chr. 27:25.*

Adiel was the father of Azmavaeth who was assigned by David to be over the king's treasures.

ADIN. *Ezra 2:15; 8:6; Neh. 7:20; 10:16.*

Adin was of the people of Israel. The men of the children of Adin who returned to Jerusalem from Babylon after Cyrus' proclamation to build the temple numbered 454. *(Ezra 2:15.) (The number given in Neh. 7:20 is 655.)* Adin's descendant Ebed, the son of Jonathan, was the chief of his fathers when Ezra led many exiled Israelites out of Babylon back to Jerusalem. *(Ezra 8:6.)* He was among those chief of the people who covenanted to marry in Israel, honor the Sabbath, pay tithes and keep the commandments. *(Neh. 10:16.)*

ADINA. *1 Chr. 11:42.*

Adina, the son of Shiza the Reubenite, was a captain of the Reubenites and is listed among the mighty men of David and was one of the valiant men of the armies. (Chart 17.)

ADINO (Jashobeam (1)). *2 Sam. 23:8; 1 Chr. 11:11.*

Adino the Eznite (also called the Tachmonite) is listed among David's mighty men. He was chief among the captains. He slew 800 at one time *(300 according to 1 Chr. 11:11 which also refers to him as Jashobeam, a Hachmonite)*. (Chart 17.)

ADLAI. *1 Chr. 27:29.*

Adlai was the father of Shaphat who was the officer assigned by king David to be over the herds that were in the valleys.

ADMATHA. *Esth. 1:14-15.*

Admatha was one of the seven princes of Persia and Media with king Ahasuerus when queen Vashti refused to come at his command. They asked what should be done to Vashti because of her refusal to obey Ahasuerus' command.

ADNA (1). *Ezra 10:30.*

Adna was a son of Pahath-moab. He and his brothers were among the Israelites who took foreign wives but separated themselves from them at Ezra's request as he feared the Lord would destroy all of Israel due to this latest iniquity.

ADNA (2). *Neh. 12:15.*

Adna, son of Harim, was one of the priests who was a chief of the fathers in the days of Joiakim.

ADNAH (1). *1 Chr. 12:20-21.*

Adnah was from the tribe of Manasseh and was a mighty man of valor, one of the captains in the host. He helped David when David went to Ziklag.

ADNAH (2). *2 Chr. 17:14.*

Adnah, of the house of Judah, was chief of the captains of thousands when Jehoshaphat was king over Judah. His men numbered 300,000.

ADONI-BEZEK. *Judg. 1:5-7.*

Adoni-bezek was the king of Bezek. When the tribes of Judah and Simeon went to fight the Canaanites, the Lord delivered the Canaanites and the Perizzites into Judah's hands. They slew 10,000 men in Bezek but Adoni-bezek fled. When they caught him, "they cut off his thumbs and his great toes." They took him to Jerusalem and he died there.

ADONIJAH (1). *2 Sam. 3:4; 1 Kgs. 1:5-53; 2:13-25; 1 Chr. 3:2.*

Adonijah, son of David and Haggith, was David's fourthborn son in Hebron. *(2 Sam. 3:4; 1 Chr. 3:2.)* As David became old and stricken in years, Adonijah exalted himself, saying he would be king. He called certain key people together, including Joab and Abiathar the priest, but he did not include Zadok the priest, Benaiah, Nathan the prophet, Shimei, nor Rei, nor the mighty men which belonged to David. Nathan reported the situation to Bath-sheba and suggested a plan whereby she and he would get word to David. When David learned what Adonijah had done, he immediately had Solomon appointed king in his stead. When Adonijah heard that David had made Solomon king, he went "and caught hold on the horns of the altar," saying "Let king Solomon swear unto me to day that he will not slay his servant with the sword." When Solomon heard this, he sent for Adonijah and said that if he proved himself to be a worthy man, not a hair of him would fall to the earth, but that if wickedness were found in him, he would die. Adonijah bowed himself before Solomon and Solomon told him to go home. *(1 Kgs. 1:5-53.)*

After David's death, Adonijah asked Bath-sheba, Solomon's mother, to ask Solomon to let him have Abishag, the fair young Shunammite who waited upon David in his last months or years, for a wife. Instead, Solomon had Adonijah put to death that very day by the hand of Benaiah. *(1 Kgs. 2:13-25.)* (Chart 8e.)

ADONIJAH (2). *2 Chr. 17:8-9.*

Adonijah, a Levite, along with other Levites and Elishama and Jehoram, the priests, was sent by king Jehoshaphat to journey with the princes of Judah throughout the cities of Judah to instruct the people out of the book of the law of the Lord.

ADONIJAH (3). *Neh. 10:16 (1, 16, 28-29).*

Adonijah was among those chief of the people who covenanted to marry in Israel, honor the Sabbath, pay tithes and keep the commandments.

ADONIKAM. *Ezra 2:1-2, 13; 8:13; Neh. 7:18.*

Adonikam was of the people of Israel. The men of the children of Adonikam who returned to Jerusalem from Babylon with Zerubbabel after Cyrus' proclamation to build the temple numbered 666. *(Ezra 2:1-2, 13; Neh. 7:18). (The number given in Neh. 7:18 is 667.)* Adonikam's "last sons" were Eliphelet, Jeiel and Shemaiah. They had 60 male members of their family with them when they were led out of exil and went back to Jerusalem with Ezra. *(Ezra 8:13.)*

ADONIRAM. *1 Kgs. 4:6.* See **Adoram**.

ADONI-ZEDEK. *Josh. 10:1-27.*

Adoni-zedek, one of the five kings of the Amorites, was king of Jerusalem. He called the other kings together and they united in battle against the city of Gibeon which had made peace with the Israelites. The men of Gibeon asked Joshua for help. Adoni-zedek's people were destroyed, partly by the sword but mostly by hailstones the Lord poured down upon them. He hid in a cave with the other four kings. Joshua had a stone rolled in front of the cave until the rest of the Amorites were destroyed and then he had the kings brought out to him. They were all slain and hung on a tree. Their bodies were then cast into the cave wherein they had hidden and the mouth of the cave was sealed with great stones.

ADORAM (Adoniram, Hadoram). *2 Sam. 20:24; 1 Kgs. 4:6; 5:14; 12:18; 2 Chr. 10:18.*

Adoram was over the tribute when David regained the throne from Absalom and the insurrection by Sheba was quelled. *(2 Sam. 20:24.)* **Adoniram**, the son of Abda, was over the tribute (levy) in Solomon's court. *(1 Kgs. 4:6; 5:14.) (Note: The Bible Dictionary states that Adoniram is sometimes abbreviated into Adoram and sometimes referred to as Hadoram.)* Adoram was sent by king Rehoboam, Solomon's son, to collect the tribute from the people. Rehoboam had told Israel that he was going to make their burdens heavy so when Adoram went to them, they stoned him to death. *(1 Kgs. 12:18; 2 Chr. 10:18.) (His name is given as **Hadoram** in 2 Chr. 10:18.)*

ADRAMMELECH (1) AND ANAMMELECH. *2 Kgs. 17:31.*

Adrammelech and Anammelech were the false gods to whom the Sepharvites burned their children in fire.

ADRAMMELECH (2). *2 Kgs. 19:37; 2 Chr. 32:21; Isa. 37:38.*

Adrammelech and Sharezer, two sons of Sennacherib, king of Assyria, killed their father as he was worshipping in the house of the false god Nisroch following his unsuccessful attempt to capture Judah. They escaped into the land of Armenia. *(2 Kgs. 19:37; Isa. 37:38.)*

When Sennacherib returned in shame after being defeated in his attempt to take Judah from king Hezekiah, two of his sons slew him. *(2 Chr. 32:21.)*

ADRIEL. *1 Sam. 18:19; 2 Sam. 21:8.*

Adriel the Meholathite was given Saul's daughter Merab for a wife. She had been promised to David. *(1 Sam. 18:19.)* Adriel was the son of Barzillai. His and Merab's five sons—along with Saul's two sons by Rizpah, Armoni and Mephibosheth—were given to the Gibeonites by David to atone for Saul's having slain the Gibeonites contrary to an oath Israel had made with them. *(2 Sam. 21:8.).* *(2 Sam. 21:8 says Michal rather than Merab, which would appear to be an error.)*

AGAG (Agagite). *Num. 24:7; 1 Sam. 15:8, 33; Esth. 3:1, 10; 8:5; 9:24.*

Agag was an Amalekite king. Balaam prophesied that the kingdom of God would ultimately be higher than the kingdom of Agag. *(Num. 24:7.)* Saul saved him alive when he was supposed to kill all of the Amalekites. Samuel had Saul bring Agag to him and Samuel "hewed Agag in pieces before the Lord in Gilgal." *(1 Sam. 15:8, 33.)*

One of Agag's descendants was Hammedath. His son Haman sought to kill Mordecai, cousin/father of queen Esther, as well as all of the other Jews in the province. *(Esth. 3:1, 10; 8:5; 9:24.)*

AGEE. *2 Sam. 23:11.*

Agee the Hararite was the father of Shammah who was one of David's mighty men.

AGUR. *Prov. 30.*

Agur the son of Jakeh prophesied that every word of God is pure. He counseled, "Add thou not unto his words, lest he reprove thee, and thou be found a liar." He requested that he be given neither poverty nor riches. He prophesied of a generation that "curseth their father, and doth not bless their mother;" who are "pure in their own eyes, and yet is not washed from their filthiness;" "whose teeth are as swords, and their jaw teeth as knives, to devour the poor from off the earth, and the needy from among men."

AHAB (1). *1 Kgs. 16:28-33; 17:1; 18; 20; 21; 22; 2 Kgs. 10:1-8, 11-14; 8:16-18, 26; 2 Chr. 18.*

Ahab was the son of Omri and reigned as king of Israel upon Omri's death. His reign began in the 38th year of the reign of Asa, king of Judah. He reigned over Israel in Samaria for 22 years. He "did evil in the sight of the Lord above all that were before him." He married Jezebel, the daughter of Ethbaal, king of the Zidonians. Ahab worshipped Baal and served him. He made an altar for Baal in the house of Baal which he built in Samaria. *(1 Kgs. 16:28-33.)* Because of Ahab's terrible wickedness, Elijah the Tishbite sealed the heavens up so there would be no rain. *(1 Kgs. 17:1.)*

In the third year of the drought, Ahab and Obadiah, the governor of Ahab's house, went different directions to find grass wherewith to save some of the animals. Obadiah met with Elijah who sent him to tell Ahab he wanted to meet with him. Elijah challenged Ahab and the prophets of Baal to a contest. The priests of Baal took a bullock and offered it as a sacrifice and called upon their god to send fire down from heaven to consume it. They failed. Elijah then called upon his God and the Lord sent down fire from heaven and it consumed the wood, the stone altar, the burnt sacrifice and even lapped up the water that had been poured in the trenches around the altar. Elijah had the prophets of Baal taken to the brook Kishon where he slew them. Elijah then sent word to Ahab to come down from Mount

Carmel because the rain was going to come and he'd have to hurry before he couldn't get down. Elijah ran before Ahab to the entrance of Jezreel. *(1 Kgs. 18.)*

Ben-hadad and the Syrians made war against Israel. They were defeated twice. However, Ahab, contrary to the will of the Lord, let Ben-hadad go free. Thus, a man who was of the sons of the prophets informed Ahab that "thy life shall go for his life, and thy people for his people." *(1 Kgs. 20.)*

Naboth the Jezreelite had a vineyard which king Ahab desired. Naboth refused to give the inheritance of his family to king Ahab. When Ahab mourned because he could not have the vineyard, queen Jezebel told Ahab she would deliver the vineyard to him. She had the elders and nobles of the city set Naboth on high among the people and then had two men bear false witness against him claiming that he had blasphemed God and the king. As a result, Naboth was taken out of the city and stoned to death. Ahab then took possession of the vineyard. The Lord sent Elijah to rebuke Ahab and to prophesy what would become of him and Jezebel because of what they had done. Elijah told Ahab that his house would become like the house of Jeroboam and the house of Baasha. "In the place where dogs licked the blood of Naboth," he said, "shall dogs lick thy blood, even thine." Elijah also said, "The dogs shall eat Jezebel by the wall of Jezreel." When Ahab humbled himself, Elijah was told by the Lord that He would bring the evil (the detruction of his house) to pass in Ahab's son's days. *(1 Kgs. 21.)*

Ahab invited Jehoshaphat, king of Judah, to join him in battle against the Syrians. Ahab received advice from 400 of his prophets who advised him the Lord would deliver Syria into his hands. Jehosphaphat asked if they could not also get input from a prophet of the Lord. Micaiah, the Lord's prophet, foretold of the defeat and death of Ahab. Ahab had Micaiah cast into prison and followed the advice of the false prophets. He was slain by a certain man who drew a bow and smote the king. He died and was buried in Samaria. Dogs licked up his blood as it was washed out of his chariot. His son Ahaziah reigned in his stead. *(1 Kgs. 22; 2 Chr. 18.)*

Ahab was the father of Joram (Jehoram) king of Israel, and of Athaliah, wife of Joram (Jehoram) king of Judah. *(2 Kgs. 8:16-18, 26.)*

Ahab had 70 sons. Jehu invited the rulers of Jezreel, the elders and those who had brought up Ahab's children to choose one of those sons to be king. But they were afraid to do so. They said they would serve Jehu. Thus, he told them to bring him the heads of all Ahab's sons. They sent them to him in Jezreel in baskets. He had them placed in two heaps at the entering in of the gate. Jehu slew all that remained of the house of Ahab in Jezreel, including his kinsfolks and his priests. Then he went to Samaria and enroute slew all 42 of the men who were the brethren of Ahaziah. When he got to Samaria, he slew all who remained who were related to Ahab. *(2 Kgs. 10:1-8, 11-14.)* (Chart 1.)

AHAB (2). *Jer. 29:21.*

Ahab was the son of Kolaiah. Because he prophesied a lie, Ahab was cursed by the Lord who said He would deliver him, along with Zedekiah the son of Maaseiah, into the hand of Nebuchadrezzar (Nebuchadnezzar) who would slay them both. *(Note: Zedekiah was the son of Josiah. Verse 25 indicates that Zephaniah was the son of Maaseiah.)*

AHAB'S (1) DAUGHTER (See Athaliah).

AHAB'S OFFICER. *1 Kgs. 22:9; 2 Chr. 18:8.*

Ahab's OFFICER was sent by Ahab to get the prophet Micaiah so he could advise him and Jehoshaphat regarding their intention to go to battle against Syria.

AHAB'S PROPHETS. *1 Kgs. 22:6.*

Ahab's Prophets (approx. 400) foretold that Ahab and Jehoshaphat would be victorious if they went to battle against the Syrians. The Lord's prophet, Micaiah, said otherwise. Ahab followed the advice of the 400 false prophets and was slain.

AHARAH. *1 Chr. 8:1.*

Aharah was the thirdborn son of Benjamin. His brothers were Bela, the firstborn; Ashbel, the secondborn; Nohar, the fourthborn; and Rapha, the fifth. *(Note: Benjamin's sons are listed with different names in other scripture verses.)* (Chart 16d.)

AHARHEL. *1 Chr. 4:8.*

Aharhel was the son of Harum.

AHASAI. *Neh. 11.13.*

Ahasai was the son of Meshellimoth the son of Immer, and was the father of Azareel. (Chart 7e.)

AHASBAI. *2 Sam. 23:34.*

Ahasbai was the father of Eliphelet who was one of David's mighty men.

AHASUERUS (1). *Ezra 4:6; Esth. 1-10.*

Ahasuerus was king over Persia prior to Darius. During his reign, the Samaritans wrote him letters of accusation against the children of Israel as the Samaritans sought to stop construction of the temple. *(Ezra 4:6.) (Note: According to the Bible Dictionary, there are three people named Ahasuerus: "one Median and two Persian kings. (1) Dan. 9:1, father of "Darius the Mede." (2) Ezra 4:6; probably the same as (3) Esth. 1:1, etc., where Ahasuerus is certainly to be identified with Xerxes.")* Ahasuerus reigned over 127 provinces from India unto Ethiopia. His wife Vashti refused to come at his command so he deposed her as queen. *(Esth. 1.)*

Ahasuerus sought a new queen. Mordecai, a Jew, brought his cousin (and adopted daughter) Esther to the king's palace and placed her in the custody of Hegai, keeper of the women. Ahasuerus learned of a plot against his life through Esther who had been informed by Mordecai. The perpetrators were discovered and hanged. *(Esth. 2.)*

Ahasuerus promoted Haman the son of Hammedatha to a high station. Haman presented a proposal to Ahasuerus whereby all the Jews in the kingdom could be destroyed. *(Esth. 3.)*

There was a law that anyone who entered the inner court without having been called by the king was to be put to death unless the king held out the golden sceptre that he or she may live. *(Esth. 4.)* When Esther went in, unbidden, to see Ahasuerus, he held out the golden sceptre to her. He accepted Esther's invitation for him and Haman to come to a banquet that she had prepared. *(Esth. 5.)*

When Ahasuerus could not sleep, he read in the book of records and chronicles and discovered that Mordecai had been the person who reported the attempt on his life. He desired to honor him. He asked Haman what he should do to honor a man that the king wanted to honor. Thinking it was he whom the king desired to honor, Haman offered some generous suggestions. Ahasuerus instructed him to so honor Mordecai. *(Esth. 6.)*

Ahazuerus and Haman went to Esther's banquet. When Ahazuerus learned of Haman's evil plot to kill Mordecai and destroy the Jews, he ordered Haman to be hung. *(Esth. 7.)* Ahasuerus placed Mordecai over the house of Haman and gave Mordecai the ring which he had taken from Haman. He then reversed the decree that called for the destruction of the Jews. *(Esth. 8.)* The king not only reversed the decree that called for the destruction of the Jews, but turned it against Haman and decreed that he and his sons should be hanged on the gallows. He then sent words of peace and truth throughout the 127 provinces of the kingdom. *(Esth. 9.).* Ahasuerus placed a tribute upon the people and advanced Mordecai to the position of second in command, next only to himself. *(Esth. 10.)*

AHASUERUS (2). *Dan. 9:1.*

Ahasuerus was the father of Darius the Mede who was king over the realm of the Chaldeans after Belshazzar, Nebuchadnezzar's son.

AHAZ (1). *2 Kgs. 15:38; 16:1-20 ; 20:11; 23:12; 1 Chr. 3:12-13; 2 Chr. 27:9; 28; Isa. 1:1-31; 7; Hosea 1:1, 6, 9; Micah 1:1.*

Ahaz was the son of Jotham. He reigned over Judah in his father's stead upon Jotham's death. *(2 Kgs. 15:38; 2 Chr. 27:9.)* He began his reign over Judah at the age of 20 years. This was in the 17th year of Pekah's reign over Israel. He reigned 16 years in Jerusalem. He did not walk uprightly before the Lord but offered his son in heathen sacrifice. King Rezin of Syria and Pekah, king of Israel, warred against Ahaz. They did not defeat him, but Rezin recovered several cities for the Syrians. Ahaz petitioned Tiglath-pileser, king of Assryria, for assistance and gave him silver and gold, etc. Tiglath-pileser assisted Ahaz and slew Rezin. Ahaz had Urijah the priest build a new altar. Ahaz destroyed the brasen sea and changed the order of sacrifice in the temple. He died and was buried in the city of David. His son Hezekiah *(1 Chr. 3:13)* reigned in his stead. *(2 Kgs. 16:1-20; 2 Chr. 28.)* Oded, a prophet of the Lord, had instructed the children of Israel to let the children of Judah go and they were freed by prophetic direction. Nevertheless, the Philistines and the Assyrians continued to afflict Judah. *(2 Chr. 28.)*

Ahaz had built a sundial. When Isaiah cried unto the Lord, he brought the shadow backward on the sundial 10 degrees as a sign to Hezekiah that the Lord would heal him. *(2 Kgs. 20:11.)*

The altars that were on the top of the upper chamber of Ahaz's home were destroyed by Josiah king of Judah. *(2 Kgs. 23:12.)*

Isaiah saw in vision Judah and Jerusalem during the days of Ahaz, Uzziah, Jotham and Hezekiah, kings of Judah. Israel was in an apostate, rebellious and corrupt state. A very small remnant remained faithful. The Lord rejected their sacrifices and feasts. Vain oblations mean nothing to the Lord. They were called upon to repent. Isaiah prophesied that Zion would be redeemed in the day of restoration. *(Isa. 1:1-31.)*

Ahaz was the son of Jotham, who was the son of Uzziah. In the days of Ahaz, the Lord instructed Isaiah to take his son Shear-jashub and deliver a message to Ahaz. He warned him that Rezin king of Syria, Pekah king of Ephraim and the son of Remaliah were planning to wage war against Judah and planned to make the son of Tabeal king, but not to fear. He prophesied that within 65 years Ephriam would be broken and no longer be a people. As a sign, the Lord revealed that a virgin would conceive and bear a son. She would call his name Immanuel. *(Isa. 7.)*

In the days of Uzziah, Jotham, Ahaz and Hezekiah, kings of Judah, the Lord instructed Hosea to marry a wife from among those who committed whoredoms. He and his family were to be a sign unto Israel. The names of his children meant: "Not having obtained mercy," and "Not my people." While the Lord said He would no longer have mercy for the house of Israel, He said He would have mercy upon the house of Judah. *(Hosea 1:1, 6, 9.)*

Micah prophesied in the days of Ahaz, in the days of his father Jotham, and in the days of Hezekiah regarding the downfall of Samaria and Jerusalem. *(Micah 1:1.)* (Chart 1.)

AHAZ (2). *1 Chr. 8:35-36; 9:41-42.*

Ahaz, of the tribe of Benjamin, was one of the sons of Micah, was a great-grandson of Jonathan, and was a great-great-grandson of Saul. His brothers were Pithon, Melech and Tarea. He begat Jehoadah (Jarah) who begat Alemeth, Azmaveth and Zimri. *(1 Chr. 8:35-36; 9:41-42.)* (Chart 16 l.)

AHAZIAH (1). *1 Kgs. 22:40, 49, 51-53; 2 Kgs. 1:1-17; 3:4-5; 2 Chr. 20:35-37.*

Ahaziah was the son of king Ahab of Israel. He reigned in Ahab's stead. He began his reign in the 17th year of Jehoshaphat's reign over Judah. He asked Jehoshaphat to let his men go on the ships with Jehoshaphat's men, but Jehoshaphat said they could not. He reigned two years, doing evil, walking in the ways of his father and mother and Jeroboam. He served Baal and worshipped him. *(1 Kgs. 22:40, 49, 51-53.)*

Ahaziah fell through a lattice and became sick. He sent messengers to Baal-zebub to inquire as to whether or not he would get better. The messengers were intercepted by the prophet Elijah who told them to remind Ahaziah that the reason they were sent to Baal-zebub was that there was no God in Israel to whom they could turn, and that Ahaziah would not get better but would die. Ahaziah sent three different groups of 50 along with their respective captains of 50 to Elijah. The first two groups were destroyed when Elijah called down fire from heaven and it consumed them. The third group pleaded that he would be mindful of them. An angel instructed Elijah to return with them to Ahaziah where he personally reminded him that there was no God in Israel and that he would not get better. Ahaziah died as Elijah said. "And Jehoram (Ahaziah's brother) reigned in his stead in the second year of Jehoram the son of Jehoshaphat king of Judah; because he had no son." *(2 Kgs. 1:1-17.)*

When Ahaziah became king upon Ahab's death, Mesha king of Moab rebelled against him. *(2 Kgs. 3:4-5.)*

Ahaziah and Jehoshaphat, near the end of Jehoshaphat's reign over Judah, joined together to make ships to go to Tarshish. Because of Ahaziah's wickedness, Eliezer prophesied against Jehoshaphat and said their work would be broken. The ships were broken and were unable to go to Tarshish. *(2 Chr. 20:35-37.)*

AHAZIAH (2) (Jehoahaz, Azariah). *2 Kgs. 8:24-29; 9:23-29; 10:12-14; 11:2; 12:18; 1 Chr. 3:10-11; 2 Chr. 21:17; 22:1-12.*

Ahaziah was the son of Jehoram (Joram) and Athaliah. He was 22 years old when he began to reign over Judah following the death of his father which was in the 12th year of the reign of his uncle Jehoram (Joram) over Judah. He reigned one year in Jerusalem. He walked in wickedness as did the rest of the house of Ahab. Ahaziah joined Joram (Jehoram) in battle against Hazael, king of Syria. When Joram was wounded and went to Jezreel to recover, Ahaziah went down to Jezreel to see him. *(2 Kgs. 8:24-29.)*

Ahaziah was warned by Joram (Jehoram) as Joram fled from Jehu that there was treachery afoot. Ahaziah also fled, but Jehu's men pursued him and slew him in his chariot. Ahaziah's servants took him to Jerusalem and buried him in the sepulchre with his fathers in the city of David. Ahaziah began his reign over Judah in the eleventh year of Joram's reign over Israel. *(2 Kgs. 9:23-29.) (Note: 2 Kgs. 8:25 states that Ahaziah began his reign over Judah in the 12th year of Joram's reign over Israel.)*

Ahaziah's brethren met Jehu at the shearing house in Samaria and were captured and slain at the command of Jehu. *(2 Kgs. 10:12-14.)*

Ahaziah's son was Joash. Joash was saved from his grandmother's destruction when his aunt, Jehosheba, took Joash and his nurse and hid them in the house of the Lord. After Ahaziah died and his posterity (except Joash) was slain, Ahaziah's mother, Joash's grandmother Athaliah, reigned as queen. *(2 Kgs. 11:2.)* After Joash (Jehoash) became king, he took all the hallowed things and the things that were in the king's house and gave them to Hazael, king of Syria, to keep him from attacking Jerusalem. *(2 Kgs. 12:18.)*

Ahaziah was the father of Joash, the son of Joram (Jehoram), and the grandson of Jehosophat. *(1 Chr. 3:10-11.)*

Jehoahaz (Ahaziah), Jehoram's youngest son, was the only one left after the Philistines and Arabians came against the house of Jehoram and Judah because of Jehoram's wickedness, taking all of the substance of the king's household, his sons and his wives. *(2 Chr. 21:17.)*

Ahaziah, Jehoram's youngest son, became king after his father's death. The Arabians had slain all his elder brothers. He was 42 years old when he began to reign over Judah. *(Note: 2 Kgs. 8:26 states he was 22 years old when he began to reign as king.)* His mother was Athaliah, the daughter (granddaughter) of Omri. He reigned for just one year, walking in wickedness. He joined with Jehoram (Joram), king of Israel, in battle against Hazael, king of Syria. When Jehoram was wounded in battle and went to Jezreel to recover, **Azariah** (Ahaziah) went to visit him. However, he was slain by Jehu, the son of Nimshi, "whom the Lord had anointed to cut off the house of Ahab." His mother, learning of his death, sought to destroy all of the royal seed and claimed the throne for herself. However, Jehoshabeath (Jehosheba), wife of Jehoiada the priest and sister to Ahaziah, rescued Ahaziah's son Joash and the child's nurse and hid them from Athaliah in the house of God for six years. *(2 Chr. 22:1-12.)* (Chart 1.)

AHAZIAH'S (1) MESSENGERS. *2 Kgs. 1:1-8.*

Ahaziah's Messengers were sent to inquire of Baal-zebub whether or not Ahaziah would recover from his disease. Enroute, they met the prophet Elijah. Elijah told them to tell Ahaziah that he would not come down from his bed but that he would die.

AHBAN. *1 Chr. 2:29.*

Ahban, a five-times-great-grandson of Judah and brother of Molid, was the son of Abishur and Abihail. (Chart 8c.)

AHER. *1 Chr. 7:12.*

Aher, a descendant of Benjamin, was the father of Hushim. (Chart 16c.)

AHI (1) . *1 Chr. 5:15.*

Ahi, a descendant of Gad and chief of the house of his fathers, was the son of Abdiel and a grandson of Guni. (Chart 13b.)

AHI (2). *1 Chr. 7:34.*

Ahi, head of his father's house, was a son of Shamer (Shomer) and a great-great-grandson of Asher. His brothers were Rohgah, Jehubbah and Aram. (Chart 14a.)

AHIAH (1). *1 Sam. 14:3.*

Ahiah was the son of Ahitub (Ichabod's brother), grandson of Phinehas and great-grandson of Eli the priest.

AHIAH (2). *1 Kgs. 4:3.*

Ahiah and Elihoreph, sons of Shisha, were scribes in Solomon's court.

AHIAH (3). *1 Chr. 8:7.* See **Ahoah.**

AHIAM. *2 Sam. 23:33; 1 Chr. 11:35.*

Ahiam, the son of Sharar the Hararite, was one of David's mighty men and one of the valiant men of the armies. (Chart 17.)

AHIAN. *1 Chr. 7:19.*

Ahian was a son of Shemida and a grandson of Gilead, great-grandson of Machir, and great-great-grandson of Manasseh. His brothers were Shechem, Likhi and Aniam. (Chart 15a.)

AHIEZER (1). *Num. 1:12, 38-39; 2:25-31; 7:66.*

Ahiezer was the son of Ammishaddai. They were of the tribe of Dan. He was appointed by the Lord to be the one to stand at the head of all of the tribe of Dan as Moses organized Israel in preparation for war. The males in the tribe of Dan who were 20 years old or older who could go to war numbered 62,700. *(Num. 1:12, 38-39.)* Ahiezer was instructed to have the tribe of Dan pitch their tents on the north side of the encampment. Next to them was the tribe of Asher and the tribe of Naphtali. Combined, those numbered with the camp of Dan totaled 157,600 men. *(Num. 2:25-31.)*

When the altar of the tabernacle was anointed and dedicated, Ahiezer made his offering on the tenth day. *(Num. 7:66.)*

AHIEZER (2). *1 Chr. 12:3.*

Ahiezer was one of David's mighty men who came to him to Ziklag to defend him against Saul and to turn the kingdom of Saul to David. He was the chief among those named. He was a son of Shemaah, the Gibeathite. His brother was Joash.

AHIHUD (1). *Num. 34:27.*

Ahihud, prince of the tribe of Asher and son of Shelomi, was assigned to divide the land of their inheritance among the tribe of Asher. (Chart 14b.)

AHIHUD (2). *1 Chr. 8:7.*

Ahihud was a son of Ehud who was a descendant of Benjamin. (Chart 16d.)

AHIJAH (1). *1 Kgs. 11:29-39; 12:15; 14:2-16; 15:29; 2 Chr. 9:29; 10:15.*

Ahijah the Shilonite was the prophet the Lord sent to Jeroboam to inform him that the Lord would rend the kingdom of Israel from Solomon and give ten tribes of Israel to him (Jeroboam). This would occur after Solomon's death during the reign of Solomon's son. *(1 Kgs. 11:29-39.)* Ahijah prophesied unto Jeroboam and the king "hearkened not unto the people" and, thus, the cause of the Lord was facilitated. *(1 Kgs. 12:15.)*

When Jeroboam's son Abijah became ill, Jeroboam sent his wife in disguise to see Ahijah to ascertain the fate of their son. Ahijah foretold the ruin of Jeroboam's house, the death of Abijah which would occur when her feet entered into the city, and the scattering of Israel because of their idolatry. *(1 Kgs. 14:2-16.) (The record of the fulfillment of the prophecy which Ahijah spoke against Jeroboam is found in 1 Kgs. 15:29.)*

The prophecies of Ahijah and Iddo against Jeroboam the son of Nebat also contain prophecies pertaining to Solomon. *(2 Chr. 9:29.)*

The prophecy Ahijah gave to Jeroboam began to be fulfilled when the kingdom was divided due to king Rehoboam's promise to increase the yoke Solomon had placed on Israel rather than reduce it as Jeroboam and all Israel had requested. *(2 Chr. 10:15.) (Also see Ahimelech (1). The Bible Dictionary indicates that Ahijah and Ahimelech may be one and the same.)*

AHIJAH (2). *1 Kgs. 15:27.*

Ahijah, father of Baasha king of Israel, was of the house of Issachar. (Chart 9.)

AHIJAH (3). *1 Chr. 2:25.*

Ahijah was a son of Jerahmeel and one of Judah's great-great-grandsons. His brothers were Ram, Bunah, Oren and Ozem. His half-brother was Onam. (Chart 8c.)

AHIJAH (4). *1 Chr. 11:36.*

Ahijah the Pelonite was one of David's mighty men and one of the valiant men of the armies. (Chart 17.)

AHIJAH (5). *1 Chr. 26:20.*

Ahijah, a Levite, was over the treasures of the house of God and over the treasures of the dedicated things when David was king.

AHIJAH (6). *Neh. 10:26.*

Ahijah was among those who were chief of the people who covenanted to marry in Israel, honor the Sabbath, pay tithes and keep the commandments.

AHIKAM. *2 Kgs. 22:12-20; 25:22; 2 Chr. 34:20; Jer. 26:24; 39:14; 40:5-16; 41:1-2; 43:6.*

Ahikam was the son of Shaphan. He was commanded by king Josiah to accompany his father and Hilkiah, the high priest, and others to inquire of the Lord concerning the book of the law which Hilkiah had found in the house of the Lord. They inquired of the prophetess Huldah who prophesied wrath upon the people because of their wickedness but blessings upon king Josiah because of his righteousness. *(2 Kgs. 22:12-20.) (2 Chr. 34:20 is a repeat of 2 Kgs. 22:12-20, but names are slightly altered.)*

Ahikam was the son of Shaphan and the father of Gedaliah, which Gedaliah Nebuchadnezzar made ruler over the people left in Judah when the rest of Israel was carried off to Babylon. *(2 Kgs. 25:22.) (Note: It was into Gedaliah's care that Nebuzar-adan, captain of Nebuchadnezzar's guard, placed the prophet Jeremiah. Jer. 39:14.)* Ahikam kept the prophet Jeremiah from being turned over to the people who wanted to put him to death for prophesying against them because of their wickedness *(Jer. 26:24)*. HIs son Gedaliah was slain by Ishmael. *(Jer. 40:5-16; 41:1-2; 43:6.)*

AHILUD. *2 Sam. 8:16; 1 Kgs. 4:3, 7, 12.*

Ahilud was the father of Jehoshaphat who was the recorder when David reigned over all Israel *(2 Sam. 8:16)* and was also the recorder in Solomon's court. His son Baana was one of twelve officers over all Israel who provided victuals for the king and his household one month each year. *(1 Kgs. 4:3, 7, 12.)*

AHIMAAZ (1). *1 Sam. 14:50.*

Ahimaaz was father of Ahinoam, Saul's wife. (Chart 16 l.)

AHIMAAZ (2). *2 Sam. 15:27-36; 17:17-21; 18:19; 1 Kgs. 4:15; 1 Chr. 6:8-9, 53; Ezra 7:1-5.*

Ahimaaz was the son of Zadok the priest. When David and his family and followers fled Jerusalem to escape from Absalom, David had Zadok take Ahimaaz back to Jerusalem with him so they could keep David informed as to what Absalom's plans were. Ahimaaz and Jonathan, the son of Abiathar, were to carry information back to David. *(2 Sam. 15:27-36.)*

Ahimaaz and Jonathan were sent to David carrying information from Hushai to let him know what advice he had given Absalom and what was happening. They were assisted by a wench who conveyed the message to them so they could carry the messsage to king David. A lad saw them and told Absalom, but they quickly hid in a well in a man's court in Bahurim. They were protected by a woman who spread a covering over the well's mouth and spread ground corn on it. When Absalom's men came and inquired about them, the woman lied and said they had gone over the brook of water. After they left, Ahimaaz and Jonathan carried their message to David. *(2 Sam. 17:17-21.)*

Ahimaaz and Cushi raced to convey to David news of the battle. Ahimaaz reached David first. However, he didn't know about Absalom's death and was unable to report it to David. Cushi reported it. *(2 Sam. 18:19.)*

Ahimaaz was one of Solomon's twelve officers over Israel who provided victuals for the king and his household one month each year. He married Basmath, one of Solomon's daughters. *(1 Kgs. 4:15.)*

Ahimaaz was the son of Zadok, the father of Azariah, the grandson of Ahitub and a ninth-great-grandson of Aaron. *(1 Chr. 6:8-9, 53.) (Note: The verses in Ezra 7:1-5 give the descendants of Aaron down through Ezra as given in 1 Chr. 6:4-15. However, there are several differences: no Ahimaaz or Johanan is named. Nor is Jehozadak listed. Instead, the names following Meraioth—Amariah, Ahitub, Zadok, Ahimaaz, Azariah and Johanan—have been deleted and Jehozadak has been replaced with Ezra. Perhaps there was a duplication of names in 1 Chronicle. It is also possible that Jehozadak and Ezra are one and the same. It is conceivable that Ahimaaz is the same as Shallum, son of Zadok or the same as Hilkiah, son of Shallum and father of Azariah.)* (Chart 7b.; 8f.)

AHIMAN (1). *Num. 13:22-33; Josh. 15:14; Judg. 1:10.*

Ahiman was a son of Anak. His family was one of the families of giants living in Caanan who caused ten of the leaders Moses had sent to scout out the land to return with a negative report. *(Num. 13:22-33.)* Ahiman and his brothers Sheshai and Talmai were driven out of the land by Caleb. *(Josh. 15:14.)* The tribe of Judah slew all three brothers. *(Judg. 1:10.)*

AHIMAN (2). *1 Chr. 9:1, 17.*

Ahiman, a Levite, was one of the porters over the work of the service of the tabernacle. He was an inhabitant of Jerusalem and his genealogy was written in the book of the kings of Israel and Judah, who were carried away to Babylon for their transgression.

AHIMELECH (1). *1 Sam. 21:1-9; 22:9-20; 30:7; Ps. 52: Subtitle.*

Ahimelech was a priest in Nob. David received help from him when he fled after being warned by Jonathan that Saul really intended to kill him. The priest feared meeting with David. Nevertheless, David assured him that he was on the king's business. Ahimelech gave him hallowed bread and also the sword of Goliath. *(1 Sam. 21:1-9.)*

Ahimelech was the son of Ahitub and the father of Abiathar. He was seen by Doeg, one of Saul's servants, visiting with David and giving him hallowed bread and Goliath's sword. Saul ordered his servants to kill all the priests in Nob. They refused; but Doeg, when ordered to kill them, slew 85 "persons that did wear a linen ephod"—including Ahimelech—and in Nob he slew both men and women, children and sucklings, oxen, asses and sheep. Ahimelech's son Abiathar escaped and fled after David. *(1 Sam. 22:9-20.)*

Ahimelech's son was Abiathar. *(1 Sam. 30:7.-Ps. 52: Subtitle.)*

This psalm was written in response to Doeg's report to Saul informing him that David was at the house of Ahimelech. *(Ps. 52: Subtitle.) (Also see Ahijah (1). The Bible Dictionary indicates that Ahimelech and Ahijah may be one and the same.)* (Chart 7b.)

AHIMELECH (2). *1 Sam. 26:6.*

Ahimelech, the Hittite, was one of David's followers.

AHIMELECH (3) (Abimelech (3)). *2 Sam. 8:17; 1 Chr. 18:16; 24:3-6, 31.*

Ahimelech was the son of Abiathar (grandson of Ahimelech) and was one of the priests when David was king over all Israel *(2 Sam. 8:17).* **Abimelech** (Ahimelech), son of Abiathar, was one of the priests when David was king. *(1 Chr. 18:16.)*

Ahimelech was of the sons of Ithamar and was the son of Abiathar. When David made the divisions of the sons of Aaron, Ithamar and Eleazar executed the office of the priests because their brothers Nadab and Abihu had died. David distributed Ithamar's division through Ahimelech, and he distributed Eleazar's division through Zadok. Ithamar had eight sons; Eleazar had 16. The lots were cast in the presence of king David, Zadok the priest, and Ahimelech and the chief of the fathers of the priests and Levites. *(1 Chr. 24:3-6, 31.)* (Chart 7b.)

AHIMOTH (Mahath (1)). *1 Chr. 6:25, 35; 2 Chr. 29:12.*

Ahimoth **(Mahath)**, of the house of Levi through Kohath, was the son of Amasai and was among those who were set over the service of song in the house of the Lord. *(1 Chr. 6:25, 35.)* When Hezekiah became king over Judah, Hezekiah had Mahath, son of Amasai, and other Levites be cleansed and then had them sanctify the house of the Lord after sanctifying themselves. *(2 Chr. 29:12.)* (Chart 7d.)

AHINADAB. *1 Kgs. 4:14.*

Ahinadab was the son of Iddo. He was one of twelve officers over Israel who provided victuals for king Solomon and his family one month each year.

AHINOAM (1). *1 Sam. 14:50.*

Ahinoam was Saul's wife. She was the daughter of Ahimaaz and the mother of Jonathan. (Chart 16 l.)

AHINOAM (2). *1 Sam. 25:43; 27:3; 30:5, 18; 2 Sam. 2:2; 3:2; 1 Chr. 3:1.*

Ahinoam was of Jezreel and was one of David's wives. *(1 Sam. 25:43.)* She and David's wife Abigail dwelt with him in Gath. *(1 Sam. 27:3.)* The Amalekites burned Ziklag and took both Ahinoam and Abigail captive along with the other people of Ziklag. David and his men slew the Amalekites and rescued the people, including his wives. *(1 Sam. 30:5,18.)* Ahinoam and Abigail went to Hebron to dwell with David. *(2 Sam. 2:2.)*

Ahinoam was the mother of Amnon, David's firstborn son in Hebron. *(2 Sam. 3:2; 1 Chr. 3:1.)*

AHIO (1). *2 Sam. 6:3; 1 Chr. 13:7.*

Ahio and Uzzah were sons of Abinadab. When David and 30,000 men of Israel went from Baale of Judah to fetch the ark of God from Abinadab in Gibeah, Ahio and Uzzah drove the new cart.

AHIO (2). *1 Chr. 8:14.*

Ahio, a descendant of Benjamin, was a son of Beriah who was a son of Elpaal who was a son of Shaharaim and his wife Hushim. (16g.)

AHIO (3). *1 Chr. 8:31; 9:35-38.*

Ahio was of the tribe of Benjamin. He was a son of the father of Gibeon. His mother was Maachah. His brothers were Abdon, Zur, Kish, Baal, Nadab, Gedor, Zacher and Mikloth. *(1 Chr. 8:31.)* Ahio's father's name was Jehiel (Abiel). His mother and brothers are named again with the addition of Ner. Zacher's name is given as Zechariah. *(1 Chr. 9:35-38.)* (Chart 16k.)

AHIRA. *Num. 1:15-16, 42-43; 2:25-29; 7:78.*

Ahira was the son of Enan. He was of the tribe of Naphtali and was one of those princes of the tribes of their fathers who were renowned of the congregation. He was appointed by the Lord to be the one to stand at the head of all of the tribe of Naphtali as Moses organized Israel in preparation for war. The males in the tribe of Naphtali who were 20 years old or older who could go to war numbered 53,400. *(Num. 1:15-16, 42-43.)* Ahira was instructed to have the tribe of Naphtali pitch their tents next to the tribe of Asher as part of the camp of Dan on the north side of the encampment. *(Num. 2:25-29.)*

When the altar of the tabernacle was anointed and dedicated, Ahira made his offering on the twelfth day. *(Num. 7:78.)* (Chart 12b.)

AHIRAM (Ahiramites). *Num. 26:38.*

Ahiram was a son of Benjamin. His descendants were the **Ahiramites**. (Also see Gera.) (Chart 16b.)

AHISAMACH. *Ex. 31:6.*

Ahisamach, of the tribe of Dan, was the father of Aholiab. (Chart 11b.)

AHISHAHAR. *1 Chr. 7:10.*

Ahishahar, son of Bilhan and grandson of Jediael, was a great-grandson of Benjamin and a mighty man of valor. His brothers were Jeush, Benjamin, Ehud, Chenaanah, Zethan and Tharshish. (Chart 16c.)

AHISHAR. *1 Kgs. 4:6.*

Ahishar was over the household in Solomon's court.

AHITHOPHEL. *2 Sam. 15:12, 31-34; 16:15, 20-23; 17:1-4, 14, 23; 23:34; 1 Chr. 27:33.*

Ahithophel was a Gilonite. He was David's counselor, but he supported Absalom in his conspiracy against his father. David requested Hushi's help in defeating whatever counsel Ahithophel gave Absalom. *(2 Sam. 15:12, 31-34.)* Ahithophel accompanied Absalom to Jerusalem and he counseled Absalom to go in unto his father's concubines whom David had left behind to take care of the house when he fled Jerusalem to escape from Absalom. "And the counsel of Ahithophel, which he counselled in those days, was as if a man had inquired at the oracle of God: so was all the counsel of Ahithophel both with David and with Absalom." *(2 Sam. 16:15, 20-23.)*

Ahithophel suggested to Absalom that he be allowed to choose 12,000 men to pursue after David, killing only David and bringing the rest of the people back to Absalom. Hushai counseled Absalom otherwise. When Ahithophel saw that his counsel was not followed, but Hushai's was instead, he went home, set his affairs in order, and hanged himself. He was buried in the sepulchre of his father. *(2 Sam. 17:1-4, 14, 23.)*

Ahithophel the Gilonite was the father of Eliam (and grandfather of Bath-sheba). *(2 Sam. 23:34.)* He was king David's counselor. *(1 Chr. 27:33.)*

AHITUB (1). *1 Sam. 14:3.*

Ahitub was the father of Ahiah, the brother of Ichabod, the son of Phinehas and the grandson of Eli.

AHITUB (2). *1 Sam. 22:9, 11-12.*

Ahitub was the father of Ahimelech the priest and grandfather of Abiathar. (Chart 7b.)

AHITUB (3) . *2 Sam. 8:17; 1 Chr. 6:7; Ezra 7:1-5.*

Ahitub was the father of Zadok the priest. *(2 Sam. 8:17.)* He was the son of Amariah and a descendant of Aaron. *(1 Chr. 6:7.)* *(Note: In the listing of Aaron's posterity, Amariah, Ahitub and Zadok are listed twice and in the same order: verses 7-8 and verses 11-12. Whether this is a duplication or whether Aaron's posterity just used the same names in the same order, it is not clear. For the purposes of this book, the names in both listings are presented here.)*

Ahitub's ancestors and descendants are listed again with several deletions and some modifications—for instance, Ahitub has been deleted and Jehozadak has been replaced with Ezra. *(Ezra 7:1-5.)* (Chart 7b.)

AHITUB (4). *1 Chr. 6:11-12; 9:11; Ezra 7:1-5; Neh. 11:11.*

Ahitub, a descendant of Aaron, was the son of Amariah and the father of Zadok. *(1 Chr. 6:11-12.)* He was the ruler of the house of God and was the father of Meraioth who was the father of Zadok. He is listed among the priests who resided in Jerusalem whose genealogy was recorded in the book of the kings of Israel and Judah who were carried away into Babylon because of transgression. *(1 Chr. 9:11; Neh. 11:11.)*

Ahitub's descendants and forefathers from Aaron through Ezra are listed with some modification from prior listings. *(Ezra 7:1-5)* (Chart 7b.)

AHLAI (1). *1 Chr. 2:31, 34.*

Ahlai was a daughter of Sheshan and an eight-times great-granddaughter of Judah. Sheshan had no sons, only daughters. Ahlai's father gave his daughter to Jarha, his Egyptian servant, for a wife. She bore Attai. (Chart 8c.)

AHLAI (2). *1 Chr. 11:41.*

Ahlai was the father of Zabad.

AHOAH. *1 Chr. 8:4, 7.*

Ahoah was a son of Bela who was a son of Benjamin. *(Note: This listing of Bela's sons differs from that in 1 Chr. 7:7.)* **Ahiah (3)** (Ahoah), Naaman and Gera were removed. (Chart 16d.)

AHOHITE. *2 Sam. 23:9, 28; 1 Chr. 27:4.*

The Ahohites, Zalmon and Eleazar (son of Dodo), were two of David's mighty men who defied the Philistines who had gathered for battle. *(2 Sam. 23:9, 28.)*. Another Ahohite, Dodai, was one of David's officers who served over the course of the second month. *(1 Chr. 27:4.)*

AHOLIAB. *Ex. 31:6; 35:30-35; 36-38.*

Aholiab was the son of Ahisamach of the tribe of Dan. He was an artisan whom the Lord inspired to help build and furnish the tabernacle. Moses was told he was given both Aholiab and Bezaleel to work on the tabernacle. *(Ex. 31:6.)* Moses told the people Aholiab and Bezaleel had been called by the Lord to be in charge of building the tabernacle. The Lord also put it into their hearts to teach others the skills necessary for building the tabernacle. *(Ex. 35:30-35.)* Aholiab and Bezaleel and others worked on the tabernacle, made the ark, the altar of burnt offerings and all things that pertained to the tabernacle. Aholiab was an engraver, a cunning workman, and an embroiderer in blue, purple, scarlet, and fine linen. *(Ex. 36-38:23.)* (Chart 11b.)

AHOLIBAMAH (1). *Gen. 36:2-5, 14, 25.*

Aholibamah, daughter of Anah, was one of Esau's wives. She bore Jeush, Jaalam, and Korah. (Charts 3b-c.; 4c.)

AHOLIBAMAH (2). *Gen. 36:41.*

Aholibamah was one of the dukes (tribal chiefs) who came of Esau. (Chart 19.)

AHUMAI. *1 Chr. 4:2.*

Ahumai, a descendant of Judah, was the son of Jahath. His brother was Lahad. (Chart 8m.)

AHUZAM. *1 Chr. 4:6.*

Ahuzam was the son of Ashur the father of Tekoa and his wife Naarah. His brothers were Hepher, Temeni and Haahashtari. (Chart 8d.)

AHUZZATH. *Gen. 26:26-31.*

AHUZZATH was a friend of Abimelech, king of Gerar. He was with Abimelech and Phichol, the chief captain of the army, when they met with Isaac and made a covenant with Isaac that Isaac would do them no harm.

AI. *Ezra 2:28; Neh. 7:32.*

Ai was of the people of Israel. The men of Ai and Beth-el who returned to Jerusalem from Babylon after Cyrus' proclamation to build the temple numbered 223. *(Note: The number of men is listed as 123 in Neh. 7:32.)*

AIAH (1). *2 Sam. 3:7.*

Aiah was the father of Rizpah who was one of Saul's concubines. (Chart 16 l.)

AIAH (2). *1 Chr. 1:40.* See **Ajah.**

AJAH (Aiah (2)). *Gen. 36:24; 1 Chr. 1.40.*

Ajah was one of Zibeon's children. His brother was Anah *(Gen. 36:24).* **Aiah** (Ajah) was one of Zibeon's sons *(1 Chr. 1:40.)* (Chart 4c.)

AKAN (Jakan). *Gen. 36:27; 1 Chr. 1:42.*

Akan *(Gen. 36:27)* **Jkan** (Akan) *(1 Chr. 1:42)* was one of the sons of Ezer. (Chart 4e.)

AKKUB (1). *1 Chr. 3:24.*

Akkub, a descendant of David, was a son of Elioenai. His brothers were Hodaiah, Eliashib, Pelaiah, Johanan, Dalaiah and Anani. (Chart 1.)

AKKUB (2). *1 Chr. 9:17; Ezra 2:42; Neh. 7:45; 11:19; 12:25.*

Akkub, a Levite, was one of the porters over the work of the service and was a keeper of the gates of the tabernacle. He was an inhabitant of Jerusalem and his genealogy was written in the book of the kings of Israel and Judah, who were carried away to Babylon for their transgression. *(1 Chr. 9:17.)*

When Cyrus, king of Persia, proclaimed that the people of God should go to Jerusalem to build the temple, the children of the porters—Akkub, Shallum, Ater, Talmon, Hatita and Shobai—numbered 139. *(Ezra 2:42.) (Note: The number is given as 138 rather than 139 in Neh. 7:45.)*

Akkub, Talmon, and the other porters numbered 172 when they returned to Jerusalem from Babylonian captivity. *(Neh. 11:19.)*

Akkub, a porter named along with Mattaniah, Bakbukiah, Obadiah, Meshullam and Talmon, kept the ward at the thresholds of the gates in the days of Joiakim, Nehemiah and Ezra. *(Neh. 12:25.)*

AKKUB (3). *Ezra 2:45, 58.*

Akkub was a Nethinim. When the Nethinims and the children of Solomon's servants left Babylon to return to Jerusalem to build the house of the Lord as proclaimed by Cyrus, king of Persia, they numbered 392.

AKKUB (4). *Neh. 8:7-8.*

Akkub was one of the men who, when Ezra read and interpreted the law of Moses to the people, helped the people to understand the law.

ALAMETH (1). *1 Chr. 7:8.*

Alameth, brother of Zemira, Joash, Eliezer, Elioenai, Omri, Jerimoth, Abiah and Anathoth, was Becher's son and Benjamin's grandson, (Chart 16c.)

ALEMETH (2). *1 Chr. 8:36; 9:42.*

Alemeth, from the tribe of Benjamin, was a son of Jehoadah (Jarah). They were descendants of Saul through Jonathan. His brothers were Azmaveth and Zimri. (Chart 16 l.)

ALIAH. *1 Chr. 1:51.* See **Alvah**.

ALIAN. *1 Chr. 1:40.* See **Alvan**.

ALLON. *1 Chr. 4:37.*

Allon was the father of Shiphi, the son of Jedaiah and a descendant of Shimei. (Chart 6a.)

ALMODAD. *Gen. 10:26.*

Almodad was a son of Joktan, a third-great-grandson of Shem and a fourth-great-grandson of Noah. (Chart 2b.)

AL-TASCHITH. *Ps. 57-59, 75:Subtitles.*

Al-taschith was David's chief Musician.

ALVAH (Aliah). *Gen. 36:40; 1 Chr. 1:51.*

Alvah (Aliah) was one of the dukes and tribal chiefs who came of Esau. (Chart 19.)

ALVAN (Alian). *Gen. 36:23; 1 Chr. 1:40.*

Alvan (Alian) was one of the sons of Shobal. (Chart 4b.)

AMAL. *1 Chr. 7:35.*

Amal was a son of Helem (Hotham) and a descendant of Asher. His brothers were Zophah, Imna and Shelesh. (Chart 14a.)

AMALEK (1). *Gen. 36:12, 16.*

Amalek was the son of Eliphaz and Timna, Eliphaz's concubine, and counted as a son of Adah, Esau's wife. He was a duke or tribal chief. (Chart 3b.)

AMALEK (2) (Amalekites). *Ex. 17:8-14; Num. 24:20; Deut. 25:Intro., 19; Judg. 5:14; 1 Sam. 15:1-3; 27:8-9; 30; 2 Sam. 8:12; 1 Chr. 4:43; 18:11.*

Amalek fought against Israel in Rephidim. As long as Moses kept his hand holding the rod of God up, the children of Israel—under Joshua's leadership—prevailed. When his hand dropped, Amalek prevailed. Aaron and Hur propped Moses' arms up and Joshua was able to "discomfit" Amalek. The Lord said He would completely destroy all remembrance of Amalek from under the heavens.

(Ex. 17:8-14.) Balaam prophesied regarding the destiny of Israel and said that "Amalek was the first of the nations; but his latter end shall be that he perish for ever." *(Num. 24:20.)* The **Amalekites** were descendants of Amalek. Israel was instructed to blot out all remembrance of Amalek from under heaven. *(Deut. 25:Intro., 19.)*

Deborah and Barak sang a song of praise because Israel had been delivered from Canaanite bondage: from Ephraim had come a "root" of them against Amalek; governors came down from Machir; and others who assisted are praised. *(Judg. 5:14.)*

The Lord, through the prophet Samuel, commanded Saul to destroy all the Amalekites, including women and children and all their animals. *(1 Sam. 15:1-3.)* David and his men invaded the land of the Amalekites along with other lands and "smote the land, and left neither man nor woman alive." *(1 Sam. 27:8-9.)*

The Amalekites invaded Ziklag and burned it with fire. They carried the women off captive, including Ahinoam and Abigail, David's wives. David pursued them, defeated them, and rescued his wives. *(1 Sam. 30.)* David dedicated to the Lord the silver and gold that he had taken from the Amalekites and others he had conquered. *(2 Sam. 8:12; 1 Chr. 18.11.)*

The last remnant of the Amalekites was destroyed by the Simeonites and the Simeonites then dwelt in their land. *(1 Chr. 4:43.)*

AMARIAH (1). *1 Chr. 6:7; Ezra 7:1-5.*

Amariah, a descendant of Aaron, was the son of Meraioth and the father of Ahitub. *(1 Chr. 6:7.)* Aaron's descendants are listed through Ezra. *(Ezra 7:1-5.)* *(Note: this listing does not include this Amariah nor the following: Ahitub, Zadok, Ahimaaz, Azariah or Johanan. Rather, it jumps to Azariah, the father of Amariah, the father of Ahitub.)* (Chart 7b.)

AMARIAH (2). *1 Chr. 6:11-14; Ezra 7:1-5.*

Amariah, a descendant of Aaron, was the son of Azariah and the father of Ahitub. His genealogy is listed. *(1 Chr. 6:11-14.)* His descendants and forefathers from Aaron through Ezra are listed again, but there are several modifications. *(Ezra 7:1-5.)* (Chart 7b.)

AMARIAH (3). *1 Chr. 23:19; 24:23, 31.*

Amariah, a Levite, was of the sons of Hebron, son of Kohath. When David numbered the Levites at the time he made Solomon king, he divided them into courses among the sons of Levi. Jeriah was the first, Amariah the second, Jahaziel the third, and Jekameam the fourth. *(1 Chr. 23:19.)* Amariah and his brothers are named again. He, with the rest of the chief fathers of the Levites, drew lots for his course in the presence of king David, Zadok, Ahimelech and other community leaders. *(1 Chr. 24:23, 31.)* (Chart 7d.)

AMARIAH (4). *2 Chr. 19:11.*

Amariah was the chief priest when Jehoshaphat was king of Judah and was over the people in "all matters of the Lord."

AMARIAH (5). *2 Chr. 31:14.*

Amariah, and others, assisted Kore, porter toward the east, in caring for the freewill offerings of God and their distribution when Hezekiah was king over Judah.

AMARIAH (6). *Ezra 10:42 (18-19, 42, 44).*

Amariah, along with other sons of Bani, was one of the men in Israel who had taken foreign wives but gave them up when Ezra feared the wrath of God would destroy Israel for this iniquity.

AMARIAH (7). *Neh. 11:4.*

Amariah, a descendant of Judah, the son of Shephatiah and the father of Zechariah, dwelled in Jerusalem after leaving Babylon. (Chart 8b.)

AMARIAH (8). *Zeph. 1:1.*

Amariah was the son of Hizkiah and the father of Gedaliah. The prophet Zephaniah was his great-grandson who prophesied in the days of Josiah son of Amon, king of Judah.

AMASA (1) (Amasai). *2 Sam. 17:25; 19:13; 20:1-13; 1 Kgs. 2:5, 32; 1 Chr. 2:17; 12:18 (1-2, 16-18).*

Amasa was the son of Ithra, an Israelite (Ishmeelite), and Abigail, David's sister. His cousin was Joab, son of Zeruiah. Absalom made Amasa captain of the host instead of Joab. *(2 Sam. 17:25.)* Amasa replaced Joab as captain of David's hosts after Joab chastised David for caring more about Absalom than for those who defended his life and kingdom. *(2 Sam. 19:13.)*

When Sheba, of the tribe of Benjamin, led all the tribes of Israel except Judah away from David, David instructed Amasa to gather all the men of Judah and return in three days. However, Amasa did not return on schedule so David told Abishai to gather men together and pursue Sheba. Amasa eventually met up with the other troops. Joab took Amasa by the beard as if to kiss him but smote him with a sword instead, killing him. He was left lying in a pool of blood in the middle of the highway until a man removed him from the road and put him in a field and covered him with a cloth so the people would move on and not stop and look at him. *(2 Sam. 20:1-13.)*

Amasa was the son of Jether (Ithra) *(1 Kgs. 2:5, 32)* and Abigail, David's sister. *(1 Chr. 2:17.)*

When the various tribes of Israel went to David at Ziklag when he became king, David went out to meet those who came from Benjamin and Judah. When David announced that if they came in peace his heart would be "knit unto" them, but that if they came to betray him, God would rebuke them, **Amasai** (Amasa), who was chief of the captains, told him they came in peace. *(1 Chr. 12:18 (1-2, 16-18.)* (Chart 8d.)

AMASA (2). *2 Chr. 28:12.*

Amasa, son of Hadlai, was one of the leaders of the children of Ephraim who supported the prophet Oded in letting the captives of Judah go so as not to incur greater wrath from the Lord upon Israel.

AMASAI (1). *1 Chr. 6:25, 35; 2 Chr. 29:12.*

Amasai, of the house of Levi through Kohath, was the son of Elkanah. His son was Mahath (Ahimoth). Amasai was the father of Mahath. (Chart 7d.)

AMASAI (2). *1 Chr. 12:18.* See **Amasa (1)**.

AMASAI (3). *1 Chr. 15:24.*

Amasai was among those who, under the direction of David, was assigned to make music before the Lord as the ark was removed from the house of Obed-edom and taken to the place which David had prepared for it to be housed. As one of the priests, he was assigned to blow the trumpet before the ark of God.

AMASHAI (See Maasiai).

AMASIAH. *2 Chr. 17:16.*

Amasiah, son of Zichri was of the house of Judah and was one of the captains of thousands when Jehoshaphat was king over Judah. He willingly offered his services to the Lord. His men numbered 200,000.

AMAZIAH (1). *2 Kgs. 12:21; 13:12; 14:1-21; 15:1, 3; 1 Chr. 3:11-12; 2 Chr. 24:26-27; 25:1-28; 26:1.*

Amaziah was the son of Joash and became king in Judah when Joash was slain by two of his servants. *(2 Kgs. 12:21.)*

The wars between Amaziah king of Judah and Joash king of Israel are recorded in the chronicles of the kings of Israel. *(2 Kgs. 13:12.)*

Amaziah, at the age of 25 years, began his reign over Judah in the second year of the reign of Joash over Israel and reigned 29 years. His mother was Jehoaddan of Jerusalem. He walked uprightly before the Lord. However, just as with his father, the "high places were not taken away: as yet the people did sacrifice and burnt incense on the high places." He slew Jozachar and Jehozabad, the two servants who killed his father. He requested a face-to-face meeting with Jehoash (Joash), king of Israel. Unfortunately, it did not go well for him. "Judah was put to the worse before Israel; and they fled every man to their tents." Amaziah was taken captive. Jehoash went to Jerusalem with his men, broke down the wall of Jerusalem, took all the gold and silver and treasures in the house of the Lord and in the king's house, along with hostages, and returned to Samaria. Amaziah lived an additional 15 years after the death of Jehoash, during which time Jeroboam reigned over Israel. When Amaziah learned of a conspiracy against him, he fled to Lachish, where he was caught and killed. His body was returned to Jerusalem and buried with his fathers in the city of David. His 16 year-old son Azariah (Uzziah) was made king by all the people of Judah. *(2 Kgs. 14:1-21.)*

Amaziah's son Azariah reigned over Judah after his father beginning in the 27th year of the reign of Jeroboam over Israel, and did that which was right in the sight of the Lord just as Amaziah had done. *(2 Kgs. 15:1, 3.) (Note: If Amaziah lived 15 years after the death of Jehoash during which time Jeroboam reigned over Israel, and if Azariah began his reign upon the death of Amaziah, Azariah would have begun his reign in the 15th year of the reign of Jeroboam rather than the 27th year.)*

Amaziah was the son of Joash, the father of Azariah, and the grandfather of Jotham. *(1 Chr. 3:11-12.)*

Amaziah reigned over Judah after Joash's death. *(2 Chr. 24:26-27.)*

A man of God counseled Amaziah, and Amaziah followed his counsel. However, Amaziah brought the gods of the children of Seir back and bowed himself down to them, incurring the wrath of the Lord. Thus, the Lord allowed him to be defeated by Joash, king of Israel. A prophet was sent to him who foretold Amaziah of his pending destruction. *(2 Chr. 25:1-28.) (Note: This is a repeat and expansion of 2 Kgs. 14:1-21.)*

His son Uzziah (Azariah) reigned in his stead. *(2 Chr. 26:1.)* (Chart 1.)

AMAZIAH (2). *1 Chr. 4:34.*

Amaziah, a descendant of Shimei, was the father of Joshah. (Chart 6a.)

AMAZIAH (3). *1 Chr. 6:45.*

Amaziah, the son of Hilkiah, was a descendant of Merari who was the son of Levi. *(Note: Merari's descendants are listed differently in 1 Chr. 6:29-30 than in 1 Chr. 6:44-47.)* (Chart 7e.)

AMAZIAH (4). *Amos 7:10-14.*

Amaziah was the priest of Beth-el. When the prophet Amos prophesied against Israel and said king Jeroboam would die by the sword, Amaziah sent word to Jeroboam that Amos conspired against him. He tried to get Amos to leave and go to the land of Judah and prophesy there.

AMI (Amon (3)). *Ezra 2:57-5; Neh. 7:59-60.*

Ami was one of Solomon's servants. The children of Solomon's servants and the Nethinims numbered 392 when they returned from Babylonian captivity. *(His name is given as **Amon** in Neh. 7:59.)*

AMITTAI. *2 Kgs. 14:25; Jonah 1:1.*

Amittai was the father of the prophet Jonah.

AMMIEL (1). *Num. 13:12, 31-33; 14:37.*

Ammiel, of the tribe of Dan, was the son of Gemalli. He was one of twelve leaders sent to scout out the land of Caanan. He returned with a negative report. *(Num. 13:12, 31-33.)* Ammiel and all of the other scouts, exept for Caleb and Joshua, "died by the plague before the Lord" because of the negative report they gave after scouting out the land of Caanan. *(Num. 14:37.)*

AMMIEL (2). *2 Sam. 9:4; 17:27.*

Ammiel, of Lodebar, was the father of Machir.

AMMIEL (3). *1 Chr. 3:5.* See **Eliam (1)**.

AMMIEL (4). *1 Chr. 26:5, 8, 12.*

Ammiel, a Levite, was the sixth son of Obed-edom. His brothers were Shemaiah, Jehozabad, Joah, Sacar, Nethaneel, Issachar and Peulthai. They, along with other Levites, were appointed by king David to be porters—to have charge of the treasures, serve as officers and judges, and to conduct the outward business over Israel. (Chart 7c.)

AMMIHUD (1). *Num. 1:10; 1 Chr. 7:26-27.*

Ammihud was the father of Elishama and was of the tribe of Ephraim, one of two tribes allotted Joseph. *(Num. 1:10.)* Ammihud was the son of Laadan. Joshua was his great-grandson. *(1 Chr. 7:26-27.)* (Chart 15d.)

AMMIHUD (2). *Num. 34:20.*

Ammihud, of the tribe of Simeon, was the father of Shemuel.

AMMIHUD (3). *Num. 34:28.*

Ammihud was the father of Pedahel who was prince of the tribe of Naphtali. (Chart 12b.)

AMMIHUD (4). *2 Sam. 13:37.*

Ammihud was the father of Talmai, king of Geshur. Absalom fled to Talmai after killing Amnon, his own half-brother.

AMMIHUD (5). *1 Chr. 9:4.*

Ammihud, a descendant of Pharez who was the son of Judah, was the father of Uthai and the son of Omri. (Chart 8b.)

AMMINADAB (1). *Ex. 6:23; Num. 1.7, 7.12, Ruth 4.18-21.*

Amminadab was the father of Naashon and Elisheba, Aaron's wife. *(Ex. 6:23.)* Amminadab was the father of Nahshon (Naashon) who was appointed by the Lord to head all the tribe of Judah as Moses organized Israel for war. *(Num. 1:7.)* He was of the tribe of Judah. *(Num. 7:12.)* He was the son of Ram, the son of Hezron. Amminadab begat Nahshon, who begat Salmon, who begat Boaz, who begat Obed, who begat Jesse, who begat king David. *(Ruth 4:18-21.)* (Charts 1.; 8d.)

AMMINADAB (2). *1 Chr. 6:22.* See **Izhar**.

AMMINADAB (3). *1 Chr. 15:10-12.*

Amminadab, a Levite, was the chief of the sons of Uzziel. He and 112 of his brethren were called by David to assemble with other Levites to prepare themselves to retrieve the ark of God from the house of Obed-edom so as to bring it to the place David had prepared for it in the city of David.

AMMISHADDAI. *Num. 1:12.*

Ammishaddai, of the tribe of Dan, was the father of Ahiezer.

AMMON (Ammonites, See Children of Ammon)

AMNON (1). *2 Sam. 3:2; 13; 1 Chr. 3:1.*

Amnon was David's firstborn son in Hebron. His mother was Ahinoam, the Jezreelitess. *(2 Sam. 3:2; 1 Chr. 3:1.)* Amnon fell in love with his half-sister Tamar whose brother was Absalom. He forced her to lie with him and then he hated her and had her shut out. When Absalom learned what had happened, he had his servants kill Amnon. *(2 Sam. 13.)* (Chart 8e.)

AMNON (2). *1 Chr. 4:20.*

Amnon, Rinnah, Ben-hanan and Tilon were sons of Shimon.

AMNON'S (1) SERVANT. *2 Sam. 13:17.*

Amnon's Servant was instructed to cast Tamar out after Amnon forced her to lie with him, and the servant was told to bolt the door after her.

AMOK. *Neh. 12:7, 20.*

Amok was one of the men (chief priests and Levites in the days of Jeshua) who went with Zerubbabel from Babylonian captivity to Jerusalem. He was the father of Eber, who was one of the priests who was a chief of the fathers in the days of Joiakim.

AMON (1). *1 Kgs. 22:26-27; 2 Chr. 18:25-26.*

Amon was the governor of Samaria. He was instructed to cast the prophet Micaiah into prison and to feed him just bread and water until Ahab returned in peace from battle against Syria.

AMON (2). *2 Kgs. 21:18-24; 22:1; 1 Chr. 3:13-14; 2 Chr. 33:20-25; Jer. 1:2; Zeph. 1:1.*

Amon, son of Manasseh, became king following Manasseh's death. He was 22 years old and reigned two years in Jerusalem. His mother was Meshullemeth. He did evil in the sight of the Lord just as his father did, but he did not repent as his father repented. His servants conspired against him and killed him in his own house. The people then killed those who had conspired against Amon. They made his son Josiah king in his stead. *(2 Kgs. 21:18-24; 2 Chr. 33:20-25.)*

Amon's wife Jedidah was the mother of Josiah and the daughter of Adaiah of Boscath. *(2 Kgs. 22:1.)*

Amon, son of Manasseh, was the father of Josiah. *(1 Chr. 3:13-14; Jer. 1:2.)* Josiah was king of Judah when Zephaniah prophesied against Judah. *(Zeph. 1:1.)* (Chart 1.)

AMON (3). *Neh. 7:59.* See **Ami**.

AMON'S (2) SERVANTS. *2 Kgs. 21:23.*

Amon's Servants conspired against him and killed him in his own house. The people rose up and slew all those who were involved in the conspiracy.

AMORITE. *Gen. 10:16; 15; Deut. 1:44; 7:1; 1 Kgs. 9:20; 2 Chr. 8:7; Ezra 9:1; Neh. 9:8; Ezek. 16:45; Amos 2:9.*

Amorites were descendants of Canaan who was a son of Ham. *(Gen. 10:16.)*

Abram was told that his seed would be strangers in a land that was not theirs and that they would be afflicted for 400 years. He was also told that in the fourth generation they would "come hither again for the iniquity of the Amorites is not yet full." The Amorites' lands were given to Abram's seed in a covenant with the Lord. *(Gen. 15.)*

Moses reminded the children of Israel that because they disobeyed the Lord, first by refusing to conquer Canaan when He told them to and then presumptuously going up into the hill to fight when they had been told not to, the Amorites were successful in destroying them in Seir. *(Deut. 1:44.)*

The Amorites were one of seven nations the Lord promised to destroy in Canaan, nations greater and mightier than the Israelites, so Israel could inherit the promised land. *(Deut. 7:1.)*

Solomon levied a tribute of bondservice upon all of the Amorites who remained among the Israelites. *(1 Kgs. 9:20.)* The people who were not of Israel who remained in the land—the Amorites, Hivites, Hittites, Perizzites and Jebusites—had to pay tribute to Solomon. *(2 Chr. 8:7.)*

After the children of Israel were delivered from Babylonian bondage, many Jews—including the priests and Levites— intermarried with and followed the abominations of the Amorites, Jebusites, Canaanites, Hittites, Perizzites, Ammonites, Moabites and Egyptians. Ezra prayed and confessed the sins of all the people, fearing the Lord would completely destroy them this time for their abominations. *(Ezra 9:1.)*

The Levites praised the Lord for His goodness to them and for the covenant the Lord had made with Abraham to give him the land of the Amorites, Canaanites, Hittites, Perizzites, Jebusites and Girgashites. *(Neh. 9:8.)*

The Amorites are referred to in the proverb the Lord gave Ezekiel comparing Jerusalem to a mother's daughter with the pagan nations being referred to as "sisters." In this proverb, the Lord told Jerusalem that "your mother was an Hittite and your father an Amorite." Just as the mother loathed her husband, so the daughter, Jerusalem, loathed her husband, the Lord. *(Ezek. 16:45.)*

The Lord reminded Israel that, just as He had destroyed the Amorites who were tall and strong, He could destroy them. *(Amos 2:9.)* (Chart 2e.)

AMOS. *Amos 1-9.*

Amos was a herdsman from Tekoa. He prophesied during the time of Uzziah (Azariah) king of Judah (who died about 740 B.C.) and in the days of Jeroboam the son of Joash, king of Israel (who died about 750 B.C.). He proclaimed the Lord's judgments that would befall Syria, the Philistines, Tyre, Edom and Ammon. Two years after Amos' prophecy, there was a big earthquake which caused the people to flee. *(Amos 1.)*

Amos prophesied the Lord would pour out judgments against Moab, Judah and Israel because of their transgressions. *(Amos 2.)*

Amos stressed that we must be in harmony with the Lord or He will not be with us. "Can two walk together except they be agreed?" The Lord will do nothing unless He first reveals His secrets unto His servants the prophets. Because Israel chose to do evil, they were encompassed about and overwhelmed by an adversary. *(Amos 3.)*

Amos taught that in spite of pestilence, famine, death, the Lord's withholding of rain and His pouring out of judgments upon the people, the children of Israel refused to return unto Him. *(Amos 4.)*

Amos urged Israel to seek the Lord, to do good, and live. The Lord knows their transgressions: they afflict the just; they take bribes; they turn aside the poor. Their sacrifices to idols is abhorrent to the Lord. *(Amos 5.)*

Amos continued to warn Israel. Woe to those who are at ease in Zion but are not grieved for the affliction of Joseph. Jacob shall be scattered because of pride. Israel shall be plagued with desolation. *(Amos 6.)*

When Amos prophesied against Israel, Amaziah the priest of Beth-el told him to go away. Amos explained that he was a herdsman and a gatherer of sycamore fruit—not a prophet nor the son of a prophet—when the Lord told him to prophesy against Israel. He prophesied that Israel would be taken captive and Jeroboam king of Israel would be slain by the sword. *(Amos 7.)*

The Lord showed Amos a basket of summer fruit and told him it indicated that "the end is come upon my people Israel; I will not again pass by them any more." There would be a "famine" of the Lord's word to His people. *(Amos 8.)*

The Lord showed Amos more judgments that would befall the children of Israel. No one can escape the eye of the Lord, no matter where they run to or hide. The Lord will sift the house of Israel among all nations. He will destroy the sinful from off the face of the earth; however, He will not destroy the house of Jacob completely. In the latter days, the Lord will again gather His people and raise up the tabernacle of David. The children of Israel will plant crops and make the area fruitful again. *(Amos 9.)*

AMOZ. *2 Kgs. 19:2; Isa. 1:1; 37:2.*

Amoz was the father of Isaiah the prophet.

AMRAM (1) (Moses' Father, Amramites). *Ex. 2:1; 6:18, 20; Num. 3:19, 27; 26:59; 1 Chr. 6:2-3; 23:12-20.*

Moses' Father (Amram) was of the house of Levi. He married a daughter of Levi. They had a son. When he was three months old, the infant's mother hid him in an ark in the bulrushes. *(Ex. 2:1.)*

Amram was a son of Kohath and a grandson of Levi. He married his father's sister, Jochebed. He and Jochebed were the parents of Aaron and Moses. He lived 137 years. *(Ex. 6:18, 20.)* Amram's wife Jochebed was his aunt. They were the parents of Aaron, Moses and Miriam. *(Num. 26:59.)*

Amram was the son of Kohath. **Amramites** were descendants of Amram. *(Num. 3:19, 27.)*

Amram's brothers were Izhar, Hebron and Uzziel. He was the father of Aaron, Moses and Miriam. *(1 Chr. 6:2-3.)*

When David numbered the Levites at the time he made Solomon king, he also divided them into courses among the sons of Levi: Gershon, Kohath and Merari. Kohath's sons were Amram, Izhar, Hebron and Uzziel. Amram's sons were Aaron and Moses. Aaron was separated from the others because he and his sons were to forever have the responsibility to sanctify the most holy things and to burn incense before the Lord. Moses' sons, Gershom and Eliezer, were named of the tribe of Levi. *(1 Chr. 23:12-20.)* (Charts 7b., 7d.)

AMRAM (2). *1 Chr. 1:41.* See **Hemdan.**

AMRAM (3). *Ezra 10:34 (18-19, 34, 44).*

Amram, a son of Bani, and his brothers were some of the men in Israel who took foreign wives but gave them up when Ezra feared the wrath of God would destroy Israel for this iniquity.

AMRAMITES (See Amram (1)).

AMRAPHEL. *Gen. 14:1.*

Amraphel was king of Shinar. He joined Chedorlaomer, king of Elam, and others in battle against Sodom and Gomorrah in which Lot, Abraham's nephew, and his family were taken captive.

AMZI (1). *1 Chr. 6:46 (44-47).*

Amzi, a descendant of Levi through Merari, was the son of Bani and the father of Hilkiah. (Chart 7e.)

AMZI (2). *Neh. 11:12.*

Amzi, an ancestor of Adaiah, the son of Zechariah and the father of Pelaliah, was one of the families chosen by lot to dwell in Jerusalem. (Chart 7g.)

ANAH (1). *Gen. 36:2, 20, 25.*

Anah, son of Seir the Horite, was the father of Aholibamah, one of Esau's wives. He also begat Dishon. He was a duke or tribal chief. (Charts 4a-f.; 19.)

ANAH (2). *Gen. 36:24; 1 Chr. 1:40-41.*

Anah was the son of Zibeon, who was the son of Seir the Horite. He was "that Anah that found the mules in the wilderness, as he fed the asses of Zibeon his father." (*Gen. 36:24.*)

Anah was a brother of Aiah (Ajah). *(1 Chr. 1:40-41.)* (Chart 4c.)

ANAIAH. *Neh. 8:1-8; 10:22.*

Anaiah was one of the men who stood on Ezra's right hand when Ezra read and interpreted the law of Moses to the people. *(Neh. 8:1-8.)* He was among those chief of the people who covenanted to marry in Israel, honor the Sabbath, pay tithes and keep the commandments. *(Neh. 10:22.)*

ANAK (Anakims). *Num. 13:22, 32-33; Deut. 1:28; 2:10-11, 20; 9:1-3; Josh. 11:21-22; 14:12-15; 15:13-14.*

Anak was the father of Ahiman, Sheshai and Talmai. He and his descendants occupied the land of Hebron. Because of their giant size, ten of the leaders Moses sent to scout out the land of Caanan gave negative reports upon their return. *(Num. 13:22, 32-33.)* **Anakims** were the descendants of Anak and dwelled in Canaan. When Moses sent spies from each tribe to scout out the land of Canaan, all but two returned with negative reports. The Anakims were very large. The scouts referred to them as giants and were afraid of them. *(Deut. 1:28.)* In addition to the Anakims, Emins and the Zamzummims and other tribes were also giants. *(Deut. 2:10-11, 20.)*

As the Israelites went into Canaan to dispossess them of their land, Moses admonished them to have no fear of the Anakims, even though they were "a people great and tall," because the Lord would fight their battles for them. *(Deut. 9:1-3.)*

Joshua cut off the Anakims so none were left in the land of the children of Israel. However, some remained in Gaza, Gath and Ashdod. *(Josh. 11:21-22.)*

Arba was a great man among the Anakims. Kirjath-arba (Hebron) was named after him. Caleb was given the land of Hebron for his inheritance because he had been faithful in helping to drive the Anakims out of the land. *(Josh. 14:12-15.)* Anak son of Arba was father of Sheshai, Ahiman and Talmai, who Caleb drove out of Hebron. *(Josh 15:13-14.)*

ANAMIM. *Gen. 10:13.*

Anamin was a son of Mizraim, a grandson of Ham, and a great-grandson of Noah. (Chart 2e.)

ANAMMELECH (See Adrammelech)

ANAN. *Neh. 10:26 (1, 26, 28-31.)*

Anan was among those chief of the people who covenanted to marry in Israel, honor the Sabbath, pay tithes and keep the commandments.

ANANI. *1 Chr. 3:24.*

Anani, a descendant of David, was a son of Elioenai. His brothers were Hodaiah, Eliashib, Pelaiah, Akkub, Johanan and Dalaiah. (Chart 1.)

ANANIAH. *Neh. 3:23.*

Ananiah was the father of Maaseiah and the grandfather of Azariah.

ANATH. *Judg. 3:31.*

Anath was the father of Shamga who was the third judge in Israel.

ANATHOTH (1). *1 Chr. 7:8.*

Anathoth was a son of Becher and a grandson of Benjamin. (Chart 16c.)

ANATHOTH (2). *Ezra 2:23 (1, 23); Neh. 7:27; 10:19 (1, 19, 28-31).*

Anathoth was of the people of Israel. The men of Anathoth who returned to Jerusalem from Babylon after Cyrus' proclamation to build the temple numbered 128. *(Ezra 2:23 [1, 23]; Neh. 7:27.)* He was among those chief of the people who covenanted to marry in Israel, honor the Sabbath, pay tithes and keep the commandments. *(Neh. 10:1, 19, 28-31.)*

ANER. *Gen. 14:13-24.*

Aner was a brother to Mamre and Eshcol. They joined Abram in Lot's rescue from King Chedorlaomer. When they returned from the slaughter of Chedorlaomer and the kings that were with him, the king of Sodom offered Abram the goods that had been retrieved. Abram took none, but suggested that Aner, Mamre and Eshcol should be allowed to take their portion.

ANETHOTHITE. *2 Sam. 23:27; 1 Chr. 27:12.*

The **Anethothite**, Abiezer, was one of David's mighty men. *(2 Sam. 23:27.)* He was a Benjamite and was assigned by David to be captain of the course of 24,000 who served for the ninth month. *(1 Chr. 27:12.)*

ANGEL OF THE LORD (1). *Gen. 16:7-11; 21:17.*

An **Angel of the Lord** found Hagar by a fountain of water after Hagar had been dealt harshly with by Sarah. The angel told her to return to her mistress and to submit herself to her. He told her the baby she was expecting was a boy and to name him Ishmael. *(Gen. 16:7-11.)*

An Angel of God spoke to Hagar from out of heaven when she and Ishmael were cast out and told her God had heard the cries of the lad. Hagar was shown a well where she was able to obtain water to give Ishmael a drink. *(Gen. 21:17.)*

ANGEL OF THE LORD (2). *Gen. 22:11-12.*

An **Angel of the Lord** intervened in Isaac's behalf when Abraham prepared to offer him as a sacrifice in obedience to the Lord's command.

ANGEL(S) OF THE LORD (3). *Gen. 32:1.*

Angels of God met Jacob after he left Laban to return to his own country.

ANGEL OF THE LORD (4). *Num. 22:23-35.*

An **Angel of the Lord** was sent to block the way of Balaam's ass when Balaam was responding to Balak's request for a curse against Israel. In the exchange that resulted, Balaam had his foot crushed against the wall and the ass' mouth was opened and the ass chastised him for smiting him. Balaam eventually saw the angel that the ass saw. The angel told him to go unto Balak, but to speak only what the angel told him to speak.

ANGEL OF THE LORD (5). *Judg. 2:1-4.*

An **Angel OF THE LORD** rebuked Israel for not serving the Lord.

ANGEL OF THE LORD (6). *Judg. 6:11-21.*

An **Angel of the Lord** appeared to Gideon and called him to deliver Israel from the hand of the Midianites.

ANGEL OF THE LORD (7). *Judg. 13:3-21.*

An **Angel of the Lord** appeared unto Manoah's wife and told her she would have a male child who would begin to deliver Israel from Philistine bondage. He gave her instructions. He appeared a second time to both Manoah and his wife. When he departed, he ascended to heaven in a flame from the altar. Manoah and his wife named their son Samson.

ANGEL OF THE LORD (8). *2 Sam. 24:16-17; 1 Chr. 21:15-16, 18, 20, 27, 30.*

An **Angel of the Lord** was sent to implement the Lord's vengence upon Israel because David had sinned in numbering Israel. Seventy thousand people died and then the Lord stayed the hand of the angel. *(2 Sam. 24:16-17; 1 Chr. 21:15-16.)* The angel of the Lord commanded Gad, David's seer, to tell David to go and build an altar in the threshingfloor of Ornan (Araunah). Ornan saw the angel of the Lord and his four sons hid themselves. David was afraid because of the sword of the angel of the Lord. *(1 Chr. 21: 18, 20, 27, 30.)*

ANGEL OF THE LORD (9). *1 Kgs. 19:5-7.*

An **Angel of the Lord** woke Elijah as he slept beneath a juniper tree and told him to eat. The angel awakened him a second time and instructed him to eat again as he had a long journey to make.

ANGEL OF THE LORD (10). *2 Kgs. 1:3, 15.*

The **Angel of the Lord** sent the prophet Elijah to intercept Ahaziah's messengers as they were enroute to inquire of Baal-zebub regarding Ahaziah's health. The Angel of the Lord instructed Elijah to accompany the third captain of 50 back to Ahaziah.

ANGEL OF THE LORD (11). *2 Kgs. 19:35; 2 Chr. 32:21; Isa. 37:36.*

An **Angel of the Lord**, in fulfillment of Isaiah's prophesy that the Assyrians would be destroyed, slew 185,000 of them while they slept in their camp.

ANGEL(S) OF THE Lord (12). *Zech. 1:9-21; 2:1-4; 3-5; 6:1-8.*

An **Angel of the Lord** explained Zechariah's vision of the red horses and the vision concerning four horns and four carpenters to him. *(Zech. 1:9-21.)*

The angel explained Zechariah's vision of the man with the measuring tape in his hand to him. *(Zech. 2:1-4.)*

In this vision, Zechariah saw Joshua the high priest (Jeshua), in filthy garments, standing before the angel of the Lord. Satan was at his right hand to accuse him. *(Zech. 3.)*

The angel of the Lord explained Zechariah's fifth vision wherein he saw a candlestick with seven lamps and seven pipes and two olive trees to him. *(Zech. 4.)*

An angel explained truths to Zechariah by using symbolical representations. *(Zech. 5.)*

An angel explained Zechariah's vision of the four chariots with horses of red, black, white, grisled and bay to him. *(Zech. 6:1-8.)*

ANIAM. *1 Chr. 7:19.*

Aniam, Ahian, Shechem and Likhi were sons of Shemida and descendants of Gilead, Machir and Manasseh. (Chart 15a.)

ANOTHER MAN. *1 Kgs. 20:37.*

Another Man was asked to smite one of the sons of the prophets after a first man refused, and he did so, wounding him.

ANTOTHIJAH. *1 Chr. 8:24-25.*

Antothijah, a descendant of Benjamin, was a son of Shashak who was a son of Beriah. (Chart 16g.)

ANUB. *1 Chr. 4:8.*

Anub was the son of Coz and the brother of Zobebah.

APHARSACHITES (See Apharsathchites)

APHARSATHCHITES (Apharsachites). *Ezra 4:9; 5:3-17; 6:6, 13.*

The **Apharsathchites** were among the various groups who were companions with the Samaritans and helped to hinder the work of rebuilding the temple in Jerusalem. *(Ezra 4:9.)* The **Apharsachites**, along with Tatnai, governor of the west side of the Euprhates River, and their friend Shethar-boznai, queried Zerubbabel, Jeshua and the prophets as to who gave them instruction to proceed with construction of the temple. They sent a letter to Darius outlining their response with a suggestion that a search be made to see if Cyrus had made such a decree. *(Ezra 5:3-17.)*

The Apharsachites Tatnai and Shethar-boznai were commanded by Darius, who had made a search and found that Cyrus had, indeed, made a decree that the temple should be built, not to hinder the work but, instead, to assist with funds and with sacrificial animals. This they quickly did. *(Ezra 6:6, 13.)*

APHARSITES. *Ezra 4:9.*

The **Apharsites** were among the various groups who were companions with the Samaritans and helped to hinder the work of rebuilding the temple in Jerusalem.

APHIAH. *1 Sam. 9:1.*

Aphiah, a Benjamite who was a mighty man of power, was the father of Bechorath and a great-great-great-grandfather of Saul. (Chart 16k.)

APHSES. *1 Chr. 24:15.*

Aphses was from the sons of Aaron. When David made the divisions of the sons of Aaron, there was one principal household for Eleazar and one taken for Ithamar. Eleazar had 16 sons and there were eight sons of Ithamar. These 24 sons who were chief of the fathers were divided by lot. Aphses drew the eighteenth lot.

APPAIM. *1 Chr. 2:30.*

Appaim was the son of Nadab. He begat Ishi. His brother was Seled. He was a five-times-great-grandson of Judah. (Chart 8c.)

ARA. *1 Chr. 7:38.*

Ara was a son of Jether. His brothers were Jephunneh and Pispah. He was a descendant of Asher. (Chart 14b.)

ARABIANS. *2 Chr. 17:11; 21:16-17; 26:7; Neh. 2:19; 4:7; Ezek. 27:21.*

Arabians (southern Arabia) are descendants of Joktan and are called Joktanites and Arabians in the Old Testament. *(See Arabians in the BD) (Note: Joktan's sons are listed in Gen. 10:26-30 and repeated in 1 Chr. 1:20-23.)* Because the Lord was with king Jehoshaphat, none of the kingdoms of the lands that were near Judah came to war against Jehoshaphat. The Arabians even brought him flocks. *(2 Chr. 17:11.)*

The Arabians and Philistines who were near the Ethiopians were stirred up by the Lord to go against Judah because of the wickedness of Jehoram, king of Judah. They took all of the substance they could find in the king's house as well as his sons and his wives. The only one left was Jehoahaz, Jehoram's youngest son. *(2 Chr. 21:16-17.)*

The Arabians and Philistines were defeated by Uzziah (Azariah), king of Judah. *(2 Chr. 26:7.)*

The Arabian Geshem, Sanballat the Horonite, and Tobiah the servant, an Ammonite, laughed and scorned Nehemiah for planning to rebuild the walls and gates of Jerusalem. *(Neh. 2:19.)* The Arabians, Ammonites and Ashdodites conspired with Sanballat and Tobiah to stop the work on the city walls. *(Neh. 4:7.)*

As Ezekiel lamented the fall of the great city of Tyrus, he bemoaned the loss of her riches and commerce, part of which involved the merchants of Arabia and all the princes of Kedar who traded lambs, rams and goats in the fairs of Tyrus. *(Ezek. 27:21.)*

ARAD (1). *Num. 21:1-3.*

Arad was king of the Canaanites. He fought against Israel and took some of them prisoner. Upon the plea of Israel to the Lord, the Lord delivered the Canaanites to Israel and they were utterly destroyed.

ARAD (2). *1 Chr. 8:15.*

Arad, a descendant of Benjamin, was a son of Beriah, who was a son of Elpaal, who was a son of Shaharaim and Hushim. (Chart 16g.)

ARAH (1). *1 Chr. 7:39.*

Arah, a descendant of Asher, was a son of Ulla. His brothers were Haniel and Rezia. (Chart 14b.)

ARAH (2). *Ezra 2:5; Neh. 7:10.*

Arah was of the people of Israel. The men of the children of Arah who returned to Jerusalem from Babylon after Cyrus' proclamation to build the temple numbered 775. *(Ezra 2:5.)* The number of men is given as 652 rather than 775 in Neh. 7:10.

ARAH (3). *Neh. 6:18.*

Arah was the father of Shechaniah who was the father-in-law of Tobiah.

ARAM (1). *Gen. 10:22-23; 1 Chr. 1:17.*

Aram was a son of Shem and a grandson of Noah. Aram's children were Uz, Hul, Gether and Mash (Meshech). *(Gen. 10:22-23.)*

Aram was a son of Shem. *(1 Chr. 1:17.)* (Chart 2b.)

ARAM (2). *Gen. 22:21.*

Aram was the son of Kemuel and the grandson of Milcah and Nahor, Abraham's brother. (Chart 2c.)

ARAM (3). *1 Chr. 7:34.*

Aram was a son of Shamer (Shomer) and a great-great-grandson of Asher. His brothers were Ahi, Rohgah and Jehubbah. (Chart 14a.)

ARAM-NAHARAIM. *Ps. 60:Subtitle.*

Aram-naharaim and Aram-zobah apparently strove with David. However, there is no other reference in the Bible to anyone with either of those names.

ARAM-ZOBAH. *Ps. 60:Subtitle.*

Aram-zobah and Aram-naharaim apparently strove with David. However, there is no other reference in the Bible to anyone with either of those names.

ARAN. *Gen. 36:28.*

Aran was a son of Dishan who was a son of Seir the Horite. (Chart 4f.)

ARAUNAH (Ornan). *2 Sam. 24:16-25; 1 Chr. 21:18-28; 2 Chr. 3:1.*

Araunah the Jebusite had a threshingplace. When David angered the Lord because he counted the men of war in Israel, three days of pestilence followed. David was instructed by the prophet Gad to go to Araunah and build an altar unto the Lord in the threshingfloor. Araunah offered to give David all he needed to make his sacrifice, but David declined to make an offering which cost him nothing. David bought the threshingfloor from Araunah and built an altar unto the Lord where upon he offered burnt offerings and peace offerings. *(2 Sam. 24:16-25.)*

Ornan (Araunah) saw the angel of the Lord standing in the threshingfloor. His four sons who were with him hid themselves. *(1 Chr. 21:18-28. This is a repeat of 2 Sam. 24:16-18, but with some modification.)*

Solomon built the house of the Lord at the site where the Lord had appeared unto David in the threshingfloor of Ornan the Jebusite at Jerusalem in mount Moriah. *(2 Chr. 3:1.)*

ARBA. *Josh. 14:15; 15:13-14.*

Arba was both a person and a city. "Arba was a great man among the Anakims." The city of Kirjath-arba (later called Hebron) was named for him. *(Note: The city is called Arbah in Gen. 35:27. It is the city where Abraham and Isaac sojourned.) (Josh. 14:15.)* Arba was the father of Anak and the grandfather of Sheshai, Ahiman and Talmai. *(Josh. 15:13-14.)*

ARBATHITE. *2 Sam. 23:31; 1 Chr. 11:32.*

The **Arbathite** Abi-albon (Abiel) was one of David's mighty men. (Chart 17.)

ARBITE. *2 Sam. 23:35.*

The **Arbite** Paarai was one of David's mighty men. (Chart 17.)

ARCHEVITES. *Ezra 4:9.*

The **Archevites** were among the various groups who were companions with the Samaritans and helped to hinder the work of rebuilding the temple in Jerusalem.

ARCHITE. *2 Sam. 15:32; 1 Chr. 27:33.*

An **Archite** named Hushai was David's friend *(2 Sam. 15:32)* and the king's companion *(1 Chr. 27:33)*.

ARD (Ardites). *Gen. 46:21; Num. 26:40.*

Ard was a son of Benjamin and a grandson of Jacob. His brothers were Belah, Becher, Ashbel, Gera, Naaman, Ehi, Rosh, Muppim and Huppim. *(Gen. 46:21.)*

Ard and Naaman are listed as sons of Bela rather than sons of Benjamin. Ard's descendants are the Ardites. *(Num. 26:40.)* (Charts 16a-b.)

ARDON. *1 Chr. 2:18.*

Ardon was one of the sons of Caleb and Azubah of the house of Judah. His brothers were Jesher and Shobab. *(Note: It is not clear in this scripture if Ardon, Jesher and Shobab were sons of Azubah or if they were sons of Jerioth.)* (Chart 8h.)

ARELI (Arelites). *Gen. 46:16; Num. 26:17.*

Areli was a son of Gad and a grandson of Jacob. *(Gen. 46:16.)* He is the father of the **Arelites**. *(Num. 26:17.)* (Chart 13a.)

ARGOB. *2 Kgs. 15:25.*

Argob, along with Arieh and fifty men of the Gileadites, assisted Pekah in his coup d'e´tat over Pekahiah wherein Pekahiah was killed and Pekah reigned in his stead.

ARIDAI . *Esth. 9:9, 13.*

Aridai was one of Haman's ten sons who was slain by the Jews and, at queen Esther's request, was hung on the gallows by king Ahasuerus.

ARIDATHA. *Esth. 9:8, 13.*

Aridatha was one of Haman's ten sons who was slain by the Jews and, at queen Esther's request, was hung on the gallows by king Ahasuerus.

ARIEH. *2 Kgs. 15:25.*

Arieh, along with Argob and fifty men of the Gileadites, assisted Pekah in his coup d'e´tat over Pekahiah wherein Pekahiah was slain and Pekah reigned in his stead.

ARIEL. *Ezra 8:16.*

Ariel was one of the chief men Ezra sent for when he gathered the people together as he was preparing to lead them to Jerusalem from Babylon and discovered there were no Levites among the group. He sent this group to Iddo and the Nethinims to request that they send them some ministers for the house of God. *(Note: The Bible Dictionary indicates Ariel is also another name for Jerusalem. It is used in that sense in Isa. 29:1, 7.)*

ARIOCH (1). *Gen. 14:1, 9.*

Arioch, king of Ellasar, joined with Chedorlaomer (king of Elam) and others in battle against Sodom and Gomorrah wherein Lot and his family were taken captive.

ARIOCH (2). *Dan. 2:14-25.*

Arioch was captain of king Nebuchadnezzar's guard. When Nebuchadnezzar had a disturbing dream (which he could not remember), the Chaldeans, Nebuchadnezzar's magicians, astrologers and sorcerers could neither interpret the dream for him nor tell him what the dream was, so Nebuchadnezzar ordered all the wise men killed. However, Daniel asked Arioch what the hurry was and requested time to inquire of the Lord. After getting an answer from the Lord, Daniel asked Arioch to take him before the king, which he did.

ARISAI. *Esth. 9:9, 13.*

Arisai was one of Haman's ten sons who was slain by the Jews and, at queen Esther's request, was hung on the gallows by king Ahasuerus.

ARKITE. *Gen. 10:17.*

Arkites were descendants of Canaan who was a son of Ham. (Chart 2e.)

ARMONI. *2 Sam. 21:8-9.*

Armoni was one of the sons of Saul and his concubine Rizpah. He and his brother Mephibosheth were given to the Gibeonites by David to be hung as an atonement for Saul's having slain the Gibeonites contrary to the oath Israel had made with them. (Chart 16 l.)

ARNAN. *1 Chr. 3:21.*

Arnan, a descendant of David, was a son of Jesaiah. (Chart 1.)

ARODI (Arod, Arodites). *Gen. 46:16; Num. 26:17.*

Arodi was a son of Gad and a grandson of Jacob. *(Gen. 46:16.)* **Arod** was the father of the **Arodites.** *(Num. 26:17.)* (Chart 13a.)

ARPHAXAD. *Gen. 10:22, 24.*

Arphaxad was a son of Shem and a grandson of Noah. He begat Salah. *(Note: There is a ten-year discrepancy between the years that add up to the date of the flood and the date of Arphaxad's birth. The flood occurred 1656 years following the Fall of Adam and Eve, according to the sum total of the years indicated for who begat whom at what age. According to the sum totals—as clarified in Moses 8:12 in the Pearl of Great Price—Shem was born 1548 years after the Fall and would have been 108 years old at the time of the flood and 110 years old when Arphaxad was born. However, in Gen. 11:10, it indicates that he was 100 years old when Arphaxad was born and that Arphaxad was born two years after the flood.)* (Charts 1., 2b.; 21.)

ARTAXERXES (Psuedo-Smerdis). *Ezra 4:7-24.*

(Note: There are three Artaxerxes in the Encyclopædia Britannica: Artaxerxes I (Longimanus) (465-425 B.C.), son of Xerxes; Artaxerxes II (404-359/358 B.C.), son of Darius II and brother to Cyrus the Younger; Artaxerxes III (Ochus) (359/358-338 B.C.), son of Artaxerxes II. There is no entry for the Artaxerxes who ruled in 521 B.C.)

Artaxerxes was king of Persia (521 B.C.) following Ahasuerus and prior to Darius. When the Samaritans and all their companions wrote a letter against Jerusalem and sent it to Artaxerxes, he responded that they should cause the children of Israel to stop building the temple and the city. Thus, as Artaxerxes instructed, the Samaritans used their power and force to make the children of Israel cease work. It ceased unto the second year of the reign of Darius king of Persia. *(Note: According to the "Profane History" in the Chronology Chart in the Bible Dictionary, there are two Artaxerxes: Psuedo-Smerdis—king of Persia around 521 B.C., as metioned in Ezra 4:7; and Longimanus—king of Persia between 465 and 425 B.C.—mentioned in other references. However, under "Artaxerxus" in the BD, all references are directed to Longimanus. If that were the case, he would have been king briefly in 521 B.C. following Ahasuerus (Cambyses, king of Persia, 529-521 B.C.) and then again in 465 B.C. after Darius I and Ahasuserus (Xerxes). Because the work ceased unto the second year of king Darius' reign, the assumption here is that this reference is to Pseudo-Smerdis since Darius reigned after him and that the other scriptures refer to Longimanus.)*

ARTAXERXES (Longimanus). *Ezra 6:14; 7:1-28; 8; Neh. 2:6-9; 5:14; 13:6.*

Artaxerxes, son of Xerxes, was king of Persia around 465-425 B.C. According to his commandment and that of Cyrus and Darius, Israel finished building the temple. *(Ezra 6:14.)*

Artaxerxes decreed in his seventh year that Ezra could leave Babylon and take any Israelite exiles, priests and Levites who wanted to go with him back to Jerusalem. He also decreed that Ezra should take all the gold and silver "thou canst find in all the province of Babylon, with the freewill offering of the people" to Jerusalem for beautifying the temple. In addition, he instructed Ezra to appoint magistrates and judges to judge the people. *(Ezra 7:1-28.)* Those who left Babylon and went with Ezra during the reign of Artaxerxes are listed. *(Ezra 8.)*

Artaxerxes allowed Nehemiah to go to Jerusalem to rebuild the walls and gates that had been burned down. He gave Nehemiah letters showing that Nehemiah had official approval to do what he went to do. *(Neh. 2:6-9.)*

Artaxerxes had been king 12 years when Nehemiah chastised the nobles and rulers in Jerusalem for engaging in usury against the people. *(Neh. 5:14.)* It was in the 32nd year of Artaxerxes king of Babylon that Nehemiah was given permission to leave the king and return to Jerusalem to rebuild the walls of the city. *(Neh. 13:6.)*

ARTAXERXES' (Longimanus') WIFE, THE QUEEN. *Neh. 2:6.*

The Queen was with Artaxerxes when he gave Nehemiah permission to go to Jerusalem to rebuild the walls and the gates to the city.

ARVADITE. *Gen. 10:18.*

Arvadites were descendants of Canaan who was a son of Ham. (Chart 2e.)

ARZA. *1 Kgs. 16:9.*

Arza was steward of king Elah's house in Tirzah. Zimri, Elah's servant, slew Elah in Arza's house.

ASA (1). *1 Kgs. 15:8-24; 1 Chr. 3:10; 2 Chr. 14-17:1; 20:32; Jer. 41:9.*

Asa was the son of Abijam, grandson of Rehoboam and great-grandson of Solomon. He reigned as king of Judah following Abijam's death. His reign began in the 20th year of king Jeroboam's reign over the rest of Israel. He reigned for 41 years in Jerusalem. His grandmother was Maachah. He was a righteous man and removed the Sodomites from the land along with the idols. He removed Maachah from her position of queen and burned her idol. He returned the items which had been dedicated unto the Lord to the temple. There was war between him and Baasha, king of Israel all their days. When Baasha came against him to battle, he enlisted the help of Ben-hadad, king of Syria. The rest of his history is recorded in the book of the chronicles of the kings of Judah. In his old age his feet were diseased. He died and was buried with his fathers in the city of David. His son Jehoshaphat reigned in his stead. *(1 Kgs. 15:8-24.)*

Asa was the son of Abia (Abijam) and the father of Jehoshaphat. *(1 Chr. 3:10.)*

Asa's father, Abijah (Abia, Abijam), died and Asa reigned in his stead. Asa did that which was right before the Lord. There was peace in the land the first 10 years of his reign. He rebuilt the cities. He defeated Zerah and the Ethiopians who came against Judah. *(2 Chr. 14.)*

The prophet Azariah went to Asa and prophesied that Judah would prosper if the people kept the commandments. Asa did away with all the false worship. Judah was joined by many people from the other tribes when they saw that the Lord was with Judah. The people gathered together in the 15th year of Asa's reign and made a covenant with the Lord. Asa removed his grandmother Maachah from being queen because she had made an idol in a grove. There were no more wars until the 35th year of Asa's reign. *(2 Chr. 15.)*

In the 36th year of Asa's reign, Baasha, king of Israel, came against Judah. Asa turned to Ben-hadad, king of Syria, for help rather than turning to the Lord. Hanani the seer came to him and chastised him and told him that because he had not relied on the Lord the king of Syria had escaped and he would henceforth have wars. Asa became angry with Hanani and cast him into prison. In the 39th year of his reign, Asa's feet became diseased. He died in the 41st year of his reign. *(2 Chr. 16.)*

Asa's son Jehoshaphat reigned in his stead. *(2 Chr. 17:1.)* He walked in the ways of Asa, doing right in the sight of the Lord. *(2 Chr. 20:32.)*

When Asa was king of Judah, he feared Baasha king of Israel so he dug a big pit. Later, when Ishmael slew Gedaliah who was governor over the remnant of Judah, the Jews, Chaldeans and men of war who were also in Mizpah, he dumped the bodies into the pit Asa had made. *(Jer. 41:9.)* (Chart 1.)

ASA (2). *1 Chr. 9:16.*

<u>Asa</u> was the son of Elkanah and the father of Berechiah. He was a Levite whose descendants dwelled in the villages of the Netophathites. His genealogy was written in the book of the kings of Israel and Jusdah who were carried away to Babylon for their transgression.

ASAHEL (1). *2 Sam. 2:18-32; 3:27-30; 23:24; 1 Chr. 2:16; 11:26; 27:7.*

<u>Asahel</u> was one of David's sister Zeruiah's three sons. His brothers were Joab and Abishai. He was "as light of foot as a wild roe." He pursued after Abner when Abner's 12 servants from the tribe of Benjamin and David's 12 servants had been engaged in a conflict wherein all of Abner's men were slain. Abner told him to turn back, and when he wouldn't, Abner slew him with a spear. He was buried in the sepulchre of his father in Beth-lehem. *(2 Sam. 2:18-32.)* Asahel's blood was avenged when Joab slew Abner. *(2 Sam. 3:27-30.)*

Asahel was one of David's mighty men *(2 Sam. 23:24)* and one of the valiant men of his armies *(1 Chr. 11:26)*.

Asahel, Abishai and Joab were sons of Zeruiah. *(1 Chr. 2:16.)*

Asahel was assigned by David to be captain over the coursefor the fourth month. His son Zebadiah was after him. His course numbered 24,000. *(1 Chr. 27:7.)* (Charts 8d.; 17.)

ASAHEL (2). *2 Chr. 17:8-9.*

Asahel, a Levite, along with other Levites and Elisham and Jehoram, the priests, was sent by king Jehoshaphat to journey with the princes of Judah throughout the cities of Judah to instruct the people out of the book of the law of the Lord.

ASAHEL (3). *2 Chr. 31:13.*

Asahel, among others, was an overseer of tithes, offerings and the "dedicated things" under the hand of Cononiah and Cononiah's brother Shimei according to the commandment of king Hezekiah and Azariah, the ruler of the house of God.

ASAHEL (4). *Ezra 10:15.*

Asahel was the father of Jonathan.

ASAHIAH (Asaiah (1)). *2 Kgs. 22:12-20; 2 Chr. 34:20-28.*

Asahiah was a servant of king Josiah. He was commanded by king Josiah to accompany the high priest Hilkiah, Shaphan and others to inquire of the Lord concerning the book of the law which Hilkiah had found in the house of the Lord. They inquired of the prophetess Huldah who prophesied wrath upon the people because of their wickedness but blessings upon king Josiah because of his righteousness. *(2 Kgs. 22:12-20.)*

Asahiah's name is given as **Asaiah**. *(2 Chr. 34:20-28. This is a repeat of 2 Kgs. 22:12-20.)*

ASAIAH (2). *1 Chr. 4:36.*

Asaiah was a descendant of Shimei who was a descendant of Jacob's son Simeon. (Chart 6a.)

ASAIAH (3). *1 Chr. 6:30, 44-45; 15:6, 11.*

Asaiah, a descendant of Levi through Merari, was the son of Haggiah. *(1 Chr. 6:30, 44-45.)* He was the chief of the sons of Merari. He and 220 of his brethren were called by David to assemble with other Levites to prepare themselves to retrieve the ark of God from the house of Obed-edom so as to bring it to the place David had prepared for it in the city of David. *(1 Chr. 15:6, 11.)* (Chart 7e.)

ASAIAH (4). *1 Chr. 9:5.*

Asaiah was a Shilonite and was the firstborn son of his father. He and his sons were chosen to dwell in Jerusalem following their captivity in Babylon. Their genealogy was recorded in the book of the kings of Israel and Judah who were carried away to Babylon for their transgression.

ASAPH (1). *2 Kgs. 18:18; Isa. 36-3.*

Asaph was the father of Hezekiah's recorder Joah.

ASAPH (2). *1 Chr. 6:39; 9:15; 15:17-19; 16:5, 7, 37; 25:1-2, 9; 2 Chr. 5:12; 20:14-17; 29:13; Ezra 2:41; 3:10; Neh. 7:44; 11:17, 22; 12:35; Ps. 50; 73-83.*

Asaph was the son of Berachiah and was of the house of Levi through Gershom. He was one of David's singers. *(1 Chr. 6:39.)*

Asaph, the father of Zichri, was a Levite whose descendants dwelt in the villages of the Netophahites. His genealogy was written in the book of the kings of Israel and Judah who were carried away to Babylon for their transgression. He and others named by name were heads of the house of their fathers and were "able men for the work of the service of the house of God." *(1 Chr. 9:15.)*

Asaph, of the tribe of Gershon; Heman, of the tribe of Kohath; and Ethan, of the tribe of Merari, were singers appointed to sound the cymbals of brass. *(1 Chr. 15:17-19.)* Asaph was appointed by David to minister before the ark of the Lord and was assigned to play the cymbals. David delivered his psalm of thanksgiving to Asaph and his brethren, who administered before the ark continually. *(1 Chr. 16:5, 7, 37.)* The musicians, Asaph and his sons along with those of Heman and Jeduthun, cast their lots and were separated by David as to their service. Those of the sons of Asaph were Zaccur (Zichri), Joseph, Nethaniah and Asarelah. "The first lot came forth for Asaph to Joseph." *(1 Chr. 25:1-2, 9.)*

The Levites who were the singers, those of Asaph, Heman and Jeduthun, with their sons and brethren, were dressed in white linen and made music to praise the Lord when the temple was finished by Solomon and the ark of the covenant was placed in the holy of holies. The glory of the Lord filled the temple. *(2 Chr. 5:12.)*

Asaph's descendants included Mattaniah, the father of Jeiel, the father of Benaiah, the father of Zechariah, the father of Jahaziel, which Jahaziel prophesied to king Jehoshaphat that the Lord would fight Judah's battle against the children of Ammon, Moab and mount Seir. *(2 Chr. 20:14-17.)*

Asaph's sons, Zechariah and Mattaniah, were among those whom Hezekiah, king of Judah, instructed to sanctify themselves so they could cleanse and sanctify the house of the Lord. *(2 Chr. 29:13.)*

When Cyrus, king of Persia, proclaimed the building of the temple in Jerusalem and the people left Babylon to return to Jerusalem, the singers, the children of Asaph, numbered 128. *(Ezra 2:41.)*

When the builders laid the foundation of the temple, the sons of Asaph with their cymbals and the priests dressed in their apparel and with trumpets, praised the Lord. *(Ezra 3:10.)*

The children of Asaph who went up out of captivity, of those whom Nebuchadnezzar had carried away captive, who returned to Jerusalem numbered 148. *(Neh. 7:44.) (Compare Ezra 2:41.)*

Asaph was the father of Zabdi (Zichri, Zaccur), who was the father of Micha, the father of Mattaniah, the father of Hashabiah, the father of Bani, the father of Uzzi. The singers, the sons of Asaph, were over the business of the house of God when the children of Israel returned to Jerusalem from Babylonian captivity. *(Neh. 11:17, 22.)*

Asaph's descendants are listed as Zaccur, Michaiah, Mattaniah, Shemaiah, Jonathan and Zechariah. *(Neh. 12:35.)*

Several psalms are attributed to Asaph. He speaks of the Second Coming of the Messiah in Psalm 50. In Psalm 83, he declares that the Lord's name is JEHOVAH and that JEHOVAH is the Most High over all the earth. *(Ps. 50; 73-83.)* (Chart 7a.)

ASAPH (3). *1 Chr. 26:1.*

<u>Asaph's</u> descendant Meshelemiah the son of Kore, along with other Levites, was assigned by David to be a porter.

ASAPH (4). *Neh. 2:8.*

<u>Asaph</u> was keeper of king Artaxerxes' forest. Nehemiah requested Artaxerxes send a letter to Asaph instructing him to give Nehemiah timber for making the gates and walls of Jerusalem.

ASAREEL. *1 Chr. 4:16.*

<u>Asareel</u> was a son of Jehaleleel. His brothers were Ziph, Ziphah and Tiria. (Chart 8n.)

ASARELAH (Jesharelah). *1 Chr. 25:2, 14.*

<u>Asarelah</u>, a Levite, was one of the musicians. He was of the sons of Asaph. The musicians—sons of Asaph, Heman and Jeduthun—drew lots and were given their duty assignments by David and the captains of the host. **Jesharelah** cast the seventh lot. He, his sons and his brethren numbered 12. (Chart 7a.)

ASENATH. *Gen. 41:45, 50-52; 46:20.*

<u>Asenath</u>, the daughter of Potipherah priest of On, was Joseph's wife, given to him by Pharaoh. She bore Joseph two sons before the famine: Manasseh and Ephraim. *(Gen. 41:45, 50-52.)* Asenath bore Manasseh and Ephraim in the land of Egypt. *(Gen. 46:20.)* (Chart 15d.)

ASHBEA. *1 Chr. 4:21.*

<u>Ashbea</u> belonged to the family of Shelah, son of Judah. The families of his house wrought fine linen. (Chart 8a.)

ASHBEL (Ashbelites). *Gen. 46:21-22; Num. 26:38; 1 Chr. 8:1.*

<u>Ashbel</u> was a son of Benjamin (and numbered unto Rachel) and a grandson of Jacob. His brothers were Belah, Becher, Gera, Naaman, Ehi, Rosh, Muppim, Huppim and Ard. *(Gen. 46:21-22.)* His descendants are the **Ashbelites**. *(Num. 26:38.)*

Ashbel was Benjamin's secondborn son. His brothers were Bela, Benjamin's firstborn; Aharah, the thirdborn; Nohah, the fourthborn; and Rapha, the fifthborn. *(1 Chr. 8:1.)* (Charts 16a-b., 16d.)

ASHDODITES. *Neh. 4:7.*

<u>Ashdodites</u>, citizens of the Philistine city of Ashdod, conspired with Sanballat and his servant Tobiah, the Arabians and the Ammonites to stop Nehemiah and the Jews from rebuilding the walls of Jerusalem.

ASHER. *Gen. 30:13; 37; 46:17; 49:1, 20; 50:8; Num. 1:13, 40-41; 2:25-27; 26:44-47; 34:27; Deut. 27:13; 33:24; Josh. 19:24-31; 21:6, 30; Judg. 1:31-32; 5:17; 6:35; 7:23; 1 Kgs. 4:16; 1 Chr. 6:62, 74; 7:30-40; 12:36; 2 Chr. 30:11; Ezek. 48:2, 34.*

<u>Asher</u> was the second son of Jacob and Zilpah, Leah's handmaid. (He was Jacob's eighth son.) *(Gen. 30:13.)*

Asher and his brothers hated their younger brother Joseph and sold him to a group of Ishmeelites, or Midianite merchantmen, for 20 pieces of silver. They dipped his coat of many colors in animal blood and gave it to their father so he would think Joseph had been killed by wild beasts. *(Gen. 37.)*

Asher begat Jimnah, Ishuah, Isui, Beriah, and Serah their sister. *(Gen. 46:17.)*

After the brothers had gone to Egypt for grain and were finally reunited with Joseph, and following their moving their entire family to Egypt, the time came when Jacob called his sons together to tell them what would befall each of them in the last days. He told Asher "his bread shall be fat, and he shall yield royal dainties." *(Gen. 49:1, 20.)*

Following Jacob's death, Asher traveled to Canaan with his brothers and a royal entourage from Egypt for his father's burial. *(Gen. 50:8.)*

From the tribe of Asher, Moses was instructed to appoint Pagiel, son of Ocran, to be the leader of his people as Israel prepared for war. The males in the tribe of Asher who were 20 years old or older who could go to war numbered 41,500. *(Num. 1:13, 40-41.)* The tribe of Asher, under the leadership of Pagiel, was instructed to pitch their tents between the tribes of Dan and Naphtali on the north side of the encampment. *(Num. 2.25-27.)*

Asher's children are listed as Jimna (Jimnah), Jesui (Isui), Beriah and Sarah (Serah). *(Note: Ishuah has been omitted.)* The males in Asher's family who were twenty years old or older as counted by Moses and Eleazar on the plains of Moab numbered 53,400. His family included the Jimnites, Jesuites, Berites, Heberites and Malchielites. *(Num. 26:44-47.)*

Asher's descendant, Ahihud, son of Shelomi, was assigned to divide Asher's inheritance among Asher's posterity. *(Num. 34:27.)*

As the children of Israel crossed over Jordan into Canaan to inherit the promised land, the tribes of Asher, Reuben, Gad, Zebulun, Dan and Naphtali were instructed to stand upon mount Ebal to curse. *(Deut. 27:13.)*

Moses blessed the tribe of Asher. *(Deut. 33:24.)*

When Joshua cast lots to divide the promised land, the tribe of Asher received the fifth lot. Boundaries of the cities of Asher's inheritance are described. *(Josh. 19:24-31.)*

The cities taken from within the bourdaries of land given to Asher, Issachar, Nephtali and the half tribe of Manasseh that were to be given to the children of Gideon are listed. *(Josh. 21:6, 30.)*

Asher did not drive the inhabitants out of the promised land and the people dwelled among the Canaanites. *(Judg. 1:31-32.)*

In Deborah's and Barak's song of praise, they rejoice that "Asher continued on the sea shore, and abode in his beaches." *(Judg. 5:17.)*

Gideon sent messengers throughout the land, including unto Asher, that they might come up to meet him so they could unite to save Israel. *(Judg. 6:35.)*

The men of Asher, Naphtali and Manasseh joined together and pursued the Midianites. *(Judg. 7:23.)*

The officers in Solomon's court are listed. Baanak the son of Hushai was in Asher and in Aloth. *(1 Kgs. 4:16.)*

The cities given to the Levites out of Asher and other areas are listed. *(1 Chr. 6:62, 74.)*

Asher's children were Imnah (Jimnah, Jimna), Isuah (Ishuah), Ishuai (Isui, Jesui), Beriah and Serah, a daughter. *(1 Chr. 7:30-40.)*

When David became king and went to Ziklag, all Israel rejoiced and sent their armies to support him. The tribe of Asher sent 40,000 men who were expert in war. *(1 Chr. 12:36.)*

When Hezekiah, king of Judah, invited all Israel to go to Jerusalem to participate in a solemn Passover, many of the children of Israel scorned and mocked the couriers. Nevertheless, some of those from Asher, Manasseh and Zebulun humbled themselves and went to Jerusalem. *(2 Chr. 30:11.)*

The Lord revealed to Ezekiel just how the land should be divided by tribes when the children of Israel are gathered in the latter days. Asher's portion will be by the border of Dan, from the east side unto the west side. The twelve gates of the city are to bear the names of the twelve sons of Jacob. One of the three west gates is to be named for Asher. *(Ezek. 48:2, 34.)* (Charts 1; 3d.; 5a.; 6a.; 7a.; 8a.; 9a.; 10a.; 11a.; 12a.; 13a.; 14a.; 15a.; 16a.)

ASHIMA. *2 Kgs. 17:30.*

<u>Ashima</u> was the false god made by the men of Hamath after they were given the lands of the Israelites.

ASHKENAZ. *Gen. 10:3.*

<u>Ashkenaz</u> was a son of Gomer, grandson of Japheth, and a great-grandson of Noah. (Chart 2a.)

ASHPENAZ. *Dan. 1:3-7.*

<u>Ashpenaz</u> was the master of king Nebuchadnezzar's eunuchs. Nebuchadnezzar instructed him to bring certain unblemished children of Israel to the palace that they might be taught in the learning and language of the Chaldeans. Daniel (Belteshazzar), Hananiah (Shadrach), Mishael (Meshach) and Azariah (Abed-nego) were among those who were chosen.

ASHRIEL (See Asriel).

ASHTAROTH (Ashtoreth). *Judg. 2:13; 10:6; 1 Sam. 7:3-4; 12:10; 31:10; 1 Kgs. 11:5.*

<u>Ashtaroth</u> (plural of **Ashtoreth**) refers to the pagan gods Israel worshipped along with Baal and the gods of Syria, Zidon, Moab, the children of Ammon and the Philistines *(Judg. 2:13; 10:6.)*

Samuel urged Israel to put away false gods. If Israel did, the Lord would deliver them out of the hand of the Philistines. Israel followed Samuel's counsel and served the Lord. *(1 Sam. 7:3-4.)*

The children of Israel acknowledged their sins of idol worship to the Lord and prayed for deliverance from their enemies. *(1 Sam. 12:10.)*

After the Philistines slew Saul and his sons, they put Saul's armor in the house of Ashtoroth and fastened his headless body to the wall of Beth-shan. *(1 Sam. 31:10.)*

In Solomon's old age, he went after Ashtoreth, the goddess of the Zidonians, and other false gods. *(1 Kgs. 11:5.)*

ASHUR. *1 Chr. 2:24; 4:5-7.*

Ashur was the son of Abiah, Hezron's wife, born after Hezron died. He was the father of Tekoa. *(1 Chr. 2:24.)* He had two wives: Helah and Naarah. Naarah bore him Ahuzam, Hepher, Temeni and Haahashtari. Helah bore Zereth, Jezoar and Ethnan. *(1 Chr. 4:5-7.)* (Charts 8c-d., 8h.; 15b.)

ASHURITES. *Ezek. 27:6.*

The **Ashurites** made benches of ivory for Tyrus, which Tyrus Ezekiel prophesied would fall.

ASHVATH. *1 Chr. 7:33.*

Ashvath was a son of Japhlet and a great-great-grandson of Asher. His brothers were Pasach and Bimhal. (Chart 14a.)

ASIEL. *1 Chr. 4:35.*

Asiel, a descendant of Shimei, was the father of Seraiah. (Chart 6a.)

ASNAH. *Ezra 2:50, 58.*

Asnah was a Nethinim. When the Nethinims and the children of Solomon's servants left Babylon to return to Jerusalem to build the house of the Lord as proclaimed by Cyrus, king of Persia, they numbered 392.

ASNAPPAR. *Ezra 4:10.* See **Esarhaddon**.

ASPATHA. *Esth. 9:7.*

Aspatha was one of Haman's ten sons who was slain by the Jews and, at queen Esther's request, was hung on the gallows by king Ahasuerus.

ASRIEL (Ashriel, Asrielites). *Num. 26:31-32; 1 Chr. 7:14.*

Asriel was a son of Gilead and a great-grandson of Manasseh. His descendants were the **Asrielites**. His brothers were Jeezer, Helek, Shechem, Shemida and Hepher. *(Num. 26:31-32.)*

Ashriel was a son (great grandson) of Manasseh. *(1 Chr. 7:14.)* (Charts 15a-b.)

ASSHUR (1). *Gen. 10:11.*

Asshur came out of the land of Shinar *(v. 10)*, which was the beginning of the kingdom of Nimrod, who was a grandson of Ham. Asshur built Nineveh, Rehoboth and Calah.

ASSHUR (2). *Gen. 10:22.*

Asshur was a son of Shem and a grandson of Noah. (Chart 2.b)

ASSHUR (3) (Also see Assyrians). *Num. 24:22-24; Ezek. 27:22-23; 32:21-23; Hosea 14:3.*

Asshur, Balaam prophesied concerning the destiny of Israel, would carry the Kenite away captive and would be afflicted by ships coming from the coast of Chittim. *(Num. 24:22-24.)*

As Ezekiel lamented the fall of the great city of Tyrus, he bemoaned the loss of her riches and commerce, part of which involved the merchants of Sheba and Raamah who traded spices, precious stones and gold in the fairs at Tyrus. Haran, Canneh and Eden were merchants of Asshur, Sheba and Chilmad and traded in blue clothes, broidered work, chests of rich apparel, bound with cords, and made of cedar. *(Ezek. 27:22-23.)*

As Ezekiel lamented for Pharaoh king of Egypt and for Egypt, herself, the Lord told him, "The strong among the mighty shall speak to him (Pharaoh) out of the midst of hell with them that help him: they are gone down, they lie uncircumcised, slain by the sword. Asshur is there and all her company: his graves are about him: all of them slain, fallen by the sword: whose graves are set in the sides of the pit, and her company is round about her grave: all of them slain, fallen by the sword, which caused terror in the land of the living." *(Ezek. 32:21-23.)*

Hosea prophesied that in the latter days, Asshur (Assyria) will not be able to save Ephraim, but Ephraim will repent and return to the Lord. *(Hosea 14:3.)*

ASSHURIM. *Gen. 25:3.*

Asshurim was a son of Dedan, a grandson of Jokshan, and a great-grandson of Abraham and Keturah. (Chart 3f.)

ASSIR (1). *Ex. 6:24; 1 Chr. 6:22.*

Assir, son of Korah, grandson of Izhar, great-grandson of Kohath and great-great-grandson of Levi, was the father of Elkanah. *(Ex. 6:24.)* Assir was the grandson of Amminadab (Izhar). *(1 Chr. 6:22.)* (Chart 7d.)

ASSIR (2). *1 Chr. 3:17.*

Assir, a descendant of David, was a son of Jeconiah (Jehoiachin). His son was Salathiel. (Chart 1.)

ASSIR (3). *1 Chr. 6:23.*

Assir was the son of Ebiasaph and the father of Tahath. He was the great-grandson of Assir, son of Korah. (Chart 7d.)

ASSYRIANS (Asshur (3)). *Ezek. 16:28-29; 23:23-29; 31:3; Hosea 5:13 (3-13); 7:11; 8:8-9; 11:5; 12:1; 14:3; Zeph. 2:13.*

Assyrians were citizens of Assyria. Assyria was one of "the two great Eastern empires before which all the old states of Syria and Palestine fell . . . Assyria, or **Asshur**, occupied the Tigris valley to the north of Babylonia." *(See Assyria in the BD.)* Jerusalem "played the whore also with the Assyrians" said the Lord to Ezekiel. *(Ezek. 16:28-29.)* Because Jerusalem followed the ways of Babylon and worshipped idols, Ezekiel prophesied the destruction of Jerusalem by all the Assyrians, the Babylonians, Chaldeans and others. *(Ezek. 23:23-29.)*

The Assyrians were compared to a mighty cedar in Lebanon, and Ezekiel prophesied that Pharaoh king of Egypt would fall just like the Assyrians. *(Ezek. 31:3.)*

The Assyrian king was Jareb. Hosea prophesied that Ephraim, Israel and Judah would fall because of iniquity. Ephraim willingly walked after filth and sought help from king Jareb instead of from the Lord. *(Hosea 5:13 [3-13].)* The Lord condemned Ephraim for "going to Assyria," "calling" to Egypt and forsaking Him. *(Hosea 7:11.)* Hosea condemned Israel and said, "Israel is swallowed up: now shall they be among the Gentiles as a vessel wherein is no pleasure. For they are gone up to Assyria, a wild ass alone by himself: Ephraim hath hired lovers." *(Hosea 8:8-9.)* The Assyrians would rule over Ephraim because Ephraim refused to return to the Lord. *(Hosea 11:5.)* The Lord condemned Ephraim for making a covenant with the Assyrians. *(Hosea 12:1.)* Hosea prophesied that in the latter days, Assyria (Asshur) will not be able to save Ephraim, but Ephraim will repent and return to the Lord. *(Hosea 14:3.)*

The prophet Zephaniah prophesied judgment to come upon the Assyrians and said the Lord would stretch out His hand from the north and destroy Assyria. *(Zeph. 2:13.)*

ASUPPIM. *1 Chr. 26:15-17.*

The sons of the house of **Asuppim** (Shuppim and Hosah) were apparently descendants of Obed-edom. As the porters were given their divisions, the lot that went to Shuppim and Hosah came forth westward.

ATARAH. *1 Chr. 2:26.*

Atarah, one of Jerahmeel's wives, was the mother of Onam. (Chart 8c.)

ATAROTH. *1 Chr. 2:54 (50-54).*

Ataroth was a son of Salma, grandson of Hur and great-grandson of Caleb. (Chart 8 l.)

ATER (1). *Ezra 2:16; Neh. 7:21; 10:17 (1, 17, 28-31).*

Ater of Hezekiah was of the people of Israel. The men of the children of Ater of Hezekiah who returned to Jerusalem from Babylon after Cyrus' proclamation to build the temple numbered 98. *(Ezra 2:16; Neh. 7:21.)* He was among those chief of the people who covenanted to marry in Israel, honor the Sabbath, pay tithes and keep the commandments. *(Neh. 10:17 [1, 17, 28-31].)*

ATER (2). *Ezra 2:42; Neh. 7:45.*

Ater was one of the porters. When Cyrus, king of Persia, proclaimed that the people of God should go to Jerusalem to build the temple, the children of the porters—Ater, Shallum, Talmon, Akkub, Hatita and Shobai—numbered 139. *(Note: The number of men is given as 138 rather than 139 in Neh. 7:45.)*

ATHAIAH. *Neh. 11:4.*

Athaiah, the son of Uzziah of the children of Judah, dwelled in Jerusalem after leaving Babylon. (Chart 8b.)

ATHALIAH (1). *2 Kgs. 8:18, 26; 11:1-3, 13-16, 20-21; 2 Chr. 21:6; 22:2, 10-12; 23:12-15; 24:7.*

Athaliah, daughter of Ahab and Jezebel and granddaughter of Omri, was the wife of Jehoram who reigned over Judah after Jehoshaphat and was also the mother of Ahaziah. *(2 Kgs. 8:18, 26.)* When Athaliah saw that Ahaziah was dead, she sought to destroy all of the royal seed, but Jehosheba hid her nephew Joash, Ahaziah's son, and the infant's nurse. Meanwhile, Athaliah claimed the throne. She reigned seven years over Judah. The people then rose up under the direction of Jehoiada, the priest, and slew her with a sword. Ahaziah's son, Joash (Jehoash), who had been hidden in the house of the Lord for six years, was made king at the age of seven years. *(2 Kgs. 11:1-3, 13-16, 20-21.)*

Ahab's daughter was the wife of Jehoram, king of Judah. *(2 Chr. 21:6.)*

Jehosheba's name is given as Jehoshabeath. *(2 Chr. 22:2, 10-12. This is a repet of 2 Kgs. 11:1-3.)*

(2 Chr. 23:12-15 is a repeat of 2 Kgs. 11:13-16, 20.)

Athalia was a wicked woman. *(2 Chr. 24:7.)* (Chart 1.)

ATHALIAH (2). *1 Chr. 8:26-27.*

Athaliah, a descendant of Benjamin, was a son of Jeroham. (Chart 16j.)

ATHALIAH (3). *Ezra 8:7.*

Athaliah, of the sons of Elam, was the father of Jeshaiah, which Jeshaiah was the chief of his fathers and went with Ezra up from Babylon to Jerusalem. He took 70 male family members with him.

ATHLAI. *Ezra 10:28 (18-19, 28, 44).*

Athlai was one of Bebai's sons who took foreign wives, causing Ezra to cry unto the Lord, fearing the Lord would destroy the remainder of Israel because of their iniquity. He and his brothers agreed to comply with Ezra's request that they put away their strange wives.

ATTAI (1). *1 Chr. 2:35-36.*

Attai was the son of Jarha, Sheshan's Egyptian servant, and Sheshan's daughter. He begat Nathan. (Chart 8c.)

ATTAI (2). *1 Chr. 12:11 (1-2, 11).*

Attai, of the tribe of Gad, was one of David's mighty men who came to him at Ziklag to defend him against Saul. (Chart 13b.)

ATTAI (3). *2 Chr. 11:20.*

Attai was one of the sons of king Rehoboam, Solomon's son, and Maachah, Absalom's daughter. His brothers were Abijah, Ziza and Shelomith. (Chart 1.)

AVIMS. *Deut. 2:23.*

The Avims, Moses reminded the children of Israel, possessed Hazerim before the Caphtorims destroyed them. Just as the Avims had been destroyed, the Caphtorims could also be destroyed.

AZALIAH. *2 Kgs. 22:3; 2 Chr. 34:8.*

Azaliah was the father of Shaphan and the son of Meshullam.

AZANIAH. *Neh. 10:9.*

Azaniah, a Levite, was the father of Jeshua.

AZARAEL. *Neh. 12:36.*

Azarael joined with Zechariah, a descendant of Asaph, and others of his brethren with their musical instruments in the dedication of the wall of Jerusalem.

AZAREEL (1). *Neh. 11:13.* See **Adiel (2)**.

AZAREEL (2). *1 Chr. 12:6 (1-2, 6).*

Azareel, a Korhite, was one of David's mighty men who came to him at Ziklag to defend him against Saul.

AZAREEL (3). *1 Chr. 25:18.*

Azareel, a Levite and musician, cast the 11th lot when the musicians were assigned their duties by king David. He, his sons and brethren numbered 12.

AZAREEL (4). *1 Chr. 27:22.*

Azareel, son of Jeroham, was prince of the tribe of Dan when David was king.

AZAREEL (5). *Ezra 10:41 (18-19, 41, 44).*

Azareel, a son of Bani, and his brothers were some of the men in Israel who took foreign wives but gave them up when Ezra feared the wrath of God would destroy Israel for this iniquity.

AZARIAH (1). *1 Kgs. 4:2.; 1 Chr. 6:4-15; Ezra 7:1-5.*

Azariah grandson of Zadok the priest, was one of the princes of Israel when Solomon was king. *(1 Kgs. 4:2.)* He was a descendant of Aaron through Eleazar and was the son of Ahimaaz who was the son of Zadok. He begat Johanan. His ancestors and posterity are listed. *(1 Chr. 6:4-15.) (Ezra 7:1-5 is a repeat of 1 Chr. 6:4-15 with modification.)* (Chart 7b.)

AZARIAH (2). *1 Kgs. 4:5.*

Azariah, son of Nathan and brother of Zabud, was over the officers in Solomon's court.

AZARIAH (3) (Uzziah (1)). *2 Kgs. 14:21-22; 15:1-7, 13, 27; 1 Chr. 3:10-12; 2 Chr. 26; Isa. 1:1-31; 6:1; 7:1; Hosea 1:1, 6-9; Amos 1:1; Zech. 14:5.*

Azariah was the son of Amaziah. The people slew his father and made him king over Judah when he was 16 years old. He built Elath and restored it to Judah. He died (about 740 B.C.) and "slept with his fathers." *(2 Kgs. 14:21-22.)*

Azariah began his reign over Judah in the 27th year of Jeroboam's reign over Israel. He reigned 52 years. His mother was Jecholiah of Jerusalem. He walked upright before the Lord except he did not remove the "high places" where the people sacrificed and burned incense. Thus, the Lord smote him with leprosy and he lived in a separate house while his son Jotham actually judged the people of the land. In the 39th year of **Uzziah's** (Azariah's) reign, Shallam reigned one month in Samaria. In the 52nd year of Uzziah's reign, Remaliah began his reign over Israel. Upon Azariah's death, he was buried in the city of David and Jotham became king in his stead. *(2 Kgs. 15:1-7, 13, 27.)*

Azariah, a descendant of Solomon through Rehoboam, was the son of Amaziah and the father of Jotham. *(1 Chr. 3:10-12.)*

Uzziah's (Azariah) mother's name is spelled Jecoliah. He sought God in the days of Zechariah, and as long as he sought the Lord, he prospered. He was victorious against the Philistines and the Arabians. The Ammonites gave gifts to him. However, he transgressed against the Lord and went into the temple and burned incense upon the altar. Thus, the Lord caused him to have leprosy. *(2 Chr. 26.) (Note: This is a repeat and expansion of 2 Kgs. 15:1-7.)*

Isaiah had a vision in which he saw that which concerned Judah and Jerusalem during the days of Uzziah (Azariah), Jotham, Ahaz and Hezekiah, kings of Judah. Israel was in an apostate, rebellious and corrupt state. A very small remnant remained faithful. The Lord rejected their sacrifices and feasts. They were called upon to repent. Isaiah prophesied that Zion would be redeemed in the day of restoration. *(Isa. 1:1-31.)*

In the year Uzziah died, Isaiah saw the Lord sitting upon a throne. *(Isa. 6:1.)*

Uzziah was the father of Jotham who was the father of Ahaz. *(Isa. 7:1.)*

In the days of Uzziah (Azariah), Jotham, Ahaz and Hezekiah, kings of Judah, the Lord instructed Hosea to marry a wife from among those who committed whoredoms. He and his family were to be a sign unto Israel. The names of his children meant: "Not having obtained mercy," and "Not my people." While the Lord said He would no longer have mercy for Israel, He said He would have mercy upon the house of Judah. *(Hosea 1:1, 6-9.)*

During the time of Uzziah king of Judah and Jeroboam king of Israel, Amos prophesied of things he saw concerning Israel and the judgments that would come upon Syria, the Philistines and others. Two years after Amos' prophecy, there was a big earthquake. *(Amos 1:1.)*

There was a big earthquake in the days of Uzziah (Azariah) which caused the people to flee. Just as people fled then, people will again flee at the Second Coming. *(Zech. 14:5.)* (Chart 1.)

AZARIAH (4). *Jer. 43:2.* See **Jaazaniah**.

AZARIAH (5). *1 Chr. 2:8.*

Azariah was the son of Ethan and a great-grandson of Judah. (Chart 8g.)

AZARIAH (6). *1 Chr. 2:38-39.*

Azariah, of the tribe of Judah, was the son of Jehu and the father of Helez. (Chart 8c.)

AZARIAH (7). *1 Chr. 6:10-11; 2 Chr. 26:16-21; Ezra 7:1-5.*

Azariah, father of Amariah, was the son of Johanan, a grandson of Azariah, and a descendant of Aaron. He "executed the priest's office in the temple that Solomon built in Jerusalem." *(1 Chr. 6:10-11.)*

Azariah the priest, plus 80 other priests of the Lord, chastised Uzziah (Azariah), king of Judah, for burning incense upon the temple altar because that was the duty of the priests. Uzziah became angry and the Lord caused him to become afflicted with leprosy. *(2 Chr. 26:16-21.)*

Azariah's descendants and forefathers from Aaron through Ezra are listed with some omissions from the listing in 1 Chr. 6:4-14. *(Ezra 7:1-5.)* (Chart 7b.)

AZARIAH (8). *1 Chr. 6:13-14; 9:11; Ezra 7:1-5.*

Azariah, a descendant of Aaron, was the son of Hilkiah and the father of Seraiah. *(1 Chr. 6:13-14.)* He is listed among the priests who lived in Jerusalem whose genealogy was recorded in the book of the kings of Israel and Judah, who were carried away captive into Babylon because of transgression. *(1 Chr. 9:11.)*

Azariah's descendants and forefathers from Aaron through Ezra are listed with some omissions and some variations from other listings. *(Ezra 7:1-5.)* (Chart 7b.)

AZARIAH (9). *2 Chr. 15:1.*

Azariah was the son of Oded. He went to king Asa and prophesied that Judah would prosper if the people would keep the commandments.

AZARIAH (10). *2 Chr. 21:2-4.*

Azariah was one of king Jehoshaphat's sons. His brothers were Jehoram (the firstborn), Jehiel, Zechariah, Azariah, Michael and Shephatiah. After Jehoram became king, he slew all his brethren plus many of the princes of Israel. *(Note. There are two sons by the name of Azariah. Since the entry would say the same for each one, they have been combined for purposes of this book.)* (Chart 1.)

AZARIAH (11). *2 Chr. 22:6.* See **Ahaziah (2)**

AZARIAH (12). *2 Chr. 23:1.*

Azariah, son of Jeroham, was one of the captains of hundreds Jehoiada the priest rallied to make Joash king over Judah and to slay Athaliah.

AZARIAH (13). *2 Chr. 23:1.*

Azariah, son of Obed, was one of the captains of hundreds Jehoiada the priest rallied to make Joash king over Judah and to slay Athaliah.

AZARIAH (14). *2 Chr. 28:12-14.*

Azariah. son of Johanan, was one of the leaders of the children of Ephraim who supported the prophet Oded in letting the captives of Judah go so as not to incur greater wrath from the Lord upon Israel.

AZARIAH (15). *2 Chr. 29:12.* See **Uzziah (2)**

AZARIAH (16). *2 Chr. 29:12; 31:10-13.*

Azariah, a Levite and a descendant of Merari, was the son of Jehalelel. When Hezekiah, king of Judah, began his reign, he had Azariah and other Levites and priests sanctify themselves and cleanse and sanctify the house of the Lord. *(2 Chr. 29:12.)* He was ruler of the house of God when Hezekiah was king of Judah and was the chief priest of the house of Zadok. *(2 Chr. 31:10-13.)*

AZARIAH (17). *Neh. 7.7.* See **Seraiah (6)**.

AZARIAH (18). *Neh 3:23; 8:7-8; 10:2 (1-2, 28-29); 12:33.*

Azariah, son of Maaseiah (and grandson of Ananiah), labored next to Benjamin and Hashub when the children of Israel rebuilt the walls and gates of Jerusalem during the time of Ezra and Nehemiah. *(Neh 3:23.)*

Azariah was one of the men who, when Ezra read and interpreted the law of Moses to the people, helped the people to understand the law. *(Neh. 8:7-8.)*

Azariah was among the priests who covenanted and sealed their covenant to marry in Israel, honor the Sabbath, pay tithes and keep the commandments. *(Neh. 10:2 [1-2, 28-29].)*

Azariah and others, along with Hoshaiah and half of the princes of Judah, were appointed by Nehemiah to one of the two great companies of people gathered for the dedication of the walls of Jerusalem. *(Neh. 12:33.)*

AZARIAH (19) (Abed-nego). *Dan. 1:6-21; 2; 3.*

Azariah, Hananiah, Mishael and Daniel were among the children of Israel who were without blemish who were brought to the palace of Nebuchadnezzar by Ashpenaz, the master of the king's eunuchs, to be taught in the learning and language of the Chaldeans. The prince of the eunuchs gave each of them a different name. Azariah was given the name of **Abed-nego**. They elected not to eat the meat and wine the king provided. After ten days they were healthier than those who ate the meat and drank the wine. At the end of three years, when the king visited with all those who were being taught, none of them could compare with these four friends. They were wiser and had greater understanding than any of the king's magicians or astrologers. *(Dan. 1:6-21.)*

When Nebuchadnezzar had a dream that troubled him, he called in his magicians, astrologers, sorcerers and the Chaldeans and demanded they not only tell him the interpretation of the dream but the dream, itself, because he could not remember it. When they could not, he sentenced all the wisemen to death. Daniel, however, requested time to inquire of the Lord. He invited his friends, Abed-nego, Shadrach and Meshach to also petition the Lord regarding the matter. The Lord revealed the dream and the interpretation of the dream to Daniel. He explained the dream to Nebuchadnezzar, saying that God had revealed to Nebuchadnezzar what would happen in the latter days. Daniel was not only rewarded by Nebuchadnezzar, who elevated him to a position where he "sat in the gate of the king," but he honored a request Daniel made regarding his friends and set Abed-nego, Shadrach and Meshach over the affairs of the province of Babylon. *(Dan. 2.)*

When Nebuchadnezzar made a golden image and commanded that everyone worship it whenever they heard music or be cast into a fiery furnace, Abed-nego, Shadrach and Meshach refused to do so. Thus, Nebuchadnezzar had his most mighty men from the army make the furnace seven times hotter than usual and bound and cast the friends into it. The fire was so hot that it killed the soldiers. Suddenly, Nebuchadnezzar saw four men, the fourth being "like the Son of God," walking freely around inside the furnace, not being harmed by the fire. He called

Abed-nego, Shadrach and Meshach forth and decreed that no one should speak anything against their God or they would be cut in pieces because no other God could deliver like their God. He then rewarded the three friends by promoting them in the province of Babylon. *(Dan. 3.)*

AZAZ. *1 Chr. 5:8.*

Azaz, of the tribe of Reuben, was the son of Shem, the father of Bela, and the grandson of Joel. (Chart 5b.)

AZAZIAH (1). *1 Chr. 15:21.*

Azaziah, a Levite, under the direction of David, was assigned to be one of the singers who would make music before the Lord. He was to excel on the harp on the Sheminith.

AZAZIAH (2). *1 Chr. 27:20.*

Azaziah was the father of Hoshea, the prince of the tribe of Ephraim when David was king.

AZAZIAH (3). *2 Chr. 31:13.*

Azaziah, among others, was an overseer of tithes, offerings and the dedicated things under the hand of Cononiah and Cononiah's brother Shimei according to the commandment of king Hezekiah and Azariah, the ruler of the house of God.

AZBUK. *Neh. 3:16.*

Azbuk was the father of Nehemiah.

AZEL. *1 Chr. 8:37-39; 9:43-44.*

Azel, son of Eleasah, was from the tribe of Benjamin. He descended through Saul through Jonathan. He had six sons: Azrikam, Bocheru, Ishmael, Sheariah, Obadiah and Hanan. His brother was Eshek. (Chart 16 l.)

AZGAD (1). *Ezra 2:12; Neh. 7:17; 10:15 (1, 15, 28-31).*

Azgad was of the people of Israel. The men of the children of Azagad who returned to Jerusalem from Babylon after Cyrus' proclamation to build the temple numbered 1,222 (2,322). *(Ezra 2:12; Neh. 7:17.)*

Azgad was among those chief of the people who covenanted to marry in Israel, honor the Sabbath, pay tithes and keep the commandments. *(Neh. 10:15 [1, 15, 28-31].)*

AZGAD (2). *Ezra 8:12 (1, 12).*

Azgad's descendant Johanan, the son of Hakkatan, was the chief of his fathers when Ezra led many exiled Israelites out of Babylon back to Jerusalem. He took 110 males with him.

AZIEL. *1 Chr. 15:20.* See **Jaaziel.**.

AZIZA. *Ezra 10:27 (18-19, 27, 44).*

Aziza was one of the sons of Zattu who took wives from among the Canaanites and other foreign groups. He and his brothers complied with Ezra's request that they separate themselves from these foreign wives lest the Lord destroy the reemainder of the children of Israel because of this iniquity.

AZMAVETH (1). *2 Sam. 23:3; 1 Chr. 11:33.*

Azmaveth the Barhumite (Baharumite) was one of David's mighty men *(2 Sam. 23:31)* and was one of the valiant men of the armies *(1 Chr. 11:33)*. (Chart 17.)

AZMAVETH (2). *1 Chr. 8:36; 9:42.*

Azmaveth, Alemeth and Zimri, descendants of Saul through Jonathan, were from the tribe of Benjamin and were sons of Jehoadah. *(1 Chr. 8:36.)* Azmaveth's father was also called Jarah. *(1 Chr. 9:42.)* (Chart 16 l.)

AZMAVETH (3). *1 Chr. 12:3.*

Azmaveth was the father of Jeziel and Pelet, two of David's mighty men who came to David at Ziklag to defend him against Saul.

AZMAVETH (4). *1 Chr. 27:25.*

Azmaveth, the son of Adiel, was assigned by king David to be over the king's treasures.

AZMAVETH (5) (Beth-azmaveth). *Ezra 2:24; Neh. 7:28.*

Azmaveth (Beth-azmaveth) was of the people of Israel. The men of the children of Azamaveth who returned to Jerusalem from Babylon after Cyrus' proclamation to build the temple numbered 42. *(Ezra 2:24; Neh. 7:28.)*

AZRIEL (1). *1 Chr. 5:24-26.*

Azriel was from the half tribe of Manasseh that was aligned with the Reubenites and Gadites. He was a famous and mighty man of valor and was head of the house of his father. He, along with others, transgressed the laws of God; thus, God allowed them to be carried away into captivity by the Assyrian kings, Pul and Tilgath-pilneser. (Chart 15c.)

AZRIEL (2). *1 Chr. 27:19.*

Azriel was the father of Jerimoth who was a prince over the tribe of Naphtali when David was king.

AZRIEL (3). *Jer. 36:26.*

Azriel was the father of Seraiah, which Seraiah, along with Jerahmeel and Shelemiah, was commanded by Jehoiakim to arrest Baruch and Jeremiah for voicing the Lord's warnings against the people.

AZRIKAM (1). *1 Chr. 3:23.*

Azrikam, a descendant of David, was a son of Neariah. His brothers were Elioenai and Hezekiah. (Chart 1.)

AZRIKAM (2). *1 Chr. 8:38.*

Azrikam, son of Azel, was from the tribe of Benjamin. He was a descendant of Saul. His brothers were Bocheru, Ishmael, Sheariah, Obadiah and Hanan. (Chart 16 l.)

AZRIKAM (3). *1 Chr. 9:14; Neh. 11:15 (1, 15).*

Azrikam, a Levite and descendant of Merari, was the son of Hashabiah and the father of Hasshub. His genealogy was written in the book of the kings of Israel and Judah, who were carried away to Babylon for their transgression. *(1 Chr. 9:14.)*

Hashub (Hasshub) and his family dwelled in Jerusalem after returning from Babylonian captivity. *(Neh. 11:15 [1, 15].)* (Chart 7e.)

AZRIKAM (4). *2 Chr. 28:7.*

Azrikam, governor of king Ahaz's house, was slain by Zichri, a mighty man of Ephraim, when the Lord allowed Judah to be brought low because of wickedness.

AZUBAH (1). *1 Kgs. 22:42; 2 Chr. 20:31-32.*

Azubah, daughter of Shilhi (and wife of Asa), was the mother of Jehoshaphat, king over Judah. (Chart 1.)

AZUBAH (2). *1 Chr. 2:18.*

Azubah was the wife of Hezron's son Caleb. She bore him the following sons: Jesher, Shobab and Ardon. (Chart 8h.)

AZUR (1). *Jer. 28:1-3.*

Azur the prophet was father of Hananiah. Hananiah falsely prophesied that the yoke of Babylon would be broken within two years. (Chart 16m.)

AZUR (2). *Ezek. 11:1.*

Azur was the father of Jaazaniah, which Jaazaniah was among 25 men who sat at the east gate of the Lord's house and gave false counsel to the people in Jerusalem.

AZZAN. *Num. 34:26.*

Azzan was the father of Paltiel and was of the tribe of Issachar. (Chart 9b.)

AZZUR. *Neh. 10:17 (1, 17, 28-31).*

Azzur was among those chief of the people who covenanted to marry in Israel, honor the Sabbath, pay tithes and keep the commandments.

AZUR (2). *Ezek. 11:1.*

Azur was the father of Jaazaniah, which Jaazaniah was among 25 men who sat at the east gate of the Lord's house and gave false counsel to the people in Jerusalem.

AZZAN. *Num. 34:26.*

Azzan was the father of Paltiel and was of the tribe of Issachar. (Chart 9b.)

AZZUR. *Neh. 10:17 (1, 17, 28-31).*

Azzur was among those chief of the people who covenanted to marry in Israel, honor the Sabbath, pay tithes and keep the commandments.

NAMES THAT BEGIN WITH "B"

BAAL (1). *1 Chr. 5:5-6.*

Baal, of the tribe of Reuben, was the son of Reaia and the father of Beerah. (Chart 5b.)

BAAL (2). *1 Chr. 8:30-32; 9:35-38.*

Baal was of the tribe of Benjamin and was the son of the father of Gibeon (Jehiel). His brothers included Abdon, Zur, Kish, Nadab, Gedor, Ahio, Zacher and Mikloth. His mother was Maachah.*1 Chr. 8:30-32.*

Baal's father was Jehiel (Abiel). His brothers are listed again with the addition of Ner. Zacher's name is given as Zechariah. *(1 Chr. 9:35-38.)* (Chart 16f.)

BAAL (3). *1 Kgs. 16:31-32.* See **Baalim.**

BAAL-BERITH. *Judg. 8:33; 9:4.*

Baal-berith was the false god the children of Israel immediately turned to upon the death of Gideon. *(Judg. 8:33.)* Abimelech, Gideon's son, using 70 pieces of silver from the house of Baal-berith, hired vain and light persons to follow him. *(Judg. 9:4.)*

BAAL-HANAN (1). *Gen. 36:38; 1 Chr. 1:50.*

Baal-hanan, son of Achbor, reigned as king in Edom upon the death of Saul of Rehoboth. *(Gen. 36:38.)* When Baal-hanan died, Hadad reigned in his stead. *(1 Chr. 1:50.)* (Chart 18.)

BAAL-HANAN (2). *1 Chr. 27:28.*

Baal-hanan the Gederite served king David by being over the olive trees and the sycamore trees that were in the low plains.

BAALIM (Baal (3), Baal-Peor, Baal-Zebub). *Num. 25:3-5; Judg. 10:6; 1 Kgs. 16:31-32; 2 Kgs. 1:1-6; Ps. 106:28; Jer. 2:8, 23; 11:13; 19:5; 32:35; Hosea 2:8-9, 13, 17; 9:10; 11:2; Zeph. 1:4.*

Baal-peor was the idol at Peor (a mountain in Moab) which the children of Israel began to worship. Moses was commanded by the Lord to slay all who had "joined unto Baal-peor." *(Num. 25:3-5.) (Note: The Bible Dictionary states that "compounds of Baal with a second word denote (1) an attribute of the god, (2) the place or manner of his worship, or (3) something that a place possesses.")*

Baalim refers to the pagan gods Israel worshipped from time to time. *(Judg. 10:6.)* **Baal** (singular of Baalim) was one of the false gods Ahab, king of Israel, worshipped when he took Jezebel, daughter of Ethbaal king of the Zidonians, to wife. Ahab worshipped the fertility and Sun-god, leading Israel into more wickedness than all the other kings before him. *(1 Kgs. 16:31-32.)*

Baal-zebub was the god of Ekron. Ahaziah sent his messengers to inquire of Baal-zebub whether or not he would recover from his disease, but they were intercepted by the prophet Elijah. *(2 Kgs. 1:1-6.) (Note: In the New Testament, Matt. 12:24, Baal-zebub is called Beelzebub.)*

The children of Israel, while wandering in the desert, began to worship Baal-peor. *(Ps. 106:28.)* The children of Israel were chastised by the prophet Jeremiah for worshipping Baal. *(Jer. 2:8, 23.)* Baal is referred to as "that shameful thing" to which Israel had set up altars *(Jer. 11:13)* and to which the children of Israel separated themselves *(Hosea 9:10)*.

The children of Israel offered their sons as burnt sacrifices to Baal; therefore, they incurred the wrath of the Lord. *(Jer. 19:5.)* The children of Israel built the high places of Baal and caused their sons and daughters to "pass through the fire unto Molech." *(Jer. 32:35.)* The Lord brought severe judgments upon Israel for her worship of Baal and Baalim. *(Hosea 2:8-9, 13, 17.)*

The Lord brought Israel out of Egypt, but Israel turned to Baalim and burned incense and sacrificed unto graven images. *(Hosea 11:2.)* At the Second Coming, the Lord will cut off the remnant of Baal. *(Zeph. 1:4.)*

BAALIS. *Jer. 40:14.*

Baalis was king of the Ammonites. He sent Ishmael to slay Gedaliah the son of Ahikam who had been made governor over the remnant of the Jews when Nebuchadnezzar carried Israel off captive to Babylon.

BAANA (1). *1 Kgs. 4:12.*

Baana, the son of Ahilud and one of twelve officers over Israel, provided victuals for king Solomon and his family one month each year.

BAANA (2). *Neh. 3:4.*

Baana was the father of Zadok, which Zadok helped repair the gates and walls of Jerusalem.

BAANAH (1). *2 Sam. 4:2, 5-12.*

Baanah and Rechab, Beerothites from the tribe of Benjamin, were two of Saul's captains and were the sons of Rimmon who crept into Ish-bosheth's house and slew him while he was sleeping. They beheaded him and took his head to David. David commanded his men to slay these two unrighteous men. After slaying them, David's men cut off their hands and feet and hanged them up over the pool in Hebron.

BAANAH (2). *2 Sam. 23:29; 1 Chr. 11:30.*

Baanah, a Netophathite, was the father of Heleb (Heled).

BAANAH (3). *1 Kgs. 4:16.*

Baanah, son of Hushai and one of twelve officers over Israel, provided victuals for king Solomon and his family one month each year.

BAANAH (4). *Ezra 2:2; Neh. 7:7; 10:27 (1, 27-31).*

Baanah was one of the people who left Babylon and went with Zerubbabel back to Jerusalem following king Cyrus' proclamation to build the temple there. *(Ezra 2:2; Neh. 7:7.)* He was among those chief of the people who covenanted to marry in Israel, honor the Sabbath, pay tithes and keep the commandments. *(Neh. 10:27 [1, 27-31].)*

BAARA. *1 Chr. 8:8.*

Baara was one of the wives of Shaharaim, a descendant of Benjamin.

BAASEIAH. *1 Chr. 6:40.*

Baaseiah, a descendant of Levi through Gershon, was the father of Michael and the son of Malchiah. (Chart 7a.)

BAASHA. *1 Kgs. 15:16-34; 16:1-7, 8-13; 21:22; 2 Kgs. 9:9; 2 Chr. 16:1-6; Jer. 41:9.*

Baasha, king over Israel, was the son of Ahijah of the house of Issachar. He slew king Nadab, son of Jeroboam, and began to reign over Israel in the third year of Asa's reign over Judah. When he went against Asa in battle, Asa enlisted the help of Ben-hadad, king of Syria. Baasha withdrew to Tirzah. He reigned over Israel in Tirzah for 24 years, doing evil in the sight of the Lord. During his reign, he smote all of the house of Jeroboam—leaving not one member of Jeroboam's family alive just as the prophet Ahijah had foretold. There was war between Baasha and Asa all their days. Baasha's evil ways continued to cause Israel to sin. *(1 Kgs. 15:16-34; 2 Chr. 16:1-6.)*

Jehu prophesied evil upon Baasha, saying that he "that dieth of Baasha in the city shall the dogs eat; and him that dieth of his in the fields shall the fowls of the air eat" just as the prophet Ahijah had prophesied against Jeroboam. The rest of his record is written in the book of the chronicles of the kings of Israel. He died and was buried in Tirzah. His son Elah reigned in his stead. Elah was slain by Zimri, captain of half his chariots, who then slew all of the house of Baasha and reigned over Israel. *(1 Kgs. 16:1-7, 8-13.)*

The Lord, through the prophet Elijah, told Ahab that He would make Ahab's house like the house of Baasha and the house of Jeroboam because "thou hast provoked me to anger, and made Israel to sin." *(1 Kgs. 21:22; 2 Kgs. 9:9.)*

When Ishmael slew Gedaliah who was governor over the remnant of Judah, the Jews, Chaldeans and men of war who were also in Mizpah, he dumped the bodies in a pit previously made by Asa when he was king of Judah and feared Baasha. *(Jer. 41:9.)* (Chart 9b.)

BABYLONIANS (Babel, Babylon). *Gen. 10:10 (8-10); 11:1-9; Ezra 4:9; Isa. 47. 48:20; Jer. 50; 51; 52; Ezek. 23:17-29.*

Babel (i.e., **Babylon**) was built by Nimrod, the son of Cush who was the son of Ham who was the son of Noah. *(Gen. 10:10 [8-10] .)* Babel received its name because the Lord confounded the languages of the people there as they sought to build a tower to heaven. *(Gen. 11:1-9.)*

The **Babylonians** were among the various groups who were companions with the Samaritans and helped to hinder the work of rebuilding the temple in Jerusalem. *(Ezra 4:9.)* Isaiah prophesied that Babylon and Chaldea would be destroyed for their iniquities. Babylon would be depopulated and its king would be destroyed. *(Isa. 47:8-9.) (Note: Babylon was overthrown by Cyrus of Persia in 539 B.C.)*

Isaiah prophesied that Israel would eventually be freed from Babylonian captivity and would flee from the Chaldeans. *(Isa. 48:20.)*

Jeremiah prophesied that Babylon would be destroyed, never to rise again. The children of Israel and the children of Judah will come together seeking the Lord and be restored again into the lands of their inheritance. The Lord will plead their cause for they were oppressed by those who took them captive. *(Jer. 50.)*

The Lord instructed Israel and Judah to flee out of the midst of Babylon, "and deliver every man his soul."(Jer. 51:6.). Jeremiah recorded all his prophecies regarding the woes to befall Babylon. *(Jer. 51:60.)*

After Nebuchadnezzar took Jerusalem captive, slew king Zedekiah's sons before his eyes and then put Zedekiah's eyes out *(Jer. 52:10-11)*, his people carried the vessels of the house of the Lord to Babylon, including the twelve brasen bulls that were under the baptismal font in the temple built by Solomon *(Jer. 52:20)*.

Because Jerusalem followed the ways of Babylon and worshipped idols, Ezekiel prophesied the destruction of Jerusalem by the Babylonians, Chaldeans and others. *(Ezek. 23:17-29.)*

BACHRITES. *Num. 26:35*. See **Becher (2)**.

BAKBAKKAR (Bakbukiah). *1 Chr. 9:15 (2, 15); Neh. 11:17; 12:9, 25.*

Bakbakkar, along with Mattaniah and Zichri (Zabdi) and others named as heads of the house of their fathers, was a Levite. The Israelites, priests, Levites and Nethenims were the first inhabitants that dwelled in their possessions in the cities. Bakbakkar's genealogy was written in the book of the kings of Israel and Judah who were carried away to Babylon for their transgression. *(1 Chr. 9:15 [2, 15].)*

Bakbukiah was the second among his brethren (i.e., Mattaniah) in attending to the thanksgiving prayer when the children of Israel returned from Babylonian captivity. *(Neh. 11:17.)*

Bakbukiah and Unni were with those Levites who went up from Babylon with Zerubbabel to Jerusalem. They were "over against them" (Mattaniah and his brethren) in their watches. Bakbukiah was one of the porters, along with Akkub, Mattaniah, Obadiah, Meshullam (Shullam, Shallum) and Talmon, who kept the ward at the thresholds of the gates in the days of Joiakim, Nehemiah and Ezra. *(Neh. 12:9, 25.)*

BAKBUK. *Ezra 2:51, 58; Neh. 7:53, 60.*

Bakbuk was a Nethinim. When the Nethinims and the children of Solomon's servants left Babylon to return to Jerusalem to build the house of the Lord as proclaimed by Cyrus, king of Persia, they numbered 392.

BAKBUKIAH. *Neh. 11:17*. See **Bakbakkar**.

BALAAM. *Num. 22:5-41; 23:1-30; 24:17; 31:8-16; Deut. 23:4-5; Josh. 13:22; 24:9-10; Neh. 13:1-2; Micah 6:5.*

Balaam was the son of Beor and a prophet from Pethor. Balak, king of Moab, sent word to him requesting help in defeating the children of Israel, saying, "For I wot that he whom thou blessest is blessed, and he whom thou cursest is cursed" *(Num. 22:6)*. God came unto Balaam and told him not to go to Balak and not to curse the people he wanted cursed because they are blessed. Balaam declined

Balak's request saying the Lord refused to give him leave to go with Balak. When Balak sent a second request, Balaam again approached the Lord for permission. The Lord told him that if the men came to call again, to go with them but "the word which I shall say unto thee, that shalt thou do." *(Num. 22:20.)* The Lord was unhappy with Balaam for going and sent an angel to block the way of Balaam's ass. In the exchange that resulted, Balaam had his foot crushed against the wall. The ass' mouth was opened and the ass chastised him for smiting him. Balaam eventually saw the angel that the ass saw. The angel told him to go unto Balak, but to speak only what the angel told him to speak. *(Num. 22:5-41.)*

Balaam had Balak build seven altars. The Lord commanded Balaam to bless Israel and he did. Balak continued to press Balaam and was instructed three times to build seven altars—seven each in three different locations. *(Num. 23:1-30.)*

Balaam was given a vision and he prophesied of the destiny of Israel. He also prophesied of the coming of the Messiah. *(Num. 24:17.)*

Balaam was slain by a sword when the army of the children of Israel warred against the Midianites. Every man was slain but the women and children were saved. Moses was angry with the leaders of his army because, through the counsel of Balaam, the women had caused the children of Israel to commit "trespass against the Lord in the matter of Peor" and had brought a plague upon the people. Thus, the people were told to slay every male child and every woman who had known man, and to only keep alive the women and children who had not known a man by lying with him. *(Num. 31:8-16.)*

Moses reminded the children of Israel that the Ammonites and Moabites, who were forbidden to enter the congregation, had once hired Balaam to curse the children of Israel but the Lord had caused Balaam to bless Israel rather than curse Israel. *(Deut. 23:4-5.)*

Balaam, son of Beor, was slain with the sword. *(Josh. 13:22.)*

When Balaam was hired by Balak to curse Israel, Joshua reminded the people, the Lord turned the curse into a blessing and delivered Israel out of Balak's hand. *(Josh. 24:9-10.)*

Balaam was hired by the Ammonites and Moabites to go against the children of Israel in ancient days. The people were reminded as they read the book of Moses that the Moabites and the Ammonites were forever forbidden to become part of the congregation of God and that the Lord had turned the curse Balak had wanted into a blessing on Israel instead. *(Neh. 13:1-2.)*

Micah told the children of Israel to reflect on the experience of Balak king of Moab with Balaam the son of Beor to recognize and know the righteousness of the Lord. *(Micah 6:5.)*

BALADAN. *2 Kgs. 20:12; Isa. 39:1.*

Baladan was the father of Berodach-baladan *(2 Kgs. 20:12)* (i.e., Merodach-baladan, *Isa. 39:1*) king of Babylon.

BALAK. *Num. 22:2-41; 23; 24:10; Micah 6:5.*

Balak was the son of Zippor and king of the Moabites. He feared the children of Israel as they pitched in the plains of Moab by Jordan near Jericho. He sent a request to Balaam pleading for help and requesting a blessing that he, Balak, would be victorious against Israel. When Balaam said he couldn't because the Lord had told him not to, Balak again pleaded with him for help. *(Num. 22:2-41.)* When Balaam finally went to Balak, he instructed Balak to build seven altars. He did so three different times. *(Num. 23.)* Balak became angry with Balaam for blessing Israel instead of cursing Israel. *(Num. 24:10.)*

Micah told the children of Israel to reflect on the experience of Balak king of Moab with Balaam the son of Beor to recognize and know the righteousness of the Lord. *(Micah 6:5.)*

BANI (1). *2 Sam. 23:36.*

Bani the Gadite was one of David's mighty men. (Chart 17.)

BANI (2). *1 Chr. 6:46.*

Bani, a descendant of Levi through Merari, was the son of Shamer and the father of Amzi. (Chart 7c.).

BANI (3). *1 Chr. 9:4.*

Bani, father of Imri, was of the children of Pharez, the son of Judah. (Chart 8b.)

BANI (4) (Binnui (1)). *Ezra 2:10; 10:29 (18-19, 29, 44); Neh. 7:1; 10:14 (1, 14, 28-31).*

Bani was of the people of Israel. The men of the children of Bani who returned to Jerusalem from Babylon after Cyrus' proclamation to build the temple numbered 642. *(Ezra 2:10.) (Note: His name is given as **Binnui** in Neh. 7:15 and the number of men is given as 648 rather than 642.)* Bani's sons—Meshullam, Malluch, Adaiah, Jashub, Sheal and Ramoth—were among the children of Israel who took foreign wives but who agreed to give up their strange wives at Ezra's request as he feared the Lord would destroy all of Israel due to this transgression. *(Ezra 10:29 [18-19, 29, 44].)* He was among those chief of the people who covenanted to marry in Israel, honor the Sabbath, pay tithes and keep the commandments. *(Neh. 10:14 [1, 14, 28-31].)*

BANI (5). *Ezra 10:38 (18-19, 38, 44).*

Bani, of the sons of Bani, and his brothers were some of the men in Israel who took foreign wives but gave them up when Ezra feared the wrath of God would destroy Israel for this iniquity.

BANI (6). *Neh. 3:17; 10:13 (1, 13, 28-31).*

Bani, a Levite, was the father of Rehum. *(Neh. 3:17.)* He was among those Levites who covenanted and sealed their covenant to marry in Israel, honor the Sabbath, pay tithes and keep the commandments. *(Neh. 10:13 [1, 13, 28-31].)*

BANI (7). *Neh. 8:7-8.*

Bani was one of the men who, when Ezra read and interpreted the law of Moses to the people, helped the people to understand the law.

BANI (8). *Neh. 9.*

Bani was a Levite. When Ezra read and interpreted the law of Moses and he and Nehemiah proclaimed the day a holy day, the Levites—Bani, Jeshua, Kadmiel, Shebaniah, Bunni, Sherebiah, Bani, Chenani, Hashabniah, Hodijah and Pethahiah—blessed and praised the Lord, reciting the Lord's goodness to Israel: the blessing of Abraham; giving the land of the Canaanites, Hittites, Amorites, Perizzites, Jebusites and Girgashites to Israel; dividing the Red Sea so they could cross it yet drowning the Egyptians who pursued them; the signs and wonders shown to Pharaoh; leading them in the wilderness and protecting them so that they had bread from heaven, water from the rock, and their shoes and clothes never wore out; accepting them whenever they repented, even when they made a molten calf. They had been given the kingdoms of Shihon, Heshbon and Bashan and the Lord had subdued the Canaanites and delivered them into the hands of the Israelites, etc. After giving praise, they made a covenant with the Lord. The princes, Levites and priests sealed the covenant.

BANI (9). *Neh. 11:22.* See **Benaiah (6)**.

BARACHEL. *Job 32:2.*

Barachel the Buzite, of the kindred of Ram, was the father of Elihu which Elihu chastised Job and his friends.

BARAK. *Judg. 4:6-22; 5.*

Barak was the son of Abinoam. Deborah summoned him and reminded him that the Lord had said He would deliver Sisera, captain of king Jabin's host, into his hands at the river Kishon. Barak said he would go after Sisera, but only if Deborah would come with him. Deborah agreed, but said there would be no honor in it for Barak because the Lord would deliver Sisera into the hand of a woman. As the battle pursued, Barak and his men from the tribes of Zebulun and Naphtali killed all of Sisera's men, but Sisera escaped to the tent of Jael. While Barak pursued Sisera, Jael slew Sisera as he slept. *(Judg. 4:6-22.)*

Barak and Deborah sang a song of praise because the Lord delivered Israel from Canaanite bondage. "And the land had rest for 40 years." *(Judg. 5.)*

BARHUMITE. *2 Sam. 23:31.*

The **Barhumite** Azmaveth was one of David's mighty men. (Chart 17.)

BARIAH. *1 Chr. 3:22.*

Bariah, a descendant of David, was a son of Shemaiah and grandson of Shechaniah. His brothers were Hattush, Igeal, Neariah and Shaphat. (Chart 1.)

BARKOS. *Ezra 2:53, 58; Neh. 7:55, 60.*

Barkos was a Nethinim. When the Nethinims and the children of Solomon's servants left Babylon to return to Jerusalem to build the house of the Lord as proclaimed by Cyrus, king of Persia, they numbered 392.

BARUCH (1). *Neh. 3:20; 10:6 (1, 6, 28-31).*

Baruch, son of Zabbai, labored next to Ezer when the children of Israel rebuilt the walls and gates of Jerusalem during the time of Ezra and Nehemiah and "earnestly repaired the other piece, from the turning of the wall unto the door of the house of Eliashib the high priest." *(Neh. 3:20.)*

Baruch was among the priests who covenanted and sealed their covenant to marry in Israel, honor the Sabbath, pay tithes and keep the commandments. *(Neh. 10:6 [1, 6, 28-31].)*

BARUCH (2). *Neh. 11:5.*

Baruch, of the children of Perez, son of Col-hozeh and father of Maaseiah, dwelled in Jerusalem after leaving Babylon. (Chart 8b.)

BARUCH (3). *Jer. 32:12-16; 36:4-19, 27-32; 43:2-6; 45.*

Baruch was the son of Neriah who was the son of Maaseiah. His brother was Seraiah. *(See Jer. 51:59.)* Jeremiah had his purchase of his uncle's son Hanameel's property recorded by Baruch in the presence of Hanameel. *(Jer. 32:12-16.)*

Baruch, in the fourth year of Jehoiakim's reign over Judah, was instructed by Jeremiah who was under arrest or in confinement, to record the prophecies Jeremiah dictated to him and to read them in the house of the Lord. In the fifth year of Jehoiakim, Baruch read the words of Jeremiah in the house of the Lord. The princes told Baruch and Jeremiah to hide. Jehoiakim sought to have Baruch and Jeremiah taken captive, but the Lord hid them. When Jehoiakim burned the "rolls," Jeremiah had Baruch write the prophecies down again and included some additional prophecies. *(Jer. 36:4-19, 27-32.)*

When Jeremiah prophesied that the remnant of Judah would find peace and safety if they remained in Judah but that they would suffer death, famine and pestilence if they went to dwell in Egypt, Johanan—son of Kareah—and Azariah (Jezaniah, Jaazaniah)—son of Hoshaiah— and "all the proud men" refused to believe Jeremiah and claimed that Baruch the son of Neriah had turned Jeremiah against them so that the Chaldeans could slay them or carry them off captive into Babylon. *(Jer. 43:2-6.)*

At the time Baruch wrote the prophesies of Jeremiah, Jeremiah promised that Baruch's life would be peserved. *(Jer. 45.)* (Chart 8b.)

BARZILLAI (1). *2 Sam. 17:27; 19:31-38; Ezra 2:61-62; Neh. 7:63-64.*

Barzillai, a Gileadite of Rogelim, along with Machir and Shobi, brought beds, food and other items to aid David and his followers when they came to Mahanaim on their flight to escape Absalom. *(2 Sam. 17:27.)*

After Absalom's death, as David returned to Jerusalem, Barzillai came down from Rogelim and went over Jordan with him. David wanted him to return to Jerusalem with him, but Barzillai declined. He was 80 years old and preferred to die in his own city and be buried by the grave of his father and mother. However, he requested that David take Chimham with him. *(2 Sam. 19:31-38.)*

Barzillai the Gileadite had a daughter who married one of the priests, and her husband and posterity were called after Barzillai. *(Ezra 2:61-62; Neh. 7:63-64.)*

BARZILLAI (2). *2 Sam. 21:8.*

Barzillai, the Meholathite, was the father of Adriel and the father-in-law of Merab, Saul's daughter.

BARZILLAI (3), THE CHILDREN OF. *Ezra 2:61-62; Neh. 7:63-64.*

Barzillai was one of the priests. However, his children could not find their names among those who were listed by their genealogy and therefore they were "as polluted" and were excluded from the priesthood. He took a wife from among the daughters of Barzillai the Gileadite and was called after their name.

BASHEMATH (Mahalath (1)). *Gen. 26:34-35; 28:9; 36:3-4.*

Bashemath was a daughter of Elon the Hittite. Esau married her when he was 40 years old. This grieved Rebekah, Esau's mother. *(Gen. 26:34-35.) (Note: Adah, another of Esau's wives, was apparently the daughter of Elon the Hittite, not Bashemath. See Gen. 36:2.)*

Mahalath (Bashemath) was the sister of Rebajoth and the daughter of Ishmael, Abraham's son by Hagar. She was a half-cousin to Esau and became one of Esau's wives. *(Gen. 28:9.)*

Bashemath (Mahalath) was Ishmael's daughter, sister of Nebajoth (Rebajoth). She bore Reuel. *(Gen. 36:3-4.)* (Charts 3b-c, e.)

BASMATH. *1 Kgs. 4:15.*

Basmath, one of Solomon's daughters, was the wife of Ahimaaz. (Charts 7b., 8f.)

BATH-SHEBA (Bath-shua). *2 Sam. 11:3-27; 12:15-18, 24; 1 Kgs. 1:11-31; 2:13-19; 1 Chr. 3:5.*

Bath-sheba, daughter of Eliam, was the wife of Uriah the Hittite. From his rooftop, David watched Bath-sheba washing herself and observed that she was very beautiful. He had her brought to him and he lay with her while Uriah was away with the army. Bath-sheba became pregnant and sent word to David. David tried to cover up his sin by trying to get her husband to come home from battle so he could sleep with her. However, when Uriah refused to go in unto his wife while the rest of Israel slept in tents, David had him placed in the forefront of battle so he would be killed. After Uriah's death and Bath-sheba's time of mourning, David took her to wife. She bore him a son, but the Lord was displeased with David. *(2 Sam. 11:3-27.)* The son Bath-sheba bore to David was very sick and died "on the seventh day." Bath-sheba bore David a second son, Solomon. *(2 Sam. 12:15-18, 24.)*

When David's son Adonijah—son of Haggith—exalted himself and made himself king in David's stead, the prophet Nathan counseled with Bath-sheba and encouraged her to inform David as to what Adonijah was doing and to remind him that he had promised her that Solomon would be the one chosen to follow David as king. She did as Nathan counseled her to do and, following Nathan's confirmation about Adonijah's activities, David had Solomon anointed king. *(1 Kgs. 1:11-31.)*

Bath-sheba was approached by Adonijah who requested she petition Solomon to give Abishag, who had helped David in his last months, to Adonijah for a wife.

Bath-shea did as he requested. In response, Solomon had Adonijah put to death that very day. *(1 Kgs. 2:13-19.)*

Bath-shua and David had four sons born to them in Jerusalem: Shimea (Shammua), Shobab, Nathan and Solomon. Bath-sheba's father was Ammiel (Eliam). *(1 Chr. 3:5.)*

BAVAI. *Neh. 3:18.*

Bavai, son of Henadad and ruler of the half part of Keilah, labored next to Hashabiah when the children of Israel rebuilt the walls and gates of Jerusalem during the time of Ezra and Nehemiah.

BAZLUTH (Bazlith). *Ezra 2:52, 58; Neh. 7:54, 60.*

Bazluth was a Nethinim. When the Nethinims and the children of Solomon's servants left Babylon to return to Jerusalem to build the house of the Lord as proclaimed by Cyrus, king of Persia, they numbered 392. *(Note: His name is spelled Bazlith in Neh. 7:54.)*

BEALIAH. *1 Chr. 12:5 (1-2, 5).*

Bealiah was one of David's mighty men who came to him at Ziklag to defend him against Saul.

BEBAI. *Ezra 2:11; 8:11; 10:28 (18-19, 28, 44); Neh. 7:16; 10:15 (1, 15, 28-31).*

Bebai was of the people of Israel. The men of the children of Bebai who returned to Jerusalem from Babylon after Cyrus' proclamation to build the temple numbered 623. *(Ezra 2:11; also Neh. 7:16. However, the number is given as 628 rather than 623.)*

Of the sons of Bebai, Zechariah the son of Bebai, was the chief of his fathers when Ezra led many exiled Israelites out of Babylon back to Jerusalem. *(Ezra 8:11.)*

Bebai's descendants—Jehohanan, Hananiah, Zabbai and Athlai—were among the people of Israel who took foreign wives, causing Ezra to cry unto the Lord, fearing the Lord would destroy the remainder of Israel because of their iniquity. *(Ezra 10:28 [18-19, 28, 44].)*

Bebai was among those chief of the people who covenanted to marry in Israel, honor the Sabbath, pay tithes and keep the commandments. *(Neh. 10:15 [1, 15, 28-31].)*

BECHER (1). *Gen. 46:21; Num. 26:38-41; 1 Chr. 7:6, 8.*

Becher was a son of Benjamin and a grandson of Jacob. His brothers were Belah, Ashbel, Gera, Naaman, Ehi, Rosh, Muppim, Huppim and Ard.*(Gen. 46:21.) (Note: Becher is not included in the listing of Benjamin's family in Num. 26:38-41; nor are Gera, Ehi, Rosh and Muppim. Other names have been included: Ahiram and Shupham. Ard and Naaman are listed as Bela's sons.)*

Becher is listed as one of three sons of Benjamin: Bela, Becher and Jediael. Becher's sons were Zemira, Joash, Eliezer, Elioenai, Omri, Jerimoth, Abiah, Anathoth and Alameth. *(1 Chr. 7:6, 8.)* (Charts 16a, c.)

BECHER (2) (Bachrites). *Num. 26:35.*

Becher was a son of Ephraim. His descendants were the **Bachrites**. (Chart 15d.)

BECHORATH. *1 Sam. 9:1.*

Bechorath, a Benjamite, was the son of Aphiah, the father of Zeror, and a great-great-grandfather of Saul. (Chart 16k.)

BEDAD. *Gen. 36:35.*

Bedad was the father of king Hadad king of Edom.

BEDAN (1). *1 Sam. 12:11.*

Bedan was one of the people the Lord had previously sent to deliver the Israelites out of the hands of their enemies. He is mentioned along with Jerubbaal (Gideon), Jephthah and Samuel. However, this is the only reference made to him.

BEDAN (2). *1 Chr. 7:17.*

Bedan was a son of Ulam, a grandson of Peresh, a great-grandson of Machir, and a great-great-grandson of Manasseh. (Chart 15b.)

BEDEIAH. *Ezra 10:35 (18-19, 35, 44).*

Bedeiah, of the sons of Bani, and his brothers were some of the men in Israel who took foreign wives but gave them up when Ezra feared the wrath of God would destroy Israel for this iniquity.

BEELIADA. *1 Chr. 14:7.* See **Eliada (1)**.

BEERA. *1 Chr. 7:37.*

Beera, a descendant of Asher, was a son of Zophah. He was one of those recognized as head of his father's house, a man of valor, a chief of the princes. (Chart 14a.)

BEERAH. *1 Chr. 5:6.*

Beerah, of the tribe of Reuben, was the son of Baal. He was prince of the Reubenites. He was carried away by Tilgathpilneser, king of Assyria. (Chart 5b.)

BEERI (1). *Gen. 26:34.*

Beeri, the Hittite, was the father of Judith and a father-in-law of Esau. (Chart 3c.)

BEERI (2). *Hosea 1:1.*

Beeri was the father of the prophet Hosea.

BEEROTH. *Ezra 2:25; Neh. 7:29.*

Beeroth was of the people of Israel. The men of the children of Beeroth, Kirjath-arim and Chephirah who returned to Jerusalem from Babylon after Cyrus' proclamation to build the temple numbered 743. *(Note: Kirjath-arim is given as Kirjath-jearim in Neh. 7:29.)*

BEEROTHITE. *2 Sam. 23:37.*

The **Beerothite** Neharai, Joab's armorbearer, was one of David's mighty men. (Chart 17.)

BEL. *Isa. 46:1, 7; Jer. 50:2; 51:44.*

Bel and Nebo are idol gods. Instead of being able to help the people, the people must carry them. *(Isa. 46:1, 7.)* Jeremiah proclaimed that Bel was confounded and unable to help Babylon: Babylon would be destroyed, never to rise again. *(Jer. 50:2.)* The Lord will destroy Bel, the nations will cease to flow unto him, and the walls of Babylon shall fall. *(Jer. 51:44.)*

BELA (1). *Gen. 36:32; 1 Chr. 1:43-44.*

Bela was the son of Beor. He reigned as king in Edom before there were any kings over the children of Israel. *(Gen. 36:32.)* He reigned over the city of Dinhabah. Upon his death, Jobab the son of Zerah reigned in his stead. (Chart 18.) *(1 Chr. 1:43-44.)*

BELA (2). *Num. 26:38.* See **Belah**.

BELA (3). *1 Chr. 5:8.*

Bela, of the tribe of Reuben, was the son of Azaz. He was one of the chiefs among the Reubenites. He was a descendant of Joel. (Chart 5b.)

BELAH (Bela (2), Belaites). *Gen. 46:21; Num. 26:38, 40; 1 Chr. 7:6-7; 8:1-5.*

Belah was a son of Benjamin and grandson of Jacob. His brothers were Becher, Ashbel, Gera, Naaman, Ehi, Rosh, Muppim, Huppim and Ard. *(Gen. 46:21.)* He **(Bela)** was the father of the **Belaites**. His sons were Ard and Naaman. *(Num. 26:38, 40.)*

Bela, son of Benjamin, was the brother of Becher and Jediael. His sons were Ezbon, Uzzi, Uzziel, Jerimoth and Iri. *(1 Chr. 7:6-7.)*

Bela was Benjamin's firstborn; Ashbel, the secondborn; Aharah, the thirdborn; Nohah, the fourthborn; and Rapha, the fifthborn. Bela's sons were Addar, Gera, Abihud, Abishua, Naaman, Ahoah, Gera, Shephuphan and Huram. *(1 Chr. 8:1-5.)* (Charts 16a-e.)

BELAITES. *Num. 26:38.* See **Belah**.

BELSHAZZAR. *Dan. 5; 7:1; 8:1.*

Belshazzar, the son of Nebuchadnezzar, became king of Babylon following his father. He and his fellow revelers praised the gods of gold, silver, brass, iron, wood and stone, and drank from the vessels of the temple. As they were doing so, a hand wrote upon the wall. When the astrologers, Chaldeans and soothsayers could not interpret the writing, the queen suggested Belshazzar call in Daniel. He did so, and Daniel provided the following interpretation: MENE, MENE: "God hath numbered thy kingdom and finished it." TEKEL: "Thou art weighed in the balances and found wanting." PERES (UPHARSIN): "Thy kingdom is divided and given to the Medes and Persians." That night, Belshazzar was slain and Darius the Mede took the kingdom. *(Note: In the JST, PERES, in Dan. 5:28, is changed to UPHARSIN.)* *(Dan. 5.)*

In the first year of Belshazzar's reign, Daniel had a dream which troubled him. *(Dan. 7:1.)*

In the third year of Belshazzar's reign, Daniel had another vision. *(Dan. 8:1.)*

BELSHAZZAR'S WIFE, THE QUEEN. *Dan. 5:10-12.*

Belshazzar's Wife, the Queen, suggested to Belshazzar when the astrologers, Chaldeans and soothsayers could not read what the hand had written upon the wall, that he call in Daniel who had been able to interpret things for his father.

BELTESHZAZZAR. *Dan. 1:7.* See **Daniel (3)**.

BEN. *1 Chr. 15:18-20.*

Ben and his brethren of the second degree were assigned, under the direction of David, to be singers along with Heman, Asaph and Ethan.

BENAIAH (1). *2 Sam. 8:18; 20:23; 23:20-23; 1 Kgs. 1:8, 26, 32-44; 2:25-46; 4:4; 1 Chr. 11:22, 25; 18:17; 27:5-6.*

Benaiah, son of Jehoiada, was one of David's rulers over the Cherethites and the Pelethites. *(2 Sam. 8:18; 20:23; 1 Chr. 18:17.)*

Benaiah, one of David's mighty men, slew two lionlike men of Moab, a lion in a pit and an Egyptian. David set him over his guard. *(2 Sam. 23:20-23; 1 Chr. 11:22, 25.)*

Benaiah, Zadok the priest, Nathan the prophet, Shimei, Rei and the mighty men loyal to David, were excluded from Adonijah's group of co-conspirators when Adonijah aspired to be king in David's stead. *(1 Kgs. 1:8, 26, 32-44.)*

Benaiah was instructed by Solomon to slay Adonijah when Adonijah desired to have Abishag, the fair, young Shunammite who had conforted David in his final months or years, for a wife. *(1 Kgs. 2:25-46.)*

Benaiah was over the host when Solomon was king. *(1 Kgs. 4:4.)*

Benaiah, son of Jehoiada, was a chief priest and he and his course of 24,000 were appointed by king David to be over the third month. His son Ammizabad was in his course. Benaiah's son Jehoiada became king David's counselor after Ahitophel. *(1 Chr. 27:5-6, 34.) (Note: Apparently, both Benaiah's father and son were named Jehoiada.)* (Chart 17.)

BENAIAH (2). *2 Sam. 23:30; 1 Chr. 11:31; 27:14.*

Benaiah the Pirathonite was one of David's mighty men *(2 Sam. 23:30)* and one of the valiant men of the armies *(1 Chr. 11:31)*. He was of the children of Ephraim and was assigned by David to be over the course of 24,000 who served for the eleventh month. *(1 Chr. 27:14.)* (Chart 17.)

BENAIAH (3). *1 Chr. 4:36.*

Benaiah, of the lineage of Simeon and a descendant of Shimei, was a prince in his family. (Chart 6a.)

BENAIAH (4). *1 Chr. 15:18-20; 16:5.*

Benaiah and his brethren of the second degree were assigned, under the direction of David, to be singers along with Heman, Asaph and Ethan. Benaiah and his brethren were assigned to play with psalteries on Alamoth. *(1 Chr. 15:18-20.)* He was a Levite, and he and his brethren were appointed by David to minister before the ark of the Lord with psalteries and harps. *(1 Chr. 16:5.)*

BENAIAH (5). *1 Chr. 15:24; 16:6.*

Benaiah was among those who, under the direction of David, was assigned to make music before the Lord as the ark was removed from the house of Obed-edom and taken to the place which David had prepared for it to be housed. As one of the priests, he was assigned to blow the trumpet before the ark of God. *(1 Chr. 15:24.)*

Benaiah and Jahaziel, the priests, were appointed by David to minister continually before the ark of the Lord with trumpets. *(1 Chr. 16:6.)*

BENAIAH (6) (Bani (9), Jonathan (8)). *2 Chr. 20:14; Neh. 11:22; 12:35.*

Benaiah, a Levite of the sons of Asaph, father of Zechariah and grandfather of Jahaziel, was the son of Jeiel who was the son of Mattaniah. *(2 Chr. 20:14.)*

Bani (Benaiah), son of Hashabiah (Jeiel), was the father of Uzzi (Zechariah) who was the overseer of the Levites at Jerusalem. *(Neh. 11:22.)*

Jonathan's (Benaiah's) son Zechariah was one of the sons of the priests with trumpets who was instructed by Nehemiah to purify themselves and then assigned to one of two great companies for the dedication of the walls of Jerusalem. *(Neh. 12:35.)* (Chart 7a.)

BENAIAH (7). *2 Chr. 31:13.*

Benaiah, among others, was an overseer of tithes, offerings and the dedicated things under the hand of Cononiah and Cononiah's brother Shimei according to the commandment of king Hezekiah and Azariah, the ruler of the house of God.

BENAIAH (8). *Ezra 10:25 (18-19, 25, 44).*

Benaiah was of the sons of Parosh. He was among those who had taken wives from among the Canaanites or other foreign groups but who agreed to Ezra's request that they separate themselves from these "strange" wives lest the Lord destroy the rest of the children of Israel.

BENAIAH (9). *Ezra 10:30 (18-19, 30, 44).*

Benaiah was a son of Pahath-moab. He and his brothers were among the Israelites who took foreign wives but separated themselves from them at Ezra's request as he feared the Lord would destroy all of Israel due to this latest iniquity.

BENAIAH (10). *Ezra 10:35 (18-19, 35, 44).*

Benaiah, a son of Bani, and his brothers were some of the men in Israel who took foreign wives but gave them up when Ezra feared the wrath of God would destroy Israel for this iniquity.

BENAIAH (11). *Ezra 10:43 (18-19, 43-44).*

Benaiah was of the sons of Nebo. He and his brothers Jeiel, Mattithiah, Zabad, Zebina, Jadau and Joel were some of the Israelite men who took foreign wives but agreed to separate themselves from them because Ezra feared the Lord's wrath would destroy all of Israel for this iniquity.

BENAIAH (12). *Ezek. 11:1.*

Benaiah was the father of Pelatiah, which Pelatiah was among 25 men who Ezekiel saw in vision sitting at the east gate of the Lord's house giving false counsel to the people in Jerusalem.

BENAMMI. *Gen. 19:38.*

Benammi was the son of Lot's younger daughter, fathered by Lot as she lay with him after getting him drunk with wine. He was the father of the children of Ammon. (Chart 2d.)

BEN-HADAD (1). *1 Kgs. 15:18-20; 20; 2 Kgs. 6:24; 8:7-15; 2 Chr. 16:2-4.*

Ben-hadad, king of Syria, "worshipper of Hadad," was the son of Tabrimon and grandson of Hezion. When Baasha king of Israel (953-930 B.C.) came against Asa king of Judah, Asa enlisted the help of Ben-hadad (930 B.C.). *(1 Kgs. 15:18-20; 2 Chr. 16:2-4.)*

Ben-hadad gathered his host together, which included 32 kings, and made war on Israel in Samaria. The Syrians were defeated twice. Ben-hadad was let go free by Ahab contrary to the will of the Lord. The man who was of the sons of the prophets told Ahab that since he had let Ben-hadad go, Ahab's life would go for Ben-hadad's life. *(1 Kgs. 20.)*

Ben-hadad gathered all his host and besieged Samaria. *(2 Kgs. 6:24.)*

Ben-hadad was sick and sent Hazael to Elisha to inquire of him whether or not he would recover. Elisha said he would recover from his illness but that he would still die and Hazael would become king. The next day, Hazael smothered Ben-hadad with a thick cloth dipped in water and reigned in his stead. *(2 Kgs. 8:7-15.)* *(Note: The Bible Dictionary indicates there are three Ben-hadads. This writer could only identify two. The reference of 1 Kgs. 20 under "Ben-hadad" indicates that scripture refers to Ben-hadad (2). However, in the Chronology Chart opposite the year 925 B.C., it indicates that that scripture refers to Ben-hadad (1)).*

BEN-HADAD (2). *2 Kgs. 13:3, 24; Jer. 49:27; Amos 1:4.*

Ben-hadad was the son of Hazael, king of Syria. Because of wickedness, the Lord delivered Israel into the hands of Hazael and Ben-hadad all their days. Hazael died and Ben-hadad reigned in his stead. The lands Ben-hadad had taken from Jehoahaz in battle were recovered by Jehoash, Jehoahaz's son. *(2 Kgs. 13:3, 24.)*

The Lord said He would kindle a fire in the walls of Damascus that would consume the palaces of Ben-hadad. *(Jer. 49:27; also Amos 1:4 with slight modification.)*

BEN-HADAD'S (1) MESSENGERS. *1 Kgs. 20:2.*

Ben-hadad's Messengers conveyed Ben-hadad's intention of war to Ahab.

BEN-HADAD'S (1) SERVANTS. *1 Kgs. 20:12, 23, 28.*

Ben-hadad's Servants were told to set themselves in array against Israel in Samaria because Ahab rejected his demands. After suffering some defeat at the hands of Israel, the servants of the king of Syria told him, "Their gods are gods of the hills; therefore, they were stronger than we; but let us fight against them in the plain and surely we shall be stronger than they." Because of this claim, the Lord told Ahab that He would deliver the Syrians into his hands.

BEN-HAIL. *2 Chr. 17:7-8.*

Ben-hail was one of the princes of Judah who king Jehoshaphat instructed to teach in the cities of Judah. He sent a number of Levites and Elishama and Jehoram, the priests, with the princes to teach Judah from the book of the law of the Lord.

BEN-HANAN. *1 Chr. 4:20.*

Ben-hanan was a son of Shimon. His brothers were Amnon, Rinnah and Tilon.

BENINU. *Neh. 10:13 (1, 13, 28-31).*

Beninu, a Levite, was among those who covenanted and sealed their covenant to marry in Israel, honor the Sabbath, pay tithes and keep the commandments. *(Note: It is possible that Beninu is a misspelling of Binnui and refers to one of the Binnui's listed.)*

BENJAMIN (1) (Ben-Oni, Benjamites). *Gen. 35:18; 42:4, 13-24, 36-38; 43; 44; 45:1; 46:21; 49:1, 27; 50:8; Num. 1:11, 36-37; 2:22-23; 26:38-41; 34:21; Deut. 27:12; 33:12; Josh. 18:11-28; 21:4, 17; Judg. 1:21; 19-20; 1 Sam. 9:1-2; 1 Kgs. 12:21; 1 Chr. 7:6-12; 8:1-2; 12:29; 27:12, 21; 2 Chr. 11:1-14; 17:17-18; Ezra 1:5; Neh. 11:1, 7-8; Ezek. 48:22-23, 32; Hosea 5:8; Obad.*

Benjamin was the second son of Rachel and Jacob. (He was Jacob's 12th son.) His mother died in childbirth. She called him **Ben-oni**. *(Gen. 35:18.)*

When Jacob sent his sons to Egypt to purchase corn during the famine, he kept Benjamin at home because he didn't want any harm to come to him. When Joseph's brothers were accused of being spies, they denied it, saying they were 12 brothers—sons of one man—that one son was no more and the youngest remained with their father in Canaan. Joseph insisted that in order to prove they were not spies, they had to go get Benjamin and bring him to Egypt. Meanwhile, Simeon was kept as collateral. Jacob refused to let them return to Egypt with Benjamin. *(Gen. 42:4, 13-24, 36-38.)*

As the famine continued, Jacob instructed his sons to return to Egypt for more grain. With Judah as spokesman, they refused to go unless they could take Benjamin, too. Jacob finally agreed. When they got to Egypt, Joseph had them taken to his house and had a feast prepared for them. To their astonishment, they were seated by age—oldest to youngest. To each was given some food. Benjamin's portion was five times as much as the others. *(Gen. 43.)*

When the brothers prepared to return to Egypt, Joseph had the steward of his house hide a silver cup in Benjamin's sack. As they traveled, the steward was sent after them to accuse them of stealing the cup. They denied the charge and Judah said that if it should be found among them, the person who had taken it should be put to death. When it was found in Benjamin's sack, Judah pleaded with them to take him instead of Benjamin, as it would kill their father if he lost Benjamin after having lost Joseph. *(Gen. 44.)*

Joseph finally revealed himself to his brothers. *(Gen. 45:1.)*

Benjamin begat Belah, Becher, Ashbel, Gera, Naaman, Ehi, Rosh, Muppim, Huppim and Ard. *(Gen. 46:21.)*

After the brothers were reunited with Joseph, and following the move of their entire family to Egypt, the time came when Jacob called his sons together to tell them what would befall each of them in the last days. He said, "Benjamin shall ravin as a wolf: in the morning he shall devour the prey, and at night he shall divide the spoil." *(Gen. 49:1, 27.)*

When Jacob died, Benjamin and his brothers traveled to Canaan to bury him. *(Gen. 50:8.)*

Moses was instructed to have Abidan, son of Gideoni, lead the tribe of Benjamin as Israel prepared for war. The males in the tribe of Benjamin who were 20 years old or older who could go to war numbered 35,400. *(Num. 1:11, 36-37.)* Abidan was instructed to have the tribe of Benjamin pitch their tents next to the tribe of Manasseh as part of the camp of Ephraim on the west side of the encampment. *(Num. 2:22-23.)*

When Moses and Eleazar numbered the males in Israel who were twenty years old and older as they camped on the plain of Moab near Jericho, those in Benjamin's family numbered 45,600. These included the Belaites, Ashbelites, Ahiramites, Shuphamites, Huphamites, Ardites and Naamites. *(Num. 26:38-41.)*

Elidad was assigned to divide the land of inheritance given to the tribe of Benjamin. *(Num. 34:21.)*

The tribes of Benjamin, Simeon, Levi, Judah, Issachar and Joseph were to stand upon mount Gerizim to bless the people as the Israelites prepared to cross over Jordan. *(Deut. 27:12.)*

Moses blessed the tribe of Benjamin. *(Deut. 33:12.)*

When Joshua cast lots to divide the land between the various tribes of Israel, Benjamin's tribe came up first. Their lot came between the children of Judah and the children of Joseph. *(Josh. 18:11-28.)*

The cities to be given to the Levites that were taken out of the tribe of Benjamin, Judah and Simeon are listed. *(Josh. 21:4, 17.)*

The children of Benjamin did not drive the Jebusites out of Canaan but allowed them to dwell among them. *(Judg. 1:21.)*

A certain Levite and his concubine stopped overnight in Gibeah, which belonged to the tribe of Benjamin. Some wicked men from the city took the Levite's concubine and abused her, causing her to die. The Levite cut her body up into 12 pieces and sent the pieces to the various tribes of Israel. When the Benjamites refused to deliver up the wicked men from Gibeah, the children of Israel came against the Benjamites and they were smitten and destroyed. *(Judg. 19-20.)*

Saul, the first king of Israel, was a **Benjamite**. *(1 Sam. 9:1-2.)*

The tribe of Benjamin joined with Rehoboam and the house of Judah against Israel. *(1 Kgs. 12:21.)*

Benjamin's posterity is listed. Only three sons are listed: Bela, Becher and Jediael. *(1 Chr. 7:6-12.)*

Benjamin's sons are listed as Bela, his firstborn; Ashbel, the second; Ahara, the third; Nohah, the fourth; and Rapha, the fifthborn. *(1 Chr. 8:1-2.) (Note: This listing of sons differs from that in other verses.)*

When David became king and went to Ziklag, all Israel rejoiced and sent their armies to support him. Even though the children of Benjamin were Saul's kindred, they sent 3,000 men. *(1 Chr. 12:29.)*

Abiezer the Anethothite was of the Benjamites. He was assigned by David to be over the course of 24,000 who served for the ninth month. Jaasiel, son of Abner, was prince over the tribe of Benjamin when David was king. *(1 Chr. 27:12, 21.)*

The houses of Benjamin and Judah went with Rehoboam when Rehoboam became king after Solomon died and the house of Israel became divided. The rest of the house of Israel went with Jeroboam. The priests and Levites and all who wished to worship the God of Israel eventually returned to Rehoboam because Jeroboam led the children of Israel into idolatry. *(2 Chr. 11:1-14.)*

When Jehoshaphat was king of Judah, Eliada of the house of Benjamin, with his 200,000 men, and Jehozabad of the house of Benjamin, with his 180,000 men, served as the captains of thousands. *(2 Chr. 17:17-18.)*

When Cyrus, king of Persia, proclaimed the building of the temple in Jerusalem, he called for those who were of God's people to go up and build the temple. The chief of the fathers of Judah and Benjamin, the priests and the Levites, rose up to go build the house of the Lord. *(Ezra 1:5.)*

Those people from the tribe of Benjamin and their overseers who were elected by lot to dwell in Jerusalem following their captivity in Babylon are listed. The men numbered 928. *(Neh. 11:1, 7-8.)*

The Lord revealed to Ezekiel just how the land should be divided by tribes when the children of Israel are gathered in the latter days. Benjamin's portion will be between the borders of Levi and Simeon, from the east side unto the west side. The twelve gates of the city are to bear the names of the twelve sons of Jacob. One of the three east gates is to be named for Benjamin. *(Ezek. 48:22-23, 32.)*

When Hosea prophesied the fall of Israel, Ephraim and Judah, he told Benjamin to blow the cornet in Gibeah and the trumpet in Ramah. *(Hosea 5:8.)*

Obadiah prophesied that Benjamin would possess Gilead. *(Obad. 1:19.)* (Charts 1.; 3d.; 5a.; 6a.; 7a.; 8a.; 9a.; 10a.; 11a.; 12a.; 13a.; 14a.; 15a.; 16a-f, j-k, m.)

BENJAMIN (2). *1 Chr. 7:10.*

Benjamin, son of Bilhan and grandson of Jediael, was a great-grandson of Benjamin and a mighty man of valor. His brothers were Jeush, Ehud, Chenaanah, Zethan, Tharshish and Ahishahar. (Chart 16c.)

BENJAMIN (3). *Ezra 10:32 (18-19, 32, 44); Neh. 3:23; 12:34.*

Benjamin (one of Harim's sons) and his brothers Eliezer, Ishijah, Malchiah, Shemaiah, Shimeon, Malluch and Shemariah, were some of the Israelite men who took wives from among the Canaanites and other foreign groups. They agreed to

Ezra's request to separate themselves from their foreign wives. *(Ezra 10:32 [18-19, 32, 44].)*

Benjamin and Hashub labored next to the priests, the men of the plain, working "over against their house" when the children of Israel rebuilt the walls and gates of Jerusalem during the time of Ezra and Nehemiah. *(Neh. 3:23.)*

Benjamin and others, along with Hoshaiah and half of the princes of Judah, were appointed by Nehemiah to one of two great companies of people gathered for the dedication of the walls of Jerusalem. *(Neh. 12:34.)*

BENJAMITES. *1 Sam. 9:1.* See **Benjamin (1)**.

BENO. *1 Chr. 24:26.*

Beno, a Levite, was a son of Merari through Jaaziah. He, with the rest of the chief fathers of the Levites, drew lots for his course in the presence of king David, Zadok, Ahimelech and other community leaders. (Chart 7e.)

BEN-ONI. *Gen. 35:18.* See **Benjamin (1)**.

BEN-ZOHETH. *1 Chr. 4:20.*

Ben-zoheth was a son of Ishi.

BEOR (1). *Gen. 36:32.*

Beor was the father of Bela, king in Edom.

BEOR (2). *Num. 22:5.*

Beor was father of the prophet Balaam.

BERA. *Gen. 14:2.*

Bera was king of Sodom. Chedorlaomer and other kings defeated him and Birsha king of Gomorrah in battle and took Lot and his family captive.

BERACHAH. *1 Chr. 12:3.*

Berachah was one of David's mighty men who came to him at Ziklag to help defend him against Saul.

BERACHIAH. *1 Chr. 6:39; 15:17, 23.*

Berachiah, of the house of Levi through Gershon, was the father of Asaph and the son of Shimea. *(1 Chr. 6:39.)*

Berachiah, father of Asaph, was assigned to be a doorkeeper for the ark, along with Elkanah, a descendant of Levi through Kohath. *(1 Chr. 15:17, 23.)* (Chart 7a.)

BERAIAH. *1 Chr. 8:21.*

Beraiah, a descendant of Benjamin, was a son of Shimhi. (Chart 16h.)

BERECHIAH (1). *1 Chr. 3:20.*

Berechiah, a descendant of David through Pedaiah, was a son of Shelomith, the daughter of Zerubbabel. His brothers were Hashubah, Ohel, Hasadiah and Jushabhesed. (Chart 1.)

BERECHIAH (2). *1 Chr. 9:16.*

Berechiah was the son of Asa. He was a Levite who dwelled in the villages of the Netophathites. His genealogy was written in the book of the kings of Israel and Judah, who were carried away to Babylon for their transgression. He was among the first inhabitants to dwell in their possessions upon returning from Babylonian captivity.

BERECHIAH (3). *2 Chr. 28:12.*

Berechiah, son of Meshillemoth, was one of the leaders of the children of Ephraim who supported the prophet Oded in letting the captives of Judah go so as not to incur greater wrath from the Lord upon Israel.

BERECHIAH (4). *Neh. 3:4; 6:18.*

Berechiah was the father of Meshullam and the son of Meshezabeel. *(Neh. 3:4.)* His granddaughter, daughter of Meshullam, married Johanan, the son of Tobiah who opposed Nehemiah and the Jews' efforts to rebuild the walls of Jerusalem. *(Neh. 6:18.)*

BERECHIAH (5). *Zech. 1:1, 7.*

Berechiah was the father of the prophet Zechariah and the son of Iddo the prophet.

BERED. *1 Chr. 7:20.*

Bered was the son of Shuthelah and the grandson of Ephraim. His son was Tahath. (Chart 15d.)

BERI. *1 Chr. 7:36.*

Beri, son of Zophah, was a grandson of Hotham and a descendant of Asher through Beriah. (Chart 14a.)

BERIAH (1) (Beriites). *Gen. 46:17; Num. 26:44-47; 1 Chr. 7:30-31.*

Beriah was a son of Asher and a grandson of Jacob. He begat Heber and Malchiel. His brothers were Jimnah (Imnah), Ishuah (Isuah) and Isui (Jesui, Ishuai). His sister was Serah. *(Gen. 46:17.)* His descendants are called **Beriites**. *(Num. 26:44-47.)*

Beriah, the son of Asher, is again listed with his siblings. He was the father of Heber and Malchiel and the grandfather of Birzavith. *(1 Chr. 7:30-31.)* (Chart 14a.)

BERIAH (2). *1 Chr. 7:23.*

Beriah was a son of Ephraim. (Chart 15d.)

BERIAH (3). *1 Chr. 8:13-16.*

Beriah, a descendant of Benjamin, was a son of Elpaal who was a son of Shaharaim and Hushim. His sons were Ahio, Shashak, Jeremoth, Zebadiah, Arad Ader, Michael, Ispah and Joha. He and Shema "were heads of the fathers of the inhabitants of Aijalon, who drove away the inhabitants of Gath." (Chart 16g.)

BERIAH (4). *1 Chr. 23:10-11.*

Beriah was one of four sons of Shimei from the tribe of Levi through Gershon who was named when David numbered the Levites and divided them into courses. Jahath was the chief, Zizah (Zina) was the second, but Jeush and Beriah were combined into one reckoning because they didn't have many sons. (Chart 7f.)

BERIITES. *Num. 26:44.* See **Beriah (1)**.

BERITH. *Judg., 9:46.*

Berith was one of the pagan gods in Shechem.

BERODACH-BALADAN (Merodach-baladan). *2 Kgs. 20:12-19; Isa. 39.*

Berodach-baladan, king of Babylon, was the son of Baladan. He sent a letter and a gift to king Hezekiah when he heard he was ill. After Hezekiah showed the Babylonians everything in his house, the prophet Isaiah prophesied that Babylon would place Judah in captivity. *(Note: His name is given as Merodach-baladan in Isa. 39.)*

BESAI. *Ezra 2:49, 58; Neh. 7:52, 60.*

Besai was a Nethinim. When the Nethinims and the children of Solomon's servants left Babylon to return to Jerusalem to build the house of the Lord as proclaimed by Cyrus, king of Persia, they numbered 392.

BESODEIAH. *Neh. 3:6.*

Besodeiah was the father of Meshullam who helped repair the gates of Jerusalem when the children of Israel rebuilt the walls and gates of Jerusalem during the time of Ezra and Nehemiah.

BETH-EL. *Ezra 2:28; Neh. 7: 32.*

Beth-el was of the people of Israel and means, "House of God." The men of Beth-el and Ai who returned to Jerusalem from Babylon after Cyrus' proclamation to build the temple numbered 223 (123).

BETH-GADER. *1 Chr. 2:51.*

Beth-gader was the son of Hareph and a great-grandson of Caleb and Ephratah. (Chart 8 l.)

BETH-LEHEM (1). *1 Chr. 2:51.*

Beth-lehem was the son of Salma and a great-grandson of Caleb and Ephratah. (Chart 8 l.)

BETH-LEHEM (2). *Ezra 2:21-22; Neh. 7:26.*

Beth-lehem was of the people of Israel. The men of the children of Beth-lehem who returned to Jerusalem from Babylon after Cyrus' proclamation to build the temple numbered 123. *(Note: The men of Beth-lehem and Netophah together is given as 188 in Neh. 7:26 whereas the total in Ezra is 179.)*

BETH-LEHEMITE. *2 Sam. 21:19.*

One of the Beth-lehemites, Elhanan son of Jaare-oregim, slew the brother of Goliath the Gittite.

BETH-RAPHA. *1 Chr. 4:12.*

Beth-rapha was a son of Eshton. His brothers were Paseah and Tehinnah.

BETHUEL. *Gen. 22:22-23; 24:15, 24, 47, 50; 25:20; 28:2, 5.*

Bethuel was a son of Nahor and Milcah and a nephew of Abraham. He was the father of Rebekah, Isaac's wife. *(Gen. 22:22-23.)*

Abraham's servant saw Rebekah, the daughter of Bethuel, and put jewelry on her and asked Laban (Rebekah's brother) and Bethel if Rebekah could be the wife of his master's son. They said yes. *(Gen. 24:15, 24, 47, 50.)*

Bethuel's daughter Rebekah married Isaac when Isaac was 40 years old. *(Gen. 25:20.)*

Isaac sent his son Jacob to Bethel to seek a wife from among Laban's daughters. *(Gen. 28:2, 5.)* (Chart 2c.)

BETH-ZUR. *1 Chr. 2:45.*

Beth-zur was the son of Maon who was the son of Shammai who was the son of Rekem who was one of the sons of Hebron. (Chart 8i.)

BEZAI. *Ezra 2:17; Neh. 7:23; 10:18 (1, 18, 28-31).*

Bezai was of the people of Israel. The men of the children of Bezai who returned to Jerusalem from Babylon after Cyrus' proclamation to build the temple numbered 323 (324). *(Ezra 2:17; Neh. 7:23.)*

Bezai was among those chief of the people who covenanted to marry in Israel, honor the Sabbath, pay tithes and keep the commandments. *(Neh. 10:18 [1, 18, 28-31].)*

BEZALEEL (1). *Ex. 31:2-5; 35:30-35; 36-38; 1 Chr. 2:20; 2 Chr. 1:5.*

Bezaleel, of the tribe of Judah, was the son of Uri, who was the son of Hur. He was an artisan who the Lord inspired in building and furnishing the tabernacle. The Lord told Moses he had filled Bezaleel with wisdom, understanding, knowledge, and in all manner of workmanship, etc. *(Ex. 31:2-5.)* Moses told the people that the Lord had called Bezaleel and Aholiab to be in charge of building the tabernacle. The Lord also put it into their hearts to teach others the skills necessary for building the tabernacle. *(Ex. 35:30-35.)* Bezaleel and Aholiab and others worked on the tabernacle, made the ark, etc., the altar of burnt offerings and all things that pertained to the tabernacle. *(Ex. 36-38.)*

Bezaleel's father was Uri; his grandfather was Hur; his great-grandfather was Caleb. *(1 Chr. 2:20.)* Bezaleel the son of Uri, the son of Hur, made the brasen altar that was before the tabernacle of the Lord. *(2 Chr. 1:5.)* (Charts 8i, 8m.)

BEZALEEL (2). *Ezra 10:30 (18-19, 30, 44).*

Bezaleel was of the sons of Pahath-moab. He and his brothers were among the Israelites who took foreign wives but separated themselves from them at Ezra's request as he feared the Lord would destroy all of Israel due to this latest iniquity.

BEZER. *1 Chr. 7:36.*

Bezer, of the tribe of Asher, was a son of Zophah and grandson of Hotham. He was head of his father's house, a mighty man of valor and a chief of the princes. (Chart 14a.)

BICHRI. *2 Sam. 20:1.*

Bichri, a Benjamite, was the father of Sheba, which Sheba led the men of Israel away from David.

BIDKAR. *2 Kgs. 9:25-26.*

Bidkar was one of Jehu's captains. He was told to cast the body of Joram (Jehoram), king of Israel, into the portion of the field of Naboth the Jezreelite in accordance to the word of the Lord. *(See 1 Kgs. 21:19.)*

BIGTHA (Bigthan, Bigthana). *Esth. 1:10; 2:21; 6:2.*

Bigtha was one of the seven chamberlains serving in the presence of Ahasuerus the king who was sent to bring queen Vashti to Ahasuerus. *(Esth. 1:10.)*

Bigthan (Bigtha), along with his accomplice Teresh, plotted to destroy the king. When Mordecai informed queen Esther and Esther informed the king, Bigthan and Teresh were hung. *(Esth. 2:21.)*

The plot by **Bigthana** and Teresh to kill the king was revealed by Mordecai as recorded in the book of records of the chronicles of the kings of Media and Persia. *(Esth. 6:2.)*

BIGVAI (1). *Ezra 2:2, 14; Neh. 7:7, 19; 10:16 (1, 16, 28-31).*

Bigvai was one of the people who left Babylon and went with Zerubbabel back to Jerusalem following king Cyrus' proclamation to build the temple there. The men of the children of Bigvai who returned to Jerusalem from Babylon numbered 2,056 (2,067). *(Ezra 2:2, 14; Neh. 7:7, 19.)*

Bigvai was among those chief of the people who covenanted to marry in Israel, honor the Sabbath, pay tithes and keep the commandments. *(Neh. 10:16 [1, 16, 28-31].)*

BIGVAI (2). *Ezra 8:14 (1, 14).*

Bigvai's descendants, Uthai and Zabbud, took 70 male family members with them when Ezra led many exiled Israelites out of Babylon back to Jerusalem.

BILDAD. *Job 2:11; 8; 18; 25; 26; 42.*

Bildad the Shuhite was one of Job's three friends who came to mourn with him when he lost his children, his servants and his animals. *(Job 2:11.)* He reproved Job. *(Job 8.)* Bildad continued to upbraid Job and told him of the awful state that awaits the wicked who know not God. *(Job 18.)*

Bildad classified man as nothing more than a worm. *(Job 25.)*

Bildad was chastised by Job for his lack of empathy. *(Job 26.)*

Bildad, Eliphaz and Zophar were chastised by the Lord because they had not "spoken of me the thing that is right, as my servant Job hath." He instructed them to make offerings and that Job would pray for them; and He would accept them because of Job. They did as the Lord commanded. *(Job 42.)*

BILGAH (1). *1 Chr. 24:14.*

Bilgah was from the sons of Aaron. When David made the divisions of the sons of Aaron, there was one principal household for Eleazar and one taken for Ithamar. Eleazar had 16 sons and there were eight sons of Ithamar. These 24 sons who were chief of the fathers were divided by lot. Bilgah drew the fifteenth lot.

BILGAH (2). *Neh. 12:5, 18.*

Bilgah was one of the men (priests and Levites) who went with Zerubbabel from Babylonian captivity to Jerusalem. Bilgah was the father of Shammua who was one of the priests who was a chief of the fathers in the days of Joiakim.

BILGAI. *Neh. 10:8 (1, 8, 28-31).*

Bilgai was among the priests who covenanted and sealed their covenant to marry in Israel, honor the Sabbath, pay tithes and keep the commandments.

BILHAH. *Gen. 29:29; 30:1-8; 35:22, 25; 37:2; 46:23-25; 1 Chr. 7:13.*

Bilhah was Rachel's maid, given to her by her father Laban when she was given in marriage to Jacob. *(Gen. 29:29.)*

Rachel, unhappy that she was barren, gave her handmaid Bilhah unto Jacob for a wife so she could have children through her. Bilhah begat two sons: Dan and Naphtali. *(Gen. 30:1-8.)*

Rachel's two sons were Dan and Naphtali. Reuben, Jacob's firstborn son by Leah, went in and lay with Bilhah. *(Gen. 35:22, 25.)*

Joseph was feeding the flock with the sons of Bilhah and Zilpah and brought Jacob "their evil report." *(Gen. 37:2.)*

Bilhah had seven sons, i.e., Dan and his son, Hushim; and Naphtali and his sons Jahzeel, Guni, Jezer and Shillem. *(Gen. 46:23-25.)* Bilhah's sons, i.e., Naphtali's sons, were Jahziel, Guni, Jezer and Shallum. *(1 Chr. 7:13.)* (Chart 3d.)

BILHAN (1). *Gen. 36:27.)*

Bilhan was a son of Ezer who was a duke of the Horites. (Chart 4e.)

BILHAN (2). *1 Chr. 7:10.*

Bilhan, the son of Jediael, was a grandson of Benjamin. His sons were Jeush, Benjamin, Ehud, Chenaanah, Zethan, Tharshish and Ahishahar. (Charts 16c, e.)

BILSHAN. *Ezra 2:2; Neh. 7:7.*

Bilshan was one of the people who left Babylon and went with Zerubbabel back to Jerusalem following king Cyrus' proclamation to build the temple there.

BIMHAL. *1 Chr. 7:33.*

Bimhal was a son of Japhlet and a great-great-grandson of Asher. His brothers were Pasach and Ashvath. (Chart 14a.)

BINEA. *1 Chr. 8:37; 9:43.*

Binea, the son of Moza, was from the tribe of Benjamin. He descended through Saul through Jonathan. He begat Rapha (Rephaiah). *(1 Chr. 8:37.)* (Chart 16 l.)

BINNUI (1). *Neh. 7:15.* See **Bani (4)**

BINNUI (2). *Ezra 8:33.*

Binnui, a Levite, was the father of Noadiah.

BINNUI (3). *Ezra 10:30 (18-19, 30, 44).*

Binnui was a son of Pahath-moab. He and his brothers were among the Israelites who took foreign wives but separated themselves from them at Ezra's request as he feared the Lord would destroy all of Israel due to this latest iniquity.

BINNUI (4). *Ezra 10:38 (18-19, 38, 44).*

Binnui and his brothers, who were of the sons of Bani, were some of the men in Israel who took foreign wives but gave them up when Ezra feared the wrath of God would destroy Israel for this iniquity.

BINNUI (5). *Neh. 3:24; 10:9 (1, 9, 28-31); 12:8.*

Binnui, son of Henadad, labored next to Azariah—from the house of Azariah to the corner of the wall—when the children of Israel rebuilt the walls and gates of Jerusalem during the time of Ezra and Nehemiah. *(Neh. 3:24.)*

Binnui was one of the Levites who covenanted to marry in Israel, honor the Sabbath day, pay tithes and keep the commandments. *(Neh. 10:9 [1, 9, 28-31].)*

Binnui and his brethren are listed among those Levites who went up from Babylon with Zerubbabel to Jerusalem. *(Neh. 12:8.)*

BIRSHA. *Gen. 14:2 (1-2, 11-12).*

Birsha was king of Gomorrah. Chedorlaomer king of Elam, joined with other kings in battle against Birsha and his ally, Bera king of Sodom, at which time Sodom and Gomorrah were defeated and Lot, Abraham's nephew, and his family were taken captive.

BIRZAVITH. *1 Chr. 7:31.*

Birzavith was the son of Malchiel and a great-grandson of Asher. (Chart 14a.)

BISHLAM. *Ezra 4:7-21.*

Bishlam, a Samaritan, along with Mithredath, Tabeel and the rest of their companions, wrote to king Artaxerxes against Jerusalem causing the king to command that the Samaritans should cause the children of Israel to cease building the temple and the city.

BITHIAH. *1 Chr. 4:18.*

Bithiah was the daughter of Pharaoh and the wife of Mered.

BIZTHA. *Esth. 1:10.*

Biztha was one of the seven chamberlains serving in the presence of Ahasuerus the king who was sent to bring queen Vashti to Ahasuerus.

BOAZ. *Ruth 2-4.*

Boaz was a kinsman of Elimelech, Naomi's deceased husband. He took Naomi's daughter-in-law Ruth to wife. He begat Obed, who begat Jesse, who begat king David. Boaz was a descendant of Pharez, son of Judah. (Charts 1.; 8d.)

BOCHERU. *1 Chr. 8:38.*

Bocheru, a son of Azel, was from the tribe of Benjamin. He was a many-times-great-grandson of Saul. His brothers were Azrikam, Ishmael, Sheariah, Obadiah and Hanan. (Chart 16 l.)

BOHAN. *Josh. 15:6; 18:17.*

Bohan was a descendant of Reuben. Apparently, there was a stone called the stone of Bohan which was a recognized landmark.

BUKKI (1). *Num. 34:22.*

Bukki was the son of Jogli and was prince of the children of the tribe of Dan. He was assigned to divide the land of inheritance given to his people. (Chart 11b.)

BUKKI (2). *1 Chr. 6:5; Ezra 7:1-5.*

Bukki was the son of Abishua and was Aaron's great-great-grandson. He begat Uzzi. *(1 Chr. 6:5.)*

Bukki's descendants and forefathers are listed *(Ezra 7:1-5)* from Aaron through Ezra with some modification from the listing in 1 Chr. 6:4-15. (Chart 7b.)

BUKKIAH. *1 Chr. 25:4, 13.*

Bukkiah, a Levite and musician, was a son of Heman. The musicians—sons of Heman, Asaph and Jeduthun—drew lots and were given their duty assignments by David and the captains of the host. Bukkiah cast the sixth lot. He, his sons and his brethren numbered 12. (Chart 7d.)

BUNAH. *1 Chr. 2:25.*

Bunah was a son of Jerahmeel and a great-great-grandson of Judah. His brothers were Ram, Oren, Ozem and Ahijah. His half-brother: Onam. (Chart 8c.)

BUNNI (1). *Neh. 9:4-38; 10:15 (1, 15, 28-31).*

Bunni was a Levite. When Ezra read and interpreted the law of Moses and he and Nehemiah proclaimed the day a holy day, the Levites—Bunni, Jeshua, Kadmiel, Shebaniah, Bani, Sherebiah, Bani, Chenani, Hashabniah, Hodijah and Pethahiah—blessed and praised the Lord, reciting the Lord's goodness to Israel: the blessing of Abraham; giving the land of the Canaanites, Hittites, Amorites, Perizzites, Jebusites and Girgashites to Israel; dividing the Red Sea so they could cross it and drowning the Egyptians who pursued them; the signs and wonders shown to Pharaoh; leading them in the wilderness and protecting them so that they had bread from heaven, water from the rock, and their shoes and clothes never wore out; accepting them whenever they repented, even when they made a molten calf. They had been given the kingdoms of Shihon, Heshbon and Bashan and the Lord had subdued the Canaanites and delivered them into the hands of the Israelites, etc. After giving praise, they made a covenant with the Lord. The princes, Levites and priests sealed the covenant. *(Neh. 9:4-38.)*

Bunni was among those chief of the people who covenanted to marry in Israel, honor the Sabbath, pay tithes and keep the commandments. *(Neh. 10:15 [1, 15, 28-31].)*

BUNNI (2). *Neh. 11:15.*

Bunni, a Levite, was the father of Hashabiah. (Chart 7e.)

BUZ (1). *Gen. 22:21.*

Buz, Abraham's nephew, was a son of Nahor and Milcah. (Chart 2c.)

BUZ (2). *1 Chr. 5:14.*

Buz, a descendant of Gad, was the father of Jahdo. (Chart 13b.)

BUZI. *Ezek. 1:3.*

Buzi was the father of Ezekiel the priest.

BUZITE. *Job 32:2.*

Buzite. Barachel, of the kindred of Ram and father of Elihu, was a Buzite.

NAMES THAT BEGIN WITH "C"

CAIN. *Gen. 4.*

Cain, son of Adam and Eve *(v. 1)*, was a tiller of the ground *(v. 2)*. His offering unto the Lord was not acceptable to the Lord so he became very angry *(v. 5)*. *(Note: No reason is given in Genesis as to why the Lord rejected Cain's offering. However, we are given an explanation in Moses 5:4-8, 18-21 in the Pearl of Great Price: Cain loved Satan more than God; and Satan commanded Cain to make an offering unto the Lord, knowing that his offering would be rejected. The Lord had instructed Adam and Eve and their posterity to make offerings of the firstling of their flocks because this offering was a similitude of the Only Begotten of the Father which would be sacrificed on the cross generations later.)* Cain became angry with Abel and slew him *(v. 8)*. The Lord condemned the earth that it would not yield its fruits for Cain. Cain was told he would be a fugitive and a vagabond in the earth *(v. 12)*. Because Cain feared that every one who found him would try to kill him, the Lord set a mark upon Cain so no one would kill him. If anyone slew Cain, vengence would be upon him sevenfold *(vs. 14-15)*. He left the presence of the Lord and went to live in the land of Nod, east of Eden *(v. 16)*. He begat a son whom he called Enoch. He built a city and called it Enoch *(vs. 17-24)*. *(Note: We learn in Moses 5:2-3, 13, 16-17, 28, that Cain was not Adam and Eve's firstborn. They had several sons and daughters prior to the birth of Cain. These sons and daughters divided two and two in the land and begot sons and daughters. They loved Satan more than God. Cain married one of his brother's daughters. He and his wife also loved Satan more than God.)* (Chart 1.)

CAINAN (Kenan). *Gen. 5:9; 5:12-14; 1 Chr. 1:1.*

Cainan, great-grandson of Adam, was the son of Enos, who was 90 years old when he begat Cainan. *(Gen. 5:9.)*

Cainan was 70 years old when he begat Mahalaleel. He begat sons and daughters and lived a total of 910 years. *(Gen. 5:12-14.)*

Kenan (Cainan) was the son of Enosh (Enos). *(1 Chr. 1:1.)* (Charts 1.; 21.)

CALCOL. *1 Chr. 2:6.*

Calcol was one of the five sons of Zerah. He was a grandson of Judah and a great-grandson of Jacob. (Charts 8d, g-h.)

CALEB (Chelubai, Carmi). *Num. 13:6, 30; 14:6-9, 29-30; 26:65; 32:12; 34:19; Deut. 1:36-38; Josh. 14:6-14; 15:13-19; 21:11-12, 13; Judg. 1:12-15, 20; 3:9; 1 Sam. 25:3; 30:14; 1 Chr. 4:15; 2:9, 18-19, 42-49; 4:1.*

Caleb, of the tribe of Judah, was the son of Jephunneh. He was one of twelve leaders sent to scout out the land of Caanan. He returned with a positive report. *(Num. 13:6, 30.)*

Caleb and Joshua were the only two scouts to give favorable reports. Because the children of Israel chose to believe the ten negative reports, the Lord said none of them who were then twenty years old or older would be allowed into the promised land except Caleb and Joshua. *(Num. 14:6-9, 29-30.)* They were the only two men who had been numbered in the wilderness of Sinai who remained to be numbered on the plains of Moab to be given an inheritance in the promised land. *(Num. 26:65.)* They were the only two men who were twenty years old and upward when they left Egypt who were to be allowed to enter and receive an inheritance in the promised land. And this was because of their righteousness. *(Num. 32:12.)*

Caleb was the prince of the tribe of Judah named by the Lord when He named a prince for each tribe and commanded they divide the land by their inheritance. *(Num. 34:19.)*

Moses reminded the children of Israel that because of lack of faith when they were commanded 40 years earlier to conquer the promised land, none of the people who were then 20 years old or older except Caleb and Joshua were being permitted to enter the promised land. *(Deut. 1:36-38.)*

Caleb was 40 years old when he was sent as a spy by Moses to scout out the promised land. When he was 85 years old, he requested Joshua give him his land of inheritance as promised by Moses. He was as strong and vigorous at age 85 as at age 40 and said the Lord would help him take the land. Moses had promised Caleb that the land he stood on would be his inheritance; thus, Joshua gave Hebron to Caleb. *(Josh. 14:6-14.)*

Hebron was taken from Arba, the father of Anak. Caleb drove Anak's three sons out of the city and promised to give his daughter Achsah to the person who took Kirjath-sepher. His nephew, Othniel, son of Kenaz, took the city and received Achsah for his wife. *(Josh. 15:13-19; Judg. 1:12-15, 20.)*

Out of Caleb's inheritance, the city of Arba was given to the Levites for their inheritance, but the fields of the city of Hebron and the villages thereof were given to Caleb. His younger brother was Kenaz. *(Josh. 21:11-12, 13.)*

Caleb's younger brother, Kenaz, was the father of Othniel. *(Judg. 3:9.)*

Nabal, a churlish and evil man of the house of Caleb, was husband to Abigail who eventually became one of David's wives. *(1 Sam. 25:3.)*

The south border of the land that was given to Caleb was invaded by the Amalekites. *(1 Sam. 30:14.)*

Caleb's sons were Iru, Elah and Naam. *(1 Chr. 4:15.)*

(Note: It would appear that Caleb the son of Jephunneh and Caleb (Chelubai) the son of Hezron are one and the same. 1 Chr. 2:42-45 refers to Caleb the brother of Jerahmeel and lists his descendants which include Mareshah the father of Hebron and Maon the son of Shammai. The Encyclopædia Britannica indicates Caleb (the son of Jephunneh) settled in Hebron and that a later descendant, Abigail's husband Nabal, lived at Maon (places obviously named after Caleb's sons). As Caleb's posterity continues to be named, 1 Chr. 2:49 states that the

daughter of Caleb (brother of Jerahmeel) was Achsah. The footnote to Josh. 15:17 references Caleb the father of Achsah to Caleb the son of Jephunneh in Num. 32:12. Therefore, all references pertaining to Caleb the son of Jephunneh and Caleb (Chelubai, Carmi) the son of Hezron are assumed here to refer to the same person.)

Chelubai (Caleb) was one of the sons of Hezron. His brothers were Jerahmeel and Ram (a progenitor of David). Caleb begat the following sons "of Azubah his wife, and of Jerioth:" Jesher, Shobab and Ardon. When Azubah died, he took Ephrath, and she bore him Hur. Other sons of Caleb were Mesha, his firstborn. Ephah, his concubine, bore him Haran and Moza. Maachah, his concubine, bore him Sheber, Tirhanah, Shaaph and Sheva. His daughter was Achsah. *(1 Chr. 2:9, 18-19, 42-49.)*

Carmi (Caleb) was the son of Hezron, father of Hur, and great-grandson of Judah. *(1 Chr. 4:1.)* (Charts 8c-d, h-k, m-n.)

CANAAN (Canaanites). *Gen. 9:22; 10:6, 18-19; 10:18-19; 12:5-6; 15:18-21; Deut. 7:1; Josh. 17:12-13; 1 Kgs. 9:16; Ezra 9:1; Neh. 9:8.*

Canaan was the son of Ham who was the son of Noah. *(Gen. 9:22.)* He was the fourth son of Ham and a grandson of Noah. His brothers were Cush, Mizraim and Phut. *(Gen. 10:6,* 18-19.) **Canaanites** were descendants of Canaan. The families of the Canaanites were spread abroad. *(Gen. 10:18-19.)*

Abram took Sarai, his wife, and Lot, his nephew, and all they had into the land of Canaan. *(Gen. 12:5-6.)*

The Canaanites' lands were given to Abram's seed through a covenant with the Lord. *(Gen. 15:18-21.)*

The Canaanites were one of the seven nations in Canaan, greater and mightier than the Israelites, whom the Lord said He would destroy so that Israel could inherit the promised land. *(Deut. 7:1.)*

The Manassites were unable to drive the Canaanites totally out of the land so they dwelled among the children of Manasseh. However, when the Manassites became strong enough, they put the Canaanites to tribute. *(Josh. 17:12-13.)*

Pharaoh, king of Egypt, burned Gezer with fire and slew the Canaanites who dwelled in the city, and then gave the city to his daughter, Solomon's wife, for a present. *(1 Kgs. 9:16.)*

After the children of Israel were delivered from Babylonian bondage, many Jews—including the priests and Levites— intermarried with and followed the abominations of the Canaanites, Hittites, Perizzites, Jebusites, Ammonites, Moabites, Egyptians and Amorites. Ezra prayed and confessed the sins of all the people, fearing the Lord would completely destroy them for their abominations this time. *(Ezra 9:1.)*

The Lord gave the land of the Canaanites, Hittites, Amorites, Perizzites, Jebusites and Girgashites to Abraham. *(Neh. 9:8.)* (Chart 2e.)

CANNEH. *Ezek. 27:23.*

Canneh, Haran and Eden, the merchants of Asshur, Sheba and Chilmad, traded at the fairs in Tyrus before Tyrus' fall, trading in blue clothes, broidered work, chests of rich apparel, bound with cords, and made of cedar.

CAPHTORIM (Caphtorims). *Gen. 10:14; Deut. 2:23.*

Caphtorim was a son of Mizraim, a grandson of Ham, and a great-grandson of Noah. *(Gen. 10:14.)* Moses reminded the children of Israel that the **Caphtorims** defeated the Avims in Hazerim and occupied their cities. The Lord would help the children of Israel defeat the Caphtorims so they could obtain the land for their inheritance. *(Deut. 2:23.)* (Chart 2e.)

CAPTAIN OF THE LORD'S HOST. *Josh. 5:13-15.*

The **Captain of the Lord's Host** appeared to Joshua when Joshua was by Jericho. He told Joshua, "Loose thy shoe from off thy foot; for the place whereon thou standest is holy."

CAPTAINS OF 50 WITH THEIR FIFTY. *2 Kgs. 1:9-15.*

Three different **Captains of 50 with Their Fifty** were sent to the prophet Elijah by Ahaziah after Elijah foretold his death. The first two captains of 50 along with their 50 were destroyed when Elijah called down fire from heaven and it consumed them. The third captain of 50 pleaded with Elijah to spare his and his men's lives. The angel of the Lord instructed Elijah to accompany this captain of 50 back to Ahaziah.

CAPTAINS OF JEHORAM'S (2) HOST. *2 Kgs. 9:5-13.*

The **Captains of Jehoram's Host** included Jehu, the son of Jehoshaphat. One of the sons of the prophets anointed Jehu king over Israel and informed him that he was to smite the house of Ahab and destroy it. The son of the prophets anointed Jehu king and the captains of the host blew their trumpets, saying, "Jehu is king."

CARCAS. *Esth. 1:10.*

Carcas was one of the seven chamberlains serving in the presence of Ahasuerus the king who was sent to bring queen Vashti to Ahasuerus.

CAREAH (Kareah). *2 Kgs. 25:23; Jer. 40:8; 41:11-16; 42:1; 43:2, 4-5.*

Careah was the father of Johanan. *(Note: His name is spelled **Kareah** beginning with Jer. 40:8, which states that he was also the father of Jonathan.)*

CARMELITE. *2 Sam. 23:35.*

The **Carmelite**, Hezrai, was one of David's mighty men. (Chart 17.)

CARMI (1) (Carmites). *Gen. 46:9; Num. 26:6.*

Carmi was one of Reuben's sons and a grandson of Jacob. *(Gen. 46:9.)* He was the father of the **Carmites**. *(Num. 26:6.)* (Chart 5a.)

CARMI (2). *Josh. 7:1; 1 Chr. 2:7.*

Carmi was the father of Achan and was of the tribe of Judah. His father was Zabdi (Zimri), the son of Zerah who was the son of Judah. Thus, he was the great-

great-grandson of Jacob. *(Josh. 7:1.)* Carmi's son Achar (Achan) was the "troubler of Israel." *(1 Chr. 2:7.)* (Chart 8g.)

CARMI (3). *1 Chr. 4:1.* See **Caleb.**

CARMITES (See Carmi (1)).

CARPENTERS, BUILDERS, MASONS AND HEWERS OF STONE.
2 Kgs. 12:10-15; 22:5-7; 2 Chr. 24:4-13.

Carpenters, Builders, Masons and Hewers of Stone were employed to repair the house of the Lord. The king's scribe and Jehoiada, the high priest, brought up the money that was found in the house of the Lord and gave it to the workmen as commanded by king Jehoash (Joash) so supplies could be purchased and repairs made. *(2 Kgs. 12:10-15.) (Note: 2 Chr. 24:4-13 is a repeat and expansion of 2 Kgs. 12:10-15.)*

King Josiah instructed the high priest Hilkiah to give workmen money so they could repair the house of the Lord. *2 Kgs. 22:5-7.*

CARSHENA. *Esth. 1:14-15.*

Carshena was one of the seven princes of Persia and Media with king Ahasuerus when queen Vashti refused to come at his command. He and his colleagues asked what should be done to Vashti because of her refusal to obey Ahasuerus' command.

CASLUHIM. *Gen. 10:14.*

Casluhim was a son of Mizraim, a grandson of Ham, and a great-grandson of Noah. Out of him came Philistim. (Chart 2e.)

CERTAIN LEVITE, A. *Judg. 19-20.*

A Certain Levite had a concubine who left him and went back to her father's house. The Levite followed after her to retrieve her. After he took his wife back and they sojourned with her father a few days, they traveled to Gibeah, where they spent the night in the home of an old man who was from mount Ephraim but who "sojourned" in Gibeah among the Benjamites. Some wicked Benjamites took the Levite's concubine and abused her and she died. The Levite cut her up into 12 pieces and "sent her into all the coast of Israel." *(Judg. 19)* The children of Israel united against the Benjamites and destroyed them when they refused to deliver up the men of Gibeah who had abused the Levite's concubine. *(Judg. 20.)*

CERTAIN LEVITE'S CONCUBINE, A. *Judg. 19-20.*

A Certain Levite's Concubine left him and returned to her father's home. The Levite followed after her to get her back. After taking his wife back, they sojourned a few days with her father. As they journeyed home, they stopped for a night in Gibeah, home of the Benjamites. Some wicked Benjamites took the concubine and abused her, causing her to die. Her husband, the Levite, cut her body up into 12 pieces and sent a piece to each tribe. *(Judg. 19.)* The children of Israel gathered together to destoy the Benjamites when they refused to deliver up the men of Gibeah who had abused and killed the Levite's concubine. *(Judg. 20.)*

CHALCOL. *1 Kgs. 4:31.*

Chalcol, a son of Mahol, was recognized as a wise man, but Solomon was wiser than he.

CHALDEES. *Gen. 11:28; 2 Kgs. 24:2; 25:4-10; 2 Chr. 36:17; Job 1:17; Isa. 13:19; 23:13; 47; 48:20; Jer. 22:25; 25:11-12; 32:1-5, 24-29; 35:11; 37:6-10; 38:2; 39:5, 8; 41:3, 18; 50; 51; 52; Ezek. 23:14-28; Dan. 1:3-4, 6; 2:1-15; 3:8-12; 4:7-9; 5:7; 9:1; Hab. 1.*

The **Chaldees** were from that portion of Babylonia which lay south and east of Babylon called Chaldea. *(See Chaldea in the BD.)* Haran, the father of Lot, died before his father Terah in Ur of the Chaldees. *(Gen. 11:28.)*

Because of the wickedness of Judah, the Lord sent bands of the Chaldees, along with other groups, against Judah to destroy it. *(2 Kgs. 24:2.)* The armies of the Chaldees captured king Zedekiah, slew his sons before his eyes, and then put Zedekiah's eyes out. They bound him with fetters of brass and carried him to Babylon. In the 19th year of Nebuchadnezzar's reign, Nebuzar-adan, captain of his guard, went to Jerusalem and burned the house of the Lord, the king's house, and all the other houses. The Chaldean army with him broke down the walls of the city and carried the remnant of Judah away, along with everything of value—including the two pillars, one sea, and 12 brasen bulls that were in the house of the Lord—leaving only those who were the poor of the land to be vine-dressers and husbandmen. *(2 Kgs. 25:4-10; Jer. 52.)*

Because of the wickedness of Judah, the Chaldees were strengthened against Judah. They burned the temple and destroyed Jerusalem, slaying men and women, old and young. Those who weren't slain were carried away captive to Babylon where they were servants until the reign of the kingdom of Persia under king Cyrus. *(2 Chr. 36:17.)*

The Chaldeans made out three bands and fell upon Job's camels and carried them away. *(Job 1:17.)*

Isaiah prophesied that Babylon would be destroyed and the glory of the Chaldees' would be as that of Sodom and Gomorrah when they were overthrown by God. *(Isa. 13:19.)* The land of the Chaldeans was founded by the Assyrians: they set up the towers, etc., but God brought it to ruin. Likewise, Isaiah prophesied, Tyre would be overthrown. *(Isa. 23:13.)* Isaiah prophesied that Chaldea and Babylon would be destroyed for their iniquities. *(Isa. 47.)* Israel would eventually flee from the Chaldeans and be freed from Babylonian captivity. *(Isa. 48:20.)*

The prophet Jeremiah pronounced the judgments of the Lord upon the kings of Judah because of their wickedness. The Lord would deliver them into the hands of the Chaldeans and into the hands of Nebuchadrezzar (Nebuchadnezzar) king of Babylon. *(Jer. 22:25.)* The children of Israel would remain captive for 70 years, afterwhich the Lord said He would punish the king of Babylon and the land of the Chaldeans. *(Jer. 25:11-12.)*

It was in the 10th year of Zedekiah's reign over Judah and the 18th year of Nebuchadrezzar's reign over Babylon that Jeremiah was imprisoned by Zedekiah for prophesying that the king would be captured by Nebuchadrezzar and the Chaldeans would burn the city. *(Jer. 32:1-5, 24-29.)*

When Nebuchadnezzar came into their lands, the Rechabites feared him and the armies of the Chaldeans and Syrians so they went to Jerusalem for protection. *(Jer. 35:11.)*

Jeremiah told Zedekiah that Egypt would not save Judah from the Chaldeans. The Chaldeans would take Jerusalem and burn it. *(Jer. 37:6-10.)* Jeremiah prophesied that if the children of Israel would go forth to the Chaldeans they would live. If they didn't, they would die. The city would be given into the hand of the Chaldeans and they would surely burn it. Zedekiah would not escape out of their hand. *(Jer. 38:2.)* When the Chaldean army and Nebuchadnezzar came against Jerusalem, Zedekiah tried to escape, but the Chaldean army went after him and brought him back to Nebuchadnezzar for judgment. They burned the king's house, the houses of the people, and broke down the walls of Jerusalem. *(Jer. 39:5, 8.)*

The Chaldeans who were found in Mizpah were slain by Ishmael and his men when Ishmael slew Gedaliah who Nebuchadnezzar had made governor over the remnant of the Jews who were not carried captive to Babylon. Because Johanan the son of Kareah (Careah), who rescued the people of Mizpah from Ishmael feared the Chaldeans, they went to dwell in Chimham by Beth-lehem preparatory to going into Egypt. *(Jer. 41:3, 18.)*

The Chaldeans and Babylon, Jeremiah prophesied, would be destroyed for their iniquity and because it is a "land of graven images, and they are mad upon their idols." (Jer. 50:38.). The Lord would raise up a group of great nations from the north against Babylon and Chaldea would become a spoil. *(Jer. 50.)* Jeremiah continued his prophecy about the judgments and destruction and desolation that would come upon Babylon and the Chaldeans: "The slain shall fall in the land of the Chaldeans." *(Jer.51:4.)* The Lord also had raised "the spirit of the kings of the Medes: for his device is against Babylon, to destroy it." *(Jer. 51:11.)*

Jerusalem "doted" upon the things the Chaldeans had and thus committed whoredoms with them. But, Ezekiel prophesied, the Chaldeans and Babylonians and others would come against Jerusalem. "Behold," said the Lord, "I will deliver thee into the hand of them whom thou hatest, into the hand of them by whom thy mind is alienated." *(Ezek. 23:14-28.)*

Nebuchadnezzar instructed Ashpenaz, the master of his eunuchs, to bring unblemished people of the children of Israel to the palace to be taught in the learning and language of the Chaldeans. Daniel and his friends—Mishael (Meshach), Hananiah (Shadrach) and Azariah (Abed-nego)—were among those chosen. *(Dan. 1:3-4, 6.)*

The Chaldeans, along with Nebuchadnezzar's magicians, astrologers and sorcerers, were called in when Nebuchadnezzar had a dream that troubled him. He demanded they not only tell him the interpretation of the dream but the dream also because he could not remember it. The Chaldeans complained that no man could do that, and when they could not, Nebuchadnezzar sentenced them all to death. Daniel, being one of the "wise men" however, requested time to inquire of the Lord. *(Dan. 2:1-15.)*

The Chaldeans reported to Nebuchadnezzar, after he created a golden image and commanded that everyone should fall down and worship it whenever they heard music, that there were certain Jews—Shadrach, Meshach and Abed-nego, specifically—who had been set over the affairs of the province of Babylon who were not worshipping the golden image as commanded. *(Dan. 3:8-12.)*

Because the Chaldeans, magicians, astrologers and soothsayers could not interpret Nebuchadnezzar's new dream for him, Nebucahadnezzar asked Daniel to interpret it for him. *(Dan. 4:7-9.)*

The Chaldeans, astrologers and soothsayers were called in when king Belshazzar saw part of a hand write upon a wall. They could not explain the writing so Belshazzar called in Daniel. *(Dan. 5:7.)*

Darius, son of Ahasuerus, was king over the realm of the Chaldeans following Belshazzar. *(Dan. 9:1.)*

The prophet Habakkuk questioned the Lord as to why He blessed the wicked Chaldeans with success in conquering Israel who, in spite of their wickedness, were still more righteous than the Chaldeans. The Lord said He had raised them up for a purpose. *(Hab. 1.)*

CHEDORLAOMER. *Gen. 14:1-18.*

Chedorlaomer was king of Elam. Chedorlaomer and the kings that were with him went to battle against the Rephaims, Zuzims, Emims, Horites, Amalekites and Amorites. King Bera, King Birsha and King Shinab, King Shemeber and King Zoar joined in battle against Chedorlaomer, Tidal, Amraphel and Arioch. King Bera of Sodom and King Birsha of Gomorrah fell and "they took all the goods of Sodom and Gomorrah, and all their victuals, and went their way." Lot, Abraham's nephew, was taken captive. Abram rescued him, and brought him and the women and the rest of the people, along with their goods, back home after the slaughter of Chedorlaomer and the kings who were with him. Abram was greeted by Melchizedek king of Salam.

CHELAL. *Ezra 10:30 (18-19, 30, 44).*

Chelal, of the sons of Pahath-moab, was among the Israelites who took foreign wives but separated themselves from them at Ezra's request as Ezra feared the Lord would destroy all of Israel due to this latest iniquity.

CHELLUH. *Ezra 10:35 (18-19, 35, 44).*

Chelluh, of the sons of Bani, was one of the men in Israel who took foreign wives but gave them up when Ezra feared the wrath of God would destroy Israel for this iniquity.

CHELUB (1). *1 Chr. 4:11.*

Chelub, father of Mehir, was the brother of Shuah and the grandfather of Eshton.

CHELUB (2). *1 Chr. 27:26.*

Chelub was the father of Ezri who served David by being over those who tilled the ground.

CHELUBAI (See Caleb).

CHEMOSH. *Judg. 11:24; 1 Kgs. 11:7; 2 Kgs. 3:27; 23:13.*

Chemosh was a pagan god worshipped by the children of Ammon. *(Judg. 11:24.)*

When Solomon grew old and had many strange wives, he worshipped Chemosh (the abomination of Moab) and Molech (the abomination of Ammon) and incurred the anger of the Lord. He built a high place for Chemosh on mount Olivet. *(1 Kgs. 11:7.)*

Mesha king of Moab gave his eldest son as a burnt offering to Chemosh when the king of Israel and those aligned with him came against Moab for rebellion against Israel. *(2 Kgs. 3:27.)*

The high places of Chemosh, Ashtoreth and Milcom, which Solomon built, were destroyed by king Josiah. *(2 Kgs. 23:13.)*

CHENAANAH (1). *1 Kgs. 22:11; 2 Chr. 18:10.*

Chenaanah was the father of Zedekiah.

CHENAANAH (2). *1 Chr. 7:10.*

Chenaanah, son of Bilhan and grandson of Jediael, was a great-grandson of Benjamin and a mighty man of valor. His brothers were Jeush, Benjamin, Ehud, Zethan, Tharshish and Ahishahar. (Chart 16c.)

CHENANI. *Neh. 9.*

Chenani was a Levite. When Ezra read and interpreted the law of Moses and he and Nehemiah proclaimed the day a holy day, the Levites—Chenani, Jeshua, Bani, Kadmiel, Shebaniah, Bunni, Sherebiah, Bani, Hashabniah, Hodijah and Pethahiah—blessed and praised the Lord, reciting the Lord's goodness to Israel: the blessing of Abraham; giving the land of the Canaanites, Hittites, Amorites, Perizzites, Jebusites and Girgashites to Israel; dividing the Red Sea so they could cross it yet drowning the Egyptians who pursued them; the signs and wonders shown to Pharaoh; leading them in the wilderness and protecting them so that they had bread from heaven, water from the rock, and shoes and clothes that never wore out; accepting them whenever they repented, even when they made a molten calf. They had been given the kingdoms of Shihon, Heshbon and Bashan and the Lord had subdued the Canaanites and delivered them into the hands of the Israelites, etc.

After giving praise, they made a covenant with the Lord. The princes, Levites and priests sealed the covenant.

CHENANIAH (1). *1 Chr. 15:16, 22, 27.*

Chenaniah was chief of the Levites. David asked him to appoint singers with instruments of music to play before the Lord as they carried the ark from Obed-edom's house to the place David had prepared to house it. Chenaniah was skilful in song and in instructing about song.

CHENANIAH (2). *1 Chr. 26:29.*

Chenaniah was of the Izharites. He and his sons were assigned over the outward business of Israel—to be officers and judges.

CHEPHIRAH. *Ezra 2:25; Neh. 7:29.*

Chephirah was of the people of Israel. The men of the children of Chephirah, Kirjath-arim (Kirjath-jearim) and Beeroth who returned to Jerusalem from Babylon after Cyrus' proclamation to build the temple numbered 743.

CHERAN. *Gen. 36:26; 1 Chr. 1:41.*

Cheran was a son of Dishon. His brothers were Hemdan (Amram), Eshban and Ithran. (Chart 4d.)

CHERETHIMS. *Ezek. 25:16*

Cherethims were allied with the Philistines; however, there is no indication as to exactly who they were. The Lord, when He had Ezekiel prophesy destruction upon the Ammonites, Moab, Edom and the Philistines, said He would "cut off the Cherethims, and destroy the remnant of the sea coast."

CHERETHITES. *1 Sam. 30:14; 2 Sam. 8:18; 15:18; 20:7; 1 Kgs. 1:44; Zeph. 2:5-7.*

The **Cherethites** were invaded by the Amalekites at the same time the Amalekites invaded and destroyed Ziklag where two of David's wives were living. *(1 Sam. 30:14.)* King David placed Benaiah, son of Jehoiada, as ruler over the Cherethites and the Pelethites. *(2 Sam. 8:18.)*

When David and his household fled from Jerusalem to escape Absalom, the Cherethites , Pelethites and Gittites were with David. *(2 Sam. 15:18.)*

The Cherethites and Pelethites went with Abishai and Joab in pursuit of Sheba who was causing an insurrection in Israel and had drawn away the tribes of Israel from David. *(2 Sam. 20:7.)*

The Cherethites and Pelethites accompanied Zadok the priest, Nathan the prophet, and Benaiah the son of Jehoiada, when they brought Solomon to Gihon to reign as the new king. *(1 Kgs. 1:44.)*

The prophet Zephaniah prophesied judgment to come upon the Cherethites, the inhabitants of the sea coast, and said the sea coast would be for the remnant of the house of Judah. *(Zeph. 2:5-7.)*

CHERUB. *Ezra 2:59-62; Neh. 7:61-64.*

Cherub, Tel-Melah, Tel-harsa, Addan (Addon) and Immer had decendants go up to Jerusalem who could not declare their lineage so they were regarded as polluted and were put from the priesthood. These included 652 children of Delaiah, Tobiah and Nekoda and the children of the priests: Habaiah, Koz and Barzillai.

CHESED. *Gen. 22:22.*

Chesed was one of Milcah and Nahor's children. (Chart 2c.)

CHILDREN OF AMMON (Ammonites). *(Note: This is listed under Ammonites in the BD.) Gen. 19:38; Deut. 2:19-21; 23:3; Judg. 11; 1 Sam. 11; 2; Sam. 10; 11:1; 12:9, 26, 31; 1 Kgs. 11:7, 33; 2 Kgs. 24:2; 1 Chr. 18:11; 19; 20:3; 2 Chr. 20:1, 22-24; 26:8; 27:5; Ezra 9:1; Neh. 2:10, 19; 4:7-8; 13:1; Jer. 40:11, 14; 41:10; 49:1-6; Ezek. 21:28; 25:2-11; Amos 1:1, 13-15; Zeph. 2:8-9.*

The **Children of Ammon** are the descendants of Benammi who was the son of Lot and Lot's younger daughter. *(Gen. 19:38.)*

Moses reminded the children of Israel that they were commanded not to battle against the children of Ammon because Lot's descendants had been given that land as an inheritance. The children of Ammon defeated the Anakims who were regarded as giants, and the Anakims had succeeded a people called Zamzummims who were also regarded as giants. *(Deut. 2:19-21.)*

Moses instructed the Israelites that the Ammonites were not to enter into the congregation of the Lord, even to their tenth generation or forever because they did not befriend them when they came out of Egypt, but had hired Balaam the son of Beor to curse them. *(Deut. 23:3.)*

Jephthah led the armies of Israel in a successful battle against the children of Ammon. *(Judg. 11.)*

Saul led the children of Israel in a successful battle against the children of Ammon at Jabesh-gilead. *(1 Sam. 11.)*

David sought to show kindness unto Hanun, king of the children of Ammon, when Hanun's father Nahash, died, because Nahash had shown kindness unto him. Unfortunately, the princes of the children of Ammon convinced Hanun that David's servants were spies and he abused David's servants by shaving off one-half of their beards and by cutting "off their garments in the middle, even to their buttocks, and sent them away." Therefore, David sent Israel against the children of Ammon. The children of Ammon hired various groups of Syrians to help them fight against Israel. Shobach was the captain of the host of Hadarezer. Joab led Israel's troops against the Syrians and Abishai led the troops against the children of Ammon. Both the Syrians and the children of Ammon were defeated. *(2 Sam. 10.)*

David sent Joab and his armies against the children of Ammon while he tarried in Jerusalem. *(2 Sam. 11:1.)*

Under the guise of war, David used the children of Ammon and their swords to slay Uriah the Hittite. Rabbah and the children of Ammon were defeated and the capital city was taken by Joab. David brought the people out who were left in the defeated cities and "put them under saws, and under harrows of iron, and under axes of iron, and made them pass through the brick-kiln." *(2 Sam. 12:9, 26, 31; 1 Chr. 20:3.)*

The abomination of the children of Ammon was Solomon's building of a high place for Chemosh. *(1 Kgs. 11:7, 33.)*

The Lord sent bands of the children of Ammon, along with bands of Chaldees, Syrians and Moabites, against Judah. *(2 Kgs. 24:2.)*

David dedicated all the silver and gold, and other things he took or received from cities, including that which he took from the children of Ammon, unto the Lord. *(1 Chr. 18:11.)*

The name of the captain of Hadarezer's host is given as Shophach rather than Shobach. The Syrians would not help the children of Ammon any more. *(1 Chr. 19 basically repeats 2 Sam. 10 .)*

The children of Ammon, along with the children of Moab and mount Seir, came to battle against Jehoshaphat, king of Judah. The prophet Jahaziel prophesied that the Lord would protect Judah and fight the battle for them. Jehoshaphat and his people fasted and prayed. While they sang and praised the Lord, the children of Ammon, Moab and mount Seir fought amongst themselves and destroyed themselves, "and none escaped." *(2 Chr. 20:1, 22-24.)*

The Ammonites gave gifts to Uzziah (Azariah), king of Judah. *(2 Chr. 26:8.)*

The Ammonites were defeated by Jotham, king of Judah, and for each of three years they paid him a hundred talents of silver plus much wheat and barley. *(2 Chr. 27:5.)*

After the children of Israel were delivered from Babylonian bondage, many Jews, including the priests and Levites, intermarried with and followed the abominations of the Ammonites, Canaanites, Hittites, Perizzites, Jebusites, Moabites, Egyptians and Amorites. Ezra prayed and confessed the sins of all the people, fearing the Lord would completely destroy them this time for their abominations. *(Ezra 9:1.)*

Tobiah the servant was an Ammonite. He and Sanballat the Horonite were grieved when they heard that Nehemiah was seeking information regarding the children of Israel. *(Neh. 2:10, 19.)* They conspired with the Ammonites, Arabians and Ashdodites to stop the work on the city walls. *(Neh. 4:7-8.)*

The people were reminded as they read the book of Moses that the Ammonites and Moabites were forever forbidden to become part of the congregation of God because they had hired Balaam against them in ancient days. Thus, they were not to intermarry with them. *(Neh. 13:1.)*

After the children of Israel were carried off captive to Babylon by Nebuchadnezzar, the Jews who were among the Ammonites, in Moab, in Edom, and in other surrounding countries, went to Gedaliah (who Nebuchadnezzar had made governor over the remnant of the Jews who were left in Judah). Johanan the son of Kareah (Careah) and the captains of the forces in the fields warned Gedaliah that Baalis, king of the Ammonites, had sent Ishmael to slay Gedaliah. *(Jer. 40:11, 14.)*

The residue of the people who were in Mizpah who Nebuzar-adan had committed to Gedaliah, including the king's daughters, were carried off captive by

Ishmael who slew Gedaliah. He intended to take them to the Ammonites. *(Jer. 41:10.)*

Jeremiah prophesied of the destruction that would befall the Ammonites. *(Jer. 49:1-6.)*

Ezekiel prophesied the destruction of the Ammonites. *(Ezek. 21:28.)* Because the Ammonites rejoiced in the desolation of Jerusalem, the capture of Judah and the profaning of the Lord's sanctuary, Ezekiel was instructed by the Lord to prophesy vengence against them. *(Ezek. 25:2-11.)*

During the time of Uzziah (Azariah) king of Judah and Jeroboam king of Israel, Amos prophesied of things he saw concerning Israel and the judgments that would come upon Ammon, Syria, Edom, the Philistines and others. Of Ammon, he said the Lord would kindle a fire in the wall of Rabbah that would devour the palaces of the city, "with shouting in the day of battle, with a tempest in the day of the whirlwind: and their king shall go into captivity, he and his princes together." *(Amos 1:1, 13-15.)*

The prophet Zephaniah prophesied judgment to come upon the children of Ammon and said they shall be as Gomorrah and Moab shall be as Sodom. *(Zeph. 2:8-9.)* (Chart 2d.)

CHILDREN OF ISRAEL, THE (Israelites). *Ex. 1:7-22; 2:23-25; 3:1-10; 4-12; 13:21-22; 14: 16, 21-22, 29; 15-16; 17:1-6; Num. 9-11; 12:16; 13; 14; 16; 21:3, 4-9, 21-24, 33-35; 25:1-5; 26; 31; 33:50-56; Deut. 1-34; 34:9; Josh. 1-24:31; Judg. 1-20 (3:8-ll, 12-30, 31; 4-5; 6:11-8:28; 8:31-9:57; 10:1-2, 3, 6-8, 13-14; 12:7, 8-10, 11-12, 13-15; 13:1-16:31); 1 Kgs. 5; 6:1; 8:6, 9, 65; 2 Kgs. 24:17-20; 1 Chr. 11; 2 Chr.28:3-15; 31:1-2; 36:10-21; Ezra 3; 6:16-22; 7:6-7, 13, 24; Neh. 8; Ps. 105-106; 135:4; Isa. 1:1-31; 8:6, 19-20; 10-11; 41:8; 43:5-6, 12; 44:3, 26-28; 47:6-9, 11; 48:3-5, 10, 20; 49:12, 22-23; 51; 52; 54; 55; 56; 58; 59:12, 19; 60:10, 12-14, 18-21; 62; 63; 65; 66; Jer. 2; 3:14; 16:3-4, 11-12, 16; 17:4, 24-27; 19:5; 20:2-5; 21:3-7; 29:10; 30:9; 32:35; 33:7, 15; 34:8-17; 35-36; 40:5, 11; 41:3; 42:8-16; 46:27-28; 50:17-20, 33-34; 51:5-6, 19-23; Ezek. 2-24; 23:25-26; 33; 11:16-20; 28; 34; 36-37; 38-39; 45; 47; 48; Dan. 1:3-4, 6-7; 9:1, 7; Hosea 1-10; 11:1-2, 12; 12:10-12, 13; 13:9-14; 14:5; Joel 3; Amos 1:1; 2:6-16; 3-6; 7:9; 8-9; Micah 2-3; 4:6-7; 5:8; 6-7; Zeph. 3; Zech. 2:4; 7-8; 10; 12-13; 14:2-3; Mal. 1-2; 3:1, 4.*

The Children of Israel refers to Jacob's posterity, specifically those born after Jacob, Joseph and all of his brethren had died, and all of that generation. Because they increased greatly in number, the king of Egypt feared them and placed them in bondage. Pharaoh ordered the Hebrew midwives to kill all male babies born, but to save the girls. When the midwives did not comply, Pharaoh ordered the people to cast all newborn male babies into the river. *(Ex. 1:7-22.)*

Pharaoh died and the children of Israel cried unto God because of their bondage. He remembered the covenant He had made with Abraham, Isaac and Jacob. *(Ex. 2:23-25.)*

The Lord appeared unto Moses in a burning bush on Mt. Horeb and told him He wanted him to go to Egypt to free the children of Israel. God planned to bring them to a land flowing with milk and honey, unto the place of the Canaanites, Hittites, Amorites, Perizzites, Hivites and Jebusites. *(Ex. 3:1-10.)*

Moses and Aaron gathered together the elders of the children of Israel and told them what the Lord had instructed them to do. The children of Israel believed Moses and Aaron. The heads of Israel's households are enumerated (*Ex. 6:14-25*). When the Lord brought numerous plagues upon Egypt, He spared the children of Israel and protected the land of Goshen against the plagues. After the death of all the Egyptians' firstborn children, Pharaoh finally told the people to leave. The children of Israel had been in Egypt 430 years. They left with about 600,000 men on foot, plus children and all their cattle and flocks. As part of their preparation to leave, the Lord instituted the Passover and gave strict instructions for its observance. *(Ex. 4-12.)*

When the children of Israel left Egypt, led by Moses, the Lord went before them in a pillar of cloud by day and in a pillar of fire by night. *(Ex. 13:21-22)*

The Israelites crossed through the Red Sea on dry land when the Lord parted the waters. *(Ex. 14:16, 21-22, 29.)*

The children of Israel and Moses sang a song of praise unto the Lord. Moses and Aaron's sister, Miriam, led the women in dance and timbrels. Nevertheless, when the waters of Marah were bitter, the Israelites murmured again. The Lord told them that if they would be diligent in keeping His commandments, He would not put the illnesses upon them which He put upon the Egyptians. *(Ex. 15.)*

The Israelites murmured for want of food and lusted after the flesh pot of Egypt. The Lord sent them manna for bread and quail for meat. They were instructed to gather just enough for each person for one day. Anything left over spoiled and had worms. However, on the sixth day, they were told to gather enough for two days as the Lord would not send any on the Sabbath. The manna held over from the sixth day did not spoil. The Lord sent the children of Israel manna for 40 years. *(Ex. 16.)*

The children of Israel thirsted and murmured for want of water. The Lord had Moses smite a rock in Horeb and water came forth. *(Ex. 17:1-6.)*

In the first month of the second year after the children of Israel had fled Egypt, the Lord commanded them again to keep the Passover. A cloud rested above the tabernacle both during the daytime and nighttime. There was also a pillar of fire at night. When the cloud covered the tabernacle, they rested; when the cloud was taken up, they journeyed. *(Num. 9.)*

The children of Israel were commanded to make silver trumpets to be used to call assemblies and to blow alarms. The cloud was taken up from the tabernacle and so the people journeyed out of the wilderness of Sinai into the wilderness of Paran. They traveled in a prescribed order: Nahshon leading the tribe of Judah; Nethaneel leading the tribe of Issachar; Eliab leading the children of Zebulun; the sons of Gershon and Merari bearing the tabernacle; Elizur leading the camp of Reuben;

Shelumiel over Simeon's posterity; Eliasaph over the children of Gad; the Kohathites bearing the sanctuary; Elishama over the children of Ephraim and Gamaliel over the children of Manasseh; Abidan over the children of Benjamin; Ahiezer over the children of Dan; Pagiel leading the children of Asher and, finally, Ahira leading the children of Naphtali. *(Num. 10.)*

When the children of Israel complained against the Lord, it displeased the Lord and He "consumed them that were in the uttermost part of the camp" with fire. Eldad and Medad, two of the men in camp, prophesied among the people. The people murmured and lusted for meat. The Lord said he would send them so much meat that it would come out their nostrils. He sent them quail. In His wrath, the Lord also sent a plague. They called the name of the place, Kibroth-hattaavah because they buried the people who lusted there. They moved to a place called Hazeroth. *(Num. 11.)*

After Moses' sister, Miriam, recovered from her seven days of leprosy, the children of Israel left Hazeroth and settled in the wilderness of Paran. *(Num. 12:16.)*

The Lord instructed Moses to send a leader from each tribe to scout out the Land of Canaan and to report back. The men chosen were Shammua of the tribe of Reuben; Shaphat of the tribe of Simeon; Caleb of the tribe of Judah; Igal of the tribe of Issachar; Oshea (Joshua) of the tribe of Ephraim; Paltri of the tribe of Benjamin; Gaddiel of the tribe of Zebulun; Gaddi of the tribe of Manasseh; Ammiel of the tribe of Dan; Sethur of the tribe of Asher; Nahbi of the tribe of Naphtali; and Geuel of the tribe of Gad. They spent 40 days scouting the area. All but Joshua and Caleb brought back negative reports, saying the land was inhabited by giants and they were as small as grasshoppers in their sight. *(Num. 13.)*

Because the scouts gave negative reports and the people believed them and murmured against Moses and Aaron, the Lord said the children would have to wander in the wilderness 40 years—one year for every day they scouted out the area—and that no one who was then twenty years old or older would be allowed to enter the promised land except for Caleb and Joshua who had given good reports. The ten men who gave evil reports of the land died by the plague before the Lord. Some of the people decided they'd go up to the land and try to conquer it contrary to the Lord's stated position. The Amalekites and Caananites who lived there came down and smote them. *(Num. 14.)*

Korah (great-grandson of Levi), Dathan, Abiram and On (grandsons of Reuben), led 250 princes of Israel, men of renown who were famous in the congregation, in rebellion against Moses and Aaron. The Lord caused the rebels to be swallowed up by the earth and the 250 princes to be consumed by fire. Another 14,700 people were destroyed by plague for rebellion. *(Num. 16.)*

As the children of Israel journeyed from mount Hor to the land of Edom, they again complained against Moses and the Lord sent fiery serpents among the people. Many of the people died. They came to Moses acknowledging they had sinned and asked him to ask the Lord to take the serpents away. The Lord instructed Mosed to make a fiery serpent and to set it upon a pole. Everyone who was bitten by a serpent was to look upon it and they would then live. Moses made a serpent of brass. As they journeyed, they defeated the Canaanites, the Amorites, and the people of Bashan. *(Num. 21:3, 4-9, 21-24, 33-35.)*

As Israel abode in Shittim, the children of Israel committed many whoredoms and bowed down to the gods of the Moabites, even unto Baal-peor. The Lord commanded Moses to slay all those who had joined unto Baal-peor. *(Num. 25:1-5.)*

Moses and Eleazar received instructions to count all the males who were twenty years old and older as they camped on the plains of Moab. They numbered 601,730 (excluding the Levites). None of those numbered, except Caleb and Joshua, had been numbered among the children of Israel in the wilderness of Sinai because the Lord had said none of those would be permitted into the promised land but would all die in the wilderness. The Levites were counted separately and numbered 23,000 counting all males from one month upward because they did not have an inheritance. They administered the priesthood. The land was to be divided by lot giving each tribe according to its numbers. *(Num. 26.)*

Moses sent an army of 12,000 men (1,000 from every tribe), to war against the Midianites. They slew every man including the kings: Evi, Rekem, Zur, Hur and Reba. Balaam, son of Beor, was also slain. When they returned with the spoils, they were instructed to slay every male child and every woman who had lain with a man. The spoils were then divided according to instructions given to Moses by the Lord. *(Num. 31.)*

The children of Israel were told to drive all of the inhabitants out of Canaan because the land was to be their's for an inheritance. Any inhabitants left would be a thorn in their sides and pricks in their eyes and would vex them. Furthermore, the time would come when the Lord would do unto them what He thought to do unto the Canaanites. *(Num. 33:50-56.)*

Moses recounted all that had transpired over the past 40 years. *(Deut. 1-34.) (See Moses' entry.)*

Joshua was chosen to lead the children of Israel after Moses. *(Deut. 34:9.)*

Joshua led Israel as they took possession of the promised land. *(Josh. 1-24:31.) (See Joshua's entry.)*

The children of Israel alternately followed the Lord and fell away. Various leaders were raised up to lead them to freedom. The Lord established judges over Israel. Because of wickedness, the children of Israel served a variety of kings for various numbers of years.

(1) Chushan-rishathaim, king of Mesopotamia, for eight years. They were delivered by Othniel, son of Kenaz. They had peace for 40 years under Othniel. *(Judg. 3:8-11.)*

(2) Eglon, king of Moab, for 18 years. They were delivered by Ehud, son of Gera, a Benjamite. They had rest for 80 years. *(Judg. 3:12-30.)*

(3) Shamgar, son of Anath, followed Ehud as a deliverer and slew 600 Philistines. *(Judg. 3:31.)*

(4) Jabin, king of Canaan, oppressed the children of Israel for 20 years. Israel was delivered by Deborah, Barak, and Jael, wife of Heber the Kenite. And the land had rest for 40 years. *(Judg. 4-5.)*

(5) Midian ruled Israel for seven years. Gideon was called to deliver them. They had "quietness" in the land for 40 years "in the days of Gideon." *(Judg. 6:11-8:28.)*

(6) Gideon's son from a concubine, Abimelech, was made king after he killed his 70 brothers. One brother, Jotham, escaped. Abimelech reigned over Israel for three years. *(Judg. 8:31-9:57.)*

(7) After Abimelech, Tola, son of Puah, rose up to defend Israel. He judged Israel 23 years. *(Judg. 10:1-2.)*

(8) Jair, a Gileadite, followed Tola, and judged Israel 22 years. *(Judg. 10:3.)*

(9) The children of Israel again served false gods, and the Lord allowed the Philistines and the children of Ammon to defeat them. They oppressed Israel for 18 years. *(Judg. 10:6-8.)*

(10) The Lord said He would deliver them no more. *(Judg. 10:13-14.)*

(11) The elders of Gilead appointed Jephthah to be their captain to fight against the children of Ammon. Jephthah judged Israel six years. *(Judg. 12:7.)*

(12) Ibzan of Bethlehem judged Israel seven years. *(Judg. 12:8-10.)*

(13) Elon, a Zebulonite, judged Israel 10 years. *(Judg. 12:11-12.)*

(14) Abdon, the son of Hillel, a Pirathonite, judged Israel eight years. *(Judg. 12:13-15.)*

(15) The children of Israel again did evil in the sight of the Lord and were in bondage to the Philistines 40 years. Samson, a Nazarite from the womb, was raised up to begin to deliver Israel from the Philistines. He judged Israel 20 years. *(Judg. 13:1-16:31.)*

Solomon had the Israelites work alongside the Sidonians in hewing timber and stones for the temple because the Sidonians were skilled craftsmen in the hewing of timber. *(1 Kgs. 5.)*

It was in the 480th year after the children of Israel left Egypt and in the fourth year of Solomon's reign that he began to build the house of the Lord. *(1 Kgs. 6:1.)*

When the temple of the Lord was completed and the ark containing the two tables of stone were placed in the holy of holies, Solomon offered a dedicatory prayer and the children of Israel worshipped and feasted for 14 days. *(1 Kgs. 8:6, 9, 65.)*

After the children of Israel were taken captive to Babylon, the king of Babylon made Zedekiah (Mattaniah) king in lieu of Jehoiachin. He reigned 11 years in Jerusalem, beginning when he was 21 years old. He did evil in the sight of the Lord. Zedekiah rebelled against the king of Babylon. *(2 Kgs. 24:17-20.)*

After Saul died, the Israelites gladly anointed David king over Israel, indicating that even when Saul was alive, it was David who led out and protected Israel. David's valiant warriors are named and their deeds are recounted. *(1 Chr. 11.)*

The children of Israel smote Judah when Ahaz was king of Judah and carried them off captive. Oded, a prophet of the Lord, instructed them to let the captives go. The following leaders from the tribe of Ephraim spoke in support of letting Judah go: Azariah the son of Johanan; Berechiah the son of Meshillemoth; Jehizkiah the son of Shallum; and Amasa the son of Hadlai. *(2 Chr.28:3-15.)* After the faithful portion of Israel attended the solemn Passover in Jerusalem which Hezekiah, king of Judah, called for, they overthrew the false worship among them, destroying the images, the altars and the groves used in worshipping false gods. They then returned to their own cities and houses. Hezekiah reinstated the appointment of the priests and Levites after their courses according to the law. *(2 Chr. 31:1-2.)*

Judah's king Zedekiah rebelled against the Lord and the people mocked the Lord's messengers, despised his words and misused his prophets. Therefore, the Lord allowed the king of the Chaldees to defeat Judah. The Chaldees burned the temple and destroyed Jerusalem. Those who escaped the sword were carried away to Babylon where they remained as servants until the reign of the kingdom of Persia under king Cyrus. *(2 Chr. 36:10-21 is a repeat and expansion of 2 Kgs. 24:17-20..)*

The children of Israel, at the instruction of Cyrus, returned to Jerusalem to rebuild the temple unto the Lord. When the seventh month came, they built an altar and made the various burnt offerings according to the law of Moses. They paid the masons and carpenters and gave meat, drink and oil to those from Tyre to bring cedar trees, etc. for the temple. When the foundation was finally laid, the people all sang and gave thanks. The priests, Levites and chief of the fathers wept and shouted aloud for joy. *(Ezra 3.)* The children of Israel rejoiced when, in the sixth year of Darius, king of Persia, they were finally able to complete the building of the temple. The priests were set in their divisions and the Levites were set in their courses so the work of the temple could commence. *(Ezra 6:16-22.)*

Around 458 B.C., during the reign of Persia's king Artaxerxes Longimanus, Artaxerxes issued a decree allowing Ezra to take some of the children of Israel, the priests, Levites, singers, porters and Nethinims back to Jerusalem with him. *(Ezra 7:6-7, 13, 24.)*

Ezra read and interpreted the law of Moses to the people. He was assisted by Mattithiah, Shema, Anaiah, Urijah, Hilkiah and Maaseiah on his right hand; and Pedaiah, Mishael, Malchiah, Hashum, Hashbadana, Zechariah and Meshullam on his left hand. Several others also helped the people understand the law. Ezra and Nehemiah, the Tirshatha (governor), proclaimed the day to be a holy day. The people gathered tree branches and made booths so they could keep the feast of the tabernacles. This was the first time they had sat under the booths since the days of Jeshua (Joshua), the son of Nun. *(Neh. 8.)*

The children of Israel were instructed to observe and keep the Lord's statues and laws. A way was prepared for them to be saved from famine by the Lord allowing Joseph to be sold into Egypt. The children of Israel sojourned in Egypt. Moses was sent to bring them out of Egypt. The plagues are outlined. *(Ps. 105.)*

The children of Israel envied Moses and Aaron, rebelled and did wickedly. Had it not been for Moses' pleading in their behalf, the Lord would have destroyed them. They began to worship Baal-peor. This provoked Moses to the point that he "spake unadvisedly with his lips." Therefore, things went "ill with Moses for their sakes." *(Ps. 106.)*

The Lord chose Jacob and Israel for his "peculiar treasure." *(Ps. 135:4.)*

Isaiah saw in a vision that which concerned Judah and Jerusalem during the days of Uzziah, Jotham, Ahaz and Hezekiah, kings of Judah. Israel was in an apostate, rebellious and corrupt state. A very small remnant remained faithful. The Lord rejected their sacrifices and feasts. They were called upon to repent. Isaiah prophesied that Zion would be redeemed in the day of restoration. *(Isa. 1:1-31.)*

Because the children of Israel trusted in Rezin and Pekah, Remaliah's son, rather than in the Lord, Isaiah warned them and counseled them to seek the Lord not peeping wizards and to turn to the law and to the testimony for guidance. *(Isa. 8:6, 19-20.)*

Isaiah prophesied the destruction of Assyria. It is a type of destruction of the wicked that will occur when the Savior comes a second time. Although only a few people will be left after the Lord comes again, a remnant of the house of Jacob will return unto the Lord. *(Isa. 10:19-22.)*

When the Savior comes a Second time, he shall judge in righteousness. He will set up an ensign unto the nations and will gather together the righteous remnant of his people from the islands of the sea and the four corners of the earth. Ephraim and Judah will no longer be at odds with each other. *(Isa. 11.)*

The Lord, through Isaiah, reminded Israel that they are His servants. *(Isa. 41:8.)*

The Lord said He would gather the seed of Israel from the east and from the west, from the north and from the south. The Lord also told Israel that "ye are my witnesses . . . that I am God." *(Isa. 43:5-6, 12.)*

The Lord will pour His spirit out upon the seed of Israel and His blessing will be upon their offspring. Isaiah prophesied that Cyrus would free the Israelites and rebuild Jerusalem. In the latter days, the Lord will gather and redeem Israel and rebuild Jerusalem. *(Isa. 44:3, 26-28.)*

Isaiah predicted Israel's Babylonian captivity. *(Isa. 47:6-9, 11.)*

The Lord knew Israel would be obstinate and stiff-necked; thus, He continually revealed his plan for them from the beginning. He chose them in the furnace of affliction. They are to go forth out of Babylonian captivity and flee from the Chaldeans. The Lord will redeem them. *(Isa. 48:3-5, 10, 20.)*

Israel shall be gathered in the last days. Kings shall be their nursing fathers and queens their nursing mothers. *(Isa. 49:12, 22-23.)* The Lord shall judge the people.

The redeemed of the Lord shall return and come with singing and every lasting joy to Zion. Mourning and sorrow shall pass away. *(Isa. 51.)* The Messiah will comfort and deal prudently with his people. He will redeem Jerusalem and bring again Zion. *(Isa. 52.)*

Israel's "children shall be taught of the Lord; and great shall be the peace of thy children." Israel shall be gathered and the stakes of Zion shall be established—her curtains shall be stretched, her cords lengthened and her stakes strengthened. The Lord will remember Israel with kindness and mercy. *(Isa. 54.)*

Israel is counseled not to purchase that which "satisfieth not," but to trust in the Lord "and eat that which is good." If Israel will come unto Him, He will make an everlasting covenant with her. Israel is counseled to seek the Lord while He may yet be found. The Lord reminded Israel, "My thoughts are not your thoughts, neither are my ways your ways." *(Isa. 55.)*

The Lord promised that all who keep the commandments, including keeping the Sabbath day, will be exalted and will be joined together with the house of Israel. *(Isa. 56.)* Isaiah taught the children of Israel about the law of the fast, with its attendant blessings, and the importance of keeping the Sabbath Day holy. *(Isa. 58.)*

The children of Israel separated themselves from God by their iniquities. Their sins testify against them, "for our transgressions are with us; and as for our iniquities, we know them." *(Isa. 59:12.)* The Redeemer will come to Zion and redeem those who repent. *(Isa. 59:20.)*

Isaiah prophesied that in the last days Israel will arise and become a mighty nation. The Gentiles will join with Israel and will serve her. The nations that fight against Zion, the city of the Lord, will be destroyed. They will finally dwell in celestial splendor. *(Isa. 60:10, 12-14, 18-21.)* Israel shall become righteous and be called by a new name which shall be given her by the Lord. Jerusalem will be a praise in the earth. They will lift up an ensign to the people. They will be a holy people, redeemed of the Lord. *(Isa. 62.)*

When the Savior comes the Second Time, it will be a day of vengence. The righteous will then praise the Lord and acknowledge him as their father. *(Isa. 63.)*

Ancient Israel was rejected by the Lord for rejecting Him. In the Millenium, the Lord's people will rejoice; children will live to be 100 years old; there will be no crying or weeping. *(Isa. 65.)*

Everything is the Lord's. He made it all. The righteous also sin. The Lord will accept a contrite heart. Isaiah prophesied that at the Second Coming, Israel, as a nation, will be born in a day and the wicked will be destroyed. *(Isa. 66.)*

The Lord chastised Israel through the prophet Jeremiah because they had rejected Him and become idol worshippers. They had also rejected the prophets. The Lord suggested that Israel should turn to her idol gods next time the people need to be saved, saying, "But where are thy gods that thou hast made thee? Let them arise if they can save thee in the time of thy trouble." *(Jer. 2.)*

Israel and Judah were like adulterous wives who left the Lord and married themselves to false gods, defiling and polluting the land through wickedness. Nevertheless, in the last days, Israel will be gathered, "one of a city, and two of a family." *(Jer. 3.14.)* Because of wickedness, mothers and fathers, sons and daughters born in Jerusalem, would die grievous deaths. Their fathers were wicked, but they are even worse than their fathers. Nevertheless, in the latter days, Israel will be gathered, even by missionary work. "The Lord said He will send fishers "and they shall fish them" and then He will send "hunters, and they shall hunt them from every mountain, and from every hill, and out of the holes of the rocks." *(Jer. 16:3-4, 11-12, 16.)*

The Lord told Jeremiah that it was because of sin that He would cause the people to serve their enemies "in a land which thou knowest not." *(Jer. 17:4.)* The people were commanded to keep the Sabbath day holy. If they did, they would be blessed; but if they didn't, they would be destroyed. *(Jer. 17:24-27.)*

The children of Israel, specifically of Judah, sacrificed their children to Baal. *(Jer. 19:5.)* They forsook the prophets and put the prophet Jeremiah in the stocks. Jeremiah prophesied that Judah would be taken captive by Babylon. *(Jer. 20:2-5.)*

Jeremiah prophesied that the children of Israel would be taken captive by Nebuchadnezzar. The Lord, Himself, would fight against Israel "with an outstretched hand and with a strong arm." *(Jer. 21:3-7.)* The children of Israel taken captive by Nebuchadnezzar would remain captive of Babylon for 70 years after which the Lord would perform good works toward them. *(Jer. 29:10.)*

In the latter days, Israel and Judah will be gathered to their own lands. "They shall serve the Lord their God, and David their king, whom I will raise up unto them" (i.e. Jesus Christ). *(Jer. 30:9.)*

The children of Israel built the high places of Baal and caused their children to "pass through the fire unto Molech." *(Jer. 32:35.)*

The children of Israel will be gathered in the last days, and the seed of David (i.e., Jesus Christ), "the Branch of righteousness," will "execute judgment and righteousness in the land.". *(Jer. 33:7, 15.)*

Jeremiah prophesied that the Jews would be removed from their land and dispersed thoughout all the kingdoms of the earth. They were chastised for not following the Lord's command to let every manservant and every maidservant who was Hebrew go free after six years: no Jew should be a servant to his brother. *(Jer. 34: 8-17.)*

The Lord chastised the people for refusing to heed His words while pointing out to them that the Rechabites had faithfully heeded the words of their fathers. Thus, the Lord promised to bring upon Judah and Jerusalem all the evils He had pronounced upon them, but blessed Jonadab and the Rechabites. *(Jer. 35.)*

In the fourth year of Jehoiakim's reign over Judah, Jeremiah had Baruch record and read the prophecies Jeremiah dictated to him. Jehoiakim burned the rolls. The

Lord promised to bring upon Jerusalem all the evils He had pronounced upon them, and that Jehoiakim would have none to sit upon the throne of David. *(Jer. 36.)*

When the children of Israel were carried off captive to Babylon, Gedaliah was made governor over the remnant of the Jews left in Judah which included the poor of the land. *(Jer. 40:5, 11.)* The Jews, including Gedaliah, who remained in Mizpah after Nebuchadnezzar carried the rest of the children of Israel off captive to Babylon, were slain by Ishmael. *(Jer. 41:3.)*

The remnant of Judah, under the leadership of Johanan, was promised peace and safety if they stayed in Judah; but, if they went to Egypt, "none of them shall remain or escape" from the destruction by sword, famine and pestilence promised by the Lord. *(Jer. 42:8-16.)*

Jeremiah prophesied that Jacob, or the house of Israel, would return from captivity in the latter days and be restored to their lands, "and Jacob shall return, and be in rest and at ease, and none shall make him afraid . . . for I will make a full end of all the nations whither I have driven thee." While the Lord will not completely destroy Israel, neither will He leave Israel "wholly unpunished." *(Jer. 46:27-28.)*

Jeremiah prophesied that scattered Israel would eventually be gathered and restored to her inheritance. "In those days, and in that time, saith the Lord, the iniquity of Israel shall be sought for, and there shall be none; and the sins of Judah, and they shall not be found: for I will pardon them whom I reserve" *(Jer. 50:17-20)*. The Lord, their Redeemer, shall plead the cause of the children of Israel and the cause of the children of Judah. *(Jer. 50:17-20, 33-34.)*

Israel and Judah have not been forsaken. The Lord told both Israel and Judah to flee from Babylon. Israel is the Lord's rod with which He will destroy all kingdoms and nations. *(Jer. 51:5-6, 19-23.)*

The prophet Ezekiel prophesied repeatedly of the judgments and destruction that would befall Israel if the people didn't repent and return to the Lord. *(Ezek. 2-24.)* "Thy remnant shall fall by the sword: they shall take thy sons and thy daughters and thy residue shall be devoured by fire. They shall also strip thee out of thy clothes and take away thy fair jewels" *(Ezek. 23:25-26.)* Sinners who repent will be blessed for their righteousness and their former sins will be forgotten. The righteous who turn to sin, will be punished for their sins and their former righteousness will be forgotten. The children of Israel thought erroneously that because Abraham, one person, had inherited certain lands from the Lord they, because of their vast numbers, would possess the land promised to them in spite of their rejection of the Lord. However, the Lord said He would lay the land to waste. Then they would know that a prophet had been among them. Jerusalem was smitten and the Jews living there were to be destroyed because of their wickedness. *(Ezek. 33.)*

Ezekiel prohesied that Israel would eventually be restored to the land of her inheritance. The Lord will seek out the children of Israel as a shepherd seeks his lost sheep. The Messiah will be their shepherd and their king. *(Ezek. 11:16-20; 28; 34;*

36-37.) The stick of Judah and the stick of Joseph shall be joined together. The two nations shall become as one *(Ezek. 37:16-22). (Note: the stick of Judah is the Holy Bible. The stick of Joseph, i.e., the stick of Ephraim, is the Book of Mormon. See D&C 27:5.)*

The Second Coming will be ushered in with a great battle when Gog and Magog come against Israel. The Lord will magnify and sanctify Himself and "will be known in the eyes of many nations," and they will know He is the Lord. *(Ezek. 38-39.)*

The children of Israel, when they are restored to the land of their inheritance, are to divide it by lot and are to keep their feasts and offer their oblations and sacrifices as instructed by the Lord. *(Ezek. 45.)*

The borders of the land the children of Israel are instructed to divide by lot are outlined to Ezekiel. *(Ezek. 47.)* The borders of each tribe's portion of the land was revealed to Ezekiel. The gates of the city shall be named for the tribes of Israel. *(Ezek. 48.)*

Nebuchadnezzar instructed Ashpenaz, the master of his eunuchs, to bring certain unblemished children of Israel, and of the king's seed, and of the princes, to the palace to be taught in the learning and language of the Chaldeans. Daniel (Belteshazzar) and his friends—Mishael (Meshach), Hananiah (Shadrach) and Azariah (Abed-nego)—were among those chosen. *(Dan. 1:3-4, 6-7.)*

In the first year of the reign of Darius over the Chaldeans, Daniel fasted and prayed and confessed the sins of Israel, acknowledging that the inhabitants of Jerusalem, the men of Judah, and all Israel had trespassed against the Lord and, thus, were in a state of confusion. *(Dan. 9:1, 7.)*

During the days of Uzziah, Jotham, Ahaz and Hezekiah, kings of Judah, and Jeroboam, king of Israel, the Lord told Hosea and his family they were to be a sign unto Israel. His wife, Gomer was chosen from among those who committed whoredoms. Their first son was named Jezreel. The Lord said He would avenge the blood of Jezreel upon the house of Jehu and would "cause to cease the kingdom of the house of Israel." Hosea's daughter was named Lo-ruhamah, which means, "Not having obtained mercy." His second son was named Lo-ammi, which means, "Not my people." Nevertheless, in the last days, the children of Israel and the children of Judah will be gathered together under one head and they will become the sons of the living God. *(Hosea 1.)*

Harsh judgments were pronounced upon Israel for worshipping false gods. In the latter days, the Lord will make a covenant with Israel and He will show them mercy and they will become His people. *(Hosea 2.)* Hosea taught that Israel would be without the Lord for a long time, but in the latter days, Israel would return and would seek the Lord and His goodness. *(Hosea 3.)* He taught that Israel had lost all truth, mercy, and knowledge of God because of wickedness. Because they rejected knowledge, the Lord rejected them. They shall be punished for their wickedness and idolatry. *(Hosea 4.)* Hosea prophesied that Israel, Ephraim and Judah would fall because of iniquity. *(Hosea 5.)*

Hosea again reminded Israel that she had defiled herself. God desired mercy more than sacrifices and knowledge of Him more than burnt offerings. *(Hosea 6.)*

The Lord condemned Israel and Ephraim. *(Hosea 7.)* Hosea continued to recite the Lord's condemnation of Israel, Ephraim and Judah, and prophesied against them because they forsook the Lord and worshipped idols. *(Hosea 8.)* Because of sin, Israel would no longer live in the Lord's land. *(Hosea 9.)* Hosea condemned Israel for worshipping false idols and said Israel shall be ashamed. He called upon Israel to repent. *(Hosea 10.)*

The Lord compared Israel to His firstborn. Israel, as a child, was called out of Egypt. They sacrified unto Baalim. Israel "compasseth me about" with deceit. *(Hosea 11:1-2, 12.)* Hosea proclaimed that the Lord speaks through prophets and uses visions and similitudes to teach His people. When the people become rich, they turn from the Lord. "Jacob fled into the country of Syria, and Israel served for a wife . . ." *(Hosea 12:10-12)*. The Lord brought Israel out of Egypt by the hand of a prophet and by a prophet He preserved Israel. *(Hosea 12:13.)*

The Lord told Israel she had destroyed herself, "but in me is thine help." There is no god but the Lord, no savior except Him. Only He will redeem them from death and ransom them from the grave. *(Hosea 13:9-14.)* In the latter days, the Lord will be as the dew unto Israel. *(Hosea 14:5.)*

Joel prophesied that in the latter days, the Lord will gather Judah and Jerusalem and plead for his people Israel. Judah and Jerusalem have been "sold" unto the Grecians. However, in the latter days the children of their captors shall be delivered unto Judah and they will "sell them to the Sabeans." *(Joel 3.)*

During the time of Uzziah king of Judah and Jeroboam king of Israel, Amos prophesied of things he saw concerning Israel and the judgments that would come upon Syria, the Philistines and others. *(Amos 1:1.)*

Amos prophesied the Lord would pour out judgments against Israel, Judah and Moab because of their transgressions. Israel's sins included despising the law of the Lord, lying, not keeping the commandments, giving wine to the Narazites and commanding the prophets not to prophesy. The Lord reminded Israel that He could destroy them just as He destroyed the powerful Amorites. *(Amos 2:6-16.)*

The Lord reminded Israel that He will do nothing save He first reveals His secrets unto His servants the prophets. We must be in harmony with the Lord or He will not be with us. Because Israel chose to do evil, they were encompassed about and overwhelmed by an adversary. *(Amos 3.)*

In spite of famines, pestilence, death, and the Lord's withholding of rain and His pouring out of judgments upon the people, the children of Israel refused to return unto him. *(Amos 4.)* Amos urged Israel to seek the Lord, to do good, and live. He reminded Israel that the Lord knows their transgressions: they afflict the just; they take bribes; they turn aside the poor. Their sacrifices to idols is abhorrent to the Lord. The Lord will cause them to go into captivity. *(Amos 5.)*

The people were at ease in Zion and put their trust in Samaria. The Lord condemned their pride. Israel shall be taken captive. Her places shall be destroyed. *(Amos 6.)* Amos prophesied the sanctuaries of Israel would be laid waste. Israel would be taken captive and the house of king Jeroboam would die by the sword. *(Amos 7:9.)*

Israel shall fall. They shall wander from sea to sea, from the north to the east, seeking the Lord, but they will not find Him. There will be a famine of "hearing the words of the Lord." *(Amos 8.)* Amos reminded Israel that no one can hide from the Lord. The Lord will sift the house of Israel among all nations. Nevertheless, in the latter days, Israel will be gathered into her own land again and will plant crops and become fruitful. *(Amos 9.)*

Israel's destruction was lamented by Micah. Nevertheless, Micah prophesied that the Lord will eventually gather the remnant of Israel—like a flock of sheep. *(Micah 2.)*

Micah prophesied against the heads of Jacob—the heads of the children of Israel—who judged for reward, the priests who taught for hire, and the prophets who divined for money. *(Micah 3.)*

Israel will be gathered in the latter days; the mountain of the house of the Lord shall be established in the top of the mountains; the Lord will reign over His people forever. *(Micah 4:6-7.)* The remnant of Jacob will triumph over the Gentiles. *(Micah 5:8.)*

Israel was reminded by Micah that in spite of the Lord's goodness to them—His leading them out of Egyptian bondage and giving them Moses, Aaron and Miriam—they had turned away from Him and followed the ways of Balak king of Moab. Instead of the Lord's statutes, they kept the statutes of Omri and followed the work of Ahab. All the Lord required of them is to "do justly, and to love mercy, and to walk humbly with thy God." *(Micah 6:8, 4, 16.)* Micah told the people to reflect on the experience of Balak with Balaam the son of Beor to recognize and know the righteousness of the Lord. *(Micah 6:5.)*

Israel's fallen state was lamented, but Micah expressed confidence that the Lord will have compassion and will show mercy on Israel and will pardon her iniquity in the latter days. *(Micah 7.)*

Zephaniah prophesied that at the Second Coming, the Lord will gather all the nations together and pour out His anger against them. All the earth shall be devoured with the fire of the Lord's jealousy. The remnant of Israel shall be gathered and there will be a righteous people. The Lord will give the people a pure language. He will reign in their midst. *(Zeph. 3.)* Zechariah prophesied that in the latter days Jerusalem shall be inhabited as towns without walls, so numerous will be the people. They will be gathered from the land of the north. The Lord will dwell in the midst of them. *(Zech. 2:4.)*

Zechariah was sent to reprove the people for their hypocrisy in the fourth year of king Darius' reign. He told the people to execute judgment; to show mercy and have compassion one to another; not to oppress the widow, the fatherless, the stranger nor the poor. However, the people would not hear the Lord's cries unto them so He did not hear their cries unto Him, but scattered them among the nations. *(Zech. 7.)*

The Lord will gather His people in the latter days. He will be in the midst of them. He will bless them with great blessings. *(Zech. 8.)* The children of Israel—Judah and Joseph—shall be sown among the people in far countries, but the Lord will eventually gather them again. He will strengthen them and they will walk in His name. *(Zech. 10.)*

When the Lord comes again, He will destroy all the nations that come against Jerusalem and Judah. The children of Israel will look upon Him "whom they have pierced, and they shall mourn for him . . ." *(Zech. 12:10.)* Zechariah prophesied that when the Savior comes again, the Jews shall be forgiven. They will ask Him about the wounds in His hands. He will respond that they are the wounds He received in the house of His friends. The remnant of the house of Israel will be tried and refined and shall be the Lord's people. *(Zech. 13.)*

Zechariah prophesied that at the Second Coming, all nations shall be gathered to battle against Jerusalem. As Jerusalem is losing the war, the Lord will go forth and fight for Israel. *(Zech. 14:2-3.)*

The Lord sent Malachi to chastise the children of Israel for offering polluted bread upon the altar and for offering blemished animals for sacrifices. They found the offerings to be "a weariness" and belittled the cermony. *(Mal. 1:7-8, 13.)*

The Lord chastised the priests for departing out of the way, corrupting the covenant of Levi, and causing others to stumble. Judah was chastised for dealing treacherously one with another and for marrying daughters of other gods. *(Mal. 2.)*

Malachi prophesied that prior to the Second Coming, the Lord would send His messenger to prepare the way. The Lord will come suddenly to His temple. He will accept the offering of Jerusalem and Judah. *(Mal. 3:1, 4.)*

CHILDREN OF SOLOMON'S SERVANTS, THE. *Ezra 2:55-58; Neh. 7:57-60.*

The **Children of Solomon's Servants** combined with the Nethinims numbered 392 when they left Babylon to return to Jerusalem to build the temple as proclaimed by Cyrus, king of Persia. They included the children of Sotai, Sophereth, Peruda (Perida), Jaalah (Jaala), Darkon, Giddel, Shephatiah, Hatil, Pochereth of Zebaim and Ami (Amon).

CHILEAB. *2 Sam. 3:3.* See **Daniel (1)**

CHILION. *Ruth 1:2-5.*

Chilion was the second son of Elimelech and Naomi. His brother was Mahlon. He married Ruth, a girl from Moab. He, his brother and father all died in Moab.

CHIMHAM. *2 Sam. 19:37-38.*

Chimham was possibly a son of Barzillai, although it doesn't state that specifically. Barzillai had accompained David across Jordan, referring to himself as "thy servant," but declined to accompany him all the way to Jerusalem because he was 80 years old. However, he requested that David allow Chimham, "thy servant," to accompany him. And David told Barzillai, "And I will do to him that which shall seem good unto thee: and whatsoever thou shalt require of me, that will I do for thee."

CHISLON. *Num. 34:21.*

Chislon was the father of Elidad and was of the tribe of Benjamin.

CHITTIM. *Num. 24:24.* See **Kittim**. *(Note: This is listed under Chittim in the BD.)*

CHOZEBA. *1 Chr. 4:22.*

(Note: The scripture refers to "the men of Chozeba," not directly to Chozeba. It is possible Chozeba was a daughter of Shelah and a granddaughter of Judah although the scripture does not state that.) (Chart 8a.)

CHUSHAN-RISHATHAIM. *Judg. 3:8-11.*

Chushan-rishathaim was the king of Mesopotamia. When Israel became wicked, the Lord allowed Chushan-rishathaim to capture Israel. They served him for eight years. However, when Othniel became judge, the Lord delivered Chushan-rishathaim into his hand. And the land had rest for 40 years.

COL-HOZEH (1). *Neh. 3:15.*

Col-hozeh was the father of Shallun who was ruler of part of Mizpah.

COL-HOZEH (2). *Neh. 11:5.*

Col-hozeh, son of Hazaiah and the father of Baruch of the children of Perez, dwelled in Jerusalem after leaving Babylon. (Chart 8b.)

CONIAH. *Jer. 22:24, 28.* See **Jehoiachin**.

CONONIAH. *2 Chr. 31:12.*

Cononiah the Levite was ruler over the offerings and tithes and the dedicated things when Hezekiah was king over Judah. His brother was Shimei.

COZ. *1 Chr. 4:8.*

Coz was the father of Anub and Zobebah and the families of Aharhel the son of Harum.

COZBI. *Num. 25:6-8, 15-18.*

Cozbi was the daughter of Zur who "was head over a people, and a chief house in Midian." She is first referred to as a Midianitish woman *(v. 6).* She is referred to by name in verse 15. Zimri brought her unto his brethren. Phinehas, the son of Eleazar and grandson of Aaron, slew them both by thrusting a javelin through them. Thus, "the plague was stayed from the children of Israel."

CUSH. *Gen. 10:6-8; 1 Chr. 1:8-10.*

Cush was a son of Ham and a grandson of Noah. His sons were Seba, Havilah, Sabtah (Sabta), Raamah, Sabtecha and Nimrod. *(Note: According to the BD, Cush is the name of Ethiopia and also refers to the dark-skinned race of Eastern Africa south of Egypt and of South Arabia.)* (Chart 2e.)

(1). *2 Sam. 18:21, 31-32.*

<u>Cushi</u> was told by Joab to report to David what he had seen. Thus, Cushi reported to David that his son Absalom was dead.

CUSHI (2). *Jer. 36:14.*

<u>Cushi</u> was the father of Shelemiah who was the father of Nethaniah who was the father of Jehudi.

CUSHI (3). *Zeph. 1:1.*

<u>Cushi</u>, father of the prophet Zephaniah, was the son of Gedaliah.

CYRUS. *2 Chr. 36:22-23; Ezra 1:1-3, 4-11; 3:7; 4:3-5; Isa. 44:28; 45:1, 13; Dan. 1:21; 6:28; 10:1, 14.*

<u>Cyrus</u> was king of Persia. After Judah had been conquered by Nebuchadnezzar and were servants to the Chaldees because of wickedness, the Lord moved Cyrus to decree the building of the temple in Jerusalem. This was in fulfillment of the words spoken by Jeremiah. *(2 Chr. 36:22-23; Ezra 1:1-3, 4-11.)* Cyrus returned all the precious things that belonged to the house of the Lord that Nebuchadnezzar had brought out of Jerusalem. *(Note· According to the Chronology Chart and listed in the "Profane History" column, Cyrus' reign over the Persian Empire began about 559 B.C. However, information in the "Jewish History" column indicates that Cyrus issued his decree for the return of the Jews to Jerusalem in 537 B.C. In Ezra, it states that it was in the first year of Cyrus' reign that he proclaimed the building of the temple. Thus, there appears to be a little discreptancy in the dates between Jewish History and the Profane History.)*

According to the grant Cyrus had given them, the children of Israel paid money to the workmen, including those of Tyre, to bring cedar trees from Lebanon to the sea of Joppa. *(Ezra 3:7.)*

Cyrus commanded the children of Israel to rebuild the temple, but the Samaritans frustrated the work all during his reign, even until the reign of Darius as king of Persia. *(Ezra 4:3-5.)*

Isaiah prophesied that the Lord would move Cyrus to rebuild Jerusalem, and that in the latter days, He, the Lord, would again rebuild Jerusalem. *(Isa. 44:28.)* Isaiah prophesied that the Lord would raise up Cyrus as king of Persia, and that Cyrus would "build my city, and he shall let go my captives." *(Isa. 45:1, 13.)*

Daniel and his friends were found to be ten times wiser than all of Nebuchadnezzar's other magicians and astrologers. "And Daniel continued even unto the first year of king Cyrus." *(Dan. 1:21.)* During the reign of Cyrus, as well as during the reign of Darius the Mede, Daniel prospered. *(Dan. 6:28.)* In the third year of the reign of Cyrus, king of Persia, Daniel was given a vision wherein he saw the Lord and was shown what would occur to his people in the latter days. *(Dan. 10:1, 14.)*

NAMES THAT BEGIN WITH "D"

DAGON. *Judg. 16:23-30; 1 Sam. 5:1-7; 1 Chr. 10:10.*

Dagon was one of the Philistines' pagan gods. Samson slew more people at his death than he did in his life when he caused the pillars to collapse as the people were gathered to worship Dagon which they credited with Samson's capture. *(Judg. 16:23-30.)*

The Philistines were plagued because they took the ark of God and placed it in the house of Dagon next to Dagon. Each morning, they found Dagon fallen on his face before the ark of the Lord. One morning they found Dagon fallen, his head and palms cut off upon the threshold. Only the stump of Dagon remained. *(1 Sam. 5:1-7.)*

After Saul was slain by the Philistines, they placed his head in the temple of Dagon. *(1 Chr. 10:10.)*

DALAIAH. *1 Chr. 3:24.*

Dalaiah, a descendant of David, was a son of Elioenai. His brothers were Hodaiah, Eliashib, Pelaiah, Akkub, Johanan and Anani. (Chart 1.)

DALPHON . *Esth. 9:7-10, 13-14.*

Dalphon was one of Haman's ten sons who was slain by the Jews and, at queen Esther's request, was hung on the gallows by king Ahasuerus.

DAN (Danites). *Gen. 30:6; 37; 46:23; 49:1, 16-17; 50:8; Ex. 31:6; Num. 1:12, 38-39; 2:25-31; 26:42-43; 34:22; Deut. 27:13; 33:22; Josh. 19:40-48; Judg. 1:34-35; 13:2, 24-25; 18; 1 Kgs. 12:28-29; 15:20; 2 Kgs. 10:29; 15:29; 1 Chr. 12:35; 27:22; 2 Chr. 16:4; Ezek. 27:19; 48:1, 32.*

Dan was the first son of Jacob and Bilhah, Rachel's handmaid. (He was Jacob's 5th son.) *(Gen. 30:6.)* He and his brothers hated their younger brother Joseph and sold him to a group of Ishmeelites, or Midianite merchantmen, for 20 pieces of silver. They dipped his coat of many colors in animal blood and gave it to their father so he would think Joseph had been killed by wild beasts. *(Gen. 37.)*

Dan begat Hushim. *(Gen. 46:23.)*

After the brothers had gone to Egypt for grain and were finally reunited with Joseph, and following the move of their entire family to Egypt, the time came when Jacob called his sons together to tell them what would befall each of them in the last days. He told Dan that he shall judge his people as one of the tribes of Israel. He would be a serpent by the way, an adder in the path that biteth the horse heels so that his rider shall fall backward. *(Gen. 49:1, 16-17.)*

Dan and his brothers went together to carry their father's body to Canaan for burial. *(Gen. 50:8.)*

Dan's descendant, Aholiab, was an artisan who was inspired of God so as to work on the building and furnishing of the tabernacle which Moses was instructed to build while the children of Israel were in the wilderness. *(Ex. 31:6.)*

When Moses was instructed to choose a leader from each tribe to stand by him as Israel prepared for war and to number all the males 20 years old and older, he was told to appoint Ahiezer, son of Ammishaddai, to lead the tribe of Dan. The males numbered in the tribe of Dan totaled 62,700. *(Num. 1:12, 38-39.)* The tribe of Dan, under the leadership of Ahiezer, was instructed to camp on the north side "far off about the tabernacle of the congregation." Next to them was the tribe of Asher, with 41,500 men, and next to them was the tribe of Naphtali with 53,400 men. The total number of men in the camp of Dan was 157,600. *(Num. 2:25-31.)*

Dan's son's name is given as Shuham (Hushim) in verse 42. His descendants were called Shuhamites. While on the plains of Moab, Moses and Eleazar counted the males in Israel who were twenty years old and older. Those of the Shuhamites numbered 64,400. *(Num. 26:42-43.)*

The prince of the tribe of Dan was Bukki. He was assigned to divide the land of their inheritance between Dan's posterity. *(Num. 34:22.)*

The tribes of Dan, Reuben, Gad, Asher, Zebulun and Naphtali were instructed to stand upon mount Ebal to curse as the children of Israel crossed over Jordan into Canaan to inherit the promised land. *(Deut. 27:13.)*

Moses blessed the tribe of Dan *(Deut. 33:22.)*

When Joshua cast lots to divide the promised land among the tribes of Israel, the seventh lot fell to the tribe of Dan. When the borders were too little for them, they smote Leshem and possessed it, calling it Dan after their father. *(Josh. 19:40-48.)* The children of Dan were unable to cast the Amorites out of Canaan and were forced into the mountain. Nevertheless, the Amorites eventually became tributaries to the children of Dan. *(Judg. 1:34-35.)*

A Danite named Manoah was told by an angel of the Lord that his barren wife would have a son who would begin to deliver Israel from forty years of Philistine bondage. Samson was born and the Spirit of the Lord began to be with him. *(Judg. 13:2, 24-25.)*

Danites were the descendants of Dan. At the time there was no king in Israel, and after the land was divided between the various tribes and each was given its inheritance to obtain, the Danites sent men to seek their inheritance. Thus far, they had not been successful in obtaining all the lands they were given. As they journeyed, they came to the home of Micah. They took his false gods and enticed his priest—whom he had consecrated himself—to go with them and become their priest. They then traveled to Laish, which they conquered. Using Micah's false gods, the Danites set up idolatry in Laish. Jonathan (Manasseh's son Gershom's son) and his sons served as priests to the tribe of Dan until the day of the captivity of the land. *(Judg. 18.)*

Jeroboam, king of Israel, made two calves of gold and set one up in Dan and the other in Beth-el. *(1 Kgs. 12:28-29.)*

Dan was beseiged by Ben-hadad's armies. *(1 Kgs. 15:20; 2 Chr. 16:4.)*

In Dan and Beth-el, Jehu continued the worship of the golden calves. *(2 Kgs. 10:29.) (Note: According to the BD, Jewish tradition records that the golden calf was carried off to Assyria by Tiglath-pileser in the days of Pekah king of Israel.) (2 Kgs. 15:29.)*

The Danites sent an army of 28,600 men to support David when he became king and went to Ziklag. *(1 Chr. 12:35.)* The prince who was over the tribe of Dan when David was king was Azareel, son of Jeroham. *(1 Chr. 27:22.)*

As Ezekiel lamented the fall of the great city of Tyrus, he bemoaned the loss of her riches and commerce, part of which involved the merchants of Dan who traded in bright iron, cassia and calamus. *(Ezek. 27:19.)*

The Lord revealed to Ezekiel just how the land should be divided by tribes when the children of Israel are gathered in the latter days. The twelve gates of the city will bear the names of Jacob's twelve sons. One of the three east side gates will be named for Dan. *(Ezek. 48:1, 32.)* (Charts 1.; 3d.; 5a.; 6a.; 7a.; 8a.; 9a.; 10a.; 11a-b.; 12a.; 13a.; 14a.; 15a.; 16a.)

DANIEL (1) (Chileab). *2 Sam. 3:3; 1 Chr. 3:1.*

Chileab was David's secondborn son in Hebron. His mother was Abigail (who had been married to Nabal previously). His name is given as **Daniel** in 1 Chr. 3:1. (Chart 8e.)

DANIEL (2). *Ezra 8:2; Neh. 10:6 (1, 6, 28-31).*

Daniel, of the sons of Ithamar, was the chief of his fathers and went with Ezra from Babylon to Jerusalem. *(Ezra 8:2.)* He was among the priests who covenanted and sealed their covenant to marry in Israel, honor the Sabbath, pay tithes and keep the commandments. *(Neh. 10:6 [1, 6, 28-31].)*

DANIEL (3) (Belteshzazzar). *Ezek. 14:14-20; 28:3; Dan. 1:3-4, 6-21; 2; 4; 5:12-29; 6; 7; 8; 9; 10; 11; 12.*

Daniel was one of three prophets whom the Lord told Ezekiel that even if he, Noah and Job ministered to the children of Israel, the children of Israel would still not follow the Lord. *(Ezek. 14:14-20.)*

The destruction of Tyrus, as prophesied by Ezekiel, was in part because the king of Tyrus, who was "wiser than Daniel," was proud and thought of himself as God. *(Ezek. 28:3.)*

Daniel, Hananiah, Mishael and Azariah were among the children of Israel who were without blemish who were brought to the palace of Nebuchadnezzar by Ashpenaz, the master of the king's eunuchs, to be taught in the learning and language of the Chaldeans. The prince of the eunuchs gave each of them a different name. Daniel was given the name **Belteshazzar**; Hananiah, Shadrach; Mishael, Meshach; and Azariah, Abed-nego. They elected not to eat the meat and wine the king provided and, after ten days, they were healthier than those who ate the meat and drank the wine. At the end of three years, when the king visited with all those who had been taught, none of them could compare with Daniel and his friends.

They were wiser and had greater understanding than any of the king's magicians or astrologers. Daniel continued until the first year of king Cyrus. *(Dan. 1:3-4, 6-21.)*

Nebuchadnezzar had a dream that troubled him, but he could not recall it in the morning. He called in his magicians, astrologers, sorcerers and the Chaldeans and demanded they not only tell him the interpretation of the dream but the dream, also. When they could not, he sentenced all the wisemen to death. Daniel, however, requested time to inquire of the Lord. He invited his friends, Shaddrach, Meshach and Abed-nego to also petition the Lord regarding the matter. The Lord revealed the dream and the interpretation of the dream to Daniel. He explained the dream to Nebuchadnezzar, saying that God had revealed to Nebuchadnezzar what would happen in the latter days. Daniel was rewarded by Nebuchadnezzar who elevated him to a position where he "sat in the gate of the king." Daniel also made a request of the king regarding his friends; and Nebuchadnezzar set Shadrach, Meshach and Abed-nego over the affairs of the province of Babylon. *(Dan. 2.)*

Nebuchadnezzar had another dream which he had Daniel interpret for him. Daniel told him it represented the king's fall and madness and his being returned to the kingdom after seven years and after learning that the Lord rules over all the earth. David counseled Nebuchadnezzar to repent by showing mercy to the poor so that his prosperity might be lengthened. *(Dan. 4.)*

When Belshazzar, son of Nebuchadnezzar, was king of Babylon, he and his fellow revelers drank from the vessels of the temple. While doing so, fingers of a man's hand wrote upon the wall. Daniel was asked to interpret the writing when none of the king's astrologers, Chaldeans and soothsayers could interpret them. Daniel gave him the interpretation and reproved the king for pride and idolatry. That night, Belshazzar was slain and Babylon was conquered. Darius the Mede became king. *(Dan. 5:12-29.)*

Darius placed 120 princes over the kingdom with three presidents over the princes. He made Daniel the first president. The other presidents and princes were jealous of Daniel and sought to destroy him by getting the king to sign a decree which stated that no one could petition any man or God, except Darius, for thirty days. When Daniel defied the order and prayed to God, these men reported it to Darius and reminded him that he had signed a decree that he could not revoke that required he cast Daniel into a den of lions. Darius was grieved, but finally complied. However, he spent the night fasting and praying that the Lord would deliver Daniel, which He did. Darius then had those men, their wives and their children cast into the lions' den. He made a decree that all peoples in his kingdom should revere the God of Daniel for "he is the living God." Daniel prospered under the reign of Darius and under the reign of Cyrus the Persian. *(Dan. 6.)*

Daniel had a dream in the first year of king Belshazzar's reign in Babylon, but he kept it to himself.

The Dream   and   the Interpretation of the Dream

Four winds of the heavens blew upon the sea. Four great, diverse beasts came up out of the sea.

Four beasts are four kings which shall arise out of the earth. However, the saints of the most High shall take the kingdom and possess it forever and ever.

The first was like a lion with eagle's wings. The wings were plucked and the lion was lifted up and made to stand upon feet like a man. It was given the heart of a man.

The second was like a bear and had three ribs in its mouth between its teeth. It was told to "arise and eat much flesh."

The third was like a leopard and had four wings of a fowl upon its back. It had four heads and was given dominion.

The fourth beast was dreadful and terrible, and exceedingly strong with teeth of iron. It devoured and broke in pieces, and stamped the rest with its feet. It was different from all the other beasts. It had ten horns. Another little horn came up among the ten horns before whom three of the ten horns were plucked up by the roots. In this little horn, there were eyes like a man's and a mouth speaking great things.

This is the fourth kingdom upon the earth. It shall be diverse from all kingdoms. It shall devour the whole earth, tread it down, and break it in pieces. Ten kings shall arise. Another shall arise. This diverse king shall subdue three kings. This horn made war with the saints and prevailed against them. He will seek to change times and laws. He shall speak great words against the Most High. He will wear down the saints and they will be given into his hand for a time.

He saw thrones cast down and the Ancient of days sat in judgment. A fiery stream issued forth from him. Thousands and thousands ministered unto him. The judgment was set and the books were opened.

The Ancient of days came, and judgment was given to the saints of the Most High. The time came that the saints possessed the kingdom.

The beast was slain and his body was destroyed and given to the burning flame. The rest of the beasts lost their dominions, but their lives were prolonged for a while.

The judgment shall sit, and they shall take away his dominion forever.

The Son of man came with the clouds of heaven to the Ancient of days. Dominion, glory, and an everlasting kingdom were given Him and all nations, people and languages should serve Him.

The kingdom shall be given to the people of the saints of the Most High, whose kingdom is an everlasting kingdom. All dominions shall serve and obey Him. (Dan. 7.)

In the third year of king Belshazzar's reign over Babylon, Daniel had another vision.

The Vision and the Interpretation of the Vision
Daniel was by the river of Ulai. A ram with two horns stood before the river. One horn was higher than the other; the higher one came last. The ram pushed west, north and southward. He became great and none could deliver out of his hand.

An angel, Gabriel, revealed the meaning of the vision to Daniel. The fulfillment of the vision would come to pass in the latter days. The ram with two horns represents the kings of Media and Persia.

A he goat came from the west and did not touch the ground.

The he goat is the king of Grecia.

The goat had a notable horn between his eyes.

The great horn is the first king.

He attacked the ram with anger, broke the rams horns and stamped upon him. None could deliver the ram from the he goat. The he goat waxed strong, the great horn was broken, and four notable ones grew instead.

Four kingdoms shall replace the one that is broken, but will not be in his power.

Out of one of them came a little horn which waxed very strong toward the south and east. It waxed great, even against the host of heaven. It cast down some of the host and stars to the ground and stamped upon them. He magnified himself to the prince of the host.

He will stand against the Prince of princes.

By him the daily sacrifice was taken away and the place of his sanctuary was cast down. An host was given him against the daily sacrifice by reason of transgression. The truth was cast down. The he goat practiced and prospered.

But, he shall be broken without hands.

The events revealed in the vision would come to pass in 2,300 days. Then the sanctuary would be cleansed.

The vision will be fulfilled at the time of the end. Many days will pass before the events seen in the vision happen.

At the end of the vision, Daniel fainted and was sick for several days. *(Dan. 8.)*

In the first year of the reign of Darius over the Chaldeans, Daniel fasted and prayed and confessed the sins of Israel. The angel Gabriel appeared to him again and revealed to him the time of the coming of the Messiah. *(Dan. 9.)*

Daniel was given a vision in the third year of Cyrus' reign as king of Persia in which he saw the Lord. He was shown what would happen to his people in the latter days. When he saw the Lord, all his strength left him. Those with him could not see the Lord, but they felt a great quaking and they fled and hid themselves. *(Dan. 10.)* Daniel's vision continued. He saw the successive kings and their conflicts, leagues and wars which will lead up to the Second Coming of Christ. The people who do wickedly shall be corrupted by flatteries, but the people who know their God shall be strong. *(Dan. 11.)* Daniel's vision concluded. Michael will deliver Israel from their troubles. That time of trouble will be greater than there had ever been in the past. There will be two resurrections: some will awaken to everlasting life and some to shame and everlasting contempt. None of the wicked will understand the meaning of Daniel's vision, but the righteous will. *(Dan. 12.) (Note: We learn in D&C 27:11 that Michael the Archangel was Adam "the father of all, the prince of all, the ancient of days.")*

DANITES (See Dan)

DARA. *1 Chr. 2:6.*

Dara was one of the five sons of Zerah. He was a grandson of Judah and a great-grandson of Jacob. (Charts 8d, g-h.)

DARDA. *1 Kgs. 4:31.*

Darda, a son of Mahol, was recognized as a wise man, but Solomon was wiser than he.

DARIUS (1). *Ezra 4:5, 24; 5:5-17; 6:1-12, 15; Hag. 1:1, 8, 15; 2:6-10; Zech. 1; 7.*

Darius, king of Persia sometime after Cyrus (apparently following Ahasuerus and Artaxerxes), was the son of Hystaspes and founder of the Persian dynasty. The work of rebuilding the temple as commanded by Cyrus was frustrated during Cyrus' reign as king even until the second year of the reign of Darius. *(Ezra 4:5, 24.)*

When Zerubbabel and Jeshua, with the help of the prophets Haggai and Zechariah, began again to build the temple, Tatnai, the governor on the west side of the Euphrates River and Shethar-boznai and their companions the Apharsachites, confronted them and asked who had commanded them to build the temple. After the Israelites responded, Tatnai and his group wrote a letter to Darius indicating that the children of Israel claimed that Cyrus had decreed that the temple should be built. They suggested that Darius make a search to see if such a decree had ever been made by Cyrus. *(Ezra 5:5-17.)*

Darius made a search and found that Cyrus had, indeed, made a decree that the temple should be built. Thus, he renewed the decree and instructed Tatnai, Shethar-boznai and the Apharsachites that they not only should not hinder the work, but that they should help with expenses and by providing animals for the burnt offerings. Anyone who altered the words of his decree was to be hung from timbers of that person's own house. The temple was completed in the sixth year of the reign of Darius. *(Ezra 6:1-12, 15.)*

In the second year of Darius' reign, the prophet Haggai instructed Zerubbabel and Joshua to build the temple. *(Hag. 1:1, 8, 15.)* In the seventh month of the second year of Darius' reign, Haggai spoke Messianically to Zerubbabel and Joshua. *(Hag. 2:6-10.)* In the eighth month of the second year of Darius' reign, Zechariah called upon Judah to repent. Also in the eleventh month of the second year, Haggai was shown in a vision that the cities of Judah and the temple will be rebuilt. *(Zech. 1.)*

In the fourth year of king Darius, Zechariah reproved the hypocisy of the people in their fasts. *(Zech. 7.)*

DARIUS (Condomannus) (2). *Neh. 12:22.*

<u>Darius</u> the Persian was the last king of Pesia, overthrown by Alexander the Great in 330 B.C. The Levites who were chief of the fathers and the priests during the days of Eliashib, Joiada, etc., were recorded to the reign of Darius the Persian.

DARIUS THE MEDE (3). *Dan. 5:30-31; 6; 9:1, 4-5; 11.*

<u>Darius the Mede</u> was about 62 years old when Babylon fell under the reign of Belshazzar and he took over the kingdom. *(Dan. 5:30-31.)*

Darius placed 120 princes over the kingdom with three presidents over the princes. He made Daniel the first president. The other presidents and princes were jealous of Daniel and sought to destroy him by getting the king to sign a decree that no one could petition any man or God, except Darius, for thirty days. When Daniel defied the order and prayed to God, these men reported it to Darius and reminded him that he had signed a decree that he could not revoke that required he cast Daniel into a den of lions. Darius was grieved, but finally complied. However, he spent the night fasting and praying that the Lord would deliver Daniel, which He did. Darius then had those men, their wives and their children cast into the lions' den. He made a decree that all peoples in his kingdom should revere the God of Daniel for "he is the living God," *(Dan. 6.)*

Darius, of the seed of the Medes, was the son of Ahasuerus and was king over the realm of the Chaldeans. In the first year of his reign, Daniel fasted and prayed to the Lord confessing the sins of Israel. *(Dan. 9:1, 4-5.)*

In the first year of the reign of Darius, Daniel was given a vision in which he saw the successive kings and their conflicts, leagues and wars which will lead up to the Second Coming of Christ. *(Dan. 11.)*

DARIUS' PRESIDENTS, PRINCES, GOVERNORS, COUNSELORS, CAPTAINS. *Dan. 6:3-24.*

<u>Darius' Presidents, Princes, Governors, Counselors and Captains</u> sought to destroy Daniel. Darius had placed 120 princes over the kingdom with three presidents over the princes. He had made Daniel the first president. The other presidents, princes, governors, counselors and captains were jealous of Daniel and conspired to get the king to sign a decree that no one could petition any man or God, except Darius, for thirty days. When Daniel defied the order and prayed to God, these men reported it to Darius and reminded him that he had signed a decree that he could not revoke that required he cast Daniel into a den of lions. Darius was grieved, but finally complied. However, he spent the night fasting and praying that the Lord would deliver Daniel, which He did. Darius had those men and their wives and children cast into the lions' den.

DARKON. *Ezra 2:56; Neh. 7:58.*

<u>Darkon</u> was one of Solomon's servants whose children returned to Jerusalem from Babylonian captivity.

DATHAN. *Num. 16:1-33; Deut. 11:6; Ps. 106:17.*

Dathan was a son of Eliab, who was a son of Reuben. He, along with his brother Abiram, On and Korah, rebelled against Moses. The Lord caused the earth to open up and they, and all their families and goods, were swallowed up. *(Num. 16:1-33.)* Dathan and his brother Abiram were swallowed up by the earth. *(Ps. 106:17.)*

Moses called to the remembrance of the Israelites what happened to Dathan and his brother Abiram because of their disobedience to the Lord. *(Deut. 11:6.)* (Chart 5a.)

DAUGHTER OF MACHIR. *1 Chr. 2:24.* See **Abiah (2)**.

DAVID. *Ruth 4:17; 1 Sam. 16:11-13, 16-23; 17; 18; 19; 20; 21; 22; 23; 24:4; 25:3-44; 26; 27; 29; 30; 2 Sam. 1; 2; 3; 4:7-12; 5:3-25; 6; 7; 8; 9; 10; 11; 12; 13; 14; 15; 16; 17; 18:31-33; 19; 20:1-6; 21; 22; 23:8-39; 24; 1 Kgs. 1; 2:2-10; 1 Chr. 3; 10:14; 11; 12; 13; 14; 15; 16; 17; 18; 19; 20; 21; 22; 23; 24; 25; 26; 28; 29; 2 Chr. 3:1; 29:25; Ezra 8:2; Ps. 51:title; 52; 54; 89:4; Ezek. 34:23-24; 37:24-25; Zech. 12:10-12.*

David was the son of Jesse, the grandson of Obed, and the great-grandson of Boaz and Ruth. *(Ruth 4:17.)* He was the youngest of Jesse's eight sons. He was the keeper of his father's sheep. The Lord directed Samuel to anoint him to be king in Saul's stead. David played the harp and was summoned to Saul's court to play for him to soothe him when the evil spirit troubled him. Saul loved David. *(1 Sam. 16:11-13, 16-23.)*

The Philistines gathered against Israel. Goliath taunted and challenged anyone in Israel to come fight against him. When David took food and supplies to three of his brothers who were in Saul's camp, he heard Goliath. David accepted Goliath's challenge. Saul doubted his ability, but David recounted how the Lord had helped him kill a lion and a bear with his bare hands and assured him that the Lord would be with him. Saul wanted to clothe him in armor, but David took it off. He met with Goliath and slew him with a sling and a stone. Then, he cut off his head and took it to Jerusalem. Saul had David brought before him. *(1 Sam. 17.)*

David was loved by Jonathan. Saul set David over all of his armies. However, when the people honored David for his "ten thousands" and Saul for his "thousand," Saul became jealous and tried to kill David with a javelin. Saul promised his elder daughter Merab to David for a wife, but when it came time that she should have been given to him, Saul gave her to Adriel, the Meholathite, for a wife. Saul's younger daughter Michal loved David and Saul hoped she would be a snare to him. He promised her to David for his wife pending his bringing Saul 100 Philistine foreskins. David brought Saul 200 foreskins and Saul gave Michal to him for a wife. Saul feared David and became David's enemy. *(1 Sam. 18.)*

Saul instructed Jonathan and all of his servants to try to kill David. Jonathan warned David. Saul again tried to kill David with a javelin while he played his harp for him. David's wife Michal saved him from her father's messengers by letting him down through a window and then making and covering an image in the bed so they would think he was asleep. David fled to Samuel and joined him and the prophets. Three sets of messengers were sent to find David and each group began to prophesy. *(1 Sam. 19.)*

David and Jonathan loved each other and made a covenant of peace one with the other. Being warned by Jonathan that Saul was indeed bent on killing him, they kissed, wept and parted. *(1 Sam. 20.)*

David fled to Nob where he received help from Ahimelech the priest. The priest feared meeting with David, but David assured him he was on the king's business. One of Saul's servants saw David with Ahimelech and told Saul. When Saul had Doeg slay all the priests in Nob—who also slew the men, women, children and animals, as well—David fled to Gath. He feared the king of Gath and so he feigned madness before him. *(1 Sam. 21.)*

David went from place to place, fleeing Saul and gathering followers. He went to Moab where he brought his mother and father to live while he was there. The prophet Gad instructed him to go to the land of Judah. When Abiathar, Ahimelech's son who escaped when Doeg slew the people in Nob, told David what had happened, David said he, David, had been the reason Abiathar's family had been slain but that Abiathar would be safe with him. *(1 Sam. 22.)*

The Lord instructed David to smite the Philistines and save Keilah. Saul heard he was in Keilah and prepared to come after him there. When David inquired of the Lord, the Lord told him that Saul would come against him in Keilah and that the men of Keilah would deliver David into his hands so David escaped to a mountain in the wilderness of Ziph. Jonathan came to him there and comforted him. The Ziphites told Saul they would deliver David to him, but David continued to evade Saul. *(1 Sam. 23.)*

When David and his men found Saul asleep in a cave, his men suggested to him that the time had come when the Lord said He would deliver his enemy into his hand. Nevertheless, David refused to stretch forth his hand against him because, he said, "he is the anointed of the Lord." *(1 Sam. 24:4.)*

David sent 10 young men to Nabal, a rich man from Maon, to ask for food. Nabal rebuffed him and refused to give him anything. Thus, David determined to slay him. However, Abigail, the wife of Nabal, quickly came to him with 200 loaves and 200 bottles of wine, plus sheep, parched corn, raisin clusters and cakes of figs, and pleaded that David not do what he was planning to do. When Nabal learned what Abigail had done, "his heart died within him, and he became as a stone," and died about ten days later. When David learned that Nabal was dead, he asked Abigail to be his wife. He also took Ahinoam for a wife. Saul gave his daughter Michal, David's wife, to Phalti for a wife. *(1 Sam. 25:3-44.)*

David had another opportunity to kill Saul as Saul lay asleep in the trenches after pursuing David. However, he just took his spear and the cruse of water from

Saul's bolster so Saul would know he could have slain him but didn't. Saul again apologized to David and they each went their separate ways. *(1 Sam. 26.)*

David fled to Achish at Gath and he lived among the Philistines for 16 months. *(1 Sam. 27.)*

David prepared to join the Philistines in battle against Saul. However, the Philistine princes demanded that Achish send David and his men away because they feared they would become adversaries in battle. *(1 Sam. 29.)*

David and his men returned to Ziklag and found that the Amalekites had burned the city and taken the people captive, including David's two wives: Ahinoam and Abigail. David had Abiathar the priest bring him the ephod, and David inquired of the Lord whether or not he should pursue the Amalekites. He and 400 of his men (200 were so faint they stayed behind), with the aid of an Egyptian who had been a slave to the Amalekites, destroyed the Amalekites and rescued David's wives. David divided the spoil with the elders of Judah and with his friends in various places. *(1 Sam. 30.)*

A man from the Amalekites came to David and claimed to have killed Saul and reported that Jonathan had also been slain. David had one of his men kill the man for having slain the Lord's anointed. He mourned and lamented over their deaths. *(2 Sam. 1.)*

David was anointed king over the house of Judah. However, Abner (Saul's cousin) took Saul's son Ish-bosheth to Mahanaim and made him king over the rest of Israel. Ish-bosheth reigned two years. David was king in Hebron over the house of Judah for seven years and six months. Twelve men from David's followers and 12 men of Benjamin, followers of Ish-bosheth and Abner, engaged in a battle and David's men slew all of the men of Benjamin. Abner and the men of Israel were beaten. From David's followers, 19 men plus Asahel died. Three hundred and sixty of Abner's men died. *(2 Sam. 2.)*

David begat six sons in Hebron: Amnon, son of Abhinoam; Chileab (Daniel), son of Abigail; Absalom, son of Maacah; Adonijah, son of Haggith; Shephatiah, son of Abital; and Ithream, son of Eglah. Abner left Ish-bosheth and joined with David. However, Joab didn't trust Abner and was angry with Abner for killing his brother, so Joab slew him. David mourned the death of Abner and cursed Joab and all Joab's father's house. David, himself, followed the funeral bier and wept. *(2 Sam. 3.)*

When Baanah and Rechab, two of Saul's captains, slew Ish-bosheth and brought his head to David, David had his men kill them for having slain a righteous person upon his own bed in his own house. He had them bury Ish-bosheth's head in the sepulchre of Abner in Hebron. *(2 Sam. 4:7-12.)*

David was anointed king over all Israel. He was 30 years old when he began to reign. He reigned for 40 years: seven years and six months over Hebron and 33 years over all the house of Israel. The Lord was with David. David left Hebron and established himself in Jerusalem, the city of David. He took more wives and concubines out of Jerusalem. He begat several more sons and daughters: Shammua, Shobab, Nathan, Solomon, Ibhar, Elishua, Nepheg, Japhia, Elishama, Eliada and Eliphalet. When the Philistines came against David, he inquired of the Lord if he should go after them. The Lord said He would deliver them into David's hand. This band of Philistines was defeated. Another group of Philistines came against David. This time the Lord said not to go up after them, but to "fetch a compass behind them, and come upon them over against the mulberry trees." Again, the Lord delivered the Philistines into David's hand. *(2 Sam. 5:3-25.)*

David took 30,000 men of Israel from Jerusalem to Gibeah to retrieve the ark of God from Abinadab. Two of Abinadab's sons drove the cart carrying the ark. When one of the sons, Uzzah, touched the ark to steady it, the Lord was angry and took his life. Thus, David feared to take the ark any further and left it in the house of Obed-edom. It remained there for three months during which time the Lord blessed Obed-edom. When this was reported back to David, David rejoiced and decided it was safe to bring the ark to Jerusalem. David danced before the Lord. Apparently, he exposed more of his body than his wife Michal, Saul's daughter, thought proper, and she chastised him. David was angry with her for being angry with him. "Therefore, Michal . . . had no child unto the day of her death." *(2 Sam. 6.) (1 Chr. 13 is a repeat of 2 Sam. 6:1-11.)*

David thought he would build a house of cedar to house the ark of God. However, the Lord sent Nathan the prophet to tell David it was not for him to build a temple, that the Lord would establish his kingdom through David's seed, and David's son would build a house for the Lord. David was also told by Nathan that David's throne would be established forever through one of his seed. *(Note: This refers to Jesus Christ who would establish his kingdom forever [Luke 1:31-33].)* David offered a prayer of thanksgiving. *(2 Sam. 7.)*

The Lord blessed David and he subdued all the adversaries of Israel. He smote the Philistines, the Moabites, the king of Zobah, the Syrians who came to aid Hadarezer, king of Zabah. Toi (Tou), king of Hamath, sent his son Joram (Hadoram) to congratulate David on his defeat of Hadarezer and had him give David many gifts of gold and silver and brass. David dedicated all these unto the Lord. David's nephew Abishai also captured the Edomites, slaying 18,000 of them and causing the rest to become servants unto David. David reigned in justice over all Israel. His sons were made chief rulers. *(2 Sam. 8.)*

David wanted to honor the house of Saul so he sought out a surviving member of Saul's family: Mephibosheth, Jonathan's lame son. He restored all of Saul's land to him. *(2 Sam. 9.)*

David wanted to show kindness unto Hanun, king of the children of Ammon, because Hanun's father, Nahash, had befriended David at one time. When Nahash, the king of the children of Ammon, died, David sent messengers to Hanun to comfort him. However, Hanun's princes counseled Hanun not to trust the messengers because they were probably spies. Therefore, Hanun's servants shaved

David's messengers and cut off their garments "in the midst hard by their buttocks," and sent them on their way. When David heard how his messengers had been insulted he sent Joab and Abishai to battle against the children of Ammon and the Syrians who were assisting the children of Ammon. When the children of Ammon saw that the Syrians fled from before Joab, they fled from before Abishai. David gathered Israel and they went to battle against the fleeing Syrians. David slew Shophach, captain of the Syrian host. The remainder of the Syrians made peace with David and became his servants and would not aid the children of Ammon any more. *(2 Sam. 10.)*

From his rooftop, David watched Bath-sheba washing herself and observed that she was very beautiful. He had her brought to him and he lay with her while her husband, Uriah, was away with the army. Bath-sheba became pregnant and sent word to David. David tried to cover up his sin by trying to get her husband to come home from battle so he could sleep with her. However, when Uriah refused to go in unto his wife while the rest of Israel slept in tents, David had him placed in the forefront of battle where he would surely be killed. After Uriah's death and Bath-sheba's time of mourning, David took her to wife. She bore him a son, but the Lord was displeased with David. *(2 Sam. 11.)*

The prophet Nathan was sent by the Lord to David. He told David a parable about the ewe lamb. Nathan told David that the Lord had given David many wives but that David was now cursed for taking Bath-sheba. *(Note: Speaking of David, the Lord said in modern-day revelation recorded in D&C 132:39: "David's wives and concubines were given unto him of me, by the hand of Nathan, my servant, and others of the prophets who had the keys of this power; and in none of these things did he sin against me save in the case of Uriah and his wife; and, therefore he hath fallen from his exaltation, and received his portion; and he shall not inherit them out of the world, for I gave them unto another, saith the Lord.")* Nathan informed David that the sword would never depart from his house because he had taken the life of Uriah. The son Bath-sheba bore him was very sick and even though David fasted and prayed for him, the Lord took him on the seventh day. Bath-sheba bore him another son, Solomon. David took the city of Rabbah, the royal city of the Ammonites, with the assistance of Joab. *(2 Sam. 12.)*

David's son Amnon forced his half-sister Tamar to lie with him. In retaliation, Absalom, Tamar's brother, had his servants kill Amnon. David was told that all of his sons had been killed by Absalom. However, Jonadab, David's nephew, informed him otherwise and comforted David. Absalom fled to Geshur and David mourned for him because he had been comforted concerning Amnon. *(2 Sam. 13.)*

David allowed Absalom to be brought back to Jerusalem following a three year absence; however, he refused to meet with him. Two years later, Joab, at Absalom's request, was able to reunite David and Absalom. Absalom bowed himself on his face to the ground before the king: and the king kissed him. *(2 Sam. 14.)*

Absalom conspired against David and gained the support of the people. Thus, David and his household fled from Jerusalem. Absalom occupied Jerusalem. David sent Zadok and Abiathar and their sons Ahimaaz and Jonathan back to Jerusalem so they could keep him informed as to Absalom's plans. He also sent Hushai to volunteer to serve Absalom so he could defeat the counsel of Ahithophel and pass information on to Zadok and Abiathar and, subsequently, on to Ahimaaz and Jonathan. *(2 Sam. 15.)*

David was informed that Mephibosheth, Jonathan's son, was seeking to be king. Shimei of the household of Saul cursed David. When Abishai wanted to stop him, David reminded him that if his own son could seek his life then Shimei could curse him and that the Lord had bidden it. *(2 Sam. 16.)*

David received information regarding the counsel Hushai had given Absalom so David, being warned of Absalom's plans, fled over Jordan. *(2 Sam. 17.)*

When David received word of Absalom's death, he wept and mourned for him and cried, "O my son Absalom, my son, my son Absalom! Would God I had died for thee, O Absalom, my son, my son!" *(2 Sam. 18:31-33.)*

Joab rebuked David for mourning the death of Absalom instead of commending those who had fought to defend his kingdom. David sent word to Zadok and Abiathar the priests to inquire why the elders of Judah had not yet brought David back to his house. He replaced Joab as captain of the hosts with Amasa. Shimei apologized to David and asked for and was given forgiveness, much to Abishai's chagrin. Mephibosheth pledged his allegiance to David. Barzillai went over Jordan to conduct David over Jordan, but declined to go to David's house with him because he was now 80 years old and he wanted to die in his own city, but he requested that David take Chimham with him. *(2 Sam. 19.)*

Sheba, a Benjamite, led all the tribes of Israel except Judah away from David. David told Amasa to assemble the men of Judah together and return in three days. However, he didn't return on schedule so David told Abishai to gather troops together and go after Sheba. *(2 Sam. 20:1-6.)*

The Lord caused a famine to come over the land because Saul had slain the Gibeonites contrary to an oath Israel had made with the Gibeonites. To atone for Saul's sin, David agreed to the Gibeonites' request that they be given seven men of Saul's sons to be hung. David gave them Armoni and Mephibosheth, Saul's sons by his concubine Rizpah, and five of his daughter Merab's sons. He took Saul's and Jonathan's bones from the men of Jabesh-gilead and brought them to the country of Benjamin in Zelah and buried them in the sepulchre of Kish, Saul's father. David became faint in battle against the Philistines and his men insisted that he not personally go to battle any more so that the light of Israel would not be quenched. *(2 Sam. 21.)*

David praised the Lord in a psalm of thanksgiving. *(2 Sam. 22.)*

The names of the men who were David's leaders are named and their deeds are extolled. *(2 Sam. 23:8-39.)*

David angered the Lord by numbering Israel, so the Lord sent the prophet Gad to present him with three options: seven years of famine *(1 Chr. 21:12 says three kyears of famine)*; three months of fleeing before his enemies; or three days of pestilence. David left it up to the Lord, and the Lord sent three days of pestilence. During those three days, 70,000 of the 1,300,000 men of war died from the pestilence. David saw an angel and repented. The prophet Gad came to him and instructed him to go to the threshingplace of Araunah (Ornan) the Jebusite, which he did. He purchased the threshingfloor from Araunah and built an altar there unto the Lord and offered burnt offerings and peace offerings. Thus, the plague was stopped. *(2 Sam. 24; also 1 Chr. 21.)* Araunah the Jebusite is referred to as Ornan the Jebusite. *(1 Chr. 21:18.)*

David grew old and stricken in years. His servants chose a young virgin, Abishag, a Shunammite, to wait upon him. His son Adonijah aspired to be king and drew Joab and Abiathar the priest to his support. Bath-sheba and Nathan the prophet informed David, and David immediately named Solomon to be king. He had Zadok the priest and Nathan anoint him such. *(1 Kgs. 1.)*

David charged Solomon to keep the commandments of the Lord and to walk in His ways at all times. He also charged him to punish Joab for the things he had done wrong and to punish Shimei for having cursed him. However, he asked Solomon to shew kindness unto the sons of Barzillai because they had befriended him in his time of need. David died and was buried in the city of David. *(1 Kgs.2:2-10.)*

David's sons who were born in Hebron are again listed. However, his second son who is listed as Chileab in 2 Sam. 3:2 is given as Daniel in 1 Chr. 3:1. David reigned seven years and six months in Hebron and 33 years in Jerusalem. He and Bath-shua (Bath-sheba) had four sons born to them in Jerusalem: Shimea (Shammua), Shobab, Nathan and Solomon. David had additional sons born to him in Jerusalem: Ibhar, Elishama, Eliphelet, Nogah (Elishua), Nepheg, Japhia and Eliada. *(Note: In these verses, it says there were nine additional sons but lists 13—two by the name of Elishama and two by the name of Eliphelet. In 2 Sam. 5:14-16, eleven sons are listed. 2 Sam. lists one son as Shammua and another as Elishua. 1 Chr. 3 lists Shimea instead of Shammua and Nogah instead of Elishua.) (1 Chr. 3.)*

Saul died for his transgressions against the Lord and the kingdom was given to David, son of Jesse. *(1 Chr. 10:14.)*

David was anointed king over Israel. He and all Israel went to Jerusalem. The inhabitants of Jebus told David he couldn't go there. Nevertheless, he took the city and declared that whoever smote the Jebusites first would be the chief and captain of his troops. His nephew Joab was the one who accomplished the task and was made chief and captain. David's valiant warriors are named and their deeds are recounted. *(1 Chr. 11.)*

The armies of the tribes of Israel gathered (and are cataloged) together with David at Hebron and all Israel rejoiced in David's becoming king. *(1 Chr. 12.)*

David married more wives at Jerusalem and begot many more sons and daughters: Shammua (Shimea), Shobab, Nathan, Solomon, Ibhar, Elishua, Elpalet, Nogah, Nepheg, Japhia, Elishama, Beeliada (Eliada) and Eliphalet. *(Note: There continues to be variation in the different listings of David's sons.)* David went to battle against the Philistines at Baal-perazim and defeated them. He burned the Philistines' gods. The Lord again delivered the Philistines unto David a second time "over against the mulberry trees." *(1 Chr. 14.)*

The account of David's retrieving the ark from the house of Obed-edom is retold with additional details: i.e., David realized that none but the Levites should carry the ark of God; also, those Levites who were the chiefs of the fathers of the Levites are named. They were told to sanctify themselves so they could bring the ark up to the place which David had had prepared. The singers and instrumentalists are named. They were to sing and minister before the Lord. David's wife, Michal, was disgusted with David when she saw him dancing and playing, "and she despised him in her heart." *(1 Chr. 15.) (See 2 Sam. 6:16.)*

David appointed certain Levites to minister before the ark of the Lord. He gave Asaph and his brethren, who sang and played instruments before the ark, a psalm of thanksgiving. *(1 Chr. 16.)*

The account of David's desire to build a temple is retold. *(1 Chr. 17 is a repeat of 2 Sam. 7.)*

David defeated and subjected many nations. *(1 Chr. 18 is a repeat of 2 Sam. 8 with some slight modification in names and numbers..)*

David's desire to befriend Nahash is recounted. *(1 Chr. 19 is a repeat of 2 Sam. 10.)*

When the time had expired that kings go out to battle, David remained in Jerusalem while Joab continued to "waste" the country of the children of Ammon. When the people and the spoils were brought out of the cities, David "cut them with saws, and with harrows of iron and with axes." War continued against the Philistines and the sons of the giant of Gath were slain by David and his servants. *(1 Chr. 20.)*

Even though David was not to build the temple unto the Lord, he prepared gold, silver, brass, iron, stone and cedar wood for the temple and charged Solomon to do the work of building it. *(1 Chr. 22.)*

When David was old, he made Solomon king over Israel. He numbered the Levites who were 30 years and upward. There were 38,000 men: 24,000 who were assigned to the work of the house of the Lord; 6,000 to be officers and judges; 4,000 porters; and 4,000 musicians. *(1 Chr. 23.)*

David divided the sons of Aaron and the rest of the sons of Levi into groups and assigned them their duties by lot. *(1 Chr. 24.)* He assigned the singers and musicians their duties by lot. *(1 Chr. 25.)* He assigned the porters their responsibilities by lot. *(1 Chr. 26.)*

David assembled the leaders of Israel and appointed Solomon to build the temple, giving him the pattern and the materials with which to build it. He exhorted Solomon and the people to keep the commandments. *(1 Chr. 28.)*

David blessed and praised the Lord as he instructed the people prior to his death. He reigned over Israel 40 years: seven years in Hebron and 33 years in Jerusalem. His son Solomon reigned in his stead. *(1 Chr. 29.)*

The Lord had appeared unto David in the threshingfloor of Ornan the Jebusite which site David had prepared. There it was that Solomon began to build the house of the Lord—in Jerusalem at Mount Moriah. *(2 Chr. 3:1.)*

Hezekiah, king of Judah, had the Levites and priests purify themselves and cleanse and purify the house of the Lord in accordance with the commandments given years earlier by David, Gad the seer and Nathan the prophet. *(2 Chr. 29:25.)*

Of the sons of David, Hattush was the chief of the fathers of David's posterity when Ezra led many exiled Israelites out of Babylon back to Jerusalem. *(Ezra 8:2.)*

Nathan came to David after David had gone in unto Bathsheba. This psalm, in which he pleads for mercy and forgiveness from the Lord, was written in response to Nathan's visit. *(Ps. 51:title.) (Note: The Bible Dictionary indicates that of the 150 psalms, 73 are attributed to David. However, 76 psalms have David's name attached to them: 3-32; 34-41; 51-65; 68-72; 86; 101; 103; 108-110; 122; 124; 131; 133; 138-145. The Bible Dictionary states that many of the psalms attributed to David were probably not written by him, but that in addition to the ones readily acknowledged to be his [3-4; 15; 18; 20-21; 24; 26; 28-29; 32; 51; 60; 62-63; 68; 101; and 110], others could possibly be of Davidic origin [BD, David]. The Bible Dictionary also states: "In some cases in which a Psalm is ascribed to David in the Hebrew, it is certain that he could not have written it, and it has been concluded that the Hebrew titles are sometimes inaccurate" [BD, Psalms].)*

Psalm 52 pertains to when Doeg the Edomite told Saul that David was at the house of Ahimelech.

Psalm 54 pertains to when the Ziphims (Ziphites) offered to deliver David to Saul.

David's seed and throne *(through the Messiah)* will be established forever. *(Psalm 89:4.)*

A descendant of the house of David—Jesus Christ, The Messiah—will gather Israel in the latter days and be their shepherd and their God. *(Ezek. 34:23-24.)*

In the last days, the Messiah, Jesus Christ, of the lineage of David, will be king over Israel. He will be their shepherd and they shall be restored to the lands of their inheritance. *(Ezek. 37:24-25.)*

When the Savior comes again and the children of Israel recognize Him as the Savior whom they crucified, there will be great mourning in the land. Each family shall mourn apart: the family of the house of David and their wives; the family of the house of Nathan and their wives, etc. *(Zech. 12:10-12.)* (Charts 1.; 8d-f.)

DAVID AND BATH-SHEBA'S SON. *2 Sam. 12:15-18.*

David and Bath-sheba's Son, conceived while Bath-sheba's husband, Uriah the Hittite, was away at battle, was very sick and died on the seventh day.

DAVID'S MEN. *1 Sam. 24:4; 25:5-40.*

DAVID'S MEN reminded David, when they found Saul asleep in a cave, that the time had come when the Lord said He would deliver his enemy into his hand. *(1 Sam. 24:4.)*

David sent 10 of his young men to Nabal, a rich man from Maon, to request food. Nabal rebuffed them. David instructed all of his men to gird on their swords and to prepare to go against Nabal. Nabal's wife, Abigail, intervened and brought them food and drink. When Nabal died shortly thereafter, David sent some of his men to Abigail to ask her to become his wife. *(1 Sam. 25:5-40.)*

DAVID'S SERVANTS. *2 Sam. 10:25.*

David's Servants were sent to Hanun, king of the Ammonites, to offer comfort and to show kindness unto him because Hanun's father, Nahash, had shown kindness unto him while Nahash was king. Unfortunately, the princes of the children of Ammon convinced Hanun that David's servants were spies and so Hanun abused David's servants by shaving off one half of their beards and by cutting "off their garments in the middle, even to their buttocks, and sent them away." The men were ashamed and when David learned of it, he had them tarry at Jericho until their beards were grown.

DAVID'S TEN CONCUBINES. *2 Sam. 15:16; 16:21-22; 20:3.*

Ten Concubines were left behind by David to keep his house when he and his household fled from Jerusalem to escape Absalom. *(2 Sam. 15:16.)* Ahithophel counseled Absalom to go in unto his father's concubines, and he did. *(2 Sam. 16:21-22.)* When David returned to Jerusalem, he put the ten concubines in a ward, "and fed them, but went not in unto them. So they were shut up unto the day of their death, living in widowhood." *(2 Sam. 20:3.)*

DEBIR. *Josh. 10:1-11, 16-27.*

Debir, one of the five kings of the Amorites, was king of Eglon. He and the other kings united in battle against Gibeon. The men of Gibeon sought help from Joshua. Debir and his people were destroyed, partly by the sword but mostly by hailstones the Lord poured down upon them. He hid in a cave with the other four kings. Joshua had a stone rolled in front of the cave until the rest of the Amorites were destroyed. Then he had the kings brought out to him. They were all slain and hung on a tree. Their bodies were then cast into the cave where the kings had hidden and the mouth of the cave was closed with great stones.

DEBORAH (1) (Rebekah's Nurse). *Gen. 24:59; 35:8.*

Rebekah's Nurse accompanied Rebekah when she traveled back to Abraham's house with Abraham's servant. *(Gen. 24:59.)*

Rebekah's nurse, **Deborah**, is mentioned by name. She died in Luz and was buried beneath Beth-el under an oak. *(Gen. 35:8.)*

DEBORAH (2). *Judg. 4:4-9; 5:31.*

Deborah, wife of Lapidoth, was a prophetess and judge in Israel. She summoned Barak to her and reminded him that the Lord had said He would deliver Sisera, captain of king Jabin's host, into his hands. Barak said he would only go after Sisera if Deborah would go with him. She agreed, but said there would be no honor in it for him because the Lord would deliver Sisera into the hand of a woman. *(Judg. 4:4-9.)*

Deborah and Barak sang a song of praise because the Lord delivered Israel from Canaanite bondage. "And the land had rest for 40 years." *(Judg. 5:31.)* (Chart 20.)

DEDAN (1). *Gen. 10:7; Ezek. 27:15, 20; 38.*

Dedan was a son of Raamah, grandson of Cush, great-grandson of Ham, and a great-great-grandson of Noah. *(Gen. 10:7.)*

As Ezekiel lamented the fall of the great city of Tyrus, he bemoaned the loss of her riches and commerce, part of which involved the merchants who were the men of Dedan who brought horns of ivory and ebony to Tyrus. Dedan also traded in precious clothes for chariots. *(Ezek. 27:15, 20.)*

In the latter days, the battle of Gog and Magog against Israel will usher in the Second Coming of the Lord. Gathered together with Gog will be Dedan, Gomer, Togarmar, Sheba and the merchants of Tarshish. *(Ezek. 38.)* (Chart 2e.)

DEDAN (2). *Gen. 25:3.*

Dedan was a son of Jokshan and a grandson of Abraham and Keturah. (Charts 3a, d, f.)

DEHAVITES. *Ezra 4:9.*

The Dehavites were among the various groups who were companions with the Samaritans and helped to hinder the work of rebuilding the temple in Jerusalem. *(According to the BD, they had been placed in Esarhaddon after the completion of Israel's captivity.)*

DEKAR'S SON. *1 Kgs. 4:9.*

Dekar's SON was one of twelve officers over Israel who provided victuals for king Solomon and his family one month each year. *(Note: There is no information explaining who Dekar was, nor what his son's name was.)*

DELAIAH (1). *1 Chr. 24:18.*

Delaiah was from the sons of Aaron. When David made the divisions of the sons of Aaron, there was one principal household for Eleazar and one taken for Ithamar. Eleazar had 16 sons: Ithamar had eight. These 24 sons who were chief of the fathers were divided by lot. Delaiah drew the twenty-third lot.

DELAIAH (2). *Neh. 6:10.*

Delaiah was the father of Shemaiah and the son of Mehetabeel.

DELAIAH (3). *Jer. 36:12, 25.*

Delaiah was the son of Shemaiah. He was in the scribe's chamber in king Jehoiakim's house with Elishama the scribe and all the princes when Michaiah told them of the prophecies of Jeremiah which he had heard Baruch read in his father

Gemariah's chamber. When the king went to burn the roll, Delaiah, Elnathan and Gemariah tried to intervene, but the king would not listen to them.

DELAIAH, THE CHILDREN OF. *Ezra 2:60; Neh. 7:61-62.*

The Children of Delaiah were among those who went up to Jerusalem from Tel-melah, Tel-harsa, Chenrub, Addan, and Immer when king Cyrus declared that the Israelites should return there and build the temple, but they could not verify that they were actually of the house of Israel. The children of Delaiah, Tobiah and Nekoda numbered 652. *(Note: In Neh. 7:61-62, the number of men listed is 642 rather than 652.)*

DELILAH. *Judg. 16:4-21.*

Delilah was a Philistine woman in the valley of Sorek whom Samson loved after his wife's death. She discovered the source of his strength, had his hair cut, and then delivered him to the Philistines.

DEUEL (Reuel (3)). *Num. 1:14; 2:14; 7:42, 47; 10:20.*

Deuel, of the tribe of Gad, was the father of Eliasaph. *(Num. 1:14.)*

His name is given as **Reuel** in Num. 2:14. *(Note: The footnote indicates that in Hebrew "d" and "r" look much alike.)*

Deuel was the father of Eliasaph. *(Num. 7;42, 47· 10·20.)*

DIBLAIM. *Hosea 1:3.*

Diblaim was the father of Gomer who was the wife of Hosea. Diblaim, Gomer, and their fellow citizens committed whoredoms and worshipped idols.

DIBRI. *Lev. 24:11.*

Dibri, of the tribe of Dan, was the father of Shelomith who was the mother whose son was brought before Moses and stoned to death for blasphemy. (Chart 11b.)

DIKLAH. *Gen. 10:27.*

Diklah was a son of Joktan, a third-great-grandson of Shem and a fourth-great-grandson of Noah. (Chart 2b.)

DINAH. *Gen. 30:21; 34; 46:15.*

Dinah was a daughter of Leah and Jacob. She is the only daughter mentioned by name. *(Gen. 30:21.)*

After Jacob settled his family in Canaan, in the city of Shalem, a city of Shechem, Dinah went out among the people to see the daughters of the land. Shechem took Dinah and defiled her by laying with her. He desired to marry her. Her brothers Simeon and Levi, however, killed Shechem, Hamor, and all the males of the land in retaliation after agreeing to let Shechem marry her if all the males would first be circumcized. *(Gen. 34.)*

Dinah was the daughter of Leah and Jacob. *(Gen. 46:15.)* (Charts 1.; 3d.; 5a.; 6a.; 7a.; 8a.; 9a.; 10a.; 11a.; 12a.; 13a.; 14a.; 15a.; 16a.)

DINAITES. *Ezra 4:9.*

The **Dinaites** were among the various groups who were companions with the Samaritans and helped to hinder the work of rebuilding the temple in Jerusalem.

(According to the BD, they were possibly from western Armenia and were placed in cities of Samaria by Tiglath-pileser.)

DISHAN. *Gen. 36:21, 28; 1 Chr. 1:38, 42.*

Dishan was a son of Seir the Horite. He was a duke or tribal chief. His children were Uz and Aran. (Charts 4a-f.; 19.)

DISHON (1). *Gen. 36:21, 26; 1 Chr. 1:38, 41.*

Dishon was the son of Seir the Horite. His brothers were Lotan, Shobal, Zibeon, Anah, Ezer and Dishan. His children were Hemdan (Amram), Eshban, Ithran and Cheran. He was a duke or tribal chief. (Charts 4a-f.; 19.)

DISHON (2). *Gen. 36:25.*

Dishon was a son of Anah, grandson of Zibeon, great-grandson of Seir the Horite, and the brother of Aholibamah, one of Esau's wives. (Chart 4c.)

DODAI. *1 Chr. 27:4.*

Dodai, an Ahohite, was one of David's officers. He and his course of 24,000 were over the course of the second month. Mikloth was also the ruler over the second course with Dodai.

DODANIM. *Gen. 10:4.*

Dodanim was a son of Javan, grandson of Japheth, and a great-grandson of Noah. (Chart 2a.)

DODAVAH. *2 Chr. 20:37.*

Dodavah of Mareshah, was the father of the prophet Eliezer.

DODO (1). *Judg. 10:1.*

Dodo, father of Puah and grandfather of Tola, was from the tribe of Issachar. (Chart 9b.)

DODO (2). *2 Sam. 23:9; 1 Chr. 11:12.*

Dodo the Ahohite was the father of Eleazar.

DODO (3). *2 Sam. 23:24; 1 Chr. 11:26.*

Dodo of Beth-lehem was the father of Elhanan.

DOEG. *1 Sam. 21:7; 22:9-19.*

Doeg, an Edomite, was one of Saul's servants, the chiefest of the herdsmen that belonged to Saul. He was in Nob when David went there and saw Ahimelech the priest. *(1 Sam. 21:7.)*

Doeg told Saul that he saw David visiting with Ahimelech. Saul ordered his servants to kill all the priests in Nob. They refused. However, Doeg, when ordered to kill them, slew 85 "persons that did wear a linen ephod" and in Nob he slew both men and women, children and sucklings, oxen, asses and sheep. *(1 Sam. 22:9-19.)*

DUMAH. *Gen. 25:14; Isa. 21:11.*

Dumah was a son of Ishmael and a grandson of Abraham and Hagar, Sarah's handmaid. *(Gen. 25:14.)*

Isaiah prophesied a message of doom to the Edomites, wherein he called it, the "burden of Dumah." *(Isa. 21:11.)* (Chart 3e.)

NAMES THAT BEGIN WITH "E"

EBAL (1). *Gen. 36:23.*

Ebal was one of the children of Shobal, son of Seir the Horite. (Chart 4b.)

EBAL (2). *1 Chr. 1:22.* See **Obal.**

EBED (1). *Judg. 9:26.*

Ebed was the father of Gaal.

EBED (2). *Ezra 8:6.*

Ebed, son of Jonathan who was of the sons of Adin, was the chief of his fathers and went with Ezra up from Babylon to Jerusalem. He took 50 males with him.

EBED-MELECH. *Jer. 38:7-13; 39:16-18.*

Ebed-melech was an Ethopian eunuch in king Zedekiah's house. When he heard that the princes had cast Jeremiah into a miry dungeon, he petitioned the king for permission to rescue Jeremiah. The king agreed and told him to take 30 men with him. Ebed-melech, using cords, let down some worn-out clothes and rotten rags to Jeremiah and told him to put them under his armholes under the cords; and the men with him proceeded to lift him up out of the dungeon. *(Jer. 38:7-13.)*

The Lord instructed Jeremiah to tell Ebed-melech that He would deliver him from the evil that would befall the city and he would not fall by the sword because he put his trust in the Lord. *(Jer. 39:16-18.)*

EBER (1). *Gen. 10:21, 24, 25; Gen. 11:14-17; Num. 24:24.*

Eber was the son of Salah, grandson of Arphaxad, a great-grandson of Shem and a great-great-grandson of Noah. He was the father of Joktan and Peleg in whose days the earth was divided. *(Gen. 10:21; 24-25.) (Note: The Bible Dictionary also says he was "the ancestor of the Hebrew people. Somestimes called Heber. The word Hebrew is a patronymic name derived from Eber.")* Eber's father was 30 years old when he begat Eber. Eber was 34 years old when he begat Peleg. He lived to be 464 years olf. *(Gen. 11:14-17.)*

Balaam prophesied concerning the destiny of Israel and said that "ships shall come from the coast of Chittim and shall afflict . . . Eber, and he also shall perish for ever." *(Num. 24:24.)* (Charts 1.; 2b.; 21.)

EBER (2). *1 Chr. 8:12 (8, 11-12).*

Eber, a descendant of Benjamin, was a son of Elpaal who was a son of Shaharaim and Hushim. (Chart 16g.)

EBER (3). *Neh. 12:20.*

Eber, son of Amok, was one of the priests who was a chief of the fathers in the days of Joiakim.

EBIASAPH. *1 Chr. 6:23.* See **Abiasaph.**

EDEN (1). *2 Chr. 29:12.* See **Iddo (2).**

EDEN (2). *2 Chr. 31:15.*

Eden and others assisted Kore, porter toward the east, in caring for the freewill offerings of God and their distribution when Hezekiah was king over Judah.

EDEN (3). *Ezek. 27:23-24.*

Eden, Haran and Canneh, the merchants of Sheba, Asshur and Chilmad, traded at the fairs in Tyrus before Tyrus' fall, trading in blue clothes, broidered work, chests of rich apparel, bound with cords, and made of cedar.

EDER. *1 Chr. 23:23-24; 24:30-31.*

Eder, a Levite, was the son of Mushi who was the son of Merari. His brothers were Mahli and Jeremoth. When David made Solomon king, he numbered the Levites and divided them into courses among the children of Levi: Gershon, Kohath and Merari. Mahli, Eder and Jeremoth were named as chief of their fathers. From the age of twenty years and upward, they and the others so named did the work for the service of the house of the Lord. *(1 Chr. 23:23-24.)* He was named as one of the chief of the fathers who cast lots with the other Levites to determine his course in the presence of king David, Zadok, Ahimelech and other leaders. *(1 Chr. 24:30-31.)* (Chart 7e.)

EDOM (1). *Gen. 25:30.* See **Esau.**

EDOM (2). *Num. 20:14, 18-21, 28; Judg. 11:17-18.*

Edom was the king of Edom. He refused to let Moses and the children of Israel pass peacefully through the land and came out against them. Thus, Moses and the children of Israel turned away and journeyed to mount Hor where Aaron subsequently died. *(Num. 20:14, 18-21, 28.)*

Jephthah reminded the king of the children of Ammon that the king of Edom would not let Moses and the children of Israel pass through his land when they came out of Egypt. Thus, they compassed it about along with the land of Moab. *(Judg. 11:17-18.)*

EDOMITES. See **Esau.**

EGLAH. *2 Sam. 3:5; 1 Chr. 3:3.*

Eglah was the mother of Ithream, David's sixthborn son in Hebron.

EGLON. *Judg. 3:12-21.*

Eglon was the king of Moab. He was very fat. After Othniel's death, Israel again became wicked and the Lord delivered them into Eglon's hand. The children of Israel served Eglon 18 years. The Lord then raised Ehud up to deliver the Israelites. Ehud killed Eglon by plunging a dagger into his belly.

EGYPTIANS. *Deut. 23:7; Ezra 9; Ezek. 16:26; 29:2-16; 30; Hosea 7:11; 12:1.*

Egyptians are citizens of Egypt where the children of Israel had been in bondage for many years. Moses instructed the Israelites that they should "not abhor an Egyptian because thou was a stranger in his land." Their children should be allowed to enter into the congregation of the Lord in their third generation. *(Deut. 23:7.)*

After the children of Israel were delivered from Babylonian bondage, many Jews, including the priests and Levites, intermarried with and followed the abominations of the Egyptians, Canaanites, Hittites, Perizzites, Jebusites, Ammonites, Moabites and Amorites. Fearing the Lord would completely destroy them this time for their abominations, Ezra prayed and confessed the sins of all the people. *(Ezra 9.)*

The Lord condemned Jerusalem and said she had committed fornication with the Egyptians. *(Ezek. 16:26.)*

Ezekiel prophesied that Egypt would be overthrown by Babylon because of her idolatry and pride and because Israel turned to her for help instead of to the Lord. Egypt had been as a staff of reed to the children of Israel. The Egyptians would be scattered among the nations. Egypt would be uninhabited for 40 years. After that, the Lord would gather the Egyptians from among the people. Ezekiel prophesied that they would be returned into the land of Pathros. Egypt would never be powerful again but would be the basest of the kingdoms. *(Ezek. 29:2-16.)*

Ezekiel prophesied that Egypt and all those who supported her would fall by the hand of Nebuchadnezzer and become desolate, and her idols would be destroyed. The Egyptians would be scattered among the nations and dispersed thoughout the countries. *(Ezek. 30.)*

Ephraim was condemned by the Lord for forsaking Him and turning to Egypt and Assyria for help. *(Hosea 7:11.)*

The Lord condemned Ephraim for carrying oil into Egypt and for making a covenant with the Assyrians. *(Hosea 12:1.)*

EHI. *Gen. 46:21.*

Ehi was a son of Benjamin the son of Jacob. His brothers were Belah (Bela), Becher, Ashbel, Gera, Naaman, Rosh, Muppim (Shupham), Huppim (Hupham) and Ard. *(Note: Benjamin's family is listed differently in Num. 26:38-41.)* (Chart 16a.)

EHUD. *Judg. 3:15-30; 4:1; 1 Chr. 7:10; 8:6.*

Ehud was the son of Gera, a Benjamite. He was left-handed. When the children of Israel cried unto the Lord, the Lord raised up Ehud to deliver them from Eglon, king of Moab. He took a gift to Eglon and using his left hand, pulled a dagger from his right thigh and killed Eglon. After making his escape, he led the children of Israel in battle against Moab. They slew about 10,000 men. Israel then had rest for 80 years. *(Judg. 3:15-30.)*

After Ehud died, the children of Israel returned to their evil ways. *(Judg. 4:1.)*

Ehud, son of Bilhan and grandson of Jediael, was a great-grandson of Benjamin and a mighty man of valor. His brothers were Jeush, Benjamin, Chenaanah, Zethan, Tharshish and Ahishahar. *(1 Chr. 7:10.)*

The names of the sons of Ehud, the heads of the fathers of the inhabitants of Geba, are listed. *(1 Chr. 8:6.) (Note: The Bible Dictionary indicates that all references to Ehud pertain to the same person. This allows for some confusion because Judg. 3:15 refers to Ehud the son of Gera, a Benjamite; 1 Chr. 7:10 refers*

to Ehud as the son of Bilhan, son of Jediael the son of Benjamin; and 1 Chr. 8:3
refers to Ehud as the son of Gera the son of Bela (who was Jediael's brother.)
(Charts 16c-e.; 20.)

EKER. *1 Chr. 2:27.*

Eker was one of the sons of Ram. He was a great-great-great-grandson of Judah.
His brothers were Maaz and Jamin. (Chart 8c.)

ELADAH. *1 Chr. 7:20.*

Eladah was the son of Tahath, the father of Tahath, and the great-great-
grandson of Ephraim. (Chart 15d.)

ELAH (1). *Gen. 36:41.*

Elah was one of the dukes (tribal chiefs) who came of Esau. (Chart 19.)

ELAH (2). *1 Kgs. 4:18.*

Elah was the father of Shimei.

ELAH (3). *1 Kgs. 16:6-14.*

Elah, son of Baasha, reigned as king of Israel upon Baasha's death. He began
his reign in the 26th year of Asa's reign as king of Judah. He reigned over Israel in
Tirzah for two years. He was slain by his servant Zimri, captain of half his chariots,
who reigned in his stead. Zimri destroyed all the house of Baasha because of the
sins of Baasha and the sins of Elah, as prophesied by Jehu the prophet. The rest of
his record is written in the chronicles of the kings of Israel. (Chart 9b.)

ELAH (4). *2 Kgs. 15:30.*

Elah was the father of Hoshea.

ELAH (5). *1 Chr. 4:15.*

Elah was a son of Caleb who was the son of Jephunneh. His brothers were Iru
and Naam. He begat Kenaz. (Chart 8n.)

ELAH (6). *1 Chr. 9:8.*

Elah, of the tribe of Benjamin, was the son of Uzzi. He and his family were
among the inhabitants of Jerusalem whose genealogy was written in the book of the
kings of Israel and Judah, who were carried away to Babylon for their transgression.
(Chart 16m.)

ELAM (1). *Gen. 10:22.*

Elam was a son of Shem and a grandson of Noah. (Chart 2b.)

ELAM (2). *1 Chr. 8:24-25.*

Elam, a descendant of Benjamin, was a son of Shashak who was a son of
Beriah. (Chart 16g.)

ELAM (3). *1 Chr. 26:3.*

Elam, a Levite, was the fifthborn son of Meshelemiah (Shelemiah), son of Kore
of the sons of Asaph. His brothers were Zechariah, Jediael, Zebadiah, Jathniel,
Jehohanan and Elioenai. They, along with others, were assigned by king David to
be porters—to have charge of the treasures, serve as officers and judges, and
conduct the outward business over Israel. (Charat 7d.)

ELAM (4). *Ezra 2:7; 10:26 (18-19, 26, 44); Neh. 7:12; 10:14 (1, 14, 28-31).*

Elam was of the people of Israel. The men of the children of Elam who returned to Jerusalem from Babylon after Cyrus' proclamation to build the temple numbered 1,254. *(Ezra 2:7; Neh. 7:12.)*

The sons of Elam who took wives from among the Canaanites and other groups were Mattaniah, Zechariah, Jehiel, Abdi, Jeremoth and Eliah. They agreed to do as Ezra said and separate themselves from their foreign wives. *(Ezra 10:26 [18-19, 26, 44].)*

Elam was among those chief of the people who covenanted to marry in Israel. The promised to honor the Sabbath, pay tithes and keep the commandments. *(Neh. 10:14 [1, 14, 28-31].)*

ELAM (5). *Ezra 2:31; Neh. 7:34.*

Elam (this "other Elam") was of the people of Israel. The men of the children of Elam who returned to Jerusalem from Babylon with Zerubbabel after Cyrus' proclamation to build the temple numbered 1,254. *(Note: The children of this Elam and Elam (4) who returned from Babylon with Zerubbabel numbered 1,254 men. The Bible lists them as two separate individuals. However, it may be that they are one and the same.)*

ELAM (6). *Ezra 8:7.*

Elam's descendant Jeshaiah, the son of Athaliah, was the chief of his fathers when Ezra led many exiled Israelites out of Babylon back to Jerusalem.

ELAM (7). *Ezra 10:2.*

Elam was the father of Jehiel and grandfather of Shechaniah.

ELAM (8). *Neh. 12:42.*

Elam, a priest and singer, joined in the dedication of the walls of Jerusalem with Nehemiah.

ELAMITES. *Ezra 4:9; Isa. 21:2; 22:6; Jer. 49:34-39; Ezek. 32:21, 24..*

The **Elamites** were among the various groups who were companions with the Samaritans and helped to hinder the work of rebuilding the temple in Jerusalem. *(Ezra 4:9.)*

Isaiah prophesied that Elam would besiege Babylon. *(Isa. 21:2.) (Note: Isaiah's prophecy, according to the Bible footnote, was fullfilled in 538 B.C., which is the year before Cyrus issued his decree for the return of the Israelites to Jerusalem.)*

Elam and Kir will attack and scourge Jerusalem. "And Elam bare the quiver . . . and Kir uncovered the shield." *(Isa. 22:6.)*

In the beginning of the reign of Zedekiah king of Judah, Jeremiah prophesied the destruction that would befall the Elamites. *(Jer. 49:34-39.)*

As Ezekiel lamented for Pharaoh king of Egypt and for Egypt, herself, the Lord told him, "The strong among the mighty shall speak to him (Pharaoh) out of the midst of hell with them that help him: they are gone down, they lie uncircumcised, slain by the sword . . . There is Elam and all her multitude round about her grave, all of them slain, fallen by the sword, which are gone down uncircumcised into the nether parts of the earth, which caused their terror in the land of the living; yet have they borne their shame with them that go down to the pit." *(Ezek. 32:21, 24.)*

ELASAH (1). *Ezra 10:22 (18-19, 22, 44).*

Elasah, one of the sons of Pashur, was among the sons of the priests who had taken foreign wives and who agreed to Ezra's request that they separate themselves from their strange wives.

ELASAH (2). *Jer. 29:3-10.*

Elasah was the son of Shaphan. After Jeconiah and the queen and their household departed Jerusalem, Jeremiah the prophet sent a letter by the hand of Elasah and Gemariah, son of Hilkiah, unto the residue of the elders, priests, prophets and people whom Nebuchadnezzar carried away captive, telling them that the Lord said they would remain captive for 70 years and to find peace there. After 70 years He would perform good works for them.

ELDAAH. *Gen. 25:4.*

Eldaah was a son of Midian and grandson of Abraham and Keturah. His brothers were Ephah, Epher, Hanoch and Abida. (Chart 3f.)

ELDAD. *Num. 11:24-27.*

Eldad was one of seventy men of the elders of the children of Israel who Moses gathered together to help share the responsibility of leading the people. When the other 68 leaders went about prophesying, Eldad and Medad remained in camp and prophesied to the people who were in camp.

ELDERS OF GILEAD. *Judg. 11:5-11.*

The **Elders of Gilead** went to Jephthah, whom they had cast out, and asked him to be the captain of Israel's army when the children of Ammon made war against them.

ELDERS OF JUDAH. *2 Kgs. 23:1-3.*

The **Elders of Judah** and the elders of Jerusalem, along with all the rest of the people, were gathered unto king Josiah, and he read to them what was written in the book of the covenant which the high priest Hilkiah had found. They all made a covenant "to walk after the Lord, and to keep his commandments and his testimonies and his statutes."

ELDERS OF MOAB AND MIDIAN (1). *Num. 22:7-14.*

The **Elders of Moab and Midian** were sent to Balaam by Balak to plead with him to come and curse the Israelites. They were told to return to their own land and report that Balaam could not come because the Lord refused to give him permission.

ELDERS OF MOAB AND MIDIAN (2). *Num. 22:15.*

These **Elders of Moab and Midian** were "more honourable" than the previous ones and were also sent to Balaam to offer him bribes and to plead with him to come to Balak and curse the Israelites as he requested.

ELEAD. *1 Chr. 7:21.*

Elead was a descendant of Ephraim through Shuthelah. The men of Gath slew Elead and Ezer "because they came down to take away their cattle." (Chart 15d.)

ELEASAH (1). *1 Chr. 2:39-40.*

Eleasah was the son of Helez and the father of Sisamai. (Chart 8c.)

ELEASAH (2). *1 Chr. 8:37, 39; 9:43.*

Eleasah, the son of Rapha (Rephaiah), was from the tribe of Benjamin. He descended through Saul through Jonathan. He begat Azel and Eshek. *(1 Chr. 8:37, 39; 9:43.)* (Chart 16 l.)

ELEAZAR (1). *Ex. 6:23, 25; 28:1; 40:12-16; Lev. 8:6-9, 13; 10:12, 16-17; Num. 3: 32; 16:37; 19; 20:25-29; 27:19-23; Deut. 10:6; Josh. 14:1; 24:33; 1 Chr. 6:3-14; 9:20; 24:1-6; Ezra 7:1-5.*

Eleazar was the third son of Aaron and Elisheba. His brothers were Nadab, Abihu and Ithamar. He married one of Putiel's daughters and they begat Phinehas. *(Ex. 6:23, 25.)*

Eleazar, along with his father and brothers, was to be consecrated and anointed to minister in the priest's office. They were to keep a light burning always in the tabernacle of the congregation *(Ex. 28:1.) (Also see Ex. 27:20-21.)* He and his father and brothers were washed and anointed and given an everlasting priesthood. *(Ex. 40:12-16.)*

Throughout Leviticus, instructions pertaining to Aaron and his sons were given to Moses who then instructed Aaron and his sons regarding their responsibilities. Aaron and his sons were washed and anointed and dressed in the holy garments. *(Lev. 8:6-9, 13.)* They were instructed to eat with leaven what remained of the offering of the Lord made by fire. Moses chastised Eleazar and Ithamar for not eating the sin offering which had been burned. *(Lev. 10:12, 16-17.)*

The Lord instructed Moses that Eleazar "shall be chief over the chief of the Levites, and have the oversight of them that keep the charge of the sanctuary." *(Num. 3: 32.)* The Lord instructed Moses to have Eleazar take up the censers of the sinners who had rebelled against Moses whom the Lord destroyed and to scatter the fire "yonder" for they were hallowed. *(Num. 16:37.)*

Eleazar was given direction for the sacrifice of a red heifer, the water of separation used for purification from sin, and for other ceremonies. *(Num. 19.)*

As the time approached for Aaron to die, the Lord instructed Moses to take Aaron and Eleazar up unto mount Hor, to strip Aaron of his garments and to put them upon Eleazar. *(Num. 20:25-29.)* Eleazar ministered in the priest's office upon the death of his father. *(Deut. 10:6.)*

Eleazar set Joshua apart to lead Israel as Moses' time to leave had come. He would receive instructions from the Lord for Joshua through the Urim and Thummim. *(Num. 27:19-23.)* Eleazar and Joshua, along with the heads of the various tribes, divided the countries by lot and distributed them to the nine-and-a-half tribes for their inheritance. *(Josh. 14:1.)*

Eleazar died and was buried in a hill in mount Ephraim which belonged to his son Phinehas. *(Josh. 24:33.)*

Eleazar, son of Aaron, begat Phinehas. His posterity is listed. *(1 Chr. 6:3-14.)*

Eleazar was the father of Phinehas. *(1 Chr. 9:20.)*

David divided the sons of Aaron and the rest of the sons of Levi into groups and assigned them their duties. Eleazar's brothers, Nadab and Abihu, had been slain earlier by the Lord and had no children. Therefore, Eleazar and Ithamar executed the priest's office. Of the sons of Eleazar, David distributed the duties through Zadok. There were more chief men among the sons of Eleazar—16—than among the sons of Ithamar—8—which was distributed through Ahimelech. They were to be the governors of the sanctuary and of the house of God. One principal household was taken for Eleazar and one for Ithamar. *(1 Chr. 24:1-6.) (Note: Twenty-four lots were drawn and the names, in order of lot, are listed in verses 7-18. However, there is no indication as to which ones are of the sons of Eleazar and which ones are of the sons of Ithamar.)*

Eleazar's descendants through Ezra are listed with some variation and omissions from the listing in 1 Chr. 6:4-14. *(Ezra 7:1-5.) (Note: The Bible Dictionary states, "All the high priests until the Maacabean period were descended from Eleazar, with the exception of those from Eli to Abiathar, inclusive, who belonged to the family of Ithamar.")* (Chart 7b.)

ELEAZAR (2). *1 Sam. 7:1-2.*

<u>Eleazar</u>, son of Abinadab, was sanctified by the men of Kirjath-jearim to keep the ark of the Lord which was kept in his father's house for 20 years after it was retrieved from the Philistines.

ELEAZAR (3). *2 Sam. 23:9; 1 Chr. 11:12.*

<u>Eleazar</u>, son of Dodo the Ahohite, was one of David's mighty men. (Chart 17.)

ELEAZAR (4). *1 Chr. 23:21-27; 24:28.*

<u>Eleazar</u>, a Levite, was a son of Mahli who was a son of Merari. His brother was Kish. He had no sons, only daughters. When he died, Kish's sons took Eleazar's daughters. When David made Solomon king, he numbered the Levites and divided them into courses among the sons of Levi: Gershon, Kohath and Merari. Eleazar and Kish, along with their cousins Mahli, Eder and Jeremoth, Mushi's sons, were named among those who were chief of the fathers. *(1 Chr. 23:21-27.)*

Eleazar, son of Mahli, had no sons. *(1 Chr. 24:28.)* (Chart 7e.)

ELEAZAR (5). *Ezra 8:33.*

<u>Eleazar</u>, a Levite, was the son of Phinehas. He was with Meremoth when the precious items that belonged in the temple which had been placed in the care of Sherebiah, Hashabiah and ten additional chief priests by Ezra were delivered to Meremoth.

ELEAZAR (6). *Ezra 10:25 (18-19, 25, 44).*

<u>Eleazar</u>, of the sons of Parosh, was among those who had taken wives from among the Canaanites or other foreign groups but who agreed to Ezra's request that

they separate themselves from these strange wives lest the Lord destroy the rest of the children of Israel.

ELEAZAR (7). *Neh. 12:42.*

Eleazar, a priest and singer, joined in the dedication of the walls of Jerusalem with Nehemiah.

ELHANAN (1). *2 Sam. 21:19; 1 Chr. 20:5.*

Elhanan, son of Jaare-oregim the Beth-lehemite, slew the brother of Goliath the Gittite in a second battle with the Philistines in Gob. *(2 Sam. 21:19.) (Note: The BD, under Goliath, states that the Goliath mentioned in this scripture is probably a different Goliath than the one David slew or that perhaps some error may have crept into the text, as this refers to Goliath the Gittite and the Goliath David slew was of Gath.)*

Elhanan's father's name is given as Jair. The name of the brother of Goliath the Gittite was Lahmi. *(1 Chr. 20:5.) (Note: 1 Chr. 20:5 is a repeat of 2 Sam. 21:19, with modification.)*

ELHANAN (2). *2 Sam. 23:24; 1 Chr. 11:26.*

Elhanan, son of Dodo of Beth-lehem, was one of David's mighty men *(2 Sam. 23:24)* and one of the valiant men of the armies *(1 Chr. 11:26)*. (Chart 17.)

ELI. *1 Sam. 1:3 thru 4:18.*

Eli was the high priest and judge who was given charge of Samuel. His two sons, Hophni and Phinehas, were wicked and brought the Lord's judgment upon Eli and all his house because Eli tolerated their iniquities. Meanwhile, Samuel was called by the Lord to be a prophet over Israel. After the Lord called Samuel repeatedly, Eli told him it was the Lord calling him and if He called him again to answer, "Speak, Lord; for thy servant heareth" *(1 Sam. 3:9)*. Hophni and Phinehas, according to the Lord's judgment, were slain in battle with the Philistines who captured the ark of God. When Eli received the report and heard mention of the ark of God, "he fell from off the seat backward by the side of the gate, and his neck brake, and he died: for he was an old man, and heavy. And he had judged Israel forty years." He was 98 years old. *(Eli was a descendant of Aaron through Ithamar. "He was probably the first high priest of this line, and the office remained in his family till the deprivation of Abiathar, when it passed back to the family of Eleazar, Aaron's eldest son." See "Eli" in the BD.)* (Charts 7b.; 20.)

ELIAB (1). *Num 1:9, 30-31; 2:2-9; 7:24.*

Eliab, son of Helon of the tribe of Zebulun, was appointed by the Lord to stand at the head of all of the tribe of Zebulun as Moses organized Israel in preparation for war. The males in his tribe who were 20 years old or older who could go to war numbered 57,400. *(Num 1:9, 30-31.)* Eliab was instructed to have the tribe of Zebulun pitch their tents with the tribe of Judah next to the tribe of Issachar on the east side of the encampment *(Num. 2:2-9.)*

Eliab made his offering the third day when the altar of the tabernacle was anointed. *(Num. 7:24.)*

ELIAB (2). *Num. 16:1; 26:8-9.*

Eliab, father of Dathan and Abiram, was a son of Reuben. *(Num. 16:1.)*

Eliab was the son of Pallu the son of Reuben. He had another son named Nemuel. *(Num. 26:8-9.)* (Chart 5a.)

ELIAB (3). *1 Chr. 6:27.* See **Elihu (1)**.

ELIAB (4). *1 Sam. 16:6; 2 Chr. 11:18.*

Eliab was Jesse's eldest son and one of David's brothers. Samuel thought he might be the one the Lord wanted him to anoint king over Israel, but the Lord told him no. *(1 Sam. 16:6.)*

Eliab's daughter Abihail became one of her nephew king Rehoboam's 18 wives. *(2 Chr. 11:18.)* (Charts 8d-f.)

ELIAB (5). *1 Chr. 12:9 (1, 9, 14).*

Eliab, of the tribe of Gad, was one of David's mighty men—one of the captains of the host who came to him at Ziklag to defend him against Saul. (Chart 13b.)

ELIAB (6). *1 Chr. 15:18-20; 16:5.*

Eliab and his brethren of the second degree were assigned, under the direction of David, to be singers along with Heman, Asaph and Ethan. Eliab and his brethren were assigned to play with psalteries on Alamoth. *(1 Chr. 15:18-20.)* Eliab was a Levite. He and his brethren were appointed by David to minister before the ark of the Lord with psalteries and harps. *(1 Chr. 16:5.)*

ELIADA (1) (Beeliada). *2 Sam. 5:16; 1 Chr. 3:5-7; 14:4-7.*

Eliada was one of David's children born in Jerusalem. His brothers were Shammua, Shobab, Nathan, Solomon, Ibhar, Elishua, Nepheg, Japhia, Elishama, and Eliphalet. *(2 Sam. 5:16.) (Note: The brothers are listed somewhat differently in 1 Chr. 3:5-7.)*

He and his brothers and half-brothers are again listed with some variations, additions and deletions. His name is given as **Beeliada**. *(1 Chr. 14:4-7.)* (Chart 8e.)

ELIADA (2). *2 Chr. 17:17.*

Eliada, of the house of Benjamin, was the captain of 200,000 men when Jehoshaphat was king of Judah.

ELIADAH. *1 Kgs. 11:23.*

Eliadah was the father of Rezon whom the Lord stirred up against Solomon and all Israel when Solomon began worshipping idols.

ELIAH (1). *1 Chr. 8:27.*

Eliah, a descendant of Benjamin, was a son of Jeroham. He and others named were heads of the fathers, by their generations, chief men who lived in Jerusalem. (Chart 16j.)

ELIAH (2). *Ezra 10:26 (18-19, 26, 44).*

Eliah, one of the sons of Elam who took wives from among the Canaanites and other groups, agreed to do as Ezra said and separate himself from foreign wives.

ELIAHBA. *2 Sam. 23:32; 1 Chr. 11:33.*

Eliahba the Shaalbonite was one of David's mighty men *(2 Sam. 23:32)* and one of the valiant men of the armies *(1 Chr. 11:33)*. (Chart 17.)

ELIAKIM (1). *2 Kgs. 18:18, 26, 37; 19:2; Isa. 22:15, 20-25; 36.*

Eliakim, son of Hilkiah, was over king Hezekiah's household in Judah. When Rab-shakeh and his men called to the king to surrender to the Assyrians, Eliakim, Shebna and Joah came out to hear Rab-shakeh's demands. They reported what he said to Hezekiah. *(2 Kgs. 18:18, 26, 37.) (Note: Isa. 36 is a retelling of 2 Kgs. 18:11-37.)*

Hezekiah sent Eliakim, along with Shebna the scribe and the elders of the priests, to speak with Isaiah the prophet regarding the Assyrian demands. *(2 Kgs. 19:2.)*

Isaiah prophesied that Eliakim, son of Hilkiah, would replace Shebna. He used language that foretold of the Messiah's holding the keys of the house of David; the glory that shall be His; that He would be fastened to a cross with a nail in the sure place, i.e., the wrist. *(Isa. 22:15, 20-25.)*

ELIAKIM (2) (Jehoiakim). *2 Kgs. 23:34-37; 24:1-6, 19; 1 Chr. 3:15; 2 Chr. 36:4-8; Jer. 1:3; 22:18-19; 25; 26; 27:1-8, 19-22; 28:4; 36; 37:1; 45; 46:2; 52:2; Dan. 1:1-2.*

Eliakim, son of Josiah and Zebudah, was king of Judah 690-598 B.C. When he was 25 years old, he was made king over Judah by Pharaoh-nechoh in place of his brother Jehoahaz who had been taken captive. His name was changed to **Jehoiakim**. Pharaoh-necho required a high tax on Judah. Jehoiakim collected it from the people. He reigned 11 years in Jerusalem and did that which was evil. *(2 Kgs. 23:34-37.) (2 Chr. 36:4-8 is a retelling of 2 Kgs. 23:34-37. However, the king of Egypt is merely referred to as Necho rather than Pharaho-nechoh.)* Because of his wickedness, the Lord allowed Jehoiakim to be defeated by Nebuchadnezzar, king of Babylon, who bound him in fetters and carried him to Babylon. His son Jehoiachin (Coniah) reigned in his stead.

While Jehoiakim was king of Judah, Nebuchadnezzar was king of Babylon. Jehoiakim became a servant to Nebuchadnezzar. After three years, Jehoiakim rebelled. However, the Lord sent others against Judah because of the sins of Manasseh: bands of the Chaldees, Syrians, Moabites and bands of the children of Ammon. When Jehoiakim died, his son Jehoiachin reigned in his stead and did evil just as Jehoiakim had done. *(2 Kgs. 24:1-6, 19.)*

Jehoiakim was the second son of Josiah. His brothers were Johanan, Zedekiah (Mattaniah) and Shallum (Jehoahaz). *(1 Chr. 3:15.)*

During the days of Jehoiakim, king of Judah, the prophet Jeremiah declared the word of the Lord unto the nations. *(Jer. 1:3.)* Jeremiah pronounced the judgments of the Lord upon the kings of Judah. Of Jehoiakim, he said, "They shall not lament for him . . . He shall be buried with the burial of an ass, drawn and cast forth beyond the gates of Jerusalem." *(Jer. 22:18-19.)*

Jeremiah reminded the people that for 23 years—from the 13th year of Josiah's reign until the fourth year of Jehoiakim's reign—the Lord had sent him and other prophets to warn them to turn away from their evil ways, but they had refused. Thus, the condemnation of the Lord was upon them: they would be carried captive to Babylon where they would remain for 70 years. After that time, many heathen nations would be overthrown. Eventually, in the latter days, all the inhabitants of the earth will be at war. *(Jer. 25.)*

In the beginning of Jehoiakim's reign, Jeremiah prophesied the destruction of the people. The priests and prophets didn't like what he said and felt he should die. The princes of Judah disagreed and reminded them that Micah the Morasthite had prophesied in the days of Hezekiah and they didn't put him to death but repented and the Lord turned away the evil He had threatened against them. Nevertheless, when Urijah also prophesied against the people, Jehoiakim sought him out and had him put to death. *(Jer. 26.)*

In the beginning of Jehoiakim's reign, Jeremiah was instructed by the Lord to send word to many nations that they were to serve Babylon. The vessels of the Lord's house which were not carried away when his son Jeconiah was carried away were to be taken to Babylon where they would remain until such time as the Lord restored the people to Jerusalem. *(Jer. 27:1-8, 19-22.)*

Jehoiakim's son Jeconiah and all the captive would be free within two years according to Hananiah's false prophesy. *(Jer. 28:4.)*

In the fourth year of Jehoiakim's reign over Judah, Jeremiah, while under arrest or in confinement, instructed Baruch to record the prophecies that he (Jeremiah) dictated to him and to read them in the house of the Lord. Jehoiakim burned the rolls, and Jeremiah had Baruch write the prophecies down again. Jeremiah added additional prophecies to these rolls. He prophesied that Jehoiakim would "have none to sit upon the throne of David: and his dead body shall be cast out in the day to the heat, and in the night to the frost." The Lord said He would punish Jehoiakim and his seed and his servants for their iniquity and would bring upon them and the inhabitants of Jerusalem all the evil He had pronounced against them. *(Jer. 36.)*

Zedekiah, Jehoiakim's brother, was placed by Nebuchadnezzar as king over Judah in place of Jehoiakim's son Coniah (Jeconiah, Jehoiachin). *(Jer. 37:1.)*

At the time Jehoiakim (Eliakim) had Jeremiah confined and Jeremiah had Baruch record his prophesies, Jeremiah promised Baruch that his life would be preserved. *(Jer. 45.)*

In the fourth year of the reign of Jehoiakim, Jeremiah prophesied the conquest of Egypt and Pharaoh-necho by Babylon and king Nebuchadrezzar. *(Jer. 46:2.)*

Just as Jehoiakim did evil before the Lord, Zedekiah also did evil before the Lord. *(Jer. 52:2.)*

In Jehoiakim's third year as king of Judah, Jerusalem was beseiged by Nebuchadnezzar and Jehoiakim was taken captive. *(Dan. 1:1-2.)* (Chart 1.)

ELIAKIM (3). *Neh. 12:41.*

Eliakim, a priest and trumpeter, joined in the dedication of the walls of Jerusalem with Nehemiah.

ELIAM (1) (Ammiel (3)). *2 Sam. 11:3; 1 Chr. 3:5.*

Eliam (Ammiel) was the father of Bath-sheba. *(2 Sam. 11:3; 1 Chr. 3:5.) (Note: According to footnotes to the text, Ammiel is the same as Eliam only with the syllables transposed.)*

ELIAM (2). *2 Sam. 23:34.*

Eliam, son of Ahithophel the Gilonite, was one of David's mighty men. (Chart 17.)

ELIASAPH (1). *Num. 1:14, 24-25; 2:14-16; 7:42; 10:20.*

Eliasaph, son of Deuel, was of the tribe of Gad and was appointed by the Lord to stand at the head of all his tribe as Moses organized Israel in preparation for war. The males in the tribe of Gad who were 20 years old or older who could go to war totaled 45,650. *(Num. 1:14, 24-25.)* Eliasaph, son of Reuel (Deuel), was instructed to have the tribe of Gad pitch their tents next to the tribe of Simeon. His host numbered 5,650. *(Num. 2:14-16.)*

When the altar of the tabernacle was anointed and dedicated, Eliasaph made his offering on the sixth day. *(Num. 7:42.)*

Eliasaph, son of Deuel, was over the host of the children of the tribes of Gad. *(Num. 10:20.)* (Chart 13b.)

ELIASAPH (2). *Num. 3:24.*

Eliasaph, son of Lael, was of the house of Gershon, son of Levi who was the grandson of Jacob. Moses was instructed by the Lord that Eliasaph was to be the leader of the Gershonites whose charge was to serve in the tabernacle. (Chart 7a.)

ELIASHIB (1). *1 Chr. 3:24.*

Eliashib, a descendant of David, was a son of Elioenai. His brothers were Hodaiah, Pelaiah, Akkub, Johanan, Dalaiah and Anani. (Chart 1.)

ELIASHIB (2). *1 Chr. 24:12.*

Eliashib was from the sons of Aaron. When David made the divisions of the sons of Aaron, there was one principal household for Eleazar, who had 16 sons, and one for Ithamar, who had eight sons. These 24 sons who were chief of the fathers were divided by lot. Eliashib drew the eleventh lot.

ELIASHIB (3). *Ezra 10:6; Neh. 3:1; 12:10-11, 22-23; 13:4-9, 28.*

Eliashib was the father of Johanan who lived during the time Ezra brought some of the children of Israel out of Babylonian captivity and led them to Jerusalem. *(Ezra 10:6.)*

Eliashib the high priest and his brethren built the sheep gate when the children of Israel rebuilt the walls and gates of Jerusalem after their return from captivity. *(Neh. 3:1.)*

Eliashib was father of Joiada, grandfather of Jonathan, great-grandfather of Jaddua, son of Joiakim, grandson of Jeshua. A record was made of those Levites who were chief of the fathers in the days of Eliashib, Joiada, Johanan (Jonathan) and Jaddua. *(Neh. 12:10-11, 22-23.)*

Eliashib had oversight of the house of God but was allied to Tobiah who supported Sanballat in his efforts to stop Nehemiah from rebuilding the walls of Jerusalem. Nehemiah cast Tobiah and his possessions from the temple and commanded that the chambers be cleansed. One of Eliashib's grandsons, a son of Joiada, was Sanballat's son-in-law. *(Neh. 13:4-9, 28.)* (Chart 7b.)

ELIASHIB (4). *Ezra 10:24 (18-19, 24, 44).*

Eliashib, one of the singers, was among those who had taken wives from among the Canaanites or other foreign groups but who agreed to Ezra's request to separate themselves from these strange wives lest the Lord destroy the rest of the children of Israel.

ELIASHIB (5). *Ezra 10:27 (18-19, 27, 44).*

Eliashib was one of the sons of Zattu who took wives from among the Canaanites and other foreign groups. He and his brothers complied with Ezra's request that they separate themselves from these foreign wives lest the Lord destroy the remainder of the children of Israel because of this iniquity.

ELIASHIB (6). *Ezra 10:36 (18-19, 27, 36, 44).*

Eliashib, a son of Bani, and his brothers were some of the men in Israel who took foreign wives but gave them up when Ezra feared the wrath of God would destroy Israel for this iniquity.

ELIATHAH. *1 Chr. 25:4, 27.*

Eliathah, a Levite and musician, was of the lineage of Kohath and was one of Heman's 14 sons. The musicians—sons of Heman, Asaph and Jeduthun—drew lots and were given their duty assignments by David and the captains of the host. Eliathah cast the 20th lot. He, his sons and his brethren numbered 12. (Chart 7d.)

ELIDAD. *Num. 34:18, 21.*

Elidad, son of Chislon of the tribe of Benjamin, was assigned to divide the land of inheritance given to his people.

ELIEL (1). *1 Chr. 5:24-26.*

Eliel was from the half tribe of Manasseh that was aligned with the Reubenites and Gadites. He was a famous and mighty man of valor and was head of the house of his father. He, along with others, transgressed the laws of God; thus, God allowed them to be carried away into captivity by the Assyrian kings, Pul and Tilgath-pilneser. (Chart 15c.)

ELIEL (2). *1 Chr. 6:34.* See **Elihu (1)**.

ELIEL (3). *1 Chr. 8:20-21.*

Eliel, a descendant of Benjamin, was a son of Shimhi. He and his brothers were heads of the fathers by their generations, chief men who dwelled in Jerusalem. (Chart 16h.)

ELIEL (4). *1 Chr. 8:22, 25.*

Eliel, a descendant of Benjamin, was a son of Shashak who was a son of Beriah. He and his brothers were heads of the fathers by their generations, chief men who dwelled in Jerusalem. (Chart 16g.)

ELIEL (5). *1 Chr. 11:46.*

Eliel the Mahavite was one of David's mighty men—one of the valiant men of the armies. (Chart 17.)

ELIEL (6). *1 Chr. 11:47.*

Eliel was one of David's mighty men—one of the valiant men of the armies. (Chart 17.)

ELIEL (7). *1 Chr. 12:11.*

Eliel, of the tribe of Gad, was one of David's mighty men who came to him at Ziklag to defend him against Saul. (Chart 13b.)

ELIEL (8). *1 Chr. 15:9.*

Eliel, a Levite, was the chief of the sons of Hebron. He and 80 of his brethren were called by David to assemble with other Levites to prepare themselves to retrieve the ark of God from the house of Obed-edom so as to bring it to the place David had prepared for it in the city of David. (Chart 7d.)

ELIEL (9). *2 Chr. 31:13.*

Eliel was one of the overseers of tithes, offerings and the dedicated things of the house of the Lord under the hand of Cononiah and Cononiah's brother Shimei according to the commandment of king Hezekiah and Azariah, the ruler of the house of God.

ELIENAI. *1 Chr. 8:20-21.*

Elienai, a descendant of Benjamin, was a son of Shimhi. He and his brothers were heads of the fathers by their generations, chief men who dwelled in Jerusalem. (Chart 16h.)

ELIEZER (1). *Gen. 15:2; 24:2.*

Eliezer was of Damascus and was the steward of Abram's house. *(Gen. 15:2.)* Eliezer promised Abram that he would not take a wife for Isaac from among the daughters of the Canaanites but would go unto the country of Abram's kindred to find him a wife. *(Gen. 24:2.)*

ELIEZER (2). *Ex. 18:2-5; 1 Chr. 23:14-17; 26:25.*

Eliezer was one of Moses and Zipporah's sons. Jethro, his grandfather, took him and his mother, Zipporah, and his brother Gershom back to Moses after Moses and the children of Israel were encamped in the wilderness. *(Ex. 18:2-5.)*

Eliezer's only son was Rehabiah. Rehabiah had many sons. When David numbered the Levites at the time he made Solomon king, he divided them into courses. Moses' sons were named of the tribe of Levi. *(1 Chr. 23:14-17.)*

Eliezer's posterity included his son Rehabiah; his grandson Jeshaiah; his great-grandson Joram; his great-great-grandson Zichri; and his great-great-great-grandson

Shelomith. Shelomith and his brethren were over the treasures of the dedicated things which king David and others had dedicated. *(1 Chr. 26:25.)* (Chart 7b.)

ELIEZER (3) (Jahaziel (1)). *1 Chr. 15:24; 16:6.*

Eliezer and Benaiah, the priests, were assigned, under the direction of David, to blow the trumpet before the ark of God as it was transported from the house of Obed-edom to the place David had prepared to house it. *(1 Chr. 15:24.)* **Jahaziel** (Eliezer) and Benaiah, the priests, blew the trumpets before the ark of God. *(1 Chr. 16:6.)*

ELIEZER (4). *1 Chr. 7:8.*

Eliezer was a son of Becher and a grandson of Benjamin. His brothers were Zemira, Joash, Elioenai, Omri, Jerimoth, Abiah, Anathoth and Alameth. (Chart 16c.)

ELIEZER (5). *1 Chr. 27:16.*

Eliezer was the son of Zichri and was prince over the tribe of Reuben when David was king.

ELIEZER (6). *2 Chr. 20:37.*

Eliezer the son of Dodavah of Mareshah prophesied against Jehoshaphat, king of Judah, because Jehoshaphat aligned himself with Israel's wicked king Ahaziah to make ships to sail to Tarshish. As a result, the ships were broken and were unable to go to Tarshish.

ELIEZER (7) . *Ezra 8:16 (15-17).*

Eliezer was one of the chief men Ezra sent for when he gathered the people together as he was preparing to lead them to Jerusalem from Babylon and discovered there were no Levites among the group. He sent this group to Iddo and the Nethinims to request that they send them some ministers for the house of God.

ELIEZER (8). *Ezra 10:18-19.*

Eliezer the son of Jeshua the son of Jozadak was one of the sons of the priests who had taken foreign wives and who agreed to put them away as instructed by Ezra.

ELIEZER (9). *Ezra 10:23 (18-19, 23, 44).*

Eliezer was one of the Levites who had taken wives from among the Canaanites or other foreign groups and who agreed to Ezra's request that they separate themselves from these strange wives lest the Lord destroy the rest of the children of Israel.

ELIEZER (10). *Ezra 10:31 (18-19, 31, 44).*

Eliezer of the sons of Harim was one of the Israelite men who took wives from among the Canaanites, etc., who agreed to Ezra's request to separate himself from foreign wives.

ELIHOENAI. *Ezra 8:4.*

Elihoenai, the son of Zerahiah of the sons of Phinehas, was the chief of his fathers and went with Ezra up from Babylon to Jerusalem taking 200 males with him.

ELIHOREPH. *1 Kgs. 4:3.*

Elihoreph and Ahiah, sons of Shisha, were scribes in Solomon's court.

ELIHU (1) (Eliab (3), Eliel (2)). *1 Sam. 1:1, 20; 1 Chr. 6:27, 34.*

Elihu, son of Tohu (Toah) and grandson of Zuph, was the father of Jeroham, grandfather of Elkanah, and great-grandfather of Samuel. *(1 Sam. 1:1, 20.)* Other names also apply to Elihu: **Eliab (3)** and **Eliel (2)**. *(1 Chr. 6:27, 34.)* (Chart 7d.)

ELIHU (2). *1 Chr. 12:20, 21.*

Elihu was from the tribe of Manasseh and was a mighty man of valor, one of the captains in the host. When David stayed confined in Ziklag because of Saul, Elihu helped David against the band of rovers.

ELIHU (3). *1 Chr. 26:7.*

Elihu, a Levite of the lineage of Obed-edom, was a son of Shemaiah. Shemaiah's other sons were Othni, Rephael, Obed, Elzabad and Semachiah. They, along with other Levites, were appointed by king David to be porters—to have charge of the treasures, serve as officers and judges, and to conduct the outward business over Israel. (Chart 7c.)

ELIHU (4). *1 Chr. 27:18.*

Elihu, one of David's brethren, was prince of the tribe of Judah when David was king.

ELIHU (5). *Job 32-37.*

Elihu, the son of Barachel the Buzite, of the kindred of Ram, angrily chastised Job and three friends: Job because he justified himself rather than God; and his three friends because they had found no answer yet they condemned Job. He was younger than the three friends who were very old, according to Elihu. He testified "that there is a spirit in man: and the inspiration of the Almighty giveth them understanding." He further cautioned them that great men are not always wise nor do the aged always understand judgment. *(Job 32.)* Speaking to Job, he taught that God is greater than man; that God speaks in dreams and visions; He ransoms souls from hell, delivering them from the "pit"—giving them life and light. *(Job 33.)* Elihu rebuked Job because he spoke "without knowledge, and his words were without wisdom." God is just. He cannot pervert judgment nor respect persons. People need to bear chastisement and not offend any more. *(Job 34.)* Our wickedness does not hurt God, but it may hurt a man. Our righteousness does not profit God, but it may profit a man. Judgment is always before God and we should, therefore, trust in Him. *(Job 35.)* The righteous will prosper and the wicked shall perish by the sword and die without knowledge. Elihu extolled the greatness of God *(Job 36)* and exhorted Job to "stand still, and consider the wondrous works of God" who controls the laws of nature and reigns in "terrible majesty." *(Job 37).*

ELIJAH (1). *1 Kgs. 17:1-24; 18; 19; 21:17-24, 28-29; 2 Kgs. 1:1-8; 2:8, 10, 11; 2 Chr. 21:12-15; Mal. 4:5-6.*

Elijah the Tishbite was a prophet in Ahab's day who sealed the heavens so there would be neither dew nor rain, "but according to my word." The ravens fed him by the brook Cherith until it dried up. The Lord sent him to Zarephath where a widowwoman would sustain him. He told the widowwoman that her barrel of meal and her cruse of oil would not waste nor fail until the day that the Lord sent rain upon the earth again. Her son became ill and died. Elijah appealed to the Lord and the child revived and lived. *(1 Kgs. 17:1-24.)*

Three years into the drought, the Lord sent Elijah to see Ahab to tell him rain would again fall upon the earth. Elijah met Obadiah, the governor of Ahab's house but a man who feared the Lord, and asked him to inform Ahab that he wanted to meet him. Ahab went to Elijah; and Elijah told him that it was Ahab who troubled Israel by following Baalim. He told him to gather all Israel unto mount Carmel along with the 450 prophets of Baal and the 400 prophets of the groves which ate at Jezebel's table. Once they were all gathered, Elijah challenged the prophets of Baal to call down fire from heaven to consume their sacrifice. They tried multiple times and met with failure each time. Elijah built an altar of 12 stones unto the Lord and had the people pour 12 barrels of water over his offering. He then called upon the Lord, and the Lord sent fire from heaven that consumed the wood, the stones, the burnt offering, the dust, and licked up the water that was in the trenches. The people then knew which god was God. Elijah had the prophets of Baal brought to the brook Kishon where he slew them. He then sent his servant to go look toward the sea seven times. After the seventh time, the servant reported seeing rain clouds. He sent word to Ahab to come down from the mount before the rain kept him from getting down. Elijah ran before Ahab to the entrance of Jezreel. *(1 Kgs. 18.)*

Jezebel warned Elijah through her messenger that she intended to kill him by noon the following day. Elijah fled to Beer-sheba and left his servant there. He then journeyed another day into the wilderness where he sat under a juniper tree and wished he could die. As he slept, an angel touched him and told him to eat. After eating and drinking he slept again, and again the angel touched him and told him to eat and drink because he had a long journey to make. He traveled 40 days and 40 nights unto Horeb, the mount of God, on the strength of what he had eaten and drunk. The Lord spoke to Elijah in a still small voice. The Lord instructed him to anoint Hazael to be king over Syria, Jehu to be king over Israel, and Elisha to be prophet in his stead. Elijah cast his mantle upon Elisha. Elisha followed Elijah and ministered unto him. *(1 Kgs. 19.)*

Elijah was sent by the Lord to rebuke Ahab after Jezebel had Naboth slain so Ahab could claim his vineyard. Elijah prophesied that Ahab and Jezebel and their posterity would all be destroyed—that in the place where dogs licked the blood of Naboth dogs would likewise lick Ahab's blood. Because Ahab humbled himself, the Lord said the destruction of his family would not occur in Ahab's day but in his son's days. *(1 Kgs. 21:17-24, 28-29.)*

When Ahaziah fell sick and sent his messengers to inquire of Baal-zebub as to whether or not he would recover from his disease, the messengers were intercepted by the prophet Elijah. Elijah told them to remind Ahaziah that the reason he had sent them to Baal-zebub was because there was no God in Israel. He also had the messengers tell him that he would not come down from his sick bed but that he would die. Elijah was described by Ahaziah's messengers as "an hairy man, and girt with a girdle of leather about his loins." Ahaziah sent three separate groups of 50 along with their captains of 50 to seek Elijah. The first two groups were destroyed when Elijah called down fire from heaven and it consumed them. The third group appealed to him to spare them. An angel of the Lord told Elijah to go with this group to see Ahaziah. Elijah told Ahaziah what he had told his messengers: he chastised him because there was no God in Israel, and he told him he would not leave his sick bed but would die. *(2 Kgs. 1:1-8.)*

Elijah, with Elisha beside him, smote the river Jordan with his mantle and the waters were divided so they could pass over on dry land. When Elisha asked that Elijah "let a double portion of thy spirit be upon me" when he was taken by the Lord, Elijah told him "if thou see me when I am taken from thee, it shall be so unto thee; but if not, if shall not be so." A chariot and horses of fire appeared and took Elijah to heaven in a whirlwind. *(2 Kgs. 2:8, 10, 11.)*

Elijah sent a message in writing to Jehoram, king of Judah, prophesying of a plague that would come upon the people and the illness and death of Jehoram because of Jehoram's wickedness. *(2 Chr. 21:12-15.)*

Prior to the Second Coming, the Lord promised to send Elijah the prophet to turn the hearts of the children to the fathers and the hearts of the fathers to their children (i.e., to restore the sealing powers of the priesthood), lest He come and smite the earth with a curse. *(Mal. 4:5-6.) (Note: Without this sealing power, families would be disbanded at death and the plan of the Lord, the plan that provides for eternal families, the Plan of Exaltation, would be null and void. This prophecy was fulfilled when Elias [Elijah], a translated being, appeared with Moses who was also translated, and conferred the keys of the priesthood on Peter, James and John. [Matt. 17:1-12.] He appeared again on April 3, 1836, along with Moses and others, in the Kirtland Ohio Temple and conferred those keys upon Joseph Smith and Oliver Cowdery. [D&C 27:12-13].)*

ELIJAH (2). *Ezra 10:21 (18-19, 21, 44).*

Elijah, one of the sons of Harim, was among those sons of the priests who had taken foreign wives and Who Agreed to Put Them Away as Instructed by Ezra.

Elijah's (1) Servant. *1 Kgs. 18:43-44; 1 Kgs. 19:3.*

Elijah's Servant was sent to look toward the sea to watch for rain clouds after Elijah slew the prophets of Baal following their contest to see whose god would send fire from heaven to consume their burnt offering. He was told to go look seven times. After the seventh time, Elijah's servant reported seeing rain clouds rising out of the sea "like a man's hand." *(1 Kgs. 18:43-44.)*

When Elijah fled from Jezebel and went to Beer-sheba, he left his servant at Beer-sheba while he traveled another day into the wilderness. *(1 Kgs. 19:3.)*

ELIKA. *2 Sam. 23:25.*

Elika the Harodite was one of David's mighty men. (Chart 17.)

ELIMELECH. *Ruth 1:1-3.*

Elimelech, an Ephrathite, was the husband of Naomi and the father of Mahlon and Chilion. Because of famine in the land, he took his family from Beth-lehem-judah to dwell in Moab, where he died.

ELIOENAI (1). *1 Chr. 3:23-24.*

Elioenai, Hezekiah and Azrikam were descendants of David and sons of Neariah. Elioenai had seven sons: Hodaiah, Eliashib, Pelaiah Akkub, Johanan, Dalaiah and Anani. (Chart 1.)

ELIOENAI (2). *1 Chr. 4:36.*

Elioenai was a descendant of Shimei of the sons of Simeon. (Chart 6a.).

ELIOENAI (3). *1 Chr. 7:8.*

Elioenai was a son of Becher and a grandson of Benjamin. His brothers were Zemira, Joash, Eliezer, Omri, Jerimoth, Abiah, Anathoth and Alameth. (Chart 16c.)

ELIOENAI (4). *1 Chr. 26:3, 12.*

Elioenai, a Levite, was the seventhborn son of Meshelemiah son of Kore of the sons of Asaph. His brothers were Zechariah, Jediael, Zebadiah, Jathniel, Elam and Jehohanan. They, along with others, were assigned by king David to be porters—to have charge of the treasures, serve as officers and judges, and conduct the outward business over Israel. (Chart 7d.)

ELIOENAI (5). *Ezra 10:22 (18-19, 22, 44).*

Elioenai, one of the sons of Pashur, was among the sons of the priests who had taken foreign wives and who agreed to Ezra's request that they separate themselves from their strange wives.

ELIOENAI (6). *Ezra 10:27 (18-19, 27, 44).*

Elioenai was one of the sons of Zattu who took wives from among the Canaanites and other foreign groups. He and his brothers complied with Ezra's request that they separate themselves from these foreign wives lest the Lord destroy the remainder of the children of Israel because of this iniquity.

ELIOENAI (7). *Neh. 12:41.*

Elioenai, a priest and trumpeter, joined in the dedication of the walls of Jerusalem with Nehemiah.

ELIPHAL. *1 Chr. 11:35.*

Eliphal, son of Ur, was one of David's mighty men. (Chart 17.)

ELIPHALET (Eliphelet, Elpalet). *2 Sam. 5:14-16; 1 Chr. 3:6-8; 14:4-7.*

Eliphalet was one of David's children born in Jerusalem. His brothers were Shammua, Shobab, Nathan, Solomon, Ibhar, Elishua, Nepheg, Japhia, Elishama and Eliada. *(2 Sam. 5:14-16.)*

His brothers are listed somewhat differently and his name is spelled **Eliphelet**. *(1 Chr. 3:6-8.) (Note: Two sons are listed with the name "Eliphelet." Since the same information would apply to both, for the purposes of this book, they are* *combined into one entry. Nevertheless, they could be "sons" from different generations.)*

His brothers are again listed with some variations, additions and deletions, i.e., Eliada's name is given as Beeliada. In addition, instead of two Eliphelets, there is one **Elpalet** and one Eliphalet. *(1 Chr. 14:4-7.)* (Chart 8e.)

ELIPHAZ (1). *Gen. 36:4, 11-12; 1 Chr. 1:36.*

Eliphaz was the son of Adah and Esau and was born in Canan. He begat Teman, Omar, Zepho, Gatam and Kenaz. His concubine Timna bore Amalek. *(Gen. 36:4, 11-12.)*

Eliphaz's son Zepho is listed as Zephi. *(1 Chr. 1:36.) (Note: This verse states that Timna and Amalek were sons of Eliphaz. However, Gen. 36:12 states that Timna was Eliphaz's concubine and she bore Amalek.)* (Charts 3b-c.)

ELIPHAZ (2). *Job 2:11; 4-5; 15; 22; 42.*

Eliphaz the Temanite was one of Job's three friends who came to mourn with him when he lost his children, his servants and his animals. *(Job 2:11.)* He reproved Job. *(Job 4-5.)* He rebuked Job and indicated that Job was a wicked man. He disputed the notion of a resurrection. *(Job 15.)* He accused Job of various sins and urged him to repent. *(Job 22.)*

Eliphaz, Bildad and Zophar were chastised by the Lord because they had not "spoken of me the thing that is right, as my servant Job hath." He instructed them to make offerings and that Job would pray for them; and He would accept them because of Job. They obeyed the Lord. *(Job 42.)*

ELIPHELEH. *1 Chr. 15:18-21.*

Elipheleh and his brethren of the second degree were assigned, under the direction of David, to be singers along with Heman, Asaph and Ethan. Elipheleh and his brethren were assigned to excel with harps on the Sheminith.

ELIPHELET (1). *2 Sam. 23:34.*

Eliphelet, the son of Ahasbai, was one of David's mighty men. (Chart 17.)

ELIPHELET (2). *1 Chr. 8:39.*

Eliphelet, thirdborn son of Eshek, was from the tribe of Benjamin, descending through Jonathan, son of Saul. His brothers were Ulam and Jehush. (Chart 16 l.)

ELIPHELET (3). *Ezra 8:13.*

Eliphelet, Jeiel and Shemaiah, of the last sons of Adonikam, were the chiefs of the fathers of their families and went with Ezra back to Jerusalem from Babylon, taking 60 males with them.

ELIPHELET (4). *Ezra 10:33 (18-19, 33, 44).*

Elilphelet, Mattenai, Mattathah, Zabad, Jeremai, Manasseh and Shimei, sons of Hashum, were among the Israelite men who took foreign wives but complied with Ezra's request that they put away their strange wives so as not to bring the wrath of God upon Israel.

ELI'S DAUGHTER-IN-LAW. *1 Sam. 4:19-21.*

Eli's Daughter-in-law, the wife of Phinehas, died in childbirth when she heard that the ark was taken and that Eli and Phinehas were dead. Prior to her death, she named her son Ichabod.

ELISHA. *1 Kgs. 19:16-21; 2 Kgs. 2:1-7, 8-11, 13-15, 19-22, 23-25; 3:11-20; 4; 5; 6; 7:1-2, 17-20; 8:1-6, 7-15; 9:1-10; 13:14-21.*

Elisha was the son of Shaphat. The Lord instructed Elijah to anoint him to be prophet in his stead. After Elijah cast his mantle upon Elisha, Elisha kissed his parents good-bye and then he followed Elijah and ministered unto him. *(1 Kgs. 19:16-21.)*

Elisha would not leave Elijah's side when the time was nigh for Elijah to be taken from the earth, but followed him to Beth-el and Jericho and to the river Jordan. *(2 Kgs. 2:1-7.)* Elijah smote the river with his mantle and it divided so they could pass over on dry land. Knowing he would be taken soon, Elijah asked Elisha what he would have him do for him. Elisha requested that he let a double portion of his spirit be upon him. Elijah said he asked a hard thing but that if he saw him when he was taken, it would be so. If he didn't see him when he was taken, it would not be so. Elisha saw him taken to heaven in a whirlwind in a chariot of fire with horses of fire. *(2 Kgs. 2:8-11.)* He took Elijah's mantle that had fallen from him and smote the waters of Jordan and they were again divided. Thus, the sons of the prophets who witnessed it knew that the spirit of Elijah rested upon Elisha. *(2 Kgs. 2:13-15.)*

Elisha healed the waters of Jericho. *(2 Kgs.2:19-22.)* As he journeyed to Beth-el, a group of little children mocked him and called him "bald head." Elisha cursed them in the name of the Lord and two she-bears came out of the wood and killed 42 of them. He then traveled on to mount Carmel and then to Samaria. *(2 Kgs. 2:23-25.)*

When Jehoram of Israel and Jehoshaphat of Judah, along with the king of Edom, went to battle against Mesha and the Moabites, Jehoshaphat had Jehoram inquire of Elisha what they should do regarding the Moabites. Elisha instructed them to fill the valley with ditches and promised them water for their stock in spite of the fact there was no water in the land and that they would be victorious against the Moabites. *(2 Kgs. 3:11-20.)*

Elisha performed five miracles: 1) he multiplied a widow's oil so creditors would not take her sons for bondsmen *(2 Kgs. 4:1-7)*; 2) he promised a Shunammite woman who had befriended him that she would have a child *(2 Kgs. 4:8-17)*; 3) when the child died, he restored his life *(2 Kgs. 4:18-37)*; 4) he healed the deadly pottage at Gilgal which the sons of the prophets were about to eat *(2 Kgs. 4:38-41)*; and 5) he multiplied the bread and grain which a man from Baal-shalisha brought to him so all the people could eat *(2 Kgs. 4:42-44)*.

Elisha was approached by Naaman the Syrian who desired to be healed from leprosy. Elisha told him to bathe in the river Jordan seven times and he'd be healed.

Naaman angrily refused but, upon the urging of his servants, reluctantly agreed and was healed. Elisha refused to accept any reward from Naaman. However, Elisha's servant Gehazi decided he wanted "somewhat" from Naaman and falsely claimed Elisha had changed his mind and now was requesting silver and a couple of changes of garments for "two young men of the sons of the prophets." When Elisha learned what Gehazi did, he told him that the leprosy which had been upon Naaman would be upon Gehazi, and it was so. *(2 Kgs. 5.)*

As some of the sons of the prophets were felling beams, an axe head fell into the water. One man lamented it to Elisha because the axe was borrowed. Elisha caused the axe head to float, and the man retrieved it. *(2 Kgs. 6: 1-7.)* Elisha revealed to the king of Israel how to conduct a war with Syria. When the Syrians came in search of Elisha, Elisha's servant feared when he saw the Syrian forces gathered against them. Elisha asked the Lord to open his servants eyes so that he could see that those "that be with us are more than they that be with them." His servant saw that they were protected by horses and chariots of fire that surrounded them. *(2 Kgs. 6:8-17.)* At Elisha's request, the Syrians were smitten with blindness. He then led them into Samaria where he requested that their sight be restored. He had the king of Israel give them food and drink and send them home. "So the bands of Syria came no more into the land of Israel." *(2 Kgs. 6:18-23.)* There was a famine in Samaria and what goods there were sold for great prices. *(2 Kgs. 6:25.)*

Elisha prophesied that on the morrow there would be incredible plenty in Samaria and that prices would be greatly reduced and it was so. He also prophesied that the "lord on whose hand the king leaned" would "see it with thine eyes, but shalt not eat thereof" because he doubted it would be so. This, also, came to pass. *(2 Kgs. 7:1-2, 17-20.)*

Elisha encouraged the Shunammite woman whose son's life had been restored to go to some other place to live because there was going to be a seven-year famine in Samaria. *(2 Kgs. 8:1-6.)*

Elisha went to Damascus and was informed that king Ben-hadad was ill. He told Hazael who had been sent to inquire of him as to what would become of the king that he would recover from his illness but that he would die. Elisha then wept because he knew that Hazael would become king when Ben-hadad died and that he would do great evil unto the children of Israel. *(2 Kgs. 8:7-15.)*

Elisha sent one of the sons of the prophets to Ramoth-gilead to anoint Jehu king over Israel and to instruct Jehu that the Lord had decreed that he should smite the house of Ahab that the entire house perish. *(2 Kgs. 9:1-10.)*

Elisha fell ill and was near death when Joash (Jehoash) king of Israel came and wept over him. Elisha had the king shoot an arrow out the window. He told him it was the arrow of the Lord's deliverance and the arrow of deliverance from Syria. He then had him take the rest of the arrows and strike the ground with them. Joash struck the ground three times. Elisha was angry with him because he should have struck the ground five or six times. Now the Israelites would only defeat the Syrians three times whereas had he struck the ground five or six times they would have completely consumed Syria. Elisha died and was buried. It came to pass that another man also died. They cast that man into the sepulchre of Elisha. When the man's body touched Elisha's bones, the man was restored to life. *(2 Kgs. 13:14-21.) (Note: Elisha's ministry lasted more than 50 years, covering the reigns of Jehoram, Jehu, Jehoahaz and Joash.)*

ELISHAH. *Gen. 10:4; Ezek. 27:7.*

Elishah was a son of Javan, grandson of Japheth, and a great-grandson of Noah. By the sons of Javan, Gomer and Japheth "were the isles of the Gentiles divided in their lands." *(Gen. 10:4.)*

Before the fall of Tyrus, Tyrus was a magnificent sea-faring city whose fine linen with broidered work from Egypt "was that which thou spreadest forth to be thy sail; blue and purple from the isles of Elishah was that which covered thee." *(Ezek. 27:7.)* (Chart 2a.)

ELISHAMA (1). *Num. 1:10, 32-33; 2:18-24; 7:48; 1 Chr. 7:26-27.*

Elishama was the son of Ammihud. They were of the tribe of Ephraim, one of two tribes allotted Joseph. He was appointed by the Lord to be the one to stand at the head of all of the tribe of Ephraim as Moses organized Israel in preparation for war. The males in the tribe of Ephraim who were 20 years of age and older who could go to war numbered 40,500. *(Num. 1:10, 32-33.)* Elishama was instructed to have the tribe of Ephraim pitch their tents on the west side of the encampment. Next to him was the tribe of Manasseh and then the tribe of Benjamin. Combined, the camp of Ephraim totaled 108,100. *(Num. 2:18-24.)*

When the altar of the tabernacle was anointed and dedicated, Elishama made his offering on the seventh day. *(Num. 7:48.)*

Elishama was the son of Ammihud and a fifth-great-grandson of Ephraim. His son was Non (Nun) and his grandson was Jehoshua (Joshua). *(1 Chr. 7:26-27.)* (Chart 15d.)

ELISHAMA (2). *2 Sam. 5:14-16; 2 Kgs. 25:25; 1 Chr. 3:6-8; 14:4-7; Jer. 41:1-2.*

Elishama was one of David's children born in Jerusalem. His brothers were Shammua, Shobab, Nathan, Solomon, Ibhar, Elishua, Nepheg, Japhia, Eliada and Eliphalet. *(2 Sam. 5:14-16.)*

Elishama's grandson Ishmael, son of Nethaniah, slew Gedaliah who had been made governor over the remnant of Judah by Nebuchadnezzar, king of Babylon. *(2 Kgs. 25:25; Jer. 41:1-2.)*

Elishama was one of David's sons. His brothers are listed with some variations. *(1 Chr. 3:6-8.) (Note: There are two sons named Elishama listed. Since both entries would state the same thing, for the purposes of this book they are combined into one entry. Nevertheless, they could be "sons" from different generations.)*

His brothers are again listed with some variations, additions and deletions. Eliada is listed as Beeliada. *(1 Chr. 14:4-7.)* (Chart 8e.)

ELISHAMA (3). *1 Chr. 2:41.*

Elishama, of the lineage of Judah, was the son of Jekamiah. (Chart 8c.)

ELISHAMA (4). *2 Chr. 17:8-9.*

Elishama and Jehoram, the priests, along with other Levites, were sent by king Jehoshaphat to journey with the princes of Judah throughout the cities of Judah to instruct the people out of the book of the law of the Lord.

ELISHAMA (5). *Jer. 36:12.*

Elishama was Jehoiakim's scribe and was in the scribe's chamber with all the princes when Michaiah told them of the prophecies of Jeremiah which he had heard Baruch read in his father Gemariah's chamber.

ELISHAPHAT. *2 Chr. 23:1.*

Elishaphat, the son of Zichri, was one of the captains of hundreds Jehoiada the priest rallied to make Joash king over Judah and to slay Athaliah.

ELISHA'S MESSENGER. *2 Kgs. 5:10.*

Elisha's Messenger met Naaman at the door and conveyed Elisha's instructions to him to bathe in the Jordan river seven times. He would then be cleansed of leprosy.

ELISHEBA. *Ex. 6:23.*

Elisheba, the daughter of Amminadab of the tribe of Judah and the sister of Naashon, was the wife of Aaron and bore him Nadab, Abihu, Eleazar and Ithamar. (Chart 7b.)

ELISHUA (Nogah). *2 Sam. 5:15; 1 Chr. 3:7; 14:4-7.*

Elishua was one of David's children born in Jerusalem. His brothers were Shammua, Shobab, Nathan, Solomon, Ibhar, Nepheg, Japhia, Elishama, Eliada and Eliphalet. *(2 Sam. 5:15.)*

Elishua's brothers are named again with some variations. Elishua's name is replaced with **Nogah**. *(1 Chr. 3:7.)*

Elishua's brothers are listed again with some variations, additions and deletions. Both Elishua and Nogah are listed this time and Eliada's name is given as Beeliada. *(1 Chr. 14:4-7.)* (Chart 8e.)

ELIZAPHAN (1). *Num. 3:30.* See **Elzaphan**.

ELIZAPHAN (2). *Num. 34:25.*

Elizaphan was the son of Parnach and was of the tribe of Zebulun. He was assigned to divide the land of their inheritance among Zebulun's posterity. (Chart 10b.)

ELIZAPHAN (3). *2 Chr. 29:13.*

Elizaphan's descendants Shimri and Jeiel were among those whom Hezekiah, king of Judah, instructed to sanctify themselves so they could cleanse and sanctify the house of the Lord.

ELIZUR. *Num. 1:5, 20-21; 2:10-16; 7:30.*

Elizur, son of Shedeur of the tribe of Reuben, was appointed by the Lord to stand at the head of all of the tribe of Reuben as Moses organized Israel in preparation for war. The males of the tribe of Reuben, 20 years and over who could go to war, numbered 46,500. *(Num. 1:5, 20-21.)* Elizur was instructed to have his armies pitch their tents on the south side of the camp. Next to him was the tribe of Simeon and then the tribe of Gad. Together, the men in the camp of Reuben numbered 151,450. *(Num. 2:10-16.)*

When the altar of the tabernacle was dedicated, Elizur made his offering on the fourth day. *(Num. 7:30.)*

ELKANAH (1). *Ex. 6:24; 1 Chr. 6:22-28, 33-37.*

Elkanah, a Levite, was a son of Korah. *(Ex. 6:24.)*

Elkanah was the son of Assir, grandson of Korah, and the father of Ebiasaph. His genealogy is given. *(1 Chr. 6:22-28, 33-37.)* (Chart 7d.)

ELKANAH (2). *1 Sam. 1:1-20; 2:20-21; 1 Chr. 6:27-28, 33-38.*

Elkanah, the son of Jeroham, was the husband of Hannah and the father of Samuel. He had two wives: Hannah and Peninnah. When "Elkanah offered, he gave to Peninnah and to all her sons and her daughters, portions: but unto Hannah he gave a worthy portion; for he loved Hannah." Hannah was barren until the Lord answered her petition to have a male child, whom she promised she would give unto the Lord. They named him Samuel. *(1 Sam. 1:1-20.)* The Lord blessed Elkanah and Hannah with three more sons and two daughters. *(1 Sam. 2:20-21.)*

Elkanah, son of Jeroham and father of Samuel (Shemuel), was of the house of Levi through Kohath. *(1 Chr. 6:27-28, 33-38.)* (Chart 7d.)

ELKANAH (3). *1 Chr. 6:25, 36.*

Elkanah, of the house of Levi through Kohath, was the son of Shaul (Joel) and the father of Amasai. (Chart 7d.)

ELKANAH (4). *1 Chr. 6:26, 35; 15:23.*

Elkanah, of the house of Levi through Kohath, was the son of Ahimoth (Mahath), and was the father of Zophai (Zuph). *(1 Chr. 6:26, 35.)*

Elkanah and Berechiah, who was a descendant of Gershon, were assigned to be the doorkeepers for the ark when David brought it out of the house of Obed-edom. *(1 Chr. 15:23.)* (Chart 7d.)

ELKANAH (5). *1 Chr. 9:16.*

Elkanah was the father of Asa. He was a Levite whose descendants dwelled in the villages of the Netophathites. His genealogy was written in the book of the kings of Israel and Judah, who were carried away to Babylon for their transgression.

ELKANAH (6). *1 Chr. 12:6 (1-2, 6, 23, 38).*

Elkanah, a Korhite, was one of David's mighty men who came to him at Ziklag to defend him against Saul and to rejoice with all Israel when David became king.

ELKANAH (7). *2 Chr. 28:7.*

Elkanah, who was next to Ahaz, king of Judah, was slain by Zichri, a mighty man of Ephraim, when the Lord allowed Judah to be brought low because of wickedness.

ELNAAM. *1 Chr. 11:46.*

Elnaam was the father of Jeribai and Joshaviah, two of David's mighty men.

ELNATHAN (1). *2 Kgs. 24:8.*

Elnathan was a grandfather of Jehoiachin, king of Judah, and father of Nehushta, Jehoiachin's mother.

ELNATHAN (2). *Ezra 8:16 (15-17).*

Elnathan was one of the chief men Ezra sent for when he gathered the people together as he was preparing to lead them to Jerusalem from Babylon and discovered there were no Levites among the group. He sent this group to Iddo and the Nethinims to request that they send them some ministers for the house of God.

ELNATHAN (3). *Ezra 8:16 (15-17).*

Elnathan was another of the chief men Ezra sent for when he gathered the people together as he was preparing to lead them to Jerusalem from Babylon and discovered there were no Levites among the group. He sent this group to Iddo and the Nethinims to request that they send them some ministers for the house of God.

ELNATHAN (4). *Ezra 8:16 (15-17).*

Elnathan, a man of understanding, was one of the men Ezra sent for when he gathered the people together as he was preparing to lead them to Jerusalem from Babylon and discovered there were no Levites among the group. He sent this group to Iddo and the Nethinims to request that they send them some ministers for the house of God. *(Note: In this scripture, there are three Elnathans named: two who were "chief men," and one who was a man of "understanding.")*

ELNATHAN (5). *Jer. 26:22; 36:12.*

Elnathan was the son of Achbor. When the prophet Urijah fled to Egypt because king Jehoiakim sought to put him to death, Elnathan and a group of men were sent to Egypt to bring Urijah back. This they did, and Urijah was slain by Jehoiakim. *(Jer. 26:22.)*

Elnathan was in the scribe's chamber in king Jehoiakim's house with Elishama the scribe and several princes when Michaiah told them of the prophecies of Jeremiah which he had heard Baruch read in his father Gemariah's chamber. When the king went to burn the roll, Elnathan, Delaiah and Gemariah tried to intervene, but the king would not listen to them. *(Jer. 36:12.)*

ELON (1). *Gen. 26:34; 36:2-4.*

Elon the Hittite was the father of Bashemath and a father-in-law of Esau. *(Gen. 26:34.) (Note: According to other scripture verses, Elon was the father of Esau's wife Adah, who bore Eliphaz, rather than the father of Bashemath, as recorded in Gen. 26:34. Instead, Bashemath's father was Ishmael.) (Gen. 36:2-4.)*

ELON (2) (Elonites). *Gen. 46:14; Num. 26:26.*

Elon was a son of Zebulun and a grandson of Jacob. *(Gen. 46:14.)* His descendents are the **Elonites**. *(Num. 26:26.)* (Chart 10a.)

ELON (3). *Judg. 12:11-12.*

<u>Elon</u> judged Israel ten years following Ibzan. He was from the tribe of Zebulun. When he died, he was buried in Aijalon in the country of Zebulun. (Chart 20.)

ELONITES. *Num. 26:26.* See **Elon (2)**.

ELPAAL. *1 Chr. 8:11, 17-18.*

<u>Elpaal</u>, descendant of Benjamin and son of Hushim and Shaharaim, was father of Eber, Misham, Shamed, Beriah, and Shema; also of Zebadiah, Meshullam, Hezeki, Heber, Ishmerai, Jezliah and Jobab. (Charts 16g, i.)

ELPALET (See Eliphalet)

ELUZAI. *1 Chr. 12:5 (1, 5).*

<u>Eluzai</u> was one of David's mighty men who came to him at Ziklag to protect him against Saul.

ELZABAD (1). *1 Chr. 12:12-15.*

<u>Elzabad</u>, of the tribe of Gad, was one of David's mighty men who came to him at Ziklag. He was one of the 12 captains of the host whose faces were like lions and who were as swift as roes, who went over Jordan in the first month and put all the people in the valleys to flight. (Chart 13b.)

ELZABAD (2). *1 Chr. 26:7 (Subtitle, 6-8).*

<u>Elzabad</u>, a Levite of the lineage of Obed-edom, was a son of Shemaiah. His brethren were strong men. His brothers were Othni, Rephael, Obed, Elihu and Semachiah. They, along with other Levites, were appointed by king David to be porters—to have charge of the treasures, serve as officers and judges, and to conduct the outward business over Israel. (Chart 7c.)

ELZAPHAN (Elizaphan (1)). *Ex. 6:22; Lev. 10:4-5; Num. 3:30; 1 Chr. 15:8.*

<u>Elzaphan</u> was a son of Uzziel, a grandson of Kohath and a great-grandson of Levi. His brothers were Mishael and Zithri. *(Ex. 6:22.)*

Elzaphan and Mishael were instructed by Moses to carry the bodies of their cousins Nadab and Abihu, who the Lord had slain by fire for performing unauthorized sacrifices, from before the sanctuary and out of the camp. They carried the bodies in their coats out of the camp. *(Lev. 10:4-5.)*

<u>Elizaphan</u> (Elzaphan), the son of Uzziel, was named as chief of the house of the fathers of the families of the Kohathites. *(Num. 3:30.)*

Shemaiah was chief of the sons of Elizaphan. He and 200 of his brethren were assembled by David along with many other Levites and instructed to sanctify themselves so they could bring up the ark of the Lord to the place which David had prepared to house it. *(1 Chr. 15:8.)* (Chart 7d.)

EMIMS. *Gen. 14:5; Deut. 2:10.*

The <u>Emims</u> in Shaveh Kiriathaim were smitten by Chedorlaomer and the kings who were with him in the 14th year of Chedorlaomer's reign. *(Gen. 14:5.)* They were displaced from the land of Ar by the Moabites. They were considered to be giants just like the Anakims. *(Deut. 2:10.)*

ENAN. *Num. 1:15.*

Enan was the father of Ahira. They were of the tribe of Naphtali. (Chart 12b.)

ENOCH (1) . *Gen. 4:17-18.*

Enoch, grandson of Adam and Eve, was the son of Cain and his wife. Cain built a city and called it Enoch. Enoch begat Irad. (Chart 1.)

ENOCH (2) (Henoch). *Gen. 5:18, 21-24; 1 Chr. 1:1.*

Enoch was the son of Jared (who was 162 years old when he begat Enoch) and a great-great-great-great-grandson of Adam. When Enoch was 65 years old he begat Methuselah. *(Gen. 5:18, 21-24.) (Note: Adam was 687 years old by this time. According to the BD, "Enoch walked with God after he begat Methuselah 300 years" and all of Enoch's days on earth were 365 years, at which time "God took him." Moses 6:21, 25-27; 7:68-69; 8, in the Pearl of Great Price indicate that Enoch was 65 years old when he first began to walk with God. After that time, he dwelled in Zion another 365 years; and that all the days of Enoch were four hundred and thirty years.)*

Henoch (Enoch) begat Methusaleh. *(1 Chr. 1:1.)* (Charts 1.; 21.)

ENOS (Enosh).. *Gen. 4:26; 5:6, 9-11; 1 Chr. 1:1.*

Enos was the son of Seth and the grandson of Adam. After his birth, the people began to call upon the name of the Lord. *(Gen. 4:26.)* He was born when his father, Seth, was 105 years old. He begat Cainan when he was 90 years old. He lived a total of 905 years, begetting sons and daughters. *(Gen. 5:6, 9-11.)*

Enosh (Enos) was the son of Sheth (Seth). *(1 Chr. 1:1.)* (Charts 1.; 21.)

EPHAH (1). *Gen. 25:4.*

Ephah was a son of Midian and a grandson of Abraham and Keturah. His brothers were Epher, Hanoch, Abida and Eldaah. (Chart 3f.)

EPHAH (2). *1 Chr. 2:46.*

Ephah was one of Caleb's concubines. She bore him Haran, Moza and Gazez. (Chart 8j.).

EPHAH (3). *1 Chr. 2:47.*

Ephah was one of the sons of Jahdai. His brothers were Regem, Jotham, Geshan, Pelet and Shaaph. He was related to Caleb and Jerahmeel, but the connection is not clear. (Chart 8j.)

EPHAI. *Jer. 40:8 (7-9).*

Ephai was a Netophathite. His sons and the captains of the forces which were in the fields went to Gedaliah after Gedaliah was made governor over the remnant of the Jews who were left in Judah after Nebuchadnezzar took the rest captive, and were counseled by Gedaliah not to fear serving the Chaldeans.

EPHER (1). *Gen. 25:4.*

Epher was a son of Midian and a grandson of Abraham and Keturah. His brothers were Ephah, Hanoch, Abida and Eldaah. (Chart 3f.)

EPHER (2). *1 Chr. 4:17.*

Epher, Jether and Mered were sons of Ezra. Their sister was Jalon. (Chart 8 o.)

EPHER (3). *1 Chr. 5:24-26.*

Epher was from the half tribe of Manasseh that was aligned with the Reubenites and Gadites. He was a famous and mighty man of valor and was head of the house of his father. He, along with others, transgressed the laws of God; thus, God allowed them to be carried away into captivity by the Assyrian kings, Pul and Tilgath-pilneser. (Chart 15c.)

EPHLAL. *1 Chr. 2:37.*

Ephlal was the son of Zabad and the father of Obed. (Chart 8c.)

EPHOD. *Num. 34:23.*

Ephod, father of Hanniel, was prince of the children of Joseph for the tribe of the children of Manasseh. (Chart 15c.)

EPHRAIM. *Gen. 41:52; 46:20; 48:5-6, 13-20; Num. 26:35-37; 34:24; Judg. 8:1; 12:1-6; 1 Chr. 5:1-2; 7:20-27; 12:30; 27:10, 14, 20; 2 Chr. 30:10-11, 18; Ps. 78:62-68; Isa. 11:11-13; Jer. 31:9; Ezek. 48:5-6, 32; Hosea 4:17; 5; 6; 7:8, 11; 8; 9; 10:6, 11; 11:3-12; 12; 13:1, 12-14; 14; Zech. 10:7.*

Ephraim was Joseph and Asenath's secondborn son. *(Gen. 41:52.)* He and Manasseh were born unto Joseph in the land of Egypt. *(Gen. 46:20.)*

Jacob told Joseph that Ephraim and Manasseh would be his just as Reuben and Simeon were his, but that any issue he begot after them would be Joseph's and would be called after the name of their brethren in their inheritance. When Joseph presented his two sons to Jacob, Jacob placed his right hand upon Ephraim and his left hand upon Manesseh and set Ephraim before Manasseh over Joseph's objections. He said that Manasseh would be great, but that Ephraim would be greater. *(Gen. 48:5-6, 13-20.)*

The males in Ephraim's family numbered 32,500 when Moses and Eleazar numbered the males in Israel who were twenty years old and older as they camped on the plains of Moab near Jericho. They included the Shuthalhites, Bachrites, Tahanites and Eranites. *(Num. 26:35-37.)*

The prince of the tribe of the children of Ephraim assigned to divide Ephraim's inheritance was Kemuel, son of Shiphtan. *(Num. 34:24.)*

The men of Ephraim chided Gideon for not enlisting their help in his fight against the Midianites. *(Judg. 8:1.)*

The men of Ephraim chastised Jephthah for not including them in the fight against the children of Ammon and threatened to burn their houses. Jephthah explained they hadn't helped them in the past so he didn't count on them this time. Jephthah and the Gileadites fought against the Ephraimites and the Manassites. Some escaped. When the Gileadites tested people they captured by having them say "Shibboleth," the Ephraimites could not say it correctly and said "Sibboleth." The Gileadites slew 42,000 Ephraimites. *(Judg. 12:1-6.)*

Because Reuben, Jacob's firstborn, defiled his father's bed, the birthright went to Joseph and subsequently to Ephraim. *(1 Chr. 5:1-2.)* Ephraim has the birthright of the firstborn. *(Jer. 31:9.) (Also see Gen. 48:20)*

Ephraim's posterity is listed. *(1 Chr. 7:20-27.)*

The children of Ephraim sent 20,800 men to Ziklag when David became king and all Israel rejoiced and sent their armies to support him. *(1 Chr. 12:30.)*

The prince and the officers from the tribe of Ephraim who were assigned by king David to serve him were Helez the Pelonite—assigned to be over the course of 24,000 who served for the seventh month; Benaiah the Pirathonite—assigned to be over the course of 24,000 who served for the eleventh month; and Hoshea, son of Azaziah, prince over the tribe of Ephraim. *(1 Chr. 27:10, 14, 20.)*

When Hezekiah, king of Judah, sent couriers throughout all Israel to invite them to come to Jerusalem to participate in a solemn Passover, many throughout the country of Ephraim and Manasseh even unto Zebulun laughed and mocked the couriers to scorn. *(2 Chr. 30:10-11, 18.)*

The Lord chose the tribe of Judah, the "mount Zion which he loved," over the tribe of Ephraim. *(Ps. 78:62-68.)*

When the Savior comes again, Ephraim will no longer envy Judah and Judah will no longer vex Ephraim. *(Isa. 11:11-13.)*

The Lord revealed to Ezekiel just how the land should be divided by tribes when the children of Israel are gathered in the latter days. Because Joseph is to receive two portions *(see Ezek. 47:13)*, Ephraim and Manasseh will each receive one portion. Ephraim will have the portion of land between the borders of Manasseh and Reuben. The twelve gates of the city are to bear the names of the twelve sons of Jacob. One of the east gates will bear the name of Joseph. *(Ezek. 48:5-6, 32.)*

Ephraim was chastised by Hosea who said Ephraim was joined to idols. He counseled the people to stay away from Ephraim. *(Hosea 4:17.)* Ephraim, Israel and Judah, Hosea prophesied, would fall because of iniquity. Ephraim willingly walked after filth and sought help from Jareb, king of Assyria. *(Hosea 5.)* Ephraim, Hosea pointed out, had committed whoredoms, and reminded the people that God desired mercy more than sacrifices and knowledge of Him more than burnt offerings. *(Hosea 6.)* Ephraim had become mixed among the people and incurred the wrath of the Lord for turning to Egypt and Assyria instead of to Him. *(Hosea 7:8, 11.)* Hosea continued to prophesy against Ephraim, Israel and Judah for forsaking the Lord and worshipping idols. The Lord had written the great things of His law to Ephraim, but they were counted as a "strange thing." *(Hosea 8.)*

Hosea prophesied that Ephraim would return to Egypt and be wanderers among the nations. *(Hosea 9.)* Ephraim shall receive shame. The Lord passed over upon her neck. *(Hosea 10:6, 11.)* Ephraim was condemned for turning away from the Lord. "Ephraim compasseth me about with lies," said the Lord. The Assyrians shall be Ephraim's king because Ephraim refused to return to the Lord. *(Hosea 11:3-12.)*

Ephraim provoked the Lord most of all and made a covenant with the Assyrians and carried oil into Egypt. Hosea proclaimed that the Lord speaks through prophets and uses visions and similitudes to teach His people. When the people become rich, they turn from the Lord. *(Hosea 12.)*

The Lord lamented the sins of Ephraim, who "exalted himself in Israel; but when he offended in Baal, he died." Ephraim sinned more and more and made molten images. "The iniquity of Ephraim is bound up; his sin is hid . . . he is an unwise son." Only the Lord can ransom the people from the grave and redeem them from death. *(Hosea 13:1, 12-14.)*

Hosea prophesied that in the latter days, Ephraim will repent and return to the Lord, recognizing that Asshur (i.e., Assyria) shall not save them. *(Hosea 14.)*

Zechariah prophesied that when the Lord gathers His people, "Ephraim shall be like a mighty man, and their heart shall rejoice as through wine: yea, their children shall see it, and be glad . . ." *(Zech. 10:7.)* (Charts 15a, d-e.)

EPHRATH (Ephratah). *1 Chr. 2:19, 50.*

Ephrath became Caleb's wife after his wife Azubah died. **Ephratah** begat Hur. (Chart 8i.)

EPHRON. *Gen. 23:8-18.*

Ephron was the son of Zohar. He was a Hittite. Abraham purchased Ephron's field and the cave of Machpelah which was in the end of the field for a burial site for Sarah.

ER (1). *Gen. 38:3, 6-7; 46:12; 1 Chr. 2:3.*

Er was Shuah and Judah's firstborn son. Judah chose Tamar to be Er's wife. Er was wicked in the sight of the Lord and the Lord slew him. *(Gen. 38:3, 6-7; 1 Chr. 2:3.)* He died in the land of Canaan. *(Gen. 46:12.)* (Charts 8a, c-d, g-h.)

ER (2). *1 Chr. 4:21.*

Er was a son of Shelah and a grandson of Judah. He was the father of Lecah. (Chart 8a.)

ERAN (Eranites). *Num. 26:36.*

Eran was the son of Shuthelah and a grandson of Ephraim. His descendants are the **Eranites**. (Chart 15d.)

ERI (Erites). *Gen. 46:16; Num. 26:16.*

Eri was a son of Gad and a grandson of Jacob. *(Gen. 46:16.)* He was the father of the **Erites**. *(Num. 26:16.)* (Chart 13a.)

ESARHADDON (Esar-haddon, Asnappar). *2 Kgs. 19:37; Ezra 4:2, 10; Isa. 37:38.*

Esarhaddon was one of king Shennacherib's sons. He was king (680-668 B.C.) after his father was murdered by two of his brothers: Adrammelech and Sharezer. *(2 Kgs. 19:37; Isa. 37:38.)*

The Samaritans falsely claimed they had sought the God of the Israelites ever since **Esar-haddon**, king of Assur, had brought them to Samaria to occupy the lands vacated by the children of Israel when they were carried off captive to

Babylon. *(Ezra 4:2, 10.) (Note: In verse ten, it states that "the great and noble Asnappar brought over, and set in the cities of Samaria" the various nations. Thus, it would appear that Asnappar and Esar-haddon are one and the same. 2 Kgs. 17:24 states that the king of Assyria brought men from Babylon and other places and placed them in the cities of Samaria instead of the children of Israel. Assur and Assyria are one and the same. The Bible Dictionary states that Esarhaddon was succeeded by his son Assurbanipal or Asnapper. The only place the name Asnappar appears is in verse 10 and would appear to refer to Esar-haddon himself who brought the people up and placed them in the cities (v. 4). The only place the name Assurbanipal appears is in the chonology chart in the Bible Dictionary in the Synchronism column for the years 667-626 B.C.)*

ESAU (Edom, Idumea). *Gen. 25:25-27, 28, 29-34; 26:34-35; 27; 28:1-9; 32; 33; 35:29; 36:1-8, 9-43; Deut. 2:4-5,22; 23:7; Josh. 24:4; Judg. 11:17; 1 Sam. 14:47; 2 Sam. 8:14; 1 Kgs. 22:41-47; 2 Kgs. 3:9; 8:20; 14:7; 1 Chr. 1:35; 2 Chr. 21:8; 25:11-12, 14-15; 28:17; Isa. 21:11; 34:5-6; Jer. 27:3; 49:7-22; Ezek. 25:12-14; 32:21, 29; 35; 36:5; Amos 1:1, 6, 11-12; Obad.; Mal. 1:2-4.*

Esau was the firstborn twin son of Isaac and Rebekah. When he was born, he "first came out red, all over like an hairy garment." The Lord had told Rebekah while the babies were yet in the womb that the elder would serve the younger: i.e., Esau would serve Jacob. Esau was a hunter and worked in the fields. His father was 60 years old when he and Jacob were born. Isaac favored Esau over Jacob because he ate of Esau's venison. Esau sold his birthright to Jacob for some bread and pottage of lentiles. Esau was called **Edom**. *(Gen. 25:25-27, 28, 29-34.) (Note: The footnote to the text indicates that Edom means red. Esau was red when he was born and the pottage he bought from Jacob with his birthright was red.)*

Esau was 40 years old when he took two Hittite women—Judith and Bashemath—as wives, much to the sorrow of his parents. *(Gen. 26:34-35.)*

When Isaac grew old and his eyesight was dim, he called Esau to him and asked him to prepare him some venison, which he loved, and to bring it to him that he might eat it and then he would give him a blessing. While Esau was hunting for and preparing the venison, his mother had Jacob take some savory meat to Isaac and, with kid skins on his arms and neck, deceive Isaac into giving him the birthright blessing. When Esau learned that the blessing had been given to Jacob, "he cried with a great and exceeding bitter cry." He asked his father for a blessing, too. He was told that the blessing would remain with Jacob. He was told that his dwelling would be the fatness of the earth and the dew of heaven; that by the sword he would live; that he would serve his brother; but "when thou shalt have the dominion, that thou shalt break his yoke from off thy neck." Esau hated Jacob and planned to kill him as soon as his father died. *(Gen. 27.)*

When Esau saw that Isaac had blessed Jacob and had told him to not take a wife from among the Canaanites but had sent him to Padan-aram to take a wife from among the daughters of their uncle Laban, he deliberately went to Ishmael and took another wife, Mahalath, from among Ishmael's daughters. *(Gen. 28:1-9.)*

As Jacob returned to the land of his fathers, he sent messengers ahead to tell Esau he was coming and wanted to be reconciled with him. The messenger returned and told Jacob that Esau was on his way with 400 men. *(Gen. 32.)*

Esau and Jacob were reconciled. He returned to Seir after being persuaded to accept Jacob's gift of many animals. *(Gen. 33.)*

Esau and Jacob buried their father Isaac. *(Gen. 35:29.)*

Esau is Edom. His wives were from among the Canaanites: Adah, the daughter of Elon the Hittite; Aholibamah, the daughter of Anah the daughter of Zibeon the Hivite; and Bashemath, Ishmael's daughter, sister of Nebajoth. Adah bore Eliphaz. Bashemath bore Reuel. Aholibamah bore Jeush, Jaalam and Korah. Esau and his families separated themselves from Jacob and his families because their riches were too much to allow them to dwell together. Esau dwelled in Seir. His generations are set forth. *(Gen. 36:1-8, 9-43.)* Esau begat Eliphaz, Reuel, Jeush, Jaalam and Korah. *(1 Chr. 1:35.)*

Moses recounted to the children of Israel how they were allowed to pass through the land of the children of Esau in peace. The Lord had given mount Seir unto Esau for a possession. *(Deut. 2:4-5,22.)*

Moses instructed the Israelites that they should "not abhor an Edomite for he is thy brother." *(Deut. 23:7.)*

The Lord gave mount Seir to Esau as a possession. *(Josh. 24:4.)*

The king of Edom refused to let the children of Israel pass through his land when Jephthah requested passage through. *(Judg. 11:17.)*

King Saul fought against Edom, Moab, the children of Ammon, the kings of Zobah and the Philistines and "vexed" them. *(1 Sam. 14:47.)*

David put garrisons in Edom and all the Edomites became his servants. *(2 Sam. 8:14.)*

Edom had no king—a deputy was acting as king—when Jehoshaphat became king over Judah. *(1 Kgs. 22:41-47.)*

The king of Edom joined with Jehoshaphat, king of Judah, and Jehoram, king of Israel, against Moab. (2 Kgs. 3:9.) Edom revolted from under the hand of Judah during the reign of Jehoram and selected a king for themselves. *(2 Kgs. 8:20.)*

Amaziah, king of Judah, slew 10,000 Edomites in the valley of salt and took the city of Selah by war shortly after becoming king. *(2 Kgs. 14:7.)*

The Edomites revolted under Jehoram's reign over Judah and made themselves a king. *(2 Chr. 21:8.)*

The Edomites were slaughtered by Amaziah, king of Judah, who then brought the gods of the children of Seir back and set them up to be his gods, incurring the wrath of the Lord upon Judah. *(2 Chr. 25:11-12, 14-15.)*

The Edomites and the Philistines, as well as Israel, smote Judah and carried away captives when Ahaz was king of Judah because Judah had become very wicked. Ahaz solicited help from king Tilgath-pineser and the Assyrians. *(2 Chr. 28:17.)*

Isaiah prophesied a message of doom to the Edomites, wherein he called it the "burden of Dumah." *(Isa. 21:11.) (Note: The Edomites descended through Isaac through Esau. Dumah was a son of Ishmael.)* The sword of the Lord will come down upon **Idumea** to judgment. *(Isa. 34:5-6.) (Note: The footnote to the text indicates that Idumea is Hebrew for Edom. The Bible Dictionary indicates that Idumea is also used to represent the world.)*

The kings of Edom, Moab, the Ammonites, Tyrus and Zidon were warned by Jeremiah in a letter that they were to serve Babylon. *(Jer. 27:3.)*

When Jeremiah prophesied of the judgment and destruction that would come upon the Edomites, he said the Lord would "bring the calamity of Esau" upon them. *(Jer. 49:7-22.)*

Because the Edomites had taken vengeance against Judah, Ezekiel was instructed by the Lord to prophesy vengeance against them. *(Ezek. 25:12-14.)*

As Ezekiel lamented for Pharaoh king of Egypt and for Egypt, herself, the Lord told him, "The strong among the mighty shall speak to him (Pharaoh) out of the midst of hell with them that help him: they are gone down, they lie uncircumcised, slain by the sword . . . There is Edom, her kings, and all her princes, which with their might are laid by them that were slain by the sword: they shall lie with the uncircumcised, and with them that go down to the pit." *(Ezek. 32:21, 29.)*

Ezekiel prophesied that, because of their hatred of Israel, the Lord's wrath would fall upon Mount Seir and all of Idumea, i.e., Edom. *(Ezek. 35.) (Note: The BD, under the heading of "Edom," states that from the time of the Maccabees, Edom was known as Idumea and that the original inhabitants were the Horites or "children of Seir.")*

The Lord spoke against the heathen and all Idumea (Edom) which had taken the land of the Israelites for their own possession. *(Ezek. 36:5.)*

When Amos prophesied during the time of Uzziah king of Judah and Jeroboam king of Israel of things he saw concerning Israel and the judgments that would come upon Edom, Syria, the Philistines and others, he said that because the Israelites had been taken captive to Edom, and because Edom pursued one another with the sword and had no pity for anyone, the Lord would send fire upon Teman which would devour the palaces of Bozrah. *(Amos 1:1, 6, 11-12.)*

Edom's doom was foretold by Obadiah. Edom had sinned in their violence against the seed of Jacob; in rejoicing in Judah's destruction; by speaking proudly in the day of distress; in gathering up the possessions of Judah; by cutting off those who tried to escape; and by delivering up those who remained. That which Edom had done would be returned upon their own heads. *(Note: According to the BD, the account of the fulfillment of this prophecy is recorded in 2 Kgs. 14:7 and 2 Chr. 25:11-12.)* In the latter days, the mount of Esau shall be judged by saviors on mount Zion and the kingdom shall be the Lord's. *(Obad.)*

Esau was Jacob's brother. The Lord loved Jacob, but He hated Esau (Edom) (because of wickedness). *(Mal. 1:2-4.)* (Charts 1.; 2c.; 3a-d.; 4c.)

ESH-BAAL. *1 Chr. 8:33; 9:39.*

Esh-baal was one of the sons of Saul. However, he is not listed among Saul's sons in 1 Sam. 14:49 nor in 1 Sam. 31:2. His brothers were Jonathan, Malchi-shua and Abinadab. (Chart 16 l.)

ESHBAN. *Gen. 36:26.*

Eshban was a son of Dishon, son of Seir the Horite. (Chart 4d.)

ESHCOL. *Gen. 14:13-24.*

Eshcol was a brother to Mamre and Aner. They joined Abram in Lot's rescue from King Chedorlaomer. When they returned from the slaughter of Chedorlaomer and the kings that were with him, the king of Sodom offered Abram the goods that had been retrieved. Abram took none, but suggested that Eshcol, Mamre and Aner should be allowed to take their portion.

ESHEK. *1 Chr. 8:39.*

Eshek was the brother of Azel and a son of Eleasah. He was from the tribe of Benjamin. He descended through Jonathan, the son of Saul. He begat Ulam, Jehush and Eliphelet. (Chart 16 l.)

ESHTAULITES. *1 Chr. 2:53.*

The **Eshtaulites** come through Shobal who was a son of Hur and grandson of Caleb. (Chart 8 l.)

ESHTEMOA (1). *1 Chr. 4:17.*

Eshtemoa was the son of Ishbah. His mother was Jalon who was a daughter of Ezra. (Chart 8 o.)

ESHTEMOA (2). *1 Chr. 4:19.*

Eshtemoa was a Maachathite. His brother was Keilah the Garmite.

ESHTON. *1 Chr. 4:11.*

Eshton was the son of Mehir, the grandson of Chelub, the father of Beth-rapha, Pasea and Tehinnah, and the grandfather of Irnahash.

ESTHER (Hadassah). *Esth. 2:7-23; 4; 5:1-8; 6:14; 7; 8; 9.*

Esther (**Hadassah**), daughter of Abihail, was the cousin of Mordecai, the Jew. When her parents died, Mordecai raised her as his own daughter. She was fair and beautiful. When king Ahasuerus desired to find a new queen to replace Vashti whom he had deposed, Mordecai, in compliance with Ahasuerus' decree that all fair young virgins should be gathered unto Shushan the palace, took Esther there and delivered her to the custody of Hegai, keeper of women. Ahasuerus chose Esther to be his queen. She was instructed by Mordecai not to reveal that she was a Jew. When Mordecai learned of plans to kill the king, he reported them to Esther who informed Ahasuerus. The perpetrators were hung. *(Esth. 2:7-23.)*

Because Mordecai would not bow down to Haman, one of Ahasuerus' leaders, Haman had gotten Ahasuerus to give him permission to destroy all the Jews. When Esther learned of the mourning and fasting by Mordecai and her kindred people, she inquired as to the reason. Mordecai requested that she petition the king in their behalf. After some hesitation, fasting and prayer, she agreed to approach the king, unbidden, putting her life in peril. *(Esth. 4.)*

The king received Esther and she invited him and Haman to a banquet she had prepared. *(Esth. 5:1-8.)* The king and Haman attended the banquet. *(Esth. 6:14.)*

Esther revealed to Ahasuerus Haman's plot to destroy all of the Jews; and Haman was hung on the gallows he had prepared for Mordecai. *(Esth. 7.)*

Esther was given the house of Haman by Ahasuerus and she set Mordecai over it. She petitioned the king to void the decree that would allow Haman's people to destroy the Jews. Ahasuerus not only reversed it but decreed that the Jews in every city could defend their lives, destroy or cause to perish anyone who assaulted them, and take their spoil for a prey. *(Esth. 8.)*

After the Jews smote all of their enemies and slew Haman's ten sons, Ahasuerus, at Esther's request, had Haman's sons hung upon the gallows. The Feast of Purim was instituted to commemorate their deliverance and victory, and Esther the queen "wrote with all authority to confirm this second letter of Purim." *(Esth. 9.)*

ETAM. *1 Chr. 4:3.*

Etam was of the lineage of Judah. The families of the father of Etam were Iezreel, Ishma, Idbash and Hazelelponi, their sister." (Chart 8m.)

ETHAN (1). *1 Kgs. 4:31; Ps. 89.*

Ethan the Ezrahite was a wise man, but Solomon was wiser than he. *(1 Kgs. 4:31.)*

This is a Messianic Psalm and a subtitle associates it with Ethan: "Maschil of Ethan the Ezrahite." *(Ps. 89.) (Note: Under Psalms in the BD, it states that Maschil means "giving instruction.")*

ETHAN (2). *1 Chr. 2:6, 8.*

Ethan was one of the five sons of Zerah. He was a grandson of Judah and a great-grandson of Jacob. He was the father of Azariah. (Charts 8d, g-h.)

ETHAN (3). *1 Chr. 6:42.* See **Joah (2)**.

ETHAN (4). *1 Chr. 6:44 (31, 44); 15:17-19.*

Ethan was a descendant of Levi through Merari and was the son of Kishi. He was among those who David set over the services of song in the house of the Lord. *(1 Chr. 6:44 [31, 44].)*

Under King David's direction, Ethan, Asaph, of the tribe of Gershon, and Heman, of the tribe of Kohath, were appointed to be singers and to sound the cymbals of brass. Ethan's father is listed as Kushaiah rather than Kishi. *(1 Chr. 15:17-19.)* (Chart 7e.)

ETHBAAL. *1 Kgs. 16:31.*

Ethbaal, king of the Baal-worshipping Zidonians, was father of Jezebel, wife of Israel's king Ahab.

ETHIOPIANS (Lubims, Sukkims). *Gen. 2:13; Num. 12:1; 2 Kgs. 19:9; 2 Chr. 12:3; Isa. 20:4-5; Jer. 13:23; Ezek. 30:4-9; Nahum 3; Zeph. 2:12.*

Ethiopians were the inhabitants in the land called Ethiopia that was compassed about by the river Gihon. Ethiopia was also known as Cush. *(Gen. 2:13.)* Moses married an Ethiopian woman and Miriam and Arron spoke against him for doing so. *(Num. 12:1.)*

Tirhakah, king of Ethiopia, came out against Hezekiah, king of Judah. *(2 Kgs. 19:9.)*

The Ethiopians (Cushites), which included modern Nubia, the **Lubims** (Libyans) and the **Sukkims** came out of Egypt with king Shishak against king Rehoboam and the children of Israel when Rehoboam and the children of Israel forsook the Lord. *(2 Chr. 12:3.)*

Isaiah prophesied that the Ethiopians would be taken captive by the king of Assyria. *(Isa. 20:4-5.)*

The Lord indicated that just as the Ethiopian cannot change the color of his skin, nor the leopard change his spots, those who are accustomed to doing evil cannot do good. *(Jer. 13:23.)*

Ezekiel prophesied that Egypt and all who supported her would fall by the hand of Nebuchadnezzer and become desolate, and her idols would be destroyed. There would be great pain in Ethiopia when the slain fell in Egypt and the multitude were dispersed. When this destruction occurs, the Lord said messengers from Him would go forth in ships "to make the careless Ethiopians afraid, and great pain shall come upon them, as in the day of Egypt." *(Ezek. 30:4-9.)*

Nahum pointed out to the people of Ninevah that Ethiopia and Egypt had helped No, but the city was still destroyed and the people taken captive. Ninevah's fate would be the same. *(Nahum 3.)*

The prophet Zephaniah prophesied judgment to come upon Ethiopia and said they would be slain by the sword. *(Zeph. 2:12.)*

ETHNAN. *1 Chr. 4:7.*

Ethnan, of the tribe of Judah, was the son of Ashur the father of Tekoa and his wife Helah. His brothers were Zereth and Jezoar. He also had several half-brothers, sons of Ashur and Naarah. (Chart 8d.)

ETHNI. *1 Chr. 6:41.*

Ethni, a Levite, was the son of Zerah, a descendant of Gershom. *(Note: Gershom's descendants are listed differently in verses 20-21.)* (Chart 7a.)

EUNUCHS IN JEZREEL. *2 Kgs. 9:32-33.*

Eunuchs in Jezreel, as instructed by Jehu, cast Jezebel out a window, causing her death in accordance to the word of the Lord. *(Note: Eunuchs were men who had been castrated and were attached to the courts of eastern rulers with the assignment to watch over the harem. They were often placed in positions of trust.)*

EVE. *Gen. 2:21-22; 3:1-8,16, 20, 21-24; 4:1-2, 25.*

Eve was Adam's wife. God took a rib from Adam and created Eve and gave her to Adam to be his wife. *(Gen. 2:21-22.)*

The serpent approached Eve and convinced her that she and Adam should partake of the fruit from the tree of the knowledge of good and evil. She got Adam to partake. Their eyes were opened and they knew they were naked. They made aprons out of fig leaves. Adam and Eve hid from the Lord when they heard His voice. Eve told the Lord that the serpent beguiled her. The Lord told Eve He would multiply her discomfort in pregnancy because of her disobedience. She was instructed to have her desires be to her husband and to follow his guidance. She is first mentioned by name in Gen. 3:20. Adam called her "Eve" "because she is the mother of all living." The Lord made coats of animal skins for them. They were driven out of the Garden of Eden. *(Gen. 3:1-8,16, 20, 21-24.) (Note: In Moses 5:11, in the Pearl of Great Price, we learn that Eve recognized the necessity of the Fall and the joys of redemption. "And Eve, his wife, heard all these things and was glad, saying: Were it not for our transgression we never should have had seed, and never should have known good and evil, and the joy of our redemption, and the eternal life which God giveth unto all the obedient.")*

Eve bore two sons, Cain and Abel. After Cain killed Abel, Eve bore another son, Seth. *(Gen. 4:1-2, 25.) (Note: Eve must have been 130 years old when she bore Seth because that's how old Adam was and they began their mortal experience together. Moses 5:2-3, 13, 16-17 tell us that Eve bore several sons and daughters prior to the births of Cain and Abel. These sons and daughters divided two and two in the land. They loved Satan more than God. They also bore sons and daughters.)* (Chart 1.)

EVI. *Num. 31:8 (1-8); Josh. 13:21.*

Evi was one of five Midianite kings slain by the children of Israel when Moses sent an army of 12,000 men to destroy the Midianites.

EVIL-MERODACH. *2 Kgs. 25:27-30; Jer. 52:31-34.*

Evil-merodach was king of Babylon (561-559 B.C.) after his father Nebuchadnezzar. He released Jehoiachin, king of Judah, from prison and showed him great favor, having him dine with him and providing a daily allowance for him for the rest of his life. *(2 Kgs. 25:27-30; Jer. 52:31-34.) (Note: The Bible Dictionary indicates that Evil-merodach was killed by his brother-in-law, Neriglissar, who then became king. Neriglissar is not mentioned in the Old Testament but is shown on the Chronology Chart in the Profane History column for the years 559-555 B.C.)*

EZBAI. *1 Chr. 11:37.*

Ezbai was the father of Naarai (Paarai).

EZBON (1) (Ozni, Oznites). *Gen. 46:16; Num. 26:16.*

Ezbon was a son of Gad and a grandson of Jacob. *(Gen. 46:16.)* **Ozni**.(Ezbon) was the father of the **Oznites**. *(Num. 26:16.)* (Chart 13a.)

EZBON (2). *1 Chr. 7:7.*

Ezbon was a son of Bela and a grandson of Benjamin. His brothers were Uzzi, Uzziel, Jerimoth and Iri. He was the head of his house and a mighty man of valor. (Chart 16c.)

EZEKIEL. *Ezek. 1:3-28; 2; 3; 4; 5; 6; 7; 8; 9; 10; 11; 12; 13; 14; 15; 16; 17; 18; 19; 20; 21; 22; 23; 24; 25; 26; 27; 28; 29; 30; 31:18; 32; 33; 34; 35; 36; 37; 38; 39; 40-48.*

Ezekiel the priest, was the son of Buzi of the family of Zadok. He prophesied for 22 years between 592-570 B.C. (BD) In the fifth year of king Jehoiachin's captivity in Babylon, Ezekiel, while among the captives by the river Chebar, received a vision from the Lord in which he saw four living creatures—each with four faces, four wheels—and the glory of God on his throne. Regarding the four faces each of the four living creatures had: one was the face of a man, one the face of a lion, one the face of an ox, and one the face of an eagle. He heard the voice of one who spoke to him. *(Ezek. 1:3-28.)*

The Lord told Ezekiel he was to carry His word to the rebellious children of Israel but not to fear them nor their words. Ezekiel saw a hand in which there was a book. The book contained lamentations, mourning and woe. *(Ezek. 2.)*

Ezekiel was commanded to take the Lord's word to the people and to warn them on behalf of the Lord. The Lord told him that He had made him a watchman unto the house of Israel. If he did not give them warning and they died in their iniquity, the Lord said He would require their blood at Ezekiel's hand. However, if he gave them warning and they still sinned, they would die in their sins but Ezekiel would have delivered his own soul. Again, if Ezekiel did not warn the righteous not to sin, and they sinned, their blood would be required at Ezekiel's hand. If they were warned and sinned, they would die in their sins, but Ezekiel would have delivered his own soul. And if the righteous, having been warned, refrained from sinning, they would "surely live," and again the Lord said, "also thou hast delivered thy soul." *(Ezek. 3.)* Ezekiel was told by the Lord that if a watchman warns the people of pending disaster and they repent, their souls shall be delivered. If they do not heed the watchman, their blood shall be upon their own heads, but he will have "delivered" his own soul. If a watchman does not warn the people and, therefore, they are destroyed, their blood will be upon the head of the watchman. The Lord said that Ezekiel was a watchman unto the house of Israel. Sinners who repent shall be saved and "none of his sins that he hath committed shall be mentioned unto him: he hath done that which is lawful and right; he shall surely live." However, those who turn away from righteousness shall be punished and "all his righteousnesses shall not be remembered, but for his iniquity that he had committed, he shall die for it." The Jews in Jerusalem enjoyed listening to the words of Ezekiel but they refused to heed them. The Lord warned that when the promised destruction came to pass, "then shall they know that a prophet hath been among them." *(Ezek. 33.)*

Ezekiel was instructed by the Lord to take a tile and draw upon it a city. He was to create a model that would represent the seige and famine that would befall Jerusalem. *(Ezek. 4.)*

Ezekiel was told to shave the hair off his head and also his beard. He was to divide the hair into thirds: one third he was to burn with fire; one third he was to smite with a knife; and the other third he was to scatter in the wind. He was to bind a few hairs together in his skirts and then cast them into the midst of the fire. This represented what the Lord said would happen to Israel: one third would die with pestilence and famine; one third would fall by the sword; and the Lord said He would scatter one third. *(Ezek. 5.)*

Ezekiel prophesied that Israel would be destroyed for her idolatry. Those of the children of Israel carried far off will die by pestilence. Those who remain nearby, will fall by the sword. Those who remain and are beseiged will die by famine. Nevertheless, the Lord promised to save a remnant of those who are scattered throughout the nations. *(Ezek. 6.)*

Ezekiel continued his prophecy concerning the destruction and desolation of Jerusalem and the children of Israel. *(Ezek. 7.)*

Ezekiel saw in vision the wickedness of Judah in Jerusalem as the people, even the elders, worshipped such idols as Tammuz the Amorite idol and the sun god of the Egyptians in the court and in the house of the Lord. *(Ezek. 8.)*

Ezekiel saw the righteous of Israel and Judah marked so they would not be destroyed. The destruction of the wicked, beginning with the "ancient men which were before the house" was to begin at the Lord's sanctuary. *(Ezek. 9.)*

Ezekiel either recorded the vision he had in Ezek. 1:4-28 a second time, or he had a repeat of the vision. There is a slight modification in this narration. Ezekiel described the four faces of each of the figures he saw as: (1) the face of a cherub; (2) the face of a man; (3) the face of a lion; and (4) the face of an eagle. *(Ezek. 10.)*

Ezekiel was shown in vision the destruction of Jerusalem and the captivity of the people. Jaazaniah the son of Azur and Pelatiah the son of Benaiah, who were princes of the people, were men who provided false and wicked counsel in Jerusalem. Ezekiel prophesied of the latter-day gathering of Israel. *(Ezek. 11.)*

The Lord instructed Ezekiel to move his "stuff" by day in the sight of the inhabitants of Jerusalem, to go forth at evening like those who go forth into captivity, and to dig through the wall in the sight of the people and carry things out through the hole so that he might be "for a sign unto the house of Israel." He did as instructed and told them he represented the scattering of the Jews from Jerusalem. He then prophesied that the house of Israel would be scattered among the nations. *(Ezek. 12.)*

Ezekiel was told to reprove both male and female false prophets who claim to speak for God when He has not spoken to them. *(Ezek. 13.)*

Ezekiel was told to warn the people that the Lord would not answer through the prophets those who worship false gods, but that "I the Lord will answer him by myself." Idol worshippers would be destroyed. The Lord said He would "set my face against that man, and will make him a sign and a proverb." Ezekiel cried repentance unto the people, but they would not listen. The Lord told Ezekiel that even if Noah, Daniel and Job were there, the only souls that would be saved are those three because the people had become so wicked. *(Ezek 14.)*

The Lord compared Israel to a useless vine that would be burned. *(Ezek. 15.)*

Ezekiel was instructed by the Lord to enumerate Israel's sins to her. Jerusalem was compared to a harlot who sold herself to every nation, engaging in all of their sins. Even as wicked as Sodom and Samaria had been, Israel was worse. Thus, Israel was rejected by the Lord. Nevertheless, the Lord promised to reestablish His covenant with her in the last days. *(Ezek. 16.)*

Ezekiel was given a parable which he was to teach the people describing to Israel how, while they were subject to Babylon, they sought help from Egypt rather than from the Lord. Eventually, the Lord will bring forth a good branch from the cedars of Lebanon. *(Ezek. 17.)*

The Lord taught Ezekiel that men shall be punished for their own sins and not anyone else's sins. The wicked who repent shall be forgiven and their sins forgotten. The righteous who turn to sin will be punished for their sins and their righteousness shall not be remembered. *(Ezek. 18.)*

Ezekiel was instructed to lament for Israel because she had been taken captive by other nations and was now planted in dry and thirsty ground. She was weak. Her fruit was dried up. "Her strong rods were broken and withered." She had "no strong rod to be a sceptre to rule." *(Ezek. 19.)*

Ezekiel was instructed by the Lord to tell the people He would no longer hear their petitions. From the time the Lord delivered the children of Israel from Egypt, through their sojourn in their wilderness and their gaining the lands of their inheritance, even up unto the current time of Ezekiel, the Lord had taught the people His truths and they had rebelled against them and defiled the Sabbath. In the latter days, when He gathers Israel out of the countries where they have been scattered, the Lord will again accept the people. *(Ezek. 20.)*

Ezekiel prophesied that Babylon would prevail against Israel and that both the righteous and the wicked would be slain by the sword. *(Ezek. 21.)*

The Lord enumerated the sins of the Jews in Jerusalem so Ezekiel could list them before the children of Israel: shedding of blood, idol worship, dishonoring parents, oppressing the stranger, vexing the fatherless and widow, profaning the Sabbath and despising holy things, bearing false witness, lewdness, sexual sins, greed, false prophets, robbery. As a result of their sins, "the house of Israel is to me become dross," said the Lord. Therefore, the house of Israel would become scattered and destroyed. *(Ezek. 22.)*

The Lord compared Samaria and Jerusalem to two sisters who were the daughters of one mother. The Lord referred to Samaria as Ahola and to Jerusalem as Aholibah. They both committed whoredoms and were as harlots, worshipping idols. As a result, the Lord destroyed both for their lewdness. *(Ezek. 23.)*

Ezekiel, on the day that Nebuchadnezzar set himself against Jerusalem, was given another parable by the Lord which he was to give unto the house of Israel. This parable talked about a pot filled with all the parts of an animal, using bones under the pot to make the pot boil. "Woe," said the Lord, "to the pot whose scum is therein, and whose scum is not gone out of it." This parable was indicative of the fact that the judgment pronounced on Jerusalem was irrevocable. "I the Lord have spoke it: it shall come to pass." As a sign to the Jews that the Lord was going to take from them the joy of their glory and the desire of their eyes, the Lord told Ezekiel He was going to take his wife—the desire of his eyes—but that he should shed no tears at her death. So it was, Ezekiel spoke to the people in the morning and his wife died that evening. *(Ezek. 24.)*

Ezekiel prophesied that the Lord's vengence would fall upon the Ammonites, Moabites, Edomites and Philistines because they rejoiced in Israel's troubles. *(Ezek. 25.)*

Ezekiel prophesied that because Tyrus rejoiced when Jerusalem fell and was destroyed, the Lord would destroy Tyrus. Nebuchadnezzar, king of Babylon, would break down her walls, slay her people and make a spoil of her riches. The isles of the sea would tremble at the fall of this great sea-faring city. *(Ezek. 26.)* The Lord instructed Ezekiel to take up a lamentation for Tyrus. Tyrus, the crown jewel of sea-faring cities, would be "broken by the seas" at which time "thy merchandise and all thy company in the midst of thee shall fall . . . thou shalt be a terror, and never shalt be any more." *(Ezek. 27.)*

Ezekiel prophesied that both Tyrus, because of her pride, and Zidon, because she was a "pricking brier" to the house of Israel, would fall and be destroyed. The house of Israel would eventually be gathered and would dwell in peace in the land the Lord gave Jacob. *(Ezek. 28.)*

Ezekiel prophesied that Egypt, because she failed to help Israel and was as a "staff of reed" to them, would be overthrown by Nebuchadnezzar. Egypt would be desolate 40 years and then be restored to her land of habitation. However, she would no longer be powerful. *(Ezek. 29.)*

Ezekiel again prophesied against Egypt and Pharaoh king of Egypt (Pharaoh-hophra) saying the Lord would scatter the Egyptians among the nations. Egypt and the lands of those who helped her would be made desolate by the hand of Nebuchadnezzar, king of Babylon. *(Ezek. 30.)*

Ezekiel prophesied that Pharaoh king of Egypt (Pharaoh-hophra) would fall just like the Assyrians, who were compared to a mighty cedar in Lebanon. "Yet shalt thou be brought down with the trees of Eden unto the nether parts of the earth". *(Ezek. 31:18.)*

Ezekiel made a lamentation for Egypt and Pharaoh because of the great destruction that would come to them. *(Ezek. 32.)*

Ezekiel prophesied against shepherds who feed themselves and not their flocks. Shepherds should seek for those sheep who are lost and scattered. In the last days, the Messiah *(Jesus Christ from the house of David)* will be the shepherd who seeks and feeds the scattered house of Israel and brings them to safety. The Lord will make a "covenant of peace" with them and "they shall dwell safely." He will cause blessings to flow unto them. *(Ezek. 34.)*

Ezekiel prophesied that, because of their hatred of Israel, the Lord's wrath would fall upon Mount Seir and all of Idumea (the world). *(Ezek. 35.)*

Ezekiel was commanded by the Lord to prophesy unto the mountains and hills that in the latter days Israel would again inhabit the land. The land will then no longer be profaned by the heathen. The land will blossom like a garden of Eden. The Lord will bless the children of Israel with a new heart "and a new spirit will I put within you." They will know He is the Lord. *(Ezek. 36.)*

Ezekiel was carried "out in the spirit of the Lord" and set down in a valley full of bones. He prophesied of the resurrection. The children of Israel will be given the land of their inheritance in the resurrection. The Lord instructed Ezekiel regarding two sets of scriptures: the stick of Judah *(the Bible)* and the stick of Joseph *(the Book of Mormon: See D&C 27:5)*. They will be joined together and "they shall be one in my hand." Israel will be gathered in the last days and the Lord will cleanse them. He will rule over them and be their God, and they will be His people. He will make a covenant of peace with them which will be an everlasting covenant. *(Ezek. 37.)*

Ezekiel prophesied that in the latter days there would be a large battle when the descendants of Gog in the land of Magog would come against Israel. This battle will usher in the Second Coming of the Savior. The Lord will come during a time of pestilence and bloodshed. All men upon the face of the earth will shake at his presence. *(Ezek. 38.)* *(Note: The footnote to the text cross-references Gog with Magog, the son of Japheth and grandson of Noah.)*

Ezekiel prophesied that Magog would be destroyed by fire and that Gog would be destroyed and buried in Israel in the valley called Hamon-gog. Those who dwell in the cities of Israel will burn their weapons of war for seven years. The house of Israel will spend seven months burying the dead. The Lord will continue to gather Jacob's posterity and they will know that He is God. *(Ezek. 39.)*

Ezekiel was taken in a vision to a city in the land of Israel wherein he was shown the "frame of a city." There was also a heavenly ministrant who showed him the form and size of the temple and all of its courts along with the chambers for the priests—the one "toward the north" was for the keepers of the charge of the altar: the sons of Zadok of the family of Levi. *(Ezek. 40.)* He was taken to the temple and shown the holy of holies. *(Ezek. 41.)* He was taken into the outward court and was shown the priests' chambers. *(Ezek. 42.)* He was taken to the east gate of the temple and the glory of the Lord filled the temple by way of the east gate. The Lord's throne is in the temple. He promised to dwell in the midst of the children of Israel forever. Ezekiel was instructed to show the plan of the temple to the house of Israel and, if they repented of their sins, he was to show them the form of the house and the ordinances thereof. He was shown the altar of the Lord and the ordinances that pertained to the altar. *(Ezek. 43.)* Ezekiel was taken back to the east gate. It was closed because the Lord had entered in by it and no one else should enter through it. No unworthy person should enter the temple. The services of the priests in the temple were explained. Those priests who had not remained faithful but had worshipped idols would be allowed to be "keepers of the charge of the house, for all the service thereof," but they would not be allowed to come near unto the holy things: those services would be done by the priests who were the sons of Zadok who had remained obedient to the Lord. The priests were to wear special clothing when working in the temple and were to change garments when leaving the temple. They were also given instructions pertaining to whom they should and should not marry. *(Ezek. 44.)* Ezekiel was instructed that the children of Israel should divide by lot their land of inheritance, reserving one portion to be used for the sanctuary and dwellings for the priests, and that the people were to keep their feasts and offer their oblations and sacrifices. *(Ezek. 45.)* He was instructed regarding the ordinances of worship and the performance of sacrificial offerings. *(Ezek. 46.)* He was shown a river running out of the house of the Lord and entering and healing the Dead Sea, which then flourished with fish and had trees on its banks. The Lord showed him the borders of the land that the children of Israel were to divide by lot as their inheritance according to their tribes, with Joseph being given two portions. *(Ezek. 47.)* He revealed to Ezekiel just how the land should be divided by tribes. The twelve gates of the city were to bear the names of the twelve sons of Jacob. The name of the city shall be "The LORD is there." *(Ezek. 48)*.

EZEKIEL'S WIFE. *Ezek. 24:15-18.*

Ezekiel's WIFE was the desire of his eyes. The Lord told Ezekiel she was going to die but that he was not to weep or mourn at her death because it was a sign to the Jews of their pending judgment. Ezekiel prophesied to the people in the morning and his wife died that evening.

EZER (1). *Gen. 36:21, 27; 1 Chr. 1:42.*

Ezer was a son of Seir the Horite. He was a duke or tribal chief. His children were Bilhan, Zaavan (Zavan) and Akan (Jakan). (Charts 4a-f.; 19.)

EZER (2). *1 Chr. 4:4.*

Ezer, of the lineage of Judah through Hur, was the father of Hushah and a son of Hazelelponi. (Chart 8m.)

EZER (3). *1 Chr. 7:21.*

Ezer was a descendant of Ephraim through Shuthelah. The men of Gath slew Ezer and Elead "because they came down to take away their cattle." (Chart 15d.)

EZER (4). *1 Chr. 12:9 (1, 8-9)*.

Ezer, of the tribe of Gad, was one of David's mighty men who came to him at Ziklag to protect him against Saul. He was one of those whose "faces were like the faces of lions, and were as swift as the roes upon the mountains." (Chart 13b.)

EZER (5). *Neh. 3:19*.

Ezer, son of Jeshua and ruler of Mizpah, labored next to Bavai when the children of Israel rebuilt the walls and gates of Jerusalem during the time of Ezra and Nehemiah.

EZER (6). *Neh. 12:42*.

Ezer, a priest and singer, joined in the dedication of the walls of Jerusalem with Nehemiah.

EZNITE. *2 Sam. 23:8*.

Eznites were a branch of the Tachmonites. "The Tachmonite that sat in the seat, chief among the captains" was Adino the Eznite, who was one of David's mighty men.

EZRA (1). *1 Chr. 4:17*.

Ezra was the father of Jether, Mered, Epher and Jalon, a daughter who bore Miriam, Shammai and Ishbah, the father of Eshtemoa. (Chart 8 o.)

EZRA (2) (Jehozadak). *1 Chr. 6:14-15; Ezra 7:1-28; 9; 10:1-17; Neh. 8:1-9; 12:1, 13, 26, 33, 36*.

(Ezra) JEHOZADAK, the son of Seraiah, was the many-times-great-grandson of Aaron. He was taken into captivity by Nebuchadnezzar when the Lord delivered Judah and Jerusalem into his hands. *(1 Chr. 6:14-15.)*

Ezra (Jehozadak) was a priest and a scribe among the Israelites. He set out to teach Israel the statutes and judgments. Artaxerxes, king of Persia, made a decree (458 B.C.) giving Ezra permission to teach, to take to Jerusalem any Jewish exiles who cared to go with him, and to take gold and silver, etc., up to Jerusalem to beautify the temple. He was told to set up magistrates and judges and to teach those who know not the laws. Ezra gathered together chief men of Israel who were still in Babylon to go up to Jerusalem with him. *(Ezra 7:1-28.) (Note: Aaron's descendants down through Ezra (Jehozadak) are chronicled. However, in 1 Chr. 6:14, Seraiah's son is given as Jehozadak. In Ezra 7:1, Seraiah's son is listed as Ezra.)*

After Ezra returned to Jerusalem with the children of Israel, the princes told him that many Jews—including the priests and Levites—had intermarried with and were following the abominations of the Canaanites, Hittites, Perizzites, Jebusites, Ammonites, Moabites, Egyptians and Amorites. Ezra prayed and confessed the sins of all the people, fearing the Lord would completely destroy them this time for their abominations. *(Ezra 9.)*

At Shechaniah's suggestion, Ezra had the people covenant to put away the strange wives they had taken from the Canaanites and others. *(Ezra 10:1-17.)*

Ezra read and interpreted the law of Moses to the people. He was assisted by Mattithiah, Shema, Anaiah, Urijah, Hilkiah and Maaseiah on his right hand; and Pedaiah, Mishael, Malchiah, Hashum, Hashbadana, Zechariah and Meshullam on his left hand. Ezra and Nehemiah, the Tirshatha (governor), proclaimed the day to be a holy day. *(Neh. 8:1-9.)*

Ezra was one of the people (priests and Levites) who went to Jerusalem out of Babylon with Zerubbabel. His son Meshullam was one of the priests who was a chief of the fathers in the days of Joiakim. The porters in the days of Ezra, Nehemiah and Joiakim are listed. Ezra and others, along with Hoshaiah and half of the princes of Judah, were appointed by Nehemiah to one of the two great companies of people gathered for the dedication of the walls of Jerusalem. Ezra went before the musicians when they went upon the wall for the dedication. *(Neh. 12:1, 13, 26, 33, 36.)* (Chart 7b.)

EZRAHITE. *1 Kgs. 4:31.*

An **Ezrahite**, Ethan, was recognized as a wise man, but Solomon was wiser than he.

EZRI. *1 Chr. 27:26.*

Ezri, son of Chelub, served David by being over those who tilled the ground.

NAMES THAT BEGIN WITH "F"

FIVE LORDS OF THE PHILISTINES. *Josh. 13:3.*

Five Lords of the Philistines were yet to be conquered: the Gazathites, Ashdothites, Eshkalonites, Gittites and Ekronites, plus the Avites.

FORTY-TWO BRETHREN OF AHAZIAH (2). *2 Kgs. 10:13-14.*

Forty-two Brethren of Ahaziah were slain at the pit of the shearing house along the way to Samaria according to the command of Jehu in compliance with the word of the Lord.

FOUR LEPROUS MEN. *2 Kgs. 7:3-11.*

Four Leprous Men decided that rather than die of famine in Samaria they would go to the camp of the Syrians saying that if they killed them, so be it, but if they didn't kill them they would live. When they got to the camp of the Syrians, they found it abandoned along with food and animals, etc. They went back to Samaria and informed the porters of the city who reported it to the king. Thus, the king's servants went and collected all the goods and returned with them to Samaria, ending the famine that was there. This fulfilled Elisha's prophecy that there would be incredible plenty in Samaria within a day's time.

FOURSCORE MEN (1). *2 Kgs. 10:24-25.*

Fourscore Men were appointed by Jehu not to let any of the worshippers of Baal escape from the house of Baal. Following Jehu's making a burnt offering, the captains and guard were told to slay all who worshipped Baal.

FOURSCORE MEN (2). *Jer. 41:5.*

Fourscore Men from Shechem, Shiloh and Samaria were intercepted by Ishmael who two days earlier had slain Gedaliah, the governor of the people (as well as the Jews, the Chaldeans, and the men of war who were in Mizpah). He began slaying these men as well, sparing ten who said they had treasures in the field of wheat, barley, oil and honey.

NAMES THAT BEGIN WITH "G"

GAAL. *Judg. 9:26-41.*

Gaal was the son of Ebed. He encouraged the men of Shechem to defy Abimelech. He and his followers fought against Abimelech but were defeated. Zebul, Abimelech's officer and ruler of the city, banned Gaal and his brethren from the city.

GABA (Geba). *Ezra 2:26; Neh. 7: 30.*

Gaba (Geba) was of the people of Israel. The men of the children of Gaba and Ramah who returned to Jerusalem from Babylon after Cyrus' proclamation to build the temple numbered 621.

GABBAI. *Neh. 11:8.*

Gabbai, of the tribe of Benjamin, was elected by lot to dwell in Jerusalem following his captivity in Babylon. (Chart 16m.)

GABRIEL. *Dan. 8:16.* See **Noah**.

GAD (1) (Gadites, Gileadites). *Gen. 30:11; 37; 46:16; 49:1, 19; 50:8; Num. 1:14, 24-25; 2:14-16; 26:18; 32; 34:14; Deut. 3:12-16; 27:13; 29:8; 33:20; Josh. 1:12 18; 4.12, 12:1-6; 13: 8-12; 22:1, 6, 26-28; Judg. 5:17; 12:4; 2 Sam. 23:36; 2 Kgs. 10:33; 1 Chr. 5:11-17, 18-22, 26; 12:8, 14, 37; Ezek. 48:27, 31.*

Gad was the first son of Jacob and Zilpah, Leah's handmaid. (He was Jacob's 7th son.) *(Gen. 30:11.)* Gad and his brothers hated their younger brother Joseph and sold him to a group of Ishmeelites, or Midianite merchantmen, for 20 pieces of silver. They dipped his coat of many colors in animal blood and gave it to their father so he would think Joseph had been killed by wild beasts. *(Gen. 37.)*

Gad's sons were Ziphion, Haggi, Shuni, Ezbon, Eri, Arodi and Areli. *(Gen. 46:16.)*

After the brothers had gone to Egypt for grain and were finally reunited with Joseph, and following the move of the entire family to Egypt, the time came when Jacob called his sons together to tell them what would befall each of them in the last days. He told Gad a troop shall overcome him, but that he shall overcome at the last. *(Gen. 49:1, 19.)*

Gad traveled with his brothers to Canaan for his father's burial as Jacob had requested being buried there. *(Gen. 50:8.)*

The Lord instructed Moses to appoint Eliasaph, son of Deuel, to head the tribe of Gad as Israel prepared for war. The males 20 years old and older in the tribe of Gad numbered 45,650 at that time. *(Num. 1:14, 24-25.)* The tribe of Gad was camped next to the tribe of Simeon who was next to the tribe of Reuben on the south side "far off about the tabernacle of the congregation." The tribe of Gad numbered 45,650. All the men in the camp of Reuben numbered 151,450. *(Num. 2:14-16.)*

While on the plains of Moab near Jericho, Moses and Eleazar were instructed to number all the males who were twenty years old and older. Those in the tribe of Gad numbered 40,500. *(Num. 26:18.)*

Gad's posterity and Reuben's posterity asked Moses if they could have the land east of Jordan for their inheritance. Moses told them that they could have it only if they would join the other tribes in conquering Canaan. They covenanted to do so. Part of the land was also given to half of Manasseh's posterity. *(Num. 32.)* The tribe of Gad, the tribe of Reuben and half the tribe of Manasseh received their inheritance on the east side of the Jordan. *(Num. 34:14.)*

Moses reminded Israel that the Lord delivered Og the king of Bashan and his lands into their hands and that his land had been divided between the Gadites, Reubenites and half the tribe of Manasseh. *(Deut. 3:12-16.)*

As the children of Israel crossed over Jordan into Canaan to inherit the promised land, the tribes of Reuben, Gad, Asher, Zebulun, Dan and Naphtali were instructed to stand upon mount Ebal to curse. *(Deut. 27:13.)*

The lands given to the tribes of Gad and Reuben and half of Manasseh were won in battle against Sihon king of Heshbon and Og king of Bashan. The tribes were counseled to keep the covenant they made with God that they might prosper in all their doings. *(Deut. 29:8.)*

Moses blessed the tribe of Gad. *(Deut. 33:20.)*

Joshua counseled the tribes of Gad, Reuben and half of Manasseh to arm themselves and help their brethren win their lands as they had promised Moses. *(Josh. 1:12-18.)* The children of Gad, Reuben and half of Manasseh did as instructed and joined the rest of Israel in battle. *(Josh. 4:12.)*

The lands given to the children of Gad, Reuben and half of Manasseh are described. *(Josh. 12:1-6.)*

The nine and a half tribes were instructed to divided their lands by lot just as the tribes of Gad, Reuben and half of Manasseh had done. *(Josh. 13: 8-12.)*

After the rest of the tribes of Israel had received their inheritances, the tribes of Gad, Reuben, and the half tribe of Manasseh, were dismissed and allowed to return to their own lands on the other side of Jordan. Joshua counseled them to stay close to the Lord and gave them a blessing. They built an altar to be a witness between the two-and-a-half tribes on the east of Jordan and the other tribes on the west side of Jordan and the generations that would follow so that in future times no one could say they had no part in the Lord. *(Josh. 22:1, 6, 26-28.)*

*(Note: The Bible Dictionary indicates that sometimes the children of Gad were known as **Gileadites**.) (Judg. 5:17; 12:4.)*

Gadites were the descendants of Gad, son of Jacob and Zilpah. Bani the Gadite was one of David's mighty men. *(2 Sam. 23:36.)*

In the days of king Jehu, the Lord began to "cut Israel short" and smote all the land of Gilead which included the lands of Gad, Reuben and Manasseh from Jordan eastward. *(2 Kgs. 10:33.)*

Gad's descendants included: Joel, Shapham, Jaanai and Shaphat. They joined the children of Reuben in battle against Jetur, Nephish and Nodab. His sons, combined with the sons of Reuben and half the tribe of Manasseh, numbered 44,760 who were skillful with "buckler and sword" and in the art of war. The Gadites, Reubenites, and half the tribe of Manasseh became wicked and transgressed the laws of God. Thus, God stirred up the Assyrian kings, Pul and Tilgath-pilneser, and they carried them away. Gad's genealogy was reckoned in the days of Jotham, king of Judah, and Jeroboam, king of Israel. *(1 Chr. 5:11-17, 18-22, 26.)*

When David became king and went to Ziklag, all Israel rejoiced and sent armies to support him. The Gadites, Reubenites and the half tribe of Manasseh sent 120,000 men with all their instruments of war. *(1 Chr. 12:8, 14, 37.)*

The Lord revealed to Ezekiel just how the land should be divided by tribes when the children of Israel are gathered in the latter days. Gad's portion is to be by the border of Zebulun, from the east side unto the west side. The twelve gates of the city are to bear the names of the twelve sons of Jacob. One of the three gates on the west side is to be named for Gad. *(Ezek. 48:27, 31.)* (Charts 1.; 3d.; 5a.; 6a.; 7a.; 8a.; 9a.; 10a.; 11a.; 12a.; 13a-b.; 14a.; 15a.; 16a.)

GAD (2). *1 Sam. 22:5; 2 Sam. 24:11-14; 1 Chr. 21.9-13; 29:29; 2 Chr. 29:25.*

Gad, a prophet in Moab, instructed David to leave Moab and flee into the land of Judah. *(1 Sam. 22:5.)*

Gad was sent to David when David angered the Lord by numbering Israel. He presented David with three choices: seven years of famine, fleeing for three months before his enemies, or three days of pestilence. *(2 Sam. 24:11-14.) (Note: 1 Chr. 21:9-13 is a repeat of 2 Sam. 24:11-14, but with some modification: i.e., three years of famine rather than seven.)*

Gad wrote a book chronicling the acts of David. *(1 Chr. 29:29.)*

Gad was king David's seer. Hezekiah, king of Judah, set the Levites in the house of the Lord with their instruments of music according to the earlier commandments of Gad, David and Nathan the prophet. *(2 Chr. 29:25.)*

GADDI. *Num. 13:11 (1-2, 11); Num. 14:37.*

Gaddi, of the tribe of Joseph through Manasseh, was the son of Susi. He was one of twelve leaders sent to scout out the land of Caanan. He returned with a negative report. *(Num. 13:11 [1-2, 11].)* He "died by the plague before the Lord" because of the negative report. *(Num. 14:37.)*

GADDIEL. *Num. 13:10 (1-2, 10); Num. 14:37.*

Gaddiel, of the tribe of Zebulun, was the son of Sodi. He was one of twelve leaders sent to scout out the land of Caanan. He returned with a negative report. *(Num. 13:10 [1-2, 10].)* He "died by the plague before the Lord" because of the negative report. *(Num. 14:37.)*

GADI. *2 Kgs. 15:14.*

Gadi was the father of Menahem, which Menahem slew Shallum and reigned in his stead.

GADITE. *2 Sam. 23:36*. See **Gad (1)**.

GAHAM. *Gen. 22:24*.

Gaham was born to Nahor (Abraham's brother) and Reumah, his concubine. (Chart 2d.)

GAHAR. *Ezra 2:47, 58; Neh. 7:49, 60*.

Gahar was a Nethinim. When the Nethinims and the children of Solomon's servants left Babylon to return to Jerusalem to build the house of the Lord as proclaimed by Cyrus, king of Persia, they numbered 392. *(Ezra 2:47, 58.)*

GALAL. *1 Chr. 9:15-16; Neh. 11:17*.

Galal was the son of Jeduthun and the father of Shemaiah. He was a Levite whose descendants dwelled in the villages of the Netophathites when they returned from Babylonian captivity. His genealogy was written in the book of the kings of Israel and Judah, who were carried away to Babylon for their transgression. *(1 Chr. 9:15-16.)*

Galal was the father of Shammua (Shemaiah). *(Neh. 11:17.)* (Chart 7h.)

GAMALIEL. *Num. 1:10, 34-35; 2:20-21; 7:54*.

Gamaliel, son of Pedahzur, was of the tribe of Manasseh. He was appointed by the Lord to be the one to stand at the head of all of the tribe of Manasseh as Moses organized Israel in preparation for war. The males in the tribe of Manasseh who were 20 years old or older who could go to war numbered 32,200. *(Num. 1:10, 34-35.)* Gamaliel was instructed to have the tribe of Manasseh pitch their tents between the armies of Ephraim and Benjamin on the west side of the encampment. *(Num. 2:20-21.)*

When the altar of the tabernacle was anointed and dedicated, Gamaliel made his offering on the eighth day. *(Num. 7:54.)*

GAMMADIMS. *Ezek. 27:11*.

Gammadims were in the towers of Tyrus, making Tyrus' beauty perfect, prior to her fall.

GAMUL. *1 Chr. 24:17*.

Gamul was from the sons of Aaron. When David made the divisions of the sons of Aaron, there was one principal household for Eleazar and one taken for Ithamar. Eleazar had 16 sons and there were eight sons of Ithamar. These 24 sons who were chief of the fathers were divided by lot. Gamul drew the twenty-second lot.

GAREB. *2 Sam. 23:38; 1 Chr. 11:40*.

Gareb, an Ithrite, was one of David's mighty men *(2 Sam. 23:38.)* and one of the valiant men of his armies (1 Chr. 11:40). (Chart 17.)

GARMITE. See **Keilah**.

GASHMU. See **Geshem**.

GATAM. *Gen. 36:11,16; 1 Chr. 1:36*.

Gatam was a son of Eliphaz, son of Adah and Esau. He was a duke or tribal chief. *(Gen. 36:11,16.) (1 Chr. 1:36.)* (Chart 3b.)

GAZEZ (1). *1 Chr. 2:46.*

Gazez was a son of Caleb and his concubine Ephah. (Chart 8j.)

GAZEZ (2). *1 Chr. 2:46.*

Gazez was the son of Haran who was the son of Caleb and his concubine Ephah. (Chart 8j.)

GAZITES. *Judg. 16:1-3.*

Gazites were citizens of Gaza. Samson visited a harlot in Gaza.

GAZZAM. *Ezra 2:48, 58; Neh. 7:51, 60.*

Gazzam was a Nethinim. When the Nethinims and the children of Solomon's servants left Babylon to return to Jerusalem to build the house of the Lord as proclaimed by Cyrus, king of Persia, they numbered 392.

GEBA. See **Gaba**.

GEBER. *1 Kgs. 4:19.*

Geber, the son of Uri, was one of the 12 officers over Israel who provided victuals for king Solomon and his family one month each year. He was the only officer in the country of Gilead, in the area of king Sihon and the area of king Og.

GEBER, SON OF. *1 Kgs. 4:13.*

The **Son of Geber** was one of 12 officers over Israel who provided victuals for king Solomon and his family one month each year. He was responsible for the towns of Jair (son of Manasseh) and the region of Argob.

GEDALIAH (1). *2 Kgs. 25:22-26; Jer. 39:14; 40:5-16; 41:1-2; 43.*

Gedaliah, son of Ahikam and grandson of Shaphan, was made ruler over the few remaining inhabitants of Jerusalem by Nebuchadnezzar, king of Babylon, when king Zedekiah was captured and taken to Babylon. When Ishmael (son of Nethaniah of the seed royal), Johanan, Seraiah (the son of Tanhumeth) and Jaazaniah came to Gedaliah, Gedaliah told them not to fear being servants of the Chaldees and that it would go well with them if they served the king of Babylon. In the seventh month of his reign, Ishmael and ten men slew Gedaliah and the Jews and the Chaldees who were with him at Mizpah. The rest of the people then fled to Egypt because they feared the Chaldees. *(2 Kgs. 25:22-26.)*

Nebuchadnezzar's captain of the guard, Nebuzar-adan, had the Babylonian princes rescue Jeremiah from the court of the prison and commit him into the care of Gedaliah. They instructed him to carry Jeremiah home. Thus, Jeremiah dwelled among the people. *(Jer. 39:14.)*

Gedaliah was made governor over the cities of Judah and the remnant who were left after Nebuchadnezzar carried the rest off to Babylon. The prophet Jeremiah was released and went to dwell in Judah among the people. The captains of the forces in the fields—Ishmael, Johanan, Jonathan, Seraiah, the sons of Ephai and Jezaniah—came to Gedaliah with their concerns. He counseled them not to fear serving the Chaldeans. Johanan and others warned Gedaliah that Baalis, king of the Ammonites, had sent Ishmael to slay him, but Gedaliah did not believe them. When

Johanan came to him secretly and offered to slay Ishmael so as to protect Gedaliah, Gedaliah said no "for thou speakest falsely of Ishmael." *(Jer. 40:5-16.)*

Gedaliah was slain by Ishmael after he and ten princes of the king ate with Gedaliah in Mizpah. Ishmael then slew the Jews, Chaldeans and men of war who were also in Mizpah. *(Jer. 41:1-2.)*

Because Johanan the son of Kareah and Azariah (Jezaniah) the son of Hoshaiah and all the proud men refused to believe the prophet Jeremiah, Jeremiah and the remnant of Judah and all the people Nebuzar-adan had left with Gedaliah were carried into Egypt. *(Jer. 43.)*

GEDALIAH (2). *1 Chr. 25:3, 9.*

Gedaliah, a Levite and musician, was a son of Jeduthun. The musicians—sons of Jeduthun, Asaph, and Heman—drew lots and were given their duty assignments by David and the captains of the host. Gedaliah cast the second lot. He, his sons and brethren numbered 12. (Chart 7h.)

GEDALIAH (3). *Ezra 10:18-19, 44.*

Gedaliah was one of the sons of the priests who had taken foreign wives and agreed to put them away as instructed by Ezra.

GEDALIAH (4). *Jer. 38:1-6.*

Gedaliah was the son of Pashur. When he, Shephatiah (son of Mattan) and Pashur (son of Malchiah) heard Jeremiah prophesy that if the people did not go forth with the Chaldeans they would die by the sword, famine and pestilence because Jerusalem would surely be taken, they asked Zedekiah if they could slay Jeremiah. The king said he could not prevail against them, so they cast Jeremiah into a miry dungeon in the home of Malchiah the son of the king.

GEDALIAH (5). *Zeph. 1:1.*

Gedaliah, son of Amariah and father of Cushi, was the grandfather of the prophet Zephaniah.

GEDERITE. *1 Chr. 27:28.*

The **Gederite** Baal-hanan served king David by being over the olive trees and the sycomore trees that were in the low plains.

GEDOR (1). *1 Chr. 4:4.*

Gedor, of the lineage of Judah and a descendant of Hur, was the son of Penuel. (Chart 8m.)

GEDOR (2). *1 Chr. 4:18.*

Gedor was a son of Jered and a grandson of Jehudijah. (Chart 8 o.)

GEDOR (3). *1 Chr. 8:31-32; 9:35-37.*

Gedor was of the tribe of Benjamin. He was a son of the father of Gibeon. His brothers were Abdon, Zur, Kish, Baal, Nadab, Ahio, Zacher and Mikloth. *(1 Chr. 8:31-32.)*

Gedor's father's name was Jehiel (Abiel). His mother was Maachah. His brothers are listed again, with the addition of Ner. Zacher's name has been changed to Zechariah. *(1 Chr. 9:35-37.)* (Chart 16k.)

GEHAZI. *2 Kgs. 4:12-37; 5:20-27; 8:4-5.*

Gehazi was Elisha's servant. He informed Elisha that the Shunammite woman had no child. She was blessed with a son according to Elisha's promise. When the son died, Elisha had Gehazi place his staff upon the face of the Shunammite woman's son but he didn't recover. Elisha then went in to see him and restored his life. *(2 Kgs. 4:12-37.)*

When Naaman, the Syrian, was cleansed of leprosy by Elisha, he offered Elisha a reward. Elisha refused to accept it. However, Gehazi followed after Naaman and falsely claimed that Elisha had changed his mind and was now requesting some silver and two changes of garments for two young men who were sons of the prophets. When Elisha learned what Gehazi had done, he told him that the leprosy which Naaman had had would now cleave unto him and unto his seed forever. Gehazi "went out from his presence a leper as white as snow." *(2 Kgs. 5:20-27.)*

At the end of a seven year famine which Elisha had prophesied would occur, the king inquired of Gehazi about all the great things that Elisha had done. Gehazi told him about Elisha's restoring a young man to life. As a result, the Shunammite woman, after being out of the country during the seven years of famine, had her lands and fruit restored to her. *(2 Kgs. 8:4-5.)*

GEMALLI. *Num. 13:12.*

Gemalli, of the tribe of Dan, was the father of Ammiel.

GEMARIAH (1). *Jer. 29:3-10.*

Gemariah was the son of Hilkiah. After Jeconiah and the queen and their household left Jerusalem, Jeremiah the prophet sent a letter by the hand of Gemariah and by the hand of Elasah, son of Shaphan, unto the residue of the elders who were carried away captive, and to the priests, etc., informing them that the Lord said they would remain captive for 70 years and to find peace there. After 70 years He would perform good works for them.

GEMARIAH (2). *Jer. 36:10-25.*

Gemariah was the son of Shaphan the scribe and the father of Michaiah. In the fourth year of Jehoiakim, Baruch read the words of Jeremiah in the house of the Lord in Gemariah's chambers. Gemariah and the other princes were sitting in the scribe's chambers when Michaiah told them the words Baruch had read. When the king went to burn the roll, Gemariah, Elnathan and Delaiah tried to intervene, but the king would not listen to them.

GENTILES. *Gen. 10:2-5; Jer. 46:1, 13-14; Micah 5; Mal. 1:7-11.*

The isles of the **Gentiles** were divided by the sons of Japheth (Noah's son), each after their family and after their tongue. *(Gen. 10:2-5.) (The Bible Dictionary states, "The word gentiles means the nations, and eventually came to be used to mean all those not of the house of Israel.")*

Jeremiah prophesied against the Gentiles and said that Pharaoh-necho king of Eygpt and his armies would be conquered by Nebuchadrezzar of Babylon. *(Jer. 46:1, 13-14.)*

Micah prohesied that the remnant of Jacob which has been scattered among all the nations shall rise with power in the latter days and triumph gloriously over the Gentiles. *(Micah 5.)*

Malachi chastised the children of Israel for offering polluted bread upon the altars and for offering blemished animals for sacrifices. In contrast, he said the Gentiles would revere the name of the Lord and would offer pure offerings. *(Mal. 1:7-11.)*

GENUBATH. *1 Kgs. 11:20.*

Genubath was the son of Hadad. His mother was the sister of Tahpenes, queen of Egypt. He was weaned and raised in Pharaoh's household among Pharaoh's sons.

GERA (1) (Also see **Ahiram**.) *Gen. 46:21; Num. 26:38.*

Gera was a son of Benjamin and a grandson of Jacob. His brothers were Belah (Bela), Becher, Ashbel, Naaman, Ehi, Rosh, Muppim (Shupham), Huppim and Ard. *(Gen. 46:21.)*

*(Note: Gera is not listed among Benjamin's family in Num. 26:38-41. Rather, the name **Ahiram** is given following Ashbel's name. Considering the placement of this name, it is possible that Gera and Ahiram are one and the same.)* (Charts 16a, e.)

GERA (2). *Judg. 3:15; 1 Chr. 8:3, 7.*

Gera, father of Ehud whom the Lord raised up to deliver Israel, was of the tribe of Benjamin. *(Judg. 3:15.)*

Gera was a son of Bela who was a son of Benjamin. Other sons of Bela were Addar, Abihud, Abishua, Naaman, Ahoah, Gera, Shephuphan and Huram. *(1 Chr. 8:3, 7.) (Note: This listing differs from that in 1 Chr. 7:7.)* Naaman, Ahiah (Ahoah) and Gera were "removed" and Ehud begat Uzza and Ahihud. (Charts 16d-e.)

GERA (3). *2 Sam. 16:5.*

Gera was a Benjamite of the house of Saul. He was the father of Shimei who cursed David and cast stones at him. (Chart 16 l.)

GERA (4). *1 Chr. 8:5.*

Gera was a son of Bela who was a son of Benjamin. Other sons of Bela were Addar, Gera, Abihud, Abishua, Naaman, Ahoah, Shephuphan and Huram. *(Note: This listing differs from that in 1 Chr. 7:7.)* Naaman, Ahiah (Ahoah) and Gera were "removed" and Ehud begat Uzza and Ahihud. *(Based on the order of names listed and the order of names of those who were "removed," it would appear the Gera referred to is the second one listed among Bela's sons [v. 5].)* (Chart 16d.)

GERSHOM (1). *Ex. 2:22; 18:3-6; Judg. 18:30; 1 Chr. 23:15-16.*

Gershom was Zipporah and Moses' son, born in Midian while Moses was living as a shepherd. *(Ex. 2:22.)* Gershom's grandfather Jethro took him and his mother, Zipporah, and his brother, Eliezer, back to Moses after Moses and the children of Israel were encamped in the wilderness. *(Ex. 18:3-6.)*

Gershom, father of Jonathan, was a son of Manasseh. *(Judg. 18:30.) (Note: The footnote to the text indicates that this actually refers to Moses, but had been altered to Manasseh.)*

When David numbered the Levites at the time he made Solomon king, he divided them into courses among the sons of Levi: Gershon, Kohath and Merari. Moses, son of Amram who was a son of Kohath, and his sons (Gershom and Eliezer) were named of the tribe of Levi. Gershom's son Shebuel was the chief of his course. *(1 Chr. 23:15-16.)* (Chart 7b.)

GERSHOM (2). *1 Chr. 6:17.* See **Gershon**.

GERSHOM (3). *Ezra 8:2.*

Gershom, of the sons of Phinehas, was the chief of his fathers and went with Ezra up from Babylon to Jerusalem during the reign of Artaxerxes.

GERSHON (Gershom (2), Gershonites). *Gen. 46:11; Ex. 6:17; Num. 3:18, 21-26; 1 Chr. 6:17, 20-21, 39-43; 23:6-11.*

Gershon was a son of Levi and a grandson of Jacob. His brothers were Kohath and Merari. *(Gen. 46:11.)* His sons were Libni and Shimi. *(Ex. 6:17.)*

Gerson's sons were Libni and Shimei (Shimi). His descendants were called **Gershonites**. When Moses numbered all the males of the Gershonites who were one month and upward, there were 7500. They were to pitch behind the tabernacle westward. Eliasaph, son of Lael, was chosen to be the leader of the Gershonites. Their assignment for the tabernacle was, among other things, the tabernacle, which included the tent, the covering thereof, and the hanging for the door of the tabernacle of the congregations. *(Num. 3:18, 21-26.)*

Gershom's (Gershon) posterity is enumerated with some modification; i.e., verses 42-43 state that Gershom's son was Jahath and that Jahath's son was Shimei. *(1 Chr. 6:17, 20-21, 39-43.)*

When David made Solomon king, he numbered the Levites and divided them into courses among the sons of Levi: Gershon, Kohath and Merari. Among the Gershonites were Laadan and Shimei. Of the sons of Laadan, Jehiel was the chief, but there was also Zetham and Joel. Three were named among the sons of Shimei: Shelomith, Haziel and Haran. *(1 Chr. 23:6-11.)* (Charts 7a-b, d-f.)

GESHAN. *1 Chr. 2:47.*

Geshan was a son of Jahdai. (Chart 8j.)

GESHEM (Gashmu). *Neh. 2:19; 6:1-6.*

Geshem was an Arabian. He, Sanballat the Horonite, and Tobiah the Ammonite, a servant, scorned and laughed at Nehemiah for planning to rebuild the walls and gates of Jerusalem. *(Neh. 2:19.)* **Gashmu** (Geshem), Sanballat and Tobiah plotted ways to get Nehemiah to come meet with them that they might destroy him and stop the work on the walls of the city. Nehemiah refused to meet with them in spite of repeated letters of request. *(Neh. 6:1-6.)*

GESHURITES. *Josh. 12:5.*

Geshurites bordered the land ruled by Og, king of Bashan, on the east of Jordan.

GETHER. *Gen. 10:23; 1 Chr. 1:17.*

Gether was a son of Aram, a grandson of Shem and a great-grandson of Noah. His brothers were Uz, Hul and Mash (Meshech). *(Gen. 10:23.)* Gether and his brothers are listed as the sons of Shem. *(1 Chr. 1:17.)* (Chart 2b.)

GEUEL. *Num. 13:15 (1-2, 15, 32).*

Geuel, of the tribe of Gad, was the son of Machi. He was one of twelve leaders sent to scout out the land of Caanan. He returned with a negative report. *(Num. 13:15 [1-2, 15, 32].)* Geuel died by the plague before the Lord because of the negative report he gave. *(Num. 14:37.)* (Chart 13b.)

GIBBAR (Gibeon). *Ezra 2:20; Neh. 7:25.*

Gibbar (Gibeon) was of the people of Israel. The men of the children of Gibbar who returned to Jerusalem from Babylon after Cyrus' proclamation to build the temple numbered 95.

GIBEA. *1 Chr. 2:49.*

Gibea was the son of Sheva and the brother of Machbenah. His grandparents were Caleb and Caleb's concubine Maachah. (Chart 8k.)

GIBEON. See **Gibbar**.

GIBEON, FATHER OF (Jehiel (1), See **Abiel (1))**

GIBEONITES (Hivites). *Josh. 9:Intro.-27; 2 Sam. 2:12-17; 20:8-9; 21:1-14; 1 Kgs. 3:4-15; 1 Chr. 8:29; 9:35; 16:39; 2 Chr. 1:3; Neh. 3:7.*

Gibeonites were **Hivites** who, fearing they would be destroyed, obtained a treaty with the Israelites through trickery and were then allowed to remain with the Israelites as servants; i.e., as hewers of wood and drawers of water for the congregation. *(Josh. 9:Intro.-27.)*

The battle between 12 servants of Abner who represented Saul and 12 servants of David under the direction of Joab took place at Gibeon. *(2 Sam. 2:12-17.)*

Joab slew Amasa with his sword at the great stone in Gibeon. *(2 Sam. 20:8-9.)*

The Gibeonites were a remnant of the Amorites. Because Saul smote the Gibeonites, contrary to the oath of Israel, the Lord sent a famine that lasted three years. When David inquired of the Gibeonites what he could do to rectify what Saul had done to them, they asked that they be given seven of Saul's sons whom they could hang. This was done. "And after that God was intreated for the land." *(2 Sam. 21:1-14.)*

Solomon offered sacrifice at Gibeon and the Lord appeared to him in a dream and promised him wisdom. *(1 Kgs. 3:4-15.)*

Gibeon may be both a person and a place as reference is made to "the father of Gibeon." However, no one by the name of Gibeon is listed among his sons. *(1 Chr. 8:29.) (Note: 1 Chr. 9:35 is also unclear as to whether or not Gibeon is both a person and a place since no one by the name of Gibeon is listed among the sons of Jehiel, who is referred to as the father of Gibeon.)*

Zadok and others ministered before the Lord "in the high place that was at Gibeon." *(1 Chr. 16:39.)*

The tabernacle of the congregation of God which Moses had made in the wilderness was in the high place at Gibeon. *(2 Chr. 1:3.)*

Melatiah, a Gibeonite, and the men from Gibeon, along with Jadon the Meronothithe and the men of Mizpah, worked next to Jehoiada and Meshullam when the children of Israel rebuilt the walls and gates of Jerusalem during the time of Ezra and Nehemiah. *(Neh. 3:7.)*

GIBLITES. *Josh. 13:1, 5.*

The **Giblites** were yet to be conquered by the Israelites as Joshua grew old.

GIDDALTI. *1 Chr. 25:4, 29.*

Giddalti, a Levite and musician, was a son of Heman who was of the lineage of Kohath. The musicians—sons of Heman, Asaph and Jeduthun—drew lots and were given their duty assignments by David and the captains of the host. Giddalti cast the 22nd lot. He, his sons and his brethren numbered 12. (Chart 7d.)

GIDDEL (1). *Ezra 2:47, 58; Neh. 7:49, 60.*

Giddel was a Nethinim. When the Nethinims and the children of Solomon's servants left Babylon to return to Jerusalem to build the house of the Lord as proclaimed by Cyrus, king of Persia, they numbered 392.

GIDDEL (2). *Ezra 2:56, 58; Neh. 7:58, 60.*

Giddel was one of Solomon's servants. The children of Solomon's servants and all the Nethinims numbered 392 when they returned to Jerusalem from out of captivity.

GIDEON (Jerubbaal, Jerubbesheth). *Judg. 6:11-40; 7; 8; 9:1; 1 Sam. 12:11; 2 Sam. 11:21.*

Gideon, the son of Joash, was called by an angel to deliver Israel. He questioned how he could do it when his family were "poor in Manasseh." He was instructed by the angel to throw down the altar of Baal that his father had, to cut down the grove that was by it, and to build an altar unto the Lord and offer a burnt offering. He did it by night, fearing the men of the city. When the men discovered what Gideon had done, they wanted to slay him. The spirit of the Lord rested upon Gideon. Using a fleece of wool, Gideon asked for a sign to verify that the Lord had really called him to deliver Israel. First, the fleece was wet with dew and the surrounding ground was dry. Then, the fleece was dry while the ground was wet. Thus, he knew the Lord had, indeed, called him to deliver Israel. He was called **Jerubbaal** because he threw down the altar of Baal. *(Judg. 6:11-40.)*

The Lord had Gideon deliver Israel with a small army of 300 men so the children of Israel wouldn't think they had delivered themselves through their own power. A man, apparently belonging to the Midianites or the Amalekites, was overheard by Gideon relating a dream to another fellow who interpreted the dream: God would deliver the host of Midian into Gideon's hand. Using trumpets and lights, Gideon's small army frightened the Midianite armies who fought among themselves, fled, and ultimately got defeated. *(Judg. 7.)*

The men (princes) of Succoth and the men of Penuel refused Gideon's request for loaves of bread for his faint army. Gideon promised them retribution. After Gideon "discomfited" Zebah and Zalmunna, kings of Midian, he returned and with "thorns of the wilderness and briers, . . . he taught the men of Succoth. And he beat down the town of Penuel, and slew all the men of the city." Gideon slew Zebah and Zalmunna, kings of Midian. Gideon declined Israel's request to be a king over them. He also declined having any of his sons become king over them. He said the Lord would rule over them. The people had peace for 40 years. Gideon had seventy sons by his many wives plus another son, Abimelech, by his concubine. Gideon died and was buried in the sepulchre of Joash, his father. The children of Israel forgot all the kindness Jerubbaal (Gideon) had shown them, and they showed none unto his family. *(Judg. 8.)*

Jerubbaal (Gideon) was the father of Abimelech. *(Judg. 9:1.)*

The prophet Samuel reminded the people that the Lord had sent Jerubbaal and other prophets to deliver them from their enemies and they didn't even appreciate it. Instead, they pleaded for a king to reign over them. *(1 Sam. 12:11.)*

Jerubbesheth's (Gideon's) son Abimelech was slain when a woman cast a piece of millstone down upon him from a wall. *(2 Sam. 11:21.)* (Chart 20.)

GIDEONI. *Num 1:11.*

Gideoni was the father of Abidan. They were of the tribe of Benjamin.

GIDEON'S CONCUBINE. *Judg. 8:31.*

Gideon's Concubine, who was in Schechem, bore Abimelech.

GILALAI. *Neh. 12:36.*

Gilalai joined Zechariah, a descendant of Asaph, and other of his brethren with their musical instruments in the dedication of the wall of Jerusalem.

GILEAD (1) (Gileadites, Peresh). *Num. 26:29-32; Judg. 5:17; 12:4; 2 Kgs. 15:25; 1 Chr. 7:14-18.*

Gilead was the son of Machir and a grandson of Manasseh. He begat Jeezer, Helek, Asriel, Shechem, Shemida and Hepher. His descendants are the **Gileadites**. *(Num. 26:29-32.)*

Gilead (i.e., the Gileadites) abode beyond Jordan. *(Judg. 5:17.) (Note: The Bible Dictionary indicates that sometimes the children of Gad were known as Gileadites.)*

The Gileadites were gathered together by Jephthah and fought against Ephraim. *(Judg. 12:4.)*

Fifty men of the Gileadites, along with Argob and Arieh, assisted Pekah in his coup d`e'tat over Pekahiah, king of Israel. *(2 Kgs. 15:25.)*

Manasseh's concubine, the Aramitess, bare Machir. Machir was the father of Gilead. Machir's wife Maachah begat two sons, **Peresh** and Sheresh. Peresh's posterity is given with the statement that "these were the sons of Gilead. Gideon's sister was Hammoleketh. *(1 Chr. 7:14-18.) (Note: If all the pronouns "his" in verse 16 refer to Peresh, it would appear Peresh and Gilead are one and the same. However, if the last "his" in the verse refers to Sheresh, then it would appear that*

Sheresh and Gilead would be one and the same. The assumption here is that all the "his" pronouns refer to Peresh.) (Charts 15a-b.)

GILEAD (2). *Judg. 11:1-2.*

Gilead was the father of Jephthah via a harlot. His wife, however, bore him other sons, who cast Jephthah out.

GILEAD (3). *1 Chr. 5:14.*

Gilead, the father of Jaroah and the son of Michael, was a descendant of Gad. (Chart 13b.)

GILEADITES. See **Gilead (1)**.

GILEAD'S (2) WIFE. *Judg. 11:2.*

Gilead's (2) Wife bore him sons who rejected their half-brother, Jephthah, son of a harlot.

GILONITES. *2 Sam. 15:12; 2 Sam. 23: 34.*

Gilonites were the citizens of Giloh. Ahithophel, David's counselor who followed Absalom in his conspiracy against David, was a Gilonite. *(2 Sam. 15:12.)*

Eliam, son of Ahithophel the Gilonite, was one of David's mighty men. *(2 Sam. 23: 34.)* (Chart 17.)

GINATH. *1 Kgs. 16:21.*

Ginath was the father of Tibni, which Tibni was made king over half the people of Israel.

GINNETHON (Ginnetho). *Neh. 10:6 (1, 6, 28-31); 12:4, 16.*

Ginnethon was among the priests who covenanted and sealed their covenant to marry in Israel, honor the Sabbath, pay tithes and keep the commandments. *(Neh. 10:6 [1, 6, 28-31].)*

Ginnetho (Ginnethon) was one of the men (priests and Levites) who accompanied Zerubbabel from Babylon to Jerusalem. His son Meshullam was one of the priests who was a chief of the fathers in the days of Joiakim. *(Neh. 12:4, 16.)*

GIRGASITES (Girgashites). *Gen. 10:16; 15:18-21; Deut. 7:1; Josh. 3:10; Neh. 9:8.*

Girgasites were descendants of Canaan who was a son of Ham. *(Gen. 10:16.)* The **Girgashites'** lands were given to Abram's seed in a covenant with the Lord. *(Gen. 15:18-21.)* They comprised one of seven nations in Canaan greater and mightier than the Israelites that the Lord promised to destroy so Israel could inherit the promised land. *(Deut. 7:1.)*

Joshua assured the Israelites that the Lord would drive the Girgashites and others out from before them. *(Josh. 3:10.)*

The Lord gave the land of the Girgashites, Canaanites, Hittites, Amorites, Perizzites and Jebusites to Abraham. *(Neh. 9:8.)* (Chart 2e.)

GISPA. *Neh. 11:21.*

Gispa was a Nethinim. When the children of Israel returned from Babylonian captivity, the Nethinims dwelled in Ophel. Gispa and Ziha were their overseers.

GITTITES. *2 Sam. 15:18; 21:19.*

The **Gittites**, along with the Cherethites and Pelethites, went with David and his household when they fled from Jerusalem to escape from Absalom. *(2 Sam. 15:18.)*

The brother of Goliath the Gittite was slain by Elhanan the son of Jaare-oregim, a Beth-lehemite. *(2 Sam. 21:19.)*

GOG (1). *1 Chr. 5:4.*

Gog, of the tribe of Reuben, was the son of Shemaiah and the father of Shimei. (Chart 5b.)

GOG (2). *Ezek. 38:2-20; 39:1-12.*

Gog is the king of Magog. The Lord told Ezekiel to set his face against "Gog, the land of Magog, the chief prince of Meshech and Tubal, and prophesy against him." Ezekiel prophesied of the invasion of Israel from the north by Gog in the latter-days and that Gog would be defeated. This battle will usher in the Second Coming of the Savior. The Lord will come during a time of pestilence and bloodshed. All men upon the face of the earth will shake at his presence. *(Ezek. 38:2-20.) (Note: The footnote cross-references Gog with Magog, the son of Japheth and grandson of Noah.)*

Gog was the chief prince of Mesheck and Tubal. Ezekiel prophesied against Gog. In the latter days, the Lord will send a fire on Magog. Ezekiel told Gog that the Lord would leave but "the sixth part of thee." Israel shall burn the weapons of war with fire for seven years. Gog and his followers shall be buried in Israel in a place called The Valley of Hamon-gog. It will take Israel seven months to bury them all. Jehovah will be recognized as King. *(Ezek. 39:1-12.) (Note: Rev. 20:7-9 records John's prophecy of another battle which will occur at the end of the thousand years during which Satan will be bound.)*

GOLIATH. *1 Sam. 17:4-54; 2 Sam. 21:16-22.*

Goliath, a giant, was a Philistine from Gath. He single-handedly challenged the hosts of Israel and said if anyone could kill him, the Philistines would be their servants. However, he taunted, if he killed the Israelite challenger, Israel would have to become the servants of the Philistines. David accepted the challenge and slew him with a sling and a stone. Then David cut off his head and took it to Jerusalem. *(1 Sam. 17:4-54.)*

Goliath had four sons (or three sons and a brother) who were slain in various battles between Israel and the Philistines: Ishbi-benob was slain by Abishai; Saph, of the sons of the giant, was slain by Sibbechai; the brother of Goliath the Gittite was slain by Elhanan; and "a man of great stature" who had six fingers on each hand and six toes on each foot, who "was born to the giant," was slain by Jonathan, David's nephew. *(2 Sam. 21:16-22.) (Note: Verse 22 says the four named were "born to the giant in Gath." However, one of the four named is called the brother of Goliath the Gittite in verse 19. The Bible Dictionary states that the reference in 2 Sam. 16-22 is probably to a different Goliath, or that some error may have crept into the text.)*

GOLIATH'S BROTHER (Lahmi). *2 Sam. 21:19; 1 Chr. 20:5.*

Goliath's Brother was slain in a battle in Gob by Elhanan, the son of Jaare-oregim (Jair), a Beth-lehemite. *(2 Sam. 21:19.) (Note: In the Bible Dictionary under Goliath, it states that the Goliath mentioned in this scripture is probably a different Goliath than the one David slew or that perhaps some error may have crept into the text.)* Goliath's brother is identified as **Lahmi**. *(1 Chr. 20:5.)*

GOMER (1). *Gen. 10:2; 1 Chr. 1:6; Ezek. 38.*

Gomer was a son of Japheth and a grandson of Noah. *(Gen. 10:2.)* He begat Ashchenaz, Riphath, Togarmah. *(1 Chr. 1:6.)*

In the latter days, the battle of Gog and Magog against Israel will usher in the Second Coming of the Lord. Gomer and Togarmar will be gathered together with Gog. *(Ezek. 38.)* (Chart 2a.)

GOMER (2). *Hosea 1:3.*

Gomer was the wife of Hosea and the daughter of Diblaim. She was an idolatrous woman. Hosea's family was to be a sign unto Israel. Gomer's first son was Jezreel, meaning, "for yet a little while;" her daughter was Lo-ruhamah, which means, "not having obtained mercy;" and her second son was Lo-ammi, which means, "not my people."

GREAT SHUNAMMITE WOMAN, A. *2 Kgs. 4:8-37; 8:1-6.*

A Great Shunammite Woman provided a chamber and meals for Elisha and his servant when they passed through Shunem. In return, Elisha promised her that she would have a son. When "the child was grown" he became ill and died. The woman went to Elisha and had him return with her. Elisha restored the child to life. *(2 Kgs. 4:8-37.)*

The Shunammite woman was counseled by Elisha to find another place for her and her household to live because there was going to be a seven-year famine. She and her family sojourned in the land of the Philistines for those seven years. At the end of that time, she returned to her own land and petitioned the king for her house and for her land. The king inquired of Gehazi, Elisha's servant, about the things Elisha had done. As Gehazi was telling him about Elisha's restoring a young man's life, the Shunammite woman and her son came to the king. When the king learned that this was the person of whom Gehazi was speaking, he ordered one of his officers to restore all that was hers to her, including all the fruits of the field since the day she left her land. *(2 Kgs. 8:1-6.)*

GREAT SHUNAMMITE WOMAN, HUSBAND OF A. *2 Kgs. 4:14-23.*

The **Husband of a Great Shunammite Woman** was old. He and his wife had no children so Elisha, in return for the wife's kindness to him, promised her a son. When the son was grown he went out into the field with his father to the reapers. He became ill. The father took him to his mother, where he died. When the mother wanted to go see Elisha, her husband asked why since it was neither the new moon nor the Sabbath.

GREAT SHUNAMMITE WOMAN, SON BORN TO A. *2 Kgs. 4:17-37.*

The <u>Son Born to a Great Shunammite Woman</u> as promised by the prophet Elisha, became ill when he was grown and died. His life was restored to him by Elisha.

GUNI (1) (Gunites). *Gen. 46:24-25; Num. 26:48; 1 Chr. 7:13.*

<u>Guni</u> was a son of Naphtali and a grandson of Jacob. His brothers were Jahzeel, Jezer and Shillem. *(Gen. 46:24-25.)* His descendants were called **Gunites**. *(Num. 26:48.)* His brothers were Jahziel (Jahzeel), Jezer and Shallum (Shillem). *(1 Chr. 7:13.)* (Chart 12a.)

GUNI (2). *1 Chr. 5:15.*

<u>Guni</u>, the father of Abdiel, was a descendant of Gad. (Chart 13b.)

NAMES THAT BEGIN WITH "H"

HAAHASHTARI. *1 Chr. 4:6.*

Haahashtari was the son of Naarah and Ashur the father of Tekoa. His brothers were Ahuzam, Hepher and Temeni. He also had half-brothers who were the sons of Ashur and Helah. (Chart 8d.)

HABAIAH, THE CHILDREN OF. *Ezra 2:1, 61-62; Neh. 7:6, 63-64.*

Habaiah was one of the priests whose children returned to Jerusalem with Zerubbabel but could not find their names among those who were listed by their genealogy and, therefore, were "as polluted" and were excluded from the priesthood.

HABAKKUK. *Hab. 1:13; 2:2, 4, 19; 3:19.*

Habakkuk *(probably prophesied around 600 B.C.)* questioned the Lord as to why He blessed the wicked Chaldeans with success in conquering Israel when Israel, in spite of her wickedness, was still more righteous than the Chaldeans. *(Hab. 1:13)*

The Lord instructed Habakkuk to make a plain record of what the Lord revealed to him and preserve it for those who would read it. He was to have patience. The Lord reminded him that the just shall live by his faith. Idols are dumb and have no power, no breath. *(Hab. 2:2, 4, 19.)*

Habakkuk praised the Lord in prayer. God is his strength. *(Hab. 3:19.)*

HABAZINIAH. *Jer. 35:3-19.*

Habaziniah, the father of Jeremiah who was the father of Jaazaniah, was a Rechabite. The Rechabites kept the word of their fathers and lived in tents and drank no wine. Thus, the Lord blessed them and said, "Jonadab the son of Rechab shall not want a man to stand before me for ever."

HACHALIAH. *Neh. 1:1; 10:1.*

Hachaliah was the father of Nehemiah.

HACHMONI. *1 Chr. 27:32.*

Hachmoni was the father of Jehiel who was with king David's sons.

HADAD (1). *1 Chr. 1:30.* See **Hadar (1)**.

HADAD (2). *Gen. 36:35; 1 Chr. 1:46-47.*

Hadad, son of Bedad, smote Midian in the field of Moab. He reigned as king in Edom upon the death of Husham. *(Gen. 36:35; 1 Chr. 1:46.)* Upon Hadad's death, Samlah of Masrekah reigned in his stead. *(1 Chr. 1:47.)* (Chart 18.)

HADAD (3). *1 Chr. 1:50.* See **Hadar (2)**.

HADAD (4). *1 Kgs. 11:14-22.*

Hadad was an Edomite and was of the king's seed in Edom. When David was in Edom and Joab the captain of the host had gone up to bury the slain in Edom, Hadad, who was still just a little child, had fled along with certain of his father's servants into Egypt. Pharaoh king of Egypt had given him a house, land and victuals, etc. Hadad found great favor in the sight of Pharaoh and Pharaoh gave him his wife's sister for a wife. The sister of Tahpenes the queen bore him a son whom they called Genubath. When Hadad heard that David and Joab were both dead, he asked Pharaoh to let him return unto his own country. Because of Solomon's worshipping of idols, Hadad was one of the men the Lord stirred up against him.

HADAD (5). See **Rimmon (1).**

(Note: According to the BD, Hadad was the name of the sun god or storm god of Syria and Edom. It is not found in the Old Testament standing alone as the name of a pagan god, but Hadad is used alone and in compound with other names as the names of various people.)

HADAD (4), WIFE of. *1 Kgs. 11:19.*

<u>Hadad's (4) Wife</u> was the sister of Tahpenes, queen of Egypt, and was given to Hadad by Pharaoh. She begat Genubath.

HADADEZER (Hadarezer). *2 Sam. 8:3-5; 10:6-16; 1 Kgs. 11:23; 1 Chr. 18:3-10; 19:16.*

<u>Hadadezer</u>, son of Rehob, was king of Zobah. David smote him at the river Euphrates and took 1000 chariots, 700 horsemen and 20,000 footmen from him. When the Syrians came to succor Hadadezer, David slew 22,000 of the Syrian men. *(2 Sam. 8:3-5.) (Note: 1 Chr. 18:3-10 is a repeat of 2 Sam. 8:3-5. However, This account says David took 7,000 horsemen rather than 700.)* David took the gold shields that were on Hadarezer's servants and took them to Jerusalem. Tou, king of Hamath, sent his son Hadoram to congratulate David on his victory over Hadarezer. *(1 Chr. 18:3-10.)*

Hadarezer (Hadadezer) joined the Syrians to fight against David and the Israelites. The captain of his host was Shobach. *(2 Sam. 10:6-16.)*

When Solomon began worshipping idols, the Lord stirred up Rezon the son of Eliadah, which fled from Hadadezer, to go against Solomon. *(1 Kgs. 11:23.)*

Shophach (Shobach), captain of Hadarezer's host, was slain by David when the Syrians fled before Israel. *(1 Chr. 19:16.)*

HADAR (1) (Hadad (1)). *Gen. 25:15; 1 Chr. 1:30.*

<u>Hadar</u> (Hadad) was a son of Ishmael and a grandson of Abraham and Hagar, Sarah's handmaid. *(Gen. 25:15; 1 Chr. 1:30.)* (Chart 3e.)

HADAR (2) (Hadad (3)). *Gen. 36:39-43; 1 Chr. 1:50-54.*

<u>Hadar</u> (Hadad), of the city of Pau (Pai), reigned as king in Edom upon the death of Baal-hanan. His wife was Mehetabel, the daughter of Matred, the daughter of Mezahab. The names of the dukes that came of Esau are listed. *(Gen. 36:39-43; 1 Chr. 1:50-54.)* (Chart 18.)

HADAREZER. See **Hadadezer.**

HADASSAH. See **Esther.**

HADID. *Ezra 2:33; Neh. 7:37.*

Hadid was of the people of Israel. The men of the children of Hadid, Lod and Ono who returned to Jerusalem from Babylon after Cyrus' proclamation to build the temple numbered 725 (721).

HADLAI. *2 Chr. 28:12.*

Hadlai was the father of Amasa who was one of the leaders of the children of Ephraim when Ahaz was king of Judah and the children of Israel carried many of Judah off captive.

HADORAM (1). *Gen. 10:27.*

Hadoram was a son of Joktan, a third-great-grandson of Shem and a fourth-great-grandson of Noah. (Chart 2b.)

HADORAM (2). *2 Chr. 10:18.* See **Adoram**.

HADORAM (3). *1 Chr. 18:10.* See **Joram (1)**.

HAGAB. *Ezra 2:46, 58.*

Hagab was a Nethinim. When the Nethinims and the children of Solomon's servants left Babylon to return to Jerusalem to build the house of the Lord as proclaimed by Cyrus, king of Persia, they numbered 392.

HAGABAH (Hagaba). *Ezra 2:45, 58; Neh. 7:48, 60.*

Hagabah (Hagaba) was a Nethinim. When the Nethinims and the children of Solomon's servants left Babylon to return to Jerusalem to build the house of the Lord as proclaimed by Cyrus, king of Persia, they numbered 392.

HAGAR. *Gen. 16:1-16; 21:9-21; 25:12-15.*

Hagar was Sarai's Egyptian handmaid. Because Sarai was barren she told Abram to go in unto Hagar that she might obtain children by her. Abram did so and Hagar conceived. Sarai was then despised in Hagar's eyes. Sarai lamented to Abram who told her to do with Hagar as she pleased. When Sarai dealt harshly with Hagar, Hagar fled. An angel found her by a fountain of water in the wilderness and told her to return to her mistress and to submit herself to her. She was also told that the Lord would multiply her seed exceedingly. She was told that she would have a son and she should call him Ishmael. *(Gen. 16:1-16.)*

Hagar and Ishmael were cast out because Ishmael mocked Sarah. Though grieved, Abraham complied with Sarah's wish that they be made to leave. God comforted Abraham and told him it would be alright. Abraham gave Hagar and Ishmael a bottle of water and some bread and sent them away. When the water was gone, Hagar put Ishmael under a bush and sat a little way off so as not to watch him die. An angel came and told her not to despair, that the Lord would make a great nation of him. God showed her a well of water. Hagar got Ishmael a wife from Egypt. *(Gen. 21:9-21.)*

The generations of Hagar's son Ishmael are recorded. *(Gen. 25:12-15.)* (Charts 3a, d-e.)

HAGARITES (Hagerites). *1 Chr. 5:10, 19-22; 27:31.*

The **Hagarites** fell by the hand of Reuben's descendants in the days of king Saul. The Reubenites, Gadites and the half tribe of Manasseh went to war against the Hagarites, Jetur, Nephish and Nodab and defeated them. *(1 Chr. 5:10, 19-22.)*

Jaziz, the **Hagerite** (Hagarite), was the officer assigned by David to be over the flocks. *(1 Chr. 27:31.)*

HAGGAI. *Ezra 5:1-3, 13; 6:2, 8, 11, 14-15; Hag. 1; 2.*

Haggai, a contemporary of Zechariah, was a prophet in Israel during the time the children of Israel were trying to rebuild the temple. With the help of the prophets, Zerubbabel and Jeshua again began the work. When confronted by Tatnai (the governor on the west side of the Euphrates River) and his group and queried as to who commanded that the temple be built, they indicated that Cyrus had made such a decree. *(Ezra 5:1-3, 13.)*

Darius discovered that Cyrus had made a decree; and he renewed the decree. "And the elders of the Jews builded, and they prospered through the prophesying of Haggai the prophet and Zechariah the son of Iddo." They finished the temple in the sixth year of king Darius. *(Ezra 6:2, 8, 11, 14-15.)*

Haggai was a prophet during the time Darius was king, Zerubbabel the son of Shealtiel was governor of Judah, and Joshua the son of Josedeck was high priest. His prophecy was spoken to Zerubbabel and Joshua approximately 520 B.C. during the second year of Darius' reign. He exhorted the people to build the house of the Lord. Because of their neglect to build the temple, blessings had been withheld. The people obeyed the words of Haggai and "did work in the house of the Lord of hosts." *(Hag. 1.)*

The Lord sent Haggai to Zerubbabel and Joshua and the people a second time. He counseled the people to be strong, even though the new temple was far less glorious than the former temple. The time will come when the Lord will fill the temple with glory and it will be more glorious than the former. He will fill the temple with peace. He warned the people that just as the touch of the unclean pollutes everything around it, the worldly spirit of the people had stopped the labors of their hands and brought them troubles and trials instead of blessings. Haggai told Zerubbabel greater things were in store for the people and that the Lord had chosen Zerubbabel as a "signet." *(Hag. 2.)*

HAGGERI. *1 Chr. 11:38.*

Haggeri was the father of Mibhar.

HAGGI (Haggites). *Gen. 46:16; Num. 26:15.*

Haggi was a son of Gad and a grandson of Jacob. *(Gen. 46:16.)* His descendants were the **Haggites.** *(Num. 26:15.)* (Chart 13a.)

HAGGIAH. *1 Chr. 6:30, 45.*

HAGGIAH was a descendant of Levi through Merari and was the son of Shimea and the father of Asaiah. *(Note: There are two lists of Merari's descendants.)* (Chart 7e.)

Haggites. See **Haggi.**

HAGGITH. *2 Sam. 3:4; 1 Chr. 3:2.*

Haggith was the mother of Adonijah, David's fourthborn son in Hebron.

HAKKATAN. *Ezra 8:12.*

Hakkatan, of the sons of Azgad, was the father of Johanan. He was the chief of his fathers and went with Ezra up from Babylon to Jerusalem taking 110 males with him.

HAKKOZ. *1 Chr. 24:10.*

Hakkoz was from the sons of Aaron. When David made the divisions of the sons of Aaron, there was one principal household for Eleazar and one taken for Ithamar. Eleazar had 16 sons: Ithamar had eight. The duties of these 24 sons who were chief of the fathers were divided by lot. Hakkoz drew the seventh lot.

HAKUPHA. *Ezra 2:51, 58; Neh. 7:53, 60.*

Hakupha was a Nethinim. When the Nethinims and the children of Solomon's servants left Babylon to return to Jerusalem to build the house of the Lord as proclaimed by Cyrus, king of Persia, they numbered 392.

HALOHESH (Hallohesh). *Neh. 3:12; 10:24.*

Halohesh was the father of Shallum. *(Neh. 3:12.)* He **(Hallohesh)** was among those chief of the people who covenanted to marry in Israel, honor the Sabbath, pay tithes and keep the commandments. *(Neh. 10:24.)*

HAM. *Gen. 5:32; 6:10-18; 7:13; 9:7-13, 22-26; 10:6; 1 Chr. 1:8; Ps. 78:51; 105:23; 106:22.*

Ham is the second of Noah's sons mentioned. Noah was 500 years old: and begat Ham, Shem and Japheth. *(Gen. 5:32.) (Note: According to Moses 8:12 in the Pearl of Great Price, Noah's sons were not triplets as implied in Genesis. "And Noah was four hundred and fifty years old, and begat Japheth; and forty-two years afterward he begat Shem of her who was the mother of Japheth, and when he was five hundred years old he begat Ham.")*

Noah begat Shem, Ham and Japheth. The earth was corrupt and filled with violence. The Lord told Noah to build and ark and take his sons and their wives into the ark. *(Gen. 6:10-18.)* Ham and his brothers, along with their wives, father and mother, entered the ark. *(Gen. 7:13.)*

God spoke to Noah and to his sons and told them he would establish his covenant with them and with their seed. They were told to multiply and replenish the earth. The rainbow is a token of the covenant God made with them. When Ham saw his father drunken and naked in his tent, he told his brothers. Shem and Japheth took a garment and, walking backwards so as not to see their father, covered him up. When Noah woke up and realized what Ham had done, he cursed Ham's son, Canaan, but blessed Shem and Japheth. He said Canaan would be their servant. *(Gen. 9:7-13, 22-26.)*

Ham's sons were Cush, Mizrain, Phut (Put) and Canaan. *(Gen. 10:6; 1 Chr. 1:8.) (Note: The Bible Dictionary indicates that Cush was the father of the dark-skinned race of eastern Africa and southern Arabia. Mizrain is the father of the*

Egyptians. Phut's descendants are the Libyans. Canaan's descendants were the inhabitants of Palestine before the arrival of the Semitic races.)

The firstborn of Egypt, the descendants of Ham, were killed when Pharaoh would not let the Israelites go free. *(Ps. 78:51.)* Egypt was the land of Ham. *(Ps. 105:23.)* The Lord wrought wondrous works in the land of Ham as well as terrible things by the Red Sea. *(Ps. 106:22.)* (Charts 1.; 2e.; 21.)

HAMAN. *Esth. 3; 4:7; 5:8-14; 6:4-14; 7; 8:1-2, 5; 9:10-14, 25.*

Haman, son of Hammedath the Agagite, was a man who king Ahasuerus promoted to a high position. Mordecai the Jew, queen Esther's cousin/father, refused to bow down to him so Haman arranged a decree to kill all the Jews in the kingdom. *(Esth. 3.)*

Because of the decree Haman had arranged to have issued, Mordecai and the rest of the Jews mourned in sackcloth. When Esther saw this, she sent Hatach to find out why. Mordecai explained the situation to him and he reported back to Queen Esther. *(Esth. 4:7.)*

Haman and the king were invited by Queen Esther to a banquet she had prepared. Still angry at Mordecai's refusal to bow down to him, Haman followed his wife's suggestion and had a gallows made so he could hang Mordecai. *(Esth. 5:8-14.)*

When the king decided to honor Mordecai for saving his life, he asked Haman for suggestions on how best to honor someone who the king desired to honor. Haman, thinking it was he himself who was to be honored, offered some generous suggestions which the king accepted. However, when it was Mordecai who received the honor, Haman mourned. Haman's wife and wisemen, recognizing that Mordecai was of the seed of the Jews, counseled him that he would not prevail against Mordecai, but would fall before him. He joined the king at Esther's banquet. *(Esth. 6:4-14.)* While at the banquet, Esther revealed Haman's plot to destroy the Jews. The king had Haman hung on the gallows Haman had prepared for Mordecai. *(Esth. 7.)*

Ahasuerus gave the house of Haman unto Esther. She, in turn, set Mordecai over Haman's house. The decree Haman had gotten Ahasuerus to make calling for the destruction of the Jews was reversed. *(Esth. 8:1-2, 5.)*

Haman's ten sons were slain by the Jews and their bodies, at Esther's request, were hung on the gallows. Thus, the wickedness that Haman had devised against the Jews was returned upon his own head. *(Esth. 9:10-14, 25.)*

HAMATHITE. *Gen. 10:18.*

Hamathites were descendants of Canaan who was a son of Ham. (Chart 2e.)

HAMMEDATHA. *Esth. 3:1, 10; 7:5; 9:10, 24.*

Hammedatha the Agagite was the father of Haman.

HAMMOLEKETH. *1 Chr. 7:18.*

HAMOLEKETH was the sister of Gilead (Peresh), a daughter of Machir and granddaughter of Manasseh. She bore Ishod, Abiezer and Mahalah. (Chart 15a.)

HAMOR. *Gen. 33:19; Gen. 34; Josh. 24:32.*

Hamor was the father of Shechem. After Jacob and Esau were reconciled, Jacob traveled to Shalem, a city of Shechem, in the land of Canaan, and bought a parcel of a field from Hamor's children for 100 pieces of money. *(Gen. 33:19.)*

After Jacob settled his family in Canaan, his daughter Dinah went out among the people to see the daughters of the land. Hamor's son Shechem took her and lay with her, thus defiling her. Shechem asked his father to get her for him for his wife. Hamor met with Jacob and told him his son wanted to marry Dinah. He suggested their groups intermarry and trade together, etc. Dinah's brothers answered this request deceitfully saying they would consent to that if all of Hamor's men would be circumcised. Hamor and Shechem and all the men agreed to that. On the third day after being circumcised, "when they were sore," Dinah's brothers, Simeon and Levi, took their swords and slew Hamor and Shechem and all the other males. *(Gen. 34.)*

After the children of Israel received their land of inheritance in Canaan, they buried Joseph's bones (which they had carried out of Egypt) in a parcel of ground which Jacob had bought from the sons of Hamor. *(Josh. 24:32.)*

HAMUEL. *1 Chr. 4:26.*

Hamuel was the son of Mishma and a descendant of Jacob through Simeon. His son was Zacchur. (Chart 6a.)

HAMUL (Hamulites). *Gen. 46:12; Num. 26:21; 1 Chr. 2:4-5.*

Hamul, a grandson of Judah and a great-grandson of Jacob, was one of Pharez's sons. *(Gen. 46:12.)* He was the father of the **Hamulites**. *(Num. 26:21.)* His grandmother was Tamar. *(1 Chr. 2:4-5.)* (Charts 8c-d, h.)

HAMUTAL. *2 Kgs. 23:31; Jer. 52:1.*

Hamutal, daughter of Jeremiah of Libnah and wife of Josiah, king of Judah, was the mother of Jehoahaz (Shallum). *(2 Kgs. 23:31.)* Hamutal, daughter of Jeremiah, was also the mother of Zedekiah (Mattaniah), king of Judah. *(Jer. 52:1.)* (Chart 1.)

HANAMEEL. *Jer. 32:7-12.*

Hanameel was the son of the prophet Jeremiah's uncle Shallum. Jeremiah bought his field, symbolizing the fact that Israel would some day return to the land of their inheritance even though they were soon to be taken captive by Nebuchadrezzar and carried away to Babylon.

HANAN (1). *1 Chr. 8:23, 25.*

Hanan, a descendant of Benjamin, was a son of Shashak who was a son of Beriah. (Chart 16g.)

HANAN (2). *1 Chr. 8:38.*

Hanan, a son of Azel, was from the tribe of Benjamin. He was a tenth-great-grandson of Saul. His brothers were Azrikam, Bocheru, Ishmael, Sheariah and Obadiah. (Chart 16 l.)

HANAN (3). *1 Chr. 11:43.*

Hanan, the son of Maachah, is listed among the mighty men of David and was one of the valiant men of the armies. (Chart 17.)

HANAN (4). *Ezra 2:46, 58; Neh. 7:49, 60.*

Hanan was a Nethinim. When the Nethinims and the children of Solomon's servants left Babylon to return to Jerusalem to build the house of the Lord as proclaimed by Cyrus, king of Persia, they numbered 392.

HANAN (5). *Neh. 8:7-8; 10:22 (1, 22, 28-31).*

Hanan was one of the men who, when Ezra read and interpreted the law of Moses to the people, helped the people to understand the law. *(Neh. 8:7-8.)* He was among those chief of the people who covenanted to marry in Israel, honor the Sabbath, pay tithes and keep the commandments. *(Neh. 10:22 [1, 22, 28-31].)*

HANAN (6). *Neh. 10:10 (1, 10, 28-31).*

Hanan, a Levite, was among those who covenanted and sealed their covenant to marry in Israel, honor the Sabbath, pay tithes and keep the commandments.

HANAN (7). *Neh. 10:26 (1, 26, 28-31).*

Hanan was among those chief of the people who covenanted to marry in Israel, honor the Sabbath, pay tithes and keep the commandments.

HANAN (8). *Neh. 13:13.*

Hanan was the son of Zaccur who was the son of Mattaniah. When Nehemiah discovered that the Levites and the singers who were supposed to be caring for the house of God had fled to the fields because they were not receiving the portions they should have been given, he chastised the people. Soon all Judah brought tithes of corn, new wine and oil, etc., into the treasuries. Nehemiah then appointed those who he counted faithful—Hanan, Pedaiah, Zadok the scribe and Shelemiah the priest—to make the distributions to their brethren.

HANAN (9). *Jer. 35:4.*

Hanan, the son of Igdaliah, was a man of God. Jeremiah the prophet took the Rechabites into the chamber of the sons of Hanan and offered them wine, which they declined in obedience to their forefathers.

HANANI (1). *1 Kgs. 16:1; 2 Chr. 16:7-10; 19:2; 20:34.*

Hanani was the father of the prophet Jehu. *(1 Kgs. 16:1; 2 Chr. 20:34.)*

Hanani the seer went to Asa, king of Judah, and reproved him for lack of faith after Asa enlisted the help of Ben-hadad, king of Syria, against Baasha, king of Israel, rather than trusting in the arm of the Lord. As a result, Asa, in his anger, had Hanani cast into prison. *(2 Chr. 16:7-10.)*

Hanani was the father of Jehu who rebuked Jehoshaphat for helping Ahab against Syria. *(2 Chr. 19:2.)*

HANANI (2). *1 Chr. 25:4, 25.*

Hanani, a Levite and musician, was a son of Heman who was of the lineage of Kohath. He had 13 brothers and three sisters. The musicians—sons of Heman, Asaph and Jeduthun—drew lots and were given their duty assignments by David and the captains of the host. Hanani cast the 18th lot. He, his sons and his brethren numbered 12. (Chart 7d.)

HANANI (3). *Ezra 10:20 (18-20, 44); Neh. 12:36.*

Hanani and Zabadiah, of the sons of Immer, were among those sons of the priests who had taken foreign wives and who agreed to put them away as instructed by Ezra. *(Ezra 10:20 [18-20, 44].)*

Hanani joined Zechariah, a descendant of Asaph, and other of his brethren with their musical instruments in the dedication of the wall of Jerusalem. *(Neh. 12:36.)*

HANANI (4). *Neh. 1:2; 7:2.*

Hanani was one of Nehemiah's brethren. He reported to Nehemiah regarding the state of Jerusalem and that of the Jews therein after their escape from captivity. *(Neh. 1:2.)*

Hanani (Nehemiah's brother) and Hananiah, the ruler of the palace, were given charge over Jerusalem by Nehemiah. *(Neh. 7:2.)*

HANANIAH (1). *1 Chr. 3:19.*

Hananiah, a descendant of David, was a son of Zerubbabel, a grandson of Pedaiah and a great-great-grandson of Jeconiah (Jehoiachin). His brother was Meshullam and his sister was Shelomith. (Chart 1.)

HANANIAH (2). *1 Chr. 8:24-25.*

Hananiah, a descendant of Benjamin, was a son of Shashak who was a son of Beriah. (Chart 16g.)

HANANIAH (3). *1 Chr. 25:4, 23.*

Hananiah, a Levite and musician, was a son of Heman who was of the lineage of Kohath. He had 13 brothers and three sisters. The musicians—sons of Heman, Asaph and Jeduthun—drew lots and were separated to the service by David and the captains of the host. Hananiah cast the 16th lot. He, his sons and his brethren numbered 12. (Chart 7d.)

HANANIAH (4). *2 Chr. 26:11.*

Hananiah was one of king Uzziah's (Azariah's) captains of the army.

HANANIAH (5). *Ezra 10:28 (18-19, 28, 44).*

Hananiah was one of Bebai's sons who took foreign wives. Ezra feared the Lord would destroy the remainder of Israel because of this iniquity and cried unto the Lord. Hananiah and his brothers agreed to comply with Ezra's request that they put away their strange wives.

HANANIAH (6). *Neh. 3:8.*

Hananiah was the son of one of the perfumers or ointment-makers. He worked next to Uzziel when the children of Israel rebuilt the walls and gates of Jerusalem during the time of Ezra and Nehemiah.

HANANIAH (7). *Neh. 3:30.*

Hananiah, son of Shelemiah, and Hanun, sixth son of Zalaph, repaired an area of the wall next to Shemaiah when the children of Israel rebuilt the walls and gates of Jerusalem during the time of Ezra and Nehemiah.

HANANIAH (8). *Neh. 7:2.*

Hananiah was the ruler of the palace. Nehemiah gave him and Hanani charge over Jerusalem.

HANANIAH (9). *Neh. 10:23 (1, 23, 28-31); 12:12.*

Hananiah was among those chief of the people who covenanted to marry in Israel, honor the Sabbath, pay tithes and keep the commandments. *(Neh. 10:23 [1, 23, 28-31].)*

Hananiah, son of Jeremiah, was one of the chief of the fathers during the days of Joiakim. *(Neh. 12:12.)*

HANANIAH (10). *Neh. 12:41.*

Hananiah, a priest and trumpeter, joined in the dedication of the walls of Jerusalem with Nehemiah.

HANANIAH (11). *Jer. 28; 36:12; 37:13.*

Hananiah the prophet was the son of Azur the prophet. In the fifth month of the fourth year of Zedekiah's reign over Judah, Hananiah falsely prophesied that the yoke of Babylon would be broken within two years. Jeremiah, as instructed by the Lord, told Hananiah that because he had taught the people to trust in a lie and had rebelled against the Lord, he would be cast from off the earth. He died in the seventh month of that same year. *(Jer. 28.)*

Hananiah was the father of Zedekiah, which Zedekiah was in the scribe's chamber in king Jehoiakim's house with Elishama the scribe and all the officers when Michaiah told them of the prophecies of Jeremiah which he had heard Baruch read in his father Gemariah's chamber. *(Jer. 36:12.)*

Hananiah was the father of Shelemiah who was the father of Irijah, which Irijah accused the prophet Jeremiah of deserting to the Chaldeans and hauled him before the princes who smote Jeremiah and cast him into the dungeon in the house of Jonathan. *(Jer. 37:13.)* (Chart 16m.)

HANANIAH (12) (Shadrach). *Dan. 1:6-21; 2; 3.*

Hananiah, Mishael, Azariah and Daniel were among the children of Israel who were without blemish who were brought to the palace of Nebuchadnezzar by Ashpenaz, the master of the king's eunuchs, to be taught in the learning and language of the Chaldeans. The prince of the eunuchs gave each of them a different name. Hananiah was given the name of **Shadrach**. They elected not to eat the meat and wine the king provided and after ten days they were healthier than those who ate the meat and drank the wine. At the end of three years, when the king visited with all those who had been taught, none of them could compare with these four friends. They were wiser and had greater understanding than any of the king's magicians or astrologers. *(Dan. 1:6-21.)*

When Nebuchadnezzar had a dream that troubled him, he called in his magicians, astrologers, sorcerers and the Chaldeans and demanded they not only tell him the interpretation of the dream but the dream, also, because he could not remember it. When they could not, he sentenced all the wisemen to death. Daniel, however, requested time to inquire of the Lord. He invited his friends, Shaddrach (Hananiah), Meshach (Mishael) and Abed-nego (Azariah) to also petition the Lord regarding the matter. The Lord revealed the dream and the interpretation of the dream to Daniel. He explained the dream to Nebuchadnezzar, saying that God had revealed to Nebuchadnezzar what would happen in the latter days. Daniel was not only rewarded by Nebuchadnezzar, who elevated him to a position where he "sat in the gate of the king," but he honored a request Daniel made regarding his friends and set Shadrach, Meshach and Abed-nego over the affairs of the province of Babylon. *(Dan. 2.)*

When Nebuchadnezzar made a golden image and commanded that everyone worship it whenever they heard music or be cast into a fiery furnace, Shadrach, Meshach and Abed-nego refused to do so. Thus, Nebuchadnezzar had his most mighty men from the army make the furnace seven times hotter than usual and bound the friends and cast them into it. The fire was so hot that it killed the soldiers. Suddenly, Nebuchadnezzar saw four men, the fourth being "like the Son of God," walking freely around inside the furnace, not being harmed by the fire. He called Shadrach, Meshach and Abed-nego forth and decreed that no one should speak anything against their God or they would be cut into pieces because no other God could deliver like their God. He then rewarded the three friends by promoting them in the province of Babylon. *(Dan. 3.)*

HANIEL. *1 Chr. 7:39.*

<u>Haniel</u>, son of Ulla, was a descendant of Asher. His brothers were Arah and Rezia. (Chart 14b.)

HANNAH. *1 Sam. 1:2-28; 2:1-11, 18-21.*

<u>Hannah</u> was one of the wives of Elkanah. Elkanah loved Hannah and gave her "a worthy portion" when he "offered." To his other wife, Peninnah, and her children he "gave portions." Because she was barren, Hannah cried unto the Lord for a male child and promised that if He gave her a son, she would give him unto the Lord all the days of his life. The Lord blessed her with a son. She named him Samuel. After she weaned him, she took him to Eli the priest and offered his services to the Lord. *(1 Sam. 1:2-28.)*

Hannah sang praises unto the Lord and made reference to the Messiah when she referred to "his anointed" *(v. 10)*. She made Samuel little coats and took them to him from year to year when they went to offer the yearly sacrifice. She and Elkanah were blessed with three more sons and two daughters. *(1 Sam. 2:1-11, 18-21.)* (Chart 7d.)

HANNIEL. *Num. 34:23.*

<u>Hanniel</u>, the son of Ephod, was of the tribe of Manasseh and was assigned to divide the land of inheritance given to the second half of the tribe of Manasseh. (Chart 15c.)

HANOCH (1) (Henoch). *Gen. 25:4; 1 Chr. 1:33.*

Hanoch (Henoch) was a son of Midian and a grandson of Abraham and Keturah. *(Gen. 25:4; 1 Chr. 1:33.)* (Chart 3f.)

HANOCH (2) (Hanochites). *Gen. 46:9; Num. 26:5.*

Hanoch was one of Reuben's sons and was a grandson of Jacob. *(Gen. 46:9.)* His descendants were the **Hanochites**. *(Num. 26:5.)* (Chart 5a.)

HANUN (1). *2 Sam. 10; 1 Chr. 19.*

Hanun was the son of Nahash, king of the children of Ammon. When Nahash died, Hanun reigned in his stead. David sought to .show kindness unto Hanun because Nahash had shown kindness unto him. Unfortunately, the princes of the children of Ammon convinced Hanun that David's servants were spies and Hanun abused David's servants by shaving off one-half of their beards and cutting "off their garments in the middle, even to their buttocks, and sent them away." Thus, David sent Israel against Hanun. Hanun recruited the Syrians to help him. Israel defeated both the Ammonites and the Syrians.

HANUN (2). *Neh 3:13.*

Hanun and the inhabitants of Zanoah repaired the valley gate when the children of Israel rebuilt the walls and gates of Jerusalem during the time of Ezra and Nehemiah.

HANUN (3). *Neh. 3:30.*

Hanun, sixth son of Zalaph, repaired an area of the wall next to Hananiah, son of Shelemiah, when the children of Israel rebuilt the walls and gates of Jerusalem during the time of Ezra and Nehemiah.

HARAN (1). *Gen. 11:26-29.*

Haran was a son of Terah and brother of Abraham and Nahor. He was a seventh-great-grandson of Shem and an eighth-great-grandson of Noah. He begat Lot, Milcah (Nahor's wife) and Iscah. He died in Ur of the Chaldees where he was born. After his death, Terah left that area with Abram, Sarah, and Lot. (Charts 2b-d.)

HARAN (2). *1 Chr. 2:46.*

Haran was one of the sons of Caleb and his concubine Ephah. He begat Gazez. (Chart 8j.)

HARAN (3). *1 Chr. 23:9.*

Haran, a Levite and son of Shimei, was of the Gershonites. He, Shelomith and Haziel, all sons of Shimei, were named by David as chiefs of the fathers of Laadan when David numbered the Levites and divided them into courses at the time he named Solomon king. (Chart 7f.)

HARAN (4). *Ezek. 27:23-24.*

Haran, Canneh and Eden, the merchants of Sheba, Asshur and Chilmad, traded at the fairs in Tyrus before Tyrus' fall, trading in blue clothes, broidered work, chests of rich apparel, bound with cords, and made of cedar. *(Note: It is not clear if Haran, Canneh and Eden were individual merchants or if they were cities that traded with Tyrus.)*

HARARITE (Harodite, Harorite). *2 Sam. 23:11, 25, 33.*

Five **Hararites**, Shammah the son of Agee the Hararite, Shammah the **Harodite**, Elika the Harodite, Shammah the Hararite, and Ahiam the son of Sharar the Hararite, were listed among the mighty men of David. *(Note: When comparing the listings of David's mighty men in 2 Sam. 23 and 1 Chr. 11, it seems possible that Shammah the son of Agee the Hararite mentioned in verse 11, Shammah the Harodite mentioned in verse 25, and Shammah the Hararite mentioned in verse 33 are one and the same person since they are not listed separately in 1 Chr. 11. In 1 Chr. 11:27, Shammoth the **Harorite** is mentioned. It is conceivable that Hararite, Harodite, and Harorite are different spellings of the same group. Shammoth and Shammah may also be different spellings referring to the same person.)*

HARBONA. *Esth. 1:10; 7:9.*

Harbona was one of the seven chamberlains serving in the presence of Ahasuerus the king who was sent to bring queen Vashti to Ahasuerus. *(Esth. 1:10.)*

Harbonah pointed out to the king the gallows made by Haman for the planned hanging of Mordecai. *(Esth. 7:9.)*

HAREPH. *1 Chr. 2:51.*

Hareph was one of the sons of Caleb and Ephratah. He begat Beth-gader. (Chart # 8 l.)

HARHAIAH. *Neh. 3:8.*

Harhaiah, of the goldsmiths, was the father of Uzziel.

HARHAS (Hasrah). *2 Kgs. 22:14; 2 Chr. 34:22.*

Harhas (Hasrah) was the father of Tikvah who was the father-in-law of Huldah the prophetess.

HARHUR. *Ezra 2:51, 58; Neh. 7:53, 60.*

Harhur was a Nethinim. When the Nethinims and the children of Solomon's servants left Babylon to return to Jerusalem to build the house of the Lord as proclaimed by Cyrus, king of Persia, they numbered 392.

HARIM (1). *1 Chr. 24:8.*

Harim was from the sons of Aaron. When David made the divisions of the sons of Aaron, there was one principal household for Eleazar and one taken for Ithamar. Eleazar had 16 sons and there were eight sons of Ithamar. These 24 sons who were chief of the fathers were divided by lot for the governors of the sanctuary and the governors of the house of God. Harim drew the third lot.

HARIM (2). *Ezra 2:32; 10:31 (18-19, 31, 44); Neh. 7: 35.*

Harim was of the people of Israel. The men of the children of Harim who returned to Jerusalem from Babylon after Cyrus' proclamation to build the temple numbered 320. *(Ezra 2:32; Neh. 7: 35.)*

Harim's sons—Eliezer, Ishijah, Malchiah, Shemaiah, Shimeon, Benjamin, Malluch and Shemariah—were some of the Israelite men who took wives from among the Canaanites and other foreign groups. They agreed to Ezra's request to separate themselves from their foreign wives. *(Ezra 10:31 [18-19, 31, 44].)*

HARIM (3). *Ezra 2:39; 10:21 (18-19, 21, 44); Neh. 7:42; 10:5 (1, 5, 28-31)*.

Harim was one of the priests. His children numbered 1,017 when they left Babylon to return to Jerusalem to build the temple as proclaimed by Cyrus, king of Persia. *(Ezra 2:39; Neh. 7:42.)*

Harim's sons—Maaseiah, Elijah, Shemaiah, Jehiel and Uzziah—were among those sons of the priests who had taken strange wives and agreed to Ezra's request that they separate themselves from them. *(Ezra 10:21 [18-19, 21, 44].)* He covenanted and sealed his covenant to marry in Israel, honor the Sabbath, pay tithes and keep the commandments. *(Neh. 10:5 [1, 5, 28-31].)*

HARIM (4). *Neh. 3:11; 10:27 (1, 27-31)*.

Harim was the father of Malchijah. *(Neh. 3:11.)*

He was among the chief of the people who covenanted to marry in Israel, honor the Sabbath, pay tithes and keep the commandments. *(Neh. 10:27 [1, 27-31].)*

HARIM (5). *Neh. 12:15*.

Harim was the father of Adna, who was one of the priests who was a chief of the fathers in the days of Joiakim.

HARIPH. See **Jorah**.

HARLOT IN GAZA. *Judg. 16:1*.

A **Harlot** in Gaza was visited by Samson.

HARNEPHER. *1 Chr. 7:36*.

Harnepher was a son of Zophah, a grandson of Hotham, and a great-great-great-grandson of Asher. His brothers were Suah, Shual, Beri, Imrah, Bezer, Hod, Shamma, Shilshah, Ithran and Beera. (Chart 14a.)

HARODITE. See **Hararite**.

HAROEH. *1 Chr. 2:52*.

Haroeh was one of the sons of Shobal. (Chart 8 l.)

HARORITE. See **Hararite**.

HARSHA. *Ezra 2:52, 58; Neh. 7:54, 60*.

Harsha was a Nethinim. When the Nethinims and the children of Solomon's servants left Babylon to return to Jerusalem to build the house of the Lord as proclaimed by Cyrus, king of Persia, they numbered 392.

HARUM. *1 Chr. 4:8*.

Harum was the parent of Aharhel.

HARUMAPH. *Neh. 3:10*.

Harumaph was the father of Jedaiah.

HARUZ. *2 Kgs. 21:19*.

Haruz of Jotbah was the father of Meshullemeth who was king Amon's mother and, thus, was also the father-in-law of Manasseh. (Chart 1.)

HASADIAH. *1 Chr. 3:20*.

Hasadiah, a descendant of David, was a son of Shelomith, the daughter of Zerubbabel. His brothers were Hashubah, Ohel, Berechiah and Jushabhesed. (Chart 1.)

HASENUAH. *1 Chr. 9:7-8.*

Hasenuah, of the tribe of Benjamin, was the father of Hodaviah. He and his family were among the inhabitants of Jerusalem whose genealogy was written in the book of the kings of Israel and Judah, who were carried away to Babylon for their transgression. They were among the first inhabitants from the tribe of Benjamin to dwell in Jerusalem after their return from Babylonian captivity. (Chart 16m.)

HASHABIAH (1). *1 Chr. 6:45; Neh. 12:21, 24.*

Hashabiah, a descendant of Levi through Merari, was the son of Amaziah and the father of Malluch. *(1 Chr. 6:45.) (Note: Merari's descendants are listed in verses 29-30 and 44-47 but the names differ.)*

Hashabiah, a descendant of Hilkiah, was one of the priests who was chief of the fathers in the days of Joiakim. Hashabiah, along with Sherebiah and Jeshua the son of Kadmiel, was a chief of the Levites. *(Neh. 12:21, 24.)* (Chart 7e.)

HASHABIAH (2). *1 Chr. 9:14; Neh. 11:15.*

Hashabiah, a Levite, was the father of Azrikam and was of the sons of Merari. His genealogy was recorded in the book of the kings of Israel and Judah, who were carried away to Babylon for their transgression. His posterity was among the Levites who dwelled in Jerusalem following their return from Babylonian captivity *(1 Chr. 9:14.)*

Hashabiah, father of Azrikam, was the son of Bunni. *(Neh. 11:15.)* (Chart 7e.)

HASHABIAH (3). *1 Chr. 25:3, 19.*

Hashabiah, a Levite and musician, was the son of Jeduthun. The musicians—sons of Jeduthun, Asaph and Heman—drew lots and were given their duty assignments by David and the captains of the host. Hashabiah cast the 12th lot. He, his sons and his brethren numbered 12. (Chart 7h.)

HASHABIAH (4). *1 Chr. 26:30.*

Hashabiah, a Levite, was a chief among the Hebronites. Hashabiah and his brethren, 1700 strong, were officers among Israel on the westward side of Jordan in things pertaining to the Lord and in the service of the king.

HASHABIAH (5). *1 Chr. 27:17.*

Hashabiah, the son of Kemuel, was the prince (ruler) of the Levites at the time of king David.

HASHABIAH (6). *Neh. 11:22.* See **Jeiel (3)**.

HASHABIAH (7). *Ezra 8:18-19, 24-30.*

Hashabiah was a descendant of Levi through Merari. When Ezra was preparing to lead the people from Babylon back to Jerusalem, he gathered them together by the river and discovered that there were no Levites among them. He assigned several chief men and men of understanding to go to Iddo and the Nethinims and request that they send them some ministers for the house of God. They brought Hashabiah "and with him Jeshaiah of the sons of Merari, and 20 of his brethren and their sons;" Sherebiah, with 18 of his sons and brethren; plus 220 Nethinims. Ezra delivered the silver, gold and precious things of the temple to Hashabiah, Sherebiah, and ten additional chief priests and charged them to deliver them to the appropriate leaders at Jerusalem. *(Note: It is possible that Hashabiah (7) and Hashabiah (8) are the same as Hasabiah (1) who is shown of Chart 7e.)*

HASHABIAH (8). *Neh. 3:17; Neh. 10:11.*

Hashabiah, ruler of the half part of Keilah, labored next to Rehum when the children of Israel rebuilt the walls and gates of Jerusalem during the time of Ezra and Nehemiah. *(Neh. 3:17.)*

Hashabiah, was among those Levites who covenanted and sealed their covenant to marry in Israel, honor the Sabbath, pay tithes and keep the commandments. *(Neh. 10:11.)*

HASHABNAH. *Neh. 10:25.*

Hashabnah was among those chief of the people who covenanted to marry in Israel, honor the Sabbath, pay tithes and keep the commandments after they returned to Jerusalem from out of Babylonian captivity.

HASHABNIAH (1). *Neh. 3:10.*

Hashabniah was the father of Hattush.

HASHABNIAH (2). *Neh. 9.*

Hashabniah was a Levite. When Ezra read and interpreted the law of Moses and he and Nehemiah proclaimed the day a holy day, the Levites—Hashabniah, Jeshua, Bani, Kadmiel, Shebaniah, Bunni, Sherebiah, Bani, Chenani, Hodijah and Pethahiah—blessed and praised the Lord, reciting the Lord's goodness to Israel: the blessing of Abraham; giving the land of the Canaanites, Hittites, Amorites, Perizzites, Jebusites and Girgashites to Israel; dividing the Red Sea so they could cross it yet drowning the Egyptians who pursued them; the signs and wonders shown to Pharaoh; leading them in the wilderness and protecting them so that they had bread from heaven, water from the rock, and shoes and clothes that never wore out; accepting them whenever they repented, even when they made a molten calf. They had been given the kingdoms of Shihon, Heshbon and Bashan and the Lord had subdued the Canaanites and delivered them into the hands of the Israelites, etc. After giving praise, they made a covenant with the Lord. The princes, Levites and priests sealed the covenant.

HASHBADANA. *Neh. 8:4.*

Hashbadana was one of the men who stood on Ezra's left hand when Ezra read and interpreted the law of Moses to the people.

HASHEN. See **Jashen**.

HASHUB (1). See **Hasshub**.

HASHUB (2). *Neh. 3:11.*

Hashub, son of Pahath-moab, and Malchijah, son of Harim, worked next to Hattush and repaired the tower of the furnaces when the children of Israel rebuilt the walls and gates of Jerusalem during the time of Ezra and Nehemiah.

HASHUB (3). *Neh. 3:23.*

Hashub and Benjamin labored next to the priests, the men of the plain, working "over against their house" when the children of Israel rebuilt the walls and gates of Jerusalem during the time of Ezra and Nehemiah.

HASHUB (4). *Neh. 10:23.*

Hashub was among those chief of the people who covenanted to marry in Israel, honor the Sabbath, pay tithes and keep the commandments.

HASHUBAH. *1 Chr. 3:20.*

Hashubah, a descendant of David, was a son of Shelomith, the daughter of Zerubbabel. His brothers were Ohel, Berechiah, Hasadiah and Jushabhesed. (Chart 1.)

HASHUM (1). *Ezra 2:19; 10:33 (18-19, 33, 44); Neh. 7:22; 10:18 (1, 18, 28-31).*

Hashum was of the people of Israel. The men of the children of Hashum who returned to Jerusalem from Babylon after Cyrus' proclamation to build the temple numbered 223 (328). *(Ezra 2:19;Neh. 7:22.)*

Hashum's sons—Mattenai, Mattathah, Zabad, Eliphelet, Jeremai, Manasseh and Shimei—were among the Israelite men who took foreign wives but complied with Ezra's request that they put away their strange wives so as not to bring the wrath of God upon Israel. *(Ezra 10:33 [18-19, 33, 44].)* Hashum was among those chief of the people who, after returning to Jerusalem from Babylonian captivity, covenanted to marry in Israel, honor the Sabbath, pay tithes and keep the commandments. *(Neh. 10:18 [1, 18, 28-31].)*

HASHUM (2). *Neh. 8:1-8.*

Hashum was one of the men who stood on Ezra's left hand when Ezra read and interpreted the law of Moses to the people.

HASHUPHA. See **Hasupha**.

HASRAH. See **Harhas**.

HASSENAAH. *Neh. 3:3.*

Hassenaah's sons built up the fish gate when the children of Israel rebuilt the walls and gates of Jerusalem during the time of Ezra and Nehemiah.

HASSHUB (Hashub (1)). *1 Chr. 9:14; Neh. 11:15.*

Hasshub, a Levite, was a descendant of Merari and was the son of Azrikam and the father of Shemaiah. His genealogy was written in the book of the kings of Israel and Judah, who were carried away to Babylon for their transgression. *(1 Chr. 9:14.)* Hashub was the father of Shemaiah, the son of Azrikam, the son of Hashabiah, the son of Bunni. *(Neh. 11:15.)* (Chart 7e.)

HASUPHA (Hashupha). *Ezra 2:43, 58; Neh. 7:46, 60.*

Hasupha (Hashupha) was a Nethinim. When the Nethinims and the children of Solomon's servants left Babylon to return to Jerusalem to build the house of the Lord as proclaimed by Cyrus, king of Persia, they numbered 392. *(Ezra 2:43, 58.)*

HATACH. *Esth. 4:5-15.*

Hatach was one of king Ahasuerus' chamberlains assigned to attend queen Esther. When Esther was made aware of the mourning and fasting by Mordecai and the Jews, she sent Hatach to Mordecai to see what was wrong. Hatach returned to Esther with his report that Haman had gotten the king to issue a decree to destroy all of the Jews in the province. Hatach continued to dispatch messages between Esther and Mordecai.

HATHATH. *1 Chr. 4:13.*

Hathath, of the tribe of Judah, was the son of Othniel and the grandson of Kenaz. (Chart 8k.)

HATIPHA. *Ezra 2:54, 58; Neh. 7:56, 60.*

Hatipha was a Nethinim. When the Nethinims and the children of Solomon's servants left Babylon to return to Jerusalem to build the house of the Lord as proclaimed by Cyrus, king of Persia, they numbered 392.

HATITA. *Ezra 2:42; Neh. 7:45.*

Hatita was one of the porters. When Cyrus, king of Persia, proclaimed that the people of God should go to Jerusalem to build the temple, the children of the porters—Hatita, Shallum, Ater, Talmon, Akkub and Shobai—numbered 139 (138).

HATTIL. *Ezra 2:57-58; Neh. 7:59-60.*

Hattil was one of Solomon's servants. When the children of Solomon's servants and the Nethinims returned to Jerusalem from Babylonian captivity to build the house of the Lord as proclaimed by Cyrus, king of Persia, they numbered 392.

HATTUSH (1). *1 Chr. 3:22; Ezra 8:2.*

Hattush, a descendant of David, was a son of Shemaiah. His brothers were Igeal, Bariah, Neariah and Shaphat. *(1 Chr. 3:22.)*

Hattush, of the sons of David, was the chief of his fathers and went with Ezra up from Babylon to Jerusalem. *(Ezra 8:2.)* (Chart 1.)

HATTUSH (2). *Neh. 3:10; 10:4 (1, 4, 28-31); 12:2.*

Hattush, son of Hashabniah, worked next to Jedaiah when the children of Israel rebuilt the walls and gates of Jerusalem during the time of Ezra and Nehemiah. *(Neh. 3:10.)*

Hattush was among the priests who covenanted and sealed their covenant to marry in Israel, honor the Sabbath, pay tithes and keep the commandments. *(Neh. 10:4 [1, 4, 28-31].)*

Hattush was one of the men (priests and Levites) who went up from Babylon to Jerusalem with Zerubbabel. *(Neh. 12:2.)*

HAVILAH (1). *Gen. 10:7.*

Havilah was one of the five sons of Cush, a grandson of Ham, and a great-grandson of Noah. (Chart 2e.)

HAVILAH (2). *Gen. 10:29; 1 Chr. 1:23.*

Havilah was the twelfth named of 13 sons of Joktan, a third-great-grandson of Shem and a fourth-great-grandson of Noah. *("The Joktanites were settled in the south of Arabia," BD, p. 699.)* (Chart 2b.)

HAZAEL. *1 Kgs. 19:15, 17; 2 Kgs. 8:7-15; 9:14-15; 10:32; 12:17-18; 13:3-5, 24; 2 Chr. 22:5-6; 24:24; Amos 1:1, 4.*

Hazael, according to the Lord's instruction to Elijah, was to be anointed king over Syria. Elijah was told that "him that escapeth the sword of Hazael shall Jehu slay: and him that escapeth from the sword of Jehu shall Elisha slay." *(1 Kgs. 19:15, 17.)*

When Elisha came to Damascus, Hazael, at the request of the Syrian king Ben-hadad, asked him whether or not Ben-hadad would recover from a disease. Elisha said he would recover but that he would also die. When Elisha wept, Hazael inquired why. Elisha told him it was because the Lord had shown him that Hazael would become king after Ben-hadad and that he would do great evil unto the children of Israel. Hazael returned and reported to Ben-hadad that Elisha had said he would recover. The next day, he took a thick, damp cloth and smothered Ben-hadad so that he died. Hazael then reigned in his stead (about 886-840 B.C.) *(2 Kgs. 8:7-15.)*

Hazael wounded Joram (Jehoram), king of Israel, in battle so Joram went to Jezreel to recover. *(2 Kgs. 9:14-15; 2 Chr. 22:5-6.)*

Hazael smote Israel in all her coasts when the Lord started to cut Israel short. *(2 Kgs. 10:32.)*

Hazael determined to go to war against Judah. However, Joash (Jehoash), king of Judah, bought him off by sending him gold and other precious things. *(2 Kgs. 12:17-18.)*

Because of Israel's wickedness, the Lord delivered Israel into the hand of Hazael and into the hand of his son, Ben-hadad, all their days. When the king of Israel, Jehoahaz, appealed to the Lord, he finally raised someone up who delivered Israel from the hands of the Syrians. Hazael died and his son Ben-hadad reigned in his stead. *(2 Kgs. 13:3-5, 24.)*

Hazael's army captured a large host of Israel with only a small company of men. *(2 Chr. 24:24.)*

Because of Hazael's wickedness, Amos prophesied of things he saw concerning Israel and the judgments that would come upon Syria, the Philistines and others during the time of Uzziah king of Judah and Jeroboam king of Israel. The Lord said He would send a fire into the house of Hazael which would devour the palaces of Ben-hadad. *(Amos 1:1, 4.)*

HAZAIAH. *Neh. 11:5.*

Hazaiah, son of Adaiah and the father of Col-hozeh of the children of Perez (Pharez)of the house of Judah, dwelled in Jerusalem after leaving Babylon. (Chart 8b.)

HAZARMAVETH. *Gen. 10:26.*

Hazarmaveth was a son of Joktan, a third-great-grandson of Shem and a fourth-great-grandson of Noah. (Chart 2b.)

HAZELELPONI. *1 Chr. 4:3.*

Hazeleponi was of the lineage of Judah and was "of the father of Etam." Her siblings included three brothers: Jezreel, Ishma and Idbash. Based on the punctuation in these scriptures, it would appear that Hazelelponi was the mother of Penuel and Ezer and descended through Hur. (Chart 8m.)

HAZIEL. *1 Chr. 23:9.*

Haziel, a Gershonite from the tribe of Levite, was a son of Shimei. He, Shelomith and Haran, all sons of Shimei, were named by David as chiefs of the fathers of Laadan when David numbered the Levites and divided them into courses at the time he named Solomon king. (Chart 7f.)

HAZO. *Gen. 22:22.*

Hazo was one of Milcah and Nahor's children. (Chart 2c.)

HAZZUB. *Nahum 2:7.*

"**Hazzub**" refers to the queen of Ninevah whom Nahum prophesied would be led away cative when Ninevah was destroyed.

HEBER (1) (Heberites). *Gen. 46:17; Num. 26:45; 1 Chr. 7:32-35.*

Heber was a son of Beriah, grandson of Asher, and a great-grandson of Jacob. His brother was Malchiel. *(Gen. 46:17.)* His descendants are called **Heberites**. *(Num. 26:45.)* He begat Japhlet, Shomer (Shamer) and Hotham (Helem) and a daughter, Shua. *(1 Chr. 7:32-35.)* (Chart 14a.)

HEBER (2). *Judg. 4:11-24.*

Heber the Kenite was the husband of Jael. He was of the children of Hobab, the father-in-law of Moses, but he had separated himself from the Kenites. There was peace between his house and Jabin the king of Hazor. Thus, when Jabin fled from before Israel, he fled to the tent of Heber's wife, Jael, who subsequently slew him by hammering a nail into his temple.

HEBER (3). *1 Chr. 4:18.*

Heber was the father of Socho. His mother was Jehudijah. (Chart 8 o.)

HEBER (4). *1 Chr. 5:13.*

Heber was a descendant of Gad. (Chart 13b.)

HEBER (5). *1 Chr. 8:17.*

Heber, of the tribe of Benjamin, was one of the sons of Elpaal. (Chart 16i.)

HEBER (6). *1 Chr. 8:22, 25.*

Heber, a descendant of Benjamin, was a son of Shashak who was a son of Beriah. (Chart 16g.)

HEBERITES. See **Heber (1)**.

HEBRON (1) (Hebronites). *Ex. 6:18; Num. 3:27-31; 1 Chr. 6:2; 15:9 (2-3, 9, 12); 23:19; 26:30.*

Hebron was a son of Kohath and a grandson of Levi. *(Ex. 6:18.)* **Hebronites** were descendants of Hebron, son of Kohath. The families of the Kohathites were to pitch on the southward side of the tabernacle and were to be in charge of the ark, the candlesticks, altar and all the service thereof. *(Num. 3:27-31.)*

Hebron's brothers were Amram (the father of Aaron and Moses), Izhar and Uzziel. *(1 Chr. 6:2.)*

Of the sons of Hebron, Eliel was the chief. David told those who were chief of the fathers of the Levites to sanctify themselves so they could bring the ark of Israel to the place David had prepared for it. *(1 Chr. 15:9 [2-3, 9, 12].)*

When David made Jonathan king, he also number the Levites and divided them into courses among the sons of Levi: Gershon, Kohath and Merari. Of the sons of Hebron, those appointed as chief of their course were Jeriah, first; Amariah, second; Jahaziel, third; and Jekameam, fourth. *(1 Chr. 23:19.)*

Hashabiah, a Levite, was a Hebronite. He and his brethren, 1700 strong, were officers among Israel on the westward side of Jordan in things pertaining to the Lord. Jerijah, another Hebronite, and his brethren numbered 2700 and were assigned to be rulers over the Reubenites, the Gadites and the half tribe of Manasseh in matters pertaining to the Lord and in the affairs of the king. *(1 Chr. 26:30.)* (Charts 7b, d.)

HEBRON (2). *1 Chr. 2:42-43.*

Hebron, of the house of Judah, was the son of Mareshah and the father of Korah, Tappuah, Rekem and Shema. These were sons of Caleb the brother of Jerahmeel. (Chart 8i.)

HEBRONITES. See **Hebron (1)**.

HEGE (Hegai). *Esth. 2:3, 8.*

Hege, king Ahasuerus' chamberlain, was keeper of the women. The maidens, including Esther, who were gathered together because of Ahasuerus' search for a queen to replace Vashti were placed in **Hegai's** (Hege's) custody.

HELAH. *1 Chr. 4:5, 7.*

Helah was a wife of Ashur who was of the tribe of Judah. She bore him Zereth, Jezoar and Ethnan. (See Chart 8d.)

HELDAI (1). *1 Chr. 27:15.*

Heldai the Netophathite was of Othniel. He was assigned by king David to be captain of the course of 24,000 that was for the twelfth month. (Chart 8k.)

HELDAI (2). *Zech. 6:10-12.*

The captive of **Heldai**, Tobijah and Jedaiah, who had come from Babylon were instructed to go into the house of Josiah the son of Zephaniah and crown Joshua (Jeshua) the son of Josedech, the high priest, in similitude of crowning Christ, i.e., the BRANCH.

HELEB (Heled). *2 Sam. 23:29; 1 Chr. 11:30.*

Heleb (Heled), the son of Baanah, a Netophathite, was one of David's mighty men *(2 Sam. 23:29)* and one of the valiant men of the armies *(1 Chr. 11:30)*. (Chart 17.)

HELEK (Helekites). *Num. 26:30.*

Helek was a son of Gilead and a great-grandson of Manasseh. His descendants were the **Helekites**. His brothers were Jeezer (Jeezerites), Asriel (Asrielites), Shechem Shechemites), Shemida (Shemidaites) and Hepher (Hepherites).

HELEM. See **Hotham**.

HELEZ (1) (Paltites, Pelonites). *2 Sam. 23:26; 1 Chr. 11:27; 27:10.*

Helez the **Paltite** (Pelonite) was one of David's mighty men *(2 Sam. 23:26)* and one of the valiant men of the armies *(1 Chr. 11:27)*.

Helez, the **Pelonite** was of the children of Ephraim. He and his course of 24,000 were assigned by David to serve for the seventh month. *(1 Chr. 27:10.)* (Chart 17.)

HELEZ (2). *1 Chr. 2:39.*

Helez was the son of Azariah and the father of Eleasah. (Chart 8c.)

HELKAI. *Neh. 12:15.*

Helkai, son of Meraioth, was one of the priests who was a chief of the fathers in the days of Joiakim.

HELON. *Num 1:9.*

Helon was the father of Eliab and was of the tribe of Zebulun.

HEMAM (Homam). *Gen. 36:22; 1 Chr. 1:39.*

Hemam (Homam) was a son of Lotan the son of Seir the Horite. His brother was Hori. (Chart 4a.)

HEMAN (1). *1 Kgs. 4:31; 1 Chr. 2:6.*

Heman, a son of Mahol (Zerah), was recognized as a wise man, but Solomon was wiser than he. His brothers were Ethan the Ezrahite, Chalcol and Darda. *(1 Kgs. 4:31.)*

Heman was one of the five sons of Zerah (Mahol). He was a grandson of Judah and a great-grandson of Jacob. His brothers were Zimri, Ethan, Calcol and Dara. *(1 Chr. 2:6.)* (Charts 8d, g-h.)

HEMAN (2). *1 Chr. 6:33; 15:17-19; 16:41-42; 25: 1, 4-5; 2 Chr. 5:12, 14; 29:14; Ps. 88:Subtitle.*

Heman, of the linage of Levi through Kohath, was the son of Joel (Vashni) and the grandson of Samuel (Shemuel). He was one of David's singers. *(1 Chr. 6:33.)*

Heman was a Levite and was the son of Joel. When David was king, Heman was one of the men David appointed to be a singer. He, Asaph (of the lineage of Gershon) and Ethan (of the lineage of Merari) were appointed to sound the cymbals of brass. *(1 Chr. 15:17-19.)*

David left Heman, Jeduthun and others before the ark of the covenant of the Lord to minister before the ark continually. *(1 Chr. 16:41-42.)*

David and the captains of the host assigned the singers and musicians their duties by lot. The lots were divided between the sons of Heman, Asaph and Jeduthun. Heman had 14 sons and three daughters. *(1 Chr. 25: 1, 4-5.)*

The Levites who were the singers—those of Heman, Asaph and Jeduthun, with their sons and brethren—were dressed in white and made music to praise the Lord when the temple was finished by Solomon and the ark of the covenant was placed in the holy of holies. The glory of the Lord filled the temple. *(2 Chr. 5:12, 14.)*

Jehiel and Shimei of the sons of Heman were among those whom Hezekiah, king of Judah, instructed to sanctify themselves so they could cleanse and sanctify the house of the Lord. *(2 Chr. 29:14.)*

This psalm to the chief Musician was for the sons of Korah with instructions of Heman the Ezrahite. *(Ps. 88:Subtitle.)* (Charts 7d-e.)

HEMATH. *1 Chr. 2:55.*

Hemath was the father of the house of Rechab. His descendants included the Kenites which included the Tirathites, Shimeathites and Suchathites. They were the families of the scribes which dwelt at Jabez.

HEMDAN (Amram (2)). *Gen. 36:26; 1 Chr. 1:41.*

Hemdan (Amram (2)) was a son of Dishon who was the son of Seir the Horite. (Chart 4d.)

HEN. *Zech. 6:14.*

Hen was the son of Zephaniah. His brother was Josiah. Speaking Messianically, Zechariah was told to take those of the captivity of Heldai, Tobijah and Jedaiah into the house of Josiah the son of Zephaniah and place crowns upon the head of Joshua, son of Josedech, in similitude of crowning Christ, i.e., the BRANCH. The Lord said, "And the crowns shall be to Helem, and to Tobijah, and to Jedaiah, and to Hen the son of Zephaniah for a memorial in the temple of the Lord." *(Note: It is possible that Hen and Josiah are one and the same, rather than brothers.)*

HENADAD (1). *Neh. 3:18.*

Henadad was the father of Bavai, the ruler of the half part of Keilah. He repaired the wall next to Hashabiah, ruler of the other half part of Keilah.

HENADAD (2). *Neh. 3:24; 10:9.*

Henadad was the father of Binnui.

HENADAD'S SONS. *Ezra 3:9.*

Henadad's Sons, their sons and their brethren the Levites, were assigned by Jeshua and Kadmiel and their sons, the sons of Judah, to put forward the work in the house of God as the children of Israel set forth to rebuild the temple in Jerusalem as instructed by Cyrus, king of Persia. *(Note: It is not clear who this particular Henadad was.)*

HENOCH. See **Hanoch**.

HEPHER (Hepherites). *Num. 26:32-33*.

Hepher was a son of Gilead and a great-grandson of Manasseh. His descendants are the **Hepherites**. His brothers were Jeezer, Helek, Asriel, Shechem and Shemida. He begat Zelophehad who only had daughters. (Charts 15a-b.)

HEPHER (2). *1 Chr. 4:6*.

Hepher was the son of Naarah and Ashur the father of Tekoa. His brothers were Ahuzam, Temeni and Haahashtari. He also had half-brothers who were the sons of Ashur and Helah. (Chart 8d.)

HEPHER (3). *1 Chr. 11:36*.

Hepher the Mecherathite was one of the valiant men of David's armies. (Chart 17.)

HEPHERITES. See **Hepher (1)**.

HEPHZIBAH. *2 Kgs. 21:1-3; Isa. 62:4*.

Hephzibah was the mother of Manasseh, king of Judah, and wife of Hezekiah. *(2 Kgs. 21:1-3.)*

"Hephzibah" is used by Isaiah to refer to Jerusalem. *(Isa. 62:4.)* (Chart 1.)

HERDMEN OF Gerar. *Gen. 26:20*.

The Herdmen of Gerar contended with Isaac's servants/herdmen and claimed the wells and water Isaac's men dug for their own.

HERESH. *1 Chr. 9:15 (2, 10, 15)*.

Heresh, head of the house of his father, was one of the Levites who dwelled in Jerusalem after returning from Babylonian captivity. His genealogy was written in the book of the kings of Israel and Judah, who were carried away to Babylon for their transgression.

HESED'S SON. *1 Kgs. 4:10*.

Hesed's Son was one of 12 officers over Israel who provided victuals for king Solomon and his family one month each year. *(Note: There is no indication as to who Hesed was.)*

HETH. *Gen. 10:15; 23; 27:46*.

Heth was a son of Canaan, a grandson of Ham, and a great-grandson of Noah. *(Gen. 10:15.)*

When Sarah died, Abraham spoke to the sons of Heth and told them that he was a stranger and a sojourner in their land. He asked if he could have a burial place amongst them, that he might bury his dead out of his sight. They told him to chose whichever sepulchre he wanted. He chose the cave of Machpelah which was in the field of Ephron the Hittite. Abraham insisted upon paying for it rather than having it just be given to him. *(Gen. 23.)*

Esau married two Hittite women. Rebekah told Isaac that she was weary of her life because of the daughters of Heth, and that if Jacob should marry one of the daughters of Heth, her life would do her no good. *(Gen. 27:46.)* (Chart 2e.)

HEZEKI. *1 Chr. 8:17*.

Hezeki, of the tribe of Benjamin, was one of the sons of Elpaal. (Chart 16i.)

HEZEKIAH (1). *2 Kgs. 16:20; 18:1-35; 19:9-37; 20; 21:1-3; 1 Chr. 3:13; 2 Chr. 28:27; 29; 30; 31; 32:1-22, 24-33; 33:1-3; Prov. 25; Isa. 1:1-31; 10:24-32; 36; 37; 38; 39; Jer. 15:4; 26:18-19; Hosea 1:1-9; Micah 1:1.*

Hezekiah, son of Ahaz, ruled in Judah after Ahaz died. *(2 Kgs. 16:20; 2 Chr. 28:27.)* He began his reign over Judah at the age of 25 in the third year of Hoshea's reign over Israel. He reigned for 29 years. His mother was Abi, the daughter of Zachariah. He reigned in righteousness, removed the high places and destroyed the idols. He also destroyed the brasen serpent made by Moses because the children of Israel worshipped it. The Lord was with him and he successfully defeated the Philistines. In the fourth year of Hezekiah, which was the seventh year of Hoshea, Shalmaneser, king of Assyria, besieged Samaria. At the end of three years, in the sixth year of Hezekiah (which was the ninth year of Hoshea), Samaria was taken and Israel was taken captive into Assyria because they refused to obey the Lord. In the fourteenth year of Hezekiah, the Assryian king Sennacherib came up against Judah and took all the fenced cities. Hezekiah agreed to pay him 300 talents of silver and 30 talents of gold. The king of Assyria sent an army against Jerusalem. One of his men, Rab-shakeh, made a blasphemous speech asking Jerusalem to surrender to the Assyrians. *(2 Kgs. 18.1-35. Also see Isa. 36.)*

Sennacherib sent a second blasphemous message to Hezekiah. Hezekiah petitioned the Lord, and the prophet Isaiah prophesied the destruction of the Assyrians. An angel of the Lord slew 185,000 Assyrians as they slept in their camp. Sennacherib returned home and dwelt in Nineveh where he was slain by two of his sons: Adrammelech and Sharezer, who then fled into the land of Armenia. A third son, Esarhaddon, reigned in his stead. *(2 Kgs. 19:9-37; Isa. 37.)*

When the prophet Isaiah told Hezekiah to put his house in order because the Lord said it was time for him to die, Hezekiah prayed to the Lord. The Lord heard him and had Isaiah return and tell him that his life would be extended by 15 years. Hezekiah asked that the shadow go back 10 degrees on the dial of Ahaz as a sign that he would get better and that his life would be extended, and it was so. *(2 Kgs. 20:1-11; Isa. 38:1-8.)* The Babylonian king, Berodach-baladan sent a letter and a present to Hezekiah when he heard he was sick. Hezekiah showed the Babylonians everything in his house. Isaiah inquired as to where the men came from and what they saw. When Hezekiah told him that they were from Babylon and that he had shown them everything in his house, Isaiah prophesied the Babylonian captivity of Judah and that Hezekiah's sons "that shall issue from thee, which thou shalt beget, shall they take away; and they shall be eunuchs in the palace of the king of Babylon." *(2 Kgs. 20:12-18; Isa. 39.)* While Hezekiah was king, he made a pool and conduit and brought water into the city. He died and his son Manasseh reigned in his stead. *(2 Kgs. 20:20-21).*

Hezekiah destroyed the high places Ahaz had built, but Manasseh rebuilt them when he became king. Hezekiah's wife, the mother of Manasseh, was Hephzibah. *(2 Kgs. 21:1-3.)*

Hezekiah was the son of Ahaz and the father of Manasseh. His genealogy is given. *(1 Chr. 3:13.)*

(Note: 2 Chr. 29 is a repeat and expansion of 2 Kgs. 18:1-5.) Hezekiah's mother's name is given as Abijah rather than Abi and her father's name is spelled Zechariah rather than Zachariah. Hezekiah had the house of the Lord cleansed and sanctified. He also had the priests and Levites sanctify themselves so they could administer in the house of the Lord. They made burnt and sin offerings, sang the psalms of David and of Asaph and praised the Lord with music. The people then brought sacrifices and thank offerings and made burnt offerings. *(2 Chr. 29.)*

Hezekiah invited all Israel to go to Jerusalem to participate in a solemn Passover. While many ridiculed the request, the righteous obeyed and there was greater joy in Jerusalem than there had been since the time of Solomon the son of David king of Israel. *(2 Chr. 30.)*

Hezekiah served faithfully in all that he did. After the solemn Passover, the faithful portion of Israel destroyed the altars and images and groves of the false gods. Hezekiah reinstated the priests and Levites in their appointed courses. The people again paid their tithes and offerings. *(2 Chr. 31.)*

(Note: This is a retelling of 2 Kgs. 19:9-37 with some modification.) When Sennacherib came against Judah, Hezekiah had the people stop the water and fountains so the Assyrians could not have water. Nevertheless, Sennacherib boasted that the gods of other nations could not save the people of those cities and so Hezekiah's people should not trust in their God, either. However, Hezekiah and the prophet Isaiah prayed to the Lord; and the Lord sent an angel who cut off all the mighty men of valor and the leaders and captains in the camp of Sennacherib's army. Sennacherib returned home in shame. His own sons slew him with the sword. In spite of some faults, Hezekiah reigned in righteousness all his days. He died and was buried in the chiefest of the sepulchres of the sons of David. His son Manasseh reigned in his stead. *(2 Chr. 32:1-22, 24-33.)*

The high places Hezekiah broke down were rebuilt by Manasseh. *(2 Chr. 33:1-3.)*

These proverbs of Solomon were "copied out" by the men of Hezekiah king of Judah. *(Prov. 25.)*

Isaiah saw in a vision that which concerned Judah and Jerusalem during the days of Hezekiah, Uzziah, Jotham and Ahaz, kings of Judah. Israel was in an apostate, rebellious and corrupt state. A very small remnant remained faithful. The Lord rejected their sacrifices and feasts. They were called upon to repent. Isaiah prophesied that Zion would be redeemed in the day of restoration. *(Isa. 1:1-31.)*

(The Bible Dictionary indicates that shortly after Hezekiah refused to pay the usual tribute to Assyria, Judah experienced two Assyrian invasions. The first one is alluded to in Isa. 10:24-32. The second is described in 2 Kgs. 18:13-19.) (Isa. 10:24-32.)

This is a retelling of when Sennacherib king of Assyria came against Hezekiah in the fourteenth year of Hezekiah's reign. Sennacherib sent Rabshakeh to Hezekiah and Rabshakeh told them to surrender because neither Pharaoh king of Egypt nor their God could protect them any more than the surrounding cities' gods could protect those cities. *(Isa. 36. Also see 2 Kgs. 18:11-37.)*

Hezekiah praises and thanks the Lord. *(Isa. 38:9-22.)*

The Lord told the prophet Jeremiah that because of the wickedness of the people, and because of what Hezekiah's son Manasseh had done in Jerusalem, He would allow Judah to be destroyed, slain, carried away captive and scattered. *(Jer. 15:4.)*

During the days of Hezekiah, Micah the Morasthite prophesied against Israel if they didn't repent. However, they did repent and the Lord withheld the promised destruction. *(Jer. 26:18-19.)*

In the days of Hezekiah, Uzziah, Jotham and Ahaz (kings of Judah) and Josiah (king of Israel) the Lord instructed Hosea to marry a wife from among those who committed whoredoms. The Lord said he and his family were to be a sign unto Israel. *(Hosea 1:1-9.)*

Micah prophesied in the days of Hezekiah, Ahaz and Jotham regarding the downfall of Samaria and Jerusalem. *(Micah 1:1.)* (Chart 1.)

HEZEKIAH (2). *1 Chr. 3:23.*

Hezekiah, a descendant of David, was a son of Neariah. His brothers were Elioenai and Azrikam. (Chart 1.)

HEZEKIAH (3). *Neh. 7:21 (6-7, 21).*

Hezekiah was the father of Ater. Ninety eight people "of the children of Ater" went up out of Babylonian captivity with Zerubbabel.

HEZEKIAH (4) (Hizkijah). *Neh. 10:17 (1, 17, 28-31).*

Hizkijah was among those chief of the people who covenanted to marry in Israel, honor the Sabbath, pay tithes and keep the commandments.

HEZION. *1 Kgs. 15:18.*

Hezion was the father of Tabrimon and grandfather of Ben-hadad who was king of Syria when Asa was king of Judah.

HEZIR (1). *1 Chr. 24:15.*

Hezir was from the sons of Aaron. When David made the divisions of the sons of Aaron, there was one principal household for Eleazar and one taken for Ithamar. Eleazar had 16 sons and there were eight sons of Ithamar. These 24 sons who were chief of the fathers were divided by lot. Hezir drew the seventeenth lot.

HEZIR (2). *Neh. 10:20 (1, 20, 28-31).*

Hezir was among those chief of the people who, when called to repentance, covenanted to marry in Israel, honor the Sabbath, pay tithes and keep the commandments.

HEZRAI (Hezro). *2 Sam. 23:35; 1 Chr. 11:35.*

Hezrai (Hezro) the Carmelite was one of David's mighty men *(2 Sam. 23:35)* and one of the valiant men of the armies *(1 Chr. 11:35)*. (Chart 17.)

HEZRON (1) (Hezronites (1)) . *Gen. 46:9; Num. 26:6.*

Hezron was one of Reuben's sons and a grandson of Jacob. *(Gen. 46:9.)* He was the father of the **Hezronites**. *(Num. 26:6.)* (Chart 5a.)

HEZRON (2) (Hezronites (2)). *Gen. 46:12; Num. 26:21; 1 Chr. 2:4, 9, 18, 21, 42; 1 Chr. 4:1.*

Hezron, grandson of Judah and great-grandson of Jacob, was one of Pharez's sons. *(Gen. 46:12.)* His descendants were also called **Hezronites**. *(Num. 26:21.)*

Hezron's grandmother was Tamar. His sons are listed as Jerahmeel, Ram and Chelubai *(v. 9)*. *(Note: Verse 18 states that Caleb was a son of Hezron. The assumption here is that Caleb and Chelubai are one and the same.)* Hezron also begat Segub . After Hezron's death, his wife Abiah, the daughter of Machir, bore him Ashur. Hezron married her when he was 60 years old. *(1 Chr. 2:4, 9, 18, 21, 42.)* *(Note: Verse 42 reaffirms that Caleb was the brother of Jerahmeel and, thus, a son of Hezron.)*

Hezron is listed among the sons of Judah. His father was Pharez. His son was Carmi. His grandson was Hur. *(1 Chr. 4:1.)* (Charts 8c-d, h, k, m.; 15b.)

HIDDAI (Hurai). *2 Sam. 23:30; 1 Chr. 11:32.*

Hiddai **(Hurai)** of the brooks of Gaash was one of David's mighty men *(2 Sam. 23:30)* and one of the valiant men of the armies *(1 Chr. 11:32)*. (Chart 17.)

HIEL. *1 Kgs. 16:34.*

Hiel was a Bethelite. He rebuilt Jericho. "He laid the foundation in Abiram, his firstborn; and set up the gates of the city in his youngest son Segub," fulfilling the curse pronounced by Joshua. *(Josh. 6:26: "Cursed be the man before the Lord, that riseth up and buildeth this city Jericho: he shall lay the foundation thereof in his firstborn, and in his youngest son shall he set up the gates of it.")*

HILKIAH (1). *2 Kgs. 18:18; 2 Kgs. 22:4-14; 2 Chr. 34:9-22; Isa. 22:20; Isa. 36:3.*

Hilkiah was the father of Eliakim. *(2 Kgs. 18:18; Isa. 22:20; 36:3.)*

Hilkiah, the high priest, was instructed by Judah's king Josiah via his scribe Shaphan to give money to workmen to repair the house of the Lord. Hilkiah had found the book of the law in the house of the Lord and gave it to Shaphan to give to the king. The king was distressed when he heard the words of the book of the law because he recognized that Judah had sinned against the Lord. He sent Hilkiah, Shaphan and others to inquire of the Lord what the future held for Judah. They went to the prophetess Huldah who prophesied wrath upon the people because of their wickedness. However, she promised blessings upon Josiah because of his righteousness. *(2 Kgs. 22:4-14; 2 Chr. 34:9-22.)*

HILKIAH (2). *1 Chr. 6:13; 9:11; Ezra 7:1-5; Neh. 11:11.*

Hilkiah was the son of Shallum and the father of Azariah. He was a descendant of Aaron through Eleazar. *(1 Chr. 6:13.)*

Hilkiah was the father of Azariah and the son of Meshullam (Shallum). He is listed among the priests who lived in Jerusalem whose genealogy was recorded in the book of the kings of Israel and Judah, who were carried away captive into Babylon because of transgression. *(1 Chr. 9:11.)*

Hilkiah's descendants and forefathers from Aaron through Ezra are listed. *(Ezra 7:1-5.) (Note: there is some variation between this listing and the one in 1 Chr. 6:4-15. Also, the name of Ezra has replaced Jehozadak.)*

Hilkiah, son of Meshullam, was the father (grandfather) of Seraiah. *(Neh. 11:11.)* (Chart 7b.)

HILKIAH (3). *1 Chr. 6:45.*

Hilkiah, a descendant of Levi through Merari, was the son of Amzi and the father of Amaziah. (Chart 7e.)

HILKIAH (4). *1 Chr. 26:11.*

Hilkiah, a Levite, was the secondborn son of Hosah who was of the lineage of Merari. His brothers included: Simri, who was made chief by his father even though he was not the firstborn; Tebaliah, the third; and Zechariah, the fourth. They, along with other Levites, were appointed by king David to be porters—to have charge of the treasures, serve as officers and judges, and to conduct the outward business over Israel. *(Note: Hilkiah apparently had more brothers as it states that "all the sons and brethren of Hosah were thirteen." However, only four are named by name and Simri was not the firstborn.)* (Chart 7a.)

HILKIAH (5). *Neh. 8:1-8; 12:7, 21.*

Hilkiah was one of the men who stood on Ezra's right hand when Ezra read and interpreted the law of Moses to the people. *(Neh. 8:1-8.)* He was one of the men (priests and Levites) who left Babylonian captivity with Zerubbabel and went to Jerusalem in the days of Jesua. He was the father of Hashabiah, who was one of the priests who was a chief of the fathers in the days of Joiakim. *(Neh. 12:7, 21.)*

HILKIAH (6). *Jer. 1:1.*

Hilkiah was the father of the prophet Jeremiah. They were of the priests who were in Anathoth in the land of Benjamin.

HILKIAH (7). *Jer. 29:3.*

Hilkiah was the father of Gemariah.

HILLEL. *Judg. 12:13.*

Hillel was the father of Abdon.

HINNOM. *Josh. 15:8; 18:16.*

Hinnom. There is no explanation as to who Hinnom was. Judah was given an inheritance that partially bordered on the valley of the son of Hinnom. The Bible Dictionary explains that the valley of Hinnom was the scene of the idolatrous worship of the fire-god Moloch, and later was used as a place of refuse. In N.T. times it was called Gehenna and was regarded by the Jews as symbolical of the place of torment. *(Josh. 15:8.)*

The valley of the son of Hinnom was the valley of giants and descended to the valley of Hinnom. *(Josh. 18:16.)*

HIRAH. *Gen. 38:1, 12, 20-22.*

Hirah was an Adullamite and a friend of Judah's. He went to Timnath with Judah unto Judah's sheepshearers. After Judah lay unknowingly with his daughter-in-law, Tamar (thinking the woman was just a harlot), Hirah was asked to go to the "harlot" and retrieve Judah's things, but the "harlot" was no where around. Upon inquiry, Hirah was informed that there was no harlot there. He reported this to Judah.

HIRAM (1) **(Huram (1))**. *2 Sam. 5:11; 1 Kgs. 5:1-12; 9:12-14, 27; 10:11; 1 Chr. 14:1; 2 Chr. 2:3-12; 8:2,18; 9:10, 21.*

Hiram was king of Tyre. After David was anointed king over all Israel, Hiram sent messengers and cedar trees, carpenters and masons to him and they built him a house. *(2 Sam. 5:11; 1 Chr. 14:1.)*

Hiram loved David and sent his servants to Solomon when he heard he had been anointed king. Solomon asked him to have his servants hew cedar trees for him to build a house to the Lord and to let Solomon's servants work alongside them because the Sidonians were skilled in the art of working with timber. The king of Tyre and Solomon made a league together. *(1 Kgs. 5:1-12.)*

Solomon gave Hiram several cities, but Hiram was not pleased with them. He sent his servants, who had knowledge of the sea, to serve with Solomon's servants in Solomon's navy. *(1 Kgs. 9:12-14, 27.)*

Hiram's navy brought gold, almug trees and precious stones to Solomon. *(1 Kgs. 10:11.)*

Huram (Hiram), in response to Solomon's request, sent Solomon timber and skilled workmen to work on the temple. *(2 Chr. 2:3-12.)*

Huram had restored certain cities to Solomon which Solomon rebuilt after completing the temple. Huram sent Solomon "by the hands of his servants, ships and servants that had knowledge of the sea" and they went with Solomon's servants to Ophir where thy gathered much wealth which they took back to Solomon. *(2 Chr. 8:2,18.)*

The servants of Huram and the servants of Solomon brought gold, algum trees and precious stones from Ophir. They traveled to Tarshish once every three years bringing back gold, silver, ivory, apes and peacocks. *(2 Chr. 9:10, 21.)*

HIRAM (2) **(Huram (3))**. *1 Kgs. 7:14-46; 2 Chr. 2:13-14; 4:11-16.*

Hiram was a widow's son of the tribe of Naphtali. His father was a man of Tyre, a worker in brass. Hiram was "filled with wisdom and understanding, and cunning to work all works in brass" and king Solomon brought him out of Tyre to work on the temple. His works included the baptismal font. *(1 Kgs. 7:14-46.)*

Huram, king of Tyre, wrote to Solomon informing him that he was sending **Huram** (Hiram), the son of a woman of the daughters of Dan, to work on the temple. *(2 Chr. 2:13-14.) (This is a repeat of 1 Kgs. 7:14-46 with modification. In 1 Kgs., it says he was of the tribe of Naphtali. In this scripture, it says he was the* *son of a woman of the daughters of Dan. Perhaps his mother was from the tribe of Dan and his father was of the tribe of Naphtali.)*

Huram made pots, shovels, basons and many other items for Solomon for the temple, finishing the work he was asked to do. *(2 Chr. 4:11-16.)* (Chart 12b.)

HITTITES. *Gen. 10:15; 15:18, 20; Ex. 3:8, 17; Deut. 7:1; 2 Sam. 11:3, 15; 23:39; 1 Kgs. 9:20-21; 10:29; 2 Kgs. 7:6; 2 Chr. 1:17; 8:7-8; Ezra 9:1-14; Neh. 9:8; Ezek. 16:45.*

The **Hittites** were descendants of Heth, the son of Canaan. *(Gen. 10:15.) (See Hittites in the BD.)*

The Hittites' lands were given to Abram's seed by the Lord in covenant. *(Gen. 15:18, 20.)* The lands of the Hittites, Canaanites, Amorites, Perizzites, Jebusites and Girgashites were given to Abraham by the Lord. *(Neh. 9:8.)*

The Lord told Moses that He would deliver the children of Israel out of Egypt and take them to the place of the Hittites, Canaanites, Amorites, Hivites, etc.—a land flowing with milk and honey. *(Ex. 3:8, 17.)* The Hittites were one of the seven nations in Canaan, greater and mightier than the Israelites, whom the Lord said He would destroy so Israel could inherit the promised land. *(Deut. 7:1.)*

Uriah the Hittite was Bath-sheba's husband whom king David arranged to have killed in battle so he could marry Bath-sheba. *(2 Sam. 11:3, 15.)* He was one of David's mighty men. *(2 Sam. 23:39.)*

Solomon levied a tribute of bondservice over all the Hittites and other people who were not of the children of Israel who remained among the Israelites. *(1 Kgs. 9:20-21; 2 Chr. 8:7-8.)*

Solomon paid for and had horses and chariots brought out of Egypt along with other fine items for all the kings of the Hittites and the kings of Syria. *(1 Kgs. 10:29; 2 Chr. 1:17.)*

The Lord caused the Syrians to hear a noise of chariots and horses and people and they fled, leaving their possessions behind, thinking the kings of Israel had enlisted the kings of the Hittites and Egyptians to come against them. *(2 Kgs. 7:6.)*

After the children of Israel were delivered from Babylonian bondage, many Jews—including the priests and Levites—intermarried with and followed the abominations of the Hittites, Canaanites, Perizzites, Jebusites, Ammonites, Moabites, Egyptians and Amorites. Ezra prayed and confessed the sins of all the people, fearing the Lord would completely destroy them this time for their abominations. *(Ezra 9:1-14.)*

The Hittites are referred to in the proverb the Lord gave Ezekiel comparing Jerusalem to a mother's daughter with the pagan nations being referred to as "sisters." In this proverb, the Lord told Jerusalem that "your mother was an Hittite and your father an Amorite." Just as the mother loathed her husband, so the daughter, Jerusalem, loathed her husband, the Lord. *(Ezek. 16:45.)*

HIVITE (Gibeonites). *Gen. 10:17; 34:2-36; Ex. 3:8, 17; Deut. 7:1; Josh. 9:7; 11:3, 19; Judg. 3:3-4; 1 Kgs. 9:20-21; 2 Chr. 8:7-8.*

Hivites were descendants of Canaan who was a son of Ham. *(Gen. 10:17.)*

Shechem, a Hivite, took Dinah, the daughter of Leah and Jacob, and lay with her and defiled her. The Hivites sought to arrange their marriage because Shechem loved her. However, Dinah's brothers conspired against them and slew Shechem and his father and others who had consented to be circumcised. *(Gen. 34:2-36.)*

The Lord told Moses that He would deliver the children of Israel out of Egypt and take them to the place of the Hivites, Hittites, Canaanites, Amorites, etc.—a land flowing with milk and honey. *(Ex. 3:8, 17.)*

The Hivites were one of seven nations the Lord said He would destroy in Canaan, nations greater and mightier than the Israelites, so Israel could inherit the promised land. *(Deut. 7:1.)*

The Hivites **(Gibeonites)** by craft, made a covenant with Israel. *(Josh. 9:7.)* *(Note: The subheading to this section of Joshua uses the name Gibeonites rather than Hivites.)*

Joshua, with the help of the Lord, went to battle against the Hivites, Hittites, Amorites, etc. The only ones to make peace with the children of Israel were the Hivites in Gibeon. Joshua and the Israelites took the rest in battle. *(Josh. 11:3, 19.)*

The Lord left the Hivites and a few other nations to prove Israel by them. *(Judg. 3:3-4.)*

Solomon levied a tribute of bondservice over all the Hivites and other people who were not of the children of Israel who continued to dwell among the Israelites. *(1 Kgs. 9:20-21; 2 Chr. 8:7-8.)* (Chart 2e.)

HIZKIAH. *Zeph. 1:1.*

Hizkiah was the father of Amariah, grandfather of Gedaliah, great-grandfather of Cushi, and great-great-grandfather of the prophet Zephaniah.

HIZKIJAH. See **Hezekiah (4)**.

HOBAB. *Num. 10:29-33; Judg. 4:11.*

Hobab was the son of Raguel (Jethro) and brother to Moses' wife, Zipporah. Moses asked him to journey with him and the children of Israel to the place the Lord was leading them, but Hobab declined, saying he wanted to return to his own land and people. Moses asked Hobab not to leave them but to be their eyes in the wilderness because he knew the area. *(Num. 10:29-33.)*

Hobab is, apparently in error, referred to as the father-in-law of Moses. *(Judg. 4:11.)* (Chart 7b.)

HOD. *1 Chr. 7:37.*

Hod was a son of Zophah, a grandson of Hotham, and a great-great-great-grandson of Asher. His brothers were Suah, Harnepher, Shual, Beri, Imrah, Bezer, Shamma, Shilshah, Ithran and Beera. (Chart 14a.)

HODAIAH. *1 Chr. 3:24.*

Hodaiah, a descendant of David, was a son of Elioenai. His brothers were Eliashib, Pelaiah, Akkub, Johanan, Dalaiah and Anani. (Chart 1.)

HODAVIAH (1). *1 Chr. 5:23-26.*

Hodaviah was from the half tribe of Manasseh that was aligned with the Reubenites and Gadites. He was a famous and mighty man of valor and was head of the house of his father. He, along with others, transgressed the laws of God; thus, God allowed them to be carried away into captivity by the Assyrian kings Pul and Tilgath-pilneser. (Chart 15c.)

HODAVIAH (2). *1 Chr. 9:7 (1-3, 7).*

Hodaviah, of the tribe of Benjamin, was the son of Hasenuah and the father of Meshullam. He and his family were among the inhabitants of Jerusalem whose genealogy was written in the book of the kings of Israel and Judah, who were carried away to Babylon for their transgression. His grandson Sallu was among those of the tribe of Benjamin who dwelled in Jerusalem following their return from Babylonian captivity. (Chart 16m.)

HODAVIAH (3) (Hodevah). *Ezra 2:40; Neh. 7:43.*

Hodaviah (Hodevah) was a Levite. His posterity through Jeshua and Kadmeil numbered 74 when they left Babylon and returned to Jerusalem with Zerubbabel to build the house of the Lord as proclaimed by Cyrus, king of Persia.

HODESH. *1 Chr. 8:9-10.*

Hodesh was one of the wives of Shaharaim, a descendant of Benjamin. She bore Jobab, Zibia, Mesha, Malcham, Jeuz, Shachia and Mirma. (Chart 16f.)

HODEVAH. *Neh. 7:43.* See **Hodaviah (3)**.

HODIAH. *1 Chr. 4:19.*

Hodiah was the sister of Naham.

HODIJAH (1). *Neh. 8:7-8; 9; 10:10 (1, 10, 28-31).*

Hodijah was one of the men who, when Ezra read and interpreted the law of Moses to the people, helped the people to understand the law. *(Neh. 8:7-8.)*

Hodijah was a Levite. When Ezra read and interpreted the law of Moses and he and Nehemiah proclaimed the day a holy day, the Levites—Hodijah, Jeshua, Bani, Kadmiel, Shebaniah, Bunni, Sherebiah, Bani, Chenani, Hashabniah and Pethahiah—blessed and praised the Lord, reciting the Lord's goodness to Israel: the blessing of Abraham; giving the land of the Canaanites, Hittites, Amorites, Perizzites, Jebusites and Girgashites to Israel; dividing the Red Sea so they could cross it yet drowning the Egyptians who pursued them; the signs and wonders shown to Pharaoh; leading them in the wilderness and protecting them so that they had bread from heaven, water from the rock, and shoes and clothes that never wore out; accepting them whenever they repented, even when they made a molten calf. They had been given the kingdoms of Shihon, Heshbon and Bashan and the Lord had subdued the Canaanites and delivered them into the hands of the Israelites. The people made a covenant with the Lord to serve Him. The princes, Levites and priests sealed the covenant. *(Neh. 9.)*

Hodijah was among those who covenanted and sealed their covenant to marry in Israel, honor the Sabbath, pay tithes and keep the commandments. *(Neh. 10:10 [1, 10, 28-31].)*

HODIJAH (2). *Neh. 10:13 (1, 13, 28-31).*

Hodijah, a Levite, was among those who covenanted and sealed their covenant to marry in Israel, honor the Sabbath, pay tithes and keep the commandments.

HODIJAH (3). *Neh. 10:18 (1, 18, 28-31).*

Hodijah was among those chief of the people who covenanted to marry in Israel, honor the Sabbath, pay tithes and keep the commandments.

HOGLAH. *Num. 26:33; 27:1-7.*

Hoglah was a daughter of Zelophehad and a great-granddaughter of Manasseh. Her sisters were Mahlah, Noah, Milcah and Tirzah. *(Num. 26:33.)*

Hoglah and her sisters petitioned Moses and Eleazar requesting they be given their father's inheritance because he had no sons and he, himself, had died in the wilderness. The Lord told Moses that Hoglah and her sisters were right and they should be given their father's inheritance. *(Num. 27:1-7.)* (Charts 15a-b.)

HOHAM. *Josh. 10:1-27.*

Hoham, one of the five kings of the Amorites, was king of Hebron. He and the other kings united in battle against the Israelites. His people were destroyed, partly by the sword but mostly by hailstones the Lord poured down upon them. He hid in a cave with the other four kings. Joshua had a stone rolled in front of the cave until the rest of the Amorites were destroyed. Then he had the kings brought out to him. They were all slain and hung on a tree and then their bodies were sealed in the cave in which they had hidden.

HOMAM. See **Hemam**.

HOPHNI. *1 Sam. 1:3; 2:12, 22-25, 31-34; 4:4, 11, 17-18.*

Hophni was a son of Eli, the high priest. His brother was Phinehas. *(1 Sam. 1:3.)* Hophni and Phinehas were wicked and the Lord rejected the house of Eli. The Lord told Eli that both of his sons would die in the same day. *(1 Sam. 2:12, 22-25, 31-34.)* Hophni and Phinehas were killed in battle against the Philistines on the same day. The ark of God was also taken. When Eli heard the report, he fell off his seat backwards and died. *(1 Sam. 4:4, 11, 17-18.)* (Chart 7b.)

HORAM. *Josh. 10:33.*

Horam, king of Gezer, came up to help the people in Lachish. He was defeated by Israel.

HORI (1). *Gen. 36:22.*

Hori was a son of Lotan and a brother of Hemam. (Chart 4a.)

HORI (2). *Num. 13:5.*

Hori, of the tribe of Simeon, was the father of Shaphat.

HORIMS. *Deut. 2:12.*

Horims, Moses reminded the children of Israel, dwelt in Seir before the children of Esau did, but the children of Esau destroyed them and lived there in their stead.

HORITES. *Gen. 14:6.*

Horites occupied mount Seir.

HORONITE. *Neh. 2:10, 19.*

Horonites were opposed to Israel rebuilding the walls and gates of Jerusalem. Sanballat was a Horonite.

HORSEMAN. *2 Kgs. 9:17-20.*

A **Horseman** was sent on order of king Joram (Jehoram) to see if the company headed by Jehu came in peace, but he did not return. A **SECOND HORSEMAN** was sent out to inquire if they came in peace, but he also failed to return.

HOSAH (1). *Chr. 16:38.*

Hosah was the wife of Jeduthun. They were the parents of one of the porters of the ark who was appointed by David to play with psalteries and harps before the ark of the Lord.

HOSAH (2). *1 Chr. 26:10, 16.*

Hosah, a Levite, was of the lineage of Merari. His sons included: Simri, Hilkiah, the secondborn; Tebaliah, the third; and Zechariah, the fourth. *(Note: Hosah had 13 sons and brethren. Simri was one of those, but he was not the firstborn. However, Hosah made him the chief.)* They, along with other Levites, were appointed by king David to be porters—to have charge of the treasures, serve as officers and judges, and to conduct the outward business over Israel. Hosah and Shuppim drew the lot westward when lots for porter were cast. (Chart 7a.)

HOSEA. *Hosea 1-14.*

Hosea was the son of Beeri. *(According to the BD, he began to prophesy during the latter part of Jeroboam II's reign and probably died before the accession of Pekah in 736 B.C.)* In the days of Uzziah, Jotham, Ahaz and Hezekiah, kings of Judah, and in the days of Jeroboam, king of Israel, the Lord instructed Hosea to take a wife of whoredoms. He married Gomer, the daughter of Diblaim. His family was to be a sign unto Israel. They had a son whom the Lord said they should name Jezreel because, the Lord said, "and for yet a little while and I will avenge the blood of Jezreel upon the house of Jehu and will cause to cease the kingdom of the house of Israel." Hosea's daughter was named Lo-ruhamah, which means, "Not having obtained mercy." His other son was named Lo-ammi, which means, "Not my people." Nevertheless, in the latter days, the children of Judah and the children of Israel will be gathered together and become the sons of the living God. *(Hosea 1.)*

Hosea counseled Israel that worshipping false gods brings severe judgments of God upon them. He prophesied that in the latter days, the Lord will show mercy upon them and they will become His people and He will be acknowledged as their God. *(Hosea 2.)*

Hosea taught that Israel would be without the Lord for a long time, but in the latter days, Israel would return and would seek the Lord and His goodness. *(Hosea 3.)*

Hosea taught that Israel had lost all truth, mercy, and knowledge of God because of wickedness. Because they rejected knowledge, God rejected them. They shall be punished for their wickedness and idolatry. *(Hosea 4.)*

Hosea prophesied that Judah, Israel and Ephraim would fall because of iniquity. *(Hosea 5.)*

Hosea urged the children of Israel to return and worship the Lord. He spoke to them about the resurrection and gave reference to the resurrection of the Savior: i.e., ". . . in the third day he will raise us up, and we shall live in his sight" *(v. 2)*. He taught that God desires mercy more than sacrifice and knowledge of Him more than burnt offerings. *(Hosea 6.)*

The Lord, through Hosea, continued his condemnation of Israel and Ephraim, who had become mixed among the people. *((Hosea 7.)*

Hosea continued to recite the Lord's condemnation of Israel, Ephraim and Judah, and prophesied against them. They had forsaken the Lord and were worshipping idols. *(Hosea 8.)*

Hosea continued his condemnation of Israel and Ephraim. Israel had gone "whoring from thy God." "Ephraim," he said, "shall return to Egypt . . . and they shall be wanderers among the nations." *(Hosea 9.)*

Hosea condemned Israel for worshipping false idols. Because of the golden calves, Samaria would suffer: the golden idols cannot deliver. This would also be a condemnation to king Jareb and Assyria. Ephraim and Israel shall be ashamed. Hosea called upon Israel to repent. *(Hosea 10.)*

The Lord, speaking through Hosea, compared Israel to His firstborn. Israel, as a child, was called out of Egypt. They sacrificed unto Baalim. Ephraim turned from the Lord. Judah, at this time, continued to be faithful. *(Hosea 11.)*

Hosea proclaimed that the Lord speaks through prophets and uses visions and similitudes to teach His people. When the people become rich, they turn from the Lord. He said Jacob fled into the country of Syria, and Israel served for a wife. Ephraim provoked the Lord most of all. Ephraim made a covenant with the Assyrians and carried oil into Egypt. The Lord will punish Judah and Jacob for their sins. *(Hosea 12.)*

The Lord, speaking through Hosea, bemoaned the sins of Ephraim, who exalted himself in Israel; but when he offended in Baal, he died. There is no other savior beside the Lord. He, alone, will ransom His people from the grave and redeem them from death. *(Hosea 13:4, 14.)*

Hosea prophesied that in the latter days, Ephraim will repent and return to the Lord. *(Hosea 14.)*

HOSHAIAH (1). *Neh. 12:32.*

Hoshaiah and half of the princes of Judah, under the leadership of Nehemiah, were assigned to one of the two great companies of singers, priests, Levites and princes for the dedication of the walls of Jerusalem.

HOSHAIAH (2). *Jer. 42:1;43:2.*

Hoshaiah was the father of Jezaniah. *(Jer. 42:1.) (Note: He was apparently a Maachathite as Jer. 40:8 states that Jezaniah was the son of a Maachathite.)*

Hoshaiah was the father of Azariah (Jezaniah). *(Jer. 43:2.) (Note: Because Jezaniah, the son of Hoshaiah, is listed earlier as going to see the prophet Jeremiah with Johanan, the son of Kareah, and this verse says Azariah, the son of Hoshaiah, went with Johanan the son of Kareah, to see Jeremiah, the assumption is that Asariah and Jezaniah are one and the same.)*

HOSHAMA. *1 Chr. 3:18.*

Hoshama, a descendant of David, was a son of Jeconiah (Jehoiachin). (Chart 1.)

HOSHEA (1). *Deut. 32:44.* See **Joshua (1)**.

HOSHEA (2). *2 Kgs. 15:30; 2 Kgs. 17:1.*

Hoshea, the son of Elah, conspired against Pekah, slew him, and reigned over Israel in his stead beginning in the 20th year of Jotham. *(2 Kgs. 15:30.) (Note: Some discrepancy seems to exist in the timeline of the various kings. 2 Kgs. 15:27-33 indicates Jotham only reigned 16 years over Judah and that he began his reign in the second year of Pekah's 20-year reign as king over Israel.)*

Hoshea began his reign in Israel in the 12th year of Ahaz, king of Judah. *(Note: These scriptures regarding the year in which he began his reign do not agree with each other.)* He reigned nine years. He reigned in wickedness. Shalmaneser, king of Assyria, took Hoshea captive and bound him in prison. In Hoshea's ninth year, the Assyrians captured Samaria and carried Israel away into Assyria and placed the people in various cities. Israel forsook the Lord, worshipped idols, served Baal, caused their sons and daughters to pass through the fire, used divination and enchantments, and rejected all that the Lord had given them. Thus, the Lord "rent Israel from the house of David" and only the tribe of Judah remained, even though Judah did not walk completely upright before the Lord, either. The king of Assyria brought in other people who occupied the lands the Lord had given to the children of Israel. *(2 Kgs. 17:1.)*

HOSHEA (3). *1 Chr. 27:20.*

Hoshea, the son of Azaziah, was prince of the tribe of Ephraim when David was king.

HOSHEA (4). *Neh. 10:23 (1, 23, 28-31).*

Hoshea was among those chief of the people who covenanted to marry in Israel, honor the Sabbath, pay tithes and keep the commandments.

HOTHAM (Helem). *1 Chr. 7:32, 35.*

Hotham was a son of Heber and a great-grandson of Asher. His siblings included Japhlet and Shomer (Shamer) and a sister, Shua. **Helem**'s (Hotham's) sons were Zophah, Imna, Shelesh and Amal. (Chart 14a.)

HOTHAN. *1 Chr. 11:44.*

Hothan was the father of Shama and Jehiel, two of David's mighty men.

HOTHIR. *1 Chr. 25:4, 28.*

Hothir, a Levite and musician, was a son of Heman who was of the lineage of Kohath. The musicians—sons of Heman, Asaph and Jeduthun—drew lots and were assigned their duties by David and the captains of the host. Hothir cast the 21st of 24 lots. He, his sons and his brethren numbered 12. (Chart 7d.)

HUL. *Gen. 10:23; 1 Chr. 1:17.*

Hul was a son of Aram, a son/grandson of Shem and a great-grandson of Noah. His brothers were Uz, Gether and Mash (Meshech). *(Gen. 10:23; 1 Chr. 1:17.).* (Chart 2b.)

HULDAH. *2 Kgs. 22:14-20; 2 Chr. 34:22-28.*

Huldah, wife of Shallum, was a prophetess in Jerusalem. King Josiah sent his high priest, Hilkiah, and his scribe, Shaphan, and others to her to inquire of the Lord concerning the book of the law which Hilkiah had found in the house of the Lord. She prophesied wrath upon the people because of their wickedness but blessings upon Josiah because he had humbled himself before the Lord.

HUPHAMITES. See **Huppim (1)**, **Hupham**.

HUPPAH. *1 Chr. 24:13.*

Huppah was from the sons of Aaron. When David made the divisions of the sons of Aaron, there was one principal household for Eleazar and one taken for Ithamar. Eleazar had 16 sons and there were eight sons of Ithamar. These 24 sons who were chief of the fathers were divided by lot. Huppah drew the thirteenth lot.

HUPPIM (1) (Hupham, Huphamites). *Gen. 46:21; Num. 26:39.*

Huppim was a son of Benjamin and a grandson of Jacob. His brothers were Belah, Becher, Ashbel, Gera, Naaman, Ehi, Rosh, Muppim and Ard. *(Gen. 46:21.) (Note: In 1 Chr. 8:1-2, Benjamin's sons are listed as "Bela, his firstborn, Ashbel the second, Aharah the third, Nobah the fourth, and Rapha the fifth.")*

Hupham (Huppim), the son of Benjamin, was the father of the **Huphamites**. *(Num. 26:39.)* (Charts 16a-b.)

HUPPIM (2). *1 Chr. 7:12.*

Huppim and Shuppim are listed among Benjamin's posterity as the children of Ir. *(Note: It is not clear who Ir is or what his exact relationship is to Benjamin. The only sons of Benjamin listed in 1 Chr. 7:6 are Bela, Becher and Jediael; and Jediael is not listed as a son in Gen. 46:21.)* (Charts 15b.; 16c.)

HUR (1). *Ex. 17:10-13; 24:13-14; 31:2-3; 1 Chr. 2:19-20; 4:1; 2 Chr. 1:5.*

Hur and Aaron propped Moses' arms up during Joshua's battle against Amalek and, thus, Joshua ultimately "discomfitted" Amalek. *(Ex. 17:10-13.)*

When the Lord told Moses to come unto Him in the mount and receive tables of stone, and a law, and commandments, he rose up "and his minister Joshua" also rose up and went with him. Moses instructed the elders of Israel to tarry where they were and said that Hur and Aaron would be with them to take care of any problems in his absence. *(Ex. 24:13-14.)*

Hur, of the tribe of Judah, was the father of Uri and the grandfather of Bezaleel, which Bezaleel, the Lord told Moses, was filled with the spirit of God in wisdom, understanding, knowledge, and in all manner of workmanship. *(Ex. 31:2-3.)*

Hur was begotten by Caleb the son of Hezron. He begat Uri who begat Bezaleel. *(1 Chr. 2:19-20.)* Hur was the father of Uri who was the father of Bezaleel who made the brasen altar that was put before the tabernacle of the Lord. *(2 Chr. 1:5.)*

Hur was the son of Carmi (Caleb) and the father of Shobal. *(1 Chr. 4:1.)* (Charts 8i, l, m.)

HUR (2). *Num. 31:8; Josh. 13:21-22.*

Hur was a Midianite king who was slain by the children of Israel when Moses sent an army of 12,000 men to destroy the Midianites.

HUR (3). *Neh. 3:9.*

Hur was the father of Rephaiah.

HUR'S SON. *1 Kgs. 4:8.*

Hur's Son was one of twelve officers over Israel who provided victuals for king Solomon and his family one month each year. *(Note: There is no information identifying this Hur more specifically.)*

HURAI. See **Hiddai**.

HURAM (1). *2 Chr. 2:3.* See **Hiram (1)**.

HURAM (2). *1 Chr. 8:5.*

Huram was a son of Bela who was a son of Benjamin. Other sons of Bela were Addar, Gera, Abihud, Abishua, Naaman, Ahoah, Gera and Shephuphan. *(1 Chr. 8:5.)* (Chart 16d.)

HURAM (3). *2 Chr. 2:13.* See **Hiram (2)**.

HURI. *1 Chr. 5:14.*

Huri, the father of Abihail and the son of Jaroah, was a descendant of Gad. (Chart 13b.)

HUSHAH. *1 Chr. 4:4.*

Hushah was of the lineage of Judah, descending through Hur, and was the son of Ezer. (Chart 8m.)

HUSHAI. *2 Sam. 15:32-37; 17; 1 Kgs. 4:16; 1 Chr. 27:33.*

Hushai, the Archite, was a friend of David's. He planned to accompany David when David fled Jerusalem to escape from Absalom. However, David had him return to Jerusalem and volunteer to be a servant unto Absalom so he could provide counsel to Absalom that would defeat the counsel of Ahitophel. He was also to pass information gleaned in Absalom's house on to Zadok and Abiathar, the priests, so they could have their sons Ahimaaz and Jonathan get the information back to David. *(2 Sam. 15:32-37.)*

Through Hushai, the Lord brought evil upon Ahithophel. Ahithophel suggested to Absalom that he be allowed to choose 12,000 men to pursue after David, killing only David and bringing the rest of the people back to Absalom. This was good advice. However, Hushai counseled Absalom otherwise and suggested that Absalom should go to battle himself. When Ahithophel saw that his counsel was not followed but Hushai's was, he went home, set his affairs in order, and hanged himself. He was buried in the sepulchre of his father. Hushai sent word back to David. *(2 Sam. 17.)*

Hushai's son Baanah was one of Solomon's twelve officers over all Israel who provided victuals for the king and his household one month each year. *(1 Kgs. 4:16.)*

Hushai the Archite was king David's companion. *(1 Chr. 27:33.)*

HUSHAM. *Gen. 36:34; 1 Chr. 1:46.*

Husham was of the land of Temani. He reigned as king in Edom upon the death of Jobab. *(Gen. 36:34.)*

Upon his death, Hadad reigned in his stead. *(1 Chr. 1:46.)* (Chart 18.)

HUSHATHITE. *2 Sam. 21:18; 23:27; 1 Chr. 27:11.*

Hushathites were part of Israel. Sibbechai the Hushathite slew Saph, a Philistine, in a battle at Gob. *(2 Sam. 21:18.)* He, Sibbecai (Sibbechai), was of the Zarhites and was assigned by king David to be over the course of 24,000 that served for the eighth month. *(1 Chr. 27:11.)*

Another Hushathite, Mebunnai, was one of David's mighty men. *(2 Sam. 23:27.)*

HUSHIM (1) (Shuham, Shuhamites). *Gen. 46:23; Num. 26:42-43.*

Hushim was the son of Dan and a grandson of Jacob. *(Gen. 46:23.)*

Shuham (Hushim), son of Dan, was the father of the **Shuhamites**. The males twenty years old and older as counted by Moses and Eleazar on the plains of Moab near Jericho numbered 64,400. *(Num. 26:42-43.)* (Chart 11a.)

HUSHIM (2). *1 Chr. 7:12.*

Hushim, a descendant of Benjamin, was the son of Aher. (Chart 16c.)

HUSHIM (3). *1 Chr. 8:8, 11.*

Hushim was one of the wives of Shaharaim, a descendant of Benjamin. She bore Abitub and Elpaal. (Chart 16g.)

HUZ. *Gen. 22:21.*

Huz was Milcah and Nahor's firstborn son. (Chart 2.c)

NAMES THAT BEGIN WITH "I"

IBHAR. *2 Sam. 5:15-16; 1 Chr. 3:6; 12:4-7.*

Ibhar was one of David's children born in Jerusalem. His brothers were Shammua, Shobab, Nathan, Solomon, Elishua, Nepheg, Japhia, Elishama, Eliada and Eliphalet. *(2 Sam. 5:15-16.)*

Ibhar's brothers are listed as: Shimea (Shammua), Shobab, Nathan, Solomon, Ibhar, Elishama, Eliphelet, Nogah (Elishua), Nepheg, Japhia, Elishama, Eliada and Eliphelet. *(1 Chr. 3:6.) (Note: There are two Elishamas and Eliphelets listed.)*

Ibhar's brothers are listed again with some variations: Shammua, Shobab, Nathan, Solomon, Elishua, Elpalet (probably the same as Eliphalet), Nogah, Nepheg, Japhia, Elishama, Beeliada (Eliada) and Eliphalet.*(Note: In past references, Nogah and Elishu replace each other. They are both listed in this reference but may be one and the same.) (1 Chr. 12:4-7.)* (Chart 8e.)

IBNEIAH. *1 Chr. 9:8 (1-3, 8).*

Ibneiah, of the tribe of Benjamin, was the son of Jeroham. He and his family were among the inhabitants of Jerusalem whose genealogy was written in the book of the kings of Israel and Judah, who were carried away to Babylon for their transgression and dwelled in Jerusalem upon their return from Babylonian captivity. (Chart 16m.)

IBNIJAH. *1 Chr. 9:8 (1-3, 8).*

Ibnijah, of the tribe of Benjamin, was the father of Reuel. He and his family were among the inhabitants of Jerusalem whose genealogy was written in the book of the kings of Israel and Judah, who were carried away to Babylon for their transgression. His descendants dwelled in Jerusalem upon their return from Babylonian captivity. (Chart 16m.)

IBRI. *1 Chr. 24:27.*

Ibri, a Levite, was a son of Merari by Jaaziah. He, with the rest of the chief fathers of the Levites, drew lots for his course in the presence of king David, Zadok, Ahimelech and other community leaders. (Chart 7e.)

IBZAN. *Judg. 12:8-11.*

Ibzan was from Bethlehem. He judged Israel seven years following Jephthah. He had 30 sons and 30 daughters. He died and was buried in Beth-lehem. Elon, a Zebulonite, succeeded him as judge in Israel. (Chart 20.)

ICHABOD. *1 Sam. 4:21.*

Ichabod was the son of Phinehas, Eli's son, and his wife. His mother died in childbirth shortly after giving him his name, saying, "The glory is departed from Israel: because the ark of God was taken, and because of her father-in-law and her husband." (Chart 7b.)

IDBASH. *1 Chr. 4:3.*

Idbash, of the lineage of Judah, descended through Hur, and was "of the father of Etam." His siblings included Jezreel and Ishma, and a sister named Hazelelponi. (Chart 8m.)

IDDO (1). *1 Kgs. 4:14; 2 Chr. 9:29.*

Iddo was the father of Ahinadab who was one of twelve officers over Israel who provided victuals for king Solomon and his family one month each year. *(1 Kgs. 4:14.)*

Iddo was a seer who had a vision that was "against Jeroboam the son of Nebat." This vision and other acts of Solomon are among lost scriptures referred to in the Old Testament. *(2 Chr. 9:29.)*

IDDO (2) (Adaiah (2), Eden (1)). *1 Chr. 6:21, 41; 2 Chr. 29:12.*

Iddo, of the tribe of Levi through Gershom, was the son of Joah and the father of Zerah. *(1 Chr. 6:21, 41.) (Note: It is possible that **Adaiah** is another name for Iddo. Verse 21 states that Iddo was the father of Zerah. Verse 41 states that Adaiah was the father of Zerah. Iddo's grandfather is listed as Zimmah in verse 20 and as Adaiah's grandfather in verse 42.)*

Eden (Iddo), a Levite of the tribe of Gershon, was the son of Joah. When Hezekiah became king of Judah, he had Eden and other Levites and priests sanctify themselves and cleanse and sanctify the house of the Lord. *(2 Chr. 29:12.)* (Chart 7a.)

IDDO (3). *1 Chr. 27:21.*

Iddo, son of Zechariah, was prince of the half tribe of Manasseh that was in Gilead when David was king. (Chart 15c.)

IDDO (4). *Ezra 5:1; Neh. 12:16; Zech. 1:1, 7.*

Iddo was the father of Zechariah the prophet. *(Ezra 5:1.)* Iddo was the father of Zechariah, who was one of the priests who was a chief of the fathers in the days of Joiakim. *(Neh. 12:16.)*

Iddo the prophet was the father of Berechiah and grandfather of Zechariah. *(Zech. 1:1, 7.)*

IDDO (5). *Ezra 8:17; Neh. 12:4, 16;*

Iddo was chief at the place Casiphia. When Ezra was preparing to lead the people from Babylon back to Jerusalem, he gathered them together by the river and discovered there were no Levites among them. He assigned several chief men and men of understanding to go to Iddo and the Nethinims and request that they send them some ministers for the house of God. *(Ezra 8:17.)*

Iddo was one of the priests and Levites who accompanied Zerubbabel from Babylon to Jerusalem. *(Neh. 12:4, 16.)*

IDUMEA. *Isa. 34: 5.* See **Esau**.

IGAL (1). *Num 13:7, 31-32; 14:37.*

Igal, of the tribe of Issachar, was the son of Joseph. He was one of twelve leaders sent to scout out the land of Caanan. He returned with a negative report.

(Num 13:7, 31-32.) Because of the negative report he gave, he "died by the plague before the Lord." *(Num. 14:37.)* (Chart 9b.)

IGAL (2) (Joel (2)). *2 Sam. 23:36; 1 Chr. 11:38.*

Igal, the son of Nathan of Zobah, was one of David's mighty men. *(2 Sam. 23:36.)*

Joel (Igal), the brother (son) of Nathan, was one of the valiant men of the armies. *(1 Chr. 11:38.)* (Chart 17.)

IGDALIAH. *Jer. 35:4.*

Igdaliah was the father of Hanan.

IGEAL. *1 Chr. 3:22.*

Igeal, a descendant of David through Shechaniah, was a son of Shemaiah. His brothers were Hattush, Bariah, Neariah and Shaphat. (Chart 1.)

IKKESH. *2 Sam. 23:26; 1 Chr. 11:28; 27:9.*

Ikkesh the Tekoite was the father of Ira. *(2 Sam. 23:26; 1 Chr. 11:28.)*

Ikkesh's son Ira was assigned by king David to serve as captain of the course of 24,000 that served for the sixth month. *(1 Chr. 27:9.)*

ILAI. See **Zalmon**.

IMLAH (Imla). *1 Kgs. 22:8; 2 Chr. 18:7.*

Imlah (Imla) was the father of the prophet Micaiah.

IMMER (1). *1 Chr. 9:12; Neh. 11:13.*

Immer, the father of Meshillemith, was one of the priests in Jerusalem whose genealogy was written in the book of the kings of Israel and Judah who were carried away captive into Babylon because of their transgression. His posterity was among those priests who were chosen to dwell in Jerusalem following their return from Babylonian captivity. *(1 Chr. 9:12.)*

Immer was the father of Meshillemoth (Meshillemith). *(Neh. 11:13.)* (Chart 7g.)

IMMER (2). *1 Chr. 24:14; Jer. 20:1.*

Immer was from the sons of Aaron. When David made the divisions of the sons of Aaron, there was one principal household for Eleazar and one taken for Ithamar. Eleazar had 16 sons: Ithamar had eight. These 24 sons who were chief of the fathers were divided by lot. Immer drew the sixteenth lot. *(1 Chr. 24:14.)*

Immer, a priest, was the father of Pashur. *(Jer. 20:1.)*

IMMER (3). *Ezra 2:37; 10:20 (18-20, 44); Neh. 7: 40.*

Immer was one of the priests. His children numbered 1,052 when they left Babylon to return to Jerusalem to build the temple as proclaimed by Cyrus, king of Persia. *(Ezra 2:37; Neh. 7: 40.)*

Immer's sons Hanani and Zebadiah had taken foreign wives and agreed to put them away as requested by Ezra. *(Ezra 10:20 [18-20, 44].)*

IMMER (4). *Ezra 2:59; Neh. 7:61.*

Immer, Tel-melah, Tel-harsa, Cherub and Addan (Addon) had decendants go up to Jerusalem who could not declare their lineage so they were regarded as polluted and were put from the priesthood.

IMMER (5). *Neh. 3:29.*

Immer was the father of Zadok.

IMNA. *1 Chr. 7:35.*

Imna was a son of Helem (Hotham) and a great-great-grandson of Asher. His brothers were Zophah, Shelesh and Amal. (Chart 14a.)

IMNAH (1). *1 Chr. 7:30.* See **Jimnah**.

IMNAH (2). *2 Chr. 31:14.*

Imnah the Levite was the father of Kore.

IMRAH. *1 Chr. 7:36-37.*

Imrah was a son of Zophah, a grandson of Hotham, and a great-great-great-grandson of Asher. His brothers were Suah, Harnepher, Shual, Beri, Bezer, Hod, Shamma, Shilshah, Ithran and Beera. (Chart 14a.)

IMRI (1). *1 Chr. 9:4.*

Imri was a descendant of Pharez, the son of Judah. He was the father of Omri and the son of Bani. (Chart 8b.)

IMRI (2). *Neh. 3:2.*

Imri was the father of Zaccur.

INFORMANT. *Gen. 14:13.*

An **Informant** who escaped when Sodom and Gomorrah fell to King Chedorlaomer and his allies, told Abram about Lot's capture.

IPHEDEIAH. *1 Chr. 8:25.*

Iphedeiah, a descendant of Benjamin, was a son of Shashak who was a son of Beriah. (Chart 16g.)

IR. *1 Chr. 7:12.*

Ir was a descendant of Benjamin. However, there is no indication as to how Ir is related to Benjamin. Shuppim and Huppim were children of Ir. *(Note: Gen. 46:21, lists Shuppim (Muppim) and Huppim as sons of Benjamin.)* (Charts 15b.; 16c.)

IRA (1). *2 Sam. 20:26.*

Ira, the Jairite, was a chief ruler about David.

IRA (2). *2 Sam. 23:26; 1 Chr. 11:28; 27:9.*

Ira, the son of Ikkesh the Tekoite, was one of David's mighty men *(2 Sam. 23:26)* and one of the valiant men of the armies *(1 Chr. 11:28)*. He was assigned by king David to serve as captain for the sixth month. There were 24,000 in his course. *(1 Chr. 27:9.)* (Chart 17.)

IRA (3). *2 Sam. 23:38; 1 Chr. 11:40.*

Ira, an Ithrite, was one of David's mighty men *(2 Sam. 23:38)* and one of the valiant men of the armies *(1 Chr. 11:40)*. (Chart 17.)

IRAD. *Gen: 4:18.*

Irad was the son of Enoch and the grandson of Caine. He begat Mehujael. (Chart 1.)

IRAM. *Gen. 36:43.*

Iram was one of the dukes (tribal chiefs) who came of Esau. (Chart 19.)

IRI. *1 Chr. 7:7.*

Iri was a son of Bela and a grandson of Benjamin. His brothers were Ezbon, Uzzi, Uzziel and Jerimoth. He was the head of his house and a might man of valor. (Chart 16c.)

IRIJAH. *Jer. 37:13-14.*

Irijah was the son of Shelemiah, who was the son of Hananiah. He was a captain of the ward in the land of Benjamin. When Jeremiah went there, Irijah accused him of deserting to the Chaldeans. Jeremiah denied the accusation, but Irijah took him before the princes, who smote Jeremiah and cast him into the dungeon in the house of Jonathan the scribe. (Chart 16m.)

IRNAHASH. *1 Chr. 4:12.*

Irnahash was the son of Tehinnah and the grandson of Eshton.

IRU. *1 Chr. 4:15.*

Iru was a son of Caleb who was the son of Jephunneh. His brothers were Elah and Naam. (Chart 8n.)

ISAAC. *Gen. 17:19 (15-19); 21:1-8; 22: 2-13; 24; 25; 26; 27; 28:1-5; 35:27-29; Ex. 2:24; 1 Chr. 1:28, 32.*

Isaac was the son of Abraham and Sarah. The Lord told Abraham that Sarah would conceive a son. He was to be called Isaac. He also told Abraham that He would establish his everlasting covenant with Isaac and his seed. Abraham was 100 years old and Sarah 90 years old. *(Gen. 17:19 [15-19].)*

Isaac was born according as the Lord had spoken. He was circumcised when he was eight days old. On the day he was weaned, Abraham gave a great feast in celebration. *(Gen. 21:1-8.)*

The Lord commanded Abraham to sacrifice Isaac. When Isaac inquired as to where the lamb for the sacrifice was, Abraham told him the Lord would provide. Abraham bound Isaac and placed him on the altar and was about to slay him when an angel of the Lord stopped him. A ram, caught in a thicket by its horns, was provided as a substitute sacrifice. *(Gen. 22: 2-13.)*

Abraham instructed his eldest servant to go unto the land of Abraham's relatives to find a wife for Isaac and not to take a wife from among the Canaanites for him. The servant traveled to the household of Nahor, Abraham's brother. He met Rebekah, Isaac's cousin, who drew water for him and his camels. Rebekah agreed to accompany him back and to become Isaac's wife. As the entourage approached Abraham's house, Isaac was in the field and saw them coming. He approached them. Rebekah dismounted and covered her face with a veil. The servant explained everything to Isaac. Isaac took Rebekah into his mother's tent and Rebekah became his wife, "and he was comforted after his mother's death." *(Gen. 24.)*

Isaac's father gave all he had to him. His half-brothers, born to Abraham's concubines, were given gifts and sent away. *(Gen. 25:5-6.)* When Abraham died,

Isaac and Ishmael buried him beside Sarah in the cave of Machpelah. *(Gen. 25:7-9.)* After Abraham's death, the Lord blessed Isaac; and he dwelled by the well Lahai-roi. *(Gen. 25:11.)* Isaac was 40 years old when Rebekah became his wife. Because she was barren, Isaac intreated the Lord in her behalf and she conceived. *(Gen. 25:20-21.)* He was 60 years old when Rebekah gave birth to twins: Esau and Jacob. *(Gen. 25:25-26.)* Isaac favored Esau over Jacob because he enjoyed eating the venison Esau provided. *(Gen. 25:28.)*

Because of a famine in the land, Isaac went unto Abimelech, king of the Philistines unto Gerar. However, the Lord told him not to go into Egypt and that he would bless him according to the promise he had made with Abraham and that his seed would multiply as the stars of heaven and that all the nations of the earth would be blessed through his seed. When asked about Rebekah, he said she was his sister so that they wouldn't kill him in order to get her. Eventually, Abimelech sensed that Rebekah was his wife. Isaac became very wealthy and had many flocks. The Philistines repeatedly stopped up the wells that Isaac's servants dug. Finally, they dug another well and the Philistines didn't strive for it. The Lord appeared unto Isaac and again promised him that He would bless him for Abraham's sake. Abimelech, together with a friend, Ahuzzath, and Phichol, his chief captain of the army, went to Isaac. They indicated that they recognized that the Lord was with Isaac and they made a covenant with him that they wouldn't hurt him and, in return, he would do them no harm. *(Gen. 26.)*

When Isaac grew old, he could not see very well. Knowing that his days were growing few, he called Esau to him and asked him to fix him some venison and to come to him that he might give him a blessing. Rebekah overheard Isaac talking to Esau so she immediately had Jacob bring her two kid goats so she could prepare them like venison. She devised a plan whereby Jacob could receive the blessing Isaac intended to give Esau. With animal skins on his arms and bare neck and by wearing some of Esau's clothes, Jacob was able to convince Isaac that he was, indeed, Esau. Isaac blessed him with the dew of heaven and the fatness of the earth, plenty of corn and wine; that the people would serve him and nations would bow down to him; that he would be lord over his brethren, and that his mother's sons would bow down to him; he blessed him that those who cursed him would be cursed and those who blessed him would be blessed. After Jacob left Isaac, Esau came bearing the venison and asking for the blessing. Upon realizing that Esau was not the one he had blessed, Isaac indicated that the one he blessed "shall be blessed." He told Esau that his dwelling would be the fatness of the earth and the dew of heaven. He also told him that he would live by the sword, that he would serve his brother, and "when thou shalt have the dominion, that thou shalt break his [Jacob's] yoke from off thy neck." *(Gen. 27.)*

Isaac blessed Jacob and instructed him not to take a wife from among the Canaanites but to go to Padan-aram and take a wife from among the daughters of his uncle Laban. *(Gen. 28:1-5.)*

Jacob came unto his father Isaac in Mamre and they sojourned there together. Isaac lived to be 180 years old and then he died. Esau and Jacob joined in burying him. *(Gen. 35:27-29.)*

God heard the groaning of the children of Israel as they suffered under Egyptian bondage and remembered the covenant he had made with Abraham, Isaac and Jacob. *(Ex. 2:24.)*

Isaac's half-brothers included: Ishmael (son of Hagar), Zimran, Jokshan, Medan, Midian, Ishbak and Shuah (sons of Keturah). *(1 Chr. 1:28, 32.)* (Charts 1.; 2b.; 3a-d.; 5a.; 8a.; 9a.; 10a.; 11a.; 12a.; 13a.; 14a.; 15a.; 16a.; 21.)

ISAAC'S SERVANTS and HERDMEN. *Gen. 26:19-22.*

Isaac's Servants and Herdmen and the herdmen of Gerar were in contention with each other. Each time Isaac's servants/herdmen dug a well and found water, the herdmen of Gerar claimed it for their own. They finally dug another well and "they strove not."

ISAIAH. *2 Kgs. 19:2-35; 20:1-11, 16-18; 2 Chr. 26:22; 32:20-21, 32; Isa. 1:1-31; 2; 3; 4; 5; 6; 7; 8; 9; 10; 11; 12; 13; 14; 15-16; 17; 18; 19; 20; 21; 22; 23; 24; 25; 26; 27; 28; 29; 30; 31; 32; 33; 34; 35; 36; 37; 38; 39; 40; 41; 42; 43; 44; 45; 46; 47; 48; 49; 50; 51; 52; 53; 54; 55; 56; 57; 58; 59; 60; 61; 62; 63; 64; 65; 66.*

Isaiah, the prophet (740-701 B.C.), was the son of Amoz. When Rab-shakeh blasphemed the Lord and asked Judah to surrender to the Assyrians, king Hezekiah sent messengers to Isaiah to get his advice. When king Sennacherib of Assyria sent another blasphemous message to Hezekiah and Hezekiah petitioned the Lord, Isaiah prophesied the destruction of the Assyrians and that a remnant of Judah would flourish. *(2 Kgs. 19:2-35; Isa. 37.)*

Isaiah told king Hezekiah he was appointed unto death. After Hezekiah pleaded with the Lord, the Lord had Isaiah tell Hezekiah his life would be extended 15 years. As a sign, Isaiah told Hezekiah that the shadow would go back 10 degrees on the dial of Ahaz. After Hezekiah showed the Babylonians everything in his house, Isaiah prophesied the Babylonian captivity of Judah. *(2 Kgs. 20:1-11, 16-18; Isa. 38:1-8; 39:3-8.)*

Isaiah recorded the rest of the acts of Uzziah (Azariah), king of Judah, in his writings. *(2 Chr. 26:22.)*

Isaiah and king Hezekiah prayed and cried to the Lord when Sennacherib, king of Assyria, came against Jerusalem. The Lord sent an angel who intervened in behalf of Judah. *(This is a repeat of 2 Kgs. 19:20-35.)* The rest of the acts of Hezekiah are recorded in the vision of Isaiah and in the book of the kings of Judah and Israel. *(2 Chr. 32:20-21, 32.)*

Isaiah had a vision wherein he saw that which concerned Judah and Jerusalem during the days of Uzziah, Jotham, Ahaz and Hezekiah, kings of Judah. Israel was a sinful nation. Her people were full of iniquity and had forsaken the Lord. A very small remnant remained faithful. The Lord rejected their sacrifices and feasts. They were called upon to repent. Isaiah prophesied that Zion would be redeemed in the day of restoration. *(Isa. 1:1-31.)*

In the last days, the "mountain of the Lord's house" (i.e., the temple) "shall be established in the top of the mountains . . . and all nations shall flow unto it" *(v. 2)*. Isaiah refers to the Millennial judgment and eventual peace. Man's idols will be destroyed and the idol worshippers, the wicked and the haughty, will be brought low. *(Isa. 2.)*

Judah and Jerusalem shall be punished for their wickedness. Children will be their princes, babes shall rule over them, the people shall be oppressed by one another, even by their neighbors. Children will be their oppressors and women will rule over them. The Lord will judge his people. Because of the wickedness of the women, they will be cursed and tormented, and the crown of their heads shall be smitten with a scab. The men shall fall by the sword and the mighty will fall in war. *(Isa. 3.)*

In the Millennial day, "the filth of the daughters of Zion" shall be washed away and the Lord will redeem Zion. Because of the scarcity of men, seven women will want to take on the name of one man so as to "take away our reproach." *(Isa. 4.)*

The Lord's vineyard—the house of Israel—will bring forth wild grapes. As a result, it shall become desolate and Israel will be scattered. The Lord condemned wealthy landowners for absorbing the farms of the small, poor farmer. Wine and strong drink are condemned. The Lord condemns those who call good evil and evil good. In spite of the people's wickedness, the hand of the Lord is still stretched out to them. He will lift up an ensign to the nations. *(Isa. 5.)*

In the year that Uzziah died, Isaiah saw the Lord. Isaiah's sins were forgiven him *(Isa. 6:7)* and he was called to prophesy *(Isa. 6:8-9)*. Even though the majority of the Jews will reject Christ's teachings, a remnant—a tenth—will return. *(Isa. 6:13.)*

In the days of Ahaz, the Lord instructed Isaiah to take his son Shear-jashub (which means, "the remnant shall return") and deliver a message to Ahaz. He warned him that Syria and Ephraim were planning to wage war against Judah, but not to fear. He prophesied that within 65 years Ephriam would be broken and no longer be a people. As a sign, the Lord revealed that a virgin would conceive and bear a son. She would call his name Immanuel. *(Isa. 7:3-14. See Matt. 1:23.)*

Isaiah had another son. His name was Maher-shalal-hash-baz (which means "to speed to the spoil, he hasteneth the prey"). Isaiah (which means "The Lord is salvation") said that he and his children were "for signs and for wonders in Israel from the Lord of hosts, which dwelleth in mount Zion." People should not seek security from alliances nor from "familiar spirits" or "wizards that peep," but from the Lord. They should turn to the law and to testimony for guidance. Isaiah's wife was a prophetess. *(Isa. 8.)*

Isaiah spoke Messianically. Those who have apostatized, who "walked in darkness" will see "a great light" *(i.e., the Savior, Jesus Christ)*. He will be the

"Prince of Peace" and will sit upon the throne of David. There will be no end to the increase of his govenment. In spite of Israel's disobedience, the Lord's hand is still stretched out to His people. *(Isa. 9.)*

Isaiah prophesied of the destruction of Assyria. It is a type of destruction of the wicked at the Second Coming of the Savior. Only a few people shall remain at the Lord's coming. *(Isa. 10:12-19.)* Nevertheless, a remnant of Jacob will return unto the Lord . *(Isa. 10:20-22.)*

Isaiah continued to prophesy of Jesus Christ (the stem of Jesse) and of his righteous Millennial reign. The Lord will raise an ensign and gather Israel from the four corners of the earth and from the islands of the sea. In that day, there will be peace—even the animals will be at peace one with another. *(Isa. 11.)*

Isaiah prophesied that in the Millennial day all men shall rejoice and praise the Lord as He dwells among them. The Lord's name is JEHOVAH. *(Isa. 12.)*

Isaiah foretold the destruction of Babylon. It is a type of the Second Coming of the Savior. There will be wrath and destruction, none of the sinners—men, women, nor children—will escape the vengence of the Lord. *(Isa. 13:9, 11, 15-16.)* At that day when the Lord cometh, "the stars of heaven and the constellations thereof shall not give their light: the sun shall be darkened in his going forth, and the moon shall not cause her light to shine." *(Isa. 13:10.)*

In approximately 720 B.C., Isaiah delivered this burden, or message of doom, regarding the Philistines, but prophesied that Israel will be gathered when the Lord comes again and He will "set them in their own land." *(Isa. 14:1.)* Isaiah also made it known that Lucifer (Satan) had been with God in the pre-existence but that because of pride and greed and a desire to exalt himself above God, he was cast out of heaven *(Isa. 14:12-20)*.

Isaiah prophesied of Moab's fate: it shall be laid waste and her people will be filled with sorrow, weeping and howling. He also prophesied that the Messiah would sit in mercy upon the throne of David, "seeking judgment, and hasting righteousness" *(Isa. 16:5)*. *(Isa. 15-16.)*

Because the children of Israel had forsaken God, they would be scattered. Nevertheless, the Lord promised to destroy the nations that spoil Israel. In the day that Israel sorrows, she will begin to repent. *(Isa. 17.)*

The Lord will raise up an ensign on the mountains unto all the inhabitants of the earth. He will send messengers to his scattered people and they will be gathered to mount Zion. *(Isa. 18.)*

Isaiah prophesied that the Lord would smite Egypt. However, in the last days, Egypt would know the Lord and would be "healed." *(Isa. 19:22.)* In that day, Egypt, Assyria and Israel would join together and be blessed. *(Isa. 19:23-25.)*

In approximately 711 B.C., the Lord instructed Isaiah to "loose the sackcloth from off thy loins" and go naked (i.e., without an upper garment, like a slave or exile) and barefoot throughout the land for three years as a sign to Egypt and Ethiopia that Assyria would overrun them and make them ashamed. *(Isa. 20.)*

Isaiah was shown in vision the cataclysmic destruction of Babylon. *(Isa. 21.)* *(Note: According to the footnote to the text, this destruction came to pass in 538 B.C., about 200 years after the death of Isaiah.)*

Isaiah prophesied that Jerusalem would be attacked and scourged and that her people would be carried away captive. The people would look to their own efforts for protection rather than to the Lord. He prophesied that Eliakim would replace Shebna as king. Isaiah then used the name Eliakim in its symbolic meaning— "God raiseth up"—to refer to the Messiah. The Messiah (Jesus Christ) would be fastened as "a nail in a sure place." *(Isa. 22.)*

Isaiah prophesied that Tyre would be overthrown. After 70 years, the Lord would visit Tyre, but any success Tyre experienced would only be what the Lord permitted "for them that dwell before the Lord, to eat sufficiently, and for durable clothing." *(Isa. 23.)*

Isaiah prophesied concerning the Second Coming. Because men defiled the earth, transgressed the laws, changed the ordinance and broke the everlasting covenant, the wicked will be burned. Only a few people will remain. At that time, the earth will shake and reel to and fro, the moon will "be confounded, and the sun ashamed." The Lord will reign in mount Zion and in Jerusalem. *(Isa. 24.)*

Isaiah praised the Lord, who was a strength to the poor and to the needy in his distress. He declared the Lord will "swallow up death in victory," i.e., will be resurrected, and will save us. *(Isa. 25.)*

Isaiah continued to praise the Lord. The Lord's name is JEHOVAH. *(Isa. 26:4.)* Because of Him all men shall be resurrected. *(Isa. 26:19.)* The Lord will punish the wicked. *(Isa. 26:21.)*

Isaiah prophesied of the gathering of Israel in the last days. *(Isa. 27.)*

Isaiah prophesied of the fate to soon befall Ephraim *(which, according to the footnote to the text, was subsequently captured by the Assyrians in 722 B.C.).* Knowledge and righteous instruction should begin with the young and taught line upon line, precept upon precept. *(Isa. 28:10, 13.)* A cornerstone, a sure foundation (Christ), is promised. *(Isa. 28:16.)*

Isaiah prophesied of the coming forth of a book. It would be as "one that hath a familiar spirit, out of the ground, and thy speech shall whisper out of the dust." *(Isa. 29:4.)* It would be "as the words of a book that is sealed, which men deliver to one that is learned, saying, Read this, I pray thee: and he saith, I cannot; for it is sealed: And the book is delivered to him that is not learned, saying, Read this, I pray thee: and he saith, I am not learned." *(Isa. 29:11-12.)* "And in that day shall the deaf hear the words of the book, and the eyes of the blind shall see out of obscurity and out of darkness." *(Isa. 29:18.)* He foretold of the apostasy and subsequent restoration of the Gospel. *(Isa. 29:13-14.).* *(Note: This prophecy was also given by Nephi in the Book of Mormon: "And it shall come to pass that the Lord God shall bring forth unto you the words of a book, and they shall be the words of them which have slumbered. And behold the book shall be sealed; and in the book shall be a revelation from God, from the beginning of the world to the ending thereof. Wherefore, because of the things which are sealed up, the things which are sealed shall not be delivered in the day of the wickedness and abominations of the people. Wherefore the book shall be kept from them . . . But behold, it shall come to pass that the Lord God shall say unto him to whom he shall deliver the book: Take these words which are not sealed and deliver them to another, that he may show them unto the learned, saying: Read this, I pray thee. And the learned shall say: Bring hither the book, and I will read them . . . And the man shall say: I cannot bring the book, for it is sealed. Then shall the learned say: I cannot read it." (2 Nephi 27:6-8, 15, 17-18). (Note: This prophecy was fulfilled in 1828 when Martin Harris, an early convert to the Church of Jesus Christ of Latter-day Saints (Mormon), showed some of the characters and translation of the Book of Mormon to Professor Charles Anthon, who was recognized for his literary attainments. Professor Anthon indicated that the translation was correct and that the characters were true characters. He gave Martin Harris a certificate certifying to that fact. However when Professor Anthon learned that Joseph Smith had received the gold plates from the angel Moroni, he took the certificate back and tore it up, claiming there was no such thing now as ministering angels. He asked to see the plates. Martin Harris informed him that he could not do that and that part of the plates were sealed. Professor Anthon then responded, "I cannot read a sealed book" (JS-H, 1:64-65).*

Because Israel rejected the seers and prophets, she would be scattered. The time would come when she would be gathered again and blessed both temporally and spiritually. When the Lord comes the second time, He will judge and destroy the wicked. *(Isa. 30.)*

Israel continued to be chastised for looking to Egypt for help rather than relying on the Lord. Both Israel and Egypt shall fall. Nevertheless, the Lord will deliver Jerusalem when He comes again. *(Isa. 31.)*

The land of Israel shall be desolate. "Upon the land of my people shall come up thorns and briers; yea, upon all the houses of joy in the joyous city: Because the palaces shall be forsaken; the multitude of the city shall be left; the forts and towers shall be for dens for ever, a joy of wild asses, a pasture of flocks; Until the spirit be poured upon us from on high, and the wilderness be a fruitful field, and the fruitful field be counted for a forest.. . ." *(Isa. 32:13-15).* After this, there shall come judgment and righteousness, peace, and the Lord's people shall dwell in peaceable habitation and quiet resting places. *(Isa. 32: 16-18.)*

Prior to the Second Coming, there will be apostasy and wickedness. The wicked will be destroyed by fire. Those who survive the fire will be those who are righteous. Zion and her stakes shall not be removed. The Lord will be our judge, lawgiver and king. *(Isa. 33.)*

Isaiah continued his prophecy regarding the Second Coming. The Lord's vengence will be upon all the nations of the world. *(Isa. 34.)*

Isaiah prohesied that in the day of restoration, the desert will blossom as a rose; the eyes of the blind shall be opened and the ears of the deaf shall be unstopped; the Lord will come; Israel shall be gathered and Zion will be built up. *(Isa. 35.)*

Isaiah's words continue to reveal that he had a thorough knowledge of the future coming of the Savior, the Second Coming, and all things pertaining to the Messiah. *(Isa. 40.)*

Through Isaiah, the Lord reminded Israel that they are His servants and that He will preserve them. Idols are nothing, merely "wind and confusion." The Lord will send one to Jerusalem that will bring good tidings. *(Isa. 41.)*

Isaiah again reminded the people that the Messiah would come and bring His law and judgment, and would be a light to the Gentiles. *(Isa. 42.)*

Through Isaiah, the Lord reminded Israel that He is God; there is no other Savior than Himself; they are His witnesses that He is God; and He will gather their seed in the latter days. *(Isa. 43.)*

The Lord, through Isaiah, continued to remind Israel that He would bless their seed. He will eventually gather and redeem Israel and rebuild Jerusalem. Isaiah prophesied that the Lord would move Cyrus, king of Persia, to rebuild Jerusalem and the temple. The Lord also reminded Israel that idols of wood are of no more worth than firewood. *(Isa. 44.)* Isaiah prophesied that the Lord would raise up Cyrus as king of Persia, and that Cyrus would "build my city, and he shall let go my captives." *(Isa. 45:1, 13.) (Note: Cyrus issued his proclamation instructing Israel to return to Jerusalem and build the temple in 537 B.C.)*

Isaiah condemned the worship of idols. They can not help anyone: they, themselves, must be carried. They cannot be compared to God. Only God can save Israel. *(Isa. 46.)*

Isaiah prophesied that Babylon and Chaldea would be destroyed for their wickedness. *(Isa. 47.) (Note: Babylon was overthrown by Cyrus of Persia in 539 B.C.)*

The Lord, through Isaiah, told Israel that He knew they would be a stubom and stiff-necked people; therefore, He had revealed His purposes to Israel from the beginning. They were chosen in the furnace of affliction, but they would eventually be freed from Babylonian captivity. *(Isa. 48.)*

Isaiah prophesied that the Messiah would be a light to the Gentiles. He will set the prisoners free. Israel will be gathered with power in the last days. The Gentiles will bring Israel's sons in their arms and carry their daughters upon their shoulders. Kings will be their nursing fathers and queens their nursing mothers. *(Isa. 49.)*

Isaiah's knowledge of the mortal life of Jesus is again demonstrated as he speaks Messianically. The Messiah will have the tongue of the learned. He shall give his back to the smiters. He won't turn away from those who spit upon him. He shall not be confounded. *(Isa. 50.)*

The Lord continued to remind Israel that in the last days He shall comfort Zion and gather Israel. The redeemed of the Lord shall return and come with singing and everlasting joy to Zion. *(Isa. 51.)*

Israel is again admonished to put on her strength. Zion will return and Israel shall be redeemed in the last days. The Messiah will deal prudently with the people and shall be exalted. *(Isa. 52.)*

Isaiah prophesied the Savior's eventual humiliation and sufferings. The Messiah will make his soul as an offering for sin. He will be despised and rejected by the people. He will be numbered with the transgressors, bear the sins of the people, and make intercession for the transgressors. *(Isa. 53.)*

In the latter days, Zion will expand her "curtains," lengthen her cords and strengthen her stakes. Israel will be gathered with great mercy and tenderness. They should not fear. The Lord will be with them and they will triumph. They shall be established in righteousness and their children shall have peace. *(Isa. 54.)*

The Lord pleads with His people not to purchase that which "satisfieth not" but to follow Him and "eat ye that which is good." They are to seek Him while He can yet be found. His ways and thoughts are not our ways and thoughts. His way is sure, "So shall my word be that goeth forth out of my mouth: it shall not return unto me void, but it shall accomplish that which I please, and it shall prosper in the thing whereto I sent it." *(Isa. 55:2-11.)*

All who keep the Sabbath and follow the Lord will be joined with the house of Israel and will receive an everlasting name. *(Isa. 56.)*

When people who are righteous die, they enter into peace and will be rewarded for their righteousness. However, the Lord said there is no peace to the wicked. *(Isa. 57.)*

The Lord set forth the law of the fast and explained the blessings that attend proper observance of the fast. Those who keep the Sabbath will be blessed. *(Isa. 58.)*

The Lord did not turn away from Israel: Israel separated herself from God through iniquity. The Redeemer will come to Zion and redeem the repentant. *(Isa. 59.)*

Isaiah prophesied that in the last days Israel will arise and became a mighty nation. The Gentiles will join with Israel and will serve her. The nations that fight against Zion, the city of the Lord, will be destroyed. They will finally dwell in celestial splendor *(Isa. 60: 10-21)*.

Isaiah prophesied of the mission of the Savior. He shall preach the gospel, proclaim liberty to the captives and free the prisoners who are bound (by sin), appoint his priests and make an everlasting covenant with his people. *(Isa. 61.)* *(Note: The fulfillment of this prophecy is found in Luke 4:18-19, 21, where Jesus quoted Isaiah [Esaias] and then said, "This day is this scripture fulfilled in your ears.")*

In the last days, Israel shall become righteous and be called by a new name which shall be given her by the Lord. Jerusalem will be a praise in the earth. They will lift up an ensign to the people. They will be a holy people, redeemed of the Lord. *(Isa. 62.)* The servants of God will pray for the Second Coming and the salvation of the righteous. *(Isa. 64.)*

When the Savior comes the Second Time, it will be a day of vengence and the day of the redeemed of the Lord. The righteous will then praise the Lord and acknowledge him as their father. *(Isa. 63:3-4, 16.)*

The Lord, through Isaiah, reminded the people that He rejected ancient Israel because they rejected Him. *(Isa. 65:1-7.)* However, He will "bring forth a seed out of Jacob and out of Judah an inheritor of my mountains: and mine elect shall inherit it, and my servants shall dwell there" and the Lord will "create new heavens and a new earth: and the former shall not be remembered, nor come into mind" *(Isa. 65:9, 17)*. The days of man shall be lengthened to a hundred years and the wolf and lamb shall feed together. *(Isa. 65:20, 25.)*

Isaiah prophesied that at the Second Coming, Israel, as a nation, will be born in a day and the wicked will be destroyed. The Gentiles will hear the gospel, and the Lord will make a new earth and new heavens. All flesh shall worship the Lord. *(Isa. 66.) (Note: The Encyclopaedia Britannica, vol. 5, p. 440, states, "There is a legend in apocryphal and rabbinical literature, that he [Isaiah] died a martyr's death by order of King Manasseh of Judah (c. 687-642), but it is unsupported by Biblical texts.")*

ISCAH. *Gen. 11:29.*

Iscah was one of Lot's children. (Charts 2c-d.)

ISHBAH. *1 Chr. 4:17.*

Ishbah was the father of Eshtemoa. His mother was Jalon, the daughter of Ezra. His siblings were Miriam and Shammai. (Chart 8 o.)

ISHBAK. *Gen. 25:2.*

Ishbak was a son of Abraham and his wife Keturah. (Charts 2b.; 3a, d, f.)

ISHBI-BENOB. *2 Sam. 21:16-17.*

Ishbi-benob, a Philistine, "was of the sons of the giant". He was slain by Abishai.

ISH-BOSHETH. *2 Sam. 2:8-31;. 4:5-12.*

Ish-bosheth was one of Saul's sons. After Saul's death, Abner, captain of Saul's hosts, took Ish-bosheth to Mahanaim and made him king over most of Israel. David, however, was anointed king over Judah. Ish-bosheth was 40 years old. He reigned over Israel two years. Ish-bosheth's servants, following Abner, went against Joab and the servants of David. Twelve of his men contended against twelve of David's servants. Abner and his men were beaten. Ultimately, 360 of Ish-bosheth's men died while David only lost 19 men plus Asahel. *(2 Sam. 2:8-31.)*

Two of Saul's servants, Rechab and Baanah (sons of Rimmon), crept into Ish-bosheth's house and slew him while he was sleeping. They cut his head off and took it to David in Hebron. David had these men slain for killing "a righteous person in his own house upon his bed." David's men buried Ish-bosheth's head in the sepulchre of Abner in Hebron. *(2 Sam. 4:5-12.)* (Chart 16 l.)

ISHI (1). *1 Chr. 2:31.*

Ishi was the son of Appiam. He begat Sheshan. He was a six-times-great-grandson of Judah. (Chart 8c.)

ISHI (2). *1 Chr. 4:20.*

Ishi was the father of Zoheth and Ben-zoheth.

ISHI (3). *1 Chr. 4:42.*

Ishi was the father of Pelatiah, Neariah, Rephaiah and Uzziel who were the captains who led a group of 500 men, including some of the sons of Simeon, to mount Seir where they smote the rest of the Amalekites who had escaped from earlier conflicts. (Chart 6b.)

ISHI (4). *1 Chr. 5:24.*

Ishi was from the half tribe of Manasseh that was aligned with the Reubenites and Gadites. He was a famous and mighty man of valor and was head of the house of his father. He, along with others, transgressed the laws of God; thus, God allowed them to be carried away into captivity by the Assyrian kings Pul and Tilgath-pilneser.

ISHIAH. *1 Chr. 7:3.*

Ishiah was the son of Izrahiah, the grandson of Uzzi, great-grandson of Tola and a great-great-grandson of Issachar. His brothers were Michael, Obadiah and Joel. (Chart 9a.)

ISHIJAH. *Ezra 10:31 (18-19, 31, 44).*

Ishijah, one of Harim's sons, and his brothers Eliezer, Malchiah, Shemaiah, Shimeon, Benjamin, Malluch and Shemariah were some of the Israelite men who took wives from among the Canaanites and other foreign groups. They agreed to Ezra's request to separate themselves from their foreign wives.

ISHMA. *1 Chr. 4:3.*

Ishma, of the lineage of Judah and a descendant of Hur, was of the father of Etam. His siblings included Jezreel and Idbash, and a sister named Hazelelponi. (Chart 8m.)

ISHMAEL (1). *Gen. 16:11-16; 17; 21:9-21; 25; 28:9; 36:3.*

Ishmael was the son of Abram and Hagar, Sarai's handmaid. The Lord told Hagar that he would be a wild man. *(Note: The footnote to the text indicates this is a metaphor for freedom-loving; probably a nomad.)* His hand would be against every man and every man's hand would be against him, but he would dwell in the presence of all his brethren. Abram was 86 years old when Ishmael was born. *(Gen. 16:11-16.)*

Ishmael, Abraham was told by the Lord, would be blessed, but the Lord would establish His covenant with Isaac. He said He "will multiply him [Ishmael] exceedingly; twelve princes shall he beget, and I will make him a great nation"

(Gen. 17:20). Ishmael was 13 years old and Abraham was 99 years old when they were circumcised as instructed by the Lord *(Gen. 17:23-26).*

Ishmael and his mother were cast out because he mocked Sarah. They were given a bottle of water and some bread. When the water was gone, his mother placed him under a bush and sat a little way off so she wouldn't have to watch him die. An angel spoke to her and told her to fear not, that the Lord would make a great nation of him. "And God opened her eyes and she saw a well of water," and they were able to fill their water bottles and quench their thirst. God was with Ishmael in the wilderness. He became an archer. His mother took a wife for him from out of Egypt. *(Gen. 21:9-21.)*

When Abraham died, Ishmael and Isaac buried their father in the cave of Machpelah beside his wife Sarah. *(Gen. 25:9-10.)* Ishmael begat 12 sons—12 princes according to their nations (as the Lord had promised earlier): Nebajoth, Kedar, Adbeel, Mibsam, Mishma, Dumah, Massa, Hadar, Tema, Jetur, Naphish and Kedemah. *(Gen. 25:13-15.)* Ishmael lived 137 years. *(Gen. 25:17.)*

Ishmael's daughter Mahalath, the sister of Nebajoth, became one of Esau's wives. *(Gen. 28:9.)*

Ishmael's daughter Bashemath (Mahalath), the sister of Nebajoth, became one of Esau's wives. *(Gen. 36:3.)* (Charts 1.; 2b.; 3a, d-e.)

ISHMAEL (2). *2 Kgs. 25:23-26; Jer. 40:8, 14-16; 41:1-15.*

Ishmael was the son of Nethaniah. He and a group of other men came to Gedaliah after he was made governor over the remnant of Judah by Nebuchadnezzar and Gedaliah told them they didn't need to fear being servants of the Chaldees. Ishmael and ten cohorts slew Gedaliah and the Jews and Chaldees who were with him at Mizpah. The people then fled to Egypt because they feared the Chaldees. Ishmael was a descendent of Elishama, king David's son. *(2 Kgs. 25:23-26.)*

(Note: The scriptural text includes a partial repeat and expansion of 2 Kgs. 25:23-26.) Johanan the son of Kareah, and all the other captains of the forces in the fields went to Gedaliah and told them that Ishmael had been sent by Baalis the king of the Ammonites to kill Gedaliah. However, Gedaliah did not believe them. *(Jer. 40:8, 14-16.)*

Ishmael, the son of Nethaniah the son of Elishama, of the seed of David, took ten princes of the king and went to Gedaliah. After eating with Gedaliah, they rose up and slew him with the sword. They also slew all the Chaldeans, the Jews and the men of war who were In Mizpah. Fourscore men from Shechem, Shiloh and Samaria came and Ishmael and his men slew all but ten of them who had treasures in the field of wheat, barley, oil and honey. He threw all the bodies into a pit that had been built previously by king Asa who feared Baasha king of Israel. He then carried the rest of the inhabitants of Mizpah off captive. However, they were rescued by Johanan and his forces. Ishmael escaped and joined the Ammonites. *(Jer. 41:1-15.)* (Chart 8e.)

ISHMAEL (3). *1 Chr. 8:38.*

Ishmael, son of Azel, was from the tribe of Benjamin and was a tenth-great-grandson of Saul. His brothers were Azrikam, Bocheru, Sheariah, Obadiah and Hanan. (Chart 16 l.)

ISHMAEL (4). *2 Chr. 19:11.*

Ishmael was the father of Zebadiah.

ISHMAEL (5). *2 Chr. 23:1.*

Ishmael, the son of Jehohanan, was one of the captains of hundreds Jehoiada the priest rallied to make Joash king over Judah and to slay Athaliah.

ISHMAEL (6). *Ezra 10:22 (18-19, 22, 44).*

Ishmael, one of the sons of Pashur, was among the sons of the priests who had taken foreign wives and who agreed to Ezra's request that they separate themselves from their strange wives.

ISHMAELITES (Ishmeelites, Midianite Merchantmen). *BD: Ishmael; Gen. 37:25, 28, 36; 39:1; Num. 25:17-18; 31; Judg. 6-7; 8:24; Ps. 83:6, 9; Isa. 10:26.*

Ishmaelites were "descendants of Ishmael and appear to have been a wandering race who lived by plunder. They had commercial relations and intermarried with the heathen nations of Canaan." *(BD: Ishmael.)*

A group of **Ishmeelites, or Midianite Merchantmen**, bought Joseph from his brothers for 20 pieces of silver. They took him to Egypt where they sold him to Potiphar who was one of Pharaoh's officers and captain of his guard. *(Gen. 37:25, 28, 36; 39:1.)*

The Lord told Israel to vex and smite the Midianites because they "beguiled" them regarding whoredoms and the worship of false gods. *(Num. 25:17-18.)*

The Lord instructed Moses to avenge the children of Israel regarding the Midianites and Moses sent forth 12,000 warriors to destroy them. They were to kill all the men, all the male children, and all the women who had lain with a man; but all the women children who had not lain with a man they were to keep alive for themselves. *(Num. 31.)*

Because Israel became wicked, the Lord allowed them to become captives of the Midianites and be ruled by them for seven years, after which time he raised up Gideon to deliver them. *(Judg. 6-7.)*

The Ishmaelites wore golden earrings which the men of Israel collected as their prey. *(Judg. 8:24.)*

The Ishmaelites were named among those groups who opposed the Lord and sought to destroy Israel. Asaph pleaded that the Lord would do unto the groups who oppose Israel what He did unto the Midianites. *(Ps. 83:6, 9.)*

Isaiah referred to the slaughter of the Midianites. *(Isa. 10:26.)*

ISHMAIAH. *1 Chr. 27:19.*

Ishmaiah, son of Obadiah, was prince of the tribe of Zebulun when David was king. (Chart 10b.)

ISHMEELITES. See **Ishmaelites**.

ISHMERAI. *1 Chr. 8:18*.

Ishmerai, a descendant of Benjamin, was one of Elpaal's sons. He was among those named as heads of the fathers, by their generations, chief men, who lived in Jerusalem. (Chart 16i.)

ISHOD. *1 Chr. 7:18*.

Ishod was the son of Hammoleketh. His brothers were Abiezer and Mahalah. (Chart 15a.)

ISHPAN. *1 Chr. 8:22, 25*.

Ishpan, a descendant of Benjamin, was a son of Shashak who was a son of Beriah. (Chart 16g.)

ISHUAH (Isuah). *Gen. 46:17; Num. 26:44-47; 1 Chr. 7:30*.

Ishuah was a son of Asher and a grandson of Jacob. His brothers were Jimnah (Jimna, Imnah), Isui (Jesui, Ishuai) and Beriah. His sister was Serah. *(Gen. 46:17.). (Note: Ishuah is not listed among Asher's sons in Num. 26:44-47. They are all listed again in 1 Chr. 7:30, but with modified spellings.)* (Chart 14a.)

ISHUI. Also see **Abinadab (3)**. *1 Sam. 14:49; 31:2; 1 Chr. 8:33*.

Ishui was one of Saul's sons. His brothers were Jonathan and Melchi-shua. His sisters were Merab and Michal. *(1 Sam. 14:49.)*

Abinadab, not Ishui, is listed among Saul's sons. *(1 Sam. 31:2.)*

Saul's sons were Jonathan, Malchi-shua, Abinadab (Ishui) and Esh-baal. *(1 Chr. 8:33.)* (Chart 16 l.)

ISMACHIAH. *2 Chr. 31:13*.

Ismachiah, among others, was an overseer of tithes, offerings and the dedicated things under the hand of Cononiah and Cononiah's brother Shimei according to the commandment of king Hezekiah and Azariah, the ruler of the house of God.

ISMAIAH. *1 Chr. 12:4 (1-2, 4, 23)*.

Ismaiah, the Gibeonite, was one of David's mighty men who came to him at Ziklag when David became king and all Israel rejoiced and sent their armies to support him and turn the kingdom of Saul to David.

ISPAH. *1 Chr. 8:16*.

Ispah, a descendant of Benjamin, was a son of Beriah who was a son of Elpaal who was a son of Shaharaim and Hushim. (Chart 16g.)

ISRAEL. See **Jacob**.

ISRAELITE MAID WHO WAS NAAMAN'S WIFE'S SERVANT. *2 Kgs. 5:2-3*.

The **Israelite Maid Who Was Naaman's Wife's Servant** told her mistress that there was a prophet in Samaria who could cure Naaman of his leprosy.

ISRAELITES. See **Children of Israel**.

ISSACHAR (1). *Gen. 30:18; 35:23; 37; 46:13; 49:1, 14-15; 50:8, 12-13; Num. 1:8, 28-29; 2:3-9; 26:23-25; 34:26; Deut. 27:12; 33:18-19; Josh. 19:17-23; 1 Chr. 7:1, 5; 12:32; 27:18; Ezek. 48:25, 33.*

Issachar was the 5th son of Leah and Jacob. (He was Jacob's 9th son.) *(Gen. 30:18.)* Issachar and his brothers, the sons of Leah, were Reuben, Simeon, Levi, Judah, Issachar and Zebulun. *(Gen. 35:23.)*

Issachar and his brothers hated their younger brother Joseph and sold him to a group of Ishmeelites, or Midianite merchantmen, for 20 pieces of silver. They dipped his coat of many colors in animal blood and gave it to their father so he would think Joseph had been killed by wild beasts. *(Gen. 37.)*

Issachar begat Tola, Phuvah, Job and Shimron. *(Gen. 46:13.)*

After the brothers had gone to Egypt for grain and were finally reunited with Joseph, and following the move of their entire family to Egypt, the time came when Jacob called his sons together to tell them what would befall each of them in the last days. He said, "Issachar is a strong ass couching down between two burdens: And he saw that rest was good, and the land that it was pleasant; and bowed his shoulder to bear, and became a servant unto tribute." *(Gen. 49:1, 14-15.)*

Following his father's death, Issachar, along with all of his brothers, traveled to Canaan for Jacob's burial. *(Gen. 50:8, 12-13.)*

Moses was instructed to have Nethaneel, son of Zuar, lead the tribe of Issachar as Israel prepared for war. The number of males who were 20 years old or older in the tribe of Issachar who could go to war totaled 54,400. *(Num. 1:8, 28-29.)* Nethaneel was instructed to have the tribe of Issachar pitch their tents between the tribes of Judah and Zebulun on the east side of the encampment. *(Num. 2:3-9.)*

Issachar's family included the Tolaites, Punites, Jashubites and the Shimronites. When Moses and Eleazar numbered the males who were twenty years old and older while they were on the plains of Moab near Jericho, there were 64,300 in Issachar's family. *(Num. 26:23-25.)*

Paltiel, son of Azzan and prince of the tribes of the children of Issachar, was assigned to divide Issachar's land of inheritance among Issachar's posterity. *(Num. 34:26.)*

As the Israelites prepared to cross over Jordan, the tribes of Issachar, Simeon, Levi, Judah, Joseph and Benjamin were to stand upon mount Gerizim to bless the people. *(Deut. 27:12.)*

Moses blessed the tribe of Issachar. *(Deut. 33:18-19.)*

Issachar's tribe received the fourth lot when Joshua cast lots to divide the promised land. *(Josh. 19:17-23.)*

Issachar's sons were Tola, Puah (Phuvah, Pua), Jashub (Job) and Shimron. Issachar's male descendants numbered 87,000 in the days of David. *(1 Chr. 7:1, 5.)*

When David became king and went to Ziklag, all Israel rejoiced and sent their armies to support him. The children of Issachar were men who had "understanding of the times, to know what Israel ought to do." They had 200 leaders, "and all their brethren were at their commandment." *(1 Chr. 12:32.)*

The prince of the tribe of Issachar when David was king was Omri, son of Michael. *(1 Chr. 27:18.)*

The Lord revealed to Ezekiel just how the land should be divided by tribes when the children of Israel are gathered in the latter days. Issachar's portion will be by the border of Simeon, from the east side unto the west side. The twelve gates of the city are to bear the names of the twelve sons of Jacob. One of the three south gates is to be named for Issachar. *(Ezek. 48:25, 33.)* (Charts 1.; 3d.; 5a.; 6a.; 7a.; 8a.; 9a-b.; 10a.; 11a.; 12a.; 13a.; 14a.; 15a.; 16a.)

ISSACHAR (2). *1 Chr. 26:5, 8, 12.*

Issachar, a Levite, was the seventh son of Obed-edom, a Levite belonging to the house of Kohath. His brothers were Shemaiah, Jehozabad, Joah, Sacar, Nethaneel, Ammiel and Peulthai. They, along with other Levites, were appointed by king David to be porters—to have charge of the treasures, serve as officers and judges, and to conduct the outward business over Israel. (Chart 7c.)

ISSHIAH (1) (Jeshaiah (2). *1 Chr. 24:21; 26:25.*

Isshiah, a Levite, was a descendant of Amram through Rehabiah who was a grandson of Moses through Eliezer. He, with the rest of the chief fathers of the Levites, drew lots for his course in the presence of king David, Zadok, Ahimelech and other community leaders. *(1 Chr. 24:21.)*

Jeshaiah (Isshiah) was the son of Rehabiah, the grandson of Eliezer and the great-grandson of Moses. His son was Joram; his grandson, Zichri; and his great-grandson, Shelomith. Shelomith and his brethren were over the treasures of the dedicated things which king David and others dedicated. *(1 Chr. 26:25.)* (Chart 7b.)

ISSHIAH (2). *1 Chr. 24:25.* See **Jesiah (2)**.

ISUI (Jesui, Jesuites, Ishuai). *Gen. 46:17; Num. 26:44-47; 1 Chr. 7:30.*

Isui was a son of Asher and a grandson of Jacob. His brothers were Jimnah (Imnah), Ishuah (Isuah) and Beriah. His sister was Serah. *(Gen. 46:17.)*

Jesui (Isui) was the father of the **Jesuites**. *(Num. 26:44-47.)*

Ishuai (Isui) and his brothers were sons of Asher. *(1 Chr. 7:30.)* (Chart 14a.)

ITHAI. See **Ittai (2)**

ITHAMAR. *Ex. 6:23; 28:1; 38:21; 40; Lev. 1-27; Num. 3:4; 4:28, 33; 7:5-8; 1 Chr. 24:1-2, 6; Ezra 8:2.*

Ithamar was one of Aaron and Elisheba's sons. His brothers were Nadab, Abihu and Eleazar. *(Ex. 6:23.)*

Ithamar and his father and brothers were to be consecrated and anointed to minister in the priest's office. They were to keep a light burning always in the tabernacle of the congregation. *(Ex. 28:1) (See Ex. 27:21).*

Ithamar counted the items connected with the tabernacle according to the commandment of Moses. *(Ex. 38:21.)*

Ithamar and his father and brothers were washed and anointed and given an everlasting priesthood. *(Ex. 40.)*

Throughout Leviticus, instructions pertaining to Aaron and his sons were given to Moses who then instructed Aaron and his sons regarding their responsibilities. Aaron and his sons were washed and anointed and dressed in the holy garments *(Lev. 8:6-9, 13)*.

Ithamar and Eleazar ministered in the office of the priest after their brothers Nadab and Abihu died "when they offered strange fire before the Lord." *(Num. 3:4.)*

The Lord appointed Ithamar to be over the Gershonites and over the families of Merari as they performed their service in the tabernacle of the congregation. *(Num. 4:28, 33.)*

Ithamar had responsibility for giving the offerings for the service of the sanctuary to the Levites. *(Num. 7:5-8.)*

David divided the sons of Aaron and the rest of the sons of Levi into groups and assigned them their duties. Ithamar's brothers, Nadab and Abihu, had been slain earlier by the Lord and had no children. Therefore, he and his brother Eleazar executed the priest's office. Of the sons of Ithamar, David distributed the duties through Ahimelech. Eleazar's duties were distributed through Zadok. There were fewer chief men among the sons of Ithamar—eight—than among the sons of Eleazar—16. They were to be the governors of the sanctuary and of the house of God. One principle household was taken for Ithamar and one for Eleazar. Twenty-four lots were drawn. *(1 Chr. 24:1-2, 6, 7-18.)*

Ithamar was the father of Daniel who was the patriarchal leader of his posterity when Ezra led many exiled Israelites out of Babylon back to Jerusalem during the reign of Artaxerxes. *(Ezra 8:2.)* (Chart 7b.)

ITHIEL (1). *Neh. 11:7.*

Ithiel, of the tribe of Benjamin, was the father of Maaseiah and the son of Jesaiah. (Chart 16m.)

ITHIEL (2). *Prov. 30:1.*

Ithiel received the prophecy of Agur the son of Jakeh which constitutes Proverbs 30.

ITHMAH. *1 Chr. 11:46.*

Ithmah the Moabite was one of David's mighty men. (Chart 17.)

ITHRA (Jether (2)). *2 Sam. 17:25; 1 Kgs. 2:5, 32; 1 Chr. 2:17.*

Ithra (Jether) was an Israelite (Ishmeelite) and the father of Amasa. His wife was Abigail, David's sister. *(2 Sam. 17:25.)* (Chart 8d.)

ITHRAN (1). *Gen. 36:26.*

Ithran was a son of Dishon who was the son of Seir the Horite. His brothers were Hemdan, Eshban and Cheran. (Chart 4d.)

ITHRAN (2). *1 Chr. 7:36-37.*

Ithran was a son of Zophah, a grandson of Hotham, and a great-great-great-grandson of Asher. His brothers were Suah, Harnepher, Shual, Beri, Imrah, Bezer, Hod, Shamma, Shilshah and Beera. (Chart 14a.)

ITHREAM. *2 Sam. 3:5; 1 Chr. 3:3.*

Ithream was David's sixthborn son in Hebron. His mother was Eglah. (Chart 8e.)

ITHRITES. *2 Sam. 23:38; 1 Chr. 2:53.*

Two **Ithrites**—ira and Gareb—were mighty men of David. *(2 Sam. 23:38.)* The Ithrites were descendants of Shobal, son of Hur (the son of Caleb). *(1 Chr. 2:53.)* (Charts 8 l.; 17.)

ITTAI (1). *2 Sam. 15:19-21.*

Ittai was a Gittite. He went with David when David fled Jerusalem to escape from Absalom. David encouraged him to go back home as he had just recently come to Jerusalem and David didn't think he should risk his life. However, Ittai responded, ". . . as my lord the king liveth, surely in what place my lord the king shall be, whether in death or life, even there also will thy servant be."

ITTAI (2) (Ithai). *2 Sam. 23:29; 1 Chr. 11:31.*

Ittai (Ithai), was a son of Ribai out of Gibeah. He was one of David's mighty men *(2 Sam. 23:29)*; one of the valiant men of the armies *(1 Chr. 11:31)*. (Chart 17.)

IZHAR (Izehar, Izeharites, Izharites, Amminadab (2)). *Ex. 6:18; Num. 3:19, 27-31; 1 Chr. 6:2, 22-28, 33-38; 26:29.*

Izhar was a son of Kohath and a grandson of Levi. His brothers were Amram (the father of Aaron and Moses), Hebron and Uzziel. *(Ex. 6:18.)* **Izeharites** were descendants of Izhar, who was a son of Kohath, a grandson of Levi and a great-grandson of Jacob (Israel). His name is spelled **Izehar**. *(Num. 3:19, 27-31.)*

Amminadab (Izhar) was the father of Korah. *(1 Chr. 6:2, 22-28, 33-38.)*

Of the **Izharites**, Chenaniah and his sons were assigned to the outward business over Israel to be officers andjudges. *(1 Chr. 26:29.)* (Charts 7b, d.)

IZRAHIAH. *1 Chr. 7:3.*

Izrahiah was the son of Uzzi, the grandson of Tola, and a great-grandson of Issachar. His sons were Michael, Obadiah, Joel and Ishiah. (Chart 9a.)

IZRAHITE. *1 Chr. 27:8.*

The **Izrahite** Shamhuth was assigned by king David to be captain of the course of 24,000 who served the king in any matter of the courses for the fifth month.

IZRI. *1 Chr. 25:11.*

Izri, a Levite and musician, cast the fourth lot when the musicians were assigned their duties by king David. He, his sons and brethren numbered 12.

NAMES THAT BEGIN WITH "J"

JAAKOBAH. *1 Chr. 4:36.*

Jaakobah was a descendant of Shimei. (Chart 6a.)

JAALAH (Jaala). *Ezra 2:56; Neh. 7:58.*

Jaalah (Jaala) was one of Solomon's servants.

JAALAM. *Gen. 36:5,18.*

Jaalam, son of Aholibamah and Esau, was a duke or tribal chief. (Charts 3b-c.; 4c.)

JAANAI. *1 Chr. 5:12, 19.*

Jaanai was a descendant of Gad. He, along with Joel, Shapham and Shaphat, joined with Reuben's descendants and the half tribe of Manasseh in battle against the Hagarites in the days of king Saul. (Chart 13b.)

JAARE-OREGIM (Jair (3)). *2 Sam. 21:19; 1 Chr. 20:5.*

Jaare-oregim (Jair), a Beth-lehemite, was the father of Elhanan.

JAASAU. *Ezra 10:37 (18-19, 37, 44).*

Jaasau, a son of Bani, and his brothers were some of the men in Israel who took foreign wives but gave them up when Ezra feared the wrath of God would destroy Israel for this iniquity.

JAASIEL. *1 Chr. 27:21.*

Jaasiel, the son of Abner, was prince of the tribe of Benjamin when David was king. (Chart 16f.)

JAAZANIAH (1) (Jezaniah, Azariah (4)). *2 Kgs. 25:23-26; Jer. 40:8; 42:1-18; 43:2.*

Jaazaniah (Jezaniah) was the son of a Maachathite. He, Johanan the son of Careah, and a group of other men came to Gedaliah after Gedaliah was made king by Nebuchadnezzar. Gedaliah told them they shouldn't fear being servants of the Chaldees. After Ishmael and his cohorts slew Gedaliah and the Jews and Chaldees who were with him at Mizpah, the rest all fled to Egypt because they feared the Chaldees. *(2 Kgs. 25:23-26; Jer. 40:8.)*

Jezaniah, the son of Hoshaiah, accompanied Johanan the son of Kareah (Careah) and the captains of the forces when they approached Jeremiah and asked him to pray to the Lord and inquire what they should do. They promised to follow whatever the Lord said. Jeremiah told them that if they remained in Judah, they would have peace and safety. But, he said they would perish by the sword, famine and pestilence if they went to Egypt and none of them would remain or escape from the evil the Lord promised to bring upon them. *(Jer. 42:1-18.)*

Azariah (Jezaniah) the son of Hoshaiah, Johanan "and all the proud men" told Jeremiah that he spoke falsely, and they carried Jeremiah and the remnant into Egypt. *(Jer. 43:2.)*

JAAZANIAH (2). *Jer. 35:3-11.*

Jaazaniah was the son of Jeremiah who was the son of Habaziniah. They were Rechabites. Jaazaniah and the rest of the Rechabites refused to partake of wine and lived in tents in accordance with the instructions they had received from their fathers. Because they feared Nebuchadrezzar and the armies of the Chaldeans and the Syrians, they left their tents and went to dwell in Jerusalem.

JAAZANIAH (3). *Ezek. 8:11-18.*

Jaazaniah was the son of Shaphan. The prophet Ezekiel saw in a vision "seventy men of the ancients of the house of Israel," among whom was Jaazaniah, worshipping falsely in the house of the Lord.

JAAZANIAH (4). *Ezek. 11:1.*

Jaazaniah was the son of Azur, one of the princes of the people. He was among 25 men who Ezekiel saw in vision sitting at the east gate of the Lord's house giving false counsel to the people in Jerusalem, saying that the city would not be destroyed and they were safe to build houses. Ezekiel was instructed by the Lord to prophesy against them.

JAAZIAH. *1 Chr. 24:26-27.*

Jaaziah appears to be a wife or concubine of Merari. The sons of Merari by Jaaziah were Beno, Shoham, Zaccur and Ibri. (Chart 7e.)

JAAZIEL (Aziel). *1 Chr. 15:18-20.*

Jaaziel and his brethren "of the second degree" were assigned, under David's direction, to be singers along with Heman, Asaph and Ethan. **Aziel** (Jaaziel) and his brethren were assigned to play with psalteries on Alamoth. (Chart 1.)

JABAL. *Gen. 4:20.*

Jabal was one of the sons born to Lamech and Adah. He was the father of such as dwell in tents and of those who have cattle. (Chart 1.)

JABESH. *2 Kgs. 15:10.*

Jabesh was the father of Shallum which Shallum slew king Zachariah.

JABESH MESSENGERS. *1 Sam. 11:3-11.*

Jabesh Messengers were sent to Saul in Gibeah to see if anyone would come and save the people in Jabesh.

JABEZ. *1 Chr. 4:9-10.*

Jabez was an honorable man. His mother named him Jabez because she bore him with sorrow. When he called on the God of Israel to keep him from evil, the Lord granted his request.

JABIN. *Josh. 11:1-13; Judg. 4:2-24.*

Jabin was king of Hazor. When he heard what Israel was doing to other kingdoms, he contacted Jobab, king of Madon, the king of Shimron and the king of Achshaph and numerous other kings and they banded together to fight against Israel. The Lord was with Israel and they defeated all of these kingdoms. "And they smote them, until they left them none remaining." *(Josh. 11:8.)* However, the only city he burned was Hazor, because Hazor was the head of the other kingdoms. *(Josh. 11:1-13.)*

Jabin was the king of Canaan reigning in Hazor. He oppressed the children of Israel for twenty years following the death of Ehud because the children of Israel again turned against the Lord. The children of Israel cried mightily unto the Lord because Sisera, captain of Hazor's host, had 900 chariots of iron. The Lord raised up Deborah the prophetess to free Israel. Sisera was killed and the children of Israel prevailed against Jabin and destroyed him. *(Judg. 4:2-24.)*

JACHAN. *1 Chr. 5:13.*

Jachan was a descendant of Gad. (Chart 13b.)

JACHIN (1) (Jarib (1), Jachinites). *Gen. 46:10; Num. 26:12; 1 Chr. 4:24.*

Jachin was one of Simeon's sons and a grandson of Jacob. His brothers were Jemuel, Jamin, Ohad and Zohar, and Shaul the son of a Canaanitish woman. *(Gen. 46:10.)*

Jachin's descendants were called **Jachinites**. His brothers were Nemuel (Jemuel), Jamin, Zerah (Zohar) and Shaul. *(Note: Ohad is not listed.) (Num. 26:12.)*

Simeon's sons are listed as Nemuel (Jemuel), Jamin, **Jarib** (Jachin), Zerah (Zohar) and Shaul. *(Note: Ohad is omitted again.) (1 Chr. 4:24.)* (Chart 6a.)

JACHIN (2). *1 Chr. 9:10 (1-3, 10); Neh. 11:10-12.*

Jachin was one of the priests in Jerusalem whose genealogy was written in the book of the kings of Israel and Judah, who were carried away captive into Babylon because of their transgression. He was one of the priests who dwelled in Jerusalem after returning from Babylonian captivity. *(1 Chr. 9:10 [1-3, 10].)*

Jachin was one of the priests elected by lot to dwell in Jerusalem following Babylonian captivity. Those who did the work of the house of the Lord were 822. *(Neh. 11:10-12.)*

JACHIN (3). *1 Chr. 24:17.*

Jachin was from the sons of Aaron. When David made the divisions of the sons of Aaron, there was one principal household for Eleazar and one taken for Ithamar. Eleazar had 16 sons and there were eight sons of Ithamar. These 24 sons who were chief of the fathers were divided by lot. Jachin drew the twenty-first lot.

JACHINITES. See **Jachin (1)**.

JACOB (Israel). *Gen. 25:23, 26-27; 27; 28:1-5, 10-22; 29; 30; 31; 32; 33; 34; 35; 37; 42:1-4, 29-38; 43:1-14; 45:25-28; 46; 47; 48; 49; 50:1-13; Ex. 2:24; Jer. 46:27-28; 51:19-23; Ezek. 28:25; 37:25; 39:25-29; Hosea 12:2-4, 12; Amos 6:8; 9:8-9, 14-15; Obad.; Micah 3; 5; 7; Mal. 1:2-3; 2:12.*

Jacob was the secondborn twin son of Isaac and Rebekah. When he was born, his hand was holding onto the heel of his brother, Esau. He was a "plain" man and dwelled in tents. His father was 60 years old when he and Esau were born. Rebekah was told by the Lord that the older twin would serve the younger. Jacob was favored over Esau by his mother. Esau sold his birthright to Jacob for some bread and pottage of lentiles. *(Gen. 25:23, 26-27.)*

When Isaac grew old and his eyesight was dim, he called Esau to him and asked him to prepare him some venison, which he loved, and to bring it to him that he might eat it and then he would give Esau a blessing. While Esau was hunting for and preparing the venison, Jacob's mother Rebekah had Jacob bring two kid goats to her so she could prepare them like venison. She had Jacob take it to Isaac, and with kid skins on his arms and neck, deceive Isaac into thinking he was Esau, thus obtaining the blessing instead of Esau. Isaac blessed Jacob and said God would give him of the dew of heaven and the fatness of the earth, with plenty of corn and wine. He blessed him that the people would serve him and nations would bow down to him; that he would be lord over his brethren, and that his mother's sons would bow down to him. He said those who cursed him would be cursed and those who blessed him would be blessed. When Esau learned that the blessing had been given to Jacob "he cried with a great and exceeding bitter cry." He asked his father for a blessing, too. He was told that the blessing would remain with Jacob. He was told that his dwelling would be the fatness of the earth and the dew of heaven; that by the sword he would live; that he would serve his brother; but that the time would come when he would break the yoke of his brother from off his neck. Esau hated Jacob and planned to kill him as soon as his father died. When Rebekah learned of this, she told Jacob to flee to Haran to her brother Laban. *(Gen. 27.)*

Isaac instructed Jacob not to take a wife from among the daughters of Canaan, but to go to Padan-aram and take a wife from the daughters of his uncle Laban, his mother's brother. He also prayed that God would bless him and bestow the blessing of Abraham upon him. As Jacob traveled to his relatives' land, he spent a night in Luz. As he slept, he had a vision wherein he saw a ladder reaching up into heaven and the Lord spoke to him and told him that He would be with him always. When he awoke, he built an altar unto the Lord using the rock he had used as a pillow. He then called the place Beth-el, and said that would be God's house. He covenanted to pay tithes of all he should ever have. *(Gen. 28:1-5, 10-22.)*

When Jacob finally reached his destination, he saw men watering their flocks at the well. He inquired as to who they were and whether or not they knew Laban. They said they did and that his daughter Rachel was approaching. Jacob watered her sheep, kissed her and told her that he was her father's brother, that he was Rebekah's son. She ran to tell her father. Jacob stayed with Laban's family a month. Laban indicated that he wanted to pay Jacob for his labor—he didn't want him to work for him for nothing. Laban had two daughters, Leah, who was "tender-eyed," and Rachel, who was "beautiful and well favoured." Jacob said he would serve him seven years if he could have Rachel for a wife. Laban agreed. At the end of the seven years, Jacob was given his bride. However, Laban tricked him and gave him Leah instead of Rachel. When Jacob confronted Laban the next morning, Laban told him to "fulfil her week" and then they would also give him Rachel because in their land it was not right that the younger should be given before the firstborn. Jacob loved Rachel more than Leah. The Lord blessed Leah because she was hated, and Leah gave Jacob four sons: Reuben, Simeon, Levi and Judah. Rachel remained barren. *(Gen. 29.)*

When Rachel complained to Jacob that she was barren, Jacob became angry with her, declaring it was not his fault that she was unable to have children. At Rachel's request, he married Bilhah, Rachel's handmaid, so Rachel could obtain children through her. Bilhah begat two sons: Dan and Naphtali. *(Gen. 30: 1-8.)* After Rachel gave Jacob her handmaid Bilhah for a wife, Leah gave Jacob her handmaid, Zilpah, so she could obtain more children through her since she had stopped bearing children herself. Zilpah begat two sons: Gad and Asher. *(Gen. 30: 9-13.)* Leah "hired" Jacob to sleep with her by giving Rachel some mandrakes her son Reuben had gotten for her. Leah conceived and had a son. She called him Issachar. She begat another son and called him Zebulun. She also bore a daughter named Dinah. *(Gen. 30: 14-21.)* Rachel was finally blessed with a son of her own. She and Jacob called him Joseph. *(Gen. 30: 22-24.)* Jacob asked Laban to send him and his wives away so they could find a place of their own. Laban asked him to stay because he knew he had done well because the Lord was with Jacob. Jacob said he would stay if Laban would agree to a proposal he would make regarding the division of the sheep and cattle. Laban agreed. They set three days' journey between the two families. However, Jacob continued to feed Laban's flocks. As time passed, Jacob's flocks and herds became stronger than Laban's. Jacob also increased in maidservants and menservants, and in other areas. *(Gen. 30: 25-43.)*

After working for Laban for 20 years, Jacob was instructed by the Lord to return unto his own land. Jacob recognized that Laban's feelings for him had changed. He left without telling Laban. After three days, Laban learned Jacob and his family had gone. He pursued them. The Lord appeared to Laban in a dream and told him not to speak good or bad to Jacob. Laban finally overtook Jacob. He asked why they had left and complained that someone had stolen his images. Jacob told him that he was afraid that Laban would use force to keep his daughters from leaving. He also told Laban that he could search every tent and, not knowing that Rachel had taken them, said that whoever had his idols should die. However, Laban could not find them. Rachel had hidden them in the camel's furniture and sat upon them, saying she could not get down because the custom of women was upon her. Jacob reminded Laban that he had worked 14 years for his wives and another six years for his flocks, and that Laban had changed his wages 10 times. Laban and Jacob covenanted not to harm one another. Laban kissed his sons and daughters goodbye and blessed them. He and Jacob parted on good terms. *(Gen. 31.)*

As Jacob neared his former home, he met some angels. In anticipation of meeting his brother Esau, he sent some messengers ahead to let Esau know he was coming and wanted to be reconciled. When they returned, they told Jacob that Esau was on the way with 400 men. Jacob was fearful and asked the Lord for a blessing to preserve him. He devised a plan whereby he might make peace with Esau. He spent the night wrestling with an angel of God. His name was changed to **Israel**.

(Gen. 32: 28.). Jacob called the place Peniel because he had seen God face to face and his life had been preserved. *(Gen. 32.)*

Jacob and Esau were reconciled. Jacob insisted that Esau accept his gift of many animals. Esau returned unto Seir. Jacob journeyed to Succoth and built a house there. Jacob came to Shalem, which was a city of Shechem, in the land of Canaan, and pitched his tent. He bought a parcel of land from the children of Hamor, Shechem's father. He then erected an altar. *(Gen. 33.)*

After Jacob settled his family in Canaan, his daughter Dinah went out among the people to see the daughters of the land. Hamor's son Shechem took her and lay with her, thus defiling her. Shechem asked his father to get her for him for his wife. Hamor met with Jacob and told him his son wanted to marry Dinah. He suggested their groups intermarry and trade together. Dinah's brothers answered this request deceitfully saying they would consent to that if all of Hamor's men would be circumcised. Hamor and Shechem and all the men agreed to that. On the third day after being circumcised, "when they were sore," Dinah's brothers, Simeon and Levi, took their swords and slew Hamor and Shechem and all the other males. When Jacob learned what his sons had done, he said, "Ye have troubled me to make me to stink among the inhabitants of the land, among the Canaanites and the Perizzites: and I being few in number, they shall gather themselves together against me, and slay me; and I shall be destroyed, I and my house." *(Gen. 34.)*

God instructed Jacob to go to Beth-el. Jacob told his family and all who were with them to get rid of their idols, to be clean and to change their garments because they were going to Beth-el where he would build an altar unto God. While there, his mother's nurse, Deborah, died and was buried under an oak. Jacob's name was changed to Israel by the Lord. *(Gen. 35: 10.)* The Lord renewed the promise he had made to Abraham and Isaac and told Jacob that kings and nations would come from his loins, and that he would give him and his seed this land. Rachel gave birth to Benjamin, Jacob's twelfth son, but died in childbirth. He buried her "in the way to Ephrath, which is Beth-lehem." Jacob visited his father, Isaac, in Hebron. Isaac died and Jacob and Esau buried him. *(Gen. 35.)*

Jacob loved Joseph more than his other children and made him a coat of many colors. His other sons hated Joseph because Jacob loved him more than he loved them. When Joseph told his brothers of the dream he had wherein their sheaves in the field made obeisance to his sheaf, they hated him even more for his dreams. *(Gen. 37:5-8.)* When Joseph told his father of a dream he had in which the sun and the moon and the eleven stars made obeisance to him, his father inquired, "Shall I and thy mother and thy brethren indeed come to bow down ourselves to thee to the earth?" *(Gen. 37:10.)* His brothers envied him for the dream, but Jacob "observed the saying." When his brothers were tending their father's flock in Shechem, Jacob sent Joseph to them and asked him to see how they were doing and to report back to him. Because of their hatred toward him, the brothers sold Joseph to some Ishmeelites (also referred to as Midianite merchantmen) who sold him to Potiphar,

Pharaoh's officer and captain of his guard. Jacob was given Joseph's blood-drenched coat and, assuming Joseph to have been slain by wild beasts, Jacob refused to be comforted. *(Gen. 37.)*

When the famine struck throughout the land, Jacob instructed ten of his sons to go to Egypt to buy corn. He kept Benjamin at home. When they returned home with the grain they informed Jacob about all that had happened to them, that each of them had found his bundle of money in the top of his sack, that Simeon was kept as collateral and that they needed to return with Benjamin. Jacob refused to let them take Benjamin. *(Gen. 42:1-4, 29-38.)*

As the famine continued, Jacob asked his sons to go to Egypt again to buy more grain. They refused unless he agreed to let them take Benjamin with them. He finally relented. *(Gen. 43:1-14.)*

When his sons returned this time, they informed Jacob that Joseph was still alive and was governor over all of the land of Egypt, and that Joseph had sent wagons to carry his father and all his father's household back to Egypt. Jacob responded, "It is enough; Joseph my son is yet alive: I will go and see him before I die." *(Gen. 45:25-28.)*

Jacob and his family (consisting of 70 people) went to Egypt. (His posterity is listed.) As they journeyed, God spoke to Israel in "the visions of the night." Jacob and Joseph were reunited. *(Gen. 46.)*

Jacob and his family, the Israelites, settled in Goshen. Jacob was presented to Pharaoh by Joseph, and Jacob blessed Pharaoh. Jacob and his household were nourished by Joseph. Jacob lived 17 years in Egypt, reaching the age of 147 years. *(Gen. 47.)*

Jacob told Joseph of the appearance of God to him in Luz. Jacob adopted Joseph's sons, Ephraim and Manasseh, as his own. When Joseph presented them to him for a blessing, Jacob laid his right hand upon the head of Ephraim, who was the younger of the boys. Joseph corrected his father, but his father refused to change hands, saying, "I know it, my son, I know it: he (Manasseh) also shall become a people, and he also shall be great: but truly his younger brother shall be greater than he, and his seed shall become a multitude of nations . . . and he set Ephraim before Manasseh." Jacob promised Joseph that God would someday bring him again unto the land of his fathers. *(Gen. 48.)*

Prior to his death, Jacob gathered all his sons together and told them what would befall them in the last days. He also gave them a charge that when he died, they were to bury him with his fathers, Abraham and Sarah, Isaac and Rebekah, and Leah, in the cave in the field of Ephron the Hittite, in the field of Machpelah in the land of Canaan. He then died. *(Gen. 49.)*

Jacob was embalmed and his sons, with Pharaoh's permission, carried his body to Canaan to be buried as he had requested. *(Gen. 50:1-13.)*

God heard the groaning of the children of Israel as they suffered under Egyptian bondage and remembered the covenant he had made with Abraham, Isaac and Jacob. *(Ex. 2:24.)*

Jeremiah prophesied that Jacob, or the house of Israel, would return from captivity in the latter days and be restored to their lands, "and Jacob shall return, and be in rest and at ease, and none shall make him afraid . . . for I will make a full end of all the nations whither I have driven thee." *(Jer. 46:27-28.)*

Jacob's posterity, Israel, is the rod with which the Lord will destroy all the kingdoms and nations of the world. *(Jer. 51:19-23.)*

Jacob's posterity, the house of Israel, will be gathered by the Lord in the latter days from among the various nations where He scattered them and they will then dwell in the land He gave to Jacob. *(Ezek. 28:25.)*

In the latter days, Jacob's posterity will be restored to the lands of their inheritance. The Lord promised that "my servant David shall be their prince for ever" *(i.e., the Messiah, Jesus Christ of the house of David, "shall be their prince for ever")*. *(Ezek. 37:25.)*

In the latter days, the Lord will bring Jacob's posterity out of captivity and gather them into their own land and they will know that He is the Lord their God. *(Ezek. 39:25-29.)*

The Lord will punish Jacob according to his ways. Reference is made to Jacob's birth when he took hold of Esau's heel when they were born. Reference is also made to when Jacob wrestled with an angel and prevailed over him. Jacob forsook the Lord and fled into the country of Syria. A prophet of the Lord brought Israel out of Egypt. *(Hosea 12:2-4, 12.)*

The Lord condemned the pride of Jacob and said He would scatter Jacob and "deliver up the city and all that is therein." *(Amos 6:8.)*

The Lord promised that even though He would sift the house of Israel among all nations, He would not destroy the house of Jacob entirely. He will preserve a remnant and, in the last days, bring them forth into their own land. *(Amos 9:8-9, 14-15.)*

Obadiah prohesied of the downfall of Edom because of Esau's posterity's violence against the house of Jacob. *(Obad.)*

Micah prophesied against the heads of Jacob who judged for reward, the priests who taught for hire, and the prophets who divined for money. *(Micah 3.)*

Micah prophesied that the remnant of Jacob which had been scattered among all the nations shall rise with power in the latter days and triumph gloriously over the Gentiles. *(Micah 5.)*

Micah lamented the fallen state of the children of Israel, but expressed confidence that the Lord will have compassion and will show mercy on them and will pardon their iniquity in the latter days, performing "the truth to Jacob and the mercy to Abraham" which the Lord had sworn unto their fathers from the days of old. *(Micah 7.)*

Jacob was Esau's brother. The Lord loved Jacob, but He hated Esau (Edom) *(because of wickedness). (Mal. 1:2-3.)*

Malachi reproved those of the house of Jacob who were wicked and said the Lord would cut them out of the tabernacles of Jacob. *(Mal. 2:12.)* (Charts 1.; 2c.; 3a-d.; 5a.; 6a.; 7a.; 8a.; 9a.; 10a.; 11a.; 12a.; 13a.; 14a.; 15a.; 16a.; 21.)

JADA. *1 Chr. 2:28, 32.*

Jada was one of the sons of Onam. His brother was Shammai. He was a great-great-great-grandson of Judah. He begat Jether and Jonathan. (Chart 8c.)

JADAU. *Ezra 10:43 (18-19, 43-44).*

Jadau was one of Nebo's sons. He and his brothers Jeiel, Mattithiah, Zabad, Zebina, Joel and Benaiah were some of the Israelite men who took foreign wives but agreed to separate themselves from them because Ezra feared the Lord's wrath would destroy all of Israel for this iniquity.

JADDUA. *Neh. 10:21 (1, 21, 28-31); 12:11, 22.*

Jaddua was among those chief of the people who covenanted to marry in Israel, honor the Sabbath, pay tithes and, henceforth, keep the commandments. *(Neh. 10:21 [1, 21, 28-31].)*

Jaddua, son of Jonathan (Johanan), was a priest. The Levites who were the chief of the fathers in the days of Eliashib, Joiada, Johanan and Jaddua were recorded up to the reign of Darius of Persia. *(Neh. 12:11, 22.)* (Chart 7b.)

JADON. *Neh. 3:7.*

Jadon was a Meronothite. He and Melatiah, the Gibeonite, labored next to Jehoiada and Meshullam on the walls and gates of Jerusalem when the children of Israel rebuilt them during the time of Ezra and Nehemiah.

JAEL. *Judg. 4:17-22; 5:24-27.*

Jael was the wife of Heber the Kenite. There was peace between the house of Heber and Jabin, king of Canaan in Hazor. When Sisera, captain of Jabin's army, fled to Jael's tent to escape Deborah and Barak and the forces from Israel, she covered him. When he fell asleep, she drove a tent nail through his temples and fastened it into the ground. When Barak came, she showed him where Sisera was. Thus, God delivered Jabin into the hands of Israel. *(Judg. 4:17-22.)* Jael was praised by Deborah and Barak for slaying Sisera. *(Judg. 5:24-27.)*

JAHATH (1). *1 Chr. 4:2.*

Jahath, of the lineage of Judah, was the son of Reaiah, the grandson of Shobal, and the father of Ahumai and Lahad. They are the families of the Zorathites. (Chart 8m.)

JAHATH (2). *1 Chr. 6:20, 42-43.*

Jahath was the son of Libni, who was the son of Gershom. He was a great-grandson to Levi. Jahath's son (grandson) was Zimmah. (Chart 7a.)

JAHATH (3). *1 Chr. 23:10-11.*

Jahath, a descendant of Gershom, was a son of Shimei. When David numbered the Levites and divided them into courses among the sons of Levi—Gershon,

Kohath and Merari—at the time he named Solomon king, those of the sons of Shimei who were named chiefs of their father's house were Jahath, Zina, Jeush and Beriah. Jahath was the chief and Zizah (Zina) the second. However, Jeush and Beriah did not have many sons so they were combined according to their father's house. (Chart 7f.)

JAHATH (4). *1 Chr. 24:22.*

Jahath, a Levite, was a descendant of Izhar through Shelomoth (Shelomith). He, with the rest of the chief fathers of the Levites, drew lots for his course in the presence of king David, Zadok, Ahimelech and other community leaders. (Chart 7d.)

JAHATH (5). *2 Chr. 34:12.*

Jahath, a Levite of the sons of Merari, and others were assigned by Josiah, king of Judah, to oversee the workmen who repaired the house of the Lord and to oversee all who performed any manner of service regarding the house of the Lord.

JAHAZIAH. *Ezra 10:15.*

Jahaziah was the son of Tikvah. He and Jonathan, son of Asahel, were assigned by Ezra the task of separating the children of Israel from their foreign wives. They were assisted by Meshullam and Shabbethai the Levite.

JAHAZIEL (1). *1 Chr. 16:6.* See **Eliezer (3)**.

JAHAZIEL (2). *1 Chr. 12:4 (1-2, 4, 23, 38).*

Jahaziel was one of David's mighty men who came to him at Ziklag to rejoice with all Israel and to turn the kingdom of Saul unto David.

JAHAZIEL (3). *1 Chr. 23:19; 24:23.*

Jahaziel, a Levite, was of the sons of Hebron, son of Kohath. When David numbered the Levites at the time he made Solomon king, he divided them into courses among the sons of Levi. Jeriah was the first, Amariah the second, Jahaziel the third, and Jekameam the fourth. *(1 Chr. 23:19.)*

Jahaziel, a Levite, was one of the sons of Hebron. His brothers were Jeriah, Amariah and Jekameam. He, with the rest of the chief fathers of the Levites, drew lots for his course in the presence of king David, Zadok, Ahimelech and other community leaders. *(1 Chr. 24:23.)* (Chart 7d.)

JAHAZIEL (4). *2 Chr. 20:14-17.*

Jahaziel was the son of Zechariah, the son of Benaiah, the son of Jeiel, the son of Mattaniah, a Levite of the sons of Asaph. He prophesied to king Jehoshaphat that the Lord would fight his battle for him when the children of Moab, Ammon and mount Seir came against Judah. (Chart 7a.)

JAHAZIEL (5). *Ezra 8:5.*

Jahaziel was of the sons of Shechaniah. Jahaziel's son was the chief of his fathers and went with Ezra up from Babylon to Jerusalem. He took 300 males with him.

JAHDAI. *1 Chr. 2:47.*

Jahdai was the parent of Regem, Jotham, Geshan, Pelet, Ephah and Shaaph. *(Note: They were related to Caleb, the brother of Jerahmeel, but it is not clear as to how they were related.)* (Chart 8j.)

JAHDIEL. *1 Chr. 5:24-26.*

Jahdiel was from the half tribe of Manasseh that was aligned with the Reubenites and Gadites. He was a famous and mighty man of valor and was head of the house of his father. He, along with others, transgressed the laws of God; thus, God allowed the people to be carried away into captivity by the Assyrian kings Pul and Tilgath-pilneser. (Chart 15c.)

JAHDO. *1 Chr. 5:14.*

Jahdo, the father of Jeshishai and the son of Buz, was a descendant of Gad. (Chart 13b.)

JAHLEEL (Jahleelites). *Gen. 46:14; Num. 26:26.*

Jahleel was a son of Zebulun and a grandson of Jacob. *(Gen. 46:14.)* His descendants are the **Jahleelites**. *(Num. 26:26.)* (Chart 10a.)

JAHMAI. *1 Chr. 7:2.*

Jahmai was a son of Tola and a grandson of Issachar. His brothers were Uzzi, Rephaiah, Jeriel, Jibsam and Shemuel. Tola's sons were heads of their father's house and were "valiant men of might in their generations." (Chart 9a.)

JAHZEEL (Jahziel, Jahzeelites). *Gen. 46:24; Num. 26:48; 1 Chr. 7:13.*

Jahzeel was a son of Naphtali and a grandson of Jacob. His brothers were Guni, Jezer and Shillem. *(Gen. 46:24.)* His descendants were called **Jahzeelites**. *(Num. 26:48.)*

The sons of Naphtali were **Jahziel** (Jahzeel), Guni, Jezer and Shallum (Shillem). *(1 Chr. 7:13.)* (Chart 12a.)

JAHZERAH. *1 Chr. 9:12.*

Jahzerah, the father of Adiel and the son of Meshullam, was one of the priests in Jerusalem whose genealogy was written in the book of the kings of Israel and Judah who were carried away captive into Babylon because of their transgression. His posterity was among those priests who dwelled in Jerusalem following their return from Babylonian captivity. (Chart 7g.)

JAHZIEL. See **Jahzeel**.

JAIR (1). *Num. 32:41; Deut. 3:14; 1 Chr. 2:21-22.*

Jair, a son of Manasseh, was given an inheritance east of Jordan and named the towns Havoth-jair. *(Num. 32:41.)*

Moses reminded the Israelites that the Lord delivered Og, king of Bashan, into their hands and that his land had been given to the Reubenites, Gadites, and half the tribe of Manasseh for an inheritance. Jair took all the country of Argob unto the coasts of Geshuri and Maachathi, and called them after his own name, Bashan-havoth-jair. *(Deut. 3:14.)*

Jair's father was Segub (son of Hezron). His mother was the daughter of Machir (son of Manasseh). *(1 Chr. 2:21-22.)* (Charts 8d.; 15b.)

JAIR (2). *Judg. 10:3-5.*

Jair, a Gileadite, judged Israel for 22 years following Tola. He had 30 sons. When he died, he was buried in Camon. (Chart 20.).

JAIR (3). *1 Chr. 20:5.* See **Jaare-oregim**.

JAIR (4). *Esth. 2:5.*

Jair, the son of Shimei the son of Kish, a Benjamite, was father of Mordecai. (Chart 16k.)

JAIRITE. *2 Sam. 20:26.*

Jairites were descendants of Jair; however, it is not clear as to which Jair. Ira, one of the chief rulers with David, was a Jairite.

JAKEH. *Prov. 30:1.*

Jakeh was the father of the prophet Agur.

JAKIM (1). *1 Chr. 8:19-21.*

Jakim, a descendant of Benjamin, was a son of Shimhi. (Chart 16h.)

JAKIM (2). *1 Chr. 24:12.*

Jakim was from the sons of Aaron. When David made the divisions of the sons of Aaron, there was one principal household for Eleazar and one taken for Ithamar. Eleazar had 16 sons and there were eight sons of Ithamar. These 24 sons who were chief of the fathers were divided by lot. Jakim drew the twelfth lot.

JALON. *1 Chr. 4:17.*

Jalon was the daughter of Ezra. Her siblings were Jether, Mered, and Epher. She bore Miriam, Shammai and Ishbah the father of Eshtemoa. (Chart 8 o.)

JAMIN (1) (Jaminites). *Gen. 46:10; Num. 26:12; 1 Chr. 4:24.*

Jamin was one of Simeon's sons and a grandson of Jacob. His brothers were Jemuel, Ohad, Jachin, Zohar and Shaul the son of a Canaanitish woman. *(Gen. 46:10.)*

Jamin's descendants were called **Jaminites**. His brothers were Nemuel (Jemuel), Jachin, Zerah (Zohar) and Shaul. Ohad is not listed. *(Num. 26:12.)*

Jamin's brothers were Nemuel, Jarib, Zerah and Shaul. *(1 Chr. 4:24.) (Note: Jarib is new and Ohad and Jachin are not listed.)* (Chart 6a.)

JAMIN (2). *1 Chr. 2:27.*

Jamin was one of the sons of Ram. He was a great-great-great-grandson of Judah. His brothers were Maaz and Eker. (Chart 8c.)

JAMIN (3). *Neh. 8:7-8.*

Jamin was one of the men who, when Ezra read and interpreted the law of Moses to the people, helped the people to understand the law.

JAMINITES. See **Jamin (1)**.

JAMLECH. *1 Chr. 4:34 (27-34).*

Jamlech was a descendant of that Shimei who had 16 sons and six daughters. (Chart 6a.)

JAPHETH. *Gen. 5:32; 6:10-18; 7:13; 9; 10:2-5; 1 Chr. 1:4-5.*

Japheth is the third of Noah's sons mentioned. Noah was 500 years old when he and his brothers, Shem and Ham, were born. *(Gen. 5:32.) (Note: The implication in Genesis is that Japheth, Shem and Ham were triplets, all born when Noah was 500 years old. However, according to Moses 8:12 in the Pearl of Great Price, they were not triplets: "And Noah was four hundred and fifty years old, and begat Japheth; and forty-two years afterward he begat Shem of her who was the mother of Japheth, and when he was five hundred years old he begat Ham.")*

Noah begat three sons. The Lord said He would establish His covenant with Noah, and that he should take his wife and his sons and their wives into the ark. *(Gen. 6:10-18.)* His family entered the ark. *(Gen. 7:13.)*

God spoke to Noah and to his sons and told them He would establish His covenant with them and with their seed. There would never be another flood to cover the whole earth. The Lord set the rainbow in the sky as a token of the covenant. They were told to mulitply and replenish the earth. *(Gen. 9:7-13.)* When Ham saw his father drunken and naked in his tent, he told his brothers. Japheth and Shem took a garment and, walking backwards so as not to see their father, covered him up. When Noah woke up and realized what Ham had done, he cursed Ham's son, Canaan, but blessed Japheth and Shem. He said "God shall enlarge Japheth, and he shall dwell in the tents of Shem; and Canaan shall be his servant." *(Gen.9:22-27).*

Japheth's posterity is named. "By these were the isles of the Gentiles divided in their lands; every one after his tongue, after their families, in their nations." *(Gen. 10:2-5; 1 Chr. 1:4-5.)* (Charts 1.; 2a.; 21.)

JAPHIA (1). *Josh. 10:3-27.*

Japhia, one of the five kings of the Amorites, was king of Lachish. He and the other kings united in battle against the Israelites. His people were destroyed, partly by the sword but mostly by hailstones the Lord poured down upon them. He hid in a cave with the other four kings. Joshua had a stone rolled in front of the cave until the rest of the Amorites were destroyed. Then he had the kings brought out to him. They were all slain and hung on a tree and their bodies were then sealed in the cave where the kings had hidden themselves.

JAPHIA (2). *2 Sam. 5:15; 1 Chr. 3:7; 14:4-7.*

Japhia was one of David's children born in Jerusalem. His brothers were Shammua, Shobab, Nathan, Solomon, Ibhar, Elishua, Nepheg, Elishama, Eliada and Eliphalet. *(2 Sam. 5:15.)*

(Note: 1 Chr. 3:7 is a repeat of 2 Sam. 5:15 with modification: Shimea is listed instead of Shammua; Nogah is listed instead of Elishua; and there are two Elishamas and two Eliphelets listed.)

(Note: 1 Chr. 14:4-7 is a repeat of 2 Sam. 5:15 and 1 Chr. 3:7 with modification. Beeliada is listed instead of Eliada.) (Chart 8e.)

JAPHLET. *1 Chr. 7:32-33.*

Japhlet was a son of Heber and a great-grandson of Asher. His siblings included Shomer and Hotham and a sister, Shua. His sons were Pasach, Bimhal and Ashvath. (Chart 14a.)

JARAH. See **Jehoadah**.

JAREB. *Hosea 5:13; 10:6.*

Jareb was king of Assyria. Ephraim was condemned by the Lord for turning to Jareb for help rather than to Him. *(Hosea 5:13.)* Hosea prophesied that a golden calf would be carried unto Asyria for a present to king Jareb. Thus, Ephraim would receive shame and Israel would be ashamed of his own counsel. *(Hosea 10:6.)*

JARED (Jered (1)). *Gen. 5:15; 1 Chr. 1:2.*

Jared was a son of Mahalaleel and a great-great-great-grandson of Adam. His father was 65 years old when he was born. Jared begat Enoch when he was 162 years old. He begat more sons and daughters and lived to be 962 years old. *(Gen. 5:15.)*

Jered was the son of Mahalaleel and the father of Henoch (Enoch). *(1 Chr. 1:2.)* (Charts 1.; 21.)

JARESIAH. *1 Chr. 8:27.*

Jaresiah, a descendant of Benjamin, was a son of Jeroham. (Chart 16j.)

JARHA. *1 Chr. 2:34-35.*

Jarha was an Egyptian servant of Sheshan. Sheshan gave his daughter Ahlai to Jarha for a wife. Jarha begat Attai. (Chart 8c.)

JARIB (1). *1 Chr. 4:24.* See **Jachin (1)**.

JARIB (2). *Ezra 8:16.*

Jarib was one of the chief men Ezra sent for when he gathered the people together as he was preparing to lead them to Jerusalem from Babylon and discovered there were no Levites among the group. He sent this group to Iddo and the Nethinims to request that they send them some ministers for the house of God.

JARIB (3). *Ezra 10:18-19.*

Jarib was one of the sons of the priests who had taken foreign wives and who agreed to put them away as instructed by Ezra.

JAROAH. *1 Chr. 5:14.*

Jaroah, the father of Huri and the son of Gilead, was a descendant of Gad. (Chart 13b.)

JASHEN (Hashen). *2 Sam. 23:32; 1 Chr. 11:34.*

Jashen's (Hashen's) sons were among David's mighty men.

JASHOBEAM (1). *1 Chr. 11:11.* See **Adino**.

JASHOBEAM (2). *1 Chr. 12:6 (1-2, 6, 23, 38).*

Jashobeam, a Korhite, was one of David's mighty men who came to him at Ziklag to rejoice with all Israel and to turn the kingdom of Saul unto David.

JASHOBEAM (3). *1 Chr. 27:2-3.*

Jashobeam, the son of Zabdiel of the children of Perez, was one of the officers who served king David. He and his course of 24,000 were over the first month.

JASHUB (1). *Num. 26:24.* See **Job (1).**

JASHUB (2). *Ezra 10:29 (18-19, 29, 44).*

Jashub, a son of Bani, was one of the Israelites who took foreign wives, causing Ezra to cry unto the Lord in behalf of Israel, fearing that the Lord would totally destroy the children of Israel due to this latest iniquity. Jashub and his brothers agreed to put away their foreign wives.

JASHUBI-LEHEM. *1 Chr. 4:22.*

Jashubi-lehem was a son of Shelah and a grandson of Judah. (Chart 8a.)

JASHUBITES. See **Job (1).**

JASIEL. *1 Chr. 11:47.*

Jasiel the Mesobaite was one of David's mighty men and one of the valiant men of the armies. (Chart 17.)

JATHNIEL. *1 Chr. 26:2.*

Jathniel, a Levite, was the fourthborn son of Meshelemiah, son of Kore of the sons of Asaph. His brothers were Zechariah, Jediael, Zebadiah, Elam, Jehohanan and Elioenai. They, along with others, were assigned by king David to be porters—to have charge of the treasures, serve as officers and judges, and conduct the outward business over Israel. (Chart 7d.)

JAVAN. *Gen. 10:2, 4; 1 Chr. 1:5, 7; Isa. 66:19; Ezek. 27:13, 19.*

Javan was a son of Japheth and a grandson of Noah. His sons were Elishah, Tarshish, Kittim and Dodanim. *(Gen. 10:2, 4; 1 Chr. 1:5, 7.)*

At the Second Coming, the Lord will send missionaries to the descendants of Javan and others. *(Isa. 66:19.)*

As Ezekiel lamented the fall of the great city of Tyrus, he bemoaned the loss of her riches and commerce, part of which involved the merchants of Javan, Tubal and Meshech, merchants who traded in "persons of men and vessels of brass in thy markets." Javan also traded in bright iron, cassia and calamus. *(Ezek. 27:13, 19.)* *(Note: The Bible Dictionary indicates that Javan is regarded as the founder of the Greek race. Thus, references to Grecia in Dan. 8:21; 10:20; 11:2, and Zech. 9:13, refer to his descendants.)* (Chart 2a.)

JAZIZ. *1 Chr. 27:31.*

Jaziz the Hagerite was the officer assigned by David to be over the flocks.

JEATERAI. *1 Chr. 6:21, 41.*

Jeaterai, of the tribe of Levi through Gershom, was the son of Zerah. *(Note: Gershom's descendants differ in verses 20-21 from verses 41-42.)* (Chart 7a.)

JEBERECHIAH. *Isa. 8:2.*

Jeberechiah was the father of that Zechariah who served as a faithful witness for Isaiah to record information regarding Maher-shalal-hash-baz. *(Note: According* *to the footnote to the scriptural text, Maher-shalal-hash-baz means "to speed to the spoil, he hasteneth the prey.")*

JEBUSITE. *Gen. 10:16; 15:18-21; Deut. 7:1; Judg. 1:21; 2 Sam. 24:16-25; 1 Kgs. 9:20-21; 1 Chr. 21:18-28; 2 Chr. 8:7-8; Ezra 9:1-5; Neh. 9:8.*

Jebusites were descendants of Canaan who was a son of Ham. *(Gen. 10:16.)* Their lands were given to Abram's seed through a covenant with the Lord. *(Gen. 15:18-21.)*

The Jebusites were one of the seven nations, greater and mightier than the Israelites, which the Lord said He would destroy in Canaan so Israel could receive the promised land. *(Deut. 7:1.)*

The children of Benjamin did not drive the Jebusites out of the land. The Jubusites continued to live among the children of Benjamin. *(Judg. 1:21.)*

When David numbered Israel, the Lord was displeased and sent the prophet Gad to him giving him three choices: seven years of famine *(1 Chr. 21:12 says "three years' famine")*; three months flight before David's enemies; three days' pestilence in the land. Following David's response, the Lord sent three days' pestilence which resulted in the death of 70,000 men. When the people repented, David was instructed to go to the threshingplace of Araunah (Ornan) the Jebusite. He purchased the threshingfloor, built an altar unto the Lord, and offered burnt offerings and peace offerings. The plague was then stayed from Israel. *(2 Sam. 24:16-25.)*

Solomon levied a tribute of bondservice upon all of the Jebusites who remained among the Israelites. *(1 Kgs. 9:20-21; 2 Chr. 8:7-8.)*

After the children of Israel were delivered from Babylonian bondage, many Jews—including the priests and Levites—intermarried with and followed the abominations of the Jebusites, Canaanites, Hittites, Perizzites, Ammonites, Moabites Egyptians and Amorites. Ezra prayed and confessed the sins of all the people, fearing the Lord would completely destroy them this time for their abominations. *(Ezra 9:1-5.)*

The Levites blessed and praised the Lord in remembrance that He gave the land of the Canaanites, Hittites, Amorites, Perizzites, Jebusites and Girgashites to Abraham. *(Neh. 9:8.)* (Chart 2e.)

JECAMIAH. *1 Chr. 3:18.*

Jecamiah, a descendant of David, was a son (grandson) of Jeconiah (Jehoiachin). (Chart 1.)

JECHOLIAH (Jecoliah). *2 Kgs. 15:2; 2 Chr. 26:3.*

Jecholiah (Jecoliah) of Jerusalem was the mother of Azariah (Uzziah) and wife of king Amaziah. (Chart 1.)

JECONIAH. See **Jehoiachin**.

JEDAIAH (1). *1 Chr. 4:37.*

Jedaiah was thefather of Allon and the son Shimri. He was a descendant of Shimei. (Chart 6a.)

JEDAIAH (2). *1 Chr. 9:10 (1-3, 10); Ezra 2:36; Neh. 7:39; 11:10-12.*

Jedaiah was one of the priests in Jerusalem whose genealogy was written in the book of the kings of Israel and Judah who were carried away captive into Babylon because of their transgression. He was among those priests selected to live in Jerusalem upon returning from Babylonian captivity. *(1 Chr. 9:10 [1-3, 10].)*

The children of Jedaiah, of the house of Jeshua, numbered 973 when they left Babylon to return to Jerusalem to build the temple as proclaimed by Cyrus, king of Persia. *(Ezra 2:36; Neh. 7:39.)*

Jedaiah was the son of Joiarib. He was one of the priests elected by lot to dwell in Jerusalem following Babylonian captivity. Those who did the work of the house of the Lord were 822. *(Neh. 11:10-12.)*

JEDAIAH (3). *1 Chr. 24:7.*

Jedaiah was from the sons of Aaron. When David made the divisions of the sons of Aaron, there was one principal household for Eleazar and one taken for Ithamar. Eleazar had 16 sons and there were eight sons of Ithamar. These 24 sons who were chief of the fathers were divided by lot. Jedaiah drew the second lot.

JEDAIAH (4). *Neh. 12:6, 19; Zech. 6:10-14.*

Jedaiah was one of the men (priests and Levites) who left Babylon captivity with Zerubbabel and returned to Jerusalem. He was the father of Uzzi who was one of the priests who was a chief of the fathers in the days of Joiakim. *(Neh. 12:6, 19.)*

The captive of Jedaiah, Heldai and Tobijah, who had come from Babylon were instructed to go into the house of Josiah the son of Zephaniah and crown Joshua (Jeshua) the high priest in similitude of crowning Christ, i.e., the BRANCH. *(Zech. 6:10-14.)*

JEDAIAH (5). *Neh. 3:10; 12:7, 21.*

Jedaiah, the son of Harumaph, worked next to Rephaiah when the children of Israel rebuilt the walls and gates of Jerusalem during the time of Ezra and Nehemiah. *(Neh. 3:10.)*

Jedaiah was one of the men (priests and Levites) who left Babylonian captivity with Zerubbabel and returned to Jerusalem. Jedaiah was the father of Nethaneel who was one of the priests who was a chief of the fathers in the days of Joiakim. *(Neh. 12:7, 21.)*

JEDIAEL (1). *1 Chr. 7:6, 10-11.*

Jediael was a son of Benjamin. *(Note: He is not listed, at least by that name, among the sons of Benjamin in other references.)* His son was Bilhan. Bilhan's sons were Jeush, Benjamin, Ehud, Chenaanah, Zethan, Tharshish and Ahishahar. (Charts 16c, e.)

JEDIAEL (2). *1 Chr. 11:45.*

Jediael, a son of Shimri and brother to Joha the Tizite, was one of the mighty men of David, one of the valiant men of the armies. (Chart 17.)

JEDIAEL (3). *1 Chr. 12:20-21.*

Jediael was from the tribe of Manasseh and was a mighty man of valor, one of the captains in the host. When David went to Ziklag and the tribes all sent their armies in support of his becoming king, Jediael helped David against the band of rovers sent by Saul to kill David.

JEDIAEL (4). *1 Chr. 26:2 (Subtitle, 2, 26).*

Jediael, a Levite, was the secondborn son of Meshelemiah, son of Kore of the sons of Asaph. His brothers were Zechariah, Zebadiah, Jathniel, Elam, Jehohanan and Elioenai. The Levites were assigned by king David to be porters—to have charge of the treasures, serve as officers and judges, and conduct the outward business over Israel. (Chart 7d.)

JEDIDAH. *2 Kgs. 22:1.*

Jedidah, the daughter of Adaiah of Boscath, was the mother of Josiah and wife of Amon.

JEDIDIAH. See **Solomon**.

JEDUTHUN. *1 Chr. 9:16; 16:38, 42; 25:1, 3; 2 Chr. 5:12; 29:14; Neh. 11:17; Ps. 39:Subtitle; 77:Subtitle.*

Jeduthun was the father of Galal. He was a Levite whose descendants dwelled in the villages of the Netophathites. His genealogy was written in the book of the kings of Israel and Judah who were carried away to Babylon for their transgression. *(1 Chr. 9:16.)*

Jeduthun's sons were the porters of the ark. Jeduthun, along with Heman, was left before the ark of the covenant of the Lord with trumpets and cymbals for those who were to minister with music. *(1 Chr. 16:38, 42.)*

The sons of Jeduthun, Asaph and Heman were separated to the service by David and the captains of the hosts. Their assignment was to "prophesy with harps, with psalteries, and with cymbals." *(1 Chr. 25:1, 3.)*

The Levites who were the singers—those of Jeduthan, Asaph and Heman, with their sons and brethren—were dressed in white and made music to praise the Lord when the temple was finished by Solomon and the ark of the covenant was placed in the holy of holies. The glory of the Lord filled the temple. *(2 Chr. 5:12.)*

Shemaiah and Uzziel were of the sons of Jeduthun and were among those who Hezekiah, king of Judah, instructed to sanctify themselves so they could cleanse and sanctify the house of the Lord. *(2 Chr. 29:14.)*

Jeduthun was the father of Galal. *(Neh. 11:17.)*

This was a psalm of David to Jeduthun, the chief Musician. *(Ps. 39:Subtitle.)*

This psalm of Asaph was to Jeduthun, the chief Musician. *(Ps. 77:Subtitle.)* (Chart 7h.)

JEEZER (Jeezerites). *Num. 26:30.*

Jeezer was a son of Gilead and great-grandson of Manasseh. His descendants were the **Jeezerites**. His brothers were Helek, Asriel, Shechem, Shemida and Hepher. (Charts 15a-b.)

JEHALELEEL. *1 Chr. 4:16.*

Jehaleleel was the father of Ziph, Ziphah, Tiria and Asareel. (Chart 8n.)

JEHALELEL. *2 Chr. 29:12.*

Jehalelel, a Levite of the house of Merari, was the father of Azariah. (Chart 7e.)

JEHDEIAH (1). *1 Chr. 24:20.*

Jehdeiah, a Levite, was a descendant of Amram through Shubael (Shebuel) who was the grandson of Moses. He, with the rest of the chief fathers of the Levites, drew lots for his course in the presence of king David, Zadok, Ahimelech and other community leaders. (Chart 7b.)

JEHDEIAH (2). *1 Chr. 27:30.*

Jehdeiah the Meronothite was assigned by David to be over the asses.

JEHEZEKEL. *1 Chr. 24:16.*

Jehezekel was from the sons of Aaron. When David made the divisions of the sons of Aaron, there was one principal household for Eleazar and one taken for Ithamar. Eleazar had 16 sons and there were eight sons of Ithamar. These 24 sons who were chief of the fathers were divided by lot. Jehezekel drew the twentieth lot.

JEHIAH. *1 Chr. 15:24.*

Jehiah, a Levite, along with Obed-edom, was a doorkeeper for the ark as it was transported from the house of Obed-edom by David and the children of Israel to the place David had prepared for it to be housed.

JEHIEL (1). *1 Chr. 9:35.* See **Abiel (1)**.

JEHIEL (2). *1 Chr. 11:44.*

Jehiel, a son of Hothan the Aroerite and brother to Shama, was one of the mighty men of David, one of the valiant men of the armies. (Chart 17.)

JEHIEL (3). *1 Chr. 15:18-20; 16:5.*

Jehiel and his brethren of the second degree were assigned, under the direction of David, to be singers along with Heman, Asaph and Ethan. Jehiel and his brethren were assigned to play with psalteries on Alamoth. *(1 Chr. 15:18-20.)*

Jehiel and his brethren were assigned by David to minister before the ark of the Lord and to play with psalteries and harps. *(1 Chr. 16:5.)*

JEHIEL (4) (Jehieli). *1 Chr. 23:8; 26:21-22; 29:8.*

Jehiel was of the sons of Laadan who was of the sons of Gershon, son of Levi. When David divided the Levites into courses, Jehiel, Zetham and Joel were named, but Jehiel was the chief of the sons of Laadan. *(1 Chr. 23:8.)*

Jehieli's (Jehiel's) sons Zetham and Joel were over the treasures of the house of the Lord. *(1 Chr. 26:21-22.)*

Jehiel the Gershonite received the precious stones that were donated to the treasure of the house of the Lord. *(1 Chr. 29:8.)* (Chart 7f.)

JEHIEL (5). *1 Chr. 27:32.*

Jehiel, the son of Hachmoni, was with king David's sons.

JEHIEL (6). *2 Chr. 21:2-4.*

Jehiel was one of Jehoshaphat's sons. His brothers were Jehoram (the firstborn), Azariah, Zechariah, Azariah, Michael and Shephatiah. After Jehoram became king, he slew all his brethren plus many of the princes of Israel. (Chart 1.)

JEHIEL (7). *2 Chr.29:14; 2 Chr. 31:13.*

Jehiel, a Levite of the sons of Heman, was among those instructed by Hezekiah, king of Judah, to santify themselves so they could cleanse and sanctify the house of the Lord. *(2 Chr.29:14.)*

Jehiel, among others, was an overseer of tithes, offerings and the dedicated things under the hand of Cononiah and Cononiah's brother Shimei according to the commandment of king Hezekiah and Azariah, the ruler of the house of God. *(2 Chr. 31:13.)* (Chart 7f.)

JEHIEL (8). *Ezra 8:9.*

Jehiel, of the sons of Joab, was the father of Obadiah.

JEHIEL (9). *Ezra 10:2, 18-19, 26, 44.*

Jehiel, a son of Elam, was the father of Shechaniah. He was one of the sons of Elam who took wives from among the Canaanites and other groups but agreed to do as Ezra said and separate themselves from their foreign wives.

JEHIEL (10). *Ezra 10:21 (18-19, 21, 44).*

Jehiel, one of the sons of Harim, was among those sons of the priests who had taken foreign wives and who agreed to put them away as instructed by Ezra.

JEHIELI. See Jehiel **(4).**

JEHIZKIAH. *2 Chr. 28:12.*

Jehizkiah, son of Shallum, was one of the leaders of the children of Ephraim who supported the prophet Oded in letting the captives of Judah go so as not to incur greater wrath from the Lord upon Israel.

JEHOADAH (Jarah). *1 Chr. 8:36; 9:42.*

Jehoadah, of the tribe of Benjamin, was the son of Ahaz and was one of Saul's descendants through Jonathan. He begat Alemeth, Azmaveth and Zimri. *(1 Chr. 8:36.)*

Jarah (Jehoadah) begat Alemeth, Azmavaeth and Zimri. *(1 Chr. 9:42.)* (Chart 16 l.)

JEHOADDAN. *2 Kgs. 14:2; 2 Chr. 25:1.*

Jehoaddan, wife of Joash king of Judah, was the mother of Amaziah, king of Judah. (Chart 1.)

JEHOAHAZ (1). *2 Kgs. 10:35; 13; 2 Chr. 25:17.*

Jehoahaz, the son of Jehu, reigned over Israel in his father's stead. *(2 Kgs. 10:35.)*

Jehoahaz began his reign over Israel in the 23rd year of the reign of Joash (Jehoash) over Judah and reigned 17 years in Samaria. He reigned in wickedness. Because of the wickedness of Israel, the Lord delivered them into the hand of Hazael of Syria, and into the hand of Beh-hadad, Hazael's son, all their days. When

Jehoahaz sought the Lord, the Lord delivered them from the hand of Syria. Nevertheless, Israel continued to sin under Jehoahaz's leadership. He died and was buried in Samaria. His son Joash (Jehoash) reigned in his stead. *(2 Kgs. 13.)*

Jehoahaz, son of Jehu, was the father of Joash (Jehoash). *(2 Chr. 25:17.)*

JEHOAHAZ (2) (Shallum (5)). *2 Kgs. 23:30-34; 2 Chr. 36:1-4; 1 Chr. 3:15; Jer. 22:11.*

Jehoahaz was a son of Josiah. The people anointed him king after his father's death. He was 23 years old when he became king. He reigned three months in Jerusalem. His mother was Hamutal. His grandfather was Jeremiah of Libnah. He did evil in the sight of the Lord. Egypt's king Pharaoh-nechoh put him in bands in Hamath so he could not reign in Jerusalem. After Pharaoh-nechoh took Jehoahaz to Egypt, he died there. His half-brother Eliakim (Jehoiakim) reigned in his stead. *(2 Kgs. 23:30-34; 2 Chr. 36:1-4 [reduced version of 2 Kgs. 23:30-34].)*

Shallum (Jehoahaz) was the fourth son of Josiah. His brothers were Johanan, Jehoiakim (Eliakim) and Zedekiah (Mattaniah). *(1 Chr. 3:15.)*

The prophet Jeremiah enumerated the judgments of the Lord that rested upon the kings of Judah. Of Shallum, "which reigned instead of Josiah his father," he said that because of wickedness he "went forth out of this place; He shall not return thither any more: but he shall die in the place whither they have led him captive, and shall see this land no more." *(Jer. 22:11.)* (Chart 1.)

JEHOASH (1). *2 Kgs. 12:1*. See **Joash (3)**.

JEHOASH (2). *2 Kgs. 14:8*. See **Joash (4)**.

JEHOHANAN (1). *1 Chr. 26:3 (Subtitle, 3, 26)*.

Jehohanan, a Levite, was the sixthborn son of Meshelemiah, son of Kore of the sons of Asaph. His brothers were Zechariah, Jediael, Zebadiah, Jathniel, Elam and Elioenai. They, along with others, were assigned by king David to be porters—to have charge of the treasures, serve as officers and judges, and conduct the outward business over Israel. (Chart 7d.)

JEHOHANAN (2). *2 Chr. 17:15; 23:1*.

Jehohanan, of the house of Judah, was one of the captains of thousands when Jehoshaphat was king over Judah. His men numbered 280,000. *(2 Chr. 17:15.)*

Jehohanan was the father of Ishmael who was one of the captains of hundreds who Jehoiada the priest rallied to make Joash king over Judah and to slay Athaliah. *(2 Chr. 23:1.)*

JEHOHANAN (3). *Ezra 10:28 (18-19, 28, 44)*.

Jehohanan, one of Bebai's sons, was one of many who took foreign wives, causing Ezra to cry unto the Lord, fearing the Lord would destroy the remainder of Israel because of their iniquity. He and his brothers agreed to comply with Ezra's request that they put away their strange wives.

JEHOHANAN (4). *Neh. 12:13; 12:42*.

Jehohanan, son of Amariah, was one of the priests who was a chief of the fathers in the days of Joiakim son of Jeshua. *(Neh. 12:13.)*

Jehohanan, a priest and singer, joined in the dedication of the walls of Jerusalem with Nehemiah. *(Neh. 12:42.)*

JEHOIACHIN (Jeconiah, Coniah). *2 Kgs. 24:6, 8-17; 25:27-30; 1 Chr. 3:16-18; 2 Chr. 36:8-10; Esth. 2:5-6; Jer. 22:24, 28; 27:20; 28:4; 29:2; 37:1; 52:31; Ezek. 1:2.*

<u>Jehoiachin</u>, king of Judah 598 B.C., was the son of Jehoiakim (Eliakim). Upon his father's death, he became king at the age of 18 years. He reigned in Jerusalem three months. His mother was Nehushta. He did evil in the sight of the Lord. Nebuchadnezzar, in his eighth year as king of Babylon, took Jehoiachin, his mother, his wives, his officers and the mighty of the land captive, leaving only the "poorest sort of the people in the land." Nebuchadnezzar then made Mattaniah (Zedekiah), Jehoiachin's uncle, king in his stead. *(2 Kgs. 24:6, 8-17; 2 Chr. 36:8-10.) (Note: 2 Kgs. 24:8 states that Jehoiachin was 18 years old when he began to reign as king of Judah. However, 2 Chr. 36:9 states that he was eight years old when he began to reign as king.)*

In the 37th year of Jehoiachin's captivity, Evil-merodach, who had become king of Babylon, released him from prison and showed him great favor in Babylon. He had him dine with him and provided him with a daily allowance for the rest of his life. *(2 Kgs. 25:27-30.)*

Jeconiah (Jehoiachin) was the father of Assir, Malchiram, Pedaiah, Shenazar, Jacamiah, Hoshama and Nedabiah. *(1 Chr. 3:16-18.)*

When Jeconiah was carried away captive by Nebuchadnezzar, Mordecai, cousin/father of Esther, was also carried away. *(Esth. 2:5-6.)*

The prophet Jeremiah pronounced the judgment of the Lord upon the kings of Judah. Because of wickedness, they would die in foreign lands, captives of their enemies, never to see Jerusalem again. The Lord said, " . . . though **Coniah** (Jehoiachin) were the signet upon my right hand, yet would I pluck thee thence . . ." *(Jer. 22:24, 28.)*

The vessels of the Lord's house which were not carried away when Jeconiah (Jehoiachin) was carried away were to be taken to Babylon where they would remain until such time as the Lord restored the people to Jerusalem. *(Jer. 27:20.)*

During the fourth year of Zedekiah's reign over Judah, Hananiah falsely prophesied that within two years the yoke of Nebuchadnezzar, king of Babylon, would be broken and Jeconiah (Jehoiachin) and all the captives would return. *(Jer. 28:4.)*

After Jeconiah (Jehoiachin) and the queen and their household left Jerusalem, Jeremiah the prophet sent a letter by the hand of Elasah, son of Shaphan, and Gemariah, son of Hilkiah, unto the elders who were carried away captive, and to the priests, the prophets and all the people who had been carried off captive, informing them that the Lord said they would remain captive for 70 years and to find peace there. After 70 years He would perform good works for them. *(Jer. 29:2.)*

Nebuchadnezzar made Zedekiah, the son of Josiah, king over Judah in lieu of Coniah (Jeconiah, Jehoiachin). *(Jer. 37:1.)*

In the 37th year of Jehoiachin's captivity, in Evil-merdach's first year as king of Babylon, Jehoiachin was brought out of prison. Evil-merdach placed Jehoiachin's throne above the rest of the kings in Babylon. Jehoiachin received food and respect the rest of his life. *(Jer. 52:31.)*

In the fifth year of Jehoiachin's captivity, Ezekiel the priest, who was also among the captives, received a vison from the Lord. *(Ezek. 1:2.) (Note: The Bible Dictionary indicates that Jehoiachin was also called Joachin.)* (Chart 1.)

JEHOIADA (1). *2 Sam. 8:18; 1 Chr. 11:22-24; 27:5-6.*

Jehoiada was the father of Benaiah. *(2 Sam. 8:18.)*

Jehoiada was the father of Benaiah, one of the three "mighties" among David's 30 mighty men. *(1 Chr. 11:22-24.)*

Jehoiada was the father of Benaiah, a chief priest. His grandson was Ammizabad. *(1 Chr. 27:5-6.)*

JEHOIADA (2). *2 Kgs. 11:4-20; 12:2, 7-12; 2 Chr. 23; 24:1-16, 20-22.*

Jehoiada was a priest in Judah when Athaliah thought she slew all of Ahaziah's seed and then ruled over Judah. However, Jehosheba, Ahaziah's sister and Jehoiada's wife, hid Joash and his nurse in the house of the Lord. In the seventh year, Jehoiada rallied the rulers and captain and the guard and instructed them to support Joash as king of Judah. They slew Athaliah and restored the crown to seven-year-old Jehoiada. Jehoiada destroyed the house of Baal and Mattan the priest of Baal. *(2 Kgs. 11:4-20; 2 Chr. 23.)*

As long as Jehoiada the priest was alive, Jehoash (Joash) did that which was right in the eyes of the Lord. Jehoash had Jehoiada and the priests collect money from the people so the temple could be repaired, and they gave the money to the carpenters, masons, hewers of stone and the builders for the repair of the Lord's house. *(2 Kgs. 12:2, 7-12. Also, see 2 Chr. 24:1-16, 20-22, which is a repeat and expansion of 2 Kgs. 12:2-12.)*

Jehoiada's wife was Jehoshabeath (Jehosheba), Athaliah's daughter and Ahaziah's sister. Jehoiada helped hide Joash and his nurse for six years in the house of God to protect him from his grandmother Athaliah who sought to slay him so she could rule Judah. *(2 Chr. 22:11-12.)*

Jehoiada chose two wives for Joash. He grew old, and died when he was 130 years. After his death, Joash became wicked, worshipped idols and slew Jehoiada's son, Zechariah the prophet. *(2 Chr. 24:1-16, 20-22.)*

JEHOIADA (3). *1 Chr. 12:27.*

Jehoiada was the leader of the Aaronites and took 3,700 men to assist David in gaining the kingdom from Saul.

JEHOIADA (4). *1 Chr. 27:34.*

Jehoiada was the son of Benaiah and David's counselor after Ahithophel.

JEHOIADA (5). *Neh. 3:6.*

Jehoiada the son of Paseah and Meshullam the son of Besodeiah repaired the old gate, laying up the beams, setting up the doors, locks and bars, when the children of Israel rebuilt the walls and gates of Jerusalem during the time of Ezra and Nehemiah.

JEHOIADA (6). *Jer. 29:26.*

Jehoiada was a priest. Shemaiah the Nehelamite sent letters to other priests claiming the Lord had made them priests in the stead of Jehoiada and challenging the authority of the prophet Jeremiah.

JEHOIAKIM. *Jer. 36:28-32.* See **Eliakim (2).**

JEHOIARIB (1) (Joiarib (1)). *1 Chr. 9:10; Neh. 11:10-12.*

Jehoiarib was one of the priests in Jerusalem whose genealogy was written in the book of the kings of Israel and Judah, who were carried away captive into Babylon because of their transgression. He was among the priests who lived in Jerusalem after returning from captivity. *(1 Chr. 9:10.)*

Joiarib (Jehoiarib) was the father of Jedaiah. *(Neh. 11:10-12.)*

JEHOIARIB (2). *1 Chr. 24:7.*

Jehoiarib was from the sons of Aaron. When David made the divisions of the sons of Aaron, there was one principal household for Eleazar and one taken for Ithamar. Eleazar had 16 sons and there were eight sons of Ithamar. These 24 sons who were chief of the fathers were divided by lot. Jehoiarib drew the first lot.

JEHONADAB (Jonadab (2)). *2 Kgs. 10:15-16; Jer. 35:6-19.*

Jehonadab was the son of Rechab. He pledged his hand to support Jehu who had been commanded by the Lord to destroy the house of Ahab. *(2 Kgs. 10:15-16.)*

Jonadab (Jehonadab) commanded his people not to build houses, but to dwell in tents and not to drink wine. His posterity obeyed his command and the Lord commended and blessed them, saying, "Jonadab the son of Rechab shall not want a man to stand before me for ever." Because they feared Nebuchadnezzar and the armies of the Chaldeans and Syrians, they went to live in Jerusalem. *(Jer. 35:6-19.)*

JEHONATHAN (1). *1 Chr. 27:25.*

Jehonathan, son of Uzziah, was assigned by David to be over the storehouses in the fields, cities, villages and castles.

JEHONATHAN (2). *2 Chr. 17:8-9.*

Jehonathan, a Levite, along with other Levites and Elishama and Jehoram, the priests, was sent by king Jehoshaphat to journey with the princes of Judah throughout the cities of Judah to instruct the people out of the book of the law of the Lord.

JEHONATHAN (3). *Neh. 12:18.*

Jehonathan, son of Shemaiah, was one of the priests who was a chief of the fathers in the days of Joiakim.

JEHORAM (1) (Joram (2)). *1 Kgs. 22:50; 2 Kgs. 8:16-25; 11:2; 12:18; 1 Chr. 3:11; 2 Chr. 21; 22:1, 11-12.*

Jehoram, son of Jehoshaphat, reigned over Judah after his father. *(1 Kgs. 22:50.)*

Jehoram began his reign over Judah in the fifth year of the reign of Israel's king Joram (Jehoram), the son of Ahab. He was 32 years old and reigned eight years in Jerusalem. He walked in evil ways, just as the kings of Israel did. Ahab's daughter, Athaliah, was his wife. During his reign, Edom revolted against Judah and made a king over themselves. **Joram** (Jehoram) died and was buried in the city of David. His son, Ahaziah, reigned in his stead beginning in the twelfth year of the reign of Israel's king Joram (Ahab's son). *(2 Kgs. 8:16-25.)*

Joram's daughter Jehosheba hid her nephew Joash from her mother Athaliah so she could not kill him. *(2 Kgs. 11:2.)*

Joram's grandson king Jehoash (Joash) gave Hazael king of Syria all the hallowed things that his fathers before him had dedicated along with his own hallowed things so Hazael would not destroy Jerusalem. *(2 Kgs. 12:18.)*

Joram (Jehoram) was the son of Jehoshaphat and the father of Ahaziah. *(1 Chr. 3:11.)*

Jehoram, the firstborn of Jehoshaphat, reigned over Judah after Jehoshapat died. He began his reign when he was 32 years old and reigned for eight years. His brothers were Azariah, Jehiel, Zechariah, Azariah, Michael and Shephatiah. After gaining power, he slew all of his brethren with the sword as well as many of the princes of Israel. His wife was the daughter of Ahab; and he followed Ahab in wickedness. Both Edom and Libnah revolted from under his hand because of his wickedness. The prophet Elijah sent him a message and told him that a plague would be upon the people and that his bowels would be diseased causing his death. The Lord stirred up the spirit of the Philistines and the Arabians who were near the Ethiopians to go against Jehoram. They carried away his substance and all his household save his youngest son, Jehoahaz (Ahaziah, Azariah). He died and was buried in the city of David. *(2 Chr. 21.)*

His youngest son, Ahaziah, reigned in his stead because the Arabians had slain all the eldest sons. His daughter Jehoshabeath (Jehosheba), wife of Jehoiada the priest, rescued Ahaziah's son Joash and Joash's nurse from being slain by Athaliah after the death of Ahaziah. *(2 Chr. 22:1, 11-12.)* (Chart 1.)

JEHORAM (2) (Joram (3)). *2 Kgs. 1:17; 3; 8:16, 25, 28-29; 9:14-26; 2 Chr. 22:5-6.*

Jehoram reigned in Israel after the death of his brother Ahaziah. He began his reign in the second year of the reign of Judah's king Jehoram (Jehoshaphat's son). *(2 Kgs. 1:17.) (Note: 2 Kgs. 8:16 states that Jehoram, Jehoshaphat's son, began his reign over Judah in the fifth year of Israel's king Jehoram's reign.)*

Jehoram, the son of Ahab, was Ahaziah's brother. *(Note: There seems to be some additional confusion. In 2 Kgs. 1:17 it says that Jehoram began his reign*

over Israel in the second year of the reign of Jehoram over Judah. In 2 Kgs. 3:1,
however, it says that Jehoram began his reign over Israel in the eighteeth year of
Jehoshaphat's reign over Judah.) He reigned 12 years. He put away the image of
Baal but still walked in evil paths, following the sins of Jeroboam. *(2 Kgs. 3:1-3.)*
When Mesha king of Moab rebelled against Israel following the death of Ahab,
Jehoram enlisted the aid of Jehoshaphat to go to battle against him. They solicited
input from the prophet Elisha who responded to their request out of respect for
Jehoshaphat. He asked them to bring him a minstrel, and while the minstrel played,
the hand of the Lord came upon Elisha. He told Jehoram, Jehoshaphat and the king
of Edom to fill the valley with ditches and the Lord would provide them water for
their stock and victory over the Moabites. *(2 Kgs. 3:4-18.)* They were told to
destroy every fenced city and every choice city, to fell every good tree and mar
every good piece of land with stones. They did as instructed and the Moabites were
defeated. *(2 Kgs. 3:19-26.)*

In **Joram's** (Jehoram's) twelfth year as king over Israel, Ahaziah, son of Judah's
king Joram, began his reign over Judah. Israel's king Joram was wounded in battle
against Hazael, king of Syria. He went down to Jezreel to recover. Ahaziah went to
Jezreel to visit him. *(2 Kgs. 8:25, 28-29.) (Note: 2 Kgs. 9:29 states that Ahaziah*
began his reign over Judah in Joram's eleventh year.)

One of the sons of the prophets was instructed by Elisha to anoint Jehu king
over Israel and to inform him that the Lord wanted him to smite the house of Ahab
so that every member of Ahab's family perished. Jehu conspired against the king.
Joram had gone to Jezreel to recover from wounds received in battle against Hazael,
king of Syria. Ahaziah went to Jezreel to see Joram. Jehu and his company rode
furiously toward Jezreel. When horsemen sent out to see if they came in peace did
not return, Joram went out. When he realized Jehu had not come in peace, he tried
to flee. He warned Ahaziah that there was treachery afoot. However Jehu shot
Joram (Jehoram) with a bow and arrow, killing him. Jehu instructed Bidkar, his
captain, to cast him in the portion of the field of Naboth the Jezreelite. Ahaziah also
tried to flee but was pursued and killed by Jehu's men. *(2 Kgs. 9:14-26.)*

Jehoram, king of Israel, was joined by Ahaziah, king of Judah, in war against
Hazael, king of Syria. The Syrians smote Jehoram (Joram) who returned to Jezreel
to recover from his wounds. *(2 Chr. 22:5-6.)*

JEHORAM (3). *2 Chr. 17:8-9.*

Jehoram and Elishama, the priests, along with other Levites, were sent by king
Jehoshaphat to journey with the princes of Judah throughout the cities of Judah to
instruct the people out of the book of the law of the Lord.

JEHORAM'S (2) SERVANTS. *2 Kgs. 3:11; 7:13-15.*

One of **Jehoram's Servants** pointed to Elisha as a prophet of God when
Jehoshaphat asked if there was not a prophet of the Lord in Israel from whom they
could make inquiry regarding their battle against Mesha king of Moab. *(2 Kgs.*
3:11.)

After the Syrians fled their camp because the noise of chariots, horses and soldiers frightened them, the king of Israel was informed by porters who had been informed by four leprous men, that there were goods to be retrieved. One of his servants suggested taking chariots and horses to the empty camp to collect the goods. A messenger returned and reported to the king about what they found. Thus, the people all went out and "spoiled the tents of the Syrians" which ended the famine in Samaria. *(2 Kgs. 7:13-15.)*

JEHOSHABEATH. See **Jehosheba**.

JEHOSHAPHAT (1). *2 Sam. 8:16; 20:24; 1Kgs. 4:3; 1 Chr. 18:15.*

Jehoshaphat the son of Ahilud was the recorder when David reigned over Israel. *(2 Sam. 8:16; 1 Chr. 18:15.)*

Jehoshaphat was the recorder when David regained the kingdom from Absalom and the insurrection by Sheba was quelled. *(2 Sam. 20:24.)*

Jehoshaphat was the recorder in Solomon's court. *(1 Kgs. 4:3.)*

JEHOSHAPHAT (2). *1 Kgs. 4:17.*

Jehoshaphat, son of Paruah, was one of twelve officers over Israel who provided victuals for king Solomon and his family one month each year.

JEHOSHAPHAT (3). *1 Kgs. 15:24; 22:1-51; 2 Kgs. 3; 8:16; 1 Chr. 3:10-11, 2 Chr. 17; 18:1-32; 19; 20; 21:1-3.*

Jehoshaphat was the son of Asa, grandson of Abijam, great-grandson of Rehoboam and great-great-grandson of Solomon. When Asa died, Jehoshaphat reigned as king of Judah in his stead. *(1 Kgs. 15:24.)*

Jehoshaphat of Judah joined Ahab of Israel in battle against Syria. When Ahab received advice from 400 of his prophets, Jehoshaphat requested that they get input from one of the Lord's prophets. The prophet Micaiah foretold of the defeat and death of Ahab. Jehoshaphat reigned in righteousness, beginning his reign in the fourth year of Ahab's reign as king over Israel. He was 35 years old when he became king. He reigned 25 years. His mother was Azubah, the daughter of Shilhi. He died and was buried in the city of David. His son Jehoram reigned in his stead. It was in the 17th year of Jehoshaphat's reign over Judah that Ahaziah began his two-year reign in Israel. *(1 Kgs. 22:1-51; Also see 2 Chr. 18:1-32, which is a repeat and expansion of 1 Kgs. 22:2-8, 32-33.)*

It was in the 18th year of Jehoshaphat's reign as king over Judah that Jehoram (Ahab's son) began his reign over Israel. *(Note: 2 Kgs. 1:17 states that Jehoram began his reign over Israel in the second year of Jehoshaphat's son Jehoram's reign over Judah.)* Jehoshaphat joined Jehoram of Israel in battle against Moab. At his request, they petitioned help from the prophet Elisha. Elisha promised them water for their stock and victory in the war. The Moabites were defeated. *(2 Kgs. 3.)*

Jehoshaphat's son Jehoram (Joram) began his reign over Judah in the fifth year of the reign of Jehoram (Joram, son of Ahab) over Israel. *(2 Kgs. 8:16.) (Again, note the discrepancy between this verse and 2 Kgs. 1:17.)*

Jehoshaphat was the son of Asa, grandson of Abia (Abijam), and father of Joram (Jehoram). *(1 Chr. 3:10-11.)*

Jehoshaphat reigned as king over Judah when Asa died. He reigned well and prospered Judah. Some of the Philistines and Arabians brought him presents. In the third year of his reign, he sent the priests traveling throughout the land to teach the people out of the book of the law of the Lord. *(2 Chr. 17.)*

Jehoshaphat went to battle wearing his robes. When the Syrian army came against him, Jehoshaphat cried out and they turned away from him as they were looking for Ahab. *(2 Chr. 18:1-32.) (Note: These verses are also a repeat and expansion of 1 Kgs. 22:2-8, 32-33.)*

Because Jehoshaphat had helped Ahab in his battle against Syria, he was chastised by Jehu the son of Hanani the seer. Nevertheless, Jehu told Jehoshaphat that there were good things found in him. Jehoshaphat brought the people back to the Lord and set up judges and administrators of justice. *(2 Chr. 19.)*

When the children of Moab, Ammon and mount Seir came against Jehoshaphat, Jehoshaphat and his people fasted and prayed to the Lord. The prophet Jahaziel, son of Zechariah, prophesied that all would be well and that the Lord would fight their battle for them. While Judah sang and praised the Lord, their enemies fought amongst themselves and destroyed themselves. Then Jehoshaphat and his people returned in peace to their own homes. Jehoshaphat was 35 years old when he began his reign over Judah. He reigned 25 years. His mother was Azubah, the daughter of Shilhi. He walked in the ways of the Lord. However, near the end of his reign, he joined with Ahaziah, a wicked king of Israel, to make ships to go to Tarshish. As a result, Eliezer, son of Dodaviah of Mareshah, prophesied against Jehoshaphat and said his works would be broken. And so it was, the ships were broken and were not able to go to Tarshish. *(2 Chr. 20.)*

Jehoshaphat died and his son Jehoram reigned in his stead. Jehoshaphat's sons were Jehoram, Azariah, Jehiel, Zechariah, Azariah, Michael and Shephatiah. *(2 Chr. 21:1-3.)* (Chart 1.)

JEHOSHAPHAT (4). *2 Kgs. 9:2.*

Jehoshaphat was the father of Jehu and the son of Nimshi.

JEHOSHAPHAT (5). *1 Chr. 15:24.*

Jehoshaphat was one of the priests assigned, under the direction of David, to blow the trumpet before the ark of God as the ark was removed from the house of Obed-edom and taken to the place which David had prepared for it to be housed.

JEHOSHEBA (Jehoshabeath). *2 Kgs. 11:2-3; 2 Chr. 22:11-12.*

Jehosheba (Jehoshabeath), wife of Jehoiada the priest, was the daughter of king Joram and Athaliah and sister of Ahaziah. After Ahaziah's death, when Athaliah sought to destroy all the royal seed, Jehosheba stole Joash (Jehoash), Ahaziah's son, away and hid him for six years in the house of the Lord so Athaliah could not slay him.

JEHOSHUA. See **Joshua**.

JEHOZABAD (1). *2 Kgs. 12:21; 2 Chr. 24:26.*

Jehozabad, son of Shomer, and Jozachar, son of Shimeath, fellow servants to king Joash (Jehoash) of Judah, conspired against the king and slew him. *(2 Kgs. 12:21.)*

Jehozabad's mother was Shimrith, a Moabitess. *(2 Chr. 24:26.)*

JEHOZABAD (2). *1 Chr. 26:4, 8, 12.*

Jehozabad, a Levite, was the secondborn son of Obed-edom. His brothers were Shemaiah, Joah, Sacar, Nethaneel, Ammiel, Issachar and Peulthai. They, along with other Levites, were appointed by king David to be porters—to have charge of the treasures, serve as officers and judges, and to conduct the outward business over Israel. (Chart 7c.)

JEHOZABAD (3). *2 Chr. 17:18.*

Jehozabad, of the house of Benjamin, was the captain of 180,000 men ready and prepared for war in behalf of Jehoshaphat king of Judah.

JEHOZADAK. See **Ezra**.

JEHU (1). *1 Kgs. 16:1-7; 2 Chr. 19:2-3; 20:34.*

Jehu, son of Hanani, prophesied evil upon Baasha and his house. The Lord said He would make Baasha's house like Jeroboam's house. "Him that dieth of Baasha in the city shall the dogs eat; and him that dieth of his in the fields shall the fowls of the air eat." *(1 Kgs. 16:1-7.)*

Jehu the son of Hanani the seer rebuked Jehoshaphat for helping ungodly Ahab in Ahab's battle against Ben-hadad, king of Syria. Nevertheless, he said there were good things to be found in Jehoshaphat. *(2 Chr. 19:2-3.)*

Jehu recorded the acts of Jehoshaphat but the book of Jehu is among the lost scriptures mentioned in the Old Testament. *(2 Chr. 20:34.)*

JEHU (2). *1 Kgs. 19:16-17; 2 Kgs. 9; 10; 15:12; 2 Chr. 22:7-9; 25:17; Hosea 1:1,.4.*

Jehu was the son of Nimshi. The Lord instructed Elijah to anoint him to be king over Israel. Elijah was told that "him that escapeth the sword of Hazael shall Jehu slay: and him that escapeth from the sword of Jehu shall Elisha slay." *(1 Kgs. 19:16-17.)*

Elisha sent one of the sons of the prophets to Ramoth-gilead and instructed him to find Jehu the son of Jehoshaphat who was the son of Nimshi and, with oil, anoint him king over Israel. *(2 Kgs. 9:2-3.)* Jehu was one of the captains of the host. He was instructed by the son of the prophets that the Lord directed that he should smite the house of Ahab so that the whole house of Ahab perished. *(2 Kgs. 9:5-8.)* He was declared king by the rest of the captains of the host. Jehu then conspired against Joram (Jehoram) king of Israel and slew him with a bow and arrow *(2 Kgs. 9:13-14, 24)*. He also pursued Ahaziah, king of Judah, and slew him in his chariot. *(2 Kgs. 9:27.)*

Jehu had the rulers of Jezreel, the elders and those who brought up Ahab's children send him the heads of Ahab's 70 sons. They sent them to him in Jezreel in baskets. He had them make two heaps "at the entering in of the gate until the morning." *(2 Kgs. 10:1-8.)* He went to Jezreel and slew all the rest of Ahab's family that were there, including his kinsfolks and his priests, and then moved on to Samaria. *(2 Kgs. 10:11.)* Enroute he slew the brethren of Ahaziah at the pit of the shearing house. *(2 Kgs. 10:12-14.)* In Samaria, he slew all that remained who were related to Ahab; thus, he totally destroyed the house of Ahab as he had been instructed to do. *(2 Kgs. 10:17.)* Jehu destroyed all the worshippers of Baal and destroyed Baal out of Israel. *(2 Kgs. 10:18-28.)* Because he had done unto the house of Ahab all that the Lord had commanded, the Lord promised him that his children of the fourth generation would sit upon the throne of Israel. Nevertheless, he still continued to worship the golden calves in Beth-el and Dan. Thus, Hazael and the Syrians were able to wax strong against Israel. Jehu reigned 28 years over Israel. He died and was buried in Samaria. His son Jehoahaz reigned in his stead. *(2 Kgs. 10:29-36.)*

Jehu's children unto the fourth generation would sit upon the throne. *(2 Kgs. 15:12.) (Note: After Jehu reigned, his son Jehoahaz reigned, then Joash, followed by his great-grandson Jeroboam, and finally by Zachariah, his great-great-grandson who reigned just 6 months before he was slain, completing the fourth generation as the Lord had promised.)*

After Jehoram, king of Israel, was wounded in battle against Hazael and the Syrians, he went to Jezreel to recover. Ahaziah, king of Judah, went to Jezreel to visit him. This allowed Jehu to have his men capture Ahaziah, who had hidden himself in Samaria, and slay him according to the judgment of the Lord. *(2 Chr. 22:7-9.)*

Jehu was the father of Jehoahaz who was father of Joash, king of Israel. *(2 Chr. 25:17.)*

Hosea was told by the Lord that the Lord would avenge the blood of Jezreel upon the house of Jehu and would cause the kingdom of the house of Israel to cease because of their wickedness. *(Hosea 1:1, 4.)*

JEHU (3). *1 Chr. 2:38.*

Jehu was the son of Obed and the father of Azariah. (Chart 8c.)

JEHU (4). *1 Chr. 4:35.*

Jehu, a descendant of Shimei, was the son of Josibiah. (Chart 6a.)

JEHU (5). *1 Chr. 12:3.*

Jehu, the Anthothite, was one of David's mighty men who came to him at Ziklag, prepared to defend him against Saul, when all Israel sent their armies in support of David as king.

JEHUBBAH. *1 Chr. 7:34.*

Jehubbah was a son of Shamer (Shomer) and a great-great-grandson of Asher. His brothers were Ahi, Rohgah and Aram. (Chart 14a.)

JEHUCAL (Jucal). *Jer. 37:3; 38:1.*

Jehucal was the son of Shelemiah. He and Zephaniah the son of Maaseiah the priest were sent to Jeremiah by king Zedekiah to ask him to pray to the Lord in behalf of the people. *(Jer. 37:3.)*

When **Jucal** (Jehucal) the son of Shelemiah, Shephatiah the son of Mattan, Gedaliah the son of Pashur who was the son of Immer, and Pashur the son of Malchiah (Melchiah) heard Jeremiah prophesy that if the people did not go forth with the Chaldeans Jerusalem would be burned, they asked Zedekiah the king if they could not slay Jeremiah. The king said he could not prevail against them, so they cast Jeremiah into a miry dungeon in the home of Malchiah the son of the king. *(Jer. 38:1.)*

JEHUDI. *Jer. 36:14, 21, 23.*

Jehudi was the son of Nethaniah who was the son of Shelemiah who was the son of Cushi. The princes sent him to Baruch to ask Baruch to bring the roll which Jeremiah had had him read before the people and read it before them. King Jehoiakim had Jehudi take the roll from the scribe's chamber and read it to him. When Jehudi had read three of four leaves, the king cut the roll up and burned it.

JEHUDIJAH. *1 Chr. 4:18.*

Jehudijah was the mother of Jered, Heber and Jekuthiel, and the grandmother of Gedor, Socho and Zanoah. (Chart 8 o.)

JEHUSH. *1 Chr. 8:39.*

Jehush was the secondborn son of Eshek. He was from the tribe of Benjamin. He descended through Jonathan, the son of Saul. His brothers were Ulam and Eliphelet. (Chart 16 l.)

JEIEL (1). *1 Chr. 5:7.*

Jeiel was one of the chiefs among the Reubenites. *(Note: His direct lineage to Reuben is not clear.)* (Chart 5b.)

JEIEL (2). *1 Chr. 15:18-20; 1 Chr. 16:5.*

Jeiel and his brethren of the second degree were assigned, under the direction of David, to be singers along with Heman, Asaph and Ethan. Jeiel and his brethren were assigned to excel wth harps on the Sheminith. Jeiel and Obed-edom were the porters for the ark. *(1 Chr. 15:18-20.)*

Jeiel and his brethren were appointed by David to minister before the ark of the Lord and to play with psalteries and harps. *(1 Chr. 16:5.)*

JEIEL (3) (Hashabiah (6), Shemaiah (15). *2 Chr. 20:14; Neh. 11:22; 12:35, 36.*

Jeiel, son of Mattaniah, a Levite of the sons of Asaph, was the father of Benaiah who was the father of Zechariah who was the father of Jahaziel. *(2 Chr. 20:14.)*

Hashabiah (Jeiel) was the father of Bani (Benaiah). *(Neh. 11:22.)*

Shemaiah (Jeiel, Hashabiah) was an ancestor of Zachariah, one of the sons of the priests who was instructed by Nehemiah to purify himself and was then assigned to one of two great companies for the dedication of the walls of Jerusalem. His son was Jonathan (Bani/Benaiah). Shemaiah participated in the dedication of the wall with his musical instrument. *(Neh. 12:35, 36.)* (Chart 7a.)

JEIEL (4). *2 Chr. 26:11.*

Jeiel was a scribe in Judah when Uzziah (Azariah) was king.

JEIEL (5). *2 Chr. 29:13.*

Jeiel was a descendant of Elizaphan. He was among those whom Hezekiah, king of Judah, instructed to sanctify themselves so they could cleanse and sanctify the house of the Lord.

JEIEL (6). *Ezra 8:13.*

Jeiel, Eliphelet and Shemaiah were of the last sons of Adonikam. They were the chiefs of their fathers. They went with Ezra back to Jerusalem from Babylon and took 60 males with them.

JEIEL (7). *Ezra 10:43-44.*

Jeiel was one of Nebo's sons. He and his brothers Mattithiah, Zabad, Zebina, Jadau, Joel and Benaiah were some of the Israelite men who took foreign wives but agreed to separate themselves from them because Ezra feared the Lord's wrath would destroy all of Israel for this iniquity.

JEKAMEAM. *1 Chr. 23:19, 24; 24:23.*

Jekameam, a Levite, was the fourth son of Hebron, son of Kohath. When David numbered the Levites at the time he made Solomon king, he divided them into courses among the sons of Levi to do the work for the service of the house of the Lord. *(1 Chr. 23:19, 24.)*

Jekameam, along with his brothers Jeriah, Amariah and Jahaziel and the rest of the chief fathers of the Levites, drew lots for his course in the presence of king David, Zadok, Ahimelech and other community leaders. *(1 Chr. 24:23.)* (Chart 7d.)

JEKAMIAH. *1 Chr. 2:41.*

Jekamiah was the son of Shallum and the father of Elishama. (Chart 8c.)

JEKUTHIEL. *1 Chr. 4:18.*

Jekuthiel was the father of Zanoah. His mother was Jehudijah. (Chart 8 o.)

JEMIMA. *Job 42:14.*

Jemima was Job's firstborn daughter after his trials when the Lord gave Job twice as much as he had had earlier. Her sisters were Kezia and Keren-happuch.

JEMUEL (Nemuel (2), Nemuelites). *Gen. 46:10; Num. 26:12; 1 Chr. 4:24.*

Jemuel was one of Simeon's sons and a grandson of Jacob. His brothers were Jamin, Ohad, Jachin, Zohar and Shaul the son of a Canaanitish woman. *(Gen. 46:10.)*

Nemuel (Jemuel) was the father of the **Nemuelites**. His siblings were Jamin, Jachin, Zerah (Zohar) and Shaul. *(Num. 26:12.)*

Nemuel's brothers were Jamin, Jarib (Jachin), Zerah and Shaul. *(1 Chr. 4:24.)* (Chart 6a.)

JEPHTHAH. *Judg. 11; Judg. 12:1-7.*

Jephthah was the son of Gilead and a harlot. He was cast out by Jephthah's other children. He was chosen captain of the armies of Israel. Jephthah sent messengers to the king of the children of Ammon inquiring why he was warring against Israel. After receiving the king's reply, Jephthah sent the messengers back to the king denying that Israel had taken the land of Moab or the land of the children of Ammon away, reminding him of some past history. He then reminded the king that they possess lands which their pagan god Chemosh had given them and that Israel would possess lands which their God gives to them. Jephthah was guided by the Spirit and defeated Ammon with a great slaughter. However, he made a rash promise that he would offer up for a burnt offering the first thing that come forth from the doors of his house to greet him upon his return home. Unfortunately, that turned out to be his daughter, his only child. With her agreement, he kept the promise to the Lord. *(Judg. 11.)*

Jepththah and the Gileadites slew 42,000 Ephraimites who came to war against them. Jephthah judged Israel six years and then died. He was buried in one of the cities of Gilead. *(Judg. 12:1-7.)* (Chart 20.)

JEPHTHAH'S DAUGHTER. *Judg. 11:34-40.*

Jephthah's Daughter was the first thing to come forth from his house to greet him upon his return from battle and, thus, became the thing which Jephthah had rashly promised he would offer as a burnt sacrifice if the Lord delivered the children of Ammon into his hands. His daughter agreed to being sacrificed but asked if she could have two months so she and her friends could go into the mountains and bewail her virginity. Following the two months, she presented herself to her father who kept his vow to the Lord. Thus, "the daughters of Israel went yearly to lament the daughter of Jephthah the Gileadite four days in a year."

JEPHUNNEH (1). *Num. 13:6.*

Jephunneh, of the tribe of Judah, was the father of Caleb, which Caleb was one of 12 spies Moses had sent to scout out the promised land. (Charts 8k, n.)

JEPHUNNEH (2). *1 Chr. 7:38.*

Jephunneh was a son of Jether. His brothers were Pispah and Ara. He was a descendant of Asher, but the connection is not clear. (Chart 14b.)

JERAH. *Gen. 10:26.*

Jerah was a son of Joktan, a third-great-grandson of Shem and a fourth-great-grandson of Noah. (Chart 2b.)

JERAHMEEL (1). *1 Chr. 2:9, 25-26, 42.*

Jerahmeel was one of the sons of Hezron. His brothers were Ram (a progenitor of David) and Chelubai (Caleb). His sons were Ram, Bunah, Oren, Ozem Ahijah and Onam. Onam's mother was Atarah. Jerahmeel had another wife, but she is not mentioned by name. (Charts 8c-d, h.)

JERAHMEEL (2). *1 Chr. 24:29.*

Jerahmeel, a Levite, was a son of Kish. He was named as one of the chief of the fathers. He, along with the other Levites who were chief of the fathers, drew lots for his course in the presence of king David, Zadok, Ahimelech and the other leaders. (Chart 7e.)

JERAHMEEL (3). *Jer. 36:26.*

Jerahmeel was the son of Hammelech (i.e., the king). Jehoiakim commanded Jerahmeel, Seraiah the son of Azriel, and Shelemiah the son of Abdeel to arrest Baruch and Jeremiah because of Jeremiah's prophecies. However, "the Lord hid them."

JERED (1). *1 Chr. 1:2.* See **Jared**.

JERED (2). *1 Chr. 4:18.*

Jered was the father of Gedor. His mother was Jehudijah. (Chart 8 o.)

JEREMAI. *Ezra 10:33 (18-19, 33, 44).*

Jeremai, one of Hashum's sons, and his brothers Mattenai, Mattathah, Zabad, Eliphelet, Manasseh and Shimei were among the Israelite men who took foreign wives but complied with Ezra's request that they put away their strange wives so as not to bring the wrath of God upon Israel.

JEREMIAH (1). *2 Kgs. 23:31; 2 Chr. 35:25; Jer. 52:1.*

Jeremiah of Libnah, father-in-law of Josiah king of Judah, was the father of Hamutal who was the mother of Jehoahaz who became king of Judah following Josiah's death. *(2 Kgs. 23:31.)*

Jeremiah lamented the death of king Josiah. *(2 Chr. 35:25.)*

Jeremiah of Libnah was the father of Hamutal who was the mother of Zedekiah (Mattaniah), king of Judah. *(Jer. 52:1.)* (Chart 1.)

JEREMIAH (2). *2 Chr. 36:19-21; Jer. 1-20; 21:1-17; 22-39; 40:1-6; 42-51; 52:1; Lam. 1-5; Dan. 9:2.*

Jeremiah prophesied over 40 years: 626-586 B.C. *(Note: Jer. 1-6 are Jeremiah's prophecies during the reign of Josiah: 626-608 B.C.)* He prophesied that Judah would be taken captive by Babylonia and would remain in captivity for seventy years. Because of Judah's wickedness, the Lord allowed the Chaldees to burn the temple and destroy Jerusalem and take the children of Israel captive where they served as servants to the Chaldees until the reign of Cyrus, king of Persia. This was to fulfil the word of the Lord by the mouth of Jeremiah, "until the land had enjoyed her sabbaths" three score and ten years. *(2 Chr. 36:19-21.)*

Jeremiah the son of Hilkiah was of the priests who were in Anathoth in the land of Benjamin. He was ordained to be a prophet unto the nations before he was born. As a mortal, he was called by the Lord in the days of Josiah, king of Judah, and also in the days of Jehoiakim, king of Judah, up until the 11th year of Zedekiah, king of Judah, to declare His word. *(Jer. 1.)*

Jeremiah chastised the children of Israel because they had rejected the prophets and the Lord and had become idol worshippers. *(Jer. 2.)*

Jeremiah urged "backsliding" Israel and Judah to return to the Lord. He prophesied that in the last days Israel will be gathered, "one of a city, and two of a family," and be brought by the Lord to Zion. *(Jer. 3.)*

Jeremiah called Israel and Judah to repentance. He lamented the miseries he knew would befall Judah. *(Jer 4.)*

Jeremiah bemoaned the hardness of the hearts of the Jews who refused to return to the Lord. He prophesied of the judgments that would be poured out upon the Jews because of their sins: the Lord would "bring a nation upon you from afar . . . like as ye have forsaken me, and served strange gods in your land, so shall ye serve strangers in a land that is not yours" *(Jer. 5:15, 19)*. He reminded them that their sins caused blessings to be withheld from them. *(Jer. 5:25.)*

Jeremiah prophesied of the great destruction that would be visited upon Jerusalem "out of the north" by a "great nation . . . raised from the sides of the earth" because everyone, even the prophets and priests, were dealing falsely. This nation would be fierce and cruel and have no mercy on Jerusalem. *(Jer. 6.)*

(Note: Jer. 7-20 are Jeremiah's prophecies during the reign of Jehoiakim: 608-597 B.C.) The Lord told Jeremiah to tell Judah that if the people repented, they would be preserved to dwell in the land the Lord had given their fathers forever and ever. Judah was told to observe what the Lord had done to Israel in Shiloh and, if they didn't repent, their lot would be the same. However, because of their wickedness—which included making burnt sacrifices of their own children—the Lord rejected that generation. *(Jer. 7.)*

Judah refused to repent and great calamities were prophesied to befall Jerusalem. *(Jer. 8.)*

In anguish, Jeremiah bemoaned the fate of Judah who the Lord said would be scattered and punished and slaughtered because of their sins and idolatry. *(Jer. 9.)*

The Lord, through Jeremiah, told the people they should not learn the ways of the heathen and they should not be afraid of false gods for those gods can do neither evil nor good. The Lord is the only true and living God. *(Jer. 10.)*

The Lord instructed Jeremiah to tell Judah and Jerusalem that if they did not obey the covenant of obedience which He had commanded them even in the days when he brought their fathers out of Egypt, they would be cursed. Because the people refused to give up their idol worship, the Lord refused to hear their prayers. *(Jer. 11:14.)* Because the men of Anathoth rejected the prophets, the Lord said their young men would die by the sword and their sons and daughters would die by famine. *(Jer. 11:22.)*

Jeremiah questioned the Lord as to why the wicked prospered and seemed happy. The Lord told Jeremiah that if the nations came to accept the Lord, to "diligently learn the ways of my people, to swear by my name . . . then shall they be built in the midst of my people." *(Jer. 12:16-17.)* However, if they refused to accept the Lord, He would "pluck up and destroy that nation." *(Jer. 12:17.)*

The Lord said He would mar the pride of Judah and Jerusalem like a marred girdle which was profitable for nothing. They were entreated to repent. They were told that if they didn't, Judah would be carried away captive and scattered "as the stubble that passeth away by the wind of the wilderness." *(Jer. 13:9-24.)*

The Lord caused a dearth upon the land so there was no water nor food for the people and no grass for the cattle. Jeremiah prayed for the people, but the Lord would not hear their cries because of their wickedness. False prophets prophesied lies in His name, saying there would be no famine, they wouldn't perish by the sword, and assured them peace. The Lord said He didn't send them and that they prophesied a false vision and divination, and a thing of nought. *(Jer. 14.)*

The Lord said that even if Moses and Samuel stood before Him to plead for the people He would not save them because of their wickedness. *(Jer. 15:1.)* Because of wickedness, because of Manasseh the son of Hezekiah king of Judah who led his people into wickedness, the Jews would suffer death, famine and captivity. The Lord would send four destroyers: "the sword to slay, and the dogs to tear, and the fowls of the heaven, and the beasts of the earth, to devour and destroy." *(Jer. 15:3.)* The Lord said He would destroy His people and cause them to be "removed" into all the kingdoms of the earth—to pass into a land they "knowest not."*(Jer. 15:4-14.)*

Jeremiah was instructed by the Lord not to take a wife nor have children in Jerusalem because all those born there would perish, as well as all those who fathered or who gave birth to children there. When the people asked why the Lord was threatening to destroy them, he was to tell them it was because their fathers had forsaken the Lord and worshipped idols and that they were even worse than their fathers. However, He also told Jeremiah that in the latter days the children of Israel who had been scatter to the north and to other lands would be gathered again "into their land that I gave unto their fathers." The gospel will be restored: they will know that His name is "The LORD." *(Jer. 16.)*

The Lord told Jeremiah that it was because of sin that He would cause the people to serve their enemies "in a land which thou knowest not." *(Jer. 17:4.)* The people were commanded to keep the Sabbath day holy. *(Jer. 17:21-22.)* If they did, they would be blessed *(Jer. 17:25)*; but if they didn't, they would be destroyed *(Jer. 17:27)*.

The Lord compared Israel to potter's clay. Just as a potter can do with the clay whatsover he chooses, so the Lord can do for or to Israel whatsoever He chooses. If they repented, He would withhold evil from them. Likewise, if they chose to do evil, He would withhold the good with which He would have blessed them. The people sought to do evil to Jeremiah. *(Jer. 18.)*

The Lord sent Jeremiah to the valley of the son of Hinnom to prophesy of the destruction that would come to Judah. Because they offered their sons as burnt offerings to Baal, the Lord said they would be destroyed and the valley would be called the valley of slaughter. The people would eat the flesh of their own sons and daughters as well as that of their friends. The people would be broken just like the potter's vessel which Jeremiah broke before them. *(Jer. 19.)*

Jeremiah was arrested by Pashur, chief governor in the house of the Lord, and was placed in stocks. He told Pashur the Lord now called him Magor-missabib. Jeremiah prophesied that the Lord would deliver all of Judah up into Babylonian captivity and that Pashur and all his friends and family would die there and be buried there. Jeremiah praised the Lord but also lamented the day he was born. *(Jer. 20.)*

(Note: Jer. 21-38 are Jeremiah's prophecies during the reign of Zedekiah: 597-586 B.C.) When king Zedekiah sent Jeremiah to inquire of the priests whether or not the Lord would protect them against Nebuchadrezzar, king of Babylonia, who was threatening war against them, Jeremiah instructed Pashur and Zepahiah, the priests, to tell Zedekiah that the Lord would not help them and that Jerusalem would be captured and destroyed by Nebuchadrezzar (Nebuchadnezzar). Additionally, Zedekiah himself would be taken captive by Nebuchadrezzar. *(Jer. 21:1-7.)*

Jeremiah was told by the Lord to command the kings and leaders of Judah to execute righteous judgment and to do no wrong. If they were obedient to this command, the throne of David would stand. If they were not, the throne of David would fall. Jeremiah enumerated the judgments of the Lord upon the heads of the kings of Judah. *(Jer. 22.)*

Jeremiah prophesied of the gathering of Israel in the latter days and of the reign of the Messiah upon the earth: "Behold, the days come, saith the Lord, that I will raise unto David a righteous Branch, and a King shall reign and prosper, and shall execute judgment and justice in the earth." He shall be called, THE LORD OUR RIGHTEOUSNESS." *(Jer. 23:5-6.)* The Lord condemned false prophets and priests who commit adultery, preach false doctrines and lies, and lead the people astray. They shall be cursed. *(Jer. 23.)*

Following the capture of Jerusalem by Nebuchadrezzar, Jeremiah was shown a vision wherein he saw two baskets of figs: one was of good figs, the other of evil figs. The good figs represented those who were carried away captive but who would be gathered back from Chaldea to again serve the Lord. The evil figs represented the residue who would be cursed and scattered throughout all the lands. *(Jer. 24.)*

Jeremiah reminded the people that for 23 years—from the 13th year of Josiah's reign until the fourth year of Jehoiakim's reign—the Lord had sent him and other prophets to warn them to turn away from their evil ways, but they had refused. Thus, the condemnation of the Lord was upon them: they would be carried captive to Babylon where they would remain for 70 years. After that time, many heathen nations would be overthrown. Eventually, all the inhabitants of the earth will be at war. *(Jer. 25.)*

In the beginning of Jehoiakim's reign, Jeremiah prophesied the destruction of the people. The priests and prophets didn't like what he said and felt he should die. The princes of Judah disagreed and reminded them that Micah the Morasthite had prophesied in the days of Hezekiah and they didn't put him to death. Instead, they had repented and the Lord turned away the evil He had threatened against them. Ahikam refused to turn Jeremiah over to the people. *(Jer. 26.)*

Jeremiah, in the beginning of Jehoiakim's reign, was instructed by the Lord to send word to many nations that they were to serve Babylon. Those who refused would be punished. The vessels of the Lord's house that were not carried away to Babylon along with Jeconiah were to be carried to Babylon where they would stay until the Lord restored Israel to Jerusalem. *(Jer. 27.)*

When Hananiah falsely prophesied during the fourth year of Zedekiah's reign over Judah that the yoke of Nebuchadnezzar and Babylon would be broken and Jeconiah and the people would return within two years, the Lord instructed Jeremiah to tell Hananiah that because he had made the people trust in a lie and had rebelled against the Lord, he would be cast off from the face of the earth. Thus, Hananiah died that same year. *(Jer. 28.)*

Jeremiah sent a letter by the hand of Elasah to the elders who were carried away captive by Nebuchadnezzar. In it, he counseled the people to find peace by having families, building houses and planting gardens. He also told them that they would remain in captivity for 70 years, after which the Lord would cause good things to happen for them. Those who remained in Jerusalem would yet be scattered. Jeremiah told Shemaiah the Nehelamite that because he had prophesied falsely, the Lord would punish him. He would "have not a man to dwell among this people; neither shall he behold the good that I will do for my people." Jeremiah sent his letter forth after Jeconiah the king and the queen and their household left Jerusalem. *(Jer. 29.)*

Jeremiah prophesied that in the latter days Israel and Judah would be restored to the lands the Lord had given their fathers; "they would serve the Lord their God, and David their king, whom I will raise up unto them" *(i.e. Jesus Christ). (Jer. 30.)*

Israel will be gathered in the last days and the Lord will make a new covenant with them. *(Jer. 31.)*

In the 10th year of Zedekiah's reign as king of Judah—which was the 18th year of Nebuchadrezzar's reign in Babylon—Jeremiah was imprisoned by Zedekiah for prophesying that Zedekiah would be taken captive by Nebuchadrezzar and that Jerusalem would be burned and destroyed by the Chaldeans. He, as instructed by the Lord, bought his uncle Shallum's son Hanameel's property in Anathoth. This recognized the fact that the children of Israel would return to their land. In the latter days, the Lord will gather Israel and make an everlasting covenant with them. *(Jer. 32.)*

Jeremiah prophesied those who fight against the Chaldeans will be defeated because the Lord had withdrawn from Israel. *(Jer. 33:5.)* However, the children of Israel will be gathered in the last days *(Jer. 33:7)*, and the seed of David *(i.e., Jesus Christ)*, "the Branch of righteousness," will "execute judgment and righteousness in the land" *(Jer. 33:15)*.

Jeremiah prophesied that Zedekiah would be delivered into the hands of his enemies. However, he told him that he would not die by the sword but would die in peace. Nevertheless, the Jews would be removed from their land and dispersed thoughout all the kingdoms of the earth. They were chastised for not following the Lord's command to let every manservant and every maidservant who was Hebrew go free after six years: no Jew should be a servant to his brother. *(Jer. 34.)*

Jeremiah commended the Rechabites for their obedience to their father's commandment to live in tents and not drink wine, and the Lord promised them blessings for their obedience. The Israelites were chastised for lack of obedience to the Lord's commandments. *(Jer. 35.)*

Jeremiah, in the fourth year of Jehoiakim's reign over Judah while under arrest or in confinement, instructed Baruch to record the prophecies he (Jeremiah) dictated to him and to read them in the house of the Lord. When Jehoiakim burned the rolls, Jeremiah had Baruch write the prophecies down again, and Jeremiah added additional prophecies to these rolls. He prophesied that Jehoiakim would "have none to sit upon the throne of David: and his dead body shall be cast out in the day to the heat, and in the night to the frost." *(Jer. 36.)*

Zedekiah, who was made king over Judah by Nebuchadnezzar, sent messengers to Jeremiah requesting him to pray unto the Lord for Judah. Jeremiah prophesied that Egypt could not save Judah and that Jerusalem would be taken and burned by the Chaldeans. Jeremiah went to the land of Benjamin where a "captain of the ward," Irijah, accused him of deserting to the Chaldeans. Jeremiah denied the accusation, but Irijah took him to the princes who smote him and cast him into a dungeon in the house of Jonathan the scribe. Zedekiah had him removed from the dungeon and asked what word there was from the Lord. Even though Jeremiah again prophesied that Zedekiah would be delivered into the hand of the king of Babylon, Zedekiah commanded that he not be returned to the house of Jonathan, but ordered that he be committed into the court of the prison as Jeremiah requested as Jeremiah feared he would die if he were returned to the house of Jonathan. *(Jer. 37.)*

Because Jeremiah prophesied that if Israel did not go with the Chaldeans Jerusalem would be captured and burned, the princes cast him into a miry dungeon in the house of Malchiah the son of the king. Ebed-melech the Ethiopian went to Zedekiah and beseeched him to let him rescue Jeremiah. Zedekiah instructed him to take 30 men and proceed to rescue the prophet. Jeremiah remained in the court of the prison until the day that Jerusalem was taken captive: "and he was there when Jerusalem was taken." *(Jer. 38.)*

(Note: Jer. 39-44 provide the prophet's history and other events after the fall of the city. BD.) When Nebuchadnezzar and the Chaldeans captured Jerusalem, slew Zedekiah's sons, put out Zedekiah's eyes, burned the city and carried all but the poor people off to Babylonia, Nebuchadnezzar instructed Nebuzar-adan, captain of his guard, to do no harm to Jeremiah but to do to Jeremiah whatsoever Jeremiah said. *(Jer. 39:1-12.)* He and the king's princes took Jeremiah out of the court of the

prison and committed him unto Gedaliah (who was the son of Ahikam the son of Shaphan) and had him take him home. Thus, Jeremiah dwelled among the people. *(Jer. 39:13-14.)*

Jeremiah was placed in the care of Gedaliah by Nebuzar-adan and dwelled among the people. *(Jer. 40:1-6.)*

Jeremiah was approached by Johanan and the captains of the forces who asked him to pray to the Lord and inquire what they should do. They promised to follow whatever the Lord said. Jeremiah told them that if they remained in Judah they would have peace and safety. But, he said, "none of them shall remain or escape" from the evil the Lord promised to bring upon them if they went to Egypt: they would perish by the sword, famine and pestilence. *(Jer. 42.)*

In spite of Jeremiah's prophecy, and in spite of Johanan's saying he would do whatever the Lord said, he carried Jeremiah and the remnant of Judah into Egypt. Jeremiah prophesied that Nebuchadrezzar would conquer Egypt and set his throne upon the stones Jeremiah had buried at the entry of Pharaoh's house. He would destroy the false idols and slay those who "are for death" and capture those who "are for captivity." *(Jer. 43.)*

Jeremiah prophesied that because the remnant of Judah that went into Egypt worshipped false gods, the Lord would destroy all but a few who would escape. Egypt's king Pharaoh-hophra would be delivered into the hands of his enemy just as Zedekiah king of Judah had been delivered into the hand of Nebuchadrezzar. *(Jer. 44.)*

At the time Baruch wrote Jeremiah's prophecies down for him in the fourth year of Jehoiakim's reign, Jeremiah prophesied that Baruch's life would be preserved. *(Jer. 45.)*

(Note: Jer. 46-51 are Jeremiah's prophecies against foreign nations.) In the fourth year of Jehoiakim king of Judah, Jeremiah prophesied that the Gentiles, including Pharaoh-necho king of Egypt and his armies, would be conquered by Nebuchadrezzar king of Babylon. He also prophesied that Jacob's posterity, the house of Israel, would be gathered in the last days. *(Jer. 46.)*

Jeremiah prophesied of the destruction that would befall the Philistines. *(Jer. 47.)*

Jeremiah prophesied of the destruction that would befall Moab because of the Moabites' loftiness, arrogance, pride, haughtiness and contempt of God's instructions. *(Jer. 48.)*

Jeremiah prophesied of the destruction that would befall the Ammonites *(Jer. 49:1-6)*; the Edomites *(Jer. 49:7-23)*; Damascus *(Jer. 49:23-27)*; Kedar *(Jer. 49:28-29)*, which would be conquered by Nebuchadrezzar; Hazor *(Jer. 49:30-33)*, which would also be conquered by Nebuchadrezzar; the Elamites *(Jer. 49:34-39)*.

Jeremiah prophesied that Babylon would be destroyed and would not rise again. Israel would eventually be gathered and "the children of Israel and the children of Judah would come "together, going and weeping: they shall go, and seek the Lord their God." *(Jer. 50:4.)* They will be restored to the lands of their inheritance *(Jer. 50:19.)*

Jeremiah continued his prophecy that judgments and destruction would come upon Babylon for her sins and her idol worship. Israel was commanded by the Lord to flee from Babylon. In the fourth year of Zedekiah's reign, Jeremiah commanded Seraiah the son of Neriah the son of Maaseiah to read to Babylon all the words of his prophecy which he had had written down which warned that Babylon would fall and never rise again. *(Jer. 51.)*

(Jer. 52 provides a historical conclusion to the book of Jeremiah. BD.) (Jer. 52:1.)

Jeremiah lamented the sad state of Israel and the terrible status of Jerusalem. Judah was captive and Jerusalem had been destroyed. *(Lam. 1-5.)*

In the first year of the reign of Darius the Mede over the realm of the Chaldeans, Daniel was given an understanding of the time of the coming of the Messiah as revealed earlier to Jeremiah the prophet. *(Dan. 9:2.) (Note: According to tradition, Jeremiah was stoned to death. BD.)*

JEREMIAH (3). *1 Chr. 5:24.*

Jeremiah was from the half tribe of Manasseh that was aligned with the Reubenites and Gadites. He was a famous and mighty man of valor and was head of the house of his father. He, along with others, transgressed the laws of God; thus, God allowed them to be carried away into captivity by the Assyrian kings Pul and Tilgath-pilneser. (Chart 15c.)

JEREMIAH (4). *1 Chr. 12:4 (1-2, 4, 23, 38).*

Jeremiah was one of David's mighty men who came to him at Ziklag to make him king and defend him against Saul.

JEREMIAH (5). *1 Chr. 12:10 (1-2, 10, 23, 38).*

Jeremiah, of the tribe of Gad, was one of David's mighty men who came to him at Ziklag to make him king and defend him against Saul. (Chart 13b.)

JEREMIAH (6). *1 Chr. 12:13 (1-2, 12, 23, 38).*

Jeremiah, of the tribe of Gad, was one of David's mighty men who came to him at Ziklag to make him king and defend him against Saul. (Chart 13b.)

JEREMIAH (7). *Neh. 10:2 (1-2, 28-31); 12:1, 12, 34.*

Jeremiah was among the priests who covenanted and sealed their covenant to marry in Israel, honor the Sabbath, pay tithes and keep the commandments. *(Neh. 10:2 [1-2, 28-31].)*

Jeremiah was one of the people (priests and Levites) who went to Jerusalem out of Babylon with Zerubbabel. His son Hananiah was one of the chief of the fathers. Jeremiah and others, along with Hoshaiah and half of the princes of Judah, were appointed by Nehemiah to one of two great companies of people gathered for the dedication of the walls of Jerusalem. *(Neh. 12:1, 12, 34.)*

JEREMIAH (8). *Jer. 35:3.*

Jeremiah was the father of Jaazaniah and the son of Habaziniah. He was one of the Rechabites who kept the counsel of Jonadab to live in tents and not drink wine.

JEREMOTH (1). *1 Chr. 8:14.*

Jeremoth, a descendant of Benjamin, was a son of Beriah who was a son of Elpaal who was a son of Shaharaim and Hushim. He was one of the heads of the fathers of the inhabitants of Aijalon who drove away the inhabitants of Gath. (Chart 16g.)

JEREMOTH (2) (Jerimoth (4)). *1 Chr. 23:23-24; 24:30.*

Jeremoth, a Levite, was the son of Mushi who was the son of Merari. His brothers were Mahli and Eder. When David made Solomon king, he numbered the Levites and divided them into courses among the children of Levi: Gershon, Kohath and Merari. Mahli, Eder and Jeremoth were named as chief of their fathers. From the age of twenty years and upward, they and the others so named did the work for the service of the house of the Lord. *(1 Chr. 23:23-24.)*

Jerimoth (Jeremoth) was one of the chief of the fathers who cast lots with the other Levites to determine his course in the presence of king David, Zadok, Ahimelech and other leaders. *(1 Chr. 24:30.)* (Chart 7e.)

JEREMOTH (3). *1 Chr. 25:22.* See **Jerimoth (5)**.

JEREMOTH (4). *Ezra 10:26 (18-19, 26, 44).*

Jeremoth was one of the sons of Elam who took wives from among the Canaanites and other groups. He agreed to separate himself from his foreign wives and instructed by Ezra.

JEREMOTH (5). *Ezra 10:27 (18-19, 27, 44).*

Jeremoth was one of the sons of Zattu who took wives from among the Canaanites and other foreign groups. He and his brothers complied with Ezra's request that they separate themselves from these foreign wives lest the Lord destroy the remainder of the children of Israel because of this iniquity.

JERIAH (Jerijah). *1 Chr. 23:19; 24:23; 26:31-32.*

Jeriah was a Levite of the sons of Hebron who was the son of Kohath. When David numbered the Levites at the time he made Solomon king, he divided them into courses. Jeriah was the first, Amariah the second, Jahaziel the third and Jekameam the fourth. *(1 Chr. 23:19.)*

Jeriah, along with his brothers and the rest of the chief fathers of the Levites, drew lots for his course in the presence of king David, Zadok, Ahimelech and other community leaders. *(1 Chr. 24:23.)*

Jerijah (Jeriah), a Hebronite, was chief among the Hebronites. He and his brethren numbered 2700 in the 40th year of the reign of king David and were assigned to be rulers over the Reubenites, the Gadites and the half tribe of Manasseh in matters pertaining to the Lord and in the affairs of the king. *(1 Chr. 26:31-32.)* (Chart 7d.)

JERIBAI. *1 Chr. 11:46.*

Jeribai and Joshaviah, sons of Elnaam, were among the mighty men of David, valiant men of the armies. (Chart 17.)

JERICHO. *Ezra 2:34; Neh. 7:36.*

Jericho, i.e., the children of Jericho who returned to Jerusalem from Babylon after Cyrus' proclamation to build the temple, numbered 345.

JERIEL. *1 Chr. 7:2.*

Jeriel was a son of Tola and a grandson of Issachar. His brothers were Uzzi, Rephaiah, Jahmai, Jibsam and Shemuel. They were heads of their father's house and were valiant men of might in their generations. (Chart 9a.)

JERIJAH. See **Jeriah**.

JERIMOTH (1). *1 Chr. 7:7.*

Jerimoth was a son of Bela (Belah) and a grandson of Benjamin. His brothers were Ezbon, Uzzi, Uzziel and Iri. He was the head of his house and a mighty man of valor. (Chart 16c.)

JERIMOTH (2). *1 Chr. 7:8.*

Jerimoth was a son of Becher and a grandson of Benjamin. His brothers were Zemira, Joash, Eliezer, Elioenai, Omri, Abiah, Anathoth and Alameth. He and his brothers were mighty men of valor and heads of the house of their fathers. (Chart 16c.)

JERIMOTH (3). *1 Chr. 12:5 (1-2, 5, 23, 38).*

Jerimoth was one of David's mighty men who came to him at Ziklag to make him king and defend him against Saul.

JERIMOTH (4). *1 Chr. 24:30.* See **Jeremoth (2)**.

JERIMOTH (5) (Jeremoth (3)). *1 Chr. 25:4, 22.*

Jerimoth, a Levite and musician, was a son of Heman who was of the lineage of Kohath. The musicians—sons of Heman, Asaph and Jeduthun—drew lots and were given their duty assignments by David and the captains of the host. **Jeremoth** (Jerimoth) cast the fifteenth lot. He, his sons and his brethren numbered 12. (Chart 7d.)

JERIMOTH (6). *1 Chr. 27:19.*

Jerimoth, son of Azriel, was a prince over the tribe of Naphtali when David was king.

JERIMOTH (7). *2 Chr. 11:18.*

Jerimoth was a son of David, a brother of Solomon, and an uncle to Rehoboam. His daughter Mahalath was one of Rehoboam's 18 wives. *(Note: He is not listed among the sons of David in 1 Chr. 3.)* (Charts 8e-f.)

JERIMOTH (8). *2 Chr. 31:13.*

Jerimoth was an overseer of tithes, offerings and the dedicated things under the hand of Cononiah and Cononiah's brother Shimei according to the commandment of king Hezekiah and Azariah, the ruler of the house of God.

JERIOTH. *1 Chr. 2:18.*

Jerioth bore children of Caleb. *(Note: The scripture states Caleb begat children of Azubah, his wife, and of Jerioth. It would appear that Jerioth was possibly a concubine.)*

JEROBOAM (1). *1 Kgs. 11:26-40; 12; 13:1-10, 33-34; 14:1-20; 2 Chr. 9:29; 10; 11:1-17; 12:15.*

Jeroboam was the son of Solomon's servant Nebat, an Ephrathite of Zereda. His mother's name was Zeruah, a widow woman. The Lord stirred him up to go against Solomon. Ahijah the prophet, a Shilonite, told him the Lord was going to rend the kingdom from Solomon and give it to him. However, he would be given just ten tribes and Solomon would retain one tribe "for my servant David's sake, and for Jerusalem's sake, the city which I have chosen out of all the tribes of Israel." He was told that this would occur in Solomon's son's days, not in Solomon's days. Jeroboam was given a promise that if he would keep the Lord's statutes and commandments, he would prosper. Solomon sought to kill Jeroboam so Jeroboam fled into Egypt unto Shishak, king of Egypt, and remained there until Solomon's death. *(1 Kgs. 11:26-40.)*

After Solomon's death, when Rehoboam, Solomon's son, went to Shechem to be made king, Jeroboam came from Egypt and spoke to Rehoboam asking him to make their yoke light and they would be glad to serve him. Rehoboam asked the old men for advice. They said he should make their yoke light so they would gladly serve him. Rehoboam then asked the young men who had grown up with him what they thought. They said to make their yoke heavy. He followed their advice. This was "for the cause of the Lord" so that what Ahijah had promised Jeroboam would come to pass. Ten tribes made Jeroboam their king. Rehoboam reigned over the tribe of Judah. Jeroboam feared that, if the people went up to the mount to worship the Lord and make sacrifice to Him, they would return to Rehoboam in Judah; therefore, he made two calves of gold and told the children of Israel to worship them instead. He made priests of the lowest of the people and of those who were not of the sons of Levi. *(1 Kgs. 12; 2 Chr. 10.)*

A man of God out of Judah came to Beth-el where Jeroboam stood by the altar to burn incense and cried against the altar. Jeroboam reached out to lay hold on him and his hand dried up. He asked the man of God to petition the Lord to restore his hand, which he did. Jeroboam invited the man of God to come to his house and eat and drink with him. The man of God declined because the Lord had instructed him accordingly. Later, when the man of God was led astray by a prophet from Beth-el and was slain by a lion for his disobedience, Jeroboam still did not turn from his evil ways. "And this thing became sin unto the house of Jeroboam, even to cut if off, and to destroy it from off the face of the earth." *(1 Kgs. 13:1-10, 33-34.)*

When Jeroboam's son Abijah became ill, Jeroboam sent his wife in disguise to inquire of the prophet Ahijah what would become of the child. Ahijah foretold the ruin of Jeroboam's house, the death of Abijah, and the scattering of Israel because of their idolatry. "The rest of the acts of Jeroboam, how he warred, and how he reigned, behold, they are written in the book of the chronicles of the kings of Israel." Jeroboam reigned 22 years and he died. His son Nadab reigned in his stead. *(1 Kgs. 14:1-20.)*

Ahijah the Shilonite prophesied against Jeroboam, and that prophecy also contains "the rest of the acts of Solomon." *(2 Chr. 9:29.)*

Jeroboam became king over the children of Israel and Rehoboam was king over Judah and Benjamin. The Lord instructed Rehoboam not to go against Jeroboam. Jeroboam led the children of Israel into idolatry so the priests and the Levites and all who set their hearts to seek the God of Israel left Jeroboam and returned to Rehoboam. *(2 Chr. 11:1-17.)*

There were wars continually between Jeroboam and Rehoboam. *(2 Chr. 12:15.)*

JEROBOAM (2). *2 Kgs. 13:13; 14:16, 23-29; 15: 1, 8; 1 Chr. 5:17; Hosea 1:1-2; Amos 1:1; 7:9-11.*

Jeroboam was the son of Joash (Jehoash). He reigned in his stead. *(2 Kgs. 13:13.)*

Jeroboam (son of Israel's king Joash) began his reign in Israel during the 15th year of the reign of Amaziah (son of Judah's king Joash) over Judah. He reigned 41 years. He walked in wickedness before the Lord. He recovered Damascus and Hamath, which belonged to Judah, for Israel. He died and his son Zachariah reigned in his stead. *(2 Kgs. 14:16, 23-29.)*

It was in Jeroboam's 27th year as king in Israel that Azariah, son of Amaziah, began his reign over Judah. Jeroboam's son Zachariah began his reign over Israel in the 38th year of Azariah's reign over Judah. *(2 Kgs. 15: 1, 8.)*

The genealogies of Reuben and Gad were "reckoned" in the days of Jeroboam, king of Israel, and Jotham, king of Judah. *(1 Chr. 5:17.)*

In the days of Jeroboam, king of Israel, and Uzziah, Jotham, Ahaz, and Hezekiah, kings of Judah, the Lord instructed Hosea to marry a wife from among those who committed whoredoms. He and his family were to be a sign unto Israel. *(Hosea 1:1-2.)*

During the time of Jeroboam king of Israel and Uzziah king of Judah, two years before a big earthquake, Amos prophesied of things he saw concerning Israel and the judgments that would come upon Syria, the Philistines and others. *(Amos 1:1.)*

Amos prophesied the captivity of Israel, the destruction of the house of Jeroboam, and Jeroboam's death by the sword. *(Amos 7:9-11.)*

JEROBOAM'S (1) WIFE. *1 Kgs. 14:2-17.*

Jeroboam's Wife is not mentioned by name. When her son Abijah became ill, Jeroboam sent her in disguise to the prophet Ahijah to inquire what would become of the child. Ahijah told her of the coming destruction of Jeroboam's house because of his idolatry and that Abijah would die as soon as her feet entered again into the city. He told her that Abijah would be the only one of Jeroboam's family who would actually be buried in a grave because there was found in him some good thing toward the Lord God of Israel in Jeroboam's household, but that others of the family would fare differently: "him that dieth of Jeroboam in the city shall the dogs eat; and him that dieth in the field shall the fowls of the air eat." He also foretold of the scattering of Israel.

JEROHAM (1). *1 Sam. 1:1; 1 Chr. 6:27, 34.*

Jeroham, the father of Elkanah, was the son of Elihu and the grandfather of Samuel. *(1 Sam. 1:1, 20.)*

Jeroham, of the house of Levi through Kohath, was a son of Eliab (Eliel, Elihu), father of Elkanah, and grandfather of Samuel. *(1 Chr. 6:27, 34.)* (Chart 7d.)

JEROHAM (2). *1 Chr. 8:27.*

Jeroham was a descendant of Benjamin. His sons were Shamsherai, Shehariah, Athaliah, Jaresiah, Eliah and Zichri. They were heads of the fathers by their generations, chief men, who lived in Jerusalem. (Chart 16j.)

JEROHAM (3). *1 Chr. 9:8 (1, 8).*

Jeroham, of the tribe of Benjamin, was the father of Ibneiah. He and his family were among the inhabitants of Jerusalem whose genealogy was written in the book of the kings of Israel and Judah who were carried away to Babylon for their transgression. He and his brethren, chiefs of the fathers, lived in Jerusalem when they returned from Babylonian captivity. (Chart 16m.)

JEROHAM (4). *1 Chr. 9:12 (1, 12-13); Neh. 11:12.*

Jeroham, the son of Pashur and the father of Adaiah, was one of the priests in Jerusalem whose genealogy was written in the book of the kings of Israel and Judah who were carried away captive into Babylon because of their transgression. When they returned from Babylonian captivity, they were heads of the houses of their fathers. They were very able men for the work of the service of the house of God. *(1 Chr. 9:12 [1, 12-13].)*

Jeroham was the father of Adaiah, the son of Pelaliah and a great-great-grandson of Pashur. *(Neh. 11:12.)* (Chart 7g.)

JEROHAM (5). *1 Chr. 12:7.*

Jeroham of Gedor, was the father of Joelah and Zebadiah, two of David's mighty men who came to him at Ziklag.

JEROHAM (6). *1 Chr. 27:22.*

Jeroham was the father of Azareel, prince of the tribe of Dan when David was king.

JEROHAM (7). *2 Chr. 23:1.*

Jeroham was the father of Azariah who was one of the captains of hundreds Jehoiada the priest rallied to make Joash king over Judah and to slay Athaliah.

JERUBBAAL. See **Gideon**.

JERUBBESHETH. See **Gideon**.

JERUSHA. *2 Kgs. 15:33; 2 Chr. 27:1.*

Jerusha was the mother of Jotham (who became king of Judah), the wife of Azariah (Uzziah), king of Judah, and the daughter of Zadok. (Chart 1.)

JESAIAH (1). *1 Chr. 3:21*.

Jesaiah, a descendant of David, was a son of Hananiah and a grandson of Zerubbabel. His brother was Pelatiah. (Chart 1.)

JESAIAH (2). *Neh. 11:7*.

Jesaiah, of the tribe of Benjamin, was the father of Ithiel. He was among those elected to dwell in Jerusalem upon returning from Babylonian captivity. (Chart 16m.)

JESHAIAH (1). *1 Chr. 25:3, 15*.

Jeshaiah, a Levite and musician, was the son of Jeduthun. The musicians—sons of Jeduthun, Asaph and Heman—drew lots and were given their duty assignments by David and the captains of the host. Jeshaiah cast the eighth lot. He, his sons and his brethren numbered 12. (Chart 7h.)

JESHAIAH (2). *1 Chr. 26:25*. See **Isshiah (1)**.

JESHAIAH (3). *Ezra 8:7*.

Jeshaiah, son of Athaliah who was of the sons of Elam, was the chief of the family of his fathers and went with Ezra up from Babylon to Jerusalem. He took 70 male family members with him.

JESHAIAH (4) *Ezra 8:18-19*.

Jeshaiah was a descendant of Levi through Merari. When Ezra was preparing to lead the people from Babylon back to Jerusalem, he gathered them together by the river and discovered that there were no Levites among them. He assigned several chief men and men of understanding to go to Iddo and the Nethinims and request they send them some ministers for the house of God. They brought Jeshaiah of the sons of Merari, and 20 of his brethren and their sons; Hashabiah; Sherebiah, with 18 of his sons and brethren; plus 220 Nethinims.

JESHARELAH. *1 Chr. 25:14*. See **Asarelah**.

JESHEBEAB. *1 Chr. 24:13*.

Jeshebeab was from the sons of Aaron. When David made the divisions of the sons of Aaron, there was one principal household for Eleazar and one taken for Ithamar. Eleazar had 16 sons and there were eight sons of Ithamar. These 24 sons who were chief of the fathers were divided by lot. Jeshebeab drew the fourteenth lot.

JESHER. *1 Chr. 2:18*.

Jesher, of the house of Judah, was one of the sons of Caleb and either Azubah or Jerioth. His brothers were Shobab and Ardon. (Chart 8h.)

JESHISHAI. *1 Chr. 5:14*.

Jeshishai, the father of Michael and the son of Jahdo, was a descendant of Gad. (Chart 13b.)

JESHOHAIAH. *1 Chr. 4:36*.

Jeshohaiah was a descendant of Simeon through Shimei. (Chart 6a.)

JESHUA (1). *Neh. 8:17*. See **Joshua (1)**.

JESHUA (2). *1 Chr. 24:11.*

Jeshua was from the sons of Aaron. When David made the divisions of the sons of Aaron, there was one principal household for Eleazar and one taken for Ithamar. Eleazar had 16 sons and there were eight sons of Ithamar. These 24 sons who were chief of the fathers were divided by lot. Jeshua drew the ninth lot.

JESHUA (3). *2 Chr. 31:14-15.*

Jeshua assisted Kore, porter toward the east, in caring for the freewill offerings of God and their distribution when Hezekiah was king over Judah.

JESHUA (4) (Joshua (4)). *Ezra 2:2, 36; 3:2, 8; 4:3; 5:2; 10:18-19, 44; Neh. 7:7, 39; 12:1, 10-11, 26; Hag. 1:1, 12, 14; 2:4; Zech. 3; 4; 6:10-14.*

Jeshua was one of the people who went with Zerubbabel back to Jerusalem following king Cyrus' proclamation to build the temple there. Jeshua was the father of Jedaiah, a priest. His children through Jedaiah numbered 973 when they left Babylon to return to Jerusalem to build the temple as proclaimed by Cyrus, king of Persia. *(Ezra 2:2, 36; Neh. 7:7, 39; 12:1.)*

Jeshua, a priest, was the son of Jozadak. He and his brethren, along with Zerubbabel and his brethren, built the altar unto God in the seventh month; and the children of Israel offered burnt offerings thereon according to the law of Moses. In the second year after their return to Jerusalem, Jeshua and Zerubbabel appointed the Levites to begin work on rebuilding the temple. *(Ezra 3:2, 8.)*

The Samaritans went to Zerubbabel and the chief of the fathers volunteering to help build the temple. Their offer was declined by Jeshua, Zerubbabel and the rest of the chiefs of the fathers. The Samaritans hindered the work and caused it to cease. *(Ezra 4:3.)*

During the second year of Darius' reign as king of Persia, the prophets Haggai and Zechariah prophesied unto the Jews in Judah and Jerusalem. As a result, with the prophets of God helping them, Jeshua and Zerubbabel began once more to build the temple. *(Ezra 5:2.)*

Of the sons of Jeshua and his brethren, Maaseiah, Eliezer, Jarib and Gedaliah were among those who had taken strange wives and who agreed to do as Ezra proclaimed they should do: put away their foreign wives. *(Ezra 10:18-19, 44.)*

Jeshua and those who were the chief of the priests are listed, as are Jeshua's descendants: Jeshua, son of Jozadak, begat Joiakim who begat Eliashib who begat Joiada who begat Jonathan who begat Jaddua. The porters in the days of Jeshua, Nehemiah and Ezra are listed. *(Neh. 12:10-11, 26.)*

Joshua (Jeshua) the high priest was the son of Josedech (Jozadak). In the second year of king Darius' reign, the prophet Haggai spoke to Joshua and Zerubbabel and exhorted the people to build the temple. They obeyed. *(Hag. 1:1, 12, 14.)*

The Lord sent Haggai to Joshua and Zerubbabel and the people a second time. He counseled them to be strong, even though the new temple was far less glorious than the former temple. The time would come when the Lord would fill the temple with glory and it would be more glorious than the former. He promised to fill the temple with peace. *(Hag. 2:4.)*

In Zechariah's fourth vision, he saw Joshua the high priest, in filthy garments, standing before the angel of the Lord. Satan was at his right hand to accuse him, but was rebuked by the Lord. *(Zech. 3.)*

In Zechariah's fifth vision, he beheld a golden candlestick which had seven lamps and seven pipes to the lamps. He also saw two olive trees beside it—one on the left side and one on the right. *(Zech. 4.) (Note: According to the BD, the olive trees represent two anointed ones, Joshua and Zerubbabel, who represent the priestly and royal rule.)*

Zechariah was instructed by the Lord to take those who had come from Babylonian captivity of Heldai, Tobijah and Jedaiah and go into the house of Josiah the son of Zephaniah and crown Joshua the high priest. *(Zech. 6:10-14.) (Note: This was a similitude of crowning Christ, i.e., the BRANCH. The Bible Dictionary explains that Jesus is another form of Joshua.)* (Chart 7b.)

JESHUA (5). *Ezra 2:6; Neh. 7:11.*

Jeshua was of the people of Israel. The men of the children of Pahath-moab of the children of Jeshua and Joab who returned to Jerusalem from Babylon after Cyrus' proclamation to build the temple numbered 2,812 (2,818).

JESHUA (6). *Ezra 2:40; 3:9; Neh. 7:43; 9; 12:8, 24.*

Jeshua was a Levite. He and Kadmiel were of the children of Hodaviah. Their children numbered 74 when they left Babylon to go to Jerusalem to build the house of the Lord as proclaimed by Cyrus, king of Persia. *(Ezra 2:40.; Neh. 7:43.)*

Jeshua, with his sons and brethren, and Kadmiel and his sons, the sons of Judah, set forward the workmen in the house of God. *(Ezra 3:9.)*

The Levites—Jeshua, Bani, Kadmiel, Shebaniah, Bunni, Sherebiah, Bani, Chenani, Hashabniah, Hodijah and Pethahiah—blessed and praised the Lord, reciting the Lord's goodness to Israel: the blessing of Abraham; giving the land of the Canaanites, Hittites, Amorites, Perizzites, Jebusites and Girgashites to Israel; dividing the Red Sea so they could cross it yet drowning the Egyptians who pursued them; the signs and wonders shown to Pharaoh; leading them in the wilderness and protecting them so that they had bread from heaven, water from the rock, and shoes and clothes that never wore out; accepting them whenever they repented, even when they made a molten calf. They had been given the kingdoms of Shihon, Heshbon and Bashan and the Lord had subdued the Canaanites and delivered them into the hands of the Israelites. After giving praise, they made a covenant with the Lord. The princes, Levites and priests sealed the covenant. *(Neh. 9.)*

Jeshua, son of Kadmiel, and his brethren are listed among those Levites who went up from Babylon with Zerubbabel to Jerusalem. He was one of those men named who was chief of the Levites. *(Neh. 12:8, 24.)*

JESHUA (7). *Neh. 8:7-8, 33; 10:9 (1, 9, 28-31).*

Jeshua, a Levite and the father of Jozabad, was one of the men who, when Ezra read and interpreted the law of Moses to the people, helped the people to understand the law. *(Neh. 8:7-8, 33.)*

Jeshua, son of Azaniah, was one of the Levites who covenanted and sealed his covenant to marry in Israel, honor the Sabbath, pay tithes and keep the commandments. *(Neh. 10:9 [1, 9, 28-31].)*

JESHUA (8). *Neh. 3:19.*

Jeshua was the father of Ezer, the ruler of Mizpah.

JESIAH (1). *1 Chr. 12:6 (1-2, 6, 23, 38).*

Jesiah, a Korhite, was one of David's mighty men who came to him at Ziklag to defend him against Saul and to rejoice with all Israel when David became king.

JESIAH (2) (Isshiah (2)). *1 Chr. 23:20; 24:25.*

Jesiah, a Levite, was of the sons of Uzziel, son of Kohath. When David made Solomon king, he numbered the Levites and divided them into courses among the children of Levi: Gershon, Kohath and Merari. Jesiah was one of two named from among the sons of Uzziel: Michah was first; Jesiah, second. *(1 Chr. 23:20.)*

Isshiah (Jesiah), a Levite, was a descendant of Uzziel. His brother was Michah. His decendants included Zechariah. He, with the rest of the chief fathers of the Levites, drew lots for his course in the presence of king David, Zadok, Ahimelech and other community leaders. *(1 Chr. 24:25.)* (Chart 7d.)

JESIMIEL. *1 Chr. 4:36.*

Jesimiel, a descendant of Shimei, was the prince in his family. (Chart 6a.)

JESSE. *Ruth 4:17; 1 Sam. 16:18; Isa. 11:1, 10; 1 Chr. 2:13-17.*

Jesse, grandson of Boaz and Ruth (Naomi's daughter-in-law), was the son of Obed and the father of king David. *(Ruth 4:17.) (The Bible Dictionary adds: "and therefore ancestor of all the kings of Judah and also of Christ.")*

Jesse's son David was a great harpist and also a mighty warrior. Saul desired that he be brought to him. *(1 Sam. 16:18.)*

In the latter days, a rod out of the stem of Jesse shall stand as an ensign of the people. *(Isa. 11:1, 10.) (Note: Modern-day revelation recorded in D&C 113:1-6, reaffirms Isaiah's statement. The stem of Jesse is Christ: he shall be a descendant of Jesse. In the latter days, the root of Jesse, [i.e., a descendant of Jesse as well as of the house of Joseph] will stand as an ensign for the gathering of the people.)*

Jesse begat Eliab, Abinadab, Shimma, Nethaneel, Raddai, Ozem and David. He also begat two daughters: Zeruiah and Abigail. He was the grandfather of Abishai, Joab and Asahel (Zeruiah's sons) and Amasa (Abigail's son). *(1 Chr. 2:13-17.)* (Charts 1.; 8d-f.)

JESUITES. See **Isui**.

JETHER (1). *Judg. 8:20.*

Jether was Gideon's firstborn. Out of fear, he refused to slay Zebah and Zalmunna, two kings of the Midianites so Gideon slew them.

JETHER (2). *1 Kgs. 2:5*. See **Ithra**.

JETHER (3). *1 Chr. 2:32*.

Jether was the son of Jada. His brother was Jonathan. He died without children. He was a great-great-great-great-grandson of Judah. (Chart 8c.)

JETHER (4). *1 Chr. 4:17*.

Jether was a son of Ezra. His siblings were Mered and Epher, and Jalon, a sister. (Chart 8 o.)

JETHER (5). *1 Chr. 7:38*.

Jether, a descendant of Asher, was the father of Jephunneh, Pispah and Ara. *(Note: It is not clear who his father was.)* (Chart 14b.)

JETHETH. *Gen. 36:40*.

Jetheth was one of the dukes (tribal chiefs) who came of Esau. (Chart 19.)

JETHRO (Reuel (2), Raguel). *Ex. 2:16, 18; 3:1; 4:18; 18; Judg. 4:11*.

Jethro (Reuel) was the priest of Midian, father of Zipporah, Moses' wife. *(Ex 2:16, 18.)* Moses tended the flocks of his father-in-law **Jethro**. *(Ex. 3:1.)*

When Moses requested leave of Jethro so he could return to his brethren in Egypt, Jethro bid him to go in peace. *(Ex. 4:18.)*

After Moses had safely led the children of Israel out of Egypt and they were camped in the wilderness, Jethro heard what the Lord had done in bringing the children of Israel out of Egypt and he brought Moses' wife, Zipporah, and their two sons to him (as Moses had sent them to him earlier). Jethro saw that Moses was trying to do too much all by himself and counseled him to be the teacher of the law and appoint others to be lesser judges and to delegate power to them; otherwise, he told Moses, he would wear away. He left and returned to his own land. *(Ex. 18.)*

Moses' father-in-law is called **Raguel**. He was the father of Hobab. *(Num. 10:29.)*

(Note: Moses' father-in-law is called Hobab in Judg. 4:11. This is apparently an error. In Num. 10:29, Hobab is referred to as the son of Raguel, Moses' father-in-law. Thus, Hobab was his brother-in-law, not another name for his father-in-law.) (Chart 7b.)

JETUR .*Gen. 25:15; 1 Chr. 5:19*.

Jetur was a son of Ishmael and a grandson of Abraham and Hagar, Sarah's handmaid. *(Gen. 25:15.)* The Reubenites, Gadites and half the tribe of Manasseh, made war with Jetur, the Hagarites, Nephish (Naphish) and Nodab (probably Kedemah). *(1 Chr. 5:19.)* (Chart 3e.)

JEUEL. *1 Chr. 9:6 (1-3, 6)*.

Jeuel was a Shilonite. His father was Zerah. He and his family were numbered among the inhabitants of Jerusalem whose genealogy was written in the book of the kings of Israel and Judah who were carried away to Babylon for their transgression. Jeuel and his brethren, 690 strong, chief of the fathers in the house of their fathers, lived in Jerusalem upon returning from Babylonian captivity.

JEUSH (1). *Gen. 36:5, 18.*

Jeush, son of Aholibamah and Esau, was born in Caanan and was a duke (tribal chief). His brothers were Jaalam and Korah. (Charts 3b-c.; 4c.)

JEUSH (2). *1 Chr. 7:10.*

Jeush, son of Bilhan and grandson of Jediael, was a great-grandson of Benjamin and a mighty man of valor. His brothers were Benjamin, Ehud, Chenaanah, Zethan, Tharshish, and Ahishahar. (Chart 16c.)

JEUSH (3). *1 Chr. 23:10-11.*

Jeush was one of four sons of Shimei from the tribe of Levi through Gershon who was named when David numbered the Levites and divided them into courses. Jahath was the chief, Zizah (Zina) was the second, but Jeush and Beriah were combined into one reckoning because they didn't have many sons. (Chart 7f.)

JEUSH (4). *2 Chr. 11:19.*

Jeush was the son of Abihail, daughter of David's brother Eliab, and king Rehoboam, David's grandson. His brothers were Shamariah and Zaham. (Chart 8d, f.)

JEUZ. *1 Chr. 8:10.*

Jeuz was a son of Hodesh and Shaharaim, a descendant of Benjamin. (Chart 16f.)

JEZANIAH (Azariah (4), See Jaazaniah (1))

JEZEBEL. *1 Kgs. 16:31; 18:4, 7-8, 19; 19:1-2; 21; 2 Kgs. 9:30-37.*

Jezebel was the daughter of Ethbaal, king of the Zidonians, Baal worshippers. She married Ahab, king of Israel. *(1 Kgs. 16:31.)*

Jezebel sought to destroy the prophets so Obadiah hid 100 of them—50 in each of two caves. Elijah requested Ahab send 450 prophets of Baal and 400 of Jezebel's prophets unto mount Carmel to meet him. *(1 Kgs. 18:4, 7-8, 19.)*

When Ahab told Jezebel that Elijah had slain all the priests of Baal, Jezebel sent a messenger to Elijah informing him that she intended to have him killed "by tomorrow about this time." *(1 Kgs. 19:1-2.)*

When Ahab mourned because he could not persuade Naboth to give him his vineyard, Jezebel told him to let his heart be merry because she would deliver the vineyard to him. She sent letters to the elders and nobles in Ahab's name, sealing them with his seal. She instructed them to set Naboth on high among the people, to have two sons of Belial bear false witness against him, and to then carry him out and stone him to death. When she received word of his death she went to Ahab and told him he could now have the vineyard. Elijah was sent by the Lord to Ahab to rebuke him and to prophesy what would become of him and Jezebel. Elijah told him, "In the place where dogs licked the blood of Naboth shall dogs lick thy blood, even thine;" and that his posterity would be cut off just as Jeroboam's and Baasha's posterities had been destroyed. He also said, "The dogs shall eat Jezebel by the wall of Jezreel." *(1 Kgs. 21.)*

When Jehu went to Jezreel and slew Jehoram and Ahaziah, Jezebel disguised herself and peered out a window and spoke to Jehu. Jehu had two or three eunuchs who were on his side throw her out the window. "So they threw her down: and some of her blood was sprinkled on the wall, and on the horses: and he trode her under foot." After eating and drinking, Jehu sent men out to bury her, but they only found her skull, feet, and the palms of her hands. Thus, the word of the Lord regarding Jezebel was fulfilled. *(2 Kgs. 9:30-37.)*

JEZEBEL'S MESSENGER. *1 Kgs. 19:2.*

Jezebel's Messenger was sent to Elijah to inform him that Jezebel intended to kill him by the same time the following day.

JEZER (Jezerites). *Gen. 46:24-25; Num. 26:49; 1 Chr. 7:13.*

Jezer, grandson of Jacob, was a son of Naphtali and Bilhah, Rachel's handmaid. His brothers were Jahzeel (Jaziel), Guni and Shillem (Shallum). *(Gen. 46:24-25; 1 Chr. 7:13.)* His descendants were called **Jezerites**. *(Num. 26:49.)* (Chart 12a.)

JEZIAH. *Ezra 10:25 (18-19, 25, 44).*

Jeziah, one of the sons of Parosh, was among those who had taken wives from among the Canaanites or other foreign groups and agreed to Ezra's request that they separate themselves from these strange wives lest the Lord destroy the rest of the children of Israel.

JEZIEL. *1 Chr. 12:3 (1-3, 23, 38).*

Jeziel, a son of Azmaveth and a brother of Pelet, was one of David's mighty men of war who came to him at Ziklag to defend him against Saul and to rejoice with all Israel when David became king.

JEZLIAH. *1 Chr. 8:18.*

Jezliah, a descendant of Benjamin, was a son of Elpaal. He, along with others who were heads of the fathers of the inhabitants of Aijalon, drove the inhabitants of Gath away. (Chart 16i.)

JEZOAR. *1 Chr. 4:7.*

Jezoar, of the house of Judah, was the son of Helah and Ashur the father of Tekoa. His brothers were Zereth and Ethnan. (Chart 8d.)

JEZRAHIAH. *Neh. 12:42.*

Jezrahiah, a priest and singer, joined in the dedication of the walls of Jerusalem with Nehemiah. He was the overseer of the singers.

JEZREEL (1). *1 Chr. 4:3.*

Jezreel, of the lineage of Judah, was of the father of Etam. His siblings included Ishma and Idbash, and a sister named Hazelelponi. (Chart 8m.)

JEZREEL (2). *Hosea 1:4.*

Jezreel, the first son of Hosea and Gomer, was so named because the Lord said, ". . . for yet a little while, I will avenge the blood of Jezreel upon the house of Jehu and will cause to cease the kingdom of the house of Israel."

JIBSAM. *1 Chr. 7:2.*

Jibsam was a son of Tola and a grandson of Issachar. His brothers were Uzzi, Rephaiah, Jeriel, Jahmai and Shemuel. (Chart 9a.)

JIDLAPH. *Gen. 22:22.*

Jidlaph was one of Milcah and Nahor's children. (Chart 2c.)

JIMNAH (Jimna, Jimnites, Imnah). *Gen. 46:17; Num. 26:44; 1 Chr. 7:30.*

Jimnah was a son of Asher and a grandson of Jacob. His brothers were Ishuah, Isui and Beriah. His sister was Serah. *(Gen. 46:17.)* He **(Jimna)** was the father of the **Jimnites**. *(Num. 26:44.)*

Imnah (Jimnah, Jimna), Isuah (Ishuah), Ishuai (Isui) and Beriah were sons of Asher. Their sister was Serah. *(1 Chr. 7:30.)* (Chart 14a.)

JOAB (1). *1 Sam. 26:6; 2 Sam. 2:13-30; 3:27-29; 8:16; 10:7-19; 11:14-21; 12:26-28; 14; 18:10-15; 19:13; 20:9-23; 24:2-9; 1 Kgs. 1:7; 2:5-34; 1 Chr. 11:6-8; 18:15; 19:8-15; 20:1; 21:2-5; 27:7, 24, 34.*

Joab was the brother of Abishai and the eldest son of Zeruiah, David's sister. *(1 Sam. 26:6.)*

Joab and the servants of David met with Abner (Saul's uncle) and the servants of Ish-bosheth. Twelve of Joab's men and 12 of Abner's men engaged in games wherein Joab's men slew all 12 of Abner's men. When Abner left, Joab's brother Asahel pursued after him to kill him. Abner kept telling him to stop the pursuit. When he wouldn't stop, Abner killed him. Joab and Abishai and David's servants gathered to battle against Abner and the children of Benjamin. However, Abner called for peace, and Joab agreed. Through it all, Abner and the tribe of Benjamin lost 360 men; David lost 19 plus Asahel. *(2 Sam. 2:13-30.)*

Joab slew Abner, who had come to join with David. He didn't trust him and he was angry with him for having slain his brother, Asahel. He and all his father's house were cursed by David for having killed Abner. *(2 Sam. 3:27-29.)*

David reigned over all Israel and he placed Joab, son of Zeruiah, over all the army. *(2 Sam. 8:16.)*

David sent Joab and the Israelite army against Hanun and the children of Ammon because Hanun had abused David's servants. The children of Ammon hired the Syrians to help them fight against the Israelites. Joab led the toops against the Syrians and had Abishai lead the troops against the children of Ammon. Joab defeated the Syrians and the children of Ammon were defeated by Abishai. *(2 Sam. 10:7-19; 1 Chr. 19:8-15.)*

Joab was instructed by David to place Uriah the Hittite in the forefront of a battle so he would be killed. When Uriah was dead, Joab sent a messenger to David to inform him about the status of the war, with the instruction to report that Uriah was dead. *(2 Sam. 11:14-21.)*

Joab conquered the royal city of the Ammonites and sent messengers to David inviting him to come and take the city so that it wouldn't be called after Joab's name but after David. *(2 Sam. 12:26-28.)*

Joab desired to reunite David and his son Absalom. Using the services of a wise woman from Tekoah, he succeeded in getting David to bring Absalom back from Geshur where Absalom had fled following his having his half-brother Amnon killed. Nevertheless, Joab was instructed to have Absalom go to his own home. He was not to see the king's face. After two years, Absalom sent for Joab but Joab did not come to him. Absalom sent for him a second time. Joab still did not respond so Absalom had his servants set Joab's fields on fire. Joab went to Absalom to inquire why he had set his fields on fire. Absalom said it was because he wouldn't come to him so he could send him to king David to inquire why he refused to see him. Joab then did what Absalom requested, and David agreed to meet with Absalom. *(2 Sam. 14.)*

A certain man observed Absalom get hung up in a tree as he pursued David. The man told Joab that he saw Absalom hanging in a tree. However, Absalom was still alive. The man refused to kill Absalom because the king had charged everyone to "deal gently for my sake with the young man, even with Absalom." Nevertheless, Joab took three darts and thrust them through the heart of Absalom as he hung in the tree. Another 10 young men who were Joab's armorbearers gathered around and slew Absalom. *(2 Sam. 18:10-15.)*

Joab was removed as captain of David's army; and David made Amasa (his sister Abigail's son) captain of the host in place of Joab. *(2 Sam. 19:13.)*

David had instructed Amasa to gather the men of Judah together and return in three days so as to go after Sheba. Amasa did not return on schedule so David sent Abishai and other men after Sheba. When Amasa joined up with the rest of the troops a little later, Joab took hold of his cousin Amasa by the beard as if to kiss him, but he ran Amasa through with a sword instead. Joab pursued Sheba to Abel of Beth-maachah and was about to attack the city when a wise woman intervened and said the people would throw Sheba's head over the wall to Joab. She did as promised and Joab and his men returned to Jerusalem. Joab was again captain over all the host of Israel. *(2 Sam. 20:9-23.)*

Contrary to the will of the Lord, and against Joab's recommendation, David instructed Joab to number the people. Therefore, Joab and the captains of the hosts went throughout the tribes of Israel and numbered them. They reported that there were 800,000 valiant men of Israel who drew the sword and 500,000 men of Judah. *(2 Sam. 24:2-9; 1 Chr. 21:2-5.)*

Joab and Abiathar the priest supported Adonijah in his bid to wrest the kingdom from David. *(1 Kgs. 1:7.)*

David charged Solomon to punish Joab for supporting Adonijah, for slaying the two captains of the hosts of Israel, and for the killings of Abner and Amasa. Solomon had Benaiah slay Joab. Joab was buried in his own house in the wilderness. *(1 Kgs. 2:5-34.)*

When David was made king, he and Israel went to Jerusalem and the Jebusites told him he couldn't come there. Nevertheless, David took the city and said that whosoever smote the Jebusites first would be made chief and captain over the armies. Joab accomplished the task and was made chief. He then repaired the rest of the city. *(1 Chr. 11:6-8.)*

Joab was over the army. *(1 Chr. 18:15.)*

Joab and his army "wasted the country of the children of Ammon" and beseiged Rabbah and destroyed it. *(1 Chr. 20:1.)*

Joab's brother Asahel was assigned by David to be over the course of 14,000 that served for the fourth month. Joab began to number Israel but did not complete the assignment because of the wrath of the Lord. Joab was the general of king David's army. *(1 Chr. 27:7, 24, 34.)* (Chart 8d.)

JOAB (2). *1 Chr. 4:14.*

Joab was the son of Seraiah and a grandson of Kenaz. He was "the father of the valley of Charashim; for they were craftsmen." (Chart 8k.)

JOAB (3). *Ezra 2:6; Neh. 7:11.*

Joab was of the people of Israel. The men of the children of Pahath-moab of the children of Jeshua and Joab who returned to Jerusalem from Babylon after Cyrus' proclamation to build the temple numbered 2,812 (2818).

JOAB (4). *Ezra 8:9.*

Joab's descendant Obadiah, the son of Jehiel, was the chief of his father's family when Ezra led many exiled Israelites out of Babylon back to Jerusalem. The sons of Joab numbered 218.

JOAB'S (1) ARMORBEARERS - TEN YOUNG MEN. *2 Sam. 18:15.*

Joab's Armorbearers gathered around Absalom as he hung in a tree and slew him. They cast him into a great pit and piled a large pile of stones on him.

JOAB'S (1) MEN, ONE OF. *2 Sam. 20:11-13.*

One of Joab's Men rallied the men to go with Joab following the slaying of Amasa. He removed Amasa's body from the middle of the highway, placed it in a field and covered it with a cloth so the people would pass on and not stop and look at it.

JOAB'S (1) MESSENGER. *2 Sam. 11:19.*

Joab's Messenger was sent to David to inform him of the events surrounding a particular battle wherein Bath-sheba's husband, Uriah the Hittite, had died.

JOAH (1). *2 Kgs. 18:18 (11-37); Isa. 36.*

Joah, the recorder, was the son of Asaph. He, along with Eliakim and Shebna, came out to hear the demands of Rab-shakeh of Assyria. They reported what Rab-shakeh said to Hezekiah.

JOAH (2) (Ethan (3)). *1 Chr. 6:21, 42; 2 Chr. 29:12.*

Joah, of the tribe of Levi through Gershom, was the son of Zimmah and the father of Iddo. *(1 Chr. 6:21, 42.) (Note: Verse 42 lists **Ethan** as the son of Zimmah while verse 21 lists Joah as the son of Zimmah. One listing of Gershon's posterity shows Zerah as the grandson of Joah; the other listing shows Zerah as the grandson of Ethan.)*

Joah's son was Eden (Iddo) *(2 Chr. 29:12.)* (Chart 7a.)

JOAH (3). *1 Chr. 26:4, 8 12.*

Joah, a Levite, was the thirdborn son of Obed-edom. His brothers were Shemaiah, Jehozabad, Sacar, Nethaneel, Ammiel, Issachar and Peulthai. They, along with other Levites, were appointed by king David to be porters—to have charge of the treasures, serve as officers and judges, and to conduct the outward business over Israel. (Chart 7c.)

JOAH (4). *2 Chr. 34:8-9.*

Joah, son of Joahaz the recorder, was sent by Judah's king Josiah (with Shaphan and Maaseiah) to Hilkiah the high priest to deliver money for workmen to repair the house of the Lord.

JOAHAZ. *2 Chr. 34:8.*

Joahaz, father of Joah, was the recorder when Josiah was king of Judah.

JOASH (1). *Judg. 6:11, 29-32; 7:14; 8:13, 29, 32.*

Joash, the Abi-ezrite, was the father of Gideon. An angel of the Lord sat under his oak tree. Joash called his son Gideon, "Jerubbaal," because he cast down the altar of Baal. *(Judg. 6:11, 29-32.)*

Joash was the father of Gideon. *(Judg. 7:14.)*

Joash was the father of Gideon (Jerubbaal). When Gideon died at an old age, he was buried in Joash's sepulchre. *(Judg. 8:13, 29, 32.)*

JOASH (2). *1 Kgs. 22:26-27; 2 Chr. 18:25-26.*

Joash, one of the sons of king Ahab, and Amon the governor of the city, were instructed to cast the prophet Micaiah into prison and to feed him just bread and water until Ahab returned in peace from battle against Syria.

JOASH (3) (Jehoash (1)). *2 Kgs. 11:2-16, 21; 12:1-21; 14:1; 1 Chr. 3:11-12; 2 Chr. 22:10-12; 23:1-11; 24.*

Joash was the son of Ahaziah. He was an infant when Ahaziah was slain and his grandmother Athaliah sought to destroy all of Ahaziah's seed. His aunt Jehosheba (Jehoshabeath) stole him away and hid him in the house of the Lord where he stayed for six years. In the seventh year of Athaliah's reign over Judah, Jehoiada the priest rallied the leaders and they slew Athaliah and made **Jehoash** (Joash) king of Judah at the tender age of seven years. *(2 Kgs. 11:2-16, 21; 2 Chr. 22:10-12 (repeat of 11:1-3); 2 Chr. 23:1-11 (repeat of 11:4-12).*

Jehoash began his reign in the seventh year of the reign of Jehu over Israel. He reigned 40 years in Jerusalem. His mother was Zibiah. Jehoash did right in the sight of the Lord all the days wherein Jehoiada instructed him. He had the house of the Lord repaired. By sending Hazael the king of Syria all the hallowed things that former kings of Judah had dedicated, his own hallowed things and all the gold in the treasures of the house of the Lord, Joash was able to purchase the safety of Jerusalem. Two of his servants—Jozachar and Jehozabad—slew him. He was buried in the city of David. His son Amaziah reigned in his stead. *(2 Kgs. 12:1-21.)* *(Note: 2 Chr. 24 is a repeat and expansion of 2 Kgs. 12.).* Jehoiada chose two wives for Joash, and Joash begat sons and daughters. After Jehoiada died, Joash and the princes of Judah worshipped idols again, incurring the wrath of the Lord. Joash even commanded his people to slay the prophet Zechariah, son of Jehoiada the priest. Thus, the Lord allowed Syria to destroy all the princes of Judah and Jerusalem from among the people. The spoil was sent to the king of Damascus. Joash's servants, Zabad (Jozachar) the son of Shimeath an Ammonitess, and Jehozabad the son of Shimrith a Moabitess, conspired against him and slew him on his bed. His son Amaziah reigned in his stead. *(2 Chr. 24.)*

Joash's son Amaziah began his reign over Judah during the second year of Jehoahaz's son Joash's reign over Israel. *(2 Kgs. 14:1.)*

Joash was the son of Ahaziah and the father of Amaziah. *(1 Chr. 3:11-12.)* (Chart 1.)

JOASH (4) (Jehoash (2)). *2 Kgs. 13:9-25; 14:1, 8-14, 16; 2 Chr. 25:17-24; Hosea 1:1; Amos 1:1.*

Joash, son of Jehoahaz, reigned in his father's stead over Israel. He began his reign in the 37th year of the reign of Joash (Jehoash) over Judah. He reigned 16 years. He reigned in wickedness just as his father had. He fought against Amaziah when Amaziah became king over Judah. When the prophet Elisha fell ill and was dying, Joash went to him and wept over him. Elisha had him shoot an arrow out the window and said it was the arrow of the Lord's deliverance of Israel from Syria. He then had him take the arrows and smite them upon the ground. Joash struck the ground three times. Elisha was angry with him and told him he should have struck the ground five or six times because now they would only be successful against Syria three times and would not totally consume their enemies as they would have otherwise. Joash ended up defeating Ben-hadad three times, recovering the cities of Israel. *(2 Kgs. 13:9-25.)*

In the second year of Jehoahaz's son Joash's reign over Israel, Judah's king Joash's son Amaziah began his reign over Judah. Amaziah requested a face-to-face meeting with **Jehoash** (Joash), king of Israel. Unfortunately, it did not go well for Amaziah. "Judah was put to the worse before Israel; and they fled every man to their tents." Amaziah was taken captive. Jehoash went to Jerusalem with his men and broke down the wall of Jerusalem and took all the gold and silver and treasures in the house of the Lord and in the king's house, along with hostages, and returned to Samaria. Jehoash died and his son Jeroboam reigned in his stead. *(2 Kgs. 14:1, 8-14, 16.) (Note: 2 Chr. 25:17-24 is a repeat and expansion of 2 Kgs. 14:8-14.)* Joash (Jehoash) was the son of Jehoahaz who was the son of Jehu. He took Amaziah king of Judah captive at Beth-shemesh and carried him back to Jerusalem and broke down the wall of the city. *(2 Chr. 25:17-24.) (Note: The Bible Dictionary states that he was one of the best kings Israel had. Elisha, Hosea and Amos all prophesied during his reign.)*

Joash was the father of Jeroboam who was king of Israel. Hosea and his family were a sign unto Israel during Jeroboam's day that the Lord would no longer have mercy on Israel. *(Hosea 1:1.)*

Joash was the father of Jeroboam. *(Amos 1:1.)*

JOASH (5). *1 Chr. 4:22.*

Joash was a son of Shelah and a grandson of Judah. (Chart 8a.)

JOASH (6). *1 Chr. 7:8.*

Joash was a son of Becher and a grandson of Benjamin. His brothers were Zemira, Eliezer, Elioenai, Omri, Jerimoth, Abiah, Anathoth and Alameth. (Chart 16c.)

JOASH (7). *1 Chr. 12:1-3, 23, 38.*

Joash, a son of Shemaah the Gibeathite and a brother of Ahiezer, was one of David's mighty men who came to him at Ziklag to defend him against Saul and to rejoice with all Israel when David became king.

JOASH (8). *1 Chr. 27:28.*

Joash was the officer assigned by king David to be over the cellars of oil.

JOASH'S (3) NURSE. *2 Kgs. 11:2; 22:11.*

Joash's Nurse was hidden by Jehosheba (Jehoshabeath), Joash's aunt, in the bedchamber in the house of the Lord along with Joash when Joash's grandmother Athaliah sought to slay him.

JOB (1) (Jashub, Jashubites). *Gen. 16:13; Num. 26:24.*

Job was a son of Issachar and a grandson of Jacob. *(Gen. 46:13.)* **Jashub's** (Job's) descendants were called **Jashubites**. *(Num. 26:24.)* (Chart 9a.)

JOB (2). *Job 1-42; Ezek. 14:14.*

Job was a righteous man who lived in the land of Uz. He was righteous and had been blessed with great riches. He had seven sons and three daughters. The Lord pointed out to Satan that Job was a perfect and upright man. Satan claimed that was only because the Lord protected him on every side. The Lord gave Satan permission to tempt and try Job, with the stipulation that Satan could have power over Job's possessions but was not to put his hand on Job himself. Satan destroyed all of Job's animals as well as all of his sons and daughters. Still, Job praised and blessed the Lord. *(Job:1.)*

Satan challenged the Lord with the claim that a man will give up his possessions and not complain against the Lord, but if he suffered physically he would curse the Lord. The Lord gave him permission to afflict Job directly. Job was smitten with boils. His wife encouraged him to curse God and die. Three friends—Eliphaz, Bildad and Zophar—came to comfort him. *(Job 2.)*

Job cursed the day he was born. *(Job 3.)*

Job was reproved by Eliphaz. *(Job 4-5.)*

Job bemoaned his grief and prayed the Almighty would answer his prayers. He asked, "Isn't there an appointed time to man upon the earth—are man's days not numbered? What is man, that thou shouldest magnify him? Why dost thou not pardon my transgression and take away mine iniquity?" *(Job 6-7.)*

Job was reproved by Bildad. *(Job 8.)*

Job acknowledged that man cannot contend against God. He recognized God's greatness and justice. Nevertheless, Job was weary of his life and discussed his afflictions with God and questioned why God even let him be born. *(Job 9-10.)*

Zophar questioned the idea that a person can find God by searching, and indicated that the hope of the wicked was "as the giving up of the ghost." *(Job 11.)*

Job claimed that the souls of all things are in the hands of the Lord and that the Lord would be his salvation. He testified of the certainty of death and also of the resurrection. *(Job 12-14.)*

Eliphaz rebuked Job, indicated Job was a wicked man, and disputed the notion of a resurrection. *(Job 15.)*

Job told his friends that they were "miserable comforters" and that, even though they scorned him, his witness was in heaven and his record was on high. He told his friends that he couldn't find one wise man among them. *(Job 16-17.)*

Bildad continued to upbraid Job and told him of the awful state that awaits the wicked who know not God. *(Job 18.)*

Job outlined the problems that had befallen him, and then testified that he knew his Redeemer lives and that "he shall stand at the latter day upon the earth: and though after my skin worms destroy this body, yet in my flesh shall I see God." *(Job 19.)*

Zophar added his condemnation of Job and reminded him that the triumph of the wicked is short and that the joy of the hypocrite is for only a moment. *(Job 20.)*

Job acknowledged that wicked men sometimes prosper in this life, but he also chided his friends and said they wrongfully imagined things against him. *(Job 21.)*

Eliphaz accused Job of various sins and urged him to repent. *(Job 22.)*

Job sought the Lord. He claimed his righteousness and testified that after the Lord had tried him, "I shall come forth as gold." He also acknowledged that wicked people often go unpunished in this life but ultimately they are punished. "They are exalted for a little while, but are gone and brought low." *(Job 23-24.)*

Bildad classified man as nothing more than a worm. *(Job 25.)*

Job chastised Bildad for his lack of emphathy, but praised the majesty and power of God. *(Job 26.)* He continued to assert his own righteousness while acknowledging that those who die in their wickedness shall tremble. *(Job 27.)* Precious stones and grains, etc., come from the earth, but wisdom cannot be purchased, "for the price of wisdom is above rubies" and "the fear of the Lord, that is widom; and to depart from evil is understanding." *(Job 28.)* Job believed that his former prosperity and greatness were due to his righteousness and the good deeds he did. *(Job 29.)* Whereas he used to be esteemed by men and children, he was now derided by the children of "fathers he would have disdained to have set with the dogs of my flock." Job cried unto the Lord that he wept for others who were in trouble, but no one seemed to be there to offer him comfort. *(Job 30.)* Job told the Lord that if he has done wrong, if he has not helped the poor, if he has made gold his hope, then he would willingly accept the penalties the Lord placed upon him. *(Job 31.)*

Elihu, the son of Barachel the Buzite of the kindred of Ram, angrily chastised Job and his three friends: Job because Elihu felt he justified himself rather than God; and his three friends because they had found no answer yet they condemned Job. *(Job 32-37.)*

The Lord spoke to Job out of the whirlwind and asked, "Where wast thou when I laid the foundations of the earth? . . . When the morning stars sang together, and all the sons of God shouted for joy?" The Lord pointed out the weakness of man as He showed His own greatness through the phenomena of nature. *(Job. 38-39.)* The Lord continued to humble Job. Job responded contritely. *(Job 40.)* The Lord's chastisement continued. *(Job 41.)*

Job was humbled and repented in dust and ashes. Previously, he had heard the Lord, but now he saw Him with his eyes. The Lord reproved Job's three friends because "ye have not spoken of me the thing that is right, as my servant Job hath." The Lord instructed them to make offerings and that Job would pray for them; and He would accept them because of Job. Job was blessed with double what he had lost earlier: twice as many sheep, camels and oxen, etc. He also was blessed with seven more sons and three more daughters: Jemima, Kezia, Keren-happuch. He lived an additional 140 years and saw his posterity even unto the fourth generation. *(Job 42.)*

The Lord told Ezekiel that even if Job, Noah and Daniel ministered to the children of Israel, the children of Israel would still not follow the Lord. *(Ezek. 14:14.)*

JOB'S (2) MESSENGERS. *Job 1:14-18.*

Four **Messengers** reported Job's losses to him. The first reported that the Sabeans fell upon the oxen as they were plowing and the asses as they were feeding and took them away, slaying all the servants save himself. The second messenger reported that the "fire of God is fallen from heaven" and all the sheep had been burned up; the servants also had been consumed and only he was saved. A third messenger reported that the Chaldeans came in three bands, captured all of the camels and slew all of the servants save himself. A fourth servant reported that a wind had come up and destroyed the house where Job's sons and daughters were dining and drinking and only he had survived.

JOB'S (2) SONS AND DAUGHTERS. *Job 1:2, 18; 42:13-14.*

Job's Sons and Daughters (seven sons and three daughters) were killed when a wind came from the wildernes and destroyed the house where they were eating and drinking. After Job's trials, the Lord again blessed him with seven more sons and three more daughters: Jemima, Kezia, Keren-happuch.

JOB'S (2) WIFE. *Job 2:9.*

Job's Wife counseled him to curse God and die when their ten children were killed, their animals were stolen and all of their servants slain.

JOBAB (1). *Gen. 10:29*.

Jobab was a son of Joktan, a third-great-grandson of Shem and a fourth-great-grandson of Noah. (Chart 2b.)

JOBAB (2). *Gen. 36:33; 1 Chr. 1:44*.

Jobab was the son of Zerah. He reigned as king in Edom upon the death of Bela. *(Gen. 36:33.)* Upon Jobab's death, Husham of the land of Temanites reigned in his stead. *(1 Chr. 1:44.)* (Chart 18.)

JOBAB (3). *1 Chr. 8:9*.

Jobab, a descendant of Benjamin, was a son of Shaharaim and his wife Hodesh. (Chart 16f.)

JOBAB (4). *1 Chr. 8:18*.

Jobab, a descendant of Benjamin, was a son of Elpaal. (Chart 16i.)

JOCHEBED (Moses' Mother). *Ex. 2:1-10; 6:20; Num. 26:59*.

Moses' Mother was of the house of Levi, as was her husband. *(She is first mentioned by name in Ex. 6:20.)* She bore a male child. Because of Pharaoh's order to kill all male Hebrew newborn babies, she hid him for three months and then made an ark of bulrushes, slime and pitch, and set the infant in it. She laid it in the river. Moses' sister watched him from a distance. When Pharaoh's daughter discovered the baby, Moses' sister volunteered to find a Hebrew nurse for the baby. Moses' mother was given the responsibility to nurse the child. As Moses grew, his mother returned him to Pharaoh's daughter and he became her son. *(Ex. 2:1-10.)*

Jochebed was the wife and aunt of Amram and the mother of Aaron and Moses. She was Amram's father's sister. *(Ex. 6:20.)*

Jochebed was born to Levi in Egypt. *(Num. 26:59.)* (Chart 7b.)

JOED. *Neh. 11:7*.

Joed, of the house of Benjamin, was the father of Meshullam and the son of Pedaiah. (Chart 16m.)

JOEL (1) (Vashni). *1 Sam. 8.2-3; 1 Chr. 6:28, 33*.

Joel was the first son of the prophet Samuel. He was a wicked judge in Israel and took bribes and perverted judgment. His brother was Abiah. *(1 Sam. 8.2-3.)*

Vashni (Joel), a descendant of Levi through Kohath, was the firstborn son of Samuel (Shemuel). His brother was Abiah. His son was Heman, one of David's singers. *(1 Chr. 6:28, 33.)* (Chart 20.)

JOEL (2). *1 Chr. 11:38*. See **Igal (2)**.

JOEL (3). *1 Chr. 4:35*.

Joel was a descendant of Shimei (Shimi). (Chart 6a.)

JOEL (4). *1 Chr. 15:7, 11-12*.

Joel was the chief of the sons of Gershom. He and 130 of his brethren were called by David to assemble with other Levites to prepare themselves to retrieve the ark of God from the house of Obed-edom so as to bring it to the place David had prepared for it in the city of David.

JOEL (5). *1 Chr. 23:8; 26:22.*

Joel, Jehiel and Zetham were named by David as chief of the fathers of the sons of Laadan (son of Gershon) when he divided the Levites into courses at the time he made Solomon king. *(1 Chr. 23:8.)*

Joel and Zetham were sons of Jehieli (Jehiel) who was a son of Laadan. They were chief fathers and were over the treasures of the house of the Lord. *(1 Chr. 26:22.)* (Chart 7f.)

JOEL (6). *1 Chr. 5:4-10.*

Joel was thefather of Shemaiah. They were descendants of Reuben. Joel was the father of Shema (Shemaiah), grandfather of Azaz, great-grandfather of Bela. In the days of Saul, they made war with the Hagarites. (Chart 5b.)

JOEL (7). *1 Chr. 5:12.*

Joel was a descendant of Gad. He was the chief leader as Gad's descendants joined Reuben's descendants in battle against the Hagarites in the days of Saul. (Chart 13b.)

JOEL (8). *2 Chr. 29:12.* See **Shaul (3)**

JOEL (9). *1 Chr. 7:3.*

Joel, a descendant of Issachar, was the son of Izrahiah, grandson of Uzzi and great-grandson of Tola. His brothers were Michael, Obadiah and Ishiah. (Chart 9a.)

JOEL (10). *1 Chr. 27:20.*

Joel, the son of Pedaiah, was prince of one of the half tribes of Manasseh when David was king. (Chart 15c.)

JOEL (11). *Ezra 10:43 (18-19, 43-44).*

Joel was one of Nebo's sons. He and his brothers Jeiel, Mattithiah, Zabad, Zebina, Jadau and Benaiah were some of the Israelite men who took foreign wives but agreed to separate themselves from them because Ezra feared the Lord's wrath would destroy all of Israel for this iniquity.

JOEL (12) *Neh. 11:9.*

Joel, son of Zichri, was elected by lot to be the overseer of the people of Benjamin who dwelled in Jerusalem following their release from captivity in Babylon. (Chart 16m.)

JOEL (13). *Joel 1-3.*

Joel was the son of Pethuel. *(Note: The Bible Dictionary states that the date of his prophecy is uncertain but could have been anywhere from 850 B.C. to sometime after the Return. His prophecy was occasioned by a severe drought and infestation of locusts. He assured the people that if they repented, they would again receive the blessings of God.)* When the word of the Lord came to him, desolation had befallen the people. They were instructed to call together a solemn assembly for the day of the Lord was at hand. *(Joel 1.)*

Joel declared that prior to the Second Coming, there will be war and desolation. The earth shall quake, the heavens tremble, the sun and moon will be darkened, and the stars will not shine. The Lord will then restore things and will pour out His spirit upon all flesh. Sons and daughters shall prophesy; old men will dream dreams; young men shall see visions. There will be wonders in the heaven and the earth: the sun will be turned into darkness, the moon into blood. There will be deliverance in mount Zion and in Jerusalem. *(Joel 2.)*

Joel continued to prophesy, and said that in the day the Lord gathers Judah and Jerusalem, all nations shall gather in war. Multitudes will stand in the valley of decision as the Second Coming—the day of the Lord—draws near. The Lord will dwell in Zion and Jerusalem shall be a holy city. *(Joel 3.)*

JOELAH. *1 Chr. 12:7 (1-2, 7, 23, 38).*

Joelah, a son of Jeroham of Gedor, was one of David's mighty men who came to him at Ziklag to defend him against Saul and to rejoice with all Israel when David became king. His brother was Zebadiah.

JOEZER. *1 Chr. 12:6 (1-2, 6, 23, 38).*

Joezer, a Korhite, was one of David's mighty men who came to him at Ziklag to defend him against Saul and to rejoice with all Israel when David became king.

JOGLI. *Num. 34:22.*

Jogli was the father of Bukki and was of the tribe of Dan. (Chart 11b.)

JOHA (1). *1 Chr. 11:45.*

Joha, a son of Shimri and brother to Jediael, was one of David's mighty men, one of the valiant men of the armies. (Chart 17.)

JOHA (2). *1 Chr. 8:16.*

Joha, a descendant of Benjamin, was a son of Beriah who was a son of Elpaal who was a son of Shaharaim and Hushim. (Chart 16g.)

JOHANAN (1). *2 Kgs. 25:23-26; Jer. 40:8, 13-16; 41:11-18; 43.*

Johanan was the son of Careah. He and a group of other men (including Ishmael) came to Gedaliah after Gedaliah was made governor over the remnant of Judah by Nebuchadnezzar. Gedaliah told them they should not fear being servants of the Chaldees. After Ishmael and ten cohorts slew Gedaliah and the Jews and Chaldees who were with him at Mizpah, the rest all fled to Egypt because they feared the Chaldees. *(2 Kgs. 25:23-26.)*

(Jer. 40:8, 13-16 is a repeat and expansion of 2 Kgs. 25:23-26.) Johanan and Jonathan, sons of Kareah (Careah), along with others, went to Gedaliah and informed him that Ishmael the son of Nethaniah had been sent by Baalis the king of the Ammonites to slay him. Gedaliah did not believe them. Johanan spoke to Gedaliah privately and offered to slay Ishmael to protect Gedaliah, but Gedaliah said no, "for thou speakest falsely of Ishmael." *(Jer. 40:8, 13-16.)*

When Johanan and the captains of the forces who were with him learned that Ishmael had slain Gedaliah, they pursued him and rescued the people he had taken captive. They traveled to Chimham by Beth-lehem, preparatory to entering Egypt because they feared the Chaldeans. *(Jer. 41:11-18.)*

Johanan and the captains of the forces approached Jeremiah and asked him to pray to the Lord and inquire what they should do. They promised to follow whatever the Lord said. Jeremiah told them that if they remained in Judah, they would have peace and safety. But, he said none of them would remain or escape from the evil the Lord promised to bring upon them if they went to Egypt. They would perish by the sword, famine and pestilence. *(Jer. 42.)*

Johanan and Azariah (Jaazaniah) the son of Hoshaiah and "all the proud men" told Jeremiah that he spoke falsely and they refused to follow the Lord's counsel. They carried Jeremiah and the remnant of Judah into Egypt. *(Jer. 43.)*

JOHANAN (2). *1 Chr. 3:15.*

Johanan was the firstborn son of Josiah. His brothers were Jehoiakim (Eliakim), Zedekiah (Mattaniah), and Shallum (Jehoahaz). (Chart 1.)

JOHANAN (3). *1 Chr. 3:24.*

Johanan, a descendant of David, was a son of Elioenai. His brothers were Hodaiah, Eliashib, Pelaiah, Akkub, Dalaiah and Anani. (Chart 1.)

JOHANAN (4). *1 Chr. 6:9-10; Ezra 7:1-5.*

Johanan was the son of Azariah, an eleventh-great-grandson of Aaron, and the father of Azariah. *(1 Chr. 6:9-10.)*

Aaron's descendants are listed through Ezra. *(Note: This listing does not include Johanan.) (Ezra 7:1-5.)* (Chart 7b.)

JOHANAN (5). *1 Chr. 12:4 (1-2, 4, 23, 38).*

Johanan was one of David's mighty men who came to him at Ziklag to defend him against Saul and to rejoice with all Israel when David became king.

JOHANAN (6). *1 Chr. 12:12 (1-2, 12, 23, 38).*

Johanan, of the tribe of Gad, was one of David's mighty men who came to him at Ziklag to defend him against Saul and to rejoice with all Israel when David became king. (Chart 13b.)

JOHANAN (7). *2 Chr. 28:12.*

Johanan was the father of Azariah who was one of the leaders of the children of Ephraim when Ahaz was king of Judah and the children of Israel carried many of Judah off captive.

JOHANAN (8). *Ezra 8:12.*

Johanan was the son of Hakkatan who was of the sons of Azgad. He was the chief of the fathers in his family. He went with Ezra up from Babylon to Jerusalem and took 110 males with him.

JOHANAN (9) (Jonathan (10)). *Ezra 10:6; Neh. 12:11, 22-23.*

Johanan was the son of Eliashib. After Ezra prayed for the children of Israel because of their marriages to foreign women, he went into the chamber of Johanan. Together, they made a proclamation throughout Judah and Jerusalem calling all those who had been in captivity to meet together within three days or forfeit all their substance and be separated from the rest of the children of Israel. *(Ezra 10:6.)*

Jonathan (Johanan), grandson of Eliashib, son of Joiada and father of Jaddua, was a priest. The Levites who were the chief of the fathers in the days of Eliashib,

Joiada, Johanan and Jaddua were recorded to the reign of Darius the Persian. *(Neh. 12:11, 22-23.)* (Chart 7b.)

JOHANAN (10). *Neh. 6:18.*

Johanan was the son of Tobiah. (Tobiah opposed Nehemiah in rebuilding the walls of Jerusalem.) Johanan married the daughter of Meshullam who was the son of Berechiah. As a result, many in Judah were supportive of Tobiah.

JOIADA. *Neh. 12:10-11, 22; 13:28.*

Joiada, son of Eliashib, father of Jonathan (Johanan) and grandfather of Jaddua, was a priest. The Levites who were the chief of the fathers in the days of Eliashib, Joiada, Johanan and Jaddua were recorded to the reign of Darius the Persian. *(Neh. 12:10-11, 22.)*

One of Joiada's sons was a son-in-law to Sanballat. *(Neh. 13:28.)* (Chart 7b.)

JOIAKIM. *Neh. 12:10-21, 26.*

Joiakim was the son of Jeshua and the father of Eliashib. The priests who were chief of their fathers during the days of Joiakim are listed. Those who were porters in the days of Joiakim, Nehemiah and Ezra are listed. (Chart 7b.)

JOIARIB (1). *Neh. 11:10.* See **Jehoiarib (1)**.

JOIARIB (2). *Ezra 8:16.*

Joiarib, a man of understanding, was one of the men Ezra sent for when he gathered the people together as he was preparing to lead them to Jerusalem from Babylon and discovered there were no Levites among the group. He sent this group to Iddo and the Nethinims to request that they send them some ministers for the house of God.

JOIARIB (3). *Neh. 11:5.*

Joiarib, son of Zechariah and father of Adaiah of the children of Perez, dwelled in Jerusalem after leaving Babylon. (Chart 8b.)

JOIARIB (4). *Neh. 12:6, 19.*

Joiarib was one of the men (priests and Levites) who went with Zerubbabel from Babylonian captivity to Jerusalem. He was the father of Mattenai who was one of the priests who was a chief of the fathers in the days of Joiakim.

JOKIM. *1 Chr. 4:22.*

Jokim was a son of Shelah and a grandson of Judah. (Chart 8a.)

JOKSHAN. *Gen. 25:2.*

Jokshan was a son of Abraham and his wife Keturah. He begat Sheba and Dedan. (Charts 2b.; 3a, d, f.)

JOKTAN (Joktanites). *Gen. 10:25-29; 1 Chr. 1:20-23; 2 Chr. 17:11.*

Joktan was the brother of Peleg, a son of Eber, a great-great-grandson of Shem and a great-great-great-grandson of Noah. His sons were Almodad, Sheleph, Hazarmaveth, Jerah, Hadoram, Uzal, Diklah, Obal, Abimael, Sheba, Ophir, Havilah and Jobab. *(Gen. 10:25-29.)*

Joktan's sons are listed again; however, Obal's name is given as Ebal. *(1 Chr. 1:20-23.)*

*(Note: According to the BD, Joktan's descendants, the **Joktanites**, are the inhabitants of southern Arabia; thus, they are also called Arabians.)* Because the Lord was with king Jehoshaphat, none of the kingdoms of the lands that were near Judah came to war against Jehoshaphat. The Arabians (Joktanites) even brought him flocks. *(2 Chr. 17:11.) (Also see Arabians)* (Charts 1.; 2b.)

JONADAB (1). *2 Sam. 13:3-36.*

Jonadab was the son of Shimeah (Shamma), David's brother, and was a friend of his cousin Amnon, David's son. He was a very subtle man. When Amnon pined for Tamar, his half-sister, Jonadab suggested that he pretend to be sick and when David came to see him to request that Tamar be sent to make him some food so that he could eat at her hand. Tamar came, and Amnon forced her to lie with him. Amnon was subsequently killed by Absalom's orders. Jonadab comforted David by informing him that, contrary to what David had been told, only Amnon had been slain, the rest of his sons were still alive. (Chart 8d.)

JONADAB (2). *Jer. 35:6.* See **Jehonadab**.

JONAH. *2 Kgs. 14:25; Jonah 1-4.*

Jonah, the prophet, was the son of Amittai and was of Gath-hepher. While Jeroboam was king, the Lord restored the coast of Israel to them as prophesied by Jonah. *(2 Kgs. 14:25.)*

The Lord instructed Jonah to go to Ninevah and cry repentance unto the people. Jonah didn't want to go to Ninevah so he fled to Joppa and boarded a ship bound for Tarshish. The Lord sent a strong wind upon the sea. The mariners feared the ship would be broken. They prayed to their gods and threw cargo overboard to lighten the ship. Meanwhile, Jonah slept. The shipmaster woke him and told him to pray to his God for deliverance. The mariners cast lots to see who was responsible for the evil that was befalling them. The lot fell upon Jonah. Upon inquiry, Jonah acknowledged he was the cause of the problem because he was fleeing from the Lord. He told them to cast him overboard. They didn't want to do that and just rowed harder. Finally, in desperation, they threw Jonah overboard. The sea calmed. The Lord had prepared a large fish to swallow Jonah. He was in the belly of the fish three days and three nights. *(Jonah 1.)*

Johan repented while in the belly of the fish and prayed to the Lord. The Lord spoke unto the fish and it vomited Jonah out upon the dry land. *(Jonah 2.)*

The Lord again instructed Jonah to go to Ninevah and cry repentance. Jonah told the people that Ninevah would be overthrown in 40 days. The people believed the word of God and repented. *(Jonah 3.)*

When the Lord did not destroy Ninevah, Jonah was upset with the Lord. The Lord chastised him, using a gourd to illustrate how Jonah had pity for the gourd which withered—a gourd he hadn't even labored for—and how much more the Lord should show mercy to the 120,000 people and their cattle for whom He had labored. *(Jonah 4.)*

JONATHAN (1). *Judg. 17:7-13; 18:30.*

Jonathan was a son of Gershom, the son of Manasseh. *(Note: The footnote to Judg. 18:30 indicates that Manasseh actually refers to Moses, but that it has been altered to Manasseh.)* He hired himself as a house-priest to Micah the Ephraimite. He and his sons were made priests to the tribe of Dan. Through them idolatrous worship was established in Dan. (Chart 7b.)

JONATHAN (2). *1 Sam. 13:2,16; 14; 18:1; 20; 23:16-18; 28:19; 31:2-13; 2 Sam. 1:17-27; 1 Chr. 8:33; 9:39-40; 10:2, 12.*

Jonathan, the son of Saul, took a thousand men and smote the garrison of the Philistines in Geba. He and Saul and their men abode in Gibeah of Benjamin while the Philistines encamped in Michmash. *(1 Sam. 13:2,16.)*

Jonathan and his armorbearer destroyed a twenty-member garrison of Philistines. Unaware of his father's instructions for no one to eat anything until evening under penalty of death, Jonathan ate some honey. When Saul decreed his death, the people rescued him. His brothers were Ishui and Melchi-shua. His sisters were Merab and Michal. His mother was Ahinoam. *(1 Sam. 14.)*

Jonathan loved David as his own soul. *(1 Sam. 18:1.)*

Jonathan and David loved each other and made a covenant of peace with one another. Jonathan devised a plan whereby when he shot an arrow into the air he could warn David whether or not his father was intent on killing him. They kissed one another, wept and parted. *(1 Sam. 20.)*

Jonathan comforted David in Ziph when Saul sought him there. He acknowledged that David would be king after Saul and that he, Jonathan, would be "next unto thee." *(1 Sam. 23:16-18.)*

Jonathan's death was prophesied. When Saul sought a revelation at the hands of the woman (witch) of En-dor, he was told by Samuel (who the witch called up) that Saul and all his sons would be with him the next day. *(1 Sam. 28:19.) (Note: The Bible Dictionary states: "The account . . . of the prophet being brought back from the dead by the witch of Endor, at King Saul's request, presents a problem. It is certain that a witch or other medium cannot by any means available to her bring up a prophet from the world of spirits. We may confidently be assured that if Samuel was present on that occasion, it was not due to conjuring of the witch. Either Samuel came in spite of and not because of the witch, or some other spirit came impersonating him.")*

Jonathan and his brothers Abinadab and Malchi-shua were slain in battle with the Philistines; and the Israelites were defeated. Saul was seriously injured and fell upon his own sword. Saul's head was cut off and paraded about. Their bodies were hung on the wall of Beth-shan. Valiant men from Jabesh-gilead, under cover of night, retrieved their bodies and burned them in Jabesh, burying their bones under a tree in Jabesh. *(1 Sam. 31:2-13; 1 Chr. 10:2, 12.)*

Jonathan's and Saul's deaths were lamented by David in song. *(2 Sam. 1:17-27.)*

Jonathan's brothers are listed as Malchi-shua, Abinadab and Esh-baal. *(1 Chr. 8:33.) (Note: 1 Sam. 14:49 lists his brothers as Ishui and Melchi-shua.)*

Saul begat Jonathan and his brothers, and Jonathan begat Merib-baal. *(1 Chr. 9:39-40.)* (Chart 16 l.)

JONATHAN (3). *2 Sam. 15:27-36; 17:17-21.*

Jonathan was the son of Abiathar the priest. When David and his family and followers fled Jerusalem to escape from Absalom, David had Abiathar take Jonathan back to Jerusalem with him so they could keep David informed as to what Absalom's plans were. Jonathan and Ahimaaz, the son of Zadok the priest, were to carry information back to David. *(2 Sam. 15:27-36.)*

Jonathan and Ahimaaz were sent to David carrying information from Hushai as to what advice he had given Absalom and what was happening. They were assisted by a wench who kept them informed, and then they informed king David. A lad saw them and told Absalom. They quickly hid in a well in a man's court in Bahurim and were protected by a woman who spread a covering over the well's mouth and spread ground corn on it. When Absalom's men came and inquired about them, the woman said they had gone over the brook of water. After they left, Jonathan and Ahimaaz carried their message to David. *(2 Sam. 17:17-21.)*

JONATHAN (4). *2 Sam. 21:20-21; 1 Chr. 20:6-7.*

Jonathan, a son of Shimea (Shamma) the brother of David, slew one of the four sons who was born to the giant in Gath: a man of great stature who had six fingers on each hand and six toes on each foot. (Chart 8d.)

JONATHAN (5). *2 Sam. 23:32; 1 Chr. 11:34.*

Jonathan was one of David's mighty men *(1 Chr. 11:34)*, the son of Shage the Hararite and one of the valiant men of the armies *(1 Chr. 11:34)*. (Chart 17.)

JONATHAN (6). *1 Chr. 2:32.*

Jonathan, a descendant of Judah, was the son of Jada. His brother was Jether. He begat Peleth and Zaza. (Chart 8c.)

JONATHAN (7). *1 Chr. 27:32.*

Jonathan, David's uncle, was a wise man and counselor and scribe to David.

JONATHAN (8). *Neh. 12:35.* See **Benaiah (6)**.

JONATHAN (9). *Ezra 8:6.*

Jonathan was of the sons of Adin. His son Ebed was the leader of his posterity when Ezra led many exiled Israelites out of Babylon back to Jerusalem.

JONATHAN (10). *Neh. 12:11.* See **Johanan (9)**.

JONATHAN (11). *Ezra 10:15.*

Jonathan the son of Asahel and Jahaziah the son of Tikvah were assigned by Ezra to the task of separating the children of Israel from their foreign wives. They were assisted by Meshullam and Shabbethai the Levite.

JONATHAN (12). *Neh. 12:14.*

Jonathan, son of Melicu, was one of the priests who was a chief of the fathers in the days of Joiakim.

JONATHAN (13). *Jer. 37:15, 20; 38:26.*

Jonathan was a scribe. His house was the prison where Jeremiah was cast into the dungeon when he went to the land of Benjamin. When Jeremiah met with Zedekiah, he requested that he not be returned to the house of Jonathan because he feared he would die there if he were returned there. Zedekiah complied and had him placed in the court of the prison. *(Jer. 37:15, 20.)*

After Zedekiah had a secret conversation with Jeremiah, he instructed Jeremiah that he not let the princes know of their conversation. If they inquired, he was to tell them that he, Jeremiah, had presented his supplication to the king that he not be returned to Jonathan's house. *(Jer. 38:26.)*

JONATHAN (14). *Jer. 40:8.*

Jonathan, son of Kareah (Careah), and his brother Johanan went with others to Gedaliah after Gedaliah was made governor over the remnant of the Jews left in Judah when Nebuchadnezzar took Judah captive. Gedaliah counseled them that they should not fear serving the Chaldeans.

JONATHAN'S (2) ARMORBEARER. *1 Sam. 14:1-14.*

Jonathan's Armorbearer and Jonathan smote a 20-member Philistine garrison over a half-acre of land.

JORAH (Hariph). *Ezra 2:18; Neh. 7:24; 10:19 (1, 19, 28-31).*

Jorah (Hariph) was of the people of Israel. The men of the children of Jorah who returned to Jerusalem from Babylon after Cyrus' proclamation to build the temple numbered 112. *(Ezra 2:18; Neh. 7:24.)*

Hariph (Jorah) was among those chief of the people who covenanted to marry in Israel, honor the Sabbath, pay tithes and keep the commandments. *(Neh. 10:19 [1, 19, 28-31].)*

JORAI. *1 Chr. 5:13.*

Jorai was a descendant of Gad. (Chart 13b.)

JORAM (1) (Hadoram (3)). *2 Sam. 8:9-10; 1 Chr. 18:10 (9-10).*

Joram (Hadoram) was the son of Toi (Tou), king of Hamath. When David smote Hadadezer, king of Zobah, Toi sent Joram to salute David and to take him gifts of silver, gold and brass.

JORAM (2). *2 Kgs. 8:21, 24.* See **Jehoram (1)**.

JORAM (3). *2 Kgs. 8:25, 28-29.* See **Jehoram (2)**.

JORAM (4). *1 Chr. 26:25.*

Joram, a Levite, was the son of Jeshaiah, the father of Zichri, the great-grandson of Eliezer and the great-great-grandson of Moses. His grandson was Shelomith. Shelomith and his brethren were over the treasures of the dedicated things which king David and others had dedicated to maintain the house of the Lord. (Chart 7b.)

JORKOAM. *1 Chr. 2:44.*

Jorkoam was the son of Raham who was the son of Shema who was one of the sons of Hebron. (Chart 8i.)

JOSABAD. *1 Chr. 12:4 (1-2, 4, 23, 38)*.

Josabad the Gederathtite was one of David's mighty men who came to him at Ziklag to defend him against Saul and to rejoice with all Israel when David became king.

JOSEDECH. See **Jozadak**.

JOSEPH (1) (Zaphnath-paaneah). *Gen. 30:24; 37, 39-50; Ex. 13:19; Num. 1:10, 32-35; 2:18-24; Deut. 27:12; 33:13-17; Josh. 24:32; Judg. 1:22; Ps. 79:67-68; 105:17-23; Exek. 47:13; 48:4-5, 32; Amos 5:6, 15; 6:6; Zech. 10.*

Joseph was the firstborn son of Rachel and Jacob. (He was Jacob's 11th son.) *(Gen. 30:24.)*

When Joseph was about 17 years old, Jacob made him a coat of many colors. Because his father loved him more than his siblings, they hated him. They hated him even more when he told them about the dreams he had.

First Dream. They were binding sheaves in the field. His sheaf arose and stood upright. His brothers sheaves stood round about and made obeisance to his sheaf. *(Gen. 37:7.)*

Second Dream. The sun and the moon and eleven stars made obeisance to him. *(Gen. 37: 9.)* His father observed what he said, but his brothers envied him.

While Joseph's siblings were tending their father's flocks in Shechem, Jacob sent him to see how they were doing and asked him to report back to him. As his brothers saw him coming, they plotted to kill him. However, his eldest brother, Reuben, sought to protect him and suggested they cast him into a pit instead, thinking he would be able to rescue him later and return him to their father. They stripped him of his coat and cast him into the pit. While Reuben was away from his brothers, they saw a company of Ishmeelites coming. Judah suggested that they sell Joseph to the Ishmeelites rather than kill him. The Ishmeelites, or Midianite merchantmen as they were also called, took Joseph to Egypt and sold him to Potiphar, an officer of Pharaoh's and captain of Pharaoh's guard. When Reuben discovered that Joseph was gone, he was distressed and rent his clothes. *(Gen. 37.)*

Joseph was sold to Potiphar. The Lord blessed Joseph; and Potiphar made him overseer of all he had. Potiphar's wife wanted Joseph to lie with her. He refused. On one occasion when she was asking him to lie with her, she took hold of his coat and he fled, leaving his coat behind in her hand. Rejected, she cried out that Joseph had tried to lie with her but had fled when she cried out. She showed his coat as evidence. Potiphar cast him into prison. The Lord blessed Joseph in prison and the prison keeper committed all the prisoners into Joseph's hand. *(Gen. 39.)*

While in prison, Joseph interpreted the dreams of Pharaoh's chief butler and chief baker.

Chief Butler's Dream. A vine was before him. In the vine were three branches. The blossoms shot forth and the clusters brought forth ripe grapes. Pharaoh's cup was in his hand. The butler took the grapes and pressed them into Pharaoh's cup and gave the cup to Pharaoh. *(Gen. 40:9-11.)*

Joseph's Interpretation. The three branches represented three days. Within three days, Pharaoh would lift up the butler's head and restore him to his place. The butler would deliver the cup to Pharaoh as he used to do. *(Gen. 40:12-13.)*

Chief Baker's Dream. He had three white baskets on his head. In the top basket was all manner of bakemeats for Pharaoh. The birds ate them out of the basket. *(Gen. 40: 16-17.)*

Joseph's Interpretation. The three baskets represented three days. Within three days, Pharaoh would lift up the baker's head from off him and would hang him on a tree. The birds would eat his flesh from off him. *(Gen. 40:18-19.)* The Pharaoh did to the butler and the baker exactly what Joseph had said he would do.

Pharaoh had two dreams and when none of the magicians nor wisemen could interpret them, the butler remembered Joseph and told Pharaoh he could interpret them. Pharaoh asked Joseph to interpret his dreams.

Pharaoh's Dream #1. Seven robust cows came out of the river and fed in a meadow. Seven ill-favored and leanfleshed cows ate up the seven robust cows. *(Gen. 41:1-4, 17-21.)*

Pharaoh's Dream #2. Seven good ears of corn grew on one stalk. Seven withered and thin ears sprang up and devoured the seven good ears. *(Gen. 41:5-7, 22-24.)*

Joseph's Interpretation. The seven healthy cows and the seven good ears of corn both represented seven years. The seven thin, ill-favored cows and the seven withered ears of corn also represented seven years—seven years of famine. There would be seven years of great plenty in Egypt. These would be followed by seven years of famine. All the years of plenty would be forgotten. Famine would consume the land. *(Gen. 41:26-31.)* Joseph recommended that Pharaoh select a wise and discreet man and set him over Egypt—have him appoint officers over the land and take up 1/5 of the land and store corn during the seven plenteous years so there would be food available during the seven years of famine. Pharaoh chose Joseph and placed him over all Egypt—second in command only to himself. He called Joseph, **Zaphnath-paaneah**. *(Gen. 41:45.)* He gave him Asenath, daughter of Potipherah priest of On, for a wife. Joseph was now thirty years old. He gathered and stored food during the seven years of plenty. He begat two sons: Manasseh and Ephraim. During the seven years of famine, all countries came to Egypt to buy corn.

Jacob sent his sons, all except Benjamin, to Egypt to buy corn. Joseph recognized his brothers but they did not recognize him. Joseph accused them of being spies. They denied it and said they were all one man's family—that there were twelve sons, but one was dead, and the youngest was at home. Joseph, speaking through an interpreter, insisted they must bring Benjamin and that one of them would have to stay in Egypt until they did so. Simeon was bound and taken away. Joseph commanded that their sacks be filled with corn and had each man's money placed in his sack. The brothers didn't discover the money until part way home and were frightened. They reported to Jacob upon their return. Jacob refused to allow them to take Benjamin back to Egypt. *(Gen. 42.)*

As the famine continued, it became necessary for Joseph's brothers to return to Egypt for more corn. They refused to go unless Jacob sent Benjamin with them. Jacob finally agreed. The brothers were taken to Joseph's house. They bowed themselves before Joseph (still not recognizing him) and made obeisance to him. Simeon was brought forth to join his brothers. Joseph had the ruler of his house take his brothers to his [Joseph's] home so they could dine with him at noon. To their astonishment, the brothers were seated at dinner according to age—oldest to youngest. *(Gen. 43.)*

As the brothers prepared to leave Egypt, Joseph again had their money put back into each sack. In Benjamin's sack, however, he had his steward hide a silver cup. Joseph then sent his steward after them to "find" the silver cup. The brothers denied having taken it and said that whoever had it should die and they would be their bondsmen. When the cup was found in Benjamin's sack, Judah offered himself in place of Benjamin because he knew it would kill their father if anything happened to Benjamin. *(Gen. 44.)* Joseph finally made himself known to his brothers and explained that God had sent him before them that they might all be preserved. They all rejoiced together. Pharaoh invited Joacob and his family to come live in Egypt and eat the fat of the land. The brothers returned to Jacob and conveyed all this to him. Jacob exclaimed, "It is enough; Joseph my son is yet alive: I will go and see him before I die." *(Gen. 45.)*

Joseph was finally reunited with his father and all his father's household. He begat Manasseh and Ephraim. *(Gen. 46:20.)* He settled his father's family in Goshen. On Pharaoh's behalf, he sold grain to the Egyptians in return for their cattle and lands. As Jacob approached the time that he knew he would die, he made Joseph promise him that he would not bury him in Egypt but would bury him among his fathers in the cave that is in the field of Machpelah in the land of Canaan. *(Gen. 47.)*

Joseph took Manasseh and Ephraim to Jacob. Jacob adopted them as his own children, saying, "And now thy two sons, Ephraim and Manasseh, which were born unto thee in the land of Egypt are mine; as Reuben and Simeon, they shall be mine." Then told Joseph that any issue which he begot after Ephraim and Manasseh, "shall be thine, and shall be called after the name of their brethren in their inheritance." *(Gen. 48:5-6.)*

Prior to Jacob's death, he gave each of his sons either some counsel or a blessing, letting them know what would befall them in the last days. To Joseph he said, "Joseph is a fruitful bough, even a fruitful bough by a well; whose branches run over the wall . . . The blessings of thy father have prevailed above the blessings of my progenitors unto the utmost bound of the everlasting hills: they shall be on the head of Joseph, and on the crown of the head of him that was separate from his brethren." *(Gen. 49:22-26.)* When Jacob died, Joseph had him embalmed and got permission from Pharaoh to carry him back to Canaan to be buried. He then returned to Egypt. Joseph lived to be 110 years old, and saw Ephraim's children of the third generation. He also saw Machir, the son of Manasseh. He had the children of Israel make an oath that they would eventually "carry up my bones from hence." *(Gen. 50:25.)* He died and was embalmed and placed in a coffin in Egypt.

When Moses left Egypt with the children of Israel, he took Joseph's bones with him. *(Ex. 13:19.)*

When Moses was instructed to number the male children who were 20 years old and older in each tribe of Israel and to name a leader for each tribe to stand by him as Israel prepared for war, he was told to choose Elishama, son of Ammihud, from the tribe of Ephraim and to appoint Gamaliel, son of Pedahzur, from the tribe of Manasseh. Thus, two tribes came from Joseph instead of just one. The males numbered in Ephraim's tribe totaled 40,500. The males numbered in Manasseh's tribe totaled 32,200. *(Num. 1:10, 32-35.)* The assigned spot for the armies of Ephraim and Manasseh was on the west side of the encampment. Next to Manasseh was the tribe of Benjamin with 35,400 men. The total men in the camp of Ephraim was 108,100. *(Num. 2:18-24.)*

As the Israelites prepared to cross over Jordan, the tribes of Simeon, Levi, Judah, Issachar, Joseph and Benjamin were to stand upon mount Gerizim to bless the people. *(Deut. 27:12.)*

Joseph's tribes were blessed by Moses. *(Deut. 33:13-17.)*

Joseph's bones were buried in Shechem, "in a parcel of ground which Jacob bought of the sons of Hamor the father of Shechem for an hundred pieces of silver: and it became the inheritance of the children of Joseph." *(Josh. 24:32.)*

The house of Joseph went up against Beth-el. Spies were sent to scout out the city. They met a man who showed them the gate to the city in return for their promise that he would be saved. *(Judg. 1:22.)*

The Lord "refused the tabernacle of Joseph," and chose the tribe of Judah, "the mount Zion which he loved," over the tribe of Ephraim. *(Ps. 78:67-68.)*

The Lord prepared a protection for his people by allowing Joseph to be sold for a servant. As a result of the famine which He sent, Israel came to live in Egypt, the land of Ham. *(Ps. 105:17-23.)*

In the latter days when the children of Israel are restored to their land of inheritance, they are to divide the land by lot according to their tribes. Joseph is to be given two portions of land. *(Ezek. 47:13.)* The Lord revealed to Ezekiel just how the land should be divided by tribes in the latter days. Joseph's son Manasseh will have the portion of land between the borders of Naphtali and Ephraim, and Ephraim will have the land between Naphtali and Reuben. The twelve gates of the city are to bear the names of the twelve sons of Jacob. One of the east gates will bear the name of Joseph. *(Ezek. 48:4-5, 32.)*

Israel was exhorted to seek the Lord that they might live; lest the Lord "break out like fire in the house of Joseph and devour it. The Lord may be gracious unto the remnant of Joseph if the people will repent and seek to do good, establishing judgment in the gate. *(Amos 5:6, 15.)* The Lord condemned those who were at ease and were not grieved for the affliction of Joseph. *(Amos 6:6.)*

Zechariah prophesied that the Lord would sow Joseph and Judah among the people in far countries, but they shall eventually remember Him. The Lord will "hiss" for them and gather them because He has redeemed them. He will bring them again out of Egypt and gather them out of Assyria and place them in the lands of Gilead and Lebanon. *(Zech. 10.)* (Charts 1.; 3d.; 5a.; 6a.; 7a.; 8a.; 9a.; 10a.; 11a.; 12a.; 13a.; 14a.; 15a, d.; 16a.)

JOSEPH (2). *Num. 13:7.*

Joseph, of the tribe of Issachar, was the father of Igal. (Chart 9b.)

JOSEPH (3). *1 Chr. 25:2, 9.*

Joseph, a Levite and one of the musicians, was of the sons of Asaph. The musicians—sons of Asaph, Heman and Jeduthun—drew lots and were given their duty assignments by David and the captains of the host. The first lot came forth for Asaph to Joseph. (Chart 7a)

JOSEPH (4). *Ezra 10:42 (18-19, 42, 44).*

Joseph, a son of Bani, and his brothers were some of the men in Israel who took foreign wives but gave them up when Ezra feared the wrath of God would destroy Israel for this iniquity.

JOSEPH (5). *Neh. 12:14.*

Joseph, son of Shebaniah, was one of the priests who was a chief of the fathers in the days of Joiakim.

JOSHAH. *1 Chr. 4:34, 38-41.*

Joshah, a descendant of Shimei and the son of Amaziah, and others named by name were princes in their families. They defeated those who dwelled in the plush pastureland on the east side of the valley of Gedor and then occupied the valley in their stead. (Chart 6a.)

JOSHAPHAT. *1 Chr. 11:43.*

Joshaphat the Mithnite was one of David's mighty men—one of the valiant men of the armies. (Chart 17.)

JOSHAVIAH. *1 Chr. 11:46.*

Joshaviah, a son of Elnaam and brother to Jeribai, was one of David's mighty men—one of the valiant men of the armies. (Chart 17.)

JOSHBEKASHAH. *1 Chr. 25:4, 24.*

Joshbekashah, a Levite and musician, was a son of Heman who was of the lineage of Kohath. The musicians—sons of Heman, Asaph and Jeduthun—drew lots and were given their assigned duties by David and the captains of the host. Joshbekashah cast the seventeenth of twenty-four lots. He, his sons and his brethren numbered 12. (Chart 7d.)

JOSHUA (1) (Oshea, Hoshea (1), Jehoshua, Jeshua (1)). *Ex. 17:9-13; 24:13-14; 32:17; 33:11; Num. 11:28-29; 13:8, 16; 14:6-9, 29-30; 26:65; 27:18-23; Deut. 1:36-38; 3:21, 28; 31:6-8, 14, 23; 32:44; 34:9; Josh. 1-14; 19:49-50; 23:1-16; 24; Judg. 2:8; 1 Chr. 7:27; Neh. 8:17.*

Joshua was instructed by Moses to gather together an army and fight against Amalek who had come against the children of Israel. As long as Moses kept his hand with the rod of God high, Joshua and his men prevailed. When Moses dropped his hand, Amalek prevailed. Aaron and Hur propped Moses' arms up and Joshua ultimately "discomfitted" Amalek. *(Ex. 17:9-13.)*

When the Lord told Moses to come unto him in the mount and receive tables of stone, and a law, and commandments, he rose up "and his minister Joshua" also rose up and went with him. The elders of Israel were instructed to tarry where they were and told that Aaron and Hur would be with them to take care of any problems in their absence. *(Ex. 24:13-14.)*

As Joshua and Moses were coming down from the mount after Moses received the tablets from the Lord, Joshua heard a noise and told Moses, "There is a noise of war in the camp." *(Ex. 32:17.)*

Joshua the son of Nun was a young man and was in the tabernacle when Moses spoke face to face with the Lord. When Moses returned to camp, Joshua stayed in the tabernacle. *(Ex. 33:11.)*

When Eldad and Medad went about prophesying, a young man ran to tell Moses. Joshua, the servant of Moses, told Moses he should forbid them. However, Moses said he wished everyone were righteous enough to prophesy and have the spirit of the Lord upon them. *(Num. 11:28-29.)*

Oshea (Joshua) the son of Nun, representing the tribe of Ephraim, was chosen as one of the leaders of the twelve tribes to scout out the land of Canaan which the Lord had promised to the children of Israel. Moses called him **Jehoshua**. *(Num. 13:8, 16.)*

Joshua and Caleb the son of Jephunneh were the only two scouts to give favorable reports regarding the land of Canaan. Because the children of Israel chose to believe the ten negative reports, the Lord said none of them who were then twenty years old or older would be allowed into the promised land except Joshua and Caleb. *(Num. 14:6-9, 29-30.)*

Joshua and Caleb were the only two males who had been numbered in the wilderness of Sinai who remained to be numbered on the plains of Moab to be given an inheritance in the promised land. *(Num. 26:65.)*

According to the instructions of the Lord to Moses, Joshua was set apart by Eleazar to be the leader of the children of Israel. *(Num. 27:18-23.)*

Moses reminded the children of Israel that because they lacked faith 40 years earlier when the Lord had intended to lead them into the land of Canaan, none of the people who at that earlier time had been twenty years old or older were permitted to enter the promised land except Joshua and Caleb who had been faithful. *(Deut. 1:36-38.)*

The Lord reminded Moses that he had commanded Joshua not to be fearful, but to trust the Lord who would fight the battles of the Israelites for them. Moses was told to charge Joshua with his assignment and to encourage and strengthen him. *(Deut. 3:21, 28.)*

Joshua and all Israel were counseled by Moses to be strong and of good courage. In compliance with the Lord's instructions, Moses took Joshua and they presented themselves in the tabernacle of the congregation so the Lord could give Joshua a charge. He told him, "Be strong and of a good courage: for thou shalt bring the children of Israel into the land which I sware unto them: and I will be with thee." *(Deut. 31:6-8, 14, 23.)*

Hoshea (Joshua) and Moses spoke the words of the song of Moses unto the children of Israel. *(Deut. 32:44.)*

"Joshua . . . was full of the spirit of wisdom; for Moses had laid his hands upon him." *(Deut. 34:9.)*

After the death of Moses, the Lord spoke to Joshua and told him to lead the people into Canaan and that He would be with them to fight their battles. He encouraged him to have courage and instructed him to meditate upon the law and keep the commandments. The Reubenites, Gadites, and the half tribe of Manasseh agreed to do all they had promised Moses they would do in helping to secure Canaan for the other tribes. *(Josh. 1.)*

Joshua sent two spies to scout out Jericho. Rehab, a harlot, received them and protected them by concealing them. The spies promised to preserve Rehab and her household. *(Josh. 2.)*

Joshua led the people to Jordan. The Lord told him that when the soles of the feet of the priests who bore the ark of the Lord touched the edge of the waters, the waters would be cut off and would "stand upon an heap." The children of Israel crossed over the Jordan on dry land. *(Josh. 3.)* The Lord had Joshua choose one man from each tribe and had them each take a stone from the river where the priests' feet stood firm. They were told to leave them in the lodging place where they lodged that night that they might stand as a memorial to their posterity of when the Lord cut off the waters of Jordan and they passed over on dry land. After the priests passed over Jordan, the waters returned to their banks. *(Josh. 4.)*

The Lord instructed Joshua to make some sharp knives and circumcise all the males of Israel. Israel observed the Passover and manna ceased on the following day. The captain of the Lord's host appeared to Joshua. *(Josh. 5.)*

The Lord had the Israelites march around Jericho once each day for six days—not making a sound—and then seven times on the seventh day, blowing their trumpets and shouting, and the walls of Jericho fell down. Only Rehab and her household were saved. *(Josh. 6.)*

The Lord allowed the people of Ai to defeat Israel because Achan, of the tribe of Judah, had kept some of the spoils from Jericho against the Lord's commandment. Joshua, puzzled that the Lord let them be defeated, inquired of the

Lord. The Lord told him Israel had sinned and how to find the offender. Achan and his household were destroyed. *(Josh. 7.)*

Joshua used an ambush and took Ai. He slew the inhabitants but kept the cattle and the spoil of the city as commanded by the Lord. He built an altar in Mount Ebal and read all the words of the law, the blessings and the cursings as written by Moses, to the people. *(Josh. 8.)*

The Gibeonites—a branch of the Hivites—using trickery, made a treaty with the Israelites so they would not destroy them. In making the treaty, Israel failed to ask counsel of the Lord. When they found out that the people were really the Hivites, they determined to honor their treaty. Nevertheless, the Hivites were told they would have to be servants to the congregation of Israel. *(Josh. 9.)*

Five kings of the Amorites united to fight against Israel. The Amorites were destroyed, partly by the sword, but mostly by hailstones which the Lord sent down upon them. The kings fled and hid in a cave at Makkedah. Joshua ordered his men to roll great stones upon the mouth of the cave so they could not get out. After the rest of the Amorites were destroyed, Joshua had the kings brought out to him. The people put their feet upon the necks of the kings and Joshua reminded his people, "for thus shall the Lord do to all your enemies against whom ye fight." Then "Joshua smote them and slew them and hanged them on five trees. . . until the evening." Their bodies were then taken down and cast into the cave wherein the kings had hidden themselves, and the entrance to the cave was sealed with a rock. *(Josh. 10.)*

Numerous other kings and their people banded together against Israel but the Lord was with Israel and they conquered the whole land, destroying many cities and nations. *(Josh. 11.)* The two kings on the east of Jordan and the 31 kings on the west of Jordan were all conquered. Their respective cities are listed. *(Josh. 12.)*

Joshua was old and stricken with years. The Lord said there was still a lot of land to be possessed. Some inhabitants, the Geshurites and Maachahites, had not been expelled but had been allowed to dwell among the Israelites. The inheritances of Reuben, Gad and half the tribe of Manasseh were confirmed. The tribe of Levi was not given an inheritance. *(Josh. 13.)* The land was divided and awarded by lot as the Lord commanded Moses. Caleb inherited Hebron as a special reward for faithfulness. Joshua was 40 years old when Moses sent him to spy out the land with the other spys. He was now 85 years old. *(Josh. 14.)*

After all the promised land had been divided and assigned by lot, the children of Israel gave Joshua Timnath-sera in mount Ephraim, which he requested for an inheritance. *(Josh. 19:49-50.)*

Joshua was now quite aged. He cautioned the people to be courageous, to keep the commandments, to love the Lord and not to marry the Canaanites who remained in the land. He reminded the children of Israel that when they serve other gods, they will be cursed and dispossessed of the lands of their inheritance. *(Josh. 23:1-16.)*

Joshua recounted with the children of Israel how the Lord had blessed and led Israel. He made a covenant with the people that they would follow the Lord. Joshua died and was buried in the border of his inheritance in Timnath-serah. He was 110 years old. *(Josh. 24.)*

Joshua the son of Nun was 110 years old when he died. *(Judg. 2:8.)*

Jehoshua (Joshua) the son of Non (Nun) was a seventh-great-grandson of Ephraim through Beriah. *(1 Chr. 7:27.)*

The children of Israel had not sat under booths since the days of **Jeshua** (Joshua) until the days of Ezra and Nehemiah. *(Neh. 8:17.)* (Chart 15d.)

JOSHUA (2). *1 Sam. 6:14, 19.*

Joshua was a Beth-shemite. The Philistines decided to return the ark of the Lord to Israel because they were being smitten and destroyed by the Lord. They brought it to the field of Joshua in Beth-shemesh and set it on the great stone of Abel which was in his field. Because the men looked into the ark, the Lord smote 50,070 men in Beth-shemesh.

JOSHUA (3). *2 Kgs. 23:8.*

Joshua was the governor of the city of Jerusalem when Josiah was king. Josiah destroyed the high places of the gates that were "in the entering in of the gate of Joshua."

JOSHUA (4). *Hag. 1:1.* See **Jeshua (4)**.

JOSIAH (1). *2 Kgs. 21:24; 22; 23; 1 Chr. 3:14; 2 Chr. 34; 35; 36:1; Jer. 1:2-5; 3:6; 22:11, 18, 24; 25; 26:1; 27:1; 35:1; 36:1; 37:1; 45:1; 46:2; Zeph. 1:1.*

Josiah (king over Judah from 641 to 610 B.C.) was the son of Amon. When Amon's servants killed Amon, the people rose up and slew those who had conspired against him. The people made Josiah king in his father's stead. *(2 Kgs. 21:24.)*

Josiah was eight years old when he became king over Judah. He reigned 31 years in Jerusalem and walked uprightly before the Lord. His mother was Jedidah. In the 18th year of his reign, he sent Shaphan to the high priest Hilkiah to ask him to give money to workmen to repair the house of the Lord. When Shaphan returned to Josiah with the book of the law which Hilkiah had found, he read it to the king. Josiah sorrowed because of the wickedness of the people and commanded Hilkiah, Ahikam, Achbor, Shaphan and Asahiah to inquire of the Lord concerning the book of the law and Judah. They inquired of the prophetess Huldah who prophesied wrath upon the people because of their wickedness. She prophesied blessings upon Josiah because of his righteousness. Josiah was told that the Lord would not bring His wrath upon the people until after Josiah died so he would not have to witness it. *(2 Kgs. 22; 2 Chr. 34:1-28.)*

Josiah read the book of the covenant to the people and they covenanted with the Lord to keep the commandments. He destroyed the objects related to Baal, overturned the worship of false gods, removed the Sodomites and destroyed the idolatrous priests. *(2 Kgs. 23:1-5; 2 Chr. 34:29-33.)* He commanded the people to keep the Passover. Never before nor after was there a king who so completely turned to the Lord with all his heart. *(2 Kgs. 23:21, 25.)* When Pharaoh-nechoh, king of Egypt, went to battle against the king of Assyria, Josiah went against him but was slain by Pharaoh-nechoh. His servants carried him back to Jerusalem where he was buried. His son Jehoahaz (Shallum) was anointed king in his stead. Three months later, his son Eliakim (Jehoiakim) was made king by Pharaoh-nechoh. Josiah's wife Hamutal was the mother of Jehoahaz. His wife Zebudah was the mother of Eliakim. *(2 Kgs. 23:29-37.)*

Josiah was the son of Amon and the father of Johanan, Jehoiakim (Eliakim), Zedekiah (Mattaniah) and Shallum (Jehoahaz). *(1 Chr. 3:14.)*

Josiah and all the people kept a solemn Passover; there had been none like it from the days of the prophet Samuel. When Necho, king of Egypt, went against the Assyrian king at Carchemish, Josiah went against Necho. Necho said he had no quarrel with Josiah and to turn away from war with him. However, Josiah didn't. He disguised himself and went to battle. He was wounded in battle by archers and died when he returned to Jerusalem. *(2 Chr. 35.)*

After Josiah's death, the people made his son Jehoahaz king in his stead. *(2 Chr. 36:1.)*

Josiah was in the 13th year of his reign as king of Judah when the Lord called Jeremiah to declare His word unto the nations. Jeremiah also declared the words of the Lord during the reign of Josiah's son Jehoiakim unto the end of the eleventh year of the reign of Josiah's son Zedekiah. *(Jer. 1:2-5.)*

Israel was "backsliding" into idolatry even in the days of Josiah when Jeremiah was called of the Lord to declare His word to the nations. *(Jer. 3:6.)*

Josiah's son Shallum (Jehoahaz) reigned briefly after his father. His son Jehoiakim (Eliakim) reigned after Shallum. Following Jehoiakim's reign, Jehoiakim's son Jehoiachin (Coniah) reigned. Because they all reigned in wickedness, Jeremiah pronounced the judgments of the Lord upon them and upon the rest of the kings of Judah. *(Jer. 22:11, 18, 24.)*

Jeremiah reminded the people that for 23 years—from the 13th year of Josiah's reign until the fourth year of Jehoiakim's reign—the Lord had sent him and other prophets to warn them to turn away from their evil ways, but they had refused. Thus, the condemnation of the Lord was upon them: they would be carried captive to Babylon where they would remain for 70 years. After that time, many heathen nations would be overthrown. Eventually, all the inhabitants of the earth would be at war. *(Jer. 25.)*

Josiah was the father of Jehoiakim. *(Jer. 26:1; 27:1; 35:1; 36:1.)*

Josiah was the father of Zedekiah (Mattaniah), whom Nebuchadnezzar made king in lieu of Coniah (Jeconiah, Jehoiachin). *(Jer. 37:1.)*

Josiah was the father of Jehoiakim. *(Jer. 45:1; 46:2.)*

Josiah, son of Amon, was king of Judah in the day Zephaniah prophesied against Judah. *(Zeph. 1:1.)* (Chart 1.)

JOSIAH (2). *Zech. 6:10-12.*

Josiah was the son of Zephaniah. Zechariah was instructed by the Lord to go into the house of Josiah and crown Joshua (Jeshua) the son of Josedech the high priest and say, "Behold the man whose name is The BRANCH . . . " *(Note: This was a similitude of crowning Christ, i.e., the BRANCH. The Bible Dictionary indicates that Jesus is another name for Joshua. See "Joshua.")*

JOSIBIAH. *1 Chr. 4:35.*

Josibiah, a descendant of Shimei was the father of Jehu and the son of Seraiah. (Chart 6a.)

JOSIPHIAH. *Ezra 8:10.*

Josiphiah was of the sons of Shelomith. His son was the leader of his posterity when Ezra led many exiled Israelites out of Babylon back to Jerusalem. He took 160 males with him.

JOTHAM (1). *Judg. 9:5-21.*

Jotham was Gideon's (Jerubbaal's) youngest son. When Abimelech slew his 70 brothers, Jotham hid himself. When he heard that the men of Shechem and the house of Millo had named Abimelech king, he told them a parabolic fable of trees choosing a king, and then he fled to Beer

JOTHAM (2). *2 Kgs. 15:5, 7, 32-38; 1 Chr. 3:12-13; 5:17; 2 Chr. 26:21-23; 27; Isa. 1:1-31; 7:1; Hosea 1:1, 6, 9; Micah 1:1.*

Jotham (king of Judah, 758-742 B.C.) was the son of king Azariah (Uzziah). He judged the people while his father was afflicted with leprosy. Upon Azariah's death, Jotham became king. He began his reign in the second year of Pekah's reign over Israel. He was 25 years old and reigned 16 years. His mother was Jerusha. He reigned in righteousness except that he did not remove the high places where the people sacrificed and burned incense. It was during this time that the Lord began to send Pekah and Rezin king of Syria against Judah to stir them up. Jotham died and was buried in the city of David. His son Ahaz reigned in his stead. *(2 Kgs. 15:5, 7, 32-38; 2 Chr. 26:21-23; 2 Chr. 27 is a repeat and expansion of 2 Kgs. 15:30-38.)*

Jotham was the son of Azariah and the father of Ahaz. *(1 Chr. 3:12-13.)*

The genealogies of Reuben and Gad were "reckoned" in the days of Jotham, king of Judah, and Jeroboam, king of Israel. *(1 Chr. 5:17.)*

(2 Chr. 27 is a repeat and expansion of 2 Kgs. 15:30-38.) Jotham built cities and castles and towers. He defeated the Ammonites and they paid him with silver, wheat and barley. But, his people behaved corruptly. He died and his son Ahaz reigned in his stead. *(2 Chr. 27.)*

Isaiah saw iin a vision that which concerned Judah and Jerusalem during the days of Jotham, Uzziah, Ahaz and Hezekiah, kings of Judah. Israel was in an apostate, rebellious and corrupt state. A very small remnant remained faithful. The Lord rejected their sacrifices and feasts. They were called upon to repent. Isaiah prophesied that Zion would be redeemed in the day of restoration. *(Isa. 1:1-31.)*

Jotham, son of Uzziah, was father of Ahaz. *(Isa. 7:1.)*

In the days of Jotham (son of Uzziah), Uzziah, Ahaz, and Hezekiah, kings of Judah, the Lord instructed Hosea to marry a wife from among those who committed whoredoms. He and his family were to be a sign unto Israel. The names of his children meant: "Not having obtained mercy," and "Not my people." While the Lord said He would no longer have mercy for the house of Israel, He said He would have mercy upon the house of Judah. *(Hosea 1:1, 6, 9.)*

In the days of Jotham, Ahaz and Hezekiah, Micah prophesied regarding that which he saw concerning Samaria and Jerusalem. *(Micah 1:1.)* (Chart 1.)

JOTHAM. *1 Chr. 2:47.*

Jotham was one of the sons of Jahdai. (Chart 8j.)

JOZABAD (1). *1 Chr. 12:20 (1-2, 20-23, 38).*

Jozabad was from the tribe of Manasseh and was a mighty man of valor, one of the captains in the host. He helped David against the band of rovers when David went to Ziklag. All Israel rejoiced when David became king. The armies were prepared to defend David against Saul and to turn the kingdom of Saul to him.

JOZABAD (2). *1 Chr. 12:20 (1-2, 20-23, 38).*

Jozabad was from the tribe of Manasseh and was a mighty man of valor, one of the captains in the host. He helped David against the band of rovers when David went to Ziklag. All Israel rejoiced when David became king. The armies were prepared to defend David against Saul and to turn the kingdom of Saul to him. *(Note: There are two separate people with the name Jozabad listed in 1 Chr. 12:20.)*

JOZABAD (3). *2 Chr. 31:13.*

Jozabad, under the hand of Cononiah and Cononiah's brother Shimei, was one of the overseers of tithes, offerings and the dedicated things according to the commandment of king Hezekiah and Azariah, the ruler of the house of God.

JOZABAD (4). *Ezra 8:33.*

Jozabad, a Levite, was the son of Jeshua. He was with Meremoth when the precious items that belonged in the temple and had been placed in the care of Sherebiah, Hashabiah and ten additional chief priests by Ezra were delivered to Meremoth.

JOZABAD (5). *Ezra 10:22 (18-19, 22, 44).*

Jozabad, one of the sons of Pashur, was among the sons of the priests who had taken foreign wives and who agreed to Ezra's request that they separate themselves from their strange wives.

JOZABAD (6). *Ezra 10:23 (18-19, 23, 44).*

Jozabad was one of the Levites who had taken wives from among the Canaanites or other foreign groups and who agreed to Ezra's request that they separate themselves from these strange wives lest the Lord destroy the rest of the children of Israel.

JOZABAD (7). *Neh. 8:7-8; 11:16.*

<u>Jozabad</u> was one of the men who, when Ezra read and interpreted the law of Moses to the people, helped the people to understand the law. *(Neh. 8:7-8.)*

Jozabad, of the chief of the Levites, along with Shabbethai, had oversight of the outward business of the house of God when the children of Israel returned to Jerusalem from Babylonian captivity. *(Neh. 11:16.)*

JOZACHAR (Zabad (2)). *2 Kgs. 12:21; 2 Chr. 24:26.*

<u>Jozachar</u> was the son of Shimeath. He and Jehozabad the son of Shomer, a fellow servant to king Joash, conspired against the king and slew him. *(2 Kgs. 12:21.)*

Zabad's (Jozachar's) mother was Shimeath. *(2 Chr. 24:26 is a repeat of 2 Kgs. 12:21.)*

JOZADAK (Josedech). *Ezra 3:2; 10:18-19, 44; Neh. 12:26; Hag. 1:1, 12, 14; 2:2, 4.*

<u>Jozadak</u> was the father of Jeshua which Jeshua returned to Jerusalem to rebuild the temple at the command of Cyrus. *(Ezra 3:2.) (Note: Jozadak is probably the same as Jehozadak, i.e., Ezra.)*

Jozadak was the father of Jeshua whose sons took strange wives, but agreed to put away their wives. *(Ezra 10:18-19, 44.)*

Jozadak was the father of Jeshua and the grandfather of Joiakim. The porters in the days of Jeshua, Nehemiah and Ezra are listed. *(Neh. 12:26.)*

Josedech (Jozadak) was the father of Joshua (Jeshua) the high priest. *(Hag. 1:1, 12, 14.)*

Josedech was the father of Joshua. *(Hag. 2:2, 4.)* (Chart 7b., "Jehozadak")

JUBAL. *Gen. 4:21.*

<u>Jubal</u> was one of the sons born to Lamech and Adah. He was the father of all who play the harp and organ. (Chart 1.)

JUCAL (Jehucal).

JUDAH (1). *Gen. 29:35; 37-38; 42-44; 45:1; 46:12; 49:1, 8-12; 50:8; Ex. 31:2-3; Num. 1:7, 26-27; 2:2-9; 26:22; 34:19; Deut. 27:12; 33:7; 1 Chr. 2:3-4; 4:1; 12:24; 27:18; 28:4; 2 Chr. 11:1-11; 17:14-16; 30:12; Ezra 1:5; Neh. 11:24; 13:10-12; Ps. 78:67-70; Jer. 40:5-7, 11; 41:3; 42-44; 50:4-8, 17-20, 33-34; 51:5-6, 19-23; Ezek. 8:17; 9:4, 9; 27:17; 48:7, 31; Dan. 9:7; Hosea 1; 4:15; 5; 6:4-6; 8; 10:11; 11:12; 12:2, 10; Joel 3; Amos 2:4-5; Micah 1:1; 5:2; Nahum 1:15; Zeph. 2:4-7; Zech.2:4-5, 12; 7; 10; 12-14; Mal. 2:11-17; 3:1, 4.*

<u>Judah</u> was the fourth son of Jacob and Leah. *(Gen. 29:35.)* Judah and his brothers hated their younger brother Joseph. They thought to kill him as he approached them in the fields. However, Reuben, the eldest son, suggested casting him into a pit (where he hoped to rescue him later). When a group of Ishmeelites, or Midianite merchantmen, approached, Judah suggested selling Joseph to them. This they did—for 20 pieces of silver. Then they dipped his coat of many colors in

animal blood and gave it to their father so he would think Joseph had been killed by wild beasts. *(Gen. 37.)*

Judah departed from his brothers and visited an Adullamite whose name was Hirah. While there, he married a Canaanite daughter named Shuah (Shua). She bore three children: Er, Onan and Shelah. He chose a wife, Tamar, for his firstborn son, Er. When Er died, Judah told his second son, Onan, to marry Tamar and raise up seed unto his brother. However, Onan did not desire to do that so when he "went in unto his brother's wife, that he spilled it on the ground." This displeased the Lord, wherefore He slew Onan. When Onan died, Judah suggested to Tamar that she remain a widow at her father's home until Shelah was old enough to marry her. Time passed and Shuah, Judah's wife, died. Judah was comforted and went unto his sheepshearers with his friend Hirah. His daughter-in-law, Tamar, posed as a harlot beside the road. Judah saw her and, not knowing who she was, asked to come in unto her. She agreed on certain conditions: that he would send her a kid from his flock; and that until he sent the kid, he would leave his signet, bracelets and staff with her for a pledge. Judah lay with her and she conceived. Three months later, Judah was informed that his daughter-in-law was with child. He told them to bring her forth to be burned. When she came to him, Tamar said the father of the child was the man whose signet, bracelets and staff she had. Judah recognized them as his and declared that she was more righteous than he because he had failed to give his son Shelah to her for a husband. He didn't lay with her any more. She bore twins: Pharez and Zarah. *(Gen. 38.)*

When the famine came, all of Joseph's brothers, with the exception of Benjamin, were sent by Jacob to Egypt to buy corn. Judah and his brothers were accused by Joseph of being spies and were instructed to bring Benjamin back to Egypt to prove that they were not spies. They were required to leave Simeon as a hostage to guarantee they would return. As they journeyed home, they discovered their money in their sacks and were afraid. Jacob would not let them take Benjamin back to Egypt. *(Gen. 42.)*

As the famine continued, Jacob instructed his sons to return to Egypt to purchase more corn. They refused, and Judah, acting as spokesman for his brothers, said they would not go unless they could take Benjamin, too. Jacob finally consented. When they got to Egypt, Joseph had his brothers taken to his house and had a feast prepared for them. To their astonishment, they were seated by age—oldest to youngest. *(Gen. 43.)*

When the brothers prepared to return to Egypt, Joseph had his steward hide a silver cup in Benjamin's sack. As they traveled, the steward was sent after them to accuse them of stealing the cup. They denied the charge; and Judah said that if it should be found among them, the person who had taken it should be put to death. When it was found in Benjamin's sack, Judah pleaded with them to take him instead of Benjamin, as it would kill their father if he lost Benjamin after having lost Joseph. *(Gen. 44.)*

Joseph finally revealed himself to his brothers. *(Gen. 45:1.)*

Judah begat Er, Onan, Shelah, Pharez and Zerah (Zarah). *(Gen. 46:12.)*

After the brothers had gone to Egypt for grain and were finally reunited with Joseph, and following the move of their entire family to Egypt, the time came when Jacob called his sons together to tell them what would befall each of them in the last days. Jacob told Judah that his brethren would praise him and his hand would be in the neck of his enemies. His father's children would bow down before him. The sceptre would not depart from Judah, "nor a lawgiver from between his feet, until Shiloh (Christ) come; and unto him shall the gathering of the people be." *(Gen. 49:1, 8-12.)*

Judah and his brothers all went together to transport Jacob's body to Canaan for burial. *(Gen. 50:8.)*

Judah's descendant, Bezaleel, was an artisan who was inspired of God in wisdom, understanding and knowledge, "and in all manner of workmanship" so as to work on the building and furnishing of the tabernacle Moses was instructed to have built while the children of Israel were in the wilderness. *(Ex. 31:2-3.)*

Moses was instructed to appointed one person to lead each of the tribes of Israel The Lord told him to appoint Nahshon, son of Amminadab, to head the tribe of Judah. Moses was further instructed to number all the males in each tribe who were 20 years old or older. The tribe of Judah numbered 74,600. *(Num. 1:7, 26-27.)*

The camp of Judah was assigned to pitch their tents on the east side "far off about the tabernacle of the congregation." Next to them was the tribe of Issachar with 54,400 men, and next to them was the tribe of Zebulun with 57,400. Combined, the camp of Judah had 186,400 men. *(Num. 2:2-9.)*

While on the plains of Moab near Jericho, Moses and Eleazar were instructed to count all the males, excluding the Levites, who were 20 years old and older. The family of Judah numbered 76,500. *(Num. 26:22.)*

The land of inheritance given to the tribe of Judah was to be divided by Caleb the son of Jephunneh. *(Num. 34:19.)*

As the Israelites prepared to cross over Jordan, the tribes of Judah, Simeon, Levi, Issachar, Joseph and Benjamin were to stand upon mount Gerizim to bless the people. *(Deut. 27:12.)*

Moses blessed the tribe of Judah. *(Deut. 33:7.)*

Judah's descendants are listed. He had five sons: three—Er, Onan and Shelah—by Shua (Shuah) the Canaanitess and two—Pharez and Zerah (Zarah)—by Tamar, his daughter-in-law. *(1 Chr. 2:3-4.)*

Judah's descendants are again named. Judah begat Pharez, who begat Hezron, who begat Carmi (Caleb), who begat Hur who begat Shobal. *(1 Chr. 4:1.)*

When David became king and went to Ziklag, all Israel rejoiced and sent their armies to support him. The tribe of Judah sent 6,800 men. *(1 Chr. 12:24.)*

Elihu, one of David's brethren, was prince of the tribe of Judah when David was king. *(1 Chr. 27:18.)*

David reminded Solomon and the people that the Lord had chosen the house of Judah to be the ruler over Israel. *(1 Chr. 28:4.)*

The houses of Judah and Benjamin went with Rehoboam when Rehoboam became king upon Solomon's death and the kingdom became divided. The rest of the house of Israel went with Jeroboam. The priests and Levites and all who wished to worship the God of Israel eventually returned to Rehoboam. *(2 Chr. 11:1-11.)*

When Jehoshaphat was king of Judah the following from the house of Judah served as the captains of thousands: Adnah was over 300,000 men, Jehohanan was over 280,000 men, and Amasiah the son of Zichri was over 200,000 men. *(2 Chr. 17:14-16.)*

When Hezekiah was king of Judah, he sent couriers throughout the land inviting the people to come to Jerusalem to participate in a solemn Passover. While many of the house of Israel scorned and mocked the couriers, "in Judah the hand of God was to give them one heart to do the commandment of the king and of the princes, by the word of the Lord." *(2 Chr. 30:12.)*

When Cyrus, king of Persia, proclaimed the building of the temple in Jerusalem, he called for those who were of God's people to go up and build the temple. The chief of the fathers of Judah and Benjamin, the priests and the Levites, rose up to go build the house of the Lord. *(Ezra 1:5.)*

Judah's descendant, Pethahiah, son of Meshezabeel of the children of Zerah, was at the king's hand in all matters concerning the children of Israel after they returned from Babylonian captivity to Jerusalem and the other cities. *(Neh. 11:24.)*

Nehemiah discovered that the Levites and the singers who were supposed to be caring for the house of God had fled to the fields because they were not receiving the portions that should have been given them. After being chastised, all Judah brought tithes of corn, new wine and oil into the treasuries. *(Neh. 13:10-12.)*

The Lord chose the tribe of Judah, "the mount Zion which he loved," over the tribe of Ephraim, and chose David to be his servant. *(Ps. 78:67-70.)*

When the children of Israel were carried off captive to Babylon by Nebuchadnezzar, Gedaliah was made governor over the remnant of the Jews left in Judah. Those who were left were the poor of the land. The Jews who were in the surrounding areas came to Gedaliah in the land of Judah. *(Jer. 40:5-7, 11.)*

The Jews who remained in Mizpah when Nebuchadnezzar carried the rest of the children of Israel off captive to Babylon were slain by Ishmael after he slew Gedaliah. *(Jer. 41:3.)*

The remnant of Judah was promised peace and safety if they stayed in Judah; but if they went to Egypt, "none of them shall remain or escape" from the destruction by sword, famine and pestilence promised by the Lord. *(Jer. 42.)*

Johanan the son of Kareah (Careah) and Azariah (Jaazaniah) the son of Hoshaiah and all the "proud men" refused to believe the prophet Jeremiah, so the remnant of Judah and all the people Nebuzar-adan had left with Gedaliah were carried into Egypt. *(Jer. 43.)*

Because the remnant of Judah who went to dwell in Egypt worshipped false gods, Jeremiah prophesied that all but a few who would escape would be destroyed just as Jerusalem had been destroyed: by sword, famine and pestilence; and the king of Egypt, Pharaoh-hophra, would be delivered into the hands of his enemies just as Zedekiah, king of Judah, had been delivered into the hands of his enemies. *(Jer. 44.)*

Jeremiah prophesied that scattered Israel would eventually be gathered and restored to her inheritance. "In those days, and in that time, saith the Lord, the iniquity of Israel shall be sought for, and there shall be none; and the sins of Judah, and they shall not be found: for I will pardon them whom I reserve." *(Jer.50:4-8, 17-20, 33-34.)*

Judah and Israel have not been forsaken. The Lord told both Judah and Israel to flee from Babylon. They will be instruments in His hands by which He will accomplish His word. *(Jer. 51:5-6, 19-23.)*

The prophet Ezekiel was shown in a vision the wickedness and abominations of the house of Judah in Jerusalem and their idol worship, even in the house of the Lord. *(Ezek. 8:17.)*

Ezekiel saw in vision the identifying of the righteous and the destruction of the wicked of the house of Judah. *(Ezek. 9:4, 9.)*

As Ezekiel lamented the fall of the great city of Tyrus, he bemoaned the loss of her riches and commerce, part of which involved the merchants of Judah and the land of Israel, who traded in wheat, honey, oil and balm. *(Ezek. 27:17.)*

The Lord revealed to Ezekiel just how the land should be divided by tribes when the children of Israel are gathered in the latter days. Judah's border will abut the borders of Reuben and Levi. The twelve gates of the city are to bear the names of the twelve sons of Jacob. Judah's name will be upon one of the three northward gates. *(Ezek. 48:7, 31.)*

In the first year of the reign of Darius over the Chaldeans, Daniel fasted and prayed and confessed the sins of Israel, acknowledging that the men of Judah, the inhabitants of Jerusalem and all Israel had trespassed against the Lord and, thus, were in a state of confusion. *(Dan. 9:7.)*

During the days of Uzziah, Jotham, Ahaz, and Hezekiah, kings of Judah, and Jeroboam, king of Israel, the Lord told Hosea and his family they were to be a sign unto Israel. His wife Gomer was chosen from among those who committed whoredoms, and his daughter was named Lo-ruhamah, which means, "Not having obtained mercy." His son was named Lo-ammi, which means, "Not my people." While the Lord said He would have no more mercy for the house of Israel, He said He would have mercy for the house of Judah; and, in the last days, the children of Israel and the children of Judah will be gathered together under one head and they will become the sons of the living God. *(Hosea 1.)*

Hosea counseled Judah not to offend, while at the same time he chastised Israel for playing the role of a harlot. *(Hosea 4:15.)*

Hosea prophesied that Judah, Israel and Ephraim would fall because of iniquity. *(Hosea 5.)*

The Lord chastised Judah and said, ". . . your goodness is as a morning cloud, and as the early dew it goeth away." God desired mercy more than sacrifice and knowledge of Him more than burnt offerings. *(Hosea 6:4-6.)*

Hosea continued to recite the Lord's condemnation of Judah, Israel and Ephraim and prophesied against them. They had forsaken the Lord. Judah had multipled fenced cities, but the Lord said He would send fire upon the cities and the fire would destroy the palaces therein. *(Hosea 8.)*

The Lord's rebuke of Judah, Ephraim and Jacob continues. *(Hosea 10:11.)*

Hosea chastised Israel and Ephraim but said, "Judah yet ruleth with God, and is faithful with the saints." *(Hosea 11:12.)*

The Lord will punish Judah and Jacob for their sins. The people were taught and knew that the Lord speaks through prophets and uses visions and similitudes to teach His people. When the people become rich, they turn from the Lord. *(Hosea 12:2, 10.)*

Joel prophesied that in the latter days, the Lord will gather Judah and Jerusalem and plead for his people Israel. Judah and Jerusalem have been "sold" unto the Grecians, but in the latter days the children of their captors shall be delivered unto Judah and they will "sell them to the Sabeans." *(Joel 3.)*

Amos prophesied the Lord would pour out judgments against Judah, Israel and Moab because of their trangressions: the Lord would send fire upon Judah and burn the palaces of Jerusalem. *(Amos 2:4-5.)*

Micah prophesied in the days of Jotham, Ahaz and Hezekiah, kings of Judah, regarding the downfall of Jerusalem and Samaria. *(Micah 1:1.)*

Micah prophesied that the Savior would be born in Bethlehem of the lineage of Judah. *(Micah 5:2.) (Note: This prophesy was fulfilled with the birth of Christ. See Matthew 1:1-16.)*

Nahum cried unto Judah to keep their solemn feasts and to perform their vows because when the Lord comes in glory the wicked will not pass through Judah again. *(Nahum 1:15.)*

The prophet Zephaniah urged the people to seek righteousness and meekness, and prophesied the fall of Ashkelon, Ashdod, Ekron, the Cherethithes and the Philistines but, he said, the coasts shall be for the remnant of the house of Judah. *(Zeph. 2:4-7.)*

Zechariah prophesied that, in the latter days, Judah will be gathered and Jerusalem shall be inhabited without walls so numerous will be the people. They will be gathered from the land of the north. The Lord will dwell in the midst of them. *(Zech.2:4-5, 12.)*

In the fourth year of Darius' reign, Zechariah was sent to reprove the people for their hypocrisy. He told the people to execute judgment; to show mercy and have compassion one to another; not to oppress the widow, the fatherless, the stranger not the poor; but the people would not hear the Lord's cries unto them so He did not hear their cries unto Him and scattered the people among the nations. *(Zech. 7.)*

Zechariah prophesied that the Lord would sow Judah and Joseph among the people in far countries. Nevertheless, the Lord will "hiss" for them, and gather them, because He has redeemed them. He will bring them again out of Egypt and gather them out of Assyria and place them in the land of Gilead and Lebanon. *(Zech. 10.)*

When the Lord comes again, He will destroy all the nations that come against Judah and Jerusalem. He will open His eyes upon Judah. The governor of Judah will be like "an hearth of fire among the wood, and like a torch of fire in a sheaf." *(Zech. 12:6).* The Lord shall save the tents of Judah first. *(Zech. 12:7.)*

Zechariah prophesied that when the Savior comes again, the Jews shall be forgiven. They will ask Him about the wounds in His hands. He will respond that they are the wounds He received in the house of His friends *(Zech. 13:6).* The remnant of the house of Israel will be tried and refined and shall be the Lord's people. *(Zech. 13:9.)*

Zechariah prophesied that at the Second Coming all nations shall be gathered in battle against Jerusalem. As Jerusalem is losing the war, the Lord will go forth and fight for Israel. The wicked shall be destroyed by plague. *(Zech. 14.)*

Malachi reproved Judah for marrying idol worshippers and for not being faithful to their wives. *(Mal. 2:11-17.)*

Malachi prophesied that prior to the Second Coming, the Lord would send His messenger to prepare the way. The Lord will come suddenly to His temple. He will accept the offering of Judah and Jerusalem. *(Mal. 3:1, 4.)* (Charts 1.; 3d., 5a.; 6a.; 7a.; 8a-d, g-h, m-o.; 9a.; 10a.; 11a.; 12a.; 13a.; 14a.; 15a.; 16a.)

JUDAH (2). *Ezra 10:23 (18-19, 23, 44); Neh. 12:8.*

Judah was one of the Levites who had taken wives from among the Canaanites or other foreign groups and who agreed to Ezra's request that they separate themselves from these strange wives lest the Lord destroy the rest of the children of Israel. *(Ezra 10:23 [18-19, 23, 44].)*

Judah and his brethren are listed among those Levites who went up from Babylon with Zerubbabel to Jerusalem. *(Neh. 12:8.)*

JUDAH (3). *Neh. 11:9.*

Judah, son of Senuah, was elected by lot to be second in command over the people of Benjamin who dwelled in Jerusalem following their release from captivity in Babylon. (Chart 16m.)

JUDAH (4). *Neh. 12:34.*

Judah and others, along with Hoshaiah and half of the princes of Judah, were appointed by Nehemiah to one of the two great companies of people gathered for the dedication of the walls of Jerusalem. This company went on the right hand toward the dung gate.

JUDAH (5). *Neh. 12:36.*

Judah was among the sons of the priests who joined Zechariah, a descendant of Asaph, and other of his brethren with their musical instruments in the dedication of the wall of Jerusalem. *(Note: Reference is made to two separate individuals named Judah in verses 34 and 36.)*

JUDITH. *Gen. 26:34.*

Judith was a daughter of Beeri the Hittite. She married Esau when he was 40 years old. This grieved Rebekah, Esau's mother. (Chart 3c.)

JUSHABHESED. *1 Chr. 3:20.*

Jushabhesed, a descendant of David, was a son of Shelomith, the daughter of Zerubbabel. His brothers were Hashubah, Ohel, Berechiah and Hasadiah. (Chart 1.)

NAMES THAT BEGIN WITH "K"

KADMIEL. *Ezra 2:40; Ezra 3:9; Neh. 7:43; Neh. 9; Neh. 10:9 (1, 9, 28-31); Neh. 12:8, 24.*

Kadmiel was a Levite. He and Jeshua were of the children of Hodaviah (Hodevah). Their children numbered 74 when they left Babylon to go to Jerusalem to build the house of the Lord as proclaimed by Cyrus, king of Persia. *(Ezra 2:40; Neh. 7:43.)*

Kadmiel and his sons, the sons of Judah, and Jeshua with his sons and brethren, set forward the workmen in the house of God: the sons of Henadad with their sons and their brethren the Levites. *(Ezra 3:9.)*

The Levites—Kadmiel, Jeshua, Bani, Shebaniah, Bunni, Sherebiah, Bani, Chenani, Hashabniah, Hodijah (probably the same as Hodevah, Hodaviah) and Pethahiah—blessed and praised the Lord, reciting the Lord's goodness to Israel: the blessing of Abraham; giving the land of the Canaanites, Hittites, Amorites, Perizzites, Jebusites and Girgashites to Israel; dividing the Red Sea so they could cross it yet drowning the Egyptians who pursued them; the signs and wonders shown to Pharaoh; leading them in the wilderness and protecting them so that they had bread from heaven, water from the rock, and shoes and clothes that never wore out; accepting them whenever they repented, even when they made a molten calf. They had been given the kingdoms of Shihon, Heshbon and Bashan and the Lord had subdued the Canaanites and delivered them into the hands of the Israelites. After giving praise, they made a covenant with the Lord. The princes, Levites and priests sealed the covenant. *(Neh. 9.)*

Kadmiel was among the Levites who covenanted and sealed their covenant to marry in Israel, honor the Sabbath, pay tithes and keep the commandments. *(Neh. 10:9 [1, 9, 28-31].)*

Kadmiel and his brethren are listed among those Levites who went up from Babylon with Zerubbabel to Jerusalem. Kadmiel was the father of Jeshua. *(Neh. 12:8, 24.)*

KADMONITES. *Gen. 15:19-21.*

The **Kadmonites'** lands were among those given to Abram's seed by the Lord in covenant.

KALLAI. *Neh. 12:20.*

Kallai, son of Sallai, was one of the priests who was a chief of the fathers in the days of Joiakim.

KAREAH. See **Careah**.

KEDAR. *Gen. 25:13; Isa. 21:16-17; 42:11; Jer. 49:28-29; Ezek. 27:21.*

Kedar was a son of Ishmael and a grandson of Abraham and Hagar, Sarah's handmaid. *(Gen. 25:13.)*

Isaiah prophesied the cataclysmic destruction of Babylon, which occured in 538 B.C. In his prophecy, he indicated that all the glory of Kedar would fail and that the "residue of the number of archers, the mighty men of the children of Kedar, shall be diminished." *(Isa. 21:16-17.)*

Isaiah referred to the Messiah and the Second Coming and said, "Let the wilderness and the cities thereof lift up their voice, the villages that Kedar doth inhabit: let the inhabitants of the rock sing, let them shout from the top of the mountains." *(Isa. 42:11.)*

Jeremiah prophesied the destruction that would befall Kedar. *(Jer. 49:28-29.)*

As Ezekiel lamented the fall of the great city of Tyrus, he bemoaned the loss of her riches and commerce, part of which involved the merchants of Arabia and all the princes of Kedar who traded lambs, rams and goats in the fairs of Tyrus. *(Ezek. 27:21.)* (Chart 3e.)

KEDEMAH (Nodab). *Gen. 25:15; 1 Chr. 5:19.*

Kedemah was a son of Ishmael and a grandson of Abraham and Hagar, Sarah's handmaid. *(Gen. 25:15.)*

The Reubenites, Gadites and half the tribe of Manasseh went to war against the Hagarites, against Jetur, Nephish and **Nodab** (Kedemah). *(1 Chr. 5:19.) (Note: The last three sons of Ishmael are given in Gen. 25:15 as Jetur, Naphish and Kedemah. In this verse it lists them as Jetur, Nephish and Nodab. It would appear that Kedemah and Nodab are one and the same.)* (Chart 3e.)

KEEPER OF THE PRISON, CAPTAIN OF THE GUARD. *Gen. 39:21-23.*

The **Keeper of the Prison** put Joseph in charge of the prisoners

KEEPERS OF THE DOOR. *2 Kgs. 23:4; 25:18-21.*

The **Keepers of the Door**, Hilkiah the high priest, and the priests of the second order were commanded by king Josiah to bring all the objects related to Baal out of the temple and to destroy them. *(2 Kgs. 23:4.)*

Three of the keepers of the door, along with Zeraiah the chief priest, Zephaniah the second priest, the principal scribe and several other men, were captured by Nebuzar-adan, captain of Nebechadnezzar's guard, and taken to Nebechadnezzar who then slew them. *(2 Kgs. 25:18-21.)*

KEILAH. *1 Chr. 4:19.*

Keilah was a Garmite and the son of Naham (probably). *(Note: It is not clear if Keilah was the son of Naham or of Naham's sister Hodiah.)*

KELAIAH (Kelita). *Ezra 10:23 (18-19, 23, 44); Neh. 8:7-8; 10:10 (1, 10, 28-31).*

Kelaiah (Kelita) was one of the Levites who had taken wives from among the Canaanites or other foreign groups and who agreed to Ezra's request that they separate themselves from these strange wives lest the Lord destroy the rest of the children of Israel. *(Ezra 10:23 [18-19, 23, 44].)*

Kelita was one of the men who, when Ezra read and interpreted the law of Moses to the people, helped the people to understand the law. *(Neh. 8:7-8.)*

Kelita was among those Levites who covenanted and sealed their covenant to marry in Israel, honor the Sabbath, pay tithes and keep the commandments. *(Neh. 10:10 [1, 10, 28-31].)*

KEMUEL (1). *Gen. 22:21-23.*

Kemuel was a brother to Huz and Buz, a son of Nahor and Milcah, and the father of Aram. Other brothers included Chesed, Hazo, Pildash, Jidlaph and Bethuel, the father of Rebekah. (Chart 2c.)

KEMUEL (2). *Num. 34:24.*

Kemuel was the son of Shiphtan and was of the tribe of Ephraim. He was assigned to divide the land of their inheritance among Ephraim's posterity. (Chart 15e.)

KEMUEL (3). *1 Chr. 27:17.*

Kemuel was the father of Hashabiah, prince of the tribe of Levi at the time of king David.

KENAZ (1). *Gen. 36:11, 15, 42.*

Kenaz was a son of Eliphaz, son of Adah and Esau. He was a duke or tribal chief. His brothers were Teman, Omar, Zepho, Gatam and Amalek (the son of Timna, Esau's concubine). (Charts 3b.; 19.)

KENAZ (2). *Josh. 15:17; Judg. 1:13; 1 Chr. 4:13.*

Kenaz , of the house of Judah, was the father of Othniel and was the younger brother of Caleb. *(Josh. 15:17; Judg. 1:13.)*

Kenaz was the father of Othniel and Seraiah. *(1 Chr. 4:13.)* (Chart 8k.)

KENAZ (3). *1 Chr. 4:15.*

Kenaz was the son of Elah and the grandson of Caleb son of Jephunneh of the house of Judah. (Chart 8n.)

KENITES. *Gen. 15:19-21; Num. 24:22; Judg. 1:16; 4:11, 17; 5:24; 1 Sam. 15:6; 27:10; 30:29; 1 Chr. 2:55.*

The **Kenites'** and other "ites" lands were given to Abram's seed by the Lord in covenant. *(Gen. 15:19-21.)*

Balaam prophesied of the destiny of Israel and said "the Kenite shall be wasted, until Asshur shall carry thee away captive." *(Num. 24:22.)*

Moses' father-in-law Jethro was a Kenite. *(Judg. 1:16.)*

Heber the Kenite was of the children of Hobab the father-in-law of Moses. *(Note: Hobab was Moses' brother-in-law, not his father-in-law. See Num. 10:29.)* Heber's wife Jael slew Sisera. *(Judg. 4:11, 17.)*

Deborah and Barak sang a song of praise and especially praised Jael. *(Judg. 5:24.)*

Saul spared the Kenites when he went against the Amalekites because they had shown kindness to the children of Israel when they came up out of Egypt. *(1 Sam. 15:6.)*

David raided the Kenites, Jerahmeelites and the south of Judah. *(1 Sam. 27:10.)*

David divided the spoils he had taken from the Kenites and the other cities with his friends and the elders of Judah. *(1 Sam. 30:29.)*

The Kenites came of Hemath, the father of Rechab and included the Tirathites, Shimeathites and Suchathites. These were the families of the scribes which dwelt at Jabez. *(1 Chr. 2:55.)*

KENIZZITES. *Gen. 15:19-21.*

The **Kenizzites**' lands were given to Abram's seed by the Lord in covenant.

KEREN-HAPPUCH. *Job 42:14.*

Keren-happuch was Job's third daughter following his trials when the Lord gave him twice as much as he had had earlier. Her sisters were Jemima and Kezia.

KEROS. *Ezra 2:44, 58; Neh. 7:47, 60.*

Keros was a Nethinim. When the Nethinims and the children of Solomon's servants left Babylon to return to Jerusalem to build the house of the Lord as proclaimed by Cyrus, king of Persia, they numbered 392.

KETURAH. *Gen. 25:1-4; 1 Chr. 1:32-33.*

Keturah was the wife Abraham took after Sarah's death. She bore the following children: Zimran, Jokshan, Medan, Midian, Ishbak and Shuah. Jokshan begat Sheba and Dedan. Dedan begat Asshurim, Letushim and Leummim. Midian begat Ephah, Epher, Hanoch (Henoch), Abida and Eldaah. These were all called the children of Keturah. *(Note: Gen. 25:1 says Abraham married Keturah after Sarah died. 1 Chr. 1:32 refers to Keturah as Abraham's concubine.)* (Charts 3a, d, f.)

KEZIA. *Job 42:14.*

Kezia was Job's second daughter following his trials when the Lord gave him twice as much as he had had earlier. Her sisters were Jemima and Keren-happuch.

KING MAACAH (Maachah, Maoch). *1 Sam. 27:2; 2 Sam. 10:6-8; 1 Kgs. 2:39; 1 Chr. 19:7-10.*

King Maacah (Maoch), king of Gath, was the father of Achish. *(1 Sam. 27:2.)*

King **Maacah** joined his forces with the children of Ammon when David went against Hanun for abusing his servants whom he had sent to comfort Hanun upon the death of his father Nahash. *(2 Sam. 10:6-8; 1 Chr. 19:7-10.)*

Maachah (Maacah, Maoch), king of Gath, was the father of Achish. *(1 Kgs. 2:39.)*

KING OF AI. *Josh. 8:23-29.*

The **King of ai** was captured by Israel, taken to Joshua and then hung. Earlier, the Lord had allowed the city of Ai to defeat a stronger group of Israelites because Achan had kept some of the spoils from Jerusalem contrary to His commandment. *(See Josh. 7).*

KING OF DEBIR. *Josh. 10:38-39.*

The **King of Debir** was defeated by Joshua; and Joshua smote him just as he had the king of Hebron and the king of Libnah.

KING OF GRECIA. *Dan. 8:21; 10:1, 13, 20.*

The **King of Grecia** was represented as a he goat in a vision Daniel had. According to the interpretation of the vision, in the latter days, Grecia will destroy Media and Persia. *(Dan. 8:21.)*

Daniel was given a vision in the third year of Cyrus' reign as king of Persia, in which he saw the Lord and others. The Lord told Daniel that "the prince of the kingdom of Persia withstood me one and twenty days: but, lo, Michael *(the arch-angel [See Adam])*, one of the chief princes, came to help me; and I remained there with the kings of Persia." He also said, " . . . and now will I return to fight with the prince of Persia: and when I am gone forth, lo, the prince of Grecia shall come." *(Dan. 10:1, 13, 20.)*

KING OF JERICHO. *Josh. 2:2-3; 6:17.*

The **King of Jericho** heard that two Israelite spies had entered Jericho and he sent word to Rahab to send the men out. When she said they had gone out the gate, he sent men to search for them. *(Josh. 2:2-3.)*

The king of Jericho and all the inhabitants of the city, except Rahab and her family, were killed when Joshua and the children of Israel caused the walls of Jericho to fall. *(Josh. 6:17.)*

KING OF LIBNAH. *Josh. 10:29-30.*

The **King of Libnah** and his people were destroyed by Joshua just as the king of Jericho and his people had been slain and destroyed.

KING OF MAKKEDAH. *Josh. 10:28.*

The **King of Makkedah** was slain and his people destroyed just as the king of Jericho was slain and his people destroyed.

KING OF MOAB. *1 Sam. 22:3-4.*

The **King of Moab** allowed David to bring his parents to Mizpeh to live until David knew what the Lord would have him do.

KING OF NINEVAH. *Jonah 3.*

The **King of Ninevah** heard about Jonah's prophecy that Ninevah would be overthrown in 40 days and repented, instructing his people to repent and fast and pray that the Lord might turn away His anger and not destroy them. Because of this, the Lord did not destroy Ninevah.

KING OF THE CHILDREN OF AMMON. *Judg. 11:12-33.*

The **King of the Children of Ammon** claimed Israel had taken away their land and he requested that Israel return it. When Jephthah refused, saying the king and his people possess the lands their god Chemosh gives them and, likewise, Israel will possess the land their God gives to them, the king made war against Israel. However, he and his people were defeated "with a very great slaughter."

KING OF TYRUS. *Ezek. 28:2-19.*

The **King of Tyrus** (or Tyre) was successful and wealthy, and the Lord said he was wiser than Daniel. However, he became proud and thought of himself as God so the Lord had Ezekiel prophesy the fall and destruction of Tyrus.

KING'S DAUGHTERS. *Jer. 41:10; 43:6.*

The **King's Daughters** *(i.e., Zedekiah's daughters)*, who had been left in Mizpah under the governorship of Gedaliah and not carried captive into Babylon by Nebuchadnezzar, were carried away captive by Ishmael after he and his cohorts slew Gedaliah. They, along with the rest of the captives, were rescued by Johanan the son of Kareah (Careah) and taken to Chimham near Beth-lehem preparatory to entering Egypt. *(Jer. 41:10.)*

Because Johanan and his captains did not believe the prophecy of Jeremiah when he said they would have peace and safety in Judah but would be destroyed if they went to live in Egypt, the king's daughters and all the other people who had been left with Gedaliah went to dwell in Egypt. *(Jer. 43:6.)*

KING'S SCRIBE AND THE HIGH PRIEST('S OFFICER). *2 Kgs. 12:10; 2 Chr. 24:11.*

The **King's Scribe and the High Priest('S Officer)** took the money found in the house of the Lord and gave it to the workmen so they could repair the house of the Lord as directed by king Jehoash (Joash).

KIR. *Isa. 22:6.*

Kir and Elam will attack and scourge Jerusalem. "And Elam bare the quiver . . . and Kir uncovered the shield." *(Note: There is no further indication as to Kir's identity.)*

KIRJATH-JEARIM (1). *1 Chr. 2:50-53.*

Kirjath-jearim was the son of Shobal the son of Hur and great-grandson of Caleb and Ephratah. (Chart 8 1.)

KIRJATH-JEARIM (2). *Jer. 26:20.*

Kirjath-jearim. *(Note: It is not clear if this Kirjath-jearim is a person or a place. Shemaiah, father of the prophet Urijah, was "of Kirjath-jearim.")*

KISH (1). *1 Sam. 9:1-2; 14:51; 1 Chr. 8:30-33; 9:35-39.*

Kish, a Benjamite, was the father of Saul and the son of Abiel. *(1 Sam. 9:1-2.)*

Kish was the father of Saul. His brother was Ner, the father of Abner. *(1 Sam. 14:51.)*

Kish was of the tribe of Benjamin. He was a son of the father of Gibeon (Jehiel, Abiel) and Maachah, his mother. His brothers were Abdon, Zur, Baal, Nadab, Gedor, Ahio, Zacher and Mikloth. *(Note: Verse 33 appears to be in error as it states that Ner begat Kish. Ner and Kish were brothers.)* Kish begat Saul, who begat Jonathan, Malchi-shua, Abinadab and Esh-baal. *(1 Chr. 8:30-33.)*

His father was Abiel (Jehiel), the father of Gibeon. His mother was Maachah. His brothers were Abdon, Zur, Baal, Ner, Nadab, Gedor, Ahio, Zechariah (Zacher) and Mikloth. *(1 Chr. 9:35-39.) (Note: Verse 39 repeats what would seem to be an erroneous statement that Ner begat Kish.)* (Charts 16k-l.)

KISH (2). *2 Chr. 29:12.* See **Kishi**.

KISH (3). *1 Chr. 23:21-22; 24:29, 31.*

Kish, a Levite, was a son of Mahli who was a son of Merari. His brother was Eleazar. Eleazar had no sons, only daughters. When Eleazar died, Kish's sons "took" Eleazar's daughters. *(1 Chr. 23:21-22.)*

Kish was the father of Jerahmeel who was named as being a chief of the fathers. He, along with the other Levites, drew lots for his course in the presence of king David, Zadok, Ahimelech and other leaders. *(1 Chr. 24:29, 31.)* (Chart 7e.)

KISH (4). *Esth. 2:5.*

Kish, a Benjamite, was the father of Shimei, who was the father of Jair, who was the father of Mordecai. (Chart 16k.)

KISHI (Kish (2), Kushaiah). *1 Chr. 6:44; 15:17; 2 Chr. 29:12, 15.*

Kishi, a descendant of Levi through Merari, was the son of Abdi and the father of Ethan. *(1 Chr. 6:44.)*

Kushaiah (Kishi) was the father of Ethan, one of the singers appointed to sound the cymbals of brass. *(1 Chr. 15:17.)*

Kish (Kishi), the son of Abdi, and other Levites sanctified themselves and then cleansed and sanctified the house of the Lord as instructed by Hezekiah, king over Judah. *(2 Chr. 29:12, 15.)* (Chart 7e.)

KITTIM (Chittim). *Gen. 10:4; Num. 24:24; 1 Chr. 1:7; Isa. 23:1, 12; Jer. 2:10; Ezek. 27:6; Dan. 11.*

Kittim was a son of Javan, grandson of Japheth, and a great-grandson of Noah. *(Gen. 10:4; 1 Chr. 1:7.)*

Balaam saw a vision regarding the Messiah and said that ships shall come from the coast of **Chittim** and afflict Asshur and Eber, "and he also shall perish for ever." *(Num. 24:24.)*

Isaiah speaks of the lands of Chittim. *(Isa. 23:1, 12.)*

The Lord bemoaned the fact that the people changed their gods to that which are not gods and doth not profit, and said to pass over to the isles of Chittim to see if this was not so. *(Jer. 2:10.)*

Ezekial lamented the fall of Tyrus and the loss of her riches and commerce which included ivory brought out of the isles of Chittim. *(Ezek. 27:6.)*

In the first year of the reign of Darius, Daniel had a vision in which he saw the successive kings and their conflicts, leagues, and wars which will lead up to the Second Coming of Christ, and indicated that the ships of Chittim will be engaged in the conflict. *(Dan. 11.)* (Chart 2a.)

KOHATH (Kohathites). *Gen. 46:11; E x. 6:18; Num. 3:17, 19, 27-31; 4:18-20, 34, 37; 10:21; Josh. 21; 1 Chr. 6:18, 22-28, 33-38, 61-70; 15:5; 23:12-20; 2 Chr. 20:19.*

Kohath was a son of Levi and a grandson of Jacob. His brothers were Gershon and Merari. *(Gen. 46:11.)* His sons were Amram, Izhar, Hebron and Uzziel. He lived to be 133 years old. *(Ex. 6:18.)*

Kohath, son of Levi, was the father of Amram (Amramites), Izhar (Izehartites), Hebron (Hebronites) and Uzziel (Uzzielites). In the wilderness of Sinai, the Lord commanded Moses to count the males, one month old and upward. Kohath's sons numbered 8,600. Moses instructed them to pitch on the south side of the tabernacle. Elizaphan, son of Uzziel, was selected to be the chief of the house of all the **Kohathites**. Their charge was the ark, table, candlestick, altars and vessels of the sanctuary. *(Num. 3:17, 19, 27-31.)*

The Lord instructed Moses to include the Kohathites among the Levites, but to have Aaron and his sons appoint each one to his service. They were not to go in unto the holy things when they were covered, "lest they die." Moses and Aaron numbered the Kohathites, who were 30 to 50 years old, by their families. Those assigned to the service in the tabernacle of the congregation numbered 2,750. *(Num. 4:18-20, 34, 37.)*

The Kohathites were responsible for bearing the sanctuary. *(Num. 10:21.)*

The families of the Levites, including the Kohathites, were, by lot, given specific cities to live in from within the various tribes as well as specific cities for refuge. *(Josh. 21.)*

Kohath's sons—Amram, Izhar, Hebron and Uzziel—are again listed as well as their posterity. Izhar is listed as Amminadab in verse 22. The cities that were given to Kohath's sons are listed, some of which were out of the cities of the half tribe of Manasseh. *(1 Chr. 6:18, 22-28, 33-38, 61-70.)*

When David gathered all Israel together to Jerusalem to bring the ark of the Lord there, he assembled the Levites. Of the sons of Kothath, there was "Uriel the chief, and his brethren an hundred and twenty." *(1 Chr. 15:5.)*

When David numbered the Levites at the time he made Solomon king, he also divided them into courses among the sons of Levi: Gershon, Kohath and Merari. Kohath's sons were Amram, Izhar, Hebron and Uzziel. Kohath's grandsons were Aaron and Moses. Aaron was separated from the others because he and his sons were to forever have the responsibility to sanctify the most holy things and to burn incense before the Lord. Moses' sons, Gershom and Eliezer, were named of the tribe of Levi. *(1 Chr. 23:12-20.)*

The Kohathites and Korhites stood up and praised the Lord when the Ammonites and others came against Judah and warred among themselves and destroyed each other. *(2 Chr. 20:19.)* (Charts 7a-e.)

KOLAIAH. *Neh. 11:7; Jer. 29:21.*

Kolaiah, of the tribe of Benjamin, was the father of Pedaiah and the son of Maaseiah. *(Neh. 11:7.)*

Kolaiah was the father of Ahab, which Ahab was destroyed by Nebuchadnezzar, king of Babylon, along with Zedekiah, son of Maaseiah, for prophesying a lie in the name of the Lord. *(Jer. 29:21.) (Note: This is apparently a misstatment: Zedekiah was the son of Josiah. Verse 25 indicates that Zephaniah was the son of Maaseiah the priest.)* (Chart 16m.)

KORAH (1). *Gen. 36:5, 14, 18.*

Korah was a son of Aholibamah and Esau born in Canaan. His brothers were Jeush and Jaalam. He was a duke or tribal chief. (Charts 3b-c.; 4c.)

KORAH (2). *Gen. 36:16 (15-16).*

Korah was one of the dukes that came of Eliphaz the son of Esau and Adah. (Chart 3b.)

KORAH (3) (Korhites, Korahites, Korathites). *Ex. 6:21, 24; Num. 16; 26:9-11; 1 Chr. 6:22-28, 33-38; 9:19; 26:1; 2 Chr. 20:19; Ps. 42; 44-48; 84-85; 87-88 Subtitles.*

Korah, a son of Izhar and brother of Nepheg and Zichri, was the grandson of Kohath and the great-grandson of Levi. His sons were Assir, Elkanah and Abiasaph (Ebiasaph). *(Ex. 6:21, 24.)*

Korah, along with Dathan and Abiram (sons of Eliab), On (the son of Peleth) and two hundred and fifty princes of the assembly who were famous among the children of Israel (seeking priestly offices) rose up against Moses. The Lord caused the earth to open up and the rebels, their families, and those who "appertained unto Korah," were swallowed up. The other 250 rebels were consumed by fire. Another 14,700 people were slain by a plague for rising up against Moses and Aaron. *(Num. 16.)*

Korah, along with Eliab's sons Nemuel, Dathan and Abiram, was swallowed up in the earth for rebelling against Moses and Aaron. However, Korah's children did not die. *(Num. 26:9-11.)*

Korah was the son of Amminadab (Izhar) and the father of Assir. *(1 Chr. 6:22-28, 33-38.)*

Korah's descendants were over the work of the service and were keepers of the gates of the tabernacle. Shallum, the son of Kore the son of Ebiasaph (Abiasaph) the son of Korah, was the chief porter. *(1 Chr. 9:19.)*

Korhites were the descendants of Korah, son of Izhar, Kohath's son. They were assigned by king David to be porters. *(1 Chr. 26:1.)*

The Korhites and Kohathites stood up and praised the Lord when the Ammonites and others came against Judah and warred among themselves and destroyed each other. *(2 Chr. 20:19.) (Note: The Bible Dictionary indicates the Korhites,* **Korahites** *and* **Korathites** *were all one and the same and that they formed a guild of musicians.)*

These psalms were directed to the chief Musician with instructions for the sons of Korah or written specifically for the sons of Korah. Psalm 88 also indicates it contained instructions of Heman the Ezrahite. *(Ps. 42; 44-48; 84-85; 87-88 Subtitles.)* (Chart 7d.)

KORAH (4). *1 Chr. 2:43.*

Korah was one of the sons of Hebron. His brothers were Tappuah, Rekem and Shema. (Chart 8i.)

KORE (1). *1 Chr. 9:19; 1 Chr. 26:1.*

Kore, a Levite, was the father of Shallum, the chief porter, and the son of Ebiasaph (Abiasaph) the son of Korah. *(1 Chr. 9:19.)*

Kore, was the father of Meshelemiah. He was of the lineage of Asaph. He and his sons were assigned by king David to be porters. *(1 Chr. 26:1.)* (Chart 7d.)

KORE (2). *2 Chr. 31:14.*

Kore, son of Imnah the Levite, was the porter toward the east, and was assigned by Hezekiah, king of Judah, to be over the freewill offerings of God and to distribute the holy things and oblations of the Lord.

KOZ. *Neh. 3:4, 21.*

Koz was the father of Urijah (Uriah) who was the father of Meremoth, one of the priests who helped build the walls and gates of Jerusalem.

KOZ, THE CHILDREN OF. *Ezra 2:61-62; Neh. 7:63-64.*

The Children of Koz could not find their names among those who were listed by their genealogy and, therefore, they were "as polluted" and were excluded from the priesthood.

KUSHAIAH. See **Kishi**.

NAMES THAT BEGIN WITH "L"

LAADAH. *1 Chr. 4:21.*

Laadah was a son of Shelah and a grandson of Judah. He was the father of Mareshah. (Chart 8a.)

LAADAN (1). *1 Chr. 7:26-27.*

Laadan was the son of Tahan, the father of Ammihud, and the great-great-great-grandson of Ephraim. His descendants included Jehoshua (Joshua) the son of Non (Nun). (Chart 15d.)

LAADAN (2). *1 Chr. 23:7-8; 26:21-22.*

Laadan was of the sons of Gershon, son of Levi. David divided the Levites into courses at the time he made Solomon king. Jehiel, Zetham and Joel of the sons of Laadan, were given their assignments. *(1 Chr. 23:7-8.)*

Laadan's son Jehieli and his grandsons Zetham and Joel, chief fathers, were over the treasures of the house of the Lord. *(1 Chr. 26:21-22.)* (Chart 7f.)

LABAN. *Gen. 24:29; 27:43; 29:15-28; 31.*

Laban was Rebekah's brother, a son of Bethuel, a grandson of Nahor and Milcah and a grandnephew of Abraham. When Rebekah told her family about Abraham's servant's arrival, Laban ran to the well to greet him. He welcomed him warmly. *(Gen. 24:29.)*

Because Esau hated Jacob and planned to kill him over the birthright blessing, Rebekah counseled Jacob to flee to Haran unto her brother Laban. *(Gen. 27:43.)*

Laban had two daughters: Leah, who was "tender-eyed," and Rachel, who was "beautiful and well favoured." Jacob stayed with Laban's family a month afterwhich Laban indicated that he wanted to pay Jacob for his labor—he didn't want him to work for him for nothing. Jacob said he would serve him seven years if he could have Rachel for a wife. Laban agreed. At the end of the seven years, Jacob was given his bride. However, Laban tricked him and gave him Leah instead of Rachel. When Jacob confronted Laban the next morning, Laban told him to "fulfil her week" and then they would also give him Rachel because in their land it was not right that the younger should be given before the firstborn. *(Gen. 29:15-28.)*

After working for Laban for 20 years, Jacob was instructed by the Lord to return unto his own land. He recognized that Laban's feelings for him had changed. He left without telling Laban. After three days, Laban learned Jacob and his family had gone. He pursued them. The Lord appeared to Laban in a dream and told him not to speak good or bad to Jacob. Laban finally overtook Jacob. He asked why they had left and complained that someone had stolen his images. Jacob told him that he was afraid that Laban would use force to keep his daughters from leaving. He also told Laban that he could search every tent and (not knowing that Rachel had taken the images) said that whoever had them should die. However, Laban could not find them. Rachel had hidden them in the camel's furniture and sat upon them, saying she could not get down because the custom of women was upon her. Jacob reminded Laban that he had worked 14 years for his wives and another six years for his flocks, and that Laban had changed his wages 10 times. Laban and Jacob covenanted not to harm one another and parted on good terms after Laban kissed his sons and daughters and blessed them. *(Gen. 31.)* (Chart 2c.)

LAD, A. *2 Sam. 17:18.*

A **Lad** saw a wench convey information from Hushai to Jonathan and Ahimaaz and told Absalom.

LAEL. *Num. 3:24.*

Lael was the father of Eliasaph and was of the tribe of Gershon, a Levite. (Chart 7a.)

LAHAD. *1 Chr. 4:2.*

Lahad, a descendant of Judah, was the son of Jahath and the father of Etam. (Chart 8m.)

LAHMI. See **Goliath's Brother**

LAISH. *1 Sam. 25:44.*

Laish, of Gallim, was the father of Phalti.

LAMECH (1). *Gen. 4:18, 19, 23-24.*

Lamech was the son of Methusael. He took two wives: Adah and Zilah. Lamech told his wives that he had killed a man, and that if Cain would be avenged sevenfold, he would be avenged seventy and sevenfold. (Chart 1.)

LAMECH (2). *Gen. 5:25-31; 1 Chr. 1:1-3.*

Lamech was the father of Noah, the son of Methuselah and the six-times-great-grandson of Adam. His father was 187 years old when he was born. He, himself, was 182 years old when he begat Noah. He lived to be 777 years old, dying when Noah was 595 years old. *(Gen. 5:25-31.) (Note: The flood occurred approximately five years later—lasting about a year.)*

Lamech's ancestors are listed with some spelling changes: Adam, Sheth (Seth), Enosh (Enos), Kenan (Cainan), Mahalaleel, Jered (Jared), Henoch (Enoch), Methuselah, Lamech. *(1 Chr. 1:1-3.) (Note: Revelation recorded in D&C 107:51 states: "Lamech was 32 years old when he was ordained under the hand of Seth.")* (Charts 1.; 21.)

LEAH. *Gen. 29:16-35; 30:9-21; 31:4, 14-15, 33; 33:1-2, 7; 35:23, 26; 49:31.*

Leah was Jacob's cousin. She was the eldest daughter of Laban, Jacob's mother Rebekah's brother. "Leah was tender eyed" but her sister Rachel "was beautiful and well favoured" and Jacob loved Rachel. Laban deceived Jacob and gave him Leah for a bride after Jacob had worked seven years in order to marry Rachel. Laban gave Leah his handmaid Zilpah to be her maid. Laban told Jacob to fulfill Leah's week and then he could also have Rachel. In their country, he explained, it was not acceptable for the younger daughter to get married before the firstborn. Rachel was unable to conceive. Leah, however, had four sons: Reuben, Simeon, Levi and

Judah. Each time she bore Jacob a son she hoped it would make Jacob love her. *(Gen. 29:16-35.)*

After Rachel gave Jacob her handmaid Bilhah for a wife, Leah gave Jacob her handmaid Zilpah so she could obtain more children through her since she had stopped bearing children herself. Zilpah begat two sons: Gad and Asher. Rachel asked Leah to share her son's mandrakes with her. Leah countered that she had taken her husband from her and now she wanted to take her son's mandrakes from her, too. Rachel offered to have Jacob lie with her in return for the mandrakes. Leah told Jacob he must come to her that night because she had "hired" him with her son's mandrakes. Leah begat Issachar. She conceived again and begat Zebulun. She also begat a daughter, Dinah. *(Gen. 30:9-21.)*

Leah and Rachel were called into the field by Jacob who was tending his flock, and informed that because Laban had turned against him and had not treated him fairly, they were going to flee. Leah and Rachel recognized that their father had taken all of their inheritance and agreed they should do as the Lord instructed. *(Gen. 31:4, 14-15, 33.)*

As they journeyed, Esau and his men approached. Jacob divided his family according to their mothers and set them in front of his group. After the handmaids and their children, came Leah and her children and then Rachel and Joseph. They bowed themselves before Esau. *(Gen. 33:1-2, 7.)*

Leah's sons were Reuben, Simeon, Levi, Judah, Issachar and Zebulun. Her handmaiden Zilpah's sons were Gad and Asher. *(Gen. 35:23, 26.)*

Leah was buried in the cave in the field of Machpelah where Abraham, Sarah, Isaac and Rebekah were buried. *(Gen. 49:31.)* (Charts 2c.; 3d.; 5a.; 6a.; 7a.; 8a.; 9a., 10a.; 11a.; 12a.; 13a.; 14a.; 15a.; 16a.)

LEBANAH (Lebana). *Ezra 2:45, 58; Neh. 7:48, 60.*

Lebanah (Lebana) was a Nethinim. When the Nethinims and the children of Solomon's servants left Babylon to return to Jerusalem to build the house of the Lord as proclaimed by Cyrus, king of Persia, they numbered 392.

LECAH. *1 Chr. 4:21, 23.*

Lecah was the son of Er, the grandson of Shelah and a great-grandson of Judah. He was one of the potters, one of those who dwelled among plants and hedges: "there they dwelt with the king for his work." (Chart 8a.)

LEHABIM. *Gen. 10:13.*

Lehabim was a son of Mizraim, a grandson of Ham and a great-grandson of Noah. (Chart 2e.)

LEMUEL. *Prov. 31.*

Lemuel was apparently a king. However, he has not been mentioned prior to Prov. 31, which is "the prophecy that his mother taught him." It stresses that a virtuous woman is to be prized "far above rubies," and urges people to plead the cause of the poor and needy. It also condemns the use of wine and strong drink. *(Note: While the name Lemuel doesn't appear any place else in the Old Testament,* *it does appear in the Book of Mormon. Lemuel was the second son of Lehi and Sarah. He and his brother Laman rebelled against the Lord. The American Indians, the Lamanites, are their descendants.)*

LETUSHIM. *Gen. 25:3.*

Letushim was a son of Dedan, a grandson of Jokshan, and a great-grandson of Abraham and Keturah. (Chart 3f.)

LEUMMIM. *Gen. 25:3.*

Leummim was a son of Dedan, a grandson of Jokshan, and a great-grandson of Abraham and Keturah. (Chart 3f.)

LEVI (Levites). *Gen. 29:34; 34:25-30; 35:23; 37; 46:11; 49:1, 5-7; 50:13; Ex. 6:16; 32:26-28; Num. 1:47-53; 3:9, 12-22, 39; 8; 18:21, 23-24; 26:51; 35:2-8; Deut. 10:8-9; 12:18-19; 14:27; 27:12, 14-26; 33:8; Josh. 21; 1 Chr. 6:1, 16-48; 12:26; 15; 23; 24; 27:17; 2 Chr. 7:6; 11:13-17; 19:8; 29:34; 31:2; 35:11; Ezra 1:5; 6:16-22; 7:7, 24; 9:1; Neh. 8:7-13; 9; 11:18; 12:22-24; 13:10; Ezek. 40:46; 43:19; 44:10-16; 45:5; 48:8-22, 31; Zech. 12:12-13; Mal. 2:4-8; 3:1-3.*

Levi was the third son of Jacob and Leah. *(Gen. 29:34.)*

Levi and his brother Simeon slew Hamor and Shechem his son with their swords because Shechem had defiled their sister Dinah. When Jacob bemoaned what they had done, their response was, "Should he deal with our sister as with an harlot?" *(Gen. 34:25-30.)*

Levi, the third son of Leah and Jacob, is named along with his brothers Reuben, Simeon, Judah, Issachar and Zebulun. *(Gen. 35:23.)*

Levi and his brothers hated their younger brother Joseph and sold him to a group of Ishmeelites, or Midianite merchantmen, for 20 pieces of silver. They dipped his coat of many colors in animal blood and gave it to their father so he would think Joseph had been killed by wild beasts. *(Gen. 37.)*

Levi begat Gershon, Kohath and Merari. *(Gen. 46:11.)*

After the brothers had gone to Egypt for grain and were finally reunited with Joseph, and following the move of their entire family to Egypt, the time came when Jacob called his sons together to tell them what would befall each of them in the last days. To Levi he said, "Simeon and Levi are brethren; instruments of cruelty are in their habitations. . . for in their anger they slew a man, and in their selfwill they digged down a wall. Cursed be their anger, for it was fierce; and their wrath, for it was cruel: I will divide them in Jacob, and scatter them in Israel." *(Gen. 49:1, 5-7.)*

Levi and his brothers traveled together to transport their father's body to Canaan for burial. *(Gen. 50:13.)*

Levi's sons were Gershon, Kohath and Merari. He lived 137 years. *(Ex. 6:16.)*

When Moses came down from the mount and the people were worshipping the golden calf, he called for all those who were on the Lord's side to come stand by him. All of the children of Levi gathered together by Moses. He instructed them to go throughout the camp and to slay "every man his brother, and every man his companion, and every man his neighbour" that had not stood on the Lord's side.

And the children of Levi did as instructed. Approximately 3,000 men fell that day. *(Ex. 32:26-28.)*

When Moses was commanded to number the males in the tribes of Israel who were 20 years old and older in preparation for war, he was told he should not number the tribe of Levi but should appoint them to keep the charge of the tabernacle of testimony. *(Num. 1:47-53.)*

The **Levites** charge was to assist the priests, Aaron and his sons. The Lord told Moses that all the firstborn in Israel were to be dedicated to him. However, where the Levites were concerned, the whole tribe was to be dedicated to the Lord, not just the firstborn. He was also instructed to number the children of the Levites, every male one month old and older. The total was 22,000. *(Num. 3:9, 12-22, 39.)*

The Levites were offered as a wave-offering on behalf of the children of Israel and became God's peculiar property, given to Him in place of the firstborn. The Lord instructed Moses to wash the Levites, consecrate them and set them apart by the laying on of hands. The Lord told Moses that He had given the Levites as a gift to Aaron and his sons from among the children of Israel, to do the service of the tabernacle. *(Num. 8.)*

The Lord gave the Levites a "tenth in Israel for an inheritance" since they were dispersed among all the children of Israel rather than having a specific area to call their own. Thus, the Lord gave them the tithe for their service in the tabernacle. *(Num. 18:21, 23-24.)*

While on the plains of Moab near Jericho, Moses and Eleazar were instructed to count all the males, excluding the Levites, who were 20 years old and older. The total was 601,730. *(Num. 26:51.)*

The other tribes were required to give the Levites six cities for refuge plus an additional 42 cities along with their suburbs. *(Num. 35:2-8.)*

Moses reviewed with the children of Israel all that had transpired and recounted that the tribe of Levi was separated from the others and assigned to bear the ark of the covenant of the Lord and to minister unto him. The Lord was their inheritance; therefore, Levi's descendants were not given a specific land of inheritance like the other tribes were given. *(Deut. 10:8-9.)* The Levites had a claim on the alms of the people at feast times. *(Deut. 12:18-19.)* Israel was reminded to never forsake the Levites inasmuch as they did not have an inheritance. *(Deut. 14:27.)*

As the Israelites prepared to cross over Jordan, the tribes of Levi, Simeon, Judah, Issachar, Joseph and Benjamin were to stand upon mount Gerizim to bless the people. The Levites were to sound a warning to all the people that they are the Lord's people but they shall be cursed if they do not obey the Lord. *(Deut. 27:12, 14-26.)*

Moses blessed the tribe of Levi and instructed them to let the Urim and Thummim be with the holy one who they proved at Massah and with whom they strove at the waters of Meribah. *(Deut.33:8.)*

The families of the Levites, i.e., Kohathites, were given, by lot, specific cities from within the various tribes wherein they could live as well as specific cities for refuge. *(Josh. 21.)*

Levi's sons—Gershom, Kohath and Merari—and their posterity are chronicled. They were set over the service of song in the house of the Lord. *(1 Chr. 6:1, 16-48.)*

When David became king and went to Ziklag, all Israel rejoiced. The tribes sent their armies to assist David. The tribe of Levi sent 4,600 men. *(1 Chr. 12:26.)*

After Abinadab's son Uzza was slain by the Lord for touching the ark when David was trying to have it transferred from Abinadab's house to the city of David, David realized that only the Levites should carry the ark of God. Thus, he assembled the children of Aaron and gave Zadok and Abiathar, the priests, plus the chiefs of the fathers of the Levites an assignment to sanctify themselves in preparation of bringing the ark up to the place which David had prepared for it. David also appointed the chief of the Levites to appoint some of their brethren to be the musicians, to sing and play music and minister before the Lord. *(1 Chr. 15.)*

When David made Solomon king, he gathered all the princes of Israel with the priests and the Levites and numbered all the Levites from the age of thirty years and upward. The Levites numbered, man by man, 38,000. Twenty-four thousand were to help with the work of the house of the Lord; 6,000 were officers and judges; 4,000 were porters and 4,000 were musicians assigned to praise the Lord with music. The Levites were divided into courses by David. The chief of the fathers are named. *(1 Chr. 23.)*

The sons of Aaron and the rest of the sons of the Levites were divided into groups and assigned their duties by lot. *(1 Chr. 24.)*

The prince of the tribe of Levi at the time of king David was Hashabiah, the son of Kemuel. *(1 Chr. 27:17.)*

When Solomon finished the temple and the people gathered to feast and make offerings for seven days, the Levites brought their musical instruments, the priests sounded their trumpets, and all Israel stood. *(2 Chr. 7:6.)*

When the house of Israel became divided under the reign of Rehoboam (son of Solomon) and Jeroboam, the Levites initally followed Jeroboam along with most of the children of Israel. (Only the houses of Judah and Benjamin remained with Rehoboam.) However, Jeroboam would not let the priests and Levites perform their religious duties and he led the children of Israel into idolatry. Eventually, the priests, Levites, and all who desired to worship the God of Israel returned to Rehoboam. *(2 Chr. 11:13-17.)*

Jehoshaphat, king of Judah, returned the people to the Lord. He set up the Levites, priests and chief of the fathers of Israel to be judges and administrators of justice. *(2 Chr. 19:8.)*

When the priests could not flay all the burnt offerings because there were too few worthy priests, the Levites assisted them until the work was ended. They "were more upright in heart to sanctify themselves than the priests." *(2 Chr. 29:34.)*

Hezekiah, king of Judah, reinstated the appointment of the courses of the priests and the Levites, according to the law of the Lord. The Levites' service was over burnt offerings and for peace offerings, to minister, give thanks and praise in the gates of the tents of the Lord. *(2 Chr. 31:2.)*

While the Levites flayed the offerings, the priests sprinkled the blood of the passover. *(2 Chr. 35:11.)*

When Cyrus, king of Persia, proclaimed the building of the temple in Jerusalem, he called for those who were of God's people to go up and build the temple. The priests and Levites and the chief of the fathers of Judah and Benjamin rose up to go build the house of the Lord. *(Ezra 1:5.)*

After much delay and hindrance from the Samaritans, the temple was finally completed in the sixth year of the reign of Darius, king of Persia. The children of Israel rejoiced and the priests were set in their divisions and the Levites were set in their courses so the work of the temple could proceed. *(Ezra 6:16-22.)*

Around 458 B.C., during the reign of Persia's king Artaxerxes Longimanus, Artaxerxes issued a decree allowing Ezra to take any of the children of Israel, the priests, Levites, singers, porters and Nethinims back to Jerusalem who desired to return there with him and made it unlawful for anyone to impose a toll, tribute or custom upon them. *(Ezra 7:7, 24.)*

After the children of Israel were delivered from Babylonian bondage, many Jews—including the priests and Levites— intermarried with and followed the abominations of the Canaanites, Hittites, Perizzites, Jebusites, Ammonites, Moabites, Egyptians and Amorites. Ezra prayed and confessed the sins of all the people, fearing the Lord would completely destroy them this time for their abominations. *(Ezra 9:1.)*

When Ezra read and interpreted the law of Moses to the people, the Levites and a group of men—Jeshua, Bani, Sherebiah, Jamin, Akkub, Shabbethai, Hodijah, Maaseiah, Kelita, Azariah, Jozabad, Hanan and Pelaiah—helped the people to understand the law. The people wept when they heard the law and the day was proclaimed a holy day, but the Levites quieted them and reminded them it was a holy day and they should not be grieved. *(Neh. 8:7-13.)*

The Levites—Jeshua, Bani, Kadmiel, Shebaniah, Bunni, Sherebiah, Bani, Chenani, Hashabniah, Hodijah and Pethahiah—blessed and praised the Lord and recited the Lord's goodness to Israel: the blessing given to Abraham; His giving the land of the Canaanites, Hittites, Amorites, Perizzites, Jebusites and Girgashites to Israel; the Red Sea was divided so they could cross it yet the Egyptians who pursued them were drowned; the signs and wonders shown to Pharaoh; His leading them in the wilderness and protecting them so that they had bread from heaven, water from the rock, and shoes and clothes that never wore out; His willingness to accept them whenever they repented, even when they made a molten calf. They had been given the kingdoms of Shihon, Heshbon and Bashan and the Lord had subdued the Canaanites and delivered them into the hands of the Israelites. After giving praise, they made a covenant with the Lord. The princes, Levites and priests sealed the covenant. *(Neh. 9.)*

When the children of Israel returned to Jerusalem from Babylonian captivity, those in the holy city numbered 284. *(Neh. 11:18.)*

The Levites who were chief of the fathers in the days of Eliashib, Joiada, Johanan and Jaddua were recorded in the book of the chronicles of the kings even until the days of Johanan the son of Eliashib. Those named chief of the Levites were Hashabiah, Sherebiah, and Jeshua the son of Kadmiel. *(Neh. 12:22-24.)*

Nehemiah discovered that the Levites and the singers who were supposed to be caring for the house of God had fled to the fields because they were not receiving the portions that should have been given them. After being chastised, all Judah brought tithes of corn, new wine and oil into the treasuries. *(Neh. 13:10.)*

Ezekiel was shown in a vision the city where the temple would be built, and the form and size of the temple and its courts. He saw the chamber toward the north which was for Levi's descendants, the priests who were the sons of Zadok. *(Ezek. 40:46.)*

Ezekiel was instructed in the ordinances of the altar for the day when the people build it to offer burnt offerings. The priests (Levites) who were of the seed of Zadok were to be given a young bullock for a sin offering. *(Ezek. 43:19.)*

The Levites who did not remain faithful when Israel went astray were not to minister in the Lord's sanctuary but were given the responsibility to be the "keepers of the charge of the house, for all the service thereof, and for all that shall be done therein. But the priests the Levites, the sons of Zadok, that kept the charge of my sanctuary when the children of Israel went astray from me, they shall come near to me to minister unto me, and they shall stand before me to offer unto me the fat and the blood, saith the Lord God: They shall enter into my sanctuary, and they shall come near to my table, to minister unto me, and they shall keep my charge." *(Ezek. 44:10-16.)*

Ezekiel was shown that the Levites, those who ministered in the house of the Lord, were to have a specific area allotted to them for their houses and for a holy place for the sanctuary. *(Ezek. 45:5.)*

The Lord revealed to Ezekiel just how the land should be divided by tribes when the children of Israel are gathered in the latter days. The tribe of Levi is to have the land between the border of Judah and the border of Benjamin. The twelve gates of the city are to bear the names of the twelve sons of Jacob. One of the three northward gates will be named for Levi. *(Ezek. 48:8-22, 31.)*

When the Savior comes again and the children of Israel recognize Him as the Savior whom they crucified, there will be great mourning in the land. Each family shall mourn apart: the family of the house of Levi and their wives apart; the family of the house of David and their wives; the family of the house of Nathan and their wives, etc. *(Zech. 12:12-13.)*

The Lord's covenant was with Levi. Malachi reproved the priests because, as the Lord's messengers, they were supposed to keep knowledge; and people should have been able to seek to know the law from them. However, the priests were not keeping their covenants nor teaching the people, but were leading them astray. *(Mal. 2:4-8.)*

Malachi prophesied that prior to the Second Coming, the Lord would send His messenger to prepare the way. The Lord will come suddenly to His temple. He will purify the sons of Levi. *(Mal. 3:1-3.)* (Charts 1., 3d.; 5a.; 6a.; 7a-b, d-e, g.; 8a.; 9a.; 10a.; 11a.; 12a.; 13a.; 14a.; 15a.; 16a.)

LIBNI (1) (Libnites). *Ex. 6:17; Num. 3:21; 1 Chr. 6:20-21, 39-43.*

Libni was a son of Gershon and a grandson of Levi. *(Ex. 6:17.)*

Libnites descended from Libni, son of Gershon, grandson of Levi, great-grandson of Jacob (Israel). One of the families of the Gershonites. *(Num. 3:21.)*

Libni was the son of Gershom (Gershon) and the father of Jahath. His posterity is listed. *(1 Chr. 6:20-21, 39-43.)* (Chart 7a.)

LIBNI (2). *1 Chr. 6:29, 46-47.*

Libni, a descendant of Levi through Merari, was the son of Mahli and the father of Shimei. *(Note: There are two different listings of Merari's descendants.)* (Chart 7c.)

LIKHI. *1 Chr. 7:19.*

Likhi, a descendant of Manasseh the son of Joseph, was the son of Shemida and grandson of Gilead. His brothers were Ahian, Shechem and Ahiam. (Chart 15a.)

LITTLE CHILDREN WHO MOCKED ELISHA. *2 Kgs. 2:23.*

Little Children came out of the city and mocked Elisha as he traveled to Beth-el, calling him "bald head." He cursed them in the name of the Lord and two she-bears came out of the wood and killed 42 of them.

LITTLE LAD, A. *1 Sam. 20:35.*

A Little Lad accompanied Jonathan the son of Saul into the field. By shooting an arrow and telling the little lad the arrow had gone beyond him, Jonathan warned David that king Saul was, indeed, bent on killing David.

LO-AMMI. *Hosea 1:9.*

Lo-ammi was the second son of the prophet Hosea and Gomer. His name means, "Not my people." This was a sign to Israel, for the Lord said, "Ye are not my people, and I will not be your God."

LOD. *Ezra 2:33; Neh. 7: 37.*

Lod was of the people of Israel. The men of the children of Lod, Hadid and Ono who returned to Jerusalem from Babylon after Cyrus' proclamation to build the temple numbered 725 (721).

LORD ON WHOSE HAND THE KING LEANED. *2 Kgs. 7:2, 17-20.*

The **Lord on Whose Hand the King Leaned** doubted that the famine would end and there would be plenty in Samaria on the morrow as prophesied by Elisha. Thus, Elisha prophesied that "thou shalt see it with thine eyes, but shalt not eat thereof." The following day there was "plenty" when the abandoned goods of the Syrians were brought into Samaria. The "Lord on Whose Hand the King Leaned" was assigned to be in charge of the gate. As the people rode through the gate, they trode upon him and he died. Thus, he saw the goods but did not get to eat of them, just as Elisha prophesied.

LO-RUHAMAH. *Hosea 1:6, 8.*

<u>Lo-ruhamah</u> was the daughter of the prophet Hosea and Gomer. Her name means, "Not having obtained mercy." This was a sign to Israel, for the Lord said He would "no more have mercy upon the house of Israel."

LOT. *Gen. 11:27-31; 12:4-5; 13:1, 5-13; 14:1-16; 19:1-8, 9-26, 30-38; Deut. 2:9,19.*

<u>Lot</u> was the son of Haran, an eighth-great-grandson of Shem and a ninth-great-grandson of Noah. After his father died, he traveled with his grandfather, Terah, and his uncle and aunt, Abram and Sarai, to the land of Canaan where they settled in a place called Haran. *(Gen. 11:27-31.)*

Lot traveled with Abram and Sarai when they left Haran and moved to Canaan. *(Gen. 12:4-5.)*

Lot traveled with Abram when they left Egypt. Abram and Lot each had many flocks and herds and the land could not handle all of them. Strife developed between Abram's herdsmen and those of Lot. Thus, Abram suggested they go separate ways. Abram told Lot to choose which of the land he wanted, that on his left hand or that to the right, and he said he would take the other. Lot chose all of the plain of Jordan, which included the cities of Sodom and Gomorrah which, at that time, were "well watered every where." Lot set his tent up near Sodom. *(Gen. 13:1, 5-13.)*

A war involving several kings developed during which the kings of Sodom and Gomorrah fell and Lot, who was dwelling in Sodom, was taken captive. A person who escaped told Abram about Lot's capture. Abram armed his trained servants and, together with Mamre, Eshcol and Aner who were confederate with him, rescued Lot and his goods along with the other people. *(Gen. 14:1-16.)*

Two angels came to Sodom. Lot invited them into his home where he made them a feast. *(Note: The Joseph Smith Translation reads "three angels," and the footnote to the text indicates they were "messengers" or "holy men.")* Some of the wicked townsmen came to Lot's house and wanted him to send these men out to them so they could sexually molest them. Lot offered, instead, to send out his two virgin daughters to them, saying, "Do ye to them as is good in your eyes: only unto these men do nothing; for therefore came they under the shadow of my roof." *(Gen. 19:1-8.) (Note: Gen. 19:11-14 in the JST sheds a different perspective on these verses: "Wherefore they said unto the man, We will have the men, and thy daughters also; and we will do with them as seemeth us good. Now this was after the wickedness of Sodom. And Lot said, Behold now, I have two daughters which have not known man; let me, I pray you, plead with my brethren that I may not bring them out unto you; and ye shall not do unto them as seemeth good in your eyes; For God will not justify his servant in this thing; wherefore, let me plead with my brethren, this once only, that unto these men ye do nothing that they may have peace in my house; for therefore came they under the shadow of my roof.")*

The men of Sodom demanded the men be given to them. The angels pulled Lot back into the house, shut the door, and smote the men at the door with blindness. They instructed Lot to gather his family together and leave the city. His sons-in-law just scoffed at him, so the angels told Lot to take his wife and two daughters and leave; "lest thou be consumed in the iniquity of the city." They were instructed not to look behind them nor to stay in the plain but were encouraged to escape to the mountain. Lot said he couldn't go to the mountain, "lest some evil take me, and I die." However, he suggested that there was a little city nearby to which he could flee. Thus, he fled to Zoar. The Lord rained fire and brimstone upon Sodom and Gomorrah. Unfortunately, Lot's wife looked back and became a pillar of salt. Lot was preserved because the Lord remembered Abraham and sent Lot out of the area before destroying the city. *(Gen. 19:9-26.)*

Lot and his two daughters left Zoar and lived in the mountain. His older daughter observed to the younger daughter that their father was old and that there were no other men around whereby they could conceive and preserve their father's seed. Thus, she suggested that they get their father drunk with wine, lay with him, and preserve his seed. This they did. The older daughter bore a son whom she called Moab. He became the father of the Moabites. The younger daughter bore a son whom she called Benammi. He is the father of the children of Ammon. *(Gen. 19:30-38.)*

Moses reminded the children of Israel they were not to distress the Moabites: the Lord had given Ar unto the children of Lot for a possession. The Lord also told them not to fight against the children of Ammon: He had given that land unto the children of Lot for a possession. *(Deut. 2:9,19.)* (Charts 2c-d.)

LOTAN. *Gen. 36:20, 22; 1 Chr. 1:38-39.*

Lotan, a son of Seir the Horite, was a duke or tribal chief. He was Timna's brother. His children were Hori and Hemam (Homam). (Charts 4a-f.; 19.)

LOT'S DAUGHTERS. *Gen. 19:8, 16, 17-32, 33-34, 37.*

Lot's Daughters were virgins. Lot offered them to the male mob in Sodom rather than give two angels (holy men, messengers) over to the men. However, they wanted the men. *(Note: The JST sheds a different perspective on this event. See the information on Lot.)* Lot's daughters left Sodom with their father and mother before it was destroyed. Unfortunately, their mother looked back and was turned into a pillar of salt. After leaving Sodom, they went to Zoar, and from there up into the mountains to dwell. The elder daughter observed to her younger sister that their father was getting old and there were no men around by whom they could preserve his seed. She suggested they get their father drunken with wine, lie with him, and conceive and bare children that they might preserve his seed. Lot's daughters got him drunk and the elder daughter went in and lay down with him. She bore a son and called him Moab. They got their father drunk with wine again and the younger sister went in and lay with him. She bore a son and called him Benammi. (Chart 2d.)

LOT'S WIFE. *Gen. 19:15-26*.

Lot's Wife left Sodom with Lot and their two daughters. They went to the city of Zoar. The angels instructed them not to look back at Sodom and Gomorrah as the cities were going to be destroyed. Lot's wife looked back and became a pillar of salt.

LUBIMS. See **Ethiopians**.

LUD. *Gen. 10:22*.

Lud was a son of Shem and a grandson of Noah. (Chart 2b.)

LUDIM. *Gen. 10:13*.

Ludim was a son of Mizraim, a grandson of Ham, and a great-grandson of Noah. (Chart 2e.)

NAMES THAT BEGIN WITH "M"

MAACAH (Maachah (2)). *2 Sam. 3:3; 1 Chr. 3:2.*

Maacah (Maachah) was the mother of David's son Absalom. Her father was Talmai, king of Geshur.

MAACAH, KING. See **King Maacah**.

MAACHAH (1). *Gen. 22:24.*

Maachah was born to Nahor (Abraham's brother) and Reumah, his concubine. (Chart 2d.)

MAACHAH (2). *1 Chr. 3:2.* See **Maacah**.

MAACHAH (3). *1 Chr. 11:43.*

MAACHAH was the father of Hanan—one of David's mighty men.

Maachah (4). *1 Kgs. 15:2, 13; 2 Chr. 11:20-21; 2 Chr. 15:16.*

Maachah, mother of Abijam (king of Judah), was wife of Rehoboam, daughter of Abishalom and daughter-in-law to Solomon. When Asa was king, he removed his grandmother from being queen because she built an idol in a grove. *(1 Kgs. 15:2, 13.)*

Maachah was the daughter of David's son Absalom (Abishalom) and wife of king Rehoboam, David's grandson. She was one of Rehoboam's 18 wives. She bore Abijah (Abijam), Attai, Ziza and Shelomith. Rehoboam loved her more than any of his other wives and concubines and planned to eventually make their son Abijah king. *(2 Chr. 11:20-21.) (Note:2 Chr. 13:2 states that Michaiah the daughter of Uriel of Gibeah was the mother of Abijah.)*

When Asa, her grandson was king, he removed her from being queen because she built an idol in a grove. *(2 Chr. 15:16.)* (Charts 1.; 8f.)

MAACHAH (5). *1 Chr. 2:48-49.*

Maachah, one of Caleb's concubines, bore Sheber, Tirhanah, Shaaph and Sheva. They also had a daughter Achsah. (Chart 8k.)

MAACHAH (6). *1 Chr. 7:15.*

Maachah was the wife of Machir who was a son of Manasseh. She was the sister of Huppim and Shuppim. She had two sons: Peresh and Sheresh. *(Note: Peresh and Gilead may be one and the same.)* (Charts 15b.; 16c.)

MAACHAH (7). *1 Chr. 8:29; 1 Chr. 9:35.*

Maachah was the wife of the "father of Gibeon." They were of the tribe of Benjamin. *(1 Chr. 8:29.)* Maachah was the wife of Jehiel (Abiel), the "father of Gibeon." *(1 Chr. 9:35.) (Note: Jehiel was the father of Kish, who was the father of Saul.)* (Chart 16k.)

MAACHAH (8). *1 Chr. 27:16.*

Maachah was the father of Shephatiah who was prince over the tribe of Simeon at the time of king David.

MAACHATHITES. *Josh 12:5-6; 2 Sam. 23:34; 2 Kgs. 25:23-24; 1 Chr. 4:19; Jer. 40:8-9.*

Maachathites occupied some of the land on the east of Jordan that was given for a possession to the Reubenites, Gadites and the half tribe of Manasseh. *(Josh 12:5-6.)*

It is not clear which Maachah was the ancestor of the Maachathites. Hanan, son of Maachah, was one of David's mighty men. *(1 Chr. 11:43.)* Eliphelet the son of Ahasbai, the son of the Maachathite, was another of David's mighty men. *(2 Sam. 23:34.)*

Another Maachathite, Jaazaniah (Jezaniah), one of the captains of the armies, went to Gedaliah with his colleagues when they heard Gedaliah had been made governor of Judah by Nebuchadnezzar. *(2 Kgs. 25:23-24; Jer. 40:8-9.)*

Eshtemoa was a Maachathite. *(1 Chr. 4:19.)*

MAADAI. *Ezra 10:34 (18-19, 34, 44).*

Maadai, a son of Bani, and his brothers were some of the men in Israel who took foreign wives but gave them up when Ezra feared the wrath of God would destroy Israel for this iniquity.

MAADIAH. *Neh. 12:5.*

Maadiah was one of the men (priests and Levites) who went with Zerubbabel from Babylonian captivity to Jerusalem.

MAAI. *Neh. 12:36.*

Maai joined Zechariah, a descendant of Asaph, and other of his brethren with their musical instruments in the dedication of the wall of Jerusalem.

MAASEIAH (1). *1 Chr. 15:18-20.*

Maaseiah and his brethren of the second degree were assigned, under the direction of David, to be singers along with Heman, Asaph and Ethan. Maaseiah and his brethren were assigned to excel with harps on the Sheminith.

MAASEIAH (2). *2 Chr. 23:1.*

Maaseiah, the son of Adaiah, was one of the captains of hundreds Jehoiada the priest rallied to slay Athaliah and make Joash king over Judah.

MAASEIAH (3). *2 Chr. 26:11.*

Maaseiah was the ruler in Judah when Uzziah (Azariah) was king.

MAASEIAH (4). *2 Chr. 28:7.*

Maaseiah was a son of Ahaz, king of Judah. He was slain by Zichri, a mighty man of Ephraim, when the Lord allowed Judah to be brought low because of wickedness.

MAASEIAH (5). *2 Chr. 34:8-9.*

Maaseiah, the governor of Jerusalem, was sent by Josiah, king of Judah, with Shaphan, son of Azaliah, and Joah, son of Joahaz, to repair the house of the Lord. They went to Hilkiah the high priest, delivered the money for the workmen and returned to the city.

MAASEIAH (6). *Ezra 10:18-19, 44.*

Maaseiah of the sons of Jeshua the son of Jozadek and his brethren, was one of the sons of the priests who had taken foreign wives and who agreed to put them away as instructed by Ezra.

MAASEIAH (7). *zra 10:21 (18-19, 21, 44).*

Maaseiah, one of the sons of Harim, was among those sons of the priests who had taken foreign wives and who agreed to put them away as instructed by Ezra.

MAASEIAH (8). *Ezra 10:22 (18-19, 22, 44).*

Maaseiah, one of the sons of Pashur, was among those sons of the priests who had taken foreign wives and who agreed to put them away as instructed by Ezra.

MAASEIAH (9). *Jer. 21:1-7; 29:25; 37:3.*

Maaseiah the priest was the father of Zephaniah. When king Zedekiah sent Jeremiah to inquire of the priests whether or not the Lord would protect them against Nebuchadrezzar, king of Babylonia, who was threatening war against them, Jeremiah instructed Pashur and Zephaniah to tell Zedekiah that the Lord would not help them and that Jerusalem would be captured and destroyed by Nebuchadrezzar. Additionally, Zedekiah himself would be taken captive by Nebuchadrezzar. *(Jer. 21:1-7.)*

Maaseiah the priest was the father of Zephaniah. *(Jer. 29:25.)*

Maaseiah was the father of Zephaniah, which Zephaniah was sent by Zedekiah to ask Jeremiah to pray for the people. *(Jer. 37:3.)*

MAASEIAH (10). *Ezra 10:30 (18-19, 30, 44).*

Maaseiah, a son of Pahath-moab, and his brothers were among the Israelites who took foreign wives but separated themselves from them when Ezra feared the Lord would destroy all of Israel because of this iniquity.

MAASEIAH (11). *Neh. 3:23.*

Maaseiah, son of Ananiah, was the father of Azariah.

MAASEIAH (12). *Neh. 8:1-4, 7-8.*

Maaseiah was one of the men who stood on Ezra's right hand when Ezra read and interpreted the law of Moses to the people. He was one of the men who, when Ezra read and interpreted the law of Moses to the people, helped the people to understand the law.

MAASEIAH (13). *Neh. 10:25 (1, 25, 28-31).*

Maaseiah was among those chief of the people who covenanted to marry in Israel, honor the Sabbath, pay tithes and keep the commandments.

MAASEIAH (14). *Neh. 11:5.*

Maaseiah, son of Baruch of the children of Perez of the lineage of Judah, dwelled in Jerusalem after leaving Babylon. (Chart 8b.)

MAASEIAH (15). *Neh. 11:7.*

Maaseiah, father of Kolaiah of the tribe of Benjamin and son of Ithiel, dwelled in Jerusalem after leaving Babylon. (Chart 16m.)

MAASEIAH (16). *Neh. 12:41-42.*

Maaseiah, a priest and trumpeter, joined in the dedication of the walls of Jerusalem with Nehemiah and others. Jezrahiah was their overseer.

MAASEIAH (17). *Neh. 12:42.*

Maaseiah, a priest and singer, joined in the dedication of the walls of Jerusalem with Nehemiah and others. Jezrahiah was their overseer. *(Note: Two people named Maaseiah are referred to in Neh. 12:41-42.)*

MAASEIAH (18). *Jer. 29:21.*

Maaseiah was the father of Zedekiah.

MAASEIAH (19). *Jer. 32:12-16; 51:59-64.*

Maaseiah was the father of Neriah and the grandfather of Baruch who recorded the prophet Jeremiah's purchase of his uncle's son Hanameel's property. *(Jer. 32:12-16.)*

Maaseiah, father of Neriah, was the grandfather of Seraiah, which Seraiah was instructed by Jeremiah in the fourth year of Zedekiah's reign to read the book of prophecies concerning Babylon in Babylon when he got there and to then throw the book in the river and tell them that Babylon would be destroyed and not rise again just as the book would not rise again. *(Jer. 51:59-64.)*

MAASEIAH (20). *Jer. 35:4.*

Maaseiah, the son of Shallum, was the keeper of the door. The prophet Jeremiah brought the Rechabites into the chamber of the sons of Hanan which was by the chamber of the princes, which was above Maaseiah's chamber.

MAASIAI (Amashai). *1 Chr. 9:12-13; Neh. 11:13.*

Maasiai, the son of Adiel, was one of the priests who was among the first inhabitants to dwell in Jerusalem following the Israelites' Babylonian captivity. He and his brethren were "very able men for the work of the service of the house of God." *(1 Chr. 9:12-13.)*

Amashai (Maasiai) was one of the chief of the fathers chosen to dwell in Jerusalem. *(Neh. 11:13.)* (Chart 7g.)

MAAZ. *1 Chr. 2:27.*

Maaz was one of the sons of Ram. He was the great-great-great-grandson of Judah. His brothers were Jamin and Eker. (Chart 8c.)

MAAZIAH (1). *1 Chr. 24:18.*

Maaziah was from the sons of Aaron. When David made the divisions of the sons of Aaron, there was one principal household for Eleazar and one taken for Ithamar. Eleazar had 16 sons and there were eight sons of Ithamar. These 24 sons who were chief of the fathers were divided by lot. Maaziah drew the 24th lot.

MAAZIAH (2). *Neh. 10:8 (1,8, 28-31).*

Maaziah was among the priests who covenanted and sealed their covenant to marry in Israel, honor the Sabbath, pay tithes and keep the commandments.

MACHBANAI. *1 Chr. 12:13.*

Machbanai, of the tribe of Gad, was one of David's mighty men who came to him at Ziklag to rejoice with all Israel when David became king and to defend him against Saul. (Chart 13b.)

MACHBENAH. *1 Chr. 2:49.*

Machbenah, of the tribe of Judah through Caleb, was the son of Sheva. (Chart 8k.)

MACHI. *Num. 13:15, 31; Num. 14:37.*

Machi, of the tribe of Gad, was the father of Geuel, which Geuel was one of the 12 men sent by Moses to spy out the land of Canaan. He returned with a negative report. *(Num. 13:15, 31.)*

Machi and all the other scouts who returned with a negative report "died by the plague before the Lord." *(Num. 14:37.)* (Chart 13b.)

MACHIR (1) (Machirites). *Gen. 50:23; Num. 26:29; 32:33, 39-42; Deut. 3:12-16; 1 Chr. 2:21; 7:14-17.*

Machir was a son of Manasseh, grandson of Joseph and great-grandson of Jacob. His children were brought up upon Joseph's knee. *(Gen. 50:23.)* His descendants are the **Machirites**. He begat Gilead. *(Num. 26:29.)*

Moses gave the land of Sihon, king of the Amorites, and the land of Og, king of Bashan, which was on the east side of Jordan, to the children of Gad, Reuben, and to half the tribe of Manasseh for an inheritance. Machir took the land of Gilead. His son Jair named the small towns he took Havothjair. Nobah took Kenath and called it Nobah after his own name. *(Num. 32:33, 39-42.)*

Moses reminded Israel that the Lord delivered Og into their hands and that his land had been given to the half the tribe of Manasseh, the Reubenites and the Gadites for an inheritance, with Machir being given the land of Gilead, specifically. His son Jair was given the country of Argob unto the coasts of Geshuri and Maachathi, which he called Bashan-havoth-jair. *(Deut. 3:12-16.)*

Machir's daughter married Hezron when Hezron was 60 years old. She bore him Segub. Segub begat Jair (Manasseh's great-great-grandson). *(1 Chr. 2:21.)*

Machir's wife was Maachah, the sister of Huppim and Shuppim. His mother was Manasseh's concubine the Aramitess. Machir was the father of Gilead, Peresh and Sheresh. *(1 Chr. 7:14-17.) (Note: Verses 14-17 leave some confusion. Verse 14 states that Machir was the father of Gilead. Verse 16 states that Machir's wife, Maachah, bore two sons to Machir: Peresh and Sheresh, and that Peresh's sons were Ulam and Rakem. Verse 17 states that the son of Ulam was Bedan, and that these were the sons of Gilead. Thus, it would appear that Peresh and Gilead are one and the same.)* (Charts 15a-b.)

MACHIR (2). *2 Sam. 9:4; 17:27.*

Machir was the son of Ammiel. Following the death of Saul and Jonathan, Mephibosheth, Jonathan's lame son, was cared for in Machir's house in Lodebar. *(2 Sam. 9:4.)*

Machir, Shobi (son of Nahash) and Barzillai (the Gileadite) brought beds, food and other items to aid David and his followers when they came to Mahanaim on their flight to escape Absalom for they knew they were hungry, weary and thirsty. *(2 Sam. 17:27.)*

MACHIR (1), DAUGHTER OF. See **Abiah (2)**.

MACHIRITES. See **Machir (1)**.

MACHNADEBAI. *Ezra 10:40 (18-19, 40, 44).*

Machnadebai, a son of Bani, and his brothers were some of the men in Israel who took foreign wives but gave them up when Ezra feared the wrath of God would destroy Israel for this iniquity.

MADAI. *Gen. 10:2.*

Madai was a son of Japheth and a grandson of Noah. (Chart 2a.)

MADMANNAH. *1 Chr. 2:49.*

Madmannah, of the house of Judah, was the son of Shaaph and the grandson of Caleb and his concubine Maachah. (Chart 8k.)

MAGBISH. *Ezra 2:30.*

Magbish was of the people of Israel. The men of the children of Magbish who returned to Jerusalem from Babylon after Cyrus' proclamation to build the temple numbered 156.

MAGDIEL. *Gen. 36:43.*

Magdiel was one of the dukes (tribal chiefs) who came of Esau. (Chart 19.)

MAGOG. *Gen. 10:2; 1 Chr. 1:5.*

Magog was a son of Japheth and a grandson of Noah. (Chart 2a.)

MAGOR-MISSABIB. See **Pashur (1)**.

MAGPIASH. *Neh. 10:20 (1, 20, 28-31).*

Magpiash was among those chief of the people who covenanted to marry in Israel, honor the Sabbath, pay tithes and keep the commandments.

MAHALAH. *1 Chr. 7:18.*

Mahalah was the son of Hammoleketh, grandson of Machir and great-grandson of Manasseh. His brothers were Ishod and Abiezer. (Chart 15a.)

MAHALALEEL (1). *Gen. 5:12-17.*

Mahalaleel was a son of Cainan and a great-great-grandson of Adam. He was 65 years old when he begat Jared. He lived a total of 895 years, during which time he begat sons and daughters. (Charts 1.; 21.)

MAHALALEEL (2). *Neh. 11:4.*

Mahalaleel, the father of Shephatiah of the children of Judah through Perez, dwelled in Jerusalem after leaving Babylon. (Chart 8b.)

MAHALATH (1). *Gen. 28:9.* See **Bashemath**.

MAHALATH (2). *2 Chr. 11:18.*

Mahalath, daughter of Jerimoth and granddaughter of David, was the wife of king Rehoboam, son of Solomon and grandson of David. *(Note: Mahalath was*

Rehoboam's cousin and one of his 18 wives. He also had 60 concubines.) (Chart 8f.)

MAHALI (Mahli (1), Mahlites). *Ex. 6:19; Num. 3:33-37; 1 Chr. 6:19, 29; 23:21; 24:26, 28-31.*

Mahali was a son of Merari of the family of Levi. His brother was Mushi. *(Ex. 6:19.)*

Mahlites and Mushites were descendants of Merari. *(Num. 3:33-37.)*

Mahli (Mahali) and Mushi were sons of Merari. Mahli was the father of Libni who was the father of Shimei, the father of Uzza, the father of Shimea, the father of Haggiah, the father of Asaiah. He was one of those appointed over the services of song in the house of the Lord. *(1 Chr. 6:19, 29.)*

When David made Solomon king, he numbered the Levites and divided them into courses among the sons of Levi: Gershon, Kohath and Merari. The sons of Merari were Mahli and Mushi. Mahli's sons were Eleazar and Kish. Mushi's sons were Mahli, Eder and Jeremoth. These are those who were named as chief of their courses. *(1 Chr. 23:21.)*

Mahli was the son of Merari. His brother was Mushi. Their sons who were the chief of the fathers are named. They drew lots with the other Levite leaders for their courses in the presence of king David, Zadok Ahimelech and other Levite leaders. Eleazar came of Mahli but had no sons. *(1 Chr. 24:26, 28-31.)* (Chart 7c.)

MAHARAI. *2 Sam. 23:28; 1 Chr. 11:30; 27:13.*

Maharai the Netophathite was one of David's mighty men *(2 Sam. 23:28)* and one of the valiant men of the armies *(1 Chr. 11:30).*

Maharai the Netophathite was of the Zarhites. He was assigned by David to be captain for the tenth month. There were 24,000 in his course. *(1 Chr. 27:13.)* (Chart 17.)

MAHATH (1). *1 Chr. 6:35; 2 Chr. 29:12.* See **Ahimoth**.

MAHATH (2). *2 Chr. 31:13.*

Mahath, among others, was an overseer of tithes, offerings and the dedicated things under the hand of Cononiah and his brother Shimei according to the commandment of king Hezekiah and Azariah, the ruler of the house of God.

MAHAZIOTH. *1 Chr. 25:4, 30.*

Mahazioth, a Levite and musician, was a son of Heman who was of the lineage of Kohath. The musicians—sons of Heman, Asaph and Jeduthun—drew lots and were assigned their duties by David and the captains of the host. Mahazioth cast the 23rd of 24 lots. He, his sons and his brethren numbered 12. (Chart 7d.)

MAHER-SHALAL-HASH-BAZ. *Isa. 8:1-3.*

Maher-shalal-hash-baz was the son of Isaiah and the prophetess. His name means "to speed to the spoil he hasteneth the prey." Isaiah stated that he and his sons "are for signs and for wonders in Israel from the Lord of hosts." Before Maher-shalal-hash-baz would be old enough to choose between good and evil, the riches of Damascus and the spoil of Samaria would be taken away.

MAHLAH. *Num. 26:33; Num. 27:1-7.*

Mahlah was a daughter of Zelophehad and a great-granddaughter of Manasseh. Her sisters were Noah, Hoglah, Milcah and Tirzah. *(Num. 26:33.)* Mahlah and her sisters petitioned Moses and Eleazar to be given their father's inheritance because he had no sons and he, himself, had died in the wilderness. The Lord told Moses the sisters were right and should be given an inheritance among their father's brethren. *(Num. 27:1-7.)* (Charts 15a-b.)

MAHLI (1). *1 Chr. 6:19, 29.* See **Mahali**.

MAHLI (2). *1 Chr. 6:47; 23:23; 24:30-31.*

Mahli was the son of Mushi who was the son of Merari. *(1 Chr. 6:47.)*

Mahli's brothers were Eder and Jeremoth. When David made Solomon king, he numbered the Levites and divided them into courses among the sons of Levi. Mahli, Eder and Jeremoth were named as chief of their fathers. From the age of twenty years and upward, they and the others named did the work for the service of the house of the Lord. *(1 Chr. 23:23.)*

Mahli and his brothers drew lots with the other Levite leaders for their courses in the presence of king David, Zadok Ahimelech and other Levite leaders. *(1 Chr.1 24:30-31.)* (Chart 7e.)

MAHLITES. See **Mahali**.

MAHLON. *Ruth 1:2-5.*

Mahlon was the first son of Elimelech and Naomi. His brother was Chileon. He married Orpah. He died in Moab.

MAHOL. See **Zarah**.

MALACHI. *Mal. 1-4.*

Malachi prophesied about 430 B.C. His prophecy is recorded in the last book in the Old Testament. It is just four chapters long. The Lord sent Malachi to chastise and condemn the children of Israel for offering polluted bread upon the altars and for offering blemished animals for sacrifices. They found it "a weariness" and belittled the ceremony. In contrast, the Gentiles would revere the name of the Lord and would offer pure offerings. *(Mal. 1.)*

Malachi reproved the priests. As the messengers of the Lord, Malach said they should keep knowledge. People should be able to seek to know the law from them. However, the priests were not keeping their own covenants nor teaching the people, but were leading them astray. He reminded the people that we are all brothers and sisters, children of one heavenly Father. He chastised them for dealing treacherously with each other and for profaning the covenant of their fathers. He also reproved them for marrying idol worshippers, i.e. "The daughters of a strange god." He stressed that the Lord hates divorce and admonished them to be faithful to their wives. *(Mal. 2.)*

Malachi prophesied that prior to the Second Coming, the Lord would send His messenger to prepare the way. The Lord will come suddenly to His temple. The Lord will be as a refiner's fire. He will purify the sons of Levi. He will accept the offering of Judah and Jerusalem. He will sit in judgment and be a witness against those who are evil. The Lord does not change. The people were instructed to pay tithes and offerings. A book of remembrance was kept. *(Mal. 3.)*

At the Second Coming, the earth shall "burn as an oven" and the wicked will be destroyed. The Sun of righteousness will arise with healing in His wings. The people were admonished to remember the law of Moses. Prior to the Second Coming, the Lord promised to send Elijah the prophet *(to restore the sealing power of the priesthood)* to turn the hearts of the children to the fathers and the hearts of the fathers to their children *(genealogy work and temple work)*, lest He come and smite the earth with a curse *(i.e., without this sealing power, families would be disbanded at death and the plan of the Lord, the plan that provides for eternal families, the Plan of Salvation would be null and void). (Mal. 4.) (Note: This prophesy was fulfilled April 3, 1836, in the temple at Kirkland, Ohio, as recorded in D&C 110:13-16: "After this vision had closed, another great and glorious vision burst upon us [Joseph Smith and Oliver Cowdery]; for Elijah the prophet, who was taken to heaven without tasting death, stood before us, and said: 'Behold, the time has fully come, which was spoken of by the mouth of Malachi—testifying that he [Elijah] should be sent, before the great and dreadful day of the Lord come—To turn the hearts of the fathers to the children, and the children to the fathers, lest the whole earth be smitten with a curse—Therefore, the keys of this dispensation are committed into your hands; and by this ye may know that the great and dreadful day of the Lord is near, even at the doors.'")*

MALCHAM. *Chr. 8:9.*

Malcham was a son of Shaharaim, a descendant of Benjamin, and Hodesh. (Chart 16f.)

MALCHIAH (1). *1 Chr. 6:40-41.*

Malchiah, a descendant of Levi through Gershon, was the father of Baaseiah and the son of Ethni who was the son of Zerah. (Chart 7a.)

MALCHIAH (2). *Neh. 11:12; Jer. 38:1.* See **Malchijah (1)**.

MALCHIAH (3). *Ezra 10:25 (18-19, 25, 44).*

Malchiah was of the sons of Parosh. He was among those who had taken wives from among the Canaanites or other foreign groups but who agreed to Ezra's request that they separate themselves from these strange wives lest the Lord destroy the rest of the children of Israel.

MALCHIAH (4). *Ezra 10:31 (18-19, 31, 44).*

Malchiah, one of Harim's sons, and his brothers Eliezer, Ishijah, Shemaiah, Shimeon, Benjamin, Malluch and Shemariah, were some of the Israelite men who took wives from among the Canaanites and other foreign groups. They agreed to Ezra's request to separate themselves from their foreign wives.

MALCHIAH (5). *Neh. 3:14.*

Malchiah the son of Rechab, the ruler of part of Beth-haccerem, repaired the dung gate when the children of Israel rebuilt the walls and gates of Jerusalem during the time of Ezra and Nehemiah.

MALCHIAH (6). *Neh. 3:31.*

Malchiah was a goldsmith's son. He labored next to the area between Meshullam and the Nethinims over "against the gate Miphkad . . . and between the going up of the corner unto the sheep gate repaired the goldsmiths and the merchants" when the children of Israel rebuilt the walls and gates of Jerusalem during the time of Ezra and Nehemiah.

MALCHIAH (7). *Neh. 8:1-8.*

Malchiah was one of the men who stood on Ezra's left hand when Ezra read and interpreted the law of Moses to the people.

MALCHIAH (8). *Jer. 38:1, 6.*

Malchiah was the son of Hammelech (i.e., the king, presumably Zedekiah). The princes cast Jeremiah into Malchiah's miry dungeon which was in the court of the prison. *(Note: Verse 26 states that Jeremiah was to say to those who sought his death, if they questioned him, that he had petitioned the king that he not be returned to Jonathan's house for fear he would die there. Perhaps Malchiah and Jonathan are one and the same.)*

MALCHIEL (Malchielites). *Gen. 46:17; Num. 26:45.*

Malchiel was a son of Beriah, grandson of Asher, and a great-grandson of Jacob. *(Gen. 46:17.)* His descendants are called **Malchielites**. *(Num. 26:45.)* (Chart 14a.)

MALCHIJAH (1) (Malchiah (2), Melchiah). *1 Chr. 9:12; Neh. 11:12; Jer. 21:1; 38:1.*

Malchijah, a descendant of Immer, was the father of Pashur and was one of the priests in Jerusalem whose genealogy was written in the book of the kings of Israel and Judah who were carried away captive into Babylon because of their transgression. *(1 Chr. 9:12.)*

Malchiah (Malchijah, **Melchiah**) was the father of Pashur. *(Neh. 11:12; Jer. 21:1; 38:1.)* (Chart 7g.)

MALCHIJAH (2). *1 Chr. 24:9.*

Malchijah was from the sons of Aaron. When David made the divisions of the sons of Aaron, there was one principal household for Eleazar and one taken for Ithamar. Eleazar had 16 sons and there were eight sons of Ithamar. These 24 sons who were chief of the fathers were divided by lot. Malchijah drew the fifth lot.

MALCHIJAH (3). *Ezra 10:25 (18-19, 25, 44).*

Malchijah was of the sons of Parosh. He was one of those who had taken wives from among the Canaanites or other foreign groups but who agreed to Ezra's request that they separate themselves from these strange wives lest the Lord destroy the rest of the children of Israel.

MALCHIJAH (4). *Neh. 3:11.*

Malchijah the son of Harim and Hashub the son of Pahath-moab worked next to Hattush and repaired the tower of the furnaces when the children of Israel rebuilt the walls and gates of Jerusalem during the time of Ezra and Nehemiah.

MALCHIJAH (5). *Neh. 10:3 (1, 3, 28-31).*

Malchijah was among the priests who covenanted and sealed their covenant to marry in Israel, honor the Sabbath, pay tithes and keep the commandments.

MALCHIJAH (6). *Neh. 12:42.*

Malchijah, a priest and singer, joined in the dedication of the walls of Jerusalem with Nehemiah.

MALCHIRAM. *1 Chr. 3:18.*

Malchiram, a descendant of David, was a son (grandson) of Jeconiah (Jehoiachin). (Chart 1.)

MALCHI-SHUA. See **Melchi-shua**.

MALLOTHI. *1 Chr. 25:4, 26.*

Mallothi, a Levite and musician, was a son of Heman who was of the lineage of Kohath. The musicians—sons of Heman, Asaph and Jeduthun—drew lots and were given their assigned duties by David and the captains of the host. Mallothi cast the 19th of 24 lots. He, his sons and his brethren numbered 12. (Chart 7d.)

MALLUCH (1). *1 Chr. 6:44-45.*

Malluch, a descendant of Levi through Merari, was the son of Hashabiah (Asaiah) and the father of Abdi. (Chart 7e.)

MALLUCH (2). *Ezra 10:29 (18-19, 29, 44).*

Malluch, a son of Bani, was one of the Israelites who took foreign wives causing Ezra to cry unto the Lord in behalf of Israel, fearing that the Lord would totally destroy the children of Israel due to this latest iniquity. Malluch and his brothers agreed to put away their foreign wives.

MALLUCH (3). *Ezra 10:32 (18-19, 32, 44).*

Malluch, one of Harim's sons, and his brothers Eliezer, Ishijah, Malchiah, Shemaiah, Shimeon, Benjamin and Shemariah, were some of the Israelite men who took wives from among the Canaanites and other foreign groups. They agreed to Ezra's request to separate themselves from their foreign wives.

MALLUCH (4). *Neh. 10:4 (1, 4, 28-31).*

Malluch was among the priests who covenanted and sealed their covenant to marry in Israel, honor the Sabbath, pay tithes and keep the commandments.

MALLUCH (5). *Neh. 10:27 (1, 27-31).*

Malluch was among those chief of the people who covenanted to marry in Israel, honor the Sabbath, pay tithes and keep the commandments.

MALLUCH (6). *Neh. 12:2.*

Malluch was one of the men (priests and Levites) who went up from Babylon to Jerusalem with Zerubbabel.

MAMRE. *Gen. 14:13-24.*

Mamre was an Amorite. He and his brothers, Eshcol and Aner, joined Abram to rescue Lot from King Chedorlaomer. When they returned from the slaughter of Chedorlaomer and the kings that were with him, the king of Sodom offered Abram the goods that had been retrieved. Abram took none, but suggested that Mamre, Aner and Eshcol should be allowed to take their portion.

MAN (1), A. *Gen. 37:15-17.*

A Man found young Joseph wandering in the fields. Jacob had sent him to find his brothers who were tending the flocks in Shechem, but Joseph couldn't find them. The man directed him to Dothan where they had gone.

MAN (2), A. *Judg. 7:13.*

A Man belonging to the Midianites or the Amalekites was overheard by Gideon relating a dream to another fellow who interpreted the dream: God would deliver the host of Midian into Gideon's hand.

MAN (3), A. *2 Sam. 1:2-16.*

A Man who was an Amalekite claimed to David that he had killed Saul. He reported that Jonathan was also slain. David had one of his men kill the man for having killed the Lord's anointed.

MAN (1), A CERTAIN. *2 Sam. 18:10-14.*

A Certain Man observed Absalom get hung up in a tree as he pursued David. The man told Joab that he saw Absalom hanging in a tree. However, Absalom was still alive. The man refused to kill Absalom because the king had charged everyone to "deal gently for my sake with the young man, even with Absalom."

MAN (2), A CERTAIN. *1 Kgs. 22:34; 2 Chr. 18:33.*

A Certain Man drew a bow and smote Ahab, king of Israel, which resulted in Ahab's death.

MAN, A DEAD. *2 Kgs. 13:21.*

A Dead Man was restored to life when his body was cast into the sepulchre wherein Elisha's body lay. When the man's body touched Elisha's bones, he revived and stood up on his feet.

MANAHATH. *Gen. 36:23.*

Manahath was one of the children of Shobal, son of Seir the Horite. (Chart 4b.)

MANAHETHITES. *1 Chr. 2:52.*

Manahethites (i.e., half the Manahethites) were descendants of Shobal who was a son of Hur and grandson of Caleb. (Chart 8 l.)

MAN, AN OLD. *Judg. 19:16-28.*

An Old Man in Gibeah offered a certain Levite and his concubine a place to lodge for the night. When some wicked men of Gibeah, Benjamites, came to his house asking for the Levite that they might "know" him, the old man pleaded in behalf of the Levite and offered them his daughter and the Levite's concubine instead. They took the concubine and abused her to her death.

MANASSEH (1) (Manassites). *Gen. 41:51; 46:20; 48:5-6, 13-20; 50:23; 26:29-34; Num. 32; 34:23; Deut. 3:12-16; 4:43; 33:17; Josh. 17:12-13; 22:1, 26-28; Judg. 1:27-28; 18:30; 1 Chr. 2:21; 5:18-26; 12:31, 37; 27:20-21; 2 Chr. 30:10-11, 18; Ezek. 48:4-5, 32.*

Manasseh was Joseph and Asenath's firstborn son. *(Gen. 41:51.)*

Manasseh and Ephraim were born in Egypt unto Joseph and Asenath, the daughter of Poti-pherah, priest of On. *(Gen. 46:20.)*

Jacob told Joseph that Manasseh and Ephraim would be his just as Reuben and Simeon were his, but that any issue he begot after them would be Joseph's. When Joseph presented his two sons to Jacob, Jacob placed his left hand upon Manasseh and his right hand upon Ephraim, giving Ephraim the birthright blessing instead of Manasseh. He said that Manasseh would be great and become a great people, but that Ephraim would be greater. *(Gen. 48:5-6, 13-20.)*

Manasseh was the father of Machir. Machir was brought up upon Joseph's knee. *(Gen. 50:23.)*

When Moses and Elcazar numbered Israel's males who were twenty years old and older as they were on the plains of Moab near Jericho, those in Manasseh's family numbered 52,700. His descendants included the Machirites, Gileadites, Jeezerites, Helekites, Asrielites, Shechemites, Shemidaites and Hepherites. *(Num. 26:29-34.)*

The posterity of Reuben and Gad asked Moses if they could have the land east of Jordan for their inheritance. They were granted their request upon covenanting to join the other tribes in conquering Canaan. Moses also gave it to half of the tribe of Manasseh. Machir, Manasseh's son, dispossessed the Amorites and settled in the land of Gilead. Manasseh's son Jair took the small towns and called them Havoth-jair. Nobah took Kenath and called it Nobah. *(Num. 32.)*

Hanniel, son of Ephod, was chosen to divide the land of inheritance given to the second half of Manasseh's posterity. *(Num. 34:23.)*

Moses reminded Israel that Og, the king of Bashan, had been delivered into their hands and that his cities and lands had been divided between the half tribe of Manasseh and the Reubenites and Gadites. *(Deut. 3:12-16.)*

Manassites were the descendants of Manasseh. The city of Golan in Bashan, which was given to part of the tribe of Manassah, was selected by Moses as commanded by the Lord to be one of the cities of refuge for people who unintentionally killed someone. *(Deut. 4:43.)*

Moses blessed the tribes of Israel. Joseph was blessed above all others: the thousands of Manasseh and the ten thousands of Ephraim. They shall gather the people together in the latter days. *(Deut. 33:17.)*

The children of Manasseh did not drive the inhabitants of Canaanan out of the land. However, when they became strong enough, they put the Canaanites to tribute. *(Josh. 17:12-13; Judg. 1:27-28.)*

After the rest of the tribes of Israel had received their inheritances, the half tribe of Manasseh and the tribes of Reuben and Gad were dismissed and allowed to return to their own lands on the other side of Jordan. They built an altar to be a witness between the two-and-a-half tribes on the east of Jordan and the other tribes on the west side of Jordan and the generations that would follow so that in future times no one could say they had no part in the Lord. *(Josh. 22:1, 26-28.)*

During the time of the judges, the children of Israel fell away into idolatry. "Jonathan, the son of Gershom, the son of Manasseh, he and his sons were priests to the tribe of Dan until the day of the captivity of the land." *(Judg. 18:30.)*

Manasseh's granddaughter, Machir's daughter, married Hezron when he was 60 years old and bore him Segub. *(1 Chr. 2:21.)*

The sons of the half tribe of Manasseh, combined with the sons of Reuben and the sons of Gad, numbered 44,760 who were skillful with "buckler and sword" and in the art of war. They made war with the Hagarites, with Jetur and Nephish (Naphish) and Nodab (Kedemah). The following were the heads of the house of their fathers: Epher, Ishi, Eliel, Azriel, Jeremiah, Hodaviah and Jahdiel. They became wicked and transgressed the laws of God. Thus, God stirred up the Assyrian kings, Pul and Tilgath-pilneser, and they carried away the half tribe of Manasseh, the tribe of Reuben and the tribe of Gad. *(1 Chr. 5:18-26.)*

When David became king and went to Ziklag, all Israel rejoiced and sent their armies to support him. The half tribe of Manasseh sent 18,000 men. The other half tribe of Manasseh, along with the Reubenites and Gadites, sent 120,000 men and their instruments of war. *(1 Chr. 12:31, 37.)*

When David was king, Hoshea, son of Azaziah, was prince of one of the half tribes of Manasseh. Iddo, son of Zechariah, was the prince of the half tribe of Manasseh that was in Gilead. *(1 Chr. 27:20-21.)*

Hezekiah, king of Judah, sent couriers throughout all Israel to invite them to come to Jerusalem to participate in a solemn Passover. Many throughout the country of Manasseh and Ephraim even unto Zebulun laughed and mocked the couriers to scorn. Some of those from Manasseh, Asher and Zebulun, however, humbled themselves and went to Jerusalem. *(2 Chr. 30:10-11, 18.)*

The Lord revealed to Ezekiel just how the land should be divided by tribes when the children of Israel are gathered in the latter days. Joseph will receive two portions *(Ezek. 47:13)*; thus, Manasseh and Ephraim will each receive one portion. Manasseh's land will be between the borders of Naphtali and Ephraim. The twelve gates of the city will bear the names of the twelve sons of Jacob. One of the east gates will bear the name of Joseph. *(Ezek. 48:4-5, 32.)* (Charts 15a, c.)

MANASSEH (2). *2 Kgs. 20:21; 21:1-18; 23:12, 26; 24:3; 1 Chr. 3:13; 2 Chr. 32:33; 33:1-20; Jer. 15:4.*

Manasseh, the son of Hezekiah, reigned over Judah after his father. *(2 Kgs. 20:21.)* He was 12 years old when he became king. He reigned 55 years in Jerusalem, doing evil in the sight of the Lord. His mother was Hephzibah. He rebuilt all the altars to Baal that his father had destroyed. He shed innocent blood and made his son to pass through the fire, used enchantments, and dealt with "familiar spirits" and wizards. He seduced his people to do more evil than even those nations the Lord destroyed had done before the children of Israel were given their lands. He caused his people to be more wicked than even the Amorites so the Lord told them that He would "forsake the remnant of mine inheritance, and deliver them into the hand of their enemies; and they shall become a prey and a spoil to all their enemies." Manasseh died and was buried in a sepulchre in the garden of his own house. His son Amon reigned in his stead. *(2 Kgs. 21:1-18; 2 Chr. 33:1-10, 20.)*

The altars Manasseh had built in the two courts of the house of the Lord were broken down and destroyed by Josiah. However, Manasseh's great wickedness had kindled the Lord's wrath against Judah and He did not turn His anger away. *(2 Kgs. 23:12, 26.)*

Judah was removed from the sight of the Lord because of the sins of Manasseh. *(2 Kgs. 24:3.)*

Manasseh was the son of Hezekiah and the father of Amon. *(1 Chr. 3:13.)*

Manasseh reigned after the death of his father Hezekiah. *(2 Chr. 32.33.)*

Because of Manasseh's wickedness, the Lord allowed the captains of the Assyrians to take him captive. Manasseh repented and called upon the Lord. He removed the strange gods and idols out of the house of the Lord and all the altars that he had built up. He commanded Judah to serve the Lord God of Israel. He died and his son Amon reigned in his stead. *(2 Chr. 33:11-20.)*

The Lord told the prophet Jeremiah that due to the wickedness of the people and what Manasseh had done in Jerusalem, He would allow Judah to be destroyed, slain, carried away captive and scattered. *(Jer. 15:4.)* (Chart 1.)

MANASSEH (3). *Ezra 10:30 (18-19, 30, 44)*.

Manasseh was a son of Pahath-moab. He and his brothers were among the Israelites who took foreign wives but separated themselves from them at Ezra's request as Ezra feared the Lord would destroy all of Israel due to this latest iniquity.

MANASSEH (4). *Ezra 10:33 (18-19, 33, 44)*.

Manasseh, one of Hashum's sons, and his brothers Mattenai, Mattathah, Zabad, Eliphelet, Jeremai and Shimei were among the Israelite men who took foreign wives but complied with Ezra's request that they put away their strange wives so as not to bring the wrath of God upon Israel.

MAN FROM BAAL-SHALISHA. *2 Kgs. 4:42-44*.

A **Man from Baal-shalisha** brought Elisha bread and grain. Elisha mulitplied it and the multitude ate of it.

MAN FROM BETH-EL, A. *Judg. 1:24-26*.

A Man from Beth-el encountered spies from the house of Joseph. They asked him to shew them the gate to the city and they would let him and his family go. He did as requested. He then went into the land of the Hittites and built a city there.

MANOAH. *Judg. 13:2-24.*

Manoah was the father of Samson and was of Zorah of the family of the Danites. His wife informed him that an angel of the Lord had told her she would conceive a son. Manoah petitioned the Lord to send the angel again that he might teach them what they should do. The angel returned. Manoah invited the angel to eat with them but the angel declined. (Chart 11b.)

MANOAH'S WIFE. *Judg. 13:2-24.*

Manoah's Wife was barren. An angel appeared to her and promised she would have a son who would begin to deliver Israel from Philistine bondage. The angel told her she was to abstain from wine and strong drink and not to eat any unclean thing. She was also told that a razor was never to touch his head as he would be a Nazarite unto God from the womb. When the child was born, she called him Samson.

MAN OF GOD. *(2 Chr. 25:7.)*

A **Man of God** went to Amaziah, king of Judah, and counseled him against letting the army of Israel accompany him to battle because the Lord was not with Israel.

MAN OF GOD OUT OF JUDAH. *1 Kgs. 13:1-32.*

A **Man of God** came out of Judah to Jeroboam where he cried against the altar in Beth-el. King Jeroboam put forth his hand to lay hold on him for doing so, and Jeroboam's hand dried up and the altar was rent and the ashes poured out from the altar as the man of God had said. Then Jeroboam aked him to petition the Lord to restore his hand; and it was so. The man of God had been instructed by the Lord to neither eat nor drink and to return home a different way than he came. Nevertheless, he was led astray by an old prophet from Beth-el and was slain by a lion for disobedience.

MAN OF GREAT STATURE. *2 Sam. 21:20-21; 1 Chr. 20:6-7.*

A Man of Great Stature, who had six fingers on each hand and six toes on each foot, was born to the giant in Gath. When he went against Israel, he was slain by Jonathan, the son of Shimea, David's brother.

MAOCH. *1 Sam. 27:2.* See **King Maacah**.

MAON. *1 Chr. 2:45.*

Maon, of the house of Judah, was the son of Shammai who was the son of Rekem who was one of the sons of Hebron. He begat Beth-zur. (Chart 8i.)

MARA. See **Naomi**.

MARESHAH (1). *1 Chr. 2:42.*

Mareshah, of the house of Judah, was the father of Hebron. (Chart 8i.)

MARESHAH (2). *1 Chr. 4:21.*

Mareshah was a son of Laadah, a grandson of Shelah and a great-grandson of Judah. (Chart 8a.)

MARINERS AND SHIPMASTER. *Jonah 1.*

Mariners and Shipmaster of a ship docked at Joppa were headed to Tarshish when Jonah booked passage on the ship. Once they got on the sea, a terrible storm developed. While Jonah slept, the mariners prayed to their god and lightened their boat by dumping cargo overboard. The shipmaster wakened Jonah and told him to pray to his God for deliverence. Eventually, the mariners and shipmaster cast lots to see who was the cause of their problem. The lot fell upon Jonah, who acknowledged that he was fleeing from the Lord and that was why they were having the storm. At Jonah's insistence, they reluctantly cast him overboard.

MARSENA. *Esth. 1:14-15.*

Marsena was one of the seven princes of Persia and Media with king Ahasuerus when queen Vashti refused to come at his command. He and his companions asked Ahasuerus what they should do to Vashti because of her refusal to obey his command.

MASH (Meshech (2)). *Gen. 10:23; 1 Chr. 1:17.*

Mash (Meshech) was a descendant of Aram, a grandson of Shem and a great-grandson of Noah. (Chart 2b.)

MASSA. *Gen. 25:14.*

Massa was a son of Ishmael and a grandson of Abraham and Hagar, Sarah's handmaid. (Chart 3e.)

MATRED. *Gen. 36:39; 1 Chr. 1:50.*

Matred, Hadar's (Hadad's) wife, was the mother of Mehetabel. (Chart 18.)

MATRI. *1 Sam. 10:21.*

Matri, of the tribe of Benjamin, was the family taken by Samuel from which he was to select a king over Israel. Saul, the son of Kish was chosen from the family of Matri.

MATTAN (1). *2 Kgs. 11:18; 2 Chr. 23:17.*

Mattan was the priest of Baal. When Jehoiada the priest made a covenant between the Lord and the king and the people in Judah that they should be the Lord's people, the people of the land went into the house of Baal and destroyed it. They slew Mattan before the altars.

MATTAN (2). *Jer. 38:1-6.*

Mattan was the father of Shephatiah, which Shephatiah along with other associates cast Jeremiah the prophet into a miry dungeon.

MATTANIAH (1). *2 Kgs. 24:17.* See **Zedekiah (2)**.

MATTANIAH (2). *1 Chr. 9:15 (2, 14-15); 2 Chr. 20:14; 29:13; Neh. 11:17, 22; 12:8, 35.*

Mattaniah, a descendant of Asaph, was the son of Micah (Micha, Michaiah). He was a Levite who dwelt in the villages of the Netophathites. His genealogy was written in the book of the kings of Israel and Judah, who were carried away to Babylon for their transgression. He was among those Levites who were the first inhabitants to dwell in their possessions upon returning from Babylonian captivity. *(1 Chr. 9:15 [2, 14-15].)*

Mattaniah, a Levite of the sons of Asaph, was the father of Jeiel (Hashabiah, Shemaiah) who was the father of Benaiah (Bani, Jonathan) who was the father of Zechariah (Uzzi) who was the father of Jahaziel. *(2 Chr. 20:14.)*

Mattaniah, along with Zechariah, was among those Levites whom Hezekiah, king of Judah, instructed to sanctify themselves so they could cleanse and sanctify the house of the Lord. *(2 Chr. 29:13.)*

Mattaniah, son of Micha, was the principal to begin the thanksgiving in prayer when the children of Israel returned to Jerusalem from Babylonian captivity. He was the father of Hashabiah (Jeiel). *(Neh. 11:17, 22.)*

Mattaniah and his brethren are listed among those Levites who went up from Babylon with Zerubbabel to Jerusalem and was over the thanksgiving. His descendant Zechariah was one of the priests' sons who was assigned by Nehemiah to take his trumpet and join one of two great companies on the walls of Jerusalem for the dedication of the walls. *(Neh. 12:8, 35.)* (Chart 7a.)

MATTANIAH (3). *Neh. 13:13.*

Mattaniah was the father of Zaccur who was the father of Hanan, which Hanan was chosen by Nehemiah to be one of the treasurers over the treasury to oversee the distribution of the portion that should go to the Levites.

MATTANIAH (4). *1 Chr. 25:4, 16.*

Mattaniah, a Levite and musician, was a son of Heman. The musicians—sons of Heman, Asaph and Jeduthun—drew lots and were given their duty assignments by David and the captains of the host. Mattaniah cast the ninth lot. He, his sons and his brethren numbered 12. (Chart 7d.)

MATTANIAH (5). *Ezra 10:26 (18-19, 26, 44).*

Mattaniah, one of the sons of Elam who took wives from among the Canaanites and other groups, agreed to do as Ezra said and separate himself from foreign wives.

MATTANIAH (6). *Ezra 10:27 (18-19, 27, 44).*

Mattaniah was one of the sons of Zattu who took wives from among the Canaanites and other foreign groups. He and his brothers complied with Ezra's request that they separate themselves from these foreign wives lest the Lord destroy the remainder of the children of Israel because of this iniquity.

MATTANIAH (7). *Ezra 10:30 (18-19, 30, 44).*

Mattaniah was a son of Pahath-moab. He and his brothers were among the Israelites who took foreign wives but separated themselves from them at Ezra's request as Ezra feared the Lord would destroy all of Israel due to this iniquity.

MATTANIAH (8). *Ezra 10:37 (18-19, 37, 44).*

Mattaniah, a son of Bani, and his brothers were some of the men in Israel who took foreign wives but gave them up when Ezra feared the wrath of God would destroy Israel for this iniquity.

MATTANIAH (9). *Neh. 12:25.*

Mattaniah, Akkub, Bakbukiah, Obadiah, Meshullam and Talmon were porters who kept the ward at the thresholds of the gates in the days of Joiakim, Nehemiah and Ezra.

MATTATHAH. *Ezra 10:33 (18-19, 33, 44).*

Mattathah, one of Hashum's sons, and his brothers—Mattenai, Zabad, Eliphelet, Jeremai, Manasseh and Shimei—were among the Israelite men who took foreign wives but complied with Ezra's request that they put away their strange wives so as not to bring the wrath of God upon Israel.

MATTENAI (1). *Ezra 10:33 (18-19, 33, 44).*

Mattenai, one of Hashum's sons, and his brothers—Mattathah, Zabad, Eliphelet, Jeremai, Manasseh and Shime—were among the Israelite men who took foreign wives but complied with Ezra's request that they put away their strange wives so as not to bring the wrath of God upon Israel.

MATTENAI (2). *Ezra 10:37 (18-19, 37, 44).*

Mattenai, a son of Bani, and his brothers were some of the men in Israel who took foreign wives but put them away when Ezra feared the wrath of God would destroy Israel for this iniquity.

MATTENAI (3). *Neh. 12:19.*

Mattenai, son of Joiarib, was one of the priests who was a chief of the fathers in the days of Joiakim.

MATTITHIAH (1). *1 Chr. 9:31.*

Mattithiah, a Levite, was the firstborn of Shallum the Korahite. "He had the set office over the things that were made in the pans."

MATTITHIAH (2). *1 Chr. 15:18-21; 16:5; 25:3, 21.*

Mattithiah and his brethren of the second degree were assigned, under the direction of David, to be singers along with Heman, Asaph and Ethan. Mattithiah and his brethren were assigned to excel wth harps on the Sheminith. *(1 Chr. 15:18-21.)*

Mattithiah, a Levite, and his brethren were appointed by David to minister before the ark of the Lord and to play with psalteries and with harps. *(1 Chr. 16:5.)*

David and the captains of the host separated to the service the musicians—the sons of Asaph, Heman and Jeduthun—and they cast lots to determine their courses. Mattithiah, of the sons of Jeduthun, cast the 14th of 24 lots. He, his sons and his brethren numbered 12. *(1 Chr. 25:3, 21.)* (Chart 7h.)

MATTITHIAH (3). *Ezra 10:43 (18-19, 43-44).*

Mattithiah was one of Nebo's sons. He and his brothers—Jeiel, Zabad, Zebina, Jadau, Joel and Benaiah—were some of the Israelite men who took foreign wives but agreed to separate themselves from them because Ezra feared the Lord's wrath would destroy all of Israel for this iniquity.

MATTITHIAH (4). *Neh. 8:1-8.*

Mattithiah was one of the men who stood on Ezra's right hand when Ezra read and interpreted the law of Moses to the people.

MEBUNNAI (Sibbecai). *2 Sam. 23:27; 1 Chr. 11:29; 27:11.*

Mebunnai (Sibbecai) the Hushathite was one of David's mighty men *(2 Sam. 23:27)* and one of the valiant men of the armies *(1 Chr. 11:29).*

Sibbecai the Hushathite, was of the Zarhites. He was assigned by king David to be over the course of 24,000 who served for the eighth month. *(1 Chr. 27:11.)* (Chart 17.)

MEDAD. *Num. 11:26-27.*

Medad was one of seventy men of the elders of the children of Israel who Moses gathered together to help share the responsibility of leading the people. Sixty-eight leaders went about prophesying, but Medad and Eldad, another of the seventy chosen elders, remained in camp and prophesied to the people there.

MEDAN. *Gen. 25:2.*

Medan was a son of Abraham and his wife Keturah. (Charts 2b.; 3a, d, f.)

MEDES. *Jer. 51:11, 28; Dan. 5:31; 6:8; 8:20-25; 9:1.*

The Medes were from the kingdom of Media which was in the part of Southwest Asia that is now Northwest Iran. Jeremiah prophesied that judgment and destruction would come upon Babylon and that "the Lord hath raised up the spirit of the kings of the Medes: for his device is against Babylon, to destroy it." *(Jer. 51:11, 28.)*

Darius the Median took over Babylon when it fell under the reign of Belshazzar, Nebuchadnezzar's son. *(Dan. 5:31.)*

The Medes and Persians had a law that when the king established a decree and signed the written document, that it could not be changed nor altered. King Darius' leaders used that law to try to destroy Daniel. *(Dan. 6:8.)*

Daniel saw in vision a ram representinig Media and Persia in the latter days and a he goat representing Grecia. The goat destroyed the ram. *(Dan. 8:20-25.)*

Darius, king over the realm of the Chaldeans, was of the seed of the Medes. *(Dan. 9:1.)*

MEHETABEEL. *Neh. 6:10.*

Mehetabeel was the father of Delaiah and the grandfather of Shemaiah.

MEHETABEL. *Gen. 36:39; 1 Chr. 1:50.*

Mehetabel was the wife of king Hadar (Hadad) of Edom. She was the daughter of Matred who was the daughter of Mezahab. (Chart 18.)

MEHIDA. *Ezra 2:52, 58; Neh. 7:54, 60.*

Mehida was a Nethinim. When the Nethinims and the children of Solomon's servants left Babylon to return to Jerusalem to build the house of the Lord as proclaimed by Cyrus, king of Persia, they numbered 392.

MEHIR. *1 Chr. 4:11.*

Mehir, the father of Eshton, was the son of Chelub the brother of Shuah.

MEHOLATHITE. *2 Sam. 21:8.*

Meholathites. Barzilla, father-in-law to Merab, Saul's daughter, was a Meholathite.

MEHUJAEL. *Gen. 4:18.*

Mehujael, a descendant of Cain, was the son of Irad. He begat Methusael. (Chart 1.)

MEHUMAN. *Esth. 1:10.*

Mehuman was one of the seven chamberlains serving in the presence of king Ahasuerus who was sent to bring queen Vashti to Ahasuerus.

MEHUNIM (Meunim). *Ezra 2:50, 58; Neh. 7:52, 60.*

Mehunim (Meunim) was a Nethinim. When the Nethinims and the children of Solomon's servants left Babylon to return to Jerusalem to build the house of the Lord as proclaimed by Cyrus, king of Persia, they numbered 392.

MELATIAH. *Neh. 3:7.*

Melatiah was a Gibeonite. He and Jadon, the Meronothite, labored next to Jehoiada and Meshullam on the walls and gates of Jerusalem when the children of Israel rebuilt them during the time of Ezra and Nehemiah.

MELCHIAH. *Jer. 21:1.* See **Malchijah (1)**.

MELCHI-SHUA (Malchi-shua). *1 Sam. 14:49; 31:2-13; 31:2-13; 1 Chr. 8:33; 9:39; 10:2, 12.*

Melchi-shua was one of Saul's sons. His brothers were Jonathan and Ishui. His sisters were Merab and Michal. *(1 Sam. 14:49.)*

Malchi-shua (Melchi-shua) was slain in battle against the Philistines along with his brothers Jonathan and Abinadab (Ishui). His father died in the same battle. Their bodies were hung on the wall of Beth-shan. Valiant men from Jabesh-gilead, under cover of night, retrieved their bodies and burned them at Jabesh, burying their bones under a tree at Jebesh. His death was foretold by Samuel, who was dead but was called up by the witch of En-dor. *(1 Sam. 31:2-13; 1 Chr. 10:2,12.) (Ssee 1 Sam. 28:19, also.) (Note: See "Samuel" for explanation regarding witch of En-dor.)*

Malchi-shua was begotten by Saul. His brothers were Jonathan, Abinadab and Esh-baal. *(1 Chr. 8:33; 9:39.)* (Chart 16 l.)

MELCHIZEDEK. *Gen. 14:18-20.*

Melchizedek was king of Salem and lived about 2000 B.C. He was the priest of the most high God. He blessed Abram following the slaughter of Chedorlaomer and Lot's rescue. Abram paid tithes to Melchizedek. *(Note: The Joseph Smith translation of these verses and passages in the Book of Mormon and the Doctrine and Covenants provide additional insight into Melchizedek: Abram paid tithes to Melchizedek of all he had taken from Sodom. Melchizedek feared God even as a child and had shut the mouths of lions and quenched fire. Melchizedek was called the King of peace by his people. "And thus, having been approved of God, he was ordained an high priest after the order of the covenant which God made with Enoch." [JST Gen. 14:17-40.] The people in Salem had become very wicked.*

Melchizedek preached repentance unto them, and they repented. Thus, he was called the prince of peace. There were many righteous kings both before and after Melchizedek, "but none were greater; therefore, of him they have more particularly made mention." [Alma 13:17-19.] Melchizedek, who had received the priesthood through the lineage of his fathers, even till Noah, bestowed it upon Abraham. [D&C 84:14.] The Melchizedek Priesthood is called so because Melchizedek was such a great high priest and out of reverence and respect for the name of the Supreme Being, to avoid the too frequent repetition of the Lord's name. [D&C 107:1-4.])

MELECH. *1 Chr. 8:35; 9:41.*

Melech, of the tribe of Benjamin through Micah, was a great-grandson of Jonathan and a great-great-grandson of Saul. His brothers were Pithon, Tarea and Ahaz. *(1 Chr. 8:35.)*

Melech was one of the sons of Micah. His brothers were Pithon, Tahrea (Tarea) and Ahaz. *(1 Chr. 9:41.)* (Chart 16 l.)

MELICU. *Neh. 12:14.*

Melicu was the father of Jonathan who was one of the priests who was a chief of the fathers in the days of Joiakim.

MELZAR. *Dan. 1:11.*

Melzar, i.e., the steward, was set over Daniel, Hananiah, Mishael and Azariah by Ashpenaz the prince of the eunuchs.

MEMUCAN. *Esth. 1:14-15.*

Memucan was one of the seven princes of Persia and Media with king Ahasuerus when queen Vashti refused to come at his command. They asked what should be done to Vashti because of her refusal to obey Ahasuerus' command. Memucan indicated that Vashti had not only wronged the king but all the people in the kingdom, as well, and that other women would begin to despise their husbands. Thus, he suggested that the king command that Vashti never come before him again and that her estate be given to another. Ahasuerus followed Memucan's recommendation.

MENAHEM. *2 Kgs. 15:14, 16-22.*

Menahem was the son of Gadi. He was from Tirza. He killed Shallum who reigned as king of Israel just one month and usurped the throne. When Tiphsah and the coasts thereof from Tirzah would not open up to him, he smote the people; and all the women who were with child "he ripped up." He began his wicked reign over Israel in the 39th year of Azariah's reign in Judah and reigned 10 years. He purchased peace with Pul, king of Assyria, by exacting a thousand talents of silver from the wealthy men in Israel. When he died, his son Pekahiah reigned in his stead.

MEN OF CHOZEBA. *1 Chr. 4:22.*

The **Men of Chozeba** were sons of Shelah and grandsons of Judah. They and others named were the potters and dwelled among the plants and hedges where they served the king. (Chart 8a.)

MEN OF PENUEL. *Judg. 8:8, 16-17.*

The **Men of Penuel** refused Gideon's request for loaves of bread for his faint army just as the men of Succoth had. Therefore, Gideon promised them retribution. After Gideon "discomfited" Zebah and Zalmunna, kings of Midian, he returned and with "thorns of the wilderness and briers, . . . he taught the men of Succoth. And he beat down the tower of Penuel, and slew all the men of the city."

MEN OF POTIPHAR'S HOUSE. *Gen. 39:14.*

The **Men of Potiphar's House** came running when Potiphar's wife cried out that Joseph had tried to lie with her.

MEN OF SUCCOTH (Princes of Succoth). *Judg. 8:5-7,16-17.*

The **Men of Succoth** refused Gideon's request for loaves of bread for his faint army. Gideon promised them retribution. After Gideon "discomfited" Zebah and Zalmunna, kings of Midian, he returned and with "thorns of the wilderness and briers, . . . he taught the men of Succoth. And he beat down the tower of Penuel, and slew all the men of the city."

MEN OF THE CITY OF JERICHO. *2 Kgs. 2:19.*

The **Men of the City of Jericho** came to Elisha and told him the water was naught and the ground was barren. Elisha then healed the waters of Jericho.

MEONOTHAI. *1 Chr. 4:14.*

Meonothai was the father of Ophrah. They were craftsmen.

MEPHIBOSHETH (1) (Merib-baal). *2 Sam. 4:4; 9; 16:3; 19:24-30; 21:7-9; 1 Chr. 8:34; 9:40.*

Mephibosheth was the son of Jonathan. He was five years old when his father was slain. As his nurse tried to flee with him to protect him, he fell and became lame. *(2 Sam. 4:4.)*

David inquired of Ziba, a servant in Saul's house, if there was not someone of Saul's house still alive to whom he could show the kindness of God unto him. Ziba told him Mephibosheth was still alive. David had him brought to him. He restored all of Saul's land to Mephibosheth, and told Mephibosheth he would have him eat at his table from then on. Ziba and all his household—15 sons and 20 servants—were servants unto Mephibosheth and tilled the land for him. Mephibosheth was lame on both feet. *(2 Sam. 9.)*

Mephibosheth thought to regain his father's kingdom when David's son Absalom gained favor in the sight of the people and turned against David, causing David to flee Jerusalem. Ziba, Mephibosheth's servant, however, took food and drink to David and his people as they tarried in the wilderness *(vs. 1-4). (2 Sam. 16:3.)*

When David regained his throne after Absalom's death, Mephibosheth came down to meet him. He pledged his allegiance to David. *(2 Sam. 19:24-30.)*

When David agreed to deliver up seven of the men of Saul's sons to the Gibeonites to atone for Saul's having slain the Gibeonites contrary to an oath Israel had made with them, he spared Jonathan's son Mephibosheth but he gave up two of Rizpah's sons and five of Merab's sons. *(2 Sam. 21:7-9.)*

Merib-baal (Mephibosheth) was the son of Jonathan and the grandson of Saul. He begat Micah. *(1 Chr. 8:34.)*

Merib-baal was the son of Jonathan. He begat Micah. *(1 Chr. 9:40.) (According to the BD, Mephibosheth and Merib-baal are one and the same.)* (Chart 16 l.)

MEPHIBOSHETH (2). *2 Sam. 21:8-9.*

Mephibosheth was one of the sons of Saul and his concubine Rizpah. He and his brother Armoni were given to the Gibeonites by David to be hung as an atonement for Saul's having slain the Gibeonites contrary to the oath Israel had made with them. (Chart 16 l.)

MEPHIBOSHETH'S (1) NURSE. *2 Sam. 4:4.*

Mephibosheth's Nurse heard that Saul and Jonathan had been slain so she fled with Jonathan's five-year-old son, Mephibosheth. In the process, he fell and became lame.

MERAB. *1 Sam. 14:49; 18:17-19; 2 Sam. 21:8.*

Merab was the firstborn of Saul's daughters. *(1 Sam. 14:49.)*

Saul promised Merab to David for a wife if David would be valiant for him and fight the Lord's battles. However, when it came time to give her to David, Saul gave her to Adriel, the Meholathite, for a wife. *(1 Sam. 18:17-19.)*

Because Saul slew the Gibeonites contrary to the oath Israel had made with them, the Lord caused a famine to come upon the land. To make an atonement, David asked the Gibeonites what they would have him do. They asked that seven men of Saul's sons be given to them so they could hang them up unto the Lord. David gave them five of Merab's and Adriel's sons along with two sons of Rizpah, the daughter of Aiah, whom she had borne unto Saul. *(2 Sam. 21:8.) (Note: In this verse, it says Michal rather than Merab. This would appear to be an error since Merab married Adriel and Michal married David.)* (Chart 16 l.)

MERAIAH. *Neh. 12:12.*

Meraiah, son of Seraiah, was one of the chief of the fathers during the days of Joiakim.

MERAIOTH (1). *1 Chr. 6:6-7; Ezra 7:3.*

Meraioth was the son of Zerahiah, a fifth-great-grandson of Aaron, and the father of Amariah. *(1 Chr. 6:6-7.)*

Meraioth's descendants and progenators are listed from Aaron through Ezra with some modification from 1 Chr. 6:4-15. *(Ezra 7:3 [1-5].)* (Chart 7b.)

MERAIOTH (2). *1 Chr. 9:11; Neh. 11:11.*

Meraioth, the son of Ahitub and the father of Zadok, was a priest who resided in Jerusalem whose genealogy was written in the book of the kings of Israel and Judah, who were carried away captive into Babylon because of their transgression. *(1 Chr. 9:11.)*

Meraioth was the son of Ahitub and the father of Zadok. *(Neh. 11:11.)* (Chart 7b.)

MERAIOTH (3). *Neh. 12:15.*

Meraioth was the father of Helkai, who was one of the priests who was a chief of the fathers in the days of Joiakim.

MERARI (Merarites). *Gen. 46:11; Ex. 6:19; Num. 3:33-37; 26:57; 1 Chr. 6:19, 29, 44-47; 9:14; 23:21 (1, 6, 21, 23-24); 24:26-30.*

Merari was a son of Levi and a grandson of Jacob. His brothers were Gershon and Kohath. *(Gen. 46:11.)*

Merari's sons were Mahali and Mushi. *(Ex. 6:19.)*

Merari's descendants included the Mahlites and Mushites. When their males one month old and older were counted by Moses, they numbered 6200. The chief of the house of the fathers of the families of Merari was Zuriel, son of Abihail. They were instructed to pitch on the northward side of the tabernacle. They were put in charge of the boards of the tabernacle, the bars, pillars, sockets, cords, etc. *(Num. 3:33-37.)*

Merari's descendants were called **Merarites**. *(Num. 26:57.)*

Merari's sons were Mahli and Mushi. Merari's descendants via Mahli are listed in verse 29. Merari's descendants via Mushi are listed in verses 44-47. *(1 Chr. 6:19, 29, 44-47.)*

Merari's genealogy was written in the book of the kings of Israel and Judah, who were carried away to Babylon for their transgression. After returning from Babylonian captivity, "Shemaiah the son of Hasshub, the son of Azrikam, the son of Hashabiah, of the sons of Merari" was among the Levites who dwelled in Jerusalem. *(1 Chr. 9:14.)*

When David made Solomon king, he numbered the Levites and divided them for the work in the service of the house of the Lord into courses among Levi's sons: Gershon, Kohath and Merari.. The chief of the fathers of the sons of Merari were Mahli, Mushi and two sons of Mahli: Eleazar and Kish. The chief of the fathers of the sons of Mushi were Mahli, Eder and Jeremoth. *(1 Chr. 23:21 [1, 6, 21, 23-24].)*

Merari's sons were Mahli and Mushi. Other descendants are named: Jaaziah, Beno, Shoham, Zaccur, Ibri, Eleazar, Kish, Jerahmeel, Mahli, Eder and Jerimoth. They were the chief of the fathers and drew lots with others of the Levites for their courses. *(1 Chr. 24:26-30.)* (Charts 7a-b, d-e.)

MERED. *1 Chr. 4:17-18.*

Mered was a son of Ezra. His siblings were Jether, Epher, and Jalon, a sister. Mered was the husband of Bithiah, the daughter of Pharaoh. (Chart 8 o.)

MEREMOTH (1). *Ezra 8:33; Neh. 3:4, 21; 10:5 (1, 5, 28-31); 12:3.*

Meremoth was the son of Uriah the priest. Ezra had delivered the silver, gold and precious things of the temple to Sherebiah, Hashabiah and ten additional chief priests and charged them to deliver them to the chief priests and chief of the fathers at Jerusalem. They delivered them into the hand of Meremoth and those Levites who were with him: Eleazar, son of Phinehas; Jozabad, son of Jeshua; and Nodiah, son of Binnui. *(Ezra 8:33.)*

Meremoth, son of Urijah (Uriah), repaired the walls next to Hassenaah when the children of Israel rebuilt the walls and gates of Jerusalem during the time of Ezra and Nehemiah. He also repaired from Eliashib the high priest's door to the end of Eliashib's house. *(Neh. 3:4, 21.)*

Meremoth was among the priests who covenanted and sealed their covenant to marry in Israel, honor the Sabbath, pay tithes and keep the commandments. *(Neh. 10:5 [1, 5, 28-31].)*

Meremoth was one of the men (priests and Levites) who left Babylon and went to Jerusalem with Zerubbabel. *(Neh. 12:3.)*

MEREMOTH (2). *Ezra 10:36 (18-19, 36, 44).*

Meremoth, a son of Bani, and his brothers were some of the men in Israel who took foreign wives but gave them up when Ezra feared the wrath of God would destroy Israel for this iniquity.

MERES. *Esth. 1:14-15.*

Meres was one of the seven princes of Persia and Media with king Ahasuerus when queen Vashti refused to come at his command. He and his companions asked Ahasuerus what they should do unto Vashti because of her refusal to obey Ahasuerus' command.

MERIB-BAAL. See **Mephibosheth (1)**.

MERODACH-BALADAN. See **Berodach-baladen**.

MERONOTHITE. *1 Chr. 27:30; Neh. 3:7.*

Meronothites. Jehdeiah, a Meronothite, was the officer assigned by David to be over the asses. *(1 Chr. 27:30.)*

Jadon the Meronothite and the men of Mizpah, along with Melatiah the Gibeonite and the men of Gibeon, worked next to Jehoiada and Meshullam when the children of Israel rebuilt the walls and gates of Jerusalem during the time of Ezra and Nehemiah. *(Neh. 3:7.)*

MESHA (1). *2 Kgs. 3:4-27.*

Mesha, king of Moab, was a sheepmaster and paid a heavy tribute to Ahab, king of Israel. After Ahab's death, he rebelled against Jehoram who became king of Israel. Jehoram, Jehoshaphat king of Judah and the king of Edom joined forces against Mesha. They asked the prophet Elisha for help. Out of respect for Jehoshaphat, Elisha complied and told them the Lord would provide them water for their stock and victory in the war. Mesha and the Moabites were defeated. When all looked lost for Mesha, he took his eldest son who "should have reigned in his stead, and offered him for a burnt offering upon the wall."

MESHA (2). *1 Chr. 2:42.*

Mesha was the firstborn son of Caleb who was the brother of Jerahmeel. He was the father of Ziph. (Chart 8i.)

MESHA (3). *1 Chr. 8:9.*

Mesha was a son of Shaharaim, a descendant of Benjamin. His mother was Hodesh. (Chart 16f.)

MESHACH. See **Mishael**.

MESHECH (1). *Gen. 10:2; Ezek. 27:13; 32:21, 26; 38:2-3; 39:1.*

Meshech was a son of Japheth and a grandson of Noah. *(Gen. 10:2.)*

As Ezekiel lamented the fall of the great city of Tyrus, he bemoaned the loss of her riches and commerce, part of which involved the merchants of Meshech, Javan and Tubal, merchants who traded in "persons of men and vessels of brass in thy markets." *(Ezek. 27:13.)*

As Ezekiel lamented for Pharaoh king of Egypt and for Egypt, herself, the Lord told him, "The strong among the mighty shall speak to him (Pharaoh) out of the midst of hell with them that help him: they are gone down, they lie uncircumcised, slain by the sword . . . There is Meschech, Tubal, and all her multitude: her graves are round about him: all of them uncircumcised, slain by the sword, though they caused their terror in the land of the living." *(Ezek. 32:21, 26.)*

The Lord told Ezekiel to set his face against "Gog, the land of Magog, the chief prince of Meshech and Tubal, and prophesy against him." *(Ezek. 38.2-3.)*

Gog was the chief prince of Meshech and Tubal. *(Ezek. 39:1.)* (Chart 2a.)

MESHECH (2). *1 Chr. 1:17.* See **Mash**.

MESHA'S (1) ELDEST SON. *2 Kgs. 3:27.*

Mesha's Eldest Son, who should have reigned over Moab after his father, was offered by his father for a burnt offering upon the wall when the battle he was waging against Israel and Judah became too much for him and he was about to meet with defeat.

MESHELEMIAH. *1 Chr. 9:21; 26:2.* See **Shallum (9)**.

MESHEZABEEL (1). *Neh. 3:4; Neh. 10:21 (1, 21, 28-31).*

Meshezabeel was the father of Berechiah and the grandfather of Meshullam who helped rebuild the walls and gates of Jerusalem. *(Neh. 3:4.)*

Meshezabeel was among those chief of the people who covenanted to marry in Israel, honor the Sabbath, pay tithes and keep the commandments. *(Neh. 10:21 [1, 21, 28-31].)*

MESHEZABEEL (2). *Neh. 11:24.*

Meshezabeel, of the children of Zerah the son of Judah, was the father of Pethahiah. (Chart 8g.)

MESHILLEMITH (Meshillemoth (1)). *1 Chr. 9:12; Neh. 11:13.*

Meshillemith, the son of Immer and the father of Meshullam, was one of the priests in Jerusalem whose genealogy was written in the book of the kings of Israel and Judah, who were carried away captive into Babylon because of their transgression. *(1 Chr. 9:12.)*

Meshillemoth (Meshillemith) was the son of Immer. *(Neh. 11:13.)* (Chart 7g.)

MESHILLEMOTH (1). See **Meshillemith**.

MESHILLEMOTH (2). *2 Chr. 28:12.*

Meshillemoth was the father of Berechiah who was one of the leaders of the children of Ephraim when Ahaz was king of Judah and the children of Israel carried many of Judah off captive.

MESHOBAB. *1 Chr. 4:34.*

MESHOBAB was a descendant of Shimei—a prince in his family. His house increased greatly. (Chart 6a.)

MESHULLAM (1). *2 Kgs. 22:3; 2 Chr. 34:12.*

Meshullam was the father of Azaliah and grandfather of Shaphan, king Josiah's scribe. *(2 Kgs. 22:3.)*

Meshullam, Zechariah (Kohathites) and other Levites having skill with musical instruments were assigned by Josiah, king of Judah, to be overseers of all who performed any manner of service, including scribes, officers and porters. *(2 Chr. 34:12.)*

MESHULLAM (2). *1 Chr. 3:19.*

Meshullam a descendant of David, was a son of Zerubbabel, a grandson of Pedaiah and a great-grandson of Jeconiah (Jehoiachin). His brother was Hananiah and his sister was Shelomith. (Chart 1.)

MESHULLAM (3). *1 Chr. 5:13.*

Meshullam was a descendant of Gad. (Chart 13b.)

MESHULLAM (4). *1 Chr. 8:17.*

Meshullam, of the tribe of Benjamin, was one of the sons of Elpaal. (Chart 16i.)

MESHULLAM (5). *1 Chr. 9:7.*

Meshullam, of the tribe of Benjamin, was the son of Hodaviah and the father of Sallu. He and his family were among the inhabitants of Jerusalem whose genealogy was written in the book of the kings of Israel and Judah, who were carried away to Babylon because of transgression. Sallu was one of the families chosen to dwell in Jerusalem upon returning from Babylonian captivity. (Chart 16m.)

MESHULLAM (6). *1 Chr. 9:8.*

Meshullam, of the tribe of Benjamin, was the son of Shephathiah. He and his family were among the inhabitants of Jerusalem whose genealogy was written in the book of the kings of Israel and Judah, who were carried away to Babylon for their transgression. (Chart 16m.)

MESHULLAM (7). *1 Chr. 9:11.* See **Shallum (7)**.

MESHULLAM (8). *1 Chr. 9:12.*

Meshullam, the father of Jahzerah and the son of Meshillemith, was one of the priests in Jerusalem whose genealogy was written in the book of the kings of Israel and Judah, who were carried away captive into Babylon because of their transgression. (Chart 7g.)

MESHULLAM (9). *Neh. 12:25.* See **Shallum (8)**.

MESHULLAM (10). *Ezra 8:16; Neh. 3:4, 30; 6:18.*

Meshullam was one of the chief men Ezra sent for when he gathered the people together as he was preparing to lead them to Jerusalem from Babylon and discovered there were no Levites among the group. He sent this group to Iddo and the Nethinims to request that they send them some ministers for the house of God. *(Ezra 8:16.)*

Meshullam was the son of Berechiah who was the son of Meshezabeel. He built next to Meremoth when the children of Israel rebuilt the walls and gates of Jerusalem during the time of Ezra and Nehemiah. Meshullam also repaired an area of the wall "over against his chamber" next to an area worked on by Hanun. *(Neh. 3:4, 30.)*

Meshullam's daughter was the wife of Johanan, the son of Tobiah. Because of this relationship, many nobles of Judah were sworn unto Tobiah even though Tobiah and Sanballat sought to stop Nehemiah and the Jews from rebuilding the walls and gates of Jerusalem. *(Neh. 6:18.)*

MESHULLAM (11). *Ezra 10:15.*

Meshullam and Shabbethai the Levite were assigned to assist Jonathan the son of Asahel and Jahaziah the son of Tikvah the task of separating the children of Israel from their foreign wives.

MESHULLAM (12). *Ezra 10:29 (18-19, 29, 44).*

Meshullam, a son of Bani, was one of the Israelites who took foreign wives, causing Ezra to cry unto the Lord in behalf of Israel, fearing that the Lord would totally destroy the children of Israel because of this iniquity. Meshullam and his brothers agreed to put away their foreign wives.

MESHULLAM (13). *Neh. 3:6.*

Meshullam was the son of Besodeiah. He and Jehoiada, son of Paseah, repaired the old gate when the children of Israel rebuilt the walls and gates of Jerusalem during the time of Ezra and Nehemiah.

MESHULLAM (14). *Neh. 8:1-8.*

Meshullam was one of the men who stood on Ezra's left hand when Ezra read and interpreted the law of Moses to the people.

MESHULLAM (15). *Neh. 10:7 (1, 7, 28-31).*

Meshullam was among the priests who covenanted and sealed their covenant to marry in Israel, honor the Sabbath, pay tithes and keep the commandments.

MESHULLAM (16). *Neh. 10:20 (1, 7, 28-31).*

Meshullam was among those chief of the people who covenanted to marry in Israel, honor the Sabbath, pay tithes and keep the commandments.

MESHULLAM (17). *Neh. 11:7.*

Meshullam, of the tribe of Benjamin, was the father of Sallu and the son of Joed. (Chart 16m.)

MESHULLAM (18). *Neh. 12:13, 33.*

Meshullam, son of Ezra, was one of the priests who was chief of the fathers during the days of Joiakim. Meshullam, Ezra and Azariah, along with Hoshaiah and half of the princes of Judah, were appointed by Nehemiah to one of the two great companies of people gathered for the dedication of the walls of Jerusalem.

MESHULLAM (19). *Neh. 12:16.*

Meshullam was a son of Ginnethon. He was one of the priests who was a chief of the fathers in the days of Joiakim.

MESHULLEMETH. *2 Kgs. 21:19.*

Meshullemeth, the daughter of Haruz of Jotbah and the wife of Manasseh, was the mother of Amon. (Chart 1.)

MESSENGER (1). *1 Sam. 23:27.*

A **Messenger** came to Saul as he chased David in the wilderness of Maon and warned him that the Philistines had invaded the land, causing Saul to temporarily give up his pursuit of David.

MESSENGER (2). *2 Kgs. 10:8 (6-8).*

A **Messenger** informed Jehu that the heads of king Ahab's 70 sons had arrived in baskets as ordered by Jehu.

MESSENGERS. *Judg. 11:12-24.*

Jephthah sent **Messengers** to the king of the children of Ammon inquiring why he was warring against Israel. After receiving the king's reply, Jephthah sent the messengers back to the king explaining Israel's position.

METHUSAEL. *Gen. 4:18.*

Methusael, a great-great-grandson of Cain, was the son of Mehujael and the father of Lamech. (Chart 1.)

METHUSELAH. *Gen. 5:21, 25-27.*

Methuselah was the son of Enoch and the five-times-great-grandson of Adam through Seth. He begat Lamech when he was 187 years old and lived to be 969 years, during which time he begat sons and daughters. *(Note: Moses 8:1-3 in the Pearl of Great Price records that Methuselah was not taken up with the righteous city of Enoch in order that the covenants of the Lord might be fulfilled. D&C 107:50, 52, 53, records that Methuselah was 100 years old when he was ordained by Adam. He ordained Noah when Noah was ten years old. Methuselah, Seth, Enos, and the other high priests along with the rest of Adam's righteous posterity gathered in the valley of Adam-ondi-Ahman three years prior to Adam's death and Adam bestowed blessings upon them.)* (Charts 1.; 21.)

MEUNIM. See **Mehunim**.

MEZAHAB. *Gen. 36:39; 1 Chr. 1:50.*

Mezahab was the grandparent of Mehetabel, wife of king Hadar (Hadad). (Chart 18.)

MIAMIN. *Ezra 10:25 (18-19, 25, 44); Neh. 12:5.*

Miamin was of the sons of Parosh. He was among those who had taken wives from among the Canaanites or other foreign groups but who agreed to Ezra's request that they separate themselves from these strange wives lest the Lord destroy the rest of the children of Israel. *(Ezra 10:25 [18-19, 25, 44].)*

Miamin was one of the men (priests and Levites) who left Babylonian captivity with Zerubbabel and went to Jerusalem. *(Neh. 12:5.)*

MIBHAR. *1 Chr. 11:38.*

Mibhar, the son of Haggeri, was one of David's mighty men. He was one of the valiant men of the armies. (Chart 17.)

MIBSAM (1). *Gen. 25:13.*

Mibsam was a son of Ishmael and a grandson of Abraham and Hagar, Sarah's handmaid. (Chart 3e.)

MIBSAM (2). *1 Chr. 4:25.*

Mibsam, son of Shallum and great-grandson of Simeon, was a great-great-grandson of Jacob and the father of Mishma. (Chart 6a.)

MIBZAR. *Gen. 36:42.*

Mibzar was one of the dukes (tribal chiefs) who came of Esau. (Chart 19.)

MICAH (1). *Judg. 17-18.*

Micah was from mount Ephraim. He had a house of pagan gods and consecrated his own priests. He consecrated a Levite from the family of Judah who had come to Ephraim and dwelled with Micah's family. *(Judg. 17.)*

The Danites, while seeking a land of inheritance which they had not been successful in obtaining thus far, came to Micah's home. They took his false gods for themselves and enticed his priest (Jonathan, the son of Gershom, the son of Manasseh, i.e., Moses) to come with them and be their priest. *(Judg. 18.)*

MICAH (2). *2 Chr. 34:20.* See **Michaiah (1).**

MICAH (3). *1 Chr. 5:5.*

Micah, of the tribe of Reuben, was the son of Shimei and the father of Reaia. (Chart 5b.)

MICAH (4). *1 Chr. 8:3-35; 9:41.*

Micah, of the tribe of Benjamin, was the son of Merib-baal, a grandson of Jonathan and a great-grandson of Saul. He begat Pithon, Melech, Tarea and Ahaz. *(1 Chr. 8:34-35.)*

Micah's sons were Pithon, Melech, Tahrea (Tarea) and Ahaz. *(1 Chr. 9:41.)* (Chart 16 l.)

MICAH (5) (Micha (2), Michaiah (2)). *1 Chr. 9:15; Neh. 11:17, 22; 12:35.*

Micah, a Levite and a descendant of Asaph, was the son of Zichri and the father of Mattaniah, which Mattaniah was among those chosen to live in Jerusalem following release from Babylonian captivity. *(1 Chr. 9:15.)*

Micha (Micah) was the son of Zabdi (Zichri), father of Mattaniah and grandfather of Hashabiah. *(Neh. 11:17, 22.)*

Michaiah (Micah) was the son of Zaccur (Zichri, Zabdi). His descendant Zechariah (Uzzi) was one of the priests' sons assigned by Nehemiah to take his trumpet and join one of two great companies on the walls of Jerusalem for the dedication of the walls. *(Neh. 12:35.)* (Chart 7a.)

MICAH (6). *Jer. 26:18; Micah 1-7.*

Micah the Morasthite prophesied during the days of king Hezekiah that if the people didn't repent, they would be destroyed. They did repent, and the Lord withheld the evil He had designed for them. *(Jer. 26:18.)*

Micah was a Morasthite who prophesied in the days of Jotham, Ahaz and Hezekiah, kings of Judah, regarding the downfall of Samaria and Jerusalem. *(Micah 1.)*

Micah lamented the destruction of Israel. Nevertheless, Micah prophesied that the Lord will eventually gather the remnant of Israel—like a flock of sheep. *(Micah 2.)*

Micah prophesied against the heads of Jacob who judged for reward, the priests who taught for hire, and the prophets who divined for money. *(Micah 3.)*

Micah prophesied that in the latter days, the house of the Lord—the temple—would be established in the top of the mountains and people would flow unto it; the Millennial era will begin and the Lord will gather Israel and will reign henceforth. *(Micah 4.)*

Micah prophesied that the Savior would be born in Bethlehem. The remnant of Jacob which has been scattered among all the nations shall rise with power in the latter days and triumph gloriously over the Gentiles. *(Micah 5.)*

Micah reminded Israel that in spite of the Lord's goodness to them—His leading them out of Egyptian bondage and giving them Moses, Aaron and Miriam—they had turned away from Him and were following the ways of Balak king of Moab. Instead of the Lord's statutes, they kept the statues of Omri and followed the work of Ahab. All the Lord required of them was to do justly, love mercy, and walk humbly with God. *(Micah 6.)*

Micah lamented the fallen state of Israel, but expressed confidence that the Lord will have compassion and show mercy on her and will pardon her iniquity in the latter days. *(Micah 7.)*

MICAH'S PRIEST. *Judg. 17:7-13; 18:3-30.*

Micah's Priest was a Levite from the family of Judah who came to the house of Micah looking for a place to stay. Micah consecrated him to be a priest over his house and "the young man was unto him as one of his sons." *(Judg. 17:7-13.)*

The Danites, seeking a land of inheritance which had eluded them thus far, came to Micah's home. They took his false gods for themselves and enticed his priest to come with them and be their priest. "And Jonathan, the son of Gershom, the son of Manasseh (i.e., Moses), he and his sons were priests to the tribe of Dan until the day of the captivity of the land." *(Judg. 18:3-30.) (Note: The footnote to this scripture indicates that, in this instance, Manasseh refers to Moses, but has been altered to Manasseh.)*

MICAIAH. *1 Kgs. 22:8-28; 2 Chr. 18:7-27.*

Micaiah was a prophet of the Lord. His father was Imlah. Ahab hated him because he always prophesied ill against him. He foretold of the defeat and death of Ahab when Ahab and Jehoshaphat were planning to go to battle against Syria. This made Ahab angry and he told his men to take Micaiah back to the city unto Amon the governor and to Joash, the king's son, and have him cast into prison and fed with just bread and water until Ahab's return from battle in peace. Micaiah responded that if he returned at all in peace, then the Lord had not spoken to him. However, everything he foretold came to pass.

MICHA (1). *2 Sam. 9:12.*

Micha was Mephibosheth's son, Jonathan's grandson, and Saul's great-grandson. (Chart 16 l.)

MICHA (2). *Neh. 11:17, 22.* See **Micah (5)**.

MICHA (3). *Neh. 10:11 (1, 11, 28-31).*

Micha, a Levite, was among those who covenanted and sealed their covenant to marry in Israel, honor the Sabbath, pay tithes and keep the commandments.

MICHAEL (1). *Num. 13:13.*

Michael, of the tribe of Asher, was the father of Sethur.

MICHAEL (2). *1 Chr. 5:13.*

Michael was a descendant of Gad. (Chart 13b.)

MICHAEL (3). *1 Chr. 5:14.*

Michael, the father of Gilead and the son of Jeshishai, was a descendant of Gad. (Chart 13b.)

MICHAEL (4). *1 Chr. 6:40.*

Michael, a descendant of Levi through Gershon, was the father of Shimea and the son of Baaseiah. (Chart 7a.)

MICHAEL (5). *1 Chr. 7:3; 27:18.*

Michael, the son of Izrahiah, was a descendant of Issachar. Izrahiah's other sons were Obadiah, Joel and Ishiah. They were chief men of their father's house. *(1 Chr. 7:3.)*

Michael's son, Omri, was prince of the tribe of Issachar when David was king. *(1 Chr. 27:18.)* (Chart 9a.)

MICHAEL (6). *1 Chr. 8:16.*

Michael, a descendant of Benjamin, was a son of Beriah, who was a son of Elpaal, who was a son of Shaharaim and Hushim. (Chart 16g.)

MICHAEL (7). *1 Chr. 12:20.*

Michael was from the tribe of Manasseh and was a mighty man of valor, one of the captains in the host. When David stayed close at Ziklag because of Saul, all Israel sent troops there to join in celebrating his becoming king and to defend him against Saul. Michael helped defend against the band of the rovers.

MICHAEL (8). *2 Chr. 21:2-4*.

Michael was one of Jehoshaphat's sons. His brothers were Jehoram, the firstborn; Azariah, Jehiel, Zechariah, Azariah and Shephatiah. After Jehoram became king, he slew all his brethren plus many of the princes of Israel. (Chart 1.)

MICHAEL (9). *Ezra 8:8*.

Michael, of the sons of Shephatiah, was the father of Zebadiah who was the chief of the fathers of his family and went with Ezra up from Babylon to Jerusalem, taking 80 male family members with him.

MICHAEL (10). *Dan. 10:13; 12:1*. See **Adam**.

MICHAH. *1 Chr. 23:20; 24:24*.

Michah, a Levite, was of the sons of Uzziel, son of Kohath. When David made Solomon king, he numbered the Levites and divided them into courses among the children of Levi: Gershon, Kohath and Merari. Michah was the first of two named from among the sons of Uzziel. Jesiah was second. *(1 Chr. 23:20.)*

Michah, a Levite, was of the sons of Uzziel. His descendants included Shamir. His brother was Isshiah. He drew lots for his course in the presence of king David, Zadok, Ahimelech and other community leaders. *(1 Chr. 24:24.)* (Chart 7d.)

MICHAIAH (1) (Micah (2)). *2 Kgs. 22:12-20; 2 Chr. 34:20-28*.

Michaiah (Micah) was the father of Achbor (Abdon), which Achbor was sent by king Josiah to inquire of Huldah the prohetess concerning the words of the book Hilkiah the high priest had found.

MICHAIAH (2). *Neh. 12:37*. See **Micah (5)**.

MICHAIAH (3). *2 Chr. 17:7-8*.

Michaiah was one of the princes of Judah who king Jehoshaphat instructed to "teach in the cities of Judah." He sent a number of Levites and Elishama and Jehoram, the priests, with the princes to teach Judah from the book of the law of the Lord.

MICHAIAH (4). *Neh. 12:41*.

Michaiah, a priest and trumpeter, joined in the dedication of the walls of Jerusalem with Nehemiah.

MICHAIAH (5). *Jer. 36:11-13*.

Michaiah was the son of Gemariah who was the son of Shaphan the scribe. After he heard Baruch read Jeremiah's prophecies, he went into king Jehoiakim's house and the scribe's chamber and declared what he had heard to all the princes and scribes present.

MICHAL. *1 Sam. 14:49; 18:20-28; 19:11-17; 25:44; 2 Sam. 3:13-15; 6:16-23; 21:8; 1 Chr. 15:29*.

Michal was the secondborn of Saul's daughters. *(1 Sam. 14:49.)*

Michal loved David. Saul gave her to David for a wife, hoping she would be a snare to him. *(1 Sam. 18:20-28.)*

Michal lowered David down through a window and made his bed up to look like he was still there when Saul sent messengers to David's house, hoping to catch and slay David. *(1 Sam. 19:11-17.)*

Michal was taken from David by Saul and given to Phalti for a wife. *(1 Sam. 25:44.)*

When Abner sent messengers to David on Ish-bosheth's behalf suggesting he make a league with him, David agreed only on condition that Ish-bosheth first return his wife Michal to him. Ish-bosheth agreed and took Michal from Phaltiel (Phalti). *(2 Sam. 3:13-15.)*

When David returned with the ark of God, dancing joyfully before the Lord, Michal thought he exposed more of his body than was proper and chastised him. In return, David was angry with her. "Therefore Michal the daughter of Saul had no child unto the day of her death." *(2 Sam. 6:16-23.)*

Instead of Michal, this scripture should read, "the five sons of Merab the daughter of Saul." *(2 Sam. 21:8.)*

The account is retold of Michal's being disgusted with David because of his dancing and playing, "and she despised him in her heart." *(1 Chr. 15:29.)* (Chart 16 l.)

MICHMAS. *Ezra 2.27, Neh. 7: 31.*

Michmas was of the people of Israel. The men of Michmas who returned to Jerusalem from Babylon after Cyrus' proclamation to build the temple numbered 122.

MICHRI. *1 Chr. 9:8.*

Michri, of the tribe of Benjamin, was the father of Uzzi. He and his family were among the inhabitants of Jerusalem whose genealogy was written in the book of the kings of Israel and Judah, who were carried away to Babylon for their transgression. (Chart 16m.)

MIDIAN. *Gen. 25:2, 4; 1 Chr. 1:32-33, 46.*

Midian was a son of Abraham and his wife Keturah. His sons were Ephah, Epher, Hanoch, Abida and Eldaah. *(Gen. 25:2, 4.)*

The sons of Midian, the son of Abraham and Keturah, were Ephah, Epher, Henoch (Hanoch), Abida and Eldaah. Midian was smitten in the field of Moab by Hadad, son of Bedad, who reigned as king in Edom after Husham before there was any king in Israel. *(1 Chr. 1:32-33, 46.)* (Charts 2b.; 3a, d, f.)

MIDIANITES. See **Ishmeelites**.

MIJAMIN (1). *1 Chr. 24:9 (3-5, 9).*

Mijamin was from the sons of Aaron. When David made the divisions of the sons of Aaron, there was one principal household for Eleazar and one taken for Ithamar. Eleazar had 16 sons and there were eight sons of Ithamar. These 24 sons who were chief of the fathers were divided by lot. Mijamin drew the sixth lot.

MIJAMIN (2). *Neh. 10:7 (1, 7, 28-31).*

Mijamin was among the priests who covenanted and sealed their covenant to marry in Israel, honor the Sabbath, pay tithes and keep the commandments.

MIKLOTH (1). *1 Chr. 8:32; 1 Chr. 9:35-38.*

Mikloth was of the tribe of Benjamin and was the father of Shimeah. *(1 Chr. 8:32.)*

Mikloth was one of the sons of Jehiel (Abiel). His brothers were Abdon, Zur, Kish (the father of Saul), Baal, Ner, Nadab, Gedor and Ahio. His mother was Maachah. He begat Shimeam (Shimeah). *(1 Chr. 9:35-38.)* (Chart 16k.)

MIKLOTH (2). *1 Chr. 27:4.*

Mikloth was part of Dodai's course and ruled with Dodai, an Ahohite, as they served king David. They were over the second month.

MIKNEIAH. *1 Chr. 15:18-21.*

Mikneiah and his brethren of the second degree were assigned, under the direction of David, to be singers along with Heman, Asaph and Ethan. Mikneiah and his brethren were assigned to excel wth harps on the Sheminith.

MILALAI. *Neh. 12:36 (31, 36).*

Milalai joined Zechariah, a descendant of Asaph, and other of his brethren with their musical instruments in the dedication of the wall of Jerusalem.

MILCAH (1). *Gen. 11:29; 22:20-23.*

Milcah was the wife of Nahor and the daughter of Haran; thus, she was also Nahor's niece as well as his wife. *(Gen. 11:29.)*

Milcah and Nahor begat: Huz, Buz, Kemuel, Chesed, Hazo, Phildash, Jidlaph, Bethuel. Milcah was the grandmother of Rebekah, Isaac's wife. *(Gen. 22:20-23.)* (Charts 2c-d.)

MILCAH (2). *Num. 26:33; 27:1-7.*

Milcah was a daughter of Zelophehad and a great-granddaughter of Manasseh. Her sisters were Mahlah, Noah, Hoglah and Tirzah. *(Num. 26:33.)*

Milcah and her sisters petitioned Moses and Eleazar to be given their father's inheritance because he had no sons and he, himself, had died in the wilderness. The Lord instructed Moses that Milcah and her sisters were correct and should be given a possession of inheritance among their father's brethren. *(Num. 27:1-7.)* (Charts 15a-b.)

MILCOM. *1 Kgs. 11:5.*

Milcom was the false god of the Ammonites that Solomon worshipped in his old age, incurring the wrath of the Lord.

MINIAMIN (1). *2 Chr. 31:15 (14-15).*

Miniamin, and others, assisted Kore, porter toward the east, in caring for the freewill offerings of God and their distribution when Hezekiah was king over Judah.

MINIAMIN (2). *Neh. 12:17.*

Miniamin was the father of Moadiah who was the father of Piltai, who was one of the priests who was a chief of the fathers in the days of Joiakim.

MINIAMIN (3). *Neh. 12:41 (38-41).*

Miniamin, a priest and trumpeter, joined in the dedication of the walls of Jerusalem with Nehemiah.

MIRIAM(1) (Moses' Sister). *Ex. 2:4-8; 15:20 (1, 20); Num. 12; 20:1; 26:59; Deut. 24:9; Micah 6:4 (1-16).*

Moses' Sister, Miriam, watched after him from a distance when he was placed in an ark in the river. When Pharaoh's daughter found him, Miriam offered to get a Hebrew woman to nurse him. Pharaoh's daughter accepted her offer and Moses' sister brought his mother to her to be Moses' nurse. *(Ex. 2:4-8.)*

Miriam, Moses and Aaron's sister, is mentioned by name. She was a prophetess. After the children of Israel passed through the Red Sea, they sang a song of praise unto the Lord. Miriam took a timbrel in her hand and led the women in dancing and playing the timbrel. *(Ex. 15:20 [1, 20].)*

Miriam and Aaron complained against Moses for marrying an Ethopian woman; and the Lord chastised them. He caused Miriam to become leprous. Moses beseeched the Lord in her behalf. The Lord said she would have it for seven days and after that she should be welcomed back into camp. *(Num. 12.)*

Miriam died and was buried in Kadesh. *(Num. 20:1.)*

Miriam's father was Amram; her mother was Jochebed, the daughter of Levi. Her brothers were Aaron and Moses. *(Num. 26:59.)*

The children of Israel were cautioned to do according to what the priests taught them and to remember what the Lord did to Miriam (caused her to become leprous) after they came out of Egypt. *(Deut. 24:9.)*

Micah chastised the children of Israel and said that in spite of the Lord's sending Moses, Aaron and Mirian to help them, and leading them out of Egyptian bondage, they still turned away from Him. *(Micah 6:4 [1-16].)* (Chart 7b.)

MIRIAM (2). *1 Chr. 4:17.*

Miriam was the daughter of Jalon and granddaughter of Ezra. Her siblings included Shammai and Ishbah, the father of Eshtemoa. (Chart 8 o.)

MIRMA. *1 Chr. 8:10.*

Mirma was a son of Shaharaim, a descendant of Benjamin. His mother was Hodesh. (Chart 16f.)

MISHAEL (1). *Ex. 6:22; Lev. 10:4-5.*

Mishael was a son of Uzziel, a cousin of Aaron and Moses, a grandson of Kohath and a great-grandson of Levi. *(Ex. 6:22.)*

Mishael and his brother, Elzaphan, were instructed by Moses to carry the bodies of Aaron's sons—Nadab and Abihu—who the Lord had slain by fire for performing unauthorized sacrifices, from before the sanctuary and out of the camp. They carried the bodies in their coats out of the camp. *(Lev. 10:4-5.)* (Chart 7d.)

MISHAEL (2). *Neh. 8:4 (1-8).*

Mishael was one of the men who stood on Ezra's left hand when Ezra read and interpreted the law of Moses to the people.

MISHAEL (3) (Meshach). *Dan. 1:6-21; 2-3.*

Mishael, Hananiah, Azariah and Daniel were among the children of Israel who were without blemish who were brought to the palace of Nebuchadnezzar by

Ashpenaz, the master of the king's eunuchs, to be taught in the learning and language of the Chaldeans. The prince of the eunuchs gave each of them a different name. Mishael was given the name of **Meshach**. They elected not to eat the meat and wine the king provided and after ten days they were healthier than those who ate the meat and drank the wine. At the end of three years, when the king visited with all those who had been being taught, none of them could compare with these four friends. They were wiser and had greater understanding than any of the king's magicians or astrologers. *(Dan. 1:6-21.)*

When Nebuchadnezzar had a dream that troubled him, he called in his magicians, astrologers, sorcerers and the Chaldeans and demanded they not only tell him the interpretation of the dream but the dream, as well, because he could not remember it. When they could not, he sentenced all the wisemen to death. Daniel, however, requested time to inquire of the Lord. He invited his friends—Shaddrach, Meshach and Abed-nego—to also petition the Lord regarding the matter. The Lord revealed the dream and the interpretation of the dream to Daniel. He explained the dream to Nebuchadnezzar, saying that God had revealed to Nebuchadnezzar what would happen in the latter days. Daniel was not only rewarded by Nebuchadnezzar, who elevated him to a position where he "sat in the gate of the king," but he honored a request Daniel made regarding his friends and set Meshach, Shadrach and Abed-nego over the affairs of the province of Babylon. *(Dan. 2.)*

When Nebuchadnezzar made a golden image and commanded that everyone worship it whenever they heard music or be cast into a fiery furnace, Meshach, Shadrach and Abed-nego refused to do so. Thus, Nebuchadnezzar had his most mighty men from the army make the furnace seven times hotter than usual and bound and cast the friends into it. The fire was so hot that it killed the soldiers. Suddenly, Nebuchadnezzar saw four men, the fourth being "like the Son of God," walking freely around inside the furnace, not being harmed by the fire. He called Meshach, Shadrach and Abed-nego forth and decreed that no one should speak any thing against their God or they would be cut in pieces because no other God could deliver like their God. He then rewarded the three friends by promoting them in the province of Babylon. *(Dan. 3.)*

MISHAM. *1 Chr. 8:12.*

Misham, a descendant of Benjamin, was a son of Elpaal, who was a son of Shaharaim and Hushim. Misham, Eber and Shamed, built Ono and Lod and the towns thereof. (Chart 16g.)

MISHMA (1). *Gen. 25:14.*

Mishma was a son of Ishmael and a grandson of Abraham and Hagar, Sarah's handmaid. (Chart 3e.)

MISHMA (2). *1 Chr. 4:25.*

Mishma, son of Mibsam, great-great-grandson of Simeon, great-great-great-grandson of Jacob, was the father of Hamuel. (Chart 6a.)

MISHMANNAH. *1 Chr. 12:10*.

Mishmannah, of the tribe of Gad, was one of David's mighty men who came to him at Ziklag to protect him against Saul and join in the celebration when David was made king. (Chart 13b.)

MISHRAITES. *1 Chr. 2:53 (50-53)*.

The **Mishraites** come through Shobal who was a son of Hur and grandson of Caleb. (Chart 8 l.)

MISPAR (Mispereth). *Ezra 2:2; Neh. 7:7*.

Mispar (Mispereth) was one of the people who left Babylon and went with Zerubbabel back to Jerusalem following king Cyrus' proclamation to build the temple there.

MITHREDATH (1). *Ezra 1:8*.

Mithredath was the treasurer under Cyrus, king of Persia. Cyrus had him bring forth the treasures that belonged to the house of the Lord which Nebuchadnezzar had brought out of Jerusalem and they were given to Sheshbazzar to take back to Jerusalem..

MITHREDATH (2). *Ezra 4:7, 21-24*.

Mithredath, Bishlam, Tabeel and the rest of their companions wrote to king Artaxerxes against Jerusalem. As a result, the king commanded the Samaritans to cause the children of Israel to cease building the temple and the city.

MIZRAIM. *Gen. 10:6, 13-14; 1 Chr. 1:11*.

Mizraim was a son of Ham and a grandson of Noah. He begat Ludim, Anamim, Lehabim, Naphtuhim, Pathrusim, Casluhim (of whom came Philistim and the Philistines) and Caphthorim. (Chart 2e.)

MIZZAH. *Gen. 36:13,17*.

Mizzah, a duke or tribal chief, was the son of Reuel, son of Bashemath and Esau. (Chart 3c.)

MOAB (Moabites). *Gen. 19:37; Deut. 2:9; 23:3; 2 Kgs. 3:4-27; 1 Chr. 18:2; 2 Chr. 20:1, 15, 22-24; Ezra 9:1, 5-6; Neh. 13:1; Jer. 48; Ezek. 25:2-11; Amos 2:1-3; Zeph. 2:8-9*.

Moab was the son of Lot's older daughter, fathered by Lot as she lay with him after getting him drunk with wine. He is the father of the Moabites. *(Gen. 19:37.)*

Moses recounted to the children of Israel how the Lord had instructed them not to distress the Moabites nor contend with them in battle because the Lord had given Ar unto the children of Lot for a possession. *Deut. 2:9*.

Moses instructed the Israelites that the Moabites were not to enter into the congregation of the Lord; even to their tenth generation or forever because they did not befriend them earlier but had hired Balaam the son of Beor to curse them. *(Deut. 23:3.)*

Mesha, a sheepmaster, was king of Moab when Ahab was king of Israel, and was required to pay a heavy tribute to Ahab. After Ahab's death when Jehoram was king over Israel, Mesha rebelled. Jehoram enlisted the help of Jehoshaphat, king of

Judah, and the king of Edom in battle against the Moabites. The Moabites were defeated. When Mesha saw that the battle was too much for him and his men, he offered his eldest son for a burnt offering upon the wall. *(2 Kgs. 3:4-27.)*

David smote Moab and the Moabites became David's servants. *(1 Chr. 18:2.)*

The children of Moab, Ammon and mount Seir joined together to go to battle against Jehoshaphat, king of Judah. Jahaziel prophesied that the Lord would protect Judah. The children of Moab, Ammon and mount Seir fought amongst themselves and destroyed themselves. No one escaped. *(2 Chr. 20:1, 15, 22-24.)*

After the children of Israel were delivered from Babylonian bondage, many Jews—including the priests and Levites—intermarried with and followed the abominations of the Moabites, Canaanites, Hittites, Perizzites, Jebusites, Ammonites, Egyptians and Amorites. Ezra prayed and confessed the sins of all the people, fearing the Lord would completely destroy them this time for their abominations. *(Ezra 9:1, 5-6.)*

The people were reminded as they read the book of Moses that the Moabites and the Ammonites were forever forbidden to become part of the congregation of God because they had hired Balaam against them in ancient days. Thus, they were not to intermarry with them. *(Neh. 13:1.)*

Jeremiah prophesied of the destruction that would befall Moab because of the Moabites' loftiness, arrogance, pride, haughtiness and contempt of God's instructions. *(Jer. 48.)*

Because the Moabites claimed the house of Judah was no different than any other nation, and because the Moabites rejoiced in the desolation of Jerusalem, the capture of Judah and the profaning of the Lord's sanctuary, Ezekiel was instructed by the Lord to prophesy vengence against them. The Lord said He would execute judgment upon them that they might know that He is the Lord. *(Ezek. 25:2-11.)*

Amos prophesied the Lord would pour out judgments against Moab, Judah and Israel because of their transgressions. Of the Moabites, Amos said the Lord would send fire upon Moab. Moab shall die with tumult, with shouting, and with the sound of the trumpet. The judge shall be cut off and all the princes shall be slain. *(Amos 2:1-3.)*

The prophet Zephaniah prophesied judgment to come upon the Moabites and said Moab shall be as Sodom. *(Zeph. 2:8-9.)* (Chart 2d.)

MOADIAH. *Neh. 12:17.*

Moadiah, son of Miniamin, was the father of Piltai who was one of the priests who was a chief of the fathers in the days of Joiakim.

MOLECH. *Lev. 18:21; 20:2-5; 1 Kgs. 11:7; 2 Kgs. 16:3 (1-3); 17:17; 21:6; 23:10; Jer. 7:31; 32:35.*

Molech was a pagan god who the people worshipped by passing children through fire; i.e., burning them in fire. The Lord commanded the people not to let any of their seed pass through the fire to Molech. *(Lev. 18:21.)*

The Lord decreed the death penalty for those who sacrificed children to Molech. *(Lev. 20:2-5.)*

Solomon had 700 wives and 300 concubines, and in his old age he "went after" their gods: Molech, the abomination of the children of Ammon; Ashtoreth, Milcom and Chemosh. *(1 Kgs. 11:7.)*

Ahaz reigned in wickedness and sacrificed his own son to Molech. *(2 Kgs. 16:3 [1-3].)*

The children of Israel caused their sons and daughters to "pass through the fire" to Molech. *(2 Kgs. 17:17.)*

Manasseh, king of Judah, sacrificed his son to Molech. *(2 Kgs. 21:6.)*

Josiah destroyed Topheth which had been built for the burning of human sacrifices so no man might make his son or daughter pass through the fire to Molech. *(2 Kgs. 23:10.)*

The high places of Tophet were built for the burning of the sons and daughters of the children of Israel. *(Jer. 7:31.)*

The children of Israel built the high places of Baal so they could cause their children to pass through the fire unto Molech. *(Jer. 32:35.)*

MOLID. *1 Chr. 2:29.*

Molid was the son of Abishur and Abihail. His brother was Ahban. He was a five-times-great-grandson of Judah. (Chart 8c.)

MORASTHITE. *Jer. 26:18; Micah 1:1.*

Morasthite. *(Note: There is no indication who the Morasthites were other than Micah, the prophet, was a Morasthite.)*

MORDECAI. *Ezra 2:2; Neh. 7:7; Esth. 2:5-23; 3:2-6; 4; 5:9-14; 6; 7:9-10; 8-10.*

Mordecai was one of the people who went with Zerubbabel back to Jerusalem following king Cyrus' proclamation to build the temple there. *(Ezra 2:2; Neh. 7:7.)*

Mordecai, a Jew, was the son of Jair who was the son of Shimei who was the son of Kish, a Benjamite. When Nebuchadnezzar carried Jerusalem and Jeconiah, king of Judah, to Babylon, Mordecai was also carried away. He brought Esther, his uncle's daughter whom he raised as his own daughter, to Shushan the palace in compliance with king Ahasuerus' decree to gather together all the fair young virgins "to the house of women" so he could choose a new queen to replace Vasti, whom he had deposed. He instructed Esther not to reveal that she was a Jew. Mordecai sat in the king's gate. He learned that two of the king's chamberlains, Bigthan and Teresh, planned to kill the king. He told Esther who, in turn, told Ahasuerus. As a result, the king had Bigthan and Teresh hung. *(Esth. 2:5-23.)*

Mordecai refused to bow down to Haman, whom king Ahasuerus had promoted to a high position, so Haman sought to destroy Mordecai and all the Jews throughout the kingdom. The king gave Haman permission to do whatsoever he wished with the Jews. *(Esth. 3:2-6.)*

When Mordecai learned about the king's decree, he and all the Jews mourned and fasted. He petitioned Esther to supplicate the king in their behalf. When she hesitated, he reminded her that she, too, was a Jew and would not escape the same fate as the rest of them if she did not change the king's mind. *(Esth. 4.)*

Haman made a gallows and planned to have Mordecai hanged. *(Esth. 5:9-14.)*

King Ahasuerus discovered that Mordecai, the person who had reported the plot against his life, had not been rewarded, and he sought input from Haman on how best to reward someone he wanted rewarded. Thinking the king wanted to honor him, Haman made some generous suggestions, which the king accepted. However, these honors were placed upon Mordecai, not Haman. *(Esth. 6.)*

When the king learned from Esther about Haman's plot to kill the Jews, he had Haman hanged on the gallows he had prepared for Mordecai. *(Esth. 7:9-10.)*

The decree calling for the destruction of the Jews was reversed and Mordecai was honored and placed over the house of Haman. Mordecai was second in command to the king. *(Esth. 8.)*

Mordecai was great in the king's house and the rulers and leaders in the provinces all helped the Jews because the "fear of Mordecai fell upon them." Mordecai wrote unto the Jews and established the Feast of Purim to commemorate their deliverance and victory. *(Esth. 9.)*

Mordecai's history is written in the chronicles of the kings of Media and Persia. He was next in command to the king. *(Esth. 10.)* (Chart 16k.)

MOSES. *Ex. 2-5; 6:1-13; 7:7-25; 8-36; 39:43; 40; Lev. 1-27; Num. 1:1-16, 50-53; 3:38; 5-9; 14; 20; 27-31; 34-36; Deut. 1-34; Judg. 18:30; 1 Chr. 23:13-15; Ps. 78, 90, 105:26; 106:16, 23, 32; 136; Jer. 15:1; Dan. 9:11; Micah 6:4.*

Moses is first mentioned by name in Ex. 2:10, but his birth and being placed in an ark in the river to be found by Pharaoh's daughter precedes that. He was watched over by his sister and nursed by his mother. He was then taken back to Pharaoh's daughter and he became her son. She named him Moses because she drew him out of the water. *(Ex. 2:2-10.)* When Moses was grown, he came upon an Egyptian smiting a Hebrew. He killed the Egyptian and hid his body in the sand. When he intervened in a dispute between two Hebrews the next day, they rebuked him and asked if he planned to kill them as he had the Egyptian. Realizing that what he had done was known to others, Moses knew he was in danger. Pharaoh sought to kill him and he fled to Midian. *(Ex. 2:11-15.)* As Moses sat by a well, the seven daughters of the priest of Midian (Jethro) came to water their father's flocks. Shepherds came and drove them away. Moses, however, stood up and helped them. Moses was invited to dwell with them. The priest gave Moses his daughter Zipporah for a wife. She bore him a son. They named him Gershom. *(Ex. 2:16-22.)*

Moses tended his father-in-law's flocks near Mt. Horeb. God called to him out of a burning bush. He instructed Moses to remove his shoes because he was standing on holy ground. The Lord told Moses that he was to bring the children of Israel out of Egypt. The Lord said the king of Egypt, Pharaoh, would undoubtedly not let them go but that He would smite Egypt and, after that, the Egyptians would let His people go. *(Note: This is a different Pharaoh than the father of the woman who raised Moses.) (Ex. 3.)*

The Lord gave Moses signs to use to get the children of Israel to recognize that God had sent him. The first sign was a rod that turned into a serpent and back into a rod. The second sign was making Moses' hand leprous and then clean again. If these signs were not sufficient, he was to take some water from the river and pour it onto the ground and it would become blood upon the dry land. *(Ex. 4:1-9.)* When Moses complained he was slow of speech, the Lord told him Aaron, his brother, was coming and could be his mouthpiece. *(Ex. 4:10-17.)* He left Midian and his father-in-law, taking his wife, Zipporah, and their sons, back to Egypt. He was to tell Pharaoh that if he didn't let his people go, the Lord would slay Pharaoh's firstborn son. *(Ex. 4:18-23.)* The Lord was angry with Moses for not circumcising his son and was about to kill Moses, but his wife took a sharp stone and circumcised their son and Moses was spared. *(Ex. 4:24-26.)* Moses and Aaron met in the wilderness and traveled to Egypt. They told the children of Israel what the Lord had told them to tell them and performed the signs as instructed, and the people believed. *(Ex. 4:27-31.)*

Moses and Aaron asked Pharaoh to let their people travel three days into the wilderness so they could made a sacrifice unto their God. In response, Pharaoh increased their burden by no longer providing the straw for the bricks, saying they must have too much free time on their hands. They were to gather the straw themselves now but their output of bricks was not to be dimished. Pharaoh's taskmasters also beat the officers of the children of Israel. The people complained bitterly to Moses and he asked the Lord why He had treated them so evily. *(Ex. 5.)*

The Lord revealed to Moses that His name is JEHOVAH and said He had appeared unto Abraham, Isaac and Jacob by the name "God Almighty." He reassured Moses that He heard the groanings of the children of Israel and He would bring them out of bondage. *(Ex. 6:1-13.)*

Moses was 80 years old when he spoke to Pharaoh. *(Ex. 7:7.)* The Lord had Moses instruct Aaron to toss down his rod and it became a serpent. Pharaoh's servants did likewise. Aaron's rod ate up their rods. *(Ex. 7:9-12.)* Moses had Aaron stretch the rod out over the waters of Egypt and the water turned to blood. Pharaoh's magicians did likewise. The fish died and the rivers stank. It lasted seven days. *(Ex. 7:15-25.)*

Moses had Aaron stretch out his rod over the waters of Egypt and frogs came forth and plagued the land. Pharaoh's magicians did likewise. At Pharaoh's request, Moses and Aaron entreated the Lord to take away the frogs, and He did. However, instead of letting the people go, Pharaoh hardened his heart more seeing there was a respite. *(Ex. 8:2-15.)* The Lord had Moses instruct Aaron to stretch forth the rod over the land and turn the dust to lice. The magicians could not duplicate this and said it was the finger of God. *(Ex. 8:16-19.)* The next plague was flies . The land of Goshen was protected from the flies. *(Ex. 8:21-31.)*

The Lord killed all the cattle of the Egyptians but spared the cattle of the Israelites. *(Ex. 9:3-7.)* The Lord had Moses sprinkle ashes of the furnace up toward heaven and He plagued the Egyptians with boils. The magicians could not duplicate this. *(Ex. 9:8-11.)* The Lord then sent hail mingled with fire, except not in Goshen where the children of Israel were. *(Ex. 9:18-34.)*

The Lord sent Locusts. *(Ex. 10:4-19.)* Next, the Lord had Moses stretch forth his hand and a thick darkness filled all of Egypt for three days, but the children of Israel had light. *(Ex. 10:21-27.)*

Moses was instructed by the Lord to have his people gather jewels of gold and silver from their neighbors in preparation for their departure from Egypt. The Lord promised one last plague—the death of each Egyptian's firstborn child. *(Ex. 11.)*

The Lord instituted the Passover. He told Moses that that month was to now be counted unto them as the first month of the year. On the 10th day of the month, they were to take an unblemished lamb of the first year and keep it until the 14th day, at which time in the evening they were to kill it and place its blood on the two side posts and upper door post of each house wherein the lamb would be eaten. They were to roast the lamb and eat it in the evening along with unleavened bread and bitter herbs. They were to eat it dressed and ready to go, with staff in hand. The firstborn of Egypt would die that same night, but He would pass over the children of Israel when He came to those doors marked with the lamb's blood. The Lord gave Moses some strict instructions regarding day, time and procedure for them to follow henceforth regarding the feast of the Passover and unleavened bread, etc. They were instructed that they were not to break even one bone in the sacrificial lamb and that no one who was uncircumcised was to eat of the Passover. When the Lord brought death to the Egyptians' firstborn, Pharaoh finally told Moses and Aaron to leave with the children of Israel. They left with about 600,000 men, besides children, plus all their flocks and cattle. The children of Israel had been in Egypt 430 years. *(Ex. 12.)*

The Lord instructed Moses to sanctify the firstborn of man and beasts unto him. The feast of unleavened bread was to be kept in the land of Canaan. Moses took Joseph's bones with him when he left Egypt, as Joseph had instructed the children of Israel to do. The Lord went before them in a pillar of cloud by day and in a pillar of fire by night. *(Ex. 13.)*

The Lord had Moses stretch his rod out over the sea and the Lord led the children of Israel through the Red Sea on dry ground. When the Egyptians tried to follow them, the Lord instructed Moses to again stretch his hand over the seas. The water returned, covering the chariots and drowning all the horsemen. *(Ex. 14.)*

Moses and the children of Israel sang a song of praise unto the Lord. When the people murmured because the waters of Marah were bitter, the Lord had Moses cast a tree into the waters and the waters were made sweet. The Lord promised the children of Israel that he would not put the diseases which he brought upon the Egyptians upon them if they would be diligent in keeping his commandments. *(Ex. 15.)*

When the children of Israel complained of hunger in the wilderness, the Lord told Moses he would send them manna and gave Moses instructions regarding the collection and storing of it. *(Ex. 16.)*

When the children of Israel murmured for want of water, the Lord instructed Moses to take his rod and some of the elders of Israel with him and go to a rock in Horeb. Moses was instructed to smite the rock and water would then pour forth. *(Ex. 17:1-6.)* As long as Moses, standing on top of the hill, held the rod of God high in his hands, the Israelites prevailed in battle against Amalek. When he let his hand down, Amalek prevailed. Aaron and Hur stayed by Moses and kept his hands up and Joshua was able to "discomfit" Amalek. *(Ex. 17:8-13.)*

After Moses had safely led the children of Israel out of Egypt and they were camped in the wilderness, Jethro, his father-in-law, heard what the Lord had done in bringing the children of Israel out of Egypt and he brought Moses' wife, Zipporah, and their two sons to him (as Moses had sent them to him earlier). Jethro saw that Moses was trying to do too much all by himself and counseled him to be the teacher of the law and appoint others to be lesser judges and to delegate power to them, otherwise, Moses would wear away, he said. He then left and returned to his own land. Moses hearkened unto his father-in-law and followed his counsel. *(Ex. 18.)*

The Lord gave Moses instructions on Mount Sinai regarding many things. He covenanted to make Israel a peculiar treasure, a kingdom of priests, and a holy nation. *(Ex. 19.)* The Lord revealed the Ten Commandments. *(Ex. 20.)* The Lord revealed his laws pertaining to servants, plural marriage, the death penalty for various offenses. *(Ex. 21.)* He revealed his laws pertaining to stealing and the destruction of people's property. Israel's adult males were commanded to be holy. *(Ex. 22.)* The Lord revealed his laws regarding integrity and godly conduct and gave instructions regarding the Sabbath day. They were instructed to have three annual feasts and details pertaining to their observance were given. He would remove sickness from among them if they served Him. The Amorites, Hittites, Perizzites, Canaanites, Hivites and the Jebusites would be cut off and gradually driven out of the land. *(Ex. 23.)* Moses, as commanded by God, sprinkled the blood of the covenant. He and Aaron, Nadab and Abihu, and seventy of the elders of Israel saw God. The Lord called Moses into His mount to receive the tables of stone and commandments. *(Ex. 24.)* Moses was given instructions regarding the building of a tabernacle and the ark of testimony. *(Ex. 25-27.)* Moses was given instructions regarding consecrating and anointing Aaron and his sons to be ministers in the priest's office. They were instructed to make a breastplate of judgment to contain twelve precious stones with the names of the tribes of Israel. The Urim and Thummim was to be carried in the breastplate. The wave offering and the heave offering were to be Aaron's and his sons forever. And the holy garments of Aaron were to be passed on to his sons after him, to be anointed and consecrated therein. *(Ex. 28-29.)* Moses received instruction regarding the altar of incense; atonement to be made with blood of sin offering; the paying of atonement money; and, the use of holy anointing oil and perfume by priests. *(Ex. 30.)* Moses was given the names of skilled artisans the Lord had inspired to work on building and furnishing the tabernacle. Israel was again commanded to keep the Lord's Sabbath holy and the death penalty was decreed for Sabbath desecration. Moses was given the stone tablets which were written with the finger of God. *(Ex. 31.)*

While Moses was in the mount with the Lord, the children of Israel asked Aaron to make them gods that they could worship. Aaron made them a golden calf. The Lord instructed Moses to quickly get back down to the people because they had corrupted themselves. The Lord told Moses that he would consume the people. Moses pleaded with the Lord and argued that if He destroyed them, people would say He had just led them out of Egypt so He could slay them. Moses reminded the Lord of His covenants with Abraham, Isaac and Israel. The Lord "repented of the evil which he thought to do unto his people." *(Ex. 32:14.)* Moses carried the two tablets which the Lord had written on with His finger. When he reached Joshua, Joshua thought the noise they heard was that of war in camp. When they neared the camp and Moses saw the golden calf, he was so angry that he cast the tables down. He burned the golden calf and ground the gold into powder which he put in the water and made the people drink. He demanded an explanation from Aaron. He ordered all the sons of Levi to gather together and told them to go from gate to gate throughout the camp and slay those who were not on the Lord's side. They slew about three thousand men. He told the people they had sinned a great sin and that he would go back up into the mount to make an atonement for them. *(Ex. 32.)* The Lord promised Moses that He would be with Israel and would drive the people out of the land. The tabernacle of the congregation was moved away from the camp. When in the tabernacle, the Lord spoke to Moses face to face, "as a man speaketh unto his friend." Moses then returned to camp. Later on, Moses saw the glory of God, but not His face. *(Ex. 33.)*

Moses made two new tables of stone. The Lord said He would write upon these tablets as He had written upon the ones Moses destroyed. Moses was on Mount Sinai 40 days and 40 nights. The Lord again instructed Moses regarding the feast of unleavened bread, about resting on the seventh day, and about the three yearly feasts: the feast of weeks, the first fruits of wheat harvest, and the feast of ingathering at the year's end. When Moses came down from the mount, the skin on his face shone and the people were afraid to come near him. He covered his face with a veil when he spoke to them. *(Ex. 34.)*

Moses again stressed the Sabbath observance. He also conveyed to the people the instructions he had received about the construction of the tabernacle. He told the children of Israel that the Lord had called Bezaleel and Aholiab to work on the tabernacle. *(Ex. 35.)*

Moses called Bezaleel and Aholiab and "every wise hearted man in whom the Lord had put wisdom and understanding to know how to work all manner of work for the service of the sanctuary," to come to him, as the Lord commanded. Moses instructed them regarding the building of the tabernacle. The people donated more supplies than necessary so Moses had them stop making donations. *(Ex. 36.)*

When the tabernacle was finished and the cloths were made and the garments for Aaron and his sons were ready, all according to the Lord's instructions, Moses blessed the people. *(Ex. 39:43.)*

Moses was instructed to anoint the tabernacle and all that was therein, and that he should hallow it and all the vessels therein, "and it shall be holy." *(Ex. 40:9.)* He was instructed to bring Aaron and his sons unto the door of the tabernacle of the congregation and wash them with water, and do all things necessary to anoint them and prepare them to be ministers unto the Lord. All the things the Lord commanded were done. The Lord was upon the tabernacle in a cloud by day and fire was on it by night. When the cloud was taken up, the children of Israel journeyed. If it was not taken up, they did not journey. *(Ex. 40.)*

The Lord set forth rules, laws, instructions and commandments that Moses was to convey to the children of Israel. Specifically: animals without blemish were to be used for sacrifices *(Lev. 1:3)*; how offerings of flour with oil and incense were to be made *(Lev. 2:1-2)*; peace offerings were to be made with animals without blemish and Israel was forbidden to eat fat or blood *(Lev. 3:1, 17)*; how sinners were to be forgiven *(Lev. 4-6)*; laws governing various sacrifices were set forth *(Lev. 7)*; instructions regarding the washing and anointing of Aaron and his sons were given and followed and Moses and Aaron offered sacrifices to make reconciliation and atonement with the Lord *(Lev. 8)*.

Moses instructed Aaron to make an atonement sacrifice. The glory of the Lord appeared to all and fire from the Lord consumed the offerings on the altar. *(Lev. 9.)* Two of Aaron's sons performed unauthorized sacrifices and were slain by fire from the Lord; instructions were then given to Aaron and his other sons not to mourn for them, not to drink wine nor strong drink, and to teach all that the Lord revealed to Moses. *(Lev. 10.)* Moses was given instruction regarding which living things may be eaten, as well as instruction regarding clean and unclean animals. *(Lev. 11.)* The Lord gave Moses instruction regarding the purification of women following childbirth, including a sin offering. *(Lev. 12.)* Laws pertaining to leprosy, lepers, and other types of uncleanness were given to Moses *(Lev. 13-15)*; laws regarding how and when the holy place must be entered by Aaron and laws regarding sacrifices, including the scapegoat, were given to Moses. *(Lev. 16-17.)* The children of Israel were instructed not to live as the Egyptians and Canaanites lived and laws regarding sexual perversions were given to Moses: sex with family members or close relations, homosexuality and bestiality are all an abomination to the Lord.

(Lev. 18.) Other laws and commandments were reaffirmed, plus the people were instructed to love their neighbors as themselves. *(Lev. 19.)* The death penalty was prescribed for certain offenses: i.e., sacrificing children to Molech, cursing father and mother, adultery, homosexuality, bestiality, spiritualism and other sexual sins. *(Lev. 20.)* Instructions pertaining to the priests and the seed of Aaron were given to Moses. *(Lev. 21-22.)* Instructions regarding various feasts were given. *(Lev. 23.)* Moses was given commandments regarding the stoning of blasphemers and an "eye for an eye and a tooth for a tooth" doctrine. *(Lev. 24.)* Land laws were given to Moses and a commandment that every seventh year was to be kept as a Sabbath year and every 50th year was to be celebrated as a jubilee in which liberty would be proclaimed throughout the land. *(Lev. 25.)* The Lord reaffirmed that temporal and spiritual blessing would be showered upon the Israelites if they kept His commandments, but that cursing and destruction would attend the Israelites if they did not. Nevertheless, the Lord would show mercy to them if they repented. *(Lev. 26.)* Moses was given instruction pertaining to how properties were to be consecrated unto the Lord. Israel was also commanded to pay tithes of their crops, flocks, and herds: one-tenth "shall be holy unto the Lord." *(Lev. 27.)*

The Lord commanded Moses to number all the males in Israel—except those belonging to the tribe of Levi—who were 20 years old and above. They numbered 603,550. He was also instructed to have one man from each tribe stand with him in battle. He was given the names of who those twelve "princes of tribes" should be. No one from the tribe of Levi was to be appointed, however, as they were to be in charge of the tabernacle of testimony and over all the vessels and things pertaining to it. *(Num. 1:1-16, 50-53.)*

The Lord instructed Moses where the other tribes of the Levites should camp around the tabernacle and then indicated that those encamped before the tabernacle toward the east were to be Moses, and Aaron and his sons. *(Num. 3:38.)*

Moses was given instruction regarding lepers, sinners, and women who have been charged with an immoral act. *(Num. 5.)*

Moses was given instruction pertaining to the law of the Nazarite. *(Num. 6.)*

When the tabernacle was dedicated, the princes of Israel made offerings over a twelve day period. At the conclusion of the offerings, the Lord spoke to Moses from the mercy seat that was upon the ark of testimony, from between the cherubims. *(Num. 7.)*

The Lord instructed Moses to wash, consecrate and set apart the Levites unto Him by the laying on of hands *(Num. 8:10). (Num. 8.)*

In the first month of the second year after they had fled Egypt, the Lord commanded the children of Israel to keep the Passover, with all its ceremonies, on the fourteenth day of that month. A cloud appeared over the tabernacle by day and night plus a pillar of fire was over the tabernacle by night. When the cloud was taken from the tabernacle, the children of Israel journeyed; when it settled over the tabernacle, they rested in their tents and didn't travel. *(Num. 9.)*

When the Lord threatened to smite the children of Israel and to disinherit them because of their disobedience and constant complaining, Moses argued that to do so would cause the other nations to gloat that the Lord could not bring to pass what He had promised them and that, therefore, the Lord had slain them in the wilderness. As a result, the Lord spared them, but said that no one who was then twenty years old or older would be allowed to enter the promised land except Joshua and Caleb, and that the children of Israel would have to remain in the wilderness for forty years, one year for each day the scouts had scouted out Caanan. The 10 scouts who returned with a negative report were killed by a plague from the Lord. *(Num. 14.)*

When the children of Israel moved to Kadesh (where Miriam subsequently died), they again murmured against Moses and Aaron because it was a place of no water nor "seed, or of figs, or of vines, or of pomegranates." The Lord instructed Moses to take the rod and gather the assembly together and speak unto the rock that was before their eyes and it would bring forth water. Rather than speak to the rock, Moses struck the rock with his rod. The rock brought forth water. The Lord was displeased because Moses struck the rock rather than speak to it, and He said, "Because ye believed me not, to sanctify me in the eyes of the children of Israel, therefore ye shall not bring this congregation into the land which I have given them." *(Num. 20:12.)* When Moses and the children of Israel desired to pass through Edom, the king of Edom refused and came out against them. Thus, the children of Israel turned away and traveled to mount Hor. As the time approached for Aaron to die, the Lord instructed Moses to take Aaron and his son Eleazar up unto mount Hor (where Aaron subsequently died) and strip Aaron of his garments and place them upon Eleazar. *(Num. 20.)*

Moses was instructed that if a man had no sons, that man's inheritance should be passed on to his daughters. He was then given the order of kinsmen who would be next in line to receive someone's inheritance. Moses was instructed to go up into mount Abarim and see the land of promise, but was told he would not get to enter it because he had not followed the Lord's instructions in the desert of Zin when he brought forth the waters of Meribab. He was also told that it was time for him to be "gatherered" unto his people as was Aaron. Moses asked the Lord to provide another leader. Joshua was called and set apart by Eleazar. *(Num. 27.)*

Instructions were given to Moses regarding sacrifices—how and when they were to be offered. *(Num. 28-29.)*

Moses was instructed to teach the children of Israel that vows and oaths must be kept. However, if a father of a daughter living at home disallows the vows of his daughter, or if a man disallows the vows of his wife, the Lord will forgive the daughter or wife of her vows. *(Num. 30.)*

The Lord had Moses send an army forth to destroy the Midianites. The army was comprised of 1,000 men from each of the twelve tribes. When they returned with the spoils, including all the women and children, Moses instructed them to slay every male child and every woman who had lain with a man to avoid having a plague upon them as in the matter of Peor (see Cozbi and Zimri). *(Num. 31.)*

Moses was instructed to assign Eleazar and Joshua to divide the land unto the tribes of Israel for their inheritances. He also was given the names of the leader in each tribe who would allocate the land within each tribe. *(Num. 34.)*

The Lord told Moses that the Levites were to possess their own cities, that there should be cities established as a place of refuse for those guilty of unintentionally killing someone, and that murderers should be executed by the revenger of blood. *(Num. 35.)*

The Lord commanded the daughters of Israel to marry within their own tribe. Israel was also told that inheritances were not to be moved from tribe to tribe. *(Num. 36.)*

Moses reviewed with the children of Israel all that had transpired since they left Egypt. *(Deut. 1-2.)* Moses saw Canaan from Mount Pisgah but was denied entrance into the promised land. Joshua was chosen to succeed Moses as the leader of the children of Israel. *(Deut. 3.)* The house of Israel will be scattered throughout all the nations when they worship false gods, but will be gathered together again in the latter days when they again seek the Lord, God. *(Deut. 4.)* Moses reviewed the Ten Commandments with the children of Israel and reminded them that God talks with man and that blessings flow from obedience. *(Deut. 5.)* Moses exhorted Israel to keep the commandments. *(Deut. 6.)* Israel was commanded to destroy seven nations of the Canaanites and Israel was forbidden to intermarry with them. If Israel would hearken unto the Lord, the Lord would remove sickness from them. *(Deut. 7.)* The Lord tested Israel in the wilderness for forty years. Manna taught them that man lives by the word of God, not by bread alone. Their clothes never wore out, nor did their feet swell. *(Deut. 8.)* Moses reminded Israel of their past rebellions and how he had gone without food and water for forty days on two occasions on their behalf as he mediated between them and the Lord. He also reminded them that other nations had been driven out of Canaan because of wickedness. *(Deut. 9.)* Moses placed the tablets of stone containing the Ten Commandments in the ark. *(Deut. 10.)* Blessings were promised Israel if they were obedient and a curse if they were not obedient. *(Deut. 11.)* Rules were again set forth as to where and how Israel was to worship. They were forbidden to eat blood *(Deut. 12)*, to worship false gods—and those who do were to be put to death—and the idolatrous cities were to be destroyed. *(Deut. 13.)* The Lord gave Israel a law of health and instructed them regarding tithing. *(Deut. 14.)* Israel received instructions regarding debts, caring for the poor, release of servants, and the firstling males of herds and flocks. *(Deut. 15.)* Israel was instructed to keep the Passover and various feasts. They were also to appoint judges and officers. The judges were cautioned not to accept gifts nor repect persons but to judge justly. *(Deut. 16.)* By the mouths of two or three witnesses a person was to be condemned to death. People who worshipped false gods were to be put to death. Priests and judges were to determine the difficult cases. Kings were instructed not to multiply horses, wives or gold but to study the laws of God daily. *(Deut. 17.)* Israel was told how the Levites were to be supported. They were also commanded to avoid divination, spiritualism and the like, as they are abominations. The Lord promised to eventually raise up a prophet (Christ) "of they brethren" who will be "like unto" Moses. *(Deut. 18.)* Three cities were to be established as safe havens for people who killed someone unintentionally. Guilt was to be determined by the mouths of two or three witnesses. False witnesses were to be punished. *(Deut. 19.)* Instructions as to how to select soldiers for battle were given. The Lord would fight their battles. The Hittites, Amorites, Canaanites, Perizzites, Hivites and Jebusites were to be completely destroyed, but the inhabitants of cities that were far off which were not of these nations, were to be approached in peace. If they accepted peace, they were to be tributaries unto the Israelites. If they chose war, the men were all to be slain but the women and children were to be spared. *(Deut. 20.)* Instructions were given on what action to take when a person was slain by unknown persons. Women captured in battle could be taken as wives or could be set free, but they could not be sold. Equity was required in dealing with wives and children under plural marriage. Rebellious sons were to be presented to the elders of the city and all the men of the city were to stone them to death. *(Deut. 21.)* Moses taught Israel about the laws pertaining to lost property, the wearing of proper clothes and caring for the interests of others. He also instructed them regarding the marrying of virgins and the penalties for sexual immorality. *(Deut. 22.)* Moses instructed Israel about who could or could not enter the congregation. He also set forth laws concerning sanitation, servants, vows, plucking in one's neighbor's vineyard or cornfield, and charging interest on loans (usury). *(Deut. 23.)* Moses continued reciting laws regarding divorce, newly married persons, making merchandise of men, children shall not be put to death for the sins of the fathers nor the fathers put to death for the sins of their children, taking of pledges, leprosy, oppression of servants, and leaving gleanings of crops. *(Deut. 24.)* Moses continued reciting the law unto the children of Israel regarding judges prescribing punishment for the wicked, marriage of a brother's widow and just weights and measures. Israel was also commanded to blot out the Amalekites completely. *(Deut. 25.)* Israel was instructed to offer to the Lord a basket of first fruits of Canaan and to keep the law of tithing. Israel convenanted to keep the Lord's commandments, and the Lord promised to make them a holy people and a great nation. *(Deut. 26.)* Moses and the elders of Israel commanded the people to keep all the commandments they received that day. On the day they passed over Jordan, they were to build an altar and worship the Lord. The tribes of Simeon, Levi, Judah, Issachar, Joseph and Benjamin were to stand upon mount Gerizim to bless the people; the tribes of Reuben, Gad, Asher, Zebulun, Dan and Naphtali were to stand upon mount Ebal to curse the people. Israel is the Lord's people, but they shall be cursed if they do not obey Him. *(Deut. 27.)* Moses recited the blessings the Lord would bestow upon Israel if they obeyed the Lord and also recounted the curses that would befall them if they were disobedient to the Lord. *(Deut. 28.)* The children of Israel made a covenant with the Lord: they would be blessed if obedient, cursed if disobedient and their land would be as brimstone and salt. *(Deut. 29.)* Moses reminded the people that scattered Israel shall be gathered from all nations when they remember the covenant. He also placed a life or death, blessing or cursing, before the people. *(Deut. 30.)* By now, Moses was 120 years old. He told all of Israel that he could not lead them into the new land. He counseled Joshua and all of Israel to be strong and to have courage. The Lord instructed Moses to have the law read to the children of Israel every seven years so that even the children who did not know anything at that time could hear the word. Moses and Joshua were instructed to present themselves to the Lord in the tabernacle of the congregation. The Lord told them that Israel would fall away and become idolatrous. Moses was instructed to write a song and teach it to the children of Israel that it may testify against them as a witness, "for it shall not be forgotten out of the mouths of their seed." *(Deut. 31.)* Moses and Joshua—referred to as Hoshea—taught the people the song of Moses. Moses was commanded to go up into the mountain Abarim, unto mount Nebo, and behold the land of promise. He would then die there and be gathered unto his people. *(Deut. 32.)* Moses blessed all of the tribes of Israel. *(Deut. 33.)* Moses went from the plains of Moab unto mount Nebo. The Lord showed him all of the land that was promised to the children of Israel. Moses then died "in the land of Moab, according to the word of the Lord, and he buried him in a valley in the land of Moab, . . . but no man knoweth of his sepulchre unto this day." Moses was 120 years old when he died. *(Deut. 34.)*

Manasseh (Moses) was the father of Gershom and the grandfather of Jonathan. *(Judg. 18:30.)* *(Note. The footnote to the text indicates that Manasseh, in this instance, actually refers to Moses.)*

When David numbered the Levites at the time he made Solomon king, he divided them into courses among the children of Levi. Moses' sons, Gershom and Eliezer, were named of the tribe of Levi. *(1 Chr. 23:13-15.)*

Psalm. 78 recounts the Lord's interaction with Moses and the children of Israel in the wilderness as well as the plagues that fell upon Egypt.

Psalm. 90 is a prayer of Moses. A thousand years in the sight of the Lord are but as yesterday and as a watch in the night.

The Lord sent Moses and Aaron to Egypt, the land of Ham. *(Ps. 105:26.)*

The children of Israel envied Moses and Aaron. Because of Israel's wickedness, the Lord would have destroyed them had Moses not intervened in their behalf. Moses became angry with the people and "spoke unadvisedly with his lips;" thus, "it went ill with Moses for their sakes." *(Ps. 106:16, 23, 32.)*

The Lord's goodness and interaction with Moses, the children of Israel, Pharaoh, king Sihon and king Og are reviewed. *(Ps. 136.)*

The Lord told the prophet Jeremiah that even if Moses and Samuel stood before Him to plead for the Jews, He would not change His mind about destroying and scattering the people because they had become so wicked. *(Jer. 15:1.)*

In the first year of the reign of Darius over the Chaldeans, Daniel fasted and prayed and confessed the sins of Israel, acknowledging that the inhabitants of Jerusalem, the men of Judah, and all Israel had trespassed against the Lord and were in a state of confusion. "Therefore the curse is poured upon us, and the oath that is written in the law of Moses the servant of God, because we have sinned against him." *(Dan. 9:11.)*

Micah chastised the children of Israel and said that in spite of the Lord's sending Moses, Aaron and Mirian to help them, and leading them out of Egyptian bondage, they still turned away from Him. *(Micah 6:4.)*

(Note: In the New Testament, Matt. 17:3, we learn that Moses and Elias (Elijah) appeared as translated beings to Jesus and three of his apostles—Peter, James and John—on the mount of transfiguration. In D&C 110:11, we learn Moses appeared to Joseph Smith and Oliver Cowdery on April 3, 1836: "After this vision closed, the heavens were again opened unto us; and Moses appeared before us, and committed unto us the keys of the gathering of Israel from the four parts of the earth, and the leading of the ten tribes from the land of the north.") (Charts 7b, d.)

MOSES' FATHER. See **Amram (1)**.

MOSES' MOTHER. See **Jochebed**.

MOSES' SISTER. See **Miriam (1)**.

MOZA (1). *1 Chr. 2:46.*

Moza was one of the sons of Caleb and his concubine Ephah. (Chart 8j.)

MOZA (2). *1 Chr. 8:36-37; 9:42-43.*

Moza, from the tribe of Benjamin, was the son of Zimri. They were descendants of Saul through Jonathan. He begat Binea. *(1 Chr. 8:36-37.)*

Moza was the son of Zimri and the father of Binea. *(1 Chr. 9:42-43.)* (Chart 16 l.)

MUPPIM (Shupham, Shuphamites). *Gen. 46:21; Num. 26:39 (38-39).*

Muppim was a son of Benjamin and a grandson of Jacob and Rachel. His brothers were Belah, Becher, Ashbel, Gera, Naaman, Ehi, Rosh, Huppim and Ard. *(Gen. 46:21.)* *(Note: The different listings of Benjamin's sons in Num. 26:38-39, 1 Chr. 7:6-12 and 1 Chr. 8:1-7, lead to some confusion as new names are added and others are missing.)*

Shupham (Muppim), son of Benjamin, was the father of the **Shuphamites**. From verses 38-40, it would appear that Shupham and Muppim are the same person.) *(Num. 26:39 [38-39].)* (Charts 16a-b.)

MUSHI (Mushites). *Ex. 6:19; Num. 3:33-37; 1 Chr. 6:19, 46-47; 23:21, 23; 24:30.*

Mushi was a son of Merari, and a grandson of Levi. His brother was Mahali. *(Ex. 6:19.)*

Mushites were descendants of Mushi, son of Merari, grandson of Levi and great-grandson of Jacob (Israel). The Muhlites and Mushites comprised the house of Merari. They were instructed to camp on the northward side of the tabernacle. Their males numbered 6200. Chief of the house of Merari was Zuriel, son of Abihail. Their charge was the boards of the tabernacle, the bars, pillars, sockets, vessels, pins and cords, thereof, "and all that serveth thereto." *(Num. 3:33-37.)*

Mushi was the father of Mahli and grandfather of Shamer. *(1 Chr. 6:19, 46-47.)*

Mushi, son of Merari, was the brother of Mahli and the father of a son named Mahli. When David made Solomon king, he numbered the Levites and divided them into courses among the sons of Levi: Gershon, Kohath and Merari. Mahli's sons were Eleazar and Kish. Mushi's sons were Mahli, Eder and Jeremoth. These are those who were named as chief of their courses. *(1 Chr. 23:21, 23.)*

Mushi's sons were Mahli, Eder and Jerimoth. *(1 Chr. 24:30.)* (Chart 7e.)

NAMES THAT BEGIN WITH "N"

NAAM. *1 Chr. 4:15.*

Naam was a son of Caleb who was the son of Jephunneh. His brothers were Iru and Elah. (Chart 8n.)

NAAMAH (1). *Gen. 4:22.*

Naamah was the daughter of Zillah and Lamech, the sister of Tubal-cain. (Chart 1.)

NAAMAH (2). *1 Kgs. 14:21, 31; 2 Chr. 12:13.*

Naamah, an Ammonitess, was the mother of Rehoboam, son of Solomon. (Chart 1.)

NAAMAN (1) (Naamites). *Gen. 46:21; Num. 26:40 (38-40); 1 Chr. 8:4, 7.*

Naaman was a son of Benjamin and a grandson of Jacob. His brothers were Belah, Becher, Ashbel, Gera, Ehi, Rosh, Muppim, Huppim and Ard. *(Gen. 46:21.)*

Naaman and Ard were sons of Bela. *(Note: Benjamin's sons are listed as Bela, Ashbel, Ahiram, Shupham and Hupham.)* Naaman's descendants are the **Naamites**. *(Num. 26:40 [38-40].)*

Naaman was a son of Bela, a son of Benjamin. Benjamin's sons are listed as Bela, Ashbel, Aharah, Nohah, Rapha. Bela's sons were Addar, Gera, Abihud, Abishua, Naaman, Aboah, Gera, Shephuphan and Huram. Naaman, Ahiah and Gera were "removed" and he (presumably Ehud) begat Uzza and Ahihud. *(1 Chr. 8:4, 7.) (Note: The various listings of Naaman's family is inconsistent and confusing. It is not clear who Ehud was. Perhaps Ehud is another name for Benjamin or for Bela.)* (Charts 16a-b, d.)

NAAMAN (2). *2 Kgs. 5:1-27.*

Naaman was the captain of the host of the king of Syria. He was a leper. An Israelite maid servant who waited on Naaman's wife suggested that the prophet in Samaria, Elisha, could heal him. Naaman went to Elisha. Elisha sent a messenger to meet him at the door and had him instruct Naaman to wash in the river Jordan seven times. Naaman was offended that Elisha had not come to meet him himself. Furthermore, he was indignant to think he should bathe in the Jordan river feeling that the waters of Damascus were better. Nevertheless, at the urging of his servants he relented and bathed in the Jordan seven times and was cleansed. He returned to Elisha and acknowledged there was no God on earth except the God in Israel and he offered to reward Elisha. Elisha refused to accept any payment. As he traveled homeward, Elisha's servant, Gehazi, followed after and falsely claimed that Elisha had changed his mind and was now requesting silver and two changes of garments for two young men of the sons of the prophets. When Elisha learned what Gehazi had done, he told him that the leporsy of Naaman would now cleave unto him.

NAAMAN'S (2) SERVANTS. *2 Kgs. 5:13.*

Naaman's Servants urged him to follow Elisha's instruction, saying that if the prophet had asked a great thing of him he would have gladly done it. How much better then to do this simple thing. Because of their counsel, Naaman did as Elisha instructed and was cleansed from leprosy.

NAAMAN'S (2) WIFE. *2 Kgs. 5:2-3.*

Naaman's Wife had an Israelite maid who informed her that there was a prophet of God in Samaria who could cure her husband's leprosy.

NAAMATHITE. *Job 2:11; 11:1; 20:1; 42:9.*

Naamathite. Job's friend Zophar was a Naamathite.

NAAMITES. See **Naaman (1)**.

NAARAH. *1 Chr. 4:5-6.*

Naarah was one of Ashur's wives. She bore him Ahuzam, Hepher, Temeni and Haahashtari.

NAARAI. See **Paarai.**

NAASHON (Nahshon, Nashshon). *Ex. 6:23; Num. 1:7, 26-27; 2:2-9; 7:12.*

Naashon was the brother of Aaron's wife, Elisheba. *(Ex. 6:23.)*

Nahshon (Naashon) was the son of Amminadab and was of the tribe of Judah. He was appointed by the Lord to be the one to stand at the head of all of the tribe of Judah as Moses organized Israel in preparation for war. The males in the tribe of Judah who were 20 years old and older who could go to war numbered 74,600. *(Num. 1:7, 26-27.)*

Nahshon was instructed to have the camp of Judah pitch their tents on the east side of the encampment. Next to them was the tribe of Issachar and then the tribe of Zebulun. Combined, the camp of Judah had 186,400 men. *(Num. 2:2-9.)*

When the altar was anointed, Nahshon made his offering for the dedication of the altar on the first day. *(Num. 7:12.)* (Charts 1.; 8d.)

NABAL. *1 Sam. 25:3-39.*

Nabal, a rich man from Maon, lived in Carmel. He was of the house of Caleb. His wife Abigail was a beautiful and intelligent woman but he was churlish and evil. He refused to give David any food. When David was bent upon destroying Nabal, Abigail quickly came to him with 200 loaves and 200 bottles of wine, plus sheep, parched corn, raisin clusters and cakes of figs, and pleaded that David not do what he was planning to do. When Nabal learned what Abigail had done "his heart died within him, and he became as a stone," and died about ten days later. David then took Abigail for his wife.

NABOTH. *1 Kgs. 21:1-13; 2 Kgs. 9:21, 25-26.*

Naboth was a Jezreelite who owned a vineyard which king Ahab desired. He refused to give the inheritance of his family to king Ahab. When Ahab mourned because he could not have the vineyard, queen Jezebel told Ahab she would deliver the vineyard to him. She had the elders and nobles of the city set Naboth on high among the people and had two men bear false witness against him claiming that he had blasphemed God and the king. As a result, Naboth was taken out of the city and stoned to death. Ahab then took possession of the vineyard. *(1 Kgs. 21:1-13.)*

Naboth was avenged when Ahab's son, Joram (Jehoram), was slain and his body was cast into the field that had belonged to Naboth. *(2 Kgs. 9:21, 25-26.)*

NACHON. *2 Sam. 6:6.*

Nachon had a threshingfloor and when the ark of God reached that point, Uzzah, one of Abinadab's sons, tried to steady the ark with his hand, angering the Lord who caused Uzzah to die.

NADAB (1). *Ex. 6:23; 24:1, 9-10; 28:1; 40:12-15; Lev. 8:6-9, 13; 10:1-2; Num. 3:2, 4; 26:61; 1 Chr. 24:1-2.*

Nadab was a son of Aaron and Elisheba. His brothers were Abihu, Eleazar and Ithamar. *(Ex. 6:23.)*

Nadab was instructed to accompany Moses, Aaron, Abihu and seventy of the elders of Irael unto the mount to worship God. They all saw the God of Israel. *(Ex. 24:1, 9-10.)*

Nadab, along with his father and brothers, was to be consecrated and anointed to minister in the priest's office. They were to keep a light burning always in the tabernacle of the congregation. *(Ex. 28:1. Also see Ex. 27:20-21.)*

Nadab and his father and brothers were washed and anointed and given an everlasting priesthood. *(Ex. 40:12-15.)*

Throughout Leviticus instructions pertaining to Aaron and his sons were given to Moses who then instructed Aaron and his sons regarding their responsibilities. Aaron and his sons were washed and anointed and dressed in the holy garments. *(Lev. 8:6-9, 13.)*

Nadab and Abihu made unauthorized sacrifices to the Lord and the Lord slew them with fire. *(Lev. 10:1-2; Num. 3:2, 4; 26:61.)* Nadab was Aaron's firstborn son. Neither he nor Abihu had any children. *(Num. 3:2, 4.)*

Nadab, Aaron's son, died before his father. He had no children. *(1 Chr. 24:1-2.)* (Chart 7b.)

NADAB (2). *1 Kgs. 14:20; 1 Kgs. 15:25-28, 31.*

Nadab, son of Jeroboam, reigned in his father's stead. *(1 Kgs. 14:20.)*

Nadab began his reign over Israel during the second year of Asa's reign over Judah. He reigned two years. He did evil in the sight of the Lord, walking in sin just as his father had done and causing Israel to sin. Nadab was slain by Baasha, son of Ahijah of the house of Issachar, and Baasha reigned in his stead. The rest of his record is written in the book of the chronicles of the kings of Israel. *(1 Kgs. 15:25-28, 31.)*

NADAB (3). *1 Chr. 2:28.*

Nadab was a son of Shammai. His brother was Abishur. He was the great-great-great-great-grandson of Judah. (Chart 8c.)

NADAB (4). *1 Chr. 8:30-32; 9:35-38.*

Nadab was of the tribe of Benjamin. He was a son of the father of Gibeon. His brothers were Abdon, Zur, Kish (the father of Saul), Baal, Gedor, Ahio, Zacher and Mikloth. *(1 Chr. 8:30-32.)*

Nadab's father was Jehiel (Abiel). His mother was Maachah. His brothers were Abdon, Zur, Kish, Baal, Ner, Gedor, Ahio, Zechariah (Zacher) and Mikloth. *(1 Chr. 9:35-38.)* (Chart 16k.)

NAHAM. *1 Chr. 4:19.*

Naham was the brother of Hodiah, his sister.

NAHARAI. *2 Sam. 23:37; 1 Chr. 11:39.*

Naharai the Beerothite (Berothite), Joab's armorbearer, was one of David's mighty men *(2 Sam. 23:37)* and one of the valiant men of the armies *(1 Chr. 11:39).* (Chart 17.)

NAHASH (1). *1 Sam. 11:1, 11; 2 Sam. 10:1; 1 Chr. 19:1-2.*

Nahash was king of the children of Ammon who came with his armies and encamped against Jabesh-gilead. When the men of Jabesh-gilead asked him to make a covenant with them wherein they would serve Nahash, Nahash said he would make a covenant with them if he could put out the right eye of each of them. Saul came to their rescue and wreaked havoc upon the Ammonites. *(1 Sam. 11:1, 11.)*

When Nahash died, his son Hanun reigned in his stead. Because Nahash had showed kindness unto David, David sought to show kindness and comfort unto Hanun. *(2 Sam. 10:1; 1 Chr. 19:1-2.)*

NAHASH (2). *2 Sam. 17:25.*

Nahash was Abigail and Zeruiah's parent. *(Note: Abigail and Zeruiah were David's sisters. David's father was Jesse [1 Chr. 2:13-16]. Therefore, it would appear that Nahash would have been their mother.)* (Chart 8d.)

NAHASH (3) OF RABBAH. *2 Sam. 17:27.*

Nahash of Rabbah was of the children of Ammon. He was the father of Shobi.

NAHATH (1). *Gen. 36:13,17.*

Nahath was a son of Reuel, son of Bashemath and Esau. He was a duke or tribal chief. (Chart 3c.)

NAHATH (2). *1 Chr. 6:26.* See **Tohu**.

NAHATH (3). *2 Chr. 31:13.*

Nahath, among others, was an overseer of tithes, offerings and the dedicated things of the house of the Lord under the hand of Cononiah and Cononiah's brother Shimei according to the commandment of king Hezekiah and Azariah, the ruler of the house of God.

NAHBI. *Num. 13:14; 14:37.*

Nahbi, of the tribe of Naphtali, was the son of Vophsi. He was one of twelve leaders sent to scout out the land of Caanan. He returned with a negative report. *(Num. 13:14.)* Because of the negative report Nahbi gave, he "died by the plague before the Lord." *(Num. 14:37.)*

NAHOR (1). *Gen. 11:22-26; 1 Chr. 1:26-27.*

Nahor was a son of Serug, a fifth-great-grandson of Shem, and a sixth-great-grandson of Noah. He begat Terah the father of Abraham. He lived 148 years. (Charts 1.; 2b.; 21.)

NAHOR (2) (Nachor). *Gen. 11:26,29; 22:20-24; 24; 29:5; Josh. 24:2.*

Nahor was a son of Terah, a brother of Abraham and Haran, a seventh-great-grandson of Shem and an eighth-great-grandson of Noah. His wife was Milcah, Haran's daughter. *(Gen. 11:26,29.)*

Nahor and Milcah begat Huz, Buz, Kemuel, Chesed, Hazo, Pildash, Jidlaph, Bethuel. He also begat several children by his concubine Reumah: Tebah, Gaham, Thahash, Maachah. *(Gen. 22:20-24.)*

Abraham sent his servant unto Nahor's house in the land of Mesopotamia to find a wife for Isaac. Nahor's granddaughter, Rebekah, was the one to whom the servant was guided. *(Gen. 24.)*

Nahor's son (grandson) was Laban. *(Gen. 29:5.)*

Nachor's (Nahor's) father and other ancestors served false gods. *(Josh. 24:2.)* (Charts 2b-d.)

NAHSHON. See Naashon.

NAHUM. *Nahum 1-3.*

Nahum was an Elkoshite. He said the Lord is slow to anger but when He comes in power the mountains will quake, the hills melt, and the earth will be burned and all that dwell therein. He cried unto Judah to keep their solemn feasts and perform their vows because the wicked would not pass through Judah again. *(Nahum 1.)*

Nahum prophesied that Nineveh would be destroyed. *(Nahum 2.)* Nahum enumerated the many sins of Nineveh and prophesied her miserable downfall. He reminded Ninevah that populous No, inspite of all the help it received from others, was led away captive. Ninevah's fate would be equally awful. *(Nahum 3.)*

NAOMI (Mara). *Ruth 1-4.*

Naomi was the wife of Elimelech. She and her husband took their two sons, Mahlon and Chilion, from Bethlehem-judah to Moab because of famine in the land. They lived there about 10 years. Her husband and sons died in Moab. She decided to return to her own country when she learned that the famine had ended. Her two daughters-in-law wanted to go with her. She discouraged them and told them to stay with their own people. One daughter-in-law, Orpah, returned to her own family. Ruth elected to go with Naomi. Naomi called herself "**Mara**," for the Lord had dealt bitterly with her. *(Ruth 1.)*

Naomi's husband's kinsman, Boaz, was very wealthy. Ruth gleaned in his fields. He was kind to her. *(Ruth 2.)* Naomi instructed Ruth to lie at the feet of Boaz. He promised, as a kinsman, to seek her to wife, but said he must first check with a person who was a nearer kinsman than he to see if he wanted Ruth for a wife as he would have first choice and first responsibility. Naomi told Ruth to "sit still" until the matter was settled. *(Ruth 3.)*

Boaz married Ruth and they had a son whom they named Obed. Naomi "laid it to her bosom, and became nurse unto it." *(Ruth 4.) (Note: Naomi was the great-great-grandmother of David.)*

NAPHISH (Nephish). *Gen. 25:15; 1 Chr. 5:19.*

Naphish was a son of Ishmael and a grandson of Abraham and Hagar, Sarah's handmaid. *(Gen. 25:15.)*

The Reubenites, Gadites and half the tribe of Manasseh, made war with the Hagarites, Jetur, **Nephish** (Naphish) and Nodab. *(1 Chr. 5:19.)* (Chart 3e.)

NAPHTALI. *Gen. 30:8; 37; 46:24; 49:1, 21; 50:8 (7-8); Ex. 1:4; Num. 1:15, 42-43; 2:29 (25-31); 26:48-50; 34:28; Deut. 27:13; 33:23; Josh. 19:32-39; Judg. 1:33; 4:6; 5:18; 1 Chr. 7:13; 12:34; 27:19; Isa. 9:1-2; Ezek. 48:3, 34.*

Naphtali was the second son of Jacob and Bilhah, Rachel's handmaid. (He was Jacob's 6th son.) *(The Bible Dictionary says he was the 5th son.) (Gen. 30:8.)*

Naphtali and his brothers hated their younger brother Joseph and sold him to a group of Ishmeelites, or Midianite merchantmen, for 20 pieces of silver. They dipped his coat of many colors in animal blood and gave it to their father so he would think Joseph had been killed by wild beasts. *(Gen. 37.)*

Naphtali begat Jahzeel, Guni, Jezer and Shillem. *(Gen. 46:24.)*

After the brothers had gone to Egypt for grain and were finally reunited with Joseph, and following the move of their entire family to Egypt, the time came when Jacob called his sons together to tell them what would befall each of them in the last days. Jacob told his son, "Naphtali is a hind let loose; he giveth goodly words." *(Gen. 49:1, 21.)*

Naphtali traveled to Canaan with his brothers to bury their father there as he had requested. *(Gen. 50:8 [7-8].)*

Naphtali and all those who went into Egypt with Jacob are listed. *(Ex. 1:4.)*

When Moses was instructed to choose a leader from each tribe to stand by him as Israel prepared for war and to number all the males 20 years old and older, he was told to appoint Ahira, son of Enan, to lead the tribe of Naphtali. The males of the tribe of Naphtali who could go to war numbered 53,400. *(Num. 1:15, 42-43.)*

Ahira was instructed to have the tribe of Naphtali pitch their tents next to the tribe of Asher as part of the camp of Dan on the north side of the encampment. *(Num. 2:29 [25-31].)*

Naphtali's posterity included the Jahzeelites, Gunites, Jezerites and Shillemites. When Moses and Eleazar counted the males in Israel while on the plains of Moab, those in Naphtali's family who were twenty years old and older numbered 45,400. *(Num. 26:48-50.)*

Pedahel, son of Ammihud, was assigned to divide the inheritance given to the tribe of Naphtali among Naphtali's posterity. *(Num. 34:28.)*

As the children of Israel crossed over Jordan into Canaan to inherit the promised land, the tribes of Naphtali, Reuben, Gad, Asher, Zebulun and Dan were instructed to stand upon mount Ebal to curse. *(Deut. 27:13.)*

Moses blessed the tribe of Naphtali. *(Deut. 33:23.)*

When Joshua cast lots to divide the promised land, the sixth lot fell to the tribe of Naphtali. *(Josh. 19:32-39.)*

Naphtali did not drive the inhabitants out of the promised land, but dwelled among the Canaanites. The Canaanites became tributaries to the tribe of Naphtali. *(Judg. 1:33.)*

Deborah the prophetess reminded Barak that the Lord had told him to take 10,000 men of the children of Naphtali and of the children of Zebulun to battle against Sisera and that the Lord had promised to deliver the enemy into his hand. *(Judg. 4:6.) (Note: The BD, under "Naphtali," indicates that Barak was the one man of note belonging to the tribe of Naphtali.)*

Naphtali's people and Zebulun's people were praised in song by Deborah and Barak for risking their lives to deliver Israel from Canaanite bondage. *(Judg. 5:18.)*

Naphtali's sons, sons of Bilhah, were Jahziel (Jahzeel), Guni, Jezer and Shallum (Shillem). *(1 Chr. 7:13.)*

When David became king and went to Ziklag, all Israel rejoiced and sent their armies to support him. The tribe of Naphtali sent 1,000 captains along with 37,000 men with shield and spear. *(1 Chr. 12:34.)*

Jerimoth, son of Azriel, was prince of the tribe of Naphtali when David was king. *(1 Chr. 27:19.)*

The people of Naphtali and Zebulun, Isaiah prophesied, would see the Savior. *(Isa. 9:1-2.) (Note: The fulfillment of that prophecy is found in Matt. 4:13-16 when Jesus heard that John had been cast into prison and left Nazareth and dwelt in Capernaum "in the borders of Zabulon and Nephthalim.")*

The Lord revealed to Ezekiel just how the land should be divided by tribes when the children of Israel are gathered in the latter days. Naphtali's portion will be by the border of Asher, from the east side even unto the west side. The twelve gates of the city are to bear the names of the twelve sons of Jacob. His gate will be one of the three westward gates. *(Ezek. 48:3, 34.)* (Charts 1.; 3d.; 5a.; 6a.; 7a.; 8a.; 9a.; 10a.; 11a.; 12a-b.; 13a.; 14a.; 15a.; 16a.)

NAPHTUHIM. *Gen. 10:13.*

Naphtuhim was a son of Mizraim, a grandson of Ham and a great-grandson of Noah. (Chart 2e.)

NASHSHON. See **Naashon**.

NATHAN (1). *2 Sam. 5:14; 1 Chr. 3:5-9; 1 Chr. 12:4-7; Zech. 12:12.*

Nathan was one of David's children born in Jerusalem. His brothers also born in Jerusalem were Shammua, Shobab, Solomon, Ibhar, Elishua, Nepheg, Japhia, Elishama, Eliada and Eliphalet. *(2 Sam. 5:14.)*

Nathan, Shimea (Shammua), Shobab and Solomon, sons of David and Bathshua, were born in Jerusalem along with Ithar, Elishama, Eliphelet, Nogah, Nepheg, Japhia, Elishama, Eliada and Eliphelet. Plus, Tamar, a sister. *(1 Chr. 3:5-9.)*

Nathan and his brothers are listed again with some variations: Shammua, Shobab, Nathan, Solomon, Ibhar, Elishua, Elpalet (Eliphalet), Nogah, Nepheg, Japhia, Elishama, Beeliada (Eliada) and Eliphalet. *(1 Chr. 12:4-7.)*

When the Savior comes again and the children of Israel recognize Him as the Savior whom they crucified, there will be great mourning in the land. Each family shall mourn apart: the family of the house of David and their wives; the family of the house of Nathan and their wives, etc. *(Zech. 12:12.)* (Chart 8e.)

NATHAN (2) (THE PROPHET). *2 Sam. 7:2-17; 12; 1 Kgs. 1:8-45; 1 Chr. 17:1-15; 29:29; 2 Chr. 9:29; 29:25; Ps. 51:subtitle.*

Nathan the Prophet was instructed by the Lord to tell David that He had not asked him to build Him a house of cedar. Nathan was also to tell David that "when thy days be fulfilled, and thou shalt sleep with thy fathers, I will set up thy seed after thee, which shall proceed out of thy bowels, and I will establish his kingdom . . . and I will stablish the throne of his kingdom for ever. I will be his father, and he shall be my son." *(2 Sam. 7:2-17.) (Note: This refers to Jesus Christ and the kingdom he would establish that would last forever.)*

The prophet Nathan was sent by the Lord to David. He told David a parable about the ewe lamb. Nathan told David that the Lord had given David many wives, but that David was now cursed for taking Bath-sheba. He informed David that the sword would never depart from his house because he had taken the life of Uriah. *(2 Sam. 12.)*

Nathan, Zadok the priest, Jehoiada, Shimei and Rei, who were strong supporters of David, were deliberately excluded by Adonijah, David's son, when he set himself up as king in David's stead and surrounded himself with many of the leaders. Nathan counseled with Bath-sheba and encouraged her to tell David what was happening. Nathan said he would then reaffirm what she told David when he spoke to him later. As a result, David declared Solomon to be king and had Nathan and Zadok the priest escort Solomon to Gihon where they anointed him king over Israel. *(1 Kgs. 1:8-45.)*

The account of David desiring to build a temple and the Lord instructing Nathan to restrain David is retold. Nathan told David that after his death the Lord would establish his kingdom forever through the seed of David "which shall be of thy sons." *(1 Chr. 17:1-15.) (Note: This refers to Jesus Christ. See Heb. 1:5-6.)*

Nathan recorded the acts of David in a book, but the record has been lost along with other books mentioned. *(1 Chr. 29:29.)*

Nathan recorded the acts of Solomon, but this record has been lost. *(2 Chr. 9:29.)*

Hezekiah, king of Judah, "set the Levites in the house of the Lord" with their instruments of music according to commandments given years earlier by the prophet Nathan. *(2 Chr. 29:25.)*

Nathan came to David after David had gone in unto Bathsheba. Psalm 51 was writen in response to Nathan's visit. *(Ps. 51:subtitle.)*

NATHAN (3). *2 Sam. 23:36; 1 Chr. 11:38.*

Nathan of Zobah was the father of Igal who was one of David's mighty men. *(2 Sam. 23:36.)*

Nathan was the brother of Joel, one of the valiant men of David's army. *(1 Chr. 11:38.) (Note: From the way names are listed in these two scriptural references, Igal and Joel are possibly one and the same person.)* (Chart 17.)

NATHAN (4). *1 Kgs. 4:5.*

Nathan was the father of Azariah (who was over the officers who provided food for Solomon and his household) and Zabud (who was the principal officer as well as the king's friend).

NATHAN (5). *1 Chr. 2:36.*

Nathan was the son of Attai and the father of Zabad. (Chart 8c.)

NATHAN (6). *Ezra 8:16.*

Nathan was one of the chief men Ezra sent for when he gathered the people together as he was preparing to lead them to Jerusalem from Babylon and discovered there were no Levites among the group. He sent this group to Iddo and the Nethinims to request that they send them some ministers for the house of God.

NATHAN (7). *Ezra 10:39 (18-19, 39, 44).*

Nathan, a son of Bani, and his brothers were some of the men in Israel who took foreign wives but gave them up when Ezra feared the wrath of God would destroy Israel for this iniquity.

NATHAN-MELECH. *2 Kgs. 23:11.*

Nathan-melech was the chamberlain. King Josiah "took away the horses that the kings of Judah had given to the sun, at the entering in of the house of the Lord, by the chamber of Nathan-melech the chamberlain, which was in the suburbs, and burned the chariots of the sun with fire."

NAZARITE. *Num. 6:2-21; Judg. 13:5; 16:17; 1 Sam. 1:11; Amos 2:11-12.*

Nazarites were men who consecrated themselves to the Lord. They made a vow to abstain from wine, from cutting their hair, and to avoid any contact with the dead. The vow might be lifelong or just for a short definite period. *(Num. 6:2-21.)*

Samson was a Nazarite. *(Judg. 13:5.)* He confided in Delilah that he was a Nazarite and that his strength lay in his not cutting his hair. *(Judg. 16:17.)*

Hannah prayed for a son and promised the Lord she would give him unto Him all the days of his life and that no razor would come upon his head. She had Samuel, and when he was weaned, she gave him to the Lord. *(1 Sam. 1:11.)*

The Lord condemned Israel for giving wine to the Nazarites and for commanding the prophets not to prophesy. *(Amos 2:11-12.)*

NEARIAH (1). *1 Chr. 3:22.*

Neariah, a descendant of David, was a son of Shemaiah. His brothers were Hattush, Igeal, Bariah and Shaphat. His sons were Elioenai, Hezekiah and Azrikam. (Chart 1.)

NEARIAH (2). *1 Chr. 4:42.*

Neariah, a son of Ishi, was one of the captains who led a group of 500 men, including some of the sons of Simeon, to mount Seir where they smote the rest of the Amalekites who had escaped from earlier conflicts. His brothers were Pelatiah, Rephaiah and Uzziel. (Chart 6b.)

NEBAI. *Neh. 10:19 (1, 19, 28-31).*

Nebai was among those chief of the people who covenanted to marry in Israel, honor the Sabbath, pay tithes and keep the commandments.

NEBAJOTH (Nebaioth). *Gen. 25:13; 1 Chr. 1:29.*

Nebajoth (Nebaioth) was the firstborn son of Ishmael and a grandson of Abraham and Hagar, Sarah's handmaid. (Chart 3e.)

NEBAT. *1 Kgs. 11:26; 15:1.*

Nebat, Solomon's servant, was the father of Jeroboam. His wife was Zeruah. *(1 Kgs. 11:26.)*

In the 18th year of Nebat's son Jeroboam's reign, Abijam began his reign over Judah. *(1 Kgs. 15:1.)*

NEBO (1). *Ezra 2:29; 10:43 (18-19, 43-44); Neh. 7: 33.*

Nebo was of the people of Israel. The men of the children of Nebo who returned to Jerusalem from Babylon after Cyrus' proclamation to build the temple numbered 52. *(Ezra 2:29; Neh. 7: 33.)*

Nebo's sons—Jeiel, Mattithiah, Zabad, Zebina, Jadau, Joel and Benaiah—were some of the Israelite men who took foreign wives but agreed to separate themselves from them because Ezra feared the Lord's wrath would destroy all of Israel for this iniquity. *(Ezra 10:43 [18-19, 43-44].)*

NEBO (2). *Isa. 46:1-7.*

Nebo and Bel were idol gods. Instead of being able to help the people, the people had to carry them.

NEBUCHADNEZZAR (Nebuchadrezzar). *2 Kgs. 24:1-17; 25:1-21; 1 Chr. 6:15; 2 Chr. 36:6-13; Ezra 1:7; 2:1; 5:12, 14; 6:5; Neh. 7:6-63; Esth. 2:6; Jer. 21:2, 7; 22:25; 25:1, 11-12; 27; 28:1-3, 11, 14; 29:1, 3, 10; 32:1-3; 34; 35:11; 37:1; 38:3; 39:1-12; 43:10, 13; 44:30; 46:2-26; 49:28-30; 50:17; 51:34-44; 52:4-30; Ezek. 24; 26:7; 29:18-20; 30; Dan. 1:1; 2; 3; 4; 5:2.*

Nebuchadnezzar was king of Babylon between 604-561 B.C. when Jehoiakim (Eliakim) was king over Judah. He beseiged and took Jerusalem and made Jehoiakim serve as his servant. Nebuchadnezzar carried many of Judah captive into Babylon. After three years, Jehoiakim rebelled against Nebuchadnezzar. When Jehoiachin, Jehoiakim's son reigned, Nebuchadnezzar, in his eighth year as king, again came against Jerusalem and beseiged the city and took Jehoiachin, his mother, his wives, his officers, and the mighty of the land captive into Babylon, leaving only "the poorest sort of the people of the land." He made Mattaniah (whom he named Zedekiah), Jehoiachin's uncle, king over Judah. *(2 Kgs. 24:1-17.) (Note: The Encyclopaedia Brittanica, Vol. VII, p. 237, Nebuchadnezzar II, states that*

Nebuchadnezzar was the oldest son and successor of Nabopolassar and ascended to the throne within three weeks of his father's death on August 16, 605 B.C. He captured Jerusalem in August of 586 B.C. and deported its prominent citizens.)

In Nebuchadnezzar's ninth year as king over Babylon, he again went against Jerusalem. The armies of the Chaldees captured king Zedekiah, slew his sons before his eyes and then put Zedekiah's eyes out. They bound him with fetters of brass and carried him to Babylon. In Nebuchadnezzar's 19th year as king, Nebuzar-adan (captain of his army) and his men burned the house of the Lord, the king's house and all the other houses in Jerusalem and broke down the walls of Jerusalem. They carried the valuables of the city and most of the remnant of Judah away, leaving only the poor of the land to be vine-dressers and husbandmen. When Nebuzar-adan brought Seraiah, the chief priest; Zephaniah, the second priest; the three keepers of the door; an officer; five of the king's men; and 60 men of the general population to Nebuchadnezzar, the king slew them; thus, Judah was carried away out of the land of their inheritance. Nebuchadnezzar appointed Gedaliah to be ruler over those few who still remained in Jerusalem. *(2 Kgs. 25:1-21.)*

Nebuchadnezzar took Jehozadak into captivity when he carried Judah and Jerusalem away captive. *(1 Chr. 6:15.)*

Nebuchadnezzar bound and fettered Jehoiakim, king of Judah, and carried him captive to Babylon. Jehoiachin, Jehoiakim's eight (or 18) year old son became king in his stead. He reigned wickedly for three months and ten days and Nebuchadnezzar had him brought to Babylon. Nebuchadnezzar then made Zedekiah (Manttaniah), Jehoiachin's uncle, king in his stead. Zedekiah did evil before the Lord and also rebelled against Nebuchadnezzar. *(2 Chr. 36:6-13.)*

The vessels of the house of the Lord that Nebuchadnezzar took out of Jerusalem, were returned by Cyrus. *(Ezra 1:7.)*

The people who Nebuchadnezzar had captured but who were allowed to return to Jerusalem under Cyrus are listed. *(Ezra 2:1.)*

After the people provoked the Lord, He allowed Nebuchadnezzar to carry them away captive to Babylon. In the first year of the reign of Cyrus, Cyrus decreed the rebuilding of the temple and sent the people and the vessels of the Lord's house back to Jerusalem. *(Ezra 5:12, 14.)* Cyrus decreed that the temple should be rebuilt and the gold and silver vessels of the house of the Lord were to be returned and placed in it. *(Ezra 6:5.)* The children of Israel who were carried into Babylonian captivity by Nebuchadnezzar but who returned to Jerusalem and Judah with Zerubbabel are listed. *(Neh. 7:6-63.)*

One of the people carried away captive by Nebuchadnezzar when he carried Judah's king away was Mordecai, cousin/father to Esther. *(Esth. 2:6.)*

Jeremiah prophesied that **Nebuchadrezzar** (Nebuchadnezzar) would take Israel captive, including king Zedekiah, and that he would "smite them with the edge of the sword" and have no mercy nor pity on them. *(Jer. 21:2, 7.)*

The prophet Jeremiah pronounced the judgments of the Lord upon the kings of Judah because of their wickedness. The Lord would deliver them into the hands of Nebuchadrezzar and into the hands of the Chaldeans. *(Jer. 22:25.)*

The first year of Nebuchadrezzar's reign as king of Babylon corresponded to the fourth year of Jehoiakim's reign as king of Judah. The children of Israel would remain captive for 70 years, afterwhich the Lord said He would punish the king of Babylon and the land of the Chaldeans. *(Jer. 25:1, 11-12.)*

In the beginning of Jehoiakim's reign, Jeremiah was instructed by the Lord to send word to many nations that they were to serve Babylon. He said he had given all these lands into the hand of Nebuchadnezzar. Those nations who refused to serve Nebuchadnezzar would be punished. The vessels of the Lord's house which were not carried away when Jeconiah was carried away were to be taken to Babylon where they would remain until such time as the Lord restored the people to Jerusalem. *(Jer. 27.)*

During the fifth month of the fourth year of the reign of Zedekiah, king of Judah, Hananiah falsely prophesied that the yoke of Babylon and Nebuchadnezzar would be broken within two years. However, the Lord had decreed that the other nations would serve Nebuchadnezzar. *(Jer. 28:1-3, 11, 14.)*

Jeremiah sent a letter via Elasah and Gemariah unto the residue of the elders, the priests, prophets and people who were carried away captive by Nebuchadnezzar, telling them that the children of Israel would remain captive of Babylon for 70 years, after which the Lord would perform good works for them. *(Jer. 29:1, 3, 10.)*

The 18th year of Nebuchadnezzar's reign was the 10th year of Zedekiah's reign over Judah. It was at this time that Zedekiah imprisoned the prophet Jeremiah for prophesying that Nebuchadnezzar would take Zedekiah prisoner and the Chaldeans would burn Jerusalem. *(Jer. 32:1-3.)*

When Nebuchadnezzar and his army fought against Jerusalem, Jeremiah prophesied that Zedekiah, king of Judah, and his princes would be delivered into the hands of Nebuchadnezzar. *(Jer. 34.)*

When Nebuchadnezzar came into their lands, the Rechabites feared him and the armies of the Chaldeans and Syrians so they went to Jerusalem for protection. *(Jer. 35:11.)*

Nebuchadnezzar made Zedekiah king of Judah in place of Coniah (Jeconiah, Jehoiachin). Jeremiah told Zedekiah that Egypt could not save Judah from the Chaldeans. The Chaldeans would take Jerusalem and burn it. *(Jer. 37:1.)*

Jeremiah prophesied that Jerusalem would surely be taken by king Nebuchadnezzar's army. *(Jer. 38:3.)*

Nebuchadnezzar came against Jerusalem in the tenth month of the ninth year of Zedekiah's reign. By the fourth month of Zedekiah's eleventh year as king, the city was broken up. Zedekiah tried to escape but was captured by the Chaldean army which turned him over to Nebuchadnezzar. Nebuchadnezzar slew Zedekiah's sons, put Zedekiah's eyes out, bound him in chains so as to carry him to Babylon, burned the king's house as well as those of the rest of the people, and broke down the walls of Jerusalem *(Jer. 39:1-8)*. Nebuchadnezzar instructed his guard to do no harm to Jeremiah, but to do unto him whatever Jeremiah said to do *(Jer. 39:11-12)*. *(Note: Helaman 6:10 in the Book of Mormon states that one of Zedekiah's sons, Mulek, was brought by the Lord to America "into the land north." Hel. 8:21 reaffirms that all but one of Zedekiah's sons were slain.)*

Because Johanan the son of Kareah (Careah) and Azariah (Jezaniah, Jaazaniah) the son of Hoshaiah and "all the proud men" refused to believe Jeremiah's prophecy that they would be blessed if they remained in Judah but would suffer death, famine and pestilence if they went into Egypt but went into Egypt anyway, Jeremiah prophesied that Babylon would conquer Egypt and that Nebuchadrezzar would "set his throne upon these stones" which Jeremiah had buried at the entry of Pharaoh's house. Nebuchadrezzar would destroy the gods of Egypt and break the images of Beth-shemesh. *(Jer. 43:10, 13.)*

Just as Nebuchadrezzar had taken Zedekiah captive, so would Pharaoh-hophra king of Egypt be delivered into the hands of his enemies because the remnant of Judah who went to dwell in Egypt refused to believe Jeremiah's prophesies and worshipped false gods. *(Jer. 44:30.)*

In the fourth year of the reign of Jehoiakim, king of Judah, when Nebuchadrezzar conquered Pharaoh-necho the king of Egypt, Jeremiah prophesied that Nebuchadrezzar would conquer Pharaoh-hophra. *(Jer. 46:2-26.)* *(Note: The footnote to the text cross-references this Pharaoh with Pharaoh-hophra.)*

When Jeremiah prophesied of the judgment and destruction that would come upon Kedar and Hazor, he prophesied they would be conquered by Nebuchadnezzar. *(Jer. 49:28-30.)*

Jeremiah prophesied that Babylon would be destroyed, never to rise again, and that the Lord would "punish the king of Babylon and his land, as I have punished the king of Assyria" because, he said, "first the king of Assyria hath devoured him; and last this Nebuchadrezzar king of Babylon hath broken his bones." *(Jer. 50:17.)*

Because "Nebuchadrezzar the king of Babylon hath devoured me, he hath crushed me, he hath made me an empty vessel . . .", Babylon would be destroyed: the Lord promised to "dry up her sea, and make her springs dry." Furthermore, Babylon would become a dwellingplace for jackals. . . and an hissing, without an inhabitant." *(Jer. 51:34-44.)*

Nebuchadrezzar beseiged Jerusalem in the ninth year of the reign of Zedekiah. In the eleventh year of Zedekiah's reign, as he tried to flee, Nebuchadrezzar's army pursued Zedekiah and took him to Nebuchadrezzar who slew Zedekiah's sons and put out Zedekiah's eyes. In the nineteenth year of Nebuchadrezzar's reign in Babylon, Nebuzar-adan, captain of Nebuchadrezzar's guard, burned the house of the Lord, the king's house and all the houses of the great men of Jerusalem, and his army carried away captive some of the poor people and the reside of those who remained in the city. However, some of the poor people were left to be vinedressers and husbandmen. The vessels of the house of the Lord were broken down and carried into Babylon, including the twelve brasen bulls that were under the bases of the baptismal font. Seraiah the chief priest and Zephaniah the second priest were among those carried away. People were carried away over a period of time: 3,023 people in the seventh year; 832 people in the 18th year of Nebuchadrezzar; 745 people in the 23rd year of Nebuchadrezzar (4,600 all together). *(Jer. 52:4-30.)*

On the day that Nebuchadnezzar set himself against Jerusalem, the Lord told Ezekiel to utter a parable unto Israel. He also told him that his wife was going to die but that he should not mourn nor weep for her because it was a sign to the Jews of their pending judgment. *(Ezek. 24.)*

Nebuchadnezzer would be allowed to destroy Tyrus, the Lord said, because Tyrus rejoiced in the sorrows and fall of Jerusalem. *(Ezek. 26:7.)*

The Lord told the prophet Ezekiel that He would give the land of Egypt unto Nebuchadrezzar as wages for his army for their great service against Tyrus. *(Ezek. 29:18-20.)*

Ezekiel prophesied that Egypt and all those who supported her would fall by the hand of Nebuchadnezzer and become desolate, and their idols would be destroyed. *(Ezek. 30.)*

Nebuchadnezzar beseiged Jerusalem in the third year of Jehoiakim's reign over Judah and took Jehoiakim captive. He also took part of the vessels of the Lord's house to into the land of Shinar and put them in the house of his god. *(See 2 Kgs. 24:1-17.)* Nebuchadnezzar instructed Ashpenaz, who was the master of his eunuchs, to bring certain unblemished children of Israel to the king's palace that they might teach them the learning and language of the Chaldeans. Daniel, Hananiah, Mishael and Azariah were among those who were selected. *(Dan. 1:1.)*

Nebuchadnezzar had a dream that troubled him, but he could not recall it in the morning. He called in his magicians, astrologers, sorcerers and the Chaldeans and demanded they not only tell him the interpretation of the dream but the dream, also. When they could not, he sentenced all the wisemen to death. Daniel, however, requested time to inquire of the Lord and the Lord revealed the dream and the interpretation of the dream to him. Daniel explained the dream to Nebuchadnezzar, saying that God had revealed to Nebuchadnezzar what would happen in the latter days.

Nebuchadnezzar's Dream and The Interpretation of the Dream

He beheld a great and terrible image.

Nebuchadnezzar's kingdom is great and powerful.

The head was of fine gold.

Nebuchadnezzar is the head of gold.

His chest and arms were of silver. His belly and thighs were of brass. His legs were of iron. His feet and toes were part iron, part clay.

Following him, an inferior kingdom will arise. A third kingdom will rule over all the earth. A fourth kingdom will be as strong as iron. It will break in pieces and bruise.

A stone, cut out without hands, smote the image's feet and broke them into pieces. The iron, clay, brass, silver and gold were then broken to pieces together and became as chaff and the wind carried them away.

> *The kingdom shall be divided: part strong, part broken. They will mingle with the seed of men, but not cleave one to another.*

The stone became a great mountain and filled the whole earth.

> *In those days, God will establish His kingdom which will never be destroyed. It will consume all these kingdoms. The Lord's kingdom will stand forever.*

Nebuchadnezzar rewarded Daniel by elevating him to a position where he "sat in the gate of the king." He also honored Daniel's request regarding his friends and he set Shadrach (Hananiah), Meshach (Mishael) and Abed-nego (Azariah) over the affairs of the province of Babylon. *(Dan. 2.)*

Nebuchadnezzar made a golden image and commanded that everyone worship it whenever they heard music. Those who did not were to be cast into a fiery furnace. Shadrach, Meshach and Abed-nego refused to worship the golden idol and were bound and cast into the furnace which Nebuchadnezzar had had his most mighty men from the army make seven times hotter than usual, so hot that it killed the men from the army. Suddenly, Nebuchadnezzar saw four men, the fourth being "like the Son of God," walking freely around inside the furnace, not being harmed by the fire. He called them forth and decreed that no one should speak anything against the God of Shadrach, Meshach and Abed-nego or they would be cut into pieces because no other God could deliver like their God. He then rewarded the three friends by promoting them in the province of Babylon. *(Dan. 3.)*

Nebuchadnezzar had another dream which Daniel interpreted for him.

The Dream and The Interpretation of the Dream

A tall tree in the midst of the earth.

> *The tree represents Nebuchadnezzar.*

It reached unto heaven and could be seen by all the earth. The leaves were fair, it bore much fruit. The tree provided food and refuge for animal, bird and all flesh. A holy one came down from heaven. The holy one said to cut down the tree and scatter the fruit . . .

> *Nebuchadnezzar would be driven from men.*

. . . but leave a stump with a band of iron and brass. Water it with the dew from heaven.

> *The stump meant Nebuchadnezzar's kingdom would be sure unto him after he knew that the heaven's rule.*

Let "his" portion be with the beasts.

> *He would dwell with the beasts in the field.*

Let "his" heart be changed from man's to that of a beast.

> *He would eat grass with the oxen.*

Let seven seasons pass over him.

He would be wet with the dew of heaven seven years.

A year following this prophecy, as Nebuchadnezzar was boasting of his power and majesty, he was driven from men and the prophecy was fulfilled. At the end of seven years, his madness left, his reason returned to him and he was restored to his kingdom. He praised the Lord. *(Dan. 4.)*

Nebuchadnezzar was the father of Belshazzar, who became king of Babylon after Nebuchadnezzar. *(Dan. 5:2.)*

NEBUCHADNEZZAR'S ASTROLOGERS, SORCERS, SOOTHSAYERS, MAGICIANS. *Dan. 1:20; 2:1-13; 4:7-9; 5:7.*

Nebuchadnezzar's Astrologers and magicians could not compare one-tenth in wisdom and understanding to Daniel and his friends. *(Dan. 1:20.)*

When Nebuchadnezzar had a dream that troubled him, he called in his magicians, astrologers, sorcerers and the Chaldeans and demanded they not only tell him the interpretation of the dream but the dream also because he could not remember it. When they could not, he sentenced them all to death. Daniel, being one of Nebuchadnezzar's wise men, however, requested time to inquire of the Lord. *(Dan. 2:1-13.)*

Because the astrologers and soothsayers, magicians and Chaldeans could not interpret Nebuchadnezzar's new dream for him, Nebucahadnezzar asked Daniel to interpret it for him. *(Dan. 4:7-9.)*

When king Belshazzar saw part of a hand write upon a wall, he called in the astrologers, Chaldeans and soothsayers. They could not explain the writing so Belshazzar called in Daniel. *(Dan. 5:7.)*

NEBUCHADNEZZAR'S COUNSELORS. *Dan. 3:24.*

Nebuchadnezzar's Counselors confirmed that only three men were placed in the fiery furnace—Shadrach, Meshach and Abed-nego—in spite of the fact that there were four men to be seen in the furnace.

NEBECHADNEZZAR'S HERALD. *Dan. 3:4-6.*

Nebuchadnezzar's Herald made known Nebuchadnezzar's decree that everyone was to fall down and worship the golden image whenever they heard music. Those who did not comply would be cast into a fiery furnace.

NEBUCHADNEZZAR'S MOST MIGHTY MEN. *Dan. 3:20.*

Nebuchadnezzar's Most Mighty Men in his army were commanded to bind Shaddrach, Meshach and Abed-nego and cast them into the burning furnace because they refused to worship the golden image. The fire was seven times hotter than usual. In fact, it was so hot that it killed the "mighty men."

NEBUCHADNEZZAR'S SERVANTS. *2 Kgs. 24:10-14.*

Nebuchadnezzar's Servants besieged Jerusalem and Nebuchadnezzar took Jehoiachin and all the inhabitants of Jerusalelm captive to Babylon.

NEBUCHADREZZAR. See **Nebuchadnezzar**.

NEBUSHASBAN. *Jer. 39:13.*

Nebushasban, Rab-saris, Nergal-sharezer, Rab-mag, and all the princes of the king of Babylon were instructed by Nebuzar-adan, the captain of Nebuchadnezzar's guard, to take Jeremiah out of the court of the prison and commit him unto Gedaliah the son of Ahikam the son of Shaphan. He was told to carry him home. Thus, Jeremiah lived among the people.

NEBUZAR-ADAN. *2 Kgs. 25:8-21; Jer. 39:9-14; 40:1-5; 41:10; 43; 52:4-30.*

Nebuzar-adan was the captain of king Nebuchadnezzar's guard. In Nebuchadnezzar's 19th year as king of Babylon, Nebuzar-adan went to Jerusalem and burned the house of the Lord, the king's house and all the other houses in Jerusalem. The army which accompanied him broke down the walls of Jerusalem. They took all the valuables and carried the remnant of Judah who were still in Jerusalem away to Babylon—all but the poor of the land who they left to be vine-dressers and husbandmen. He took Seraiah, the chief priest; Zephaniah, the second priest; the three keepers of the door; an officer; five men who "were in the king's presence;" the principal scribe and 60 men of the people of the land and brought them to Riblah to the king of Babylon, who slew them. Thus, Judah was carried away. *(2 Kgs. 25:8-21; Jer. 52:4-30.)*

Nebuzar-adan, the captain of the guard, carried away captive all the remnant of those who remained in Jerusalem except for the poor, which had nothing, and he gave them vineyards and fields. Nebuchadnezzar instructed him to do no harm to Jeremiah, but to do to Jeremiah whatsoever Jeremiah said. He and the king's princes took Jeremiah out of the court of the prison and committed him unto Gedaliah the son of Ahikam the son of Shaphan, and had him take him home. Thus, Jeremiah dwelled among the people. *(Jer. 39:9-14.)*

Nebuzar-adan loosed the chains with which Jeremiah had been bound and told him he could go whereever he chose. He encouraged him to go back to Gedaliah who had been made governor over the remnant of Judah which had been left in Judah. He gave him "victuals and a reward" and then released him. *(Jer. 40:1-5.)*

The residue of the people in Mizpah who Nebuzar-adan committed to Gedaliah were carried off captive by Ishmael who slew Gedaliah. *(Jer. 41:10.)*

Because Johanan the son of Kareah (Careah) and Azariah (Jezaniah, Jaazaniah) the son of Hoshaiah and all the "proud men" refused to believe the prophet Jeremiah, the remnant of Judah and all the people Nebuzar-adan had left with Gedaliah were carried into Egypt. *(Jer. 43.)*

NECHO. See **Pharaoh-nechoh**.

NEDABIAH. *1 Chr. 3:18.*

Nedabiah, a descendant of David, was a son (grandson) of Jeconiah (Jehoiachin). (Chart 1.)

NEHEMIAH (1). *Ezra 2:2; Neh. 7:7.*

Nehemiah was one of the people who went with Zerubbabel back to Jerusalem following king Cyrus' proclamation to build the temple there.

NEHEMIAH (2). *Neh. 1-2; 4-6; 8:9; 10:1, 28-31; 12:26, 27-43; 13:8-31.*

(Note: The Bible Dictionary divides the book of Nehemiah into four parts: chapters 1-7:73 include Nehemiah's first visit to Jerusalem and the rebuilding of the walls. However, Neh. 7:7 apparently pertains to a different Nehemiah who is mentioned in Ezra 2:2 and not this Nehemiah. Chapters 7:73-10:39 tell of the religious and social reforms. Chapters 11:1-13:3 provide a listing of people involved with the dedication of the wall. Chapter 13:4-31 tells of Nehemiah's second visit to Jerusalem following a 12 year absence and the additional reforms that he made.)

Nehemiah was the son of Hachaliah. He had been the king's cupbearer. He mourned, fasted and prayed for the Jews in Jerusalem. *(Neh. 1.)*

Artaxerxes agreed to Nehemiah's request to return to Jerusalem so that he could rebuild the walls and gates of the city. Nehemiah was opposed in his efforts by Sanballat the Horonite and his servant Tobiah. *(Neh. 2.)*

Because enemies sought to prevent the Jews from building the walls of Jerusalem, Nehemiah armed the laborers but kept the work going. *(Neh. 4.)*

Due to various circumstances, many Jews were in bondage to their brethren. They were freed under Nehemiah's direction, restored to their lands, and the taking of usury was discontinued. From the 20th year to the 32nd year of Artaxerxes' reign, Nehemiah served as the governor in the land of Judah. He reported that neither he nor his brethren had "eaten the bread of the governor" and that he had "continued in the work of this wall." *(Neh. 5.)*

Nehemiah was repeatedly approached by Sanballat and his servant Tobiah to entice him to meet with them that they might do him harm and stop the work on the city wall. However, Nehemiah refused to be persuaded by their intrigue. *(Neh. 6.)*

Nehemiah, the Tirshatha (or governor), and Ezra the priest and scribe, declared the day a holy day as Ezra read and interpreted the law of Moses to the people. *(Neh. 8:9.)*

Nehemiah, son of Hachaliah, was among the people who covenanted to marry in Israel, honor the Sabbath day, keep the commandments and pay tithes. *(Neh. 10:1, 28-31.)*

The porters in the days of Nehemiah, Ezra and Joiakim the son of Jeshua the son of Jozadak, are listed. Nehemiah divided the singers, priests, Levites and princes into two great companies for the dedication of the walls of Jerusalem. Ezra went before one of the great companies and Nehemiah went with the other company. *(Neh. 12:26, 27-43.)*

Nehemiah returned to Jerusalem and cast Tobiah and his household goods out of the chamber in the courts of the house of God. He restored the Levites' portions to them, placed treasurers over the treasuries, corrected other abuses and reinstituted proper Sabbath observance. *(Neh. 13:8-31.)*

NEHEMIAH (3). *Neh. 3:16.*

Nehemiah, son of Azbuk, ruler of the half part of Beth-zur, labored next to Shallun when the children of Israel rebuilt the walls and gates of Jerusalem during the time of Ezra and Nehemiah.

NEHUM. See **Rehum (1)**.

NEHUSHTA. *2 Kgs. 24:8-15.*

Nehushta, wife of Jehoiakim and daughter of Elnathan of Jerusalem, was the mother of Jehoiachin. She was carried away captive into Babylon by Nebuchadnezzar along with king Jehoichin and the rest of the people in Jerusalem. (Chart 1.)

NEHUSHTAN. *2 Kgs. 18:4.*

Nehushtan was the name Hezekiah gave to the brasen serpent that Moses had made. Hezekiah destroyed it because the children of Israel burned incense to it.

NEIGHBOR OF ONE OF THE SONS OF THE PROPHETS.

1 Kgs. 20:35-36.

A **Neighbor of a Certain Man of the Sons of the Prophets** was asked to smite one of the sons of the prophets. He declined. The man who was one of the sons of the prophets told him that as soon as he departed he would be killed by a lion because he wouldn't smite him, and it was so.

NEKODA (1). *Ezra 2:48, 58; Neh. 7:50, 60.*

Nekoda was a Nethinim. When the Nethinims and the children of Solomon's servants left Babylon to return to Jerusalem to build the house of the Lord as proclaimed by Cyrus, king of Persia, they numbered 392.

NEKODA, THE CHILDREN OF. *Ezra 2:60; Neh. 7:62.*

The Children of Nekoda were among those who went up to Jerusalem from Tel-melah, Tel-harsa, Chenrub, Addan, and Immer when king Cyrus declared that the Israelites should return there and build the temple, but they could not verify that they were actually of the house of Israel. The children of Delaiah, Tobiah and Nekoda numbered 652 (642).

NEMUEL (1). *Num. 26:9.*

Nemuel was a son of Eliab and was of the tribe of Reuben. His brothers Dathan and Abiram strove against Moses and Aaron and were swallowed up by the earth. (Chart 5a.)

NEMUEL (2). *Num. 26:12.* See **Jemuel**.

NEMUELITES. See **Jemuel**.

NEPHEG (1). *Ex. 6:21.*

Nepheg, great-grandson of Levi and grandson of Kohath, was a son of Izhar. (Chart 7d.)

NEPHEG (2). *2 Sam. 5:15; 1 Chr. 3:7; 12:4-7.*

Nepheg was one of David's children born in Jerusalem. His brothers were Shammua, Shobab, Nathan, Solomon, Ibhar, Elishua, Japhia, Elishama, Eliada and Eliphalet. *(2 Sam. 5:15.)*

1 Chr. 3:7 is a repeat of 2 Sam. 5:15 except the brothers are listed somewhat differently: Shimea (Shammua), Shobab, Nathan, Solomon, Ibhar, Elishama, Eliphelet, Nogah (Elishua), Nepheg, Japhia, Elishama, Eliada and Eliphelet. *(1 Chr. 3:7.)*

His brothers are listed again with some variations: Shammua, Shobab, Nathan, Solomon, Ibhar, Elishua, Elpalet, Nogah, Nepheg, Japhia, Elishama, Beeliada (Eliada) and Eliphalet. *(1 Chr. 12:4-7.)* (Chart 8e.)

NEPHISH. See **Naphish**.

NEPHUSIM (Nephishesim). *Ezra 2:50, 58; Neh. 7:52, 60.*

Nephusim (Nephishesim) was a Nethinim. When the Nethinims and the children of Solomon's servants left Babylon to return to Jerusalem to build the house of the Lord as proclaimed by Cyrus, king of Persia, they numbered 392.

NER. *1 Sam. 10:14; 14:50-51; 1 Chr. 8:33; 9:35-39.*

Ner was Saul's uncle. *(He is first referred to by name in 1 Sam. 14:50.)* Saul and his servant reported back to Ner that they could not find the asses they had gone to search for and gave him a report of their visit to Samuel. *(1 Sam. 10:14.)*

Ner's son was Abner, captain of Saul's host. Ner and Kish, Saul's father, were sons of Abiel. *(1 Sam. 14:50-51.)*

This verse states that Ner begat Kish. *(1 Chr. 8:33). (Note: This is apparently an error as 1 Sam. 9:1 states that Abiel was the father of Kish who was the father of Saul, and 1 Sam. 14:51 states that Abiel was the father of Ner. Other verses also state that Ner was Saul's uncle. Thus, Ner and Kish were brothers.)*

Ner's father was Jehiel (Abiel) and his mother was Maachah. His siblings were Abdon, Zur, Kish, Baal, Nadab, Gedor, Ahio, Zechariah (Zacher) and Mikloth. *(Note: Verse 39 again erroneously states that Ner begat Kish, the father of Saul.) (1 Chr. 9:35-39.)* (Chart 16k.)

NERGAL. *2 Kgs. 17:30.*

Nergal was the false god made by the men of Cuth after they were given the lands of the Israelites.

NERGAL-SHAREZER. *Jer. 39:3, 13.*

Nergal-sharezer was one of the Babylonian princes who came in and sat in the middle gate of Jerusalem when Nebuchadnezzar and the Chaldean army took the city, slew Zedekiah's sons, put Zedekiah's eyes out and carried him to Babylon, burned the houses and broke down the walls of Jerusalem. Nergal-sharezer, Nebushasban, Rab-saris, Rab-mag, and all the king of Babylon's princes were instructed by Nebuzar-adan, the captain of Nebuchadnezzar's guard, to take Jeremiah out of the court of the prison and commit him unto Gedaliah the son of Ahikam the son of Shaphan who was told to carry him home. Thus, Jeremiah lived among the people.

NERIAH. *Jer. 32:12-16; 36:4, 32; 43:3, 6; 45:1; 51:59.*

Neriah was the father of Baruch and the son of Maaseiah. Baruch recorded Jeremiah's purchase of his uncle's son Hanameel's property, signifying the eventual return of Israel to the lands of her inheritance. *(Jer. 32:12-16.)*

Neriah was the father of Baruch. *(Jer. 36:4, 32; 43:3, 6; 45:1.)*

Neriah, the son of Maaseiah, was the father of Seraiah, which Seraiah was instructed by Jeremiah in the fourth year of Zedekiah when they were carried off captive to Babylon to read the words of his prophecy in Babylon and to then cast the book into the Euphrates River and declare that Babylon would be destroyed and not rise again, just like the book would not rise again. *(Jer. 51:59.)* (Chart 8b.)

NETHANEEL (1). *Num. 1:8, 28-29; 2:5 (3-9); 7:18.*

Nethaneel was the son of Zuar and was of the tribe of Issachar. He was appointed by the Lord to be the one to stand at the head of all of the tribe of Issachar as Moses organized Israel in preparation for war. The males 20 years old and older in the tribe of Issachar who could go to war numbered 54,400. *(Num. 1:8, 28-29.)*

Nethaneel was instructed to have his men camp next to the tribe of Judah on the east side of the encampment. *(Num. 2:5 [3-9].)*

When the altar of the tabernacle was anointed, Nethaneel made his offering on the second day. *(Num. 7:18.)* (Chart 9b.)

NETHANEEL (2). *1 Chr. 2:14.*

Nethaneel was Jesse's fourth son and one of David's elder brothers.
(Charts 8d-e.)

NETHANEEL (3). *1 Chr. 15:24.*

Nethaneel was among those who, under the direction of David, was assigned to make music before the Lord as the ark was removed from the house of Obed-edom and taken to the place which David had prepared for it to be housed. He was one of the priests and was assigned to blow the trumpet before the ark of God.

NETHANEEL (4). *1 Chr. 24:6.*

Nethaneel, a Levite and scribe at the time of David, was the father of Shemaiah.

NETHANEEL (5). *1 Chr. 26:4.*

Nethaneel, a Levite, was the fifthborn son of Obed-edom. His brothers were Shemaiah, Jehozabad, Joah, Sacar, Ammiel, Issachar and Peulthai. They, along with other Levites, were appointed by king David to be porters—to have charge of the treasures, serve as officers and judges, and to conduct the outward business over Israel. (Chart 7c.)

NETHANEEL (6). *2 Chr. 17:7-8.*

Nethaneel was one of the princes of Judah who king Jehoshaphat instructed to "teach in the cities of Judah." He and the princes were accompanied by a number of Levites and Elishama and Jehoram, the priests, as they taught Judah from the book of the law of the Lord.

NETHANEEL (7). *Ezra 10:22 (18-19, 22, 44); Neh. 12:36.*

Nethaneel, one of the sons of Pashur, was among the sons of the priests who had taken foreign wives and who agreed to Ezra's request that they separate themselves from their strange wives. *(Ezra 10:22 [18-19, 22, 44].)*

Nethaneel joined with Zechariah, a descendant of Asaph, and other of his brethren with their musical instruments in the dedication of the wall of Jerusalem. *(Neh. 12:36.)*

NETHANEEL (8). *Neh. 12:21.*

Nethaneel, son of Jedaiah, was one of the priests who was a chief of the fathers in the days of Joiakim.

NETHANIAH (1). *2 Kgs. 25:23-24; Jer. 40:8, 14-15; 41:1.*

Nethaniah was the father of Ishmael, which Ishmael was counseled by Gedaliah not to fear being a servant of the Chaldeans. *(2 Kgs. 25:23-24; Jer. 40:8, 14-15.)*

Nethaniah was the father of Ishmael and the son of Elishama, of the seed of David. *(Jer. 41:1.)* (Chart 8e.)

NETHANIAH (2). *1 Chr. 25:2, 12.*

Nethaniah, a Levite, was one of the musicians. He was of the sons of Asaph. The musicians—sons of Asaph, Heman and Jeduthun—drew lots and were given their duty assignments by David and the captains of the host. Nethaniah cast the fifth lot. He, his sons and his brethren, numbered 12. (Chart 7a.)

NETHANIAH (3). *2 Chr. 17:8-9.*

Nethaniah, a Levite, along with other Levites and Elisham and Jehoram, the priests, was sent by king Jehoshaphat to journey with the princes of Judah throughout the cities of Judah to instruct the people out of the book of the law of the Lord.

NETHANIAH (4). *Jer. 36:14.*

Nethaniah, son of Shelemiah and grandson of Cushi, was the father of Jehudi.

NETHINIMS. *1 Chr. 9:2; Ezra 2:43-54, 58; 7:7, 24; 8:17; Neh. 3:26; 7:46-56, 60; 11:21.*

Nethinims, priests, Levites and the Israelites, "were the first inhabitants who dwelt in their possessions in their cities after returning from Babylonian captivity. *(1 Chr. 9:2.)*

The various groups who were in captivity but who returned to Jerusalem are listed. The Nethinims and the children of Solomon's servants numbered 392 when they left Babylon to go to Jerusalem to build the temple as decreed by Cyrus, king of Persia. Nethinims, according to the footnote to the text, were servants of the temple who attended the Levites in their sacred service. *(Ezra 2:43-54, 58; Neh. 7:46-56, 60.)*

Around 458 B.C., Artaxerxes issued a decree allowing Ezra to take any of the children of Israel—the priests, the Nethinims, Levites, singers and porters—back to Jerusalem who desired to return there with him. He further decreed that it would be unlawful for anyone to impose any toll, tribute or custom upon any of them. *(Ezra 7:7, 24.)*

When Ezra was preparing to lead the people from Babylon back to Jerusalem, he gathered them together by the river and discovered that there were no Levites among them. He assigned several chief men and men of understanding to go to Iddo and the Nethinims and request that they send them some ministers for the house of God. They returned with Hashabiah, along with Jeshaiah of the sons of Merari and 20 of his brethren and their sons; Sherebiah, with 18 of his sons and brethren; plus 220 Nethinims. *(Ezra 8:17.)*

When the children of Israel repaired the walls and gates of Jerusalem under the direction of Ezra and Nehemiah, the Nethinims dwelt in Ophel and labored in the area "against the water gate toward the east." *(Neh. 3:26.)*

When the children of Israel returned from Babylonian captivity, they dwelled in Ophel. Ziha and Gispa were their overseers. *(Neh. 11:21.)*

NETOPHAH. *Ezra 2:22; Neh. 7:26.*

Netophah was of the people of Israel. The men of the children of Netophah who returned to Jerusalem from Babylon after Cyrus' proclamation to build the temple numbered 56. The total number of children of Beth-lehem and Netophah combined was 179 (188).

NETOPHATHITE. *2 Sam. 23:28-29; 2 Kgs. 25:23; 1 Chr. 9:14-16; 27:13, 15; Jer. 40:8.*

Two **Netophathites**—maharai the Netophathite and Heleb the son of Baanah, a Netophathite—are listed among David's mighty men. *(2 Sam. 23:28-29.)*

Seraiah, son of Tanhumeth the Netophathite, along with several other men, went to Gedaliah, ruler over Judah, who told them not to fear being servants to the Chaldees. After Ishmael slew Gedaliah, the rest fled to Egypt because they feared the Chaldees. *(2 Kgs. 25:23.)*

The inhabitants of Jerusalem were listed in the book of the kings of Israel and Judah, who were carried away to Babylon for their transgression. Levites dwelling in the villages of the Netophathites included Shemaiah, Bakbakkar, Heresh, Galal, Mattaniah, Obadiah and Berechiah. *(1 Chr. 9:14-16.)*

Maharai the Netophathite was of the Zarhites. He was assigned by David to be captain for the tenth month. Heldai the Netophathite was of Othniel and was assigned to be captain for the twelfth month. Each had 24,000 in his course. *(1 Chr. 27:13, 15.)*

Ephai was a Netophathite. He and others went to Gedaliah after he was made governor over the remnant of the Jews who were left in Judah after Nebuchadnezzar took the rest captive, and was counseled by Gedaliah not to fear serving the Chaldeans. *(Jer. 40:8.)* (Chart 8 l.)

NEZIAH. *Ezra 2:54, 58; Neh. 7:56, 60.*

Neziah was a Nethinim. When the Nethinims and the children of Solomon's servants left Babylon to return to Jerusalem to build the house of the Lord as proclaimed by Cyrus, king of Persia, they numbered 392.

NIBHAZ. *2 Kgs. 17:31.*

Nibhaz and Tartak were false gods made by the Avites after they were given the lands of the Israelites.

NIMROD. *Gen. 10:8-10; 1 Chr. 1:10; Micah 5:6.*

Nimrod was a son of Cush, grandson of Ham, and a great-grandson of Noah. He began to be a "mighty one in the earth" and a "mighty hunter before the Lord." The beginning of his kingdom was Babel, Erech, Accad, and Calneh in the land of Shinar. *(Gen. 10:8-10.)*

Nimrod was a son of Cush. "He began to be mighty upon the earth." *(1 Chr. 1:10.)*

In the last days, the children of Israel shall triumph over the Gentiles. "And they shall waste the land of Assyria with the sword, and the land of Nimrod in the entrances thereof. . ." *(Micah 5:6.)* (Chart 2e.)

NIMSHI. *1 Kgs. 19:16; 2 Kgs. 9:2; 2 Chr. 22:7.*

Nimshi was the father of Jehu who, according to the Lord's instruction to Elijah, was to be anointed king over Israel. *(1 Kgs. 19:16.)*

Nimshi was the father of Jehoshaphat who was the father of Jehu. *(2 Kgs. 9:2.)*

Jehu was the son (grandson) of Nimshi. *(2 Chr. 22:7.)*

NINEVAH, PEOPLE OF. *Jonah 3.*

The **People of Ninevah** were not doing what the Lord would have them do, so the Lord sent Jonah to cry repentance unto them. They believed the word of the Lord when they heard Jonah's prophesy that Ninevah would be overthrown in 40 days and repented and prayed to God, hoping He would not destroy their city. When God saw their repentance, He turned away the evil He had threatened to bring upon them. *(Note: According to the BD, Ninevah, the capital of Assyria, was built by Nimrod according to tradition. Although Gen. 10:8-12, indicates that Nimrod built many cities in the land of Shinar—Babel, Erech, Accad and Calneh—and that "out of that land went forth Asshur, and builded Nineveh." Perhaps Asshur was a descendant of Ninrod, in which case the building of Ninevah would be attributed to Nimrod.)*

NISROCH. *2 Kgs. 19:37; Isa. 37:38.*

Nisroch was one of the Assyrian king's false gods. King Sennacherib was worshipping in the house of Nisroch when two of his sons slew him with the sword.

NOADIAH (1). *Ezra 8:33.*

Noadiah, a Levite, was the son of Binnui. He was with Meremoth when the precious items that belonged in the temple which had been placed in the care of Sherebiah, Hashabiah and ten additional chief priests by Ezra were delivered to Meremoth.

NOADIAH (2). *Neh. 6:14.*

Noadiah was a prophetess who was aligned with Sanballat against Nehemiah. Nehemiah prayed that God would think upon the work of Sanballat, Tobiah, the prophetess Noadiah, and the rest of the prophets who would have put him in fear.

NOAH (1) (Gabriel). *Gen. 5:28-29, 32; 6:9-22; 7:2-3, 6-24; 8:3-22; 9:1-6, 9-17, 21-27, 28-29; Isa. 54:9; Ezek. 14:14, 20; Dan. 8:16; 9:21-27.*

<u>Noah</u> was the son of Lamech and the seven-times-great-grandson of Adam. His father was 182 years old when he was born. He begat Shem, Ham, and Japheth when he was 500 years old. *(Gen. 5:28-29, 32.) (Note: Shem, Ham and Japheth were not triplets as inplied in this scripture. Moses 8:12 in the Pearl of Great Price provides clarification: "And Noah was four hundred and fifty years old, and begat Japheth; and forty-two years afterward he begat Shem of her who was the mother of Japheth, and when he was five hundred years old he begat Ham.")*

Noah was a just man and he walked with God. He begat three sons. All the earth became corrupt and violent before God. The Lord told Noah he was going to destroy all flesh along with the earth. He instructed Noah to build an ark and told him exactly how to build it. It was to be built of gopher wood. It was to have rooms in it. Noah was to cover it with pitch both inside and out. The ark was to be 300 cubits long and 50 cubits wide and 30 cubits high. It was to have a window "and in a cubit shalt thou finish it above," and it was to have a door in one side. The ark also was to have three floors—"lower, second, and third stories." *(Note: A cubit was about 18 to 22 inches long, the length of the arm from the end of the middle finger to the elbow. Thus, the ark would have been approximately 450' to 550' long by 75' to 91.66' wide by 45' to 55' high.)* The Lord told Noah he was going to flood the earth. Nevertheless, he would establish his covenant with Noah. Noah was told that he and his wife and their three sons and their wives would be preserved in the ark. He was instructed to bring two of every living thing of flesh into the ark—male and female. This Noah did. *(Gen. 6:9-22.)*

Noah was told to take seven pair of every clean beast and fowl, but only two pair of every unclean beast. Noah was 600 years old when the flood covered the earth. The flood began on the 17th day of the second month *(that would be February 17th according to today's calendar)*. It rained for 40 days and 40 nights. *(Gen. 7:2-3, 6-24.)*

The waters prevailed upon the earth 150 days at which time "the waters were abated" and the ark rested upon the mountains of Ararat on the 17th day of the 7th month. *(Note: That would be July 17th according to today's calendar. Also, the dictionary defines abate: to make less in amount, degree, force; to terminate. It is interesting to note that it is 150 days from February 17th (our second month) to July 17th (our seventh month) according to today's calendar.)* The mountain tops were seen on the first day of the tenth month. On the first day of the first month in the six hundredth and first year, the ground was dry. On the 27th day of the second month, the earth was dried. Noah was commanded to take his family and all the animals and leave the ark. They were instructed to multiply upon the earth. Noah built an altar and took of every clean beast and every clean fowl and offered burnt offerings. The Lord was pleased and said He would not curse the ground any more for man's sake, nor would He smite every living thing again. *(Gen. 8:3-22.)*

Noah was given charge over all living things upon the earth. All things that move would be meat for him just as the plants were given to him. However, they were not to eat the blood of the animals. The death penalty for murder was decreed. *(Gen. 9:1-6.)* The Lord established his covenant with Noah that the earth would never be completely covered with a flood again. He set the bow (rainbow) in the cloud as a token of his covenant. *(Gen. 9:9-17.)* Noah became drunken with wine and fell asleep, uncovered, in his tent. His son, Ham, saw his nakedness and told his brothers. His brothers, not looking at their father, covered Noah up. Noah cursed Canaan, Ham's son, because of what Ham did. He blessed Shem and Japheth. *(Gen. 9:21-27.)* Noah lived 350 years after the flood for a total of 950 years. *(Gen. 9:28-29.)*

Just as the Lord promised Noah that the waters would never cover the whole earth again, even so, in the latter days the Lord would keep His promise to gather Israel and have mercy on her. *(Isa. 54:9.)*

The Lord told Ezekiel that even if Noah, Daniel and Job ministered to the children of Israel, the children of Israel would still not follow the Lord. *(Ezek. 14:14, 20.)*

Gabriel, an angel, revealed the interpretation of Daniel's vision to him. *(Dan. 8:16.) (Note: Modern-day revelation tells us that Gabriel is Noah. "He stands next in authority to Adam in the Priesthood; he was called of God to this office, and was the father of all living in this day, and to him was given the dominion. These men held keys first on earth, and then in heaven." Teachings of the Prophet Joseph Smith, p. 157).*

As Daniel was fasting and praying and acknowledging the sins of Israel, Gabriel came to him again and revealed the time of the coming of the Messiah who shall make atonement for iniquity. *(Dan. 9:21-27.) (Note: Additional clarifying information regarding Noah is found in Moses 8:18-20, 25-27. "And in those days there were giants on the earth, and they sought Noah to take away his life; but the Lord was with Noah, and the power of the Lord was upon him. And the Lord ordained Noah after his own order, and commanded him that he should go forth and declare his Gospel unto the children of men, even as it was given unto Enoch. And it came to pass that Noah called upon the children of men that they should repent; but they hearkened not unto his words; And it repented Noah, and his heart was pained that the Lord had made man on the earth, and it grieved him at the heart. And the Lord said: 'I will destroy man whom I have created, from the face of the earth, both man and beast, and the creeping things, and the fowls of the air; for it repenteth Noah that I have created them, and that I have made them; and he hath called upon me; for they have sought his life.' And thus Noah found grace in the eyes of the Lord; for Noah was a just man, and perfect in his generation; and he walked with God, as did also his three sons, Shem, Ham, and Japheth." D&C 107:52 tells us that "Noah was ten years old when he was ordained under the hand of Methuselah.")* (Charts 1.; 2a-e.; 21.)

NOAH (2). *Num. 26:33; 27:1-7.*

<u>Noah</u> was a daughter of Zelophehad and a great-granddaughter of Manasseh. Her sisters were Mahlah, Hoglah, Milcah and Tirzah. *(Num. 26:33.)*

Noah and her sisters petitioned Moses and Eleazar to be given their father's inheritance because he had no sons and he, himself, had died in the wilderness. The Lord told Moses that Zelophehad's daughters were correct and their father's inheritance should pass unto them. *(Num. 27:1-7.)* (Charts 15a-b.)

NOBAH. *Num. 32:42.*

Nobah, a descendant of Manasseh, was given an inheritance east of Jordan. He "took Kenath and the villages thereof, and called it Nobah, after his own name." (Chart 15c.)

NODAB. See **Kedemah**.

NOGAH. See **Elishua**.

NOHAH. *1 Chr. 8:2.*

Nohah is listed as the fourthborn son of Benjamin in this scripture. His brothers were Bela, the firstborn; Ashbel, the secondborn; Aharah, the third; and Rapha, the fifth. *(Note: Benjamin's sons are listed with different names in other scriptures.)* (Chart 16d.)

NUN (Non). *Ex. 33:11; 1 Chr. 7:27.*

Nun was the father of Joshua. *(Ex. 33:11.)*

Non (Nun), a sixth-great-grandson of Ephraim through Beriah, was the son of Elishama and the father of Jehoshua (Joshua). *(1 Chr. 7:27.)* (Chart 15d.)

NAMES THAT BEGIN WITH "O"

OBADIAH (1). *1 Kgs. 18:3-16.*

Obadiah was the governor of Ahab's house, but he feared the Lord. When Jezebel slew the prophets of the Lord, Obadiah hid 100 of them in caves—50 to a cave—and fed them bread and water. When Elijah asked him to tell Ahab that he wanted to see him, Obadiah feared Ahab would slay him because no one had been able to find Elijah. If Elijah disappeared again, Ahab would slay Obadiah. Elijah assured him that he would meet Ahab when he came. Therefore, Obadaiah did as Elijah requested.

OBADIAH (2). *1 Chr. 3:21.*

Obadiah was a descendant of David. (Chart 1.)

OBADIAH (3). *1 Chr. 7:3-5.*

Obadiah, the son of Izrahiah, was the grandson of Uzzi, great-grandson of Tola and great-great-grandson of Issachar. His brothers were Michael, Joel and Ishiah. They and their father were chief men, valiant men of might. They had many wives and daughters and their bands of soldiers numbered 36,000 men. (Chart 9a.)

OBADIAH (4). *1 Chr. 8:38.*

Obadiah, a son of Azel, was from the tribe of Benjamin. He was a tenth-great-grandson of Saul. His brothers were Azrikam, Bocheru, Ishmael, Sheariah and Hanan. (Chart 16 l.)

OBADIAH (5) (Abda, Unni). *1 Chr. 9:16; Neh. 11:17; 12:9; 12:25.*

Obadiah was the son of Shemaiah the son of Galal the son of Jeduthun. He was a Levite who dwelled in the villages of the Netophathites after returning from Babylonian captivity. His genealogy was written in the book of the kings of Israel and Judah, who were carried away to Babylon for their transgression. *(1 Chr. 9:16.)*

Abda (Obadiah) and Bakbukiah assisted Mattaniah with the thanksgiving prayer. *(Neh. 11:17.) (Note: Shemaiah's name is sgiven as Shammua.)*

Unni (Obadiah) and Bakbukiah assisted Mattaniah with the thanksgiving prayer. *(Neh. 12:9.)*

Obadiah was one of the porters, along with Akkub, Mattaniah, Bakbukiah, Meshullam (Shullam) and Talmon, who kept the ward at the thresholds of the gates in the days of Joiakim, Nehemiah and Ezra. *(Neh. 12:25.)* (Chart 7h.)

OBADIAH (6). *1 Chr. 12:9 (1-2, 9, 23, 38).*

Obadiah, of the tribe of Gad, was one of David's mighty men who came to him at Ziklag to rejoice with all Israel when David became king and to turn the kingdom of Saul unto David. He was one of the captains of the hosts, the least of which numbered 100 and the greatest which numbered 1,000 men. (Chart 13b.)

OBADIAH (7). *1 Chr. 27:19.*

Obadiah was the father of Ishmaiah, the ruler over the tribe of Zebulun when David was king. (Chart 10b.)

OBADIAH (8). *2 Chr. 17:7-8.*

Obadiah was one of the princes of Judah who king Jehoshaphat instructed to "teach in the cities of Judah" from the book of the law of the Lord, accompanied by Elishama and Jehoram, the priests, and a number of Levites.

OBADIAH (9). *2 Chr. 34:12.*

Obadiah, a Levite of the sons of Merari, and others were assigned by Josiah, king of Judah, to oversee the workmen who repaired the house of the Lord.

OBADIAH (10). *Ezra 8:9.*

Obadiah, son of Jehiel of the sons of Joab, the leader of his family, went with Ezra up from Babylon to Jerusalem taking 218 males with him.

OBADIAH (11). *Neh. 10:5 (1, 5, 28-31).*

Obadiah was among the priests who covenanted and sealed their covenant to marry in Israel, honor the Sabbath, pay tithes and keep the commandments.

OBADIAH (12). *Obad. 1.*

Obadiah prophesied the downfall of Edom and said that in the latter days, "saviours shall come up on mount Zion to judge the mount of Esau; and the kingdom shall be the Lord's." *(Note: According to the BD, Obadiah was a prophet who foretold the doom of Edom but nothing is known of his personal history. The prophecy contained in the book of Obadiah was spoken directly after some capture of Jerusalem. This could have been Jerusalem's capture by the Philistines and Arabians during the reign of Jehoram in 848-844 B.C., or their capture by the Chaldeans in 586 B.C., during which the Edomites had shown hostility toward Judah (see Edom). Obadiah foretold the punishment of Edom. The record of the fulfillment of this prophecy is found in 2 Kgs. 14:7 and 2 Chr. 25:11-12. Also according to the BD, "saviours" on mount Zion refers to the doctrine of salvation for the dead.)*

OBAL (Ebal (2)). *Gen. 10:28; 1 Chr. 1:22.*

Obal (Ebal) was a son of Joktan, a third-great-grandson of Shem and a fourth-great-grandson of Noah. (Chart 2b.)

OBED (1). *Ruth 4:17, 21-22; 1 Chr. 2:12.*

Obed, the father of Jesse and the grandfather of king David, was the son of Boaz and Ruth. (Charts 1.; 8d.)

OBED (2). *1 Chr. 2:37-38; 2 Chr. 23:1.*

Obed was the son of Ephlal and the father of Jehu. *(1 Chr. 2:37-38.)*

Obed was the grandfather of Azariah who was one of the captains of hundreds Jehoiada the priest rallied to slay Athaliah and make Joash king over Judah. *(2 Chr. 23:1.)* (Chart 8c.)

OBED (3). *1 Chr. 11:47.*

Obed was one of David's mighty men, one of the valiant men of the armies. (Chart 17.)

OBED (4). *1 Chr. 26:7.*

Obed, a Levite of the lineage of Obed-edom, was a son of Shemaiah. Shemaiah's other sons were Othni, Rephael, Elzabad, Elihu and Semachiah. They, along with other Levites, were appointed by king David to be porters—to have charge of the treasures, serve as officers and judges, and to conduct the outward business over Israel. (Chart 7c.)

OBED-EDOM. *2 Sam. 6:10-12; 1 Chr. 13:12-14; 15:18, 21, 24-25; 16:5, 38; 26:4-15; 2 Chr. 25:24.*

Obed-edom was a Levite belonging to the family of Kohath. He housed the ark of God after Uzzah died (having touched the ark of God) because David feared the Lord and didn't dare take it any further. The ark of God remained in the house of Obed-edom for three months *(BD says 6 mos.)*, during which time the Lord blessed him and all his household. *(2 Sam. 6:10-12; 1 Chr. 13:12-14.)*

Under the direction of David, the Levites appointed singers and musicians to play before the Lord. Obed-edom was among those of the second degree who were appointed. He was one of the porters. He was assigned to play "with harps on the Sheminith to excel." He was one of the doorkeepers for the ark. The people came and carried the ark out of the house of Obed-edom. *(1 Chr. 15:18, 21, 24-25.)*

Obed-edom, a Levite, and his brethren were appointed by David to minister before the ark of the Lord with psalteries and harps. He and his brethren were porters. *(1 Chr. 16:5,38.)*

Obed-edom's sons were Shemaiah, the firstborn; Jehozabad, the second; Joah, the third; Sacar, the fourth; Nethaneel, the fifth; Ammiel, the sixth; Issachar, the seventh; and Peulthai, the eighth. They, along with other Levites, were assigned by king David to be porters: to have charge of the treasures, serve as officers and judges, and conduct the outward business over Israel. His sons through Shemaiah were Othni, Rephael, Obed, Elzabad, Elihu and Semachiah. There were 62 men from Obed-edom who were "able men for strength for the service." Obed-edom drew the lot southward; "and to his sons the house of Asuppim." *(1 Chr. 26:4-15.)*

All the vessels that were found in the house of God with Obed-edom, along with hostages and the treasures of king Amaziah's house, were taken by Joash king of Israel when he captured Amaziah and returned to Samaria.

(2 Chr. 25:24.) (Chart 7c.)

OBIL. *1 Chr. 27:30.*

Obil the Ishmaelite was the officer assigned by David to be over the camels.

OCRAN. *Num. 1:13.*

Ocran was the father of Pagiel. They were of the tribe of Asher.

ODED (1). *2 Chr. 15:1, 8.*

Oded (abt. 955 B.C.) was a prophet and the father of Azariah who went to king Asa and prophesied that Judah would prosper if she would keep the commandments. Asa put away the abominable idols when he heard the prophecy of Oded.

ODED (2). *2 Chr. 28:9-15.*

Oded (abt. 742 B.C.) was a prophet of the Lord who, when the children of Israel defeated Judah and brought many back captive, instructed them to let the captives go because the Lord was not pleased with Israel. With the support of several of the heads of the children of Ephraim, the children of Israel complied with Oded's instructions.

OFFICERS IN ISRAEL. *Josh. 3:2-3.*

The **Officers in Israel** went throughout the camps of Israel commanding the people to follow the ark of the covenant as they prepared to cross over Jordan.

OG. *Num. 21:33-35; 32:33; Deut. 1:4; 3:1-16; 4:47; 29:7; 31:4; Josh. 2:10 (1-10); 9:10 (3-11); 12:4 (1-6); 13:12, 30-31; 1 Kgs. 4:19; Neh. 9:22; Ps. 135:11-12; 136:19-21.*

Og, king of Bashan, one of the giant races of Rephaim, went out against the children of Israel and was delivered into their hands. *(Num. 21:33-35.)* His land was given to one of the half tribes of Manasseh. *(Num. 32:33; Josh. 13:12, 30-31.)*

Moses recounted to the children of Israel that the Lord had delivered Og and others into their hands. *(Deut. 1:4.)* He reminded Israel that the Lord delivered Og into their hands and that his land had been divided between the Reubenites, Gadites and the half tribe of Manasseh. *(Deut. 3:1-16.)* The children of Israel possessed the land of Og as well as that of other kings who had been delivered into their hands. *(Deut. 4:47.)* Moses reminded Israel that when Og, king of Bashan, and Sihon, king of Heshbon, came against them, the children of Israel defeated them in battle. *(Deut. 29:7.)*

Moses counseled the children of Israel to follow Joshua and go into the promised land and not fear the people. He said the Lord would do the same thing to those people as He did to Og and Sihon, kings of the Amorites. *(Deut. 31:4.)*

The defeat of Og and Sihon had reached the people in Jericho, Rahab said, as well as word of the Lord's drying up the Red Sea, and she hid the spies who had come to check out the city. *(Josh. 2:10 [1-10].)*

The Gibeonites heard what the Lord had done to Og and Sihon and, using deceit, obtained a league with Israel. *(Josh. 9:10 [3-11].)*

The two kings on the east of Jordan, Og and Sihon, and 31 on the west of Jordan who were conquered by Israel are listed. Og's people were of the remnant of the giants who lived in Ashtaroth and Edrei. *(Josh. 12:4 [1-6].)*

Solomon assigned officers to be over various parts of the land. Geber the son of Uri was in the country of Gilead which included the lands formerly belonging to Og and Sihon. *(1 Kgs. 4:19.)*

The Lord's goodness to Israel was acknowledge and praised. He had delivered the land of Og king of Bashan, the land of Sihon, and the land of the king of Heshbon unto Israel. *(Neh. 9:22.)*

The Lord smote Og and Sihon, king of the Amorites, and all the kingdoms of Canaan, and their lands were given to Israel for an inheritance. *(Ps. 135:11-12.)*

A song of praise was offered to the Lord because He slew Og and Sihon and gave their lands to the Israelites. *(Ps. 136:19-21.)*

OHAD. *Gen. 46:10.*

Ohad was one of Simeon's sons and a grandson of Jacob. His brothers were Jemuel, Jamin, Jachin, Zohar and Shaul. *(Note: Ohad is not listed among Simeon's sons in Numbers 26:12-13, nor in 1 Chr. 4:24.)* (Chart 6a.)

OHEL. *1 Chr. 3:20.*

Ohel, a descendant of David, was a son of Shelomith, the daughter of Zerubbabel. His brothers were Hashubah, Berechiah, Hasadiah and Jushabhesed. (Chart 1.)

OLD PROPHET IN BETH-EL. *1 Kgs. 13:11-32.*

An **Old Prophet in Beth-el** heard about the man of God out of Judah and invited him to eat and drink with him. When the man of God refused, saying the Lord had told him not to eat or drink, etc., the old prophet in Beth-el said he was also a prophet and that an angel spoke unto him by the word of the Lord and told him to bring the man of God back to his house that he may eat and drink. So the man of God was led astray and did as the old prophet in Beth-el said. When the man of God was slain by a lion, the old prophet went and gathered up the carcase of the man of God and buried it in a sepulchre and instructed his sons that when he died, they should bury him "in the sepulchre wherein the man of God is buried; lay my bones beside his bones" because what the man of God had said would all surely come to pass.

OLD PROPHET IN BETH-EL, SONS OF THE. *1 Kgs. 13:11, 31.*

The **Sons of the Old Prophet in Beth-el** informed their father about the man of God who had come from Judah and cried against the altar in Beth-el. They told their father where he had gone and, at his request, saddled his ass for him. After the death of the man of God, the old prophet instructed his sons that when he died they were to bury his bones beside the bones of the man of God because all the words of the man of God would surely come to pass.

OMAR. *Gen. 36:11, 15-16.*

Omar was a son of Eliphaz, son of Adah and Esau. He was a duke or tribal chief. (Chart 3b.)

OMRI (1). *1 Kgs. 16:16-28; 2 Kgs. 8:26; 2 Chr. 22:2; Micah 6:16.*

Omri was captain of the host of Israel and was the father of Ahab. When king Elah, Baasha's son, was slain by Zimri and Zimri began to reign, slaying all of Baasha's family and friends, the people made Omri king over Israel. Zimri committed suicide by fire. The people of Israel divided into two parts: half followed Tibni, the son of Ginath, and half followed Omri. Omri's followers prevailed and Timni died. Then Omri reigned over Israel. His reign began in the 31st year of the reign of Asa, king of Judah. He reigned over Israel 12 years, six of which he reigned out of Tirzah. Omri bought the hill Samaria from Shemer and built a city which he called Samaria on the hill. He was more wicked than all that were before him. The rest of his record is written in the chronicles of the kings of Israel. He died and was buried in Samaria. His son Ahab reigned in his stead. *(1 Kgs. 16:16-28.)*

Omri's daughter (i.e., granddaughter) was Athaliah. His grandson (great-grandson) was Ahaziah, who reigned as king of Judah after his father Joram's death. *(2 Kgs. 8:26.)*

Omri was the father (grandfather) of Athaliah, wife of king Jehoram (Joram) of Judah. *(2 Chr. 22:2.)*

Micah reminded the people that the Lord was displeased with them because they followed the statutes of Omri and the wicked works of Ahab. *(Micah 6:16.)* (Chart 1.)

OMRI (2). *1 Chr. 7:8.*

Omri and his brothers (Zemira, Joash, Eliezer, Elioenai, Jerimoth, Abiah, Anathoth and Alameth) were sons of Becher, grandsons of Benjamin. (Chart 16c.)

OMRI (3). *1 Chr. 9:4.*

Omri was a descendant of Pharez, the son of Judah. He was the father of Ammihud and the son of Imri. (Chart 8b.)

OMRI (4). *1 Chr. 27:18.*

Omri, son of Michael, was prince (i.e., ruler) of the tribe of Issachar when David was king. (Chart 9a.)

ON. *Num. 16:1-33.*

On was the son of Peleth, who was a son of Reuben. He, along with Korah (grandson of Kohath), Dathan and Abiram (great-grandsons of Reuben), rebelled against Moses. Ultimately, those rebels who "appertained unto Korah, and all their goods" were swallowed up by the earth. (Chart 5a.)

ONAM (1). *Gen. 36:23.*

Onam was one of the children of Shobal. (Chart 4b.)

ONAM (2). *1 Chr. 2:26, 28.*

Onam was a son of Jerahmeel and Atarah. He was a great-great-grandson of Judah. His half-brothers were Ram, Bunah, Oren, Ozem and Ahijah. He begat Shammai and Jada. (Chart 8c.)

ONAN. *Gen. 38:4, 8-10; 46:12; Num. 26:19; 1 Chr. 2:3.*

Onan was Judah and Shuah's secondborn son. When Er died, Judah instructed Onan to take Er's widow, Tamar, to be his wife and bear seed for Er. Onan didn't want to and tried to circumvent his father's instruction by "spilling" his "seed" on the floor. The Lord was displeased with Onan and slew him. *(Gen. 38:4, 8-10.)*

Onan and Er died in Canaan. *(Gen. 46:12; Num. 26:19.)* Onan, Er and Shelah were sons of Judah and Shua the Canaanitess. *(1 Chr. 2:3.)* (Charts 8a, c-d, g-h.)

ONO. *Ezra 2:33; Neh. 7: 37.*

Ono was of the people of Israel. The men of the children of Ono, Lod and Hadid who returned to Jerusalem from Babylon after Cyrus' proclamation to build the temple numbered 725 (721).

OPHIR. *Gen. 10:29.*

Ophir was a son of Joktan, a third-great-grandson of Shem and a fourth-great-grandson of Noah. (Chart 2b.)

OPHRAH. *1 Chr. 4:14.*

Ophrah, a descendant of Judah, was the son of Meonothai and seems to be related to Othniel, son of Kenaz, but the connection is not indicated.

OREB. *Judg. 7:25.*

Oreb was a Midianite prince. Gideon's army slew him upon the rock Oreb and brought his head to Gideon on the other side of Jordan.

OREN. *1 Chr. 2:25.*

Oren was one of Jerahmeel's sons and one of Judah's great-great-grandsons. His brothers were Ram, Bunah, Ozem and Ahijah. His half-brother was Onam. (Chart 8c.)

ORNAN. See **Araunah**.

ORPAH. *Ruth 1:4-14.*

Orpah was the widowed daughter-in-law of Naomi and Elimelech. When Naomi decided to return to her own people, Orpah wanted to go with her. However, Noami discouraged her and encouraged her to return to her family that she might remarry and have a family. Thus, Orpah kissed her good-bye and returned to Moab.

OSHEA. See **Joshua (1)**.

OTHNI. *1 Chr. 26:7.*

Othni, a Levite, was a son of Shemaiah and grandson of Obed-edom. Shemaiah's other sons were Rephael, Obed, Elzabad, Elihu and Semachiah. They, along with other Levites, were appointed by king David to be porters—to have charge of the treasures, serve as officers and judges, and to conduct the outward business over Israel. (Chart 7c.)

OTHNIEL. *Josh. 15:17; Judg. 1:13; 3:9-11; 1 Chr. 4:13; 27:15.*

Othniel was the son of Kenaz and a nephew of Caleb. He captured the city of Kirjath-sepher and was given Achsah, Caleb's daughter, for a wife. *(Josh. 15:17; Judg. 1:13.)*

Othniel was made a judge over Israel. Under his leadership, the Israelites were freed from eight years of bondage to Chushan-rishathaim, king of Mesopotamia. Othniel went to war against the king and the Lord delivered him into Othniel's hands. The land had rest for 40 years and Othniel died. *(Judg. 3:9-11.)*

Othniel's son was Hathath. *(1 Chr. 4:13.)*

Othniel's descendant was Heldai the Nethphathite. He was assigned by David to be the captain for the twelfth month. There were 24,000 in his course. *(1 Chr. 27:15.)* (Charts 8k.; 20.)

OZEM (1). *1 Chr. 2:15.*

Ozem was Jesse's sixth son and one of David's elder brothers. (Chart 8d-e.)

OZEM (2). *1 Chr. 2:25.*

Ozem was one of Jerahmeel's sons and one of Judah's great-great-grandsons. His brothers were Ram, Bunah, Oren and Ahijah. His half-brother was Onam. (Chart 8c.)

OZNITES. See **Ezbon (1)**.

NAMES THAT BEGIN WITH "P"

PAARAI (Naarai). *2 Sam. 23:35; 1 Chr. 11:37.*

Paarai (Naarai) the Arbite (son of Ezbai), one of David's mighty men *(2 Sam. 23:35), was* one of the valiant men of the armies *(1 Chr. 11:37).* (Chart 17.)

PADON. *Ezra 2:44, 58; Neh. 7:47, 60.*

Padon was a Nethinim. When the Nethinims and the children of Solomon's servants left Babylon to return to Jerusalem to build the house of the Lord as proclaimed by Cyrus, king of Persia, they numbered 392.

PAGIEL. *Num. 1:13, 40-41; 2:27 (25-31); 7:72.*

Pagiel was the son of Ocran. They were of the tribe of Asher. He was appointed by the Lord to be the one to stand at the head of all of the tribe of Asher as Moses organized Israel in preparation for war. The males who were 20 years old or older in the tribe of Asher who could go to war numbered 41,500. *(Num. 1:13, 40-41.)*

Pagiel was instructed to have his tribe pitch their tents between the tribes of Dan and Naphtali on the north side of the encampment. *(Num. 2:27 [25-31].)*

When the altar of the tabernacle was anointed and dedicated, Pagiel made his offering on the eleventh day. *(Num. 7:72.)*

PAHATH-MOAB. *Ezra 2:6; 8:4; 10:30 (18-19, 30, 44); Neh. 3:11; 7:11; 10:14 (1, 14, 28-31).*

Pahath-moab was of the people of Israel. The men of the children of Pahath-moab of the children of Jeshua and Joab who returned to Jerusalem from Babylon after Cyrus' proclamation to build the temple numbered 2,812 (2,818). *(Ezra 2:6; Neh. 7:11.)*

Pahath-moab's descendant Zerahiah, the son of Elihoenai, was the leader of his posterity and accompanied Ezra when Ezra led many exiled Israelites out of Babylon back to Jerusalem. *(Ezra 8:4.)* Pahath-moab's sons—Adna, Chelal, Benaiah, Maaseiah, Mattaniah, Bezaleel, Binnui and Manasseh—were among the children of Israel who took foreign wives but gave them up at Ezra's request. *(Ezra 10:30 (18-19, 30, 44).)*

Pahath-moab was the father of Hashub, which Hashub helped repair the tower of the furnaces and helped repair the walls and gates of Jerusalem. *(Neh. 3:11.)*

Pahath-moab was among those chief of the people who covenanted to marry in Israel, honor the Sabbath, pay tithes and keep the commandments. *(Neh. 10:14 [1, 14, 28-31].)*

PALAL. *Neh. 3:25.*

Palal, son of Uzai, labored next to Binnui when the children of Israel rebuilt the walls and gates of Jerusalem during the time of Ezra and Nehemiah.

PALLU. See **Phallu.**

PALLUITES. See **Phallu.**

PALTI. *Num. 13:9; 14:37.*

Palti, of the tribe of Benjamin, was the son of Raphu. He was one of twelve leaders sent to scout out the land of Caanan. He returned with a negative report. *(Num. 13:9.)* Because of the negative report he gave, he "died by the plague before the Lord." *(Num. 14:37.)* (Chart 16f.)

PALTIEL. *Num. 34:26.*

Paltiel was the son of Azzan of the tribe of Issachar. He was assigned to divide the land of their inheritance among the tribe of Issachar. (Chart 9b.)

PALTITE. See **Helez (1)**.

PARMASHTA. *Esth. 9:9.*

Parsmashta was one of Haman's ten sons who was slain by the Jews and, at queen Esther's request, hung on the gallows by king Ahasuerus.

PARNACH. *Num. 34:25.*

Parnach was the father of Elizaphan and was of the tribe of Zebulun. (Chart 10b.)

PAROSH. *Ezra 2:3; 10:25 (18-19, 25, 44); Neh. 3:25; 7:8; 10:14 (1, 14, 28 31).*

Parosh was of the people of Israel. The men of the children of Parosh who returned to Jerusalem from Babylon after Cyrus' proclamation to build the temple numbered 2,172. *(Ezra 2:3; Neh. 7:8.)*

Of the sons of Parosh, Ramiah, Jeziah, Malchiah, Miamin, Eleazar, Malchijah and Benaiah had taken wives from among the Canaanites and other groups. They agreed to Ezra's request to put away these foreign wives lest the Lord destroy the rest of the children of Israel. *(Ezra 10:25 [18-19, 25, 44].)*

Parosh was the father of Pedaiah, which Pedaiah helped repair the walls of Jerusalem after returning from Babylonian captivity. *(Neh. 3:25.)*

Parosh, one of the chief of the people, covenanted to marry in Israel, honor the Sabbath, pay tithes and keep the commandments. *(Neh. 10:14 [1, 14, 28-31].)*

PARSHANDATH. *Esth. 9:7.*

Parshandath was one of Haman's ten sons who was slain by the Jews and, at queen Esther's request, hung on the gallows by king Ahasuerus.

PARUAH. *1 Kgs. 4:17.*

Paruah was the father of Jehoshaphat.

PASACH. *1 Chr. 7:33.*

Pasach was a son of Japhlet and a great-great-grandson of Asher. His brothers were Bimhal and Ashvath. (Chart 14a.)

PASEAH (1). *1 Chr. 4:12.*

Paseah was a son of Eshton. His brothers were Beth-rapha and Tehinnah.

PASEAH (2) (Phaseah). *Ezra 2:49, 58; Neh. 3:6; 7:51, 60.*

Paseah's (Phaseah's) children were Nethinims. When the Nethinims and the children of Solomon's servants left Babylon to return to Jerusalem to build the house of the Lord as proclaimed by Cyrus, king of Persia, they numbered 392. *(Ezra 2:49, 58; Neh. 7:51, 60.)*

Paseah was the father of Jehoiada who helped repair the walls and gates when the children of Israel rebuilt the walls and gates of Jerusalem during the time of Ezra and Nehemiah. *(Neh. 3:6.)*

PASHUR (1) **(Magor-missabib)**. *1 Chr. 9:12 (1-2, 12); Neh. 11:12; Jer. 20:1-6; 21:1-7; 38:1.*

Pashur, the son of Malchijah and the father of Jeroham, was one of the priests in Jerusalem whose genealogy was written in the book of the kings of Israel and Judah, who were carried away captive into Babylon because of their transgression and who was among the first inhabitants to dwell in Jerusalem upon returning from Babylonian captivity. *(1 Chr. 9:12 [1-2, 12].)*

Pashur, son of Malchiah (Malchijah), was the great-great-grandfather of Jeroham, not his father. He was father of Zechariah, who was the father of Amzi, who was the father of Pelaliah, who was the father of Jeroham. *(Neh. 11:12.)*

Pashur was the son of Immer the priest. *(Note: The footnote to the text refers us to Jer. 21:1 and Jer. 38:1 which state that Pashur was the son of Melchiah, Malchiah, respectively.)* Pashur was the chief governor in the house of the Lord. He smote Jeremiah and placed him in the stocks. Because of his wickedness, the Lord called him **Magor-missabib**, which means "Terror all around." Jeremiah prophesied that all Judah would be carried away captive into Babylon and that Pashur and his family and friends would die there and be buried there. *(Jer. 20:1-6.)*

When king Zedekiah sent Pashur (son of Melchiah) and Zephaniah the priest to Jeremiah to inquire as to whether or not the Lord would protect them against Nebuchadrezzar (Nebuchadnezzar), king of Babylonia, who was threatening war against them, Jeremiah instructed them to tell Zedekiah that the Lord would not help them and that Jerusalem would be captured and destroyed by Nebuchadrezzar. Additionally, Zedekiah himself would be taken captive by Nebuchadrezzar. *(Jer. 21:1-7.)*

Pashur was the father of Gedaliah and the son of Malchiah. He and the other princes went to king Zedekiah and requested they be allowed to put Jeremiah to death for prophesying that the people would live if they would surrender to the Chaldeans; otherwise, the city would be burned. Zedekiah said he could not prevail against the princes so they took Jeremiah and cast him into a miry dungeon in the house of Malchiah the son of the king. *(Jer. 38:1.)* (Chart 7g.)

PASHUR (2). *Ezra 2:38; 10:22 (18-19, 22, 44); Neh. 7:41; 10:3 (1, 3, 8. 28-31).*

Pashur was one of the priests. His children numbered 1,247 when they left Babylon to return to Jerusalem to build the temple as proclaimed by Cyrus, king of Persia. *(Ezra 2:38; Neh. 7:41.)*

Pashur's sons—Elionenai, Maaseiah, Ishmael, Nethaneel, Jozabad and Elasha—were among those sons of the priests who took foreign wives and agreed to Ezra's request that they separate themselves from these strange wives. *(Ezra 10:22 [18-19, 22, 44].)*

Pashur was among the priests who covenanted and sealed their covenant to marry in Israel, honor the Sabbath, pay tithes and keep the commandments. *(Neh. 10:3 [1, 3, 8. 28-31].)*

PATHRUSIM. *Gen. 10:14.*

Pathrusim was a son of Mizraim, grandson of Ham and a great-grandson of Noah. (Chart 2e.)

PEDAHEL. *Num. 34:28.*

Pedahel was the son of Ammihud and was of the tribe of Naphtali. He was assigned to divide the land of their inheritance among the tribe of Naphtali. (Chart 12b.)

PEDAHZUR. *Num. 1:10.*

Pedahzur was the father of Gamaliel and was of the tribe of Manasseh, one of two tribes allotted Joseph.

PEDAIAH (1). *2 Kgs. 23:36.*

Pedaiah, of Rumah, was the father of Zebudah who was one of the wives of king Josiah and the mother of Jehoiakim (Eliakim). (Chart 1.)

PEDAIAH (2). *1 Chr. 3:18.*

Pedaiah, a descendant of David, was a son (grandson) of Jeconiah (Jehoiachin). He begat Zerubbabel and Shimei. *(Note: The footnote to this passage indicates that this verse states that Zerubbabel was the grandson of Jeconiah through Pedaiah but that elsewhere Zerubbabel is called the son of Shealtiel.)* (Chart 1.)

PEDAIAH (3). *1 Chr. 27:20.*

Pedaiah was the father of Joel who was prince of one of the half tribes of Manasseh when David was king. (Chart 15c.)

PEDAIAH (4). *Neh. 3:25.*

Pedaiah, son of Parosh, labored next to Palal when the children of Israel rebuilt the walls and gates of Jerusalem during the time of Ezra and Nehemiah.

PEDAIAH (5). *Neh. 8:4 (1-8); 13:13.*

Pedaiah was one of the men who stood on Ezra's left hand when Ezra read and interpreted the law of Moses to the people. *(Neh. 8:4 [1-8].)*

Pedaiah, a Levite, along with Shelemiah the priest and Zadok the scribe and others who were counted faithful, was assigned by Nehemiah to help distribute to the Levites and singers the portions that should have been given to them. *(Neh. 13:13.)*

PEDAIAH (6). *Neh. 11:7.*

Pedaiah, of the tribe of Benjamin, was the father of Joed and the son of Kolaiah. (Chart 16m.)

PEKAH. *2 Kgs. 15:25-32, 37; 16:1, 5; 2 Chr. 28:6-8; Isa. 7.*

Pekah was the son of Remaliah and was one of the captains of king Pekahiah's host. He, along with Argob, Arieh, and fifty men of the Gileadites, killed Pekahiah and then usurped the throne. He began his wicked reign over Israel in the 52nd year of the reign of Azariah over Judah and reigned 20 years. Jotham began his reign in the second year of Pekah's reign. Ahaz, Jotham's son, reigned in Judah after Jotham's death. In those days, Pekah, along with Rezin, king of Syria, went against Judah. Hoshea, the son of Elah, conspired against Pekah and slew him and reigned in his stead. *(2 Kgs. 15:25-32, 37.)*

It was in the 17th year of the reign of Pekah over Israel that Ahaz began his reign over Judah. Pekah and Rezin king of Syria went to war against Ahaz, but they could not defeat him. *(2 Kgs. 16:1, 5.)*

Pekah, king of Israel, was victorious over Ahaz, king of Judah, killing 120,000 valiant men in one day because of Judah's wickedness. Maaseiah, the king's son, was slain, as was Azrikam, the governor of the house, and Elkanah, who was next to the king. Israel took 200,000 women, sons and daughters of Judah captive. *(2 Chr. 28:6-8.)*

When Pekah and Rezin were planning to wage war against Judah and set the son of Tabeal up as king, the Lord Instructed Isaiah to take his son Shear-jashub and deliver a message to Ahaz. Ahaz was told he should take heed and fear not because Pekah and Rezin would not succeed. In fact, within 65 years, Ephraim would no longer even be a people but would be broken. *(Isa. 7.)*

PEKAHIAH. *2 Kgs. 15:22-26.*

Pekahiah was the son of Menahem. He reigned over Israel in Samaria upon Menahem's death, beginning his reign in the 50th year of the reign of Azariah over Judah. He reigned two years and did that which was evil in the sight of the Lord. He was slain by Pekah, one of his captains, who smote him in Samaria in the palace of the king's house with the help of Argob, Arieh, and fifty men of the Gileadites who staged a coup d'e'tat. Pekah reigned in his stead.

PELAIAH (1). *1 Chr. 3:24.*

Pelaiah, a descendant of David, was a son of Elioenai. His brothers were Hodaiah, Eliashib, Akkub, Johanan, Dalaiah and Anani. (Chart 1.)

PELAIAH (2). *Neh. 8:7-8; 10:10 (1, 10, 28-31).*

Pelaiah was one of the men who, when Ezra read and interpreted the law of Moses to the people, helped the people to understand the law. *(Neh. 8:7-8.)*

Pelaiah was among those Levites who covenanted and sealed their covenant to marry in Israel, honor the Sabbath, pay tithes and keep the commandments. *(Neh. 10:10 [1, 10, 28-31].)*

PELALIAH. *Neh. 11:12.*

Pelaliah, son of Amzi, was the father of Jeroham and the grandfather of Adaiah. He and his brethren did the work of the house of the Lord. (Chart 7g.)

PELATIAH (1). *1 Chr. 3:21.*

Pelatiah, a descendant of David, was a son of Hananiah and a grandson of Zerubbabel. His brother was Jesaiah. (Chart 1.)

PELATIAH (2). *1 Chr. 4:42.*

Pelatiah, a son of Ishi, was one of the captains who led a group of 500 men, including some of the sons of Simeon, to mount Seir where they smote the Amalekites who had escaped from earlier conflicts. His brothers were Neariah, Rephaiah and Uzziel. (Chart 6b.)

PELATIAH (3). *Neh. 10:22 (1, 22, 28-31).*

Pelatiah was among those chief of the people who covenanted to marry in Israel, honor the Sabbath, pay tithes and keep the commandments.

PELATIAH (4). *Ezek. 11:1-4, 13.*

Pelatiah was the son of Benaiah, one of the princes of the people. He was among 25 men who sat at the east gate of the Lord's house and gave false counsel to the people in Jerusalem, saying that the city would not be destroyed and they were safe to build houses. Ezekiel was instructed by the Lord to prophesy against them. When Ezekiel prophesied against Pelatiah and the others who were giving false counsel, Pelatiah died.

PELEG. *Gen. 10:25; 11:18-19; 1 Chr. 1:19, 24-27.*

Peleg, a brother to Joktan, was a son of Eber, a great-great-grandson of Shem and a great-great-great-grandson of Noah. It was in his day that the earth was divided. *(Gen. 10:25; 1 Chr. 1:19.) (Note: Speaking of when the Savior comes again, the Lord told Joseph Smith, "And the land of Jerusalem and the land of Zion shall be turned back into their own place, and the earth shall be like as it was in the days before it was divided." D&C 133:24.)*

Peleg was 30 years old when he begat Reu. He lived 239 years. *(Gen. 11:18-19.)* He was Abraham's great-great-great-grandfather. *(1 Chr. 1:24-27.)* (Charts 1.; 2b.; 21.)

PELET (1). *1 Chr. 2:47.*

Pelet was a son of Jahdai. (Chart 8j.)

PELET (2). *1 Chr. 12:3 (1-3, 23, 38).*

Pelet, a son of Azmaveth and brother of Jeziel, was one of David's mighty men who came to him at Ziklag to defend him against Saul and to rejoice with all Israel when David became king.

PELETH (1). *Num. 16:1.*

Peleth, a son of Reuben, was the father of On who rebelled against Moses and was swallowed up by the earth. (Chart 5a.)

PELETH (2). *1 Chr. 2:33.*

Peleth was a son of Jonathan. His brother was Zaza. He was a five-times-great-grandson of Judah through Jerahmeel. (Chart 8c.)

PELETHITES. *2 Sam. 8:18; 8:18; 15:18 (12-18); 20:7 (6-7); 1 Kgs. 1:44.*

The **Pelethites**, along with the Cherethites, were under the leadership of Benaiah, a chief priest and son of Jehoiada. *(2 Sam. 8:18.)*

When David and his household fled from Jerusalem to escape from Absalom, the Pelethites, Cherethites and Gittites were with David. *(2 Sam. 15:18 [12-18].)*

The Pelethites and the Cherethites went with Abishai and Joab's men as they pursued Sheba who had caused an insurrection in Israel. *(2 Sam. 20:7 [6-7].)*

The Pelethites and Cherethites accompanied Zadok the priest, Nathan the prophet, and Benaiah the son of Jehoiada, when they brought Solomon to Gihon to reign as the new king. *(1 Kgs. 1:44.)*

PELONITE. See **Helez (1)**.

PENINNAH. *1 Sam. 1:2,4-5.*

Peninnah was one of Elkanah's wives. She had children but Hannah, another wife, was barren. When "Elkanah offered, he gave to Peninnah and to all her sons and her daughters, portions: but unto Hannah he gave a worthy portion; for he loved Hannah." (Chart 7d.)

PENUEL (1). *1 Chr. 4:4.*

Penuel was of the lineage of Judah through Hur and was the father of Gedor. His mother was Hazelelponi. (Chart m.)

PENUEL (2). *1 Chr. 8:25 (14-16, 25).*

Penuel, a descendant of Benjamin, was a son of Shashak who was a son of Beriah. (Chart 16g.)

PERESH. See **Gilead (1)**.

PEREZ. See **Pharez**.

PERIDA. See **Peruda**.

PERIZZITES. *Gen. 15:20 (18-21); Deut. 7:1; Josh. 3:10; 17:15 (14-15); 1 Kgs. 9:20-21; 2 Chr. 8:7; Ezra 9:1; Neh. 9:8.*

The **Perizzites'** lands were given to Abram's seed by the Lord in covenant. *(Gen. 15:20 [18-21].)*

The Perizzites were one of the seven nations in Canaan, greater and mightier than the Israelites, whom the Lord said He would destroy so Israel could inherit the promised land. *(Deut. 7:1.)* Joshua promised the children of Israel that the Lord would "without fail" drive the Perizzites, Canaanites, Hivites, Hittites, Girgashites, Amorites and Jebusites out from before them. *(Josh. 3:10.)*

When Joseph's posterity complained that the land they received was not sufficient for their numbers, Joshua told them to "get thee up to the wood country, and cut down for thyself there in the land of the Perizzites and of the giants, if mount Ephraim be too narrow for thee." *(Josh. 17:15 [14-15].)*

Solomon levied a tribute of bondservice over all the people who were not of Israel who remained in the land—the Perizzites, Hittites, Amorites, Hivites and Jebusites. *(1 Kgs. 9:20-21; 2 Chr. 8:7.)*

After the children of Israel were delivered from Babylonian bondage, many Jews, including the priests and Levites, intermarried with and followed the abominations of the Perizzites, Canaanites, Hittites, Jebusites, Ammonites, Moabites, Egyptians and Amorites. Ezra prayed and confessed the sins of all the people, fearing the Lord would completely desroy them this time for their abominations. *(Ezra 9:1.)*

The Lord gave the land of the Perizzites, Canaanites, Hittites, Amorites, Jebusites and Girgashites to Abraham. *(Neh. 9:8.) (Note: The Bible Dictionary indicates that Perizzites were villagers, a people of Palestine. It was apparently a general name for Canaanite tribes who had no fortified towns.)*

PERSIANS. *Dan. 6:8; 8:20; 10:1, 13, 20.*

The **Persians** and Medes had a law that when the king established a decree and signed the written document, that it could not be changed nor altered. King Darius' leaders used that law to try to destroy Daniel. *(Dan. 6:8.) (Note: The Bible Dictionary states that "the Persians were a tribe who in the 8th century B.C. inhabited a district east of Elam. Cyrus united the Medes and Persians, conquered Babylon in 538 B.C. and founded the Persian Empire." Webster's New World Dictionary states that Pesia was "the former official name of Iran.")*

Daniel saw in vision a ram with two horns. The horns represented Persia and Media who, in the latter days, would be destroyed by Grecia. *(Dan. 8:20.)*

Daniel was given a vision in the third year of Cyrus' reign as king of Persia, in which he saw the Lord and others. The Lord told Daniel that "the prince of the kingdom of Persia withstood me one and twenty days: but, lo, Michael, one of the chief princes, came to help me; and I remained there with the kings of Persia." He also said, " . . . and now will I return to fight with the prince of Persia: and when I am gone forth, lo, the prince of Grecia shall come." *(Dan. 10:1, 13, 20.)*

PERUDA (Perida). *Ezra 2:55, 58; Neh. 7:57, 60.*

Peruda (Perida) was one of Solomon's servants. The children of Solomon's servants and those of the Nethinims numbered 392.

PETHAHIAH (1). *1 Chr. 24:16 (1-5, 16).*

Pethahiah was from the sons of Aaron. When David made the divisions of the sons of Aaron for the governing of the sanctuary and the house of God, there was one principal household for Eleazar and one taken for Ithamar. Eleazar had 16 sons and there were eight sons of Ithamar. These 24 sons who were chief of the fathers were divided by lot. Pethahiah drew the19th lot.

PETHAHIAH (2). *Ezra 10:23 (18-19, 23, 44); Neh. 9.*

Pethahiah was one of the Levites who had taken wives from among the Canaanites or other foreign groups and who agreed to Ezra's request that they separate themselves from these strange wives lest the Lord destroy the rest of the children of Israel. *(Ezra 10:23 [18-19, 23, 44].)*

When Ezra read and interpreted the law of Moses and he and Nehemiah proclaimed the day a holy day, the Levites—Pethahiah, Jeshua, Bani, Kadmiel, Shebaniah, Bunni, Sherebiah, Bani, Chenani, Hashabniah and Hodijah—blessed and praised the Lord, reciting the Lord's goodness to Israel: the blessing of Abraham; giving the land of the Canaanites, Hittites, Amorites, Perizzites, Jebusites and Girgashites to Israel; dividing the Red Sea so they could cross it yet drowning the Egyptians who pursued them; the signs and wonders shown to Pharaoh; leading them in the wilderness and protecting them so that they had bread from heaven, water from the rock, and shoes and clothes that never wore out; accepting them whenever they repented, even when they made a molten calf. They had been given the kingdoms of Shihon, Heshbon and Bashan and the Lord had subdued the Canaanites and delivered them into the hands of the Israelites, etc. After giving praise, they made a covenant with the Lord. The princes, Levites and priests sealed the covenant. *(Neh. 9.)*

PETHAHIAH (3). *Neh. 11:24.*

Pethahiah was the son of Meshezabeel, of the children of Zerah the son of Judah. He was at the king's hand in all matters concerning the children of Israel after they returned from Babylonian captivity to Jerusalem and the other cities. (Chart 8g.)

PETHUEL. *Joel 1:1.*

Pethuel was the father of the prophet Joel.

PEULTHAI. *1 Chr. 26:5 (sub-title, 4-5).*

Peulthai, a Levite belonging to the family of Kohath, was the eighth son of Obed-edom. His brothers were Shemaiah, Jehozabad, Joah, Sacar, Nethaneel, Ammiel and Issachar. They, with others, were appointed by king David to be porters—to have charge of the treasures, serve as officers and judges, and to conduct the outward business over Israel. (Chart 7c.)

PHALLU (Pallu, Palluites). *Gen. 46:9; Num. 26:5-8.*

Phallu was one of Reuben's sons and a grandson of Jacob. *(Gen. 46:9.)* He **(Pallu)** was the father of the **Palluites**. He begat Eliab. *(Num. 26:5-8.)* (Chart 5a.)

PHALTI. *1 Sam. 25:44.*

Phalti, the son of Laish, was of Gallim. Saul gave his daughter Michal, David's wife, to Phalti to be his wife.

PHARAOH (1). *Gen. 12:15 (14-20).*

Pharaoh was the ruler of Egypt. When Abram and Sarai went there, the Egyptians and Pharaoh's princes saw that Sarai was very fair. When she said she was Abram's sister, she was taken into Pharaoh's house. Abram was treated well because of her. However, the Lord plagued Pharaoh because of Sarai. Pharaoh demanded to know why Abram had said Sarai was his sister and not his wife. Pharaoh commanded his men concerning Abram and Sarai and they were sent away. *(Note: See "Abraham" for additional information from Abraham 2:22-25 in the Pearl of Great Price.)*

PHARAOH (2). *Gen. 37:36; 40:1-3, 20-23; 41:1-45; 45:17-18.*

Pharaoh was the leader of Egypt. Potiphar, who bought Joseph from a group of Ishmeelites or Midianite merchantmen, was one of his officers and captain of his guard. *(Gen. 37:36.)*

Pharaoh cast his chief Butler and chief Baker into prison. In accordance to the dreams which Joseph interpreted for them, Pharaoh did restore the butler to his former place and he hanged the baker. *(Gen. 40:1-3, 20-23.)*

Pharaoh had two dreams and none of his magicians nor wisemen could interpret them. The chief butler recalled that Joseph had given him and the former chief baker correct interpretations of their dreams and conveyed that to Pharaoh. Pharaoh sent for Joseph and told him his dreams.

Pharaoh's Dreams: Dream 1. Seven robust cows came out of the river and fed in a meadow. Seven ill-favored and leanfleshed cows ate up the seven robust cows. Dream 2. Seven good ears of corn grew on one stalk. Seven withered and thin ears sprang up and devoured the seven good ears. *(Gen. 41:1-24.)*

Joseph's Interpretation: The seven healthy cows and the seven good ears of corn both represent seven years. The seven thin, ill-favored cows and the seven withered ears of corn also represent seven years—seven years of famine. There would be seven years of great plenty in Egypt. These would be followed by seven years of famine. All the years of plenty would be forgotten. Famine would consume the land. *(Gen. 41:25-31.)*

Pharaoh elevated Joseph to second in command, just behind himself, over all of Egypt. He also gave Asenath, the daughter of Potipherah priest of On, to Joseph for a wife. *(Gen. 41:37-45.)*

Pharaoh invited Jacob and all Joseph's brothers and their children and families to come live in Egypt and "eat the fat of the land." *(Gen. 45:17-18.)*

PHARAOH (3). *Ex. 1:8-22; 2:5-10, 23.*

Pharaoh was a new king over Egypt. He had not known Joseph. He feared the children of Israel because of their vast numbers so he placed them in bondage. To control their growth, he ordered that all newborn male babies should be killed by the midwives. The midwives did not obey that order. Pharaoh then ordered the people to cast all newborn Hebrew male babies into the river. *(Ex. 1:8-22.)*

Pharaoh's daughter found Moses in an ark in the bulrushes and raised him as her son. Pharaoh, king of Egypt, died. *(Ex. 2:5-10, 23.)*

PHARAOH (4). *Ex. 3:10; 5; 7; 8:6, 7, 17, 24; 9:6, 10, 23; 10:13, 22; 11:5; 12:29, 31-32, 40; 14:3, 9, 28; Neh. 9:10; Ps. 136:15.*

Pharaoh was king of Egypt when the Lord sent Moses back to Egypt to free the children of Israel. *(Ex. 3:10.)*

Moses and Aaron asked Pharaoh to let their people travel three days into the wilderness so they could make a sacrifice unto their God. In response, Pharaoh increased their burden by no longer providing the straw for the bricks. They were told to gather it themselves but that their brick output was not to be diminished. Pharaoh's taskmasters beat the officers of the children of Israel. The people complained to Moses and Moses inquired of the Lord why He had treated them so evily. *(Ex. 5.)*

When Moses and Aaron spoke to Pharaoh and Aaron's rod turned into a serpent, Pharaoh called in his magicians and they did the same with their rods. Pharaoh hardened his heart and would not let the people go. *(Ex. 7.)*

Moses and Aaron caused frogs to come out of the rivers and plague the land. *(Ex. 8:6.)* Pharaoh's magicians duplicated that plague. *(Ex. 8:7.)* However, Pharaoh now called Moses and Aaron in and said if the Lord would take away the frogs , he would let the people go. When the Lord took away the frogs, Pharaoh saw this as a respite and again hardened his heart. The Lord then sent lice to plague the Egyptians. *(Ex. 8:17.)* In spite of additional plagues of lice, flies *(Ex. 8:24)*, destruction of cattle *(Ex. 9:6)*, boils *(Ex. 9:10)*, hail and fire *(Ex. 9:23)*, locusts *(Ex. 10:13)* and thick darkness *(Ex. 10:22)*, Pharaoh continued to harden his heart and refused to let the children of Israel go. The Lord told Moses that He would smite all the firstborn in the land of Egypt and they would die, from the firstborn of Pharaoh to the firstborn of the maidservants and the firstborn of the beasts. *(Ex. 11:5.)*

At midnight on the appointed day, the Lord smote the firstborn of all Egypt. *(Ex. 12:29.)* Pharaoh called for Moses and Aaron and told them to take all their people and all their flocks and leave. *(Ex. 12:31-32.)* The children of Israel had been in Egypt 430 years. *(Ex. 12:40.)*

Pharaoh hardened his heart, and he and his armies pursued Moses and the children of Israel as they crossed through the Red Sea on dry ground. However, the waters returned and covered them. *(Ex. 14:3, 9, 28.)* The Lord overthrew Pharaoh and his armies in the Red Sea as they sought to overtake Moses and the children of Israel. *(Ps. 136:15.)*

The children of Israel acknowledged the signs and wonders the Lord had shown to Pharaoh. *(Neh. 9:10.)*

PHARAOH (5). *1 Kgs. 3:1; 7:8; 9:16, 24.*

Pharaoh, king of Egypt, made a marriage alliance with Solomon, who married Pharaoh's daughter. *(1 Kgs. 3:1.)* His daughter was Solomon's wife. *(1 Kgs. 7:8.)*

Pharaoh took over Gezer and burned it with fire, slaying the Canaanites who dwelled in the city, and he gave the city to his daughter, Solomon's wife, for a present. Pharaoh's daughter came up out of the city of David unto the house Solomon had built for her. *(1 Kgs. 9:16, 24.)*

PHARAOH (6) (Shishak). *1 Kgs. 11:40; 14:25-26; 2 Chr. 12:2-9.*

Pharaoh (Shishak) was king of Egypt. After the Lord's prophet Ahijah told Jeroboam that he would make him king over ten of the tribes of Israel, Solomon sought to kill him and Jeroboam fled unto Shishak where he remained until the death of Solomon. *(1 Kgs. 11:40.)*

In the fifth year of the reign of Rehoboam, Shishak came up against Jerusalem. and took the treasures from the temple. *(1 Kgs. 14:25-26.)*

When Rehoboam transgressed against the Lord, taking all Israel with him, the Lord allowed his enemies to prevail against him. Upon repentance, the Lord gave them partial deliverance but still allowed Shishak to spoil Jerusalem. Shishak took all the treasures of the Lord's house as well as all of the king's treasures. *(2 Chr.*

12:2-9.) (Note: The Bible Dictionary states that a pictorial representation of his victory over Rehoboam has been discovered on the wall of the temple of Karnak.)

PHARAOH (7). *1 Chr. 4:18.*

Pharaoh was the father of Bithiah who was the wife of Mered. *(Note: It is not clear as to which Pharaoh this refers.)*

PHARAOH (8) (So, King of Egypt). *2 Kgs. 17:4; 18:21; Isa. 36:6.*

Pharaoh (So) was king of Egypt when Hoshea was king of Israel and Shalmaneser was king of Assyria. *(2 Kgs. 17:4.)*

Tartan, Rabsaris and Rab-shakeh were sent by Lachish to king Hezekiah to urge him to surrender to them, saying Pharaoh king of Egypt was like a bruised reed and could not save him and his people. *(2 Kgs. 18:21.) (Note: According to the Chronology Chart in the BD, it would appear that So was the Pharaoh referred to by Rabshakeh.)*

Asssyria's king Sennacherib sent Rab-shakeh to king Hezekiah, saying Judah could not depend on being saved by Egypt any more than it could trust in the staff of a broken reed. *(Isa. 36:6.)*

PHARAOH (9) NECHOH (Necho). *2 Kgs. 23:29-34; 2 Chr. 35:20-24; 36:3-4; Jer. 25:19; 46:2-26; 47:1.*

Pharaoh-nechoh (Necho), king of Egypt (610-595 B.C.), went up against the king of Asyria. Josiah, king of Judah, went against him and was slain by him. Jehoahaz, Josiah's son reigned in his stead. Pharaoh-nechoh took him prisoner and took him to Egypt where Jehoahaz died. He made Jehoahaz's brother Eliahim king over Judah. He changed Eliahim's name to Jehoiakim. Jehoiakim taxed the people and gave the money to Pharaoh-nechoh. *(2 Kgs. 23:29-34; 2 Chr. 35:20-24; 36:3-4.)*

In the latter days, the Lord shall send a sword among all the nations, including among Pharaoh king of Egypt, and his people. *(Jer. 25:19.)*

The prophet Jeremiah prophesied the conquest of Egypt and Pharaoh-necho by Nebechadrezzar, king of Babylon. This was fulfilled in the fourth year of the reign of Jehoiakim the king of Judah. *(Jer. 46:2-26.)*

Prior to Pharaoh's smiting Gaza, Jeremiah had prophesied against the Philistines. *(Jer. 47:1.)*

PHARAOH (10) (Pharaoh-hophra). *Jer. 37:4-10; 43:9-10; 44:30; Ezek. 17:17; 29:2-16; 30:21-22; 31:2-18.; 32.*

Pharaoh, Egypt's king (589-570 B.C.) came to help Judah when Zedekiah was king over Judah and the Chaldeans had beseiged Jerusalem. Jeremiah prophesied that Egypt's armies could not save Judah from Babylon. Egypt's armies would return into their own lands and, even if Egypt smote the whole army of the Chaldeans, they would still rise up and burn Jerusalem. *(Jer. 37:4-10.)*

Because Johanan the son of Kareah (Careah) and Azariah (Jezaniah) the son of Hoshaiah and "all the proud men" refused to believe Jeremiah's prophecy that they would be blessed if they remained in Judah but would suffer death, famine and pestilence if they went into Egypt and went into Egypt anyway, Jeremiah prophesied that Babylon would conquer Egypt and that Nebuchadrezzar would "set his throne upon these stones" which Jeremiah had buried at the entry of Pharaoh's house. Nebuchadrezzar would destroy the gods of Egypt and break the images of Beth-shemesh. *(Jer. 43:9-10.)*

Pharaoh's name is given as **Pharaoh-hophra**. Jeremiah prophesied that because the remnant of Judah which went to dwell in Egypt refused to follow the Lord and worshipped false gods, they would be destroyed. Pharaoh-hophra would be delivered into the hands of his enemies just as Zedekiah king of Judah had been delivered into the hands of his enemies. *(Jer. 44:30.)*

The Lord condemned Jerusalem for seeking help from Egypt rather than from the Lord and said that Egypt's Pharaoh with his mighty army and great company could not save Jerusalem from the consequences of the Lord's wrath. *(Ezek. 17:17.)*

Pharaoh king of Egypt was told by Ezekiel that Egypt would be overthrown by Babylon because of her idolatry and pride and because Israel turned to her for help instead of to the Lord. Egypt would be as a staff of reed to the house of Israel and would be scattered among the nations 40 years, afterwhich the Lord would gather the Egyptians from among the people where they had been scattered. Ezekiel prophesied that they would be returned into the land of Pathros. Egypt would never be powerful again but would be a "base" kingdom. *(Ezek. 29:2-16.)*

Ezekiel proclaimed that the Lord was against Pharaoh king of Egypt, and would "break his arms, the strong, and that which was broken" and that He would cause the sword to fall out of his hand. The Lord said that the "broken arm of Pharaoh" would not be bound up to be healed. *(Ezek. 30:21-22.)*

Ezekiel prophesied that Pharaoh king of Egypt would fall just like the Assyrians, who were compared to a mighty cedar in Lebanon. "Yet shalt thou be brought down with the trees of Eden unto the nether parts of the earth." *(Ezek. 31:2-18.)*

Ezekiel was told by the Lord to take up a lamentation for Pharaoh king of Egypt because of his pending fall. "Yea," said the Lord, "I will make many people amazed at thee (Pharaoh), and their kings shall be horribly afraid for thee, when I shall brandish my sword before them; and they shall tremble at every moment, every man for his own life, in the day of thy fall." *(Ezek. 32:10.)* He would be brought low by the sword of the king of Babylon . . . "And he shall be laid in the midst of the uncircumcised with them that are slain with the sword, even Pharaoh and all his multitude." *(Ezek. 32:1-32.)*

PHARAOH'S CHIEF BAKER. *Gen. 40:1-4, 16-23.*

Pharaoh's Chief Baker offended the king and was cast into prison along with the chief butler. He dreamed a dream. When he saw that Joseph had given the butler a favorable interpretation of his dream, he told Joseph about his own dream.

Chief Baker's Dream: He dreamed he had three white baskets on his head. In the top basket was all manner of bakemeats for Pharaoh. The birds ate them out of the basket.

Joseph's Interpretation: The three baskets represent three days. Within three days, Pharaoh would lift up the baker's head from off him and would hang him on a tree. The birds would eat his flesh from off him.

The Pharaoh did to the baker as Joseph said he would.

PHARAOH'S CHIEF BUTLER. *Gen. 40:1-15, 20-23.*

Pharaoh's Chief Butler offended the king and was cast into prison. He dreamed a dream and Joseph interpreted it for him.

Chief Butler's Dream: A vine was before him. In the vine were three branches. The blossoms shot forth and the clusters brought forth ripe grapes. Pharaoh's cup was in his hand. The butler took the grapes and pressed them into Pharaoh's cup and gave the cup to Pharaoh.

Joseph's Interpretation: The three branches represent three days. Within three days, Pharaoh would lift up the butler's head and restore him to his place. The butler would deliver the cup to Pharaoh as he used to do.

Joseph's prediction was fulfilled. The butler forgot Joseph and did not mention him to Pharaoh as he had promised to do.

PHARAOH'S (3) DAUGHTER. *Ex. 2:5-10*

Pharaoh's Daughter found Moses floating in the river in an ark. She accepted his sister's offer to find a Hebrew nurse for the baby. She charged his mother to be his nurse. When the child grew and no longer needed a nurse, he was returned to Pharaoh's daughter and he became her son. She named him Moses because she drew him out of the water.

PHARAOH'S (5) DAUGHTER. *1 Kgs. 3:1; 9:16; 2 Chr. 8:11.*

Pharaoh's Daughter was given to Solomon for a wife. *(1 Kgs. 3:1.)* Pharaoh gave his daughter the city of Gezer for a present. *(1 Kgs. 9:16.)*

Solomon brought his wife, the daughter of Pharaoh, out of the city of David unto the house he built for her. *(2 Chr. 8:11.)*

PHARAOH'S (1) PRINCES. *Gen. 12:15.*

Pharaoh's Princes saw that Sarai (Sarah, Abraham's wife) was fair and commended her to Pharaoh.

PHAREZ (Perez, Pharzites). *Gen. 38:29-30; 46:12; Num. 26:20; 1 Chr. 2:4-5; 9:4; 27:3; Neh. 11:4-6.*

Pharez was the firstborn twin of Tamar begotten by her father-in-law Judah. His twin brother was Zarah. *(Gen. 38:29-30.)* He begat Hezron and Hamul. *(Gen. 46:12.)* He was the father of the **Pharzites**. *(Num. 26:20.)*

Pharez was the son of Tamar and Judah. He was the father of Hezron and Hamul. *(1 Chr. 2:4-5.)* His descendants included Uthai the son of Ammihud, son of Omri, son of Imri the son of Bani. *(1 Chr. 9:4.)*

Perez (probably the same as Pharez) was the father (or ancestor) of the chief of all the captains of the host who served king David the first month. *(1 Chr. 27:3.)*

The descendants of Perez, who was of the house of Judah, who dwelled in Jerusalem after their captivity in Babylon included 468 valiant men. *(Neh. 11:4-6.)* (Charts 1.; 8a-d, g-h, m.)

PHAROSH. *Ezra 8:3 (1, 3).*

Pharosh was of the sons of Shechaniah. His descendant Zechariah was the leader of his posterity when Ezra led many exiled Israelites out of Babylon back to Jerusalem.

PHARZITES. See **Pharez**.

PHASEAH. See **Paseah (2)**.

PHICHOL. *Gen. 21:22, 32; 26:26-31.*

Phichol was king Abimelech's chief captain. He was with Abimelech and Abraham when they made their covenant with each other. He and Abimelech returned into the land of the Philistines. *(Gen. 21:22, 32.)*

Phichol was with king Abimelech again when the king met with Isaac and made a covenant with him that Isaac would do them no harm. *(Gen. 26:26-31.)*

PHILISTIM. *Gen. 10:14; 1 Chr. 1:12.*

Philistim came out of Casluhim, son of Mizraim. (Chart 2e.)

PHILISTINE LAD. *Judg. 16:26.*

A **Philistine Lad** guided Samson's hands to the pillars that supported the house where the Philistines were making sport of him. Samson caused the pillars to collapse.

PHILISTINE MAN. *Judg. 16:19.*

A **Philistine Man** was summoned by Delilah to cut off Samson's hair while he slept.

PHILISTINES. *Gen. 21:32,34; Judg. 13:1-5; 14:1-5, 15, 17-20; 15; 16; 1 Sam. 4-7; 13:3; 14; 17; 23; 27:1, 7; 28:1-2; 29; 31; 2 Sam. 5:17-25; 1 Chr. 10; 14:8-16; 18:1, 11; 20:5; 2 Chr. 17:11; 21:16-17; 26:6-7; 28:18; Jer. 47; Ezek. 16:57 (44-57); 25:15-17; Amos 1:8 (1, 6-8); Obad. 1:19; Zeph. 2:5.*

The **Philistines** were a tribe that originally came from Caphtor and occupied the rich lowland on the Mediterranean coast from Joppa to the Egyptian desert prior to the days of Abraham. *(See Philistines in the BD.)* Abimelech and Phichol, his chief captain, made a covenant with Abraham, and then Abimelech and Phichol returned into the land of the Philistines. Abraham sojourned in the Philistines' land many days. *(Gen. 21:32,34.)*

Because of wickedness, the Lord delivered Israel into the hands of the Philistines for 40 years. He then raised up Samson to begin to deliver the children of Israel from Philistine bondage. *(Judg. 13:1-5.)*

Samson married a Philistine woman. After Samson's wife deceived him into revealing the explanation to a riddle, Samson slew 30 Philistines in Ashkelon. Samson's wife was given to another man. *(Judg. 14:1-5, 15, 17-20.)*

Samson burned the corn of the Philistines. The Philistines, in turn, burned Samson's wife and his father-in-law so Samson slaughtered several of them.

Because they were under Philistine rule, Judah bound Samson and delivered him to the Philistines. However, he broke the cords that bound him and, using the jawbone of an ass, slew 1,000 Philistines at Lehi. *(Judg. 15.)*

Samson fell in love with Delilah. She found out the source of his strength, had his hair cut, and delivered him into the hands of the Philistines. They put his eyes out and bound him with fetters of brass. When the Philistines decided to make sport with him, Samson asked the lad that held him by the hand to let him feel the pillars that the house stood upon. Samson caused the pillars to collapse, killing himself and about 3,000 men and women who were upon the roof. Thus, he slew more Philistines at his death than he did in life. *(Judg. 16.)*

The Lord allowed Israel to be smitten by the Philistines. The prophet Eli's two sons, Hophni and Phinehas, were slain in battle on the same day and the Philistines captured the ark of the covenant of the Lord. *(1 Sam. 4.)* The Philistines were then plagued and slain because they had the ark. *(1 Sam. 5.)* They decided to return the ark of the Lord to Israel to prevent further disasters being visited upon themselves. They took it to Beth-shemesh and delivered it up to Joshua in his field. Because the men of Beth-shemesh looked into the ark of the Lord, the Lord smote 50,070 of the men in Beth-shemesh. The people then sent messengers to Kiriath-jearim asking them to come and get the ark that the Philistines had brought to them. *(1 Sam. 6.)*

The Philistines were subdued by the children of Israel. *(1 Sam. 7.)* Jonathan, Saul's son, smote a Philistine garrison. The Philistines came out after Saul. Saul made an unauthorized burnt offering unto the Lord in Samuel's absence. *(1 Sam. 13:3.)* Jonathan attacked and defeated another Philistine garrison. The Philistines fled from before Saul and his men. *(1 Sam. 14.)* The Philistines engaged in war against Israel. Their champion warrior was Goliath, a giant from Gath. Using a sling and a stone, David slew Goliath. Thus, Israel defeated the Philistines. *(1 Sam. 17.)* The Philistines came against Keilah, and David and his followers were sent by the Lord to deliver Keilah. As Saul pursued David into the wilderness of Maon, a messenger came to him and informed him that the Philistines had invaded the land; thus, Saul temporarily gave up his pursuit of David and went to battle with the Philistines. *(1 Sam. 23.)* David fled to Achish at Gath and lived among the Philistines for 16 months. *(1 Sam. 27:1, 7.)*

The Philistines gathered together for battle against Saul. David was with them. *(1 Sam. 28:1-2.)* As they prepared for battle, the Philistine princes demanded that Achish send David and his men away because they feared they would become adversaries to them when they battled Saul and the Israelites. *(1 Sam. 29.)*. The Philistines killed Jonathan, Abinadab and Malchi-shua, Saul's sons, in battle. They seriously wounded Saul. Fearing what the Philistines would do to him, when his armorbearer would not kill him, Saul fell upon his own sword rather than let the Philistines abuse him. When the Philistines found Saul, they cut off his head and sent it about the land. They fastened his body and those of his sons on the wall of Beth-shan in the temple of Dagon. The valiant men of Jabesh-gilead went at night and retrieved their bodies. They brought them to Jabesh and burned them, burying their bones under a tree at Jabesh. *(1 Sam. 31; 1 Chr. 10:1-12.)*

When the Philistines heard that David had been anointed king over all Israel they decided to come against him. Nevertheless, the Lord delivered two different groups of Philistines into David's hands. *(2 Sam. 5:17-25; 1 Chr. 14:8-16.)*

The Philistines were smitten and subdued by David. The precious things retrieved from the Philistines were dedicated unto the Lord. *(1 Chr. 18:1, 11.)*

The Philistines were defeated again and the children of the giant of Gath were slain. *(1 Chr. 20:5.)*

Because the Lord was with king Jehoshaphat, none of the kingdoms of the lands that were around Judah made war against Jehoshaphat. Some of the Philistines even brought him presents and tribute silver. *(2 Chr. 17:11.)*

Because of the wickedness of Jehoram, king of Judah, the Lord stirred up the Philistines against Jehoram. They and the Arabians came against Judah and took all the substance they could find in the king's house plus his sons and his wives. Only Jehoahaz, the youngest son, was left. *(2 Chr. 21:16-17.)*

The Philistines and the Arabians were defeated by Uzziah (Azariah), king of Judah. *(2 Chr. 26:6-7.)*

When Judah, under the reign of king Ahaz, became so very wicked, the Lord allowed Judah to be defeated by the Philistines and the Edomites as well as by the children of Israel. The Philistines took many of the cities of the low country and those of the south of Judah. *(2 Chr. 28:18.)*

Jeremiah prophesied the destruction that would befall the Philistines. *(Jer. 47.)*

The Philistines are referred to in the proverb the Lord gave Ezekiel comparing Jerusalem to a mother's daughter with the pagan nations being referred to as sisters. The Lord indicated that Jerusalem was more wicked than the Philistines and the other nations. *(Ezek. 16:57 [44-57].)*

Because the Philistines dealt by revenge against Jerusalem, Ezekiel was instructed by the Lord to prophesy vengence against them. *(Ezek. 25:15-17.)*

During the time of Uzziah king of Judah and Jeroboam king of Israel, Amos prophesied of things he saw concerning Israel and the judgments that would come upon the Philistines, Syria and others. Of the Philistines, Amos said the Lord would send a wall of fire on the walls of Gaza, which would devour the palaces thereof. The Lord would also cut off the inhabitant from Ashdod, "and him that holdeth the sceptre from Ashkelon, and I will turn mine hand against Ekron: and the remnant of the Philistines shall perish." *(Amos 1:8 (1, 6-8).)*

Obadia prophesied that the lands of the Philistines—including the fields of Ephraim and Samaria—would be possessed by the people of the plains. *(Obad. 1:19.)*

The prophet Zephaniah prophesied judgment to come upon Canaan, the land of the Philistines, and said the Lord would "destroy thee, that there shall be no inhabitant." *(Zeph. 2:5.)*

PHILISTINE WOMAN. *Judg. 14:1-20; 15:6.*

Philistine Woman. Samson fell in love with and married a Philistine woman. She enticed him into explaining a riddle he had put forth. While Samson was away slaying 30 men in Ashkelon, his wife was given to another man, "his companion, whom he had used as his friend." *(Judg. 14:1-20.)*

Her father was a Timnite. *(Judg. 15:6.)*

PHINEHAS (1). *Ex. 6:25; Num. 25:7-13, 15; 31:6; Josh. 22:13-34; 24:33; Judg. 20:28; 1 Chr. 6:4, 50; 9:20; Ezra 7:1-5; Ps. 106:30.*

Phinehas was the son of Eleazar and the grandson of Aaron. His maternal grandfather was Putiel. *(Ex. 6:25.)*

Phinehas followed Zimri into the tent when Zimri brought the Midianitish woman, Cozbi, unto his brethren, and saved the children of Israel from the plague by thrusting a javelin through Zimri and Cozbi. The Lord was pleased with Phinehas for being zealous "for his God" and the Lord gave unto him and unto his posterity a covenant of peace—the covenant of an everlasting priesthood. *(Num. 25:7-13, 15.)*

Phinehas was sent by Moses to war with the holy instruments and trumpets. *(Num. 31:6.)*

Phinehas and ten princes in Israel, each a chief of a tribe of Israel, were sent to the tribes of Reuben, Gad and the half tribe of Manasseh on the east side of Jordan because those two-and-a half tribes had built an altar and the children of Israel on the west side of Jordan feared they had fallen away from the Lord. Phinehas and the delegation reminded the tribes of Reuben, Gad and the half tribe of Manasseh that the Lord's wrath fell upon others beside Achan when Achan sinned and, thus, they feared for their own welfare if these tribes had fallen away as evidenced by their having built an altar. After learning that the altar was only a witness between the tribes on the two sides of Jordan that the Lord is God, Phinehas and the tribal princes were satisfied and returned to their own lands with a favorable report. *(Josh. 22:13-34.)*

Phinehas' father, Eleazar, was buried in a hill that belonged to Phinehas. *(Josh. 24:33.)*

When some wicked Benjamites living in Gibeah abused and killed a certain Levite's concubine and the other Benjamites refused to deliver the wicked men up to the tribes of Israel, Phinehas inquired of the Lord whether or not he should go again to battle against the children of Benjamin and the Lord told him to go—that they would be delivered into his hand on the morrow. *(Judg. 20:28.)*

Phinehas, son of Eleazar, begat Abishua. His genealogy is given. *(1 Chr. 6:4, 50.)* Phinehas' descendants through Ezra are listed with some modification from the listing in 1 Chr. 6:4-15. *(Ezra 7:1-5.)*

When Phinehas was ruler over the porters, the Lord was with him. *(1 Chr. 9:20.)*

Phinehas executed judgment and so the plague was stayed. *(Ps. 106:30.) (See Num. 25:7-13.)* (Chart 7b.)

PHINEHAS (2). *1 Sam. 1:3; 2:12, 22-25, 31-34; 4.*

Phinehas was a son of Eli, the high priest. *(1 Sam. 1:3.)* He and his brother Hophni were wicked. Because Eli tolerated their wickedness, the Lord rejected the house of Eli and told him that both of his sons would die in the same day. *(1 Sam. 2:12, 22-25, 31-34.)*

Phinehas and Hophni were killed in battle against the Philistines on the same day. The ark of God was also captured. When Eli heard, he fell off his seat backwards and died. Phinehas' wife died in childbirth when she heard that Phinehas and Eli were dead and that the ark had been taken. Phinehas' sono was named Ichabod. *(1 Sam. 4.)* (Chart 7b.)

PHINEHAS (3). *Ezra 8:2.*

Phinehas' descendant Gershom was the leader of his posterity when Ezra led many exiled Israelites out of Babylon back to Jerusalem when Artaxerxes was king of Babylon. Ezra discovered that none of the sons of Levi was among this group *(Ezra 8:15)*.

PHINEHAS (4). *Ezra 8:33.*

Phinehas, a Levite, was the father of Eleazar, which Eleazar was with Meremoth and other Levites as the gold, silver and vessels brought by Ezra from Babylon were weighed in the house of God.

PHURAH. *Judg. 7:10.*

Phurah was Gideon's servant. He accompanied Gideon to scout out the Midianites and the Amalekites whom the Lord said He would deliver into Gideon's hands.

PHUT (Put). *Gen. 10:6; 1 Chr. 1:8; Nahum 3:9-19.*

Phut (Put) was a son of Ham and a grandson of Noah. His brothers were Cush, Mizraim and Canaan. *(Gen. 10:6; 1 Chr. 1:8.)*

Nahum pointed out to the people of Ninevah that Put and Lubim had helped No, but the city was still destroyed and the people taken captive. Ninevah's fate would be the same. *(Nahum 3:9-19.)* (Chart 2e.)

PHUVAH (Pua, Puah, Punites). *Gen. 46:13; Num. 26:23; 1 Chr. 7:1.*

Phuvah (Puah) was a son of Issachar. His brothers were Tola, Job (Jashub) and Shimron. *(Gen. 46:13; 1 Chr. 7:1.)* **Pua**'s (Phuvah's) descendants were called **Punites**. *(Num. 26:23.)* (Chart 9a.)

PILDASH. *Gen. 22:22.*

Pildash was one of Nahor and Milcah's children. (Chart 2c.)

PILEHA. *Neh. 10:24 (1, 24, 28-31).*

Pileha was among those chief of the people who covenanted to marry in Israel, honor the Sabbath, pay tithes and keep the commandments.

PILTAI. *Neh. 12:17.*

Piltai, son of Moadiah, was one of the priests who was a chief of the fathers in the days of Joiakim.

PINON. *Gen. 36:41.*

Pinon was one of the dukes (tribal chiefs) who came of Esau. (Chart 19.)

PIRAM. *Josh. 10:1-27.*

Piram, one of the five kings of the Amorites, was king of Jarmuth. He and the other kings united in battle against the Israelites. His people were destroyed, partly by the sword but mostly by hailstones the Lord poured down upon them. He hid in a cave with the other four kings. Joshua had a stone rolled in front of the cave until the rest of the Amorites were destroyed. Then he had the kings brought out to him. They were all slain and hung on a tree. Their bodies were then cast into the cave wherein they had hidden themselves and the cave was sealed shut.

PIRATHONITE. *Judg. 12:13; 2 Sam. 23:30; 1 Chr. 27:14.*

Pirathonites were one of the groups of Israelites. Abdon, son of Hillel, was a Pirathonite who judged Israel eight years. *(Judg. 12:13.)*

Benaiah the Pirathonite was one of David's mighty men. *(2 Sam. 23:30.)* He was of the children of Ephraim and was assigned by David to be captain for the course of 24,000 that served for the eleventh month. *(1 Chr. 27:14.)*

PISPAH. *1 Chr. 7:38.*

Pispah was a son of Jether. His brothers were Jephunneh and Ara. He was a descendant of Asher. (Chart 14b.)

PITHON. *1 Chr. 8:35; 1 Chr. 9:41.*

Pithon, of the tribe of Benjamin, was one of the sons of Micah, was a great-grandson of Jonathan and a great-great-grandson of Saul. His brothers were Melech, Tarea (Tahrea) and Ahaz. (Chart 16 l.)

POCHERETH OF ZEBAIM. *Ezra 2:57-58; Neh. 7:59-60.*

Pochereth of Zebaim was one of Solomon's servants. The children of Solomon's servants and the Nethinims numbered 392 when they went up out of capitivity after having been carried away by Nebuchadnezzar.

PORATHA. *Esth. 9:8, 10.*

Poratha was one of Haman's ten sons who was slain by the Jews and, at queen Esther's request, hung on the gallows by king Ahasuerus.

PORTER. *2 Kgs. 7:10-11.*

The **Porter** of the city of Samaria was informed by four leprous men that the Syrian camp was void of people but full of goods. The porters informed the king. Thus, the king had the goods retrieved and the famine in Samaria was ended.

POTIPHAR. *Gen. 37:36; 39:1, 4, 19-20.*

Potiphar was one of Pharaoh's officers in Egypt and captain of Pharaoh's guard. He bought Joseph from a group of Ishmeelites or Midianite merchantmen. *(Gen. 37:36.)*

Potiphar purchased Joseph from the Ishmeelites and made him overseer of all he had. When his wife claimed Joseph tried to lie with her, Potiphar was angry and had Joseph put into prison. *(Gen. 39:1, 4, 19-20.)*

POTIPHAR'S WIFE. *Gen. 39:7-20.*

Potiphar's Wife tried to get Joseph to lie with her. When he repeatedly refused and fled from her, leaving his coat in her hand, she cried that he had tried to lie with her. Because of her lies, Potiphar had Joseph cast into prison.

POTIPHERAH. *Gen. 41:45.*

Potipherah was priest of On and father of Asenath, Joseph's wife, whom Pharaoh gave unto Joseph.

PRIESTS. *Ezra 8:30; 9:1; 10:18-19; Neh. 3:28; 11:12.*

The **Priests** and the Levites carried the silver, gold and precious vessels to Jerusalem unto the house of God and delivered them there. *(Ezra 8:30.)*

Many of the people of Israel, including priests and Levites, intermarried with the Canaanites, Hittites and other abominable groups, causing Ezra to pray to the Lord, confessing the sins of all the people. *(Ezra 9:1.)*

Those of the sons of the priests who had taken strange wives covenanted to put them away and separate themselves from them. *(Ezra 10:18-19.)*

When the children of Israel repaired the walls and gates of Jerusalem under the direction of Ezra and Nehemiah, the priests labored on the area that was over the horse gate. *(Neh. 3:28.)*

The priests who did the work of the house in Jerusalem following their captivity in Babylon totaled 822. *(Neh. 11:12.)*

PRIESTS OF THE SECOND ORDER (Zephaniah). *2 Kgs. 23:4; 25:18-21; Jer. 21:1-7; 29:25-29; 52:24-27.*

The **Priests of the Second Order**; Hilkiah, the high priest; and the keepers of the door were commanded by king Josiah to bring all the objects related to Baal out of the temple and destroy them. *(2 Kgs. 23:4.)*

Zephaniah was the second priest. He and three of the keepers of the door; Zeraiah, the chief priest; the principal scribe and several other men were captured by Nebuzar-adan, captain of Nebechadnezzar's guard, and taken to Nebechadnezzar who then slew them. *(2 Kgs. 25:18-21; Jer. 52:24-27.)*

Zephaniah was the son of Maaseiah the priest. When king Zedekiah sent Jeremiah to inquire of the priests whether or not the Lord would protect them against Nebuchadrezzar, king of Babylonia, who was threatening war against them, Jeremiah instructed Pashur and Zephaniah to tell Zedekiah that the Lord would not help them and that Jerusalem would be captured and destroyed by Nebuchadrezzar. Additionally, Zedekiah himself would be taken captive by Nebuchadrezzar. *(Jer. 21:1-7.)*

Shemaiah the Nehelamite sent a letter to Zephaniah and other priests claiming the Lord had made him priest in place of Jehoiada and that they should be officers in the house of the Lord. The letter also claimed Jeremiah was a false prophet. Zephaniah read the letter to Jeremiah who was instructed by the Lord to prophesy against Shemaiah because of his deceit. *(Jer. 29:25-29.)*

PRINCES OF SUCCOTH. See **Men of Succoth**.

PROPHET, A. *Judg. 6:8*.

A **Prophet** of the Lord was sent to Israel to chastise them for their rebellion when they cried unto Him because of the Midianites.

PROPHETESS, THE. *Isa. 8:3*.

The **Prophetess** was the wife of Isaiah and the mother of Maher-shalal-hash-baz.

PROPHET OF GOD. *2 Chr. 25:15*.

A **Prophet of God** was sent to Amaziah who chastised him for worshipping the gods of other people which gods could not even deliver those people from out of Amaziah's hand. He foretold Amaziah of his pending destruction for worshipping these false gods.

PROPHET OF THE LORD. *1 Kgs. 20:13, 22, 28*.

A **Prophet of the Lord** came to Ahab and told him that the Lord would deliver the Syrians into his hand even though the Syrians' numbers were much greater than Israel's numbers because they boasted they could beat them on the plains since their God was just God of the hills.. The prophet told Ahab that the king of Syria would come against him again at the return of the year.

PROPHETS OF BAAL. *1 Kgs. 18:19-40*.

Prophets of Baal. Ahab had 450 prophets of Baal. Elijah challenged them to a contest to see whose god would send fire from heaven to consume their burnt offering. The prophets of Baal called upon Baal from morning until noon, but there was no answer. They cut themselves with knives and lancets until the blood gushed out upon them and continued to call upon Baal until the time of the offering of the evening sacrifice. Still no answer from Baal. Elijah taunted them by saying, "Cry aloud: for he is a god; either he is talking, or he is pursuing, or he is in a journey, or peradventure he sleepeth, and must be awaked." When Elijah called upon the Lord, fire came from heaven and consumed his sacrifice along with the wood, the stones and dust, and even lapped up the water that was in the trenches around the altar. Elijah had the prophets of Baal taken down from Mount Carmel to the brook Kishon where he slew them.

PUA. See **Phuvah**.

PUAH (1). *Ex. 1:15-21*.

Puah was a Hebrew midwife. Because she feared God, she did not obey Pharaoh's command to kill all Hebrew newborn sons. The Lord blessed her with descendants.

PUAH (2). *Judg. 10:1*.

Puah was the son of Dodo and the father of Tola, which Tola judged Israel following Abimelech. (Chart 9b.)

PUHITES. *1 Chr. 2:53*.

The **Puhites** came through Kirjath-jearim, son of Shobal who was a son of Hur and grandson of Caleb. (Chart 8 l.)

PUL (1). Also see **Telgath-pilneser**. *2 Kgs. 15:19-20; 1 Chr. 5:26.*

Pul was the king of Assyria from whom Menahem, king of Israel, "purchased" peace for a thousand talents of silver which he got by exacting the money from wealthy Israelites. *(2 Kgs. 15:19-20.)*

Pul and Tilgath-pilneser, kings of Assyria, carried the Reubenites, Gadites and the half tribe of Manasseh into captivity. *(1 Chr. 5:26.) (Note: The Bible Dictionary indicates that Pul and Tilgath-pilneser may be one and the same person.)*

PUL (2) (Put). *Isa. 66:19.*

Pul, Tarshish, Lud, Tubal, Javan and the isles far off will, in the latter days, have missionaries sent unto them by the Lord that His glory may be declared unto the Gentiles. *(The Bible Dictionary indicates this Pul may refer to Put.)*

PUNITES . See **Phuvah**.

PUT. See **Phut**.

PUTIEL. *Ex. 6:25.*

Putiel was the father of Eleazar's wife, Aaron's daughter-in-law.

NAMES THAT BEGIN WITH "Q"

QUEEN OF SHEBA. *1 Kgs. 10:1-13; 2 Chr. 9:1-12.*

The **Queen of Sheba** heard about Solomon's great wisdom and wealth and came to see for herself if what she had heard was true. After visiting with Solomon, the queen of Sheba acknowledged that "the half was not told me." She gave him gifts of gold and spices. Solomon gave unto her all her desire, "whatsoever she asked." And then she and her servants returned to their own country.

NAMES THAT BEGIN WITH "R"

RAAMAH. *Gen. 10:7; Ezek. 27:22.*

Raamah was a son of Cush, a grandson of Ham, and a great-grandson of Noah. *(Gen. 10:7.)* As Ezekiel lamented the fall of the great city of Tyrus, he bemoaned the loss of her riches and commerce, part of which involved the merchants of Raamah and Sheba who traded spices, precious stones and gold in the fairs at Tyrus. *(Ezek. 27:22.)* (Chart 2e.)

RAAMIAH. See **Reelaiah**.

RAB-MAG. *Jer. 39:3, 13.*

Rab-mag was one of the Babylonian princes who came in and sat in the middle gate of Jerusalem when Nebuchadnezzar and the Chaldean army took the city, slew Zedekiah's sons, put Zedekiah's eyes out and carried him to Babylon, burned the houses and broke down the walls of Jerusalem. Rab-mag, Nebushasban, Rab-saris, Nergal-sharezer, and all the king of Babylon's princes were instructed by Nebuzar-adan the captain of Nebuchadnezzar's guard to take Jeremiah out of the court of the prison and commit him unto Gedaliah the son of Ahikam the son of Shaphan. They were told to carry him home; thus, Jeremiah lived among the people.

RABSARIS (1). *2 Kgs. 18:17-37.*

Rabsaris was one of the men king Sennacherib of Assyria sent with Rab-shakeh and Tartan and his hosts against Jerusalem and king Hezekiah. They delivered a blasphemous speech to Hezekiah.

RAB-SARIS (2). *Jer. 39:3, 13.*

Rab-saris was one of the Babylonian princes who came in and sat in the middle gate of Jerusalem when Nebuchadnezzar and the Chaldean army took the city, slew Zedekiah's sons, put Zedekiah's eyes out and carried him to Babylon, burned the houses and broke down the walls of Jerusalem. Rab-saris, Nebushasban, Nergal-sharezer, Rab-mag, and all the king of Babylon's princes were instructed by Nebuzar-adan the captain of Nebuchadnezzar's guard to take Jeremiah out of the court of the prison and commit him unto Gedaliah the son of Ahikam the son of Shaphan. They were told to carry him home; thus, Jeremiah lived among the people.

RAB-SHAKEH (Rabshakeh). *2 Kgs. 18:17-37; 19:4, 8-13; Isa. 36; 37.*

Rab-shakeh was one of the men king Sennacherib of Assyria sent with his hosts against Jerusalem and king Hezekiah. In a blasphemous speech, Rab-shakeh arrogantly asked Jerusalem to surrender to the Assyrians and claimed their God could not save them any more than the gods of neighboring cities could save those cities. *(2 Kgs. 18:17-37; Isa. 36.)*

Rab-shakeh taunted Judah as he sought Judah's surrender and said that neither the king of Egypt nor their own God could save them any more than the gods of the neighboring cities could save those cities. *(2 Kgs. 19:4, 8-13; Isa. 37.)*

RACHEL (Rahel). *Gen. 29:6-31; 30:1-8, 14-21, 22-24; 31:4-14, 19, 22-35; 33:1-2, 7; 35:16-19, 24-25; 46:19-25; 48:7; 1 Sam. 10:2; Jer. 31:15-17.*

Rachel was Jacob's cousin. She was the daughter of Laban, Jacob's mother's brother. She first met Jacob by the well as she went there to water her father's sheep. Jacob watered them for her and told her who he was. He fell in love with Rachel and was willing to work for Laban seven years in order to have her for his wife. Laban deceived Jacob and gave him Leah, Rachel's elder sister, instead. However, after Jacob fulfilled Leah's week, Laban also gave Rachel to Jacob for a wife. Jacob loved Rachel more than Leah. "Leah was tender eyed; but Rachel was beautiful and well favoured" *(Gen. 29:16)*. Rachel's father gave her his handmaid Bilhah to be her maid. Rachel was barren. *(Gen. 29:6-31.)*

Rachel, unhappy that she was barren, gave her handmaid Bilhah unto Jacob for a wife so she could have children through her. Bilhah begat two sons: Dan and Naphtali. Rachel asked Leah to share her son's mandrakes with her. Leah countered that she had taken her husband from her and now she wanted to take her son's mandrakes from her too. Rachel offered to have Jacob lie with her in return for the mandrakes. Rachel was finally blessed with a son. She named him Joseph. *(Gen. 30:1-8, 14-21, 22-24.)*

Jacob reviewed with Rachel and Leah their father's unfair dealings with him and told them God had instructed him to take his family back to his own kindred and land. They wondered if there was any portion of inheritance for them in their father's house. Jacob took his family and left Laban without telling him they were going. Laban discovered they were gone and pursued them. When Laban caught up with them he asked for an explanation and also wanted to know why they had stolen his gods. Not knowing Rachel had taken them, Jacob said that whoever had them should die. Laban searched the tents for his gods but did not find them. Rachel had hidden her father's idols in the camel's furniture and sat upon them. She apologized for not getting down to greet him but said that "the custom of women" was upon her. *(Gen. 31:4-14, 19, 22-35.)*

As Jacob and his family traveled home, Esau and a group of 400 men came to meet them. Jacob divided his family according to their mothers, with the handmaidens and their children in front, then Leah and her children, and finally Rachel and Joseph. They all greeted Esau with a bow. *(Gen. 33:1-2, 7.)*

Rachel and Jacob had a second son, Benjamin. It was a difficult labor. Rachel called him Ben-oni. She died in childbirth and was buried "in the way to Ephrath, which is Beth-lehem." In addition to the two sons Rachel had, her handmaid Bilhah had two sons: Dan and Naphtali, which were accounted unto Rachel as her sons. *(Gen. 35:16-19, 24-25.)*

Rachel bore Joseph and Benjamin. Their sons are listed. Bilhah bore Dan and Naphtali. Their sons are listed. All the sons (and grandsons) accounted unto Rachel were 14. *(Gen. 46:19-25.)*

Rachel died in the land of Canaan and was buried "in the way of Ephrath; the same is Bethlehem." *(Gen. 48:7.)*

One of the signs the prophet Samuel gave Saul when he anointed him to be captain over the Lord's inheritance was that Saul would find two men by Rachel's sepulchre and they would tell him that the asses he was seeking were found. *(1 Sam. 10:2.)*

Rachel's name is given as **Rahel**. Israel will be gathered in the latter days and Rachel's "weeping for her children . . . because they were not" will cease and she will be comforted. *(Jer. 31:15-17.)* (Charts 2c.; 3d.)

RADDAI. *1 Chr. 2:14.*

Raddai, Jesse's fifth son, was one of David's elder brothers. (Charts 8d-e.)

RAGUEL. See **Jethro**.

RAHAB. *Josh 2:1-21; 6:17, 22-23, 25.*

Rahab was a harlot in Jericho who received and concealed the two Israelite spies Joshua sent to scout out the land. When the king sent word for her to send the men out, she said they had left by the gate, but they were hidden on her roof. In return for her helping them, she asked the spies that she and her family be spared when the Israelites destroyed Jericho. They agreed to her request. *(Josh 2:1-21.)*

Prior to destroying Jericho, Joshua had the two spies bring Rahab and her family out. *(Josh. 6:17, 22-23, 25.)*

RAHAM. *1 Chr. 2:44.*

Raham was the son of Shema who was one of the sons of Hebron. He begat Jorkoam. (Chart 8i.)

RAHEL. See **Rachel**.

RAKEM. *1 Chr. 7:16.*

Rakem was a son of Peresh (who may be the same as Gilead), a grandson of Machir, and a great-grandson of Manasseh. His brother was Ulam. (Chart 15b.)

RAM (1). *Ruth 4:19; 1 Chr. 2:9-15, 21, 24, 42.*

Ram was the son of Hezron, a grandson of Pharez and a great-grandson of Judah. He begat Amminadab, Aaron's father-in-law. *(Ruth 4:19.)*

Ram's brothers were Jerahmeel, Chelubai (Caleb), Segub and Ashur. Jesse, the father of David came through Ram's line. Ram begat Amminadab who begat Nahshon (Naashon), who begat Salma (Salmon), who begat Boaz, who begat Obed, who begat Jesse, who begat David. *(1 Chr. 2:9-15, 21, 24, 42.)* (Charts 1.; 8c-d, h.)

RAM (2). *1 Chr. 2:25-27.*

Ram was Jerahmeel's firstborn son. He was the great-great-grandson of Judah. His brothers were Bunah, Oren, Ozem and Ahijah. His half-brother was Onam. Ram begat Maaz, Jamin and Eker. (Chart 8c.)

RAM (3). *Job 32:2.*

Ram was an ancestor of Barachel the Buzite the father of Elihu.

RAMAH. *Ezra 2:26; Neh. 7:30.*

Ramah was of the people of Israel. The men of the children of Ramah and Gaba who returned to Jerusalem from Babylon after Cyrus' proclamation to build the temple numbered 621.

RAMATHITE. *1 Chr. 27:27.*

Ramathite. Shimei, who served king David by being over the vineyards, was a Ramathite.

RAMIAH. *Ezra 10:25 (18-19, 25, 44).*

Ramiah was of the sons of Parosh. He was among those who had taken wives from among the Canaanites or other foreign groups but who agreed to Ezra's request that they separate themselves from these strange wives lest the Lord destroy the rest of the children of Israel.

RAMOTH. *Ezra 10:29 (18-19, 29, 44).*

Ramoth, a son of Bani, was one of the Israelites who took foreign wives, causing Ezra to cry unto the Lord in behalf of Israel, fearing that the Lord would totally destroy the children of Israel due to this latest iniquity. Ramoth and his brothers agreed to put away their foreign wives.

RAPHA (1). *1 Chr. 8:2.*

Rapha was the fifthborn son of Benjamin. His brothers were Bela, the firstborn; Ashbel, the secondborn; Aharah, the third; and Nohah, the fourth. *(Note: Benjamin's sons are listed with different names in other scriptures.)* (Chart 16d.)

RAPHA (2) (Rephaiah (4)). *1 Chr. 8:37; 9:43.*

Rapha (Rephaiah), the son of Binea, was from the tribe of Benjamin. He descended through Saul through Jonathan. He begat Eleasah. *(1 Chr. 8:37; 9:43.)* (Chart 16 l.)

RAPHU. *Num. 13:9 16, 31-33; 14:37.*

Raphu, of the tribe of Benjamin, was the father of Palti, which Palti was sent by Moses as one of the 12 spies to search the land of Canaan. He returned with a negative report. *(Num. 13:9 16, 31-33.)* Those who returned with a negative report died by the plague before the Lord. *(Num. 14:37.)* (Chart 16f.)

REAIA. *1 Chr. 5:5.*

Reaia, of the tribe of Reuben, was the son of Micah and the father of Baal. (Chart 5b.)

REAIAH (1). *1 Chr. 4:2.*

Reaiah, a descendant of Judah, was the son of Shobal and the father of Jahath. (Chart 8m.)

REAIAH (2). *Ezra 2:47, 58; Neh. 7:50, 60.*

Reaiah was a Nethinim. When the Nethinims and the children of Solomon's servants left Babylon to return to Jerusalem to build the house of the Lord as proclaimed by Cyrus, king of Persia, they numbered 392.

REBA. *Num. 31:8; Josh. 13:21.*

Reba was one of five Midianite kings slain by the children of Israel when Moses sent an army of 12,000 men to destroy the Midianites.

REBEKAH. *Gen. 22:23; 24:15-67; 25:21-26, 26:7-8, 35. 28; 27; 28:5; 29:12; 49:31.*

Rebekah was the daughter of Bethuel, sister of Laban, the granddaughter of Nahor and Milcah, and the grandniece of Abraham. *(Gen. 22:23.)*

When Abraham's servant went to Mesopotamia to find a wife for Isaac, Rebekah gave him water and offered to water his camels as well. Her actions were a signal from the Lord to the servant that she was the one appointed to be Isaac's wife. She agreed to return with the servant unto Abraham's house. She took her nurse and some damsels with her. As they neared the end of their return journey, she saw Isaac approaching the caravan. She got off the camel and covered herself with a veil. Isaac took her into his mother's tent and Rebekah became his wife. *(Gen. 24:15-67.)*

Because Rebekah was barren, Isaac entreated the Lord in her behalf and she conceived. She gave birth to twins: Esau and Jacob, Esau being born first. Prior to their birth, the Lord told Rebekah that she would have twins—that the posterity of one would be stronger than the posterity of the other—and that the elder would serve the younger. Rebekah favored Jacob over Esau. Her husband Isaac was 60 years old when the babies were born. *(Gen. 25:21-26, 28.)*

When the men of Gerar inquired of Isaac regarding Rebekah, he said she was his sister rather than his wife for fear the men would kill him in order to have Rebekah. However, king Abimelech saw Isaac "sporting" with Rebekah and told him that surely Rebekah was his wife, and he inquired as to the deceit. Rebekah and Isaac were grieved with Esau's taking wives from among the Hittite women. *(Gen. 26:7-8, 35.)*

When Rebekah overheard Isaac's plans to give the birthright blessing to Esau, she had Jacob pretend to be Esau and trick Isaac into giving the blessing to him instead. This he did. When Esau learned that the blessing had been given to Jacob, he hated Jacob and planned to kill him as soon as his father died. When Rebekah learned of his plan, she instructed Jacob to flee to Haran unto her brother Laban until such time that it would be safe for him to return. Rebekah was "weary" of her life because of Esau's wives. She told Isaac that if Jacob were to marry any of the daughters of Heth, her life would have been in vain. *(Gen. 27.)*

Rebekah, mother of Jacob and Esau, was Laban's sister. Isaac and Rebekah sent Jacob to Laban to find a wife. *(Gen. 28:5.)*

When Jacob met Rachel, he told her that he was Rebekah's son. *(Gen. 29:12.)*

Rebekah was buried in the cave in the field of Machpelah along with Abraham, Sarah and Isaac. *(Gen. 49:31.)* (Chart 2c.)

REBEKAH'S NURSE. See **Deborah (1)**.

RECHAB (1). *2 Sam. 4:2, 5-12.*

Rechab, a Beerothite from the tribe of Benjamin, was one of Saul's captains and one of Rimmon's sons. He and his brother, Baanah, crept into Saul's son Ish-bosheth's house and slew him while he was sleeping. They beheaded him and took his head to David. David commanded his men to slay these two unrighteous men. After slaying them, David's men cut off their hands and feet and hanged them up over the pool in Hebron.

RECHAB (2) (Rechabites). *2 Kgs. 10:15; 1 Chr. 2:55; Jer. 35:2, 6-19.*

Rechab was the father of Jehonadab (Jonadab). *(2 Kgs. 10:15.)*

The families of the scribes which dwelt at Jabez included the Tirathites, Shimeathites and Suchathites. They were Kenites who came of Hemath, the father of the house of Rechab. *(1 Chr. 2:55.)*

Rechab's descendants were called **Rechabites**. Because they kept the counsel of his son Jonadab to live in tents and drink no wine, they were commended and blessed by the Lord for their obedience. The Lord said, "Jonadab the son of Rechab shall not want a man to stand before me for ever." Because they feared Nebuchadnezzar and the armies of the Chaldeans and Syrians, they went to live in Jerusalem. *(Jer. 35.2, 6-19.)*

RECHAB (3). *Neh. 3:14.*

Rechab, ruler of part of Beth-haccerem, was the father of Malchiah, which Malchiah repaired the dung gate.

RECHABITES. See **Rechab (2)**.

RECHAH. *1 Chr. 4:12.*

The "men of **Rechah**" included Eshton and his sons Beth-rapha, Paseah and Tehinnah, the father of Irnahash.

REELAIAH (Raamiah). *Ezra 2:2; Neh. 7:7.*

REELAIAH (Raamiah) was one of the people who went with Zerubbabel back to Jerusalem following king Cyrus' proclamation to build the temple there.

REGEM. *1 Chr. 2:47.*

Regem was one of the sons of Jahdai. (Chart 8j.)

REGEM-MELECH. *Zech. 7:2-7.*

Regem-melech and Sherezer and their men were sent unto the house of the Lord to pray. Zechariah was moved to reprove them for their hypocrisy because they weren't really fasting and praying unto the Lord.

REHABIAH. *1 Chr. 23:17 (6, 14, 15, 17); 24:21, 31; 26:25.*

Rehabiah was the son of Eliezer and the grandson of Moses. He had no brothers but many sons. When David numbered the Levites at the time he made Solomon king, he divided them into courses among the sons of Levi. Moses' sons were named of the tribe of Levi. Rehabiah was the chief of his course. *(1 Chr. 23:17 [6, 14, 15, 17].)*

Rehabiah, a Levite, was a descendant of Amram and an ancestor of Isshiah. He, and others of the tribe of Levi, cast lots for his course in the presence of king David,

Zadok, Ahimelech and the chief of the fathers of the priests and Levites. *(1 Chr. 24:21, 31.)*

Rehabiah's son was Jeshaiah. *(1 Chr. 26:25.)* (Chart 7b.)

REHOB (1). *2 Sam. 8:3.*

Rehob was the father of Hadadezer.

REHOB (2). *Neh. 10:11 (1, 11, 28-31).*

Rehob, a Levite, was among those who covenanted and sealed their covenant to marry in Israel, honor the Sabbath, pay tithes and keep the commandments.

REHOBOAM. *1 Kgs. 11:43; 12:1-24; 14:21-31; 15:1, 6; 1 Chr. 3:10; 2 Chr. 9:31; 10; 11:1-4; 12; 13:7.*

Rehoboam was Solomon's son who reigned after Solomon's death. *(1 Kgs. 11:43; 2 Chr. 9:31.)*

Rehoboam went to Shechem to be made king. Jeroboam came from Egypt and spoke to Rehoboam asking him to make their yoke light. If Rehoboam did, Jeroboam said they would be glad to serve him. Rehoboam asked the old men for advice and they said he should make their yoke light so they would be happy to serve him. Rehoboam then asked the young men who had grown up with him what they thought. They said to make their yoke heavy. He followed their advice. This was "for the cause of the Lord" so that the promise Ahijah had made to Jeroboam would come to pass. Ten tribes followed Jeroboam. Rehoboam reigned over the tribe of Judah. Rehoboam sent Adoram (Hadoram), who was over the tribute, to collect from the people. The people stoned Adoram to death so Rehoboam fled to Jerusalem. Rehoboam gathered an army together of the house of Judah and the tribe of Benjamin to fight against Israel so as to regain the kingdom. However, the Lord spoke to Rehoboam through Shemaiah, "the man of God," and told him not to fight against the children of Israel, his brethren. He followed Shemaiah's counsel. *(1 Kgs. 12:1-24; 2 Chr. 10; 2 Chr. 11:1-4 is a repeat of 1 Kgs. 12:21-24.)*

Rehoboam was 41 years old when he began to reign over Judah. He reigned 17 years. His mother was Naamah, an Ammonitess. Rehoboam built "high places, and images, and groves, on every high hill, and under every green tree. And there were also sodomites in the land: and they did according to all the abominations of the nations which the Lord cast out before the children of Israel." During the fifth year of his reign, Shishak, king of Egypt, came against Rehoboam and took the treasures from the temple. There was war between Rehoboam and Jeroboam all their days. The rest of the acts of Rehoboam are recorded in the book of the chronicles of the kings of Judah. He died and was buried with his fathers in the city of David. His son Abijam (Abijah) reigned in his stead. *(1 Kgs. 14:21-31; Also see 2 Chr. 12.)*

Rehoboam's wife was Maachah, the daughter of Abishalom (Absalom). Rehoboam and Jeroboam were at war with each other all the days of Abijam's life. *(1 Kgs. 15:1, 6.)*

Rehoboam's father was Solomon. His son was Abia (Abijam, Abijah). *(1 Chr. 3:10.)*

The priests and the Levites and all who set their hearts to seek the God of Israel left Jeroboam and went to Rehoboam as Jeroboam led the children of Israel into idolatry. Rehoboam and his people walked in the way of David and Solomon three years. Rehoboam had 18 wives and 60 concubines. He begat 28 sons and 60 daughters. Of all his wives, he loved Maachah, the daughter of Absalom, the best. He made her son Abijah the chief ruler among them because he planned to eventually make Abijah king. He dispersed his children throughout all the countries of Judah and Benjamin. *(2 Chr. 11:5-23.)*

(2 Chr. 12 is a retelling of 1 Kgs. 14:25-31, with slight modification.) Rehoboam forsook the law of the Lord and took all Israel with him. In the fifth year of Rehoboam's reign, the Lord allowed Shishak, king of Egypt to go against Jerusalem. Shishak took the fenced cities that pertained to Judah. The prophet Shemaiah chastised Rehoboam and the princes of Judah, who were gathered together at Jerusalem, and told them that the Lord had forsaken them because they had forsaken the Lord. Therefore, they had been left in the hand of Shishak. The king and the princes humbled themselves so the Lord had Shemaiah tell them He would not destroy them, but would grant them some deliverance. Nevertheless, they would be the servants of Shishak. Rehoboam strengthened himself in Jerusalem and reigned 17 years, beginning when he was 41 years old. His mother Naamah was an Ammonitess. He did evil because he did not seek the Lord with his heart. He died and was buried in the city of David. His son Abijah reigned in his stead. *(2 Chr. 12.)*

The people had rebelled against Rehoboam when he was young and tenderhearted and Abijah condemned them for following Jeroboam, the son of Solomon's servant Nebat. *(2 Chr. 13:7.)* (Charts 1.; 8f.)

REHUM (1) (Nehum). *Ezra 2:2; Neh. 7:7; 12:3.*

Rehum (Nehum) was one of the people who left Babylon and went with Zerubbabel back to Jerusalem following king Cyrus' proclamation to build the temple there.

REHUM (2). *Ezra 4:8-9, 17-23.*

Rehum, a Samaritan, was the chancellor. He and Shimshai, the scribe, wrote a letter against Jerusalem and the Samaritans sent it to Artaxerxes, king of Persia. When they received Artaxerxes' return letter commanding them to cause the construction to cease, they and their companions went to Jerusalem and, using force and power, stopped the building of the temple.

REHUM (3). *Neh. 3:17; 10:25 (1, 25, 28-31).*

Rehum, a Levite, son of Bani, labored between Nehemiah, son of Azbuk, and Hashabiah, ruler of the half part of Keilah, when the children of Israel rebuilt the walls and gates of Jerusalem during the time of Ezra and Nehemiah. *(Neh. 3:17.)*

Rehum was among those chief of the people who covenanted to marry in Israel, honor the Sabbath, pay tithes and keep the commandments. *(Neh. 10:25 [1, 25, 28-31].)*

REI. *1 Kgs. 1:8.*

Rei, along with Zadok the priest, Benaiah the son of Jehoiada, Nathan the prophet, and Shimei, did not support Adonijah in his attempt to take the kingdom away from David.

REKEM (1). *Num. 31:8; Josh. 13:21.*

Rekem was one of five Midianite kings slain by the children of Israel when Moses sent an army of 12,000 men to destroy the Midianites.

REKEM (2). *1 Chr. 2:43.*

Rekem was one of the sons of Hebron. His brothers were Korah, Tappuah and Shema. (Chart 8i.)

REMALIAH. *2 Kgs. 15:25; 2 Chr. 28:6; Isa. 7:1.*

Remaliah was the father of Pekah, which Pekah and cohorts slew Pekahiah, king over Israel. *(2 Kgs. 15:25.)*

Remaliah was the father of Pekah, king of Israel. *(2 Chr. 28:6; Isa. 7:1.)*

REPHAEL. *1 Chr. 26:7 (4, 6-7, 12).*

Rephael, a Levite of the lineage of Obed-edom, was a son of Shemaiah. Shemaiah's other sons were Othni, Obed, Elzabad, Elihu and Semachiah. They, along with other Levites, were appointed by king David to be porters—to have charge of the treasures, serve as officers and judges, and to conduct the outward business over Israel. (Chart 7c.)

REPHAH. *1 Chr. 7:25.*

Rephah was the son of Beriah and the grandson of Ephraim. (Chart 15d.)

REPHAIAH (1). *1 Chr. 3:21.*

Rephaiah, a descendant of David, was a son of Jesaiah. (Chart 1.)

REPHAIAH (2). *1 Chr. 4:42-43.*

Rephaiah, son of Ishi, was one of the captains who led a group of 500 men, including some of the sons of Simeon, to mount Seir where they smote the rest of the Amalekites who had escaped from earlier conflicts. His brothers were Pelatiah, Neariah and Uzziel. (Chart 6b.)

REPHAIAH (3). *1 Chr. 7:2.*

Rephaiah was the son of Tola and the grandson of Issachar. His brothers were Uzzi, Jeriel, Jahmai, Jibsam and Shemuel. (Chart 9a.)

REPHAIAH (4). *1 Chr. 9:43.* See **Rapha (2)**.

REPHAIAH (5). *Neh. 3:9.*

Rephaiah was the son of Hur, the ruler of the half part of Jerusalem. He worked next to Hananiah when the children of Israel rebuilt the walls and gates of Jerusalem during the time of Ezra and Nehemiah.

REPHAIMS. *Gen. 14:5, 11-12; 15:19-21; Josh. 12:4; 13:12.*

The **Rephaims** were in Ashteroth Karnaim and were smitten by Chedorlaomer and the kings who were with him at the time they conquered Sodom and Gomorrah and took Lot captive. *(Gen. 14:5, 11-12.)*

The Rephaims' lands were among the lands given to Abram's seed by the Lord in covenant. *(Gen. 15:19-21.)*

The Rephaims were apparently giants, as the land given to the children of Israel included "the coast of Og king of Bashan, which was of the remnant of the giants, that dwelt at Ashtaroth and at Edrei." *(Josh. 12:4; 13:12.)*

RESHEPH. *1 Chr. 7:25.*

Resheph was a son f Beriah, grandson of Ephraim, and the father of Telah. (Chart 15d.)

REU. *Gen. 11:18-21.*

Reu was the son of Peleg, a third-great-grandson of Shem and a fourth-great-grandson of Noah. He begat Serug. He lived 239 years. (Charts 1.; 2b.; 21.)

REUBEN (Reubenites). *Gen. 29:32; 30:14; 35:22-26; 37; 42:22; 46:9; 49:1, 3-4; 50:8; Num. 1:5, 20-21; 2:10-16; 26:5-7; 32; Deut. 3:12-17; 27:13; 29:7-9; 33:6; Josh. 4:12; 13:15-23; 18:7; 22:1-28; 1 Chr. 5:1-8, 18-22, 25-26; 12:37; 27:16; Ezek. 48:6, 31.*

Reuben was the firstborn son of Jacob and Leah. *(Gen. 29:32.)*

Reuben found mandrake in the field and brought some to his mother, Leah. *(Gen. 30:14.) (Note: The dictionary states that mandrake was a poisonous plant that was formerly used in medicine for its narcotic and emetic properties. Because they thought the root resembled the human shape, there was also a belief that it held magical powers.)*

Reuben lay with Bilhah, Jacob's concubine. His brothers and half-brothers are listed. *(Gen. 35:22-26.)*

Reuben and his brothers despised Joseph because their father loved him more than he loved them. When Joseph was sent by Jacob to see how they were doing as they tended the flocks in Shechem, the brothers discussed killing him. However, when Reuben heard about it, he suggested that instead of killing Joseph they could just cast him into a nearby pit. He planned to return to the pit later, rescue Joseph, and return him to their father. Unbeknownst to him, however, when a group of Ishmeelites or Midianite merchantmen approached, the brothers, following a suggestion by Judah, decided to sell Joseph to them. Thus, when Reuben returned to get Joseph, he was gone. As Reuben wondered what he should do, the brothers decided to dip Joseph's coat of many colors in animal blood and give it to their father so he would assume Joseph had been killed by wild beasts. *(Gen. 37.)*

When the brothers went to Egypt to purchase food during the famine, Joseph, through his interpreter, accused them of being spies. The brothers anguished over the accusation and felt guilty because of what they had done to Joseph. Reuben reminded his brothers that he had told them not to sin against the child. *(Gen. 42:22.)*

Reuben begat Hanoch, Phallu (Pallu), Hezron and Carmi. *(Gen. 46:9.)*

After the brothers had gone to Egypt for grain and were finally reunited with Joseph, and following their moving their entire family to Egypt, the time came when Jacob called his sons together to tell them what would befall each of them in the last days. To Reuben, he said, "Reuben, thou art my firstborn, my might and the beginning of my strength, the excellency of dignity, and the excellency of power: Unstable as water, thou shalt not excel; because thou wentest up to thy father's bed; then defiledst thou it: he went up to my couch." *(Gen. 49:1, 3-4.)*

The brothers all went together to carry their father's body back to Canaan to be buried. *(Gen. 50:8.)*

The Lord instructed Moses to appointed Elizur, son of Shedeur, to head the tribe of Reuben as they prepared for war. The males of the tribe of Reuben who were 20 years old and over numbered 46,500. *(Num. 1:5, 20-21.)*

The camp of the armies of Reuben was "far off about the tabernacle of the congregation" on the south side of the tabernacle. The tribes of Simeon and Gad were pitched next to the tribe of Reuben. Thus, the men in the camp of Reuben numbered 151,450. *(Num. 2:10-16.)*

While on the plains of Moab near Jericho, Moses and Eleazar were instructed by the Lord to count all the males, excluding the Levites, who were 20 years old and older. These included the families of Hanoch (Hanochites), Pallu (Pallluites), Hezron (Hezronites) and Carmi (Carmites). The **Reubenites** numbered 43,730. *(Num. 26:5-7.)*

Reuben's posterity and Gad's posterity asked Moses if they could have the land east of Jordan for their inheritance. Moses told them that they could have it only if they would join the other tribes in conquering Canaan. They covenanted to do so. The land was divided between the Reubenites, Gadites and half of Manasseh's tribe. *(Num. 32.)*

Moses reminded Israel that the Lord delivered Og, king of Bashan, and Sihon, king of Heshbon, into their hands and their land had been divided between the Reubenites, Gadites and half of the tribe of Manasseh. *(Deut. 3:12-17.)*

As the children of Israel crossed over Jordan into Canaan to inherit the promised land, the tribes of Reuben, Gad, Asher, Zebulun, Dan and Naphtali were instructed to stand upon mount Ebal to curse. *(Deut. 27:13.)*

Moses reiterated that the lands of Sihon and Og had been given to the tribes of Reuben, Gad and half of Manasseh. He instructed the Reubenites, Gadites, and the half tribe of Manasseh to keep the words of the covenants so they may prosper in all that they do. *(Deut. 29:7-9.)*

Prior to Moses' being taken up by the Lord, he blessed the tribes of Israel. Of Reuben, he said, "Let Reuben live, and not die; and let not his men be few." *(Deut. 33:6.)*

The children of Reuben and Gad and the half tribe of Manasseh passed over Jordan, armed before the children of Israel, as Moses spoke to them. *(Josh. 4:12.)*

The land given to Reuben's posterity for an inheritance is outlined. *(Josh. 13:15-23.)*

Reuben's inheritance, and that of Gad and the half tribe of Manasseh, was on the east side of Jordan. *(Josh. 18:7.)*

After the rest of the tribes of Israel had received their inheritances, the tribes of Reuben, Gad and the half tribe of Manasseh were dismissed and allowed to return to their own lands on the other side of Jordan.They built an altar to be a witness between the two-and-a-half tribes on the east of Jordan and the other tribes on the west side of Jordan and the generations that would follow so no one in future times could say they had no part in the Lord. *(Josh. 22:1-28.)*

Reuben defiled his father's bed and lost the birthright which was given to the sons of Joseph. His sons were Hanoch, Pallu, Hezron and Carmi. His posterity included Joel, Joel's son Shemaiah, Shemaiah's son Micah, Micah's son Reaia, Reaia's son Baal, Baal's son Beerah. Chief among the descendants of Reuben were Jeiel and Zechariah and Bela the son of Azaz who was the son of Shema who was the son of Joel. Beerah, prince of the Reubenites, was carried away captive by Tilgathpilneser, king of Assyria. Reuben's genealogy was reckoned in the days of Jotham, king of Judah, and Jeroboam, king of Israel. His sons combined with the sons of Gad and half the tribe of Manasseh, numbered 44,760 who were skillful with buckler and sword and in the art of war. They made war with the Hagarites, with Jetur and Nephish and Nodab. The Reubenites, Gadites, and half the tribe of Manasseh became wicked and transgressed the laws of God. Thus, God stirred up the Assyrian kings Pul and Tilgath-pilneser and they carried them away. *(1 Chr. 5:1-8, 18-22, 25-26.)*

When David became king and went to Ziklag, all Israel rejoiced. The tribes sent their armies to assist David. The Reubenites, Gadites and the half tribe of Manasseh sent 120,000 men. *(1 Chr. 12:37.)*

Ruler of the Reubenites when David was king and the princes of the tribes of Israel were set forth was Eliezer, the son of Zichri. *(1 Chr. 27:16.)*

The Lord revealed to Ezekiel just how the land should be divided by tribes when the children of Israel are gathered in the latter days. Reuben's portion will be by the border of Ephraim, from the east side even unto the west side. The twelve gates of the city will bear the names of the twelve sons of Jacob. One of the three gates northward will be named for Reuben. *(Ezek. 48:6, 31.)* (Charts 1.; 3d.; 5a-b.; 6a.; 7a.; 8a.; 9a.; 10a.; 11a.; 12a.; 13a.; 14a.; 15a.; 16a.)

REUEL (1). *Gen. 36:4-5, 13; 1 Chr. 1:35, 37.*

Reuel was a son of Bashemath and Esau. His half-brothers were Eliphaz, Jeush, Jaalam and Korah. He begat Nahath, Zerah, Shammah and Mizzah. *(Gen. 36:4-5, 13; 1 Chr. 1:35, 37.)* (Chart 3b-c.)

REUEL (2). *Ex. 2:18.* See **Jethro**.

REUEL (3). *Num. 2:14.* See **Deuel**.

REUEL (4). *1 Chr. 9:8.*

Reuel, of the tribe of Benjamin, was the father of Shephathiah and the son of Ibnijah. His family's genealogy was written in the book of the kings of Israel and Judah who were carried away to Babylon for their transgression. He was among those of Benjamin who were the first inhabitants to dwell in Jerusalem after returning from captivity. (Chart 16m.)

REUMAH. *Gen. 22:24.*

Reumah, Nahor's concubine, bore: Tebah, Gaham, Thahash, Maachah. (Chart 2d.)

REZIA. *1 Chr. 7:39.*

Rezia, a descendant of Asher, was a son of Ulla. His brothers were Arah and Haniel. (Chart 14b.)

REZIN (1). *2 Kgs. 15:37; 2 Kgs. 16:5-9; 2 Chr. 28:5; Isa. 7:1-9; 8:6; 9:11.*

Rezin was the king of Syria who, along with Pekah, king of Israel, was stirred up by the Lord to go against Judah in the days of Jotham, king of Judah. *(2 Kgs. 15:37.)*

When Rezin went against Judah in the days of Ahaz, king of Judah, Ahaz solicited the help of Tiglath-pileser, king of Assyria. Tiglath-pileser defeated Damascus and killed Rezin. *(2 Kgs. 16:5-9.)*

Ahaz was delivered into the hands of Rezin who was the king of Syria. *(2 Chr. 28:5.)*

When Rezin, king of Syria, and Pekah, king of Ephraim, were planning to wage war against Judah and set the son of Tabeal up as king, the Lord Instructed Isaiah to take his son Shear-jashub and deliver a message to Ahaz. Ahaz was told to fear not, that it would not come to pass. In fact, within 65 years, Ephraim would no longer even be a people but would be broken. *(Isa. 7:1-9.)*

Isaiah chastised the people for rejoicing in Rezin and in Pekah, Remaliah's son. *(Isa. 8:6.)*

Isaiah prophesied that Rezin's enemies would band together and the Lord would set them against him. *(Isa. 9:11.)*

REZIN (2). *Ezra 2:48, 58; Neh. 7:50, 60.*

Rezin was a Nethinim. When the children of the Nethinims and the children of Solomon's servants left Babylon to return to Jerusalem to build the house of the Lord as proclaimed by Cyrus, king of Persia, they numbered 392.

REZON. *1 Kgs. 11:23-25.*

Rezon was the son of Eliadah. He fled from his lord Hadadezer king of Zobah and gathered together supporters. The Lord stirred him up to be an adversary unto Solomon and all Israel because they had turned to false idols. Rezon abhorred Israel and reigned over Syria.

RIBAI. *2 Sam. 23:29; 1 Chr. 11:31.*

Ribai was of the children of Benjamin and was out of Gibeah. He was the father of Ittai, one of David's mighty men. *(2 Sam. 23:29; 1 Chr. 11:31.)*

RIMMON (1) (Hadadrimmon). *2 Kgs. 5:18; Zech. 12:11.*

Rimmon was the Syrian god of wind, rain and storm. *(2 Kgs. 5:18.)*

He is also the sun god Hadad, referred to as Hadadrimmon. *(Zech. 12:11.)* *(Note: The Bible Dictionary indicates that among the Babylonians he was the god of the air, wind, thunder and rain.)*

RIMMON (2). *2 Sam. 4:2, 5-7.*

Rimmon was a Beerothite of the tribe of Benjamin. He was the father of Baanah and Rechab who slew Ish-bosheth, Saul's son.

RINNAH. *1 Chr. 4:20.*

Rinnah was a son of Shimon. His brothers were Amnon, Ben-hanan and Tilon.

RIPHATH. *Gen. 10:3.*

Riphath was a son of Gomer, grandson of Japheth, and a great-grandson of Noah. (Chart 2a.)

RIZPAH. *2 Sam. 3:7; 21:8.*

Rizpah, one of Saul's concubines, was the daughter of Aiah. Ish-bosheth accused Abner of going in unto Rizpah. *(2 Sam. 3:7.)*

Because Saul slew the Gibeonites contrary to the oath Israel had made with them, the Lord caused a famine to come upon the land. To make an atonement, David asked the Gibeonites what they would have him do. They asked that seven men of Saul's sons be given to them that they could hang them up unto the Lord. David gave them two sons of Rizpah and Saul—Armoni and Mephibosheth—plus five of Merab's and Adriel's sons. *(Note: The scripture says Michal, but Merab married Adriel, Michal married David.) (2 Sam. 21:8.)* (Chart 16 l.)

ROHGAH. *1 Chr. 7:34.*

Rohgah was a son of Shamer (Shomer) and a great-great-grandson of Asher. His brothers were Ahi, Jehubbah and Aram. (Chart 14a.)

ROMAMTI-EZER. *1 Chr. 25:4, 31.*

Romamti-ezer, of the lineage of Kohath, was a Levite and musician and was a son of Heman, the king's seer in the words of God. The musicians—sons of Heman, Asaph and Jeduthun—drew lots and were given their duty assignments by David and the captains of the host. Romamti-ezer cast the 24th of 24 lots. He, his sons and his brethren numbered 12. (Chart 7d.)

ROSH. *Gen. 46:21.*

Rosh was a son of Benjamin and a grandson of Jacob. His brothers were Belah, Becher, Ashbel, Gera, Naaman, Ehi, Muppim, Huppim and Ard. *(Note: Rosh is not listed among Benjamin's family in Num. 26:38-41.)* (Chart 16a.)

RULER OF HIS (JOSEPH'S (1)) HOUSE. *Gen. 43:16.*

The **Ruler of His (Joseph's) House** was instructed by Joseph to bring his brothers to his home and to prepare a dinner for them so they could dine with him at noon.

RULERS IN JEZREEL, ELDERS, CARETAKERS OF AHAB'S. CHILDREN. *2 Kgs. 10:1-7.*

The **Rulers of Jezreel, Elders and Caretakers of Ahab's Children** were invited by Jehu to choose one of Ahab's sons to be king. They feared to do so and pledged allegiance to Jehu. He had them send him the heads of Ahab's 70 sons. They sent them to him in Jezreel in baskets.

RULERS OVER HUNDREDS, THE CAPTAINS AND THE GUARD. *2 Kgs. 11:4-19.*

The **Rulers over Hundreds, the Captains and the Guard** were shown the boy king Joash by the priest Jehoiada. They made a covenant with Jehoiada to support Joash as king. Then, as instructed by Jehoiada, they slew Athalia, who was reigning as queen over Judah. Thus, they restored the crown to Joash.

RUTH. *Ruth 1-4.*

Ruth was the widowed daughter-in-law of Naomi and Elimeleck. She insisted upon staying with her widowed mother-in-law when Naomi returned to Bethlehem-judah following the famine. *(Ruth 1.)*

Naomi's husband's kinsman, Boaz, was very wealthy. Ruth gleaned in his fields. He was kind to her. *(Ruth 2.)*

Naomi instructed Ruth to lie at the feet of Boaz. He promised, as a kinsman, to seek her to wife, but said he must first check with a person who was a nearer kinsman than he to see if he wanted Ruth for a wife, as he would have first choice and first responsibility. Naomi told Ruth to "sit still" until the matter was settled. *(Ruth 3.)*

The next-in-line kinsman declined to marry Ruth so Boaz took her to wife. She bore a son named Obed. Through him came king David. *(Ruth 4.)* (Chart 1.)

NAMES THAT BEGIN WITH "S"

SABEANS. *Job 1:15 (14-15); Isa. 45:14; Ezek. 23:42 (Subtitle, 42-44); Joel 3:8.*

Sabeans, an Arab tribe, fell upon Job's servants. They slew all but one servant and stole his oxen and asses. *(Job 1:15 [14-15].)*

Isaiah prophesied that the Egyptians, Ethiopians and Sabeans, "men of stature," would fall down before Cyrus and acknowledge that there is no God besides the God of Israel. *(Isa. 45:14.)*

Samaria (Aholah) and Jerusalem (Aholibah) committed whoredoms by worshipping idols and aligning themselves with those of a common sort, "and with men of the common sort were brought Sabeans (or drunkards) from the wilderness, which put bracelets upon their hands, and beautiful crowns upon their heads." *(Ezek. 23:42 [Subtitle, 42-44].)*

Joel prophesied that, while Judah and Jerusalem have been "sold" unto the Grecians, in the latter days the children of their captors shall be delivered unto Judah and they will "sell them to the Sabeans." *(Joel 3:8.)*

SABTAH. *Gen. 10:7.*

Sabtah was a son of Cush, a grandson of Ham, and a great-grandson of Noah. (Chart 2e.)

SABTECHA. *Gen. 10:7.*

Sabtecha was a son of Cush, grandson of Ham, and a great-grandson of Noah. (Chart 2e.)

SACAR (1). *1 Chr. 11:35.* See **Sharar**.

SACAR (2). *1 Chr. 26:4 (Subtitle, 4, 6, 12).*

Sacar, a Levite, was the fourth son of Obed-edom. His brothers were Shemaiah, Jehozabad, Joah, Nethaneel, Ammiel, Issachar and Peulthai. They, along with other Levites, were appointed by king David to be porters—to have charge of the treasures, serve as officers and judges, and to conduct the outward business over Israel. (Chart 7c.)

SALAH (Shelah). *Gen. 10:24; 1 Chr. 1:18.*

SALAH (Shelah) was a son of Arphaxad, a grandson of Shem and a great-grandson of Noah. He begat Eber. (Charts 1.; 2b.; 21.)

SALATHIEL. *1 Chr. 3:17.*

Salathiel, a descendant of David, was the son of Assir and a grandson of Jeconiah (Jehoiachin). (Chart 1.)

SALLAI (1). *Neh. 11:8.*

Sallai, of the tribe of Benjamin, was elected by lot to dwell in Jerusalem following his captivity in Babylon. (Chart 16m.)

SALLAI (2). *Neh. 12:20.*

<u>Sallai</u> was the father of Kallai, which Kallai was one of the priests who was a chief of the fathers in the days of Joiakim.

SALLU (1). *1 Chr. 9:7.*

<u>Sallu</u> was of the tribe of Benjamin. He was the son of Meshullam, the son of Hodaviah, the son of Hasenuah. His family's genealogy was written in the book of the kings of Israel and Judah who were carried away to Babylon for their transgression. He was among those of the tribe of Benjamin to dwell in Jerusalem after returning from captivity. (Chart 16m.)

SALLU (2). *Neh. 11:7.*

<u>Sallu</u> of the tribe of Benjamin was elected by lot to dwell in Jerusalem following his captivity in Babylon. He was the son of Meshullam, the son of Joed, the son of Pedaiah. (Chart 16m.)

SALLU (3). *Neh. 12:7.*

<u>Sallu</u> was one of the men (priests and Levites) who went with Zerubbabel from Babylonian captivity to Jerusalem.

SALMA (1). *1 Chr. 2:11.* See **Salmon**.

SALMA (2). *1 Chr. 2:51 (50-51, 54).*

<u>Salma</u> was one of the sons of Caleb and Ephratah. He begat Beth-lehem. His posterity includes the Netophathites, Ataroth, the house of Joab, half of the Manahethites and the Zorites. (Chart 8 l.)

SALMON (Salma). *Ruth 4:20 (18-22); 1 Chr. 2:11 (9-12, 15).*

<u>Salmon</u> (Salma) was the son of Nahshon (Naashon), grandson of Amminadab, (Aaron's father-in-law), and father of Boaz. His great-great-grandson was king David. (Charts 1.; 8d.)

SALU. *Num. 25:14.*

<u>Salu</u> was the father of Zimri and was of the house of the Simeonites.

SAMARIA (Samaritans). *1 Kgs. 16:24; 16:24; 2 Kgs. 17:24; Ezra 4:Subheading, 1-24; Ezek. 23:4-10; Hosea 13:16; Micah 1:1.*

<u>Samaria</u> is a city. Omri, king over Israel, bought the hill Samaria of Shemer and built a city on the hill, calling it Samaria. When the Old Testament refers to the inhabitants of this city, it sometimes just says, "Samaria." Thus, Samaria is both a place and a people. *(1 Kgs. 16:24.)*

Samaritans were adversaries of the children of Israel. When the children of Israel were carried captive out of their lands, the king of Assyria brought men from Babylon, Cuthah, Ava, Hamath and Sepharvaim and placed them in the cities of Samaria instead of the children of Israel. They became the Samaritans. *(2 Kgs. 17:24.)*

When the children of Israel returned to Jerusalem as commanded by Cyrus, king of Persia, to rebuild the temple, the Samaritans offered to help with the building, but their offer was declined. They went about hindering the work and causing the construction to cease. *(Ezra 4:Subheading, 1-24.)*

The Lord compared Samaria and Jerusalem to two daughters of one mother, both of whom committed whoredoms in Egypt. Samaria's name was Aholah. Jerusalem was given the name Aholibah. Aholah (Samaria) doted on the Assyrians. Thus, the Lord destroyed Samaria for her lewdness and delivered her into the hands of the Assyrians. *(Ezek. 23:4-10.)*

Hosea prohesied that the golden calves of Beth-aven shall cause Samaria to fear. The golden calves cannot deliver. He also said, "Her king is cut off as the foam upon the water." *(Hosea 10:5, 7.)*

Hosea prophesied that Samaria would become desolate because she rebelled against the Lord. The people would fall by the sword. *(Hosea 13:16.)*

Micah prophesied in the days of Jotham, Ahaz and Hezekiah regarding the downfall of Samaria and Jerusalem. *(Micah 1:1.)*

SAMGAR-NEBO. *Jer. 39:3, 13-14.*

Samgar-nebo was one of the Babylonian princes who came in and sat in the middle gate of Jerusalem when Nebuchadnezzar and the Chaldean army took the city, slew Zedekiah's sons, put Zedekiah's eyes out and carried him to Babylon, burned the houses and broke down the walls of Jerusalem. The Babylonian princes were assigned to take Jeremiah out of the prison court and commit him into the care of Gedaliah.

SAMLAH OF MASREKAH. *Gen. 36:36; 1 Chr. 1:48.*

Samlah was of Masrekah. He reigned as king in Edom upon the death of Hadad. *(Gen. 36:36.)*

When Samlah was dead, Shaul of Rehoboth reigned in his stead. *(1 Chr. 1:48.)* (Chart 18.)

SAMSON. *Judg. 13:24 (2-5, 24); 14; 15; 16.*

Samson was the son of Manoah and was the twelfth judge of Israel. An angel told Manoah's wife, who was barren, that she would bear a son. He was to be a Nazarite unto God from the womb and no razor was to touch his head. He would begin to deliver Israel from the Philistines. *(Judg. 13:24 [2-5, 24].)*

Samson fell in love with a Philistine woman, whom he married. While in Timnath with his mother and father, Samson killed a lion with his bare hands. His wife enticed him into explaining a riddle he had put forth. While Samson was away slaying 30 men in Ashkelon, his wife was given to another man. *(Judg. 14.)*

Samson burned the corn of the Philistines. The Philistines in turn, burned Samson's wife and his father-in-law so Samson slaughtered several of them. Because they were under Philistine rule, Judah bound Samson and delivered him to the Philistines. However, he broke the cords that bound him and, using the jawbone of an ass, slew 1,000 Philistines at Lehi. *(Judg. 15.)*

Samson visited a harlot in Gaza. The Gazites laid in wait for him in the city gates. Samson carried the doors to the city gates away. He fell in love with Delilah. She found out the source of his strength, had his hair cut, and delivered him into the hands of the Philistines. They put his eyes out and bound him with fetters of brass.

When the Philistines decided to make sport with him, Samson asked the lad that held him by the hand to let him feel the pillars that the house stood upon. Samson caused the pillars to collapse, killing himself and about 3,000 men and women who were upon the roof. Thus, he slew more at his death than he did in life. He judged Israel 20 years. *(Judg. 16.)* (Charts 11b.; 20.)

SAMUEL (Shemuel (2)). *1 Sam. 1:20-28; 2:18-19; 3:1-21; 7:3-17; 8:2-19; 9:17-27; 10:1-8; 12; 13 (1-15); 15; 16:1-13; 19:18; 25:1; 28:5-20; 1 Chr. 6:28, 33; 9:22; 11:3; 26:28; 29:29; 2 Chr. 35:18; Ps. 99:6; Jer. 15:1.*

<u>Samuel</u> was the son of Hannah and Elkenah who was the son of Jeroham, the son of Elihu, the son of Tohu, the son of Zuph. He was given to Hannah in answer to her supplication for a male child when she was barren. In turn, Hannah promised to give him to the Lord as soon as he was weaned. *(1 Sam. 1:20-28.)*

Even though he was just a child, Samuel ministered before the Lord. His mother brought him a homemade coat from year to year as she and Elkenah came to make their offering. *(1 Sam. 2:18-19.)*

There were no open visions in those days, but the word of the Lord was precious. The Lord called to Samuel three times. Each time, Samuel responded to Eli, thinking he had called him. Finally, Eli told him that if the Lord called him again to respond, "Speak, Lord; for thy servant heareth." Samuel did as instructed. The Lord appeared to Samuel. All Israel recognized that Samuel was "established to be a prophet of the Lord." *(1 Sam. 3:1-21.)*

Samuel exhorted Israel to forsake Ashtaroth and Baalim and to serve the Lord. He gathered all Israel together at Mizpeh and prayed for them. The Philistines came against them at Mizpeh. The Lord thundered a great thunder and the Philistines were discomfited. Israel pursued them and defeated them. From year to year, he made a circuit traveling from city to city judging Israel, returning to Ramah where he lived. *(1 Sam. 7:3-17.)*

His firstborn son was named Joel. His secondborn son was Abiah. Samuel's sons did not walk in his footsteps but chose wickedness, taking bribes and perverting judgment. Thus, the elders of Israel asked Samuel for a king. Troubled, Samuel took their request to the Lord who told him to give them a king: they had not rejected Samuel, they had rejected the Lord. Samuel tried to discourage the people in their request by explaining what manner of king would reign over them, but they insisted. *(1 Sam. 8:2-19.)*

The Lord disclosed to Samuel that Saul was to be selected as king. He entertained Saul in his home. As he prepared to send Saul away, Samuel asked him to wait a moment so he could show him "the word of God." *(1 Sam. 9:17-27.)*

Samuel anointed Saul to be captain over the Lord's inheritance. He gave Saul three signs by which he would know that God was with him. He instructed Saul to go to Gilgal and wait for him. He said he would be there in seven days to show Saul what he was to do. Samuel called the people together and presented Saul to them after first chastising them for rejecting the Lord. *(1 Sam. 10:1-8.)*

Samuel testified of his own just dealings in Israel. He rehearsed with them the righteous acts of the Lord which He had done unto them and unto their fathers and reproved the people for their ingratitude. He exhorted them to keep the commandments lest the Lord consume them and their king. *(1 Sam. 12.)*

Shortly after Saul was made king, he was at war with the Philistines and found himself in a situation where he was supposed to wait for Samuel to come to offer a sacrifice. He waited seven days, the appointed time set by Samuel *(1 Sam. 10:8).* When Samuel didn't come when Saul thought he should, he took it upon himself to make a burnt offering unto the Lord. When Samuel learned what Saul had done, he was grieved and told Saul that his kingdom would not continue but would be given unto another. *(1 Sam. 13 [1-15].)*

Samuel conveyed some instructions to Saul from the Lord wherein he told Saul that he was to destroy the Amalekites—to kill all the men, women and children as well as every ox, sheep, camel and ass. When Saul failed to do as instructed, Samuel told him that the Lord had now rejected him as king and that "to obey is better than sacrifice, and to hearken than the fat of rams" *(v.22). (1 Sam. 15.)*

The Lord instructed Samuel to choose David, son of Jesse, and anoint him king. *(1 Sam. 16:1-13.)*

Samuel and David went to dwell in Naioth when David fled to Samuel because Saul was trying to kill him. *(1 Sam. 19:18.)*

Samuel died and was buried in his house at Ramah, and all Israel gathered together and lamented his death. *(1 Sam. 25:1.)*

Samuel, called up by the witch at En-dor, told Saul he and his sons would be with him the following day. *(1 Sam. 28:5-20.) (Note: The Bible Dictionary indicates that inasmuch as witches nor other mediums cannot bring up prophets from the world of spirits, if Samuel was present on the occasion referred to in these verses, either he appeared in spite of and not because of the witch, or that some other spirit came impersonating him.)*

Samuel's (**Shemuel**'s) sons were Vashni (Joel) and Abiah. *(1 Chr. 6:28, 33.)*

Samuel and David ordained the porters in the gates for their service. *(1 Chr. 9:22.)*

According to the word of the Lord by Samuel, David was anointed king over Israel. *(1 Chr. 11:3.)*

All the things Samuel, Saul, Abner and Joab had dedicated for the house of God were placed under the hand of Shelomith and his brethren. *(1 Chr. 26:28.)*

The book of Samuel contains the acts of David, along with the books of Nathan and Gad, which scriptures have been lost. *(1 Chr. 29:29.)*

No passover compared to the passovers from the days of Samuel until the passover kept by Josiah. *(2 Chr. 35:18.)*

Samuel, Moses and Aaron are among those prophets and priests whom the Lord answered when they called upon His name. *(Ps. 99:6.)*

The Lord told the prophet Jeremiah that even if Samuel and Moses stood before Him to plead for the Jews, He would not change His mind about destroying and scattering the people because they had become so wicked. *(Jer. 15:1.)* (Charts 7d.; 20.)

SANBALLAT. *Neh. 2:10, 19; 4:1-8;6:1-14; 13:28.*

Sanballat was a Horonite. He and Tobiah the servant, along with others, laughed and scorned Nehemiah when they learned that he proposed to rebuild the city walls and gates of Jerusalem. *(Neh. 2:10, 19.)*

Sanballat stirred up his brethren and the army of Samaria against Nehemiah and those who were rebuilding the walls of Jerusalem. They conspired to stop the work. *(Neh. 4:1-8.)*

Sanballat engaged in intrigue to stop Nehemiah and the construction of the wall. However, Nehemiah refused to meet with him in spite of repeated requests. Sanballat and Tobiah hired Shemaiah to falsely prophesy against Nehemiah to get Nehemiah to sin against the Lord by hiding in the temple for protection, but Nehemiah refused to be deceived. *(Neh. 6:1-14.)*

Sanballat's son-in-law was one of the sons of Joiada, the son of Eliashib the high priest. Nehemiah chased him from Jerusalem because of his marriage to a heathen woman. *(Neh. 13:28.)*

SAPH (Sippai). *2 Sam. 21:18; 1 Chr. 20:4.*

Saph was a Philistine and "was of the sons of the giant." He was slain by Sibbechai the Hushathite in a battle at Gob. *(2 Sam. 21:18.)*

Sibbechai slew **Sippai** (Saph). *(1 Chr. 20:4 is a repeat of 2 Sam. 21:18.)*

SARAH (1). *Gen. 17:15.* See **Sarai**.

SARAH (2). *Num. 26:46.* See **Serah**.

SARAI (Sarah (1)). *Gen. 11:29-31; 12:5, 10-20; 12:10-20; 16:1-6; 17:15-19; 18:6, 9-15; 20; 21:2-3, 9-10; 23:1-2, 19; Isa. 51:2.*

Sarai was Abram's wife. She was barren. She traveled from Ur of the Chaldees with Abram, Lot and Terah to go to the land of Canaan. They dwelled for a time in Haran. *(Gen. 11:29-31.) (Note: The following scripture from the book of Abraham in the Pearl of Great Price gives a slightly different perspective on this incident. Abraham 2:3-5 indicates that Abraham was instructed by the Lord to leave Ur and his kindred and go to a different land. Abram says he took Sarai, Lot and his wife, and "my father followed after me, unto the land which we denominated Haran." His father had been an idol worshipper and after arriving in Haran, he "turned again unto his idolatry," and remained in Haran while the Lord led Abraham and his group to the land of Canaan.)*

Sarai, Abram and Lot left Haran and went into the land of Canaan when she was 65 years old and Abraham was 75 years old. *(Gen. 12:5, 10-20.)*

Because of a famine in the land, Abram moved to Egypt for a time. He told his wife that because she was "a fair woman to look upon" that the Egyptians would kill him to get her. Thus, he told her to say she was his sister so that he could live for her sake and it would be well with her. Sarai was taken into Pharaoh's house. The

Lord plagued Pharaoh's house because of Sarai. When Pharaoh discovered that Sarai was Abram's wife, he told Abram to take her away; and Abram and Sarai were sent on their way. *(Gen. 12:10-20.)*

(Note: Abraham 2:22-25 sheds a little different light on that same episode. These verses say that the Lord warned Abraham that because Sarai "is a very fair woman to look upon" that the Egyptians would kill Abram but save Sarai alive. Thus, the Lord instructed Abram to say that Sarai was his sister, so that his "soul shall live." Thus, Abram told Sarai to say that she was his sister "that it may be well with me for thy sake.")

Sarai was barren. In order to allow Abram to have seed and her to have children, Sarai urged Abram to go in unto her maid, Hagar, that she "may obtain children by her." Abram did as Sarai asked. When Hagar became pregnant, Sarai was despised in her eyes. Sarai lamented to Abram and he told her to do with Hagar as she felt to do. Sarai dealt "hardly" with Hagar, so Hagar fled. *(Gen. 16:1-6.)*

Sarai's name was changed by the Lord to **Sarah**. The Lord told Abraham that Sarah would be blessed with a son. In spite of Abraham's doubts due to Sarah's age (90 years old), the Lord reaffirmed that Sarah would have a son. Abraham was told to name him Isaac. *(Gen. 17:15-19.)*

The Lord and three men appeared to Abraham as he sat in his tent door. After inviting them to stay and be refreshed and fed. Sarah was instructed by Abraham to quickly prepare some cakes for them. The men inquired about Sarah. They again said that Sarah would have a son. When Sarah overheard this comment, she laughed "within herself" because she and Abraham "were old and well stricken in age." The Lord asked why Sarah laughed. "Is anything too hard for the Lord?" She denied having laughed because she was afraid. The Lord said, "Nay, but thou didst laugh." *(Gen. 18:6, 9-15.)*

Sarah and Abraham traveled to Gerar. They told Abimelech, king of Gerar, that Sarah was Abraham's sister. Abimelech took Sarah, but was visited by the Lord in a dream and told that Sarah was Abraham's wife and to restore her to him. This he did. Abraham explained that Sarah was indeed his sister—his half-sister: they shared the same father but not the same mother *(v. 12)*. *(Gen. 20.)*

Sarah conceived and bare a son. They called him Isaac. Sarah asked Abraham to cast Hagar and Ishmael out because Ishmael mocked her. She insisted that Ishmael not be an heir with Isaac. The Lord told Abraham to hearked unto Sarah and do as she asked. *(Gen. 21:2-3, 9-10.)*

Sarah was 127 years old when she died in Hebron in the land of Canaan. She was buried in the cave of the field of Machpelah in Hebron, property Abraham purchased from Ephron. *(Gen. 23:1-2, 19.) (Note: Abraham lived an additional 38 years.)*

The Lord, through Isaiah, tells His people to look to Abraham and Sarah for the promised blessings He made. In the latter days, the Lord will comfort His people. *(Isa. 51:2.)* (Charts 2b.; 3a, d.)

SARAPH. *1 Chr. 4:22.*

<u>Saraph</u> was a son of Shelah and a grandson of Judah. He had dominion in Moab. (Chart 8a.)

SARDITES. See **Sered**.

SARGON. *Isa. 20:1-2.*

<u>Sargon</u> was king of Assyria from 722 to 705 B.C. He sent Tartan against the city of Ashdod. Tartan took the city in approximately 711 B.C. During this time, the Lord sent Isaiah forth to prophesy.

SARSCHIM. *Jer. 39:3.*

<u>Sarschim</u> was one of the Babylonian princes who came in and sat in the middle gate of Jerusalem when Nebuchadnezzar and the Chaldean army took the city, slew Zedekiah's sons, put Zedekiah's eyes out and carried him to Babylon, burned the houses and broke down the walls of Jerusalem. The Babylonian princes were assigned to take Jeremiah from the court of the prison and place him in the charge of Gedaliah.

SAUL (1) (Shaul (1)). *Gen. 36:37; 1 Chr. 1:48-49.*

<u>Saul</u> of Rehoboth reigned as king in Edom upon the death of Samlah. *(Gen. 36:37.)*

Shaul (Saul) reigned as king in Edom upon the death of Samlah. Upon his death, Baal-hanan reigned. *(1 Chr. 1:48-49.)* (Chart 18.)

SAUL (2). *1 Sam. 9; 10; 11; 13; 14; 15; 16; 17; 18; 19; 20:30-33; 21-23; 24; 25:44; 26; 28; 31; 1 Chr. 8:33; 9:39; 10.*

<u>Saul</u>, a Benjamite, was the son of Kish, and was selected by the Lord to be anointed king over Israel by Samuel in response to the pleas of the children of Israel. He was a tall young man, taller than all others from his shoulders up. He was a good and choice person. As Saul searched for his father's lost asses, he sought guidance from Samuel. Samuel had him eat dinner with him, and then had him tarry a while longer so he could tell him what the Lord had in store for him. *(1 Sam. 9.)*

Saul was anointed by Samuel to be captain over the Lord's inheritance. He was also given three signs by which he would know that God was with him: 1) two men by Rachel's sepulchre would speak to him regarding his father's lost asses; 2) he would meet three men going up to God to Beth-el, they would salute him and give him two loaves of bread; 3) he would meet a company of prophets with musical instruments and they would prophesy. He would then prophesy with them. The Lord blessed him with a new heart and he prophesied among the prophets. Samuel called the people together at Mizpah and Saul was chosen king. *(1 Sam. 10.)*

The Ammonites encamped against the Israelites of Jabesh-gilead and offered a peace proposal that stipulated that in order to have peace, the Israelites would have to agree to let the Ammonites put out all their right eyes. Saul rescued them, wreaking havoc upon the Ammonites. His kingship was renewed in Gilgal. *(1 Sam. 11.)*

Contrary to the Lord's laws, Saul offered a burnt offering rather than wait for Samuel to come. The Lord rejected him and chose another person to be captain over His people. *(1 Sam. 13.)*

During a battle with the Philistines, Saul instructed the people to eat nothing until evening. The penalty of disobedience was death. His son Jonathan did not hear the instruction and ate some honey. His father decreed he should die. The people refused to allowed Saul to kill him. Saul vexed Israel's enemies on every side. Saul's sons were Jonathan, Ishui and Melchi-shua, and his daughters were Merab and Michal. His wife was Ahinoam who was the daughter of Ahimaaz. The captain of his host was his cousin Abner, son of his Uncle Ner. *(1 Sam. 14.)*

The Lord, through Samuel, commanded Saul to destroy the Amalekites and all that they had—men, women, children—as well as all animals. However, Saul spared king Agag and kept all the best animals. Thus, the Lord rejected Saul as king of Israel. Samuel reminded Saul that "to obey is better than sacrifice, and to hearken than the fat of rams." Samuel never came to see Saul again until the day of his death. *(1 Sam. 15.)*

Saul became vexed and troubled. A servant suggested he bring in a harpist to soothe him. He was informed that Jesse had a son who played the harp. Therefore, Saul invited David to come and play for him. Saul loved him and he became Saul's armorbearer. *(1 Sam. 16.)*

Saul and the men of Israel were gathered against the Philistines. Goliath of Gath boldly challenged Israel, saying that if anyone of Israel could defeat him, then the Philistines would serve Israel. However, if he killed the Israelite, all Israel would have to serve them. David volunteered to defend Israel. When David went to battle against Goliath, Saul clothed him in heavy armor, but David declined to use it. *(1 Sam. 17.)*

Saul set David over his armies. When the people danced and sang in praise of Saul who had killed his thousands and David his ten thousands, Saul became jealous and determined to kill David. Saul gave his daughter Michal to David for a wife, hoping she would prove to be a snare to him. *(1 Sam. 18.)*

While David played the harp for Saul, Saul tried to kill him by throwing a javelin at him *(1 Sam. 19.)*

Saul became angry with his son Jonathan because he said he gave David leave to miss the three-day dinner associated with the new moon so he cast a javelin at Jonathan. *(1 Sam. 20:30-33.)*

Saul pursued David from place to place and had his servant Doeg slay the priests in Nob because Ahimelech helped David. *(1 Sam. 21-23.)*

Saul apologized to David and said he knew the kingdom of Israel would be established in David's hand after David spared his life and merely cut off Saul's skirt while Saul was asleep in a cave. *(1 Sam. 24.)*

Saul gave his daughter Michal, David's wife, to Phalti to be his wife. *(1 Sam. 25:44.)*

Saul's life was spared again by David when Saul was asleep in the trenches following a day of pursuing David. David merely took Saul's spear and cruse of water from his bolster so Saul would know that David could have killed him but didn't. Saul apologized to David and praised him; and they went their separate ways. *(1 Sam. 26.)*

Saul requested a revelation from the witch of En-dor. She called up Samuel, who was dead, who told Saul that on the following day he and his sons would all be with him and that Israel would be delivered into the hands of the Philistines. *(1 Sam. 28.) (Note: The Bible Dictionary indicates that inasmuch as witches nor other mediums cannot bring up prophets from the world of spirits, if Samuel was present on the occasion referred to in these verses, either he appeared in spite of and not because of the witch, or that some other spirit came impersonating him.)*

The Philistines defeated the Israelites and slew Jonathan, Abinadab and Malchi-shua, Saul's sons, and seriously wounded Saul. *(Note:1 Sam. 14:49, lists Saul's sons as Jonathan, Ishui and Melchi-shua.)* Rather than let the Philistines capture and abuse him, Saul asked his armorbearer to slay him. He refused; so, Saul fell upon his own sword and died. When the Philistines found him, they cut off his head and paraded it about (and fastened it in the temple of Dagon). They hung his armor in the house of Ashtaroth and hung his body and those of his sons on the wall of Beth-shan. Valiant men from Jabesh-shan, under cover of night, retrieved their bodies and took them to Jabesh where they burned them and buried their bones under a tree at Jabesh. *(1 Sam. 31; 1 Chr. 10.)*

Saul begat Jonathan, Malchi-shua, Abinadab and Esh-baal. *(1 Chr. 8:33; 1 Chr. 9:39.) (Note: This is the first time Esh-baal has been mentioned. Ishui is not mentioned.)* (Charts 16k-l.)

SAUL'S (2) ARMORBEARER. *1 Sam. 31:4-5; 1 Chr. 10:4-5.*

Saul's Armorbearer refused to thrust his sword through the badly wounded king; therefore, Saul did it to himself. When the armorbearer saw that Saul was dead, he fell upon his own sword and died with him.

SAUL'S (2) SERVANT(S). *1 Sam. 9:3-27; 10:14; 11:7-9; 16:14-18.*

Saul's Servant went with Saul to search for his father's lost asses. They had trouble finding the asses and the servant suggested to Saul that they seek help from Samuel. Saul and the servant joined Samuel and thirty guests for dinner. The next morning, Samuel had Saul bid the servant pass on ahead so he could show Saul the word of God. *(1 Sam. 9:3-27.)*

Saul and his servant reported back to Saul's uncle that they could not find the asses and told of their visit to Samuel. *(1 Sam. 10:14.)*

When messengers from Jabesh came seeking someone to come save them, Saul sent messengers thoughout Israel to garner help for Jabesh. These messengers reported back to Saul and to the messengers from Jabesh that they would have a lot of help the next day. *(1 Sam. 11:7-9.)*

When Saul was troubled by an evil spirit, his servants suggested that he have a harp player come and play for him to soothe his mind. One servant suggested Jesse's son David should be asked to play for Saul. *(1 Sam. 16:14-18.)*

SEBA. *Gen. 10:7.*

Seba was a son of Cush, a grandson of Ham, and a great-grandson of Noah. (Chart 2e.)

SEGUB (1). *1 Kgs. 16:34.*

Segub was the youngest son of Hiel the Bethelite who rebuilt Jericho in fulfillment of the curse pronounced by Joshua. *(See Josh. 6:26.)*

SEGUB (2). *1 Chr. 2:21-22.*

Segub, father of Jair, was a son of Hezron. His mother was the daughter of Machir. He was a great-grandson of Manasseh as well as a great-grandson of Judah. (Charts 8c-d, h.; 15b.)

SEIR THE HORITE (Hori). *Gen. 36:20-21; 1 Chr. 1:38; 2 Chr. 20:22-24; 25:11-14.*

Seir the Horite inhabited the land of Edom. His sons were Lotan, Shobal, Zibeon, Anah, Dishon, Ezer and Dishan. *(Gen. 36:20-21; 1 Chr. 1:38.)*

The children of mount Seir (originally inhabited by Horites according to the BD), the children of Moab and Ammon joined together to go to battle against Jehoshaphat, king of Judah. Jehoshaphat and his people fasted and prayed to the Lord. The prophet Jahaziel prophesied that the Lord would deliver Judah and fight her battle. While Judah sang and praised the Lord, the children of mount Seir, Moab and Ammon fought amongst themselves and destroyed themselves, "and none escaped." *(2 Chr. 20:22-24.)*

Ten thousand of the children of Seir were slain by Amaziah, king of Judah. Another 10,000 were taken captive and cast off a cliff to their deaths. After defeating the Edomites, Amaziah brought the gods of the children of Seir back to Judah and set them up to be his gods. *(2 Chr. 25:11-14.)* (Charts 4a-f.)

SELED. *1 Chr. 2:30.*

Seled was the son of Nadab. His brother was Appaim. He had no children. He was a five-times-great-grandson of Judah. (Chart 8c.)

SEMACHIAH. *1 Chr. 26:7 (subtitle, 6-7).*

Semachiah, a Levite of the lineage of Obed-edom, was a son of Shemaiah. Shemaiah's other sons were Othni, Rephael, Obed, Elzabad and Elihu. They, along with other Levites, were appointed by king David to be porters—to have charge of the treasures, serve as officers and judges, and to conduct the outward business over Israel. (Chart 7c.)

SENAAH. *Ezra 2:35; Neh. 7: 38.*

Senaah was of the people of Israel. The men of the children of Senaah who returned to Jerusalem from Babylon after Cyrus' proclamation to build the temple numbered 3,630 (3,930).

SENNACHERIB. *2 Kgs. 18:13, 17-35; 19:8-37; 2 Chr. 32:1-22; Isa. 36; 37:8-38.*

Sennacherib was king of Assyria (705-681 B.C.). When Hezekiah was in his fourteenth year as king of Judah, Sennacherib came against Judah and took all her fenced cities. Hezekiah gave him the gold and silver he demanded. Later, Sennacherib sent a large army against Jerusalem. One of his men, Rab-shakeh, made a blasphemous speech asking Jerusalem to surrender to the Assyrians. *(2 Kgs. 18:13-37; Isa. 36.)*

Sennacherib sent a second blasphemous message to Hezekiah. Sennacherib boasted that the gods of other nations could not save the people of those cities and so Hezekiah's people should not trust in their God either. Hezekiah petitioned the Lord, and the prophet Isaiah prophesied the destruction of the Assyrians. An angel of the Lord slew 185,000 Assyrians as they slept in their camp. Sennacherib returned home and dwelt in Nineveh where he was slain by his sons Adrammelech and Sharezer. A third son, Esarhaddon, reigned in his stead. *(2 Kgs. 19:8-37; Isa. 37:8-38.)*

When Sennacherib came against Judah, Hezekiah had the people stop the water and fountains so the Assyrians could not have water. *(2 Chr. 32:1-22 retells the incident recorded in 2 Kgs. 19:8-37 with the preceding elaboration.)*

SENUAH. *Neh. 11:9.*

Senuah was the father of Judah, which Judah was second to Joel over the Benjamites who dwelled in Jerusalem after they returned from Babylonian captivity. (Chart 16m.)

SEORIM. *1 Chr. 24:8.*

Seorim was from the sons of Aaron. When David made the divisions of the sons of Aaron, there was one principal household for Eleazar and one taken for Ithamar. Eleazar had 16 sons and there were eight sons of Ithamar. These 24 sons who were chief of the fathers were divided by lot. Seorim drew the fourth lot.

SERAH (Sarah (2)). *Gen. 46:17; Num. 26:46; 1 Chr. 7:30.*

Serah (Sarah) was the daughter of Asher (and granddaughter of Jacob). Her brothers were Jimnah (Jimna, Imnah), Ishuah (Isuah), Isui (Jesui, Ishuai) and Beriah. *(Gen. 46:17; Num. 26:46; 1 Chr. 7:30.) (Note: Ishuah is not listed in Num. 26:46.)* (Chart 14a.)

SERAIAH (1) (Shavsha). *2 Sam. 8:17.; 1 Chr. 18:16.*

Seraiah (Shavsha) was the scribe when David was king.

SERAIAH (2). *2 Kgs. 25:18-21; 1 Chr. 6:14-15; Ezra 7:1-5; Neh. 11:11; Jer. 52:24-27.*

Seraiah was the chief priest when Zedekiah was king over Judah and Nebechadnezzar carried Judah away captive to Babylon. Seraiah and Zephaniah, the second priest, three keepers of the door, seven men near to the king, the principal scribe of the host and 60 men of the people, along with several others, were taken to Nebuchdnezzar who slew them. *(2 Kgs. 25:18-21; Jer. 52:24-27.)*

Seraiah was the son of Azariah. He was a many-times-great-grandson of Aaron. He begat Jehozadak who was taken into captivity when the Lord delivered Judah and Jerusalem into the hands of Nebuchadnezzar. *(1 Chr. 6:14-15.)*

Seraiah, the father of Ezra (Jehozadak), was a many-times great-grandson of Aaron. Aaron's descendants through Ezra are listed. *(Ezra 7:1-5.) (Note: there is some variation between this listing and the one in 1 Chr. 6:4-15. Neither Johanan nor Ahimaaz is listed. In addition, the names: Amariah, Ahitub, Zadok and Azariah which are listed between Meraioth and Azariah in 1 Chronicles seem to be a duplication and have been omitted from the listing in Ezra. Jehozadak is not named in this listing. Rather, Ezra is listed as the son of Seraiah.)*

Seraiah was the son (grandson) of Hilkiah, and was the ruler of the house of God when the children of Israel returned to Jerusalem following their Babylonian captivity. *(Neh. 11:11.)* (Chart 7b.)

SERAIAH (3). *2 Kgs. 25:23-26; Jer. 40:8-9.*

Seraiah was the son of Tanhumeth the Netophathite. He and a group of other men came to Gedaliah after Gedaliah was made governor over Judah by Nebuchadnezzar and he told them they shouldn't fear being servants of the Chaldees. After Ishmael and his cohorts slew Gedaliah and the Jews and Chaldees who were with him at Mizpah, the rest all fled to Egypt because they feared the Chaldees.

SERAIAH (4). *1 Chr. 4:13-14.*

Seraiah was a son of Kenaz, the brother of Othniel and the nephew of Caleb son of Jephunneh. He begat Joab. They were craftsmen. (Chart 8k.)

SERAIAH (5). *1 Chr. 4:35.*

Seraiah, a descendant of Shimei, was the father of Josibiah and son of Asiel. (Chart 6a.)

SERAIAH (6) (Azariah (17)). *Ezra 2:2.; Neh. 7:7; 10:2 (1-2, 28-31); 12:1, 12.*

Seraiah (Azariah) was one of the people who went with Zerubbabel back to Jerusalem following king Cyrus' proclamation to build the temple there. *(Ezra 2:2; Neh. 7:7.)*

Seraiah was among the priests who covenanted and sealed their covenant to marry in Israel, honor the Sabbath, pay tithes and keep the commandments. *(Neh. 10:2 [1-2, 28-31].)*

Seraiah was one of the priests and Levites who went with Zerubbabel out of captivity. His son Meraiah was a chief of the fathers in the days of Joiakim. *(Neh. 12:1, 12.)*

SERAIAH (7). *Jer. 36:26.*

Seraiah was the son of Azriel. Jehoiakim commanded Seraiah, Jerahmeel and Shelemiah the son of Abdeel, to arrest Baruch and Jeremiah because of Jeremiah's prophecies. However, "the Lord hid them."

SERAIAH (8). *Jer. 51:59-64.*

Seraiah was the son of Neriah who was the son of Maaseiah. *(Note: Seraiah and Baruch may have been brothers as Baruch was also the son of Neriah. See Jer. 45:1. It is also conceivable that Seraiah and Baruch could be one and the same.)* In the fourth year of Zedekiah's reign when Judah was taken to Babylon, Jeremiah instructed Seraiah that when he went to Babylon he was to read all the words Jeremiah had written prophesying the destruction of Babylon. After reading the words of the book, he was to attach a stone to it and throw it into the Euphrates River and say, "Thus shall Babylon sink, and shall not rise from the evil that I *(the Lord)* will bring upon her." (Chart 8b.)

SERED (Sardites). *Gen. 46:14; Num. 26:26.*

Sered was a son of Zebulun and a grandson of Jacob. *(Gen. 46:14.)* His descendants are the **Sardites**. *(Num. 26:26.)* (Chart 10a.)

SERUG. *Gen. 11:20-22.*

Serug was the son of Reu, a fourth-great-grandson of Shem and a fifth-great-grandson of Noah. He begat Nahor when he was 30 years old. He lived 230 years. (Charts 1.; 2b.; 21.)

SETH (Sheth). *Gen. 4:25-26; 5:3-8; 1 Chr. 1:1.*

Seth is the third son of Adam and Eve who is mentioned by name. He begat a son whom he called Enos. *(Gen. 4:25-26.)*

Seth was born when Adam was 130 years old. Seth begat his son, Enos, when he was 105 years old. He lived a total of 912 years, during which time he had sons and daughters. *(Gen. 5:3-8.)*

Sheth (Seth) was the son of Adam. His son was Enosh (Enos). *(1 Chr. 1:1.) (Note: Moses 6:1-3, 9-11, 16, in the Pearl of Great Price records that Seth never rebelled against God. He had a son whom he named Enos. Adam taught that God created man in his own image, in the image of his own body, male and female, and called their name Adam. He begat Seth when he was 130 years old. He died when he was 930 years old. Seth was 105 when he begat Enos. Seth lived to be 912 years old. D&C 107:42-43 provides some additional information: Seth was ordained at the age of 69 by Adam. Seth was in the express image of his father, so much like Adam that the only way to distinguish them was by age.)* (Charts 1.; 21.)

SETHUR. *Num. 13:13, 16, 31-33; 14:37.*

Sethur, of the tribe of Asher, was the son of Michael. He was one of twelve leaders sent to scout out the land of Caanan. He returned with a negative report. *(Num. 13:13, 16, 31-33.)* Because of the negative report he gave, he "died by the plague before the Lord." *(Num. 14:37.)*

SHAALBONITE. *2 Sam. 23:32.*

Shaalbonite. Eliahba the Shaalbonite was one of David's mighty men. (Chart 17.)

SHAAPH (1). *1 Chr. 2:47.*

Shaaph, of the house of Judah, was one of the sons of Jahdai. (Chart 8j.)

SHAAPH (2). *1 Chr. 2:49*.

Shaaph was one of the sons of Caleb and his concubine Maachah. He begat Madmannah. (Chart 8k.)

SHAASHGAZ. *Esth. 2:14*.

Shaashgaz was king Ahasuerus' chamberlain who kept the concubines in the second house of the women, to which Esther went after spending 12 months in the first house of women.

SHABBETHAI (1). *Ezra 10:15*.

Shabbethai the Levite and Meshullam were assigned to assist Jonathan, son of Asahel, and Jahaziah, son of Tikvah, the task of separating the children of Israel from their foreign wives.

SHABBETHAI (2). *Neh. 8:7-8*.

Shabbethai was one of the men who, when Ezra read and interpreted the law of Moses to the people, helped the people understand the law.

SHABBETHAI (3). *Neh. 11:16*.

Shabbethai, of the chief of the Levites, along with Jozabad, had the oversight of the outward business of the temple when the children of Israel returned to Jerusalem from Babylonian captivity.

SHACHIA. *1 Chr. 8:10*.

Shachia, a descendant of Benjamin, was a son of Shaharaim and Hodesh. (Chart 16f.)

SHADRACH. See **Hananiah (12)**.

SHAGE. *1 Chr. 11:34*.

Shage the Hararite was the father of Jonathan, one of the valiant men of David's army. (Chart 17.)

SHAHARAIM. *1 Chr. 8:8-10*.

Shaharaim was a descendant of Benjamin, although the exact connection is not clear in this scripture. Two of his wives were Hushim and Baara. He also had a wife named Hodesh by whom he begat Jobab, Zibia, Mesha, Malcham, Jeuz, Shachia and Mirma. (Charts 16f-g.)

SHALLUM (1) (Shillem, Shillemites). *Gen. 46:24; Num. 26:49; 1 Chr. 7:13*.

Shillem was a son of Naphtali and a grandson of Jacob and Bilhah, Rachel's handmaid. His brothers were Jahzeel, Guni and Jezer. *(Gen. 46:24.)* His descendants were called **Shillemites**. *(Num. 26:49.)*

Shallum's (Shillem's) brothers were Jahziel (Jahzeel), Guni and Jezer. *(1 Chr. 7:13.)* (Chart 12a.)

SHALLUM (2). *2 Kgs. 15:10, 13-14*.

Shallum was the son of Jabesh. He conspired against king Zachariah, killed him, and reigned over Israel in his stead. He began his reign in the 39th year of Uzziah's (Azariah) reign over Judah. He reigned just 1 month when Menahem, the son of Gadi, came up from Tirzah, slew him and reigned in his stead.

SHALLUM (3). *2 Kgs. 22:14; 2 Chr. 34:22.*

Shallum, son of Tikvah (Tikvath), was the husband of the prophetess Huldah. *(Note: The Greek translation of the O.T. [Septuagint] apparently refers to Shallum as the son of Huldah, according to the BD.)*

SHALLUM (4). *1 Chr. 2:40-41.*

Shallum, a descendant of Judah through Jerahmeel, was the son of Sisamai and the father of Jekamiah. (Chart 8c.)

SHALLUM (5). *1 Chr. 3:15; Jer. 22:11.* See **Jehoahaz (2)**.

SHALLUM (6). *1 Chr. 4:25.*

Shallum was the son of Shaul, a grandson of Simeon, and a great-grandson of Jacob. His son was Mibsam. (Chart 6a.)

SHALLUM (7) (Meshullam (7)). *1 Chr. 6:12-13; 9:11 (2, 10-11); Ezra 7:1-5; Neh. 11:11.*

Shallum was the son of Zadok. He begat Hilkiah and was a many-times-great-grandson of Aaron. *(1 Chr. 6:12-13.)*

Meshullam (Shallum) was the father of Hilkiah and the son of Zadok. He is listed among the priests who lived in Jerusalem whose genealogy was recorded in the book of the kings of Israel and Judah, who were carried away captive into Babylon because of wickedness. His grandson Azariah was among those priests who first dwelled in their possessions in Jerusalem upon returning from Babylonian captivity. *(1 Chr. 9:11 [2, 10-11].)*

Shallum's ancestors and descendants from Aaron through Ezra are recorded. *(Ezra 7:1-5.) (Note: there is some variation between this listing and the one in 1 Chr. 6:4-15.)*

Meshullam was the father of Hilkiah and the son of Zadok. *(Neh. 11:11.)* (Chart 7b.)

SHALLUM (8) (Meshullam (9)). *1 Chr. 9:17 (2, 17); Ezra 2:42; Neh. 7:45; 12:25.*

Shallum was a Levite and the chief porter. Other porters were Akkub, Talmon, Ahiman and their brethren. They were over the work of the service and were keepers of the gates of the tabernacle. He was among the first inhabitants to dwell in their possessions in their cities after returning from Babylonian captivity. *(1 Chr. 9:17 [2, 17].)*

When Cyrus, king of Persia, proclaimed that the people of God should go to Jerusalem to build the temple, the children of the porters—Shallum, Ater, Talmon, Akkub, Hatita and Shobai—numbered 139 (138). *(Ezra 2:42; Neh. 7:45.)*

Meshullam (Shallum), Akkub, Mattaniah, Bakbukiah, Obadiah and Talmon were porters who kept the ward at the thresholds of the gates in the days of Joiakim, Nehemiah and Ezra. *(Neh. 12:25.)*

SHALLUM (9) (Meshelemiah, Shelemiah (1)). *1 Chr. 9:19, 21, 31; 26:1-2, 9, 14.*

Shallum, son of Kore, the son of Ebiasaph, the son of Korah, was one of the porters who had oversight of the gates of the house of the Lord. Zechariah, son of **Meshelemiah** (Shallum), was porter of the door of the tabernacle of the congregation. Mattithiah (Zechariah), Shallum's firstborn, had the set office over the things that were made in pans. *(1 Chr. 9:19, 21, 31.)*

Meshelemiah (Shallum) was the son of Kore and was of the lineage of Asaph (Ebiasaph). His sons were Zechariah, firstborn; Jediael, secondborn; Zebadiah, thirdborn; Jathniel, fourthborn; Elam, fifthborn; Jehohanan, sixthborn; and Elioenai, seventhborn. They were assigned to be porters and to have charge of the treasures, serve as officers and judges, and conduct the outward business over Israel, along with others who were assigned to be porters. There were 18 sons and brethren of Meshelemiah who were called to the service. **Shelemiah** (Meshelemiah) drew the lot eastward. His son Zechariah drew the lot northward. *(1 Chr. 26:1-2, 9, 14.)* *(Note: According to the Bible Dictionary, Shallum (9) and Meshelemiah (Shelemiah) are the same. If so, then Zechariah, Meshelemiah's son [1 Chr. 9:21], and Mattithiah, Shallum's firstborn [1 Chr. 9:31], must be one and the same.)* (Chart 7d.)

SHALLUM (10). *2 Chr. 28:12.*

Shallum was the father of Jehizkiah who was one of the leaders of the children of Ephraim when Ahaz was king of Judah and the children of Israel carried many of Judah off captive.

SHALLUM (11). *Ezra 10:24 (18-19, 24, 44).*

Shallum was one of the porters. He was among those who had taken wives from among the Canaanites or other foreign groups but who agreed to Ezra's request that they separate themselves from these strange wives lest the Lord destroy the rest of the children of Israel.

SHALLUM (12). *Ezra 10:42 (18-19, 42, 44).*

Shallum, a son of Bani, and his brothers were some of the men in Israel who took foreign wives but gave them up when Ezra feared the wrath of God would destroy Israel for this iniquity.

SHALLUM (13). *Neh. 3:12.*

Shallum, son of Halohesh, ruler of the half part of Jerusalem, and his daughters worked next to Malchiajah and Hashub when the children of Israel rebuilt the walls and gates of Jerusalem during the time of Ezra and Nehemiah.

SHALLUM (14). *Jer. 32:7-12.*

Shallum was the father of Hanameel and the uncle of the prophet Jeremiah. Jeremiah bought Hanameel's field, symbolizing the fact that Israel would some day return to the land of their inheritance even though they were soon to be taken captive by Nebuchadrezzar and carried away to Babylon.

SHALLUM (15). *Jer. 35:4.*

Shallum was the father of Maaseiah who was the keeper of the door.

SHALLUN. *Neh. 3:15.*

Shallun, son of Col-hozeh, the ruler of part of Mizpah, repaired the gate of the fountain and the wall of the pool of Siloah by the king's garden when the children

of Israel rebuilt the walls and gates of Jerusalem during the time of Ezra and
Nehemiah.

SHALMAI. *Ezra 2:46, 58; Neh. 7:48, 60.*

Shalmai was a Nethinim. When the Nethinims and the children of Solomon's
servants left Babylon to return to Jerusalem to build the house of the Lord as
proclaimed by Cyrus, king of Persia, they numbered 392.

SHALMANESER. *2 Kgs. 17:3-6, 24-30; 18:9.*

Shalmaneser was king of Asssyria (727-722 B.C.). He took Hoshea, king of
Israel, prisoner and bound him in prison. In the ninth year of Hoshea, the king of
Assyria took Samaria and carried Israel into Assyria and placed other people in the
lands the Lord had given to Israel. The people who were placed in Samaria and
other cities of the Israelites feared not the Lord and the Lord sent in lions which
slew some of them. They asked the king to send in someone who could teach them
about the Lord of that land. The king sent in one of the priests whom they had
carried away from Samaria to teach them how they should fear the Lord.
Nevertheless, each nation built their own gods: Succoth-benoth (Babylon); Nergal
(Cuth); Ashima (Hamath); Nibhaz and Tartak (the Avites); Adrammelech and
Anammelech (Sepharvaim). *(2 Kgs. 17:3-6, 24-30.)*

It was in the fourth year of king Hezekiah—the seventh year of Hoshea, king of
Israel—when Shalmaneser besieged Samaria. At the end of three years, he took the
city and carried Israel away unto Assyria and put other peoples in the cities the Lord
had given to the children of Israel because the children of Israel would not obey the
voice of the Lord their God. *(2 Kgs. 18:9.)*

SHAMA. *1 Chr. 11:44.*

Shama, a son of Hothan the Aroerite and brother to Jehiel, was one of David's
mighty men. (Chart 17.)

SHAMARIAH. *2 Chr. 11:19.*

Shemariah was a son of Abihail (daughter of David's brother Eliab) and king
Rehoboam (David's grandson). His brothers were Jeush and Zaham. (Charts 8d, f.)

SHAMED. *1 Chr. 8:12.*

Shamed, a descendant of Benjamin, was a son of Elpaal, who was a son of
Shaharaim and Hushim. He built Ono and Lod with the towns thereof. (Chart 16g.)

SHAMER (1). *1 Chr. 6:46.*

Shamer, a descendant of Levi, was a son of Mahli, grandson of Mushi, and a
great-grandson of Merari. (Chart 7e.)

SHAMER (2). *1 Chr. 7:34.* See **Shomer (2)**.

SHAMGAR. *Judg. 3:31.*

Shamgar, the son of Anath, followed Ehud as the third judge in Israel. He slew
600 Philistines with an ox goad and delivered Israel. (Chart 20.)

SHAMHUTH. *1 Chr. 27:8.*

Shamhuth, the Izrahite, was assigned by king David to be the fifth captain for
the fifth month. There were 24,000 in his course.

SHAMIR. *1 Chr. 24:24 (19-20, 24, 31)*.

Shamir, a Levite, was a descendant of Uzziel through Michah. He, with the rest of the chief fathers of the Levites, drew lots for his course in the presence of king David, Zadok, Ahimelech and other community leaders. (Chart 7d.)

SHAMMA. *1 Chr. 7:37*.

Shamma was a son of Zophah, a grandson of Hotham, and a great-great-great-grandson of Asher. His brothers were Suah, Harnepher, Shual, Beri, Imrah, Bezer, Hod, Shilshah, Ithran and Beera. (Chart 14a.)

SHAMMAH (1). *Gen. 36:13,17*.

Shammah was a son of Reuel the son of Esau and Bashemath. He was a duke or tribal chief. (Chart 3c.)

SHAMMAH (2) (Shimea (1), Shimeah (1), Shimma). *1 Sam. 16:9; 2 Sam. 13:3, 32; 21:21; 1 Chr. 2:13*.

Shammah was Jesse's third son and one of David's elder brothers. Samuel was told by the Lord that Shammah was not the one He had chosen to replace Saul as king. *(1 Sam. 16:9.)*

Shimeah (Shammah) was David's brother and father of Jonadab. *(2 Sam. 13:3, 32.)*

Shimea (Shammah) was the father of Jonathan and a brother of David. *(2 Sam. 21:21.)*

Shimma (Shammah) was Jesse's thirdborn son. *(1 Chr. 2:13.)* (Charts 8d-e.)

SHAMMAH (3) (Shammoth). *2 Sam. 23:11, 25, 33; 1 Chr. 11:27*.

Shammah, son of Agee the Hararite, was one of David's mighty men. *(2 Sam. 23:11, 25, 33.) (Note: Shammah is mentioned three times as though there were three different men named Shammah. Two are "Hararites." One is "Harodite." It is possible that they are all one and the same and that Hararite and Harodite are varied spellings of the same name.)*

Shammoth (Shammah) the Harorite was one of the valiant men of the armies. *(1 Chr. 11:27.) (Note: There is only one Shammah among this listing.)* (Chart 17.)

SHAMMAI (1). *1 Chr. 2:28*.

Shammai was one of the sons of Onam. His brother was Jada. He was a great-great-great-grandson of Judah. His sons were Nadab and Abishur. (Chart 8c.)

SHAMMAI (2). *1 Chr. 2:44-45*.

Shammai, son of Rekem who was one of the sons of Hebron, begat Maon. He was a fifth-great-grandson of Judah. (Chart 8i.)

SHAMMAI (3). *1 Chr. 4:17*.

Shammai was a son of Jalon who was the daughter of Ezra. His siblings were Miriam and Ishbah. (Chart 8 o.)

SHAMMOTH. See Shammah (3).

SHAMMUA (1). *Num. 13:4 (1-2, 4); 14:37*.

Shammua, of the tribe of Reuben, was a son of Zaccur. He was one of twelve leaders sent to scout out the land of Caanan. He returned with a negative report.

(Num. 13:4 [1-2, 4].) Because of the negative report he gave, he "died by the plague before the Lord." *(Num. 14:37.)*

SHAMMUA (2) (Shimea (2)) . *2 Sam. 5:14; 1 Chr. 3:5; 14:4-7.*

Shammua was born to David in Jerusalem. His brothers were Shobab, Nathan, Solomon, Ibhar, Elishua, Nepheg, Japhia, Elishama, Eliada and Eliphalet. *(2 Sam. 5:14.)*

Shimea (Shammua), Shobab, Nathan and Solomon, were sons of David and Bath-sheba. *(1 Chr. 3:5.)*

His brothers are listed again with some variations: Shammua, Shobab, Nathan, Solomon, Ibhar, Elishua, Elpalet, Nogah, Nepheg, Japhia, Elishama, Beeliada and Eliphalet. *(1 Chr. 14:4-7.) (Note: Based on earlier references, it is possible that Elpalet and Eliphalet are one and the same; that Nogah and Elishua are one and the same even though they are listed separately in this reference; and that Beeliada is the same as Eliada.)* (Chart 8e.)

SHAMMUA (3). *Neh. 11:17.* See **Shemaiah (6)**.

Shammua (4). *Neh. 12:18 (12, 18).*

Shammua, son of Bilgah, was one of the priests who was a chief of the fathers in the days of Joiakim.

SHAMSHERAI. *1 Chr. 8:26-27.*

Shamsherai, a descendant of Benjamin, was a son of Jeroham. He and his brothers were heads of the fathers by their generations, chief men, who dwelled in Jerusalem. (Chart 16j.)

SHAPHAM. *1 Chr. 5:12.*

Shapham was a descendant of Gad. He was second in command to Joel, who was the chief leader, as Gad's descendants joined Reuben's descendants in battle against the Hagarites in the days of Saul. (Chart 13b.)

SHAPHAN (1). *2 Kgs. 22:3-20; 25:22; 2 Chr. 34:8-28; Jer. 26:24; 36:10-13; 39:14; 40:5-11; 41:2; 43:6.*

Shaphan, son of Azaliah, was king Josiah's scribe. Josiah sent him to the house of the Lord to instruct Hilkiah, the high priest, to give money to workmen to repair the house of the Lord. He returned to Josiah with the book of the law which Hilkiah had found. Josiah sent Shaphan, Hilkiah and others to inquire of the Lord about the book of the law and the implications for Judah. They inquired of the prophetess Huldah, who prophesied wrath upon the people because of their wickedness. However, Huldah prophesied blessings upon Josiah because of his righteousness. *(2 Kgs. 22:3-20; 2 Chr. 34:8-28.)*

Shaphan was the father of Ahikam and the grandfather of Gedaliah, which Gedaliah was made governor over the remnant of Israel left in Jerusalem when Nebuchadnezzar carried the rest off captive to Babylon. *(2 Kgs. 25:22.)*

Shaphan was the father of Ahikam. *(Jer. 26:24.)*

Shaphan the scribe was the father of Gemariah and the grandfather of Michaiah. Baruch, in the fifth year of Jehoiakim's reign, read Jeremiah's prophecies in

Gemariah's chambers, among other places. Michaiah then declared to the princes who were assembled in the scribe's chamber the words he had heard Baruch read. *(Jer. 36:10-13.) (Note: The Shaphan referred to in Jer. 36:10 is cross referenced with Shaphan the father of Ahikam, Jer. 26:24.)*

Shaphan was the father of Ahikam and the grandfather of Gedaliah, which Gedaliah was given charge of Jeremiah by Nebuchadnezzar's guards. *(Jer. 39:14.)*

Shaphan was the father of Ahikam and grandfather of Gedaliah. *(Jer. 40:5-11.)*

Shaphan was the father of Ahikam and the grandfather of Gedaliah, which Gedaliah was slain by Ishmael. *(Jer. 41:2.)*

Shaphan was the father of Ahikam who was the father of Gedaliah. Following the death of Gedaliah, Johanan, son of Kareah (Careah), and the captains of the forces carried all of the people, including the king's daughters, etc., who remained in Judah into Egypt. *(Jer. 43:6.)*

SHAPHAN (2). *Jer. 29:3*

Shaphan was the father of Elasah.

SHAPHAN (3). *Ezek. 8:11.*

Shaphan was the father of Jaazaniah which Jaazaniah was one of the seventy "ancients of the house of Israel" who worshipped falsely in the house of the Lord as seen in vision by Ezekiel.

SHAPHAT (1). *Num. 13:5, 16, 31-33; 14:37.*

Shaphat, of the tribe of Simeon, was the son of Hori. He was one of twelve leaders sent to scout out the land of Caanan. He returned with a negative report. *(Num. 13:5, 16, 31-33.)* Because of the negative report he gave, he "died by the plague before the Lord." *(Num. 14:37.)*

SHAPHAT (2). *1 Kgs. 19:16.*

Shaphat, of Abel-meholah, was the father of Elisha who was anointed to be prophet in Elijah's stead.

SHAPHAT (3). *1 Chr. 3:22.*

Shaphat, a descendant of David, was a son of Shemaiah and a grandson of Shechaniah. His brothers were Hattush, Igeal, Bariah and Neariah. (Chart 1.)

SHAPHAT (4) . *1 Chr. 5:12.*

Shaphat was a descendant of Gad. He, along with Joel, Shapham and Jaanai, joined with Reuben's descendants in battle against the Hagarites in the days of king Saul. (Chart 13b.)

SHAPHAT (5). *1 Chr. 27:29.*

Shaphat, the son of Adlai, was the officer assigned by king David to be over the herds that were in the valleys.

SHARAI. *Ezra 10:40 (18-19, 40, 44).*

Sharai, a son of Bani, and his brothers were some of the men in Israel who took foreign wives but gave them up when Ezra feared the wrath of God would destroy Israel for this iniquity.

SHARAR (Sacar (1)). *2 Sam. 23:33; 1 Chr. 11:35.*

<u>Sharar</u> **(Sacar)** the Hararite was the father of Ahiam, one of David's mighty men. (Chart 17.)

SHAREZER. *2 Kgs. 19:37; 2 Chr. 32:21; Isa. 37:38.*

<u>Sharezer</u> and Adrammelech, two of the sons of king Sennacherib of Assyria, killed their father as he was worshipping in the house of the false god Nisroch following his unsuccessful attempt to capture Judah. They escaped into the land of Armenia. Their brother Esarhaddon ruled over Assyria after Sennacherib's death. *(2 Kgs. 19:37; Isa. 37:38.)*

When Sennacherib returned in shame after being defeated in his attempt to take Judah from king Hezekiah, two of his sons slew him. *(2 Chr. 32:21.) (Note: Sharezer and Adrammelech are not mentioned by name. This verse merely states that Sennacherib was slain by those who "came forth of his own bowels.")*

SHARONITE. *1 Chr. 27:29.*

<u>Sharonites</u> were citizens of Sharon. Shitrai, the Sharonite, was the officer assigned by king David to be over the herds that fed in Sharon.

SHASHAI. *Ezra 10:40 (18-19, 40, 44).*

<u>Shashai</u>, a son of Bani, and his brothers were some of the men in Israel who took foreign wives but gave them up when Ezra feared the wrath of God would destroy Israel for this iniquity.

SHASHAK. *1 Chr. 8:14.*

<u>Shashak</u>, a descendant of Benjamin, was a son of Beriah who was a son of Elpaal who was a son of Shaharaim and Hushim. He was head of the fathers in his generation, one of the chief men who dwelled in Jerusalem. (Chart 16g.)

SHAUL (1). *1 Chr. 1:48-49.* See **Saul (1)**.

SHAUL (2) (Shaulites). *Gen. 46:10; Num. 26:13; 1 Chr. 4:24-25.*

<u>Shaul</u>, one of Simeon's sons by a Canaanitish woman, was a grandson of Jacob. *(Gen. 46:10.)* His descendants are called **Shaulites**. *(Num. 26:13.)*

Shaul, Nemuel, Jamin, Jarib and Zerah were sons of Simeon. Shaul's son was Shallum. *(1 Chr. 4:24-25.)* (Chart 6a.)

SHAUL (3) (Joel (8)). *1 Chr. 6:24 (22-28), 36 (33-38); 2 Chr. 29:12.*

<u>Shaul</u> **(Joel)** , of the house of Levi through Kohath, was the son of Uzziah (Azariah). He was the father of Elkanah. *(1 Chr. 6:24 [22-28], 36 [33-38].)*

Joel, a Levite, was the son of Azariah. When Hezekiah became king over Judah, Hezekiah had Joel and other Levites cleanse and sanctify the house of the Lord after sanctifying themselves. *(2 Chr. 29:12.)* (Chart 7d.)

SHAVSHA. *1 Chr. 18:16.* See **Seraiah (1)**.

SHEAL. *Ezra 10:29 (18-19, 29, 44).*

<u>Sheal</u>, a son of Bani, was one of the Israelites who took foreign wives, causing Ezra to cry unto the Lord in behalf of Israel for fear the Lord would totally destroy the children of Israel due to this latest iniquity. Sheal and his brothers agreed to put away their foreign wives.

SHEALTIEL. *Ezra 3:2, 8; Neh. 12:1; Hag. 1:1, 12, 14; 2:2, 23.*

Shealtiel was the father of Zerubbabel. (Zerubbabel returned to Jerusalem to rebuild the temple at the command of Cyrus.) *(Ezra 3:2, 8.)*

Shealtiel was the father of Zerubbabel, governor of Judah. *(Neh. 12:1; Hag. 1:1, 12, 14; 2:2, 23.)*

SHEARIAH. *1 Chr. 8:38.*

Sheariah, a son of Azel, was from the tribe of Benjamin. He was a tenth-great-grandson of Saul. His brothers were Azrikam, Bocheru, Ishmael, Obadiah and Hanan. (Chart 16 l.)

SHEAR-JASHUB. *Isa. 7:3-7.*

Shear-jashub was the son of Isaiah. His name means: "the remnant shall return." Isaiah was instructed to take Shear-jashub with him when Isaiah delivered a message to Ahaz, king of Judah, warning Ahaz that Syria and Ephraim were planning to war against him, but to fear not because it would not come to pass.

SHEBA (1). *Gen. 10:7; 1 Chr. 1:9; Ezek. 27:22-23; 38.*

Sheba was a son of Raamah, grandson of Cush, great-grandson of Ham, and a great great grandson of Noah. His brother was Dedan. *(Gen. 10:7; 1 Chr. 1:9.)*

As Ezekiel lamented the fall of the great city of Tyrus, he bemoaned the loss of her riches and commerce, part of which involved the merchants of Sheba and Raamah who traded spices, precious stones and gold in the fairs at Tyrus. Haran, Canneh and Eden were merchants of Sheba, Asshur and Chilmad and traded in blue clothes, broidered work, chests of rich apparel, bound with cords, and made of cedar. *(Ezek. 27:22-23.)*

In the latter days, the battle of Gog and Magog against Israel will usher in the Second Coming of the Lord. Gathered together with Gog will be Sheba, Gomer, Togarmar, Dedan and the merchants of Tarshish. *(Ezek. 38.)* (Chart 2e.)

SHEBA (2). *Gen. 10:25-29; 1 Chr. 1:19-23.*

Sheba was a son of Joktan and a nephew of Peleg. He was a third-great-grandson of Shem and a fourth-great-grandson of Noah. His brothers were Almodad, Sheleph, Hazarmaveth, Jerah, Hadoram, Uzal, Diklah, Obal (Ebal), Abimael, Ophir, Havilah and Jobab. *(Note: The Bible Dictionary indictes that Sheba's descendants gave their name to a portion of southern Arabia, now called Arabia Felix. The queen of Sheba is cross-referenced with this Sheba.)* (Chart 2b.)

SHEBA (3). *Gen. 25:3.*

Sheba was a son of Jokshan and a grandson of Abraham and Keturah. (Chart 3a, d, f.)

SHEBA (4). *2 Sam. 20:1-2.*

Sheba, son of Bichri, a Benjamite, was a wicked man who led all the tribes of Israel, save the tribe of Judah, away from David.

SHEBA (5). *1 Chr. 5:13.*

Sheba was a descendant of Gad. (Chart 13b.)

SHEBA (6). *Job 6:19.*

(Note: It is not clear if this Sheba is a place or a person. Job merely refers to the caravans of Sheba.)

SHEBANIAH (1). *1 Chr. 15:24.*

Shebaniah was one of those who, under the direction of David, was assigned to make music before the Lord as the ark was removed from the house of Obed-edom and taken to the place which David had prepared for it to be housed. He was one of the priests and was assigned to blow the trumpet before the ark of God.

SHEBANIAH (2). *Neh. 9.*

Shebaniah was a Levite. When Ezra read and interpreted the law of Moses and he and Nehemiah proclaimed the day a holy day, the Levites—Shebaniah, Jeshua, Kadmiel, Bani, Bunni, Sherebiah, Bani, Chenani, Hashabniah, Hodijah and Pethahiah—blessed and praised the Lord, reciting the Lord's goodness to Israel: His blessing of Abraham; His giving the land of the Canaanites, Hittites, Amorites, Perizzites, Jebusites and Girgashites to Israel; His dividing the Red Sea so they could cross it yet drowning the Egyptians who pursued them; the signs and wonders He showed to Pharaoh; His leading them in the wilderness and protecting them so they had bread from heaven, water from the rock, and shoes and clothes that never wore out; His accepting them whenever they repented, even when they made a molten calf. They had been given the kingdoms of Shihon, Heshbon and Bashan and the Lord had subdued the Canaanites and delivered them into the hands of the Israelites. After giving praise, they made a covenant with the Lord. The princes, Levites and priests sealed the covenant.

SHEBANIAH (3). *Neh. 10:4 (1, 4, 28-31); 12:14.*

Shebaniah was among the priests who covenanted and sealed their covenant to marry in Israel, honor the Sabbath, pay tithes and keep the commandments. *(Neh. 10:4 [1, 4, 28-31].)*

Shebaniah was the father of Joseph, one of the priests who was chief of the fathers in the days of Joiakim. *(Neh. 12:14.)*

SHEBANIAH (4). *Neh. 10:10 (1, 10, 28-31).*

Shebaniah, a Levite, was among those who covenanted and sealed their covenant to marry in Israel, honor the Sabbath, pay tithes and keep the commandments.

SHEBANIAH (5). *Neh. 10:12 (1, 12, 28-31).*

Shebaniah, a Levite, was among those who covenanted and sealed their covenant to marry in Israel, honor the Sabbath, pay tithes and keep the commandments.

SHEBER. *1 Chr. 2:48.*

Sheber was one of the sons of Caleb and his concubine Maachah. (Chart 8k.)

SHEBNA. *2 Kgs. 18:18 (13-37); 19:2; Isa. 22:15, 20; 36.*

Shebna was the scribe in king Hezekiah's day. He, along with Eliakim and Joah, came out to hear the demands of Rab-shakeh of Assyria. They reported Rab-shakeh's blasphemous remarks to Hezekiah. *(2 Kgs. 18:18 [13-37]; Isa. 36.)*

Hezekiah sent Shebna with Eliakim and the elders of the priests to consult with the prophet Isaiah. *(2 Kgs. 19:2.)*

Isaiah prophesied that Eliakim, son of Hilkiah, would replace Shebna. *(Isa. 22:15, 20.) (Note: The footnote to the text explains the symbolism of Isaiah's prophecy. The symbolic name "Eliakim" becomes representative of the Messiah, the Savior, and means "God shall cease to arise.")*

SHEBUEL (1) (Shubael (1)). *1 Chr. 23:16 (6, 16); 24:20, 31; 26:24-26.*

Shebuel was the son of Gershom who was the son of Moses. When David numbered the Levites and divided them into courses among the sons of Levi, Shebuel was the chief of his course. *(1 Chr. 23:16 [6, 16].)*

Shubael (Shebuel), a Levite, was a descendant of Amram. His descendant was Jehdeiah. He drew lots for his course in the presence of king David, Zadok, Ahimelech and other community leaders. *(1 Chr. 24.20, 31.)*

Shebuel was ruler of the treasures. His cousins, descendants of his uncle Eliezer, were over all the treasures of the dedicated things which David and others had dedicated. *(1 Chr. 26:24-26.)* (Chart 7b.)

SHEBUEL (2) (Shubael (2)). *1 Chr. 25:4, 20.*

Shebuel, a Levite and musician, was a son of Heman. The musicians—sons of Heman, Asaph and Jeduthun—drew lots and were given their duty assignments by David and the captains of the host. Shubael (Shebuel) cast the 13th lot. He, his sons and his brethren numbered 12. (Chart 7d.)

SHECHANIAH (1). *1 Chr. 3:21-22; Neh. 3:29.*

Shechaniah, a descendant of David, was the father of Shemaiah. (Chart 1.)

SHECHANIAH (2). *1 Chr. 24:11 (1, 4, 11).*

Shechaniah was from the sons of Aaron. When David made the divisions of the sons of Aaron, there was one principal household for Eleazar and one taken for Ithamar. Eleazar had 16 sons and there were eight sons of Ithamar. These 24 sons who were chief of the fathers were divided by lot. Shechaniah drew the tenth lot.

SHECANIAH (3). *2 Chr. 31:15 (14-15).*

Shecaniah, and others, assisted Kore, porter toward the east, in caring for the freewill offerings of God and their distribution when Hezekiah was king over Judah.

SHECHANIAH (4). *Ezra 10:2.*

Shechaniah the son of Jehiel, one of the sons of Elam, suggested to Ezra that he have all the children of Israel covenant to put away their foreign wives so as not to incur the wrath of God upon them due to their having taken strange wives.

SHECHANIAH (5). *Neh. 6:18.*

Shechaniah, son of Arah, was the father-in-law of Tobiah.

SHECHANIAH (6). *Neh. 12:3 (1, 3).*

Shechaniah was one of the men (priests and Levites) who went up from Babylon to Jerusalem with Zerubbabel.

SHECHANIAH'S DESCENDANT. *Ezra 8:3, 5 (1, 3, 5).*

Schechaniah's Descendant Zechariah, of the sons of Pharosh, was the chief of his fathers when Ezra led many exiled Israelites out of Babylon back to Jerusalem. He went with Ezra and took 150 males with him as reckoned by genealogy *(v. 3)*. Shechaniah's descendant, the son of Jahaziel, was the chief of his fathers when Ezra led many exiled Israelites out of Babylon back to Jerusalem. He also went with Ezra and took 300 males with him as reckoned by genealogy *(v. 5)*.

SHECHEM (1). *Gen. 33:19; 34.*

Shechem was the son of Hamor. Jacob bought a parcel of a field from the children of Hamor. *(Gen. 33:19.)*

After Jacob settled his family in Canaan, his daughter Dinah went out among the people to see the daughters of the land. Shechem took her and lay with her, thus defiling her. Shechem asked his father to get her for him for his wife. Hamor met with Jacob and told him his son wanted to marry Dinah. He suggested their groups intermarry and trade together. Dinah's brothers answered this request deceitfully saying they would consent to that if all of Hamor's men would be circumcised. Shechem and his father and all the other men agreed to that. On the third day after being circumcised, "when they were sore," Dinah's brothers, Simeon and Levi, took their swords and slew Shechem and Hamor and all the other males. *(Gen. 34.)*

SHECHEM (2) (Shechemites). *Num. 26:31.*

Shechem was a son of Gilead and a great-grandson of Manasseh. His descendants were the **Shechemites**. His brothers were Jeezer, Helek, Asriel, Shemida and Hepher. (Charts 15a-b.)

SHECHEM (3). *1 Chr. 7:19.*

Shechem was a son of Shemida, grandson of Gilead and a great-great-grandson of Manasseh. (Chart 15a.)

SHEDEUR. *Num. 1:5.*

Shedeur was the father of Elizur and was of the tribe of Reuben.

SHEHARIAH. *1 Chr. 8:26-27.*

Shehariah, a descendant of Benjamin, was a son of Jeroham. A chief man, he dwelled in Jerusalem and was head of his fathers by his generation. (Chart 16j.)

SHELAH (1). *1 Chr. 1:18.* See **Salah**.

Shelah (2) (Shelanites). *Gen. 38:5, 11, 14, 26; 46:12; Num. 26:20; 1 Chr. 4:21-22.*

Shelah was Judah and Shuah's third son whom she bore in Chezib. When Er and Onan, Shelah's older brothers, were slain by the Lord, Judah suggested to Er's widow, Tamar, that she remain a widow at her father's place until Shelah was old enough to marry her. However, when Shelah became of age, Judah failed to give him to her for a husband. *(Gen. 38:5, 11, 14, 26.)*

Shelah was one of Judah's sons and a grandson of Jacob. *(Gen. 46:12.)* He was the father of the **Shelanites**. *(Num. 26:20.)*

Shelah begat Er the father of Lecah, and Laadah the father of Mareshah, "and the families of the house of them that wrought fine linen, of the house of Ashbea, and Jokim, and the men of Chozeba, and Joash, and Saraph, who had the dominion in Moab, and Jashubi-lehem." They were potters and worked with the king's plants and hedges. *(1 Chr. 4:21-22.)* (Charts 8a, c-d, g-h.)

SHELEMIAH (1) (Meshelemiah). *1 Chr. 26:14*. See **Shallum (9)**.

Shelemiah (2). *Ezra 10:39 (18-19, 39, 44)*.

SHELEMIAH, a son of Bani, and his brothers were some of the men in Israel who took foreign wives but gave them up when Ezra feared the wrath of God would destroy Israel for this iniquity.

SHELEMIAH (3). *Ezra 10:41 (18-19, 41, 44)*.

Shelemiah, a son of Bani, and his brothers were some of the men in Israel who took foreign wives but gave them up when Ezra feared the wrath of God would destroy Israel for this iniquity.

SHELEMIAH (4), *Neh. 3:30*.

Shelemiah was the father of Hananiah.

SHELEMIAH (5). *Neh. 13:13*.

Shelemiah the priest, along with Zadok the scribe and others, was counted as faithful by Nehemiah and was assigned to help distribute to the Levites and singers the shares they were to have.

SHELEMIAH (6). *Jer. 36:14*.

Shelemiah, the son of Cushi, was the father of Nethaniah and the grandfather of Jehudi, which Jehudi was sent by the princes unto Baruch to request he come and bring the roll and read it to them.

SHELEMIAH (7). *Jer. 36:26*.

Shelemiah was the son of Abdeel. Jehoiakim commanded him, Jerahmeel (the king's son) and Seraiah (son of Azriel) to arrest Baruch and Jeremiah for pronouncing the Lord's warnings against the people. However, the Lord "hid" Baruch and Jeremiah.

SHELEMIAH (8). *Jer. 37:3; 38:1-6*.

Shelemiah was the father of Jehucal, which Jehucal was sent by Zedekiah to ask Jeremiah to pray for the people. *(Jer. 37:3.)*

Shelemiah was the father of Jucal (Jehucal), which Jucal and his colleagues asked Zedekiah if they could slay Jeremiah for prophesying that Jerusalem would be captured and burned if the people did not go with the Chaldeans. *(Jer. 38:1-6.)*

SHELEMIAH (9). *Jer. 37:13-15*.

Shelemiah was the son of Hananiah and the father of Irijah, which Irijah accused the prophet Jeremiah of deserting to the Chaldeans and hauled him before the princes who smote Jeremiah and cast him into the dungeon in the house of Jonathan. (Chart 16m.)

SHELEPH. *Gen. 10:26.*

Sheleph was a son of Joktan, a third-great-grandson of Shem and a fourth-great-grandson of Noah. (Chart 2b.)

SHELESH. *1 Chr. 7:35.*

Shelesh was a son of Helem (Hotham) and a great-great-grandson of Asher. His brothers were Zophah, Imna and Amal. They were men who were "heads of their father's house, choice and mighty men of valour, chief of the princes." (Chart 14a.)

SHELOMI. *Num. 34:27.*

Shelomi was the father of Ahihud and was of the tribe of Asher. (Chart 14b.)

SHELOMITH (1). *Lev. 24:10-11.*

Shelomith, the daughter of Dibri of the tribe of Dan and wife of an Egyptian, was an Israelitish woman whose son was stoned to death for blasphemy. (Chart 11b.)

SHELOMITH (2). *1 Chr. 3:19.*

Shelomith, a descendant of David, was a daughter of Zerubbabel, a granddaughter of Pedaiah and a great-granddaughter of Jeconiah (Jehoiachin). Her brothers were Meshullam and Hananiah. (Chart 1.)

SHELOMITH (3). *1 Chr. 23:9.*

Shelomith, a Levite and son of Shimei, was of the Gershonites. He, Haziel and Haran, all sons of Shimei, were named by David as chiefs of the fathers of Laadan when David numbered the Levites and divided them into courses at the time he named Solomon king. (Chart 7f.)

SHELOMITH (4) (Shelomoth). *1 Chr. 23:18 (6, 18); 24:22.*

Shelomith, a Levite, was of the sons of Izhar, son of Kohath. When David numbered the Levites at the time he made Solomon king, he divided them into courses among the sons of Levi. Shelomith was the chief of the sons of Izhar. They did the work for the service of the house of the Lord. *(1 Chr. 23:18 [6, 18].)*

Shelomoth (Shelomith), a Levite, was a descendant of Izhar and an ancestor of Jahath. He drew lots for his course in the presence of king David, Zadok, Ahimelech and other community leaders. *(1 Chr. 24:22.)* (Chart 7d.)

SHELOMITH (5). *1 Chr. 26:25-28.*

Shelomith, a Levite, was the son of Zichri of the lineage of Eliezer, son of Moses. He and his brethren were over all the treasures of the dedicated things which king David and others dedicated, including those dedicated by Samuel the seer, Saul, Abner and Joab. (Chart 7b.)

SHELOMITH (6). *2 Chr. 11:20.*

Shelomith was a son of king Rehoboam (Solomon's son) and Maachah (Absalom's daughter). His brothers were Abijah, Attai and Ziza. (Chart 1.)

SHELOMITH (7). *Ezra 8:10.*

Shelomith's descendant, the son of Josiphiah, was the leader of his posterity when Ezra led many exiled Israelites out of Babylon back to Jerusalem.

SHELOMOTH. See **Shelomith (4)**.

SHELUMIEL. *Num 1:6, 22-23 (5-6, 22-23); 2:12 (10-16); 7:36.*

Shelumiel, son of Zurishaddai of the tribe of Simeon, was appointed by the Lord to stand at the head of all of the tribe of Simeon as Moses organized Israel in preparation for war. The males 20 years of age and older in the tribe of Simeon who could go to war totaled 59,300. *(Num 1:6, 22-23 [5-6, 22-23].)*

Shelumiel was instructed to have his men pitch their camp next to Reuben on the south side of the encampment. *(Num. 2:12 (10-16).)*

When the altar of the tabernacle was anointed and dedicated, Shelumiel made his offering on the fifth day. *(Num. 7:36.)*

SHEM. *Gen. 5:32; 6:18; 8:16; 9:7-13, 22-26; 10:22 (21-22); 11:10-11; 1 Chr. 1:17.*

Shem is the first of Noah's sons mentioned in the Old Testament. Noah was 500 years old when Shem, Ham, and Japheth were born. *(Gen. 5:32.) (Note: The following passage from Moses 8:12, in the "Pearl of Great Price" clarifies this scripture. "And Noah was 450 years old, and begat Japheth; and 42 years afterward he begat Shem of her who was the mother of Japheth, and when he was 500 years old he begat Ham.")*

The Lord told Noah to take his wife and his sons and their wives into the ark with him. *(Gen. 6:18.)*

The Lord told Noah to take his wife and his sons and their wives and leave the ark. *(Gen. 8:16.)*

God spoke to Noah and to his sons and told them He would establish His covenant with them and with their seed. They were told to multiply and replenish the earth. God set His rainbow in the sky as a token of a covenant between Him and the earth. When Ham saw his father, drunken and naked in his tent, he told his brothers. Shem and Japheth took a garment and, walking backwards so as not to see their father, covered him up. When Noah woke up and realized what Ham had done, he cursed Ham's son Canaan but blessed Shem and Japheth. He said Canaan would be their servant. *(Gen. 9:7-13, 22-26.)*

Shem begat Elam, Asshur, Arphaxad, Lud and Aram. *(Gen. 10:22 [21-22].)*

Shem was 100 years old when he begat Arphaxad two years after the flood. He lived to be 600 years old. *(Gen. 11:10-11.) (Note: There is a ten-year discrepancy between the years that add up to the date of the flood and the date of Arphaxad's birth. The flood occurred 1656 years after the Fall, according to the sum total of the years indicated for who begat whom at what age. According to the sum totals [as clarified in Moses 8:12], Shem was born 1548 years after the Fall and would have been 108 years old at the time of the flood rather than 98 years old and 110 years old when Arphaxad was born. However, Gen. 11:10 indicates that Shem was 100 years old when Arphaxad was born and that Arphaxad was born two years after the flood.)*

Shem lived 600 years. *(Gen. 11:10-11.)*

Shem was the father of Elam, Asshur, Arphaxad, Lud, Aram, Uz, Hul, Gether and Meshech. *(1 Chr. 1:17.) (Note: Gen. 10:23 states that Aram begat Uz, Hul, Gether and Mash [Meshech]. Thus, Shem would be their grandfather rather than their father. The Bible Dictionary states that Shem was the traditional ancestor of the Shemitic or Semitic races which include the Arabs, Hebrews, Phoenicians, Aramaeans or Syrians, Babylonians and Assyrians.)* (Charts 1.; 2b-d.; 21.)

SHEMA (1). *1 Chr. 2:43.*

Shema was one of the sons of Hebron. His brothers were Korah, Tappuah and Rekem. Shema begat Raham the father of Jorkoam. (Chart 8i.)

SHEMA (2). See **Shemaiah (4)**. *1 Chr. 5:8.*

Shema, of the tribe of Reuben, was the son of Joel and the father of Azaz. *(Note: It is possible that Shema (2) is the same person as Shemaiah (4).)* (Chart 5b.)

SHEMA (3). *1 Chr. 8:13.*

Shema, a descendant of Benjamin, was a son of Elpaal, who was a son of Shaharaim and Hushim. Shema and his brother Beriah were heads of the fathers of the inhabitants of Aijalon, who drove away the inhabitants of Gath. (Chart 16g.)

SHEMA (4). *Neh. 8:4 (1-8).*

Shema was one of the men who stood on Ezra's right hand when Ezra read and interpreted the law of Moses to the people.

SHEMAAH. *1 Chr. 12:3.*

Shemaah, the Gibeathite, was the father of Ahiezer and Joash, two of David's mighty men who came to David at Ziklag to join him in battle against Saul and to rejoice with all Israel when David became king.

SHEMAIAH (1). *1 Kgs. 12:22-24; 2 Chr. 11:2-4; 12:5-8, 15.*

Shemaiah was a man of God sent to Rehoboam to tell him that he should not go to battle against Jeroboam and the children of Israel. *(1 Kgs. 12:22-24; 2 Chr. 11:2-4.)*

Shemaiah went to Rehoboam and to the princes of Judah and told them that the Lord had left them in the hand of Shishak, king of Egypt, because they had forsaken the Lord. Upon their repentance, the Lord told Shemaiah that He would not destroy them, but would grant them a partial deliverance. They would be Shishak's servants. The prophet Shemaiah's writings are among the lost scriptures of the Old Testament. *(2 Chr. 12:5-8, 15.)*

SHEMAIAH (2). *1 Chr. 3:22; 2 Chr. 31:14; Neh. 3:29.*

Shemaiah, a descendant of David, was a son of Shechaniah. His sons were Hattush, Igeal, Bariah, Neariah and Shaphat. *(1 Chr. 3:22.)*

Shemaiah, and others, assisted Kore, porter toward the east, in caring for the freewill offerings of God and their distribution when Hezekiah was king over Judah. *(2 Chr. 31:14.)*

Shemaiah, son of Shechaniah, was keeper of the east gate and labored next to Zadok when the children of Israel rebuilt the walls and gates of Jerusalem during the time of Ezra and Nehemiah. *(Neh. 3:29.)* (Chart 1.)

SHEMAIAH (3). *1 Chr. 4:37.*

Shemaiah was the father of Shimri and a descendant of Shimei. *(Note: The Bible Dictionary suggests the possibility that Shemaiah is the same as Shimei.)* (Chart 6a.)

SHEMAIAH (4). See **Shema (2)**.*1 Chr. 5:4.*

Shemaiah, of the tribe of Reuben, was the son of Joel and the father of Gog. *(Note: It is possible that Shemaiah is the same person as Shema.)* (Chart 5b.)

SHEMAIAH (5). *1 Chr. 9:14 (13-14); Neh. 11:15 (1, 4, 15).*

Shemaiah, a Levite, was a descendant of Merari and was the son of Hasshub. His genealogy was written in the book of the kings of Israel and Judah who were carried away to Babylon for their transgression. He was one of the men ably prepared for the service of the house of God upon returning from Babylonian captivity. *(1 Chr. 9:14 [13-14].)*

Shemaiah was one of the families who, after leaving Babylonian captivity, was elected by lot to dwell in Jerusalem. His father was Hashub (Hasshub). *(Neh. 11:15 [1, 4, 15].)* (Chart 7e.)

SHEMAIAH (6) (Shammua (3)). *1 Chr. 9:16 (13, 16), 2 Chr. 29:14; Neh. 11:17.*

Shemaiah, father of Obadiah, was the son of Galal who was the son of Jeduthun. He was a Levite whose descendants dwelled in the villages of the Netophathites. His genealogy was written in the book of the kings of Israel and Judah who were carried away to Babylon for their transgression. He was one of the men ably prepared for the work of the service of the house of God. *(1 Chr. 9:16 [13, 16].)*

Shemaiah was of the sons of Jeduthun. He was among those instructed by Hezekiah, king of Judah, to santify themselves so they could cleanse and sanctify the house of the Lord. *(2 Chr. 29:14.)*

Shammua (Shemaiah) was the son of Galal and the father of Abda (Obadiah), which Abda assisted Mattaniah in beginning the thanksgiving with prayer. *(Neh. 11:17.)* (Chart 7h.)

SHEMAIAH (7). *1 Chr. 15:8, 11.*

Shemaiah, a Levite, was the chief of the sons of Elizaphan. He and 200 of his brethren were called by David to assemble with other Levites to prepare themselves to retrieve the ark of God from the house of Obed-edom so as to bring it to the place David had prepared for it in the city of David.

SHEMAIAH (8). *1 Chr. 24:6.*

Shemaiah, a Levite, was the son of Nethaneel the scribe. When the divisions of the sons of Aaron were made and the 24 lots chosen, Shemaiah wrote them before the king, the princes, Zadok the priest, Ahimelech, and before the chief of the fathers of the priests and Levites: one principal household for Eleazar and one for Ithamar.

SHEMAIAH (9). *1 Chr. 26:4-8 (Subtitle, 4-8)*.

Shemaiah, a Levite, was the firstborn son of Obed-edom. His brothers were Jehozabad, Joah, Sacar, Nethaneel, Ammiel, Issachar, and Peulthai. They, along with other Levites, were appointed by king David to be porters—to have charge of the treasures, serve as officers and judges, and to conduct the outward business over Israel. Shemaiah also had several sons: Othni, Rephael, Obed, Elzabad, Elihu, and Semachiah. They ruled thoughout the house of their father and were mighty men of valor. (Chart 7c.)

SHEMAIAH (10). *2 Chr. 17:8-9 (7-9)*.

Shemaiah, a Levite, along with other Levites and Elisham and Jehoram, the priests, was sent by king Jehoshaphat to journey with the princes of Judah throughout the cities of Judah to instruct the people out of the book of the law of the Lord.

SHEMAIAH (11). *Ezra 8:13, 16*.

Shemaiah, Eliphelet and Jeiel, were of the last sons of Adonikam. They were the chief of the fathers. They took 60 males with them when they went with Ezra back to Jerusalem from Babylon. Shemaiah was one of the chief men Ezra sent for when he gathered the people together as he was preparing to lead them to Jerusalem from Babylon and discovered there were none of the sons of Levi among the group. He sent this group to Iddo and the Nethinims to request that they send them some ministers for the house of God.

SHEMAIAH (12). *Ezra 10:21 (18-19, 21, 44); Neh. 10:8 (1, 8, 28-31)*.

Shemaiah, one of the sons of Harim, was among those sons of the priests who took foreign wives but who agreed to put them away as instructed by Ezra. His brothers were Maaseiah, Elijah, Jahiel and Uzziah. *(Ezra 10:21 [18-19, 21, 44].)*

Shemaiah was among the priests who covenanted and sealed their covenant to marry in Israel, honor the Sabbath, pay tithes and keep the commandments. *(Neh. 10:8 [1, 8, 28-31].)*

SHEMAIAH (13). *Ezra 10:31 (19, 31, 44)*.

Shemaiah (one of Harim's sons) and his brothers—Eliezer, Ishijah, Malchiah, Shimeon, Benjamin, Malluch and Shemariah—were some of the Israelite men who took wives from among the Canaanites and other foreign groups. They agreed to Ezra's request to separate themselves from their foreign wives.

SHEMAIAH (14). *Neh. 6:10*.

Shemaiah, son of Delaiah and grandson of Mehetabeel, was hired by Sanballat and Tobiah to prophesy against Nehemiah. He tried to get Nehemiah to hide in the temple, but Nehemiah refused.

SHEMAIAH (15). Also see **Jeiel (3)**. *Neh. 12:6, 18, 31-42*.

Shemaiah was one of the men (priests and Levites) who left Babylonian captivity with Zerubbabel and went to Jerusalelm. He was the father of Jehonathan, who was one of the priests who was a chief of the fathers in the days of Joiakim. Shemaiah and other singers and musicians, along with Hoshaiah and half of the princes of Judah, were appointed by Nehemiah to one of the two great companies of people gathered for the dedication of the walls of Jerusalem. (Chart 7a.)

SHEMAIAH (16). *Jer. 26:20.*

Shemaiah of Kirjath-jearim, was the father of the prophet Urijah, which prophet was slain by king Jehoiakim for preaching against the wickedness of Israel.

SHEMAIAH (17). *Jer. 29:24-32.*

Shemaiah the Nehelamite claimed to be the Lord's prophet in the stead of Jehoiada the priest. He claimed Jeremiah was a false prophet. As a result, the Lord cursed him and told him that "he shall not have a man to dwell among this people; neither shall he behold the good that I will do for my people."

SHEMAIAH (18). *Jer. 36:12.*

Shemaiah was the father of Delaiah, which Delaiah was with the other princes in the scribe's chamber when Michaiah declared unto them all the words of the book he had heard from Baruch.

SHEMARIAH (1). *1 Chr. 12:5.*

Shemariah was one of David's mighty men who came to him at Ziklag to protect him from Saul and to rejoice with all Israel when David was made king.

SHEMARIAH (2). *Ezra 10:32 (18-19, 32, 44).*

Shemariah, one of Harim's sons, and his brothers—Eliezer, Ishijah, Malchiah, Shemaiah, Shimeon, Benjamin and Malluch—were some of the Israelite men who took wives from among the Canaanites and other foreign groups. They agreed to Ezra's request to separate themselves from their foreign wives.

SHEMARIAH (3). *Ezra 10:41 (18-19, 41, 44).*

Shemariah, a son of Bani, and his brothers were some of the men in Israel who took foreign wives but gave them up when Ezra feared the wrath of God would destroy Israel for this iniquity.

SHEMEBER. *Gen. 14:2-4.*

Shemeber was king of Zeboiim. Chedorlaomer, king of Elam; Amraphel, king of Shinar; Arioch, king of Ellasar; and Tidal, king of nations, made war against Shemeber and against the kings of Sodom and Gomorrah and others. They served Chedorlaomer 12 years and then they rebelled.

SHEMER. *1 Kgs. 16:24.*

Shemer owned the hill Samaria. Omri, king of Israel, bought Samaria from Shemer for two talents of silver.

SHEMIDA (Shemidaites). *Num. 26:32 (28-32); 1 Chr. 7:19.*

Shemida was a son of Gilead, a great-grandson of Manasseh, and a great-great-grandson of Joseph. His descendants were the **Shemidaites**. His brothers were Jeezer, Helek, Asriel, Shechem and Hepher. *(Num. 26:32 [28-32].)*

Shemida's sons were Ahian, Shechem, Likhi and Aniam. *(1 Chr. 7:19.)* (Charts 15a-b.)

SHEMIRAMOTH (1). *1 Chr. 15:18-20, 25; 16:5 (4-5)*.

Shemiramoth and his brethren of the second degree were assigned, under the direction of David, to be singers along with Heman, Asaph and Ethan. Shemiramoth and his brethren were assigned to play with psalteries on Alamoth as the ark was brought from the house of Obed-edom unto Jerusalem to the place David had prepared for it. *(1 Chr. 15:18-20, 25.)*

Shemiramoth and his brethren were assigned by David to minister before the ark of the Lord and to play with psalteries and harps. *(1 Chr. 16:5 [4-5].)*

SHEMIRAMOTH (2). *2 Chr. 17:8-9 (7-9)*.

Shemiramoth, a Levite, along with other Levites and Elisham and Jehoram, the priests, was sent by king Jehoshaphat to journey with the princes of Judah throughout the cities of Judah to instruct the people out of the book of the law of the Lord.

SHEMUEL (1). *Num. 34:20 (17-20)*.

Shemuel was the son of Ammihud of the tribe of Simeon. He was assigned to divide the land of inheritance given to his tribe.

SHEMUEL (2). *1 Chr. 6:33*. See **Samuel**.

SHEMUEL (3). *1 Chr. 7:2*.

Shemuel was a son of Tola and a grandson of Issachar. His brothers were Uzzi, Rephaiah, Jeriel, Jahmai and Jibsam. They were "valiant men of might in their generations." (Chart 9a.)

SHENAZAR. *1 Chr. 3:18 (17-18)*.

Shenazar, a descendant of David, was a son (grandson) of Jeconiah (Jehoiachin). (Chart 1.)

SHEPHATHIAH. *1 Chr. 9:8 (1-2, 8)*.

Shephathiah, of the tribe of Benjamin, was the father of Meshullam and the son of Reuel. He and his family were among the inhabitants of Jerusalem whose genealogy was written in the book of the kings of Israel and Judah who were carried away to Babylon for their transgression. His family was among the first inhabitants to dwell in Jerusalem after returning from Babylonian captivity. (Chart 16m.)

SHEPHATIAH (1). *2 Sam. 3:4; 1 Chr. 3:3*.

Shephatiah, the son of David and Abital, was David's fifthborn son in Hebron. (Chart 8e.)

SHEPHATIAH (2). *1 Chr. 12:5 (1-2, 5, 23, 38)*.

Shephatiah the Haruphite was one of David's mighty men who came to him at Ziklag to defend him against Saul and to rejoice with all Israel when David was made king.

SHEPHATIAH (3). *1 Chr. 27:16*.

Shephatiah, son of Maachah, was prince over the tribe of Simeon at the time of king David.

SHEPHATIAH (4). *2 Chr. 21:2-4.*

Shephatiah was one of Jehoshaphat's sons. His brothers were Jehoram, Azariah, Jehiel, Zechariah, Azariah and Michael. After Jehoram became king, he slew all his brethren plus many of the princes of Israel. (Chart 1.)

SHEPHATIAH (5). *Ezra 2:4; Neh. 7:9.*

Shephatiah was of the people of Israel. The men of the children of Shephatiah who returned to Jerusalem from Babylon after Cyrus' proclamation to build the temple numbered 372.

SHEPHATIAH (6). *Ezra 2:57-58; Neh. 7:59-60.*

Shephatiah was one of Solomon's servants. The children of Solomon's servants and the Nethinims who went up out of captivity numbered 392.

SHEPHATIAH (7). *Neh. 11:4.*

Shephatiah, the son of Mahalaleel and the father of Amariah of the children of Judah, was chosen by lot to dwell in Jerusalem after leaving Babylon. (Chart 8b.)

SHEPHATIAH (8). *Jer. 38:1-6.*

Shephatiah was the son of Mattan. When he, Gedaliah (son of Pashur), Jucal (son of Shelemiah), and Pashur (son of Malchiah) heard Jeremiah prophesy that if the people did not go forth with the Chaldeans, Jerusalem would be burned, they asked Zedekiah the king if they could slay Jeremiah. The king said he could not prevail against them, so they cast Jeremiah into a miry dungeon in the home of Malchiah the son of the king.

SHEPHATIAH'S DESCENDANT. *Ezra 8:8.*

Shephatiah's Descendant Zebadiah, the son of Michael, was the chief of his fathers when Ezra led many exiled Israelites out of Babylon back to Jerusalem. He took 80 males with him. *(Note: It is not clear as to which Shephatiah this refers.)*

SHEPHERDS IN MIDIAN. *Ex. 2:17.*

The Shepherds in Midian drove Jethro's flocks away when his seven daughters brought them to be watered. Moses assisted the women and watered their flocks.

SHEPHO (Shephi). *Gen. 36:23; 1 Chr. 1:40.*

Shepho (Shephi) was one of the children of Shobal, son of Seir the Horite. (Chart 4b.)

SHEPHUPHAN. *1 Chr. 8:5.*

Shephuphan was a son of Bela who was a son of Benjamin. His brothers were Addar, Gera, Abihud, Abishua, Naaman, Gera and Huram. *(Note: This listing differs from that in 1 Chr. 7:7.)* (Chart 16d.)

SHERAH. *1 Chr. 7:24.*

Sherah was the daughter of Ephraim. (Chart 15d.)

SHEREBIAH (1). *Ezra 8:18-19, 24-30.*

Sherebiah was a descendant of Levi through Mahli. When Ezra was preparing to lead the people from Babylon back to Jerusalem, he gathered them together by the river and discovered there were no Levites among them. He assigned several chief men and men of understanding to go to Iddo and the Nethinims and request that they send them some ministers for the house of God. They brought Sherebiah, with 18 of his sons and brethren; Hashabiah along with Jeshaiah of the sons of Merari, and 20 of his brethren and their sons; plus 220 Nethinims, back with them. Ezra delivered the silver, gold and precious things of the temple to Sherebiah, Hashabiah and ten additional chief priests and charged them to deliver them to the chief priests and those in charge at Jerusalem.

SHEREBIAH (2). *Neh. 8:7-9; 9; 10:12 (1, 12, 28-31); 12:8, 24.*

Sherebiah was one of the men who, when Ezra read and interpreted the law of Moses to the people, helped the people to understand the law. The day was proclaimed a holy day. *(Neh. 8:7-9.)*

When Ezra read and interpreted the law of Moses and he and Nehemiah proclaimed the day a holy day, the Levites—Sherebiah, Jeshua, Kadmiel, Bani, Shebaniah, Bunni, Bani, Chenani, Hashabniah, Hodijah and Pethahiah—blessed and praised the Lord, reciting the Lord's goodness to Israel: His blessing of Abraham; His giving the land of the Canaanites, Hittites, Amorites, Perizzites, Jebusites and Girgashites to Israel; His dividing the Red Sea so they could cross it yet drowning the Egyptians who pursued them; the signs and wonders He showed to Pharaoh; His leading them in the wilderness and protecting them so that they had bread from heaven, water from the rock, and shoes and clothes that never wore out; His accepting them whenever they repented, even when they made a molten calf. They had been given the kingdoms of Shihon, Heshbon and Bashan and the Lord had subdued the Canaanites and delivered them into the hands of the Israelites. They made a covenant with the Lord and the princes, Levites and priests sealed the covenant. *(Neh. 9.)*

Sherebiah was among those who covenanted and sealed their covenant to marry in Israel, honor the Sabbath, pay tithes and keep the commandments. *(Neh. 10:12 [1, 12, 28-31].)*

Sherebiah and his brethren were among those Levites who went up from Babylon with Zerubbabel to Jerusalem. Sherebiah, Hashabiah and Jeshua the son of Kadmiel, were among the men who were chief of the Levites. *(Neh. 12:8, 24.)*

SHERESH. *1 Chr. 7:16.*

Sheresh was a son of Maachah and Machir. His brother was Peresh. (Chart 15b.)

SHEREZER. *Zech. 7:2-7.*

Sherezer and Regem-melech and their men were sent unto the house of the Lord to pray. Zechariah was moved to reprove them for their hypocrisy because they weren't really fasting and praying unto the Lord.

SHESHAI. *Num. 13:22, 31-33; Josh. 15:14; Judg. 1:10.*

Sheshai was a son of Anak. He was one of the families living in Caanan who caused ten of the leaders sent by Moses to scout out the land to return with a negative report. The sons of Anak were men of great stature. *(Num. 13:22, 31-33.)*

Sheshai and his brothers Ahiman and Talmai were driven out of the land by Caleb. *(Josh. 15:14.)*

The tribe of Judah slew Sheshai and his brothers. *(Judg. 1:10.)*

SHESHAN. *1 Chr. 2:31, 34-35.*

Sheshan was the son of Ishi. He was a seven-times-great-grandson of Judah. He begat Ahlai, a daughter. Sheshan had no sons. He gave his daughter to his Egyptian servant Jarha for a wife. (Chart 8c.)

SHESHBAZZAR. See **Zerubbabel**.

SHETH. See **Seth**.

SHETHAR. *Esth. 1:14-15.*

Shethar was one of the seven princes of Persia and Media with king Ahasuerus when queen Vashti refused to come at his command. He and his colleagues inquired as to what should be done to Vashti because of her refusal to obey Ahasuerus' command.

SHETHAR-BOZNAI. *Ezra 5:3-17; 6:6-13.*

Shethar-boznai was a contemporary of Tatnai, governor of the west side of the Euphrates River. They and their companions, the Apharsachites, confronted Zerubbabel, Jeshua and the prophets while they were working on the temple. After inquiring as to who had commanded them to build the temple, they sent a letter to Darius with their response, indicating that Cyrus had decreed they should build the temple. *(Ezra 5:3-17.)*

After Darius found that Cyrus had, indeed, made a decree that the temple should be built, he renewed the decree and instructed Tatnai, Shethar-boznai and the Apharsachites to let the work of the temple proceed and to assist with funds and with sacrificial animals. They quickly did as instructed. *(Ezra 6:6-13.)*

SHEVA (1). *2 Sam. 20:25.*

Sheva was David's scribe.

SHEVA (2). *1 Chr. 2:49.*

Sheva was one of the sons of Caleb and his concubine Maachah. He begat Machbenah and Gibea. (Chart 8k.)

SHILHI. *1 Kgs. 22:42; 2 Chr. 20:31.*

Shilhi was the father of Azubah (the mother of Jehoshaphat) and grandfather of Jehoshaphat, which Jehoshaphat began to reign over Judah in the fourth year of Ahab's reign over Israel. *(1 Kgs. 22:42.)*

Shilhi was the father of Azubah. *(2 Chr. 20:31.)* (Chart 1.)

SHILLEM. See **Shallum (1)**.

SHILLEMITES. See **Shallam (1)**.

SHILONI. *Neh. 11:5.*

Shiloni, of the children of Perez, was a five-times-great-grandfather of Maaseiah, which Maaseiah dwelled in Jerusalem after leaving Babylon. (Chart 8b.)

SHILONITE. *1 Kgs. 11:29; 1 Chr. 9:5-6.*

Shilonite. The prophet Ahijah was a Shilonite. *(1 Kgs. 11:29.)*

The Shilonites who had been carried away to Babylon for their transgressions but who dwelled in Jerusalem following their captivity were Asaiah and his sons, and Jeuel and their brethren of the sons of Zerah—six hundred and ninety. *(1 Chr. 9:5-6.)*

SHILSHAH. *1 Chr. 7: 36.*

Shilshah was a son of Zophah, a grandson of Hotham, and a great-great-great-grandson of Asher. His brothers were Suah, Harnepher, Shual, Beri, Imrah, Bezer, Hod, Shamma, Ithran and Beera. (Chart 14a.)

SHIMEA (1). *2 Sam. 21:21.* See **Shammah (2).**

SHIMEA (2). *1 Chr. 3:5.* See **Shammua (2).**

SHIMEA (3). *1 Chr. 6:39-40.*

Shemea, a descendant of Levi through Gershon, was the father of Berachiah and the son of Michael. (Chart 7a.)

SHIMEA (4). *1 Chr. 6:29-30, 45-46.*

Shimea, a descendant of Levi through Merari, was the son of Uzza and the father of Haggiah. (Chart 7e.)

SHIMEAH (1). *2 Sam. 13:3, 32.* See **Shammah (2).**

SHIMEAH (2) (Shimeam). *1 Chr. 8:32; 9:38.*

Shimeah was of the tribe of Benjamin and was the son of Mikloth. *(1 Chr. 8:32.)*

Shimeam (Shimeah) was a grandson of Abiel (Jehiel). His father and Kish were brothers; thus, he was a cousin of Saul. *(1 Chr. 9:38.)* (Chart 16k.)

SHIMEAM. See **Shimeah (2).**

SHIMEATH. *2 Kgs. 12:21; 2 Chr. 24:26.*

Shimeath, an Ammonitess, was the mother of Jozachar, which Jozachar was one of the servants of king Joash who slew him. *(2 Kgs. 12:21.)*

Shimeath was the mother of Zabad (Jozachar). *(2 Chr. 24:26.)*

SHIMEATHITES. *1 Chr. 2:55.*

Shimeathites were one of the families of the scribes. They were Kenites who came of Hemath, father of the house of Rechab.

SHIMEI (1). *Num. 3:18.* See **Shimi.**

SHIMEI (2). *2 Sam. 16:5-11; 19:16-23; 1 Kgs. 2:8-9, 36-46.*

Shimei was the son of Gera. He was a Benjamite and of the house of Saul. When David fled Jerusalem to escape from his son Absalom, he came to Bahurim. Shimei cursed him and threw stones at him. When Abishai wanted to slay him for cursing and throwing stones at David, David reminded him that if his own son could seek his life, then Shimei could certainly curse him, "for the Lord hath bidden him." *(2 Sam. 16:5-11.)*

When David was conducted back over Jordan, Shimei came to him and asked forgiveness. Abishai wanted to slay him for having cursed David, but David chose to pardon him. *(2 Sam. 19:16-23.)*

David charged Solomon to punish Shimei for having cursed him. He, himself, had promised not to put Shimei to death with the sword for having cursed him. Nevertheless, he still wanted Solomon to punish Shimei. Solomon had Shimei brought to him. He instructed him to build a house in Jerusalem and to stay there, "For it shall be, that on the day thou goest out, and passest over the brook Kidron, thou shalt know for certain that thou shalt surely die." Shimei agreed. However, three years later, Shimei went to Gath to seek two run-away servants. It was reported to Solomon. Solomon summoned Shimei to him and reminded him that he was not supposed to leave Jerusalem. He then had Benaiah slay him. *(1 Kgs. 2:8-9, 36-46.)* (Chart 16m.)

SHIMEI (3). *1 Kgs. 1:8.*

Shimei was among those—Zadok the priest, Benaiah, Nathan the prophet and Rei—who were not with Adonijah when Adonijah elevated himself to be king in David's stead.

SHIMEI (4). *1 Kgs. 4:18 (7-18).*

Shimei was the son of Elah and was one of twelve officers over Israel who provided victuals for king Solomon and his family one month each year.

SHIMEI (5). *1 Chr. 3:19.*

Shimei, a descendant of David, was a son of Pedaiah and a grandson (great-great-grandson) of Jeconiah (Jehoiachin). His brother was Zerubbabel. (Chart 1.)

SHIMEI (6). *1 Chr. 4:26-43.*

Shimei was the son of Zacchur and a six-times-great-grandson of Jacob through Simeon. He had 22 children—16 sons and six daughters. They came in the days of Hezekiah, king of Judah, and smote the tents and the inhabitants who were there and dwelt in their rooms "because there was pasture there for their flocks." (Chart 6a.)

SHIMEI (7). *1 Chr. 5:4.*

Shimei, of the tribe of Reuben, was the son of Gog and the father of Micah. (Chart 5b.)

SHIMEI (8). *1 Chr. 6:29.*

Shimei, a descendant of Levi through Merari, was the son of Libni and the father of Uzza. (Chart 7e.)

SHIMEI (9). *1 Chr. 6:42.*

Shimei was the son of Jahath who was a son of Gershom (Gershon). (Chart 7a.)

SHIMEI (10). *1 Chr. 23:7-11.*

Shimei was of the lineage of Gershon, son of Levi. When David named Solomon king, he also numbered the Levites and divided them into courses among the sons of Levi: Gershon, Kohath and Merari. Of the Gershonites there was Shimei and Laadan. Of Laadan there were three sons: Jehiel, Zetham and Joel. Of Shimei there were three sons: Shelomith, Haziel and Haran. *(Note: It is not clear if there are two different Shimei's here. Verse 9 lists three sons of Shimei and states they were the chief of the fathers of Laadan. Verse 10 then lists four different sons of Shimei: Jahath, Zina [Zizah] Jeush and Beriah.)* (Chart 7e.)

SHIMEI (11). *1 Chr. 25:17 (1, 7-8, 17); 2 Chr.29:14.*

<u>Shimei</u>, a Levite and musician, cast the 10th lot when the musicians were assigned their duties by king David. He, his sons and brethren numbered 12. *(1 Chr. 25:17 [1, 7-8, 17].) (Note: Shimei, Izri and Azareel cast lots but are not listed in verses 2-4 when the sons of Asaph, Heman and Jeduthun are named. Three of the sons who are named, however, are not listed among those who cast lots: Zeri, Uzziel, and an unnamed son of Jeduthun. Thus, it is possible that the three who cast lots who are not named are the same as the three who are named but didn't cast lots. They may have just been given different names in these verses.)*

Shimei was of the sons of Heman. He was among those instructed by Hezekiah, king of Judah, to sanctify themselves so they could cleanse and sanctify the house of the Lord. *(2 Chr.29:14.)* (Chart 7f.)

SHIMEI (12). *1 Chr. 27:27.*

<u>Shimei</u> the Ramathite served David by being over the vineyards.

SHIMEI (13). *2 Chr. 31:12.*

<u>Shimei</u> was a brother of Cononiah who was over the tithes and offerings. Shimei was next in authority.

SHIMEI (14). *Ezra 10:23 (2-3, 18-19, 23, 44).*

<u>Shimei</u> was one of the Levites who had taken wives from among the Canaanites or other foreign groups and who agreed to Ezra's request that they separate themselves from these strange wives lest the Lord destroy the rest of the children of Israel.

SHIMEI (15). *Ezra 10:33 (2-3, 19, 33, 44).*

<u>Shimei</u>, one of Hashum's sons, and his brothers—Mattenai, Mattathah, Zabad, Eliphelet, Jeremai and Manasseh—were among the Israelite men who took foreign wives but complied with Ezra's request that they put away their strange wives so as not to bring the wrath of God upon Israel.

SHIMEI (16). *Ezra 10:38 (2-3, 19, 38, 44).*

<u>Shimei</u>, a son of Bani, and his brothers were some of the men in Israel who took foreign wives but gave them up when Ezra feared the wrath of God would destroy Israel for this iniquity.

SHIMEI (17). *Esth. 2:5.*

<u>Shimei</u>, a descendant of Benjamin, was son of Kish, father of Jair and grandfather of Mordecai. (Chart 16k.)

SHIMEI (18). *Zech. 12:13 (10-13).*

<u>Shimei</u>. When the Savior comes again and the children of Israel recognize Him as the Savior whom they crucified, there will be great mourning in the land. Each family shall mourn apart: the family of the house of Shimei; the family of the house of Levi; the family of the house of David and their wives; the family of the house of Nathan and their wives, etc. *(Note: There is no indication which Shimei is referred to in this passage.)*

SHIMEON. *Ezra 10:31 (2-3, 19, 31, 44)*.

Shimeon (one of Harim's sons) and his brothers Eliezer, Ishijah, Malchiah, Shemaiah, Benjamin, Malluch and Shemariah were some of the Israelite men who took wives from among the Canaanites and other foreign groups. They agreed to Ezra's request to separate themselves from their foreign wives.

SHIMHI. *1 Chr. 8:19-21*.

Shimhi, a descendant of Benjamin, was the father of Jakim, Zichri, Zabdi, Elienai, Zilthai, Eliel, Adaiah, Beraiah and Shimrath. They were heads of the fathers by their generations, chief men who lived in Jerusalem. (Chart 16h.)

SHIMI (Shimei (1), Shimites). *Ex. 6:17; Num. 3:18, 21*.

Shimi was a son of Gershon and a grandson of Levi. His brother was Libni. *(Ex. 6:17.)*

Shimites descended from **Shimei** (Shimi), son of Gershon, grandson of Levi, great-grandson of Jacob (Israel). *(Num. 3:18, 21.)* (Chart 7a.)

SHIMMA. *1 Chr. 2:13*. See **Shammah (2)**.

SHIMON. *1 Chr. 4:20*.

Shimon was the father of Amnon, Rinnah, Ben-hanan and Tilon.

SHIMRATH. *1 Chr. 8:21*.

Shimrath, a descendant of Benjamin, was a son of Shimhi. (Chart 16h.)

SHIMRI (1). *1 Chr. 11:45*.

Shimri was father of Jediael and Joha, two of David's mighty men. (Chart 17.)

SHIMRI (2). *1 Chr. 4:37*.

Shimri, of the lineage of Simeon, was the father of Jedaiah, the son of Shemaiah and a descendant of Shimei. (Chart 6a.)

SHIMRI (3). *2 Chr. 29:13*.

Shimri was a descendant of Elizaphan. He was among those whom Hezekiah, king of Judah, instructed to sanctify themselves so they could cleanse and sanctify the house of the Lord.

SHIMRITH. *2 Chr. 24:26*.

Shimrith, a Moabitess, was the mother of Jehozabad, one of king Joash's servants who slew him. *(Note: Her husband was apparently Shomer, who was the father of Jehozabad. See 2 Kgs. 12:21.)*

SHIMRON (Shimronites). *Gen. 46:13; Num. 26:24*.

Shimron was a son of Issachar and a grandson of Jacob. *(Gen. 46:13.)* His descendants were the **Shimronites**. *(Num. 26:24.)* (Chart 9a.)

SHIMSHAI. *Ezra 4:8-9*.

Shimshai, a scribe, and Rehum, the chancellor, wrote the letter against Jerusalem that the Samaritans sent to Artaxerxes, king of Persia. When they received Artaxerxes' return letter commanding them to cause the construction to cease, they and their companions went to Jerusalem and, using force and power, stopped the building of the temple.

SHINAB. *Gen. 14:2.*

Shinab was king of Admah. Chedorlaomer, king of Elam, and his colleagues warred against Shinab and his fellow kings—Bera of Sodom, Birsha of Gomorrah, Shinab of Admah, and Shemeber of Zeboiim. They served Chedorlaomer 12 years and then rebelled.

SHIPHI. *1 Chr. 4:37.*

Shiphi, of the lineage of Simeon, was the son of Allon, a descendant of Shimei. (Chart 6a.)

SHIPHMITE. *1 Chr. 27:27.*

Shiphmites. Zabdi, who served king David by being over the increase of the vineyards for the wine cellars, was a Shiphmite. *(Note: There is no indication as to who the Shiphmites were.)*

SHIPHRAH. *Ex. 1:15-21.*

Shiphrah was a Hebrew midwife. Because she feared God, she did not comply with Pharaoh's command to kill all Hebrew newborn sons. The Lord blessed her with descendants.

SHIPHTAN. *Num. 34:24.*

Shiphtan, of the tribe of Ephraim, was the father of Kemuel. (Chart 15e.)

SHISHA. *1 Kgs. 4:3.*

Shisha was the father of Elihoreph and Ahiah who were scribes in Solomon's court.

SHISHAK. See **Pharaoh (6)**.

SHITRAI. *1 Chr. 27:29.*

Shitrai the Sharonite was the officer assigned by king David to be over the herds that fed in Sharon.

SHIZA. *1 Chr. 11:42.*

Shiza the Reubenite was the father of Adina, which Adina was one of David's Mighty Men. (Chart 17.)

SHOBAB (1). *2 Sam. 5:14; 1 Chr. 3:5; 14:4-7.*

Shobab was one of David's children born in Jerusalem. His brothers were Shammua, Nathan, Solomon, Ibhar, Elishua, Nepheg, Japhia, Elishama, Eliada and Eliphalet. *(2 Sam. 5:14.)*

Shobab, Shammua (Shimea), Nathan and Solomon were sons of David and Bath-shua (Bath-sheba). *(1 Chr. 3:5.)*

His brothers are listed again with some variations: Shammua, Shobab, Nathan, Solomon, Ibhar, Elishua, Elpalet, Nogah, Nepheg, Japhia, Elishama, Beeliada (Eliada) and Eliphalet. *(1 Chr. 14:4-7.) (Note: Elpalet and Nogah are not included in the other listings.)* (Chart 8e.)

SHOBAB (2). *1 Chr. 2:18.*

Shobab was one of the sons of Caleb and Azubah of the house of Judah. His brothers were Jesher and Ardon. *(Note: It is not clear whether these were sons of Azubah or of Jerioth.)* (Chart 8h.)

SHOBACH (Shophach). *2 Sam. 10:16-18; 1 Chr. 19:16-18.*

Shobach (Shophach), a Syrian, was captain of the host of Hadarezer, king of Zoba. Shobach and his troops joined forces with the children of Ammon when David went to battle against them for abusing his messengers whom he had sent to comfort Hanun upon the death of his father Nahash. Shobach was killed along with the men of 700 chariots (7,000 men which fought in chariots) and 40,000 horsemen (footmen).

SHOBAI. *Ezra 2:42; Neh. 7:45.*

Shobai was one of the porters. When Cyrus, king of Persia, proclaimed that the people of God should go to Jerusalem to build the temple, the children of the porters—Shobai, Shallum, Ater, Talmon, Akkub and Hatita—numbered 139 (138).

SHOBAL (1). *Gen. 36:20, 23; 1 Chr. 1:38, 40.*

Shobal was a son of Seir the Horite. He was a duke or tribal chief. His children were Alvan (Alian), Manahath, Ebal, Shepho (Shephi) and Onam. (Charts 4a-f. 19.)

SHOBAL (2). *1 Chr. 2:50-54; 4:1.*

Shobal was one of the sons of Hur who was the son of Caleb and Ephratah. He begat Kirjath-jearim. The following groups descended from Shobal: half of the Manahethites, the families of Kirjath-jearim, the Ithrites, the Puhites, the Shumathites, the Mishraites, the Zareathites and the Eshtaulites. *(1 Chr. 2:50-54.)*

Shobal was the son of Hur. He was the father of Reaiah, the grandfather of Jahath and the great-grandfather of Ahumai and Lahad. They are the families of the Zorathites. *(1 Chr. 4:1.)* (Charts 8 l-m.)

SHOBEK. *Neh. 10:24 (1, 24, 28-31).*

Shobek was among those chief of the people who covenanted to marry in Israel, honor the Sabbath, pay tithes and keep the commandments.

SHOBI. *2 Sam. 17:27.*

Shobi was the son of Nahash of Rabbah of the children of Ammon. He, Machir and Barzillai brought beds, food and other items to aid David and his followers when they came to Mahanaim on their flight to escape Absalom.

SHOHAM. *1 Chr. 24:27, 31.*

Shoham, a Levite, was a son of Merari through Jaaziah. He, with the rest of the chief fathers of the Levites, drew lots for his course in the presence of king David, Zadok, Ahimelech and other community leaders. (Chart 7e.)

SHOMER (1). *2 Kgs. 12:21.*

Shomer was the father of Jehozabad. His wife was apparently Shimrith, a Moabitess, the mother of Jehozabad. *(See 2 Chr. 24:26.)*

SHOMER (2) (Shamer (2)). *1 Chr. 7:32, 34.*

Shomer was a son of Heber and a great-grandson of Asher. His siblings included Japhlet, Hotham and a sister, Shua. **Shamer**'s (Shomer's) sons were Ahi, Rohgah, Jehubbah and Aram. (Chart 14a.)

SHOPHACH. See **Shobach**.

SHUA (1). *1 Chr. 2:3.* See **Shuah (2)**.

SHUA (2). *1 Chr. 7:32.*

Shua was the daughter of Heber and a great-granddaughter of Asher. (Chart 14a.)

SHUAH (1). *Gen. 25:2.*

Shuah was a son of Abraham and his wife Keturah. (Charts 3a, d, f.)

SHUAH (2) (Shua (1)). *Gen. 38:2-5; 1 Chr. 2:3.*

Shuah (Shua) was Judah's Canaanite wife. She bore him three sons: Er, Onan and Shelah. (Chart 8c.)

SHUAH (3). *1 Chr. 4:11.*

Shuah was the brother of Chelub.

SHUAL. *1 Chr. 7:36.*

Shual was a son of Zophah, a grandson of Hotham, and a great-great-great-grandson of Asher. His brothers were Suah, Harnepher, Beri, Imrah, Bezer, Hod, Shamma, Shilshah, Ithran and Beera. (Chart 14a.)

SHUBAEL (1). *1 Chr. 24:20.* See **Shebuel (1)**.

SHUBAEL (2). *1 Chr. 25:4.* See **Shebuel (2)**.

SHUHAM. See **Hushim (1)**.

SHUHAMITES. See **Hushim (1)**.

SHUHITE. See **Bildad**.

SHUMATHITES. See **Shobal (2)**.

SHUNAMMITE. See **Abishag**.

SHUNI (Shunites). *Gen. 46:16; Num 26:15.*

Shuni was a son of Gad and a grandson of Jacob. *(Gen. 46:16.)* His descendants were the **Shunites**. *(Num 26:15.)* (Chart 13a.)

SHUNITES. See **Shuni**.

SHUPHAM. See **Muppim**.

SHUPHAMITES. See **Muppim**.

SHUPPIM (1). *1 Chr. 7:12.*

Shuppim was a descendant of Benjamin. He and Huppim were children of Ir. (Charts 15b.; 16c.)

SHUPPIM (2). *1 Chr. 26:16.*

Shuppim was a descendant of Levi through Merari. He was a porter. His lot came forth westward with the gate Shallecheth.

SHUTHALHITES. See **Shuthelah (1)**.

SHUTHELAH (1) (Shuthalhites). *Num. 26:35; 1 Chr. 7:20.*

Shuthelah was a son of Ephraim. His descendants were the **Shuthalhites**. *(Num. 26:35.)* He was the father of Bered. *(1 Chr. 7:20.)* (Chart 15d.)

SHUTHELAH (2). *1 Chr. 7:21.*

Shuthelah, son of Zabad, was a fifth-great-grandson of Ephraim. (Chart 15d.)

SIAHA (Sia). *Ezra 2:44, 58; Neh. 7:47, 60.*

Siaha (Sia) was a Nethinim. When the Nethinims and the children of Solomon's servants left Babylon to return to Jerusalem to build the house of the Lord as proclaimed by Cyrus, king of Persia, they numbered 392.

SIBBECAI. See **Mebunnai**.

SIBBECHAI. *2 Sam. 21:18; 1 Chr. 20:4.*

Sibbechai the Hushathite slew Saph (Sippai), a Philistine who was of the sons of the giant. *(Note: Sibbechai and Sibbecai may be one and the same. See Mebunnai.)*

SIDON (Zidon). *Gen. 10:15; 1 Chr. 1:13.*

Sidon (Zidon) was the firstborn son of Canaan, a grandson of Ham and a great-grandson of Noah. His brother was Heth. (Chart 2e.)

SIDONIANS (Zidonians). *Josh. 13:4 (1, 4); 1 Kgs. 5:6-12; 16:31; Ezek. 28:21-24; 32:21, 30.*

The Sidonians were to the south of the Canaanites and bordered Mearah, which was yet to be conquered as Joshua grew old. *(Josh. 13:4 (1, 4).)*

The Sidonians were skilled craftsman in the art of working with timber. When Hiram king of Tyre learned Solomon had been ordained king, he sent his servants to Solomon because of his great love for David. Solomon requested Hiram have his people hew cedar trees for him to build a house unto the Lord because of their great skill and craftmanship. They made a league together. *(1 Kgs. 5:6-12.)*

The Zidonians (Sidonians) were Baal worshippers. Ahab, king of Israel, was married to Jezebel, the daughter of Ethbaal, king of the Zidonians. *(1 Kgs. 16:31.)*

Ezekiel was commanded by the Lord to prophesy the destruction of Zidon because Zidon despised the house of Israel and was "a pricking brier" unto Israel. *(Ezek. 28:21-24.)*

As Ezekiel lamented for Pharaoh king of Egypt and for Egypt, herself, the Lord told him, "The strong among the mighty shall speak to him (Pharaoh) out of the midst of hell with them that help him: they are gone down, they lie uncircumcised, slain by the sword . . . There be the princes of the north, all of them, and all the Zidonians, which are gone down with the slain; with their terror they are ashamed of their might; and they lie uncircumcised with them that be slain by the sword, and bear their shame with them that go down to the pit." *(Ezek. 32:21, 30.)*

SIHON (Zihon). *Num. 21:21-30; 32:33; Deut. 1:4-6; 2:1-23; 2:24-36; 3:2, 6; Josh. 2:10 (1-21); 9:10 (3-15); 12:2 (1-3); 13:10, 21 (1-21); Judg. 11:19-22; Neh. 9:22; 1 Kgs. 4:19; Psalm 135:11-12 (1, 10-12); Psalm 136:19-21 (1, 18-21).*

Sihon was king of the Amorites. Sihon would not allow the Israelites to pass though his land peacefully and gathered his people against Israel. The Lord delivered them into the hands of Israel even though they had been powerful enough to dispossess the Moabites of all their lands earlier. *(Num. 21:21-30; Judg. 11:19-22.)*

The land of Sihon and the land of Og, king of Bashan, which were on the east side of Jordan, were given to the children of Gad, Reuben and half of the tribe of Manasseh for an inheritance. *(Num. 32:33.)*

After Sihon had been slain, Moses reviewed with the Israelites all that had occurred during the previous 40 years. *(Deut. 1:4-6; 2:1-23.)*

Moses reminded Israel that the Lord delivered **Zihon** (Sihon) the Amorite, king of Heshbon, and his land into their hands, as well as Og and his land. *(Deut. 2:24-36; 3:2, 6.)*

Word of the slaying of Sihon and Og reached the people of Jericho. Rahab helped the spies sent by Joshua to scout out the city. In return, she made them promise to save her and her family. *(Josh. 2:10 [1-21].)*

Because of the slaying of Sihon and Og, the Gibeonites craftily obtained a league with Israel so they would not be destroyed. *(Josh. 9:10 [3-15].)*

Sihon was slain and his lands were taken by the children of Israel. *(Josh. 12:2 [1-3].)*

Joshua was old and stricken in age and the Lord instructed him to finish getting the lands divided for the inheritance of the children of Israel. The lands beyond Jordan that had belonged to Sihon and Og had been given to the tribes of Gad, Reuben and the half tribe of Manasseh. *(Josh. 13:10, 21 [1-21].)*

Israel was reminded that the Lord, in His goodness, had delivered the lands of Sihon and Og into their hands. *(Neh. 9:22.)*

The officer in Solomon's court who was assigned over the land that had belonged to Sihon and Og was Uri's son Geber. *(1 Kgs. 4:19.)*

Israel was admonished to praise the Lord who smote Sihon and Og and all the kingdoms of Canaan and gave their lands to Israel for an inheritance. *(Psalm 135:11-12 [1, 10-12].)*

Israel was admonished to thank the Lord who slew Sihon and Og and other famous kings and gave their lands to them for an inheritance. *(Psalm 136:19-21 [1, 18-21].)*

SIMEON (Simeonites). *Gen. 29:33; 34:25-31; 35:23; 37; 42:24, 36 (9-36); 43:23; 46:10; 48:5; 49:5-7 (1, 5-7); 50:8; Ex. 1:2-5; Num. 1:6, 22-23 (2-5, 6, 22-23); 2:12 (10-16); 7:36; 10:19; 13:5 (2, 5); 26:12-14; 34:20 (18, 20); Deut. 27:12; Josh. 19:1-9; 21:4; Judg. 1:3, 17; 1 Chr. 4:24-43; 6:65; 12:25 (23, 25); 27:16; 2 Chr. 34:6 (1-3, 6); Ezek. 48:24, 33.*

Simeon was the second son of Jacob and Leah. *(Gen. 29:33.)*

Simeon and his brother Levi slew Hamor and Shechem his son with their swords because Shechem had defiled their sister Dinah, even though they had all agreed to let Shechem marry Dinah if he and all the men would get circumcised. When Jacob bemoaned what they had done, their response was, "Should he deal with our sister as with an harlot?" *(Gen. 34:25-31.)*

Simeon was the second son of Leah. His brothers were Reuben, Levi, Judah, Issachar and Zebulun. *(Gen. 35:23.)*

Simeon and his brothers hated their younger brother Joseph and sold him to a group of Ishmeelites, or Midianite merchantmen, for 20 pieces of silver. They dipped his coat of many colors in animal blood and gave it to their father so he would think Joseph had been killed by wild beasts. *(Gen. 37.)*

When Jacob's sons went to Egypt for food during the famine, Joseph, through his interpreter, accused them of being spies and insisted they had to bring their youngest brother Benjamin to Egypt to prove they were telling the truth when they said they were all one man's sons. Simeon was bound and taken from before them, to be kept as collateral until they returned with Benjamin. When Jacob learned that Simeon had not returned from Egypt, he was very grieved and did not wish to let Benjamin go back to Egypt with his brothers. *(Gen. 42:24, 36 [9-36].)*

When the brothers returned to Egypt with Benjamin, Joseph told them to fear not, and had Simeon brought out to rejoin his brothers. *(Gen. 43:23.)*

Simeon begat Jemuel (Nemuel), Jamin, Ohad *(not listed among his sons in Num. 26:12-14)*, Jachin, Zohar (Zerah), and Shaul the son of a Canaanitish woman. *(Gen. 46:10.)*

Just as Simeon and Reuben were Jacob's own sons, Jacob adopted Ephraim and Manasseh as his own two sons. *(Gen. 48:5.)*

After the brothers had gone to Egypt for grain and were finally reunited with Joseph, and following the move of their entire family to Egypt, the time came when Jacob called his sons together to tell them what would befall each of them in the last days. To Simeon, he said, "Simeon and Levi are brethren; instruments of cruelty are in their habitations. . . for in their anger they slew a man, and in their selfwill they digged down a wall. Cursed be their anger, for it was fierce; and their wrath, for it was cruel: I will divide them in Jacob, and scatter them in Israel." *(Gen. 49:5-7 [1, 5-7].)*

Simeon and his brothers all went together to carry their father's body to Canaan to be buried. *(Gen. 50:8.)*

The names of the children of Israel, including Simeon, who went into Egypt with Jacob, are listed. *(Ex. 1:2-5.)*

The Lord instructed Moses to appoint Shelumiel, son of Zuerishaddai, to lead the tribe of Simeon as Israel prepared for war. The males 20 years of age and older in the tribe of Simeon numbered 59,300 at this time. *(Num. 1:6, 22-23 [2-5, 6, 22-23].)*

The camp of the tribe of Simeon was pitched next to the camp of Reuben "far off about the tabernacle of the congregation" on the south side. Next to them was camped the tribe of Gad. Together, the camp of Reuben numbered 151,450 men. *(Num. 2:12 [10-16].)*

The "prince of the children of Simeon" who made the offering for the tabernacle at its dedication was Shelumiel. *(Num. 7:36.)*

The person over the host of the tribe of the children of Simeon was Shelumiel the son of Zurishaddai. *(Num. 10:19.)*

When Moses sent 12 spies to search out the land of Canaan, Simeon's tribe was represented by Shaphat the son of Hori. He returned with a negative report (and was subsequently slain by the Lord for giving a negative report). *(Num. 13:5 [2, 5].)*

While on the plains of Moab near Jericho, Moses and Eleazar were instructed to count all the males, excluding the Levites, who were 20 years old and older. The **Simeonites** (all the families that decended from Simeon) numbered 22,200 and included the Nemuelites, Jaminites, Jachinites, Zarhites and the Shaulites. *(Num. 26:12-14.)*

Shemuel the son of Ammihud, was chosen from Simeon's tribe to divide their land of inheritance among Simeon's posterity. *(Num. 34:20 [18, 20].)*

As the Israelites prepared to cross over Jordan, the tribes of Simeon, Levi, Judah, Issachar, Joseph and Benjamin were to stand upon mount Gerizim to bless the people. *(Deut. 27:12.)*

When Joshua divided the promised land by casting lots, Simeon's tribe came up second. They were given a portion of the land that was given to Judah because Judah's tribe had too much for them. *(Josh. 19:1-9.)*

Thirteen cities came out of the tribes of Simeon, Judah and Benjamin for the Kohathites and the children of Aaron. *(Josh. 21:4.)*

Simeon assisted Judah in fighting against the Canaanites so the children of Judah could obtain their inheritance. Then Judah assisted Simeon against the Canaanites that inhabited Zephath so the children of Simeon could obtain their inheritance. *(Judg. 1:3, 17.)*

Simeon's sons were Nemuel (Jemuel), Jamin, Jarib (Jachin), Zerah (Zohar) and Shaul. His posterity is listed. *(1 Chr. 4:24-43.)*

Certain cities from the tribes of Simeon, Judah and Benjamin were given by lot to the Levites. *(1 Chr. 6:65.)*

When David became king and went to Ziklag, all Israel rejoiced. The tribes sent their armies to assist David. The tribe of Simeon sent 7,100 men. *(1 Chr. 12:25 [23, 25].)*

When the princes of the tribes of Israel at the time of king David were named, Shephatiah, the son of Maachah, was prince over the tribe of Simeon. *(1 Chr. 27:16.)*

The cities belonging to Simeon and others were cleansed from their idolatry, and their altars, idols and groves were destroyed by king Josiah. *(2 Chr. 34:6 [1-3, 6].)*

The Lord revealed to Ezekiel just how the land should be divided by tribes when the children of Israel are gathered in the latter days. Simeon's portion will be by the border of Benjamin, from the east side unto the west side. The twelve gates of the city will bear the names of the twelve sons of Jacob. Simeon's gate will be one of the three gates on the south side of the city. *(Ezek. 48:24, 33.)* (Charts 1.; 3d., 5a.; 6a-b.; 7a.; 8a.; 9a.; 10a.; 11a.; 12a.; 13a.; 14a.; 15a.; 16.)

SIMRI. *1 Chr. 26:10-12.*

Simri, a Levite, was a son of Hosah who was of the lineage of Merari. Although he was not Hosah's firstborn, his father made him chief. His brothers included: Hilkiah, the secondborn; Tebaliah, the third; and Zechariah, the fourth. They, along with other Levites, were appointed by king David to be porters—to have charge of the treasures, serve as officers and judges, and to conduct the outward business over Israel. *(Note: Simri apparently had more brothers as it states that "all the sons and brethren of Hosah were thirteen." However, only four are named by name and Simri was not the firstborn.)* (Chart 7a.)

SINITE. *Gen. 10:17.*

Sinites were descendants of Canaan who was a son of Ham. (Chart 2e.)

SIPPAI. See **Saph.**

SISAMAI. *1 Chr. 2:40.*

Sisamai was the son of Eleasah and the father of Shallum. (Chart 8c.)

SISERA. *Judg. 4:2-21; 1 Sam. 12:9; Ps. 83:9.*

Sisera was the captain of Jabin's Canaanite army. When Deborah and Barak led the Israelites into battle against Sisera, he fled into the tent of Jael, who was the wife of Heber the Kenite. Jael hid him under a cover and then pounded a tent nail into his temples "and fastened it into the ground." Thus, he died; and Israel was freed. *(Judg. 4:2-21.)*

When the children of Israel forgot the Lord, He delivered them into the hands of Sisera (captain of the host of Hazor), the Philistines and the Moabites. *(1 Sam. 12:9.)*

This psalm of Asaph petitions the Lord to do unto their enemies as He did previously to Sisera and Jabin at the brook of Kison. *(Ps. 83:9.)*

SISERA'S CHILDREN. *Ezra 2:53, 58; Neh. 7:55, 60.*

Sisera's Children were among the Nethinims. When the Nethinims and the children of Solomon's servants left Babylon to return to Jerusalem to build the house of the Lord as proclaimed by Cyrus, king of Persia, they numbered 392. *(Note: It is not clear if the Sisera referred to here is the same Sisera referred to in the references for Sisera above.)*

SO. See **Pharoah (8).**

SOCHO. *1 Chr. 4:18.*

Socho was the son of Heber. His grandmother was Jehudijah. (Chart 8 o.)

SODI. *Num. 13:10, 16, 31-33; 14:37.*

Sodi, of the tribe of Zebulun, was the father of Gaddiel, one of the 12 spies sent by Moses to scout out the land of Canaan. He returned with a negative report. *(Num. 13:10, 16, 31-33.)* Because of the negative report he gave, he "died by the plague before the Lord." *(Num. 14:37.)*

SODOMITE MEN. *Gen. 19:4-11.*

Sodomite Men tried to get Lot to give them two men—angels, according to the scripture—so they could sexually abuse them. Lot refused. When they tried to get into the house, the angels smote the men with blindness.

SOLOMON (Jedidiah). *2 Sam. 5:14-16; 12:24-25; 1 Kgs. 1:10, 17, 30-43, 50-53; 2; 3:1, 3, 5-15, 16-27; 4:1-19, 21, 29; 5; 6:1, 38; 7:1, 13-14; 8; 9; 10; 11; 1 Chr. 3:5, 10; 14:4-7; 22:5-10; 23:1; 28; 29:22, 28; 2 Chr. 1:7-12 (5, 6, 7-12); 2; 3; 4; 5; 6; 7; 8; 9: 1-28, 30-31; Neh. 13:26; Ps. 72; Prov. 1-29; Eccl. 1-12; Song of Solomon; Jer. 52:20 (12-20).*

Solomon was one of David's children born in Jerusalem. His brothers who were also born in Jerusalem were Shammua, Shobab, Nathan, Ibhar, Elishua, Nepheg, Japhia, Elishama, Eliada and Eliphalet. *(2 Sam. 5:14-16.)*

Solomon was the second son born to David and Bath-sheba. The Lord loved him. David also called him **Jedidiah** "because of the Lord." *(2 Sam. 12:24-25.)*

When David's son Adonijah exalted himself and drew the support of Joab and Abiathar the priest, he deliberately avoided soliciting the support of his brother Solomon and other loyal supporters of David. Nathan the prophet encouraged Bath-sheba to inform David as to what was happening and to remind him that he had indicated that Solomon was to reign after him. David reaffirmed that Solomon was to reign after him and he had Zadok the priest and Nathan the prophet anoint Solomon king over Israel. Adonijah was then afraid of Solomon and asked him not to kill him. Solomon told him if he was a worthy man, no harm would befall him but that if wickedness was found in him, he would die. He then told Adonijah to go home. *(1 Kgs. 1:10, 17, 30-43, 50-53.)*

David charged Solomon to keep the commandments, to walk in the ways of the Lord and to keep His statues. He also charged him to punish Joab for the things he had done wrong and to punish Shimei for having cursed him. However, he asked Solomon to shew kindness unto the sons of Barzillai because they had befriended him in his time of need. After Bath-sheba approached Solomon at Adonijah's request to petition that Abishag, who had cared for David when he was old and stricken in years, be given to Adonijah for a wife, Solomon had Benaiah fall upon Adonijah and kill him. He sent Abiathar the priest into exile and set Zadok the priest in his place. Solomon had Benaiah slay Joab for all his previous misdeeds and he placed Benaiah in his position over the host. He ordered Shimei to build a house in Jerusalem and to stay there. If he ever ventured past the brook of Kidron, he would be put to death. Three years later, when Shimei left Jerusalem and traveled to Gath in search of two run away servants, Solomon had Benaiah slay him. *(1 Kgs. 2.)*

Solomon made a marriage alliance with the Pharaoh and took Pharaoh's daughter for a wife. He made sacrifices and burnt incense in the high places. After Solomon was anointed king, he told the Lord who appeared to him in a dream that he was but "a little child." The Lord asked what Solomon would have Him give him. Solomon asked for an understanding heart that he might judge the people wisely. The Lord did as requested. Two women, harlots, came and aked him to decide whose child was dead and whose child was the one still living. He suggested dividing the living child in two and giving half to one and half to the other. The child's actual mother declined and said to give the child to the other woman rather than slay it. The second woman was willing to have the child cut in two. Solomon gave the child to the rightful mother. *(1 Kgs. 3:1, 3, 5-15, 16-27.)*

The princes and officers of Solomon's court are listed. The boundaries of his kingdom are outlined. God blessed him with great wisdom. *(1 Kgs. 4:1-19, 21, 29.)*

Solomon asked Hiram king of Tyre for help in getting timber to build the temple because the Sidonians were skilled craftsmen in the art of hewing timber. Working alongside the Sidonians, the Israelites hewed stones and cut timber for the temple. *(1 Kgs. 5.)*

It was in his fourth year as king of Israel—in the 481st year since the children of Israel left Egypt—that Solomon began building the house of the Lord. It took seven years to build. *(1 Kgs. 6:1, 38.)*

Solomon spent 13 years building his own house. He brought Hiram out of Tyre to make the pillars, the molten sea, the ten bases, and other parts of the temple because Hiram was skilled in working with brass. *(1 Kgs. 7:1, 13-14.)*

When the temple was completed, Solomon assembled all the people—the elders of Israel and all the heads of the tribes—and he had the ark containing the two tablets of stone placed in the holy of holies. The glory of the Lord filled the house of the Lord. Solomon offered a dedicatory prayer. The people sacrificed and worshipped for 14 days. *(1 Kgs. 8.)*

When the temple was completed, the Lord appeared unto Solomon a second time. The Lord promised Solomon and the children of Israel great blessings if they worshipped Him, but great cursings if they turned away from Him. Solomon gave Hiram king of Tyre several cities, but Hiram was not pleased with them. Solomon levied a tribute upon the non-Israelites: the Amorites, Hittites, Perizzites, Hivites and Jebusites. He did not levy any tribute upon the children of Israel. "They were men of war, and his servants, and his princes, and his captain, and rulers of his chariots, and his horsemen, these were the chief of the officers that were over Solomon's work." Solomon made a navy of ships. Hiram sent his servants to serve in the navy alongside Solomon's servants because Hiram's shipmen had knowledge of the sea. *(1 Kgs. 9.)*

Word of Solomon's great wisdom and great wealth spread abroad and the queen of Sheba came to see for herself if what she had heard was true. She gave him gifts of gold and spices. He gave unto her all she desired. She was impressed that he was much wiser and much wealthier than she had even heard. His riches and wisdom exceeded all the kings of the earth. And all the earth sought him to hear the wisdom God put into his heart. *(1 Kgs. 10:1-28; 2 Chr. 9: 1-28.)*

Solomon married outside of Israel and "loved many strange women:" the daughter of Pharaoh, women of the Moabites, Ammonites, Edomites, Zidonians and Hittites. He had 700 wives, princesses, and 300 concubines. When he was old, his wives turned his heart after false gods: Ashtoreth, the goddess of the Zidonians; Milcom, the abomination of the Ammonites; Chemosh, the abomination of Moab; Molech, the abomination of the children of Ammon. "And likewise did he for all his strange wives, which burnt incense and sacrificed unto their gods." The Lord was angry with Solomon and told him He would rend the kingdom from him and give it unto another; albeit, He would only give ten tribes unto another and leave one tribe with Solomon's son for David's sake and for Jerusalem's sake which He had chosen to put His name upon. The Lord stirred up adversaries against Solomon: Hadad, Rezon, Jeroboam. Solomon reigned over Israel for 40 years. He died and was buried in the city of David his father. His son Rehoboam reigned in his stead. *(1 Kgs. 11.)*

Solomon, Shammua (Shimea), Shobab and Nathan were sons of David and Bath-sheba born in Jerusalem. Solomon's son was Rehoboam. *(1 Chr. 3:5, 10.)*

Solomon's brothers are listed again with some variations: Shammua, Shobab, Nathan, Solomon, Ibhar, Elishua, Elpalet, Nogah, Nepheg, Japhia, Elishama, Beeliada (Eliada) and Eliphalet. *(1 Chr. 14:4-7.) (Note: Elpalet and Nogah are not included in other listings.)*

David indicated that because Solomon was "young and tender" he, David, needed to make preparation for the magnificent house that Solomon was to build to the Lord. He charged Solomon to build a house unto the Lord. He also commanded all the princes of Israel to help Solomon. *(1 Chr. 22:5-10.)*

David made Solomon king over Israel. *(1 Chr. 23:1.)*

Solomon was appointed by David to build the temple. He then gave Solomon the pattern and the materials with which to build it. Solomon and the people were exhorted by David to keep the commandments. *(1 Chr. 28.)*

The people "made Solomon the son of David king the second time" and he reigned in his father's stead following David's death. *(1 Chr. 29:22, 28.)*

Solomon offered 1,000 burnt offerings unto the Lord upon the brasen altars. God appeared to Solomon and asked Solomon what he desired. Solomon asked that he might have wisdom and knowledge. God granted him his desire and blessed him with riches. *(2 Chr. 1:7-12 [5, 6, 7-12].)*

Solomon petitioned Huram (Hiram), king of Tyre, for timber for the temple and for workmen. Huram complied with his request. Solomon numbered all the foreigners in the land according to the numbering David had numbered Israel. There numbered 153,600. Of those, he set 70,000 of them to be bearers of burdens, 80,000 to be hewers in the mountain, and 3,600 were overseers of the workers. *(2 Chr. 2.)*

Solomon began construction on the temple, making the veil and the pillars, using much gold and many precious stones. The site was the place where the Lord had appeared unto David in the threshingfloor of Ornan the Jebusite at Jerusalem in mount Moriah. *(2 Chr. 3.)*

Solomon made the baptismal font. It stood upon 12 oxen: three looking in each direction—north, east, south and west. They faced away from the font, "and all their hinder parts were inward." *(2 Chr. 4.)*

Solomon finished the work of the temple and assembled the elders of Israel and the heads of the tribes, the chief of the fathers of the children of Israel, and they brought the ark of the covenant of the Lord and placed it in the holy of holies in the temple. The people praised the Lord with the trumpeters and the singers making music. The glory of the Lord filled the temple. *(2 Chr. 5.)*

Solomon blessed the congregation and offered a dedicatory prayer for the temple, praying for mercy and blessings for Israel. *(2 Chr. 6.)*

When Solomon made sacrifices unto the Lord in the temple, at the end of his praying, fire came down from heaven and consumed the burnt offering and the sacrifices. They sacrificed and rejoiced for seven days and made a solemn assembly on the eighth day. After the dedication of the altar and the feasting, Solomon sent the people home. The Lord appeared unto Solomon at night and told him He accepted the temple for His own house. He also told Solomon that if He the Lord sent pestilence upon the people, if they truly repented and called upon His name, He would forgive their sin and heal their land. However, if the people forsook His statues and commandments, then He would pluck them up by the roots out of the land. *(2 Chr. 7.)*

Following the 20 years it took Solomon to build the temple and his own home, he built cities. He had the people who were not of Israel—the remaining Hittites, Amorites, Perizzites, Hivites and Jebusites—pay tribute. The children of Israel paid no tribute but were soldiers and chief of his captains, etc. Solomon offered sacrifices according to the commandment of Moses and he appointed the priests and Levites to serve the Lord according to the order of his father David. *(2 Chr. 8.)*

Solomon reigned over Israel in Jerusalem 40 years and died. His son Rehoboam reigned in his stead. *(2 Chr. 9: 30-31.)*

Nehemiah reminded the people that even though Solomon was beloved of God, and even though there was no king like him among the many nations, he sinned by marrying women who were not of the house of Israel and received the rebuke of God. *(Neh. 13:26.)*

This was David's Psalm for Solomon who, in this psalm, is made a type of Christ. *(Ps. 72.)*

Solomon's wisdom is expounded. He states, "The fear of the Lord is the beginning of knowledge and wisdom" *(Prov. 1:7; 9:10; 15:33)*; wisdom is better than rubies or gold *(Prov. 8:11; 16:16)*; wisdom existed in the pre-existence*(Prov. 8:22-23, 30-31, 35)*. He elaborates upon the evils of pride *(Prov. 15:25; 16:5, 18)*, lying, deceit, talebearers, boastfulness, unvirtuous women, wine and strong drink

(Prov. 20:1; 23:20-21, 29-32). He also counseled about children *(Prov. 13:24; 22:6)*; the blessing of a good wife, and caring for the poor. *(See Prov. 1-29.)*

Solomon's name is not directly stated as the writer of Ecclesiastes. It refers to the Preacher, the son of David, king in Jerusalem. However, it also states, "I am come to great estate, and have gotten more wisdom than all they that have been before me in Jerusalem." *(Eccl. 1:16.)* This undoubtedly refers to Solomon. He expounded upon wisdom, ". . . wisdom excelleth folly, as far as light excelleth darkness" *(Eccl. 2:13)*; "Wisdom is better than strength . . . Wisdom is better than weapons of war: but one sinner destroyeth much good" *(Eccl. 9:16, 18)*; upon the judgment that would eventually come *(Eccl. 8:12-13; 11:9)*; and that there is a time for everything *(Eccl. 3:1-8).* He apparently had a vision wherein he "beheld all the works of God." *(Eccl. 8:17.)* He counseled that we should "Fear God, and keep his commandments: for this is the whole duty of man." *(Eccl. 12:13.) (Note: The Bible Dictionary gives this insight, "The book of Ecclesiates seems permeated with a pessimistic flavor, but must be read in the light of one of its key phrases: "under the sun" (Eccl. 1:9), meaning "from a worldly point of view.") (Eccl. 1-12.)*

(Note: The footnote to Song of Solomon says, "The JST manuscript states that 'The Songs of Solomon are not inspired writings.'" In Joseph Smith's "New Translation" of the Bible, it states that "The Song of Solomon was eliminated from the Inspired Version.")

When Nebuchadrezzar carried Judah off captive to Babylon, his guard also carried the vessels of the house of the Lord to Babylon, including the twelve brasen bulls that were under the baptismal font in the temple Solomon built. *(Jer. 52:20 [12-20].)* (Chart 7b.; 8e-f.)

SON OF AN ISRAELITISH WOMAN. *Lev. 24:10-16, 23.*

The **Son of an Israelitish Woman** and an Egyptian father (i.e., the son of Shelomith and her husband) fought with an Israelite man and blasphemed the name of the Lord. The Lord instructed Moses that he and any other person who blasphemed the name of the Lord should be stoned to death. The children of Israel did as Moses commanded and the man was stoned to death.

SONS OF THE PROPHETS. *1 Kgs. 20:35-42; 2 Kgs. 2; 9:1-10.*

A certain man of the **Sons of the Prophets** asked his neighbor to smite him. The neighbor refused. The man told him that as soon as he departed from him he would be slain by a lion. He asked another man to smite him and he did. Then, being bruised, he disguised himself with ashes upon his face and spoke with king Ahab. He told him that because he had let Ben-hadad go free, the Lord said it would be the king's life for Beh-hadad's life and "thy people for his people." *(1 Kgs. 20:35-42.)*

(Note: There were sons of the prophets in many cities. They are all included under the single heading of "Sons of the Prophets.") The sons of the prophets who were at Beth-el asked Elisha, "Knowest thou that the Lord will take away thy master from thy head to day?" Elisha told them yes. *(2 Kgs. 2:3.)* The sons of the prophets at Jericho also came to Elisha and asked him the same question. He again told them

he knew. *(2 Kgs. 2:5.)* A group of fifty sons of the prophets watched from a distance as Elijah parted the water and he and Elisha crossed the Jordan river on dry land. *(2 Kgs. 2:7-8.)* They watched Elisha part the waters and return on dry land after Elijah was taken to heaven and they knew the mantle of Elijah had fallen upon Elisha. They wanted to go in search of Elijah in case the Spirit of the Lord had taken him and left him upon some mountain or cast him into some valley. Elisha told them not to search for him. Nevertheless, they continued to pester him so he finally told them to go. They looked for him for three days but could not find him. *(2 Kgs. 2:14-17.)*

Elisha instructed one of the sons of the prophets to go to Ramoth-gilead and anoint Jehu king of Israel, to give him certain instructions and then to get out quickly. He did as instructed and prophesied that the house of Ahab would perish and Jezebel would be eaten by dogs. *(2 Kgs. 9:1-10.)*

SOPHERETH. *Ezra 2:55, 58; Neh. 7:57, 60.*

Sophereth was one of Solomon's servants. The children of Solomon's servants and the Nethinims numbered 392 when they returned from Babylonian captivity to build the house of the Lord as proclaimed by Cyrus, king of Persia.

SOTAI. *Ezra 2:55, 58; Neh. 7:57, 60.*

Sotai was one of Solomon's servants. The children of Solomon's servants and the Nethinims numbered 392 when they returned from Babylonian captivity to build the house of the Lord as proclaimed by Cyrus, king of Persia.

SPIES FROM THE HOUSE OF JOSEPH (1). *Judg. 1:24 (22-25).*

Spies were sent from the house of Joseph to scout out Beth-el. They met a man who showed them the gate to the city in return for their promise that he would be saved. They smote the city with the edge of the sword, but they let go the man and all his family.

STEWARD OF JOSEPH'S (1) HOUSE. *Gen. 43:19-22; 44:1-12.*

The **Steward of Joseph's House** met Joseph's brothers when they went to Egypt the second time to buy more grain. They quickly tried to explain to him how, on their last trip as they returned home, they found the money they had paid for grain in the mouths of their sacks, and that they had it with them so as to return it along with more money to buy more grain. *(Gen. 43:19-22.)*

Joseph commanded the steward of his house to again put the money his brothers paid for grain in the mouth of each sack and to also plant a silver cup in Benjamin's sack. He was then instructed to follow after them and accuse them of stealing the silver cup. He did as Joseph commanded him. *(Gen. 44:1-12.)*

SUAH. *1 Chr. 7:36-37.*

Suah was a son of Zophah, a grandson of Hotham, and a great-great-great-grandson of Asher. His brothers were Harnepher, Shual, Beri, Imrah, Bezer, Hod, Shamma, Shilshah, Ithran and Beera. (Chart 14a.)

SUCCOTH-BENOTH. *2 Kgs. 17:30.*

<u>Succoth-benoth</u> was a false god made by the men of Babylon after they were given the lands of the Israelites. *(Note: The Bible Dictionary states that she was regarded as the goddess of wisdom, the lady of the deep, and the wife of Bel-Merodach.)*

SUCHATHITES. *1 Chr. 2:55.*

<u>Suchathites</u> were one of the families of the scribes. They were Kenites who came of Hemath, father of the house of Rechab.

SUKKIMS. See **Ethiopians**.

SUSANCHITES. *Ezra 4:9.*

The <u>Susanchites</u> were among the various groups who were companions with the Samaritans and helped to hinder the work of rebuilding the temple in Jerusalem.

SUSI. *Num. 13:11.*

<u>Susi</u>, of the tribe of Joseph through Manasseh, was the father of Gaddi.

SYRIANS. *2 Sam. 8:5-6; 10:6-19; 1 Kgs. 20; 21; 2 Kgs. 5; 6; 7; 9:15; 1 Chr. 18:5-6.; 19:6-19; 2 Chr. 1:17; 22:6; 28:5, 18; Jer. 35:11; Ezek. 16:57 (47-48, 51-52, 57); 27:16; Amos 1:5 (1, 5).*

When the <u>Syrians</u> of Damascus went to succor Hadadezer of Zobah after David smote him and took his chariots, horsemen and footmen, David slew 22,000 Syrian men. He put garrisons in Syria, and the Syrians became servants to David. *(2 Sam. 8:5-6; 1 Chr. 18:5-6.)*

Hanun, king of the children of Ammon, hired the Syrians of Beth-rehob and the Syrians of Zoba and of king Maacah, and also of Ish-tob, to join him in battle against David and the Israelites. Joab led the troops against the Syrians while Abishai led the troops against the children of Ammon. David's army slew the men of 700 chariots (7,000 men in chariots) of the Syrians and 40,000 horsemen (footmen). Shobach (Shophach), captain of the Syrian host, was killed. Thus, the Syrians feared to help the children of Ammon any more. *(2 Sam. 10:6-19; 1 Chr. 19:6-19.)*

The Syrians under the leadership of Ben-hadad made war against Israel and were defeated twice. King Ahab let Ben-hadad go contrary to the will of the Lord. Thus, a certain man of the sons of the prophets prophesied to Ahab that his life would go for Ben-hadad's life, and the lives of his people would go for the lives of the Syrians. *(1 Kgs. 20.)*

Jehoshaphat of Judah and Ahab of Israel combined forces and went against the Syrians. Ahab's prophets foretold of success, but Micaiah, the prophet of the Lord, foretold the defeat and death of Ahab. The Syrians were victorious and Ahab was killed. *(1 Kgs. 21.)*

Naaman, a Syrian, came to Elisha to be healed of leprosy. One little Israelite maid whom the Syrians had brought captive to Syria waited upon Naaman's wife. She suggested that Naaman go to Elisha to be cured. Naaman was reluctant to follow Elisha's instructions, but finally did so at the urging of his servants and was healed. *(2 Kgs. 5.)*

When Elisha counseled the king of Israel how to conduct a war with the Syrians, the Syrians decided to go after Elisha. However, at Elisha's petition, the Syrians were smitten with blindness and Elisha guided them to Samaria where he bid their sight be restored. He told the Israelite king to give them food and drink. They went home, and "the bands of Syria came no more into the land of Israel" *(2 Kgs. 6:8-23)*—at least for a while. However, it came to pass after this that Ben-hadad, king of Syria, again went up and besieged Samaria. *(2 Kgs. 6:24.)*

While the Syrians were encamped against Israel, the Lord caused them to hear a noise of chariots and horses, and even the noise of a great army, and they fled, leaving all their possessions in camp. Four lepers informed the king of Israel that the Syrian camp was empty of people but that there were a lot of goods there. Israel took all the spoils which ended the famine in Samaria. *(2 Kgs. 7.)*

The Syrians, under the leadership of king Hazael, wounded Joram (Jehoram), king of Israel in battle. *(2 Kgs. 9:15; 2 Chr. 22:6.)*

Solomon bought horses from Egypt for all the kings of Syria and all the kings of the Hittites. *(2 Chr. 1:17.)*

Because of the wickedness of Ahaz, king of Judah, the Lord delivered Judah into the hand of Rezin, king of Syria, who smote them and carried many away into captivity. *(2 Chr. 28:5, 18.)*

When Nebuchadnezzar came into their lands, the Rechabites feared him and the armies of the Syrians and Chaldeans so they went to Jerusalem for protection. *(Jer. 35:11.)*

The Syrians are referred to in the proverb the Lord gave Ezekiel comparing Jerusalem to a mother's daughter with the pagan nations being referred to as "sisters." The Lord indicated that Jerusalem was more wicked than Syria and the other nations. *(Ezek. 16:57 [47-48, 51-52, 57].)*

As Ezekiel lamented the fall of the great city of Tyrus, he bemoaned the loss of her riches and commerce, part of which involved the merchants of Syria whose wares were "emeralds, purple, and broidered work, and fine linen, and coral, and agate." *(Ezek. 27:16.)*

When Amos prophesied during the time of Uzziah king of Judah and Jeroboam king of Israel of things he saw concerning Israel and the judgments that would come upon Syria, the Philistines and others, he said the people of Syria would go into captivity unto Kir. *(Amos 1:5 [1, 5].)*

NAMES THAT BEGIN WITH "T"

TABBAOTH. *Ezra 2:43, 58; Neh. 7:46, 60.*

Tabbaoth was a Nethinim. When the Nethinims and the children of Solomon's servants left Babylon to return to Jerusalem to build the house of the Lord as proclaimed by Cyrus, king of Persia, they numbered 392.

TABEAL, SON OF. *Isa. 7:6.*

The **Son of Tabeal** was being groomed by Pekah, king of Israel, and Rezin, king of Syria, to be set upon the throne of Judah. However, the Lord had Isaiah warn Judah and tell them that it would not come to pass. *(Note: There is no information as to who Tabeal, himself, was.)*

TABEEL. *Ezra 4:7, 21-24.*

Tabeel, a Samaritan, along with Bishlam, Mithredath and the rest of their companions, wrote to king Artaxerxes against Jerusalem causing the king to command the Samaritans to cause the children of Israel to cease building the temple and the city.

TABRIMON. *1 Kgs. 15:18.*

Tabrimon was the father of Ben-hadad, king of Syria, and the son of Hezion.

TACHMONITE. *2 Sam. 23:8.*

Tachmonite. "The Tachmonite that sat in the seat, chief among the captains" was Adino the Eznite, who was one of David's mighty men. (Chart 17.)

TAHAN (1) (Tahanites). *Num. 26:35.*

Tahan and his brothers, Shuthelah and Becher, were sons of Ephraim. Tahan's descendants were the **Tahanites**. (Chart 15d.)

TAHAN (2). *1 Chr. 7:25 (20-27).*

Tahan, son of Telah, was a great-great-grandson of Ephraim and the father of Laadan. (Chart 15d.)

TAHATH (1). *1 Chr. 6:24, 37.*

Tahath, one of Levi's descendants through Kohath, was the son of Assir and the father of Uriel. (Chart 7d.)

TAHATH (2). *1 Chr. 7:20.*

Tahath was the son of Bered and a great-grandson of Ephraim. His son was Eladah. (Chart 15d.)

TAHATH (3). *1 Chr. 7:20.*

Tahath was the son of Eladah, the father of Zabad, and a great-great-great-grandson of Ephraim. (Chart 15d.)

TAHPENES. *1 Kgs. 11:19.*

Tahpenes, the queen, was the wife of Pharaoh, king of Egypt. She weaned her sister's son Genubath in Pharoah's house and raised Genubath in Pharaoh's household among his sons.

TAHREA. See **Tarea**.

TALMAI (1). *Num. 13:22; Josh. 15:14; Judg. 1:10.*

Talmai was a son of Anak, one of the families of giants living in Caanan who caused ten of the leaders Moses sent to scout out the land to return with a negative report. *(Num. 13:22.)*

Talmai and his brothers Ahiman and Sheshai were driven out of the land by Caleb. *(Josh. 15:14.)*

The tribe of Judah slew Talmai and his brothers. *(Judg. 1:10.)*

TALMAI (2). *2 Sam. 3:3; 1 Chr. 3:2.*

Talmai was king of Geshur, father of David's wife Maacah (Maachah) and grandfather of Absalom (David's thirdborn son).

TALMON. *1 Chr. 9:17; Ezra 2:42; Neh. 7:45; 11:19; 12:25.*

Talmon, a Levite, was one of the porters over the work of the service and a keeper of the gates of the tabernacle. He was an inhabitant of Jerusalem and his genealogy was written in the book of the kings of Israel and Judah, who were carried away to Babylon for their transgression. He was among the first inhabitants to live in Jerusalem upon returning from Babylonian captivity. *(1 Chr. 9:17.)*

Whon Cyrus, king of Persia, proclaimed that the people of God should go to Jerusalem to build the temple, the children of the porters—Talmon, Shallum, Ater, Akkub, Hatita and Shobai—numbered 139 (138). *(Ezra 2:42; Neh. 7:45.)*

Talmon, Akkub, and the other porters numbered 172 when they returned to Jerusalem from Babylonian captivity. *(Neh. 11:19.)*

Talmon, along with Akkub, Mattaniah, Bakbukiah, Obadiah and Meshullam, kept the ward at the thresholds of the gates in the days of Joiakim, Nehemiah and Ezra. *(Neh. 12:25.)*

TAMAH. See **Thamah**.

TAMAR(1). *Gen. 38:6-30; Ruth 4:12; 1 Chr. 2:4.*

Tamar was the wife and widow of Er, Judah's firstborn son. Judah instructed his son Onan to take Tamar to wife and raise seed unto Er. Onan did not wish to give seed to his brother and circumvented Judah's order. Judah then promised Tamar that when his son Shelah grew up he would give him to her to be a husband. When Judah failed to give Shelah to her for a husband as he had promised, Tamar covered her face with a veil and pretended to be a harlot. Judah bought her services for a kid from his flock. He left his signet, bracelet and staff as collateral until he could deliver the kid. When Judah lay with her, she conceived. When Judah heard that his daughter-in-law was three months with child, he ordered that she be brought forth and burned. However, when she appeared, she told them that the father was the man whose signet, bracelet and staff she had. Judah recognized them as his and declared that she was more righteous than he because he had failed to give Shelah to her. He never lay with her again. Tamar delivered twins: Pharez and Zarah (Zerah). *(Gen. 38:6-30.) (Note: The Bible Dictionary indicates she was the wife of Er and Onan. However, the scriptures are not clear on whether or not Onan actually took her for a wife. In Gen. 38:8-10, it says that Onan didn't want to raise up seed to his brother and that when he went unto Tamar that "he spilled it on the ground, lest that he should give seed to his brother." This displeased the Lord and the Lord slew Onan. Judah counseled Tamar to remain a widow until Shelah was old enough to become her husband.)*

The people wished Boaz well as he contemplated taking the widow Ruth for a wife, and hoped that his house might "be like the house of Pharez, whom Tamar bare unto Judah." *(Ruth 4:12.)*

Tamar bore Judah two sons: Pharez and Zerah (Zarah). *(1 Chr. 2:4.)*

TAMAR (2). *2 Sam. 13:1-29; 1 Chr. 3:9.*

Tamar, daughter of David and Maacah, was the very fair sister of Absalom. David's son Amnon, son of Ahinoam, loved her *(2 Sam. 13:1)* and used force to lie with her. Then Amnon hated her and had her shut out. *(2 Sam. 12:14-15.)* She put ashes on her head and tore her garment. Absalom counseled her, "But hold now thy peace, my sister: he is thy brother; regard not this thing." *(2 Sam. 13:19-20)*. Tamar remained in her brother Absalom's house. However, Absalom had his servants kill Amnon in retaliation. *(2 Sam. 13:29.)*

Tamar was David's daughter. *(1 Chr. 3:9.)* (Chart 8e.)

TAMAR (3). *2 Sam. 14:27.*

Tamar was the attractive daughter of Absalom. She had three brothers. *(Note: This scripture presents some confusion. 2 Sam. 18:18 quotes Absalom as saying, "I have no son to keep my name in remembrance. Also, this verse says Absalom had one daughter and her name was Tamar. 2 Chr. 11:20 says Absalom's daughter was Maachah.)*

TAMMUZ. *Ezek. 8:14.*

Tammuz was an Amorite idol, the Babylonian god of spring slain by summer heat, *(or the god of summer slain by winter cold, according to the BD)*. Ezekiel was shown in a vision the women of the children of Israel weeping for Tammuz at the door of the gate to the Lord's house.

TANHUMETH. *2 Kgs. 25:23; Jer. 40:8.*

Tanhumeth, the Netophathite, was the father of Seraiah, which Seraiah and his colleagues (captains of the army) went to Gedaliah after Nebuchadnezzar made Gedaliah governor over the remnant left in Judah.

TAPHATH. *1 Kgs. 4:11.*

Taphath was the daughter of Solomon and the wife of the son of Abinadab. (Chart 8f.)

TAPPUAH. *1 Chr. 2:43.*

Tappuah was one of the sons of Hebron. His brothers were Korah, Rekem and Shema. (Chart 8i.)

TAREA (Tahrea). *1 Chr. 8:35; 9:41.*

Tarea (Tahrea) was of the tribe of Benjamin. He was one of the sons of Micah, a great-grandson of Jonathan and a great-great-grandson of Saul. His brothers were Pithon, Melech and Ahaz. (Chart 16 l.)

TARPELITES. *Ezra 4:9.*

The **Tarpelites** were among the various groups who were companions with the Samaritans and helped to hinder the work of rebuilding the temple in Jerusalem.

TARSHISH (1). *Gen. 10:4; Ezek. 27:12.*

Tarshish was a son of Javan, grandson of Japheth, and a great-grandson of Noah. *(Gen. 10:4.)*

Knowing that Tyrus was going to fall, Ezekiel lamented and reminded the people of Tyrus that "Tarshish was thy merchant by reason of the multitude of all kind of riches; with silver, iron, tin, and lead, they traded in thy fairs." *(Ezek. 27:12.) (Note: The footnote cross-references Tarshish with Tharshish in 1 Kgs. 10:22. It is not clear if the citizens of Tharshish are descendants of this Tarshish or not. However, the other names referred to in verses 13-15—Javan, Tubal, Meshech, Togarmah and Dedan—are all either grandsons or great-grandsons of Noah as mentioned in Gen. 10:2-4, so it seems likely that the people of Tarshish referred to here are the descendants of Javan's son Tarshish.)* (Chart 2a.)

TARSHISH (2). *Esth. 1:14-15.*

Tarshish was one of the seven princes of Persia and Media with king Ahasuerus when queen Vashti refused to come at his command. They asked what they should do unto Vashti, according to the law, because of her refusal to obey Ahasuerus' command.

TARTAK AND NIBHAZ. *2 Kgs. 17:31.*

Tartak and Nibhaz were the false gods made by the Avites after they were given the lands of the Israelites.

TARTAN. *2 Kgs. 18:17; Isa. 20:1.*

Tartan was one of the men king Sennacherib of Assyria sent with his hosts against Jerusalem and king Hezekiah. *(2 Kgs. 18:17.)*

Sargon, king of Assyria, sent Tartan against Ashdod around 711 B.C. Tartan took Ashdod. *(Isa. 20:1.)*

TATNAI. *Ezra 5:3-17; 6:6-13.*

Tatnai was the governor on the west side of the Erphrates River, which included Syria and Cilicia, at the time that Zerubbabel and Jeshua, with the help of the prophets Haggai and Zechariah, were engaged in building the temple during the first years of the reign of Darius I, king of Persia. He and Shethar-boznai and their companions, the Apharsachites, confronted them. After inquiring as to who had commanded them to build the temple, they sent a letter to Darius with their response, indicating that Cyrus had decreed they should build the temple with the suggestion that Darius make a search to see if Cyrus had made such a decree. *(Ezra 5:3-17.)*

After Darius found that Cyrus had, indeed, made a decree that the temple should be built, he renewed the decree and instructed Tatnai, Shethar-boznai and the Apharsachites to let the work of the temple proceed and to assist with funds and with sacrificial animals. They "speedily" did as instructed. *(Ezra 6:6-13.)*

TEBAH. *Gen. 22:24.*

Tebah, Abraham's nephew, was born to Nahor and Reumah, his concubine. (Chart 2d.)

TEBALIAH. *1 Chr. 26:11.*

Tebaliah, a Levite, was the thirdborn son of Hosah who was of the lineage of Merari. His brothers included: Simri, who was made chief by his father even though he was not the firstborn; Hilkiah, the second; Zechariah, the fourth. They, along with other Levites, were appointed by king David to be porters—to have charge of the treasures, serve as officers and judges, and to conduct the outward business over Israel. *(Note: Tebaliah apparently had more brothers as it states that "all the sons and brethren of Hosah were thirteen." However, only four are named by name and Simri was not the firstborn.)* (Chart 7a.)

TEHINNAH. *1 Chr. 4:12.*

Tehinnah was a son of Eshton and the father of Irnahash. His brothers were Beth-rapha and Paseah. *(Note: The scripture says, "These are the men of Rechah." However, it is not clear what that means.)*

TEKOA. *1 Chr. 2:24; 4:5-6.*

Tekoa was a child of Ashur and a grandchild of Hezron and Abiah. *(1 Chr. 2:24.) (Note: There is no indication as to whether Tekoa was a son or a daughter.)*

Tekoa was the child of Ashur, which Ashur had two wives: Helah and Naarah. Helah's and Naarah's sons are listed. *(1 Chr. 4:5-6.) (Note: Tekoa is not named among any of Ashur's sons so it is possible Tekoa was a daughter. It is also not clear as to who was the mother of Tekoa.)* (Charts 8d.; 15b.)

TEKOITE. *2 Sam. 23:26; 1 Chr. 27:9; Neh. 3:5, 27.*

A **Tekoite**, Ira, son of Ikkesh, was one of David's mighty men. *(2 Sam. 23:26.)*

Ira, the son of Ikkesh the Tekoite, was assigned by king David to be over the course of 24,000 who were to serve for the sixth month. *(1 Chr. 27:9.)*

The Tekoites worked on the walls of Jerusalem next to Zadok the son of Baana when the children of Israel rebuilt the walls and gates of Jerusalem during the time of Ezra and Nehemiah. However, they didn't really apply themselves to the task. The Tekoites also labored on an area that extended to the wall of Ophel where the Nethinims labored and dwelled. *(Neh. 3:5, 27.)*

TELAH. *1 Chr. 7:25.*

Telah, son of Resheph, was a great-grandson of Ephraim and the father of Tahan. (Chart 15d.)

TELEM. *Ezra 10:24 (19, 24, 44).*

Telem was one of the porters. He was among those who had taken wives from among the Canaanites or other foreign groups but who agreed to Ezra's request that they separate themselves from these strange wives lest the Lord destroy the rest of the children of Israel.

TEL-HARSA. *Ezra 2:59; Neh. 7:61*.

Tel-harsa, Tel-melah, Cherub, Addan (Addon) and Immer had people go up to Jerusalem who could not declare their lineage so they were regarded as polluted and were put from the priesthood. These included 652 children of Delaiah, Tobiah and Nekoda and the children of the priests: Habaiah, Koz and Barzillai.

TEL-MELAH. *Ezra 2:59; Neh. 7:61*.

Tel-melah, Tel-harsa, Cherub, Addan (Addon) and Immer had people go up to Jerusalem who could not declare their lineage so they were regarded as polluted and were put from the priesthood. These included 652 children of Delaiah, Tobiah and Nekoda and the children of the priests: Habaiah, Koz and Barzillai.

TEMA (1). *Gen. 25:15*.

Tema was a son of Ishmael and a grandson of Abraham and Hagar, Sarah's handmaid. (Chart 3e.)

TEMA (2). *Job 6:19*.

Tema. *(Note: It is not clear if this Tema is a person or a place. Job refers to the caravans of Tema.)*

TEMAN (1). *Gen. 36:11, 15, 42*.

Teman was a son of Eliphaz, son of Adah and Esau. He was a duke or tribal chief. (Charts 3b.; 19.)

TEMANI (Temanite). *Gen. 36:34; Job 2:11; 4:1; 15:1; 22:1; 42:7*.

Temani. *(Note: It is not clear if this Temani is a person or a place.)* "Husham of the land of Temani reigned in his *(Jobab's)* stead." *(Gen. 36:34.)*

Eliphaz, one of Job's three friends, was a **Temanite**. *(Job 2:11; 4:1; 15:1; 22:1; 42:7.)*

TEMENI. *1 Chr. 4:6*.

Temeni was the son of Ashur (the father of Tekoa) and his wife Naarah. His brothers were Ahuzam, Hepher and Haahashtari. His half-brothers were Zereth, Jezoar and Ethnan. (Chart 8d.)

TEN PRINCES IN ISRAEL. *Josh. 22:14*.

Ten Princes in Israel, the chief house of each tribe, were chosen and assigned to go with Phinehas, the son of Eleazar the priest, to the tribes of Reuben, Gad and the half tribe of Manasseh on the east side of Jordan because the children of Israel were concerned that these tribes had fallen away from the Lord. They had built an altar on the east side of Jordan, and the rest of Israel feared they would all come under condemnation from the Lord.

TEN YOUNG MEN. See **Joab's Armorbearers**.

TERAH. *Gen. 11:24-26, 31-32; Josh. 24:2; 1 Chr. 1:26 (1-28)*.

Terah was a son of Nahor, a sixth-great-grandson of Shem, and a seventh-great-grandson of Noah. He begat Abram (Abraham), Nahor and Haran. Terah took Abram and his wife, Sarai, and Lot (Haran's son) and left Ur of the Chaldees and moved to Canaan. He lived in Haran until his death there. He lived 205 years. *(Gen. 11:24-26, 31-32.) (Note: The following scriptures from the Pearl of Great Price* *enlarge our understanding of Terah. Abr. 1:12, 27, 30, states that Terah was led away into adolatry and sought to take away Abraham's life by offering him for a sacrifice. However, a famine in the land caused Terah to be "sorely tormented" and "he repented of the evil which he had determined against me, to take away my life." Abr. 2: 3-4, 5, indicates that Abraham was instructed by the Lord to leave Ur and to go to the land of Canaan. Abram says he took Sarai, Lot and his wife, and "my father followed after me, unto the land which we denominated Haran." Terah worshipped idols and after arriving in Haran, he "turned again unto his idolatry.")*

Terah, the father of Abraham and Nachor (Nahor), Josuah reminded the people, had previously dwelled on the other side of the flood, and had served other gods. *(Josh. 24:2.)*

Terah's genealogy from Adam to Abraham is chronicled. He was the son of Nahor and the father of Abraham. *(1 Chr. 1:26 [1-28].)* (Charts 1.; 2b-d.; 21.)

TERESH. *Esth. 2:21; 6:2.*

Teresh, one of king Ahasuerus' chamberlains, along with his accomplice Bigthan, plotted to destroy the king. When Mordecai informed queen Esther and Esther informed the king, Teresh and Bigthan were hung. *(Esth. 2:21.)*

The plot by Teresh and Bigthan to kill Ahasuerus was revealed by Mordecai as recorded in the book of records of the chronicles. *(Esth. 6:2.)*

THAHASH. *Gen. 22:24.*

Thahash was born to Nahor and Reumah, his concubine. (Chart 2d.)

THAMAH (Tamah). *Ezra 2:53, 58; Neh. 7:55, 60.*

Thamah (Tamah) was a Nethinim. When the Nethinims and the children of Solomon's servants left Babylon to return to Jerusalem to build the house of the Lord as proclaimed by Cyrus, king of Persia, they numbered 392.

THARSHISH. *1 Chr. 7:10.*

Tharshish, son of Bilhan and grandson of Jediael, was a great-grandson of Benjamin and a mighty man of valor. His brothers were Jeush, Benjamin, Ehud, Chenaanah, Zethan and Ahishahar. (Chart 16c.)

THIRTY-ONE KINGS. *Josh. 12:9-34.*

Thirty-one Kings and their kingdoms on the west side of Jordan were destroyed by Joshua and the Israelites. Some kings are mentioned by name, most are just mentioned by their kingdoms. They are: (1) The king of Jericho; (2) king of Ai; (3) Adoni-Zedek, king of Jerusalem; (4) Hoham, king of Hebron; (5) Piram, king of Jarmuth; (6) Japhia, king of Lachish; (7) Debir, king of Eglon; (8) Horam, king of Gezer; (9) king of Debir; (10) king of Geder; (11) king of Hormah; (12) king of Arad; (13) king of Libnah; (14) king of Adullam; (15) king of Makkedah; (16) king of Beth-el; (17) king of Tappuah; (18) king of Hepher; (19) king of Aphek; (20) king of Lasharon; (21) Jobab, king of Madon; (22) Jabin, king of Hazor; (23) king of Shimron-meron; (24) king of Achshaph; (25) king of Taanach; (26) king of Megiddo; (27) king of Kedesh; (28) king of Jokneam of Carmel; (29) king of Dor; (30) king of the nations of Gilgal; (31) king of Tirzah.

THIRTY-TWO KINGS. *1 Kgs. 20:1, 20-21, 23, 29-30.*

Thirty-two Kings joined Ben-hadad, king of Syria, in war against Ahab and the Israelites in Samaria. They were defeated twice.

THREE MEN. *Gen. 18:2 (1-2).*

Three Men stood by the Lord when the Lord appeared to Abraham in the doorway of his tent in the plains of Mamre.

THREE SETS OF MESSENGERS. *1 Sam. 19:20-21.*

Three Sets of Messengers were sent by Saul to find David so he could kill him. Each time when the messengers found David with Samuel and the prophets, the "Spirit of God was upon the messengers" and they also began to prophesy.

TIBNI. *1 Kgs. 16:21-22.*

Tibni was the son of Ginath. After the death of Elah who was slain by Zimri, half of Israel wanted Tibni to be king; half wanted Omri to be king. Omri's followers prevailed and Tibni died.

TIDAL. *Gen. 14:1.*

Tidal was king of nations. He, king Chedorlaomer, king Amraphel and king Arioch made war against the kings of Sodom, Gomorrah, Admah, Zeboiim and Bela.

TIGLATH-PILESER (Tilgath-pilneser, also see **Pul)**. *2 Kgs. 15:29; 16:7-9; 1 Chr. 5:26; 2 Chr. 28:20.*

Tiglath-pileser was king of Assyria (747-734 B.C.) in the days of Pekah, king of Israel. Tiglath-pileser took Ijon, Abel-beth-maachah, Janoah, Kedesh, Hazor, Gilead, Galilee, and all the land of Naphtali and carried the people captive to Assyria. *(2 Kgs. 15:29.)*

Tiglath-pileser came to Ahaz's aid against Syria. He accepted the silver and gold from the house of the Lord, etc., offered to him by Ahaz. He went up against Damascus, carried the people off captive to Kir, and slew Rezin. *(2 Kgs. 16:7-9.)*

The spirit of Tiglath-pileser and the spirit of **Pul**, kings of Assyria, were stirred up by the Lord and they carried the Reubenites, Gadites, and the half tribe of Manasseh away captive. *(1 Chr. 5:26.) (Note: Tiglath-pileser and Pul may be one and the same person according to the BD.)*

When Ahaz, king of Judah, and his people were being attacked by the children of Israel, the Edomites, the Philistines and Syria, Ahaz petitioned **Tilgath-pilneser** (Tiglath-pileser) for help. However, Tilgath-pilneser "came unto him, and distressed him, but strengthened him not." Ahaz then took treasures from out of the house of the Lord and out of his own house and gave them to Tilgath-pilneser, "but he helped him not." *(2 Chr. 28:20.)*

TIKVAH (1) (Tikvath). *2 Kgs. 22:14; 2 Chr. 34:22.*

Tikvah (Tikvath), the son of Harhas (Hasrah), was the father of Shallum and father-in-law of the prophetess Huldah.

TIKVAH (2). *Ezra 10:15.*

Tikvah was the father of Jahaziah.

TIKVATH. See **Tikvah (1)**.

TILGATH-PILNESER. See **Tiglath-pileser**.

TILON. *1 Chr. 4:20*.

Tilon was a son of Shimon. His brothers were Amnon, Rinnah and Ben-hanan.

TIMNA. *Gen. 36:12; 1 Chr. 1:36*.

Timna was Esau's son Elilphaz's concubine. She bore Amalek. She was the sister of Lotan, son of Seir. *(Gen. 36:12.)*

Timna is apparently mistakenly listed as one of Eliphaz's sons. *(1 Chr. 1:36.)* (Charts 3b.; 4a-f.)

TIMNAH. *Gen. 36:40*.

Timnah was one of the dukes (tribal chiefs) who came of Esau. (Chart 19.)

TIMNITE. *Judg. 15:6*.

Timnites were one of the groups within the Philistines. Samson married a Philistine woman whose father was a Timnite.

TIRAS. *Gen. 10:2*.

Tiras was a son of Japheth and a grandson of Noah. (Chart 2a.)

TIRATHITES. *1 Chr. 2:55*.

Tirathites were one of the families of the scribes living in Jabez. They were Kenites who came of Hemath, father of the house of Rechab.

TIRHAKAH. *2 Kgs. 19:9; Isa. 37:9*.

Tirhakah was king of Ethiopia. When Rab-shakeh (the Assyrian king Sennacherib's captain) heard that Tirhakah had come out to fight against him, he sent messengers again to Hezekiah, king of Judah, trying to get him to surrender to Assyria rather than trust in God for deliverance.

TIRHANAH. *1 Chr. 2:48*.

Tirhanah was one of the sons of Caleb and his concubine Maachah. (Chart 8k.)

TIRIA. *1 Chr. 4:16*.

Tiria was a son of Jehaleleel. His brothers were Ziph, Ziphah and Asareel. *(Note: It would appear that Tiria's father Jehaleleel and, therefore, Tiria, was related to Caleb, but the relationship is unclear.)* (Chart 8n.)

TIRSHATHA. *Ezra 2:63; Neh. 7:65*.

Tirshath was the Persian title for a local or provincial governor. When the children of some of the priests could not find their names among the genealogies that had been recorded, the Tirshath instructed them not to eat of the most holy things until such time as "there stood up a priest with Urim and with Thummim."

TIRZAH. *Num. 26:33; 27:1-7*.

Tirzah was a daughter of Zelophehad and a great-granddaughter of Manasseh. Her sisters were Mahlah, Noah, Hoglah and Milcah. She had no brothers. She and her sisters petitioned Moses and Eleazar to be given their father's inheritance because he had no sons and he, himself, had died in the wilderness. The Lord told Moses that if a man had no sons, his inheritance should pass on to his daughters. (Charts 15a-b.)

TISHBITE. *1 Kgs. 17:1.*

Tishbite. Elijah the prophet was a Tishbite.

TOAH. See **Tohu**.

TOB-ADONIJAH. *2 Chr. 17:8-9.*

Tob-adonijah, a Levite, along with other Levites and Elishama and Jehoram, the priests, was sent by king Jehoshaphat to journey with the princes of Judah throughout the cities of Judah to instruct the people out of the book of the law of the Lord.

TOBIAH. *Neh. 2:10; 4:3-8; 6; 13:4-9.*

Tobiah, a servant to Sanballat, was an Ammonite. It grieved both Tobiah and Sanballat that Nehemiah inquired about the welfare of the children of Israel. *(Neh. 2:10.)*

Tobiah supported Sanballat in his conspiracy to stop Nehemiah and his people from building the walls and gates of Jerusalem. *(Neh. 4:3-8.)*

Tobiah, Sanballat and Geshem plotted ways to stop Nehemiah and the construction of the walls of Jerusalem. Tobiah carried letters from Sanballat to Nehemiah. However, Nehemiah would not be persuaded to meet with them as he knew it was a trick. They even hired Shemaiah to try to persuade Nehemiah to hide in the temple, which he refused to do. Nevertheless, Tobiah had a large following in Judah because he was the son-in-law of Shechaniah who was the son of Arah. Additionally, Tobiah's son Johanan had married the daughter of Meshullam who was the son of Berechiah. *(Neh. 6.)*

Tobiah was allied with Eliashib the priest and had defiled the house of God. Nehemiah ejected him and his household goods from his dwelling place in the temple and commanded that the chambers be cleansed. *(Neh. 13:4-9.)*

TOBIAH, THE CHILDREN OF. *Ezra 2:60; Neh. 7:62.*

The Children of Tobiah were among those who went up to Jerusalem from Tel-melah, Tel-harsa, Chenrub, Addan and Immer when king Cyrus declared that the Israelites should return there and build the temple, but they could not verify that they were actually of the house of Israel; thus, they were regarded as polluted and were put from the priesthood. The children of Delaiah, Tobiah and Nekoda numbered 652 (642). *(Note: There is no information to indicate whether or not this Tobiah and the one cited above are one and the same.)*

TOBIJAH (1). *2 Chr. 17:8-9.*

Tobijah, a Levite, along with other Levites and Elishama and Jehoram, the priests, was sent by king Jehoshaphat to journey with the princes of Judah throughout the cities of Judah to instruct the people out of the book of the law of the Lord.

TOBIJAH (2). *Zech. 6:10-14.*

The captive of **Tobijah**, Heldai and Jedaiah who had come from Babylon were instructed to go into the house of Josiah the son of Zephaniah and crown Joshua

(Jeshua) the high priest. *(Note: This was a similitude of crowning Christ, i.e., the BRANCH.)*

TOGARMAH. *Gen. 10:3; Ezek. 27:14; 38.*

Togarmah was a son of Gomer, grandson of Japheth, and a great-grandson of Noah. *(Gen. 10:3.)*

As Ezekiel lamented the fall of the great city of Tyrus, he bemoaned the loss of her riches and commerce, part of which involved the merchants of those who were of the house of Togarmah, merchants who traded in horses, horsemen and mules. *(Ezek. 27:14.)*

In the latter days, the battle of Gog and Magog against Israel will usher in the Second Coming of the Lord. Gathered together with Gog will be Togarmah, Gomer, Sheba, Dedan and the merchants of Tarshish. *(Ezek. 38.)* (Chart 2a.)

TOHU (Toah, Nahath (2)). *1 Sam. 1:1; 1 Chr. 6:26-27, 34.*

Tohu (Nahath (2), Toah), son of Zuph (Zophai), was father of Elihu (Eliel, Eliab) and the great-great-grandfather of Samuel. *(1 Sam. 1:1.)* (Chart 7d.)

TOI (Tou) . *2 Sam. 8:9-10; 1 Chr. 18:9-10.*

Toi (Tou) was king of Hamath. He was glad when he heard that David had smitten Hadadezer because he, himself, had had battles with him. He sent his son Joram (Hadoram) to David to salute him and to take him gifts of silver, gold and brass.

TOLA (1) (Tolaites). *Gen. 46:13; Num. 26:23; 1 Chr. 7:1-2.*

Tola was one of Issachar's sons (and a grandson of Jacob). His brothers were Phuvah, Job and Shimron. *(Gen. 46:13.)*

Tola's descendants were called **Tolaites**. His brothers were Pua (Phuvah), Jashub (Job), and Shimron. *(Num. 26:23.)*

Tola, brother of Puah (Phuvah, Pua), Jashub (Job) and Shimron, was the father of Uzzi, Rephaiah, Jeriel, Jahmai, Jibsam and Shemuel. In the days of David, his sons numbered 22,600. *(1 Chr. 7:1-2.)* (Chart 9a.)

TOLA (2). *Judg. 10:1-2.*

Tola, of the lineage of Issachar, was the son of Puah who was the son of Dodo. He followed Abimelech and judged Israel 23 years. He died and was buried in Shamir. (Charts 9b.; 20.)

TOLAITES. See **Tola (1)**.

TOU. See **Toi**.

TUBAL. *Gen. 10:2; Ezek. 27:13; 32:21, 26; 38:2-3; 39:1.*

Tubal was a son of Japheth and a grandson of Noah. *(Gen. 10:2.)*

As Ezekiel lamented the fall of the great city of Tyrus, he bemoaned the loss of her riches and commerce, part of which involved the merchants of Tubal, Javan and Meshech, merchants who traded in "persons of men and vessels of brass in thy markets." *(Ezek. 27:13.)*

As Ezekiel lamented for Pharaoh king of Egypt and for Egypt, herself, the Lord told him, "The strong among the mighty shall speak to him (Pharaoh) out of the midst of hell with them that help him: they are gone down, they lie uncircumcised, slain by the sword . . . There is Meschech, Tubal, and all her multitude: her graves are round about him: all of them uncircumcised, slain by the sword, though they caused their terror in the land of the living." *(Ezek. 32:21, 26.)*

The Lord told Ezekiel to set his face against "Gog, the land of Magog, the chief prince of Meshech and Tubal, and prophesy against him." *(Ezek. 38:2-3.)*

The chief prince of Tubal and Meshech was Gog. *(Ezek. 39:1.)* (Chart 2a.)

TUBAL-CAIN. *Gen. 4:22.*

Tubal-cain was the son of Zillah and Lamech. He was an instructor of every artificer in brass and iron. (Chart 1.)

TWO ANGELS. *Gen. 19:1, 11-12.*

Two Angels approached Lot as Lot sat in the gate of Sodom. When the men of Sodom tried to get these two men so they could abuse them sexually, the angels smote them with blindness. They instructed Lot to leave with his family and told him that Sodom was going to be destroyed. *(Note: The JST and the footnote to the text indicate that there were three messengers or angels.)*

TWO HUNDRED AND FIFTY PRINCES. *Num. 16:2, 35.*

Two-hundred and Fifty Princes, famous in the congregation and men of renown and seeking priestly offices, following the leadership of Korah, Dathan, Abiram and On, rose up against Moses and Aaron. The Lord destroyed them by fire.

TWO ISRAELITE SPIES. *Josh. 2:1-24; 6:22-23.*

Two Israelite Spies were sent by Joshua to scout out the city of Jericho. They were received and concealed by the harlot Rahab. They granted her request that when the city got destroyed, she and her family would be spared. They gave Joshua a favorable report. *(Josh. 2:1-24.)*

Prior to destroying Jericho, Joshua had the two spies bring Rahab and her family out. *(Josh. 6:22-23.)*

TWO OF ABRAHAM'S YOUNG MEN. *Gen. 22:3, 5,19.*

Two of Abraham's Young Men were asked to accompany Abraham and Isaac when Abraham took Isaac away to sacrifice him as commanded by the Lord. They were asked to remain with the ass while Abraham and Isaac went off to worship. After the Lord spared Isaac and provided a substitute sacrifice, these young men journeyed with Abraham to Beer-sheba where they all dwelt.

TWO SERVANTS OF BALAAM. *Num. 22:22.*

Two Servants of Balaam accompanied him as he traveled to meet Balak.

TWO SERVANTS OF SHIMEI (1). *1 Kgs. 2:39.*

Two Servants of Shimei ran away to the king of Gath. When Shimei passed beyond the brook of Kidron to retrieve them, Solomon had Shimei put to death as he had been told never to go beyond the brook of Kidron.

TWO SONS OF A WIDOW WOMAN. *2 Kgs. 4:1-7.*

<u>Two Sons Of a Widow Woman</u> were in danger of being taken by creditors to be bondsmen. They were spared when the prophet Elisha multiplied the woman's oil. The sons borrowed empty vessels from all the neighbors and she filled them with oil. Elisha had her sell the oil to pay off her debt. She and her sons were told they could live on the remainder of the profits.

TWO WOMEN (harlots). *1 Kgs. 3:16-27.*

<u>Two Women (Harlots)</u> came to Solomon and asked him to determine the maternity of a living child. Each claimed the child was hers. When Solomon suggested cutting the child in half—giving half to each woman—the real mother declined and said to give the child to the other woman rather than slay it. Solomon gave the child to the rightful mother.

NAMES THAT BEGIN WITH "U"

UCAL. *Prov. 30:1.*

Ucal, along with Ithiel, received the words of Agur the son of Jakeh, even the prophecy that constitutes Proverbs 30. Every word of God is pure. God is a shield unto all who put their trust in Him *(v. 5)*.

UEL. *Ezra 10:34 (19, 34, 44).*

Uel, of the sons of Bani, and his brothers were some of the men in Israel who took foreign wives but gave them up when Ezra feared the wrath of God would destroy Israel for this iniquity.

ULAM (1). *1 Chr. 7:16-17.*

Ulam was a son of Peresh, a grandson of Machir, and a great-grandson of Manasseh. His brother was Rakem and his son was Bedan. *(Note: It is not clear if his father was Peresh or Sheresh. The assumption here is that the pronoun "his" refers to Peresh each time it is used in verse 16.)* (Chart 15b.)

ULAM (2). *1 Chr. 8:39-40.*

Ulam was the firstborn son of Eshek. He was from the tribe of Benjamin. He descended through Jonathan, the son of Saul. His brothers were Jehush and Eliphelet. His sons "were mighty men of valour, archers, and had many sons, and sons' sons." (Chart 16 l.)

ULLA. *1 Chr. 7:39.*

Ulla, of the tribe of Asher, was the father of Arah, Haniel and Rezia. *(Note: Ulla is listed as a descendant of Asher as though he were tied in with Zophah. However, the direct lineage is not clear.)* (Chart 14b.)

UNNI. *1 Chr. 15:18-20.*

Unni, a Levite, and his brethren of the second degree were assigned, under the direction of David, to be singers along with Heman, Asaph and Ethan. Unni and his brethren were assigned to play with psalteries on Alamoth.

UR. *1 Chr. 11:35.*

Ur was the father of Eliphal, one of David's mighty men. (Chart 17.)

URI (1). *Ex. 31:2; 1 Chr. 2:20; 2 Chr. 1:5.*

Uri, of the tribe of Judah, was the son of Hur and the father of Bezaleel, which Bezaleel was blessed with knowledge, wisdom and skill for the workmanship for the tabernacle. *(Ex. 31:2.)*

Uri, son of Hur, begat Bezaleel. *(1 Chr. 2:20.)*

Uri's son Bezaleel made the brasen altar that was before the tabernacle of the Lord. *(2 Chr. 1:5.)* (Charts 8i, m.)

URI (2). *1 Kgs. 4:19.*

Uri was the father of Geber, the officer in the land of Gilead.

URI (3). *Ezra 10:24 (18-19, 24, 44)*.

Uri was one of the porters. He was among those who had taken wives from among the Canaanites or other foreign groups but who agreed to Ezra's request that they separate themselves from these strange wives lest the Lord destroy the rest of the children of Israel.

URIAH (1). *2 Sam. 11:3-24; 23:39*.

Uriah the Hittite was Bath-sheba's husband. From his rooftop, David watched Bath-sheba washing herself and observed that she was very beautiful. He had her brought to him and he lay with her while Uriah was away with the army. Bath-sheba became pregnant and sent word to David. David tried to cover up his sin by sending for Uriah and sending him home to sleep with Bath-sheba. However, Uriah said he could not go to his home and wife while "the ark, and Israel, and Judah, abide in tents." David suggested to Uriah that he tarry for a day or two. He had him eat and drink and made him drunk, but still Uriah did not go home to Bath-sheba. Therefore, David wrote a letter to Joab and sent it by the hand of Uriah wherein he instructed Joab to place Uriah in the forefront of the hottest battle. Joab was to withdraw and allow Uriah to be smitten and die. Joab did not do exactly as instructed. Joab assigned him to a place where other valiant men were. Several men died, including Uriah. Joab sent a messenger to David to inform him of their battle losses, and instructed him to end his message by informing David that Uriah the Hittite was also dead. *(2 Sam. 11:3-24.)*

Uriah was one of David's mighty men. *(2 Sam. 23:39.)* (Chart 17.)

URIAH (2) (Urijah (2)). *Ezra 8:33; Neh. 3:4, 21; Isa. 8:2*.

Uriah, the priest, was father of Meremoth. *(Ezra 8:33.)*

Urijah (Uriah) was the father of Meremoth and the son of Koz. *(Neh. 3:4, 21.)*

Uriah the priest and Zechariah the son of Jeberechiah were two "faithful witnesses" Isaiah took with him to record information the Lord told him to record concerning his son Maher-shalal-hash-baz. *(Isa. 8:2.)*

URIEL (1) (Zephaniah 2). *1 Chr. 6:24, 36; 15:5, 11*.

Uriel (Zephaniah), one of Levi's descendants through Kohath, was the son of Tahath and the father of Uzziah (Azariah). *(1 Chr. 6:24, 36.)*

Uriel was the chief of the sons of Kohath. He and 120 of his brethren were called by David to assemble with other Levites to prepare themselves to retrieve the ark of God from the house of Obed-edom so as to bring it to the place David had prepared for it in the city of David. *(1 Chr. 15:5, 11.)* (Chart 7d.)

URIEL (2). *2 Chr. 13:2*.

Uriel of Gibeah was the father of Michaiah the mother of Abijah (Abijam), king in Judah. *(Note: 2 Chr. 11:20 states that Maachah, daughter of Absalom was the mother of Abijah.)*

URIJAH (1). *2 Kgs. 16:10-16*.

Urijah was the priest when Ahaz was king over Judah. At Ahaz's command, he built a new altar, according to the pattern Ahaz sent to him.

URIJAH (2). *Neh. 3:4, 21.* See **Uriah (2)**.

URIJAH (3). *Neh. 8:1-8.*

Urijah was one of the men who stood on Ezra's right hand when Ezra read and interpreted the law of Moses to the people.

URIJAH (4). *Jer. 26:20-23.*

Urijah was the son of Shemaiah of Kirjath-jearim. He prophesied against the children of Israel just as Jeremiah did. When king Jehoiakim determined to put him to death for his preaching, he fled to Egypt. Jehoiakim sent Elnathan, son of Achbor, along with some other men, to Egypt to capture Urijah. They did so. When they brought him back, Jehoiakim slew Urijah and threw his body into a grave of the common people.

UTHAI (1). *1 Chr. 9:4.*

Uthai, a descendant of Pharez, the son of Judah, was the son of Ammihud. He was among the first inhabitants to dwell in Jerusalem upon returning from Babylonian captivity. (Chart 8b.)

UTHAI (2). *Ezra 8:14.*

Uthai and Zabbud were of the sons of Bigvai. They were the chiefs of their fathers and went with Ezra back to Jerusalem from Babylon. They took 70 males with them.

UZ (1). *Gen. 10:23 (22-23); 1 Chr. 1:17.*

Uz was a son of Aram, a grandson of Shem and a great-grandson of Noah. (Chart 2b.)

UZ (2). *Gen. 36:28.*

Uz, one of the dukes of the Horites, was a son of Dishan. His brother was Aran. (Chart 4f.)

UZAI. *Neh. 3:25.*

Uzai was the father of Palal, which Palal repaired the portion of the wall of Jerusalem that was "over against the turning of the wall, and the tower which lieth out from the king's house, that was by the court of the prison."

UZAL. *Gen. 10:27.*

Uzal was a son of Joktan, a third-great-grandson of Shem and a fourth-great-grandson of Noah. (Chart 2b.)

UZZA (1). *1 Chr. 13:7-10.* See **Uzzah**.

UZZA (2). *1 Chr. 6:29-30.*

Uzza, a descendant of Levi through Merari, was a son of Shimei and the father of Shimea. (Chart 7e.)

UZZA (3). *1 Chr. 8:7 (6-7).*

Uzza, a descendant of Benjamin, was a son of Ehud. (Chart 16d.)

UZZA (4). *Ezra 2:49, 58; Neh. 7:51, 60.*

Uzza was a Nethinim. When the Nethinims and the children of Solomon's servants left Babylon to return to Jerusalem to build the house of the Lord as proclaimed by Cyrus, king of Persia, they numbered 392.

UZZAH (Uzza (1)). *2 Sam. 6:3, 6-7 (1-3, 6-7); 1 Chr. 13:7-10.*

Uzzah was one of Abinadab's sons. When David and 30,000 men of Israel went from Baale of Judah to fetch the ark of God from Abinadab in Gibeah, Uzzah (Uzza) and his brother, Ahio, drove the new cart. Uzzah put his hand on the ark to steady it as they came to Nachon's threshingfloor. This angered the Lord; and the Lord smote him and he died.

UZZI (1). *1 Chr. 6:5; Ezra 7:1-5.*

Uzzi was the son of Bukki and was a third-great-grandson of Aaron. He begat Zerahiah. *(1 Chr. 6:5.)*

Uzzi's descendants and forefathers are listed from Aaron through Ezra with some modification from 1 Chr. 6:4-15. *(Ezra 7:1-5.)* (Chart 7b.)

UZZI (2). *1 Chr. 7:2-3.*

Uzzi, a son of Tola and grandson of Issachar, was the father of Izrahiah. His brothers were Rephaiah, Jeriel, Jahmai, Jibsam and Shemuel. (Chart 9a.)

UZZI (3). *1 Chr. 7:7.*

Uzzi was a son of Bela and a grandson of Benjamin. His brothers were Ezbon, Uzziel, Jerimoth and Iri. He was the head of his house and a mighty man of valor. (Chart 16c.)

UZZI (4). *1 Chr. 9:8.*

Uzzi, of the tribe of Benjamin, was the father of Elah and the son of Michri. He and his family were among the inhabitants of Jerusalem whose genealogy was written in the book of the kings of Israel and Judah, who were carried away to Babylon for their transgression. (Chart 16m.)

UZZI (5). *Neh. 11:22.* See **Zechariah (11)**.

UZZI (6). *Neh. 12:19, 42.*

Uzzi, son of Jedaiah, was one of the priests who was a chief of the fathers in the days of Joiakim. He was one of the singers who joined in the dedication of the walls of Jerusalem with Nehemiah.

UZZIA. *1 Chr. 11:44.*

Uzzia the Ashterathite was one of David's mighty men. (Chart 17.)

UZZIAH (1). See **Azariah (3)**.

UZZIAH (2) (Azariah (15)). *1 Chr. 6:24, 36; 2 Chr. 29:12.*

Uzziah (Azariah), of the house of Levi through Kohath, was the son of Uriel (Zephaniah). His son was Joel (Shaul). *(1 Chr. 6:24, 36.)*

Joel (Shaul) was the son of Azariah (Uzziah). He and his brethren sanctified themselves and, in compliance with the king's commandment and by the word of the Lord, cleansed the house of the Lord. *(2 Chr. 29:12.)* (Chart 7d.)

UZZIAH (3). *1 Chr. 27:25.*

Uzziah was the father of Jehonathan who was assigned by David to be over the storehouses in the fields, cities, villages and castles.

UZZIAH (4). *Ezra 10:21 (19, 21, 44)*.

Uzziah, one of the sons of Harim, was among those sons of the priests who had taken foreign wives and who agreed to put them away as instructed by Ezra.

UZZIAH (5). *Neh. 11:4*.

Uzziah, the son of Zechariah and the father of Athaiah of the children of Judah, dwelled in Jerusalem after leaving Babylon. (Chart 8b.)

UZZIEL (1) (Uzzielites). *Ex. 6:18; Num. 3:27-31; 1 Chr. 6:2; 15:10; 23:20*.

Uzziel was a son of Kohath and a grandson of Levi. He was an uncle to Aaron and Moses. His brothers were Amram, Izhar and Hebron. *(Ex. 6:18; 1 Chr. 6:2.)*

Uzziel was the father of Elizaphan. His descendants were the **Uzzielites**. *(Num. 3:27-31.)*

Uzziel's descendant, Amminadab, was chief of Uzziel's sons at the time David was king. *(1 Chr. 15:10.)*

When David made Solomon king, he also numbered the Levites and divided them into courses for the work of the house of the Lord. Among the sons of Kohath, son of Levi, two of the sons of Uzziel were named: Michah, first; Jesiah, second. *(1 Chr. 23:20.)* (Charts 7b, d.)

UZZIEL (2). *1 Chr. 4:42*.

Uzziel, son of Ishi, was one of the captains who led a group of 500 men of the sons of Simeon to mount Seir in the days of Hezekiah king of Judah and smote the rest of the Amalekites who had escaped from earlier conflicts. His brothers were Pelatiah, Neariah and Rephaiah. (Chart 6b.)

UZZIEL (3). *1 Chr. 7:7*.

Uzziel was a son of Bela and a grandson of Benjamin. His brothers were Ezbon, Uzzi, Jerimoth and Iri. He was the head of the house of his fathers and a mighty man of valor. (Chart 16c.)

UZZIEL (4). *1 Chr. 25:4, 16*.

Uzziel, a Levite and musician, was a son of Heman. The musicians—sons of Heman, Asaph and Jeduthun—drew lots and were separated to the service by David and the captains of the host. *(Note: No lot number is given for Uzziel nor for one of the sons of Jeduthun—who was not named—nor for Zeri, another of Jeduthun's sons . However, there were three lots cast by people not named in verses 2-4: Izri [v. 11], Shimei [v. 17], Azareel [v. 18]. Perhaps, those names are just different names for the three who were not given lot assignments: Uzziel, Zeri and the unnamed son of Jeduthun.)* (Chart 7d.)

UZZIEL (5). *2 Chr. 29:14*.

Uzziel, of the sons of Jeduthun, was among those instructed by Hezekiah, king of Judah, to sanctify themselves so they could cleanse and sanctify the house of the Lord. (Chart 7f.)

UZZIEL (6). *Neh. 3:8.*

<u>Uzziel</u>, son of Harhaiah, was one of the goldsmiths. He worked next to Melatiah and Jadon when the children of Israel rebuilt the walls and gates of Jerusalem during the time of Ezra and Nehemiah.

UZZIELITES. See **Uzziel (1)**.

NAMES THAT BEGIN WITH "V"

VAJEZATHA. *Esth. 9:9.*

Vajezatha was one of Haman's ten sons who was slain by the Jews and, at queen Esther's request, hung on the gallows by king Ahasuerus.

VANIAH. *Ezra 10:36 (18-19, 36, 44).*

Vaniah, a son of Bani, and his brothers were some of the men in Israel who took foreign wives but gave them up when Ezra feared the wrath of God would destroy Israel for this iniquity.

VASHNI. See **Joel (1)**.

VASHTI. *Esth. 1:9-2:1; 2:17.*

Vashti, wife of Ahasuerus, was queen of Persia and Media. When Ahasuerus commanded that Vashti come before him and his guests so he could show off her beauty, she refused to come. Thus, following advice from Memucan, one of the seven princes of Persia and Media, he deposed Vashti as queen. *(Esth. 1:9-2:1.)*

Vashti was replaced by Esther as queen. *(Esth. 2:17.)*

VOPHSI. *Num. 13:14.*

Vophsi, of the tribe of Naphtali, was the father of Nahbi, one of the 12 spies sent out by Moses to scout out the land of Canaan.

NAMES THAT BEGIN WITH "W"

WATCHMAN. *2 Kgs. 9:17-20.*

The **Watchman** on the tower in Jezreel where Jehoram, king of Israel, was recovering from injuries in his battle with Hazael of Syria, saw Jehu and his company approaching. The king had him send a horseman out to see if the company came in peace. The horseman didn't return and the king had the watchman send out a second horseman, who also did not return. Then the watchman reported that it looked like the driving of Jehu "for he driveth furiously."

WENCH, A. *2 Sam. 17:17-20.*

A **Wench** conveyed information from Hushai (David's friend) to Jonathan (son of Abiathar the priest) and Ahimaaz (son of Zadok the priest) when they were trying to get information to David about the counsel Hushai had given Absalom and what Absalom's plans were.

WIDOW, A. *1 Kgs. 7:14 (13-14); 2 Chr. 2:14.*

A **Widow** was the mother of Hiram of Tyre. (He was of the tribe of Naphtali.) *(1 Kgs. 7:14 [13-14].)*

She was of the daughters of Dan. *(2 Chr. 2:14.)* (Chart 11b.; 12b.)

WIDOWWOMAN OF ZAREPHATH. *1 Kgs. 17:9-24.*

A **Widowwoman of Zarephath** was prepared by the Lord to sustain Elijah after Elijah sealed the heavens so there would be no rain and after the ravens fed him by the brook Cherith until it dried up. Elijah promised her that her barrel of meal nor her cruse of oil would fail until the Lord sent rain upon the earth again. Elijah restored her son to life.

WIDOWWOMAN OF ZAREPHATH, SON OF. *1 Kgs. 17:12-23.*

The **Son of the Widowwoman of Zarephath** died and Elijah restored him to life.

WISE MEN, SORCERERS AND MAGICIANS. *Ex. 7:11-12, 20-22; 8:18-19.*

The **Wise Men, Sorcerers and Magicians** in Pharaoh's court were able to duplicate several of Moses' and Aaron's feats, i.e., turn rods into serpents, the waters into blood. *(Ex. 7:11-12, 20-22.)*

They could not duplicate bringing forth lice and told Pharaoh that it was the finger of God. *(Ex. 8:18-19.)*

WISE WOMAN FROM TEKOAH, A. *2 Sam. 14:2-21.*

A **Wise Woman from Tekoah** was sent for by Joab as he perceived that David's heart was turned toward Absalom and he desired to unite them following their three years of separation following the slaying of Amnon by Absalom. The woman, speaking the words Joab told her to speak to David, succeeded in getting David to agree to have Absalom return from his exile.

WISE WOMAN IN ABEL, A. *2 Sam. 20:16-22 (14-22)*.

A **Wise Woman** intervened when Abishai and Joab and their men pursued Sheba to Abel of Beth-maachah to put down the insurrection he was causing. Rather than having the soldiers destroy a whole city, she said the people would throw Sheba's head to them over the wall. She rallied the people in the city and they threw Sheba's head over the wall to Joab. Thus, the resurrection was put down and the city was saved.

WOMAN, A. *2 Kgs. 6:26-29 (24-29)*.

A **Woman** cried for help from the king of Israel. This was at a time when there was apparently a famine in the land. She claimed that another woman had suggested that she give this other woman her son so they could eat him "today" and then "tomorrow" they could eat her son. They boiled her son and did eat, but, she said, the other woman hid her son so they could not eat him.

WOMAN, A CERTAIN. *Judg. 9: 53 (50-54)*.

A **Certain Woman** dropped a piece of millstone on Abimelech's head and broke his skull because he and his followers were trying to burn the people as they took refuge in the tower of Thebez. Abimelech did not want it said that he was killed by a woman so he had his armorbearer kill him with his sword.

WOMAN OF THE WIVES OF THE SONS OF THE PROPHETS, A CERTAIN. *2 Kgs. 4:1-7*.

A **Certain Woman of the Wives of the Sons of the Prophets**, a widow, cried unto Elisha for help because creditors were threatening to take her sons for bondsmen. Elisha multiplied the oil she had and told her to sell it so she could pay off her debt. The remainder she and her sons were to live on.

WOMAN IN BAHURIM, A. *2 Sam. 17:19-20 (17-21)*.

A **Woman in Bahurim** hid Jonathan and Ahimaaz in a well when a lad reported to Absalom that they were in the city and were being given information helpful to David.

WOMAN AT EN-DOR. *1 Sam. 28:7-25*.

The **Woman at En-dor**, referred to as the witch of En-dor, foretold Saul of his death, the death of his sons, and of the defeat of Israel by the Philistines. She called up Samuel who was dead. He told Saul that he and his sons would die the following day. *(Note: The Bible Dictionary states: "The account . . . of the prohet being brought back from the dead by the witch of Endor, at King Saul's request, presents a problem. It is certain that a witch or other medium cannot by any means available to her bring up a prophet from the world of spirits. We may confidently be assured that if Samuel was present on that occasion, it was not due to conjuring of the witch. Either Samuel came in spite of and not because of the witch, or some other spirit came impersonating him.")*

NAMES THAT BEGIN WITH "Y"

YOUNG MAN. *Gen. 18:7.*

A **Young Man** was asked by Abraham to quickly dress the calf he had selected and make a feast for the Lord and the three men who were with him.

YOUNG MEN OF THE PRINCES OF THE PROVINCES. *1 Kgs. 20:14 (13-21).*

The **Young Men of the Princes of the Provinces** were those with whom the Lord would defeat the Syrians in their war against Israel. They numbered 232. The rest of the children of Israel numbered 7,000. They defeated the Syrians.

NAMES THAT BEGIN WITH "Z"

ZAAVAN (Zavan). *Gen. 36:27; 1 Chr. 1:42.*

Zaavan (Zavan), a grandson of Seir the Horite, was a son of Ezer. His brothers were Bilhan and Akan (Jakan). (Chart 4e.)

ZABAD (1). *1 Chr. 2:36-37; 11:41.*

Zabad was the son of Nathan and the father of Ephlal. *(1 Chr. 2:36-37.)*

Zabad, great-grandson of Ahlai, was one of David's mighty men. *(1 Chr. 11:41.)* (Charts 8c.; 17.)

ZABAD (2). *2 Chr. 24:26.* See **Jozachar**.

ZABAD (3). *1 Chr. 7:21.*

Zabad was the son of Tahath, the father of Shuthelah, and a fourth-great-grandson of Ephraim. Zabad, Shuthelah, Ezer and Elead were slain by the men of Gath, because they came down to take away their cattle. (Chart 15d.)

ZABAD (4). *Ezra 10:27 (18-19, 27, 44).*

Zabad was one of the sons of Zattu who took wives from among the Canaanites and other foreign groups. He and his brothers complied with Ezra's request that they separate themselves from these foreign wives lest the Lord destroy the remainder of the children of Israel because of this iniquity.

ZABAD (5). *Ezra 10:33, 44.*

Zabad, one of Hashum's sons, and his brothers—Mattenai, Mattathah, Eliphelet, Jeremai, Manasseh and Shimei—were among the Israelite men who took foreign wives but complied with Ezra's request that they put away their strange wives so as not to bring the wrath of God upon Israel.

ZABAD (6). *Ezra 10:43-44.*

Zabad was one of Nebo's sons. He and his brothers—Jeiel, Mattithiah, Zebina, Jadau, Joel and Benaiah—were some of the Israelite men who took foreign wives but agreed to separate themselves from them because Ezra feared the Lord's wrath would destroy all of Israel for this iniquity.

ZABBAI (1). *Ezra 10:28 (18-19, 28, 44).*

Zabbai was one of Bebai's sons who took foreign wives, causing Ezra to cry unto the Lord for fear the Lord would destroy the remainder of Israel because of their iniquity. He and his brothers agreed to comply with Ezra's request that they put away their strange wives.

ZABBAI (2). *Neh. 3:20.*

Zabbai was the father of Baruch, which Baruch repaired the wall of Jerusalem "from the turning of the wall unto the door of the house of Eliashib the high priest."

ZABBUD. *Ezra 8:14.*

Zabbud and Uthai were of the sons of Bigvai. They were the chiefs of their fathers and went with Ezra back to Jerusalem from Babylon, taking 70 males with them.

ZABDI (1) (Zimri (3)). *Josh. 7:1; 1 Chr. 2:6.*

Zabdi, of the tribe of Judah, was the father of Carmi and a son of Zerah. They were of the tribe of Judah. *(Josh. 7:1.)*

Zimri (Zabdi) was one of the five sons of Zerah. He was a grandson of Judah and a great-grandson of Jacob. *(1 Chr. 2:6.)* (Charts 8d, g-h.)

ZABDI (2). *1 Chr. 8:19-21.*

Zabdi, a descendant of Benjamin, was a son of Shimhi, head of his fathers in his generation. (Chart 16h.)

ZABDI (3). *Neh. 11:17.* See **Zichri (5)**.

ZABDI (4). *1 Chr. 27:27.*

Zabdi the Shiphmite served David by being over the increase of the vineyards for the wine cellars.

ZABDIEL (1). *1 Chr. 27:2.*

Zabdiel was the father of Jashobeam, one of the officers who served king David.

ZABDIEL (2). *Neh. 11:14.*

Zabdiel, son of one of the great men, was the overseer of the priests in Jerusalem when the children of Israel returned from Babylonian captivity.

ZABUD. *1 Kgs. 4:5.*

Zabud was a son of Nathan and the brother of Azariah. He was the principal officer in Solomon's court and the king's friend.

ZACCAI. *Ezra 2:9; Neh. 7:14.*

Zaccai was of the people of Israel. The men of the children of Zaccai who returned to Jerusalem from Babylon after Cyrus' proclamation to build the temple numbered 760.

ZACCHUR. *1 Chr. 4:26.*

Zacchur was the son of Hamuel and a five-times-great-grandson of Jacob through Simeon. His son was Shimei. (Chart 6a.)

ZACCUR (1). *Num. 13:4 (2-4).*

Zaccur, of the tribe of Reuben, was the father of Shammua, which Shummua was one of the 12 spies Moses sent out to scout out the land of Canaan.

ZACCUR (2). *1 Chr. 25:2, 10.* See **Zichri (5)**.

ZACCUR (3). *1 Chr. 24:27, 31.*

Zaccur, a Levite, was a son of Merari through Jaaziah. He, with the rest of the chief fathers of the Levites, drew lots for his course in the presence of king David, Zadok, Ahimelech and other community leaders. (Chart 7e.)

ZACCUR (4). *Neh. 3:2.*

Zaccur, the son of Imri, labored next to the men from Jericho who built next to Eliashib the high priest when the children of Israel rebuilt the walls and gates of Jerusalem during the time of Ezra and Nehemiah.

ZACCUR (5). *Neh. 10:12 (1, 12, 28-31).*

Zaccur, a Levite, was among those who covenanted and sealed their covenant to marry in Israel, honor the Sabbath, pay tithes and keep the commandments.

ZACCUR (6). *Neh. 13:13.*

Zaccur, son of Mattaniah, was the father of Hanan, which Hanan was made one of the treasurers over the treasuries by Nehemiah.

ZACHARIAH (1). *2 Kgs. 14:29; 15:8-10.*

Zachariah, the son of Jeroboam, reigned over Israel after his father. *(2 Kgs. 14:29.)*

Zachariah began his reign over Israel in Samaria in the 38th year of Azariah's reign over Judah. He did evil in the sight of the Lord and ruled just six months when he was killed by Shallum, who usurped the crown. *(2 Kgs. 15:8-10.)*

ZACHARIAH (2) (Zechariah (1)). *2 Kgs. 18:2 (1-2); 2 Chr. 29:1.*

Zachariah was the father of Abi (mother of Hezekiah, king of Judah) and father-in-law of Ahaz. *(2 Kgs. 18:2 [1-2].)*

Zechariah (Zacheriah) was the father of Abijah (Abi) and grandfather of Hezekiah. *(2 Chr. 29:1.)*

ZACHER (Zechariah (3)). *1 Chr. 8:31-32 (29-32); 9:35-37.*

Zacher (Zechariah) was of the tribe of Benjamin. He was a son of the father of Gibeon (Jehiel). His mother was Maachah. His brothers were Abdon, Zur, Kish, Baal, (Ner), Nadab, Gedor, Ahio and Mikloth. *(1 Chr. 9:35-37.)* (Chart 16k.)

ZADOK (1). *2 Sam. 8:17; 15:24-36; 17:15-17; 18:19, 22, 27; 19:11; 20:25; 1 Kgs. 1: 8 (5, 8, 26, 32-45); 2:35; 4:2, 4; 1 Chr. 6:8 (4-15, 53); 15:11 (2, 11-12); 16:39 (37-40); 18:16; 24:3-4, 31; 27:17; 29:22; 2 Chr. 31:10; Ezra 7:1-5; Ezek. 40:46 (2-49); 43:19; 44:10-16; 48:11 (9-12, 22, 31).*

Zadok was the son of Ahitub and was one of the priests when David reigned over all Israel. *(2 Sam. 8:17.)*

Zadok and Abiathar, the priests, were with David when he and his household fled from Jerusalem to escape from Absalom. They carried the ark of God with them. David told them to return the ark to the city and to inform him as to the will of God: should he or should he not return from the wilderness. He instructed them to take their sons, Ahimaaz and Jonathan, with them. David instructed his friend, Hushai, to also go back to the city, volunteer to be a servant unto Absalom, and not only defeat the counsel Ahithophel would be giving Absalom, but feed information he gleaned to Zadok and Abiathar. Ahimaaz, Zadok's son, and Jonathan, Abiathar's son, were to carry information back to David. *(2 Sam. 15:24-36.)*

Zadok and Abiathar received a report back from Hushai which they passed on to Jonathan and Ahimaaz via a wench. *(2 Sam. 17:15-17.)*

Zadok's son Ahimaaz ran ahead of Cushi to give a message to David; however, he didn't know Absalom was dead so he couldn't convey the message. *(2 Sam. 18:19, 22, 27.)*

Zadok and Abiathar were queried by David as to why the elers of Judah were the last to bring the king back to his house following the death of Absalom. *(2 Sam. 19:11.)*

Zadok and Abiathar were the priests in Israel. *(2 Sam. 20:25.)*

When David's son Adonijah set himself up as king in David's stead, he gathered many of the leaders around him, but he deliberately did not include Zadok, Benaiah, Nathan the prophet, Shimei and Rei, who were faithful to David. When David was informed as to what Adonijah was doing, he named his son Solomon to be king and had Zadok the priest and Nathan the prophet anoint him such. *(1 Kgs. 1: 8 [5, 8, 26, 32-45].)*

Abiathar, who had supported Adonijah, was rejected as high priest and Solomon put Zadok in as high priest. *(1 Kgs. 2:35.)*

Zadok was the father of Azariah, one of Solomon's princes. Zadok and Abiathar (until he was rejected) were priests in Solomon's court. *(1 Kgs. 4:2, 4.)*

Zadok was the son of Ahitub, an eighth-great-grandson of Aaron and the father of Ahimaaz. His family line is given. *(1 Chr. 6:8, [4-15, 53].)*

After the Lord smote Uzza for touching the ark of God with his hand in an attempt to steady it, David realized that only the Levites should carry the ark. Thus, he assembled the chiefs of the sons of the Levites and hundreds of their brethren and instructed them and Zadok and Abiathar, the priests, to sanctify themselves so they could bring the ark of God "unto the place that I *[David]* have prepared for it." *(1 Chr. 15:11 [2, 11-12].)*

David left Zadok and the other priests before the tabernacle so they could make burnt offerings continually unto the Lord while the singers gave thanks to the Lord with their singing and instruments. *(1 Chr. 16:39 [37-40].)*

Zadok, the son of Ahitub, and Abimelech, the son of Abiathar, were the priests when David reigned over Israel. *(1 Chr. 18:16.)*

Zadok was of the sons of Eleazar, who was a son of Aaron. Ahimelech was of the sons of Ithamar, who was a son of Aaron. When David made the divisions of the sons of Aaron, he distributed them through Zadok of the sons of Eleazar and through Ahimelech of the sons of Ithamar. (Nadab and Abihu had been slain earlier by the Lord.) There were 16 chief men of the sons of Eleazar and eight chief men of the sons of Ithamar. They were divided by lot. The rest of the sons of Levi also cast lots over against their brethren in the presence of Zadok, Ahimelech and king David. *(1 Chr. 24:3-4, 31.)*

Zadok was prince of the tribe of Aaron at the time of David. *(1 Chr. 27:17.)*

The people anointed Zadok to be priest at the same time they anointed Solomon a second time to be king. *(1 Chr. 29:22.)*

The chief priest of the house of Zadok was Azariah. *(2 Chr. 31:10.)*

Zadok's ancestors and descendants from Aaron down through Ezra are listed. *(Ezra 7:1-5.) (Note: There are several differences from other listings. See 1 Chr. 6:4-15.)*

Ezekiel was shown in a vision the city where the temple would be, the form and size of the temple, and its courts. He saw the chamber that was for the priests who were the sons of Zadok, descendants of Levi, "which come near to the Lord to minister unto him." *(Ezek. 40:46 [2-49].)*

The priests who were of the seed of Zadok were to be given a young bullock for a sin offering according to instructions given to Ezekiel regarding the ordinances of the altar for the day when the people build it to offer burnt offerings. *(Ezek. 43:19.)*

The Levites who did not remain faithful when Israel went astray were not to be ministers in the Lord's sanctuary but were given the responsibility to be the "keepers of the charge of the house, for all the service thereof, and for all that shall be done therein. But the priests the Levites, the sons of Zadok, that kept the charge of my sanctuary when the children of Israel went astray from me, they shall come near to me to minister unto me, and they shall stand before me to offer unto me the fat and the blood, saith the Lord God: They shall enter into my sanctuary, and they shall come near to my table, to minister unto me, and they shall keep my charge." *(Ezek. 44:10-16.)*

The oblation of land that shall be for the priests is for those priests of the sons of Zadok who kept the Lord's charge and did not go astray like the children of Israel and the Levites went astray. The Lord revealed to Ezekiel just how the land should be divided by tribes when the children of Israel are gathered in the latter days. The priests of Levi (through Zadok) are to have the portion between Judah and Benjamin. The 12 gates of the city are to bear the names of the 12 sons of Jacob. Levi's gate will be one of the three northward gates. *(Ezek. 48:11 [9-12, 22, 31].)* (Chart 7b.)

ZADOK (2). *2 Kgs. 15:33; 2 Chr. 27:1.*

Zadok was the father of Jerusha (Jerushah); father-in-law of Uzziah; and the grandfather of Jotham, king of Judah. (Chart 1)

ZADOK (3). *1 Chr. 6:12-13; 9:11; Ezra 7:1-5; Neh. 11:11.*

Zadok, the son of Ahitub, was a many-times-great-grandson of Aaron and the father of Shallum. *(1 Chr. 6:12-13.)*

Zadok was the son of Meraioth, the grandson of Ahitub, and the father of Meshullam (Shallum). He is listed among the priests who lived in Jerusalem whose genealogy was recorded in the book of the kings of Israel and Judah who were carried away to Babylon because of transgression. *(1 Chr. 9:11.)*

Zadok's descendants and forefathers from Aaron through Ezra are listed. *(Ezra 7:1-5.) (Note: there is some variation between this listing and the one in 1 Chr. 6:4-15.)*

Zadok was the father of Meshullam and the son of Meraioth. *(Neh. 11:11.) (Note: Zadok (1) and Zadod (3) may be one and the same, depending on which ancestral listing is correct.)* (Chart 7b.)

ZADOK (4). *1 Chr. 12:27-28.*

Zadok, a young man of valor, took 22 captains from his father's house with him and went to Ziklag in support of David when he became king. All Israel rejoiced over David and sent their troops to support him. They were armed and ready for war in order to turn the kingdom of Saul over to David. *(Note: The Bible Dictionary indicates Zadok (4) may be the same as Zadok (1).)*

ZADOK (5). *Neh. 3:4.*

Zadok was the son of Baana. He worked on the walls of Jerusalem next to Meshullam when the children of Israel rebuilt the walls and gates during the time of Ezra and Nehemiah.

ZADOK (6). *Neh. 3:29.*

Zadok, son of Immer, repaired the area over against his house, next to the priests, when the children of Israel rebuilt the walls and gates of Jerusalem during the time of Ezra and Nehemiah.

ZADOK (7). *Neh. 10:21 (1, 21, 28-29).*

Zadok was among those chief of the people who covenanted to marry in Israel, honor the Sabbath, pay tithes and keep the commandments.

ZADOK (8). *Neh. 13:13.*

Zadok the scribe, along with Shelemiah the priest and others, was made treasurer over the treasuries by Nehemiah and was counted as faithful. He was assigned to help distribute to the Levites and singers the shares they were to have.

ZAHAM. *2 Chr. 11:19 (18-19).*

Zaham was the son of Abihail, daughter of David's brother Eliab, and king Rehoboam, David's grandson. His brothers were Jeush and Shamariah. (Charts 8d, f.)

ZALAPH. *Neh. 3:30.*

Zalaph was the father of Hanun (his sixth son), which Hanun helped repair the wall of Jerusalem.

ZALMON (Ilai). *2 Sam. 23:28; 1 Chr. 11:29.*

Zalmon (Ilai) the Ahohite was one of David's mighty men *(2 Sam. 23:28)* and one of the valiant men of the armies *(1 Chr. 11:29).* (Chart 17.)

ZALMUNNA. *Judg. 8:5-21.*

Zalmunna was one of the kings of Midian that Gideon pursued. He and Zebah, another king of Midian, lost 120,000 men by the sword and were in Karkos with about 15,000 men—all that were left of their host. Gideon took the two kings of Midian and "discomfited" all the host. Because Zalmunna and Zebah had slain Gideon's brethren, Gideon slew them "and took away the ornaments that were on their camels' necks."

ZAMZUMMIMS. *Deut. 2:20.*

Zamzummims were considered to be giants. They lived in the land the Lord gave unto the children of Ammon before the Anakims, who were also regarded as giants. The Anakims were succeeded in the land by the Ammonites.

ZANOAH. *1 Chr. 4:18.*

Zanoah was the son of Jekuthiel. His grandmother was Jehudijah. (Chart 80.)

ZAPHNATH-PAANEAH. See **Joseph (1)**.

ZARAH (Zerah (3), Mahol, Zarhites (2)). *Gen. 38:30 (24-30);46:12; Num. 26:20; 1 Kgs. 4:31; 1 Chr. 2:4, 6; Neh. 11:24.*

Zarah was the secondborn twin of Tamar begotten by her father-in-law Judah. At the time of delivery, one twin protruded a hand. The midwife tied a scarlet thread around his hand, saying, "This came out first." However, Pharez was actually born first and Zarah was born second. *(Gen. 38:30 [24-30].)*

Zerah (Zarah) was one of Judah's sons. His brothers were Er, Onan, Shelah and Pharez. *(Gen. 46:12.)*

Zerah was the father of the **Zarhites**. *(Num. 26:20.) (Note: Simeon also had a son named Zerah and his descendants were also called Zarhites.)*

Mahol's (Zerah's) sons were Ethan the Ezrahite, Heman, Chalcol and Darda. They were recognized as wise men, but Solomon was wiser than all of them. *(1 Kgs. 4:31.)*

Zerah and Pharez were the twin sons of Tamar and Judah. Zerah had five sons: Zimri, Ethan, Heman, Calcol (Chalcol) and Dara (Darda). *(1 Chr. 2:4, 6.)*

Zerah's descendant Pethahiah, son of Meshezabeel, was at the king's hand in all matters concerning the people after the children of Israel returned from Babylonian captivity to Jerusalem and other cities. *(Neh. 11:24.)* (Charts 8a, c-d, g-h.)

ZAREATHITES. See **Shobal (2)**.

ZARHITES (1). *Num. 26:13.* See **Zohar (2)**.

ZARHITES (2). *Num. 26:20.* See **Zarah**.

ZATTHU. *Neh. 10:14 (1, 14, 28-31).*

Zatthu was among those chief of the people who covenanted to marry in Israel, honor the Sabbath, pay tithes and keep the commandments.

ZATTU. *Ezra 2:8 (1, 8);10:27 (18-19, 27, 44); Neh. 7:13.*

Zattu was of the people of Israel. The children of Zattu who returned to Jerusalem from Babylon after Cyrus' proclamation to build the temple numbered 945 (845). *(Ezra 2:8 [1, 8]; Neh. 7:13.)*

Zattu's descendants—Elioenai, Eliashib, Mattaniah, Jeremoth, Zabad and Aziza—were some of the people of Israel who took wives from among the Canaanites and other foreign groups. They complied with Ezra's request that they separate themselves from these foreign wives lest the Lord destroy the rest of the children of Israel because of this iniquity. *(Ezra 10:27 [18-19, 27, 44].)*

ZAVAN. See **Zaavan**.

ZAZA. *1 Chr. 2:33.*

Zaza was a son of Jonathan. His brother was Peleth. He was a five-times-great-grandson of Judah. (Chart 8c.)

ZEBADIAH (1). *1 Chr. 8:15.*

Zebadiah, a descendant of Benjamin, was a son of Beriah, who was a son of Elpaal, who was a son of Shaharaim and Hushim. He and others listed were chief men, heads of the fathers by their generations and dwelled in Jerusalem. (Chart 16g.)

ZEBADIAH (2). *1 Chr. 8:17.*

Zebadiah, of the tribe of Benjamin, was one of the sons of Elpaal. He and others listed were chief men, heads of the fathers by their generations and dwelled in Jerusalem. (Chart 16i.)

ZEBADIAH (3). *1 Chr. 12:7 (1-2, 7, 23, 38).*

Zebadiah, a son of Jeroham of Gedor, was one of David's mighty men who came to him at Ziklag to defend him against Saul and turn the kingdom over to David. His brother was Joelah.

ZEBADIAH (4). *1 Chr. 26:2 (Subtitle, 2).*

Zebadiah, a Levite, was the thirdborn son of Meshelemiah, son of Kore of the sons of Asaph. His brothers were Zechariah, Jediael, Jathniel, Elam, Jehohanan, and Elioenai. They, along with others, were assigned by king David to be porters—to have charge of the treasures, serve as officers and judges, and conduct the outward business over Israel. (Chart 7d.)

ZEBADIAH (5). *1 Chr. 27:7.*

Zebadiah was the son of Asahel, son of Zeruiah, David's sister. He was the fourth captain for the fourth month after his father. There were 24,000 in his course. (Chart 8d.)

ZEBADIAH (6). *2 Chr. 17:8-9.*

Zebadiah, a Levite, along with other Levites and Elishama and Jehoram, the priests, was sent by king Jehoshaphat to journey with the princes of Judah throughout the cities of Judah to instruct the people out of the book of the law of the Lord.

ZEBADIAH (7). *2 Chr. 19:11.*

Zebadiah, the son of Ishmael, was "ruler of the house of Judah, for all the king's matters," when Jehoshaphat was king of Judah.

ZEBADIAH (8). *Ezra 8:8 (1, 8).*

Zebadiah, son of Michael who was of the sons of Shephatiah, was the chief of his fathers and went with Ezra up from Babylon to Jerusalem, taking 80 males with him.

ZEBADIAH (9). *Ezra 10:20 (18-20, 44).*

Zebadiah, of the sons of Immer, was among those sons of the priests who had taken foreign wives and who agreed to put them away as instructed by Ezra.

ZEBAH. *Judg. 8:5-21.*

Zebah was one of the kings of Midian that Gideon pursued. He and Zalmunna, another king of Midian, lost 120,000 men by the sword and were in Karkos with about 15,000 men—all that were left of their host. Gideon took the two kings of

Midian and "discomfited" all the host. Because Zeba and Zalmunna had slain Gideon's brethren, Gideon slew them "and took away the ornaments that were on their camels' necks."

ZEBINA. *Ezra 10:43-44.*

Zebina was one of Nebo's sons. He and his brothers—Jeiel, Mattithiah, Zabad, Jadau, Joel and Benaiah—were some of the Israelite men who took foreign wives but agreed to separate themselves from them because Ezra feared the Lord's wrath would destroy all of Israel for this iniquity.

ZEBUDAH. *2 Kgs. 23:36.*

Zebudah was the mother of Jehoiakim (Eliakim, king in Jerusalem), the daughter of Pedaiah, and one of the wives of Josiah. (Chart 1.)

ZEBUL. *Judg. 9:28-41.*

Zebul was uler of Shechem and one of Abimelech's officers. He sent messengers to Abimelech informing him of Gaal's gathering against him. When Gaal and his brethren were defeated by Abimelech, Zebul banned them from living in Shechem.

ZEBULUN (Zebulunites). *Gen. 30:20; 37; 46:14; 49:1, 13; 50:8, 13; Num. 1:9, 30-31; 2:7 (3-9); 26:26-27; 34:25; Deut. 27:13; 33:18; Josh. 19:10-16; 21:7, 34; Judg. 1:30; 4:6, 10; 5:14, 18 (1, 14, 18); 6:35; 1 Chr. 12:33, 38; 27:19; 2 Chr. 30:10-11, 18; Ezek. 48:26, 33.*

Zebulun was the 6th son of Leah and Jacob. (He was Jacob's 10th son.) *(Gen. 30:20.)*

Zebulun and his brothers hated their younger brother Joseph and sold him to a group of Ishmeelites, or Midianite merchantmen, for 20 pieces of silver. They dipped his coat of many colors in animal blood and gave it to their father so he would think Joseph had been killed by wild beasts. *(Gen. 37.)*

Zebulun begat Sered, Elon and Jahleel. *(Gen. 46:14.)*

After the brothers had gone to Egypt for grain and were finally reunited with Joseph, and following the move of Jacob's entire family to Egypt, the time came when Jacob called his sons together to tell them what would befall each of them in the last days. He said, "Zebulun shall dwell at the haven of the sea; and he shall be for an haven of ships; and his border shall be unto Zidon." *(Gen. 49:1, 13.)*

Following his father's death, Zebulun and his brothers carried his body to Canaan for burial. *(Gen. 50:8, 13.)*

Moses was instructed to have Eliab, son of Helon, lead the tribe of Zebulun as Israel prepared for war. The males in the tribe of Zebulun who were 20 years old or older who could go to war numbered 57,400. *(Num. 1:9, 30-31.)*

Eliab was instructed to have the tribe of Zebulun pitch their tents next to the tribe of Issachar as part of the camp of Judah on the east side of the encampment. *(Num. 2:7 [3-9].)*

Zebulun's family, the **Zebulunites**, included the Sardites, Elonites and the Jahleelites. The males who were twenty years old and older as numbered by Moses and Eleazar on the plains of Moab were 60,500. *(Num. 26:26-27.)*

Elizaphan, son of Parnach, was assigned to divide Zebulun's land of inheritance between Zebulun's posterity. *(Num. 34:25.)*

As the children of Israel crossed over Jordan into Canaan to inherit the promised land, the tribes of Reuben, Gad, Asher, Zebulun, Dan and Naphtali were instructed to stand upon mount Ebal to curse. *(Deut. 27:13.)*

Moses blessed the tribe of Zebulun. *(Deut. 33:18.)*

When Joshua cast lots to divide the promised land, Zebulun's tribe came up third. The boundaries of Zebulun's inheritance are given. *(Josh. 19:10-16.)*

From the tribes of Zebulun, Gad and Reuben, the children of Merari were given 12 cities for their inheritance. *(Josh. 21:7, 34.)*

Zebulun did not drive the inhabitants out of Kitron nor Nahalol, but the Canaanites lived among them and became tributaries. *(Judg. 1:30.)*

Ten thousand men of the children of Zebulun and Naphtali were supposed to be enlisted by Barak to help deliver Israel from the Canaanites. Barak enlisted the men after Deborah agreed to accompany him. *(Judg. 4:6, 10.)*

Zebulun's posterity, the scribes, were praised in song, along with others, by Deborah and Barak for freeing Israel from Canaanite bondage. Zebulun and Naphtali had jeopardized their lives "unto the death in the high places of the field." *(Judg. 5:14, 18 [1, 14, 18].)*

Messengers were sent unto Zebulun and throughout the land by Gideon calling them to come up to meet him that he might form an army. *(Judg. 6:35.)*

When David became king and went to Ziklag, all Israel rejoiced and sent their armies to support him. The tribe of Zebulun sent 50,000 men who were expert in war, along with all their equipment. *(1 Chr. 12:33, 38.)*

The prince of the tribe of Zebulun when David was king was Ishmaiah, the son of Obadiah. *(1 Chr. 27:19.)*

Hezekiah, king of Judah, sent couriers throughout all of Israel to invite them to come to Jerusalem to participate in a solemn Passover. Many throughout the country of Ephraim and Manasseh even unto Zebulun laughed and mocked the couriers to scorn. Nevertheless, some of those from Asher, Manasseh and Zebulun humbled themselves and went to Jerusalem and ate the Passover, even though they had not cleansed themselves appropriately. Nevertheless, Hezekiah prayed that the Lord would pardon all whose heart sought the Lord. *(2 Chr. 30:10-11, 18.)*

The Lord revealed to Ezekiel just how the land should be divided by tribes when the children of Israel are gathered in the latter days. Zebulun's portion will be by the border of Issachar, from the east side unto the west side. The 12 gates of the city are to bear the names of the 12 sons of Jacob. One of the three south gates will be named for Zebulun. *(Ezek. 48:26, 33.)* (Charts 1.; 3d.; 5a.; 6a.; 7a.; 8a.; 9a.; 10a-b.; 11a.; 12a.; 13a.; 14a.; 15a.; 16a.)

ZECHARIAH (1). *2 Chr. 29:1.* See **Zachariah (2)**.

ZECHARIAH (2). *1 Chr. 5:7.*

Zechariah was one of the chiefs among the Reubenites. His direct lineage to Reuben is not clear. (Chart 5b.)

ZECHARIAH (3). *1 Chr. 9:35-38.* See **Zacher**.

ZECHARIAH (4). *1 Chr. 9:21 (2-3, 21); 26:2, 14.*

Zechariah was a son of Meshelemiah and was porter of the door of the tabernacle of the congregation. He and others named and their children had the oversight of the gates of the house of the Lord by wards. He was among those who were the first inhabitants to dwell in Jerusalem after returning from Babylonian captivity *(1 Chr. 9:23-21).*

Zechariah was the firstborn son of Meshelemiah (Shelemiah). His brothers were Jediael, Zebadiah, Jathniel, Elam, Jehohanan, and Elioenai. They were assigned by king David to be porters to have charge of the treasures, serve as officers and judges and conduct the outward business over Israel—along with other Levites so assigned. He drew the lot northward. He was a "wise counsellor." *(1 Chr. 26:2, 14.)* (Chart 7d.)

ZECHARIAH (5). *1 Chr. 15:18-20; 16:5.*

Zechariah and his brethren of the second degree were assigned, under the direction of David, to be singers along with Heman, Asaph and Ethan. Zechariah and his brethren were assigned to play with psalteries on Alamoth. *(1 Chr. 15:18-20.)* He was appointed by David to minister before the ark of the Lord and was assigned to play the psalteries and harps. *(1 Chr. 16:5.)*

ZECHARIAH (6). *1 Chr. 15:24, 31.*

Zechariah was among those who, under the direction of David, was assigned to make music before the Lord as the ark was removed from the house of Obed-edom and taken to the place which David had prepared for it to be housed. As one of the priests, he was assigned to blow the trumpet before the ark of God.

ZECHARIAH (7). *1 Chr. 24:25.*

Zechariah, a Levite, was a descendant of Uzziel through Isshiah (Jesiah) who was a brother of Michah. He, with the rest of the chief fathers of the Levites, drew lots for his course in the presence of king David, Zadok, Ahimelech and other community leaders. (Chart 7d.)

ZECHARIAH (8). *1 Chr. 26:11 (Subtitle, 10-11, 26).*

Zechariah, a Levite, was the fourth son of Hosah who was of the lineage of Merari. His brothers included: Simri, who was made chief by his father even though he was not the firstborn; Hilkiah, the second; Tebaliah, the third. They, along with other Levites, were appointed by king David to be porters—to have charge of the treasures, serve as officers and judges, and to conduct the outward business over Israel. *(Note: He apparently had more brothers as it states that "all the sons and brethren of Hosah were thirteen." However, only four are named by name and Simri was not the firstborn.)* (Chart 7a.)

ZECHARIAH (9). *1 Chr. 27:21 (1, 16, 21).*

Zechariah was the father of Iddo who was prince of the half tribe of Manasseh that was in Gilead when David was king. (Chart 15c.)

ZECHARIAH (10). *2 Chr. 17:7-9.*

Zechariah was one of the princes of Judah who king Jehoshaphat instructed to "teach in the cities of Judah." He sent a number of Levites and Elishama and Jehoram, the priests, with the princes to teach Judah from the book of the law of the Lord.

ZECHARIAH (11) (Uzzi (5). *2 Chr. 20:14; 29:13; Neh. 11:22; 12:35, 41.*

Zechariah, a descendant of Levi through Gershom, was the father of Jahaziel and the son of Benaiah, the son of Jeiel, the son of Mattaniah, a Levite of the sons of Asaph. *(2 Chr. 20:14.)*

He was among those whom Hezekiah, king of Judah, instructed to sanctify themselves so they could cleanse and sanctify the house of the Lord. *(2 Chr. 29:13.)*

Uzzi (Zechriah)—the son of Bani (Benaiah), the son of Hashabiah (Jeiel) who was the son of Mattaniah, the son of Micha of the sons of Asaph—was the overseer of the Levites at Jerusalem when the children of Israel returned from Babylonian captivity. *(Neh. 11:22.)*

Zechariah, the son of Jonathan (Benaiah, Bani)—a musician and trumpeter—was one of the sons of the priests who was instructed by Nehemiah to purify himself and was then assigned to one of two great companies for the dedication of the walls of Jerusalem. *(Neh. 12:35, 41.)* (Chart 7a.)

ZECHARIAH (12). *2 Chr. 21:2-4.*

Zechariah was one of Jehoshaphat's sons. His brothers were Jehoram, the firstborn; Azariah, Jehiel, Azariah, Michael and Shephatiah. After Jehoram became king upon his father's death, he slew all his brethren plus many of the princes of Israel. (Chart 1.)

ZECHARIAH (13). *2 Chr. 24:20-22.*

Zechariah the prophet was the son of Jehoiada the priest. After Jehoiada died and Joash, king of Judah, began worshipping idols, Zechariah was stoned to death by order of Joash.

ZECHARIAH (14). *2 Chr. 26:5, 16-21.*

Zechariah had "understanding in the visions of God." During the days of Zechariah, Uzziah (Azariah), king of Judah, sought God. After the death of Zechariah, however, the king became lifted up in his own eyes and the Lord cursed him with leprosy.

ZECHARIAH (15). *2 Chr. 34:12.*

Zechariah, a Levite of the sons of the Kohathites, and others were assigned by Josiah, king of Judah, to oversee the workmen who repaired the house of the Lord.

ZECHARIAH (16). *Ezra 5:1-3, 13; 6:14 (1-3, 14); Neh. 12:16 (12, 16); Zech. 1-14.*

<u>Zechariah</u>, the son of Iddo and a contemporary of Haggai, was a prophet in Israel (520-518 B.C.) during the time the children of Israel were trying to rebuild the temple. With the help of Zechariah and Haggai, Zerubbabel and Jeshua again began the work. When confronted by Tatnai, the governor on the west side of the Euphrates River, and his group, and queried as to who commanded that the temple be built, they indicated that Cyrus had made such a decree. *(Ezra 5:1-3, 13.)*

Darius discovered that Cyrus had, indeed, made a decree and he renewed the decree. "And the elders of the Jews builded, and they prospered through the prophesying of Haggai the prophet and Zechariah the son of Iddo." They finished the temple in the sixth year of king Darius. *(Ezra 6:14 [1-3, 14].)*

Zechariah was one of the priests who was a chief of the fathers in the days of Juiakim. *(Neh. 12:16 [12, 16].)*

In the second year of king Darius' reign, Zechariah, son of Berechiah who was the son of Iddo, called upon Judah to repent. He was shown two visions. An angel explained them to him.

<u>Vision One</u>. He saw a man riding upon a red horse. He stood among the myrtle trees. Behind him were three red horses, speckled and white. *(Zech. 1:8.)* <u>Interpretation of Vision One</u>. These are they whom the Lord hath sent to walk to and fro throughout the earth. They answered and said they had walked the earth, but now all the earth "sitteth still" and is at rest. *(Zech. 1:10-11.)* The Lord's indignation had been upon the people 70 years. The heathen had helped the Lord afflict Judah, but the Lord was displeased at their feeling at ease. The cities of Judah and the temple would be rebuilt.

<u>Vision Two</u>. He saw four horns. He saw four carpenters. *(Zech. 1:18, 20.)* <u>Interpretation of Vision Two</u> The four horns are the horns that scattered Judah, Israel and Jerusalem. The four carpenters "are come to fray them, to cast out the horns of the Gentiles" which scattered Judah. *(Zech. 1:19, 21.)*

Zechariah had a <u>third vision</u> wherein he saw an angel with a measuring line in his hand to measure Jerusalem. Another angel joined him. In the latter days, Jerusalem shall be inhabited without walls, so numerous will be the people. They will be gathered from the land of the north. The Lord will dwell in the midst of them. *(Zech. 2.)*

Zechariah prophesied of the Messiah, i.e., the BRANCH. At the Second Coming, the iniquity of the land will be removed in one day. He had a <u>fourth vision</u>. In this vision, Zechariah saw Joshua the high priest standing before the angel of the Lord. Satan was at his right hand to accuse him. Satan was rebuked. *(Zech. 3.)*

In Zechariah's <u>fifth vision</u>, he beheld a golden candlestick with a bowl on top with seven lamps and seven pipes to the seven lamps. He also saw two olive trees by it, one on the left side and one of the right. The seven lamps and the seven pipes to the lamps represent the servants of the Lord which run to and fro throughout the whole earth. The two olive trees represent two anointed ones who stand before the

Lord. *(Zech. 4.) (Note: The Bible Dictionary explains that the oil is the symbol of the spirit, through whom, [not by might or power], all Israel's work and destiny shall be accomplished. This spirit is dispensed through the two anointed ones representing the priestly and royal rule: Joshua and Zerubbabel.)*

Using symbolical representations, an angel revealed truths to Zechariah. He condemned stealing and lying. Symbols: (a) Zechariah beheld a flying roll. *(Zech. 5:1.)* (b) Zechariah was shown an ephah going forth. *(Zech. 5:6.)* (c) There was a talent of lead. (d) Zechariah saw two women with wind in their wings—wings like a stork—and they lifted up the ephah between heaven and earth. *(Zech. 5:9.)* Meaning: (a) The angel said the flying roll represented the curse that "goeth forth over the face of the whole earth." He said that everyone who "stealeth" and "sweareth" shall be cut off. *(Zech. 5:3.)* (b) The ephah "is their [i.e. the sins of the world] resemblance throughout all the earth." *(Zech. 5:6.)* (c) Of the talent of lead, he said, "This is a woman that sitteth in the midst of the ephah . . . This is wickedness." *(Zech. 5:7-8.)* (d) The sins of the world shall be established on their own base in the land of Shinar. *(Zech. 5:11.)*

Zechariah had another vision.

Vision. Four chariots came from between two brass mountains. Red horses were in the first chariot. Black horses were in the second chariot. White horses were in the third chariot. Grisled and bay horses were in the fourth. *(Zech. 6:1-3.)*

Interpretation. The four chariots represent four ministering angels of the Lord. The black horses go into the north country. The white horses follow after the black. The grisled go forth toward the south country; and the bay went forth to and fro throughout the whole earth. *(Zech. 6:5-7.)*

Zechariah was instructed by the Lord to take those of the captivity of Heldai, Tobijah and Jedaiah who came from Babylon and go into the house of Josiah the son of Zephaniah and crown Joshua (Jeshua) the high priest. *(Zech. 6:10-12.) (Note: This was a similitude of crowning Christ, i.e., the BRANCH. The Bible Dictionary states that the name Joshua occurs in the O.T. under various forms: Jehoshua, Hoshea, Jeshua, Jesus.)*

Zechariah was sent to reprove the people for their hypocrisy in the fourth year of king Darius' reign. He told the people to execute judgment; to show mercy and have compassion one to another; not to oppress the widow, the fatherless, the stranger nor the poor. The people refused to heed his counsel. *(Zech. 7.)*

He prophesied that in the latter days the Lord will gather His people; Jerusalem shall be restored; He will be their God; people will live to an old age; and greater blessings will be poured out upon the people than in the past. *(Zech. 8.)*

Speaking Messianically, Zechariah said, ". . . behold, thy King cometh unto thee: he is just, and having salvation; lowly, and riding upon an ass, and upon a colt the foal of an ass." *(Zech. 9:9.) (Note: We read of the fulfillment of this prophecy in Mark 11:7 and Luke 19:35 in the New Testament. "And they brought the colt to Jesus, and cast their garments on him; and he sat upon him." "And they brought him to Jesus: and they cast their garments upon the colt, and they set Jesus thereon.")*

Zechariah prophesied that the Lord would sow Judah and Joseph among the people in far countries. The Lord will "hiss" for them, and gather them because He has redeemed them. He will bring them again out of Egypt, and gather them out of Assyria, and place them in the lands of Gilead and Lebanon. *(Zech. 10:8-10.)*

Zechariah spoke Messianically, indicating the Lord *(Jesus Christ)* would be betrayed for thirty pieces of silver. The silver would be cast unto the potter in the house of the Lord. *(Zech. 11.) (Note: The fulfillment of this prophesy is recorded in Matt. 27:3-10. "Then Judah, which had betrayed him, when he saw that he was condemned, repented himself, and brought again the thirty pieces of silver to the chief priests and elders . . . And they (the chief priests) took counsel, and bought with them the potter's field, to bury strangers in."*

Zechariah acknowledged the Lord created man, the heavens and the earth. When the Lord comes again, He will destroy all the nations that come against Jerusalem and Judah. The Jews shall look upon the Savior, "whom they have pierced" *(Zech. 12:10)*, and mourn for Him. Every family shall mourn apart: the family of David and their wives; the house of Nathan and their wives; the house of Levi and their wives, etc. *(Zech. 12.)*

When the Savior comes again, the Jews shall be forgiven. They will ask Him about the wounds in His hands. He will respond that they are the wounds He received in the house of His friends. *(Zech. 13:6.)* The remnant of the house of Israel will be tried and refined and shall be the Lord's people. *(Zech. 13.)*

Zechariah prophesied that at the Second Coming all nations shall be gathered in battle against Jerusalem. As Jerusalem is losing the war, the Lord will go forth and fight for Israel. His feet will stand upon the Mount of Olives. Living waters shall flow from Jerusalem. The Lord will be king over the whole earth. Plagues shall come upon all the wicked. *(Zech. 14.)*

ZECHARIAH (17). *Ezra 8:3 (1-3)*.

Zechariah, of the sons of Pharosh, of the sons of Shechaniah, was the chief of his fathers and went with Ezra up from Babylon to Jerusalem. He took 150 males with him.

ZECHARIAH (18). *Ezra 8:11 (1, 11)*.

Zacheriah, son of Bebai, was chief of his fathers and went with Ezra up from Babylon to Jerusalem. He took 28 males with him.

ZECHARIAH (19). *Ezra 8:16 (15-17); Neh. 8:1-8; Isa. 8:2*.

Zechariah was one of the chief men Ezra sent for when he gathered the people together as he was preparing to lead them to Jerusalem from Babylon and discovered there were no Levites among the group. He sent this group to Iddo and the Nethinims to request that they send them some ministers for the house of God. *(Ezra 8:15-17.)*

He was one of the men who stood on Ezra's left hand when Ezra read and interpreted the law of Moses to the people. *(Neh. 8:1-8.)*

When the Lord told Isaiah to record information concerning his son Maher-shalal-hash-baz, he took "faithful witnesses to record, Uriah the priest, and Zechariah the son of Jeberechiah." *(Isa. 8:2.) (Note: It is not clear if the Zechariah referred to in Isa. 8:2 is the same as the one referred to in Ezra 8:16, but it is likely since both Uriah the priest and this Zechariah are referred to together here and each was referred to originally in Ezra 8.)*

ZECHARIAH (20). *Ezra 10:26 (18-19, 26, 44).*

Zechariah was one of the sons of Elam who took wives from among the Canaanites and other groups. He and his brothers agreed to do as Ezra said and separate themselves from their foreign wives.

ZECHARIAH (21). *Neh. 11:4.*

Zechariah, the son of Amariah and the father of Uzziah of the children of Judah, dwelled in Jerusalem after leaving Babylon. (Chart 8b.)

ZECHARIAH (22). *Neh. 11:5.*

Zechariah, son of Shiloni and father of Joiabrib of the children of Perez, dwelled in Jerusalem after leaving Babylon. (Chart 8b.)

ZECHARIAH (23). *Neh. 11:12.*

Zechariah was the son of Pashur; the father of Amzi; the grandfather of Pelaliah; and a great-great-grandfather of Adaiah, which Adaiah was chosen by lot to dwell in Jerusalem after returning from Babylonian captivity. He and his brethren did the work of the house of the Lord. *(Note: Zechariah, Amzi and Pelaliah are not included in the listing of Adaiah's ancestors in 1 Chr. 9:12.)* (Chart 7g.)

ZEDEKIAH (1). *1 Kgs. 22:11, 24-25; 2 Chr. 18:10, 23-24.*

Zedekiah was the son of Chenaanah and was one of Ahab's men. He made himself some horns of iron and said that the Lord had said that with these they would push the Syrians until they had consumed them. When the prophet Micaiah foretold evil concerning Ahab, Zedekiah went forth and smote Micaiah on the cheek. He demanded, "Which way went the Spirit of the Lord from me to speak to thee?" Micaiah said, "Behold, thou shalt see in that day, when thou shalt go into an inner chamber to hide thyself."

ZEDEKIAH (2) (Mattaniah (1)). *2 Kgs. 24:17-20; 25:2-7; 1 Chr. 3:15; 2 Chr. 36:10-13, 14-20; Jer. 1:3; 21:1-7; 24:8-9; 27:1-3, 12; 28; 29:3, 21; 32:1-5, 28-29; 34:2-6, 21; 37-38; 39:1-8; 44:30; 49:34-35; 51:59; 52:1-11.*

Zedekiah (Mattaniah) was a son of Josiah and Hamutal. His brother was Jehoahaz. His balf-brothers were Johanan and Jehoiakim (Eliakim). He was the half-uncle of Jehoiachin, king of Judah. Nebuchadnezzar made Mattaniah king in place of Jehoiachin and changed his name to **Zedekiah**. He was 21 years old when he began to reign over Judah and reigned 11 years in Jerusalem. He did evil in the sight of the Lord. Zedekiah rebelled against the king of Babylon. *(2 Kgs. 24:17-20; Jer. 52:1-11.)*

Zedekiah and Jerusalem were beseiged by Nebuchadnezzar from the ninth year of his reign until early in the eleventh year of his reign. Famine prevailed and his men of war deserted. Zedekiah was captured, his sons slain before his eyes, and then his eyes were put out and he was carried bound and captive to Babylon. *(2 Kgs. 25:2-7.)*

Zedekiah was the third son of Josiah. His brothers were Johanan, Jehoiakim (Eliakim) and Shallum (Jehoahaz). *(1 Chr. 3:15.)*

He refused to humble himself before the prophet Jeremiah. He also rebelled against king Nebuchadnezzar. *(This is a repeat of 2 Kgs. 24:17-20 with modification.)* The Lord sent messengers to the people but they just mocked the messengers. Therefore, the Lord allowed the king of the Chaldees to defeat Judah. The Chaldees burned the temple and destroyed Jerusalem. Those who escaped the sword were carried away to Babylon where they remained as servants until the reign of the kingdom of Persia. *(2 Chr. 36:10-13, 14-20.)*

When Zedekiah was in his eleventh year of reign over Judah, Jerusalem was carried away captive into Babylon. *(Jer. 1:3.) (Note: The prophet Jeremiah had declared the word of God for over a period of 40 years (626-586 B.C.) warning the people to return to God, but they failed to heed the Lord.)*

Zedekiah requested word from Jeremiah as to whether or not the Lord would help them in their battle against Nebuchadnezzar. Jeremiah reported back, however, that the Lord would help defeat Zedekiah because of his wickedness, and he would be taken captive by Nebuchadnezzar. *(Jer. 21:1-7.)*

The Lord compared Zedekiah to evil figs that cannot be eaten but need to be removed. He said He would deliver Zedekiah, his princes and the residue of Jerusalem to be dispersed into all the kingdoms of the earth. They would be a reproach and a proverb, a taunt and a curse everywhere they were driven. *(Jer. 24:8-9.)*

In the beginning of Jehoiakim's reign, Jeremiah was instructed by the Lord to send word to many nations that they were to serve Babylon. He was to send word "by the hand of the messengers which come to Jerusalem unto Zedekiah king of Judah." *(Jer. 27:3.)* Jeremiah counseled Zedekiah to follow not after false prophets. Zedekiah should allow himself and his people to come under the yoke of the king of Babylon and live. *(Jer. 27:1-3, 12.)*

During the fifth month of the fourth year of Zedekiah's reign over Judah, Hananiah the son of Azur the prophet prophesied falsely that the yoke of Babylon would be broken within two years. Jeremiah, as instructed by the Lord, told Hananiah that he had spoken a lie and would be cast from off the earth for teaching rebellion against the Lord. Hananiah died "in the seventh month" of that same year. *(Jer. 28.)*

Zedekiah sent Hilkiah unto Babylon to Nebuchadnezzar. *(Note: Verse 21 indicates that Zedekiah was the son of Maaseiah. This would appear to be an error since other verses indicate that Josiah was the father of Zedekiah. Verse 25 indicates that Zephaniah was the son of Maaseiah.)* Because Zedekiah prophesied falsely in the name of the Lord, the Lord cursed him and said He would deliver him, along with Ahab, son of Kolaiah, into the hand of Nebuchadrezzar (Nebuchadnezzar) who would slay them both. *(Jer. 29:3, 21.)*

The 10th year of Zedekiah's reign over Judah was the 18th year of Nebuchadrezzar's reign over Babylon. It was at this time that Zedekiah imprisoned the prophet Jeremiah for prophesying that Nebuchadrezzar would take Zedekiah prisoner and the Chaldeans would burn Jerusalem. *(Jer. 32:1-5, 28-29.)*

Jeremiah prophesied that Zedekiah would be delivered into the hands of his enemies and they would burn the city. However, he told him that he would not die by the sword, but would die in peace. *(Jer. 34:2-6, 21.)*

Zedekiah reigned over Judah instead of Coniah (Jechoniah, Jehoiachin). Nebuchadnezzar placed him as king over Judah. Zedekiah sent Jehucal the son of Shelemiah and Zephaniah the son of Maaseiah to Jeremiah to ask him to pray unto the Lord on behalf of Judah. Jeremiah prophesied that Egypt's Pharaoh would not save Judah from the Chaldeans. The Chaldeans would rise up and burn Jerusalem. When Jeremiah was cast into the dungeon by Irijah, Zedekiah transferred him to the court of the prison. *(Jer. 37.)*

Zedekiah was approached by the princes who requested they be allowed to slay Jeremiah for prophesying the destruction of Jerusalem if the people did not go forth with the Chaldeans. He said he could not prevail against them, so they cast Jeremiah into the dungeon of Malchiah the son of Hammelech (i.e., the king). Ebed-melech, an Ethiopian, told Zedekiah that the princes had done evil and asked Zedekiah to let him rescue Jeremiah. Zedekiah told him to take 30 men and proceed with the rescue. Zedekiah conversed privately with Jeremiah and received Jeremiah's counsel, instructing Jeremiah not to let the princes know of their conversation with a promise he would not die nor would he be returned to those who sought his life. Zedekiah then placed Jeremiah in the court of the prison where he was until the day that Jerusalem was taken captive. *(Jer. 38.) (Note: In verse 6, it says Jeremiah was cast into the dungeon of Malchiah. In verse 26, it indicates Jeremiah petitioned the king that he not be returned to Jonathan's house where he would surely die. Thus, it is possible that Malchiah and Jonathan are one and the same, or that the wrong name was recorded in one of the verses.)*

In the tenth month of the ninth year of Zedekiah's reign, Nebuchadnezzar came against Jerusalem. By the fourth month of Zedekiah's eleventh year as king, the city was broken up. Zedekiah tried to escape but was captured by the Chaldean army which turned him over to Nebuchadnezzar. Nebuchadnezzar slew Zedekiah's sons, put Zedekiah's eyes out, bound him in chains so as to carry him to Babylon, burned the king's house as well as those of the rest of the people, and broke down the walls of Jerusalem. *(Jer. 39:1-8.) (Note: This is a retelling of 2 Kgs. 25:2-7. Also, Hel. 6:10 and Hel. 8:21 in the Book of Mormon state that one son, Mulek, escaped and was brought by the Lord to the Americas into "the land north.").*

Just as Zedekiah was delivered into the hands of his enemies, so would Pharaoh-hophra king of Egypt be delivered into the hands of his enemies and the remnant of Judah who went to dwell in Egypt would be destroyed because they worshipped false gods. *(Jer. 44:30.)*

In the beginning of the reign of Zedekiah as king of Judah, Jeremiah prophesied of the judgment and destruction that would befall Elam. *(Jer. 49:34-35.)*

When Zedekiah went captive into Babylon, Seraiah, the son of Neriah, also went into Babylon. Jeremiah gave Seraiah instructions regarding the words he *[Jeremiah]* had written. He was to read the words, prophesy against the people, bind a stone to the book and throw it into the river. He was to tell the people that Babylon would sink like the book and not rise again. *(Jer. 51:59.)* (Chart 1.)

ZEDEKIAH (3). *1 Chr. 3:16.*

Zedekiah's parentage is not clear in this verse as to whether he was the son of Jehoiakim or the son of Jeconiah (Jehoiachin) (Chart 1.)

ZEDEKIAH (4). *Jer. 36:12.*

Zedekiah was the son of Hananiah. He was in the scribe's chamber in king Jehoiakim's house with Elishama the scribe and all the princes when Michaiah told them of the prophecies of Jeremiah which he had heard Baruch read in his father Gemariah's chamber. (Chart 16m.)

ZEDEKIAH (2), SONS OF. *2 Kgs. 25:7; Jer. 39:6; 52:10.*

The **Sons of Zedekiah** tried to escape from Jerusalem when Nebuchadnezzar, the Babylonian princes and the Chaldean army came against them, but they were captured by the army and taken to Nebuchadnezzar. Zedekiah's sons were slain before his eyes. *(Note: Hel. 6:10 and Hel. 8:21 in the Book of Mormon state that one son, Mulek, escaped and was brought by the Lord to the America's into "the land north.")*

ZEEB. *Judg. 7:25.*

Zeeb was a Midianite prince. Gideon's army slew him at the winepress of Zeeb and brought his head to Gideon on the other side of Jordan.

ZELEK. *2 Sam. 23:37; 1 Chr. 11:39.*

Zelek the Ammonite was one of David's mighty men *(2 Sam. 23:37)* and one of the valiant men of the armies *(1 Chr. 11:39)*. (Chart 17.)

ZELOPHEHAD. *Num. 26:33; 27:1-7; 36:6-7; 1 Chr. 7:15.*

Zelophehad was a son of Hepher, a grandson of Gilead, a great-grandson of Machir, and a great-great-grandson of Manasseh. He begat no sons but had the following daughters: Mahlah, Noah, Hoglah, Milcah and Tirzah. *(Num. 26:33.)*

Zelophehad died in the wilderness and his daughters approached Moses and Eleazar to request that his inheritance be passed on to them because he had no sons. Moses took the matter to the Lord and was instructed that they were right: if a man had no sons, his inheritance should be passed on to his daughters. *(Num. 27:1-7.)*

When questioned about what would happen to Zelophehad's inheritance if his daughters married sons from other tribes, Moses stated that the daughters who received inheritances should marry within the tribe of their father. No inheritance was to pass to a different tribe. *(Num. 36:6-7.)*

Zelophehad descended from Machir and only had daughters. *(1 Chr. 7:15.)* (Charts 15a-b.)

ZEMARITE. *Gen. 10:18.*

Zemarites were descendants of Canaan who was a son of Ham. (Chart 2e.)

ZEMIRA. *1 Chr. 7:8.*

Zemira, son of Becher, was a grandson of Benjamin. His brothers were Joash, Eliezer, Elioenai, Omri, Jerimoth, Abiah, Anathoth and Alameth. (Chart 16c.)

ZEPHANIAH (1). *2 Kgs. 25:18-21; Jer. 21:1; 29:25, 29; 37:3; 52:24-27.*

Zephaniah was the second priest after Seraiah, the chief priest. Zephaniah, Seraiah, the three keepers of the door, and others (including 60 men of the people of the land), were taken by Nebuzar-adan out of Judah to Babylon to Riblah where they were smitten and killed and "Judah was carried away out of their land." *(2 Kgs. 25:18-21; Jer. 52:24-27.)*

Zephaniah, son of Maaseiah the priest, was one of the priests Zedekiah sent to Jeremiah to have him inquire of the Lord as to whether or not the Lord would deliver Judah from Nebuchadnezzar. *(Jer. 21:1.)*

Zephaniah reported to Jeremiah what Shemaiah the Nehelamite was saying, i.e., that Jeremiah was a false prophet. *(Jer. 29:25, 29.)*

Zephaniah was the son of Maaseiah the priest. Zedekiah sent him and Jehucal the son of Shelemiah to Jeremiah to ask him to pray for the people. *(Jer. 37:3.)*

ZEPHANIAH (2). *1 Chr. 6:36.* See **Uriel**.

Zephaniah (3). *Zeph. 1-3.*

Zephaniah, son of Cushi, prophesied (639-608 B.C.) in the days of Josiah son of Amon, king of Judah. He foretold of the destruction of Judah, which is a type of the Second Coming. The Lord will consume all things. *(Zeph. 1:2.)* The day of the Lord's sacrifice *(Zeph. 1:8)* will be a day of wrath *(Zeph. 1:15)*.

Zephaniah urged the people to seek righteousness and meekness. He prophesied of judgment to fall upon Ashkelon, Ashdod, Ekron, the Cherethites, Philistines, Moabites and the children of Ammon, the Ethiopians, Assyrians and Ninevah. *(Zeph. 2.)*

Zephaniah prophesied that at the Second Coming, the Lord will gather all the nations together and pour out His anger against them. All the earth shall be devoured with the fire of the Lord's jealousy. *(Zeph. 3:8.)* The Lord will then give the people a pure language. *(Zeph. 3:9.)* The remnant of Israel shall be a righteous people. *(Zeph. 3:13.)* The Lord will reign in their midst. *(Zeph. 3:15-17.)*

ZEPHANIAH (4). *Zech. 6:10, 14.*

Zephaniah was the father of Josiah and Hen.

ZEPHO (Zephi). *Gen. 36:11,15; 1 Chr. 1:36.*

Zepho (Zephi) was a son of Eliphaz, son of Adah and Esau. He was a duke or tribal chief. (Chart 3b.)

ZEPHON. See **Ziphion**.

ZERAH (1). *Gen. 36:13, 17; 1 Chr. 1:37.*

Zerah was a son of Reuel, son of Bashemath and Esau. He was a duke or tribal chief. His brothers were Nahath, Shammah and Mizzah. (Chart 3c.)

ZERAH (2). *Gen. 36:33; 1 Chr. 1:44.*

Zerah of Bozrah was the father of king Jobab who reigned in Edom following the death of Bela.

ZERAH (3). *Gen. 46:12; Num. 26:20; 1 Chr. 2:4, 6.* See **Zarah**.

ZERAH (4). *Num. 26:13.* See **Zohar (2)**.

ZERAH (5). *Josh. 7:1-25.*

Zerah, of the tribe of Judah, was the father of Zabdi (Zimri), the grandfather of Carmi and the great-grandfather of Achan, which Archan partook of the "accursed thing" (i.e., kept some of the spoils) when Jericho was destroyed. (Charts 8a, c-d, g-h.)

ZERAH (6). *1 Chr. 6:21, 31-32, 41.*

Zerah, of the tribe of Levi through Gershom, was the son of Iddo (Adaiah). He was one of the men whom David set over the song of the house of the Lord. He ministered before the dwelling place of the tabernacle with singing. (Chart 7a.)

ZERAH (7). *1 Chr. 9:6.*

Zerah, a Shilonite, was the father of Jeuel. Jeuel and 690 of his brethern were chosen to live in Jerusalem following their captivity in Babylon.

ZERAH (8). *2 Chr. 14:9-13.*

Zerah was an Ethiopian who came with his host of 1,000,000 plus 300 chariots against Asa, king of Judah. Asa pleaded with the Lord for help and the Lord "smote the Ethiopians before Asa and before Judah."

ZERAHIAH (1). *1 Chr. 6:6; Ezra 7:1-5.*

Zerahiah, the son of Uzzi, was a fourth-great-grandson of Aaron and the father of Meraioth. *(1 Chr. 6:6.)*

Zerahiah's descendants and ancestors are listed from Aaron through Ezra with some modification from 1 Chr. 6:4-15. *(Ezra 7:1-5.)* (Chart 7b.)

ZERAHIAH (2). *Ezra 8:4.*

Zerahiah was the father of Elihoenai and was of the sons of Phinehas. His son Elihoenai was the chief of his fathers and went with Ezra up from Babylon to Jerusalem.

ZERESH. *Esth. 5:10, 14; 6:13.*

Zeresh was Haman's wife. When Haman mourned because Mordecai would not bow down to him, she suggested he build a gallows and hang Mordecai. *(Esth. 5:10, 14.)*

Zeresh and Haman's wisemen counseled him that if Mordecai was of the seed of the Jews "before whom thou hast begun to fall," then he would not prevail against him but would surely fall before him. *(Esth. 6:13.)*

ZERETH. *1 Chr. 4:7.*

Zereth, of the tribe of Judah, was a son of Helah and Ashur the father of Tekoa. His brothers were Jezoar and Ethnan. *(Note: He also had several half-brothers: sons of Ashur and Naarah.)* (Chart 8d.)

ZERI. *1 Chr. 25:3.*

Zeri, a Levite and musician, was a son of Jeduthun. The musicians—sons of Jeduthun, Asaph and Heman—drew lots and were given their duty assignments by David and the captains of the host. *(Note: There is no lot number listed for Zeri and Uzziel named in verses 3-4. However, lots 4, 10 and 11 were cast by sons not named in those verses: Izri, Shimei and Azareel. Perhaps Zeri and Izri are one and the same; Azareel and Uzziel are one and the same; and Shimei is the unnamed sixth son of Jeduthun.)* (Chart 7h.)

ZEROR. *1 Sam. 9:1-2.*

Zeror, a Benjamite, was the father of Abiel, the son of Bechorath and the great-grandfather of Saul. (Chart 16k.)

ZERUAH. *1 Kgs. 11:26.*

Zeruah, a widow woman whose husband's name was Nebat, was the mother of Jeroboam, one of Solomon's servants.

ZERUBBABEL (Sheshbazzar). *1 Chr. 3:19; Ezra 1:8-11; 2:2; 3:2, 8-9; 4:2-4, 24; 5:2 (1-2, 14-16); Neh. 7:7-65; 12:1; Hag. 1:1, 12, 14; 2:2-4, 9, 21-23; Zech. 4:6-10.*

Zerubbabel, a descendant of David, was a son of Pedaiah and a grandson of Jeconiah (Jehoiachin). His sons were Meshullam and Hananiah and his daughter was Shelomith. *(1 Chr. 3:19.) (Note: The footnote to this passage states that Zerubbabel is identified as the grandson of Jeconiah through Pedaiah in this verse but as the son of Shealtiel elsewhere.)*

Sheshbazzar (Zerubbabel) was the prince of Judah. Cyrus, king of Persia, had Mithredath, the treasurer, return and number unto Sheshbazzar the treasures that belonged to the house of the Lord. Sheshbazzar took them from Babylon to Jerusalem. *(Ezra 1:8-11.)*

Zerubbabel was one of the people who Nebuchadnezzar had brought to Babylon from Jerusalem who returned following Cyrus' proclamation to build the temple. Those who went with him—including the following: Jeshua, Nehemiah, Seraiah (Azariah), Reelaiah (Raamiah), (Nahamani), Mordecai, Bilshan, Mispar (Mispereth), Bigvai, Rehum (Nehum) and Baanah—are listed. *(Ezra 2:2; Neh. 7:7.) (Note: The variations in Nehemiah are bracketed.)*

Zerubbabel was the son of Shealtiel. He and his brethren, along with Jeshua and his brethren the priests, built an altar unto God in the seventh month; and the children of Israel offered burnt offerings thereon according to the law of Moses. In the second year after their return to Jerusalem, Zerubbabel and Jeshua appointed the Levites to begin work on rebuilding the temple. *(Ezra 3:2, 8-9.)*

The Samaritans went to Zerubbabel and the chief of the fathers and volunteered to help build the temple. Their offer was declined. The Samaritans hindered the work and caused it to cease until the second year of Darius' reign as king of Persia. *(Ezra 4:2-4, 24.)*

The prophets Haggai and Zechariah prophesied unto the Jews in Judah and Jerusalem. Thus, with the prophets of God helping them, Zerubbabel (Sheshbazzar) and Jeshua again began to build the temple. Sheshbazzar had been made governor by Cyrus. Cyrus had the vessels of gold and silver that Nebuchadnezzar had taken from the temple in Jerusalem removed from the temple of Babylon. He had them delivered to Sheshbazzar (Zerubbabel). He had Sheshbazzar take them to Jerusalem to be placed in the temple there. Sheshbazzar laid the foundation of the house of God in Jerusalem as commanded by Cyrus. This was part of what Tatnai, governor of the west side of the Euphrates River, reported in a letter to Darius regarding who the Israelites said had commanded them to build the temple in Jerusalem. *(Ezra 5:2 [1-2, 14-16].)*

The priests and Levites who followed Zerubbabel, the son of Shealtiel, to Jerusalem out of Babylon are listed. *(Neh. 12:1.) (Also see Ezra 2:2.)*

Zerubbabel was governor of Judah. In the second year of king Darius' reign, the prophet Haggai spoke to Zerubbabel and Joshua (Jeshua) the high priest and exhorted the people to build the temple, and they did. *(Hag. 1:1, 12, 14.)*

The Lord sent Haggai to Zerubbabel and Joshua and the people a second time. He counseled the people to be strong, even though the new temple was far less glorious than the former temple. The time will come, Haggai said, when the Lord will fill the temple with glory and it will be more glorious than the former. He will fill the temple with peace. Haggai told Zerubbabel greater things were in store for the people and that the Lord had chosen Zerubbabel as a "signet." *(Hag. 2:2-4, 9, 21-23.)*

Zerubbabel was told by Zechariah that he, Zerubbabel, would lay the foundation and finish building the house of the Lord. *(Zech. 4:6-10.) (Note: Zechariah had a vision wherein he saw two olive trees, one on the left and one on the right side of a golden candlestick. The two olive trees represent two anointed ones who stand before the Lord: i.e., Zerubbabel and Joshua who represent the royal and priestly rule. See Zechariah in the BD.)* (Chart 1.)

ZERUIAH. *1 Sam. 26:6; 2 Sam. 2:18; 1 Chr. 2:16.*

Zeruiah was the mother of Abishai and Joab. *(1 Sam. 26:6.)*

Zeruiah had three sons: Joab, Abishai and Asahel. *(2 Sam. 2:18.)*

Zeruiah's sons were Abishai, Joab and Asahel. Her sister was Abigail. David was one of her brothers. *(1 Chr. 2:16.)* (Charts 8d-e.)

ZETHAM. *1 Chr. 23:8 (6-8); 26:22.*

Zetham was of the sons of Gershon, son of Levi. When David divided the Levites into courses at the time he made Solomon king, three of those who were of the sons of Laadan were named: Jehiel, Zetham and Joel. *(1 Chr. 23:8 (6-8).)*

Zethan and his brother Joel were sons of Jehieli (Jehiel) They were over the treasures of the house of the Lord. *(1 Chr. 26:22.)* (Chart 7f.)

ZETHAN. *1 Chr. 7:10.*

Zethan, son of Bilhan and grandson of Jediael, was a great-grandson of Benjamin and a mighty man of valor. His brothers were Jeush, Benjamin, Ehud, Chenaanah, Tharshish and Ahishahar. (Chart 16c.)

ZETHAR. *Esth. 1:10.*

Zethar was one of the seven chamberlains serving in the presence of Ahasuerus the king who was sent to bring queen Vashti to Ahasuerus.

ZIA. *1 Chr. 5:13.*

Zia was a descendant of Gad. (Chart 13b.)

ZIBA. *2 Sam. 9:2-12; 16:1-4.*

Ziba was a servant in Saul's house. David sent for him and inquired if there was anyone of Saul's house still alive that David could show kindness unto him. Ziba informed him that Jonathan had a lame son, Mephibosheth, who was still alive. David restored Saul's lands to Mephibosheth and instructed Ziba that he, his 15 sons and 20 servants were to till the land and bring in the fruits for their master, and all that were of his house were to be servants unto Mephibosheth. *(2 Sam. 9:2-12.)*

When David fled from Jerusalem to escape from Absalom, Ziba met him with a couple of asses saddled. They were carrying 200 loaves of bread, summer fruit and wine for David and his men. When David inquired as to where Mephibosheth was, Ziba informed him that he was in Jerusalem and had declared, "Today shall the house of Israel restore me the kingdom of my father." David told Ziba that he and his household were all that belonged to Mephibosheth. Ziba asked that he might find grace in David's sight. *(2 Sam. 16:1-4.)*

ZIBEON THE HIVITE. *Gen. 36:2, 20, 24.*

Zibeon the Hivite, son of Seir the Horite, was the father of Anah (one of Esau's fathers-in-law), and grandfather of Aholibamah (one of Esau's wives). He also was the father of Ajah (Aiah). He was a duke or tribal chief in the land of Edom. (Charts 4a-f.; 19.)

ZIBIA. *1 Chr. 8:9.*

Zibia was a son of Hodesh and Shaharaim, a descendant of Benjamin. (Chart 16f.)

ZIBIAH. *2 Kgs. 12:1; 2 Chr. 24:1.*

Zibiah of Beersheba was the mother of Jehoash (Joash), king of Judah. *(2 Kgs. 12:1.) (Note: Jehoash's father was king Ahaziah.)*

ZICHRI (1). *Ex. 6:21.*

Zichri was a son of Izhar, a grandson of Kohath and a great-grandson of Levi. (Chart 7d.)

ZICHRI (2). *1 Chr. 8:19-21.*

Zichri, a descendant of Benjamin, was a son of Shimhi. (Chart 16h.)

ZICHRI (3). *1 Chr. 8:23, 25.*

Zichri, a descendant of Benjamin, was a son of Shashak who was a son of Beriah. (Chart 16g.)

ZICHRI (4). *1 Chr. 8:27.*

Zichri, a descendant of Benjamin, was a son of Jeroham. (Chart 16j.)

ZICHRI (5) (Zaccur (2), Zabdi (3)). *1 Chr. 9:15; 25:2, 10; Neh. 11:17; 12:35.*

Zichri, the son of Asaph and the father of Micah, was a Levite whose descendants dwelt in the villages of the Netophathites. His genealogy was written in the book of the kings of Israel and Judah, who were carried away to Babylon for their transgression. *(1 Chr. 9:15.)*

Zaccur (Zichri), a Levite, was one of the musicians. He was of the sons of Asaph. The musicians—sons of Asaph, Heman and Jeduthun—drew lots and were given their duty assignments by David and the captains of the host. Zaccur cast the third lot. He, his brethren and their sons numbered 12. *(1 Chr. 25:2, 10.)*

Zabdi (Zichri) was the son of Asaph and the father of Micha (Micah). *(Neh. 11:17.)*

Zaccur (Zichri) was the son of Asaph and the father of Michaiah (Micah, Micha). His descendant Zechariah was among the priests' sons who were assigned by Nehemiah to take their trumpets and go with one of two great companies of people up on the walls of Jerusalem to participate in the dedication of the walls. *(Neh. 12:35.)* (Chart 7a.)

ZICHRI (6). *1 Chr. 26:25.*

Zichri, a Levite, was the son of Joram, the father of Shelomith, and a great-great-great-grandson of Moses. Shelomith and his brethren were over the treasures of the dedicated things which king David and others dedicated. (Chart 7b.)

ZICHRI (7). *1 Chr. 27:16.*

Zichri, the father of Eliezer, was of the tribe of Reuben.

ZICHRI (8). *2 Chr. 17:16.*

Zichri, of the house of Judah, was the father of Amasiah who was captain of 200,000 men when Jehoshaphat was king of Judah.

ZICHRI (9). *2 Chr. 23:1.*

Zichri was the father of Elishaphat who was one of the captains of hundreds Jehoiada the priest rallied to slay Athaliah and make Joash king over Judah.

ZICHRI (10). *2 Chr. 28:7.*

Zichri, a mighty man of Ephraim, slew Maaseiah (son of Ahaz, king of Judah), Azrikam (governor of the house) and Elkanah (who was next to the king) because of the wickedness of Ahaz and his people.

ZICHRI (11). *Neh. 11:9.*

Zichri, of the lineage of Benjamin, was the father of Joel. (Chart 16m.)

ZICHRI (12). *Neh. 12:17.*

Zichri, son of Abijah, was one of the priests who was a chief of the fathers in the days of Joiakim.

ZIDKIJAH. *Neh. 10:1, 28-31.*

Zidkijah was among those who covenanted to marry in Israel, honor the Sabbath day, pay tithes and keep the commandments.

ZIHA. *Ezra 2:43, 58; Neh. 7:46, 60; 11:21.*

Ziha was a Nethinim. When the Nethinims and the children of Solomon's servants left Babylon to return to Jerusalem to build the house of the Lord as proclaimed by Cyrus, king of Persia, they numbered 392. *(Ezra 2:43, 58; Neh. 7:46, 60.)*

When the children of Israel returned from Babylonian captivity, the Nethinims dwelled in Ophel. Ziha and Gispa were their overseers. *(Neh. 11:21.)*

ZILLAH. *Gen. 4:19, 22.*

Zillah was Lamech's second wife. She bore a son, Tubal-cain, and a daughter, Naamah. (Chart 1.)

ZILPAH. *Gen. 29:24; 30:9-13.*

Zilpah, Laban's maid, was given to Leah for a handmaiden when Laban gave his daughter Leah in marriage to Jacob. *(Gen. 29:24.)*

After Rachel gave Jacob her handmaid Bilhah for a wife, Leah gave Jacob her handmaid Zilpah so she could obtain more children through her since she had stopped bearing children herself. Zilpah begat two sons: Gad and Asher. *(Gen. 30:9-13.)* (Chart 3d.)

ZILTHAI (1). *1 Chr. 8:20-21.*

Zilthai, a descendant of Benjamin, was a son of Shimhi. (Chart 16h.)

ZILTHAI (2). *1 Chr. 12:20, 23.*

Zilthai, from the tribe of Manasseh, was one of the captains of thousands who went to Ziklag to defend David and turn the kingdom of Saul to David. He and his host helped David against the band of rovers.

ZIMMAH. *1 Chr. 6:20-21, 42-43; 2 Chr. 29:12.*

Zimmah, father of Joah (Ethan), was the son of Shimei who was the son of Jahath, the son of Libni, son of Gershom who was the son of Levi. *(1 Chr. 6:20-21, 42-43.)*

Zimmah, a Levite and descendant of Gershon, was the father of Joah. *(2 Chr. 29:12.)* (Chart 7a.)

ZIMRAN. *Gen. 25:2.*

Zimran was a son of Abraham and his wife Keturah. (Charts 2b.; 3a, d, f.)

ZIMRI (1). *Num. 25:14 (6-8, 14).*

Zimri was the son of Salu and was a prince of a chief house among the Simeonites. He is first just referred to as "one of the chidren of Israel" *(v. 6)*. It is not until verse 14 that he is referred to by name. He brought a Midianitish woman, Cozbi, unto his brethren. He and Cozbi were subsequently slain by Phinehas, the son of Eleazar and grandson of Aaron, by a javelin which he thrust through both of them. Thus, "the plague was stayed from the children of Israel."

ZIMRI (2). *1 Kgs. 16:9-20.*

Zimri was the servant of Elah, king of Israel, and captain of half his chariots. He slew Elah and reigned in his stead. He immediately slew all the house of Baasha, killing every one of Elah's immediate family, his kinsmen and his friends. Zimri had reigned just seven days when the people heard what he had done and made Omri, the captain of the host, king over Israel. When Omri and the people besieged Tirzah where Zimri was, Zimri went into the palace of the king's house, set fire to it, and died. The rest of his record "and his treason that he wrought" is written in the book of the chronicles of the kings of Israel.

ZIMRI (3). *1 Chr. 2:6.* See **Zabdi (1).**

ZIMRI (4). *1 Chr. 8:36; 9:42.*

Zimri, from the tribe of Benjamin, was a son of Jehoadah (Jarah). They were descendants of Saul through Jonathan. His brothers were Alemeth and Azmaveth. He begat Moza. (Chart 16 l.)

ZINA (Zizah). *1 Chr. 23:10-11.*

Zina was a son of Shimei. When David made Solomon king, he also numbered the Levites and divided them into courses among the sons of Levi—Gershon, Kohath and Merari. Of the sons of Shimei, son of Gershon, were Jahath, Zina, Jeush and Beriah. Jahath was the chief, **Zizah** (Zina) the second, and Jeush and Beriah were reckoned as one because they didn't have many sons. (Chart 7f.)

ZIPH (1). *1 Chr. 2:42.*

Ziph was the son of Mesha the son of Caleb. (Chart 8i.)

ZIPH (2). *1 Chr. 4:16.*

Ziph was a son of Jehaleleel. His brothers were Ziphah, Tiria and Asareel. (Chart 8n.)

ZIPHAH. *1 Chr. 4:16.*

Ziphah was a son of Jehaleleel. His brothers were Ziph, Tiria and Asareel. (Chart 8n.)

ZIPHIMS. See **Siphites.**

ZIPHION (Zephon, Zephonites). *Gen. 46:16; Num. 26:15.*

Ziphion (Zephon) was the son of Gad (and the father of the **Zephonites**). His brothers were Haggi, Shuni, Ezbon (Ozni), Eri, Arodi and Areli. (Chart 13a.)

ZIPHITES (Ziphims). *1 Sam. 23:19-20; Psalm 54:Subtitle.*

Ziphites were citizens of Ziph. They offered to deliver David into king Saul's hands. *(1 Sam. 23:19-20.)*

The **Ziphims** (Ziphites) informed Saul that David was hiding with them. *(Psalm 54:Subtitle.)*

ZIPPOR. *Num. 22:2, 4, 10.*

Zippor was the father of Balak, king of the Moabites.

ZIPPORAH. *Ex. 2:21-22; 4:20, 24-26; 18:2-6.*

Zipporah was Moses' wife and one of Jethro's seven daughters. She bore Moses a son whom they named Gershom. *(Ex. 2:21-22.)*

Zipporah and her sons went with Moses when he returned to Egypt to free the children of Israel. As they journeyed, the Lord was angry with Moses because he had not had his son circumcised and was going to kill him. Zipporah took a sharp stone and circumcised her son, and the Lord spared Moses. *(Ex. 4:20, 24-26.)*

At some point, Moses had apparently had Zipporah take his children and return to her father. When Jethro learned that the Lord had led the children of Israel out of Egypt and they were safely encamped in the wilderness, he brought Zipporah and her sons, Gershom and Eliezer, back to Moses. *(Ex. 18:2-6.)* (Chart 7b.)

ZITHRI. *Ex. 6:22.*

Zithri was a son of Uzziel, a grandson of Kohath and a great-grandson of Levi. (Chart 7d.)

ZIZA (1). *1 Chr. 4:37.*

Ziza, a descendant of Simeon through Shimei, was the son of Shiphi. (Chart 6a.)

ZIZA (2). *2 Chr. 11:20.*

Ziza was one of the sons of king Rehoboam, Solomon's son, and Maachah, Absalom's daughter. His brothers were Abijah, Attai and Shelomith. (Chart 1.)

ZIZAH. See **Zina**.

ZOAR. *Gen. 14:2 (1-2, 12, 14-16).*

Zoar (king of Bela), Bera (king of Sodom), Birsha (king of Gomorrah), Shinab (king of Admah) and Shemeber (king of Zeboiim) warred against Chedorlaomer and the kings allied with him. *(Note: Sodom and Gomorrah fell and Lot, Abraham's nephew, was captured and subsequently rescued by Abraham.)*

ZOBEBAH. *1 Chr. 4:8.*

Zobebah was the son of Coz and the brother of Anub.

ZOHAR (1). *Gen. 23:8.*

Zohar was the father of Ephron, which Ephron sold the cave at Machpelah to Abraham for a burial place for Sarah.

ZOHAR(2) (Zerah (4), Zarhites (1)). *Gen. 46:10; Num. 26:13; 1 Chr. 4:24.*

Zohar was Simeon's son and a grandson of Jacob. His brothers were Jemuel, Jamin, Ohad, Jachin, Zohar and Shaul, son of a Canaanite woman. *(Gen. 46:10.)*

Zarhites were descendants of **Zerah** (Zohar). *(Num. 26:13.)*

Simeon's sons were Nemuel (Jemuel), Jamin, Jarib (Jachin), Zerah (Zohar) and Shaul. *(1 Chr. 4:24.)* (Chart 6a.)

ZOHETH. *1 Chr. 4:20.*

Zoheth was a son of Ishi.

ZOPHAH. *1 Chr. 7:35-36.*

Zophah was a son of Helem (Hotham) and a great-great-grandson of Asher. His brothers were Imna, Shelesh and Amal. His sons were Suah, Harnepher, Shual, Beri, Imrah, Bezer, Hod, Shamma, Shilshah, Ithran and Beera. (Chart 14a.)

ZOPHAI. See **Zuph**.

ZOPHAR. *Job 2:11; 11; 20; 42.*

Zophar the Naamathite was one of Job's three friends who came to mourn with him when he lost his children, his servants and his animals. *(Job 2:11.)*

Zophar questioned whether or not a person could find God by searching. He counseled Job not to let wickedness dwell in his tabernacle and to put away any wickedness. He indicated that the hope of the wicked is as the giving up of the ghost. *(Job 11.)*

Zophar added his condemnation of Job to that of his colleagues and told him that the triumph of the wicked is short and the joy of the hypocrite is for only a moment. *(Job 20.)*

Zophar, Eliphaz and Bildad were chastised by the Lord because they had not "spoken of me the thing that is right, as my servant Job hath." He instructed them to make offerings and that Job would pray for them; and He would accept them because of Job. They went and did as the Lord commanded. *(Job 42.)*

ZORAH. *Judg. 13:2, 24.*

Zorah was of the family of the Danites. His descendants included Manoah and his son Samson. (Chart 11b.)

ZORATHITES. *1 Chr. 4:2.*

Zorathites included Shobal (of the lineage of Judah) and his descendants: Reaiah, Jahath, Ahumai and Lahad.

ZORITES. *1 Chr. 2:54.*

Zorites were of the house of Salma, son of Hur and grandson of Caleb. (Chart 8 l.)

ZUAR. *Num. 1:8.*

Zuar was the father of Nethaneel and was of the tribe of Issachar. (Chart 9b.)

ZUPH (Zophai). *1 Sam. 1:1; 1 Chr. 6:26, 35.*

Zuph was an Ephrathite. He was the father of Tohu and the great-great-great-grandfather of Samuel. *(1 Sam. 1:1.)*

Zophai (Zuph), father of Nahath (Tohu, Toah) was of the house of Levi through Kohath and was the son of Elkanah. *(1 Chr. 6:26, 35.)* (Chart 7d.)

ZUR (1). *Num. 25:15 (7-8, 15); 31:8; Josh. 13:21.*

Zur, head over a people and a chief house in Midian, was the father of Cozbi, which Cozbi was slain by Phinehas (Aaron's grandson) to stay the plague of the Lord from the children of Israel. *(Num. 25:15 [7-8, 15].)*

Zur was slain by the children of Israel when Moses sent an army of 12,000 men (1,000 from each tribe) to destroy the Midianites. *(Num. 31:8.)*

The Lord told Joshua that much land still needed to be possessed, and reviewed with him what Moses had done. He reminded him, among other things, that Moses had slain the princes of Midian, including Zur. *(Josh. 13:21.)*

ZUR (2). *1 Chr. 8:30-32; 1 Chr. 9:36.*

Zur was of the tribe of Benjamin and was a son of the father of Gibeon. His brothers were Abdon, Kish, Baal, Nadab, Gedor, Ahio, Zacher and Mikloth. *(1 Chr. 8:30-32.)*

Zur was the secondborn son of Jehiel (the father of Gibeon, Abiel). His mother was Maachah. His brothers were Abdon, Kish, Baal, Ner, Nadab, Gedor, Ahio, Zechariah (Zacher) and Mikloth. *(1 Chr. 9:36.)* (Chart 16k.)

ZURIEL. *Num. 3:35-37.*

Zuriel was the son of Abihail and was chief of the house of the fathers of the families of Merari. He and his people were assigned to pitch on the northward side of the tabernacle and were responsible for the boards, bars, pillars, sockets, and all the vessels used in the tabernacle.

ZURISHADDAI. *Num. 1:6.*

Zurishaddai, of the tribe of Simeon, was the father of Shelumiel.

Charts

Showing Lineage
and timelines

CHART 1.

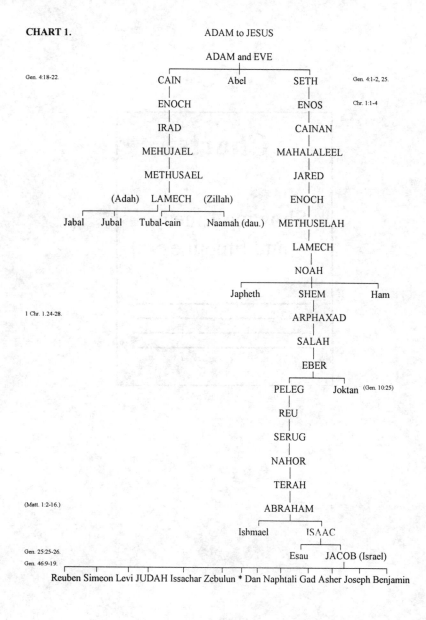

ADAM to JESUS

ADAM and EVE

Gen. 4:18-22.

CAIN   Abel   SETH   Gen. 4:1-2, 25.

ENOCH   ENOS   Chr. 1:1-4

IRAD   CAINAN

MEHUJAEL   MAHALALEEL

METHUSAEL   JARED

(Adah) LAMECH (Zillah)   ENOCH

Jabal   Jubal   Tubal-cain   Naamah (dau.)   METHUSELAH

LAMECH

NOAH

Japheth   SHEM   Ham

1 Chr. 1.24-28.

ARPHAXAD

SALAH

EBER

PELEG   Joktan   (Gen. 10:25)

REU

SERUG

NAHOR

TERAH

(Matt. 1:2-16.)

ABRAHAM

Ishmael   ISAAC

Gen. 25:25-26.   Esau   JACOB (Israel)
Gen. 46:9-19.

Reuben Simeon Levi JUDAH Issachar Zebulun * Dan Naphtali Gad Asher Joseph Benjamin

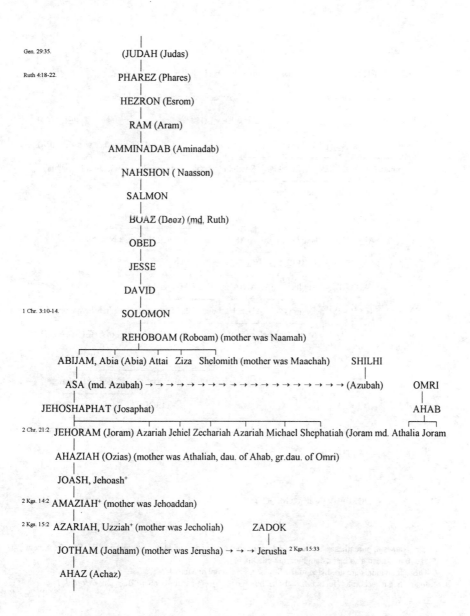

Gen. 29:35.   (JUDAH (Judas)

Ruth 4:18-22.   PHAREZ (Phares)

HEZRON (Esrom)

RAM (Aram)

AMMINADAB (Aminadab)

NAHSHON (Naasson)

SALMON

BOAZ (Booz) (md, Ruth)

OBED

JESSE

DAVID

1 Chr. 3:10-14.   SOLOMON

REHOBOAM (Roboam) (mother was Naamah)

ABIJAM, Abia (Abia) Attai Ziza Shelomith (mother was Maachah)   SHILHI

ASA (md. Azubah) → (Azubah)   OMRI

JEHOSHAPHAT (Josaphat)   AHAB

2 Chr. 21:2 JEHORAM (Joram) Azariah Jehiel Zechariah Azariah Michael Shephatiah (Joram md. Athalia Joram

AHAZIAH (Ozias) (mother was Athaliah, dau. of Ahab, gr.dau. of Omri)

JOASH, Jehoash[+]

2 Kgs. 14:2 AMAZIAH[+] (mother was Jehoaddan)

2 Kgs. 15:2 AZARIAH, Uzziah[+] (mother was Jecholiah)   ZADOK

JOTHAM (Joatham) (mother was Jerusha) → → → Jerusha 2 Kgs. 15:33

AHAZ (Achaz)

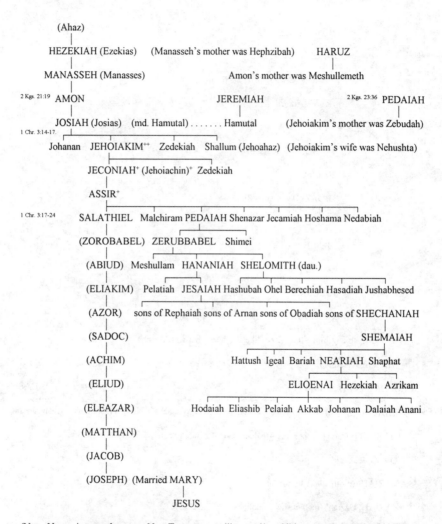

(Ahaz)
|
HEZEKIAH (Ezekias)   (Manasseh's mother was Hephzibah)   HARUZ
| |
MANASSEH (Manasses)   Amon's mother was Meshullemeth
|
2 Kgs. 21:19 AMON   JEREMIAH   2 Kgs. 23:36 PEDAIAH
| |
JOSIAH (Josias)   (md. Hamutal) . . . . Hamutal   (Jehoiakim's mother was Zebudah)
1 Chr. 3:14-17.
Johanan JEHOIAKIM[++] Zedekiah Shallum (Jehoahaz) (Jehoiakim's wife was Nehushta)

JECONIAH[+] (Jehoiachin)[+] Zedekiah

ASSIR[+]

1 Chr. 3:17-24 SALATHIEL Malchiram PEDAIAH Shenazar Jecamiah Hoshama Nedabiah

(ZOROBABEL) ZERUBBABEL   Shimei

(ABIUD) Meshullam HANANIAH SHELOMITH (dau.)

(ELIAKIM) Pelatiah JESAIAH Hashubah Ohel Berechiah Hasadiah Jushabhesed

(AZOR)   sons of Rephaiah sons of Arnan sons of Obadiah sons of SHECHANIAH

(SADOC)   SHEMAIAH

(ACHIM)   Hattush Igeal Bariah NEARIAH Shaphat

(ELIUD)   ELIOENAI Hezekiah Azrikam

(ELEAZAR)   Hodaiah Eliashib Pelaiah Akkab Johanan Dalaiah Anani

(MATTHAN)

(JACOB)

(JOSEPH) (Married MARY)
|
JESUS

(Note: Names in parentheses are New Testament spellings and/or additions not given in the Old Testament.)
* Jacob and Leah also had a daughter named Dinah.
[+] These individuals are not listed in the Savior's genealogy in Matt. 1:2-17.
[++] Josias begat Jechonias (Jehoiakim) about the time they were carried away to Babylon. *(Matt. 1:11.)*

CHART 2a.

NOAH

Gen. 10:2-4.

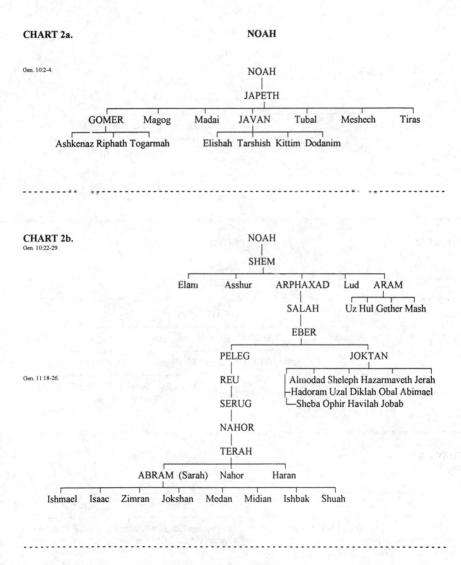

NOAH
|
JAPETH

GOMER   Magog   Madai   JAVAN   Tubal   Meshech   Tiras

Ashkenaz Riphath Togarmah   Elishah Tarshish Kittim Dodanim

- -

CHART 2b.
Gen. 10:22-29.

NOAH
|
SHEM

Elam   Asshur   ARPHAXAD   Lud   ARAM
|
SALAH   Uz Hul Gether Mash
|
EBER

PELEG   JOKTAN

Gen. 11:18-26.

REU   Almodad Sheleph Hazarmaveth Jerah
| ⎯Hadoram Uzal Diklah Obal Abimael
SERUG   ⎯Sheba Ophir Havilah Jobab
|
NAHOR
|
TERAH

ABRAM (Sarah)   Nahor   Haran

Ishmael   Isaac   Zimran   Jokshan   Medan   Midian   Ishbak   Shuah

- -

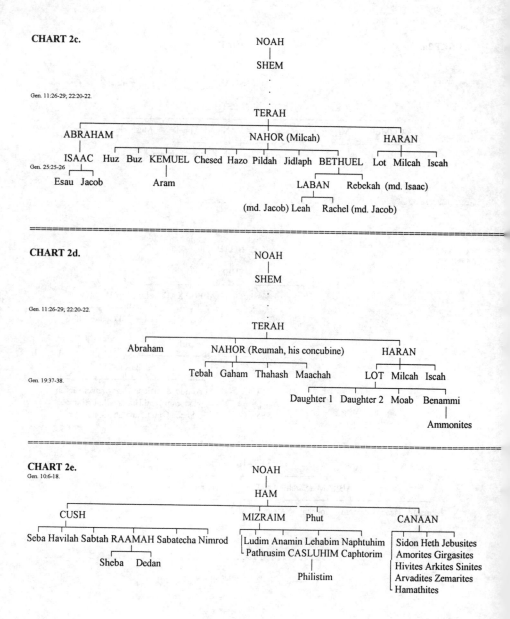

CHART 2c.

NOAH

SHEM

Gen. 11:26-29; 22:20-22.

TERAH

ABRAHAM   NAHOR (Milcah)   HARAN

ISAAC   Huz   Buz   KEMUEL   Chesed   Hazo   Pildah   Jidlaph   BETHUEL   Lot   Milcah   Iscah

Gen. 25:25-26

Esau   Jacob   Aram   LABAN   Rebekah   (md. Isaac)

(md. Jacob) Leah   Rachel (md. Jacob)

CHART 2d.

NOAH

SHEM

Gen. 11:26-29; 22:20-22.

TERAH

Abraham   NAHOR (Reumah, his concubine)   HARAN

Tebah   Gaham   Thahash   Maachah   LOT   Milcah   Iscah

Gen. 19:37-38.

Daughter 1   Daughter 2   Moab   Benammi

Ammonites

CHART 2e.
Gen. 10:6-18.

NOAH

HAM

CUSH   MIZRAIM   Phut   CANAAN

Seba Havilah Sabtah RAAMAH Sabatecha Nimrod   Ludim Anamin Lehabim Naphtuhim   Sidon Heth Jebusites

Sheba   Dedan   Pathrusim CASLUHIM Caphtorim   Amorites Girgasites

Philistim   Hivites Arkites Sinites

Arvadites Zemarites

Hamathites

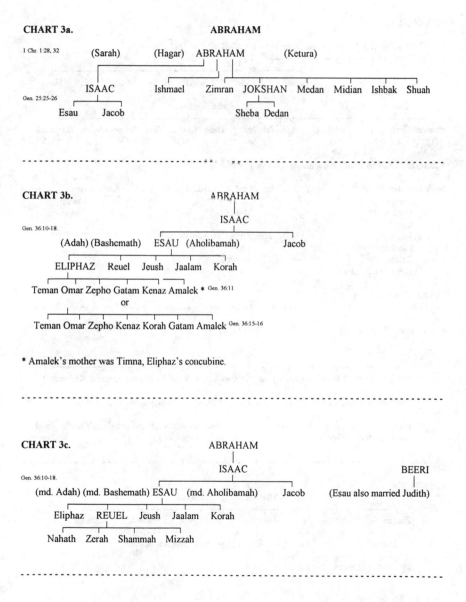

CHART 3a.   ABRAHAM

1 Chr. 1:28, 32   (Sarah)   (Hagar)   ABRAHAM   (Ketura)

        ISAAC   Ishmael   Zimran   JOKSHAN   Medan   Midian   Ishbak   Shuah

Gen. 25:25-26

     Esau   Jacob   Sheba Dedan

CHART 3b.   ABRAHAM

                        ISAAC

Gen. 36:10-18.

     (Adah) (Bashemath)   ESAU   (Aholibamah)   Jacob

   ELIPHAZ   Reuel   Jeush   Jaalam   Korah

Teman Omar Zepho Gatam Kenaz Amalek * ^{Gen. 36:11}

             or

Teman Omar Zepho Kenaz Korah Gatam Amalek ^{Gen. 36:15-16}

* Amalek's mother was Timna, Eliphaz's concubine.

CHART 3c.   ABRAHAM

                       ISAAC   BEERI

Gen. 36:10-18.

(md. Adah) (md. Bashemath) ESAU   (md. Aholibamah)   Jacob   (Esau also married Judith)

   Eliphaz   REUEL   Jeush   Jaalam   Korah

   Nahath   Zerah   Shammah   Mizzah

CHART 3d.

1 Chr. 1:28, 32

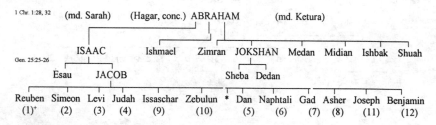

Gen. 25:25-26

Reuben Simeon Levi Judah Issaschar Zebulun * Dan Naphtali Gad Asher Joseph Benjamin
(1)[+]   (2)   (3)   (4)   (9)   (10)   (5)   (6)   (7)   (8)   (11)   (12)

* Jacob and Leah also had a daughter named Dinah, whom Leah bore after Zebulun.

Note: Leah bore: Zilpah, Leah's handmaid, bore: Rachel bore:
    Reuben   Gad   Joseph
    Simeon   Asher   Benjamin
    Levi
    Judah   Bilhah, Rachel's handmaid, bore: (Gen. 29:32 thru 30:24, 35:18)
    Issachar   Dan
    Zebulun   Naphtali
    Dinah (a daughter)

[+] Order of birth.

- -

CHART 3e.   ABRAHAM (Hagar)

Gen. 25:13-15
                                      ISHMAEL

Nebajoth Kedar Adbeel Mibsam Mishma Dumah Massa Hadar Tema Jetur Naphish Kedemah *

* Ishmael also had a daughter, Mahalath (*Gen. 28:9*), who became one of Esau's wives.

Ishmael and Isaac were half-brothers. Therefore, Ishmael was Jacob and Esau's half-uncle. Jacob and Esau were half-cousins to Mahalath (Bashemath). *(Gen. 36:3.)*

- -

CHART 3f.
Gen. 25:1-4

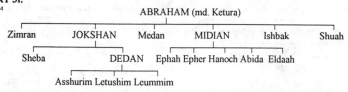

ABRAHAM (md. Ketura)

Zimran   JOKSHAN   Medan   MIDIAN   Ishbak   Shuah

    Sheba   DEDAN   Ephah Epher Hanoch Abida Eldaah

         Asshurim Letushim Leummim

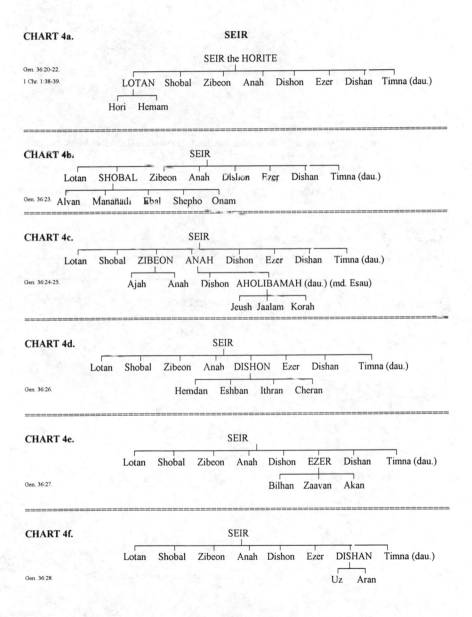

CHART 4a.

Gen. 36:20-22.
1 Chr. 1:38-39.

SEIR

SEIR the HORITE

LOTAN Shobal Zibeon Anah Dishon Ezer Dishan Timna (dau.)

Hori Hemam

CHART 4b.

Gen. 36:23.

SEIR

Lotan SHOBAL Zibeon Anah Dishon Ezer Dishan Timna (dau.)

Alvan Manahath Ebal Shepho Onam

CHART 4c.

Gen. 36:24-25.

SEIR

Lotan Shobal ZIBEON ANAH Dishon Ezer Dishan Timna (dau.)

Ajah Anah Dishon AHOLIBAMAH (dau.) (md. Esau)

Jeush Jaalam Korah

CHART 4d.

Gen. 36:26.

SEIR

Lotan Shobal Zibeon Anah DISHON Ezer Dishan Timna (dau.)

Hemdan Eshban Ithran Cheran

CHART 4e.

Gen. 36:27.

SEIR

Lotan Shobal Zibeon Anah Dishon EZER Dishan Timna (dau.)

Bilhan Zaavan Akan

CHART 4f.

Gen. 36:28.

SEIR

Lotan Shobal Zibeon Anah Dishon Ezer DISHAN Timna (dau.)

Uz Aran

CHART 5a.   REUBEN

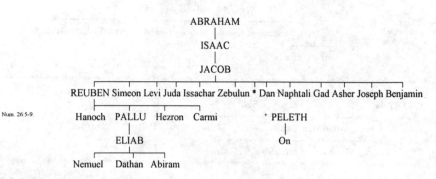

ABRAHAM
|
ISAAC
|
JACOB

REUBEN Simeon Levi Juda Issachar Zebulun * Dan Naphtali Gad Asher Joseph Benjamin

Num. 26:5-9.   Hanoch   PALLU   Hezron   Carmi   † PELETH
| |
ELIAB   On
|
Nemuel   Dathan   Abiram

* Jacob and Leah had a daughter named Dinah.

† Num. 16:1, indicates Reuben also had a son (or grandson) named Peleth, and Peleth had a son named On.

===

CHART 5b.   **DESCENDANTS OF REUBEN**

REUBEN

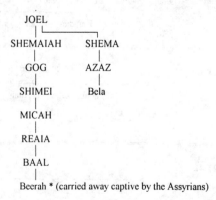

·
·
·
JOEL

1 Chr. 5:4-8

SHEMAIAH   SHEMA
| |
GOG   AZAZ
| |
SHIMEI   Bela
|
MICAH
|
REAIA
|
BAAL
|
Beerah * (carried away captive by the Assyrians)

* Beerah's brethren "by their families" were Jeiel, Zechariah and Bela, son of Azaz.

CHART 6a. SIMEON

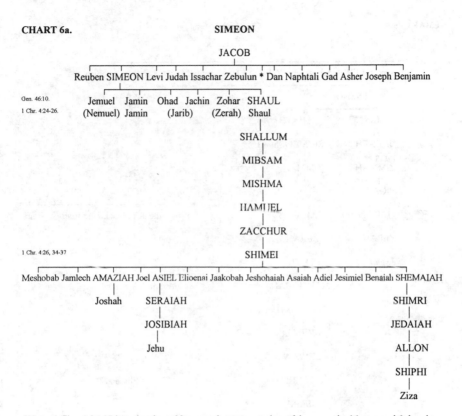

JACOB

Reuben SIMEON Levi Judah Issachar Zebulun * Dan Naphtali Gad Asher Joseph Benjamin

Gen. 46:10.

1 Chr. 4:24-26.

Jemuel Jamin Ohad Jachin Zohar SHAUL
(Nemuel) Jamin (Jarib) (Zerah) Shaul

SHALLUM

MIBSAM

MISHMA

HAMUEL

ZACCHUR

1 Chr. 4:26, 34-37

SHIMEI

Meshobab Jamlech AMAZIAH Joel ASIEL Elioenai Jaakobah Jeshohaiah Asaiah Adiel Jesimiel Benaiah SHEMAIAH

Joshah SERAIAH SHIMRI

JOSIBIAH JEDAIAH

Jehu ALLON

SHIPHI

Ziza

(Note: 1 Chr. 4:34-37 lists the above 22 names, but it is not clear if these are the 16 sons and 6 daughters or not, but it would appear so. It is also not clear which are sons and which are daughters.)

* Jacob and Leah also had a daughter named Dinah.

CHART 6b. ADDITIONAL DESCENDANTS OF SIMEON

1 Chr. 4:42.

ISHI

Pelatiah Neariah Rephaiah Uzziel

These were also, apparently, "of the sons of Simeon."

CHART 7a.   **LEVI**

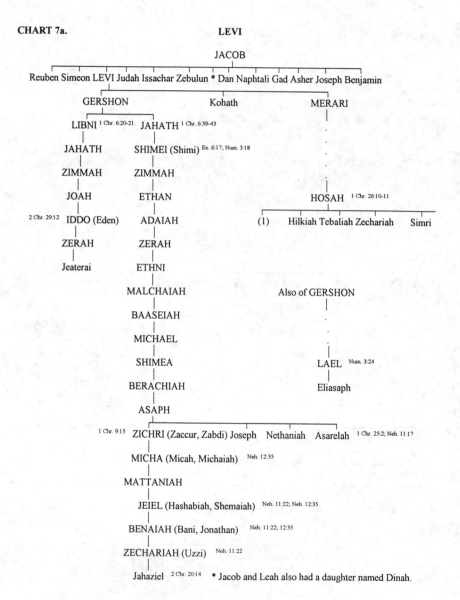

JACOB

Reuben Simeon LEVI Judah Issachar Zebulun * Dan Naphtali Gad Asher Joseph Benjamin

GERSHON   Kohath   MERARI

LIBNI [1 Chr. 6:20-21.] JAHATH [1 Chr. 6:39-43]

JAHATH   SHIMEI (Shimi) [Ex. 6:17; Num. 3:18]

ZIMMAH   ZIMMAH

JOAH   ETHAN   HOSAH [1 Chr. 26:10-11]

[2 Chr. 29:12] IDDO (Eden) ADAIAH   (1)   Hilkiah Tebaliah Zechariah   Simri

ZERAH   ZERAH

Jeaterai   ETHNI

              MALCHAIAH   Also of GERSHON

              BAASEIAH

              MICHAEL

              SHIMEA   LAEL [Num. 3:24]

              BERACHIAH   Eliasaph

              ASAPH

[1 Chr. 9:15] ZICHRI (Zaccur, Zabdi) Joseph Nethaniah Asarelah [1 Chr. 25:2; Neh. 11:17]

              MICHA (Micah, Michaiah) [Neh. 12:35]

              MATTANIAH

              JEIEL (Hashabiah, Shemaiah) [Neh. 11:22; Neh. 12:35]

              BENAIAH (Bani, Jonathan) [Neh. 11:22; 12:35]

              ZECHARIAH (Uzzi) [Neh. 11:22]

              Jahaziel [2 Chr. 20:14]   * Jacob and Leah also had a daughter named Dinah.

CHART 7b.

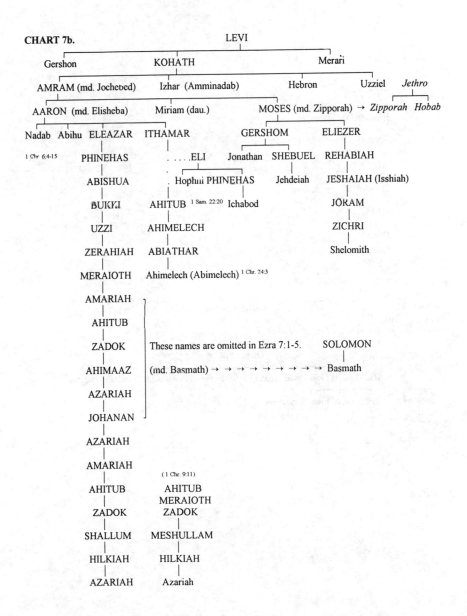

LEVI

Gershon — KOHATH — Merari

AMRAM (md. Jocheved) — Izhar (Amminadab) — Hebron — Uzziel — *Jethro*

AARON (md. Elisheba) — Miriam (dau.) — MOSES (md. Zipporah) → *Zipporah Hobab*

Nadab Abihu ELEAZAR ITHAMAR   GERSHOM   ELIEZER

1 Chr 6:4-15

PHINEHAS   . . . . .ELI   Jonathan SHEBUEL REHABIAH

ABISHUA   . Hophni PHINEHAS   Jehdeiah JESHAIAH (Isshiah)

BUKKI   AHITUB ¹ Sam. 22:20 Ichabod   JORAM

UZZI   AHIMELECH   ZICHRI

ZERAHIAH   ABIATHAR   Shelomith

MERAIOTH   Ahimelech (Abimelech) ¹ Chr. 24:3

AMARIAH

AHITUB

ZADOK   These names are omitted in Ezra 7:1-5.   SOLOMON

AHIMAAZ   (md. Basmath) → → → → → → → → → Basmath

AZARIAH

JOHANAN

AZARIAH

AMARIAH   (1 Chr. 9:11)

AHITUB   AHITUB
              MERAIOTH
ZADOK   ZADOK

SHALLUM   MESHULLAM

HILKIAH   HILKIAH

AZARIAH   Azariah

|
SERAIAH
|
JEHOZADAK (Ezra)
|
JESHUA   Ezra 3:2; Neh. 12:10-11
|
JOIAKIM
|
ELIASHIB
|
JOIADA
|
JONATHAN
|
Jaddua

CHART 7c.   **OBED-EDOM**

(Note: Obed-edom was of the family of Kohath.)

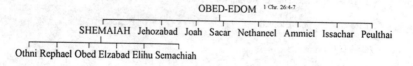

OBED-EDOM   1 Chr. 26:4-7

SHEMAIAH   Jehozabad Joah Sacar Nethaneel Ammiel Issachar Peulthai

Othni Rephael Obed Elzabad Elihu Semachiah

CHART 7d.

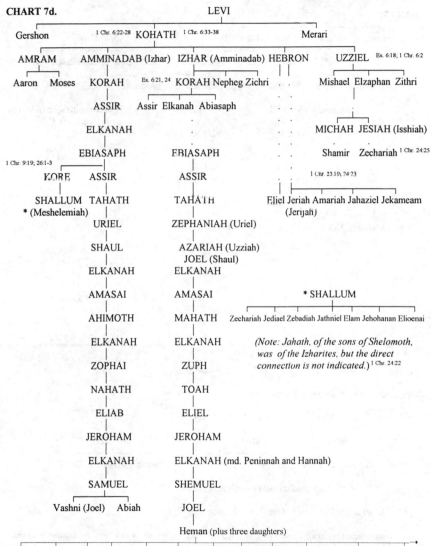

LEVI

Gershon   1 Chr. 6:22-28 KOHATH   1 Chr. 6:33-38   Merari

AMRAM   AMMINADAB (Izhar)   IZHAR (Amminadab) HEBRON   UZZIEL Ex. 6:18; 1 Chr. 6:2

Aaron   Moses   KORAH   Ex. 6:21, 24 KORAH Nepheg Zichri   . .   Mishael Elzaphan Zithri

ASSIR   Assir Elkanah Abiasaph   . .

ELKANAH   . .   MICHAH JESIAH (Isshiah)

EBIASAPH   EBIASAPH   . .   Shamir   Zechariah 1 Chr. 24:25

1 Chr. 9:19; 26:1-3

KORE   ASSIR   ASSIR   . .   1 Chr. 23:19; 24:23

SHALLUM TAHATH   TAHATH   Eliel Jeriah Amariah Jahaziel Jekameam
* (Meshelemiah) | (Jerijah)

URIEL   ZEPHANIAH (Uriel)

SHAUL   AZARIAH (Uzziah)
                JOEL (Shaul)

ELKANAH   ELKANAH

AMASAI   AMASAI   * SHALLUM

AHIMOTH   MAHATH   Zechariah Jediael Zebadiah Jathniel Elam Jehohanan Elioenai

ELKANAH   ELKANAH   *(Note: Jahath, of the sons of Shelomoth,*
                            was of the Izharites, but the direct
ZOPHAI   ZUPH   *connection is not indicated.)* 1 Chr. 24:22

NAHATH   TOAH

ELIAB   ELIEL

JEROHAM   JEROHAM

ELKANAH   ELKANAH (md. Peninnah and Hannah)

SAMUEL   SHEMUEL

Vashni (Joel) Abiah   JOEL

Heman (plus three daughters)

Bukkiah Mattaniah Uzziel Shebuel Jerimoth Hananiah Hanani Eliathah Giddalti Romanti-ezer Joshbekashah Mallothi
Hothir Mahazioth

CHART 7e.

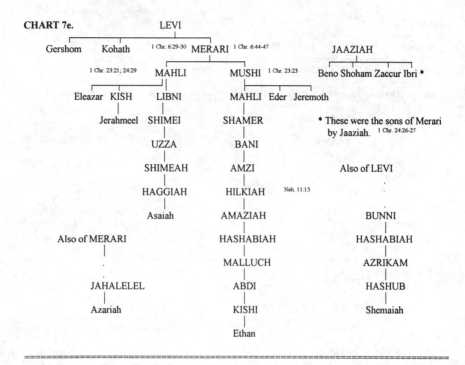

```
                              LEVI
          ┌────────────┬──────────────┼───────────────────────────┐
      Gershom       Kohath    1 Chr. 6:29-30  MERARI  1 Chr. 6:44-47    JAAZIAH
                                    │                              ┌───┬───┬───┬───┐
              1 Chr. 23:21; 24:29  MAHLI        MUSHI  1 Chr. 23:23   Beno Shoham Zaccur Ibri *
              ┌──────┬──────┐      ┌──────┬──────┐
          Eleazar KISH   LIBNI   MAHLI  Eder Jeremoth   * These were the sons of Merari
              │           │        │                      by Jaaziah.  1 Chr. 24:26-27
          Jerahmeel    SHIMEI   SHAMER
                          │        │
                         UZZA     BANI
                          │        │                     Also of LEVI
                       SHIMEAH    AMZI                        :
                          │        │
                       HAGGIAH   HILKIAH  Neh. 11:15
                          │        │                        BUNNI
                        Asaiah  AMAZIAH                       │
                                   │                       HASHABIAH
        Also of MERARI         HASHABIAH                      │
              │                    │                       AZRIKAM
              .                 MALLUCH                       │
                                   │                       HASHUB
          JAHALELEL             ABDI                          │
              │                    │                       Shemaiah
          Azariah              KISHI
                                   │
                                 Ethan
```

===

CHART 7f.   **LAADAN**

(Note: Laadan was a descendant of Gershom.)

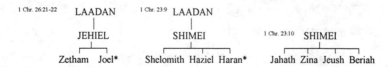

```
1 Chr. 26:21-22  LAADAN    1 Chr. 23:9  LAADAN
                    │                      │                1 Chr. 23:10  SHIMEI
                 JEHIEL                  SHIMEI                          ┌───┬────┬─────┬─────┐
              ┌────┬─────┐          ┌────────┬──────┬──────┐        Jahath Zina Jeush Beriah
          Zetham  Joel*        Shelomith Haziel Haran*
```

1 Chr. 23:4   * "These were the chief of the fathers of Laadan."

2 Chr. 29:14   Jehiel and Shimei were "of the sons of Heman."

(Note: Some confusion occurs between 1 Chr. 26:21:22 and 2 Chr. 29:14 inasmuch as Laadan is of the tribe of Gershon and Heman is of the tribe of Kohath.)

CHART 7g. ADDITIONAL DESCENDANTS OF LEVI

(Note: The following are priests. They are grouped with descendants of Eleazar, son of Aaron of the lineage of Kohath, but the exact line through which they descended is not indicated.)

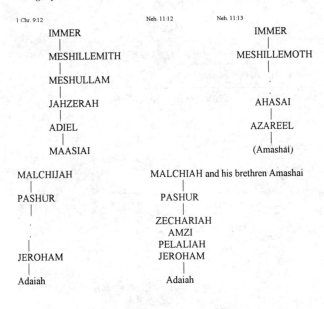

1 Chr. 9:12

IMMER
|
MESHILLEMITH
|
MESHULLAM
|
JAHZERAH
|
ADIEL
|
MAASIAI

Neh. 11:12

Neh. 11:13

IMMER
|
MESHILLEMOTH
|
.
AHASAI
|
AZAREEL
|
(Amashai)

MALCHIJAH
|
PASHUR
|
.
|
JEROHAM
|
Adaiah

MALCHIAH and his brethren Amashai
|
PASHUR
|
ZECHARIAH
AMZI
PELALIAH
JEROHAM
|
Adaiah

CHART 7h.

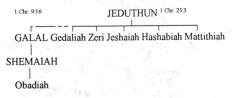

1 Chr. 9:16   JEDUTHUN 1 Chr. 25:3

GALAL Gedaliah Zeri Jeshaiah Hashabiah Mattithiah
|
SHEMAIAH
|
Obadiah

2 Chr. 29:14   (Uzziel was also of the sons of Jeduthun.)

CHART 8a.   **JUDAH**

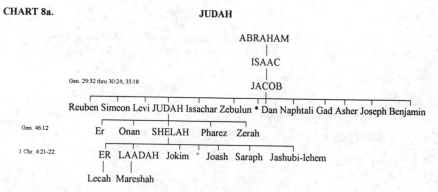

ABRAHAM
|
ISAAC
|
Gen. 29:32 thru 30:24; 35:18   JACOB

Reuben Simeon Levi JUDAH Issachar Zebulun * Dan Naphtali Gad Asher Joseph Benjamin

Gen. 46:12   Er   Onan   SHELAH   Pharez   Zerah

1 Chr. 4:21-22   ER LAADAH Jokim † Joash Saraph Jashubi-lehem

Lecah Mareshah

* Jacob and Leah also had a daughter named Dinah.

† Shelah was the father of the families of those who wrought fine linen of the house of Ashbea and of the men of Chozeba.

==

CHART 8b.   **JUDAH**
|
PHAREZ (PEREZ)

1 Chr. 9:4   Neh. 11:4   Neh. 11:5-6
| | |
.   .   SHILONI
| | |
BANI   MAHALALEEL   ZECHARIAH
| | |
IMRI   SHEPHATIAH   JOIARIB
| | |
OMRI   AMARIAH   ADAIAH
| | |
AMMIHUD   ZECHARIAH   HAZAIAH
| | |
Uthai   UZZIAH   COL-HOZEH
                   | |
                   Athaiah   BARUCH
                                      |
                                      MAASEIAH
                                      |
                                      NERIAH

Jer. 32:12 Baruch   Seraiah Jer. 51:59

CHART 8c.

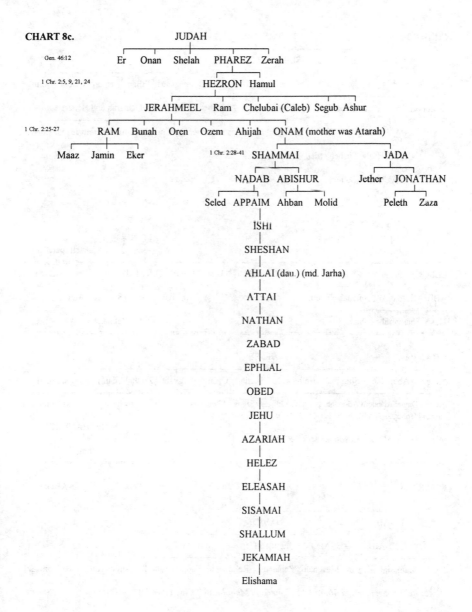

JUDAH

Gen. 46:12 — Er   Onan   Shelah   PHAREZ   Zerah

1 Chr. 2:5, 9, 21, 24 — HEZRON   Hamul

JERAHMEEL   Ram   Chelubai (Caleb)   Segub   Ashur

1 Chr. 2:25-27 — RAM   Bunah   Oren   Ozem   Ahijah   ONAM (mother was Atarah)

Maaz   Jamin   Eker

1 Chr. 2:28-41   SHAMMAI   JADA

NADAB   ABISHUR   Jether   JONATHAN

Seled   APPAIM   Ahban   Molid   Peleth   Zaza

ISHI

SHESHAN

AHLAI (dau.) (md. Jarha)

ATTAI

NATHAN

ZABAD

EPHLAL

OBED

JEHU

AZARIAH

HELEZ

ELEASAH

SISAMAI

SHALLUM

JEKAMIAH

Elishama

CHART 8d.

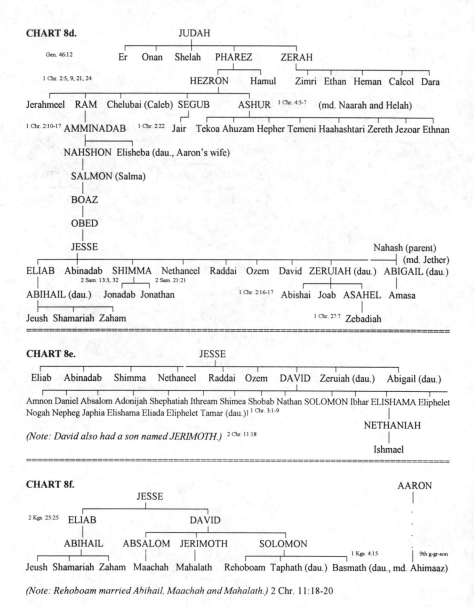

CHART 8e.

JESSE

Eliab   Abinadab   Shimma   Nethaneel   Raddai   Ozem   **DAVID**   Zeruiah (dau.)   Abigail (dau.)

Amnon Daniel Absalom Adonijah Shephatiah Ithream Shimea Shobab Nathan SOLOMON Ibhar ELISHAMA Eliphelet
Nogah Nepheg Japhia Elishama Eliada Eliphelet Tamar (dau.)] 1 Chr. 3:1-9

ELISHAMA
|
NETHANIAH
|
Ishmael

(Note: David also had a son named JERIMOTH.) 2 Chr. 11:18

CHART 8f.

AARON
|
.
.
.

JESSE

2 Kgs. 25:25   **ELIAB**   **DAVID**

ABIHAIL   ABSALOM   JERIMOTH   SOLOMON   9th g-gr-son

Jeush Shamariah Zaham   Maachah   Mahalath   Rehoboam Taphath (dau.) Basmath (dau., md. Ahimaaz)

1 Kgs. 4:15

(Note: Rehoboam married Abihail, Maachah and Mahalath.) 2 Chr. 11:18-20

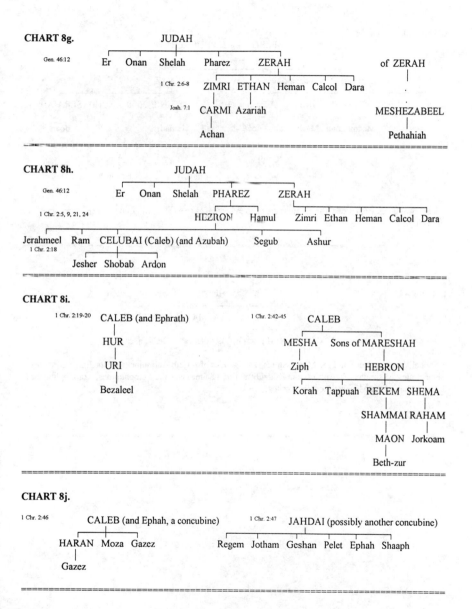

CHART 8g.

Gen. 46:12

JUDAH

Er Onan Shelah Pharez ZERAH of ZERAH

1 Chr. 2:6-8

ZIMRI ETHAN Heman Calcol Dara

Josh. 7:1

CARMI Azariah MESHEZABEEL

Achan Pethahiah

CHART 8h.

Gen. 46:12

JUDAH

Er Onan Shelah PHAREZ ZERAH

1 Chr. 2:5, 9, 21, 24

HEZRON Hamul Zimri Ethan Heman Calcol Dara

Jerahmeel Ram CELUBAI (Caleb) (and Azubah) Segub Ashur
1 Chr. 2:18

Jesher Shobab Ardon

CHART 8i.

1 Chr. 2:19-20

CALEB (and Ephrath)

1 Chr. 2:42-45

CALEB

HUR MESHA Sons of MARESHAH

URI Ziph HEBRON

Bezaleel Korah Tappuah REKEM SHEMA

SHAMMAI RAHAM

MAON Jorkoam

Beth-zur

CHART 8j.

1 Chr. 2:46

CALEB (and Ephah, a concubine)

1 Chr. 2:47

JAHDAI (possibly another concubine)

HARAN Moza Gazez Regem Jotham Geshan Pelet Ephah Shaaph

Gazez

CHART 8k.

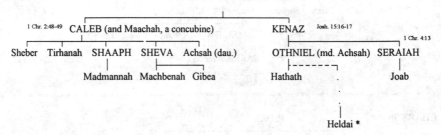

HEZRON — JEPHUNNEH

1 Chr. 2:48-49   CALEB (and Maachah, a concubine)   KENAZ   Josh. 15:16-17

                                                                         1 Chr. 4:13

Sheber   Tirhanah   SHAAPH   SHEVA   Achsah (dau.)   OTHNIEL (md. Achsah)   SERAIAH

                Madmannah   Machbenah   Gibea   Hathath   .   Joab

                                                                 Heldai *

*Heldai was a descendant of Othniel, but there is no indication as to whether or not he descended through Hathath.

CHART 8 l.

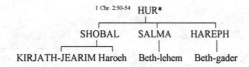

1 Chr. 2:50-54   HUR*

           SHOBAL   SALMA   HAREPH

KIRJATH-JEARIM   Haroeh   Beth-lehem   Beth-gader

* Shobal's sons included half the Manahethites. The families of Kirjath-jearim included the Ithrites, Puhites, Shumathites, Mishraites, Zareathites and Eshtaulites. From Salma came the Netophathites, Ataroth, house of Joab and half of the Manahethites, the Zorites.

CHART 8m.

1 Chr. 4:1-4

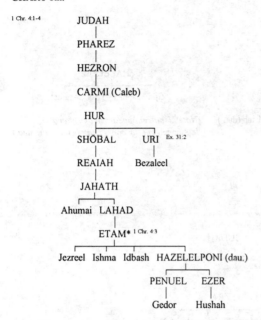

JUDAH
|
PHAREZ
|
HEZRON
|
CARMI (Caleb)
|
HUR
|
SHOBAL   URI   Ex. 31:2
| |
REAIAH   Bezaleel
|
JAHATH
|
Ahumai   LAHAD
|
ETAM*   1 Chr. 4:3
|
Jezreel Ishma Idbash HAZELELPONI (dau.)
|
PENUEL   EZER
| |
Gedor   Hushah

(Note: It is not clear whether Etam descended through Lahad or not, but he was a descendant of Hur.)

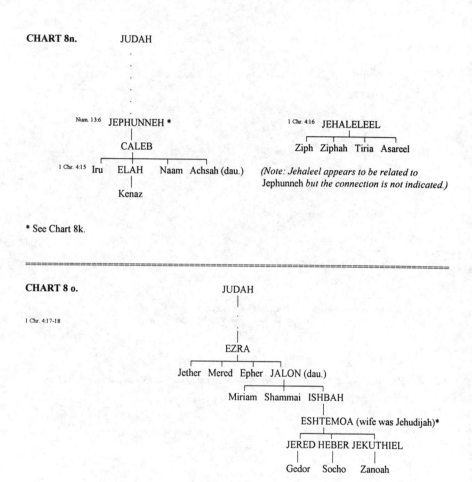

CHART 8n.   JUDAH

Num. 13:6 JEPHUNNEH *

CALEB

1 Chr. 4:15 Iru   ELAH   Naam   Achsah (dau.)

Kenaz

1 Chr. 4:16 JEHALELEEL

Ziph Ziphah Tiria Asareel

(Note: Jehaleel appears to be related to Jephunneh but the connection is not indicated.)

* See Chart 8k.

CHART 8 o.   JUDAH

1 Chr. 4:17-18

EZRA

Jether Mered Epher JALON (dau.)

Miriam Shammai ISHBAH

ESHTEMOA (wife was Jehudijah)*

JERED HEBER JEKUTHIEL

Gedor Socho Zanoah

* *(Note: It is not clear just whose wife Jehudijah was. It would appear that the pronoun "his" refers to Ezra. However, the next sentence in the scripture says, "These are the sons of Bithiah the daughter of Pharoah which Mered took.")*

CHART 9a. ISSACHAR

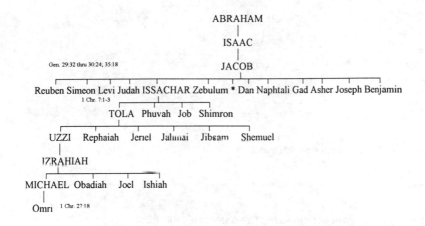

ABRAHAM
|
ISAAC
|
Gen. 29:32 thru 30:24; 35:18   JACOB

Reuben Simeon Levi Judah ISSACHAR Zebulum * Dan Naphtali Gad Asher Joseph Benjamin
1 Chr. 7:1-3

TOLA Phuvah Job Shimron

UZZI Rephaiah Jeriel Jahmai Jibsam Shemuel

IZRAHIAH

MICHAEL Obadiah Joel Ishiah

Omri   1 Chr. 27:18

* Leah and Jacob also had a daughter named Dinah.

CHART 9b.

Additional descendants of Issachar, but whose direct connections are not indicated:

Num. 1:8 ZUAR   Num. 12:7 JOSEPH   1 Kgs. 15:27; 16:6 AHIJAH   Judg. 10:1 DODO   Num. 34:26 AZZAN
| | | | |
Nethaneel   Igal   BAASHA   PUAH   Paltiel
                                                    | |
                                                  Elah   Tola

CHART 10a.   **ZEBULUM**

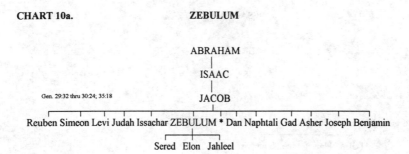

Gen. 29:32 thru 30:24; 35:18

ABRAHAM
|
ISAAC
|
JACOB

Reuben Simeon Levi Judah Issachar ZEBULUM * Dan Naphtali Gad Asher Joseph Benjamin

Sered   Elon   Jahleel

* Jacob and Leah also had a daughter named Dinah.

==

CHART 10b.   **ADDIDTIONAL DESCENDANTS OF ZEBULUM**

PARNACH Num. 34:25   OBADIAH 1 Chr. 27:19
| |
Elizaphan   Ishmaiah

CHART 11a.   **DAN**

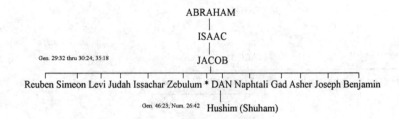

ABRAHAM
|
ISAAC
|
Gen. 29:32 thru 30:24; 35:18   JACOB

Reuben Simeon Levi Judah Issachar Zebulum * DAN Naphtali Gad Asher Joseph Benjamin
|
Gen. 46:23; Num. 26:42   Hushim (Shuham)

* Jacob and Leah also had a daughter named Dinah.

===

CHART 11b.   **ADDITIONAL DESCENDANTS OF DAN**

Additional descendants of Dan, but whose direct connections are not indicated:

Ex. 31:6 AHISAMACH	Lev. 24:11 DIBRI	Num. 34:22 JOGLI	Judg. 13:2 ZORAH	2 Chr. 2:14 WIDOW
Aholiab	Shelomith (dau.)	Bukki	.	Hiram
			.	
			MANOAH	
			Samson	

CHART 12a.   NAPHTALI

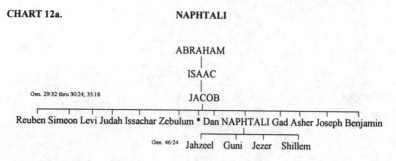

Gen. 29:32 thru 30:24; 35:18

ABRAHAM
|
ISAAC
|
JACOB

Reuben Simeon Levi Judah Issachar Zebulum * Dan NAPHTALI Gad Asher Joseph Benjamin

Gen. 46:24 Jahzeel Guni Jezer Shillem

* Jacob and Leah had a daughter named Dinah.

===

CHART 12b.   **ADDITIONAL DESCENDANTS OF NAPHTALI**

Additional descendants of Naphtali, but whose direct connection is not indicated:

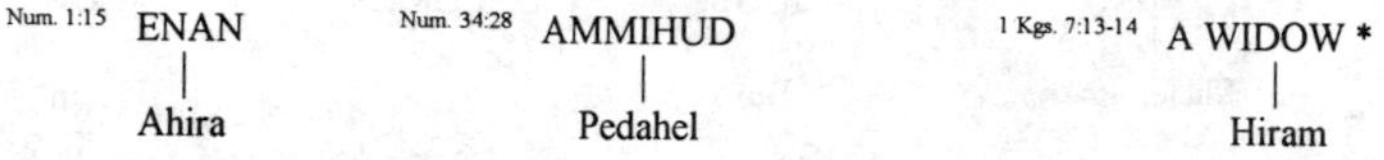

Num. 1:15 ENAN   Num. 34:28 AMMIHUD   1 Kgs. 7:13-14 A WIDOW *
| | |
Ahira   Pedahel   Hiram

* The widow was apparently from the tribe of Dan, but her son was of the tribe of Naphtali. Her husband was a man of Tyre.

CHART 13a.   **GAD**

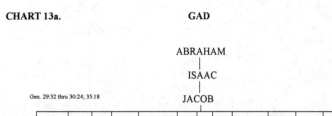

ABRAHAM
|
ISAAC
|
Gen. 29:32 thru 30:24; 35:18   JACOB

Reuben Simeon Levi Judah Issachar Zebulum * Dan Naphtali GAD Asher Joseph Benjamin

Gen. 46:16   Ziphion Haggi Shuni Ezbon Eri Arodi Areli
(Ozni)

* Jacob and Leah had a daughter named Dinah.

==

CHART 13b.   **ADDITIONAL DESCENDANTS OF GAD**

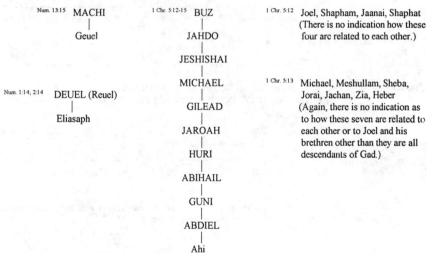

Num. 13:15 MACHI	1 Chr. 5:12-15 BUZ	1 Chr. 5:12 Joel, Shapham, Jaanai, Shaphat
Geuel	JAHDO	(There is no indication how these four are related to each other.)
	JESHISHAI	
	MICHAEL	1 Chr. 5:13 Michael, Meshullam, Sheba,
Num. 1:14; 2:14 DEUEL (Reuel)		Jorai, Jachan, Zia, Heber
	GILEAD	(Again, there is no indication as
Eliasaph		to how these seven are related to
	JAROAH	each other or to Joel and his
	HURI	brethren other than they are all
	ABIHAIL	descendants of Gad.)
	GUNI	
	ABDIEL	
	Ahi	

1 Chr. 12:9-13 Eleven men of the sons of Gad, captains of the host, took their men and assisted David at Ziklag: Ezer, Obadiah, Eliab, Mishmannah, Jeremiah, Attai, Eliel, Johanan, Elzabad, Jeremiah and Machbanai.

CHART 14a.   **ASHER**

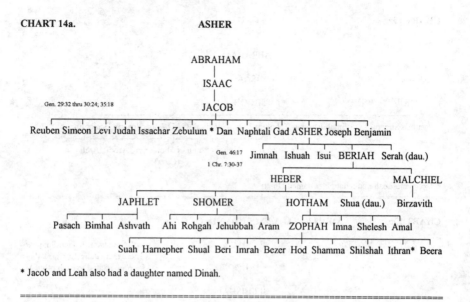

* Jacob and Leah also had a daughter named Dinah.

CHART 14b.   **ADDITIONAL DESCENDANTS OF ASHER,**
                BUT THE EXACT CONNECTION IS NOT INDICATED.

Num. 34:27 **SHELOMI**   1 Chr. 7:38 **JETHER***   1 Chr. 7:39 **ULLA**

Ahihud   Jephunneh Pispah Ara   Arah Haniel Rezia

(Note: The name "Jether" is sometimes interchanged with Ithra. It is conceivable that Jether and Ithran, the son of Zophah, [which could be "Ithra", too] are one and the same).

CHART 15a.   **JOSEPH**

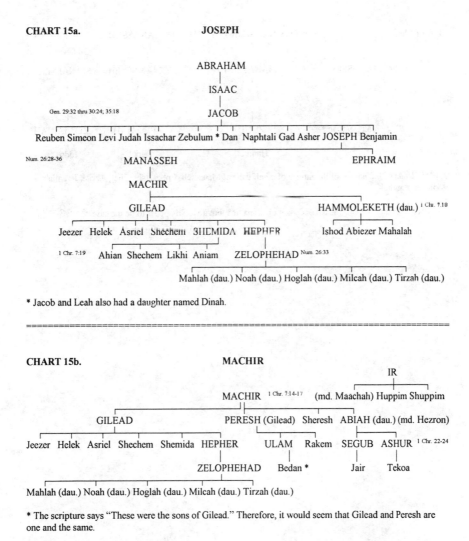

ABRAHAM
|
ISAAC
|
Gen. 29:32 thru 30:24; 35:18   JACOB

Reuben Simeon Levi Judah Issachar Zebulum * Dan Naphtali Gad Asher JOSEPH Benjamin

Num. 26:28-36   MANASSEH   EPHRAIM

MACHIR

GILEAD   HAMMOLEKETH (dau.) ¹ Chr. 7:18

Jeezer Helek Asriel Shechem SHEMIDA HEPHER   Ishod Abiezer Mahalah

1 Chr. 7:19   Ahian Shechem Likhi Aniam   ZELOPHEHAD Num. 26:33

Mahlah (dau.) Noah (dau.) Hoglah (dau.) Milcah (dau.) Tirzah (dau.)

* Jacob and Leah also had a daughter named Dinah.

CHART 15b.   **MACHIR**

IR

MACHIR ¹ Chr. 7:14-17   (md. Maachah) Huppim Shuppim

GILEAD   PERESH (Gilead) Sheresh ABIAH (dau.) (md. Hezron)

Jeezer Helek Asriel Shechem Shemida HEPHER   ULAM Rakem SEGUB ASHUR ¹ Chr. 22-24

ZELOPHEHAD   Bedan *   Jair   Tekoa

Mahlah (dau.) Noah (dau.) Hoglah (dau.) Milcah (dau.) Tirzah (dau.)

* The scripture says "These were the sons of Gilead." Therefore, it would seem that Gilead and Peresh are one and the same.

CHART 15c.   **ADDITIONAL DESCENDANTS OF MANASSEH**

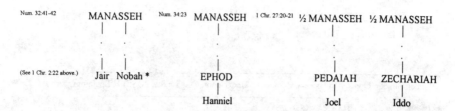

Num. 32:41-42   MANASSEH   Num. 34:23   MANASSEH   1 Chr. 27:20-21   ½ MANASSEH   ½ MANASSEH

(See 1 Chr. 2:22 above.)   Jair   Nobah *   EPHOD   PEDAIAH   ZECHARIAH

                                                 Hanniel   Joel   Iddo

1 Chr. 5:24. Heads of the houses of the fathers of a half tribe of Manasseh: Epher, Ishi, Eliel, Azriel, Jeremiah, Hodaviah, Jahdiel.

* It is not clear that Nobah was a descendant of Manasseh, but it would appear to be the case. Num. 32:42

CHART 15d.   **EPRHAIM**

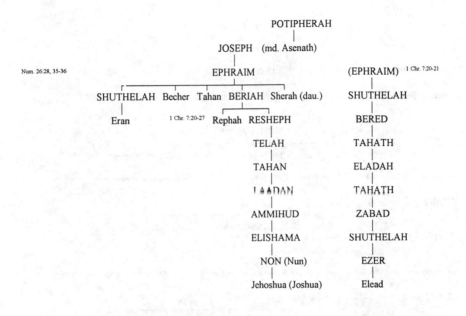

POTIPHERAH

JOSEPH (md. Asenath)

Num. 26:28, 35-36   EPHRAIM   (EPHRAIM) ¹ Chr. 7:20-21

SHUTHELAH   Becher   Tahan   BERIAH   Sherah (dau.)   SHUTHELAH

Eran   1 Chr. 7:20-27   Rephah   RESHEPH   BERED

TELAH   TAHATH

TAHAN   ELADAH

LAADAN   TAHATH

AMMIHUD   ZABAD

ELISHAMA   SHUTHELAH

NON (Nun)   EZER

Jehoshua (Joshua)   Elead

===

CHART 15e.   **ADDITIONAL DESCENDANTS OF EPHRAIM**

The following are also of the lineage of Ephraim, but the direct connection is not indicated:

Num. 34:24   EPHRAIM

SHIPHTAN

Kemuel

CHART 16a.   **BENJAMIN**

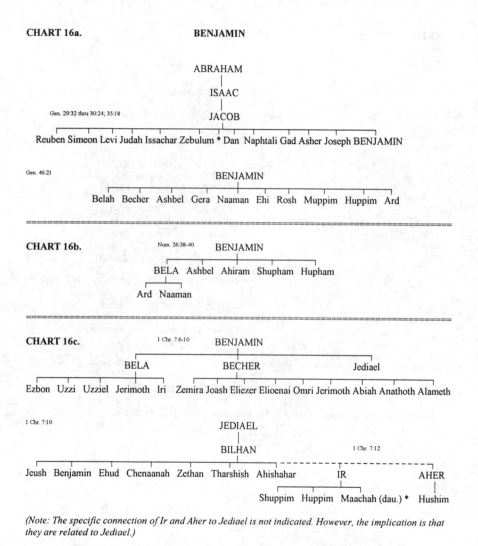

ABRAHAM
|
ISAAC
|
Gen. 29:32 thru 30:24; 35:18   JACOB

Reuben Simeon Levi Judah Issachar Zebulum * Dan Naphtali Gad Asher Joseph BENJAMIN

Gen. 46:21   BENJAMIN

Belah Becher Ashbel Gera Naaman Ehi Rosh Muppim Huppim Ard

CHART 16b.   Num. 26:38-40   **BENJAMIN**

BELA Ashbel Ahiram Shupham Hupham

Ard Naaman

CHART 16c.   1 Chr. 7:6-10   **BENJAMIN**

BELA   BECHER   Jediael

Ezbon Uzzi Uzziel Jerimoth Iri   Zemira Joash Eliezer Elioenai Omri Jerimoth Abiah Anathoth Alameth

1 Chr. 7:10   JEDIAEL
|
BILHAN   1 Chr. 7:12

Jeush Benjamin Ehud Chenaanah Zethan Tharshish Ahishahar   IR   AHER

Shuppim Huppim Maachah (dau.) *   Hushim

(Note: The specific connection of Ir and Aher to Jediael is not indicated. However, the implication is that they are related to Jediael.)

* Maachah married Machir the son of Manasseh (son of Joseph).

CHART 16d.

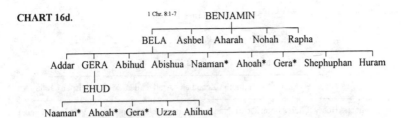

1 Chr. 8:1-7   BENJAMIN

BELA   Ashbel   Aharah   Nohah   Rapha

Addar   GERA   Abihud   Abishua   Naaman*   Ahoah*   Gera*   Shephuphan   Huram

EHUD

Naaman*   Ahoah*   Gera*   Uzza   Ahihud

* Naaman, Ahiah and Gera were "removed" to Manahath, and he (Ehud, presumedly) begat Uzza and Ahihud.

(Note: The BD indicates that all references to Ehud pertain to the same person. Some confusion results because Judg. 3:15 refers to Ehud as the son of Gera, a Benjamite; 1 Chr. 7:10 refers to Ehud as the son of Bilhan, son of Jediael the son of Benjamin; and 1 Chr. 8:3 refers to Ehud as the son of Gera, the son of Bela the son of Benjamin [Bela and Jediael were brothers]. Thus, it is not clear whether Ehud descended through Bela(h) or through Jediael. See below.)

CHART 16e.

Judg. 3:15   BENJAMIN   1 Chr. 7:10   BENJAMIN   1 Chr. 8:3   BENJAMIN

GERA   JEDIAEL   BELA

Ehud   BILHAN   GERA

                              Ehud   Ehud

CHART 16f.   BENJAMIN   BENJAMIN

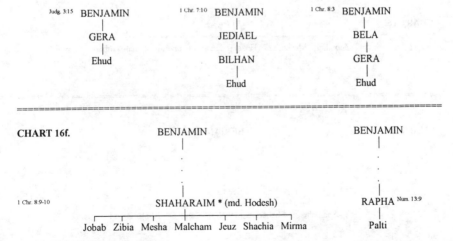

1 Chr. 8:9-10   SHAHARAIM * (md. Hodesh)   RAPHA Num. 13:9

Jobab   Zibia   Mesha   Malcham   Jeuz   Shachia   Mirma   Palti

* Shaharaim and Ehud may be one and the same, since 1 Chr. 8:8 indicates that Shaharaim was the one who begat children after sending some of them away.

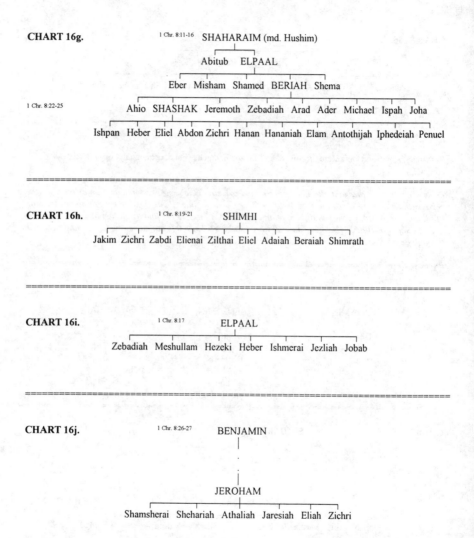

CHART 16g.   1 Chr. 8:11-16   SHAHARAIM (md. Hushim)

                              Abitub   ELPAAL

                  Eber Misham Shamed BERIAH Shema

1 Chr. 8:22-25

            Ahio SHASHAK Jeremoth Zebadiah Arad Ader Michael Ispah Joha

  Ishpan Heber Eliel Abdon Zichri Hanan Hananiah Elam Antothijah Iphedeiah Penuel

CHART 16h.   1 Chr. 8:19-21   SHIMHI

  Jakim Zichri Zabdi Elienai Zilthai Eliel Adaiah Beraiah Shimrath

CHART 16i.   1 Chr. 8:17   ELPAAL

  Zebadiah Meshullam Hezeki Heber Ishmerai Jezliah Jobab

CHART 16j.   1 Chr. 8:26-27   BENJAMIN

                                JEROHAM

  Shamsherai Shehariah Athaliah Jaresiah Eliah Zichri

CHART 16k.

1 Sam. 9:1

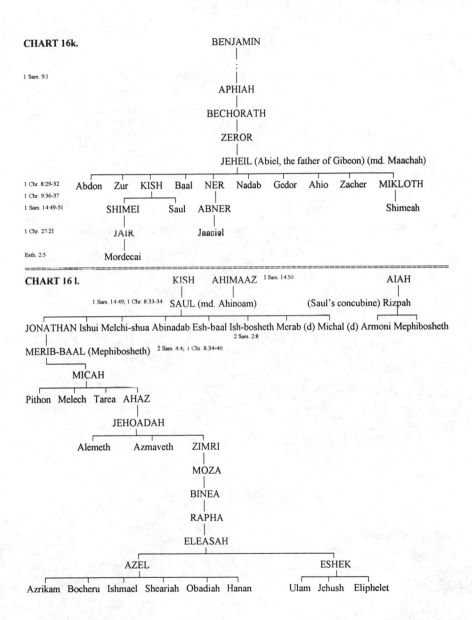

BENJAMIN

APHIAH

BECHORATH

ZEROR

JEHEIL (Abiel, the father of Gibeon) (md. Maachah)

1 Chr. 8:29-32
1 Chr. 9:36-37   Abdon   Zur   KISH   Baal   NER   Nadab   Gedor   Ahio   Zacher   MIKLOTH
1 Sam. 14:49-51   SHIMEI   Saul   ABNER   Shimeah

1 Chr. 27:21   JAIR   Jaasiel

Esth. 2:5   Mordecai

CHART 16 l.   KISH   AHIMAAZ 1 Sam. 14:50   AIAH

1 Sam. 14:49; 1 Chr. 8:33-34   SAUL (md. Ahinoam)   (Saul's concubine) Rizpah

JONATHAN Ishui Melchi-shua Abinadab Esh-baal Ish-bosheth Merab (d) Michal (d) Armoni Mephibosheth
                                                    2 Sam. 2:8

MERIB-BAAL (Mephibosheth) 2 Sam. 4:4; 1 Chr. 8:34-40

     MICAH

Pithon Melech Tarea AHAZ

          JEHOADAH

     Alemeth   Azmaveth   ZIMRI

               MOZA

               BINEA

               RAPHA

               ELEASAH

          AZEL   ESHEK

Azrikam Bocheru Ishmael Sheariah Obadiah Hanan   Ulam Jehush Eliphelet

CHART 16m.   BENJAMIN
                                            |

Additional descendants of Benjamin are given, but their direct connection is not indicated.

1 Chr. 9:7-8   IBNIJAH   MICHRI   JEROHAM   HASENUAH
                   | | | |
                 REUEL   UZZI   Ibneiah   HODAVIAH
                   | | |
              SHEPHATHIAH   Elah   MESHULLAM
                   | |
               Meshullam   Sallu

Neh. 11:7-9   JESAIAH   Gabbai   Sallai   ZICHRI   SENUAH
                 | | |
               ITHIEL   Joel   Judah
                 |
             MAASEIAH
                 |
              KOLAIAH
                 |
              PEDAIAH
                 |
               JOED
                 |
             MESHULLAM
                 |
               Sallu

Jer. 28:1   GIBEON   2 Sam. 16:5   SAUL
               | .
               .   .
               .   .
             AZUR   .
Jer. 37:13 | GERA
          HANANIAH |
               | Jer. 36:12   Shimei
     SHELEMIAH Zedekiah
          |
        Irijah

CHART 17.   **MIGHTY MEN OF DAVID**
                              (2 Sam. 23 & 1 Chr. 11)

2 Samuel 23:8-39		1 Chronicles 11	
08	Adino the Eznite, the Tachmonite (Chief among the captains)	11	Jashobeam, an Hachmonite, (Chief of the captains)
09	Eleazar, son of Dodo, the Ahohite (One of the three mighty men)	12	Eleazar, son of Dodo, the Ahohite (One of the three mighties)
11	Shammah, son of Agee the Hararite		
18	Abishai, brother of Joab, son of Zeruiah (Chief among three)	20	Abishai, brother of Joab (Chief of the three)
20	Benaiah, son of Jehoiada (Had the name among three mighty men)	22	Benaiah, son of Jehoiada (He was named among the three)
24	Asahel, brother of Joab	26	Asahel, brother of Joab
24	Elhanan, son of Dodo of Beth-lehem	26	Elhanan, son of Dodo of Beth-lehem
25	Shammah, the Harodite	27	Shammoth, the Harorite
25	Elika, the Harodite		
26	Helez, the Paltite	27	Helez, the Pelonite
26	Ira, son of Ikkesh the Tekoite	28	Ira, son of Ikkesh the Tekoite
27	Abiezer, the Anethothite	28	Abi-ezer, the Antothite
27	Mebunnai, the Hushathite	29	Sibbecai, the Hushathite
28	Zalmon, the Ahohite	29	Ilai, the Ahohite
28	Maharai, the Nethophathite	30	Maharai, the Nethhophathite
29	Heleb, son of Baanah, a Netophathite	30	Heled, son of Baanah the Netophathite
29	Ittai, son of Ribai out of Gibeah of Benjamin	31	Ithai, son of Ribai of Gibeah of Benjamin
30	Benaiah, the Pirathonite	31	Benaiah, the Pirathonite
30	Hiddai of the brooks of Gaash	32	Hurai of the brooks of Gaash
31	Abi-albon, the Arbathite	32	Abiel, the Arbathite
31	Azmaveth, the Barhumite	33	Azmaveth, the Baharumite
32	Eliahba, the Shaalbonite of sons of Jashan	33	Eliahba, the Shaalbonite
32	Jonathan	34	Jonathan, son of Shage the Hararite
33	Shammah, the Hararite		
33	Ahiam, son of Sharar the Hararite	35	Ahiam, son of Sacar the Hararite
34	Eliphelet, son of Ahasbai, son of the Maachathite	35	Eliphal, son of Ur
		36	Hepher, the Mecherathite
34	Eliam, son of Ahithophel the Gilonite	36	Ahijah, the Pelonite
35	Hezrai, the Carmelite	37	Hezro, the Carmelite
35	Paarai, the Arbite	37	Naarai, son of Ezbai
36	Igal, son of Nathan of Zobah	38	Joel, brother of Nathan
36	Bani, the Gadite	38	Mibhar, son of Haggeri
37	Zelek, the Ammonite	39	Zelek, the Ammonite
37	Naharai, the Beerothite, armorbearer to Joab the son of Zeruiah	39	Naharai, the Berothite, armorbearer of Joab the son of Zeruiah
38	Ira, an Ithrite	40	Ira, the Ithrite
38	Gareb, an Ithrite	40	Gareb, the Ithrite
39	Uriah, the Hittite	41	Uriah, the Hittite
		41	Zabad, son of Ahlai
		42	Adina, son of Shiza the Reubenite

43   Hanan, son of Maachah
43   Joshaphat, the Mithnite
44   Uzzia, the Ashterathite
44   Shama, son of Hothan the Aroerite

44   Jehiel, son of Hothan the Aroerite
45   Jediael, son of Shimri
45   Joha the Tizite, son of Shimri, brother of
         Jediael
46   Eliel, the Mahavite
46   Jeribai, son of Elnaam
46   Joshaviah, son of Elnaam, brother of
         Jeribai
46   Ithmah, the Moabite
47   Eliel
47   Obed
47   Jasiel, the Mesobaite

CHART 18.   KINGS OF EDOM

1. Bela, son of Beor
2. Jobab, son of Zerah
3. Husham, of the land of the Temanites
4. Hadad, son of Bedad   MEZAHAB
5. Samlah, of Masrekah |
6. Shaul, of Rebohoth   MATRED (dau.)
7. Baal-hanan, son of Achbor |
8. Hadar, (city was Pai), wife was Mehetabel . . . . Mehetabel

CHART 19.   DUKES OF EDOM   DUKES OF THE HORITES

	DUKES OF EDOM		DUKES OF THE HORITES
1.	Timnah	1.	Lotan
2.	Alvah	2.	Shobal
3.	Jetheth	3.	Zibeon
4.	Aholibamah	4	Anah
5.	Elah	5.	Dishon
6.	Pinon	6.	Ezer
7.	Kenaz	7.	Dishan
8.	Teman		
9.	Mibzar		
10.	Magdiel		
11.	Iram		

CHART 20.   JUDGES IN ISRAEL

Judg. 3:9	1.	OTHNIEL (son of Kenaz, Caleb's younger brother)
Judg. 3:15	2.	EHUD (son of Gera)
Judg. 3:31	3.	SHAMGAR (son of Anath)
Judg. 4:4	4.	DEBORAH
Judg. 6-8	5.	GIDEON
Judg. 9:6		ABIMELECH (son of Gideon is made king)
Judg. 10:1	6.	TOLA (son of Puah) is called to judge Israel
Judg. 10:3	7.	JAIR (a Gileadite)
Judg. 12:7	8.	JEPHTHAH (a Gileadite)
Judg. 12:8	9.	IBZAN (of Beth-lehem)
Judg. 12:11	10.	ELON (a Zebulonite)
Judg. 12:13	11.	ABDON (son of Hillel)
Judg. 13-16	12.	SAMSON (judged Israel 20 years)
I Sam. 1:1-4:18	13.	ELI (judged Israel 40 years)
1 Sam. 2:18-8:4	14.	SAMUEL
1 Sam. 8:1	15	JOEL ⎤ (Samuel made his sons judges. They perverted judgment
	16.	ABIAH ⎦

The people asked for a king. They were given Saul.

CHART 2

	0	50	100	150	200	250	300	350	400	450	500	550	600	650	700	750	800	850	900	950	1000

ADAM — Adam was 130 years old when he begot Seth. Adam lived 930 years.

SETH — Seth was 105 years old when he begot Enos. Seth lived 912 years.

ENOS — Enos was 90 years old when he begot Cainan. Enos lived 905 years.

CAINAN — Cainan was 70 years old when he begot Mahalaleel. Cainan lived 910 years.

MAHALALEEL — Mahalaleel was 65 years old when he begot Jared. Mahalaleel lived 895 years.

JARED — Jared was 162 years old when he begot Enoch. Jared lived 962 years.

ENOCH — Enoch was 65 years old when he begot Meth[usalah]. Enoch lived 430 years.

METHUSALAH — Methusalah was 187 years old whe[n]. Methusalah lived 969 yea[rs].

LAMECH — Lamech was

NOAH

JAPHETH

SHEM

HAM

ARPHAXAD

SALAH

EBER

PELEG

REU

SERUG

NAHOR

TERAH

ABRAHAM

ISAAC

JACOB

> * Note: There is a 10-year discrepancy between the years that add up to the date of the flood and the date of Arphaxad's birth. The flood occurred 1656 years after the Fall, according to the sum total of the years indicated for who begat whom at what age. According to the sum totals (as clarified in Moses 8:12), Shem was born 1548 years after the Fall and would have been 108 years old at the time of the flood and 110 years old when Arphaxad was born. However, Gen. 11:10 indicates that Shem was 100 years old when Arphaxad was born two years after the flood.

Adam to Jacob

1050 1100 1150 1200 1250 1300 1350 1400 1450 1500 1550 1600 1650 1700 1750 1800 1850 1900 1950 2000 2050 2100 2150 2200 2250

1656—The year of the flood

...got Lamech.

...rs old when he begot Noah.
...nech lived 777 years.

Noah was 450 years old when he begot Japheth; 492 when he begot Shem; and 500 years old when he begot Ham.
Noah lived 950 years.

The scriptures do not indicate how long Japheth lived.

Shem was 100 years old when he begot Arphaxad.*
Shem lived 600 years.

The scriptures do not indicate how long Ham lived.

Arphaxad was 35 years old when he begot Salah.
Arphaxad lived 438 years.

Salah was 30 years old when he begot Eber.
Salah lived 433 years.

Eber was 34 years old when he begot Peleg.
Eber lived 464 years.

Peleg was 30 years old when he begot Reu.
Peleg lived 239 years.

Reu was 32 years old when he begot Serug.
Reu lived 239 years.

Serug was 30 years old when he begot Nahor.
Serug lived 230 years.

Nahor was 29 years old when he begot Terah.
Nahor lived 148 years.

Terah was 70 years old when he begot Abraham.
Terah lived 205 years.

Abraham lived 175 years.   Abraham was 100 years old when he begot Isaac.

Isaac lived 180 years.   Isaac was 60 years old when he begot Jacob.

Jacob lived 147 years.